INEQUALITY AND SOCIETY

W.W. Norton & Company has been independent since its founding in 1923, when William Warder Norton and Mary D. Herter Norton first published lectures delivered at the People's Institute, the adult education division of New York City's Cooper Union. The firm soon expanded its program beyond the Institute, publishing books by celebrated academics from America and abroad. By mid-century, the two major pillars of Norton's publishing program—trade books and college texts—were firmly established. In the 1950s, the Norton family transferred control of the company to its employees, and today—with a staff of four hundred and a comparable number of trade, college, and professional titles published each year—W.W. Norton & Company stands as the largest and oldest publishing house owned wholly by its employees.

EDITOR: *Karl Bakeman*
MANAGING EDITOR, COLLEGE: *Marian Johnson*
PROJECT EDITOR: *Melissa Atkin*
EDITORIAL ASSISTANTS: *Kate Feighery* and *Sarah Johnson*
COPY EDITOR: *Candace Levy*
PRODUCTION MANAGER: *Eric Pier-Hocking*
DESIGN DIRECTOR: *Rubina Yeh*
BOOK DESIGNER: *Guenet Abraham*
COMPOSITION: *Matrix Publishing Services, Inc.*
MANUFACTURING: *Courier Companies—Westford division.*

LIBRARY OF CONGRESS CATALOGING-IN-PUBLICATION DATA
Manza, Jeff.
   Inequality and society : social science perspectives on social stratification / Jeff Manza and Michael Sauder. — 1st ed.
       p. cm.
   Includes bibliographical references.
   ISBN 978-0-393-97725-7 (pbk.)
   1. Equality. 2. Income distribution. 3. Social structure. I. Sauder, Michael. II. Title.

HM821.M353 2009
305.5′12—dc22   2009005150

W.W. Norton & Company, Inc., 500 Fifth Avenue,
New York, NY 10110
www.wwnorton.com
W.W. Norton & Company, Ltd., Castle House,
75/76 Wells Street, London W1T3QT

1 2 3 4 5 6 7 8 9 0

CONTENTS

Preface and Acknowledgements

Rising income and wealth inequality, persistent divisions between genders and racial and ethnic groups, and stubbornly high rates of poverty motivate the study of social stratification. As students and citizens, we continually face questions about whether the communities and societies we inhabit provide opportunities and distribute rewards justly. While social-science theory and research on inequality cannot unambiguously answer these questions, they do provide the tools to think about them in a deeper and more systematic way.

Being able to think critically about inequality is important for everyone, because societal inequalities are largely the result of our conscious choices, including the public policies of governments. In bringing this anthology of key classical and contemporary writings together, our central objective has been to provide students with the resources to understand the multiple dimensions of social inequality, including their political component. For too long, the field of research on social and economic inequality has been separated from the political pathways through which it is reproduced. We take direct aim at that separation with this volume, including scholarship exploring the political and policy underpinnings of American "exceptionalism" in regards to social inequality.

We have been assembling the final parts of this book during an extraordinarily dramatic period of change in the global economy, with a simultaneous crisis in the financial sector and a growing recession marked by rising unemployment and insecurity about the future. The last three decades have been marked by very uneven growth across the globe; and some of the foundations of the system of inequality it has produced are now in the process of being unsettled. While it is not possible to know at this writing (February 2009) how deep and enduring the economic downturn will be, it underscores how and why understanding more about the system of inequality in the United States and around the world is so important. The mass media is full of stories about individuals and families coping with the downturn. While some of the very rich are being forced to sell their fancy vacation homes or expensive jewelry to try to maintain their standard of living, for most Americans the economic downturn is far more threatening, especially because the social safety net in the United States contains many holes in its basic fabric.

We aim this reader at advanced undergraduate students in sociology and allied fields. It does not offer the breadth of the state-of-the-art contemporary research contained in David Grusky's magisterial collection, *Social Stratification*, which is a vital text for graduate students and scholars already in the field. Rather, we provide a sophisticated but accessible set of readings for serious undergraduate or entry-level graduate courses examining the system of inequality or any of its key dimensions. As teachers, we are committed to challenging our students to read and think about important scholarship—classical and contemporary—that frames current debates. At the same time, we also recognize that some kinds of contemporary research centering on results from complicated statistical models will exceed the grasp of many students entering the field.

Our approach to editing the included selections attempts, as much as possible, to avoid making excessive cuts that disrupt the flow of the authors' arguments or evidence. At the same time, we are forced, in consideration of length, to make choice cuts in some of these selections. We think in all cases we have captured the essence of the authors' ideas, but we certainly welcome feedback from readers.

We wish to thank our wonderful editors at W. W. Norton for their hard work and many insights and contributions on the project. It was Stephen Dunn who first identified and supported the project, then handed it to Karl Bakeman who brought it home with patience, thoughtful guidance, and good humor. Kate Feighery, Melissa Atkin, and the production staff were a pleasure to work with as we completed our effort. Our gratitude for the support and encouragement of our colleagues at Northwestern (where we began the project together) and New York University and the University of Iowa (where Manza and Sauder respectively finished it) is considerable. We owe a special thanks to Bill Domhoff, who prepared an original and exciting chapter for this volume on very short notice. Dan Clawson provided us with an English language translation of a paper originally published in French. Mike Hout, Devah Pager, Clem Brooks, and Leslie McCall provided advice at various stages on the project. Our families provided both advice and love to the editors. Last but certainly not least, wonderful students in our various inequality courses over the years have helped us in many ways, perhaps without realizing they were being used as guinea pigs as we developed our ideas about what topics and theories were most pressing and important for a project like this one. This past year, Manza even had the experience of having his older daughter Dana Hafter-Manza, now a college student herself, attend some of his lectures drawing from the book's material and provide blunt feedback about its inadequacies as only a daughter can do.

Jeff Manza
New York University

Michael Sauder
University of Iowa

Inequality and Society: An Introduction

JEFF MANZA

Some of us have more than others. This has always been the case. Inequality is a universal feature of all known human societies. But the amounts and types of inequality have varied a great deal in different times and places. Primitive hunting and gathering societies, for example, typically shared their (limited) food supplies and resources among all members of the group more or less equitably, although decision-making powers were wielded by tribal chiefs, and medicine men (known as shaman) had relatively privileged positions. In these primitive communities, mere survival was often in question, and there was little, if any, surplus left over after basic necessities were met and thus no significant opportunities for some individuals to gain at the expense of others. By contrast, the agrarian settlements and societies of the Middle Ages often produced more than was needed for survival, and, as a consequence, a handful of households were able to accumulate (sometimes considerable) fortunes, as were traders in early urban settlements. Political rule in agrarian societies was generally authoritarian, with power concentrated either in the hands of local or regional landowners or increasingly centralized under kings as modern states began to emerge. The tiny stratum of privileged economic and political elites in agrarian societies generally lived entirely apart from the rest of the population, and there were no significant "middle" classes like those of capitalist societies today. The resources and life chances possessed by the masses of agricultural laborers ("serfs") did not vary a great deal, at least within particular geographic regions, over the course of many centuries.

If we fast-forward to the rich capitalist societies of today, such as the United States, we find a more complex picture. There are vast inequalities between the very richest individuals and families and the poorest, but there is also a large middle class that enjoys some of the benefits of economic growth and surplus wealth. At the very top are individuals and families enjoying extraordinary wealth, unprecedented in human history. *Fortune* magazine does an annual survey of the richest people in America, and another on the richest in the world. Topping *Fortune*'s analysis of the richest individuals in the world on August 31, 2007, were Microsoft founder and former chair Bill Gates, and Mexican telephone mogul Carlos Slim Helú, each possessing approximately $60 billion in wealth. Individual fortunes of this magnitude have happened only once before, during the late nineteenth and early twentieth centuries (an earlier epoch of global financial and economic boom). The richest of the famous moguls—sometimes known as "robber barons"—in that era was John D. Rockefeller, whose fortune likely exceeded $100 billion (in inflation-adjusted dollars) at its peak.[1]

The pace at which the wealthy are getting wealthier has grown remarkably in recent years. One way we can see this is to look at the change in the amount of money required to be on *Fortune*'s annual list of the four hundred richest Americans. In 1982, a mere $210 million (in inflation-adjusted 2007 dollars) was required to be among the richest four hundred. To simply make the very bottom of the list of the four hundred richest Americans today, however, $1.3 billion is now required. In other words, one needs more than *six* times as much wealth to be in that exclusive club today as twenty-five years ago. And indeed, across the globe the rich have gotten richer and today collectively control an enormous share of the world's wealth. One recent study

---

1 The exact size of Rockefeller's fortune at its peak around 1913 is difficult to estimate with any precision. Rockefeller's biographer Ron Chernow estimates that his fortune peaked at a value of around $25 billion (in 1998 inflation-adjusted dollars), although other estimates put it over $100 billion (when the value of his philanthropy is included). See Louis Uchitelle, "The Richest of the Rich, Proud of a New Gilded Age," *New York Times*, July 15, 2007, www.nytimes.com/2007/07/15/business/15gilded. html (accessed July 15, 2007). Three other fortunes of the Gilded era may also have exceeded the Gates/Slim Helú fortunes: those of Cornelius Vanderbilt, John Jacob Astor, and Stephen Girard.

estimates that the top 1 percent of the world's population controls about 32 percent all the world's wealth, whereas the bottom 30 percent of the world's population controls less than 1 percent.[2] The global financial crisis and stock market decline, beginning in the fall of 2008, however, have eroded some of the fortunes held at the top.

Below the top, an educated upper middle class, made up of people working in salaried jobs in professional and managerial occupations, has grown steadily in size over the past hundred years. Depending on exactly how we define this group, it has increased from somewhere around 1 percent of the U.S. population at the turn of the twentieth century to 15 percent or more early in the twenty-first century. Professionals, business executives, and business managers typically receive incomes sufficient to own attractive homes and expensive cars, to be able to travel extensively, and to provide their children with many educational and cultural advantages. Their educational credentials and knowledge make it much easier for professionals and managers to build stable career paths, even in a 21st-century economy in which few stay with a single firm their entire working life. Many of the workers directly supervised by professionals and managers—nurses, paralegals, technicians, office managers, secretaries, salespeople, and others—work in safe, clean environments and receive incomes that put them in the broader "middle class," even if they cannot afford the lifestyles of their bosses.

When we turn our attention to the vast majority of American society below the very top and the upper middle class, however, the picture darkens considerably. For the more than 70 percent of Americans without a college degree, the economic environment is increasingly challenging. In the transition from a largely industrial economy to the postindustrial economies of the twenty-first century, there has been a drastic reduction in the number of well-paying blue-collar jobs, and a corresponding decline in opportunities overall for this group. If we want to understand inequality in America today, the lives and well-being of the non-college-educated majority require special attention. For this group, entering the labor market has become more difficult, as has finding a secure occupational niche. Instability is also very high; even those who find a decent job at one point cannot be sure to still have that job in a few years. America has one of the highest rates of economic instability among the rich countries in the

2 James B. Davies, Susanna Sandström, Anthony Shorrocks, and Edward N. Wolff, "Estimating the Level and Distribution of Global Household Wealth," World Institute for Development Economics Research of the United Nations University, WIDER Research Paper, 2007/77 (November 2007): 27, www.wider.unu.edu/publications/working-papers/research-papers/2007/en_GB/rp2007-77 (accessed April 2008).

world. It is a distinct possibility that at some point in their lives, those without a college education will experience one or more significant bouts of unemployment that will drain their savings and threaten their well-being.

Another important aspect of inequality in America is that the economic gains of the past three decades have not been shared by most of its population. Although household income in the very middle (at the 50th percentile, or median) has grown slightly faster than inflation since the early 1970s, the share of income received by the "median" family has slipped. The trends over the past thirty years stand in stark contrast to the pattern of the thirty years before that (from the end of World War II through the mid 1970s), when the middle class not only shared equally in the benefits of economic growth but actually saw its share of national income *increase* relative to those of the very rich.

For those at the very bottom, the situation is even bleaker. Recent economic gains have done little to improve living standards for poor Americans, while changes in public policy have eroded access to many government benefits that can make life more secure for the poorest of families. To be sure, poverty rates, while fluctuating from year to year, have not shown an overall increase during the era of rising inequality. This is an important point, one that is sometimes overlooked in discussions of rising inequality. Generally low unemployment rates in America since the mid 1990s have helped the adults in the poorest families boost their employment income and have unquestionably prevented even worse outcomes from occurring. Yet many of those jobs are dead-end, paying low wages and offering few opportunities for advancement. And poverty rates in America remain very high by comparison with other rich capitalist countries. Moreover, changes in the criminal justice system since the early 1970s have given rise to high criminal conviction rates and "mass" incarceration (with over two million Americans currently housed in prisons and jails, and some seventeen million Americans with felony convictions on their records). Skyrocketing rates of felony convictions, during a period when crime has been mostly stable or declining, has made life more difficult for many poor families and their children. And, finally, the poor are much more likely today to live in neighborhoods with a high percentage of other poor families. Such neighborhoods with concentrated poverty are likely to have high crime rates, dangerous environmental conditions, and typically lack jobs and sometimes even basic services.

This book examines many of the most important types of inequality in the United States, and compares the United States to other countries across the globe. It brings together a number of important pieces of research and theoretical writings on inequality that have been produced by sociologists, economists, political scientists, and philosophers. Our aim is to provide a multilayered understanding, in which inequalities between individuals and groups (especially those based on race, gender, and class) are linked to public policies and situated in a global economic context. Sociologists have developed a concept for the ways in which inequalities are interconnected: the stratification system. *Stratification* refers to the full range and sources of inequality: inequalities arising from economic markets as well as between groups and those rooted in, or reinforced by, social and political institutions as well as global social and economic trends. Although no single theory of stratification can account for its multiple dimensions, when we think about inequality as an interconnected stratification system we are compelled to explore how the parts fit together.

Although the political sources of inequality are sometimes acknowledged as important components of the stratification system as a whole, the ways in which political inequality reinforces social and economic inequality is frequently overlooked. Consider the following example. A household with two children headed by a single mother without a college education is more likely to be poor than is a similar household headed by a college-educated couple in all societies today. Yet there can be enormous variation among countries in the percentage of such single-mother households that actually live below the poverty line. In 2000, about 6 percent of children in these households were estimated to live in poverty in Denmark, 22 percent in Switzerland, 31 percent in Germany, but about 50 percent of children in such families in the United States were estimated to live below the poverty line.[3] These are large and substantial differences. One of our key innovations in this book is to link important social and economic aspects of inequality to political institutions and public policies. We have thus included a variety of readings that take up facets of public policy and political representation alongside other major aspects of inequality in order to provide a fuller view of the American stratification system.

Some of the readings collected here are classics, while others represent influential and/or significant pieces of contemporary scholarship. The selections are grouped together in a way that facilitates linkages among them, although we imagine most readers will focus on a subset of the readings. In the rest of this introduction, I provide a brief summary of the book's framework, and some suggestions about how to approach the readings.

---

3 These estimates are derived from data collected by the extraordinary Luxumburg Income Study (LIS) Key Figures, www.lisproject.org/keyfigures/childpovrates.htm (accessed April 2008).

||| UNDERSTANDING INEQUALITY

Why should we study inequality? We are intrinsically fascinated by the lives of the rich and famous and perhaps concerned, as citizens, with the sources and justice of the distribution of wealth and poverty. But understanding the patterning of inequality in a country like the United States also helps us understand, in fundamental ways, the very nature of the society and world we live in. For one thing, inequality in any one domain can have a number of important "spillover" consequences. For example, economic inequality skews the distribution of non-monetary rewards and benefits, like access to health care. In highly unequal societies like the United States, the rich get state-of-the-art treatment but absorb far more than their pro-rata share of medical care, whereas the poor are often less healthy than they would be with the same income in a more egalitarian society. The maldistribution of medical care helps account for why the United States has a higher rate of infant mortality—and does worse on other well-measured health outcomes—than virtually all other rich countries, even though we devote a far higher portion of our gross national product to health care than anyone else.

There are three important starting points for trying to understand the kinds of inequalities we find in the United States and throughout the world, both in the past and at the present. First, as we have already noted, there is enormous *variation* in the stratification systems of different societies. Looking around the world today, we find large differences in the levels of inequality different societies permit. Socialist countries—such as Cuba today and the countries of Eastern Europe and the former Soviet Union before 1989—minimized private enterprise and regulate wages and living standards through centralized government planning. Although there were significant inequalities in the privileges enjoyed by party members and other elites (known as the *nomenklatura*) versus everyone else in socialist countries, these societies generally had much lower overall levels of inequality than found in contemporary capitalist countries. In continental western Europe, a more regulated capitalist market economy and more generous welfare states have led to a significant reduction in levels of poverty and inequality, especially compared to the United States. Many of the countries with the highest levels of inequality today are countries experiencing rapid social or economic change, such as Russia, China, South Africa, and several countries in South America. In these places, a tiny stratum of the super-rich control levels of wealth similar to those found among the wealthiest Americans and Europeans. But large majorities of the populations in these countries have seen only limited benefits from economic restructuring and indeed may face rising costs for basic goods (especially housing) that offset much of whatever increased household income they have gained. Understanding inequality thus requires exploring how different national and regional contexts produce different patterns of inequality.

The second starting point lies in recognizing there are a wide variety of *different* inequalities in any society. There are economic inequalities (such as income and wealth), political inequalities (such as power), and social inequalities (such as those based on race, ethnicity, religion, and gender and the different kinds of social status and prestige they give rise to). Social inequalities in particular are elusive and historically contingent. For example, different racial and ethnic groups are found in virtually all contemporary societies, but whether and how those differences matter for the patterning of inequality depend on a great deal on public policies regulating economic and political life. In the contemporary United States, African Americans and Latinos face discrimination in the labor market, a racially segregated housing market, and harassment by police and higher rates of incarceration in the criminal justice system. The practice and legal foundation of discrimination, however, has not stayed the same over time: it underwent enormous changes with the adoption of civil rights legislation in the 1960s. Those measures, and affirmative action programs developed later, have helped spur the growth of a black middle class by increasing opportunities for some African Americans to attend top universities and gain entry to desired economic opportunities that would have seemed nearly unimaginable sixty years ago. Or, to take another example, in the late nineteenth century, immigrants from Ireland and southern Europe faced enormous hostility and negative stereotyping. Indeed, some historians have argued that immigrant groups like the Irish, Italians, and Slavs had to become "white" to end discrimination and integrate into the American mainstream. This was a protracted process. But between the late nineteenth century and World War II, all of these groups did become white and thus gained a measure of economic and political equality with more established northern Europeans.

Our third starting point is that the *relationship* among different types of inequalities—and how they change over time—is critical for understanding the bigger picture. The study of how different kinds of inequalities are linked is what forms the *stratification system* of any society. One type of inequality may exacerbate other types of inequalities, depending on the context. For example, differences in the amount of income or wealth a family possesses will influence the educational achievements of its children, irrespective of how hard children work in school. Conversely. the existence of class and/or racial inequality can in some contexts reduce gender inequality, by providing a ready-made supply of low-wage domestic workers who can, in turn, free up educated women from time-consuming domestic chores such as housework and raising children. For a long time, scholarship on inequality did not systematically examine these interactions, but they have become the focus of much recent research.

These three themes—the *variations* in stratification systems, the *multiple sources* of inequality, and the *relationships* among inequalities—define the challenges we face in understanding inequality and the stratification system of a society like the United States.

||| CLASSICAL THEORIES OF INEQUALITY

Part I of this book starts with some classic treatments of inequality and social stratification, works that continue to shape debates right up to the present. Adam Smith's (1723–1790) influential writings on the division of labor inspired Karl Marx's (1818–1883) elaboration of the sources and consequences of class divisions in capitalist and other societies. For Smith, a division of labor between individuals and the development of markets to efficiently allocate the fruits of that labor allow for a vast increase in wealth and productivity. Marx developed a radically different conception of the meaning of the division of labor and the consequences of the rise of market capitalism. For Marx, the rise of the division of labor creates the possibility for some people to exploit others. His concept of "class" provided both a set of analytical tools for understanding major inequalities across different types of societies, as well as the foundation of a theory of history based on the idea that *class struggles* are the crucial mechanism for the transition from one type of society to another. Whether or not we agree with the model of revolution and historical change he developed, Marx has served as a critical touchstone for the development of subsequent research and theory on stratification systems. This is true even though most later scholars and writers on inequality do not situate themselves in the Marxist tradition.

For many sociologists, the writings of the German sociologist Max Weber (1864–1920) provides one basis for moving beyond Marx. Weber called attention to the limitations of an analysis of inequality centered solely on class, noting that other kinds of social attributes, most importantly those based on honor or "status," could also serve as wellsprings of inequality. Status inequality, for Weber, is especially consequential as individuals with similar status situations or identities coalesce into what he called "status groups." The most important of these status group memberships are those involving race or ethnicity, although many other types of statuses have provided the foundation for group memberships in different societies. Weber also pioneered the idea that alongside Marx's notion of exploitation, we need to pay attention to the ways in which groups mobilize to restrict the opportunities of other, less powerful groups.

Marx's focus on class inequality did not contain much room within it for a complex theory of how race, ethnicity, and/or gender provide the basis for both meaningful identities and group-based conflicts. Weber's insights, by contrast, were paralleled in the work of scholars beginning to theorize and study the origins and types of racial and gender inequality. In the remarkable work of sociologist W. E. B. Du Bois (1868–1963), social divisions such as those based on race (and the ideas they give rise to) are the result of political struggles rather than on any biological characteristic of individuals or groups. In his historical writings, especially his monumental study of the post–Civil War era, Du Bois developed the notion that the politics of racial struggle— not class—lay at the center of the peculiar development of American political institutions. Although he was explicitly concerned with the dynamics of race in America, Du Bois's ideas have obvious parallels to, and heavily influenced, later scholarship on ethnic and gender inequality.

Another line of critique aimed at Marx came from sociological writers after World War II drawn to "functionalist" theories of societies. The key idea of functionalist sociology was that societies evolve in response to critical needs of social order. In their 1945 manifesto, one of the most widely discussed (and debated) works about inequality ever written by sociologists, Kingsley Davis and Wilbert Moore argued (without direct attribution) that Marxist claims that inequality was an artificial human construction that could be abolished in some future communist society were impossible. Inequality, they asserted, is a *necessary* condition of all known human societies, and for good reason. It provides individuals with the incentives to work and produce and, even more important, motivates the most talented members of society to prepare themselves to perform the most important tasks (and perform them well). Although the kind of functionalist reasoning employed by Davis and Moore has largely fallen out of fashion in the contemporary social sciences, the argument they develop about why inequality is universal remains a core point of departure for contemporary debates.

One aspect of Marx's writings on inequality that has sometimes been lost in contemporary scholarship is his insistence on connecting social and economic trends to political power. But Marx's theory of politics was also impoverished in a number of ways. Writing in the middle decades of the nineteenth century, Marx envisioned a particular kind of capitalist state, which would guard the economic interests of the dominant class. He and Engels famously argued in *The Communist Manifesto* that "the modern state is but an executive committee for managing the common affairs of the whole bourgeoisie." The possibility of significant political reforms of capitalism in the interests of the working class was simply not something that Marx anticipated. The rise of welfare state—those institutions of government that provide income support and services (such as health care) to most or all citizens—fundamentally challenges a view of the state as primarily devoted to protecting upper-class interests. The way goods and services are distributed within a capitalist society, and the role of public policy in responding to inequality, significantly alters those relationships.

In his famous essay on the rise of modern citizenship and the welfare state, T.H. Marshall argued in 1950 that the establishment of civil rights from the eighteenth century onward laid the foundation for the establishment of political rights and democracy in the late nineteenth century. Political citizenship in turn fostered the conditions for the emergence of the "social rights" of citizenship, as labor unions and social democratic parties across Europe and North America fought for a universal right to a decent standard of living. Among others, public programs for old age pensions, national health insurance, unemployment insurance, and public housing formidably altered the system of inequality within capitalist societies. Marshall's theorization of the role of the welfare state in upending traditional patterns of inequality and empowering citizens from below has helped give rise to a vast research literature on the welfare state that continues up to the present. This literature has established conclusively that greater levels of effort toward a welfare state reduce poverty and inequality under capitalism in ways that Marx did not anticipate.

These classical writings provide the point of departure for contemporary social science understandings of inequality. While the theoretical ideas of the authors like Smith, Marx, Weber, Du Bois, Marshall, and others continue to find new generations of readers and to inform how we understand the stratification system, recent scholarship has also pushed in new and exciting directions. The rest of the book draws from some of that research, organized into several parts. In the remainder of this introduction, I provide a brief description of the main themes guiding the organization of the book.

||| CONTEMPORARY RESEARCH ON INEQUALITY

Who Gets What? Who Does What?

The most basic question about inequality concerns the uneven distribution of rewards, especially economic rewards. Four types of interconnected inequalities have been the subject of systematic social science investigation: (1) income, (2) wealth, (3) consumption, and (4) opportunities. Inequalities of income and wealth are central, but these are also fundamentally different concepts. *Income* refers to the receipt of money or goods over a particular accounting period (such as hourly, weekly, monthly, or yearly). For most of us, it is our income that allows us to acquire goods and services, and defines our well-being. There are multiple sources of income: earned income from a regular job, income received from investments or ownership of income-generating properties or businesses, income transfers from the government (such as Social Security), income received from family or friends (including inheritances), and illegal or "underground" earnings (such as from crime or informal and untaxed work or business activity). The *source* of income—aside from the amount—is critical. Occupations vary widely in the level of income they provide to individuals; professional and managerial occupations generally pay far higher incomes and provide better employment security than do routine white-collar jobs or skilled and nonskilled manual jobs. Yet that is not the whole story. A part-time college instructor may have the same *current* income as the unionized janitor who cleans up at the end of the day, but the instructor has the potential to earn far more income over the long term than does the janitor. The sociological concept of class attempts to capture these varying life chances by making distinctions based on both life chances and current income to provide a richer conception of class.

In examining the "who gets what" question, much research has paid special attention to recent *trends* in income inequality. In the United States, there has been a particularly rapid growth in income and wealth inequality over the past thirty years. The basic trends can be seen in Figure 1. Income inequality narrowed after World War II; the lines in the figure represent different income levels and show signs of a slight convergence. But beginning in the

FIGURE 1 **FAMILY INCOMES BY INCOME PERCENTILE, 1947–2006**

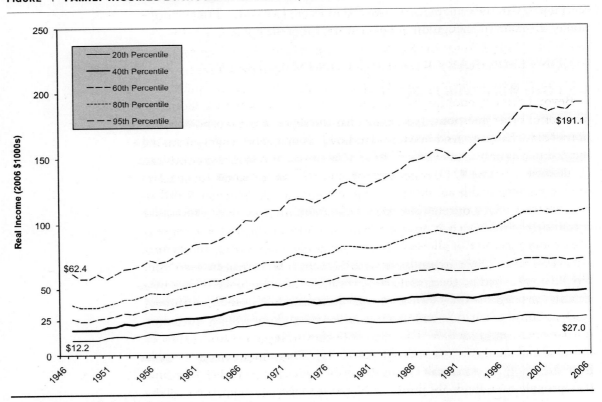

SOURCE: U.S. Census Bureau, Current Population Survey, 1947–2006.

1970s, the lines begin to diverge, a pattern that continues (with a slight pause in the late 1990s) up to the present. Much of the recent trend has been driven by the increasing share of income received by the very highest earning households (such as the top 5 percent, 1 percent, and even smaller proportions of the top 1 percent). Several readings highlight these historical patterns. In their breakthrough work on income trends, based on a detailed analysis of tax returns, economists Thomas Piketty and Emanual Saez show that growth in top incomes has ebbed and flowed over the course of the twentieth century, reaching new heights in the recent period. They found that the top one tenth of 1 percent (0.1 percent) of American households experienced a decline in their share of total income between 1929 and World War II from 8 percent to about 4 percent, as a result of the combined shocks of the Great Depression and the war on capital holdings. This relatively lower share of income received by the richest of the rich persisted until the late 1970s, when it began going up again; by 2000, it had reached nearly the same 8 percent level as seen in the late 1920s. Piketty and Saez's analysis shows a similar trajectory for the larger group of the top 1 percent of Americans (who by the end of the twentieth century were receiving around 20 percent of total national income).

Beyond the big question of why the very rich have gotten richer are a number of other questions: How much has the share of income going to all households changed? And in particular, how has inequality changed among important groups in American society? Three distinct historical periods can be identified. Before 1929, American society was very inegalitarian. In addition to the large share of income going to the very top, incomes for those households at the bottom were very low. Beginning in the 1930s—as a result of the Great Depression, the expansion of the public sector during the New Deal era, and the major increases in income taxes during World War II (when taxes on the wealthy were raised as high as 90 percent)—the shares of income received by the middle class, the working class, and the poor rose steadily through the early 1970s. The gains of economic growth in this era were not only widely shared but actually flowed downward in greater proportions to households below the top 20 percent. A number of factors combined to reinforce this shift. Changes in the South with industrialization, the decline of small farming, and the civil rights legislation that ended Jim Crow and brought African Americans into the economic mainstream were vitally important. Significantly stronger unions than in the period either before or since the 1945–75 period helped unionized and non-unionized workers alike win improved wages and benefits. These economic gains were spread widely enough to narrow the differentials between many important groups (although not all, as the gap between men and women did not shift during this period).

Beginning in the 1970s, however, this pattern of narrowing differentials between top and bottom began to reverse itself. Not only did the share of income going to the very top begin to increase, but also the shares received by the middle class and the poor began to decline. Both overall inequality grew, and the gaps between most groups widened. (Here again, however, gender proved a partial exception, as the gap between the earnings of men and women narrowed from the 1970s to the 1990s, especially among younger and better educated women and their male counterparts).

Income is one critical measure of economic inequality, but it is not the only one. Data on actual consumption patterns—what households are in fact able to buy—provide a different perspective on well-being. While the incomes received by middle-class families stagnated from the mid 1970s onward, changes in finance and the easy availability of credit made it possible for a long period of time for consumption to exceed earnings. Interestingly, this has also been true for poor families, although primarily because other family members or friends provide money or goods or because some income is unreported. Even very poor families are often able to acquire goods like telephones, televisions, and cars, items that at some point in the past were not in existence or available only to the rich. Still, the gap between the poor and the middle class in terms of consumption remains very large.

Wealth—by which we mean the net value of the assets owned by individuals or family—is another important indictor of long-term household resources. Trends in wealth inequality parallel those of income (rising, falling, and then rising again over the past one hundred years), although at any moment the gap in wealth between rich and poor is much larger than the gap in either income or consumption. The most commonly owned wealth asset is real estate. About 70 percent of Americans currently own the primary residence in which they live. Because homes tend to appreciate over time, home ownership has been one way that even modest-income households can accumulate wealth. A smaller subset of the population owns "net financial assets" (NFAs)—savings, investments, and other convertible assets less outstanding debts. Upper-class families possess vast NFAs, whereas most families possess little or no NFAs. Disparity in wealth is greatest in regard to NFAs, and the gap between the wealthiest households and everyone else has widened enormously over the past thirty years. Total wealth differences (housing assets plus NFAs) between individuals and groups are often far larger than income differences. For example, while the top 1 percent of households were receiving approximately 20 percent of the income in 2000, they owned more than 40 percent of all wealth.[4]

Although the importance of current income is fairly obvious—it is what provides us with resources to meet our daily needs and, if we are lucky, indulge in luxuries beyond our basic needs—the importance of wealth is a little more subtle. Wealth can be converted to income, but it is also a critical source of intergenerational inequality, as affluent parents can pass on to their children substantial resources that have no relationship to the children's own

---

4 Timothy Smeeding, "Poor People in Rich Nations: The United States in Comparative Perspective," *Journal of Economic Perspectives* 20 (2006):69–90.

accomplishments. Further, wealth can provide resources to invest in children's well-being or to cushion against unexpected bad luck, such as the loss of a job, ill health, or family member needing full-time care.

The final aspect of the question of who gets what that analysts of inequality have studied widely is how what one owns translates into opportunities (for individuals or their children). One of the more robust insights on the question of opportunity is what is widely known as the "Matthew effect," taken from the biblical gospel of Matthew, which holds loosely speaking that "he who has shall have more."[5] This idea is fairly straightforward for economic assets: rich individuals or families can invest their wealth in ways that produce more income, or give their children advantages and inheritances which give them a leg up in life. But following the lead of Pierre Bourdieu, sociologists have generalized the economic notion of capital to consider how individuals receive can acquire different kinds of social and cultural assets that, like economic capital, can be "invested" to seek hire returns in schools, employment situations, and in finding a desirable partner. Three kinds of non-economic capital have been seen as especially important: "cultural capital" (the kinds of cultural knowledge and linguistic competence an individual can deploy); "social capital" (who you know, the social networks that one can draw upon), and "symbolic capital" (the kinds of prestige and authority an individual possesses).

Because families are important transmission belts of *both* economic *and* non-economic capital, sociologists have long been interested in how opportunities are transmitted from one generation to the next, or more precisely, how social origins (as represented by one's family position) are related to destinations (where one ends up in the stratification system). The degree of "openness" in a social system is sometimes viewed as a critical measure of societal fairness: in a society where someone from a disadvantaged background has a decent chance of attaining positions of power or influence, social inequality does not lock-in disadvantage. On the other hand, if social background (and the kinds of economic and non-economic capital passed from parents to children) is so powerful that we can predict destinations from origins with a very degree of reliability, than the embedded power of inequality is very high indeed. The study of opportunity across generations, or *social mobility*, has thus occupied a great deal of attention, and controversy, in the study of inequality.

---

5 "For unto every one that hath shall be given, and he shall have abundance: but from him that hath not shall be taken away even that which he hath." Matthew 25:29, King James Version.

While the question of who gets what relates primarily to income and wealth for consumption (and the implications and future opportunities), the question of who does what focuses our attention on a different set of problems. The fundamental distinction is between compensated work (such as paid employment in a job) and uncompensated labor (such as housework and caring work). Feminist sociologists long ago established that the narrow focus on the world of paid work—so characteristic of social science research in the first half of the twentieth century—ignored an important second dimension of the question of who does what. We labor in our jobs, but also in our households. There continues to be a large disparity in the division of labor on the "second shift" between men and women in terms of child care, elder care, cooking, routine housework, and other household chores. These differences are themselves a powerful source of gender-based inequality. But they also generate a set of side consequences that bear on inequalities in the world of work, by making it more difficult for women with additional responsibilities to compete with men who do not.

Within the world of paid work itself, one important question is how are different jobs structured? What makes a "good" versus a "bad" job? A critical variable is the level of autonomy and discretion in occupations. In high-trust occupations, such as in professions and in management positions, incumbents work without much supervision and are trusted with important responsibilities and company secrets. They are generally able to control the pace of their work effort and even their work hours. To be sure, however, individuals in these occupations may work long hours, but they do so without the same kinds of scrutiny of other occupational locations. In the professions, in particular, *knowledge* can serve as a basis of power, one in which professionals can dominate their clients. Professionals are able to secure market advantages and obtain relatively high salaries.

By contrast, in low-trust occupations, continual monitoring of effort and lack of autonomy are defining features of the daily grind. The working day is highly regulated by the clock, and tasks and the pace of work is controlled by supervisors. The classical distinction between blue-collar and white-collar work captures some of this distinction, although changes in the occupational structure over the past hundred years have given rise to many forms of "routine" white-collar jobs with low discretion and trust.

Poverty and Inequality

Finally, we need to think about the linkages between poverty and inequality. Although inequality has risen, rates of poverty have not increased in most countries, including the United States. At one level, this is paradoxical: if the rich are getting richer, the poor surely must be getting poorer? Actually, however, the data suggest something slightly different: the incomes of poor households have held steady in (real) dollars, even as their *share* of national income has declined. The proportion of families and individuals living in poverty has fluctuated, depending especially on the health of the economy, but has not systematically increased. Nevertheless, there were still some 36.5 million people in America in 2007 living below the official (government) poverty line (12.3 percent of the population). This estimate of the size of the poverty population is based on a government measure, first devised in the mid 1960s, that most poverty researchers believe understates its real size. Poverty, in short, remains a critical problem in American society.

Poverty is important to inequality as a whole in a number of ways. First off, because living in poverty harms adults and children in many ways, it is an intrinsically important problem to study. Indeed, an industry of social science research has been devoted to dissecting the "poverty problem." But poverty is also linked to other types of inequality. The existence of a large poor population benefits middle- and upper-class individuals and families by providing the servants, maids, gardeners, cooks, and child-care and elder-care workers that have removed much of the drudgery of daily life. Without poor people to fill those jobs at low wages (or a government sector to provide it), middle-class families in particular would have very different lives. A large poor population also constrains wages for other workers who are just above the poverty line, by providing the foundation for a large "reserve army" of unemployed or underemployed people. In all of these ways, the link from poverty to inequality is important to study.

||| GROUP-BASED INEQUALITIES

Part III of the book contains a wide range of research on how the stratification system in the United States today is organized, in part on the basis of categories arising out of group memberships. The most important of these groups are those based on race, ethnicity, gender, and class. Group membership can be a critical source of advantage or disadvantage. Being a member of a high-status group eases access to opportunities, whereas membership in lower-status groups confers important disadvantages. These are not mere accidents, but rather the result of organized social and political arrangements that reinforce the importance of categorical inequalities.

There are several ways in which the social sources of group inequality have been theorized. Subjective approaches emphasize the importance of stereotypes arising from more general prejudices that people have about members of other groups. We are routinely bombarded with media images and ideas that reinforce the idea that racial minorities are different from whites—for example, they are likely to be portrayed as poorer or more criminal than they really are. The stereotyping of women as more suited for jobs in the caring sector than men is another example. Other models of the sources of such attitudes see them as rooted in competition: in those contexts in which groups are of sufficient size to compete with one another for opportunities, there are incentives for more powerful groups to respond to the threat posed by weaker groups by stereotyping them and then using those stereotypes to create formal or informal barriers to advancement or integration. In these competitive environments, such as when there are not enough good jobs for all who want one, a dominant group has incentives to promote such images.

But merely having negative images of a group is not, by itself, sufficient to create an unequal playing field. Max Weber's notion of social closure proves especially useful as a way of understanding how conflicts between dominant and subordinate groups come to be manifest in the social structure. *Closure* is the idea that organized groups will seek to create special opportunities for themselves and restrict opportunities for others. There are both formal and informal systems of social closure. Formal systems include legal barriers to entry (such as when a profession gains a legal monopoly over certain kinds of services), or explicit rules limiting the opportunities of subordinate groups (such as laws limiting women's inheritance of property, or universities adopting explicit rules about the admission of minority students). Today, however, most of these formal barriers on the basis of characteristics of individuals or groups have been abolished. We live in an era in which the ideal of meritocracy—that the best person, regardless of any personal characteristics, should be able to secure jobs or admission to education or other desired opportunities—has become dominant. But informal systems of closure, involving less explicit but nonetheless powerful forms of discrimination continue to operate. One important example can be seen in the ways in which large corporations formally open their doors to hire women and minorities but maintain systems of promotion and evaluation in a manner that disadvantages these groups. While there are many lower-level women and minorities working at large companies today, few have risen into positions of top management (which largely remains the preserve of white men). It would take quite a leap of faith to believe that merit is the primary reason this pattern persists.

With the election of Barack Obama as President of the United States in 2008, the most important executive post in the country is now held by a minority. Yet women and minorities continue to be significantly under-represented in the ranks of top management. Why? This question has been widely studied and debated. The dominant hypothesis remains that of discrimination (overt or subtle). But other ideas have been advanced also. One line of research suggests that even when minorities are able to gain access to desired positions, they often face particular hurdles to overcome to advance further. They may find it more difficult to find mentors or associates who will pull them up through the ranks. When they stand out because of their small numbers (in contrast to their peers who are members of the dominant group), they may be subject to greater scrutiny. Small mistakes that might have gone unnoticed if committed by white men are magnified in importance. The pressure to perform, and be consistently excellent, makes the work situation different (and potentially more demanding) for members of minority groups. Further, because they also may not share the same kinds of background experiences and participate in the same activities as their white or male colleagues, simple misunderstandings or difficulties in communicating are more common. And finally, career ladders continue to be structured around older notions of work–family life. For women who have children, even short disruptions in their careers can have crippling long-term consequences.

Class Analysis

Group-based processes of exclusion and discrimination provide one major source of enduring inequality, while class-based inequalities arising out of the operation of the market provides another. Marx's concept of class holds that under any mode of production two classes (one dominant, one subordinate) constitute the primary source of division. Under capitalism, Marx argued that the distinction between owners and workers had primary importance. It has long been clear, however, that only a much broader notion of class can provide a meaningful description of contemporary capitalist societies. Various middle-class groupings—managers and professionals, the self-employed—are not usefully lumped together with factory workers or the baristas at a national coffee chain.

But to ask the question, What is "middle" about the middle class? is to raise a whole host of problems for developing a "class analysis" of contemporary societies. There is no clear agreement on all of these problems, but the influential (and competing) models of neo-Marxist sociologist Erik Olin Wright and neo-Weberian sociologists Robert Erikson and John Goldthorpe—the two leading variants in the literature today—converge on a number of critical points.[6] Both Wright and Erikson/Goldthorpe treat class as rooted in income-generating labor market activities. In other words, work situation, rather than education level or income, is the defining characteristic of what we should mean by class. Each schema divides the working population into a number of classes—twelve according to Wright, and three, seven, or eleven in the collapsed or expanded versions of Erikson and Goldthorpe. One important distinction is between those individuals who own their own businesses, or are self-employed, and those who work for someone else. Among the employed, both analysts draw distinctions between those who have a type of expertise or skill that gives them some sort of market sinecure and those who do not and between those whose jobs entail supervising others or require employer trust from those that do not.

To be sure, some of these assets are worth more than others, and they can be combined in ways that reinforce their value. So the lawyer (with high skill/credential assets) who also owns her own law firm (or is a senior partner in a firm) that employs others to work under her is likely to command a far higher income than the lawyer working beneath other lawyers and supervisors (such as in a district attorney's office or as an associate in a law firm). Such complexities make the development of a precise and rigorous map of the class structure—with each individual placed in one and only one class location—difficult.

Both Wright's and Erikson and Goldthorpe's theories of class are deeply structural in the sense that they identify class locations by reference to types of assets and employment situation rather than to actual behavior. Classes, in other words, exist whether or not they ever engage in any sort of collective action to defend or promote their common interests. But in the classical notion of class, class is not simply a "thing" that exists on paper but—at least in certain crucial historical situations—is capable of acting as a group (or what Marx called "class struggle"). Great historical examples have included the struggle to extend the right to vote to nonpropertied workers and the movement to build unions and social democratic or labor parties. Such moments of independent collective action on the basis of classwide interests have, however, eroded significantly since World War II, rarely appearing beyond particular local situations or grievances or occasional (and often symbolic) large-scale demonstrations.

---

6 See Erik Olin Wright, *Class Counts* (New York: Cambridge University Press, 1997); Robert Erikson and John Goldthorpe, *Constant Flux* (Oxford: Clarendon Press, 1992), Chapter 2.

Some Peculiarities of Race and Gender Inequality in America

The classical theories of stratification have their clearest application in the case of class analysis. Indeed, following from Marx, many of the classical analysts of stratification were concerned first and foremost with problems of class inequality. But group conflicts on the basis of race/ethnicity and gender have some distinctive properties as well, and these must be part of any such discussion. Here are a few examples. The study of occupational segregation—the job ghettos where members of disadvantaged groups are far more likely employed—has been a staple of research on how labor markets work and disadvantage perpetuated. There are many examples. Many jobs remain typed as "male" or "female," with the latter paying lower wages relative to the skill and education levels of the job. Further, even where inroads have been made in desegregating entry into desirable jobs, gender "nitches" favoring men often persist. Forty years since the beginning of the modern women's movement, only twelve of the *Fortune* 500 companies (the biggest companies in America) are led by women (as of 2008).

Race and gender inequalities have been changing in some very important ways in recent decades. The rise of the civil rights movement in the 1950s and 1960s helped spur the creation of civil rights legislation and affirmative action policies that aided both racial minorities and women, and the women's movement spurred further change. In education the impact has been especially large. The entrance of minorities and women into professional fields once dominated by white men has been a startling change over the past forty years. To take one example, before 1970, the percentage of women entering ABA-approved law schools was less than 5 percent; by 2004, 48 percent of entering law students were women. Similar growth in the proportion of women in a wide range of professional and managerial fields—and to a less extent racial and ethnic minorities—can be found. But progress has, in some respects, slowed in recent years. For example, the black–white income gap, after narrowing significantly between the 1960s and the early 1980s, has remained quite stubbornly large since there. The gender gap in earnings has similarly stalled, although among younger men and women it has continued to decline.

Immigration

Rates of immigration are rising all over the world, and in most places debates over immigrants and their place in the stratification system of their new country is both sociologically important and politically contentious. This is no less true in the United States. Two critical questions are often debated. First, to what extent do immigrants displace American workers, or more generally does the presence of a growing pool of immigrant workers depress wages? Economists have divided on this question, although even studies finding the biggest effects offer estimates of wage loss to American workers as very modest (around 5 percent or less). Second, to what extent is rising immigration changing the social and political mix of poor populations? Because immigrants cannot vote until they obtain citizenship, the lack of political voice of a growing segment of the poor and working class is becoming increasingly important. This frequently neglected question has begun to be of concern, especially in many urban communities where immigrant populations are concentrated.

Immigration also plays a critical role in the maintenance (or even growth) of inequality in a couple of ways. First, immigrants provide a large low-wage labor pool. Although some immigrants are software engineers or physicists, in recent decades the vast bulk have come to the United States with skills or credentials that do not easily translate into middle-class jobs, and thus must instead settle for jobs at the bottom of the labor market. Much of the work in the agricultural sector, for example, is performed by immigrant labor. Americans enjoy one of the richest and most varied diets in the world (perhaps too rich, if rising rates of obesity are any indication). This would not be possible without a large immigrant labor force. Second, the growth of a luxury economy is fueled by immigrants who perform tasks such as child care, house cleaning, gardening, and food preparation and service. American households are far more likely today to have someone clean their houses for them, have their children in child care, or eat out regularly than they did a generation ago. This rising luxury consumption, which is reaching increasingly far down the income ladder, is again being fueled by immigrant labor.

Issues surrounding immigration are especially heated in the United States right now, as they are in many other rich countries. The controversies repeat an earlier historical pattern. Although we are virtually all immigrants or the children of immigrants (most by choice; descendants of slaves not), the historical pattern suggests that we become less welcoming once the size of the immigrant population grows large enough to pose an economic threat to native-born citizens. Just as nativist sentiment produced sharp political tensions after Word War I, so too are we entering a period in which contention over immigration is growing. However the current political contest plays itself out, there can be little question of the larger significance of immigration for the system of inequality.

‖ POLITICAL INEQUALITY AND PUBLIC POLICY

The political institutions of any society can both generate inequality or provide a source of its amelioration. Earlier I noted the important paradox that single parents with low education levels are much more likely to head a family living below the poverty line in the United States than in other rich countries. Why? Because other countries have a more generous and comprehensive welfare state than in the United States. We make political choices that produce such outcomes. The political system is very much part of the stratification system.

One way governments affect inequality is by taxing the rich more extensively than the middle class and the poor. Another is by operating a complex of programs known collectively as the welfare state. The welfare state includes those institutions that provide income transfers on the basis of either a social insurance model (such as Social Security) or means-tested benefits (such as food stamps or welfare). It also provides services such as health care (such as Medicare and Medicaid) and those designed to support low-wage workers (publicly subsidized child care, health insurance, job training and placement programs). A consistent body of evidence demonstrates that more generous welfare states reduce poverty and inequality, smooth out income fluctuations, reduce old-age poverty, and equalize health outcomes. In many postindustrial capitalist countries, market-based inequalities are growing sharply, but are reduced by welfare state interventions.

There are a number of ways in which the United States is unique, even among the liberal democratic countries most similar to the United States (e.g., Canada, Australia, and Britain). The tax system and welfare state institutions in America do less to reduce poverty and inequality than in any other rich country. We can see this in Figure 2.[7] The figure shows two sets of data. The top bar for each country estimates percent of the population that would live in poverty if there were no government programs. The bottom bar takes into account all taxes, income transfers, and services provided by the government in question. Whereas pregovernment levels of inequality are high in

---

7 Figure 2 is based on an analysis of household-level income data matched with data on government spending conducted by the Luxumburg Income Study (LIS), as reported in U.S. Department of Labor, www.dol.gov/esa/whd/flsa. The data reported here are from 2000 but similar results would be found for more recent years.

FIGURE 2 **PERCENTAGE OF POOR CHILDREN BEFORE AND AFTER GOVERNMENT**

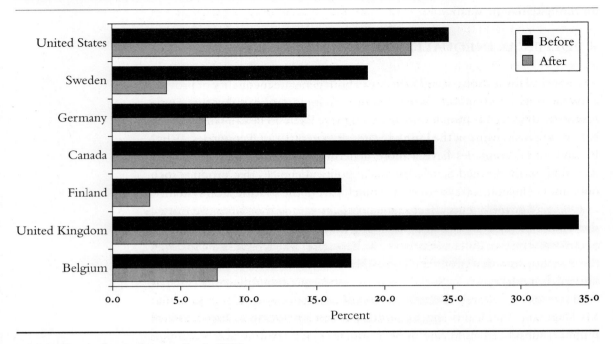

SOURCE: Luxumbourg Income Study, 2000.

most countries, once government programs are factored in the poverty rate falls dramatically. However, this is much less true in the United states. Here the welfare state fails to compensate for most of the inequalities and poverty produced by the market. The two bars are not very different. We have the highest rate of poverty among the rich democracies, not so much because of market forces (although these are a factor), but because public policy does less to reduce poverty than anywhere else.

The American welfare state stands out in the rich democracies for its low levels of public spending; the United States currently devotes about 14 percent of its gross domestic product (GDP) on social spending programs, versus an average of 26.5 percent in western European welfare states, and 18 percent in other Anglo-American democracies. To put these figures in perspective note that a 1 percent increase in the proportion of the GDP devoted to social programs translates to about $130 billion in new social spending (enough, for example, to provide adequate health insurance for everyone). We could point to many other examples of how U.S. public policy reinforces inequality: repeated tax cuts that disproportionately benefit the super-rich at a time when high-income households are already absorbing unprecedented shares of national income and the pointed refusal of Congress and the White House to adjust the federal minimum wage during the decade after 1997, leading to a 20 percent decline in real value (minimum wage declined overall by some 36 percent in real value between 1979 and 2006).[8]

What might account for these outcomes? Why is the United States a welfare state laggard, in spite of having among the highest per capita income in the world? Although political inequalities are present in all democratic societies, the American political system stands out as unique in the extent to which it enables some voices to be heard more readily than others. No other rich democratic country allows as much money into the political system, and the rate of increase in the flow of money in recent years has been shockingly high. No other rich democracy has as low a rate of voter participation as the United States or such large disparities in participation rates by income and class. And few other democratic countries have as decentralized a political system as the United States, giving powerful actors multiple opportunities to veto redistributive legislation they do not like. And finally, American citizens stand out in comparison to those of other countries in being reluctant to support social programs for the poor, as studies of public opinion have demonstrated. Each of these factors requires some attention.

Participatory Inequalities

Large, persisting disparities in participation among citizens eligible, both in elections and in many other types of political activities, is a hallmark of American politics. These disparities represent an important source of political inequality in their own right, but also have important consequences for government policy. Writing in 1949, V. O. Key asserted, "The blunt truth is that politicians are under no compulsion to pay much heed to classes and groups of citizens that do not vote."[9] In democracies in which almost everyone votes there are fewer group differences. The United States, by contrast, has skewed rates of political participation. Well-resourced groups (for example, professionals or whites) will turn out at a 25 to 30 percent higher rate than will a low-resourced group (such as unskilled workers or Hispanics).

---

8 See U.S. Department of Labor, Compliance Assistance—Fair Labor Standards Act (FLSA), www.dol.gov/esa/whd/flsa (accessed April 2008).

9 V. O. Key, *Southern Politics in State and Nation* (New York: Knopf, 1949). p. 527.

Why does the United States have such high rates of group disparity in turn out? In the social science literature on who votes, there are two broad streams of explanation: individual-level explanations (such as education level, race/ ethnicity, class, religion, community, and knowledge/interest in politics), and political and institutional explanations. Sociodemographic attributes of individuals such as education are powerful individual-level predictors, but they cannot account for the relatively low rate of voter turnout in the United States because such factors are present in all societies (and indeed the American population as a whole had far less education in the late nineteenth century than today, but turnout rates were far higher). Political and institutional explanations, by contrast, point to the role of mobilizing activities by parties and political organizations and election rules, such as voter registration requirements, holding national elections on a working day. There is much more variation across countries, and such factors provide a more useful understanding of the puzzle of the low voting rate in American politics.

The problem of unequal participation extends beyond voting to other types of political engagement. Research on *all* forms of political participation— including working on a political campaign, participating in a protest event, writing a letter to an elected official, civic volunteerism of any kind—finds large inequalities between resource-rich groups and disadvantaged groups. The definitive study in this area remains that of Sidney Verba, Kay Lehman Scholzman, and Henry Brady, who found evidence of larger disparities in most other types of political activity than in voting. For example, although 17 percent of individuals earning over $75,000 a year in 1989 reported working on a political campaign, only 4 percent of those earning under $15,000 did so. About 73 percent of the former reported being a member of a political organization, but only 29 percent of the latter did so. And 50 percent of the affluent group had written to an elected official at least once in the previous year, but only 25 percent of the low-income group had done so.[10]

The Party System

The institutional arrangements that shape and define the party system in the United States provide another key source of political inequality. The electoral rules established by the U.S. Constitution makes it essentially impossible for third parties to become viable. This key fact can largely be attributed to a single feature of the American constitutional order: a "first-past-the-post" electoral

---

10 Sidney Verba, Kay Lehman Scholzman, and Henry Brady, *Voice and Equality* (Cambridge, MA: Harvard University Press, 1995).

system in which the candidate (and party) winning the most votes in a single district wins the seat. This "majoritarian" system has proved remarkably durable in enforcing major party hegemony. The reasons are not hard to fathom. While the proportional representation systems found in most European democracies allow minority parties to gain representation in legislative bodies, in the United States only the candidate/party winning the most votes in legislative districts wins the seat. A new party seeking to build support cannot do so gradually by electing a few representatives and building a national reputation.

The two-party system had first become firmly established by 1840, with the Democratic Party and the Whig Party being dominant. There has been only one successful example of a third party entering the political system and displacing one of the dominant parties since then—the Republican Party breakthrough in the 1850s and 1860 (when Abraham Lincoln won the presidency on a Republican ticket), as the country fell into the crisis leading up to the Civil War. Since that time, American political history is littered with failed third-party efforts, even though many were launched by serious people with, in some cases, significant resources.[11]

The stranglehold of the two-party system since the Civil War prevented a politically viable social democratic or labor party explicitly concerned with egalitarian outcomes from emerging. In this, the United States is unlike all other rich democratic countries. In fact, the now vast "American exceptionalism" literature first emerged as an effort to explain the failure of a socialist party to develop in the United States. The existence of a strong left party is important for two reasons. First, research on comparative politics consistently finds that strong left parties facilitate more generous welfare states. The path to welfare state generosity through party strength is twofold: when left parties control governments they can redirect taxing and spending policies toward redistributive outcomes; but even when out of government, strong left parties provide important electoral competition that can push centrist and conservative parties toward greater generosity.

Powerful left parties are also important for shaping public opinion and for keeping issues relating to poverty and inequality on the policy agenda. Parties do more than just seek votes; they also organize voters and political ideologies

---

11 The most important of these party efforts were those of the Populists at the end of the nineteenth century, the Socialist and Communist parties in the first half of the twentieth century, the midwestern Progressive and Farmer-Labor parties in the 1930s, and in the recent era of increased third-party activism a plethora of efforts by Libertarians, Ross Perot's Reform Party, the Greens, and others. For an overview, see Micah L. Sifry, *Spoiling for a Fight: Third Party Politics in America* (New York: Routledge, 2002).

in a coherent spectrum, providing citizens with information that reminds them of egalitarian ideas and values, as the extensive literature on the cognitive bases of political beliefs suggests. When the party system includes strong left parties, political debates in the media are much more likely to include pro-equality viewpoints, and media coverage of groups and individuals making egalitarian arguments grows.

In the United States, however, such views are only more haphazardly present in ordinary political debate. The narrowness of the party system does not mean that egalitarian political ideas have always been absent from American politics. At times since the 1890s, and in certain parts of the country, the Democratic Party has operated as a kind of social democratic party, with organized labor and liberal groups having varying degrees of influence inside the party. But the Democratic Party has also, throughout its history, been strongly influenced by its strong southern wing, following the Civil War and the identification of the Republican Party with the cause of racial equality. The southern Democrats were deeply hostile to any policies challenging the Jim Crow system, which greatly narrowed the range of acceptable possibilities for egalitarian public policies even in those eras, such as the 1930s and 1960s, when momentum for equality peaked.

Political Money

Another source of political inequality is the unique role of money in the financing of American politics. Dramatic increases in the availability of money in the American political system in recent decades have often prompted concern among observers of American politics and sometimes among the very politicians living inside the money system. Rising inequality and strong income growth at the top have given the rich more resources to "invest" in politics, and they have. The basic facts are startling enough. Campaign finance data (Figure 3) suggests that since 1978, there has been a nearly 10-fold increase in real dollars contributed by business interests to candidates for American national elections as well as a steady and seemingly inexorable growth in contributions from affluent individuals. One would be hard-pressed to imagine that contributors give large amounts and get nothing in return, although specifying those impacts has proved tricky for researchers.

Where does this extraordinary flow of political money come from? The reporting of campaign contributions is now quite systematic, so we can develop a basic survey. Contributions come from individual donors or from political action committees (PACs) organized by a wide range of individual

FIGURE 3 **TRENDS IN NATIONAL ELECTION CAMPAIGN FINANCE, 1978–2006**

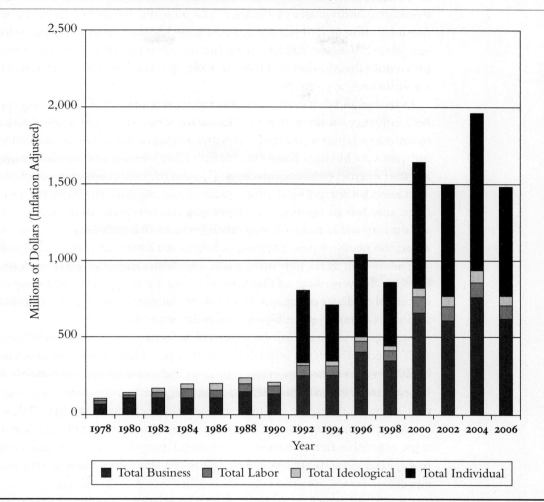

SOURCE: Author's Compilation, Federal Election Commission Reports (www.fec.gov) and Center for Responsive Politics (www.opensecrets.org). Individual contribution data available for 1992 on.

businesses, business associations, unions, and professional associations, as well as ideological groups such as the National Rifle Association (NRA) and Emily's List (a PAC that supports women candidates for office). PAC contributions can be reasonably divided into three broad categories: business related, labor, and ideological (with the latter running the gamut from far left to far right). In addition to money given by organized PACs, individuals account for a large proportion of total donations, the vast majority of which are made by affluent individuals or families.[12] Combining the rising amounts being given by affluent individuals with the growing disparities between business and labor PACs, we find that from the standpoint of who gives there can be little doubt that the signals imparted to elected officials overwhelmingly favor the affluent.

How and in what ways does political money matter? Theories of "investor" influence on the parties and legislation have, as I noted, proved difficult to definitively test and prove. It is not often that there is hard evidence of outright vote buying. The primary effect of money can be thought of as shaping four distinct political outcomes: (1) who runs for political office (making a serious run for political office increasingly requires the capacity to raise huge amounts of money), (2) who wins (underfunded challengers face an almost impossible task), (3) the voting patterns of legislators (who may think about the needs of past, present, or hoped-for future donors), and (4) other outcomes such as facilitating access to legislators through the interest group process. At every stage of this process, there are compelling arguments and empirical evidence to suggest money skews outcomes; but equally important, in no area is money plausibly viewed as the single decisive factor.

Stronger arguments can be mounted for more subtle forms of influence, such as access to elected officials that money provides. Donors are much more likely to receive the opportunity to press their case to elected officials they have donated to than those who do not give. Such access may shape legislation at the margins, for example through the creation of special hidden tax breaks or exemptions inserted into legislation that can, in the aggregate, be quite expensive and deleterious to the overall purpose of a bill. Access ensures that special interests are listened to. But access alone does not drive the policy agenda.

Of perhaps equal or greater concern in relation to political money is its impact on agenda-setting organizations. Increasingly centralized corporate

---

12 For example, in 2002, the Center for Responsive Politics was able to categorize about 70 percent of such donations for the 2000 election cycle, finding that individuals associated with business interests contributed a total of $533.7 million to election campaigns, compared with less than $1 million contributed by individuals associated with organized labor. Survey data on individual-level giving to political campaigns are consistent with this finding; patterns of significant giving are heavily skewed toward individuals from affluent households. For example, Verba et al. found that 56 percent of households with incomes over $125,000 in 1989 donated to a political campaign (the average amount of all donations was $1,183), but just 6 percent of households with incomes below $15,000 did so (the average donation was $86). See Verba, Scholzman, and Brady, *Voice and Equality*, pp. 191–196.

control over the media and the decline of independent media weakens advocacy of progressive causes such as calls for more equality. The remarkable growth in the resources flowing into conservative think tanks and foundations is perhaps even more important. Starting in the 1970s, business organizations and conservative foundations began providing resources on a heretofore unprecedented scale in support of policy formation organizations inside the Beltway. The growing capacity of these policy organizations to intervene in political debates, get their representatives into the media, and provide policy advice to presidents and Congress is well established. By all accounts, such organizations play a significant role in setting the policy agenda. To the extent that the policy organizations with the greatest resources are disproportionately promoting a conservative policy agenda—as numerous studies have found—they contribute to a larger environment in which many egalitarian policy ideas are simply not on the agenda for discussion.[13]

||| GLOBAL INEQUALITIES

The system of inequality in the United States, as in other countries, is heavily influenced by being situated in a global economy in which high levels of poverty and inequality are found. In Part V, several key aspects of the global system of inequality are examined. One of the most important widely discussed subjects in recent years is how the changing patterns of the global economy are influencing inequality in different countries, as well as the distribution of wealth between countries. Three changes in recent decades define the current era of rising globalization. First, there has been a steady increase in "flows" across borders: more trade between countries, higher rates of migration across borders (rising rates of immigration into the United States mirror the pattern found in many other rich countries), and—perhaps most important—capital for investment that is increasingly unconstrained by national borders. Many firms have found it profitable to relocate their operations from higher-wage wealthy countries to places in which they can find workers at a fraction of the cost. Truly multinational corporations, with operations in numerous countries, increasingly populate the peaks of the modern world economy. Workers travel across borders in growing numbers in pursuit

---

13 The absence of competing and similarly endowed policy organizations promoting progressive ideas has remained something of a mystery. Foundations supporting programs aimed at helping the poor and progressive civic activism have resources that far exceed that of conservative foundations supporting right-wing think tanks and policy organizations. But these organizations have not invested in ideas to nearly the same degree as the leading conservative foundations.

of economic opportunities. The global financial sector has become interconnected such that when something significant happens in the financial market of one country it will influence developments in many other parts of the world.

Second, alongside increased flows of trade, capital, and people have been changes in the hierarchy of countries across the globe (and the corresponding incomes and wealth of citizens in those countries). Some countries—especially countries in Southeast Asia like South Korea, Taiwan, Singapore, and more recently Brazil, Russia, China, and India—have and/or are expecting booming economic growth. Other countries, including most countries in Africa, have stagnated or even seen economic declines. Because the two largest countries in the world—China and India, with nearly one third of the world's population—are getting richer, as evidenced by rising household incomes and increasingly powerful domestic and global companies, overall global inequality has declined in recent decades. But the pattern of change has been uneven.

Third, the global economy has often been seen as a source of internal social and economic change, contributing to rising *intra*-country inequality in recent years. In this sense, the seemingly rosy picture of declining *between*-country inequality risks masking other inequality-producing aspects of globalization. The United States is far from alone in experiencing rising domestic inequality. The global economy has produced a class of global entrepreneurs who manage business or financial empires across borders, and receive extremely high levels of compensation to do so. It encourages companies to shift higher-wage manufacturing jobs to parts of the world in which wages are low. It creates opportunities for some but disadvantages for many others. The overall impact of globalization on intra-country inequalities is complicated, interacting in ways that make assessment difficult.

Finally, the rise of an increasingly global economy is often thought to threaten the autonomy of national governments. The idea is that if the government in a country like Germany or the United States were to raise taxes too high, let government budget deficits get too big, or provide overly generous government benefits for individuals, increasingly mobile international companies would be reluctant to maintain their investments in the German or American economy. Such a scenario would put powerful pressures on the government to conform to a lower-tax, lower-spending preference for companies seeking good investment returns.

This theory has, however, only partially borne out by developments over the last twenty years. Three outcomes appear consistent with the globalization thesis. Unemployment levels are on average higher in the last twenty years than they were in the twenty years before that. Unions—the backbone of the social forces that helped create the welfare state in the first place—are in decline, frequently sharp decline, in almost all countries. And there has been a movement toward more "workfare" and service spending in the mix of programs supported by welfare states rather than cash grants (or "welfare") programs. But the evidence that globalization undermines the capacity of governments to maintain generous welfare states has not yet occurred. Over- all welfare state spending has not retrenched; while there is some evidence of year-to-year fluctuation in spending (depending on the rate of such factors as unemployment), the overall trend is clear: with but a couple of exceptions, countries have maintained generous levels of welfare state spending, even in the face of globalization.

‖| DOES INEQUALITY MATTER?

The final section of the book is devoted to explorations of questions about how and why inequality matters. There are a variety of ways in which we might think about whether, or to what extent inequality matters. The high levels of inequality in the United States, compared to other rich democratic countries, means that the poor have fewer resources to acquire needed goods and services than they would in more egalitarian countries (and in the United States, the rich have vastly more to spend than the rich in other countries). This is a vitally important fact in its own right. The further down the income distribution, the more difficult it becomes for families to meet basic needs.

Another important consequence has been that economic prosperity has not been shared. While all Americans benefited in economic growth between the end of World War II and the early 1970s, that pattern has not held more recently. The very highest earning households have absorbed the bulk of the income being generated, whereas the college-educated population has seen more modest gains, and everyone else has largely stagnated.

But beyond the consequences of rising inequality for household well-being and shared prosperity, what else can be said? A few issues are worth paying attention to. One is political. Rising wealth at the top makes it easier for afflu- ent individuals to "invest" in the political system, and the interests and con- cerns of the rich are unlikely to be those of the rest of the population.

Inequality of income and wealth may be linked to a variety of other kinds of outcomes that raise concerns. Rich families can purchase better education and intellectual enrichment for their children than poor families, raising the possibility that meritocracy may be undermined by unequal inputs into the training and development of children. Medical care appears at least in part to be more unevenly distributed in inegalitarian societies; the rich receive more than their pro-rata share of health care, and hospitals and other medical facilities may be oriented more toward the needs and interests of their (more profitable) affluent clients. Rising inequality tends to create pockets of concentrated poverty, where survival may depend on the acquisition of a capacity for "street smarts" and even violence which is frowned upon in middle-class settings.

Another consequence of inequality is its consequences for happiness and satisfaction. To the extent that people look up to those who have more than they do, they never feel completely satisfied with the possessions they do own. Most Americans want bigger houses, faster cars, fancier jewelry, and so forth. One important consequence of this for many American families has been a willingness to take on high levels of debt to try to attain such lifestyles. The size of the debt burden carried by American families was one factor in the financial crisis that began in the fall of 2008. "Luxury fever," as the economist Robert Frank calls it, also affects subjective well-being—we are never fully satisfied with what we have. Even though America has higher average incomes than virtually all other countries in the world, we are no happier as a consequence. International surveys show that Americans are not as satisfied as would be expected based on average income levels.

||| CONCLUDING THOUGHTS

As students of inequality, we want to try to understand the vast and multifaceted ways in which inequalities have developed and how they operate to create a system of stratification. The organizing approach of this book is to highlight not just the brute facts of inequality between individuals and groups, and how these are changing in the current era of rising inequality, but also to situate these facts in historical and political context. Looking around the world, we find strong vibrant economies in societies with widely differing levels of inequality. More egalitarian countries, like many of those in Western Europe, manage to provide both high average incomes and at the same time, low rates of poverty. These outcomes are the result of conscious policy choices. It is not so much that America has higher rates of poverty and inequality because of the structure of its economy—although that is one factor—but also because, relative to our peer nations, we have political institutions and public policies that foster, rather than blunt, the forces of inequality.

It is for this reason that our approach in this book is to highlight the role of politics, and a political analysis of inequality, alongside the questions that social scientists more typically ask about stratification systems. This does not mean that classical approaches can be neglected. Indeed, we start by examining classic theories of inequality because these theoretical ideas provide an important point of departure for contemporary understandings.

At the same time, however, much intellectual progress has also been made in the past half century, as indeed we would expect. The classics of the field focused heavily on class inequality but often treated capitalism as an undifferentiated economic system. More recently, however, it has become clear that there is wide variation across time and space in how different types of capitalisms produce different kinds of stratification systems. Much attention has been focused on questions of class inequality and on rising levels of inequality and wealth in an effort to chart the sources of the changes that underpin these phenomena. We have developed much better and more sensitive tools for measuring economic inequality and broader theories for understanding how economic inequalities manifest themselves in other ways.

If there is one overriding conclusion that this survey into the state of inequality and the stratification system in America leads us to, it is that nothing is set in stone. There have been striking changes in the types of inequalities found around the world and in the United States over the past 150 years. A similar pattern can be expected to continue into the future. Indeed, the financial crisis that began in the fall of 2008 may well lead to significant changes in stratification systems in the United States and across the globe in the near future. Although the study of the sources and consequences of inequalities cannot by itself resolve the normative and philosophical questions of how much inequality is desirable or justifiable, it does provide a critical basis for thinking about some of the most pressing social questions of our age.

PART I

CLASSICAL WORKS ON
SOCIAL STRATIFICATION
AND INEQUALITY

INTRODUCTION TO PART I

Classical theories of inequality can be traced to the beginnings of the modern political economy. In the period between 1750 and 1950, the foundations for contemporary scholarship were laid. In this part of the book, we present some of the most important of these classical treatments. We start with selections from the famous work of Adam Smith (1723–1790), *The Wealth of Nations*, first published in 1776. Smith is celebrated today for his contribution to the origins of the discipline of economics and his early advocacy and popularization of free markets, free trade, and limited government at a time when such ideas were in their infancy. Smith was a more complicated thinker than he is typically given credit for (his first book, for example, was a study of the origins of human morality). It is striking that *The Wealth of Nations* opens with a discussion of the foundations of the emerging economic order (industrial capitalism) by introducing the idea of division of labor as its key innovation. In the chapters reprinted here, Smith argues that human productivity rises immensely when it is organized on a basis of specialized tasks. The division of labor arises out of a natural human propensity to "truck, barter, and exchange," which impels us to strive continually to produce more for exchange. In a later section of *The Wealth of Nations*, however, Smith acknowledges that the growth of division of labor reduces the cognitive challenges of work and thus has the potential to make workers "stupid and ignorant."

Smith's work on the division of labor was also important because of its influence on Karl Marx's (1818–1883) analysis of the sources and consequences of class divisions in capitalist and other societies. While for Smith the hallmark of the division of labor allows for a vast increase in wealth and productivity, Marx developed a radically different conception of the meaning of the division of labor and the impact of the rise of market capitalism. Marx's concept of "class" provided both a set of analytical tools for understanding major inequalities within different types of societies across human history and also a means of understanding the transition through "class struggles" from one type of society to another, which is most famously advanced in *The Communist Manifesto*, co-authored with his life-long collaborator Friedrich Engels (1819–1895). The other selections from Marx included here examine the inner workings of capitalism and how exploitation is developed ("Wage Labour and Capital"), Marx's thoughts on the nature of class power in the realm of politics (from *The German Ideology*, also co-authored with Engels), and his brief statement of his theory of historical materialism (from the preface to his 1859 book titled *A Contribution to the Critique of Political Economy*). The latter very short statement, if read carefully, suggests a different image of how class power unfolds than that advanced earlier by Marx and Engels in *The Communist Manifesto*. Those differences—between class struggle as the motor of history versus history as driven by internal conflicts within "mode of production"—are worth exploring in some detail.

In his landmark essay "Class, Status, Party," the great German sociologist Max Weber (1864–1920) called attention to the limitations of an analysis of inequality centered solely on class, notably that of Karl Marx. Weber noted that other kinds of social attributes, most important those based on honor or "status," could also serve as wellsprings of inequality. Status inequality, for Weber, was especially consequential because individuals with similar status situations or identities coalesce into what he called "status groups." The most important of these status group memberships are those involving race or ethnicity, but other kinds of status can be the basis for groups to form.

Writing at the same time in the United States, Thorstein Veblen (1857–1929) placed even greater emphasis on the decisive influence of status differences. Citing the nearly universal impulse of humans to invidiously compare themselves to their peers, Veblen highlights the extents to which people go to *demonstrate* both their wealth ("conspicuous consumption") and the time they spend not engaging in productive activity ("conspicuous leisure"). Veblen concludes that the quest for social honor is actually what drives our desire for wealth and power rather than the other way around, a view that moves the study of status to the center of stratification research.

The other selections from Weber, (taken from his 1920 magnum opus, *Economy and Society*), highlight his important work on the processes through which status groups seek to secure and monopolize access to desired goods, resources, or opportunities. Weber called these processes "social closure," to emphasize how they involve literally closing of opportunities for subordinate groups. Weber's notion of closure provides a way of understanding a wide range of different types of group inequalities, and it has become increasingly influential in recent years.

Weber's insight about the importance of status groups and processes of exclusion based on group membership paralleled the work of scholars who were beginning to theorize and study the origins and types of racial and gender inequality. One question that later authors treated was the question of group identity. In the remarkable work of sociologist W. E. B. Du Bois (1868–1963), the sense of "self" of members of a subordinate group (such as blacks in America) is shaped by what he calls a "double consciousness": the awareness of being both a looked-down-upon member of a larger society coupled with pride in being a member of a particular subgroup. Du Bois argued that social divisions such as those based on race (and the ideas they give rise to) are the result of political struggles rather of any biological characteristic of individuals or groups. In the second Du Bois essay included here, written late in his life (1950), he summarizes a number of the central themes of work on how racial divisions shaped American society and remained "the problem of the century."

The excerpt from Simone de Beauvoir's *The Second Sex* represents one of the first systematic arguments for the social construction of gender. Grounding her argument in a long historical perspective, de Beauvoir argues that the social bases of gender categories—as opposed to biological ones—are crucial to our understanding of gender relationships. Specifically, she contends that men, as a group, have been constructed as active subjects in the world while women have been cast as objects, as the passive "other" to men. Her argument anticipates that of later feminists.

A line of critique aimed at Karl Marx, but from a very different standpoint from that of Weber, came from sociological writers after World War II who were committed to "functionalist" theories of societies. The key idea of functionalist sociology was that societies evolve in response to critical needs of social order. In their famous 1945 paper—one of the most widely discussed (and criticized) works about inequality ever written by sociologists—Kingsley Davis and Wilbert Moore argue (without direct attribution) that Marxist claims that inequality was an artificial human construction that could be abolished in some future communist society were impossible. Inequality, they assert, is a *necessary* condition of all known human societies, and for good reason. It provides individuals with the incentives to work and produce and, even more significant, motivates the most talented members of society to prepare themselves to perform the most important tasks (and to perform them well).

Another aspect of Marx's writings on inequality that later scholars expanded on concerns his view of politics and the capitalist state. In his well-known essay on the rise of modern citizenship, T.H. Marshall argued in 1950 that the establishment of civil rights from the eighteenth century onward laid the foundation for the establishment of political rights and democracy in the late nineteenth century. Political citizenship in turn fostered the conditions for the emergence of the "social rights" of citizenship, as labor unions and social democratic parties across Europe and North America fought for the universal right to a decent standard of living. Among others, public programs for old age pensions, national health insurance, unemployment insurance, and public housing formidably altered the system of inequality within capitalist societies. Marshall's theorization of the role of the welfare state in upending traditional patterns of inequality and empowering citizens from below has given rise to a vast literature on the welfare state that continues up to the present.

Weber's insights about the multidimensional nature of stratification were illustrated and extended by C. Wright Mills (1916–1962) in his essay "The Sociology of Stratification," the final selection in this part. An American sociologist writing in the 1950s, Mills demonstrates the contemporary importance of inequalities based on class, status, and power, while noting the important role that a fourth dimension—occupation—plays in determining life chances. Although these dimensions dictate the objective structure of inequality in modern society, Mills encourages us to consider the influence of the subjective aspects of stratification; such a focus draws our attention to the degree to which the political commitments of individuals diverge from their objective positions in society and the consequences of this divergence.

I

The Division of Labour★

ADAM SMITH

The greatest improvement in the productive powers of labour, and the greater part of the skill, dexterity, and judgment with which it is anywhere directed, or applied, seem to have been the effects of the division of labour.

The effects of the division of labour, in the general business of society, will be more easily understood by considering in what manner it operates in some particular manufactures. It is commonly supposed to be carried furthest in some very trifling ones; not perhaps that it really is carried further in them than in others of more importance: but in those trifling manufactures which are destined to supply the small wants of but a small number of people, the whole number of workmen must necessarily be small; and those employed in every different branch of the work can often be collected into the same work-house, and placed at once under the view of the spectator. In those great manufactures, on the contrary, which are destined to supply the great wants of the great body of the people, every different branch of the work employs so great

---

★ First published in 1776; from *The Wealth of Nations*.

a number of workmen that it is impossible to collect them all into the same workhouse. We can seldom see more, at one time, than those employed in one single branch. Though in such manufactures, therefore, the work may really be divided into a much greater number of parts than in those of a more trifling nature, the division is not near so obvious, and has accordingly been much less observed.

To take an example, therefore, from a very trifling manufacture; but one in which the division of labour has been very often taken notice of, the trade of the pin-maker: a workman not educated to this business (which the division of labour has rendered a distinct trade), nor acquainted with the use of the machinery employed in it (to the invention of which the same division of labour has probably given occasion), could scarce, perhaps, with his utmost industry, make one pin in a day, and certainly could not make twenty. But in the way in which this business is now carried on, not only the whole work is a peculiar trade, but it is divided into a number of branches, of which the greater part are likewise peculiar trades. One man draws out the wire, another straights it, a third cuts it, a fourth points it, a fifth grinds it at the top for receiving the head; to make the head requires two or three distinct operations; to put it on is a peculiar business, to whiten the pins is another; it is even a trade by itself to put them into the paper; and the important business of making a pin is, in this manner, divided into about eighteen distinct operations, which in some manufactories, are all performed by distinct hands, though in others the same man will sometimes perform two or three of them. I have seen a small manufactory of this kind where ten men only were employed, and where some of them consequently performed two or three distinct operations. But though they were very poor, and therefore but indifferently accommodated with the necessary machinery, they could, when they exerted themselves, make among them about twelve pounds of pins in a day. There are in a pound upwards of four thousand pins of a middling size. Those ten persons, therefore, could make among them upwards of forty-eight thousand pins in a day. Each person, therefore, making a tenth part of forty-eight thousand pins, might be considered as making four thousand eight hundred pins in a day. But if they had all wrought separately and independently, and without any of them having been educated to this peculiar business, they certainly could not each of them have made twenty, perhaps not one pin in a day; that is, certainly, not the two hundred and fortieth, perhaps not the four thousand eight hundredth part of what they are at present capable of performing, in consequence of a proper division and combination of their different operations.

In every other art and manufacture, the effects of the division of labour are similar to what they are in this very trifling one; though, in many of them, the labour can neither be so much subdivided, nor reduced to so great a simplicity of operation. The division of labour, however, so far as it can be introduced, occasions, in every art, a proportionable increase of the productive powers of labour. The separation of different trades and employments from one another seems to have taken place in consequence of this advantage. This separation, too, is generally carried furthest in those countries which enjoy the highest degree of industry and improvement; what is the work of one man in a rude state of society being generally that of several in an improved one. In every improved society, the farmer is generally nothing but a farmer; the manufacturer, nothing but a manufacturer. The labour, too, which is necessary to produce any one complete manufacture is almost always divided among a great number of hands. How many different trades are employed in each branch of the linen and woollen manufactures from the growers of the flax and the wool, to the bleachers and smoothers of the linen, or to the dyers and dressers of the cloth! The nature of agriculture, indeed, does not admit of so many subdivisions of labour, nor of so complete a separation of one business from another, as manufactures. It is impossible to separate so entirely the business of the grazier from that of the corn-farmer as the trade of the carpenter is commonly separated from that of the smith. The spinner is almost always a distinct person from the weaver; but the ploughman, the harrower, the sower of the seed, and the reaper of the corn, are often the same. The occasions for those different sorts of labour returning with the different seasons of the year, it is impossible that one man should be constantly employed in any one of them. This impossibility of making so complete and entire a separation of all the different branches of labour employed in agriculture is perhaps the reason why the improvement of the productive powers of labour in this art does not always keep pace with their improvement in manufactures. The most opulent nations, indeed, generally excel all their neighbours in agriculture as well as in manufactures; but they are commonly more distinguished by their superiority in the latter than in the former. Their lands are in general better cultivated, and having more labour and expense bestowed upon them, produce more in proportion to the extent and natural fertility of the ground. But this superiority of produce is seldom much more than in proportion to the superiority of labour and expense. In agriculture, the labour of the rich country is not always much more productive than that of the poor; or, at least, it is never so much more productive as it commonly is in manufactures. The corn of the rich country, therefore, will not always, in the same degree of goodness, come cheaper to market than that of the poor. The corn of Poland, in the same degree of goodness, is as cheap as that of France, notwithstanding the superior opulence and improvement of the latter country. The corn of France is, in the corn provinces, fully as good, and in most years nearly about the same price with the corn of England, though, in opulence and improvement, France is perhaps inferior to England. The corn-lands of England, however, are better cultivated than those of France, and the corn-lands of France are said to be much better cultivated than those of Poland. But though the poor country, notwithstanding the inferiority of its cultivation, can, in some measure, rival the rich in the cheapness and goodness of its corn, it can pretend to no such competition in its manufactures; at least if those manufactures suit the soil, climate, and situation of the rich country. The silks of France are better and cheaper than those of England, because the silk manufacture, at least under the present high duties upon the importation of raw silk, does not so well suit the climate of England as that of France. But the hardware and the coarse woollens of England are beyond all comparison superior to those of France, and much cheaper too in the same degree of goodness. In Poland there are said to be scarce any manufactures of any kind, a few of those coarser household manufactures excepted, without which no country can well subsist.

This great increase of the quantity of work which, in consequence of the division of labour, the same number of people are capable of performing, is owing to three different circumstances; first, to the increase of dexterity in every particular workman; secondly, to the saving of the time which is commonly lost in passing from one species of work to another; and lastly, to the invention of a great number of machines which facilitate and abridge labour, and enable one man to do the work of many.

First, the improvement of the dexterity of the workman necessarily increases the quantity of the work he can perform; and the division of labour, by reducing every man's business to some one simple operation, and by making this operation the sole employment of his life, necessarily increases very much the dexterity of the workman. A common smith, who, though accustomed to handle the hammer, has never been used to make nails, if upon some particular occasion he is obliged to attempt it, will scarce, I am assured, be able to make above two or three hundred nails in a day, and those too very bad ones. A smith who has been accustomed to make nails, but whose sole or principal business has not been that of a nailer, can seldom with his utmost diligence make more than eight hundred or a thousand nails in a day. I have seen several boys under twenty years of age who had never exercised any other trade but that of making nails, and who, when they

exerted themselves, could make, each of them, upwards of two thousand three hundred nails in a day. The making of a nail, however, is by no means one of the simplest operations. The same person blows the bellows, stirs or mends the fire as there is occasion, heats the iron, and forges every part of the nail: in forging the head too he is obliged to change his tools. The different operations into which the making of a pin, or of a metal button is subdivided, are all of them much more simple, and the dexterity of the person, of whose life it has been the sole business to perform them, is usually much greater. The rapidity with which some of the operations of those manufacturers are performed, exceeds what the human hand could, by those who had never seen them, be supposed capable of acquiring.

Secondly, the advantage which is gained by saving the time commonly lost in passing from one sort of work to another is much greater than we should at first view be apt to imagine it. It is impossible to pass very quickly from one kind of work to another that is carried on in a different place and with quite different tools. A country weaver, who cultivates a small farm, must lose a good deal of time in passing from his loom to the field, and from the field to his loom. When the two trades can be carried on in the same workhouse, the loss of time is no doubt much less. It is even in this case, however, very considerable. A man commonly saunters a little in turning his hand from one sort of employment to another. When he first begins the new work he is seldom very keen and hearty; his mind, as they say, does not go to it, and for some time he rather trifles than applies to good purpose. The habit of sauntering and of indolent careless application, which is naturally, or rather necessarily acquired by every country workman who is obliged to change his work and his tools every half hour, and to apply his hand in twenty different ways almost every day of his life, renders him almost always slothful and lazy, and incapable of any vigorous application even on the most pressing occasions. Independent, therefore, of his deficiency in point of dexterity, this cause alone must always reduce considerably the quantity of work which he is capable of performing.

Thirdly, and lastly, everybody must be sensible how much labour is facilitated and abridged by the application of proper machinery. It is unnecessary to give any example. I shall only observe, therefore, that the invention of all those machines by which labour is so much facilitated and abridged seems to have been originally owing to the division of labour. Men are much more likely to discover easier and readier methods of attaining any object when the whole attention of their minds is directed towards that single object than when it is dissipated among a great variety of things. But in consequence of the division of labour, the whole of every man's attention comes naturally to be directed towards some one very simple object. It is naturally to be expected, therefore, that some one or other of those who are employed in each particular branch of labour should soon find out easier and readier methods of performing their own particular work, wherever the nature of it admits of such improvement. A great part of the machines made use of in those manufactures in which labour is most subdivided, were originally the inventions of common workmen, who, being each of them employed in some very simple operation, naturally turned their thoughts towards finding out easier and readier methods of performing it. Whoever has been much accustomed to visit such manufactures must frequently have been shown very pretty machines, which were the inventions of such workmen in order to facilitate and quicken their own particular part of the work. In the first fire-engines, a boy was constantly employed to open and shut alternately the communication between the boiler and the cylinder, according as the piston either ascended or descended. One of those boys, who loved to play with his companions, observed that, by tying a string from the handle of the valve which opened this communication to another part of the machine, the valve would open and shut without his assistance, and leave him at liberty to divert himself with his playfellows. One of the greatest improvements that has been made upon this machine, since it was first invented, was in this manner the discovery of a boy who wanted to save his own labour.

All the improvements in machinery, however, have by no means been the inventions of those who had occasion to use the machines. Many improvements have been made by the ingenuity of the makers of the machines, when to make them became the business of a peculiar trade; and some by that of those who are called philosophers or men of speculation, whose trade it is not to do anything, but to observe everything; and who, upon that account, are often capable of combining together the powers of the most distant and dissimilar objects.

In the progress of society, philosophy or speculation becomes, like every other employment, the principal or sole trade and occupation of a particular class of citizens. Like every other employment too, it is subdivided into a great number of different branches, each of which affords occupation to a peculiar tribe or class of philosophers; and this subdivision of employment in philosophy, as well as in every other business, improves dexterity, and saves time. Each individual becomes more expert in his own peculiar branch, more work is done upon the whole, and the quantity of science is considerably increased by it.

It is the great multiplication of the productions of all the different arts, in consequence of the division of labour, which occasions, in a well-governed society, that universal opulence which extends itself to the lowest ranks of the people. Every workman has a great quantity of his own work to dispose of beyond what he himself has occasion for; and every other workman being exactly in the same situation, he is enabled to exchange a great quantity of his own goods for a great quantity, or, what comes to the same thing, for the price of a great quantity of theirs. He supplies them abundantly with what they have occasion for, and they accommodate him as amply with what he has occasion for, and a general plenty diffuses itself through all the different ranks of the society.

Observe the accommodation of the most common artificer or day-labourer in a civilised and thriving country, and you will perceive that the number of people of whose industry a part, though but a small part, has been employed in procuring him this accommodation, exceeds all computation. The woollen coat, for example, which covers the day-labourer, as coarse and rough as it may appear, is the produce of the joint labour of a great multitude of workmen. The shepherd, the sorter of the wool, the wool-comber or carder, the dyer, the scribbler, the spinner, the weaver, the fuller, the dresser, with many others, must all join their different arts in order to complete even this homely production. How many merchants and carriers, besides, must have been employed in transporting the materials from some of those workmen to others who often live in a very distant part of the country! How much commerce and navigation in particular, how many ship-builders, sailors, sail-makers, rope-makers, must have been employed in order to bring together the different drugs made use of by the dyer, which often come from the remotest corners of the world! What a variety of labour, too, is necessary in order to produce the tools of the meanest of those workmen! To say nothing of such complicated machines as the ship of the sailor, the mill of the fuller, or even the loom of the weaver, let us consider only what a variety of labour is requisite in order to form that very simple machine, the shears with which the shepherd clips the wool. The miner, the builder of the furnace for smelting the ore, the seller of the timber, the burner of the charcoal to be made use of in the smelting-house, the brick-maker, the brick-layer, the workmen who attend the furnace, the mill-wright, the forger, the smith, must all of them join their different arts in order to produce them. Were we to examine, in the same manner, all the different parts of his dress and household furniture, the coarse linen shirt which he wears next his skin, the shoes which cover his feet, the bed which he lies on, and all the different parts which compose it, the kitchen-grate at which he prepares his victuals, the coals which he makes use of for that purpose, dug from the bowels of the earth, and brought to him perhaps by a long sea and a long land carriage, all the other utensils of his kitchen, all the furniture of his table, the knives and forks, the earthen or pewter plates upon which he serves up and divides his victuals, the different hands employed in preparing his bread and his beer, the glass window which lets in the heat and the light, and keeps out the wind and the rain, with all the knowledge and art requisite for preparing that beautiful and happy invention, without which these northern parts of the world could scarce have afforded a very comfortable habitation, together with the tools of all the different workmen employed in producing those different conveniences; if we examine, I say, all these things, and consider what a variety of labour is employed about each of them, we shall be sensible that, without the assistance and co-operation of many thousands, the very meanest person in a civilised country could not be provided, even according to what we very falsely imagine the easy and simple manner in which he is commonly accommodated. Compared, indeed, with the more extravagant luxury of the great, his accommodation must no doubt appear extremely simple and easy; and yet it may be true, perhaps, that the accommodation of a European prince does not always so much exceed that of an industrious and frugal peasant as the accommodation of the latter exceeds that of many an African king, the absolute master of the lives and liberties of ten thousand naked savages.

THE PRINCIPLE WHICH GIVES OCCASION TO THE DIVISION OF LABOUR

This division of labour, from which so many advantages are derived, is not originally the effect of any human wisdom, which foresees and intends that general opulence to which it gives occasion. It is the necessary, though very slow and gradual consequence of certain propensity in human nature which has in view no such extensive utility; the propensity to truck, barter, and exchange one thing for another.

Whether this propensity be one of those original principles in human nature of which no further account can be given; or whether, as seems more probable, it be the necessary consequence of the faculties of reason and speech, it belongs not to our present subject to inquire. It is common to all men, and to be found in no other race of animals, which seem to know neither this nor any other species of contracts. Two greyhounds, in running down the same hare, have sometimes the appearance of acting in some sort of concert. Each turns her towards his companion, or endeavours to intercept her when his companion turns her towards himself. This, however, is not the effect of any contract, but of the accidental concurrence of their passions in the same object at that particular time. Nobody ever saw a dog make a fair and deliberate exchange of one bone for another with another dog. Nobody ever saw one animal by its gestures and natural cries signify to another, this is mine, that yours; I am willing to give this for that. When an animal wants to obtain something either of a man or of another animal, it has no other means of persuasion but to gain the favour of those whose service it requires. A puppy fawns upon its dam, and a spaniel endeavours by a thousand attractions to engage the attention of its master who is at dinner, when it wants to be fed by him. Man sometimes uses the same arts with his brethren, and when he has no other means of engaging them to act according to his inclinations, endeavours by every servile and fawning attention to obtain their good will. He has not time, however, to do this upon every occasion. In civilised society he stands at all times in need of the cooperation and assistance of great multitudes, while his whole life is scarce sufficient to gain the friendship of a few persons. In almost every other race of animals each individual, when it is grown up to maturity, is entirely independent, and in its natural state has occasion for the assistance of no other living creature. But man has almost constant occasion for the help of his brethren, and it is in vein for him to expect it from their benevolence only. He will be more likely to prevail if he can interest their self-love in his favour, and show them that it is for their own advantage to do for him what he requires of them. Whoever offers to another a bargain of any kind, proposes to do this. Give me that which I want, and you shall have this which you want, is the meaning of every such offer; and it is in this manner that we obtain from one another the far greater part of those good offices which we stand in need of. It is not from the benevolence of the butcher, the brewer, or the baker that we expect our dinner, but from their regard to their own interest. We address ourselves, not to their humanity but to their self-love, and never talk to them of our own necessities but of their advantages. Nobody but a beggar chooses to depend chiefly

upon the benevolence of his fellow-citizens. Even a beggar does not depend upon it entirely. The charity of well-disposed people, indeed, supplies him with the whole fund of his subsistence. But though this principle ultimately provides him with all the necessaries of life which he has occasion for, it neither does nor can provide him with them as he has occasion for them. The greater part of his occasional wants are supplied in the same manner as those of other people, by treaty, by barter, and by purchase. With the money which one man gives him he purchases food. The old clothes which another bestows upon him he exchanges for other old clothes which suit him better, or for lodging, or for food, or for money, with which he can buy either food, clothes, or lodging, as he has occasion.

As it is by treaty, by barter, and by purchase that we obtain from one another the greater part of those mutual good offices which we stand in need of, so it is this same trucking disposition which originally gives occasion to the division of labour. In a tribe of hunters or shepherds a particular person makes bows and arrows, for example, with more readiness and dexterity than any other. He frequently exchanges them for cattle or for venison with his companions; and he finds at last that he can in this manner get more cattle and venison than if he himself went to the field to catch them. From a regard to his own interest, therefore, the making of bows and arrows grows to be his chief business, and he becomes a sort of armourer. Another excels in making the frames and covers of their little huts or movable houses. He is accustomed to be of use in this way to his neighbours, who reward him in the same manner with cattle and with venison, till at last he finds it his interest to dedicate himself entirely to this employment, and to become a sort of house-carpenter. In the same manner a third becomes a smith or a brazier, a fourth a tanner or dresser of hides or skins, the principal part of the clothing of savages. And thus the certainty of being able to exchange all that surplus part of the produce of his own labour, which is over and above his own consumption, for such parts of the produce of other men's labour as he may have occasion for, encourages every man to apply himself to a particular occupation, and to cultivate and bring to perfection whatever talent or genius he may possess for that particular species of business.

The difference of natural talents in different men is, in reality, much less than we are aware of; and the very different genius which appears to distinguish men of different professions, when grown up to maturity, is not upon many occasions so much the cause as the effect of the division of labour. The difference between the most dissimilar characters, between a philosopher and a common street porter, for example, seems to arise not so much from nature as from habit, custom, and education. When they came into the world, and for the first six or eight years of their existence, they were perhaps very much alike, and neither their parents nor playfellows could perceive any remarkable difference. About that age, or soon after, they come to be employed in very different occupations. The difference of talents comes then to be taken notice of, and widens by degrees, till at last the vanity of the philosopher is willing to acknowledge scarce any resemblance. But without the disposition to truck, barter, and exchange, every man must have procured to himself every

necessary and conveniency of life which he wanted. All must have had the same duties to perform, and the same work to do, and there could have been no such difference of employment as could alone give occasion to any great difference of talents.

As it is this disposition which forms that difference of talents, so remarkable among men of different professions, so it is this same disposition which renders that difference useful. Many tribes of animals acknowledged to be all of the same species derive from nature a much more remarkable distinction of genius, than what, antecedent to custom and education, appears to take place among men. By nature a philosopher is not in genius and disposition half so different from a street porter, as a mastiff is from a greyhound, or a greyhound from a spaniel, or this last from a shepherd's dog. Those different tribes of animals, however, though all of the same species, are of scarce any use to one another. The strength of the mastiff is not, in the least, supported either by the swiftness of the greyhound, or by the sagacity of the spaniel, or by the docility of the shepherd's dog. The effects of those different geniuses and talents, for want of the power or disposition to barter and exchange, cannot be brought into a common stock, and do not in the least contribute to the better accommodation and conveniency of the species. Each animal is still obliged to support and defend itself, separately and independently, and derives no sort of advantage from that variety of talents with which nature has distinguished its fellows. Among men, on the contrary, the most dissimilar geniuses are of use to one another; the different produces of their respective talents, by the general disposition to truck, barter, and exchange, being brought, as it were, into a common stock, where every man may purchase whatever part of the produce of other men's talents he has occasion for.

THE EXPENSES
OF THE SOVEREIGN

★ ★ ★

In the progress of the division of labour, the employment of the far greater part of those who live by labour, that is, of the great body of the people, comes to be confined to a few very simple operations, frequently to one or two. But the understandings of the greater part of men are necessarily formed by their ordinary employments. The man whose whole life is spent in performing a few simple operations, of which the effects are perhaps always the same, or very nearly the same, has no occasion to exert his understanding or to exercise his invention in finding out expedients for removing difficulties which never occur. He naturally loses, therefore, the habit of such exertion, and generally becomes as stupid and ignorant as it is possible for a human creature to become. The torpor of his mind renders him not only incapable of relishing or bearing a part in any rational conversation, but of conceiving any generous, noble, or tender sentiment, and consequently of forming any just judgment concerning many even of the ordinary duties of private life. Of the great and extensive interests of his country he is altogether incapable of judging, and unless very particular pains have been taken to render him otherwise, he is equally incapable of defending his country in war. The uniformity of his

stationary life naturally corrupts the courage of his mind, and makes him regard with abhorrence the irregular, uncertain, and adventurous life of a soldier. It corrupts even the activity of his body, and renders him incapable of exerting his strength with vigour and perseverance in any other employment than that to which he has been bred. His dexterity at his own particular trade seems, in this manner, to be acquired at the expense of his intellectual, social, and martial virtues. But in every improved and civilised society this is the state into which the labouring poor, that is, the great body of the people, must necessarily fall, unless government takes some pains to prevent it.

It is otherwise in the barbarous societies, as they are commonly called, of hunters, of shepherds, and even of husbandmen in that rude state of husbandry which precedes the improvement of manufactures and the extension of foreign commerce. In such societies the varied occupations of every man oblige every man to exert his capacity and to invent expedients for removing difficulties which are continually occurring. Invention is kept alive, and the mind is not suffered to fall into that drowsy stupidity which, in a civilised society, seems to benumb the understanding of almost all the inferior ranks of people. In those barbarous societies, as they are called, every man, it has already been observed, is a warrior. Every man, too, is in some measure a statesman, and can form a tolerable judgment concerning the interest of the society and the conduct of those who govern it. How far their chiefs are good judges in peace, or good leaders in war, is obvious to the observation of almost every single man among them. In such a society, indeed, no man can well acquire that improved and refined understanding which a few men sometimes possess in a more civilised state. Though in a rude society there is a good deal of variety in the occupations of every individual, there is not a great deal in those of the whole society. Every man does, or is capable of doing, almost every thing which any other man does, or is capable of doing. Every man has a considerable degree of knowledge, ingenuity, and invention: but scarce any man has a great degree. The degree, however, which is commonly possessed, is generally sufficient for conducting the whole simple business of the society. In a civilised state, on the contrary, though there is little variety in the occupations of the greater part of individuals, there is an almost infinite variety in those of the whole society. These varied occupations present an almost infinite variety of objects to the contemplation of those few, who, being attached to no particular occupation themselves, have leisure and inclination to examine the occupations of other people. The contemplation of so great a variety of objects necessarily exercises their minds in endless comparisons and combinations, and renders their understandings, in an extraordinary degree, both acute and comprehensive. Unless those few, however, happen to be placed in some very particular situations, their great abilities, though honourable to themselves, may contribute very little to the good government or happiness of their society. Notwithstanding the great abilities of those few, all the nobler parts of the human character may be, in a great measure, obliterated and extinguished in the great body of the people.

The education of the common people requires, perhaps, in a civilised and commer-cial society the attention of the public more than that of people of some rank and fortune. People of some rank and fortune are generally eighteen or nineteen years of age before they enter upon that particular business, profession, or trade, by which they propose to distinguish themselves in the world. They have before that full time to acquire, or at least to fit themselves for afterwards acquiring, every accomplishment which can recommend them to the public esteem, or render them worthy of it. Their parents or guardians are generally sufficiently anxious that they should be so accomplished, and are, in most cases, willing enough to lay out the expense which is necessary for that purpose. If they are not always properly educated, it is seldom from the want of expense laid out upon their education, but from the improper application of that expense. It is seldom from the want of masters, but from the negligence and incapacity of the masters who are to be had, and from the difficulty, or rather from the impossibility, which there is in the present state of things of finding any better. The employments, too, in which people of some rank or fortune spend the greater part of their lives are not, like those of the common people, simple and uniform. They are almost all of them extremely complicated, and such as exercise the head more than the hands. The understandings of those who are engaged in such employments can seldom grow torpid for want of exercise. The employments of people of some rank and fortune, besides, are seldom such as harass them from morning to night. They generally have a good deal of leisure, during which they may perfect themselves in every branch either of useful or ornamental knowledge of which they may have laid the foundation, or for which they may have acquired some taste in the earlier part of life.

It is otherwise with the common people. They have little time to spare for education. Their parents can scarce afford to maintain them even in infancy. As soon as they are able to work they must apply to some trade by which they can earn their subsistence. That trade, too, is generally so simple and uniform as to give little exercise to the understanding, while, at the same time, their labour is both so constant and so severe, that it leaves them little leisure and less inclination to apply to, or even to think of anything else.

But though the common people cannot, in any civilised society, be so well instructed as people of some rank and fortune, the most essential parts of education, however, to read, write, and account, can be acquired at so early a period of life that the greater part even of those who are to be bred to the lowest occupations have time to acquire them before they can be employed in those occupations. For a very small expense the public can facilitate, can encourage, and can even impose upon almost the whole body of the people the necessity of acquiring those most essential parts of education.

★ ★ ★

2

From *Wage-Labour and Capital**

KARL MARX

‖ I

From various quarters we have been reproached with not having presented the *economic relations* which constitute the material foundation of the present class struggles and national struggles. We have designedly touched upon these relations only where they directly forced themselves to the front in political conflicts.

★ ★ ★

Now, after our readers have seen the class struggle develop in colossal political forms in 1848, the time has come to deal more closely with the economic relations themselves on which the existence of the bourgeoisie and its class rule, as well as the slavery of the workers, are founded.

★ ★ ★

Now, therefore, for the first question: *What are wages? How are they determined?*

* First published in 1849; from *The Marx-Engels Reader, 2nd Edition*, edited by Robert C. Tucker.

If workers were asked: "How much are your wages?" one would reply: "I get a mark a day from my employer"; another, "I get two marks," and so on. According to the different trades to which they belong, they would mention different sums of money which they receive from their respective employers for the performance of a particular piece of work, for example, weaving a yard of linen or typesetting a printed sheet. In spite of the variety of their statements, they would all agree on one point: wages are the sum of money paid by the capitalist for a particular labour time or for a particular output of labour.

The capitalist, it seems, therefore, *buys* their labour with money. They *sell* him their labour for money. But this is merely the appearance. In reality what they sell to the capitalist for money is their labour *power*. The capitalist buys this labour power for a day, a week, a month, etc. And after he has bought it, he uses it by having the workers work for the stipulated time. For the same sum with which the capitalist has bought their labour power, for example, two marks, he could have bought two pounds of sugar or a definite amount of any other commodity. The two marks, with which he bought two pounds of sugar, are the *price* of the two pounds of sugar. The two marks, with which he bought twelve hours' use of labour power, are the price of twelve hours' labour. Labour power, therefore, is a commodity, neither more nor less than sugar. The former is measured by the clock, the latter by the scales.

★ ★ ★

Labour power is, therefore, a commodity which its possessor, the wage-worker, sells to capital. Why does he sell it? In order to live.

But the exercise of labour power, labour, is the worker's own life-activity, the manifestation of his own life. And this *life-activity* he sells to another person in order to secure the necessary *means of subsistence*. Thus his life-activity is for him only a means to enable him to exist. He works in order to live. He does not even reckon labour as part of his life, it is rather a sacrifice of his life. It is a commodity which he has made over to another. Hence, also, the product of his activity is not the object of his activity. What he produces for himself is not the silk that he weaves, not the gold that he draws from the mine, not the palace that he builds. What he produces for himself is *wages*, and silk, gold, palace resolve themselves for him into a definite quantity of the means of subsistence, perhaps into a cotton jacket, some copper coins and a lodging in a cellar. And the worker, who for twelve hours weaves, spins, drills, turns, builds, shovels, breaks stones, carries loads, etc.—does he consider this twelve hours' weaving, spinning, drilling, turning, building, shovelling, stone breaking as a manifestation of his life, as life? On the contrary, life begins for him where this activity ceases, at table, in the public house, in bed. The twelve hours' labour, on the other hand, has no meaning for him as weaving, spinning, drilling, etc., but as *earnings*, which bring him to the table, to the public house, into bed. If the silk worm were to spin in order to continue its existence as a caterpillar, it would be a complete wage-worker. Labour power was not always a *commodity*. Labour was not always wage labour, that is, *free labour*. The *slave* did not sell his labour power to the slave owner, any more than the ox sells its services to the peasant. The slave, together with his labour power, is sold once and for all to his owner. He is a commodity which can pass from the hand of one owner to that of another. He is *himself* a commodity, but the labour power is not *his* commodity. The *serf* sells only a part of his labour power. He does not receive a wage from the owner of the land; rather the owner of the land receives a tribute from him.

The serf belongs to the land and turns over to the owner of the land the fruits thereof. The *free labourer*, on the other hand, sells himself and, indeed, sells himself piecemeal. He sells at auction eight, ten, twelve, fifteen hours of his life, day after day, to the highest bidder, to the owner of the raw materials, instruments of labour and means of subsistence, that is, to the capitalist. The worker belongs neither to an owner nor to the land, but eight, ten, twelve, fifteen hours of his daily life belong to him who buys them. The worker leaves the capitalist to whom he hires himself whenever he likes, and the capitalist discharges him whenever he thinks fit, as soon as he no longer gets any profit out of him, or not the anticipated profit. But the worker, whose sole source of livelihood is the sale of his labour power, cannot leave the *whole class of purchasers, that is, the capitalist class*, without renouncing his existence. He belongs not to this or that capitalist but to the *capitalist class*, and, moreover, it is his business to dispose of himself, that is, to find a purchaser within this capitalist class.

★ ★ ★

Wages will rise and fall according to the relation of supply and demand, according to the turn taken by the competition between the buyers of labour power, the capitalists, and the sellers of labour power, the workers. The fluctuations in wages correspond in general to the fluctuations in prices of commodities. *Within these fluctuations, however, the price of labour will be determined by the cost of production, by the labour time necessary to produce this commodity—labour power.*

What, then, is the cost of production of labour power?

It is the cost required for maintaining the worker as a worker and of developing him into a worker.

The less the period of training, therefore, that any work requires the smaller is the cost of production of the worker and the lower is the price of his labour, his wages. In those branches of industry in which hardly any period of apprenticeship is required and where the mere bodily existence of the worker suffices, the cost necessary for his production is almost confined to the commodities necessary for keeping him alive and capable of working. The *price of his labour* will, therefore, be determined by the *price of the necessary means of subsistence*.

Another consideration, however, also comes in. The manufacturer in calculating his cost of production and, accordingly, the price of the products takes into account the wear and tear of the instruments of labour. If, for example, a machine costs him 1,000 marks and wears out in ten years, he adds 100 marks annually to the price of the commodities so as to be able to replace the worn-out machine by a new one at the end of ten years. In the same way, in calculating the cost of production of simple labour power, there must be included the cost of reproduction, whereby the race of workers is enabled to multiply and to replace worn-out workers by new ones. Thus the depreciation of the worker is taken into account in the same way as the depreciation of the machine.

The cost of production of simple labour power, therefore, amounts to the *cost of existence and reproduction of the worker*. The price of this cost of existence and reproduction constitutes wages. Wages so determined are called the *wage minimum*. This wage minimum, like the determination of the price of commodities by the cost of production in general, does not hold good for the *single individual* but for the *species*. Individual workers, millions of workers, do not get enough to be able to exist and reproduce themselves; *but the wages of the whole working class level down, within their fluctuations, to this minimum*.

Now that we have arrived at an understanding of the most general laws which regulate wages like the price of any other commodity, we can go into our subject more specifically.

||| III

Capital consists of raw materials, instruments of labour and means of subsistence of all kinds, which are utilised in order to produce new raw materials, new instruments of labour and new means of subsistence. All these component parts of capital are creations of labour, products of labour, *accumulated labour*. Accumulated labour which serves as a means of new production is capital.

So say the economists.

What is a Negro slave? A man of the black race. The one explanation is as good as the other.

A Negro is a Negro. He only becomes a slave in certain relations. A cotton-spinning jenny is a machine for spinning cotton. It becomes *capital* only in certain relations. Torn from these relationships it is no more capital than gold in itself is *money* or sugar the price of sugar.

In production, men not only act on nature but also on one another. They produce only by co-operating in a certain way and mutually exchanging their activities. In order to produce, they enter into definite connections and relations with one another and only within these social connections and relations does their action on nature, does production, take place.

These social relations into which the producers enter with one another, the conditions under which they exchange their activities and participate in the whole act of production, will naturally vary according to the character of the means of production. With the invention of a new instrument of warfare, firearms, the whole internal organisation of the army necessarily changed; the relationships within which individuals can constitute an army and act as an army were transformed and the relations of different armies to one another also changed.

Thus the social relations within which individuals produce, *the social relations of production, change, are transformed, with the change and development of the material means of production, the productive forces. The relations of production in their totality constitute what are called the social relations, society, and, specifically, a society at a definite stage of historical development*, a society with a peculiar, distinctive character. *Ancient* society, *feudal* society, *bourgeois* society are such totalities of production relations, each of which at the same time denotes a special stage of development in the history of mankind.

Capital, also, is a social relation of production. *It is a bourgeois production relation*, a production relation of bourgeois society. Are not the means of subsistence, the instruments of labour, the raw materials of which capital consists, produced and accumulated under given social conditions, in definite social relations? Are they not utilised for new production under given social conditions, in definite social relations? And is it not just this definite social character which turns the products serving for new production into *capital*?

Capital consists not only of means of subsistence, instruments of labour and raw materials, not only of material products; it consists just as much of *exchange values*. All the products of which it consists are *commodities*. Capital is, therefore, not only a sum of material products; it is a sum of commodities, of exchange values, *of social magnitudes*.

Capital remains the same, whether we put cotton in place of wool, rice in place of wheat or steamships in place of railways, provided only that the cotton, the rice, the steamships—the body of capital—have the same exchange value, the same price as the wool, the wheat, the railways in which it was previously incorporated. The body of capital can change continually without the capital suffering the slightest alteration.

But while all capital is a sum of commodities, that is, of exchange values, not every sum of commodities, of exchange values, is capital.

Every sum of exchange values is an exchange value. Every separate exchange value is a sum of exchange values. For instance, a house that is worth 1,000 marks is an exchange value of 1,000 marks. A piece of paper worth a pfennig is a sum of exchange values of one-hundred hundredths of a pfennig. Products which are exchangeable for others are commodities. The particular ratio in which they are exchangeable constitutes their *exchange value* or, expressed in money, their *price*. The quantity of these products can change nothing in their quality of being *commodities* or representing an *exchange value* or having a definite price. Whether a tree is large or small it is a tree. Whether we exchange iron for other products in ounces or in hundred-weights, does this make any difference in its character as commodity, as exchange value? It is a commodity of greater or lesser value, of higher or lower price, depending upon the quantity.

How, then, does any amount of commodities, of exchange value, become capital?

By maintaining and multiplying itself as an independent social *power*, that is, as the power *of a portion of society*, by means of its *exchange for direct, living labour power*. The existence of a class which possesses nothing but its capacity to labour is a necessary prerequisite of capital.

It is only the domination of accumulated, past, materialised labour over direct, living labour that turns accumulated labour into capital.

Capital does not consist in accumulated labour serving living labour as a means for new production. It consists in living labour serving accumulated labour as a means of maintaining and multiplying the exchange value of the latter.

What takes place in the exchange between capitalist and wage-worker?

The worker receives means of subsistence in exchange for his labour power, but the capitalist receives in exchange for his means of subsistence labour, the productive activity of the worker, the creative power whereby the worker not only replaces what he consumes but *gives to the accumulated labour a greater value than it previously possessed.* The worker receives a part of the available means of subsistence from the capitalist. For what purpose do these means of subsistence serve him? For immediate consumption. As soon, however, as I consume the means of subsistence, they are irretrievably lost to me unless I use the time during which I am kept alive by them in order to produce new means of subsistence, in order during consumption to create by my labour new values in place of the values which perish in being consumed. But it is just this noble reproductive power that the worker surrenders to the capitalist in exchange for means of subsistence received. He has, therefore, lost it for himself.

Let us take an example: a tenant farmer gives his day labourer five silver groschen a day. For these five silver groschen the labourer works all day on the farmer's field and thus secures him a return of ten silver groschen. The farmer not only gets the value replaced that he has to give the day labourer; he doubles it. He has therefore employed, consumed, the five silver groschen that he gave to the labourer in a fruitful, productive manner. He has bought with the five silver groschen just that labour and power of the labourer which produces agricultural products of double value and makes ten silver groschen out of five. The day labourer, on the other hand, receives in place of his productive power, the effect of which he has bargained away to the farmer, five silver groschen, which he exchanges for means of subsistence, and these he consumes with greater or less rapidity. The five silver groschen have, therefore, been consumed in a double way, *reproductively* for capital, for they have been exchanged for labour power which produced ten silver groschen, *unproductively* for the worker, for they have been exchanged for means of subsistence which have disappeared forever and the value of which he can only recover by repeating the same exchange with the farmer. *Thus capital presupposes wage labour; wage labour presupposes capital. They reciprocally condition the existence of each other; they reciprocally bring forth each other.*

Does a worker in a cotton factory produce merely cotton textiles? No, he produces capital. He produces values which serve afresh to command his labour and by means of it to create new values.

Capital can only increase by exchanging itself for labour power, by calling wage labour to life. The labour power of the wage-worker can only be exchanged for capital by increasing capital, by strengthening the power whose slave it is. *Hence, increase of capital is increase of the proletariat, that is, of the working class.*

The interests of the capitalist and those of the worker are, therefore, *one and the same,* assert the bourgeois and their economists. Indeed! The worker perishes if capital does not employ him. Capital perishes if it does not exploit labour power, and in order to exploit it, it must buy it. The faster capital intended for production, productive capital, increases, the more, therefore, industry prospers, the more the bourgeoisie enriches itself and the better business is, the more workers does the capitalist need, the more dearly does the worker sell himself.

The indispensable condition for a tolerable situation of the worker is, *therefore, the fastest possible growth of productive capital.*

But what is the growth of productive capital? Growth of the power of accumulated labour over living labour. Growth of the domination of the bourgeoisie over the working class. If wage labour produces the wealth of others that rules over it, the power that is hostile to it, capital, then the means of employment, the means of subsistence, flow back to it from this hostile power, on condition that it makes itself afresh into a part of capital, into the lever which hurls capital anew into an accelerated movement of growth.

To say that the interests of capital, and those of the workers are one and the same is only to say that capital and wage labour are two sides of one and the same relation. The one conditions the other, just as usurer and squanderer condition each other.

As long as the wage-worker is a wage-worker his lot depends upon capital. That is the much-vaunted community of interests between worker and capitalist.

‖ IV

If capital grows, the mass of wage labour grows, the number of wage-workers grows; in a word, the domination of capital extends over a greater number of individuals. ★ ★ ★

★ ★ ★

To say that the worker has an interest in the rapid growth of capital is only to say that the more rapidly the worker increases the wealth of others, the richer will be the crumbs that fall to him, the greater is the number of workers that can be employed and called into existence, the more can the mass of slaves dependent on capital be increased.

We have thus seen that:

Even the *most favourable situation* for the working class, the *most rapid possible growth of capital*, however much it may improve the material existence of the worker, does not remove the antagonism between his interests and the interests of the bourgeoisie, the interests of the capitalists. *Profit and wages* remain as before in *inverse porportion.*

If capital is growing rapidly, wages may rise; the profit of capital rises incomparably more rapidly. The material position of the worker has improved, but at the cost of his social position. The social gulf that divides him from the capitalist has widened.

Finally:

To say that the most favourable condition for wage labour is the most rapid possible growth of productive capital is only to say that the more rapidly the working class increases and enlarges the power that is hostile to it, the wealth that does not belong to it and that rules over it, the more favourable will be the conditions under which it is allowed to labour anew at increasing bourgeois wealth, at enlarging the power of capital, content with forging for itself the golden chains by which the bourgeoisie drags it in its train.

‖ V

Are *growth of productive capital and rise of wages* really so inseparably connected as the bourgeois economists maintain? We must not take their word for it. We must not even believe them when they say that the fatter capital is, the better will its slave be fed. The bourgeoisie is too enlightened, it calculates too well, to share the prejudices of the feudal lord who makes a display by the brilliance of his retinue. The conditions of existence of the bourgeoisie compel it to calculate.

We must, therefore, examine more closely:

How does the growth of productive capital affect wages?

If, on the whole, the productive capital of bourgeois society grows, a *more manifold* accumulation of labour takes place. The capitals increase in number and extent. The *numerical increase* of the capitals increases the *competition between the capitalists*. The *increasing extent* of the capitals provides the means for *bringing more powerful labour armies with more gigantic instruments of war into the industrial battlefield.*

One capitalist can drive another from the field and capture his capital only by selling more cheaply. In order to be able to sell more cheaply without ruining himself, he must produce more cheaply, that is, raise the productive power of labour as much as possible. But the productive power of labour is raised, above all, by *a greater division of labour*, by a more universal introduction and continual improvement of *machinery*. The greater the labour army among whom labour is divided, the more gigantic the scale on which machinery is introduced, the more does the cost of production proportionately decrease, the more fruitful is labour. Hence, a general rivalry arises among the capitalists to increase the division of labour and machinery and to exploit them on the greatest possible scale.

If, now, by a greater division of labour, by the utilisation of new machines and their improvement, by more profitable and extensive exploitation of natural forces, one capitalist has found the means of producing with the same amount of labour or of accumulated labour a greater amount of products, of commodities, than his competitors, if he can, for example, produce a whole yard of linen in the same labour time in which his competitors weave half a yard, how will this capitalist operate?

He could continue to sell half a yard of linen at the old market price; this would, however, be no means of driving his opponents from the field and of enlarging his own sales. But in the same measure in which his production has expanded, his need to sell has also increased. The more powerful and costly means of production that he has called into life enable him, indeed, to sell his commodities more cheaply, they *compel* him, however, at the same time *to sell more commodities*, to conquer a much *larger* market for his commodities; consequently, our capitalist will sell his half yard of linen more cheaply than his competitors.

The capitalist will not, however, sell a whole yard as cheaply as his competitors sell half a yard, although the production of the whole yard does not cost him more than the half yard costs the others. Otherwise he would not gain anything extra but only get back the cost of production by the exchange. His possibly greater income would be derived from the fact of having set a larger capital into motion, but not from having made more of his capital than the others. Moreover, he attains the object he wishes to attain, if he puts the price of his goods only a small percentage lower than that of his competitors. He drives them from the field, he wrests from them at least a part of their sales, by *underselling* them. And, finally, it will be remembered that the current price always stands *above or below the cost of production*, according to whether the sale of the commodity occurs in a favourable or unfavourable industrial season. The percentage at which the capitalist who has employed new and more fruitful means of production sells above his real cost of production will vary, depending upon whether the market price of a yard of linen stands below or above its hitherto customary cost of production.

However, the *privileged position* of our capitalist is not of long duration; other competing capitalists introduce the same machines, the same division of labour, introduce them on the same or on a larger scale, and this introduction will become so general that the price of linen *is reduced* not only *below its old*, but *below its new cost of production*.

The capitalists find themselves, therefore, in the same position relative to one another as *before* the introduction of the new means of production, and if they are able to supply by these means double the production at the same price, they are *now* forced to supply the double product *below* the old price. On the basis of this new cost of production, the same game begins again. More division of labour, more machinery, enlarged scale of exploitation of machinery and division of labour. And again competition brings the same counteraction against this result.

We see how in this way the mode of production and the means of production are continually transformed, revolutionised, *how the division of labour is necessarily followed by greater division of labour, the application of machinery by still greater application of machinery, work on a large scale by work on a still larger scale.*

That is the law which again and again throws bourgeois production out of its old course and which compels capital to intensify the productive forces of labour, *because* it has intensified them, it, the law which gives capital no rest and continually whispers in its ear: "Go on! Go on!"

This law is none other than that which, within the fluctuations of trade periods, necessarily *levels out* the price of a commodity to its *cost of production*.

However powerful the means of production which a capitalist brings into the field, competition will make these means of production universal and from the moment when it has made them universal, the only result of the greater fruitfulness of his capital is that he must now supply *for the same price* ten, twenty, a hundred times as much as before. But, as he must sell perhaps a thousand times as much as before in order to outweigh the lower selling price by the greater amount of the product sold, because a more extensive sale is now necessary, not only in order to make more profit but in order to replace the cost of production—the instrument of production itself, as we have seen, becomes more and more expensive—and because this mass sale becomes a question of life and death not only for him but also for his rivals, the old struggle begins again *all the more violently the more fruitful the already discovered means of production are. The division of labour and the application of machinery, therefore, will go on anew on an incomparably greater scale.*

Whatever the power of the means of production employed may be, competition seeks to rob capital of the golden fruits of this power by bringing the price of the commodities back to the cost of production, by thus making cheaper production—the supply of ever greater amounts of products for the same total price—an imperative law to the same extent as production can be cheapened, that is, as more can be produced with the same amount of labour. Thus the capitalist would have won nothing by his own exertions but the obligation to supply more in the same labour time, in a word, *more difficult conditions for the augmentation of the value of his capital.* While, therefore, competition continually pursues him with its law of the cost of production and every weapon that he forges against his rivals recoils against himself, the capitalist continually tries to get the better of competition by incessantly introducing new machines, more expensive, it is true, but producing more cheaply, and new division of labour in place of the old, and by not waiting until competition has rendered the new ones obsolete.

If now we picture to ourselves this feverish simultaneous agitation on the *whole world market,* it will be comprehensible how the growth, accumulation and concentration of capital results in an uninterrupted division of labour, and in the application of new and the perfecting of old machinery precipitately and on an ever more gigantic scale.

But how do these circumstances, which are inseparable from the growth of productive capital, affect the determination of wages?

The greater *division of labour* enables *one* worker to do the work of five, ten or twenty; it therefore multiplies competition among the workers fivefold, tenfold and twentyfold. The workers do not only compete by one selling himself cheaper than another; they compete by *one* doing the work of five, ten, twenty; and the *division of labour,* introduced by capital and continually increased, compels the workers to compete among themselves in this way.

Further, as the *division of labour* increases, labour *is simplified.* The special skill of the worker becomes worthless. He becomes trans-formed into a simple, monotonous productive force that does not have to use intense bodily or intellectual faculties. His labour becomes a labour that anyone can perform. Hence, competitors crowd upon him on all sides, and besides we remind the reader that the more simple and easily learned the labour is, the lower the cost of production needed to master it, the lower do wages sink, for, like the price of every other commodity, they are determined by the cost of production.

Therefore, as labour becomes more unsatisfying, more repulsive, competition increases and wages decrease. The worker tries to keep up the amount of his wages by working more, whether by working longer hours or by producing more in one hour. Driven by want, therefore, he still further increases the evil effects of the division of labour. The result is that *the more he works the less wages he receives,* and for the simple reason that he competes to that extent with his fellow workers, hence makes them into so many competitors; who offer themselves on just the same bad terms as he does himself, and that, therefore, in the last resort he *competes with himself, with himself as a member of the working class.*

Machinery brings about the same results on a much greater scale, by replacing skilled workers by unskilled, men by women, adults by children. It brings about the same results, where it is newly introduced, by throwing the hand workers on to the streets in masses, and, where it is developed, improved and replaced by more productive machinery, by discharging workers in smaller batches. We have portrayed above, in a hasty sketch, the industrial war of the capitalists among themselves; *this war has the peculiarity that its battles are won less by recruiting than by discharging the army of labour. The generals, the capitalists, compete with one another as to who can discharge most soldiers of industry.*

The economists tell us, it is true, that the workers rendered superfluous by machinery find *new* branches of employment.

They dare not assert directly that the same workers who are discharged find places in the new branches of labour. The facts cry out too loudly against this lie. They really only assert that new means of employment will open up for *other component sections of the working class*, for instance, for the portion of the young generation of workers that was ready to enter the branch of industry which has gone under. That is, of course, a great consolation for the disinherited workers. The worshipful capitalists will never want for fresh exploitable flesh and blood, and will let the dead bury their dead. This is a consolation which the bourgeois give themselves rather than one which they give the workers. If the whole class of wage-workers were to be abolished owing to machinery, how dreadful that would be for capital which, without wage labour, ceases to be capital!

Let us suppose, however, that those directly driven out of their jobs by machinery, and the entire section of the new generation that was already on the watch for this employment, *find a new occupation*. Does any one imagine that it will be as highly paid as that which has been lost? *That would contradict all the laws of economics.* We have seen how modern industry always brings with it the substitution of a more simple, subordinate occupation for the more complex and higher one.

How, then, could a mass of workers who have been thrown out of one branch of industry owing to machinery find refuge in another, unless the latter is *lower, worse paid?*

The workers who work in the manufacture of machinery itself have been cited as an exception. As soon as more machinery is demanded and used in industry, it is said, there must necessarily be an increase of machines, consequently of the manufacture of machines, and consequently of the employment of workers in the manufacture of machines; and the workers engaged in this branch of industry are claimed to be skilled, even educated workers.

Since the year 1840 this assertion, which even before was only half true, has lost all semblance of truth because ever more versatile machines have been employed in the manufacture of machinery, no more and no less than in the manufacture of cotton yarn, and the workers employed in the machine factories, confronted by highly elaborate machines, can only play the part of highly unelaborate machines.

But in place of the man who has been discharged owing to the machine, the factory employs maybe *three* children and *one* woman. And did not the man's wages have to suffice for the three children and a woman? Did not the minimum of wages have to suffice to maintain and to propagate the race? What, then, does this favourite bourgeois phrase prove? Nothing more than that now four times as many workers' lives are used up in order to gain a livelihood for *one* worker's family.

Let us sum up: *The more productive capital grows, the more the division of labour and the application of machinery expands. The more the division of labour and the application of machinery expands, the more competition among the workers expands and the more their wages contract.*

In addition, the working class gains recruits from the *higher strata of society* also; a mass of petty industrialists and small rentiers are hurled down into its ranks and have nothing better to do than urgently stretch out their arms alongside those of the workers. Thus the forest of uplifted arms demanding work becomes ever thicker, while the arms themselves become ever thinner.

That the small industrialist cannot survive in a contest one of the first conditions of which is to produce on an ever greater scale, that is, precisely to be a large and not a small industrialist, is self-evident.

That the interest on capital decreases in the same measure as the mass and number of capitals increase, as capital grows; that, therefore, the small rentier can no longer live on his interest but must throw himself into industry, and, consequently, help to swell the ranks of the small industrialists and thereby of candidates for the proletariat—all this surely requires no further explanation.

Finally, as the capitalists are compelled, by the movement described above, to exploit the already existing gigantic means of production on a larger scale and to set in motion all the mainsprings of credit to this end, there is a corresponding increase in industrial earthquakes, in which the trading world can only maintain itself by sacrificing a part of wealth, of products and even of productive forces to the gods of the nether world—in a word, *crises* increase. They become more frequent and more violent, if only because, as the mass of production, and consequently the need for extended markets, grows, the world market becomes more and more contracted, fewer and fewer new markets remain available for exploitation, since every preceding crisis has subjected to world trade a market hitherto unconquered or only superficially exploited. But capital does not *live* only on labour. A lord, at once aristocratic and barbarous, it drags with it into the grave the corpses of its slaves, whole hecatombs of workers who perish in the crises. Thus we see: *if capital grows rapidly, competition among the workers grows incomparably more rapidly, that is, the means of employment, the means of subsistence, of the working class decrease proportionately so much the more, and, nevertheless, the rapid growth of capital is the most favourable condition for wage labour.*

Manifesto of the Communist Party*

KARL MARX AND FRIEDRICH ENGELS

* * *

I. BOURGEOIS AND PROLETARIANS[1]

The history of all hitherto existing society is the history of class struggles.

Freeman and slave, patrician and plebeian, lord and serf, guild-master and journeyman, in a word, oppressor and oppressed, stood in constant opposition to one another, carried on an uninterrupted, now hidden, now open fight, a fight that each time ended, either in a revolutionary re-constitution of society at large, or in the common ruin of the contending classes.

In the earlier epochs of history, we find almost everywhere a complicated arrangement of society into various orders, a manifold gradation of social rank. In ancient Rome we have patricians, knights, plebeians, slaves; in the Middle Ages, feudal lords, vassals, guild-masters, journeymen, apprentices,

---

* First published in 1848; from *The Marx-Engels Reader, 2nd Edition*, edited by Robert C. Tucker.

1 By bourgeoisie is meant the class of modern Capitalists, owners of the means of social production and employers of wage-labour. By proletariat, the class of modern wage-labourers who, having no means of production of their own, are reduced to selling their labour-power in order to live [*Engels's English edition of 1888*].

serfs; in almost all of these classes, again, subordinate gradations.

The modern bourgeois society that has sprouted from the ruins of feudal society has not done away with class antagonisms. It has but established new classes, new conditions of oppression, new forms of struggle in place of the old ones.

Our epoch, the epoch of the bourgeoisie, possesses, however, this distinctive feature: it has simplified the class antagonisms: Society as a whole is more and more splitting up into two great hostile camps, into two great classes directly facing each other: Bourgeoisie and Proletariat.

From the serfs of the Middle Ages sprang the chartered burghers of the earliest towns. From these burgesses the first elements of the bourgeoisie were developed.

The discovery of America, the rounding of the Cape, opened up fresh ground for the rising bourgeoisie. The East-Indian and Chinese markets, the colonisation of America, trade with the colonies, the increase in the means of exchange and in commodities generally, gave to commerce, to navigation, to industry, an impulse never before known, and thereby, to the revolutionary element in the tottering feudal society, a rapid development.

The feudal system of industry, under which industrial production was monopolised by closed guilds, now no longer sufficed for the growing wants of the new markets. The manufacturing system took its place. The guild-masters were pushed on one side by the manufacturing middle class; division of labour between the different corporate guilds vanished in the face of division of labour in each single workshop.

Meantime the markets kept ever growing, the demand ever rising. Even manufacture no longer sufficed. Thereupon, steam and machinery revolutionised industrial production. The place of manufacture was taken by the giant, Modern Industry, the place of the industrial middle class, by industrial millionaires, the leaders of whole industrial armies, the modern bourgeois.

Modern industry has established the world-market, for which the discovery of America paved the way. This market has given an immense development to commerce, to navigation, to communication by land. This development has, in its turn, reacted on the extension of industry; and in proportion as industry, commerce, navigation, railways extended, in the same proportion the bourgeoisie developed, increased its capital, and pushed into the background every class handed down from the Middle Ages.

We see, therefore, how the modern bourgeoisie is itself the product of a long course of development, of a series of revolutions in the modes of production and of exchange.

Each step in the development of the bourgeoisie was accompanied by a corresponding political advance of that class. An oppressed class under the sway of the feudal nobility, an armed and self-governing association in the mediaeval commune; here independent urban republic (as in Italy and Germany), there taxable "third estate" of the monarchy (as in France), afterwards, in the period of manufacture proper, serving either the semi-feudal or the absolute monarchy as a counterpoise against the nobility, and, in fact, cornerstone of the great monarchies in general, the bourgeoisie has at last, since the establishment of Modern Industry and of the world-market, conquered for itself, in the modern representative State, exclusive political sway. The executive of the modern State is but a committee for managing the common affairs of the whole bourgeoisie.

The bourgeoisie, historically, has played a most revolutionary part.

The bourgeoisie, wherever it has got the upper hand, has put an end to all feudal, patriarchal, idyllic relations. It has pitilessly torn asunder the motley feudal ties that bound man to his "natural superiors," and has left remaining no other nexus between man and man than naked self-interest, than callous "cash payment." It has drowned the most heavenly ecstasies of religious fervour, of chivalrous enthusiasm, of philistine sentimentalism, in the icy water of egotistical calculation. It has resolved personal worth into exchange value, and in place of the numberless indefeasible chartered freedoms, has set up that single, unconscionable freedom—Free Trade. In one word, for exploitation, veiled by religious and political illusions, it has substituted naked, shameless, direct, brutal exploitation.

The bourgeoisie has stripped of its halo every occupation hitherto honoured and looked up to with reverent awe. It has converted the physician, the lawyer, the priest, the poet, the man of science, into its paid wage-labourers.

The bourgeoisie has torn away from the family its sentimental veil, and has reduced the family relation to a mere money relation.

The bourgeoisie has disclosed how it came to pass that the brutal display of vigour in the Middle Ages, which Reactionists so much admire, found its fitting complement in the most slothful indolence. It has been the first to show what man's activity can bring about. It has accomplished wonders far surpassing Egyptian pyramids, Roman aqueducts, and Gothic cathedrals; it has conducted expeditions that put in the shade all former Exoduses of nations and crusades.

The bourgeoisie cannot exist without constantly revolutionising the instruments of production, and thereby the relations of production, and with them the whole relations of society. Conservation of the old modes of production in unaltered form, was, on the contrary, the first condition of existence for all earlier industrial classes. Constant revolutionising of production, uninterrupted disturbance of all social conditions, everlasting uncertainty and agitation distinguish the bourgeois epoch from all earlier ones. All fixed, fast-frozen relations, with their train of ancient and venerable prejudices and opinions, are swept away, all new-formed ones become antiquated before they can ossify. All that is solid melts into air, all that is holy is profaned, and man is at last compelled to face with sober senses, his real conditions of life, and his relations with his kind.

The need of a constantly expanding market for its products chases the bourgeoisie over the whole surface of the globe. It must nestle everywhere, settle everywhere, establish connexions everywhere.

The bourgeoisie has through its exploitation of the world-market given a cosmopolitan character to production and consumption in every country. To the great chagrin of Reactionists, it has drawn from under the feet of industry the national ground on which it stood. All old-established national industries have been destroyed or are daily being destroyed. They are dislodged by new industries, whose introduction becomes a life and death question for all civilised nations, by industries that no longer work up indigenous raw material, but raw material drawn from the remotest zones; industries whose products are consumed, not only at home, but in every quarter of the globe. In place of the old wants, satisfied by the productions of the country, we find new wants, requiring for their satisfaction the products of distant lands and climes. In place of the old local and national seclusion and self-sufficiency, we have intercourse in every direction, universal interdependence of nations. And as in material, so also in intellectual production. The intellectual creations of individual nations become common property. National one-sidedness and narrow-mindedness become more and more impossible, and from the numerous national and local literatures, there arises a world literature.

The bourgeoisie, by the rapid improvement of all instruments of production, by the immensely facilitated means of communication, draws all, even the most barbarian, nations into civilisation. The cheap prices of its commodities are the heavy artillery with which it batters down all Chinese walls, with which it forces the barbarians' intensely obstinate hatred of foreigners to capitulate. It compels all nations, on pain of extinction, to adopt the bourgeois mode of production; it compels them to introduce what it calls civilisation into their midst, *i.e.*, to become bourgeois themselves. In one word, it creates a world after its own image.

The bourgeoisie has subjected the country to the rule of the towns. It has created enormous cities, has greatly increased the urban population as compared with the rural, and has thus rescued a considerable part of the population from the idiocy of rural life. Just as it has made the country dependent on the towns, so it has made barbarian and semi-barbarian countries dependent on the civilised ones, nations of peasants on nations of bourgeois, the East on the West.

The bourgeoisie keeps more and more doing away with the scattered state of the population, of the means of production, and of property. It has agglomerated population, centralised means of production, and has concentrated property in a few hands. The necessary consequence of this was political centralisation. Independent, or but loosely connected provinces, with separate interests, laws, governments and systems of taxation, became lumped together into one nation, with one government, one code of laws, one national class-interest, one frontier and one customs-tariff.

The bourgeoisie, during its rule of scarce one hundred years, has created more massive and more colossal productive forces than have all preceding generations together. Subjection of Nature's forces to man, machinery, application of chemistry to industry and agriculture, steam-navigation, railways, electric telegraphs, clearing of whole continents for cultivation, canalisation of rivers, whole populations conjured out of the ground—what earlier century had even a presentiment that such productive forces slumbered in the lap of social labour?

We see then: the means of production and of exchange, on whose foundation the bourgeoisie built itself up, were generated in feudal society. At a certain stage in the development of these means of production and of exchange, the conditions under which feudal society produced and exchanged, the feudal organisation of agriculture and manufacturing industry, in one word, the feudal relations of property became no longer compatible with the already developed productive forces; they became so many fetters. They had to be burst asunder; they were burst asunder.

Into their place stepped free competition, accompanied by a social and political constitution adapted to it, and by the economical and political sway of the bourgeois class.

A similar movement is going on before our own eyes. Modern bourgeois society with its relations of production, of exchange and of property, a society that has conjured up such gigantic means of production and of exchange, is like the sorcerer, who is no longer able to control the powers of the nether world whom he has called up by his spells. For many a decade past the history of industry and commerce is but the history of the revolt of modern productive forces against modern conditions of production, against the property relations that are the conditions for the existence of the bourgeoisie and of its rule. It is enough to mention the commercial crises that by their periodical return put on its trial, each time more threateningly, the existence of the entire bourgeois society. In these crises a great part not only of the existing products, but also of the previously created productive forces, are periodically destroyed. In these crises there breaks out an epidemic that, in all earlier epochs, would have seemed an absurdity—the epidemic of over-production. Society suddenly finds itself put back into a state of momentary barbarism; it appears as if a famine, a universal war of devastation had cut off the supply of every means of subsistence;

industry and commerce seem to be destroyed; and why? Because there is too much civilisation, too much means of subsistence, too much industry, too much commerce. The productive forces at the disposal of society no longer tend to further the development of the conditions of bourgeois property; on the contrary, they have become too powerful for these conditions, by which they are fettered, and so soon as they overcome these fetters, they bring disorder into the whole of bourgeois society, endanger the existence of bourgeois property. The conditions of bourgeois society are too narrow to comprise the wealth created by them. And how does the bourgeoisie get over these crises? On the one hand by enforced destruction of a mass of productive forces; on the other, by the conquest of new markets, and by the more thorough exploitation of the old ones. That is to say, by paving the way for more extensive and more destructive crises, and by diminishing the means whereby crises are prevented.

The weapons with which the bourgeoisie felled feudalism to the ground are now turned against the bourgeoisie itself.

But not only has the bourgeoisie forged the weapons that bring death to itself; it has also called into existence the men who are to wield those weapons—the modern working class—the proletarians.

In proportion as the bourgeoisie, *i.e.*, capital, is developed, in the same proportion is the proletariat, the modern working class, developed—a class of labourers, who live only so long as they find work, and who find work only so long as their labour increases capital. These labourers, who must sell themselves piece-meal, are a commodity, like every other article of commerce, and are consequently exposed to all the vicissitudes of competition, to all the fluctuations of the market.

Owing to the extensive use of machinery and to division of labour, the work of the proletarians has lost all individual character, and consequently, all charm for the workman. He becomes an appendage of the machine, and it is only the most simple, most monotonous, and most easily acquired knack, that is required of him. Hence, the cost of production of a workman is restricted, almost entirely, to the means of subsistence that he requires for his maintenance, and for the propagation of his race. But the price of a commodity, and therefore also of labour, is equal to its cost of production. In proportion, therefore, as the repulsiveness of the work increases, the wage decreases. Nay more, in proportion as the use of machinery and division of labour increases, in the same proportion the burden of toil also increases, whether by prolongation of the working hours, by increase of the work exacted in a given time or by increased speed of the machinery, etc.

Modern industry has converted the little workshop of the patriarchal master into the great factory of the industrial capitalist. Masses of labourers, crowded into the factory, are organised like soldiers. As privates of the industrial army they are placed under the command of a perfect hierarchy of officers and sergeants. Not only are they slaves of the bourgeois class, and of the bourgeois State; they are daily and hourly enslaved by the machine, by the overlooker, and, above all, by the individual bourgeois manufacturer himself. The more openly this despotism proclaims gain to be its end and aim, the more petty, the more hateful and the more embittering it is.

The less the skill and exertion of strength implied in manual labour, in other words, the more modern industry becomes developed, the more is the labour of men superseded by that of women. Differences of age and sex have no longer any distinctive social validity for the working class. All are instruments of labour, more or less expensive to use, according to their age and sex.

No sooner is the exploitation of the labourer by the manufacturer, so far, at an end, that he receives his wages in cash, than he is set upon by the other portions of the bourgeoisie, the landlord, the shopkeeper, the pawnbroker, etc.

The lower strata of the middle class—the small tradespeople, shopkeepers, and retired tradesmen generally, the handicraftsmen and peasants—all these sink gradually into the proletariat, partly because their diminutive capital does not suffice for the scale on which Modern Industry is carried on, and is swamped in the competition with the large capitalists, partly because their specialised skill is rendered worthless by new methods of production. Thus the proletariat is recruited from all classes of the population.

The proletariat goes through various stages of development. With its birth begins its struggle with the bourgeoisie. At first the contest is carried on by individual labourers, then by the workpeople of a factory, then by the operatives of one trade, in one locality, against the individual bourgeois who directly exploits them. They direct their attacks not against the bourgeois conditions of production, but against the instruments of production themselves; they destroy imported wares that compete with their labour, they smash to pieces machinery, they set factories ablaze, they seek to restore by force the vanished status of the workman of the Middle Ages.

At this stage the labourers still form an incoherent mass scattered over the whole country, and broken up by their mutual competition. If anywhere they unite to form more compact bodies, this is not yet the consequence of their own active union, but of the union of the bourgeoisie, which class, in order to attain its own political ends, is compelled to set the whole proletariat in motion, and is moreover yet, for a time, able to do so. At this stage, therefore, the proletarians do not fight their enemies, but the enemies of their enemies, the remnants of absolute monarchy, the landowners, the non-industrial bourgeois, the petty bourgeoisie. Thus the whole historical movement is concentrated in the hands of the bourgeoisie; every victory so obtained is a victory for the bourgeoisie.

But with the development of industry the proletariat not only increases in number; it becomes concentrated in greater masses, its strength grows, and it feels that strength more. The various interests and conditions of life within the ranks of the proletariat are more and more equalised, in proportion as machinery obliterates all distinctions of labour, and nearly everywhere reduces wages to the same low level. The growing competition among the bourgeois, and the resulting commercial crises, make the wages of the workers ever more fluctuating. The unceasing improvement of machinery, ever more rapidly developing, makes their livelihood more and more precarious; the collisions between individual workmen and individual bourgeois take more and more the character of collisions between two classes. Thereupon the workers begin to form combi-

nations (Trades Unions) against the bourgeois; they club together in order to keep up the rate of wages; they found permanent associations in order to make provision beforehand for these occasional revolts. Here and there the contest breaks out into riots.

Now and then the workers are victorious, but only for a time. The real fruit of their battles lies, not in the immediate result, but in the ever-expanding union of the workers. This union is helped on by the improved means of communication that are created by modern industry and that place the workers of different localities in contact with one another. It was just this contact that was needed to centralise the numerous local struggles, all of the same character, into one national struggle between classes. But every class struggle is a political struggle. And that union, to attain which the burghers of the Middle Ages, with their miserable highways, required centuries, the modern proletarians, thanks to railways, achieve in a few years.

This organisation of the proletarians into a class, and consequently into a political party, is continually being upset again by the competition between the workers themselves. But it ever rises up again, stronger, firmer, mightier. It compels legislative recognition of particular interests of the workers, by taking advantage of the divisions among the bourgeoisie itself. Thus the ten-hours' bill in England was carried.

Altogether collisions between the classes of the old society further, in many ways, the course of development of the proletariat. The bourgeoisie finds itself involved in a constant battle. At first with the aristocracy; later on, with those portions of the bourgeoisie itself, whose interests have become antagonistic to the progress of industry; at all times, with the bourgeoisie of foreign countries. In all these battles it sees itself compelled to appeal to the proletariat, to ask for its help, and thus, to drag it into the political arena. The bourgeoisie itself, therefore, supplies the proletariat with its own elements of political and general education, in other words, it furnishes the proletariat with weapons for fighting the bourgeoisie.

Further, as we have already seen, entire sections of the ruling classes are, by the advance of industry, precipitated into the proletariat, or are at least threatened in their conditions of existence. These also supply the proletariat with fresh elements of enlightenment and progress.

Finally, in times when the class struggle nears the decisive hour, the process of dissolution going on within the ruling class, in fact within the whole range of society, assumes such a violent, glaring character, that a small section of the ruling class cuts itself adrift, and joins the revolutionary class, the class that holds the future in its hands. Just as, therefore, at an earlier period, a section of the nobility went over to the bourgeoisie, so now a portion of the bourgeoisie goes over to the proletariat, and in particular, a portion of the bourgeois ideologists, who have raised themselves to the level of comprehending theoretically the historical movement as a whole.

Of all the classes that stand face to face with the bourgeoisie today, the proletariat alone is a really revolutionary class. The other classes decay and finally disappear in the face of Modern Industry; the proletariat is its special and essential product.

The lower middle class, the small manufacturer, the shopkeeper, the artisan, the peasant, all these fight against the bourgeoisie, to save from extinction their existence as fractions of the middle class. They are therefore not revolutionary, but conservative. Nay more, they are reactionary, for they try to roll back the wheel of history. If by chance they are revolutionary, they are so only in view of their impending transfer into the proletariat, they thus defend not their present, but their future interests, they desert their own standpoint to place themselves at that of the proletariat.

The "dangerous class," the social scum, that passively rotting mass thrown off by the lowest layers of old society, may, here and there, be swept into the movement by a proletarian revolution; its conditions of life, however, prepare it far more for the part of a bribed tool of reactionary intrigue.

In the conditions of the proletariat, those of old society at large are already virtually swamped. The proletarian is without property; his relation to his wife and children has no longer anything in common with the bourgeois family-relations; modern industrial labour, modern subjection to capital, the same in England as in France, in America as in Germany, has stripped him of every trace of national character. Law, morality, religion, are to him so many bourgeois prejudices, behind which lurk in ambush just as many bourgeois interests.

All the preceding classes that got the upper hand, sought to fortify their already acquired status by subjecting society at large to their conditions of appropriation. The proletarians cannot become masters of the productive forces of society, except by abolishing their own previous mode of appropriation, and thereby also every other previous mode of appropriation. They have nothing of their own to secure and to fortify; their mission is to destroy all previous securities for, and insurances of, individual property.

All previous historical movements were movements of minorities, or in the interests of minorities. The proletarian movement is the self-conscious, independent movement of the immense majority, in the interests of the immense majority. The proletariat, the lowest stratum of our present society, cannot stir, cannot raise itself up, without the whole superincumbent strata of official society being sprung into the air.

Though not in substance, yet in form, the struggle of the proletariat with the bourgeoisie is at first a national struggle. The proletariat of each country must, of course, first of all settle matters with its own bourgeoisie.

In depicting the most general phases of the development of the proletariat, we traced the more or less veiled civil war, raging within existing society, up to the point where that war breaks out into open revolution, and where the violent overthrow of the bourgeoisie lays the foundation for the sway of the proletariat.

Hitherto, every form of society has been based, as we have already seen, on the antagonism of oppressing and oppressed classes. But in order to oppress a class, certain conditions must be assured to it under which it can, at least, continue its slavish existence. The serf, in the period of serfdom, raised himself to membership in the commune, just as the petty bourgeois, under the yoke of feudal absolutism, managed to develop into a bourgeois. The modern labourer, on the contrary, instead of rising with the progress of industry, sinks deeper and deeper below the conditions of existence of his own class. He becomes a pauper, and pauperism develops more rapidly than population and wealth. And here it becomes evident, that the bourgeoisie is unfit any longer to be the ruling class in society, and to impose its conditions of existence upon society as an over-riding law. It is unfit to rule because it is incompetent to assure an existence to its slave within his slavery, because it cannot help letting him sink into such a state, that it has to feed him, instead of being fed by him. Society can no longer live under this bourgeoisie, in other words, its existence is no longer compatible with society.

The essential condition for the existence, and for the sway of the bourgeois class, is the formation and augmentation of capital; the condition for capital is wage-labour. Wage-labour rests exclusively on competition between the labourers. The advance of industry, whose involuntary promoter is the bourgeoisie, replaces the isolation of the labourers, due to competition, by their revolutionary combination, due to association. The development of Modern Industry, therefore, cuts from under its feet the very foundation on which the bourgeoisie produces and appropriates products. What the bourgeoisie, therefore, produces, above all, is its own gravediggers. Its fall and the victory of the proletariat are equally inevitable.

★ ★ ★

The German Ideology★

KARL MARX AND FRIEDRICH ENGELS

★ ★ ★

The ideas of the ruling class are in every epoch the ruling ideas: i.e., the class which is the ruling *material* force of society, is at the same time its ruling *intellectual* force. The class which has the means of material production at its disposal, has control at the same time over the means of mental production, so that thereby, generally speaking, the ideas of those who lack the means of mental production are subject to it. The ruling ideas are nothing more than the ideal expression of the dominant material relationships, the dominant material relationships grasped as ideas; hence of the relationships which make the one class the ruling one, therefore, the ideas of its dominance. The individuals composing the ruling class possess among other things consciousness, and therefore think. Insofar, therefore, as they rule as a class and determine the extent and compass of an epoch, it is self-evident that they do this in its whole range, hence among other things rule also as thinkers, as producers of ideas, and regulate the production and distribution of the ideas of their age: thus their ideas are the ruling ideas of the epoch. For instance, in an age

★ First published in 1846; from *The Marx-Engels Reader, 2nd Edition,* edited by Robert C. Tucker.

and in a country where royal power, aristocracy and bourgeoisie are contending for mastery and where, therefore, mastery is shared, the doctrine of the separation of powers proves to be the dominant idea and is expressed as an "eternal law."

The division of labour, which we have already seen above as one of the chief forces of history up till now, manifests itself also in the ruling class as the division of mental and material labour, so that inside this class one part appears as the thinkers of the class (its active, conceptive ideologists, who make the perfecting of the illusion of the class about itself their chief source of livelihood), while the others' attitude to these ideas and illusions is more passive and receptive, because they are in reality the active members of this class and have less time to make up illusions and ideas about themselves. Within this class this cleavage can even develop into a certain opposition and hostility between the two parts, which, however, in the case of a practical collision, in which the class itself is endangered, automatically comes to nothing, in which case there also vanishes the semblance that the ruling ideas were not the ideas of the ruling class and had a power distinct from the power of this class. The existence of revolutionary ideas in a particular period presupposes the existence of a revolutionary class; about the premises for the latter sufficient has already been said above.

If now in considering the course of history we detach the ideas of the ruling class from the ruling class itself and attribute to them an independent existence, if we confine ourselves to saying that these or those ideas were dominant at a given time, without bothering ourselves about the conditions of production and the producers of these ideas, if we thus ignore the individuals and world conditions which are the source of the ideas, we can say, for instance, that during the time that the aristocracy was dominant, the concepts honour, loyalty, etc., were dominant, during the dominance of the bourgeoisie the concepts freedom, equality, etc. The ruling class itself on the whole imagines this to be so. This conception of history, which is common to all historians, particularly since the eighteenth century, will necessarily come up against the phenomenon that increasingly abstract ideas hold sway, i.e., ideas which increasingly take on the form of universality. For each new class which puts itself in the place of one ruling before it, is compelled, merely in order to carry through its aim, to represent its interest as the common interest of all the members of society, that is, expressed in ideal form: it has to give its ideas the form of universality, and represent them as the only rational, universally valid ones. The class making a revolution appears from the very start, if only because it is opposed to a *class,* not as a class but as the representative of the whole of society; it appears as the whole mass of society confronting the one ruling class. It can do this because, to start with, its interest really is more connected with the common interest of all other non-ruling classes, because under the pressure of hitherto existing conditions its interest has not yet been able to develop as the particular interest of a particular class. Its victory, therefore, benefits also many individuals of the other classes which are not winning a dominant position, but only insofar as it now puts these individuals in a position to raise themselves into the ruling class. When the

French bourgeoisie overthrew the power of the aristocracy, it thereby made it possible for many proletarians to raise themselves above the proletariat, but only insofar as they became bourgeois. Every new class, therefore, achieves its hegemony only on a broader basis than that of the class ruling previously, whereas the opposition of the non-ruling class against the new ruling class later develops all the more sharply and profoundly. Both these things determine the fact that the struggle to be waged against this new ruling class, in its turn, aims at a more decided and radical negation of the previous conditions of society than could all previous classes which sought to rule.

This whole semblance, that the rule of a certain class is only the rule of certain ideas, comes to a natural end, of course, as soon as class rule in general ceases to be the form in which society is organised, that is to say, as soon as it is no longer necessary to represent a particular interest as general or the "general interest" as ruling.

Once the ruling ideas have been separated from the ruling individuals and, above all, from the relationships which result from a given stage of the mode of production, and in this way the conclusion has been reached that history is always under the sway of ideas, it is very easy to abstract from these various ideas "*the* idea," the notion, etc., as the dominant force in history, and thus to understand all these separate ideas and concepts as "forms of self-determination" on the part of *the* concept developing in history.

★ ★ ★

Preface to *A Contribution to the Critique of Political Economy**

KARL MARX

* * *

In the social production of their life, men enter into definite relations that are indispensable and independent of their will, relations of production which correspond to a definite stage of development of their material productive forces. The sum total of these relations of production constitutes the economic structure of society, the real foundation, on which rises a legal and political superstructure and to which correspond definite forms of social consciousness. The mode of production of material life conditions the social, political and intellectual life process in general. It is not the consciousness of men that determines their being, but, on the contrary, their social being that determines their consciousness. At a certain stage of their development, the material productive forces of society come in conflict with the existing relations of production, or—what is but a legal expression for the same thing—with the property relations within which they have been at work hitherto. From forms of development of the productive forces these relations turn into their fetters. Then begins an epoch of social revolution. [With the change of the economic

---

* First published in 1859; from *The Marx-Engels Reader, 2nd Edition,* edited by Robert C. Tucker.

foundation the entire immense superstructure is more or less rapidly transformed. In considering such transformations a distinction should always be made between the material transformation of the economic conditions of production, which can be determined with the precision of natural science, and the legal, political, religious, aesthetic or philosophic—in short, ideological forms in which men become conscious of this conflict and fight it out. Just as our opinion of an individual is not based on what he thinks of himself, so can we not judge of such a period of transformation by its own consciousness; on the contrary, this consciousness must be explained rather from the contradictions of material life, from the existing conflict between the social productive forces and the relations of production. No social order ever perishes before all the productive forces for which there is room in it have developed; and new, higher relations of production never appear before the material conditions of their existence have matured in the womb of the old society itself. Therefore mankind always sets itself only such tasks as it can solve; since, looking at the matter more closely, it will always be found that the task itself arises only when the material conditions for its solution already exist or are at least in the process of formation. In broad outlines Asiatic, ancient, feudal, and modern bourgeois modes of production can be designated as progressive epochs in the economic formation of society. The bourgeois relations of production are the last antagonistic form of the social process of production—antagonistic not in the sense of individual antagonism, but of one arising from the social conditions of life of the individuals; at the same time the productive forces developing in the womb of bourgeois society create the material conditions for the solution of that antagonism. This social formation brings, therefore, the prehistory of human society to a close.

★ ★ ★

3

Class, Status, Party*

MAX WEBER

A. ECONOMICALLY DETERMINED POWER AND THE STATUS ORDER

The structure of every legal order directly influences the distribution of power, economic or otherwise, within its respective community. This is true of all legal orders and not only that of the state. In general, we understand by "power" the chance of a man or a number of men to realize their own will in a social action even against the resistance of others who are participating in the action.

"Economically conditioned" power is not, of course, identical with "power" as such. On the contrary, the emergence of economic power may be the consequence of power existing on other grounds. Man does not strive for power only in order to enrich himself economically. Power, including economic power, may be valued for its own sake. Very frequently the striving for power is also conditioned by the social honor it entails. Not all power, however, entails social honor: The typical American Boss, as well as the typical

* First published in 1920; *From Max Weber: Essays in Sociology*, edited by H. H. Gerth and C. Wright Mills.

big speculator, deliberately relinquishes social honor. Quite generally, "mere economic" power, and especially "naked" money power, is by no means a recognized basis of social honor. Nor is power the only basis of social honor. Indeed, social honor, or prestige, may even be the basis of economic power, and very frequently has been. Power, as well as honor, may be guaranteed by the legal order, but, at least normally, it is not their primary source. The legal order is rather an additional factor that enhances the chance to hold power or honor; but it can not always secure them.

The way in which social honor is distributed in a community between typical groups participating in this distribution we call the "status order." The social order and the economic order are related in a similar manner to the legal order. However, the economic order merely defines the way in which economic goods and services are distributed and used. Of course, the status order is strongly influenced by it, and in turn reacts upon it.

Now: "classes," "status groups," and "parties" are phenomena of the distribution of power within a community.

B. DETERMINATION OF CLASS SITUATION BY MARKET SITUATION

In our terminology, "classes" are not communities; they merely represent possible, and frequent, bases for social action. We may speak of a "class" when (1) a number of people have in common a specific causal component of their life chances, insofar as (2) this component is represented exclusively by economic interests in the possession of goods and opportunities for income, and (3) is represented under the conditions of the commodity or labor markets. This is "class situation."

It is the most elemental economic fact that the way in which the disposition over material property is distributed among a plurality of people, meeting competitively in the market for the purpose of exchange, in itself creates specific life chances. The mode of distribution, in accord with the law of marginal utility, excludes the non-wealthy from competing for highly valued goods; it favors the owners and, in fact, gives to them a monopoly to acquire such goods. Other things being equal, the mode of distribution monopolizes the opportunities for profitable deals for all those who, provided with goods, do not necessarily have to exchange them. It increases, at least generally, their power in the price struggle with those who, being propertyless, have nothing to offer but their labor or the resulting products, and who are compelled to get rid of these products in order to subsist at all. The mode of distribution gives to the propertied a monopoly on the possibility of transferring property from the sphere of use as "wealth" to the sphere of "capital," that is, it gives them the entrepreneurial function and all chances to share directly or indirectly in returns on capital. All this holds true within the area in which pure market conditions prevail. "Property" and "lack of property" are, therefore, the basic categories of all class situations. It does not matter whether these two categories become effective in the competitive struggles of the consumers or of the producers.

Within these categories, however, class situations are further differentiated: on the one hand, according to the kind of property that is usable for returns; and, on the other hand, according to the kind of services that can be offered in the market. Ownership of dwellings; workshops; warehouses; stores; agriculturally usable land in large or small holdings—a quantitative difference with possibly qualitative consequences; ownership of mines; cattle; men (slaves); disposition over mobile instruments of production, or capital goods of all sorts, especially money or objects that can easily be exchanged for money; disposition over products of one's own labor or of others' labor differing according to their various distances from consumability; disposition over transferable monopolies of any kind—all these distinctions differentiate the class situations of the propertied just as does the "meaning" which they can give to the use of property, especially to property which has money equivalence. Accordingly, the propertied, for instance, may belong to the class of rentiers or to the class of entrepreneurs.

Those who have no property but who offer services are differentiated just as much according to their kinds of services as according to the way in which they make use of these services, in a continuous or discontinuous relation to a recipient. But always this is the generic connotation of the concept of class: that the kind of chance in the *market* is the decisive moment which presents a common condition for the individual's fate. Class situation is, in this sense, ultimately market situation. The effect of naked possession *per se*, which among cattle breeders gives the non-owning slave or serf into the

power of the cattle owner, is only a fore-runner of real "class" formation. However, in the cattle loan and in the naked severity of the law of debts in such communities for the first time mere "possession" as such emerges as decisive for the fate of the individual; this is much in contrast to crop-raising communities, which are based on labor. The creditor-debtor relation becomes the basis of "class situations" first in the cities, where a "credit market," however primitive, with rates of interest increasing according to the extent of dearth and factual monopolization of lending in the hands of a plutocracy could develop. Therewith "class struggles" begin.

Those men whose fate is not determined by the chance of using goods or services for themselves on the market, e.g., slaves, are not, however, a class in the technical sense of the term. They are, rather, a status group.

C. SOCIAL ACTION FLOWING FROM CLASS INTEREST

According to our terminology, the factor that creates "class" is unambiguously economic interest, and indeed, only those interests involved in the existence of the market. Nevertheless, the concept of class-interest is an ambiguous one: even as an empirical concept it is ambiguous as soon as one understands by it something other than the factual direction of interests following with a certain probability from the class situation for a certain average of those people subjected to the class situation. The class situation and other circumstances remaining the same, the direction in which the individual worker, for instance, is likely to pursue his interests may vary widely, according to whether he is constitutionally qualified for the task at hand to a high, to an average, or to a low degree. In the same way, the direction of interests may vary according to whether or not social action of a larger or smaller portion of those commonly affected by the class situation, or even an association among them, e.g., a trade union, has grown out of the class situation, from which the individual may expect promising results for himself. The emergence of an association or even of mere social action from a common class situation is by no means a universal phenomenon.

The class situation may be restricted in its efforts to the generation of essentially *similar* reactions, that is to say, within our terminology, of "mass behavior." However, it may not even have this result. Furthermore, often merely amorphous social action emerges. For example, the "grumbling" of workers known in ancient Oriental ethics: The moral disapproval of the work-master's conduct, which in its practical significance was probably equivalent to an increasingly typical phenomenon of precisely the latest industrial development, namely, the slowdown of laborers by virtue of tacit agreement. The degree in which "social action" and possibly associations emerge from the mass behavior of the members of a class is linked to general cultural conditions, especially to those of an intellectual sort. It is also linked to the extent of the contrasts that have already evolved, and is especially linked to the transparency of the connections between the causes and the consequences of the class situation. For however different life chances may be,

this fact in itself, according to all experience, by no means gives birth to "class action" (social action by the members of a class). For that, the real conditions and the results of the class situation must be distinctly recognizable. For only then the contrast of life chances can be felt not as an absolutely given fact to be accepted, but as a resultant from either (1) the given distribution of property, or (2) the structure of the concrete economic order. It is only then that people may react against the class structure not only through acts of intermittent and irrational protest, but in the form of rational association. There have been "class situations" of the first category (1), of a specifically naked and transparent sort, in the urban centers of Antiquity and during the Middle Ages; especially then when great fortunes were accumulated by factually monopolized trading in local industrial products or in foodstuffs; furthermore, under certain conditions, in the rural economy of the most diverse periods, when agriculture was increasingly exploited in a profit-making manner. The most important historical example of the second category (2) is the class situation of the modern proletariat.

D. TYPES OF CLASS STRUGGLE

Thus every class may be the carrier of any one of the innumerable possible forms of class action, but this is not necessarily so. In any case, a class does not in itself constitute a group (*Gemeinschaft*). To treat "class" conceptually as being equivalent to "group" leads to distortion. That men in the same class situation regularly react in mass actions to such tangible situations as economic ones in the direction of those interests that are most adequate to their average number is an important and after all simple fact for the understanding of historical events. However, this fact must not lead to that kind of pseudo-scientific operation with the concepts of class and class interests which is so frequent these days and which has found its most classic expression in the statement of a talented author, that the individual may be in error concerning his interests but that the class is infallible about its interests.

If classes as such are not groups, nevertheless class situations emerge only on the basis of social action. However, social action that brings forth class situations is not basically action among members of the identical class; it is an action among members of different classes. Social actions that directly determine the class situation of the worker and the entrepreneur are: the labor market, the commodities market, and the capitalistic enterprise. But, in its turn, the existence of a capitalistic enterprise presupposes that a very specific kind of social action exists to protect the possession of goods *per se,* and especially the power of individuals to dispose, in principle freely, over the means of production: a certain kind of legal order. Each kind of class situation, and above all when it rests upon the power of property *per se,* will become most clearly efficacious when all other determinants of reciprocal relations are, as far as possible, eliminated in their significance. It is in this way that the use of the power of property in the market obtains its most sovereign importance.

Now status groups hinder the strict carrying through of the sheer market principle. In

the present context they are of interest only from this one point of view. Before we briefly consider them, note that not much of a general nature can be said about the more specific kinds of antagonism between classes (in our meaning of the term). The great shift, which has been going on continuously in the past, and up to our times, may be summarized, although at a cost of some precision: the struggle in which class situations are effective has progressively shifted from consumption credit toward, first, competitive struggles in the commodity market and then toward wage disputes on the labor market. The class struggles of Antiquity—to the extent that they were genuine class struggles and not struggles between status groups—were initially carried on by peasants and perhaps also artisans threatened by debt bondage and struggling against urban creditors. For debt bondage is the normal result of the differentiation of wealth in commercial cities, especially in seaport cities. A similar situation has existed among cattle breeders. Debt relationships as such produced class action up to the days of Catilina. Along with this, and with an increase in provision of grain for the city by transporting it from the outside, the struggle over the means of sustenance emerged. It centered in the first place around the provision of bread and determination of the price of bread. It lasted throughout Antiquity and the entire Middle Ages. The propertyless flocked together against those who actually and supposedly were interested in the dearth of bread. This fight spread until it involved all those commodities essential to the way of life and to handicraft production. There were only incipient discussions of wage disputes in Antiquity and in the Middle Ages. But they have been slowly increasing up into modern times. In the earlier periods they were completely secondary to slave rebellions as well as to conflicts in the commodity market.

The propertyless of Antiquity and of the Middle Ages protested against monopolies, pre-emption, forestalling, and the withholding of goods from the market in order to raise prices. Today the central issue is the determination of the price of labor. The transition is represented by the fight for access to the market and for the determination of the price of products. Such fights went on between merchants and workers in the putting-out system of domestic handicraft during the transition to modern times. Since it is quite a general phenomenon we must mention here that the class antagonisms that are conditioned through the market situations are usually most bitter between those who actually and directly participate as opponents in price wars. It is not the rentier, the share-holder, and the banker who suffer the ill will of the worker, but almost exclusively the manufacturer and the business executives who are the direct opponents of workers in wage conflicts. This is so in spite of the fact that it is precisely the cash boxes of the rentier, the shareholder, and the banker into which the more or less unearned gains flow, rather than into the pockets of the manufacturers or of the business executives. This simple state of affairs has very frequently been decisive for the role the class situation has played in the formation of political parties. For example, it has made possible the varieties of patriarchal socialism and the frequent attempts—formerly, at least—of threatened status groups to form alliances with the proletariat against the bourgeoisie.

E. STATUS HONOR

In contrast to classes, *Stände* (*status groups*) are normally groups. They are, however, often of an amorphous kind. In contrast to the purely economically determined "class situation," we wish to designate as *status situation* every typical component of the life of men that is determined by a specific, positive or negative, social estimation of *honor*. This honor may be connected with any quality shared by a plurality, and, of course, it can be knit to a class situation: class distinctions are linked in the most varied ways with status distinctions. Property as such is not always recognized as a status qualification, but in the long run it is, and with extraordinary regularity. In the subsistence economy of neighborhood associations, it is often simply the richest who is the "chieftain." However, this often is only an honorific preference. For example, in the so-called pure modern democracy, that is, one devoid of any expressly ordered status privileges for individuals, it may be that only the families coming under approximately the same tax class dance with one another. This example is reported of certain smaller Swiss cities. But status honor need not necessarily be linked with a class situation. On the contrary, it normally stands in sharp opposition to the pretensions of sheer property.

Both propertied and propertyless people can belong to the same status group, and frequently they do with very tangible consequences. This equality of social esteem may, however, in the long run become quite precarious. The equality of status among American gentlemen, for instance, is expressed by the fact that outside the subordination determined by the different functions of business, it would be considered strictly repugnant—wherever the old tradition still prevails—if even the richest boss, while playing billiards or cards in his club would not treat his clerk as in every sense fully his equal in birthright, but would bestow upon him the condescending status-conscious "benevolence" which the German boss can never dissever from his attitude. This is one of the most important reasons why in America the German clubs have never been able to attain the attraction that the American clubs have.

In content, status honor is normally expressed by the fact that above all else a specific *style of life* is expected from all those who wish to belong to the circle. Linked with this expectation are restrictions on social intercourse (that is, intercourse which is not subservient to economic or any other purposes). These restrictions may confine normal marriages to within the status circle and may lead to complete endogamous closure. Whenever this is not a mere individual and socially irrelevant imitation of another style of life, but consensual action of this closing character, the status development is under way.

In its characteristic form, stratification by status groups on the basis of conventional styles of life evolves at the present time in the United States out of the traditional democracy. For example, only the resident of a certain street ("the Street") is considered as belonging to "society," is qualified for social intercourse, and is visited and invited. Above all, this dif-

ferentiation evolves in such a way as to make for strict submission to the fashion that is dominant at a given time in society. This submission to fashion also exists among men in America to a degree unknown in Germany; it appears as an indication of the fact that a given man puts forward a *claim* to qualify as a gentleman. This submission decides, at least *prima facie*, that he will be treated as such. And this recognition becomes just as important for his employment chances in swank establishments, and above all, for social intercourse and marriage with "esteemed" families, as the qualification for dueling among Germans. As for the rest, status honor is usurped by certain families resident for a long time, and, of course, correspondingly wealthy (e.g. F.F.V., the First Families of Virginia), or by the actual or alleged descendants of the "Indian Princess" Pocahontas, of the Pilgrim fathers, or of the Knickerbockers, the members of almost inaccessible sects and all sorts of circles setting themselves apart by means of any other characteristics and badges. In this case stratification is purely conventional and rests largely on usurpation (as does almost all status honor in its beginning). But the road to legal privilege, positive or negative, is easily traveled as soon as a certain stratification of the social order has in fact been "lived in" and has achieved stability by virtue of a stable distribution of economic power.

F. ETHNIC SEGREGATION AND CASTE

Where the consequences have been realized to their full extent, the status group evolves into a closed caste. Status distinctions are then guaranteed not merely by conventions and laws, but also by religious sanctions. This occurs in such a way that every physical contact with a member of any caste that is considered to be lower by the members of a higher caste is considered as making for a ritualistic impurity and a stigma which must be expiated by a religious act. In addition, individual castes develop quite distinct cults and gods.

In general, however, the status structure reaches such extreme consequences only where there are underlying differences which are held to be "ethnic." The caste is, indeed, the normal form in which ethnic communities that believe in blood relationship and exclude exogamous marriage and social intercourse usually associate with one another. ★ ★ ★ Such a caste situation is part of the phenomenon of pariah peoples and is found all over the world. These people form communities, acquire specific occupational traditions of handicrafts or of other arts, and cultivate a belief in their ethnic community. They live in a diaspora strictly segregated from all personal intercourse, except that of an unavoidable sort, and their situation is legally precarious. Yet, by virtue of their economic indispensability, they are tolerated, indeed frequently privileged, and they live interspersed in the political communities. The Jews are the most impressive historical example.

A status segregation grown into a caste differs in its structure from a mere ethnic segregation: the caste structure transforms the horizontal and unconnected coexistences of ethnically segregated groups into a vertical social system of super- and subordination. Correctly formulated: a comprehensive association integrates the ethnically divided communities into one political unit. They differ precisely in this way: ethnic co-existence, based on mutual repulsion and disdain, allows each ethnic community to consider its own honor as the highest one; the caste structure brings about a social subordination and an acknowledgement of "more honor" in favor of the privileged caste and status groups. This is due to the fact that in the caste structure ethnic distinctions as such have become "functional" distinctions within the political association (warriors, priests, artisans that are politically important for war and for building, and so on). But even pariah peoples who are most despised (for example, the Jews) are usually apt to continue cultivating the belief in their own specific "honor," a belief that is equally peculiar to ethnic and to status groups.

However, with the negatively privileged status groups the sense of dignity takes a specific deviation. A sense of dignity is the precipitation in individuals of social honor and of conventional demands which a positively privileged status group raises for the deportment of its members. The sense of dignity that characterizes positively privileged status groups is naturally related to their "being" which does not transcend itself, that is, it is related to their "beauty and excellence" (καλοκάγαθία). Their kingdom is "of this world." They live for the present and by exploiting their great past. The sense of dignity of the negatively privileged strata naturally refers to a future lying beyond the present, whether it is of this life or of another. In other words, it must be nurtured by the belief in a providential mission and by a belief in a specific honor before

God. The chosen people's dignity is nurtured by a belief either that in the beyond "the last will be the first," or that in this life a Messiah will appear to bring forth into the light of the world which has cast them out the hidden honor of the pariah people. This simple state of affairs, and not the resentment which is so strongly emphasized in Nietzsche's much-admired construction in the *Genealogy of Morals*, is the source of the religiosity cultivated by pariah status groups ★ ★ ★; moreover, resentment applies only to a limited extent; for one of Nietzsche's main examples, Buddhism, it is not at all applicable.

For the rest, the development of status groups from ethnic segregations is by no means the normal phenomenon. On the contrary. Since objective "racial differences" are by no means behind every subjective sentiment of an ethnic community, the question of an ultimately racial foundation of status structure is rightly a question of the concrete individual case. Very frequently a status group is instrumental in the production of a thoroughbred anthropological type. Certainly status groups are to a high degree effective in producing extreme types, for they select personally qualified individuals (e.g. the knighthood selects those who are fit for warfare, physically and psychically). But individual selection is far from being the only, or the predominant, way in which status groups are formed: political membership or class situation has at all times been at least as frequently decisive. And today the class situation is by far the predominant factor. After all, the possibility of a style of life expected for members of a status group is usually conditioned economically.

⦀ G. STATUS PRIVILEGES

For all practical purposes, stratification by status goes hand in hand with a monopolization of ideal and material goods or opportunities, in a manner we have come to know as typical. Besides the specific status honor, which always rests upon distance and exclusiveness, honorific preferences may consist of the privilege of wearing special costumes, of eating special dishes taboo to others, of carrying arms—which is most obvious in its consequences—, the right to be a dilettante, for example, to play certain musical instruments. However, material monopolies provide the most effective motives for the exclusiveness of a status group; although, in themselves, they are rarely sufficient, almost always they come into play to some extent. Within a status circle there is the question of intermarriage: the interest of the families in the monopolization of potential bridegrooms is at least of equal importance and is parallel to the interest in the monopolization of daughters. The daughters of the members must be provided for. With an increased closure of the status group, the conventional preferential opportunities for special employment grow into a legal monopoly of special offices for the members. Certain goods become objects for monopolization by status groups, typically, entailed estates, and frequently also the possession of serfs or bondsmen and finally, special trades. This monopolization occurs positively when the status group is exclusively entitled to own and to manage them; and negatively when, in order to maintain its specific way of life, the status group must *not* own and manage them. For the decisive role of a style of life in status honor means that status groups are the specific bearers of all conventions. In whatever way it may be manifest, all stylization of life either originates in status groups or is at least conserved by them. Even if the principles of status conventions differ greatly, they reveal certain typical traits, especially among the most privileged strata. Quite generally, among privileged status groups there is a status disqualification that operates against the performance of common physical labor. This disqualification is now "setting in" in America against the old tradition of esteem for labor. Very frequently every rational economic pursuit, and especially entrepreneurial activity, is looked upon as a disqualification of status. Artistic and literary activity is also considered degrading work as soon as it is exploited for income, or at least when it is connected with hard physical exertion. An example is the sculptor working like a mason in his dusty smock as over against the painter in his salon-like studio and those forms of musical practice that are acceptable to the status group.

H. ECONOMIC CONDITIONS AND EFFECTS OF STATUS STRATIFICATION

The frequent disqualification of the gainfully employed as such is a direct result of the principle of status stratification, and of course, of this principle's opposition to a distribution of power which is regulated exclusively through the market. These two factors operate along with various individual ones, which will be touched upon below.

We have seen above that the market and its processes knows no personal distinctions: "functional" interests dominate it. It knows nothing of honor. The status order means precisely the reverse: stratification in terms of honor and styles of life peculiar to status groups as such. The status order would be threatened at its very root if mere economic acquisition and naked economic power still bearing the stigma of its extra-status origin could bestow upon anyone who has won them the same or even greater honor as the vested interests claim for themselves. After all, given equality of status honor, property *per se* represents an addition even if it is not overtly acknowledged to be such. Therefore all groups having interest in the status order react with special sharpness precisely against the pretensions of purely economic acquisition. In most cases they react the more vigorously the more they feel themselves threatened. Calderon's respectful treatment of the peasant, for instance, as opposed to Shakespeare's simultaneous ostensible disdain of the *canaille* illustrates the different way in which a firmly structured status order reacts as compared with a status order that has become economically precarious. This is an example of a state of affairs that recurs everywhere. Precisely because of the rigorous reactions against the claims of property *per se,* the "parvenu" is never accepted, personally and without reservation, by the privileged status groups, no matter how completely his style of life has been adjusted to theirs. They will only accept his descendants who have been educated in the conventions of their status group and who have never besmirched its honor by their own economic labor.

As to the general *effect* of the status order, only one consequence can be stated, but it is a very important one: the hindrance of the free development of the market. This occurs first for those goods that status groups directly withhold from free exchange by monopolization, which may be effected either legally or conventionally. For example, in many Hellenic cities during the "status era" and also originally in Rome, the inherited estate (as shown by the old formula for placing spendthrifts under a guardian) was monopolized, as were the estates of knights, peasants, priests, and especially the clientele of the craft and merchant guilds. The market is restricted, and the power of naked property *per se*, which gives its stamp to class formation, is pushed into the background. The results of this process can be most varied. Of course, they do not necessarily weaken the contrasts in the economic situation. Frequently they strengthen these contrasts, and in any case, where stratification by status permeates a community as strongly as was the case in all political communities of Antiquity and of the Middle Ages, one can never speak of a genuinely free market competition as we understand it today. There are wider effects than this direct exclusion of special goods from the market. From the conflict between the status order and the purely economic order mentioned above, it follows that in most instances the notion of honor peculiar to status absolutely abhors that which is essential to the market: hard bargaining. Honor abhors hard bargaining among peers and occasionally it taboos it for the members of a status group in general. Therefore, everywhere some status groups, and usually the most influ-ential, consider almost any kind of overt participation in economic acquisition as absolutely stigmatizing.

With some over-simplification, one might thus say that classes are stratified according to their relations to the production and acquisition of goods; whereas status groups are stratified according to the principles of their *consumption* of goods as represented by special styles of life.

An "occupational status group," too, is a status group proper. For normally, it successfully claims social honor only by virtue of the special style of life which may be determined by it. The differences between classes and status groups frequently overlap. It is precisely those status communities most strictly segregated in terms of honor (viz. the Indian castes) who today show, although within very rigid limits, a relatively high degree of indifference to pecuniary income. However, the Brahmins seek such income in many different ways.

As to the general economic conditions making for the predominance of stratification by status, only the following can be said. When the bases of the acquisition and distribution of goods are relatively stable, stratification by status is favored. Every technological repercussion and economic transformation threatens stratification by status and pushes the class situation into the foreground. Epochs and countries in which the naked class situation is of predominant significance are regularly the periods of technical and economic transformations. And every slowing down of the change in economic stratification leads, in due course, to the growth of status structures and makes for a resuscitation of the important role of social honor.

⫴ I. PARTIES

Whereas the genuine place of classes is within the economic order, the place of status groups is within the social order, that is, within the sphere of the distribution of honor. From within these spheres, classes and status groups influence one another and the legal order and are in turn influenced by it. "*Parties*" reside in the sphere of power. Their action is oriented toward the acquisition of social power, that is to say, toward influencing social action no matter what its content may be. In principle, parties may exist in a social club as well as in a state. As over against the actions of classes and status groups, for which this is not necessarily the case, party-oriented social action always involves association. For it is always directed toward a goal which is striven for in a planned manner. This goal may be a cause (the party may aim at realizing a program for ideal or material purposes), or the goal may be personal (sinecures, power, and from these, honor for the leader and the followers of the party). Usually the party aims at all these simultaneously. Parties are, therefore, only possible within groups that have an associational character, that is, some rational order and a staff of persons available who are ready to enforce it. For parties aim precisely at influencing this staff, and if possible, to recruit from it party members.

In any individual case, parties may represent interests determined through class situation or status situation, and they may recruit their following respectively from one or the other. But they need be neither purely class nor purely status parties; in fact, they are more likely to be mixed types, and sometimes they are neither.

They may represent ephemeral or enduring structures. Their means of attaining power may be quite varied, ranging from naked violence of any sort to canvassing for votes with coarse or subtle means: money, social influence, the force of speech, suggestion, clumsy hoax, and so on to the rougher or more artful tactics of obstruction in parliamentary bodies.

The sociological structure of parties differs in a basic way according to the kind of social action which they struggle to influence; that means, they differ according to whether or not the community is stratified by status or by classes. Above all else, they vary according to the structure of domination. For their leaders normally deal with its conquest. In our general terminology, parties are not only products of modern forms of domination. We shall also designate as parties the ancient and medieval ones, despite the fact that they differ basically from modern parties. Since a party always struggles for political control (*Herrschaft*), its organization too is frequently strict and "authoritarian." Because of these variations between the forms of domination, it is impossible to say anything about the structure of parties without discussing them first. ★ ★ ★

★ ★ ★ We should add one more general observation about classes, status groups and parties: The fact that they presuppose a larger association, especially the framework of a polity, does not mean that they are confined to it. On the contrary, at all times it has been the order of the day that such association (even when it aims at the use of military force in common) reaches beyond the state boundaries. This can be seen in the [interlocal] solidarity of interests of oligarchs and democrats in Hellas, of Guelphs and

Ghibellines in the Middle Ages, and within the Calvinist party during the age of religious struggles; and all the way up to the solidarity of landlords (International Congresses of Agriculture), princes (Holy Alliance, Karlsbad Decrees [of 1819]), socialist workers, conservatives (the longing of Prussian conservatives for Russian intervention in 1850). But their aim is not necessarily the establishment of a new territorial dominion. In the main they aim to influence the existing polity.

Open and Closed Relationships*

MAX WEBER

A social relationship, regardless of whether it is communal or associative in character, will be spoken of as "open" to outsiders if and insofar as its system of order does not deny participation to anyone who wishes to join and is actually in a position to do so. A relationship will, on the other hand, be called "closed" against outsiders so far as, according to its subjective meaning and its binding rules, participation of certain persons is excluded, limited, or subjected to conditions. Whether a relationship is open or closed may be determined traditionally, affectually, or rationally in terms of values or of expediency. It is especially likely to be closed, for rational reasons, in the following type of situation: a social relationship may provide the parties to it with opportunities for the satisfaction of spiritual or material interests, whether absolutely or instrumentally, or whether it is achieved through co-operative action or by a compromise of interests. If the participants expect that the admission of others will lead to an improvement of their situation, an improvement in degree, in kind, in the security or the value of the satisfaction, their interest will be in

* First published in 1920; from *Economy and Society*, translated and edited by Gunther Roth and Hans Wittich.

keeping the relationship open. If, on the other hand, their expectations are of improving their position by monopolistic tactics, their interest is in a closed relationship.

★ ★ ★

One frequent economic determinant is the competition for a livelihood—offices, clients and other remunerative opportunities. When the number of competitors increases in relation to the profit span, the participants become interested in curbing competition. Usually one group of competitors takes some externally identifiable characteristic of another group of (actual or potential) competitors—race, language, religion, local or social origin, descent, residence, etc.—as a pretext for attempting their exclusion. It does not matter which characteristic is chosen in the individual case: whatever suggests itself most easily is seized upon. Such group action may provoke a corresponding reaction on the part of those against whom it is directed.

In spite of their continued competition against one another, the jointly acting competitors now form an "interest group" toward outsiders; there is a growing tendency to set up some kind of association with rational regulations; if the monopolistic interests persist, the time comes when the competitors, or another group whom they can influence (for example, a political community), establish a legal order that limits competition through formal monopolies; from then on, certain persons are available as "organs" to protect the monopolistic practices, if need be, with force. In such a case, the interest group has developed into a *"legally privileged group"* (*Rechtsgemeinschaft*) and the

participants have become *"privileged members"* (*Rechtsgenossen*). Such closure, as we want to call it, is an ever-recurring process; it is the source of property in land as well as of all guild and other group monopolies.

The tendency toward the monopolization of specific, usually economic opportunities is always the driving force in such cases as: "cooperative organization," which always means closed monopolistic groups, for example, of fishermen taking their name from a certain fishing area; the establishment of an association of engineering graduates, which seeks to secure a legal, or at least factual, monopoly over certain positions; the exclusion of outsiders from sharing in the fields and commons of a village; "patriotic" associations of shop clerks; the *ministeriales*, knights, university graduates and craftsmen of a given region or locality; ex-soldiers entitled to civil service positions—all these groups first engage in some joint action (*Gemeinschaftshandeln*) and later perhaps an explicit association. This monopolization is directed against competitors who share some positive or negative characteristics; its purpose is always the closure of social and economic opportunities to *outsiders*. Its extent may vary widely, especially so far as the group member shares in the apportionment of monopolistic advantages. These may remain open to all monopoly holders, who can therefore freely compete with one another; witness the holders of occupational patents (graduates entitled to certain positions or master-craftsmen privileged with regard to customers and the employment of apprentices). However, such opportunities may also be "closed" to *insiders*. This can be done in various ways: (a) Positions may be rotated: the short-run appointment of some holders of office benefices had this purpose; (b) Grants may be revocable, such as the individual disposition over fields in a strictly organized rural commune, for example, the Russian *mir*; (c) Grants may be for life, as is the rule for all prebends, offices, monopolies of master-craftsmen, rights in using the commons, and originally also for the apportionment of fields in most village communes; (d) The member and his heirs may get definite grants with the stipulation that they cannot be given to others or only to group members: witness the κλῆπος (the warrior prebend of Antiquity), the service fiefs of the *ministeriales*, and monopolies on hereditary offices and crafts; (e) Finally, only the number of shares may be limited, but the holder may freely dispose of his own without the knowledge or permission of the other group members, as in a stock-holding company. These different stages of internal closure will be called stages in the *appropriation* of the social and economic opportunities that have been monopolized by the group.

If the appropriated monopolistic opportunities are released for exchange outside the group, thus becoming completely "free" property, the old monopolistic association is doomed. Its remnants are the appropriated powers of disposition which appear on the market as "acquired rights" of individuals. For all property in natural resources developed historically out of the gradual appropriation of the monopolistic shares of group members. In contrast to the present, not only concrete goods but also social and economic opportunities of all kinds were the object of appropriation. Of course, manner, degree, and ease of the appropriation vary widely with the technical nature of the object and of the opportunities, which may lend themselves to appropriation in very different degrees. For example, a person subsisting by, or gaining an income from, the cultivation of a given field is bound to a concrete and clearly delimited material object, but this is not the case with customers. Appropriation is not motivated by the fact that the object produces a yield only through amelioration, hence that to some extent it is the product of the user's labor, for this is even more true of an acquired clientele, although in a different manner; rather, customers cannot be "registered" as easily as real estate. It is quite natural that the extent of an appropriation depends upon such differences among objects. Here, however, we want to emphasize that the process is in principle the same in both cases, even though the pace of appropriation may vary: monopolized social and economic opportunities are "closed" even to insiders. Hence, groups differ in varying degrees with regard to external or internal "openness" or "closure."

★ ★ ★

GROUP STRUCTURES AND ECONOMIC INTERESTS: MONOPOLIST VERSUS EXPANSIONIST TENDENCIES

This monopolistic tendency takes on specific forms when groups are formed by persons with shared qualities *acquired* through upbringing, apprenticeship and training. These characteristics may be economic qualifications of some kind, the holding of the same or of similar offices, a knightly or ascetic way of life, etc. If in such a case an association results from social action, it tends toward the *guild*. Full members make a vocation out of monopolizing the disposition of spiritual, intellectual, social and economic goods, duties and positions. Only those are admitted to the unrestricted practice of the vocation who (1) have completed a novitiate in order to acquire the proper training, (2) have proven their qualification, and (3) sometimes have passed through further waiting periods and met additional requirements. This development follows a typical pattern in groups ranging from the juvenile student fraternities, through knightly associations and craft-guilds, to the qualifications required of the modern officials and employees. It is true that the interest in guaranteeing an efficient performance may everywhere have some importance; the participants may desire it for idealistic or materialistic reasons in spite of their possibly continuing competition with one another: local craftsmen may desire it for the sake of their business reputation, *ministeriales* and knights of a given association for the sake of their professional reputation and also their own military security, and ascetic groups for fear that the gods and demons may turn their wrath against all members because of faulty manipulations. (For example, in almost all primitive tribes, persons who sang falsely during a ritual dance were originally slain in expiation of such an offense.) But normally this concern for efficient performance recedes behind the interest in limiting the supply of candidates for the benefices and honors of a given occupation. The novitiates, waiting periods, masterpieces and other demands, particularly the expensive entertainment of group members, are more often conomic than professional tests of qualification.

Such monopolistic tendencies and similar economic considerations have often played a significant role in *impeding* the expansion of a group. For example, Attic democracy increasingly sought to limit the number of those who could share in the advantages of citizenship, and thus limited its own political expansion. The Quaker propaganda was brought to a standstill by an ultimately similar constellation of economic interests. The Islamic missionary ardor, originally a religious obligation, found its limits in the conquering warriors' desire to have a non-Islamic, and hence underprivileged, population that could provide for the maintenance of the privileged believers—the type case for many similar phenomena.

On the other hand, it is a typical occurrence that individuals live by representing group interests or, in some other manner, ideologically or economically from the existence of a group. Hence social action may be propagated, perpetuated and transformed into an association in cases in which this might not have happened otherwise. This kind of interest may have the most diverse intellectual roots: In the 19th century the Romantic ideologists and their epigoni awakened numerous declining language groups of "interesting" peoples to the purposive cultivation of their language. German secondary and university teachers helped save small Slavic language groups, about whom they felt the intellectual need to write books.

However, such purely ideological group existence is a less effective lever than economic interest. If a group pays somebody to act as a continuous and deliberate "organ" of their common interests, or if such interest representation pays in other respects, an association comes into being that provides a strong guarantee for the continuance of concerted action under all circumstances. Henceforth, some persons are professionally interested in the retention of the existing, and the recruitment of new, members. It does not matter here whether they are paid to represent (hidden or naked) sexual interests or other "non-material" or, finally, economic interests (trade unions, management associations and similar organizations), whether they are public speakers paid by the piece or salaried secretaries. The pattern of intermittent and irrational action is replaced by a systematic rational "enterprise," which continues to function long after the original enthusiasm of the participants for their ideals has vanished.

In various ways capitalist interests proper may have a stake in the propagation of certain group activities. For example, [in Imperial Germany] the owners of German "Gothic" type fonts want to preserve this "patriotic" kind of lettering [instead of using Latin *Antiqua*]; similarly, innkeepers who permit Social Democratic meetings even though their premises are kept off limits for military personnel have a stake in the size of the party's membership. Everybody can think of many examples of this type for every kind of social action.

Whether we deal with employees or capitalist employers, all these instances of economic interest have one feature in common: The interest in the substance of the shared ideals necessarily recedes behind the interest in the persistence or propaganda of the group, irrespective of the content of its activities. A most impressive example is the complete disappearance of ideological substance in the American parties, but the greatest example, of course,

is the age-old connection between capitalist interests and the expansion of political communities. On the one hand, these communities can exert an extraordinary influence on the economy, on the other they can extract tremendous revenues, so that the capitalist interests can profit most from them: directly by rendering paid services or making advances on expected revenues, and indirectly through the exploitation of objects within the realm of the political community. In Antiquity and at the beginning of modern history the focus of capitalist acquisition centered on such politically determined "imperialist" profits, and today again capitalism moves increasingly in this direction. Every expansion of a country's power sphere increases the profit potential of the respective capitalist interests.

These economic interests, which favor the expansion of a group, may not only be counteracted by the monopolistic tendencies discussed above, but also by other economic interests that originate in a group's closure and exclusiveness. We have already stated in general terms that voluntary organizations tend to transcend their rational primary purpose and to create relationships among the participants that may have quite different goals: As a rule, an overarching communal relationship (*übergreifende Vergemeinschaftung*) attaches itself to the association (*Vergesellschaftung*). Of course, this is not always true; it occurs only in cases in which social action presupposes some personal, not merely business, contacts. For example, a person can acquire stocks irrespective of his personal qualities, merely by virtue of an economic transaction, and generally without the knowledge and consent of the other stockholders. A similar orientation prevails in all those associations that make membership dependent upon a purely formal condition or achievement and do not examine the individual himself. This occurs very often in certain purely economic groups and also in some voluntary political organizations; in general, this orientation is everywhere the more likely, the more rational and specialized the group purpose is. However, there are many associations in which admission presupposes, expressly or silently, qualifications and in which those overarching communal relationships arise. This, of course, happens particularly when the members make admission dependent upon an investigation and approval of the candidate's personal qualities. At least as a rule, the candidate is scrutinized not only with regard to his usefulness for the organization but also "existentially," with regard to personal characteristics esteemed by the members.

We cannot classify here the various modes of association according to the degree of their exclusiveness. It suffices to say that such selectness exists in associations of the most diverse kinds. Not only a religious sect, but also a social club, for instance, a veterans' association or even a bowling club, as a rule admit nobody who is personally objectionable to the members. This very fact "legitimizes" the new member toward the outside, far beyond the qualities that are important to the group's purpose. Membership provides him with advantageous connections, again far beyond the specific goals of the organization. Hence, it is very common that persons belong to an organization although they are not really interested in its purpose, merely for the sake of those economically valuable legitimations and connections that accrue from mem-

bership. Taken by themselves, these motives may contain a strong incentive for joining and hence enlarging the group, but the opposite effect is created by the members' interest in monopolizing those advantages and in increasing their economic value through restriction to the smallest possible circle. The smaller and the more exclusive such a circle is, the higher will be both the economic value and the social prestige of membership.

Finally, we must briefly deal with another frequent relationship between the economy and group activities: the deliberate offer of economic advantages in the interest of preserving and expanding a primarily non-economic group. This happens particularly when several similar groups compete for membership: witness political parties and religious communities. American sects, for instance, arrange artistic, athletic and other entertainment and lower the conditions for divorced persons remarrying; the unlimited underbidding of marriage regulations was only recently curbed by regular cartelization. In addition to arranging excursions and similar activities, religious and political parties establish youth groups and women chapters and participate eagerly in purely municipal or other basically non-political activities, which enable them to grant economic favors to local private interests. To a very large extent, the invasion of municipal, co-operative or other agencies by such groups has a direct economic motivation: it helps them to maintain their functionaries through office benefices and social status and to shift the operating costs to these other agencies. Suitable for this purpose are jobs in municipalities, producers' and consumers' co-operatives, health insurance funds, trade unions and similar organizations; and on a vast scale, of course, political offices and benefices or other prestigious or remunerative positions that can be secured from the political authorities—professorships included. If a group is sufficiently large in a system of parliamentary government, it can procure such support for its leaders and members, just like the political parties, for which this is essential.

In the present context we want to emphasize only the general fact that non-economic groups also establish economic organizations, especially for propaganda purposes. Many charitable activities of religious groups have such a purpose, and this is even more true of the Christian, Liberal, Socialist and Patriotic trade unions and mutual benefit funds, of savings and insurance institutes and, on a massive scale, of the consumers' and producers' co-operatives. Some Italian co-operatives, for instance, demanded the certification of confession before hiring a worker. In Germany [before 1918] the Poles organized credit lending, mortgage payments and farm acquisition in an unusually impressive fashion; during the Revolution of 1905/6 the various Russian parties immediately pursued similarly modern policies. Sometimes

commercial enterprises are established: banks, hotels (like the socialist *Hôtellerie du Peuple* in Ostende) and even factories (also in Belgium). If this happens, the dominant groups in a political community, particularly the civil service, resort to similar methods in order to stay in power, and organize everything from economically advantageous "patriotic" associations and activities to state-controlled loan associations (such as the *Preussenkasse*). The technical details of such propagandistic methods do not concern us here.

In this section we merely wanted to state in general terms, and to illustrate with some typical examples, the coexistence and opposition of expansionist and monopolist economic interests within diverse groups. We must forego any further details since this would require a special study of the various kinds of associations. Instead, we must deal briefly with the most frequent relationship between group activities and the economy: the fact that an extraordinarily large number of groups have secondary economic interests. Normally, these groups must have developed some kind of rational association; exceptions are those that develop out of the household ★ ★ ★.

4

The Theory of the Leisure Class★

THORSTEIN VEBLEN

▌▌▌ PECUNIARY EMULATION

★ ★ ★

Wherever the institution of private property is found, even in a slightly developed form, the economic process bears the character of a struggle between men for the possession of goods. It has been customary in economic theory, and especially among those economists who adhere with least faltering to the body of modernised classical doctrines, to construe this struggle for wealth as being substantially a struggle for subsistence. Such is, no doubt, its character in large part during the earlier and less efficient phases of industry. Such is also its character in all cases where the "niggardliness of nature" is so strict as to afford but a scanty livelihood to the community in return for strenuous and unremitting application to the business of getting the means of subsistence. But in all progressing communities an advance is presently made beyond

---

★ First published in 1899.

this early stage of technological development. Industrial efficiency is presently carried to such a pitch as to afford something appreciably more than a bare livelihood to those engaged in the industrial process. It has not been unusual for economic theory to speak of the further struggle for wealth on this new industrial basis as a competition for an increase of the comforts of life,—primarily for an increase of the physical comforts which the consumption of goods affords.

The end of acquisition and accumulation is conventionally held to be the consumption of the goods accumulated—whether it is consumption directly by the owner of the goods or by the household attached to him and for this purpose identified with him in theory. This is at least felt to be the economically legitimate end of acquisition, which alone it is incumbent on the theory to take account of. Such consumption may of course be conceived to serve the consumer's physical wants—his physical comfort—or his so-called higher wants—spiritual, aesthetic, intellectual, or what not; the latter class of wants being served indirectly by an expenditure of goods, after the fashion familiar to all economic readers.

But it is only when taken in a sense far removed from its naïve meaning that consumption of goods can be said to afford the incentive from which accumulation invariably proceeds. The motive that lies at the root of ownership is emulation; and the same motive of emulation continues active in the further development of the institution to which it has given rise and in the development of all those features of the social structure which this institution of ownership touches. The possession of wealth confers

honour; it is an invidious distinction. Nothing equally cogent can be said for the consumption of goods, nor for any other conceivable incentive to acquisition, and especially not for any incentive to the accumulation of wealth.

It is of course not to be overlooked that in a community where nearly all goods are private property the necessity of earning a livelihood is a powerful and ever-present incentive for the poorer members of the community. The need of subsistence and of an increase of physical comfort may for a time be the dominant motive of acquisition for those classes who are habitually employed at manual labour, whose subsistence is on a precarious footing, who possess little and ordinarily accumulate little; but it will appear in the course of the discussion that even in the case of these impecunious classes the predominance of the motive of physical want is not so decided as has sometimes been assumed. On the other hand, so far as regards those members and classes of the community who are chiefly concerned in the accumulation of wealth, the incentive of subsistence or of physical comfort never plays a considerable part. Ownership began and grew into a human institution on grounds unrelated to the subsistence minimum. The dominant incentive was from the outset the invidious distinction attaching to wealth, and, save temporarily and by exception, no other motive has usurped the primacy at any later stage of the development.

★ ★ ★

★ ★ ★ A certain standard of wealth in the one case, and of prowess in the other, is a necessary condition of reputability, and anything in excess of this normal amount is meritorious.

Those members of the community who fall short of this, somewhat indefinite, normal degree of prowess or of property suffer in the esteem of their fellow-men; and consequently they suffer also in their own esteem, since the usual basis of self-respect is the respect accorded by one's neighbours. Only individuals with an aberrant temperament can in the long run retain their self-esteem in the face of the disesteem of their fellows. Apparent exceptions to the rule are met with, especially among people with strong religious convictions. But these apparent exceptions are scarcely real exceptions, since such persons commonly fall back on the putative approbation of some supernatural witness of their deeds.

So soon as the possession of property becomes the basis of popular esteem, therefore, it becomes also a requisite to that complacency which we call self-respect. In any community where goods are held in severalty it is necessary, in order to his own peace of mind, that an individual should possess as large a portion of goods as others with whom he is accustomed to class himself; and it is extremely gratifying to possess something more than others. But as fast as a person makes new acquisitions, and becomes accustomed to the resulting new standard of wealth, the new standard forthwith ceases to afford appreciably greater satisfaction than the earlier standard did. The tendency in any case is constantly to make the present pecuniary standard the point of departure for a fresh increase of wealth; and this in turn gives rise to a new standard of sufficiency and a new pecuniary classification of one's self as compared with one's neighbours. So far as concerns the present question, the end sought by accumulation is to

rank high in comparison with the rest of the community in point of pecuniary strength. So long as the comparison is distinctly unfavourable to himself, the normal, average individual will live in chronic dissatisfaction with his present lot; and when he has reached what may be called the normal pecuniary standard of the community; or of his class in the community, this chronic dissatisfaction will give place to a restless straining to place a wider and ever-widening pecuniary interval between himself and this average standard. The invidious comparison can never become so favourable to the individual making it that he would not gladly rate himself still higher relatively to his competitors in the struggle for pecuniary reputability.

In the nature of the case, the desire for wealth can scarcely be satiated in any individual instance, and evidently a satiation of the average or general desire for wealth is out of the question. However widely, or equally, or "fairly," it may be distributed, no general increase of the community's wealth can make any approach to satiating this need, the ground of which is the desire of every one to excel every one else in the accumulation of goods. If, as is sometimes assumed, the incentive to accumulation were the want of subsistence or of physical comfort, then the aggregate economic wants of a community might conceivably be satisfied at some point in the advance of industrial efficiency; but since the struggle is substantially a race for reputability on the basis of an invidious comparison, no approach to a definitive attainment is possible.

What has just been said must not be taken to mean that there are no other incentives to acquisition and accumulation than this desire to excel in pecuniary standing and so gain the esteem and envy of one's fellow-men. The desire for added comfort and security from want is present as a motive at every stage of the process of accumulation in a modern industrial community; although the standard of sufficiency in these respects is in turn greatly affected by the habit of pecuniary emulation. To a great extent this emulation shapes the methods and selects the objects of expenditure for personal comfort and decent livelihood.

Besides this, the power conferred by wealth also affords a motive to accumulation. That propensity for purposeful activity and that repugnance to all futility of effort which belong to man by virtue of his character as an agent do not desert him when he emerges from the naïve communal culture where the dominant note of life is the unanalysed and undifferentiated solidarity of the individual with the group with which his life is bound up. When he enters upon the predatory stage, where self-seeking in the narrower sense becomes the dominant note, this propensity goes with him still, as the pervasive trait that shapes his scheme of life. The propensity for achievement and the repugnance to futility remain the underlying economic motive. The propensity changes only in the form of its expression and in the proximate objects to which it directs the man's activity. Under the régime of individual ownership the most available means of visibly achieving a purpose is that afforded by the acquisition and accumulation of goods; and as the self-regarding antithesis between man and man reaches fuller consciousness, the propensity for achievement—the instinct of workmanship—tends more and more to shape itself into a straining to

excel others in pecuniary achievement. Relative success, tested by an invidious pecuniary comparison with other men, becomes the conventional end of action. The currently accepted legitimate end of effort becomes the achievement of a favourable comparison with other men; and therefore the repugnance to futility to a good extent coalesces with the incentive of emulation. It acts to accentuate the struggle for pecuniary reputability by visiting with a sharper disapproval all shortcoming and all evidence of short-coming in point of pecuniary success. Purposeful effort comes to mean, primarily, effort directed to or resulting in a more creditable showing of accumulated wealth. Among the motives which lead men to accumulate wealth, the primacy, both in scope and intensity, therefore, continues to belong to this motive of pecuniary emulation.

★ ★ ★

||| CONSPICUOUS LEISURE

If its working were not disturbed by other economic forces or other features of the emulative process, the immediate effect of such a pecuniary struggle as has just been described in outline would be to make men industrious and frugal. This result actually follows, in some measure, so far as regards the lower classes, whose ordinary means of acquiring goods is productive labour. This is more especially true of the labouring classes in a sedentary community which is at an agricultural stage of industry, in which there is a considerable subdivision of property, and whose laws and customs secure to these classes a more or less definite share of the product of their industry. These lower classes can in any case not avoid labour, and the imputation of labour is therefore not greatly derogatory to them, at least not within their class. Rather, since labour is their recognised and accepted mode of life, they take some emulative pride in a reputation for efficiency in their work, this being often the only line of emulation that is open to them. For those for whom acquisition and emulation is possible only within the field of productive efficiency and thrift, the struggle for pecuniary reputability will in some measure work out in an increase of diligence and parsimony. But certain secondary features of the emulative process, yet to be spoken of, come in to very materially circumscribe and modify emulation in these directions among the pecuniarily inferior classes as well as among the superior class.

But it is otherwise with the superior pecuniary class, with which we are here immediately concerned. For this class also the incentive to diligence and thrift is not absent; but its action is so greatly qualified by the secondary demands of pecuniary emulation, that any inclination in this direction is practically overborne and any incentive to diligence tends to be of no effect. The most imperative of these secondary demands of emulation, as well as the one of widest scope, is the requirement of abstention from productive work. This is true in an especial degree for the barbarian stage of culture. During the predatory culture labour comes to be associated in men's habits of thought with weakness and subjection to a master. It is therefore a mark of inferiority, and therefore comes to be accounted unworthy of man in his best estate. By virtue of this tradition labour is felt to be debasing, and this tradition has never died out. On the contrary, with the advance

of social differentiation it has acquired the axiomatic force due to ancient and unquestioned prescription.

In order to gain and to hold the esteem of men it is not sufficient merely to possess wealth or power. The wealth or power must be put in evidence, for esteem is awarded only on evidence. And not only does the evidence of wealth serve to impress one's importance on others and to keep their sense of his importance alive and alert, but it is of scarcely less use in building up and preserving one's self-complacency. In all but the lowest stages of culture the normally constituted man is comforted and upheld in his self-respect by "decent surroundings" and by exemption from "menial offices." Enforced departure from his habitual standard of decency, either in the paraphernalia of life or in the kind and amount of his everyday activity, is felt to be a slight upon his human dignity, even apart from all conscious consideration of the approval or disapproval, of his fellows.

The archaic theoretical distinction between the base and the honourable in the manner of a man's life retains very much of its ancient force even to-day. So much so that there are few of the better class who are not possessed of an instinctive repugnance for the vulgar forms of labour. We have a realising sense of ceremonial uncleanness attaching in an especial degree to the occupations which are associated in our habits of thought with menial service. It is felt by all persons of refined taste that a spiritual contamination is inseparable from certain offices that are conventionally required of servants. Vulgar surroundings, mean (that is to say, inexpensive) habitations, and vulgarly productive occupations are unhesitatingly condemned and avoided. They are incompatible with life on a satisfactory spiritual plane—with "high thinking." From the days of the Greek philosophers to the present, a degree of leisure and of exemption from contact with such industrial processes as serve the immediate every day purposes of human life has ever been recognised by thoughtful men as a prerequisite to a worthy or beautiful, or even a blameless, human life. In itself and in its consequences the life of leisure is beautiful and ennobling in all civilised men's eyes.

This direct, subjective value of leisure and of other evidences of wealth is no doubt in great part secondary and derivative. It is in part a reflex of the utility of leisure as a means of gaining the respect of others, and in part it is the result of a mental substitution. The performance of labour has been accepted as a conventional evidence of inferior force; therefore it comes itself, by a mental short-cut, to be regarded as intrinsically base.

★ ★ ★

It has already been remarked that the term "leisure," as here used, does not connote indolence or quiescence. What it connotes is non-productive consumption of time. Time is consumed non-productively (1) from a sense of the unworthiness of productive work, and (2) as an evidence of pecuniary ability to afford a life of idleness. But the whole of the life of the gentleman of leisure is not spent before the eyes of the spectators who are to be impressed with that spectacle of honorific leisure which in the ideal scheme makes up his life. For some part of the time his life is perforce withdrawn from the public eye, and of this portion which is spent in private the gentleman of leisure should, for the

sake of his good name, be able to give a convincing account. He should find some means of putting in evidence the leisure that is not spent in the sight of the spectators. This can be done only indirectly, through the exhibition of some tangible, lasting results of the leisure so spent—in a manner analogous to the familiar exhibition of tangible, lasting products of the labour performed for the gentleman of leisure by handicraftsmen and servants in his employ.

The lasting evidence of productive labour is its material product—commonly some article of consumption. In the case of exploit it is similarly possible and usual to procure some tangible result that may serve for exhibition in the way of trophy or booty. At a later phase of the development it is customary to assume some badge or insignia of honour that will serve as a conventionally accepted mark of exploit, and which at the same time indicates the quantity or degree of exploit of which it is the symbol. As the population increases in density, and as human relations grow more complex and numerous, all the details of life undergo a process of elaboration and selection; and in this process of elaboration the use of trophies develops into a system of rank, titles, degrees and insignia, typical examples of which are heraldic devices, medals, and honorary decorations.

As seen from the economic point of view, leisure, considered as an employment, is closely allied in kind with the life of exploit; and the achievements which characterise a life of leisure, and which remain as its decorous criteria, have much in common with the trophies of exploit. But leisure in the narrower sense, as distinct from exploit and from any ostensibly productive employment of effort on objects which are of no intrinsic use, does not commonly leave a material product. The criteria of a past performance of leisure therefore commonly take the form of "immaterial" goods. Such immaterial evidences of past leisure are quasi-scholarly or quasi-artistic accomplishments and a knowledge of processes and incidents which do not conduce directly to the furtherance of human life. So, for instance, in our time there is the knowledge of the dead languages and the occult sciences; of correct spelling; of syntax and prosody; of the various forms of domestic music and other household art; of the latest proprieties of dress, furniture, and equipage; of games, sports, and fancy-bred animals, such as dogs and race-horses. In all these branches of knowledge the initial motive from which their acquisition proceeded at the outset, and through which they first came into vogue, may have been something quite different from the wish to show that one's time had not been spent in industrial employment; but unless these accomplishments had approved themselves as serviceable evidence of an unproductive expenditure of time, they would not have survived and held their place as conventional accomplishments of the leisure class.

These accomplishments may, in some sense, be classed as branches of learning. Beside and beyond these there is a further range of social facts which shade off from the region of learning into that of physical habit and dexterity. Such are what is known as manners and breeding, polite usage, decorum, and formal and ceremonial observances generally. This class of facts are even more immediately and obtrusively presented to the observation, and they are therefore more widely and more imperatively

insisted on as required evidences of a reputable degree of leisure. ★ ★ ★

★ ★ ★

Conspicuous consumption of valuable goods is a means of reputability to the gentleman of leisure. As wealth accumulates on his hands, his own unaided effort will not avail to sufficiently put his opulence in evidence by this method. The aid of friends and competitors is therefore brought in by resorting to the giving of valuable presents and expensive feasts and entertainments. Presents and feasts had probably another origin than that of naïve ostentation, but they acquired their utility for this purpose very early, and they have retained that character to the present; so that their utility in this respect has now long been the substantial ground on which these usages rest. Costly entertainments, such as the potlatch or the ball, are peculiarly adapted to serve this end. The competitor with whom the entertainer wishes to institute a comparison is, by this method, made to serve as a means to the end. He consumes vicariously for his host at the same time that he is a witness to the consumption of that excess of good things which his host is unable to dispose of single-handed, and he is also made to witness his host's facility in etiquette.

In the giving of costly entertainments other motives, of a more genial kind, are of course also present. The custom of festive gatherings probably originated in motives of conviviality and religion; these motives are also present in the later development, but they do not continue to be the sole motives. The latter-day leisure-class festivities and entertainments may continue in some slight degree to serve the religious need and in a higher degree the needs of recreation and conviviality, but they also serve an invidious purpose; and they serve it none the less effectually for having a colourable non-invidious ground in these more avowable motives. But the economic effect of these social amenities is not therefore lessened, either in the vicarious consumption of goods or in the exhibition of difficult and costly achievements in etiquette.

As wealth accumulates, the leisure class develops further in function and structure, and there arises a differentiation within the class. There is a more or less elaborate system of rank and grades. This differentiation is furthered by the inheritance of wealth and the consequent inheritance of gentility. With the inheritance of gentility goes the inheritance of obligatory leisure; and gentility of a sufficient potency to entail a life of leisure may be inherited without the complement of wealth required to maintain a dignified leisure. Gentle blood may be transmitted without goods enough to afford a reputably free consumption at one's ease. Hence results a class of impecunious gentlemen of leisure, incidentally referred to already. These half-caste gentlemen of leisure fall into a system of hierarchical gradations. Those who stand near the higher and the highest grades of the wealthy leisure class, in point of birth, or in point of wealth, or both, outrank the remoter-born and the pecuniarily weaker. These lower grades, especially the impecunious, or marginal, gentlemen of leisure, affiliate themselves by a system of dependence or fealty to the great ones; by so doing they gain an increment of repute, or of the means with which to lead a life of leisure, from their patron. They become his courtiers or retainers, servants; and being

fed and countenanced by their patron they are indices of his rank and vicarious consumers of his superfluous wealth. Many of these affiliated gentlemen of leisure are at the same time lesser men of substance in their own right; so that some of them are scarcely at all, others only partially, to be rated as vicarious consumers. So many of them, however, as make up the retainers and hangers-on of the patron may be classed as vicarious consumers without qualification. Many of these again, and also many of the other aristocracy of less degree, have in turn attached to their persons a more or less comprehensive group of vicarious consumers in the persons of their wives and children, their servants, retainers, etc.

Throughout this graduated scheme of vicarious leisure and vicarious consumption the rule holds that these offices must be performed in some such manner, or under some such circumstance or insignia, as shall point plainly to the master to whom this leisure or consumption pertains, and to whom therefore the resulting increment of good repute of right inures. The consumption and leisure executed by these persons for their master or patron represents an investment on his part with a view to an increase of good fame. As regards feasts and largesses this is obvious enough, and the imputation of repute to the host or patron here takes place immediately, on the ground of common notoriety. Where leisure and consumption is performed vicariously by henchmen and retainers, imputation of the resulting repute to the patron is effected by their residing near his person so that it may be plain to all men from what source they draw. As the group whose good esteem is to be secured in this way grows larger, more patent means are required to indicate the imputation of merit for the leisure performed, and to this end uniforms, badges, and liveries come into vogue. The wearing of uniforms or liveries implies a considerable degree of dependence, and may even be said to be a mark of servitude, real or ostensible. The wearers of uniforms and liveries may be roughly divided into two classes—the free and the servile, or the noble and the ignoble. The services performed by them are likewise divisible into noble and ignoble. Of course the distinction is not observed with strict consistency in practice; the less debasing of the base services and the less honorific of the noble functions are not infrequently merged in the same person. But the general distinction is not on that account to be overlooked. What may add some perplexity is the fact that this fundamental distinction between noble and ignoble, which rests on the nature of the ostensible service performed, is traversed by a secondary distinction into honorific and humiliating, resting on the rank of the person for whom the service is performed or whose livery is worn. So, those offices which are by right the proper employment of the leisure class are noble; such are government, fighting, hunting, the care of arms and accoutrements, and the like,—in short, those which may be classed as ostensibly predatory employments. On the other hand, those employments which properly fall to the industrious class are ignoble; such as handicraft or other productive labour, menial services, and the like. But a base service performed for a person of very high degree may become a very honorific office; as for instance the office of a Maid of Honour or of a Lady in Waiting to the Queen, or the King's Master of the Horse or his Keeper of the Hounds. The two offices last named suggest a principle of some general bearing. Whenever, as in these cases, the menial service in question has to do directly with the primary leisure employments of fighting and hunting, it easily acquires a reflected honorific character. In this way great honour may come to attach to an employment which in its own nature belongs to the baser sort.

In the later development of peaceable industry, the usage of employing an idle corps of uniformed men-at-arms gradually lapses. Vicarious consumption by dependents bearing the insignia of their patron or master narrows down to a corps of liveried menials. In a heightened degree, therefore, the livery comes to be a badge of servitude, or rather of servility. Something of a honorific character always attached to the livery of the armed retainer, but this honorific character disappears when the livery becomes the exclusive badge of the menial. The livery becomes obnoxious to nearly all who are required to wear it. We are yet so little removed from a state of effective slavery as still to be fully sensitive to the sting of any imputation of servility. This antipathy asserts itself even in the case of the liveries or uniforms which some corporations prescribe as the distinctive dress of their employees. In this country the aversion even goes the length of discrediting—in a mild and uncertain way—those government employments, military and civil, which require the wearing of a livery or uniform.

With the disappearance of servitude, the number of vicarious consumers attached to any one gentleman tends, on the whole, to decrease. The like is of course true, and perhaps in a still higher degree, of the number of dependents who perform vicarious leisure for him. In a general way, though not wholly nor consistently, these two groups coincide. The dependent who was first delegated for these duties was the wife, or the chief wife; and, as would be expected in the later development of the institution, when the number of persons by whom these duties are customarily performed gradually narrows, the wife remains the last. In the higher grades of society a large volume of both these kinds of service is required; and here the wife is of course still assisted in the work by a more or less numerous corps of menials. But as we descend the social scale, the point is presently reached where the duties of vicarious leisure and consumption devolve upon the wife alone. In the communities of the Western culture, this point is at present found among the lower middle class.

And here occurs a curious inversion. It is a fact of common observation that in this lower middle class there is no pretence of leisure on the part of the head of the household. Through force of circumstances it has fallen into disuse. But the middle-class wife still carries on the business of vicarious leisure, for the good name of the household and its master. In descending the social scale in any modern industrial community, the primary fact—the conspicuous leisure of the master of the household—disappears at a relatively high point. The head of the middle-class household has been reduced by economic circumstances to turn his hand to gaining a livelihood by occupations which often partake largely of the character of industry, as in the case of the ordinary business man

of to-day. But the derivative fact—the vicarious leisure and consumption rendered by the wife, and the auxiliary vicarious performance of leisure by menials—remains in vogue as a conventionality which the demands of reputability will not suffer to be slighted. It is by no means an uncommon spectacle to find a man applying himself to work with the utmost assiduity, in order that his wife may in due form render for him that degree of vicarious leisure which the common sense of the time demands.

The leisure rendered by the wife in such cases is, of course, not a simple manifestation of idleness or indolence. It almost invariably occurs disguised under some form of work or household duties or social amenities, which prove on analysis to serve little or no ulterior end beyond showing that she does not and need not occupy herself with anything that is gainful or that is of substantial use. As has already been noticed under the head of manners, the greater part of the customary round of domestic cares to which the middle-class housewife gives her time and effort is of this character. Not that the results of her attention to household matters, of a decorative and mundificatory character, are not pleasing to the sense of men trained in middle-class proprieties; but the taste to which these effects of household adornment and tidiness appeal is a taste which has been formed under the selective guidance of a canon of propriety that demands just these evidences of wasted effort. The effects are pleasing to us chiefly because we have been taught to find them pleasing. There goes into these domestic duties much solicitude for a proper combination of form and colour, and for other ends that are to be classed as æsthetic in the proper sense of the term; and it is not denied that effects having some substantial æsthetic value are sometimes attained. Pretty much all that is here insisted on is that, as regards these amenities of life, the housewife's efforts are under the guidance of traditions that have been shaped by the law of conspicuously wasteful expenditure of time and substance. If beauty or comfort is achieved,—and it is a more or less fortuitous circumstance if they are,—they must be achieved by means and methods that commend themselves to the great economic law of wasted effort. The more reputable, "presentable" portion of middle-class household paraphernalia are, on the one hand, items of conspicuous consumption, and on the other hand, apparatus for putting in evidence the vicarious leisure rendered by the housewife.

The requirement of vicarious consumption at the hands of the wife continues in force even at a lower point in the pecuniary scale than the requirement of vicarious leisure. At a point below which little if any pretence of wasted effort, in ceremonial cleanness and the like, is observable, and where there is assuredly no conscious attempt at ostensible leisure, decency still requires the wife to consume some goods conspicuously for the reputability of the household and its head. So that, as the latter-day outcome of this evolution of an archaic institution, the wife, who was at the outset the drudge and chattel of the man, both in fact and in theory,—the producer of goods for him to consume,—has become the ceremonial consumer of goods which he produces. But she still quite unmistakably remains his chattel in theory; for the habitual rendering of vicarious leisure and consumption is the abiding mark of the unfree servant.

This vicarious consumption practised by the household of the middle and lower classes can not be counted as a direct expression of the leisure-class scheme of life, since the household of this pecuniary grade does not belong within the leisure class. It is rather that the leisure-class scheme of life here comes to an expression at the second remove. The leisure class stands at the head of the social structure in point of reputability; and its manner of life and its standards of worth therefore afford the norm of reputability for the community. The observance of these standards, in some degree of approximation, becomes incumbent upon all classes lower in the scale. In modern civilized communities the lines of demarcation between social classes have grown vague and transient, and wherever this happens the norm of reputability imposed by the upper class extends its coercive influence with but slight hindrance down through the social structure to the lowest strata. The result is that the members of each stratum accept as their ideal of decency the scheme of life in vogue in the next higher stratum, and bend their energies to live up to that ideal. On pain of forfeiting their good name and their self-respect in case of failure, they must conform to the accepted code, at least in appearance.

The basis on which good repute in any highly organised industrial community ultimately rests is pecuniary strength; and the means of showing pecuniary strength, and so of gaining or retaining a good name, are leisure and a conspicuous consumption of goods. Accordingly, both of these methods are in vogue as far down the scale as it remains possible; and in the lower strata in which the two methods are employed, both offices are in great part delegated to the wife and children of the household. Lower still, where any degree of leisure, even ostensible, has become impracticable for the wife, the conspicuous consumption of goods remains and is carried on by the wife and children. The man of the household also can do something in this direction, and, indeed, he commonly does; but with a still lower descent into the levels of indigence—along the margin of the slums— the man, and presently also the children, virtually cease to consume valuable goods for appearances, and the woman remains virtually the sole exponent of the household's pecuniary decency. No class of society, not even the most abjectly poor, foregoes all customary conspicuous consumption. The last items of this category of consumption are not given up except under stress of the direst necessity. Very much of squalor and discomfort will be endured before the last trinket or the last pretence of pecuniary decency is put away. There is no class and no country that has yielded so abjectly before the pressure of physical want as to deny themselves all gratification of this higher or spiritual need.

From the foregoing survey of the growth of conspicuous leisure and consumption, it appears that the utility of both alike for the purposes of reputability lies in the element of waste that is common to both. In the one case it is a waste of time and effort, in the other it is a waste of goods. Both are methods of demonstrating the possession of wealth, and the two are conventionally accepted as equivalents. The choice between them is a question of advertising expediency simply, except so far as it may be affected by other standards of propriety, springing from a different source. On grounds of expediency the preference may be given to the one or the other at different stages of the economic development. The question is, which of the two methods will most effectively reach the persons whose convictions it is desired to affect. Usage has answered this question in different ways under different circumstances.

★ ★ ★

5

Of Our Spiritual Strivings*

W. E. B. DU BOIS

Between me and the other world there is ever an unasked question: unasked by some through feelings of delicacy; by others through the difficulty of rightly framing it. All, nevertheless, flutter round it. They approach me in a half-hesitant sort of way, eye me curiously or compassionately, and then, instead of saying directly, How does it feel to be a problem? they say, I know an excellent colored man in my town; or, I fought at Mechanicsville; or, Do not these Southern outrages make your blood boil? At these I smile, or am interested, or reduce the boiling to a simmer, as the occasion may require. To the real question, How does it feel to be a problem? I answer seldom a word.

And yet, being a problem is a strange experience,—peculiar even for one who has never been anything else, save perhaps in babyhood and in Europe. It is in the early days of rollicking boyhood that the revelation first bursts upon one, all in a day, as it were. I remember well when the shadow swept

---

* First published in 1903; from *The Souls of Black Folk*.

across me. I was a little thing, away up in the hills of New England, where the dark Housatonic winds between Hoosac and Taghkanic to the sea. In a wee wooden schoolhouse, something put it into the boys' and girls' heads to buy gorgeous visiting-cards—ten cents a package—and exchange. The exchange was merry, till one girl, a tall newcomer, refused my card,—refused it peremptorily, with a glance. Then it dawned upon me with a certain suddenness that I was different from the others; or like, mayhap, in heart and life and longing, but shut out from their world by a vast veil. I had thereafter no desire to tear down that veil, to creep through; I held all beyond it in common contempt, and lived above it in a region of blue sky and great wandering shadows. That sky was bluest when I could beat my mates at examination time, or beat them at a foot-race, or even beat their stringy heads. Alas, with the years all this fine contempt began to fade; for the worlds I longed for, and all their dazzling opportunities, were theirs, not mine. But they should not keep these prizes, I said; some, all, I would wrest from them. Just how I would do it I could never decide: by reading law, by healing the sick, by telling the wonderful tales that swam in my head,—some way. With other black boys the strife was not so fiercely sunny: their youth shrunk into tasteless sycophancy, or into silent hatred of the pale world about them and mocking distrust of everything white; or wasted itself in a bitter cry, Why did God make me an outcast and a stranger in mine own house? The shades of the prison-house closed round about us all: walls strait and stubborn to the whitest, but relentlessly narrow, tall, and unscalable to sons of night who must plod darkly on in res-

ignation, or beat unavailing palms against the stone, or steadily, half hopelessly, watch the streak of blue above.

After the Egyptian and Indian, the Greek and Roman, the Teuton and Mongolian, the Negro is a sort of seventh son, born with a veil, and gifted with second-sight in this American world,—a world which yields him no true self-consciousness, but only lets him see himself through the revelation of the other world. It is a peculiar sensation, this double-consciousness, this sense of always looking at one's self through the eyes of others, of measuring one's soul by the tape of a world that looks on in amused contempt and pity. One ever feels his two-ness,—an American, a Negro; two souls, two thoughts, two unreconciled strivings; two warring ideals in one dark body, whose dogged strength alone keeps it from being torn asunder.

The history of the American Negro is the history of this strife,—this longing to attain self-conscious manhood, to merge his double self into a better and truer self. In this merging he wishes neither of the older selves to be lost. He would not Africanize America, for America has too much to teach the world and Africa. He would not bleach his Negro soul in a flood of white Americanism, for he knows that Negro blood has a message for the world. He simply wishes to make it possible for a man to be both a Negro and an American, without being cursed and spit upon by his fellows, without having the doors of Opportunity closed roughly in his face.

This, then, is the end of his striving: to be a co-worker in the kingdom of culture, to escape both death and isolation, to husband and use his best powers and his latent genius. These powers of body and mind have in the past been strangely wasted, dispersed, or forgotten. The shadow of a mighty Negro past flits through the tale of Ethiopia the Shadowy and of Egypt the Sphinx. Throughout history, the powers of single black men flash here and there like falling stars, and die sometimes before the world has rightly gauged their brightness. Here in America, in the few days since Emancipation, the black man's turning hither and thither in hesitant and doubtful striving has often made his very strength to lose effectiveness, to seem like absence of power, like weakness. And yet it is not weakness,—it is the contradiction of double aims. The double-aimed struggle of the black artisan—on the one hand to escape white contempt for a nation of mere hewers of wood and drawers of water, and on the other hand to plough and nail and dig for a poverty-stricken horde—could only result in making him a poor craftsman, for he had but half a heart in either cause. By the poverty and ignorance of his people, the Negro minister or doctor was tempted toward quackery and demagogy; and by the criticism of the other world, toward ideals that made him ashamed of his lowly tasks. The would-be black *savant* was confronted by the paradox that the knowledge his people needed was a twice-told tale to his white neighbors, while the knowledge which would teach the white world was Greek to his own flesh and blood. The innate love of harmony and beauty that set the ruder souls of his people a-dancing and a-singing raised but confusion and doubt in the soul of the black artist; for the beauty revealed to him was the soul-beauty of a race which his larger audience despised, and he could not articulate the message of another people. This waste of double

aims, this seeking to satisfy two unreconciled ideals, has wrought sad havoc with the courage and faith and deeds of ten thousand thousand people,—has sent them often wooing false gods and invoking false means of salvation, and at times has even seemed about to make them ashamed of themselves.

Away back in the days of bondage they thought to see in one divine event the end of all doubt and disappointment; few men ever worshipped Freedom with half such unquestioning faith as did the American Negro for two centuries. To him, so far as he thought and dreamed, slavery was indeed the sum of all villainies, the cause of all sorrow, the root of all prejudice; Emancipation was the key to a promised land of sweeter beauty than ever stretched before the eyes of wearied Israelites. In song and exhortation swelled one refrain—Liberty; in his tears and curses the God he implored had Freedom in his right hand. At last it came,—suddenly, fearfully, like a dream. With one wild carnival of blood and passion came the message in his own plaintive cadences:—

"Shout O children!
Shout, you're free!
For God has bought your liberty!"

Years have passed away since then,—ten, twenty, forty; forty years of national life, forty years of renewal and development, and yet the swarthy spectre sits in its accustomed seat at the Nation's feast. In vain do we cry to this our vastest social problem:—

"Take any shape but that, and my firm nerves
Shall never tremble!"

The Nation has not yet found peace from its sins; the freedman has not yet found in freedom his promised land. Whatever of good may have come in these years of change, the shadow of a deep disappointment rests upon the Negro people,—a disappointment all the more bitter because the unattained ideal was unbounded save by the simple ignorance of a lowly people.

The first decade was merely a prolongation of the vain search for freedom, the boon that seemed ever barely to elude their grasp,—like a tantalizing will-o'-the-wisp, maddening and misleading the headless host. The holocaust of war, the terrors of the Ku-Klux Klan, the lies of carpet-baggers, the disorganization of industry, and the contradictory advice of friends and foes, left the bewildered serf with no new watch-word beyond the old cry for freedom. As the time flew, however, he began to grasp a new idea. The ideal of liberty demanded for its attainment powerful means, and these the Fifteenth Amendment gave him. The ballot, which before he had looked upon as a visible sign of freedom, he now regarded as the chief means of gaining and perfecting the liberty with which war had partially endowed him. And why not? Had not votes made war and emancipated millions? Had not votes enfranchised the freedmen? Was anything impossible to a power that had done all this? A million black men started with renewed zeal to vote themselves into the kingdom. So the decade flew away, the revolution of 1876 came, and left the half-free serf weary, wondering, but still inspired. Slowly but steadily, in the following years, a new vision began gradually to replace the dream of political power,—a powerful movement, the rise of another ideal to guide the unguided, another

pillar of fire by night after a clouded day. It was the ideal of "book-learning"; the curiosity, born of compulsory ignorance, to know and test the power of the cabalistic letters of the white man, the longing to know. Here at last seemed to have been discovered the mountain path to Canaan; longer than the highway of Emancipation and law, steep and rugged, but straight, leading to heights high enough to overlook life.

Up the new path the advance guard toiled, slowly, heavily, doggedly; only those who have watched and guided the faltering feet, the misty minds, the dull understandings, of the dark pupils of these schools know how faithfully, how piteously, this people strove to learn. It was weary work. The cold statistician wrote down the inches of progress here and there, noted also where here and there a foot had slipped or some one had fallen. To the tired climbers, the horizon was ever dark, the mists were often cold, the Canaan was always dim and far away. If, however, the vistas disclosed as yet no goal, no resting-place, little but flattery and criticism, the journey at least gave leisure for reflection and self-examination; it changed the child of Emancipation to the youth with dawning self-consciousness, self-realization, self-respect. In those sombre forests of his striving his own soul rose before him, and he saw himself,—darkly as through a veil; and yet he saw in himself some faint revelation of his power, of his mission. He began to have a dim feeling that, to attain his place in the world, he must be himself, and not another. For the first time he sought to analyze the burden he bore upon his back, that dead-weight of social degradation partially masked behind a half-named Negro problem. He felt his poverty; without a cent, without a home, without land, tools, or savings, he had entered into competition with rich, landed, skilled neighbors. To be a poor man is hard, but to be a poor race in a land of dollars is the very bottom of hardships. He felt the weight of his ignorance,—not simply of letters, but of life, of business, of the humanities; the accumulated sloth and shirking and awkwardness of decades and centuries shackled his hands and feet. Nor was his burden all poverty and ignorance. The red stain of bastardy, which two centuries of systematic legal defilement of Negro women had stamped upon his race, meant not only the loss of ancient African chastity, but also the hereditary weight of a mass of corruption from white adulterers, threatening almost the obliteration of the Negro home.

A people thus handicapped ought not to be asked to race with the world, but rather allowed to give all its time and thought to its own social problems. But alas! while sociologists gleefully count his bastards and his prostitutes, the very soul of the toiling, sweating black man is darkened by the shadow of a vast despair. Men call the shadow prejudice, and learnedly explain it as the natural defence of culture against barbarism, learning against ignorance, purity against crime, the "higher" against the "lower" races. To which the Negro cries Amen! and swears that to so much of this strange prejudice as is founded on just homage to civilization, culture, righteousness, and progress, he humbly bows and meekly does obeisance. But before that nameless prejudice that leaps beyond all this he stands helpless, dismayed, and well-nigh speechless; before that personal disrespect and mockery, the ridicule and systematic humiliation, the distortion of fact and wanton license

of fancy, the cynical ignoring of the better and the boisterous welcoming of the worse, the all-pervading desire to inculcate disdain for everything black, from Toussaint to the devil,—before this there rises a sickening despair that would disarm and discourage any nation save that black host to whom "discouragement" is an unwritten word.

But the facing of so vast a prejudice could not but bring the inevitable self-questioning, self-disparagement, and lowering of ideals which ever accompany repression and breed in an atmosphere of contempt and hate. Whisperings and portents came borne upon the four winds: Lo! we are diseased and dying, cried the dark hosts; we cannot write, our voting is vain; what need of education, since we must always cook and serve? And the Nation echoed and enforced this self-criticism, saying: Be content to be servants, and nothing more; what need of higher culture for half-men? Away with the black man's ballot, by force or fraud,—and behold the suicide of a race! Nevertheless, out of the evil came something of good,—the more careful adjustment of education to real life, the clearer perception of the Negroes' social responsibilities, and the sobering realization of the meaning of progress.

So dawned the time of *Sturm und Drang*: storm and stress to-day rocks our little boat on the mad waters of the world-sea; there is within and without the sound of conflict, the burning of body and rending of soul; inspiration strives with doubt, and faith with vain questionings. The bright ideals of the past,—physical freedom, political power, the trainng of brains and the training of hands,—all these in turn have waxed and waned, until even the last grows dim and overcast. Are they all wrong,—all false? No, not that, but each alone was over-simple and incomplete,—the dreams of a credulous race-childhood, or the fond imaginings of the other world which does not know and does not want to know our power. To be really true, all these ideals must be melted and welded into one. The training of the schools we need to-day more than ever,—the training of deft hands, quick eyes and ears, and above all the broader, deeper, higher culture of gifted minds and pure hearts. The power of the ballot we need in sheer self-defence,—else what shall save us from a second slavery? Freedom, too, the long-sought, we still seek,—the freedom of life and limb, the freedom to work and think, the freedom to love and aspire. Work, culture, liberty,—all these we need, not singly but together, not successively but together, each growing and aiding each, and all striving toward that vaster ideal that swims before the Negro people, the ideal of human brotherhood, gained through the unifying ideal of Race; the ideal of fostering and developing the traits and talents of the Negro, not in opposition to or contempt for other races, but rather in large conformity to the greater ideals of the American Republic, in order that some day on American soil two world-races may give each to each those characteristics both so sadly lack. We the darker ones come even now not altogether empty-handed: there are today no truer exponents of the pure human spirit of the Declaration of Independence than the American Negroes; there is no true American music but the wild sweet melodies of the Negro slave; the American fairy tales and folk-lore are Indian and African; and, all in all, we black men seem the sole oasis of simple faith and reverence in a dusty desert of dollars and smartness. Will America be poorer if she replace her brutal dyspeptic blundering with light-hearted but determined Negro humility? or her coarse and cruel wit with loving jovial good-humor? or her vulgar music with the soul of the Sorrow Songs?

Merely a concrete test of the underlying principles of the great republic is the Negro Problem, and the spiritual striving of the freedmen's sons is the travail of souls whose burden is almost beyond the measure of their strength, but who bear it in the name of an historic race, in the name of this the land of their fathers' fathers, and in the name of human opportunity.

★ ★ ★

The Problem of the Twentieth Century is the Problem of the Color Line★

W. E. B. DU BOIS

We are just finishing the first half of the Twentieth Century. I remember its birth in 1901. There was the usual discussion as to whether the century began in 1900 or 1901; but, of course, 1901 was correct. We expected great things . . . peace; the season of war among nations had passed; progress was the order . . . everything going forward to bigger and better things. And then, not so openly expressed, but even more firmly believed, the rule of white Europe and America over black, brown and yellow peoples.

I was 32 years of age in 1901, married, and a father, and teaching at Atlanta University with a program covering a hundred years of study and investigation into the condition of American Negroes. Our subject of study at that time was education: the college-bred Negro in 1900, the Negro common school in 1901. My own attitude toward the Twentieth Century was expressed in an article which I wrote in the Atlantic Monthly in 1901. It said:

> The problem of the Twentieth Century is the problem of the color-line . . . I have seen a land right merry with the sun, where children sing, and rolling hills lie like passioned women wanton with harvest. And there in

---

★ Reprinted from the *Pittsburgh Courier*, January 14, 1950.

the King's Highway sat, and sits, a figure veiled and bowed, by which the Traveler's footsteps hasten as they go. On the tainted air broods fair. Three centuries' thought have been the raising and unveiling of that bowed human soul; and now behold, my fellows, a century now for the duty and the deed! The problem of the Twentieth Century is the problem of the color-line.

This is what we hoped, to this we Negroes looked forward; peace, progress and the breaking of the color line. What has been the result? We know it all too well . . . war, hate, the revolt of the colored peoples and the fear of more war.

In the meantime, where are we; those 15,000,000 citizens of the United States who are descended from the slaves, brought here between 1600 and 1900? We formed in 1901, a separate group because of legal enslavement and emancipation into caste conditions, with the attendant poverty, ignorance, disease and crime. We were an inner group and not an integral part of the American nation; but we were exerting ourselves to fight for integration.

The burden of our fight was in seven different lines. We wanted education; we wanted particularly the right to vote and civil rights; we wanted work with adequate wage; housing, without segregation or slums; a free press to fight our battles, and (although in those days we dare not say it) social equality.

In 1901 our education was in perilous condition, despite what we and our white friends had done for thirty years. The Atlanta University Conference said in its resolutions of 1901:

We call the attention of the nation to the fact that less than one million of the three million Negro children of school age are at present regularly attending school, and these attend a session which lasts only a few months. We are today deliberately rearing millions of our citizens in ignorance and at the same time limiting the rights of citizenship by educational qualifications. This is unjust.

More particularly in civil rights, we were oppressed. We not only did not get justice in the courts, but we were subject to peculiar and galling sorts of injustice in daily life. In the latter half of the Nineteenth Century, where we first get something like statistics, no less than 3,000 Negroes were lynched without trial. And in addition to that we were subject continuously to mob violence and judicial lynching.

In political life we had, for twenty-five years, been disfranchised by violence, law and public opinion. The 14th and 15th amendments were deliberately violated and the literature of the day in book, pamphlet and daily press, was widely of opinion that the Negro was not ready for the ballot, could not use it intelligently, and that no action was called for to stop his political power from being exercised by Southern whites like Tillman and Vardaman.

We did not have the right or opportunity to work at an income which would sustain a decent and modern standard of life. Because of a past of chattel slavery, we were for the most part common laborers and servants, and a very considerable proportion were still unable to leave the plantations where they worked all their lives for next to nothing.

There were a few who were educated for the professions and we had many good artisans; that number was not increasing as it should have been, nor were new artisans being adequately trained. Industrial training was popular, but funds to implement it were too limited, and we were excluded from unions and the new mass industry.

We were housed in slums and segregated districts where crime and disease multiplied, and when we tried to move to better and healthier quarters we were met by segregation ordinance if not by mobs. We not only had no social equality, but we did not openly ask for it. It seemed a shameful thing to beg people to receive us as equals and as human beings; that was something we argued "that came and could not be fetched." And that meant not simply that we could not marry white women or legitimize mulatto bastards, but we could not stop in a decent hotel, nor eat in a public restaurant nor attend the theatre, nor accept an invitation to a private white home, nor travel in a decent railway coach. When the "public" was invited, this did not include us and admission to colleges often involved special consideration if not blunt refusal.

Finally we had poor press . . . a few struggling papers with little news and inadequately expressed opinion, with small circulation or influence and almost no advertising.

This was our plight in 1901. It was discouraging, but not hopeless. There is no question but that we had made progress, and there also was no doubt but what that progress was not enough to satisfy us or to settle our problems.

We could look back on a quarter century of struggle which had its results. We had schools; we had teachers; a few had forced themselves into the leading colleges and were tolerated if not welcomed. We voted in Northern cities,

owned many decent homes and were fighting for further progress. Leaders like Booker Washington had received wide popular approval and a Negro literature had begun to appear.

But what we needed was organized effort along the whole front, based on broad lines of complete emancipation. This came with the Niagara Movement in 1906 and the NAACP in 1909. In 1910 came the Crisis magazine and the real battle was on.

What have we gained and accomplished? The advance has not been equal on all fronts, nor complete on any. We have not progressed with closed ranks like a trained army, but rather with serried and broken ranks, with wide gaps and even temporary retreats. But we have advanced. Of that there can be no atom of doubt.

First of all in education; most Negro children today are in school and most adults can read and write. Unfortunately this literacy is not as great as the census says. The draft showed that at least a third of our youth are illiterate. But education is steadily rising. Six thousand Bachelor degrees are awarded to Negroes each year and Doctorates in philosophy and medicine are not uncommon. Nevertheless as a group, American Negroes are still in the lower ranks of learning and adaptability to modern conditions. They do not read widely, their travel is limited and their experience through contact with the modern world is curtailed by law and custom.

Secondly, in civil rights, the Negro has perhaps made his greatest advance. Mob violence and lynching have markedly decreased. Three thousand Negroes were lynched in the last half of the Nineteenth Century and five hundred in the first half of the Twentieth. Today lynching is comparatively rare. Mob violence also has decreased, but is still in evidence, and summary and unjust court proceedings have taken the place of open and illegal acts. But the Negro has established, in the courts, his legal citizenship and his right to be included in the Bill of Rights. The question still remains of "equal but separate" public accommodations, and that is being attacked. Even the institution of "jim-crow" in travel is tottering. The infraction of the marriage situation by law and custom is yet to be brought before the courts and public opinion in a forcible way.

Third, the right to vote on the part of the Negro is being gradually established under the 14th and 15th amendments. It was not really until 1915 that the Supreme Court upheld this right of Negro citizens and even today the penalties of the 14th amendment have never been enforced. There are 7,000,000 possible voters among American Negroes and of these it is a question if more than 2,000,000 actually cast their votes. This is partly from the national inertia, which keeps half of all American voters away from the polls; but even more from the question as to what practical ends the Negro shall cast his vote.

He is thinking usually in terms of what he can do by voting to better his condition and he seldom gets a chance to vote on this matter. On the wider implications of political democracy he has not yet entered; particularly he does not see the economic foundations of present civilization and the necessity of his attacking the rule of corporate wealth in order to free the labor group to which he belongs.

Fourth, there is the question of occupation. There are our submerged classes of farm labor and tenants: our city laborers, washerwomen and scrubwomen and the mass of lower-paid servants. These classes still form a majority of American Negroes and they are on the edge of poverty, with the ignorance, disease and crime that always accompany such poverty.

If we measure the median income of Americans, it is $3,000 for whites and $2,000 for Negroes. In Southern cities, 7 per cent of the white families and 30 per cent of the colored families receive less than $1,000 a year. On the other hand the class differentiation by income among Negroes is notable: the number of semi-skilled and skilled artisans has increased or will as membership in labor unions. Professional men have increased, especially teachers and less notably, physicians, dentists and lawyers.

The number of Negroes in business has increased; mostly in small retail businesses, but to a considerable extent in enterprises like insurance, real estate and small banking, where the color line gives Negroes certain advantages and where, too, there is a certain element of gambling. Also beyond the line of gambling, numbers of Negroes have made small fortunes in anti-social enterprises. All this means that there has arisen in the Negro group a distinct stratification from poor to rich. Recently I polled 450 Negro families belonging to a select organization forty-five years old. Of these families 127 received over $10,000 a year and a score of these over $25,000; 200 families received from $5,000 to $10,000 a year and eighty-six less than $5,000.

This is the start of a tendency which will grow; we are beginning to follow the American pattern of accumulating individual wealth and of considering that this will eventually settle the race problem. On the other hand, the whole trend of the thought of our age is toward social welfare; the prevention of poverty by more equitable distribution of wealth, and business for general welfare rather than private profit. There are few signs that these ideals are guiding Negro development today. We seem to be adopting increasingly the ideal of American culture.

Housing, has, of course, been a point of bitter pressure among Negroes, because the attempt to segregate the race in its living conditions has not only kept the more fortunate ones from progress, but it has confined vast numbers of Negro people to the very parts of cities and country districts where they have fewest opportunities and least social contacts. They must live largely in slums, in contact with criminals and with fewest of the social advantages of government and human contact. The fight against segregation has been carried on in the courts and shows much progress against city ordinances, against covenants which make segregation hereditary.

Literature and art have made progress among Negroes, but with curious handicaps. An art expression is normally evoked by the conscious and unconscious demand of people for portrayal of their own emotion and experience. But in the case of the American Negroes, the audience, which embodies the demand and which pays sometimes enormous price for satisfaction, is not the Negro group, but the white group. And the pattern of what the white group wants does not necessarily agree with the natural desire of Negroes.

The whole of Negro literature is therefore curiously divided. We have writers who have written, not really about Negroes, but about the things which white people, and not the highest class of whites, like to hear about Negroes. And those who have expressed what the Negro himself thinks and feels, are those whose books sell to few, even of their own people; and whom most folk do not know. This has not made for the authentic literature which the early part of this century seemed to promise. To be sure, it can be said that American literature to-day has a considerable amount of Negro expression and influence, although not as much as once we hoped.

Despite all this we have an increasing number of excellent Negro writers who make the promise for the future great by their real accomplishment. We have done something in sculpture and painting, but in drama and music we have markedly advanced. All the world listens to our singers, sings our music and dances to our rhythms.

In science, our handicaps are still great. Turner, a great entomologist, was worked to death for lack of laboratory; just never had the recognition he richly deserved, and Carver was prisoner of his inferiority complex. Notwithstanding this, our real accomplishment in biology and medicine; in history and law; and in the social sciences has been notable and widely acclaimed. To this in no little degree is due our physical survival, our falling death rate and our increased confidence in our selves and in our destiny.

The expression of Negro wish and desire through a free press has greatly improved as compared with 1900. We have a half dozen large weekly papers with circulations of a hundred thousand or more. Their news coverage is immense, even if not discriminating. But here again, the influence of the American press on us has been devastating. The predominance of advertising over opinion, the desire for income rather than literary excellence and the use of deliberate propaganda, had made our press less of a power than it could be, and leaves wide chance for improvement in the future.

In comparison with other institutions, the Negro church during the Twentieth Century has lost ground. It is no longer the dominating influence that it used to be, the center of social activity and of economic experiment. Nevertheless, it is still a powerful institution in the lives of numerical majority of American Negroes if not upon the dominant intellectual classes. There has been a considerable increase in organized work for social progress through the church, but there has also been a large increase of expenditure for buildings, furnishings, and salaries; and it is not easy to find any increase in moral stamina or conscientious discrimination within church circles.

The scandal of deliberate bribery in election of Bishops and in the holding of positions in the churches without a hierarchy has been widespread. It is a critical problem now as to just what part in the future the church among Negroes is going to hold.

Finally there comes the question of social equality, which, despite efforts on the part of thinkers, white and black, is after all the main and fundamental problem of race in the United States. Unless a human being is going to have all human rights, including not only work, but friendship, and if mutually desired, marriage and children, unless these avenues are open and free, there can be no real equality and no cultural integration.

It has hitherto seemed utterly impossible that any such solution of the Negro problem in America could take place. The situation was quite similar to the problem of the lower classes of laborers, serfs and servants in European nations during the Sixteenth, Seventeenth and Eighteenth centuries. All nations had to consist of two separate parts and the only relations between them was employment and philanthropy.

That problem has been partly solved by modern democracy, but modern democracy cannot succeed unless the peoples of different races and religions are also integrated into the democratic whole. Against this large numbers of Americans have always fought and are still fighting, but the progress despite this has been notable. There are places in the United States, especially in large cities like New York and Chicago, where the social differences between the races has, to a large extent, been nullified and there is a meeting on terms of equality which would have been thought impossible a half century ago.

On the other hand, in the South, despite religion, education and reason, the color line, although perhaps shaken, still stands, stark and unbending, and to the minds of most good people, eternal. Here lies the area of the last battle for the complete rights of American Negroes.

Within the race itself today there are disquieting signs. The effort of Negroes to become Americans of equal status with other Americans is leading them to a state of mind by which they not only accept what is good in America, but what is bad and threatening so long as the Negro can share equally. This is peculiarly dangerous at this epoch in the development of world culture.

After two world wars of unprecedented loss of life, cruelty and destruction, we are faced by the fact that the industrial organization of our present civilization has in it something fundamentally wrong. It went to pieces in the first world war because of the determination of certain great powers excluded from world rule to share in that rule, by acquisition of the labor and materials of colonial peoples. The attempt to recover from the cataclysm resulted in the collapse of our industrial system, and a second world war.

In spite of the propaganda which has gone on, which represents America as the leading democratic state, we Negroes know perfectly well, and ought to know even better than most, that America is not a successful democracy and that until it is, it is going to drag down the world. This nation is ruled by corporate wealth to a degree which is frightening. One thousand persons own the United States and their power outweighs the voice of the mass of American citizens. This must be cured, not by revolution, not by war and violence, but by reason and knowledge.

Most of the world is today turning toward the welfare state; turning against the idea of production for individual profit toward the idea of production for use and for the welfare of the mass of citizen. No matter how difficult such a course is, it is the only course that is going to save the world and this we American Negroes have got to realize.

We may find it easy now to get publicity, reward, and attention by going along with the reactionary propaganda and war hysteria which is convulsing this nation, but in the long run America will not thank its black children if they help it go the wrong way, or retard its progress.

6

*The Second Sex**

SIMONE DE BEAUVOIR

★ ★ ★

This has always been a man's world; and none of the reasons hitherto brought forward in explanation of this fact has seemed adequate. But we shall be able to understand how the hierarchy of the sexes was established by reviewing the data of prehistoric research and ethnography in the light of existentialist philosophy. I have already stated that when two human categories are together, each aspires to impose its sovereignty upon the other. If both are able to resist this imposition, there is created between them a reciprocal relation, sometimes in enmity, sometimes in amity, always in a state of tension. If one of the two is in some way privileged, has some advantage, this one prevails over the other and undertakes to keep it in subjection. It is therefore understandable that man would wish to dominate woman; but what advantage has enabled him to carry out his will?

---

* First published in 1949; translated by H.M. Parshley.

The accounts of the primitive forms of human society provided by ethnographers are extremely contradictory, the more so as they are better informed and less systematized. It is peculiarly difficult to form an idea of woman's situation in the pre-agricultural period. We do not even know whether woman's musculature or her respiratory apparatus, under conditions different from those of today, were not as well developed as in man. She had hard work to do, and in particular it was she who carried the burdens. This last fact is of doubtful significance; it is likely that if she was assigned this function, it was because a man kept his hands free on the trail in order to defend himself against possible aggressors, animal or human; his role was the more dangerous and the one that demanded more vigor. It would appear, nevertheless, that in many cases the women were strong and tough enough to take part in the warriors' expeditions. We need recall only the tales of Herodotus and the more recent accounts of the amazons of Dahomey to realize that woman has shared in warfare—and with no less ferocity and cruelty than man; but even so, man's superior strength must have been of tremendous importance in the age of the club and the wild beast. In any case, however strong the women were, the bondage of reproduction was a terrible handicap in the struggle against a hostile world. Pregnancy, childbirth, and menstruation reduced their capacity for work and made them at times wholly dependent upon the men for protection and food. As there was obviously no birth control, and as nature failed to provide women with sterile periods like other mammalian females, closely spaced maternities must have absorbed most of their strength and their

time, so that they were incapable of providing for the children they brought into the world. Here we have a first fact heavily freighted with consequences: the early days of the human species were difficult; the gathering, hunting, and fishing peoples got only meager products from the soil and those with great effort; too many children were born for the group's resources; the extravagant fertility of woman prevented her from active participation in the increase of these resources while she created new needs to an indefinite extent. Necessary as she was for the perpetuation of the species, she perpetuated it too generously, and so it was man who had to assure equilibrium between reproduction and production. Even in times when humanity most needed births, when maternity was most venerated, manual labor was the primary necessity, and woman was never permitted to take first place. The primitive hordes had no permanence in property or territory, and hence set no store by posterity; children were for them a burden, not a prized possession. Infanticide was common among the nomads, and many of the newborn that escaped massacre died from lack of care in the general state of indifference.

The woman who gave birth, therefore, did not know the pride of creation; she felt herself the plaything of obscure forces, and the painful ordeal of childbirth seemed a useless or even troublesome accident. But in any case giving birth and suckling are not *activities*, they are natural functions; no project is involved; and that is why woman found in them no reason for a lofty affirmation of her existence—she submitted passively to her biologic fate. The domestic labors that fell to her lot because they were reconcilable with the cares of maternity imprisoned her in repetition and immanence;[1] they were repeated from day to day in an identical form, which was perpetuated almost without change from century to century; they produced nothing new.

Man's case was radically different; he furnished support for the group, not in the manner of worker bees by a simple vital process, through biological behavior, but by means of acts that transcended his animal nature. *Homo faber* has from the beginning of time been an inventor: the stick and the club with which he armed himself to knock down fruits and to slaughter animals became forthwith instruments for enlarging his grasp upon the world. He did not limit himself to bringing home the fish he caught in the sea: first he had to conquer the watery realm by means of the dugout canoe fashioned from a tree-trunk; to get at the riches of the world he annexed the world itself. In this activity he put his power to the test; he set up goals and opened up roads toward them; in brief, he found self-realization as an existent. To maintain, he created; he burst out of the present, he opened the future. This is the reason why fishing and hunting expeditions had a sacred character. Their successes were celebrated with festivals and triumphs, and therein man gave recognition to his human estate. Today he still manifests this pride when he has built a dam or a skyscraper or an atomic pile. He has worked not merely to conserve the world as given; he has broken through its frontiers, he has laid down the foundations of a new future.

Early man's activity had another dimension that gave it supreme dignity: it was often dangerous. If blood were but a nourishing fluid, it would be valued no higher than milk; but the hunter was no butcher, for in the struggle against wild animals he ran grave risks. The warrior put his life in jeopardy to elevate the prestige of the horde, the clan to which he belonged. And in this he proved dramatically that life is not the supreme value for man, but on the contrary that it should be made to serve ends more important than itself. The worst curse that was laid upon woman was that she should be excluded from these warlike forays. For it is not in giving life but in risking life that man is raised above the animal; that is why superiority has been accorded in humanity not to the sex that brings forth but to that which kills.

Here we have the key to the whole mystery. On the biological level a species is maintained only by creating itself anew; but this creation results only in repeating the same Life in more individuals. But man assures the repetition of Life while transcending Life through Existence; by this transcendence he creates values that deprive pure repetition of all value. In the animal, the freedom and variety of male activities are vain because no project is involved. Except for his service to the species, what he does is immaterial. Whereas in serving the species, the human male also remodels the face of the earth, he creates new instruments, he invents, he shapes the future. In setting himself up as sovereign, he is supported by the complicity of woman herself. For she, too, is an existent, she feels the urge

---

1 This word, frequently used by the author, always signifies, as here, the opposite or negation of transcendence, such as confinement or restriction to a narrow round of uncreative and repetitious duties; it is in contrast to the freedom to engage in projects of ever widening scope that marks the untrammeled existent [*translator's note*].

to surpass, and her project is not mere repetition but transcendence toward a different future—in her heart of hearts she finds confirmation of the masculine pretensions. She joins the men in the festivals that celebrate the successes and the victories of the males. Her misfortune is to have been biologically destined for the repetition of Life, when even in her own view Life does not carry within itself its reasons for being, reasons that are more important than the life itself.

Certain passages in the argument employed by Hegel in defining the relation of master to slave apply much better to the relation of man to woman. The advantage of the master, he says, comes from his affirmation of Spirit as against Life through the fact that he risks his own life; but in fact the conquered slave has known this same risk. Whereas woman is basically an existent who gives Life and does not risk *her* life; between her and the male there has been no combat. Hegel's definition would seem to apply especially well to her. He says: "The other consciousness is the dependent consciousness for whom the essential reality is the animal type of life; that is to say, a mode of living bestowed by another entity." But this relation is to be distinguished from the relation of subjugation because woman also aspires to and recognizes the values that are concretely attained by the male. He it is who opens up the future to which she also reaches out. In truth women have never set up female values in opposition to male values; it is man who, desirous of maintaining masculine prerogatives, has invented that divergence. Men have presumed to create a feminine domain—the kingdom of life, of immanence—only in order to lock up women therein. But it is regardless of sex that the existent seeks self-justification through transcendence—the very submission of women is proof of that statement. What they demand today is to be recognized as existents by the same right as men and not to subordinate existence to life, the human being to its animality.

An existentialist perspective has enabled us, then, to understand how the biological and economic condition of the primitive horde must have led to male supremacy. The female, to a greater extent than the male, is the prey of the species; and the human race has always sought to escape its specific destiny. The support of life became for man an activity and a project through the invention of the tool; but in maternity woman remained closely bound to her body, like an animal. It is because humanity calls itself in question in the matter of living—that is to say, values the reasons for living above mere life—that, confronting woman, man assumes mastery. Man's design is not to repeat himself in time: it is to take control of the instant and mold the future. It is male activity that in creating values has made of existence itself a value; this activity has prevailed over the confused forces of life; it has subdued Nature and Woman. We must now see how this situation has been perpetuated and how it has evolved through the ages. What place has humanity made for this portion of itself which, while included within it, is defined as the Other? What rights have been conceded to it? How have men defined it?

★ ★ ★

If we cast a general glance over this history, we see several conclusions that stand out from it. And this one first of all: the whole of feminine history has been man-made. Just as in America there is no Negro problem, but rather a white problem;[2] just as "anti-semitism is not a Jewish problem: it is our problem";[3] so the woman problem has always been a man's problem. We have seen why men had moral prestige along with physical strength from the start; they created values, mores, religions; never have women disputed this empire with them. Some isolated individuals—Sappho, Christine de Pisan, Mary Wollstonecraft, Olympe de Gouges—have protested against the harshness of their destiny, and occasionally mass demonstrations have been made; but neither the Roman matrons uniting against the Oppian law nor the Anglo-Saxon suffragettes could have succeeded with their pressure unless the men had been quite disposed to submit to it. Men have always held the lot of woman in their hands; and they have determined what it should be, not according to her interest, but rather with regard to their own projects, their fears, and their needs. When they revered the Goddess Mother, it was because they feared Nature; when the bronze tool allowed them to face Nature boldly, they instituted the patriarchate; then it became the conflict between family and State that defined woman's status; the Christian's attitude toward God, the world, and his own flesh was reflected in the situation to which he consigned her; what was called in the Middle Ages "the quarrel of women" was a quarrel between clerics and laymen over marriage and celibacy; it was the social regime founded on private property that entailed the guardianship of the married woman, and it is the technological evolution accomplished by men that has emancipated

the women of today. It was a transformation in masculine ethics that brought about a reduction in family size through birth control and partially freed woman from bondage to maternity. Feminism itself was never an autonomous movement: it was in part an instrument in the hands of politicians, in part an epiphenomenon reflecting a deeper social drama. Never have women constituted a separate caste, nor in truth have they ever as a sex sought to play a historic role. The doctrines that object to the advent of woman considered as flesh, life, immanence, the Other, are masculine ideologies in no way expressing feminine aspirations. The majority of women resign themselves to their lot without attempting to take any action; those who have tried to change it have intended not to be confined within the limits of their peculiarity and cause it to triumph, but to rise above it. When they have intervened in the course of world affairs, it has been in accord with men, in masculine perspectives.

This intervention, in general, has been secondary and episodic. The classes in which women enjoyed some economic independence and took part in production were the oppressed classes, and as women workers they were enslaved even more than the male workers. In the ruling classes woman was a parasite and as such was subjected to masculine laws. In both cases it was practically impossible for woman to take action. The law and the mores did not always coincide, and between them the equilibrium was established in such a manner that woman was never concretely free. In the ancient Roman Republic economic conditions

2 Cf. Gunnar Myrdal: *The American Dilemma.* (New York: Harper & Brothers, 1944).

3 Cf. J.-P. Sartre: *Réflexions sur la question juive.* (Paris: Les Temps Modernes, 1945).

gave the matron concrete powers, but she had no legal independence. Conditions were often similar for woman in peasant civilizations and among the lower commercial middle class: mistress-servant in the house, but socially a minor. Inversely, in epochs of social disintegration woman is set free; but in ceasing to be man's vassal, she loses her fief; she has only a negative liberty, which is expressed in license and dissipation. So it was with woman during the decline of Rome, the Renaissance, the eighteenth century, the Directory (1795–9). Sometimes she succeeded in keeping busy, but found herself enslaved; or she was set free and no longer knew what to do with herself. One remarkable fact among others is that the married woman had her place in society but enjoyed no rights therein; whereas the unmarried female, honest woman or prostitute, had all the legal capacities of a man, but up to this century was more or less excluded from social life.

From this opposition of legal rights and social custom has resulted, among other things, this curious paradox: free love is not forbidden by law, whereas adultery is an offense; but very often the young girl who "goes wrong" is dishonored, whereas the misconduct of the wife is viewed indulgently; and in consequence many young women from the seventeenth century to our own day have married in order to be able to take lovers freely. By means of this ingenious system the great mass of women is held closely in leading strings: exceptional circumstances are required if a feminine personality is to succeed in asserting itself between these two series of restraints, theoretical or concrete. The women who have accomplished works comparable to those of men are those exalted by the power of social institutions above all sexual

differentiation. Queen Isabella, Queen Elizabeth, Catherine the Great were neither male nor female—they were sovereigns. It is remarkable that their femininity, when socially abolished, should have no longer meant inferiority: the proportion of queens who had great reigns is infinitely above that of great kings. Religion works the same transformation: Catherine of Siena, St. Theresa, quite beyond any physiological consideration, were sainted souls; the life they led, secular and mystic, their acts, and their writings rose to heights that few men have ever reached.

It is quite conceivable that if other women fail to make a deep impression upon the world, it is because they are tied down in their situation. They can hardly take a hand in affairs in other than a negative and oblique manner. Judith, Charlotte Corday, Vera Zasulich were assassins; the *Frondeuses* were conspirators; during the Revolution, during the Commune, women battled beside the men against the established order. Against a liberty without rights, without powers, woman has been permitted to rise in refusal and revolt, while being forbidden to participate in positively constructive effort; at the most she may succeed in joining men's enterprises through an indirect road. Aspasia, Mme de Maintenon, the Princess des Ursins were counselors who were listened to seriously—yet somebody had to be willing to listen to them. Men are glad to exaggerate the extent of these influences when they wish to convince woman that she has chosen the better part; but as a matter of fact, feminine voices are silent when it comes to concrete action. They have been able to stir up wars, not to propose battle tactics; they have directed politics hardly more than in the degree that politics is reduced to intrigue; the true control of the world has never been in the hands of women; they have not brought their influence to bear upon technique or economy, they have not made and unmade states, they have not discovered new worlds. Through them certain events have been set off, but the women have been pretexts rather than agents. The suicide of Lucretia has had value only as a symbol. Martyrdom remains open to the oppressed; during the Christian persecutions, on the morrow of social or national defeats, women have played this part of witness; but never has a martyr changed the face of the world. Even when women have started things and made demonstrations, these moves have taken on weight only when a masculine decision has effectively extended them. The American women grouped around Harriet Beecher Stowe aroused public opinion violently against slavery; but the true reasons for the War of Secession were not of a sentimental order. The "woman's day" of March 8, 1917 may perhaps have precipitated the Russian Revolution—but it was only a signal.

Most female heroines are oddities: adventuresses and originals notable less for the importance of their acts than for the singularity of their fates. Thus if we compare Joan of Arc, Mme Roland, Flora Tristan, with Richelieu, Danton, Lenin, we see that their greatness is primarily subjective: they are exemplary figures rather than historical agents. The great man springs from the masses and he is propelled onward by circumstances; the masses of women are on the margin of history, and cir-

cumstances are an obstacle for each individual, not a springboard. In order to change the face of the world, it is first necessary to be firmly anchored in it; but the women who are firmly rooted in society are those who are in subjection to it; unless designated for action by divine authority—and then they have shown themselves to be as capable as men—the ambitious woman and the heroine are strange monsters. It is only since women have begun to feel themselves at home on the earth that we have seen a Rosa Luxemburg, a Mme Curie appear. They brilliantly demonstrate that it is not the inferiority of women that has caused their historical insignificance: it is rather their historical insignificance that has doomed them to inferiority.[4]

This fact is glaringly clear in the domain in which women have best succeeded in asserting themselves—that is, the domain of culture. Their lot has been deeply bound up with that of arts and letters; among the ancient Germans the functions of prophetess and priestess were already appropriate to women. Because of woman's marginal position in the world, men will turn to her when they strive through culture to go beyond the boundaries of their universe and gain access to something other than what they have known. Courtly mysticism, humanist curiosity, the taste for beauty which flourished in the Italian Renaissance, the preciosity of the seventeenth century, the progressive idealism of the eighteenth—all brought about under different forms an exaltation of femininity. Woman was thus the guiding star of poetry, the subject matter of the work of art; her leisure

4 It is remarkable that out of a thousand statues in Paris (excepting the queens that for a purely architectural reason form the corbel of the Luxembourg) there should be only ten raised to women. Three are consecrated to Joan of Arc. The others are statues of Mme de Ségur, George Sand, Sarah Bernhardt, Mme Boucicaut and the Baroness de Hirsch, Maria Deraismes, and Rosa Bonheur.

allowed her to consecrate herself to the pleasures of the spirit: inspiration, critic, and public of the writer, she became his rival; she it was who often made prevail a mode of sensibility, an ethic that fed masculine hearts, and thus she intervened in her own destiny—the education of women was in large part a feminine conquest. And yet, however important this collective role of the intellectual woman may have been, the individual contributions have been in general of less value. It is because she has not been engaged in action that woman has had a privileged place in the domains of thought and of art; but art and thought have their living springs in action. To be situated at the margin of the world is not a position favorable for one who aims at creating anew: here again, to emerge beyond the given, it is necessary first to be deeply rooted in it. Personal accomplishment is almost impossible in the human categories that are maintained collectively in an inferior situation. "Where would you have one go, with skirts on?" Marie Bashkirtsev wanted to know. And Stendhal said: "All the geniuses who are born *women* are lost to the public good." To tell the truth, one is not born a genius: one becomes a genius; and the feminine situation has up to the present rendered this becoming practically impossible.

The antifeminists obtain from the study of history two contradictory arguments: (1) women have never created anything great; and (2) the situation of woman has never prevented the flowering of great feminine personalities. There is bad faith in these two statements; the successes of a privileged few do not counterbalance or excuse the systematic lowering of the collective level; and that these successes are rare and limited proves precisely that circumstances are unfavorable for them. As has been maintained by Christine de Pisan, Poulain de la Barre, Condorcet, John Stuart Mill, and Stendhal, in no domain has woman ever really had her chance. That is why a great many women today demand a new status; and once again their demand is not that they be exalted in their femininity: they wish that in themselves, as in humanity in general, transcendence may prevail over immanence; they wish to be accorded at last the abstract rights and concrete possibilities without the concurrence of which liberty is only a mockery.[5]

This wish is on the way to fulfillment. But the period in which we live is a period of transition; this world, which has always belonged to the men, is still in their hands; the institutions and the values of the patriarchal civilization still survive in large part. Abstract rights are far from being completely granted everywhere to women: in Switzerland they do not yet vote; in France the law of 1942 maintains in attenuated form the privileges of the husband. And abstract rights, as I have just been saying, have never sufficed to assure to woman a definite hold on the world: true equality between the two sexes does not exist even today.

In the first place, the burdens of marriage weigh much more heavily upon woman than upon man. We have noted that servitude to maternity has been reduced by the use—admitted or clandestine—of birth control; but

---

5 Here again the antifeminists take an equivocal line. Now, regarding abstract liberty as nothing, they expatiate on the great concrete role that the enslaved woman can play in the world—what then, is she asking for? Again, they disregard the fact that negative license opens no concrete possibilities, and they reproach women who are abstractly emancipated for not having produced evidence of their abilities.

the practice has not spread everywhere nor is it invariably used. Abortion being officially forbidden, many women either risk their health in unsupervised efforts to abort or find themselves overwhelmed by their numerous pregnancies. The care of children like the upkeep of the home is still undertaken almost exclusively by woman. Especially in France the antifeminist tradition is so tenacious that a man would feel that he was lowering himself by helping with tasks hitherto assigned to women. The result is that it is more difficult for woman than for man to reconcile her family life with her role as worker. Whenever society demands this effort, her life is much harder than her husband's.

Consider for example the lot of peasant women. In France they make up the majority of women engaged in productive labor; and they are generally married. Customs vary in different regions: the Norman peasant woman presides at meals, whereas the Corsican woman does not sit at table with the men; but everywhere, playing a most important part in the domestic economy, she shares the man's responsibilities, interests, and property; she is respected and often is in effective control— her situation recalls that of woman in the old agricultural communities. She often has more moral prestige than her husband, but she lives in fact a much harder life. She has exclusive care of garden, sheepfold, pigpen, and so on, and shares in the hard labor of stablework, planting, plowing, weeding, and haying; she spades, reaps, picks grapes, and sometimes helps load and unload wagons with hay, wood, and so forth. She cooks, keeps house, does washing, mending, and the like. She takes on the heavy duties of maternity and child care. She gets up at dawn, feeds the poultry and other small livestock, serves breakfast to the men, goes to work in field, wood, or garden; she draws water, serves a second meal, washes the dishes, works in the fields until time for dinner, and afterward spends the evening mending, cleaning, shelling corn, and what not. Having no time to care for her own health, even when pregnant, she soon gets misshapen; she is prematurely withered and worn out, gnawed by sickness. The compensations man finds in occasional social life are denied to her: he goes in town on Sundays and market days, meets other men, drinks and plays cards in cafés, goes hunting and fishing. She stays at home on the farm and knows no leisure. Only the well-off peasant women, who have servants or can avoid field labor, lead a well-balanced life: they are socially honored and at home exert a great deal of authority without being crushed by work. But for the most part rural labor reduces woman to the condition of a beast of burden.

The businesswoman and the female employer who runs a small enterprise have always been among the privileged; they are the only women recognized since the Middle Ages by the Code as having civil rights and powers. Female grocers, dairy dealers, landladies, tobacconists have a position equivalent to man's; as spinsters or widows, they can in themselves constitute a legal firm; married, they have the same independence as their husbands. Fortunately their work can be carried on in the place where they live, and usually it is not too absorbing.

Things are quite otherwise for the woman worker or employee, the secretary, the saleswoman, all of whom go to work outside the home. It is much more difficult for them to combine their employment with household duties, which would seem to require at least three and a half hours a day, with six hours on Sunday—a good deal to add to the hours in factory or office. As for the learned professions, even if lawyers, doctors, and professors obtain some housekeeping help, the home and children are for them also a burden that is a heavy handicap. In America domestic work is simplified by ingenious gadgets; but the elegant appearance required of the workingwoman imposes upon her another obligation, and she remains responsible for house and children.

Furthermore, the woman who seeks independence through work has less favorable possibilities than her masculine competitors. Her wages in most jobs are lower than those of men; her tasks are less specialized and therefore not so well paid as those of skilled laborers; and for equal work she does not get equal pay. Because of the fact that she is a newcomer in the universe of males, she has fewer chances for success than they have. Men and women alike hate to be under the orders of a woman; they always show more confidence in a man; to be a woman is, if not a defect, at least a peculiarity. In order to "arrive," it is well for a woman to make sure of masculine backing. Men unquestionably occupy the most advantageous places, hold the most important posts. It is essential to empha-

size the fact that men and women, economically speaking, constitute two castes.[6]

The fact that governs woman's actual condition is the obstinate survival of extremely antique traditions into the new civilization that is just appearing in vague outline. That is what is misunderstood by hasty observers who regard woman as not up to the possibilities now offered to her or again who see in these possibilities only dangerous temptations. The truth is that her situation is out of equilibrium, and for that reason it is very difficult for her to adapt herself to it. We open the factories, the offices, the faculties to woman, but we continue to hold that marriage is for her a most honorable career, freeing her from the need of any other participation in the collective life. As in primitive civilizations, the act of love is on her part a service for which she has the right to be more or less directly paid. Except in the Soviet Union,[7] modern woman is everywhere permitted to regard her body as capital for exploitation. Prostitution is tolerated,[8] gallantry encouraged. And the married woman is empowered to see to it that her husband supports her; in addition she is clothed in a social dignity far superior to that of the spinster. The mores are far from conceding to the latter sexual possibilities equivalent to

6 In America the great fortunes often fall finally into women's hands: younger than their husbands, they survive them and inherit from them; but by that time they are aged and rarely have the initiative to make new investments; they are enjoyers of income rather than proprietors. It is really men who handle the capital funds. At any rate, these privileged rich women make up only a tiny minority. In America, much more than in Europe, it is almost impossible for a woman to reach a high position as lawyer, doctor, etc.

7 At least according to official doctrine.

8 In Anglo-Saxon countries prostitution has never been regulated. Up to 1900 English and American common law did not regard it as an offense except when it made public scandal and

created disorder. Since that date repression has been more or less rigorously imposed, more or less successfully, in England and in the various states of the United States, where legislation in the matter is very diverse. In France, after a long campaign for abolition, the law of April 13, 1946 ordered the closing of licensed brothels and the intensifying of the struggle against procuring: "Holding that the existence of these houses is incompatible with the essential principles of human dignity and the role awarded to woman in modern society." But prostitution continues none the less to carry on. It is evident that the situation cannot be modified by negative and hypocritical measures.

those of the bachelor male; in particular maternity is practically forbidden her, the unmarried mother remaining an object of scandal. How, indeed, could the myth of Cinderella[9] not keep all its validity? Everything still encourages the young girl to expect fortune and happiness from some Prince Charming rather than to attempt by herself their difficult and uncertain conquest. In particular she can hope to rise, thanks to him, into a caste superior to her own, a miracle that could not be bought by the labor of her lifetime. But such a hope is a thing of evil because it divides her strength and her interests; this division is perhaps woman's greatest handicap. Parents still raise their daughter with a view to marriage rather than to furthering her personal development; she sees so many advantages in it that she herself wishes for it; the result is that she is often less specially trained, less solidly grounded than her brothers, she is less deeply involved in her profession. In this way she dooms herself to remain in its lower levels, to be inferior; and the vicious circle is formed: this professional inferiority reinforces her desire to find a husband.

Every benefit always has as its bad side some burden; but if the burden is too heavy, the benefit seems no longer to be anything more than a servitude. For the majority of laborers, labor is today a thankless drudgery, but in the case of woman this is not compensated for by a definite conquest of her social dignity, her freedom of behavior, or her economic independence; it is natural enough for many woman workers and employees to see in the right to work only an obligation from which marriage will deliver

them. Because of the fact that she has taken on awareness of self, however, and because she can also free herself from marriage through a job, woman no longer accepts domestic subjection with docility. What she would hope is that the reconciliation of family life with a job should not require of her an exhausting, difficult performance. Even then, as long as the temptations of convenience exist—in the economic inequality that favors certain individuals and the recognized right of woman to sell herself to one of these privileged men—she will need to make a greater moral effort than would a man in choosing the road of independence. It has not been sufficiently realized that the temptation is also an obstacle, and even one of the most dangerous. Here it is accompanied by a hoax, since in fact there will be only one winner out of thousands in the lottery of marriage. The present epoch invites, even compels women to work; but it flashes before their eyes paradises of idleness and delight: it exalts the winners far above those who remain tied down to earth.

The privileged place held by men in economic life, their social usefulness, the prestige of marriage, the value of masculine backing, all this makes women wish ardently to please men. Women are still, for the most part, in a state of subjection. It follows that woman sees herself and makes her choices not in accordance with her true nature in itself, but as man defines her. So we must first go on to describe woman such as men have fancied her in their dreams, for what-in-men's-eyes-she-seems-to-be is one of the necessary factors in her real situation.

9 Cf. Philip Wylie: *Generation of Vipers* (Boston: Farrar, Straus & Co., 1942).

7

Some Principles of Stratification*

KINGSLEY DAVIS AND WILBERT E. MOORE

In a previous paper some concepts for handling the phenomena of social inequality were presented.[1] In the present paper a further step in stratification theory is undertaken—an attempt to show the relationship between stratification and the rest of the social order.[2] Starting from the proposition that no society is "classless," or unstratified, an effort is made to explain, in functional terms, the universal necessity which calls forth stratification in any social system. Next, an attempt is made to explain the roughly uniform distribution of prestige as between the major types of positions in every society. Since, however, there occur between one society and another great differences in the

---

* First published in 1945; from *American Sociological Review*, Volume 10, Issue 2.

1 Kingsley Davis, "A Conceptual Analysis of Stratification," *American Sociological Review*, 7: 309–321, June, 1942.

2 The writers regret (and beg indulgence) that the present essay, a condensation of a longer study, covers so much in such short space that adequate evidence and qualification cannot be given and that as a result what is actually very tentative is presented in an unfortunately dogmatic manner.

degree and kind of stratification, some attention is also given to the varieties of social inequality and the variable factors that give rise to them.

Clearly, the present task requires two different lines of analysis—one to understand the universal, the other to understand the variable features of stratification. Naturally each line of inquiry aids the other and is indispensable, and in the treatment that follows the two will be interwoven, although, because of space limitations, the emphasis will be on the universals.

Throughout, it will be necessary to keep in mind one thing—namely, that the discussion relates to the system of positions, not to the individuals occupying those positions. It is one thing to ask why different positions carry different degrees of prestige, and quite another to ask how certain individuals get into those positions. Although, as the argument will try to show, both questions are related, it is essential to keep them separate in our thinking. Most of the literature on stratification has tried to answer the second question (particularly with regard to the ease or difficulty of mobility between strata) without tackling the first. The first question, however, is logically prior and, in the case of any particular individual or group, factually prior.

THE FUNCTIONAL NECESSITY OF STRATIFICATION

Curiously, however, the main functional necessity explaining the universal presence of stratification is precisely the requirement faced by any society of placing and motivating individuals in the social structure. As a functioning mechanism a society must somehow distribute its members in social positions and induce them to perform the duties of these positions. It must thus concern itself with motivation at two different levels: to instill in the proper individuals the desire to fill certain positions, and, once in these positions, the desire to perform the duties attached to them. Even though the social order may be relatively static in form, there is a continuous process of metabolism as new individuals are born into it, shift with age, and die off. Their absorption into the positional system must somehow be arranged and motivated. This is true whether the system is competitive or non-competitive. A competitive system gives greater importance to the motivation to achieve positions, whereas a non-competitive system gives perhaps greater importance to the motivation to perform the duties of the positions; but in any system both types of motivation are required.

If the duties associated with the various positions were all equally pleasant to the human organism, all equally important to societal survival, and all equally in need of the same ability or talent, it would make no difference who got into which positions, and the problem of social placement would be greatly reduced. But actually it does make a great deal of difference who gets into which positions, not only because some positions are inherently more agreeable than others, but also because some require special talents or training and some are functionally more important than others. Also, it is essential that the duties of the positions be performed with the diligence that their importance requires. Inevitably, then, a society must have, first, some kind of rewards that it can use as inducements, and, second, some way of distributing these rewards differentially according to positions. The rewards and their distribution become a part of the social order, and thus give rise to stratification.

One may ask what kind of rewards a society has at its disposal in distributing its personnel and securing essential services. It has, first of all, the things that contribute to sustenance and comfort. It has, second, the things that contribute to humor and diversion. And it has, finally, the things that contribute to self respect and ego expansion. The last, because of the peculiarly social character of the self, is largely a function of the opinion of others, but it nonetheless ranks in importance with the first two. In any social system all three kinds of rewards must be dispensed differentially according to positions.

In a sense the rewards are "built into" the position. They consist in the "rights" associated with the position, plus what may be called its accompaniments or perquisites. Often the rights, and sometimes the accompaniments, are functionally related to the duties of the position. (Rights as viewed by the incumbent are usually duties as viewed by other members of the community.) However, there may be a host of subsidiary rights and perquisites that are not essential to the function of the position and have only an indirect and symbolic connection with its duties, but which still may be of considerable importance in inducing people to seek the positions and fulfill the essential duties.

If the rights and perquisites of different positions in a society must be unequal, then the society must be stratified, because that is precisely what stratification means. Social inequality is thus an unconsciously evolved device by which societies insure that the most important positions are conscientiously filled by the most qualified persons. Hence every society, no matter how simple or complex, must differentiate persons in terms of both prestige and esteem, and must therefore possess a certain amount of institutionalized inequality.

It does not follow that the amount or type of inequality need be the same in all societies. This is largely a function of factors that will be discussed presently.

THE TWO DETERMINANTS OF POSITIONAL RANK

Granting the general function that inequality subserves, one can specify the two factors that determine the relative rank of different positions. In general those positions convey the best reward, and hence have the highest rank, which (a) have the greatest importance for the society and (b) require the greatest training or talent. The first factor concerns function and is a matter of relative significance; the second concerns means and is a matter of scarcity.

Differential Functional Importance

Actually a society does not need to reward positions in proportion to their functional importance. It merely needs to give sufficient reward to them to insure that they will be filled competently. In other words, it must see that less essential positions do not compete successfully with more essential ones. If a position is easily filled, it need not be heavily rewarded, even though important. On the other hand, if it is important but hard to fill, the reward must be high enough to get it filled anyway. Functional importance is therefore a necessary but not a sufficient cause of high rank being assigned to a position.[3]

Differential Scarcity of Personnel

Practically all positions, no matter how acquired, require some form of skill or capacity for performance. This is implicit in the very notion of position, which implies that the incumbent must, by virtue of his incumbency, accomplish certain things.

There are, ultimately, only two ways in which a person's qualifications come about: through inherent capacity or through training. Obviously, in concrete activities both are always necessary, but from a practical standpoint the scarcity may lie primarily in one or the other, as well as in both, Some positions require innate talents of such high degree that the persons who fill them are bound to be rare. In many cases, however, talent is fairly abundant in the population but the training process is so long, costly, and elaborate that relatively few can qualify. Modern medicine, for example, is within the mental capacity of most individuals, but a medical education is so burdensome and expensive that virtually none would undertake it if the position of the M.D. did not carry a reward commensurate with the sacrifice.

If the talents required for a position are abundant and the training easy, the method of acquiring the position may have little to do with its duties. There may be, in fact, a virtually accidental relationship. But if the skills required are scarce by reason of the rarity of talent or the costliness of training, the position, if functionally important, must have an attractive power that will draw the necessary skills in competition with other positions. This means, in effect, that the position must be high in the social scale—must command great prestige, high salary, ample leisure, and the like.

How Variations Are to Be Understood

In so far as there is a difference between one system of stratification and another, it is attributable to whatever factors affect the two determinants of differential reward—namely, functional importance and scarcity of personnel. Positions important in one society may not be important in another, because the conditions faced by the societies, or their degree of internal development, may be different. The same conditions, in turn, may affect the question of scarcity; for in some societies the stage

---

3 Unfortunately, functional importance is difficult to establish. To use the position's prestige to establish it, as is often unconsciously done, constitutes circular reasoning from our point of view. There are, however, two independent clues: (a) the degree to which a position is functionally unique, there being no other positions that can perform the same function satisfactorily; (b) the degree to which other positions are dependent on the one in question. Both clues are best exemplified in organized systems of positions built around one major function. Thus, in most complex societies the religious, political, economic, and educational functions are handled by dis- tinct structures not easily interchangeable. In addition, each structure possesses many different positions, some clearly dependent on, if not subordinate to, others. In sum, when an institutional nucleus becomes differentiated around one main function, and at the same time organizes a large portion of the population into its relationships, the *key* positions in it are of the highest functional importance. The absence of such specialization does not prove functional unimportance, for the whole society may be relatively unspecialized; but it is safe to assume that the more important functions receive the first and clearest structural differentiation.

of development, or the external situation, may wholly obviate the necessity of certain kinds of skill or talent. Any particular system of stratification, then, can be understood as a product of the special conditions affecting the two aforementioned grounds of differential reward.

MAJOR SOCIETAL FUNCTIONS AND STRATIFICATION

Religion

The reason why religion is necessary is apparently to be found in the fact that human society achieves its unity primarily through the possession by its members of certain ultimate values and ends in common. Although these values and ends are subjective, they influence behavior, and their integration enables the society to operate as a system. Derived neither from inherited nor from external nature, they have evolved as a part of culture by communication and moral pressure. They must, however, appear to the members of the society to have some reality, and it is the role of religious belief and ritual to supply and reinforce this appearance of reality. Through belief and ritual the common ends and values are connected with an imaginary world symbolized by concrete sacred objects, which world in turn is related in a meaningful way to the facts and trials of the individual's life. Through the worship of the sacred objects and the beings they symbolize, and the acceptance of supernatural prescriptions that are at the same time codes of behavior, a powerful control over human conduct is exercised, guiding it along lines sustaining the institutional structure and conforming to the ultimate ends and values.

If this conception of the role of religion is true, one can understand why in every known society the religious activities tend to be under the charge of particular persons, who tend thereby to enjoy greater rewards than the ordinary societal member. Certain of the rewards and special privileges may attach to only the highest religious functionaries, but others usually apply, if such exists, to the entire sacerdotal class.

Moreover, there is a peculiar relation between the duties of the religious official and the special privileges he enjoys. If the supernatural world governs the destinies of men more ultimately than does the real world, its earthly representative, the person through whom one may communicate with the supernatural, must be a powerful individual. He is a keeper of sacred tradition, a skilled performer of the ritual, and an interpreter of lore and myth. He is in such close contact with the gods that he is viewed as possessing some of their characteristics. He is, in short, a bit sacred, and hence free from some of the more vulgar necessities and controls.

It is no accident, therefore, that religious functionaries have been associated with the very highest positions of power, as in theocratic regimes. Indeed, looking at it from this point of view, one may wonder why it is that they do not get *entire* control over their societies. The factors that prevent this are worthy of note.

In the first place, the amount of technical competence necessary for the performance of religious duties is small. Scientific or artistic capacity is not required. Anyone can set himself up as enjoying an intimate relation with deities, and nobody can successfully dispute him. Therefore, the factor of scarcity of personnel does not operate in the technical sense.

One may assert, on the other hand, that religious ritual is often elaborate and religious lore abstruse, and that priestly ministrations require tact, if not intelligence. This is true, but the technical requirements of the profession are for the most part adventitious, not related to the end in the same way that science is related to air travel. The priest can never be free from competition, since the criteria of whether or not one has genuine contact with the supernatural are never strictly clear. It is this competition that debases the priestly position below what might be expected at first glance. That is why priestly prestige is highest in those societies where membership in the profession is rigidly controlled by the priestly guild itself. That is why, in part at least, elaborate devices are utilized to stress the identification of the person with his office—spectacular costume, abnormal conduct, special diet, segregated residence, celibacy, conspicuous leisure, and the like. In fact, the priest is always in danger of becoming somewhat discredited—as happens in a secularized society—because in a world of stubborn fact, ritual and sacred knowledge alone will not grow crops or build houses. Furthermore, unless he is protected by a professional guild, the priest's identification with the supernatural tends to preclude his acquisition of abundant wordly goods.

As between one society and another it seems that the highest general position awarded the priest occurs in the medieval type of social order. Here there is enough economic production to afford a surplus, which can be used to support a numerous and highly organized priesthood; and yet the populace is unlettered and therefore credulous to a high degree. Perhaps the most extreme example is to be found in the Buddhism of Tibet, but others are encountered in the Catholicism of feudal Europe, the Inca regime of Peru, the Brahminism of India, and the Mayan priesthood of Yucatan. On the other hand, if the society is so crude as to have no surplus and little differentiation, so that every priest must be also a cultivator or hunter, the separation of the priestly status from the others has hardly gone far enough for priestly prestige to mean much. When the priest actually has high prestige under these circumstances, it is because he also performs other important functions (usually political and medical).

In an extremely advanced society built on scientific technology, the priesthood tends to lose status, because sacred tradition and supernaturalism drop into the background. The ultimate values and common ends of the society tend to be expressed in less anthropomorphic ways, by officials who occupy fundamentally political, economic, or educational rather than religious positions. Nevertheless, it is easily possible for intellectuals to exaggerate the degree to which the priesthood in a presumably secular milieu has lost prestige. When the matter is closely examined the urban proletariat, as well as the rural citizenry, proves to be surprisingly god-fearing and priest-ridden. No society has become so completely secularized as to liquidate entirely the belief in transcendental ends and supernatural entities. Even in a secularized society some system must exist for the integration of ultimate values, for their ritualistic expression, and for the emotional adjustments required by disappointment, death, and disaster.

Government

Like religion, government plays a unique and indispensable part in society. But in contrast to religion, which provides integration in terms of sentiments, beliefs, and rituals, it organizes the society in terms of law and authority. Furthermore, it orients the society to the actual rather than the unseen world.

The main functions of government are, internally, the ultimate enforcement of norms, the final arbitration of conflicting interests, and the overall planning and direction of society; and externally, the handling of war and diplomacy. To carry out these functions it acts as the agent of the entire people, enjoys a monopoly of force, and controls all individuals within its territory.

Political action, by definition, implies authority. An official can command because he has authority, and the citizen must obey because he is subject to that authority. For this reason stratification is inherent in the nature of political relationships.

So clear is the power embodied in political position that political inequality is sometimes thought to comprise all inequality. But it can be shown that there are other bases of stratification, that the following controls operate in practice to keep political power from becoming complete: (a) The fact that the actual holders of political office, and especially those determining top policy must necessarily be few in number compared to the total population. (b) The fact that the rulers represent the interest of the group rather than of themselves, and are therefore restricted in their behavior by rules and mores designed to enforce this limitation of interest. (c) The fact that the holder of political office has his authority by virtue of his office and nothing else, and therefore any special knowledge, talent, or capacity he may claim is purely incidental, so that he often has to depend upon others for technical assistance.

In view of these limiting factors, it is not strange that the rulers often have less power and prestige than a literal enumeration of their formal rights would lead one to expect.

Wealth, Property, and Labor

Every position that secures for its incumbent a livelihood is, by definition, economically rewarded. For this reason there is an economic aspect to those positions (e.g. political and religious) the main function of which is not economic. It therefore becomes convenient for the society to use unequal economic returns as a principal means of controlling the entrance of persons into positions and stimulating the performance of their duties. The amount of the economic return therefore becomes one of the main indices of social status.

It should be stressed, however, that a position does not bring power and prestige *because* it draws a high income. Rather, it draws a high income because it is functionally important and the available personnel is for one reason or another scarce. It is therefore superficial and erroneous to regard high income as the cause of a man's power and prestige, just as it is erroneous to think that a man's fever is the cause of his disease.

The economic source of power and prestige is not income primarily, but the ownership of capital goods (including patents, good will, and professional reputation). Such ownership should be distinguished from the possession of consumers' goods, which is an index rather than a cause of social standing. In other words, the ownership of producers' goods is properly speaking, a source of income like other positions, the income itself remaining an index. Even in situations where social values are widely commercialized and earnings are the readiest method of judging social position, income does not confer prestige on a position so much as it induces people to compete for the position. It is true that a man who has a high income as a result of one position may find this money helpful in climbing into another position as well, but this again reflects the effect of his initial, economically advantageous status, which exercises its influence through the medium of money.

In a system of private property in productive enterprise, an income above what an individual spends can give rise to possession of capital wealth. Presumably such possession is a reward for the proper management of one's finances originally and of the productive enterprise later. But as social differentiation becomes highly advanced and yet the institution of inheritance persists, the phenomenon of pure ownership, and reward for pure ownership, emerges. In such a case it is difficult to prove that the position is functionally important or that the scarcity involved is anything other than extrinsic and accidental. It is for this reason, doubtless, that the institution of private property in productive goods becomes more subject to criticism as social development proceeds toward industrialization. It is only this pure, that is, strictly legal and functionless ownership, however, that is open to attack; for some form of active ownership, whether private or public, is indispensable.

One kind of ownership of production goods consists in rights over the labor of others. The most extremely concentrated and exclusive of such rights are found in slavery, but the essential principle remains in serfdom, peonage, encomienda, and indenture. Naturally this kind of ownership has the greatest significance for stratification, because it necessarily entails an unequal relationship.

But property in capital goods inevitably introduces a compulsive element even into the nominally free contractual relationship. Indeed, in some respects the authority of the contractual employer is greater than that of the feudal landlord, inasmuch as the latter is more limited by traditional reciprocities. Even the classical economics recognized that competitors would fare unequally, but it did not pursue this fact to its necessary conclusion that, however it might be acquired, unequal control of goods and services must give unequal advantage to the parties to a contract.

Technical Knowledge

The function of finding means to single goals, without any concern with the choice between goals, is the exclusively technical sphere. The explanation of why positions requiring great technical skill receive fairly high rewards is easy to see, for it is the simplest case of the rewards being so distributed as to draw talent and motivate training. Why they seldom if ever receive the highest rewards is also clear: the importance of technical knowledge from a societal point of view is never so great as the integration of goals, which takes place on the religious, political, and economic levels. Since the technological level is concerned solely with means, a purely technical position must ultimately be subordinate to other positions that are religious, political, or economic in character.

Nevertheless, the distinction between expert and layman in any social order is fundamental, and cannot be entirely reduced to other terms. Methods of recruitment, as well as of reward, sometimes lead to the erroneous interpretation that technical positions are economically determined. Actually, however, the acquisition of knowledge and skill cannot be accomplished by purchase, although the opportunity to learn may be. The control of the avenues of training may inhere as a sort of property right in certain families or classes, giving them power and prestige in consequence. Such a situation adds an artificial scarcity to the natural scarcity of skills and talents. On the other hand, it is possible for an opposite situation to arise. The rewards of technical position may be so great that a condition of excess supply is created, leading to at least temporary devaluation of the rewards. Thus "unemployment in the learned professions" may result in a debasement of the prestige of those positions. Such adjustments and readjustments are constantly occurring in changing societies; and it is always well to bear in mind that the efficiency of a stratified structure may be affected by the modes of recruitment for positions. The social order itself, however, sets limits to the inflation or deflation of the prestige of experts: an over-supply tends to debase the rewards and discourage recruitment or produce revolution, whereas an under-supply tends to increase the rewards or weaken the society in competition with other societies.

Particular systems of stratification show a wide range with respect to the exact position of technically competent persons. This range is perhaps most evident in the degree of specialization. Extreme division of labor tends to create many specialists without high prestige since the training is short and the required native capacity relatively small. On the other hand it also tends to accentuate the high position of the true experts—scientists, engineers, and administrators—by increasing their authority relative to other functionally important positions. But the idea of a technocratic social order or a government or priesthood of engineers or social scientists neglects the limitations of knowledge and skills as a basic for performing social functions. To the extent that the social structure is truly specialized the prestige of the technical person must also be circumscribed.

VARIATION IN STRATIFIED SYSTEMS

The generalized principles of stratification here suggested form a necessary preliminary to a consideration of types of stratified systems, because it is in terms of these principles that the types must be described. This can be seen by trying to delineate types according to certain modes of variation. For instance, some of the most important modes (together with the polar types in terms of them) seem to be as follows:

(a) The Degree of Specialization

The degree of specialization affects the fineness and multiplicity of the gradations in power and prestige. It also influences the extent to which particular functions may be emphasized in the invidious system, since a given function cannot receive much emphasis in the hierarchy until it has achieved structural separation from the other functions. Finally, the amount of specialization influences the bases of selection. Polar types: *Specialized, Unspecialized.*

(b) The Nature of the Functional Emphasis

In general when emphasis is put on sacred matters, a rigidity is introduced that tends to limit specialization and hence the development of technology. In addition, a brake is placed on social mobility, and on the development of bureaucracy. When the preoccupation with the sacred is withdrawn, leaving greater scope for purely secular preoccupations, a great development, and rise in status, of economic and technological positions seemingly takes place. Curiously, a concomitant rise in political position is not likely, because it has usually been allied with the religious and stands to gain little by the decline of the latter. It is also possible for a society to emphasize family functions—as in relatively undifferentiated societies where high mortality requires high fertility and kinship forms the main basis of social organization. Main types: *Familistic, Authoritarian* (*Theocratic* or sacred, and *Totalitarian* or secular), *Capitalistic.*

(c) The Magnitude of Invidious Differences

What may be called the amount of social distance between positions, taking into account the entire scale, is something that should lend itself to quantitative measurement. Considerable differences apparently exist between different societies in this regard, and also between parts of the same society. Polar types: *Equalitarian, Inequalitarian.*

(d) The Degree of Opportunity

The familiar question of the amount of mobility is different from the question of the comparative equality or inequality of rewards posed above, because the two criteria may vary independently up to a point. For instance, the tremendous divergences in monetary income in the United States are far greater than those found in primitive societies, yet the equality of opportunity to move from one rung to the other in the social scale may also be greater in the United States than in a hereditary tribal kingdom. Polar types: *Mobile* (open), *Immobile* (closed).

(e) The Degree of Stratum Solidarity

Again, the degree of "class solidarity" (or the presence of specific organizations to promote class interests) may vary to some extent independently of the other criteria, and hence is an important principle in classifying systems of stratification. Polar types: *Class organized, Class unorganized.*

||| EXTERNAL CONDITIONS

What state any particular system of stratification is in with reference to each of these modes of variation depends on two things: (1) its state with reference to the other ranges of variation, and (2) the conditions outside the system of stratification which nevertheless influence that system. Among the latter are the following:

(a) The Stage of Cultural Development

As the cultural heritage grows, increased specialization becomes necessary, which in turn contributes to the enhancement of mobility, a decline of stratum solidarity, and a change of functional emphasis.

(b) Situation with Respect to Other Societies

The presence or absence of open conflict with other societies, of free trade relations or cultural diffusion, all influence the class structure to some extent. A chronic state of warfare tends to place emphasis upon the military functions, especially when the opponents are more or less equal. Free trade, on the other hand, strengthens the hand of the trader at the expense of the warrior and priest. Free movement of ideas generally has an equalitarian effect. Migration and conquest create special circumstances.

(c) Size of the Society

A small society limits the degree to which functional specialization can go, the degree of segregation of different strata, and the magnitude of inequality.

||| COMPOSITE TYPES

Much of the literature on stratification has attempted to classify concrete systems into a certain number of types. This task is deceptively simple, however, and should come at the end of an analysis of elements and principles, rather than at the beginning. If the preceding discussion has any validity, it indicates that there are a number of modes of variation between different systems, and that any one system is a composite of the society's status with reference to all these modes of variation. The danger of trying to classify whole societies under such rubrics as *caste, feudal,* or *open class* is that one or two criteria are selected and others ignored, the result being an unsatisfactory solution to the problem posed. The present discussion has been offered as a possible approach to the more systematic classification of composite types.

8

Citizenship and Social Class*

T.H. MARSHALL

THE DEVELOPMENT OF CITIZENSHIP TO THE END OF THE NINETEENTH CENTURY

I shall be running true to type as a sociologist if I begin by saying that I propose to divide citizenship into three parts. But the analysis is, in this case, dictated by history even more clearly than by logic. I shall call these three parts, or elements, civil, political and social. The civil element is composed of the rights necessary for individual freedom—liberty of the person, freedom of speech, thought and faith, the right to own property and to conclude valid contracts, and the right to justice. The last is of a different order from the others, because it is the right to defend and assert all one's rights on terms of equality with others and by due process of law. This shows us that the institutions most directly associated with civil rights are the courts of justice. By the

---

* First published in 1950.

political element I mean the right to participate in the exercise of political power, as a member of a body invested with political authority or as an elector of the members of such a body. The corresponding institutions are parliament and councils of local government. By the social element I mean the whole range from the right to a modicum of economic welfare and security to the right to share to the full in the social heritage and to live the life of a civilised being according to the standards prevailing in the society. The institutions most closely connected with it are the educational system and the social services.

In early times these three strands were wound into a single thread. The rights were blended because the institutions were amalgamated. As Maitland said: 'The further back we trace our history the more impossible it is for us to draw strict lines of demarcation between the various functions of the State: the same institution is a legislative assembly, a governmental council and a court of law. . . . Everywhere, as we pass from the ancient to the modern, we see what the fashionable philosophy calls differentiation.' Maitland is speaking here of the fusion of political and civil institutions and rights. But a man's social rights, too, were part of the same amalgam, and derived from the status which also determined the kind of justice he could get and where he could get it, and the way in which he could take part in the administration of the affairs of the community of which he was a member. But this status was not one of citizenship in our modern sense. In feudal society status was the hallmark of class and the measure of inequality. There was no uniform collection of rights and duties with which all men—noble and common, free and serf—were endowed by

virtue of their membership of the society. There was, in this sense, no principle of the equality of citizens to set against the principle of the inequality of classes. In the medieval towns, on the other hand, examples of genuine and equal citizenship can be found. But its specific rights and duties were strictly local, whereas the citizenship whose history I wish to trace is, by definition, national.

★ ★ ★

THE EARLY IMPACT OF CITIZENSHIP ON SOCIAL CLASS

★ ★ ★ My aim has been to trace in outline the development of citizenship in England to the end of the nineteenth century. For this purpose I have divided citizenship into three elements, civil, political and social. I have tried to show that civil rights came first, and were established in something like their modern form before the first Reform Act was passed in 1832. Political rights came next, and their extension was one of the main features of the nineteenth century, although the principle of universal political citizenship was not recognised until 1918. Social rights, on the other hand, sank to vanishing point in the eighteenth and early nineteenth centuries. Their revival began with the development of public elementary education, but it was not until the twentieth century that they attained to equal partnership with the other two elements in citizenship.

★ ★ ★

Citizenship is a status bestowed on those who are full members of a community. All who possess the status are equal with respect to the rights and duties with which the status is endowed. There is no universal principle that determines what those rights and duties shall be, but societies in which citizenship is a developing institution create an image of an ideal citizenship against which achievement can be measured and towards which aspiration can be directed. The urge forward along the path thus plotted is an urge towards a fuller measure of equality, an enrichment of the stuff of which the status is made and an increase in the number of those on whom the status is bestowed. Social class, on the other hand, is a system of inequality. And it too, like citizenship, can be based on a set of ideals, beliefs and values. It is therefore reasonable to expect that the impact of citizenship on social class should take the form of a conflict between opposing principles. If I am right in my contention that citizenship has been a developing institution in England at least since the latter part of the seventeenth century, then it is clear that its growth coincides with the rise of capitalism, which is a system, not of equality, but of inequality. Here is something that needs explaining. How is it that these two opposing principles could grow and flourish side by side in the same soil? What made it possible for them to be reconciled with one another and to become, for a time at least, allies instead of antagonists? The question is a pertinent one, for it is clear that, in the twentieth century, citizenship and the capitalist class system have been at war.

★ ★ ★

★ ★ ★ Citizenship, even in its early forms, was a principle of equality, and that during this period it was a developing institution. Starting at the point where all men were free and, in theory, capable of enjoying rights, it grew by enriching the body of rights which they were capable of enjoying. But these rights did not conflict with the inequalities of capitalist society; they were, on the contrary, necessary to the maintenance of that particular form of inequality. The explanation lies in the fact that the core of citizenship at this stage was composed of civil rights. And civil rights were indispensable to a competitive market economy. They gave to each man, as part of his individual status, the power to engage as an independent unit in the economic struggle and made it possible to deny to him social protection on the ground that he was equipped with the means to protect himself. Maine's famous dictum that 'the movement of the progressive societies has hitherto been a movement from Status to Contract' expresses a profound truth which has been elaborated, with varying terminology, by many sociologists, but it requires qualification. For both status and contract are present in all but the most primitive societies. Maine himself admitted this when, later in the same book, he wrote that the earliest feudal communities, as contrasted with their archaic predecessors, were 'neither bound together by mere sentiment nor recruited by a fiction. The tie which united them was Contract.' But the contractual element in feudalism coexisted with a class system based on status and, as contract hardened into custom, it helped to perpetuate class status. Custom retained the form of mutual undertakings, but not the reality of a free agreement. Modern contract did not grow out of feudal contract; it marks a new development to whose progress feudalism was an obstacle that had to be swept aside. For modern contract is essentially an agreement between men who are free and equal in status, though not necessarily in power. Status was not eliminated from the social system. Differential status, associated with class, function and family, was replaced by the single uniform status of citizenship, which provided the foundation of equality on which the structure of inequality could be built.

★ ★ ★ This status was clearly an aid, and not a menace, to capitalism and the free-market economy, because it was dominated by civil rights, which confer the legal capacity to strive for the things one would like to possess but do not guarantee the possession of any of them. A property right is not a right to possess property, but a right to acquire it, if you can, and to protect it, if you can get it. But, if you use these arguments to explain to a pauper that his property rights are the same as those of a millionaire, he will probably accuse you of quibbling. Similarly, the right to freedom of speech has little real substance if, from lack of education, you have nothing to say that is worth saying, and no means of making yourself heard if you say it. But these blatant inequalities are not due to defects in civil rights, but to lack of social rights, and social rights in the mid-nineteenth century were in the doldrums. The Poor Law was an aid, not a menace, to capitalism, because it relieved industry of all social responsibility outside the contract of employment, while sharpening the edge of competition in the labour market. Elementary schooling was also an aid, because it increased the value of the worker without educating him above his station.

★ ★ ★

★ ★ ★ Thus although citizenship, even by the end of the nineteenth century, had done little to reduce social inequality, it had helped to guide progress into the path which led directly to the egalitarian policies of the twentieth century.

It also had an integrating effect, or, at least, was an important ingredient in a integrating process. ★ ★ ★ Citizenship requires ★ ★ ★ a direct sense of community membership based on loyalty to a civilisation which is a common possession. It is a loyalty of free men endowed with rights and protected by a common law. Its growth is stimulated both by the struggle to win those rights and by their enjoyment when won. We see this clearly in the eighteenth century, which saw the birth, not only of modern civil rights, but also of modern national consciousness. The familiar instruments of modern democracy were fashioned by the upper classes and then handed down, step by step, to the lower: political journalism for the intelligentsia was followed by newspapers for all who could read, public meetings, propaganda campaigns and associations for the furtherance of public causes. Repressive measures and taxes were quite unable to stop the flood. And with it came a patriotic nationalism, expressing the unity underlying these controversial outbursts. ★ ★ ★

This growing national consciousness, this awakening public opinion, and these first stirrings of a sense of community membership and common heritage did not have any material effect on class structure and social inequality for the simple and obvious reason that, even at the end of the nineteenth century, the mass of the working people did not wield effective political power. By that time the franchise was fairly wide, but those who had recently received the vote had not yet learned how to use it. The political rights of citizenship, unlike the civil rights, were full of potential danger to the capitalist system, although those who were cautiously extending them down the social scale probably did not realise quite how great the danger was. They could hardly be expected to foresee what vast changes could be brought about by the peaceful use of political power, without a violent and bloody revolution. The planned society and the welfare state had not yet risen over the horizon or come within the view of the practical politician. The foundations of the market economy and the contractual system seemed strong enough to stand against any probable assault. In fact, there were some grounds for expecting that the working classes, as they became educated, would accept the basic principles of the system and be content to rely for their protection and progress on the civil rights of citizenship, which contained no obvious menace to competitive capitalism. Such a view was encouraged by the fact that one of the main achievements of political power in the later nineteenth century was the recognition of the right of collective bargaining. This meant that social progress was being sought by strengthening civil rights, not by creating social rights; through the use of contract in the open market, not through a minimum wage and social security.

But this interpretation underrates the significance of this extension of civil rights in the economic sphere. For civil rights were in origin intensely individual, and that is why they harmonised with the individualistic phase of capitalism. By the device of incorporation groups were enabled to act legally as individu-

als. This important development did not go unchallenged, and limited liability was widely denounced as an infringement of individual responsibility. But the position of trade unions was even more anomalous, because they did not seek or obtain incorporation. They can, therefore, exercise vital civil rights collectively on behalf of their members without formal collective responsibility, while the individual responsibility of the workers in relation to contract is largely unenforceable. These civil rights became, for the workers, an instrument for raising their social and economic status, that is to say, for establishing the claim that they, as citizens, were entitled to certain social rights. But the normal method of establishing social rights is by the exercise of political power, for social rights imply an absolute right to a certain standard of civilisation which is conditional only on the discharge of the general duties of citizenship. Their content does not depend on the economic value of the individual claimant. There is therefore a significant difference between a genuine collective bargain through which economic forces in a free market seek to achieve equilibrium and the use of collective civil rights to assert basic claims to the elements of social justice. Thus the acceptance of collective bargaining was not simply a natural extension of civil rights; it represented the transfer of an important process from the political to the civil sphere of citizenship. But 'transfer' is, perhaps, a misleading term, for at the time when this happened the workers either did not possess, or had not yet learned to use, the political right of the franchise. Since then they have obtained and made full use of that right. Trade unionism has, therefore, created a secondary system of industrial citizenship parallel with and supplementary to the system of political citizenship.

★ ★ ★

SOCIAL RIGHTS IN THE TWENTIETH CENTURY

The period of which I have hitherto been speaking was one during which the growth of citizenship, substantial and impressive though it was, had little direct effect on social inequality. Civil rights gave legal powers whose use was drastically curtailed by class prejudice and lack of economic opportunity. Political rights gave potential power whose exercise demanded experience, organisation and a change of ideas as to the proper functions of government. All these took time to develop. Social rights were at a minimum and were not woven into the fabric of citizenship. The common purpose of statutory and voluntary effort was to abate the nuisance of poverty without disturbing the pattern of inequality of which poverty was the most obviously unpleasant consequence.

A new period opened at the end of the nineteenth century, conveniently marked by Booth's survey of Life and Labour of the People in London and the Royal Commission on the Aged Poor. It saw the first big advance in social rights, and this involved significant changes in the egalitarian principles expressed in citizenship. But there were other forces at work as well. A rise of money incomes unevenly distributed over the social classes altered the economic distance which separated these classes from one another, diminishing the gap between skilled and unskilled labour and between skilled labour

and non-manual workers, while the steady increase in small savings blurred the class distinction between the capitalist and the propertyless proletarian. Secondly, a system of direct taxation, ever more steeply graduated, compressed the whole scale of disposable incomes. Thirdly, mass production for the home market and a growing interest on the part of industry in the needs and tastes of the common people enabled the less well-to-do to enjoy a material civilisation which differed less markedly in quality from that of the rich than it had ever done before. All this profoundly altered the setting in which the progress of citizenship took place. Social integration spread from the sphere of sentiment and patriotism into that of material enjoyment. The components of a civilised and cultured life, formerly the monopoly of the few, were brought progressively within reach of the many, who were encouraged thereby to stretch out their hands towards those that still eluded their grasp. The diminution of inequality strengthened the demand for its abolition, at least with regard to the essentials of social welfare.

These aspirations have in part been met by incorporating social rights in the status of citizenship and thus creating a universal right to real income which is not proportionate to the market value of the claimant. Class–abatement is still the aim of social rights, but it has acquired a new meaning. It is no longer merely an attempt to abate the obvious nuisance of destitution in the lowest ranks of society. It has assumed the guise of action modifying the whole pattern of social inequality. It is no longer content to raise the floor-level in the basement of the social edifice, leaving the superstructure as it was. It has begun to remodel the whole building, and it might even end by converting a skyscraper into a bungalow. It is therefore important to consider whether any such ultimate aim is implicit in the nature of this development, or whether, as I put it at the outset, there are natural limits to the contemporary drive towards greater social and economic equality. ★ ★ ★

★ ★ ★

I said earlier that in the twentieth century citizenship and the capitalist class system have been at war. Perhaps the phrase is rather too strong, but it is quite clear that the former has imposed modifications on the latter. But we should not be justified in assuming that although status is a principle that conflicts with contract, the stratified status system which is creeping into citizenship is an alien element in the economic world outside. Social rights in their modern form imply an invasion of contract by status, the subordination of market price to social justice, the replacement of the free bargain by the declaration of rights. ★ ★ ★

★ ★ ★

The Sociology of Stratification*

C. WRIGHT MILLS

In New York City, some people taxi home at night from Madison Avenue offices to Sutton Place; others leave a factory loft in Brooklyn and subway home to East Harlem. In Detroit there is Grosse Pointe, with environs, and there is Hamtramck, without environs; in a thousand small towns the people live on either side of the railroad track. In Moscow, high party members ride cautiously in black cars to well-policed suburbs; other people walk home from factories to cramped apartments. And in the shadow of swank Washington, D. C., apartment houses, there are the dark alley dwellings.

In almost any community in every nation there is a high and a low, and in many societies, a big in-between.

If we go behind what we can thus casually observe while standing on street corners, and begin seriously to observe in detail the 24-hour cycle of behavior and experience, the 12-month cycle, the life-long biography of people in various cities and nations, we will soon be forced to classify. We might well

---

* Written in 1951; first published in 1963; from *Power, Politics, and People: The Collected Essays of C. Wright Mills*, edited by Irving Louis Horowitz.

decide to make our classification of people in terms of the social distribution of valued things and experiences; to find out just which people regularly expect to and do receive how many of the available valued things and experiences, and, on every level, why. Such a classification is the basis of all work in stratification.

In any society of which we know some people seem to get most of such values, some least, others being in between. The student of stratification is bent on understanding such ranking of people, and in finding out exactly in what respects these ranks differ and why. Each ranking or stratum in a society may be viewed as a stratum by virtue of the fact that all of its members have similar chances to gain the things and experiences that are generally valued, whatever they may be: things like cars, money, toys, houses, etc.; experiences, like being given respect, being educated to certain levels, being treated kindly, etc. To belong to one stratum or to another is to share with the other people in this stratum similar chances to receive such values.

If, again, we go behind these strata of people having similar life-chances, and begin to analyze each stratum and the reasons for its formation and persistence, sooner or later we will come upon at least four factors that seem to be quite important keys to the general phenomena. We call these "dimensions of stratification." Each is a way of ranking people with respect to their different chances to obtain values, and together, if properly understood, they enable us to explain these differing chances. These four dimensions are occupation, class, status and power.

I

By an occupation we understand a set of activities pursued more or less regularly as a major source of income.

From the individual's standpoint, occupational activities refer to types of skill that are marketable. These skills range from arranging mathematical symbols for $1000 a day to arranging dirt with a shovel for $1000 a year.

From the standpoint of society, occupations as activities are functions: they result in certain end products—various goods and services—and are accordingly classified into industrial groups.

As specific activities, occupations thus (1) entail various types and levels of skill, and (2) their exercise fulfills certain functions within an industrial division of labor.

In the United States today the most publicly obvious strata consist of members of similar occupations. However it has been and may now be in other kinds of societies, in contemporary U.S.A. occupations are the most ostensible and the most available "way into" an understanding of stratification. For, most people spend the most alert hours of most of their days in occupational work. What kind of work they do not only monopolizes their wakeful hours of adult life but sets what they can afford to buy: most people who receive any direct income at all do so by virtue of some occupation.

As sources of income, occupations are thus connected with *class* position. Since occupations also normally carry an expected quota of prestige, on and off the job, they are relevant to *status* position. They also involve certain degrees of *power* over other people, directly in terms of the job, and indirectly in other social areas. Occupations are thus tied to class, status, and power as well as to skill and function; to understand the occupations composing any social stratum, we must consider them in terms of each of these interrelated dimensions.

The most decisive occupational shift in the twentieth century has been the decline of the independent entrepreneurs ("the old middle class" of businessmen, farmers, and fee professionals) and the rise of the salaried employees ("the new middle class" of managers and salaried professionals, of office people and sales employees). During the last two generations the old middle class has bounded from 6 to 25 per cent, while the wage workers as a whole have levelled off, in fact declining from 61 to 55 per cent. In the course of the following remarks we will pay brief attention by way of illustration to these three occupational levels in the cities of the United States.

II

"Class situation" in its simplest, objective sense has to do with the amount and source of income. A class is a set of people who share similar life choices because of their similar class situations.

Today, occupation rather than property is the source of income for most of those who receive any direct income: the possibilities of selling their services in the labor market, rather than of profitably buying and selling their property and its yields, now determine the class-chances of over four fifths of the American people. All the things money can buy and many that men dream about are theirs by virtue of occupational level. In these occupations men work for someone else on someone else's property. This is the clue to many differences between the older, nineteenth century world of the small propertied entrepreneur and the occupational structure of the new society. If the old middle class of free enterprisers once fought big property structures in the name of small, free properties, the new middle class of white-collar employees, like the wage-workers in latter-day capitalism, has been, from the beginning, dependent upon large properties for job security.

Wage-workers in the factory and on the farm are on the propertyless bottom of the occupational structure, depending upon the equipment owned by others, earning wages for the time they spend at work. In terms of property, the white-collar people are *not* "in between Capital and Labor;" they are in exactly the same property-class position as the wage-workers. They have no direct fiscal tie to the means of production, no prime claim upon the proceeds from property. Like factory workers—and day laborers for that matter—they work for those who do own such means of livelihood.

Yet if bookkeepers and coal miners, insurance agents and farm laborers, doctors in a clinic and crane operators in an open pit have this condition in common, certainly their class situations are not the same. To understand the variety of modern class positions, we must go beyond the common fact of source of income and consider as well the amount of income.

In the middle thirties the three urban strata, entrepreneurs, white-collar, and wage-workers, formed a distinct scale with respect to median family income: white-collar employees had a median income of $2,008; entrepreneurs, $1,665; urban wage-workers, $1,175. Although the median income of white-collar workers was higher than that of the entrepreneurs, larger proportions of the entrepreneurs received both high-level and low-level incomes. The distribution of their income was spread more than that of the white collar.

The wartime boom in incomes, in fact, spread the incomes of all occupational groups, but not evenly. The spread occurred mainly among urban entrepreneurs. As an income level, the old middle class in the city is becoming less an evenly graded income group, and more a collection of different strata, with a large proportion of lumpen-bourgeoisie who receive very low incomes, and a small, prosperous bourgeoisie with very high incomes.

In the late forties (1948, median family income) the income of all white-collar workers was $4,058, that of all urban wage-workers, $3,317. These averages, however, should not obscure the overlap of specific groups within each stratum: the lower white-collar people—sales-employees and office workers—earned almost the same as skilled workers and foremen,[1] but more than semiskilled urban wage-workers.

In terms of property, white-collar people are in the same position as wage-workers; in terms of occupational income, they are "somewhere in the middle." Once they were considerably above the wage-workers; they have become less so; in the middle of the century they still have an edge

but, rather than adding new income distinctions within the new middle-class group, the overall rise in incomes is making the new middle class a more homogeneous income group.

Distributions of property and income are important economically because if they are not wide enough, purchasing power may not be sufficient to take the production that is possible or desirable. Such distributions are also important because they underpin the class structure and thus the chances of the various ranks of the people to obtain desired values. Everything from the chance to stay alive during the first year after birth to the chance to view fine art; the chance to remain healthy and if sick to get well again quickly; the chance to avoid becoming a juvenile delinquent; and very crucially, the chance to complete an intermediary or higher educational grade—these are among the chances that are crucially influenced by one's position in the class structure of a modern society.

These varying, unequal chances are factual probabilities of the class structure. It does not follow from such facts that people in similar class situations will necessarily become conscious of themselves as a class or come to feel that they belong together. Nor does it follow that they will necessarily become aware of any common interests they may objectively share, or that they will become organized in some way, in a movement or in a party, in an attempt to realize such interests. Nor does it follow that they will necessarily become antagonistic to people in other class situations and struggle with them. All these—class-consciousness and awareness

---

1 It is impossible to isolate the salaried foremen from the skilled urban wage-workers in these figures. If we could do so, the income of lower white-collar workers would be closer to that of semi-skilled workers.

of common interests, organizations and class-struggle—have existed in various times and places and, in various forms, do now exist as mental and political fact. But they do not follow logically or historically from the objective fact of class structure. In any given case, whether or not they arise from objective class situations is a matter for fresh empirical study.

||| III

Prestige involves at least two persons: one to *claim* it and another to *honor* the claim. The bases on which various people raise prestige claims, and the reasons others honor these claims, include property and birth, occupation and education, income and power—in fact almost anything that may invidiously distinguish one person from another. In the status system of a society these claims are organized as rules and expectations which regulate who successfully claims prestige, from whom, in what ways, and on what basis. The level of self-esteem enjoyed by given individuals is more or less set by this status system.

There are, thus, six items to which we must pay attention: From the claimant's side: (1) the status claim, (2) the way in which this claim is raised or expressed, (3) the basis on which the claim is raised. And correspondingly—from the bestower's side: (4) the status bestowal or deferences given, (5) the way in which these deferences are given, (6) the basis of the bestowal, which may or may not be the same as the basis on which the claim is raised. An extraordinary range of social phenomena are pointed to by these terms.

Claims for prestige are expressed in all those mannerisms, conventions and ways of consumption that make up the styles of life characterizing people on various status levels. The "things that are done" and the "things that just aren't done" are the status conventions of different strata. Members of higher status groups may dress in distinct ways, follow "fashions" with varying degrees of regularity, eat at certain times and places with certain people. In varying degrees, they maintain an elegance of person and specific modes of address, have dinners together, and are glad to see their sons and daughters intermarry. "Society" in American cities, debutante systems, the management of welfare activities—these often regiment the status activities of upper circles, where exclusiveness, distance, coldness, and condescending benevolence toward outsiders are characteristic.

Claims for prestige and the bestowal of prestige are often based on birth. The Negro child, irrespective of individual "achievement," will not receive the deference which the white child may successfully claim. The immigrant, especially a member of a recent mass immigration, will not be as likely to receive the deference given the Old American, immigrant groups being generally stratified according to how long they, and their forebears, have been in America. Within "the native-born white of native parentage," certain "Old Families" receive more deference than do other families. In each case—race, nationality and family—prestige is based on, or at least limited by, descent, which is perhaps most obviously a basis of prestige at the top and at the bottom of the social ladder. European nobilities and rigidly excluded racial minorities represent the acme of status by descent, the one high, the other low.

Upper-class position typically carries great prestige, all the more so if the source of the money is property. Yet if the possession of wealth in modern industrial societies leads to increased prestige, rich men who are too fresh from lower class levels may experience great difficulty in "buying their ways" into upper-status circles. Often, in fact, impoverished descendants of once high level Old Families receive more deference from more people than do wealthy men without appropriate grandparents. The facts of the *nouveau riche* (high class without high prestige) and the broken-down aristocrat (high prestige without high class) refute the complete identification of upper-prestige and upper-class position, even though, in due course, the broken-down aristocrat often becomes simply broken-down, and the son of the *nouveau riche*, a man of "clean, old wealth." The possession of wealth also allows the purchase of an environment which in time often leads to the development of those "intrinsic" qualities of individuals and families that are required for higher prestige. When we say that American prestige has been fluid, one thing we mean is that high economic class position has led rather quickly to high prestige. A feudal aristocracy, based on old property and long descent, has not existed here. Veblen's *The Theory of the Leisure Class* was focused primarily upon the U. S. post-civil war period and the expressions of prestige claims raised in lavish economic ways by the *nouveau riche* of meat, railroads, and steel.

The prestige of the middle strata in America is based on many principles other than descent and property. The shift to a society of employees has made *occupation* and *education* crucially important. Insofar as occupation determines the level of income, and different styles of life require different income levels, occupation limits the style of life. In a more direct way, different occupations require different levels and types of education, and education also limits the style of life and thus the status successfully claimed.

Some occupations are reserved for members of upper-status levels, others are "beneath their honor." In some societies, in fact, having no work to do brings the highest prestige, prestige being an aspect of property class, the female dependents of high-class husbands becoming specialists in the display of expensive idleness. But only those who do not need to work, yet have more income than those who must, are likely to obtain prestige from idleness. For those for whom work is necessary but not available, "leisure" brings disgrace. And income from property does not always bring more prestige than income from work; the amount and the ways the income is used are more important than its source. A small rentier may not enjoy esteem equal to that of a moderately paid doctor.

Among the employed, those occupations which pay more, involve more mental activities, and some power to supervise others seems to place people on higher prestige levels. But sheer power does not always lend prestige: the political boss gives up prestige, except among his machine members, for power; constitutional monarchs, on the other hand, may gain ceremonial prestige but give up political power. In offices and factories, skilled foremen and office supervisors expect and typically receive an esteem which lifts them above unskilled workers and typists. But the policeman's power to direct street masses does not bring prestige, except among little boys.

The type of education, as well as the amount, is an important basis for prestige: "Finishing schools" and "Prep schools" turn out women and men accomplished in a style of life which guarantees deference in some circles. In others, the amount of intellectual skill acquired through education is a key point for estimation. Yet skill alone is not as uniform a basis for prestige as is skill connected with highly esteemed occupations.

The extent to which claims for prestige are honored and by whom they are honored, may vary widely. Some of those from whom an individual claims prestige may honor his claims, others may not; some deferences that are given may express genuine feelings of esteem; others may be expedient strategies for ulterior ends. A society may, in fact, contain many hierarchies of prestige, each with its own typical bases and areas of bestowal, or one hierarchy in which everyone uniformly "knows his place" and is always in it. It is in the latter that prestige groups are most likely to be uniform and continuous.

Imagine a society in which everyone's prestige is absolutely set and unambivalent; every man's claims for prestige are balanced by the prestige he receives, and both his expression of claims and the ways these claims are honored by others are set forth in understood stereotypes. Moreover, the bases of the claims coincide with the reasons they are honored; those who claim prestige on the specific basis of property or birth are honored because of their property or birth. So the exact volume and types of deference expected between any two individuals are always known, expected, and given; and each

individual's level and type of self-esteem are steady features of his inner life.

Now imagine the opposite society, in which prestige is highly unstable and ambivalent: the individual's claims are not usually honored by others. The way claims are expressed are not understood or acknowledged by those from whom deference is expected, and when others do bestow prestige, they do so unclearly. One man claims prestige on the basis of his income, but even if he is given prestige, it is not because of his income but rather, for example, because of his education or appearance. All the controlling devices by which the volume and type of deference might be directed are out of joint or simply do not exist. So the prestige system is no system, but a maze of misunderstanding, of sudden frustration and sudden indulgence, and the individual, as his self-esteem fluctuates, is under strain and full of anxiety.

American society in the middle of the twentieth century does not fit either of these projections absolutely, but it seems fairly clear that it is closer to the unstable and ambivalent model. This is not to say that there is no prestige system in the United States; given occupational groupings, even though caught in status ambivalence, do enjoy typical levels of prestige. It is to say, however, that the enjoyment of prestige is often disturbed and uneasy, that the basis of prestige, the expressions of prestige claims, and the ways these claims are honored, are now subject to great strain, a strain which often throws men and women into a virtual status panic.

As with income, so with prestige: U.S. white-collar groups are differentiated socially, perhaps more decisively than wage-workers and entrepreneurs. Wage earners certainly do form an income pyramid and a prestige gradation, as do entrepreneurs and rentiers; but the new middle class, in terms of income and prestige, is a superimposed pyramid, reaching from almost the bottom of the first to almost the top of the second.

People in white-collar occupations claim higher prestige than wage-workers, and, as a general rule, can cash in their claims with wage-workers as well as with the anonymous public. This fact has been seized upon, with much justification, as the defining characteristic of the white-collar strata, and although there are definite indications in the United States of a decline in their prestige, still, on a nation-wide basis, the majority of even the lower white-collar employees—office workers and salespeople—enjoy a middle prestige place.

The historic bases of the white-collar employees' prestige, apart from superior income, have included (1) the similarity of their place and type of work to those of the old middle-classes which has permitted them to borrow prestige. (2) As their relations with entrepreneur and with esteemed customer have become more impersonal, they have borrowed prestige from the firm itself. (3) The stylization of their appearance, in particular the fact that most white-collar jobs have permitted the wearing of street clothes on the job, has figured in their prestige claims, as have (4) the skills required in most white-collar jobs, and in many of them the variety of operations performed and the degree of autonomy exercised in deciding work procedures. Furthermore, (5) the time taken to learn these skills and (6) the way in which they have been acquired by formal education and by close contact with the higher-ups in charge has been

important. (7) White-collar employees have monopolized high school education—even in 1940 they had completed 12 grades to the 8 grades for wage-workers and entrepreneurs. They have also (8) enjoyed status by descent: in terms of race, Negro white-collar employees exist only in isolated instances—and, more importantly, in terms of nativity, in 1930 only about 9 per cent of white-collar workers, but 16 per cent of free enterprisers and 21 per cent of wage-workers, were foreign born. Finally, as an underlying fact, (9) the limited size of the white-collar group, compared to wage-workers, has led to successful claims to greater prestige.

||| IV

To be powerful is to be able to realize one's will, even against the resistance of others. The power position of groups and of individuals typically depends upon factors of class, status, and occupation, often in intricate interrelations.

Given occupations involve specific powers over other people in the actual course of work; but also outside the job area, by virtue of their relations to institutions of property as well as the typical income they afford, occupations lend power. Some occupations require the direct exercise of supervision over other employees and workers, and many white-collar employees are closely attached to this managerial cadre. They are the assistants of authority: the power they exercise is a derived power, but they do exercise it.

Property classes may involve power over job markets and commodity markets, directly and indirectly; they may also support power, because of their property, over the state. As Franz Neumann has neatly indicated, each of these powers may be organized for execution, in employers association, cartel, and pressure group. From the underside of the property situation, propertyless wage workers may have trade unions and consumers co-ops which may be in a struggle with the organized powers of property on each of these three fronts.

When we speak of the power of classes, occupations and status groups, however, we usually refer more or less specifically to political power. This means the power of such groups to influence or to determine the policies and activities of the state. The most direct means of exercising such power and the sign of its existence are organizations, either composed of members of certain strata, or acting in behalf of their interests, or both. The power of various strata often implies a political willfulness, a "class-consciousness" on the part of members of these strata. But not always: there can be, as in the case of "un-organized, grumbling workers," a common mentality among those in common strata without organizations. And there can be, as in the case of some "pressure groups," an organization representing the interests of those in similar strata without any common mentality being notable among them.

The accumulation of political power by any stratum is generally dependent upon a triangle of factors: willful mentality, objective opportunity, and the state of organization. The opportunity is limited by the group's structural positions within the stratification of the society; the will is dependent upon the group's awareness of its interests and ways of realizing them. And both structural position and awareness interplay with organizations, which strengthen awareness, and are made politically relevant by structural position.

‖ V

What is at issue in theories of stratification and political power is (1) the objective position of various strata with reference to other strata of modern society, and (2) the political content and direction of their mentalities. Questions concerning either of these issues can be stated in such a way as to allow, and in fact demand, observational answers only if adequate conceptions of stratification and political mentality are clearly set forth.

Often the "mentality" of strata is allowed to take predominance over the objective position.

It is, for example, frequently asserted that "there are no classes in the United States" because "psychology is of the essence of classes" or, as Alfred Bingham has put it, that "class groupings are always nebulous, and in the last analysis only the vague thing called class-consciousness counts." It is said that people in the United States are not aware of themselves as members of classes, do not identify themselves with their appropriate economic level, do not often organize in terms of these brackets or vote along the lines they provide. America, in this reasoning, is a sandheap of "middle-class individuals."

But this is to confuse psychological feelings with other kinds of social and economic reality. The fact that men are not "class conscious" at all times and in all places does not mean that "there are no classes" or that "in America everybody is middle class." The economic and social facts are one thing. Psychological feelings may or may not be associated with them in rationally expected ways. Both are important, and if psychological feelings and political outlooks do not correspond to economic or occupational class, we must try to find out why, rather than throw out the economic baby with the psychological bath, and so fail to understand how either fits into the national tub. No matter what people believe, class structure as an economic arrangement influences their life chances according to their positions in it. If they do not grasp the causes of their conduct this does not mean that the social analyst must ignore or deny them.

If political mentalities are not in line with objectively defined strata, that lack of correspondence is a problem to be explained; in fact, it is the grand problem of the psychology of social strata. The general problem of stratification and political mentality thus has to do with the extent to which the members of objectively defined strata are homogeneous in their political alertness, outlook, and allegiances, and with the degree to which their political mentality and actions are in line with the interests demanded by the juxtaposition of their objective position and their accepted values.

To understand the occupation, class, and status positions of a set of people is not necessarily to know whether or not they (1) will become class-conscious, feeling that they belong together or that they can best realize their rational interests by combining; (2) will have "collective attitudes" of any sort, including those toward themselves, their common situation; (3) will organize themselves, or be open to organization by others, into associations, movements, or political parties; or (4) will become hostile toward other strata and struggle against them. These social, political, and psychological characteristics may or may not occur on the basis of similar objective situations. In any given case, such possibilities must be explored, and "subjective" attributes must *not be used as criteria* for class inclusion, but rather, as Max Weber has made clear, stated as probabilities on the basis of objectively defined situations.

Implicit in this way of stating the issues of stratification lies a model of social movements and political dynamics. The important differences among people are differences that shape their biographies and ideas; within any given stratum, of course, individuals differ, but if their stratum has been adequately understood, we ought to be able to expect certain psychological traits to recur. Our principles of stratification enable us to do this. The probability that people will have a similar mentality and ideology, and that they will join together for action, is increased the more homogeneous they are with respect to class, occupation, and prestige. Other factors do, of course, affect the probability that ideology, organization, and consciousness will occur among those in objectively similar strata. But psychological factors are likely to be associated with *strata*, which consist of people who are characterized by an intersection of the *several* dimensions we have been using: class, occupation, status, and power. The task is to sort out these dimensions of stratification in a systematic way, paying attention to each separately and then to its relation to each of the other dimensions.

★ ★ ★

PART II

WHO GETS WHAT?

INTRODUCTION TO PART II

The chapters in this part turn our attention to an examination of contemporary research on inequality in relation to the question: Who gets what? Among the most heavily debated questions in the social sciences in recent years has been the magnitude and extent of trends in inequality. In the United States, as we noted in the introduction, there has been a particularly rapid growth in income and wealth inequality over the past thirty years. The first four chapters map income trends. Patterns in wealth inequality are related to, but also independent of, trends in income. The next two chapters explore aspects of wealth inequality in the United States. Two chapters examine one of the great concerns about inequality: its impact on the poverty in the United States. Finally, three chapters explore issues of social mobility.

In their chapter examining income trends for all Americans, sociologists Claude Fischer, Michael Hout, and Jon Stiles take the long view. Examining census data over the past hundred years, they found that three distinct historical periods of inequality can be identified. Before 1929, American society was quite inegalitarian. In addition to the large share of income going to the very top, incomes for those households at the bottom were very low, and the proportion of families with what we call middle-class incomes today was modest. During the 1930s, owing to the Great Depression and the expansion of the public sector during the New Deal era, things began to change. During World War II, taxes on the wealthy were raised significantly, constraining income growth at the top. Economic growth and shared prosperity in the post-war era, continuing all the way into the early 1970s, led to a great expansion of the American middle class. The shares of income received by all groups below the very top (that is, the middle class, the working class, and the poor) rose in this period relative to the rich. In other words, the gains of economic growth were not only were widely shared but actually flowed in slightly greater amounts to households below the top 20 percent. The authors note a number of reasons for this shift, including, most intriguing, the changes in the South as a result of industrialization and the decline of small farming. Beginning in the 1970s, this pattern of narrowing differentials between top and bottom began to reverse itself. Not only did the share of income going to the very top begin to increase but the shares received by the middle class and the poor began to decline (although, the authors note, incomes did increase in absolute and inflation-adjusted dollars).

In their widely cited work on income trends among the highest earners, economists Thomas Piketty and Emanuel Saez, carefully document changes since the 1910s. They show that growth in top incomes has ebbed and flowed over the course of the twentieth century, peaking first right before World War I and again in the 1920s, receding until the late 1970s, and recently approaching its previous highs. Because they analyzed tax return microdata, Piketty and Saez were able to parse out the income shares of very tiny ultrarich groups (the top 1 percent, the top 0.5 percent, and even the top 0.1 percent).

The chapter by Peter Gottschalk and Sheldon Danziger provides a detailed overview of recent trends in inequality among groups. They show that overall inequality has grown, as have the gaps between most (but not all) groups. Using a variety of inequality measures—individual wage rates, individual annual earnings, family annual earnings, and family income adjusted for size—they provide a comprehensive picture of the society-wide growth of inequality over the past twenty-five years. They also document how the growth in overall inequality is reflected both in the increase in wage and earning differences *between* categories of workers (most significantly, categories based on race, education, and experience) and the increase in differences *within* these groups. One partial exception to the general trend is the gap between the earnings of men and of women, which Gottschalk and Danziger show have narrowed among recent cohorts. But the gender pay gap has not reduced equally across the board. The chapter by Francine Blau and Lawrence Kahn further documents and dissects trends in the gender gap. They note that among recent cohorts the gender gap in pay has narrowed and that highly educated women have made substantial gains. But older and less well educated women continue to lag relative to their male counterparts. Persisting gender inequalities such as this suggest that powerful barriers remain and are yet to be addressed.

Although income is one critical measure of economic inequality, wealth tracks other important resource inequalities. *Wealth* refers to the capital resources possessed by an individual or family. The chapter by Lisa Keister provides an overview of some of the most important aspects of the contemporary distribution of wealth in America. She shows that here too the trend has been toward rising wealth inequality. The most commonly owned wealth asset is real estate. A little over 70 percent of Americans currently own the primary residence in which they live, although troubles in the home mortgage industry beginning in the fall of 2007 are currently pushing the percentage down. Because homes tend to appreciate over time, home ownership has been one way that even modest-income households can accumulate wealth. A smaller subset of the population owns net financial assets (NFAs) (that is, the total value of savings, investments, and other convertible assets less outstanding debts). Upper-class families possess vast NFAs, while most families possess little or no NFAs (although private pension accounts are growing, and nearly half of Americans own stocks through participation in a pension program). Disparity in wealth is greatest in regard to NFAs, and Keister shows how this gap between the wealthiest households and everyone else has widened enormously over the past thirty years.

Dalton Conley focuses on a particular aspect of wealth inequality: that between blacks and whites. He notes that African Americans are systematically disadvantaged in the wealth accumulation process relative to whites; as a consequence the black–white wealth gap is far larger than the income gap. Conley argues that historical factors, including residential segregation on the basis of race (in which blacks historically have been limited in what neighborhoods they can purchase homes in), have made it difficult for African American families to accumulate wealth at the same rate as whites, even as they narrow the gap in earnings.

The next two chapters examine the problem of poverty in America. Economist Rebecca Blank provides a broad overview of the demography of poverty. Looking at the changing face of poverty, Blank discredits long-held stereotypes about the characteristics of the poor, drawing attention to the actual composition of the disadvantaged: for instance, more than 40 percent of those living in poverty are children, nearly 50 percent are white, and only 10 percent live inside the urban ghettos that are so often associated with being poor in America. Blank goes on to show that while the majority of people who fall into poverty do so because of a temporary decline in income and remain poor for only a short time (less than three years), those who do spend sustained periods of time living in poverty are disproportionately children. Blank contends that recognizing the heterogeneity of the poor and dismissing misconceptions about the composition of this group might affect willingness to address the problem of poverty as well as the effectiveness of political programs.

The chapter by Maya Federman and her colleagues provides a startling snapshot of the deprivations of poor families in America. Drawing on nine national surveys of poor and non-poor households, the authors provide very specific data on how the living conditions of the poor compare to those of other groups. Here we see the stark, ground-level consequences that lie behind poverty statistics, consequences that include susceptibility to crime, low-quality housing, lack of discretionary income and basic services, high health risks, and diminished educational opportunities. The authors created an index of overall deprivation and estimate that, on average, the poor experience five to six times the deprivation of the non-poor.

Following the exploration of poverty, the final set of readings in Part II examine the question of social mobility—the process through which individual origins are related to individuals' destinations. The chapter by Richard Breen and David Rottman provides both a superb introduction to the different meanings of social mobility (and the analytic problems of studying it), as well some evidence about comparative rates of social mobility in Europe.

One critical question relating to the patterns of social mobility concerns the manner in which jobs are secured in the first place. Sociologist Mark Granovetter revolutionized our understanding of these processes in the early 1970s, when he published a short book called *Getting a Job*. Granovetter noted that the neo-classical economic model of the labor market—in which jobs are advertised and individuals apply and an employer selects the most qualified— hardly applies to how many jobs are actually filled. He introduced the critical idea that those of us who have particular kinds of social networks are advantaged over others with similar backgrounds and resources in informal searching for jobs. The most important networks are broad, bringing us into contact with people in different organizational and social settings who might be able to give us a leg up at some point. Cultivating what Granovetter calls weak network relationships is a critical strategy, and those with starting advantages (like having a well-connected family or growing up in a well-organized, tight-knit neighborhood) are more likely to have, or be able to develop, such networks. The role of networks in finding good jobs has been widely studied since Granovetter's classic contribution in the mid-1970s. Indeed, these ideas have become part of the standard networking strategy for the career-building of enterprising citizens.

The final chapter in this part of the book is by Erik Olin Wright and Rachel Dwyer, who examine recent trends in labor market mobility for low-skilled workers. Wright and Dwyer find that upper mobility for individuals over the course of their working lives has become increasingly difficult. Gaining access to an entry-level job no longer provides many opportunities for advancement, even in an era in which overall rates of unemployment is very low. This finding is important for understanding how the structure of social mobility is changing in the current era of high inequality.

The Distribution of Income and Wealth

10

What Americans Had: Differences in Living Standards*

CLAUDE FISCHER AND MICHAEL HOUT (WITH JON STILES)

Americans are loath to describe themselves in terms of social class. Compared to the British, for example, Americans are far less likely to say that their society is composed of "haves" and "have-nots."[1] In many respects, American culture is exceptionally egalitarian; foreign visitors have long remarked on the political equality among Americans—at least, among free, white, male Americans—and noted, occasionally in horror, how little deference "common" people give to their "betters."[2] But American egalitarianism has coexisted with great economic inequality. America in 2000 was the most

---

* First published in 2006; from *Century of Difference*.

1 For example, in August 1988, Gallup asked national samples of Americans and Britons: "Do you yourself think that [America/Britain] is divided into haves and have-nots, or don't you?" Twenty-six percent of Americans and 73 percent of Britons said "yes, divided" (Gallup Report #275 [August], 8). In early 2003, 41 percent of Americans agreed; Ludwig, "Is America Divided into Haves and Have-nots?" Gallup Poll, available to subscribers at: http://www.gallup.com (accessed September 8, 2004).

2 We refer to not only the classic "visitors," such as de Tocqueville and Trollope, but many others as well. For overviews, see, for example, Woodward, *The Old World's New World*; Simmons, *Star-Spangled Eden*; and Handlin and Handlin, *From the Outer World* (full bibliographic information available in the reference section).

economically unequal nation in the developed world: it had the greatest division in wealth between haves and have-nots, and that division had grown over the previous thirty years.[3] The widening of inequality was jarring; three-fifths of Americans surveyed in 2003 said that "money and wealth should be more evenly distributed"; even Alan Greenspan, chairman of the Federal Reserve Board for almost twenty years and a closely followed economic guru, noted in 2004 that America's level of inequality "is not the type of thing which a democratic society . . . can really accept without addressing." Wide economic disparities tend to go along with high rates of social problems, civic alienation, and discontent and with low rates of economic growth.[4]

In this chapter, we ★ ★ ★ assess inequality in Americans' standards of living over the twentieth century.[5] We look at their annual incomes, financial assets, and consumption, and also at their subjective evaluations of their economic positions. We measure the gaps between the better- and the worse-off, and we track how those gaps coincided with other axes of difference, especially race, region, and education.

Americans became increasingly similar in their living standards through much of the century, but the equalizing trend stalled and then reversed around 1970. Americans then became more and more divided economically, and that division increasingly followed educational differences. Moreover, surveys show that Americans sensed the widening economic divisions among them.

||| LIVING STANDARDS IN 2000

Rich and poor Americans have little personal contact with one another. The British travel writer Jonathan Rabin dramatized this disjuncture in his depiction of the "air people" and the "street people" of Manhattan.[6] The air people live high above the street in condominium buildings guarded by doormen and work in offices similarly elevated and guarded. The street people include not only the homeless but also the hard-pressed; they live in buildings that require them to walk in, walk up, and be wary. They also work exposed to the street, in construction, maintenance, and service jobs. Well-dressed and well-coiffed air people encounter

---

3 The distinctiveness of the United States is well documented. A recent report is Gottschalk and Smeeding, "Empirical Evidence on Income Inequality in Industrialized Countries."

4 On the 2003 survey, see Ludwig, "Is America Divided?" Greenspan is quoted in Peter Grier, "Rich-Poor Gap Gaining Attention," *Christian Science Monitor*, June 14, 2005. On the consequences of inequality, see, for example, Williams and Collins, "U.S. Socioeconomic and Racial Differences in Health"; Hagan and Peterson, *Crime and Inequality*; Harper and Steffensmeier, "The Differing Effects of Economic Inequality"; Muller, "Democracy, Economic Development, and Income Inequality"; You and Khagram, "A Comparative Study of Inequality and Corruption"; Kenworthy, *Egalitarian Capitalism*; Hagerty, "Social Comparisons of Income"; Rahn and Rudolph, "A Tale of Political Trust in American Cities";

and Fischer et al., *Inequality by Design*. Some of these claims— notably those about the association between inequality in a community and ill health—have stirred methodological debates (Beckfield, "Does Inequality Harm Health?"). Gary Burtless and Christopher Jencks ("American Inequality and Its Consequences") present a more cautious appraisal of the effects of inequality. A good source on these issues is Neckerman, *Social Inequality*. The briefest summary of what we know is that inequality does no good and probably does some ill to a community and a nation.

5 An earlier and more detailed version of this chapter is available as a working paper, "Differences Among Americans in Living Standards," at: http://ucdata.berkeley.edu:7101/ rsfcensus/wp.html.

6 Rabin, *Hunting Mister Heartbreak*.

street people in the theater district when they exit from shows they have paid perhaps hundreds of dollars to see and search out taxis and limousines to carry them back to their homes in the air. On the sidewalk, they must work their way past panhandlers pleading for "spare change" to buy a bed for the night. These face-to-face encounters of people from the two ends of the income distribution are rare and perhaps melodramatic, but they highlight the reality of differences in living standards across all of America, not only in Manhattan. Away from the big cities, even such passing encounters are rare, since many Americans live in class-segregated communities ★ ★ ★.

Just how divided were Americans in their living standards in 2000? There are at least three aspects of living standards: income, wealth, and consumption.[7] Consider, first, *annual income*, which includes not only earnings from wages or self-employment but also returns such as interest, dividends, capital gains, rents, business profits, and Social Security payments. In 2000 households with joint annual incomes that put them in the highest one-fifth of American households ranked by income averaged about

$140,000 each before taxes; the one-fifth right in the middle averaged $42,000; and the lowest one-fifth of households averaged about $10,000. Using our by-now familiar eighty-fifty-twenty-percentile comparisons, the household that stood at exactly the eightieth percentile of income had about twice the income of the household at the fiftieth, and that one, in turn, had about twice the income of the household at the twentieth percentile.[8] Were these large or small differences? By international standards, they were quite large: the United States had the widest income gaps of any advanced Western society.[9]

Americans varied even more in *accumulated net wealth*—assets such as savings, stocks, pensions, and homes, minus debts. In 1998 the wealthiest one-fifth of families had an average net worth of over $1.1 million; the middle one-fifth averaged $61,000 in assets; and the least wealthy *two*-fifths of American families were worth, on average, $1,000 apiece. Thus, the richest one-fifth of families owned more than four-fifths of all the family wealth in the country, while the poorest two-fifths of families owned one-fifth of 1 percent of the national wealth. And as with

7 Our income data come largely from the IPUMS. Wealth and consumption spending data are largely from the Consumer Expenditure Survey (Harris and John Sabelhaus, *Consumer Expenditure Survey Family-Level Extracts*). Consumer goods data again come largely from the IPUMS. Another category of living standards we discuss later is public goods.

8 These gaps were, of course, many times wider at the extremes. For example, the household at the ninety-fifth percentile had an income in 2000 about fourteen times that of the household at the tenth; DeNavas and Cleveland, "Money Income in the United States: 2000," table C.

9 The Luxembourg Income Study regularly tracks and compares income distributions in many nations. In its latest tabulations, the United States was substantially more unequal than other nations. For example, the ratio of the eightieth to the

twentieth percentile in disposable income was, in 1997, 3.0 for the United States, 2.8 for the United Kingdom (1995), 2.4 for Canada (1997), 2.2 for France, and 2.1 for Germany (1994); Luxembourg Income Study, "Income Inequality Measures." Even taking into account differences in living costs, the American variation was greater than that elsewhere. Indeed, though affluent and middle-class American families had more buying power than families elsewhere, American families with below-average incomes had less buying power than comparable families in most other advanced nations; Gottschalk and Smeeding, "Empirical Evidence on Income Inequality in Industrialized Countries"; Smeeding and Rainwater, "Comparing Living Standards Across Nations." For a general discussion of American inequality in historical and cross-national contexts, see Fischer et al., *Inequality by Design*.

income, wealth inequality was greater in the United States than in Europe.[10]

People's standards of living can also be measured by their *consumption* and the *goods* they own. At the turn of the century, all but a few households had full kitchen facilities and color televisions; 91 percent had a car or truck. Other goods appeared more often in affluent than in modest homes but were still common. For example, 90 percent of households with incomes over $50,000 had clothes washers, but so did 60 percent of those with incomes under $15,000; 90 percent of the former had stereo equipment, but so did over 50 percent of the latter. The affluent and the poor differed more in their possession of other goods, such as central air conditioning—two-thirds versus one-third—and dishwashers—80 percent versus 20 percent.[11] Still, the near-universality of household goods such as refrigerators, cars, and televisions suggests that differences in consumption were not as great as differences in income or wealth.[12]

Beyond money, assets, and goods, living standards include, in the end, the quality of life, measured perhaps by longevity, health, and security. At the end of the century, Americans varied notably in these respects. For example, people in households earning under $10,000 suffered about twenty-eight days per year of disability, compared to ten days for those with $35,000 or more; moreover, 17 percent of children were reported to be living in "food insecure" homes.[13] In the late 1990s, 66 percent of urban Americans with family incomes under $15,000 reported that there were places in their neighborhood where they were afraid to walk at night, but only 42 percent of those with incomes over $60,000 felt that way.[14] And again, the variation among Americans along these dimensions—the divide between those doing well and those getting along marginally—exceeded that of citizens in other Western nations.[15] In the pages that follow, we take up separately the expansion and division in income, wealth, and consumption over the twentieth century.

INCOME DIFFERENCES OVER THE TWENTIETH CENTURY

The twentieth century was, with the notable exception of the 1930s, one of prodigious economic advancement in America. While working fewer hours, Americans easily quadrupled

---

10 The last detailed data on twentieth-century wealth covered 1998; see Wolff, "Recent Trends in Wealth Ownership"; Keister and Moller, "Wealth Inequality in the United States"; and Spilerman, "Wealth and Stratification Processes."

11 Numbers drawn and calculated from U.S. Bureau of the Census, *Statistical Abstract of the United States,* 2002, tables 946 and 947.

12 Michael Cox and Richard Alm (*Myths of Rich and Poor*) are among a group of scholars who point to such consumption as evidence of *declining* inequality.

13 Numbers drawn from U.S. Bureau of the Census, *Statistical Abstract of the United States 2000,* tables 177, 211, and 233,

which notes: "Food secure means that a household had access at all times to enough food for an active healthy life, with no need for recourse to emergency food sources or other extraordinary coping behaviors to meet their basic food needs."

14 Calculated from the General Social Survey "fear" item for 1998 and 2000. This comparison includes only respondents living in metropolitan areas. Overall, the percentages were 49 and 30.

15 For example, the World Health Organization (*World Health Report 2000*) calculated an index of "equality of child survival" based on local-area variability. The United States ranked thirty-second in the world.

their real earnings.[16] But the pace of improvement varied for different groups of Americans. There were periods when the "have-less" quickly closed the gap with the "have-more," and periods when the have-less fell further behind. The data are spotty up to about 1960—there is some evidence on wages, some on total household income, some on capital gains, some on taxes paid—and their exact interpretation is debated. Nonetheless, the general trend is clear: as average family incomes soared through the first two-thirds of the century, variation in incomes shrank. The span closed sharply around World War I and again around World War II, then closed slowly over the next decade. (The major wars contracted the range of income because they typically led to wage controls, higher taxes, and concessions to organized labor. Other political events, such as programs for income security and health services, also helped compress incomes.) Consequently, Americans differed much less in annual income in the 1960s than in the 1900s.[17] In the last third of the century, however, average family income grew little; variation in income widened as high-income Americans pulled away from the rest.

Figure 1 displays the shares of the nation's income of high-earning, middling, and poorer families over the twentieth century. It displays the percentage of all family income in a year that went to the one-fifth of families with the highest income, the percentage that went to the next *two*-fifths, and then what went to the lowest-income *two*-fifths.[18] (For lack of data, we cannot use our eighty-fifty-twenty scheme to cover the whole century.) Until the 1970s, the top fifth's share of family income shrank as the middle two-fifths took more and the bottom two-fifths took a little bit more. Then the trend reversed: by 2000, the distribution had returned to roughly the 1940 level of inequality. Why it had done so, and to what effect, have been fiercely argued. We examine a few of these debates after looking more closely at the trends of the last half-century, a period for which we have more data.

Annual Incomes, 1949 to 1999

We start with the total income provided by all the related members living in a household, including households of one person, from 1949 through 1999.[19] (The decennial census-takers asked about incomes in the year before the census, which explains the odd years.) We use income before taxes, so the numbers reflect neither fluctuations in tax rates nor changes in tax credits granted to the poor. We take inflation into account by correcting for changes in

---

16 Lebergott, *The American Economy*, and Cox and Alm, "Time Well Spent," provide overviews.

17 Key references include Williamson and Lindert, *American Inequality*; Soltow, "Wealth and Income Distribution"; Lebergott, *The American Economy*; Piketty and Saez, "Income Inequality in the United States"; Goldin and Katz, "Decreasing (and Then Increasing) Inequality in America"; Plotnick et al., "The Twentieth-Century Record of Inequality and Poverty in the United States."

18 The pre-1970 numbers are estimates provided by Lebergott in *The American Economy*, 498; the rest are from U.S. Bureau of the Census, "Historical Income Tables—Households," table H-2. The percentage gained by the top 5 percent ranged from a high of 36 percent in 1900 to a low of 16 percent in 1980, then up to 22 percent in 2000.

19 We exclude those living in group quarters and unrelated individuals sharing a household with a family. For a household of only nonrelatives, the head is included as a resident of a one-person household.

FIGURE 1 SHARES OF THE NATIONAL INCOME, BY INCOME SEGMENT

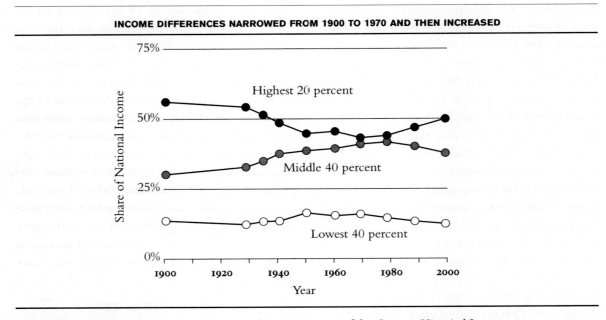

INCOME DIFFERENCES NARROWED FROM 1900 TO 1970 AND THEN INCREASED

SOURCES: Liebergott, *The American Economy*, 498; U.S. Bureau of the Census, *Historical Income Tables—Households*.

the cost of living, so that all the numbers are expressed in 1999 dollars. Because we are interested in people's standards of living, we also adjust the income figures for the size of the family. We want to know how much income individuals had per family member. However, since at least the publication of the popular book *Cheaper by the Dozen* (1948; not to be confused with a later, different movie of the same name), it has been clear that financial demands on fam-

ilies do not increase in a simple, linear way: two children are not twice as expensive as one child. Research has established that an effective way to capture a family's standard of living is to divide its dollars by the *square root* of the number of family members.[20] So, for example, when a first child arrives to a couple, the family has grown by 50 percent, from two to three. But their per-person expenses have grown, by this standard formula, only 22 percent.[21] We follow this con-

---

20 See Atkinson, Rainwater, and Smeeding, *Income Distributions in OECD Countries*; Smeeding, "Changing Income Inequality in OECD Countries." Although our adjustments are far less complex than those made by other scholars (note especially Slesnick, *Consumption and Social Welfare*), we do take into account the basic reality that family needs increase with the number of family members, but at a negatively accelerat-

ing rate. And since family size is highly associated with stage in the life cycle (Slesniek, *Consumption and Social Welfare*, 148), this adjustment captures much of the life-cycle variation as well, allowing us to hold roughly constant changes in the demographic profile of the American population.

21 That is, the increase from the square root of two to the square root of three.

vention but express the results of our calculations as the living standard in 1999 dollars for someone in a *family of four*.[22] So when we refer to a person's "adjusted family income," we mean his or her family's total income adjusted for both inflation and size of family and expressed for ease of communication as if he or she lived in a family of four.[23] In 1949 the median American had an adjusted family-of-four income of about $19,000 (in 1999 dollars); in 1999 the median American had an adjusted family-of-four income of about $53,000.

In comparing incomes—for example, between the 1999 median of $53,000 and the 1949 median of $19,400—we use the ratio (2.8) rather than the arithmetic difference ($33,600). ★ ★ ★ The standard academic practice is to use ratios for comparison. Where the choice between subtraction and division makes a substantive difference in interpretation, we point it out.

Now we can map the half-century history of income differences. The left side of figure 2 shows how adjusted family-of-four income, in a ratio scale, grew for the median American (the one at the fiftieth percentile—the open-circles line), for the relatively affluent American (the eightieth percentile—the top line), and for the relatively moneyless American (the twentieth percentile—the bottom line).[24] The median

American's income grew rapidly from 1949 to 1969, but grew much more slowly afterwards. (Median *family income* grew some after 1969 even though median earnings for individual workers grew not at all ★ ★ ★ because more wives worked and they worked longer hours.) The gaps between the three levels of income seem, by visual inspection, to widen after 1969, too. The right side of figure 2 confirms that impression by displaying the eighty-to-twenty ratio for each year. In 1949 the eightieth-percentile American had $4.00 in adjusted family-of-four income for each $1 the twentieth-percentile American had; in 1969 the ratio had dropped to $3.13; and in 1999 it was back up to almost $3.75 to $1. (Comparing by subtraction, however, shows a steadily widening gap, from a $25,000 to a $70,000 eighty-to-twenty difference.) The great equalizing trend of the century made what has been called the "U-turn" toward inequality around 1970.

Why family incomes diverged in the last thirty years of the century is a matter of heated debate in the academic journals and even in the general media. We cannot resolve those debates here, but there is consensus that most of the answer lies in the patterns of men's earnings ★ ★ ★. Beyond earnings, changes in family structure and living arrangements contributed

22 We first calculate an adjusted per-person income, or what some economists call "equivalent personal income" for each individual, by (1) taking the total income of all related members of the individual's household, (2) dividing that figure by the square root of the number of related members of the household, and (3) calculating what it would be for a family of four. Step 3 is the simple exercise of doubling the result of step 2, because the square root of four is two.

23 This procedure also removes historical changes in family size as a factor in comparing family incomes.

24 Many analyses of inequality look at comparisons of the ninetieth versus the tenth percentile. We use eightieth-twentieth for a couple of reasons. One is that we found inconsistencies between census and CPS data at the tenth percentile, originating in the fact that the CPS found more people at very low income levels. Also, the eightieth-twentieth comparison is consistent with our other analyses in this book.

FIGURE 2 **ADJUSTED FAMILY INCOME, BY YEAR**

THE INCOME GAP NARROWED AS INCOMES ROSE BETWEEN 1949 AND 1969, THEN WIDENED AGAIN

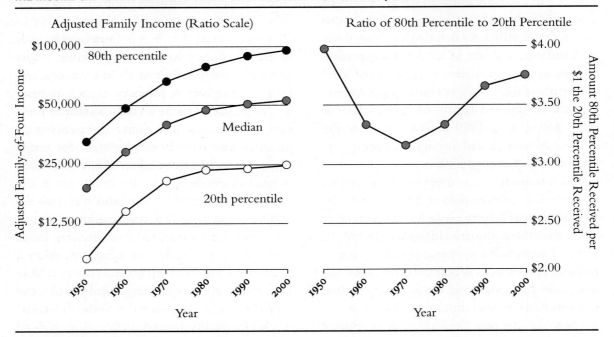

SOURCE: IPUMS (Integrated Public Use Microdata Series).
NOTES: Families include primary individuals; incomes are adjusted for inflation using the consumer price index (resarch series for urban consumers), with 1999 as the base year, and for family size by dividing income by the square root of family size and then multiplying by two for the equivalent of a family of four.

to the U-turn. More women went further in school, married men who also were well educated, and increasingly took well-paying jobs. Two-career couples thus moved further ahead of couples with wives who were homemakers or part-time workers and ahead of singles and single parents. Also, wealthy families rode the

stock market upward in the 1990s, earning considerable investment income.[25]

Whatever the explanations for the U-turn depicted in figure 2, it is clear that Americans at the end of the twentieth century were more divided in terms of income than they had been for a generation, and also that this increasing

25 See, for example, Fligstein, *Architecture of Markets*; Lichter, "Poverty and Inequality Among Children"; Campbell and Allen, "Identifying Shifts in Policy Regimes"; Kenworthy, "Do Social-Welfare Policies Reduce Poverty?"; Chevan and Stokes, "Growth in Family Income Inequality"; Karoly and Burtless, "Demographic Change, Rising Earnings Inequality."

divergence reversed at least two prior generations' worth of the convergence we see in figure 1. The inequality trend, by the way, continued into the 2000s.[26] But not all groups of Americans were equally affected by growing inequality; the most dramatic exception were the elderly.

Thanks largely to Social Security and Medicare, income differences among the elderly kept dropping. In 1949 the elderly American at the eightieth percentile of income among the elderly brought in $9 to each $1 of the twentieth-percentile elderly American. That ratio dropped to under $5 in 1969 and continued to drop slightly afterwards. Younger Americans, in contrast, notably parents of young children and the children themselves, experienced the sharpest U-turn. Income differences narrowed before 1970 but widened sharply after 1970. The eighty-to-twenty ratio for children rose from three-to-one in 1969 to four-to-one in 1999, a substantial widening of income inequality.[27]] Thus, the late-century trends depicted in figure

1 and 2 would be even more acute if we left out senior citizens.

Differences between Groups

We have described the narrowing and widening of income differences between those of high income and those of low income. We turn now to how differences in income lined up with other lines of division among Americans. Was income increasingly or decreasingly connected to those other splits? Did, for example, the income gap between blacks and whites widen or narrow?

Figure 3 answers that question. In 1949 the median European American had an adjusted family-of-four income of $20,500 compared to just $8,600 for the median African American; the ratio is 2.4-to-1. By 1999 median incomes had grown for both, and the European-African ratio had declined steadily to 1.6-to-1.[28] (Arithmetically, the difference *grew* from around $12,000 to about $21,000.) Over the half-

---

26 U.S. Bureau of the Census, *Income, Poverty, and Health Insurance*, 36.

27 Table A contrasts the trends in income inequality for the elderly and for children:

TABLE A. RATIO OF EIGHTIETH- TO TWENTIETH-PERCENTILE ADJUSTED FAMILY-OF-FOUR INCOME

	1949	1959	1969	1979	1989	1999
Among the elderly	8.7	4.9	4.6	3.6	3.8	3.7
Among children age zero to seventeen	3.6	3.0	2.9	3.3	3.8	3.9

SOURCE: Authors' compilation.

Some economists and policymakers have criticized the formula used to adjust seniors' Social Security checks for inflation, saying that the formula exaggerates inflation's effects and thus raises their incomes too rapidly. Our inflation adjuster is the research series. If the Social Security Administration had used it instead of the formula it did, Social Security benefits would not have risen as fast, and inequality among seniors

might have increased during the years of greatest inflation (1974 to 1975 and 1977 to 1981).

28 "Others" gained even more ground relative to whites, but that change is hard to interpret given that who the "others" were changed after 1965, especially with the strong influx of middle-class families from Asia.

FIGURE 3 **ADJUSTED FAMILY-OF-FOUR INCOME MEDIANS, BY ANCESTRY**

BLACK-WHITE DIFFERENCES IN FAMILY INCOME NARROWED, 1969 TO 1999

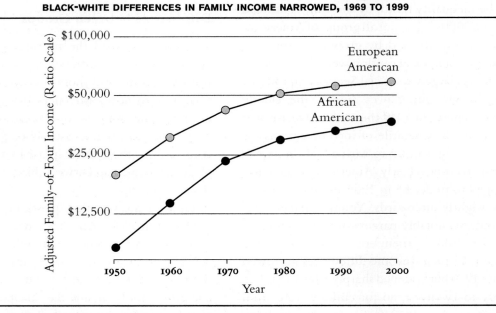

SOURCE: IPUMS (Integrated Public Use Microdata Series).

century, low-income blacks, in particular, made the most rapid advance, shortening their lag behind low-income whites.[29] (Hispanics, however, fell further behind whites, and the foreign-born fell increasingly behind the native-born, both surely reflecting the influx of low-wage immigrants.)[30]

Southerners rapidly caught up with Americans from other regions between 1949 and 1979. In 1949 nonsoutherners had about $1.70 of adjusted income for each dollar of southerners' income; by 1979 the gap had shrunk to $1.15. (Even as an arithmetic difference, the gap had narrowed.)[31] Then, after 1979, there

29 Between 1949 and 1999, the adjusted family income of the twentieth-percentile black increased 480 percent; the incomes of average and wealthy blacks grew 415 percent. The adjusted family incomes of all levels of whites increased about 290 percent.

30 The conclusion about Hispanics is not based on our data but on median family incomes collected by the Current Population Survey and reported by the Census Bureau (*Statistical Abstract of the United States, 2000,* table 743). Between 1972 and 1999, the median non-Hispanic white family's inflation-adjusted income rose 23 percent, while that of the Hispanic family rose 3 percent, with a rise in the ratio of non-Hispanics to Hispanics from $1.40 to $1.70. Adjusting for family size

might mute this widening gap, but not enough to negate the point. As for the foreign-born, in 1949 the median native-born American's adjusted family income was 90 cents per dollar of that of the median foreign-born (who was likely to be an older European-American immigrant); by 1990 the median native-born's income was $1.20 per dollar of that of the (now-increasingly Latin or Asian) foreign-born.

31 In 1949 the median southerner had a family-of-four adjusted income that was $8,800 less than that of Americans from other regions (that is, the average of the medians of the other regions); in 1979 the arithmetic difference was $7,200; in 1999 it was $6,800.

was little net change in the relative position of southerners.[32] Looking at the variation in incomes *within* regions reveals how much low- and moderate-income southerners gained on high-income southerners between 1949 and 1969; that gain accounts for most of the convergence between Americans of lower and higher incomes nationally.[33]

Similarly, rural Americans' incomes rose relative to those of city-dwellers. Suburban residents, however, outstripped both of them. In 1949 median city and suburban people each had incomes 60 percent greater than those of people in nonmetropolitan areas. In 1999 suburbanites had incomes 50 percent greater than those of city residents, who, in turn, had incomes only 10 percent greater than those of nonmetropolitan residents. At mid-century, then, Americans living in metropolitan areas, whether in the center or in the suburbs, had about the same income and considerably more than rural Americans; by 2000 nonmetropolitan residents had caught up with center-city residents, but both were considerably behind suburbanites.[34]

---

32 In 1999 the median northeasterner earned $1.20 on the southerner's dollar. The West fell notably behind the Northeast and the Midwest after 1980, most likely reflecting the inflow of low-income immigrants. The median incomes are shown in Table B:

TABLE B. MEDIAN ADJUSTED FAMILY-OF-FOUR INCOME

	1949	1959	1969	1979	1989	1999
Northeast	$22,200	$33,200	$44,600	$49,600	$59,400	$56,000
Midwest	21,200	30,800	42,400	50,400	51,200	54,000
South	13,200	22,400	34,000	42,800	46,200	46,800
West	22,800	33,200	43,400	50,000	53,200	50,000

SOURCE: Authors' compilation.

---

33 There is another way to view this change. Between 1949 and 1969, the twentieth, fiftieth, and eightieth percentiles in each region all roughly doubled their adjusted family income, except in the South. There the fiftieth percentile increased two and a half times, and the twentieth percentile increased three and a third times.

34 Analysis of nonmetropolitan, center-city, and suburban differences is complicated by missing data for many cases after 1980 ★ ★ ★. Nevertheless, the general trends are strong enough to be reliable. Table C shows the rounded figures:

TABLE C. MEDIAN ADJUSTED FAMILY-OF-FOUR INCOME

	1949	1959	1969	1979	1989	1999
Nonmetropolitan	$15,200	$24,500	$34,250	$39,800	$40,300	$41,700
Metropolitan center city	24,100	31,900	40,400	44,200	46,000	46,300
Nonmetropolitan outside center city	24,800	35,600	48,000	54,500	63,500	69,300

SOURCE: Authors' compilation.

FIGURE 4 **ADJUSTED FAMILY-OF-FOUR INCOME MEDIANS, BY EDUCATION**

EDUCATION INCREASINGLY DIVIDED FAMILIES BY INCOME

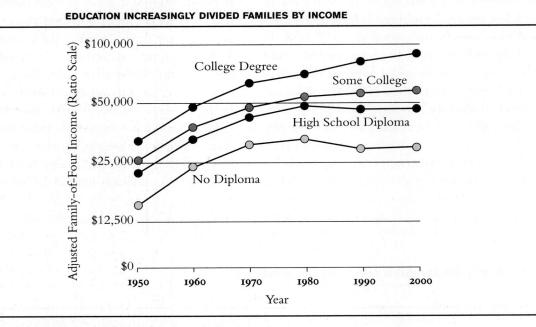

SOURCE: IPUMS (Integrated Public Use Microdata Series).
NOTE: Head of household's education is substituted for children's education.

The regional and urban–rural convergences can probably be explained by the migration of both business and people after 1950. Much of American industry in the northern cities closed down or left town; investment moved to the South and to rural areas. At the same time, Americans with relatively few marketable skills for a modernizing economy left the rural South for the center cities of the North.[35] And well-off Americans found homes in the suburbs. ★ ★ ★

During this same half-century, income differences by education grew. Figure 4 displays the median adjusted family-of-four income by level of education (or, for children, by the household head's education). The figure shows dramatic changes, especially since 1980, as college graduates did increasingly well and those with less than a BA degree stagnated or fell behind. From 1949 to 1969, college graduates' incomes remained about a constant ratio of others' incomes. College graduates in 1969 reported $1.30 of adjusted family-of-four income for each dollar reported by those with some college, about $1.50 per dollar of high

---

35 See Kim, "Economic Integration and Convergence," plus subsequent discussion in the *Journal of Economic History* 59(3, 1999): 773–88.

school graduates, and about $2.05 per dollar of high school dropouts. Then everyone fell further behind the college graduates. By the end of the century, the ratios had become $1.50, $1.80, and $3.20, growing 15, 25, and 55 percent, respectively, for those with some college, a high school diploma, and no diploma. The college grads had moved the furthest ahead, but the gaps between all the educational groups widened.

Educational attainment became substantially more critical as a ticket to family income over only twenty years. Part of the story is the growing demand in the labor market for workers with advanced schooling ★ ★ ★. But there was probably more involved. During these years, growing proportions of poorly educated men went to jail, an experience that devastated their chances of eventually finding well-paid employment.[36] Also, ★ ★ ★ education increasingly determined who married whom and thus the chances of having an income-generating spouse. Better-educated Americans' incomes more often rested on two earners. Then the increasing pattern of high earners marrying high earners further contributed to the education "premium." It also probably contributed to growing income disparities—higher eighty-to-twenty ratios—*within* specific educational groups, for instance, within the set of college graduates.[37]

Summary

Through most of the twentieth century, the spread in family and individual annual incomes narrowed, as did the income differences between blacks and whites, southerners and northerners, and rural and urban Americans. After 1970, however, differences widened between very-well-off and less-well-off Americans. (We should note that the gap between the *extremely* rich and the merely rich also widened greatly.)[38] Scholars point to various forces behind this growing income inequality, including the growing importance of schooling, but also at work were the rise in single-parent families, two-career couples, and immigration and a lagging minimum wage.[39] The axes of difference that strongly lined up with income differences shifted: by 2000, black versus white, South versus North, rural versus urban, and older versus younger all mattered less in determining income than they had earlier in the century, while suburban versus city and, especially, level of education mattered considerably more.[40]

36 By one estimate, in 1999, 15 percent of white men age thirty to thirty-four who had dropped out of high school had ever been imprisoned, and *60 percent* of similar black men had. These men, especially the black men, had slim hopes for finding quality jobs; see Western and Pettit, "Beyond Crime and Punishment."

37 Among college graduates, the eighty-to-twenty ratio increased from 2.47 in 1970 to 2.98 in 1999. Similar substantial increases occurred within other educational groups. On marriage patterns, see Kalmijn, "Intermarriage and Homogamy"; Schwartz and Mare, "Trends in Educational Assortative Marriage"; and DiPrete and Buchmann, "Gender-Specific Trends in the Value of Education."

38 The share of the national income garnered by the top one-tenth of 1 percent "more than doubled [after] 1980 to 7.4 percent in 2002. The share of income earned by the rest of the top 10 percent rose far less and the share earned by the bottom 90 percent fell"; David Cay Johnston, "Richest Are Leaving Even the Rich Far Behind," *New York Times*, June 5, 2005, A1.

39 For general discussion, see, for example, Karoly and Burtless, "Demographic Change, Rising Earnings Inequality"; Danziger and Gottschalk, *America Unequal and Uneven Tides;* Hout, Arum, and Voss, "The Political Economy of Inequality in the Age of Extremes."

40 In 1949 Americans age thirty to forty-four had $1.82 of adjusted family income for each dollar of those age sixty-five or older. In 1999 the ratio was down to $1.30.

⫴ WEALTH

Although wealth is tied closely to annual income, it is a different, broader component of people's standards of living. Many Americans with a low annual income have considerable wealth—for example, some retirees own valuable homes and stock portfolios—and many Americans with high annual incomes have little wealth—for example, some self-employed entrepreneurs can have a good year but carry large debts. Wealth differences among Americans do not simply mirror differences in income.[41] Furthermore, variations in wealth have their own consequences.

A person's wealth, or "net worth," is composed of his or her assets—a home, savings accounts, stock portfolios, bonds, insurance, and similar possessions that can be cashed out—minus debts, such as mortgages and consumer loans. Researchers differ about whether to include *potential* assets, such as future Social Security and pension payouts, and personal possessions, such as appliances and furniture. Edward Wolff, a leading expert on wealth, focuses only on those assets that can be easily converted into money at close to their real value.[42] We follow his lead. Also, some items that compose wealth—goods such as houses and cars—play a double role: people both "consume" them and hold them for possible cash or collateral value. In the next section, we look at goods; here our focus is on the liquid or potentially liquid assets people hold.

Such liquid assets are important above and beyond annual incomes. Most of the critical moments in people's lives depend on their assets (or their parents' assets) more than on their annual incomes: assets more substantially determine how well people make it through critical life transitions, such as college, weddings, funerals, homeownership, career launch, unemployment, medical emergencies, children's career launches, and retirement. Also, people's sense of financial security probably rests at least as much on their assets as on their paychecks. Looking at wealth yields a different story about the diversity of living standards than does looking at income. For example, blacks made notable progress in catching up to whites in annual income but remained far behind in wealth. In the mid-1990s, the median white received $1.60 in adjusted family-of-four income for every dollar the median black received, but the median white family had *$8.30* of net worth for each dollar the median black family had. (Excluding homes yields a $33-to-$1 ratio.) If data on Americans' wealth were not so much harder to obtain than data on their incomes—the latter are included in almost every government and private poll, the former only in occasional and complex surveys—social scientists would probably have studied wealth much more. Another limitation is that researchers are largely constrained to relatively recent data.[43]

Differences between rich and poor are much greater in wealth than in annual income. As we saw, in 2000 the American at the eightieth

---

41 Lisa Keister (*Wealth in America*) reports a correlation of .25 between wealth and income when income from investments is excluded.

42 Wolff, "Recent Trends in Wealth Ownership." See also Davies and Shorroks, "The Distribution of Wealth."

43 On the importance of wealth compared to income, see, for example, Conley, *Being Black, Living in the Red.* On our estimate of black net worth, see Wolff, "Racial Wealth Disparities," table 7. See also Keister, *Wealth in America;* and Spilerman, "Wealth and Stratification Processes."

percentile of income had an adjusted family-of-four income of $3.75 to each dollar of the American at the twentieth percentile. But the American household at the eightieth percentile of wealth had effectively an *infinite* net worth relative to that of the American at the twentieth percentile, because the least wealthy one-fifth of American households were in the red. Even compared to the *median*, the eightieth percentile's wealth advantage stands out: $6.70 to every dollar of net worth for the fiftieth percentile.[44]

The major reason differences in wealth are several times wider than annual income differences is that income differences accumulate year after year as high-income families put savings into assets that both earn money and appreciate over time, while low-income families make so little that their debts compound over time. High interest rates typically amplify financial assets while inflation wears away the buying power of wages. Gifts and bequests from parents to children allow this process of compound growth to

stretch over generations, not just over one lifetime. By one informed estimate, 40 percent of wealth accumulation is the result of inheritance or inter vivos gifts.[45] Wealthy parents help their children up the ladder in other ways as well, such as buying them a good education and providing a security net for risky business or career ventures. In addition, families' decisions about how to save and invest, their financial skills, the number of earners they have, how long those earners have worked, and other personal traits contribute to variations in wealth—as does, certainly, good or bad luck.[46] Basically, wealth tends to foster more wealth, and poverty tends to foster more poverty, widening the economic differences.

Wealth at the End of the Century

In 1998 the median American household was worth $61,000.[47] Equity in the home was the major component; without it, the median household was worth $18,000. But the median hides tremendous variation. At the top, American

---

44 Compared to an adjusted family income eighty-to-fifty ratio of $1.80. Wolff ("Recent Trends in Wealth Ownership") notes that in 1998, 18 percent of households had zero or negative net worth. The eighty-to-fifty ratio is interpolated from his table 2.

45 That informed estimate is in Davies and Shorroks, "The Distribution of Wealth." Keister's analysis of the determinants of net assets among Americans in their thirties, "Family Background and the Racial Wealth Gap," shows that, holding constant all sorts of personal and family characteristics, parents' incomes and the receipt of an inheritance significantly increased respondents' wealth. Dalton Conley ("Capital for College") shows that parental assets, net of their income and other factors, improved their children's chances of attending and graduating from college; see also Keister, *Wealth in America*. Wolff ("Inheritances and Wealth Inequality") found that bequests and gifts *reduce* inequality, because what low-income people receive is *proportionately* greater relative to their current wealth than is true of wealthier recipients. Wolff qualifies this finding methodologically in various ways, however, and points out that, given poorer persons' lower savings rates, their inheritances are less likely to promote future wealth.

46 For a review of factors that influence wealth accumulation—in the context of the black-white gap—see Scholz and Levine, "U.S. Black-White Wealth Inequality."

47 We use 1998 Consumer Expenditure Survey (CES) data because it is the last dataset in the century we could use. For analysis of the CES, we draw on the Bureau of Labor Statistics datasets prepared by the National Bureau of Economic Research. The CES is a study conducted by the BLS that asks respondents (about five thousand during each administration) to provide detailed information on their assets and their spending, using both detailed interviews and diaries (see http://www.bls.gov/cex/home.htm). The version of the data we used is drawn from extracts of the survey developed by the Congressional Budget Office (CBO) and available from the NBER (Harris and Sabelhaus, "Consumer Expenditure Survey Family-Level Extracts"). Although the CES began in 1980, we start with 1984 in part because that is when the sample became national rather than urban only and in part because other procedural changes made pre-1984 data hard to compare with later data.

households ranking between the eightieth and ninetieth percentiles were worth an average of over $340,000, and those in the top *1* percent over $10 million. At the lower end, about one-fifth of American households had zero net worth or were in the red. Setting aside home equity, about one-quarter of American households had no or negative net worth.[48]

We turn now to closer examination of specific assets and their distributions, standardizing again for inflation and family size and starting with the central asset, the house. In 2000 the average American homeowner lived in a house with a family-of-four value of about $134,000. But there was quite a range. The eightieth-percentile homeowner's house was worth (adjusted to a family-of-four) about $246,000, which was 3.4 times the house value of the twentieth-percentile homeowner, at $72,000.[49] Not included in this comparison are the roughly one-third of Americans who were not homeowners and therefore had zero home value. Differences in liquid wealth were yet greater. Take savings accounts: in the period 1996 to 1998, the twentieth-percentile saver had nothing in a savings account; the median saver had an adjusted account of about $15; and the eightieth-percentile saver had one of over $4,000. In checking accounts, the twentieth-percentile American once again had zero, the median had

$300, and the eightieth-percentile over $2,000. The contrast in stocks and bonds was even wider because most Americans, including the median one, had none. Wealth inequality far overshadowed income inequality.

★ ★ ★

||| CONSUMPTION

Some analysts argue that the best way to assess people's standards of living is not by their pay stubs or portfolios, but by what they buy. It is also argued that many people underreport (accidentally or not) their incomes and wealth to census- and survey-takers. In a 1988 national survey, for example, respondents who reported incomes under $5,000 also reported spending, on average, over four times as much money as they said they earned. Some welfare and disability recipients hide income; some middle-class families report themselves as less well-off than they are; and some wealthy people overlook a few sources of income.[50]

An entirely different reason for the income-outgo discrepancy is that many people spend their savings or borrow to sustain their standard of living. Indeed, people typically base their spending on long-term calculations rather than their immediate income. A young professional couple may, for example, spend more than they

48 Wolff, "Recent Trends in Wealth Ownership," tables 1 and 3.
49 These calculations were based on the "Consumer Expenditure Survey Family Level Extracts: 1981:1 to 1998:2," created by John Sabelhaus and continued by Ed Harris of the CBO and distributed by the NBER.
50 On the 1988 national survey, see Brown, *American Standards of Living*, 372, 461; see also Lebergott, *Consumer Expenditures*, ch. 1. On the validity issue, see, for the poor, Edin and Lein,

Making Ends Meet, and, more generally, U.S. Bureau of the Census, "Money Income in the United States, 1998," appendix E. Recent census surveys have counted 89 percent of the comparable total income and 99 percent of wages and salaries, as has the Bureau of Economic Analysis using sources other than household interviews. The implication is that unearned income, such as investment returns and side businesses, is the bulk of the understated income.

earn early in their careers because they can reasonably anticipate rapid increases in earnings (and perhaps the receipt of an inheritance); a middle-aged couple may restrain their spending to ensure their long-term health care (and perhaps to leave an inheritance).[51] Some of the reckoning works out. If a student's borrowing for college education or newlyweds' borrowing for a house pays off, if the economy does well, and if perhaps parents pitch in, borrowers get out of debt. For others, borrowing is a repeated act of desperation. If the investment or the economy sours, if kin are also strapped and make their own requests, if the indebted's ship never comes in, then they never get out of the red.[52] Typically, the poor borrow for immediate consumption and the rich save for investment, and typically, young families go into debt and retirees spend down their assets. Consequently, Americans differ less in what they consume than in their incomes and wealth.

Yet another argument for looking at spending rather than income or wealth is that Americans received increasing value for their dollars over the century. For example, in 1909 the average manufacturing worker had to labor a half-hour to afford a pound of bread and almost an hour to afford a half-gallon of milk delivered to the door; in 1970 his grandson needed to work five minutes for the bread and twelve minutes for the milk.[53] Moreover, the quality of the bread and milk—their freshness, cleanliness, and variety—improved considerably. If we want to know how standards of living changed, goes the argument, we should look at how much people spend and what they buy.

If we do, we see narrower differences than we have seen earlier. In 1998 the eighty-to-twenty ratio for adjusted family-of-four spending was only $2.50 to $1 (versus $3.75 for income and much more for assets). Table 1 shows that the twentieth-percentile spender reported buying about $4,000 worth of food a year for the standard family of four and the eightieth-percentile spender bought about $8,600 worth, for an eighty-to-twenty food ratio of just $2.13 to $1.[54] There is only so much one can spend on food, and there is only so little one can get by on, so the consumption differences there are not great, and they consist more in quality than quantity (filet mignon versus hamburger). As we move to housing, then clothing, and finally recreation, however, we see that the differences in spending widen. For recreation, the eightieth-percentile spender paid out $5.39 for each $1 spent by the twentieth-percentile consumer.

Consumption differences were smaller than the income or wealth differences. Nonetheless, 20 percent of American families in the 1990s reported failing to pay for some essential

---

51 For general discussions of income versus consumption, see, for example, Slesnick, "Consumption, Needs, and Inequality," and *Consumption and Social Welfare*; Federman et al., "What Does It Mean to Be Poor in America?"; Jencks and Mayer, "Do Official Poverty Rates Provide Useful Information . . . ?"; Jorgenson, "Did We Lose the War on Poverty?"; Cox and Alm, *Myths of Rich and Poor*; and Cutler and Katz, "Rising Inequality?"

52 On debt, see, for example, Sullivan et al., *Fragile Middle Class*.

On kin ties, see Goldstein and Warren, "Socioeconomic Reach and Heterogeneity in the Extended Family."

53 Calculations of work time based on U.S. Bureau of the Census, *Historical Statistics of the United States*, 170, 210, and 213.

54 As for income and wealth, we correct for inflation and divide by the square root of the size of the family, then multiply by two to get a family-of-four equivalent. Daniel Slesnick (*Consumption and Social Welfare*) shows how sensitive trend analyses of consumption are to estimates of household "need."

TABLE 1 **ADJUSTED FAMILY-OF-FOUR SPENDING ON CATEGORIES OF GOODS, BY PERCENTILE RANK, 1998**

	20th Percentile	50th Percentile	80th Percentile	80:20 Ratio
Food	$4,046	$6,094	$8,614	2.13
Housing	5,772	9,186	16,120	2.79
Clothing	610	1,356	2,498	4.10
Recreation	816	2,062	4,402	5.39

SOURCE: Center for Economic Studies.

NOTE: Numbers represent family spending, adjusted for inflation, divided by the square root of the size of the family, and multiplied by two.

expense, such as a utility bill, rent, or a doctor's fee. Ten percent of American households reported some "insecurity" in having enough food, and 4 percent reported some hunger. And these counts do *not* include the homeless. At the same time, many Americans at the other end spent enough on mansions, yachts, and jewelry to inspire 1990s books such as *Luxury Fever* and *The Overspent American.*[55]

Ownership of basic consumer goods was also more evenly spread than income or wealth. At the last turn of the century, virtually every American household had, for example, a refrigerator and a color television set, and 90 percent had a car or truck. They varied more on other items. Nearly 80 percent owned washing machines, and a bit more than half owned a dishwasher, a computer, or cell phones.[56]

One way to understand ownership patterns for such goods is in terms of diffusion. When a new consumer good, such as televisions or computers, first appears, only some people—

usually those who are well-off or avant-garde, or both—get it. Then, because prices drop and familiarity increases, ownership "diffuses" across the population until virtually everyone has it. In this process, differences in ownership rates first widen and then narrow. Thus, what ownership tells us about differences in standards of living depends or where that good is in its diffusion history. For the basic items—not only refrigerators and automobiles but also indoor plumbing and television—there was considerable homogeneity in 2000. The wealthy may have driven BMWs and watched thirty-two-inch rear-projection television, and the working class may have driven old cars and watched TV on seventeen-inch screens, but both groups had the commodities. Skeptics in the debate over poverty in America point out that most of those who are defined as poor by their annual incomes nonetheless own such goods. More alarmed debaters respond that, socially and psychologically, poverty is a relative matter. The poor

55 On failure to pay essential bills, see Bauman; "Extended Measures of Well-being." On food insecurity and hunger, see U.S. Bureau of the Census, *Statistical Abstract of the United States, 2000*, table 233.

56 U.S. Bureau of the Census, *Statistical Abstract of the United States, 2003*, tables 996, 997. These numbers are for 2001; the prior data were for 1997.

may have indoor plumbing, but if their children lacked computers in 2000, they remained socially disadvantaged—in this example, on the wrong side of the "digital divide." We return to an evaluation of relative need after looking at the historical trends in consumption.

Long-Term Trends in Spending

Consumption expanded dramatically for all Americans between 1900 and 2000—indeed, probably on a historically incomparable scale. But did that mean that differences in standards of living narrowed or widened? Consider, first, *spending* patterns. One way to assess living standards is to examine how people apportion their spending. When they live on the margin, people spend almost all their money on the basics, and

the most basic is food; when people live well, they spend much of their money on discretionary extras, and one of the most discretionary is recreation. Therefore, the proportion that a family spends on recreation versus food indexes its standard of living.[57] Over the twentieth century, Americans spent less of each consumer dollar on food (half as much by the end of the century) and more on recreation (twice as much as before). Figure 5 draws on two different but consistent sources: occasional national surveys asking respondents how they spent their money and national economic data tracking the buying and selling of goods.[58] The key force pushing food spending down was, of course, declines in the real cost of food. Much of the money Americans saved on food went to "feeding" the fam-

FIGURE 5   CONSUMER EXPENDITURES FOR FOOD AND RECREATION, BY YEAR

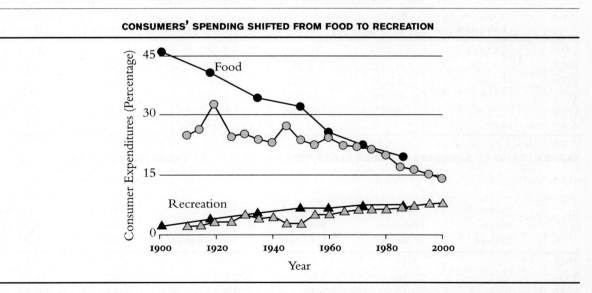

SOURCES: Household surveys: Jacobs and Shipp, "How Family Spending Has Changed in the United States." National accounts: U.S. Bureau of the Census, *Historical Statistics of the United States*, 316–21; U.S. Bureau of the Census, *Statistical Abstract of the United States*, 2003, table 667, Excel spreadsheet supplement.

NOTE: Black data points indicate that the data come from surveys of urban consumers; white data points indicate that the data come from national accounts.

ily car, which by the end of the century took about as much of the household budget as food did; some part of that car budget should also be counted as recreation.

The same household survey data displayed in the figure also speak to class differences in spending patterns. Although much "noisier" than the income and wealth data, the household surveys suggest that class differences in spending narrowed through the middle part of the century until about 1973, and then class differences stopped narrowing or even widened.[59]

57 Dora Costa ("American Living Standards") develops an economic model for using recreational spending as a mark of living standards. We use a simpler but similar procedure.

58 The household survey numbers are drawn from Jacobs and Shipp, "How Family Spending Has Changed in the United States," and refer only to urban wage-earning and clerical families. (This makes it difficult to integrate more recent CES data. The CES shows 14 percent spending on food and 5 percent spending on recreation in 2000, but these results cannot be "stitched" together with the older data.) "Recre-

ation" refers to "entertainment and reading." The national accounts data through 1955 are drawn from the U.S. Bureau of the Census, *Historical Statistics of the United States*, 316–21, and U.S. Bureau of the Census, *Statistical Abstract of the United States*, 2003, table 667. Although various details make the sources somewhat different from each other, and comparisons of the two types of data complex, the overall trend lines are clear.

59 The numbers referred to are presented in the tables below. Our calculations are simple but nonetheless suggestive.

TABLE A. ANNUAL AMOUNT SPENT ON FOOD AND RECREATION ADJUSTED TO A FAMILY OF FOUR, BY CLASS AND YEAR (IN 2000 DOLLARS)

	Food			Recreation		
	Laborers	Wage-Earners	Salaried Workers	Laborers	Wage-Earners	Salaried Workers
1918	$4,966	$5,480	$6,886	$440	$620	$1,194
1935	5,394	6,242	8,212	806	1,058	2,520
1950	8,362	9,384	10,742	1,720	2,262	2,970
1973	7,764	8,216	9,972	3,382	3,948	5,508
1988	7,108	7,902	9,190	4,260	5,244	8,550

TABLE B. RATIO OF SPENDING BETWEEN CLASS GROUPS, BY TYPE OF SPENDING AND YEAR

	Food			Recreation		
	Salaried: Wage-Earner	Wage-Earner: Laborer	Salaried Worker: Laborer	Salaried Worker Wage-Earner	Wage-Earner: Laborer	Salaried Worker: Laborer
1918	1.26	1.10	1.39	1.92	1.41	2.71
1935	1.32	1.16	1.52	2.38	1.31	3.13
1950	1.14	1.12	1.28	1.31	1.31	1.73
1973	1.21	1.06	1.28	1.39	1.17	1.63
1988	1.16	1.11	1.29	1.63	1.23	2.01

SOURCE: Authors' compilation.

We return to the Consumer Expenditure Surveys of 1984 through 1998 for more comprehensive data on how Americans spent money over the last fifteen years of the twentieth century.[60] The proportions spent on food and recreation, which we use as indicators of standard of living, changed little, and the gap between high and low spenders on recreation barely widened. Black-white differences on food spending narrowed noticeably, and differences on recreational spending narrowed marginally. Differences by the education of the head of household stayed roughly the same. We can say that the long-term convergence of black and white consumption continued into the 1990s (the end of that decade was especially beneficial to blacks) and that the class differences that had widened after 1970 stayed about the same after the mid-1980s.[61]

Several researchers have examined late-twentieth-century spending more comprehensively than we could here. Details differ among them, and with us, but some general conclusions emerge. Inequality in consumer spending continued declining from World War II to about 1973. From then to 2000, spending inequality grew again, but at a slower pace than did income or wealth inequality (perhaps because of expanded borrowing). Then the economic boom of the late 1990s stalled the trend toward more consumption inequality.[62]

Trends in What People Owned

The single most critical "good" Americans own is also their single greatest investment, a home. The proportion of American families who owned their own homes jumped in the

We use Claire Brown's *American Standards of Living*, which compiles household expenditure studies from 1918 through 1988. She distinguishes spending by urban laborers, wage-earners, and salaried workers (all white). The table shows how much each group spent on average on food and recreation over the century, adjusted as follows: (1) we correct for cost of living, using the BLS "inflation calculator" (http://stats.bls.gov/), which is for urban costs; (2) we divide each spending amount by the square root of the *average size of family for that class group* in that year; and (3) we multiply by two to get a family-of-four equivalent. Table A shows the dollar amounts, and Table B the ratios between groups. Note that differences in food spending changed modestly, although they did narrow between salaried workers and laborers between 1918 and 1950. Differences in recreational spending changed more, with the gaps narrowing substantially to 1973 and then widening by 1988.

60 Around 1986, the eightieth-percentile respondent in recreation spending spent 4.2 percent more on recreation than the twentieth-percentile respondent (five-year-moving averages); around 1996 the difference was 4.5 percent. Differences had not narrowed. In that sense, the centurylong convergence was stalled.

61 Whites' percentage of spending devoted to food stayed at 13 percent from the mid-1980s to the mid-1990s; blacks' percentage dropped from 18.5 percent to 16 percent. Both groups' spending on recreation increased very slightly, leaving the difference the same. Slesnick (*Consumption and Social*

Welfare, ch. 6) finds a drop in consumption inequality by region from 1947 to 1973 and little net change afterwards. He reports little in the way of between-group trends for race or gender of household head.

62 Studies of consumption are difficult because they involve rare and "noisy" data (a typical condition with the Consumer Expenditure Survey) and require numerous judgment calls and estimates. (For example, how should one count the "spending" represented by an owned house? By a paid-off car? How should one calculate the needs of a young person versus an old one?) Slesnick (*Consumption and Social Welfare*) finds a drop in inequality from World War II to 1973 and then essentially no trend through 1995. He thus rejects claims of widening inequality based on income trends. His calculations, however, seem notably sensitive to his assumptions. For example, he calculates that the percentage of elderly who were poor dropped from 13 percent in 1947 to 0.6 percent in 1994 (page 182); few scholars would credit that 0.6 percent. Dirk Krueger and Fabrizio Perri ("Does Income Inequality Lead to Consumption Inequality?") find that consumption inequality increased in the 1980s but almost leveled off in the 1990s, in part, they suggest, because people increasingly borrowed money to offset fluctuations in their incomes. David Johnson, Timothy Smeeding, and Barbara Boyle Torrey ("United States Inequality Through the Prisms of Income and Consumption," especially table 3) also find that spending inequality grew in the 1980s and leveled off in the 1990s.

FIGURE 6 **HOUSEHOLDS WITH KEY DOMESTIC GOODS, BY YEAR**

SOME CONSUMER GOODS, BUT NOT HOME OWNERSHIP,
BECAME NEARLY UNIVERSAL

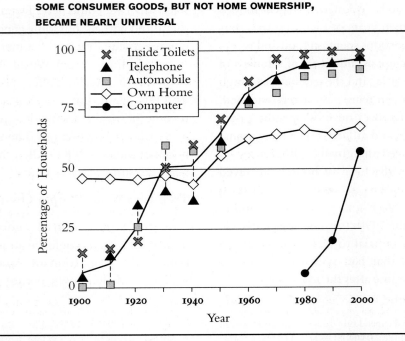

SOURCES: U.S. Bureau of the Census, *Historical Statistics of the United States*; U.S. Bureau of the Census, *Statistical Abstracts of the United States*; Liebergott, *The American Economy*, http://factfinder.census.gov; and interpolations.

NOTE: The gray line shows the average of toilet, telephone, and automobile; the data points for the individual items are connected to the line.

middle of the century. We see that displayed in figure 6 by the nearly horizontal line. A bit under half of American households owned their homes in the first part of the century; that figure jumped to over 60 percent by 1960 and stayed about there afterwards.[63] Ownership of other goods, however, increased greatly. Three

that are summarized together in the gray line in figure 6—having an inside toilet, a telephone, and an automobile—diffused in similar ways. Each was rare in 1900 but had become nearly universal by 2000. The computer, introduced late in the century, was showing a similar, albeit more rapid, diffusion.[64]

63 Ownership is heavily conditioned by the age of the head of the household and by marital status. For Americans age forty-five to sixty-four, the prime earning years, the historical trend line is the same except that it is shifted upward, with ownership rates leveling off at 80 percent in the last third of the century. The trend diverged for married-couple house-

holds and other households after 1960: rates for the married rose into the low 80 percent range in 1990s, compared to 65 percent for all households combined.

64 The numbers in this section are drawn from census data (U.S. Bureau of the Census, *Historical Statistics of the United States*, and *Statistical Abstract of the United States, 2003*, and Lebergott,

As noted earlier, as new products diffuse, differences in ownership widen and then later shrink. We can see this process in tracking black-white differences. (Few long-term data track Americans' ownership of goods by the education, occupation, or income of the owner, but the United States has long gathered many statistics by race.) In 1890, 14 percent of whites and 5 percent of blacks had toilets—a nine-point difference; by 1940, as indoor plumbing spread, blacks lagged thirty-seven points behind whites (26 versus 63 percent), but by 2000 indoor toilets were effectively universal, so the difference was about zero. In 1900 virtually no one had a car; in 1935, 60 percent of white families had cars, but only 20 percent of black families did—a forty-point gap; in 1999, 95 percent of whites and 80 percent of blacks had a car, bringing the difference down to fifteen points.[65]

Through such diffusion, Americans of all backgrounds came to own these sorts of goods by the end of the century. In 1960 rural residents, blacks, the poorly educated, and southerners were notably less likely than other Americans to have full plumbing facilities in their homes; by 1990 the differences were gone.[66] Telephone and automobile ownership did not become universal, but the differences

between groups still shrank. For example, the difference in automobile ownership between high school graduates and high school dropouts shrank from nine points in 1960 to four points in 1990.[67]

Evaluating Consumption Inequality

Thus, at the dawn of the twenty-first century Americans were all pretty similar in their ownership of nineteenth- and early-twentieth-century inventions. Certainly, wealthier Americans had more bathrooms, newer cars, and fancier phones, but almost everyone had the minimum. Even television, a mid-twentieth-century invention, was universal, meaning, for example, that almost everyone could share a common experience such as watching the Super Bowl in color. But do such commonalities mean that standards of living had generally converged? Is the growing inequality in income and wealth after 1970—and by some measures in spending—contradicted when we look at consumption of goods? Not necessarily. Consider three issues: new goods, improving goods, and public goods.

For new goods, take the example of the personal computer. Over the last quarter of the century, ownership of this new technology increasingly *divided* Americans. Figure 6 shows

---

The American Economy, 272, 289–90); a few estimates are calculated by interpolation or modeling (for example, the early estimates for telephones are based on the number of telephones per household). For more on the diffusion of the automobile and telephone, see Fischer, *America Calling.*

65 The historical racial estimates are from Lebergott, *The American Economy*, 99, 290. Other estimates are from the IPUMS, except for 1999, which is from the Annual Housing Survey (U.S. Bureau of the Census, *Annual Housing Survey*).

66 IPUMS and U.S. Bureau of the Census, *Annual Housing Survey*. For example, in 1960 only 71 percent of southerners,

compared to 93 percent of northeasterners, had full plumbing; in 1999, 99 percent of both did.

67 These numbers come from the IPUMS dataset and refer to individuals living in households with such facilities. A roughly thirty-point difference between whites and blacks and between college graduates and high school dropouts in having telephone service in 1960 became around a ten-point difference in 1990. The 1990 data on cars are adjusted to reflect the counts of cars found in 1960, 1970, and 1980 data by subtracting out estimated "truck-only" households.

the rapid spread of computer ownership from 5 percent in 1980 to 60 percent in 2000. By 2000, ownership had become highly divided according to education: 78 percent of college-graduate households had one, 47 percent of high school graduate households, and 23 percent of high school dropout households. Similarly, ancestry and regional differences in computer ownership widened as it diffused.[68] Chances are that the future of computers will resemble that of the earlier technologies. As they passed the halfway mark, differences shrank. ★ ★ ★ Nonetheless, the brief history of the personal computer reinforces one argument about goods and inequality: as old goods lose their power to mark distinctions, new products emerge that gain the power to distinguish.[69]

On improving goods, consider homeownership. As displayed in figure 6, ownership rates stayed relatively flat, 46 percent, between 1900 and 1940; rose rapidly between 1940 and 1960, largely owing to New Deal–era government assistance to young adults; and then flattened out again at 66 percent. Even among people in their peak years for capital accumulation, those age forty-five to sixty-four, ownership rates lev-

eled off at 80 percent. Ownership rates did *not* converge by social class, and indeed, the class difference widened a bit in the later decades. In 1960, for example, college graduates were four percentage points likelier to own their dwellings than high school graduates (72 versus 68 percent); in 2000 they were five points likelier (73 versus 68 percent).[70] Homeownership did not follow the same diffusion pattern as did household goods. There are key differences between owning homes and owning, say, televisions. For one, as we noted earlier, homes are simultaneously investment and consumption. As an investment, their desirability varies over time. (Around the earlier turn of the century, homeownership was a conservative investment strategy that working-class rather than middle-class families often pursued.) For another, the real price of homes does not follow the price history of other commodities. Goods such as telephones and automobiles spread in great measure because their real costs decline; the same is true of manufactured goods generally. Housing, however, continues to rise in cost. Between 1918 and 1988, Americans' spending on shelter (in constant dollars) roughly tripled.[71]

---

68 Computer ownership data come from six supplements of the Current Population Survey.

69 See the discussion of consumption as comparative distinction in, for example, Douglas and Isherwood, *The World of Goods*; Rainwater, *What Money Buys*; Frank, *Luxury Fever*; and McCracken, *Culture and Consumption*.

70 The 1960 numbers are from the IPUMS; the 2000 numbers are from the CES website.

71 Between 1983 and 1999, for example, the cost of televisions declined by 45 percent, the cost of interstate telephone calls dropped by 28 percent, and the cost of new cars rose by 28 percent, but the cost of homeownership rose 88 percent. On the history of home owning, see, for example, Tobey, Wetherell, and Brigham, "Moving Out and Settling In"; Tobey, *Technology as Freedom*, ch. 4; Chevan, "The Growth of Home-

ownership"; Harris, "Working-Class Homeownership"; Luria, "Wealth, Capital, and Power"; Thernstrom, *The Other Bostonians*. The recent price changes are from U.S. Bureau of the Census, *Statistical Abstract of the United States, 2000,* table 770; the cost of homeownership is calculated as "rental equivalent" and does not include insurance. The 1918 to 1988 comparison is from Brown, *American Standards of Living*, 455. Many have noted that, over the years, the size and quality of the housing Americans could buy increased; in per-footage or per-amenity terms, housing costs may not have nearly tripled (see, for example, Cox and Alm, "Time Well Spent"). This point does not negate the comparison we are making between types of goods. First, other commodities also improve in quality—for example, automobiles have improved dramatically in speed, safety, and comfort.

With larger-package goods, such as homes—and probably health care and higher education as well—costs do not decline much as a result of scale increases, and thus access does not diffuse as much. Thus, some of the basics become more available to more people—basic shelter with heat and water, simple vaccines, community college—but the ante, the middle-class standard, keeps going up, perpetuating distinctions, if not widening them.

Finally, there are *public goods*, an entirely different realm of consumption, but a critical one. When, for example, people search for a new house, they carefully weigh aspects of the neighborhood such as the local schools, traffic, health facilities, air quality, and safety. Public goods are a key part of the package. Other public goods, such as water and sewage treatment facilities, have been largely responsible for extending and equalizing life spans ★ ★ ★.

It is especially difficult to measure the distribution of such public goods, that is, to say anything about growing or waning public goods inequality.[72] (One effort to count "public consumption," such as the use of schools and roads, into household incomes reports an increase in inequality between 1989 and 2000).[73] But any full accounting of living standards would need to include public consumption as well as the consumption of private goods such as televisions, cars, and shoes.

The evidence we have on overall consumption suggests that over the course of the century more and more Americans shared in what is now seen as a "middle American" lifestyle, with basic facilities, new appliances, and other goods, especially private ones, that are part of the "good life." But the evidence suggests as well that this economic convergence seemed to stall—and perhaps even reverse, as was the

---

Second, rising standards also raise the cost of the minimum "housing package" people can buy. Because of legal, market, and cultural "floors," they cannot realistically buy, say, two-room houses without running water, electricity, and standard ceiling heights.

72 We tried. For example, the Annual Housing Survey (AHS) provides respondents' ratings of various aspects of their neighborhoods over a quarter-century. Conducted by the Census Bureau for HUD and renamed the American Housing Survey in 1983—it was administered annually from 1973 to 1981 and biannually afterwards—the AHS covers about five thousand households in major metropolitan areas. Over four waves, forty-six metropolitan areas are covered, with about a dozen in any given survey. Because of this sampling procedure and because of various changes in procedures, year-to-year and even decade-to-decade comparability is difficult.

The AHS asked respondents a series of questions about neighborhood conditions, one of which was whether it had crime. "Yes" answers rose strongly from 17 percent in 1974 to a peak of 24 percent in 1991, and then dropped rapidly to 14 percent in 1999—roughly in tune with nationwide crime statistics. During the rise, black-white differences and city-suburban differences widened; during the dramatic decline

in crime of the 1990s, racial and place differences stabilized, but educational differences still widened. The General Social Survey asked a similar question: was there anywhere in their neighborhoods where respondents were afraid to walk? Between 1973 and 2000, the percentage who said "no" varied from a low of 52 to a high of 63, with little net change over the quarter-century. The results differed some from those of the AHS, but once again, educational groups seemed to diverge over the quarter-century in a similar way: high school dropouts were slightly less likely to feel secure, and high school graduates more likely. Other results from the AHS are mixed, however. For example, AHS respondents' ratings of the quality of their neighborhoods and homes seemed to converge. This is a limited exercise, and more comprehensive research needs to be done on the distribution—and changes in the distribution—of public goods.

73 Wolff, Zacharias, and Caner, "Household Wealth, Public Consumption, and Economic Well-being." This heroic effort to estimate individual households' use of public goods is unable to take into account within-state differences in the value of goods such as roads or health care, and thus cannot tell us whether, say, the closing of public clinics in particular locations is widening inequality.

case with income and wealth—in the last quarter or so of the twentieth century. Equalization stalled not only in terms of several objective counts, such as spending patterns, but also in the sense that much of consumption was relative: as some goods became universal (for example, televisions), lines of division appeared around newer goods (for example, computers). It is also important to understand that *how* Americans differed in consumption changed: regional and racial differences largely narrowed, but differences by education generally widened.

★ ★ ★

||| CONCLUSION

Although Americans at the end of the century were aware of widening economic differences among them, Americans have generally worried less about economic inequality than have citizens of other affluent nations, and they have been less willing to endorse government action to balance inequalities. What Americans care about more than economic equality of outcome is equal opportunity to get wealthy.[74]

This stance fits their optimism: even in the job-tight year of 2003, one-third of Americans (and half of young Americans) thought it likely that they would become rich.[75] In this vein, some analysts argue that the growing inequality after 1970 matters little so long as opportunities to move up the ladder have also expanded. However, upward mobility did *not* increase and may even have decreased in the last few decades of the twentieth century.[76]

The economy at the end of the twentieth century was a major source of social division in the United States. Americans differed from one another economically more than they did socially or culturally. The cornucopia of America's productivity distributed consumer goods widely, so that differences in consumption were not nearly as wide as differences in annual income and accumulated wealth. Over most of the twentieth century, the least well-off in America—notably, the rural, southern, and black poor—made the greatest economic gains, narrowing historic differences. The two world wars, the Great Depression, and the New Deal welfare state combined to level economic

---

74 On American ideas about economic equality, see Hochschild, *What's Fair*; Rainwater, *What Money Buys*; Gans, *Middle American Individualism*; Smith, "Social Inequality in Cross-National Perspective"; Kelley and Evans, "The Legitimation of Inequality"; and Verba and Orren, *Equality in America*. On attitudes toward redressing inequality, see these sources and Ladd and Bowman, *Attitudes Toward Economic Inequality*. From 1978 through 2000, the GSS asked adults to place themselves on a seven-point scale ranging from support for the position that "government should reduce income differences" (coded 1) to support for the position that it should not (coded 7). Respondents' average position on EQWLTH was 3.8 in 1978–80, 3.5 in 1990–91—moving toward government action—and 3.9 during the boom years of 1998–2000, reversing that mini-trend.
75 David M. Moore, "Half of Young People Expect to Get

Rich," Gallup Poll News Service, March 11, 2003, available to subscribers at: http://www.gallup.com. The median respondent defined "rich" as an income of $122,000 and assets of $1 million.
76 Bradbury and Katz, "Issues in Economics." On consumption inequality, see Johnson et al., "United States Inequality." Also, there is evidence that the college attendance of youth became more strongly tied to their parents' affluence over these years, a trend that would dampen mobility (Kane, "College-Going and Inequality"). In a 2005 special report, *The Economist* ("Ever Higher Society") summarized several studies all pointing to either no change or a decline in upward mobility; see a similar account in David Wessel, "Escalator Ride: As Rich-Poor Gap Widens in the U.S., Class Mobility Stalls," *Wall Street Journal*, May 13, 2005, A1.

distinctions substantially by midcentury. But the new economy, the new family patterns, and the new politics that emerged in the 1970s rewidened economic divisions among Americans, particularly ★ ★ ★ along lines of education. The wealthy and the college-educated drew further away from the rest. And even Americans' subjective sense of economic well-being expressed the late-century polarization.

||| REFERENCES

Atkinson, Anthony B., Lee Rainwater, and Timothy Smeeding. 1995. *Income Distributions in OECD Countries: Evidence from the Luxembourg Income Study.* Washington, D.C.: OECD Publications and Information Center.

Bauman, Kurt J. 1999. "Extended Measures of Well-being: Meeting Basic Needs." *Current Population Reports* P70-67 (June). Washington: U.S. Bureau of the Census.

Beckfield, Jason. 2004. "Does Inequality Harm Health? New Cross-National Evidence." *Journal of Health and Social Behavior* 45 (September): 231–48.

Bradbury, Katherine, and Jane Katz. 2002. "Issues in Economics: Are Lifetime Incomes Growing More Unequal?" *Regional Review* (Federal Reserve Bank of Boston) Q4: 3–5.

Brittingham, Angela, and G. Patricia de la Cruz. 2004. "Ancestry: 2000." Census 2000 Brief (June). U.S. Bureau of the Census. Washington: U.S. Government Printing Office. Available at: http://www.census.gov/prod/2004pubs/c2kbr-35.pdf.

Brown, Claire. 1994. *American Standards of Living, 1918–1988.* Cambridge, Mass.: Blackwell.

Burtless, Gary, and Christopher Jencks. 2003. "American Inequality and Its Consequences." Luxembourg Income Study Working Paper Series, working paper 339. Syracuse, N.Y.: Syracuse University, Maxwell School of Citizenship and Public Affairs.

Campbell, John L., and Michael Patrick Allen. 2001. "Identifying Shifts in Policy Regimes: Cluster and Interrupted Time-Series Analyses of U.S. Income Taxes." *Social Science History* 25 (Summer): 187–216.

Chevan, Albert, and Randall Stokes. 2000. "Growth in Family Income Inequality, 1979–1990: Industrial Restructuring and Demographic Change." *Demography* 36 (August): 365–80.

Conley, Dalton. 1999. *Being Black, Living in the Red: Race, Wealth, and Social Policy in America.* Berkeley: University of California Press.

———. 2001. "Capital for College: Parental Assets and Postsecondary Schooling." *Sociology of Education* 74 (January): 59–72.

Costa, Dora. 1999. "American Living Standards: Evidence from Recreational Expenditures." Working paper 7148. Cambridge, Mass.: National Bureau of Economic Research.

———. 2000. "The Wage and the Length of the Workday." *Journal of Labor Economics* 18 (January): 156–68.

———. 2001. *The Evolution of Retirement.* Chicago: University of Chicago Press.

Cox, W. Michael, and Richard Alm. 1997. "Time Well Spent: The Declining Real Cost of Living in America." Annual Report of the Federal Reserve Bank of Dallas. Dallas: Federal Reserve.

————. 1999. *Myths of Rich and Poor: Why We're Better Off Than We Think.* New York: Basic Books.

Cutler, David M., and Lawrence F. Katz. 1992. "Rising Inequality? Changes in the Distribution of Income and Consumption in the 1980s." *American Economic Review* 82(May): 546–51.

Danziger, Sheldon, and Peter Gottschalk, eds. 1994. *Uneven Tides: Rising Inequality in America.* New York: Russell Sage Foundation.

————. 1995. *America Unequal.* Cambridge, Mass.: Harvard University Press.

Davies, James B., and Anthony F. Shorroks. 2000. "The Distribution of Wealth." In *Handbook of Income Distribution*, vol. 1, edited by Anthony B. Atkinson and Francois Bourguignon. New York: Elsevier.

DeNavas, Carmen, and Robert I. Cleveland. 2001. "Money Income in the United States: 2000." *Current Population Reports* P60-213 (September). Washington: U.S. Bureau of the Census.

DiPrete, Thomas A., and Claudia Buchmann. 2006. "Gender-Specific Trends in the Value of Education and the Emerging Gender Gap in College Completion." *Demography* 43(February): 1–24.

Douglas, Mary, and Baron Isherwood. 1996. *The World of Goods: Towards an Anthropology of Consumption.* London: Routledge. (Orig. pub. in 1979.)

Edin, Kathryn, and Laura Lein. 1997. *Making Ends Meet: How Single Mothers Survive Welfare and Low-Wage Work.* New York: Russell Sage Foundation.

Federman, Maya, Thesia I. Garner, Kathleen Short, W. Bowman Cutter IV, John Kiely, David Levine, Duane McDough, and Marilyn McMillen. 1996. "What Does It Mean to Be Poor in America?" *Monthly Labor Review* 119(May): 3–17.

Fischer, Claude S. 1992. *America Calling: A Social History of the Telephone to 1940.* Berkeley: University of California Press.

Fischer, Claude S., Michael Hout, Martin Sanchez Jankowski, Samuel R. Lucas, Ann Swidler, and Kim Voss. 1996. *Inequality by Design: Cracking the Bell Curve Myth.* Princeton, N.J.: Princeton University Press.

Fligstein, Neil. 2001. *The Architecture of Markets: An Economic Sociology of Twenty-first-Century Capitalist Societies.* Princeton, N.J.: Princeton University Press.

Frank, Robert H. 1999. *Luxury Fever: Why Money Fails to Satisfy in an Era of Excess.* New York: Free Press.

Goldin, Claudia, and Lawrence F. Katz. 1999. "The Returns to Skill in the United States Across the Twentieth Century." Working paper 7126. Cambridge, Mass.: National Bureau of Economic Research.

————. 2000. "Education and Income in the Early Twentieth Century: Evidence from the Prairies." *Journal of Economic History* 60(September): 782–819.

————. 2001. "Decreasing (and Then Increasing) Inequality in America: A Tale of Two Half-Centuries." In *The Causes and Consequences of Increasing Inequality*, edited by Finish Welch. Chicago: University of Chicago Press.

Goldstein, Joshua R., and John Robert Warren. 2000. "Socioeconomic Reach and Heterogeneity in the Extended Family: Contours and Consequences." *Social Science Research* 29(September): 382–402.

Gottschalk, Peter, and Timothy M. Smeeding. 2000. "Empirical Evidence on Income Inequality in Industrialized Countries." In *Handbook of Income Distribution*, vol. 1, edited by Anthony B. Atkinson and Francois Bourguignon. New York: Elsevier.

Hagan, John, and Ruth D. Peterson, eds. 1995. *Crime and Inequality*. Palo Alto, Calif.: Stanford University Press.

Hagerty, Michael. 2000. "Social Comparisons of Income in One's Community: Evidence from National Surveys of Income and Happiness." *Journal of Personality and Social Psychology* 78(April): 764–71.

Handlin, Oscar, and Lillian Handlin, eds. 1997. *From the Outer World*. Cambridge, Mass.: Harvard University Press.

Harper, Miles D., and Darrell Steffensmeier. 1992. "The Differing Effects of Economic Inequality and Black and White Rates of Violence." *Social Forces* 70(June): 1035–54.

Harris, Ed, and John Sabelhaus. 2000. "Consumer Expenditure Survey Family-Level Extracts—1980:1, 1998:2 (computer files). Washington: Congressional Budget Office.

Hochschild, Arlie. 1989. *The Second Shift*. New York: Viking.

———. 1997. *The Time Bind*. New York: Metropolitan.

Hout, Michael, Richard Arum, and Kim Voss. 1996. "The Political Economy of Inequality in the Age of Extremes." *Demography* 33(November): 421–25.

Jacobs, Eva, and Stephanie Shipp. 1990. "How Family Spending Has Changed in the United States." *Monthly Labor Review* 113(March): 20–27.

Jencks, Christopher, and Susan E. Mayer. 1996. "Do Official Poverty Rates Provide Useful Information About Trends in Children's Economic Welfare?" Unpublished paper. Northwestern University, Center for Urban Affairs (May 30).

Johnson, David S., Timothy M. Smeeding, and Barbara Boyle Torrey. 2004. "United States Inequality Through the Prisms of Income and Consumption." Paper presented to the conference "The Link Between Income and Consumption Inequality." Madrid, Spain (March 26–27).

Jorgenson, Dale W. 1998. "Did We Lose the War on Poverty?" *Journal of Economic Perspectives* 12(Winter): 79–96.

Kalmijn, Matthijs. 1991. "Shifting Boundaries: Trends in Religious and Educational Homogamy." *American Sociological Review* 56(December): 786–800.

———. 1998. "Intermarriage and Homogamy: Causes, Patterns, Trends." *Annual Review of Sociology* 24: 395–421.

Kane, Thomas J. 2004. "College-Going and Inequality." In *Social Inequality*, edited by Kathryn M. Neckerman. New York: Russell Sage Foundation.

Karoly, Lynn A., and Gary Burtless. 1995. "Demographic Change, Rising Earnings Inequality, and the Distribution of Well-being, 1959–1989." *Demography* 32 (August): 479–505.

Keister, Lisa A. 2000. *Wealth in America: Trends in Wealth Inequality*. New York: Cambridge University Press.

Keister, Lisa A., and Stephanie Moller. 2000. "Wealth Inequality in the United States." *Annual Review of Sociology* 26: 63–81.

Kelley, Jonathan, and M. D. R. Evans. 1993. "The Legitimation of Inequality: Occupational Earnings in Nine Nations." *American Journal of Sociology* 99 (July): 75–125.

Kenworthy, Lane. 1999. "Do Social-Welfare Policies Reduce Poverty? A Cross-National Assessment." *Social Forces* 77 (March): 1119–39.

———. 2004. *Egalitarian Capitalism*. New York: Russell Sage Foundation.

Kim, Sukkoo. 1998. "Economic Integration and Convergence: U.S. Regions, 1840–1987." *Journal of Economic History* 58(3): 659–83.

Krueger, Dirk, and Fabrizio Perri. 2002. "Does Income Inequality Lead to Consumption Inequality? Evidence and Theory." Working paper 9202. Cambridge, Mass.: National Bureau of Economic Research. Available at: http://www.nber.org/papers/w9202.

Ladd, Everett, and Karlyn H. Bowman. 1998. *Attitudes Toward Economic Inequality*. Washington, D.C.: American Enterprise Institute Press.

Lebergott, Stanley. 1971. "Changes in Unemployment 1800–1960." In *The Reinterpretation of American Economic History*, edited by Robert W. Fogel and Stanley L. Engerman. New York: Harper & Row.

———. 1976. *The American Economy: Income, Wealth, and Want*. Princeton, N.J.: Princeton University Press.

———. 1996. *Consumer Expenditures: New Measures and Old Motives*. Princeton, N.J.: Princeton University Press.

Ludwig, Jack. 2003. "Is America Divided into Haves and Have Nots?" The Gallup Poll. Available at: http://www.gallup.com (accessed September 8, 2004).

Luria, Daniel D. 1976. "Wealth, Capital, and Power." The Social Meaning of Homeownership." *Journal of Interdisciplinary History* 7(Autumn): 261–82.

McCracken, Grant. 1990. *Culture and Consumption*. Bloomington: Indiana University Press.

Muller, Edward N. 1998. "Democracy, Economic Development, and Income Inequality." *American Sociological Review* 53 (February): 50–68.

Neckerman, Kathryn M., ed. 2004. *Social Inequality*. New York: Russell Sage Foundation.

Piketty, Thomas, and Emmanual Saez. 2001. "Income Inequality in the United States, 1913–1998." Working paper 8467. Cambridge, Mass.: National Bureau of Economic Research (September).

Rabin, Jonathan. 1991. *Hunting Mister Heartbreak*. New York: Burlingame Books.

Rahn, Wendy M., and Thomas J. Rudolph. 2005. "A Tale of Political Trust in American

Cities." *Public Opinion Quarterly* 69(Winter): 508–29.

Scholz, John Karl, and Kara Levine. 2004. "U.S. Black-White Wealth Inequality." In *Social Inequality*, edited by Kathryn Neckerman. New York: Russell Sage Foundation.

Schwartz, Christine R., and Robert D. Mare. 2005. "Trends in Educational Assortative Marriage from 1940 to 2003." *Demography* 42(November): 621–46.

Simmons, James C. 2000. *Star-Spangled Eden.* New York: Carroll & Graf.

Slesnick, Daniel T. 1994. "Consumption, Needs, and Inequality." *International Economic Review* 35(August): 677–703.

———. 2001. *Consumption and Social Welfare: Living Standards and Their Distribution in the United States.* New York: Cambridge University Press.

Smeeding, Timothy M., and Lee Rainwater. 2001. "Comparing Living Standards Across Nations: Real Incomes at the Top, the Bottom, and the Middle." Working paper 266. Luxembourg: Luxembourg Income Study.

Smith, Tom W. 1990a. "Classifying Protestant Denominations." *Review of Religious Research* 31(March): 225–45.

———. 1990b. "Social Inequality in Cross-National Perspective." In *Attitudes to Inequality and the Role of Government*, edited by Duane F. Alwin et al. Rijswijk: Sociaal en Cultureel Planbureua; Samsom, Neth.: Alphen aan des Rijn.

Spilerman, Seymour. 2000. "Wealth and Stratification Processes." *Annual Review of Sociology* 26:497–24.

Thernstrom, Stephan. 1973. *The Other Bostonians: Poverty and Progress in the American Metropolis, 1880–1970.* Cambridge, Mass.: Harvard University Press.

Tobey, Ronald C., Charles Wetherell, and Jay Brigham. 1990. "Moving Out and Settling In: Residential Mobility, Home Owning, and the Public Enframing of Citizenship, 1921–1950." *American Historical Review* 95(December): 1395–1423.

United States Bureau of the Census. 1959. *Occupational Trends, 1900–1950.* Washington: U.S. Government Printing Office.

———. 1977. *Historical Statistics of the United States, 1790–1970.* Washington: U.S. Government Printing Office.

———. 1999. "Money Income in the United States, 1998." *Current Population Reports*, series P60–206. Washington: U.S. Bureau of the Census. Available at: http://www.census.gov/prod/99pubs/p60-206.pdf.

———. 2001a. *Annual Housing Survey, 1999: National Microdata* (computer file). Washington: U.S. Department of Commerce, Bureau of the Census. Distributed by Inter-University Consortium for Political and Social Research, Ann Arbor, Mich.

———. 2001b. *Statistical Abstract of the United States, 2000* (CD-ROM). Washington: U.S. Government Printing Office.

———. 2001c. *Mapping Census 2000: The Geography of U.S. Diversity.* Washington: U.S. Government Printing Office.

———. 2002. *Supplemental Survey Data Report,* "2002." Available at: http://www.census.gov/acs/www/Downloads/ACS/Paper41.pdf.

———. 2003. *Statistical Abstract of the United States, 2002* (CD-ROM). Washington: U.S. Government Printing Office.

———. 2004a. *Statistical Abstract of the United States, 2003* (CD-ROM). Washington: U.S. Government Printing Office.

———. 2004b. "Historical Income Tables—Households." Available at: http://www.census.gov/hhes/income/histinc/h02.html (last revised July 8, 2004).

———. 2004c. "Population by Race and Hispanic or Latino Origin." Available at: http://www.census.gov/population/www/cen2000/phc-t1.html (last revised September 29, 2004).

———. 2005a. *Income, Poverty, and Health Insurance Coverage in the United States, 2003.* Washington: U.S. Government Printing Office.

———. 2005b. "Geographical Mobility / Migration." Available at: http://www.census.gov/population/www/socdemo/migrate.html (last revised June 22, 2005; accessed January 9, 2006).

———. 2005c. "Historical Income Tables—Income Inequality," table IE-6. Available at: http://www.census.gov/hhes/www/income/histinc/ie6.html (last revised May 13, 2005; accessed 2001).

———. 2005d. "Families and Living Arrangements." Table HH-4, Households by Size: 1960 to Present. Available at: http://www.census.gov/population/socdemo/hh-fam/hh4.pdf (release date June 29, 2005).

———. N.d. "State and County QuickFacts: Metropolitan Statistical Area," available at: http://quickfacts.census.gov/qfd/meta/long_metro.htm.

———. N.d. "Population and Ranking Tables of the Older Population; Table 6, Counties Ranked." Available at: http://www.census.gov/population/cen2000/phc-t13/tab06.pdf (accessed May 25, 2006).

Verba, Sidney, and Gary R. Orren. 1985. *Equality in America: The View from the Top.* Cambridge, Mass.: Harvard University Press.

Western, Bruce, and Becky Pettit. 2002. "Beyond Crime and Punishment: Prisons and Inequality." *Contexts* 1(Fall): 37–43.

Williams, David R., and Chiquita Collins. 1995. "U.S. Socioeconomic and Racial Differences in Health: Patterns and Explanations." *Annual Review of Sociology* 21: 349–86.

Williamson, Joel. 1995. *The New People: Miscegenation and Mulattoes in the United States.* Baton Rouge: Louisiana State University Press. (Orig. pub. in 1980.)

Wolff, Edward N. 2000. "Recent Trends in Wealth Ownership, 1983–1998." Working paper 300. Annandale-on-Hudson, N.Y.: Bard College, Jerome Levy Economics Institute.

———. 2001. "Racial Wealth Disparities: Is the Gap Closing?" Public Policy Brief 66. Annandale-on-Hudson, N.Y.: Bard College, Jerome Levy Economics Institute.

————. 2003. "Inheritances and Wealth Inequality, 1989–1998." *American Economic Review* 92 (May): 260–64.

Wolff, Edward N., Ajit Zacharias, and Asena Caner. 2003. "Household Wealth, Public Consumption, and Economic Well-being in the United States." Working paper 386. Annandale-on-Hudson, N.Y.: Bard College, Jerome Levy Economics Institute.

Woodward, C. Vann. 1991. *The Old World's New World*. New York: Oxford University Press.

You, Jong-Sung, and Sanjeev Khagram. 2005. "A Comparative Study of Inequality and Corruption." *American Sociological Review* 70 (February): 136–57.

The Evolution of Top Incomes: A Historical and International Perspective*

THOMAS PIKETTY AND EMMANUEL SAEZ

This paper summarizes the main findings and perspectives emerging from a collective research project on the dynamics of income and wealth distribution. The primary objective of this project is to construct a high-quality, long-run, international database on income and wealth concentration, using historical tax statistics. ★ ★ ★

★ ★ ★

II. TOP INCOME SHARES RESULTS

Figure 1, panel A, presents the income share of the top decile in the United States from 1917 to 2002. The overall pattern of the top decile share over the century is U-shaped. The share of the top decile fluctuates around 40 to 45 percent during the interwar period. It declines substantially to just above

---

* First published in 2006; from *American Economic Association Papers and Proceedings*, Volume 96, Number 2.

FIGURE 1 **TOP INCOME SHARES IN THE UNITED STATES, 1913–2002**

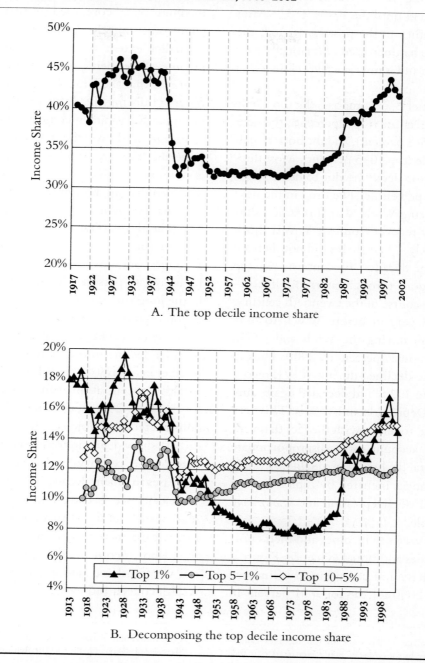

A. The top decile income share

B. Decomposing the top decile income share

NOTE: Income is defined as market income, excluding government transfers and realized capital gains.
SOURCES: Piketty and Saez (2003) and Atkinson and Piketty (2006).

30 percent during World War II and stays flat at 31 to 32 percent until the 1970s. ★ ★ ★ After decades of stability in the postwar period, the top decile share has increased dramatically over the last 25 years and is now at a level close to the pre-war level.

Figure 1, panel B, decomposes the top decile into the top percentile (top 1 percent), the next 4 percent (top 5–1 percent), and the bottom half of the top decile (top 10–5 percent). Most fluctuations of the top decile are due to fluctuations within the top percentile. The drop in the next two groups during World War II is far less dramatic and they recover from the WWII shock relatively quickly. Their shares did not increase much in recent decades. In contrast, the top percentile has gone through enormous fluctuations along the course of the twentieth century, from about 18 percent before WWI, to only about 8 percent during the 1960s and 1970s, and back to almost 17 percent by 2000. The top percentile share declined during WWI, recovered during the 1920s and declined again during the Great Depression and WWII. This very specific timing, together with the fact that very high incomes account for a disproportionate share of the total decline in inequality, strongly suggests the shocks incurred by capital owners from 1914 to 1945 (Depression and wars) have played a key role.[1]

Looking at very top incomes and their composition provides additional evidence. Figure 2 displays the share and composition of income from 1916 to 2000 for the top 0.01 percent in the United States. Until the 1970s, very top incomes were composed primarily of capital income (mostly dividend income) and to a smaller extent business income, the wage income share being very modest. Figure 2 confirms that the large decline of top incomes observed during the 1914–1960 period is predominantly a capital income phenomenon.

Figure 2 shows the income composition pattern at the very top has changed considerably between 1960 and 2000. Salary income has been driving up top incomes and has now become the main source of income at the very top. The dramatic evolution of the composition of top incomes seems robust. National accounts data show the share of capital income in aggregate personal income has been stable in the long run. Therefore, the secular decline of top capital incomes is the consequence of a decreased concentration of capital income and not of a decline in the share of capital income in the economy as a whole. Estimates of wealth concentration from estate tax returns for the 1916–2000 period in the United States, constructed by Wojciech Kopczuk and Saez (2004) show a precipitous decline in the first part of the century with only very modest increases in recent decades (Figure 4, panel B). This evidence is consistent with the income share series and shows that the dramatic recent increase in income concentration is primarily a labor income phenomenon, and this has not yet translated into a dramatic increase in wealth concentration.

---

[1] The negative effect of the wars on top incomes can be explained, in part, by the large tax increases enacted to finance the wars. During both wars, the corporate income tax (as well as the individual income tax) was drastically increased and this reduced, mechanically, the distributions to stockholders.

FIGURE 2 **THE TOP-0.1-PERCENT INCOME SHARE AND COMPOSITION IN THE UNITED STATES, 1916–2000**

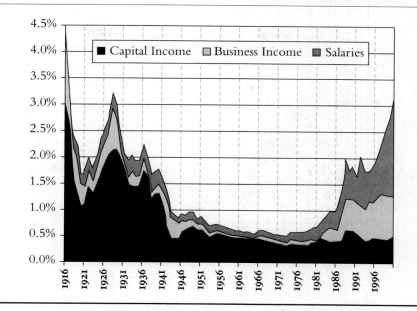

NOTE: The figure displays the top-0.1-percent income share (top curve) and its composition (excluding capital gains).

SOURCE: Piketty and Saez (2003).

The dramatic decline in top-income shares in the first part of the twentieth century took place in almost all countries that have been studied. Figure 3, panel A, displays the top-0.1-percent income share in three English-speaking countries: the United States, United Kingdom, and Canada. Panel B displays the top 0.1 percent for France and Japan. All countries experience a sharp drop in the first part of the century. The timing and size of the decline varies across countries. For example, the decline in Japan is entirely concentrated in the immediate prewar and war years. As in the United States, income composition series for each of those countries shows that this decrease is primarily a capital

income phenomenon due to the fall of top capital incomes.

Figure 3 shows a sharp contrast between English-speaking countries and others in recent decades. The United States, United Kingdom, and Canada display a substantial increase in the top-0.1-percent income share over the last 25 years. This increase is largest in the United States, but the timing is remarkably similar across the three countries. In contrast, France and Japan do not experience any noticeable increase in the top-0.1-percent income share. As a result, income concentration is much lower in those countries than in the English-speaking countries.

FIGURE 3 **TOP-0.1-PERCENT INCOME SHARES ACROSS COUNTRIES**

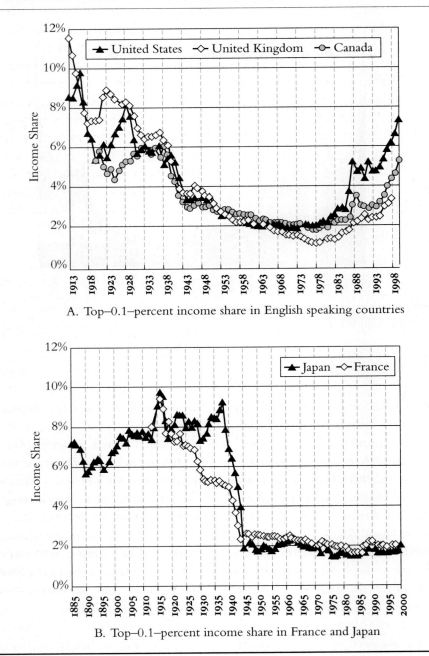

A. Top–0.1–percent income share in English speaking countries

B. Top–0.1–percent income share in France and Japan

SOURCES: United States, Piketty and Saez (2003); United Kingdom, Atkinson (2006); Canada, Saez and Veall (2005); France, Piketty (2003); Japan, Moriguchi and Saez (2005).

III. EXPLAINING THE RESULTS AND FUTURE RESEARCH

The fact that the drop in income concentration in the first part of the twentieth century is primarily due to the fall in top capital incomes, and that the fall took place mostly during wartime and the Great Depression in most of those countries, suggests an obvious explanation. For the most part, income inequality dropped because capital owners incurred severe shocks to their capital holdings during the 1914 to 1945 period such as destruction, inflation, bankruptcies, and fiscal shocks for financing the wars. This interpretation is confirmed by available wealth and estate data for countries such as France, the United States, and Japan. Note that the idea that capital owners incurred large shocks during the 1914–1945 period and that this had a big impact on income distribution is certainly not new (Kuznets, 1953). What is new is there is not much else going on.

The more challenging part needing explanation is the nonrecovery of top capital incomes during the post-1945 period. The proposed explanation is that the 1914 to 1945 capital shocks had a permanent impact because the introduction of progressive income and estate taxation (there was virtually no tax progressivity prior to 1914 and top rates increased enormously between 1914 and 1945) made it impossible for top capital holders to recover fully. Simple simulations suggest the long-run impact of tax progressivity on wealth concen-

tration is large enough to explain the magnitude of the observed changes (Piketty, 2003).

Those explanations about the dynamics of capital income concentration could possibly be tested by looking at the case of countries that either did not experience large pre-1945 shocks and/or did not implement significant and sustained progressive income tax systems. Switzerland stayed out of the wars and never implemented very progressive wealth or income taxation. As displayed in Figure 4, in contrast to other countries such as the United States, top wealth shares in Switzerland hardly declined from 1913 to the 1960s.

It would be interesting to consider (a) countries that avoided the war or Depression shocks but developed progressive taxation, such as Ireland and Sweden; and (b) countries that experienced the shocks but did not develop progressive taxation. No European country falls clearly into this latter category.[2] Atkinson and Piketty (2006) show that there was no significant drop in top income shares in Ireland during World War II, and top income shares were quite similar in the early 1920s and the late 1940s. Top income shares did fall significantly in the postwar decades, however, when Ireland implemented progressive taxation with very high top rates. Those results suggest the large war shocks may not be necessary to drive down top income shares, and the change in the tax structure might be the most important determinant of long-run income concentration. In future work, it should be possible to develop

---

2 Japan and Germany experienced a dramatic decline in income concentration during WWII. Top income shares did not recover at all in Japan (Moriguchi and Saez, 2005) but did so to some extent in Germany (Atkinson and Piketty, 2006). A systematic comparison of tax systems in Japan and Germany in the postwar period could thus be informative.

FIGURE 4 **TOP-1-PERCENT WEALTH SHARE IN SWITZERLAND AND THE UNITED STATES**

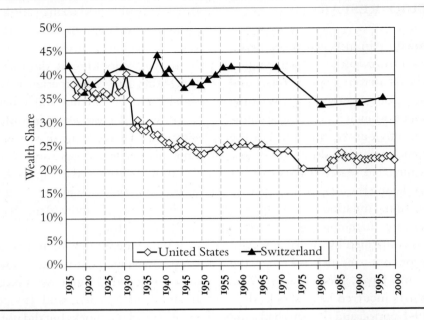

SOURCES: United States, Kopczuk and Saez (2004); Switzerland, Atkinson and Piketty (2006).

precise series of tax burdens by income fractiles and income sources for each country and use regression analysis to provide more convincing tests of those explanations. Other factors, such as fertility or the norms about estate division between heirs, could also have significant impacts on long-run wealth distribution.

During the post-1970 period, one observes a major divergence between rich countries. While top income shares have remained fairly stable in continental European countries or Japan over the past three decades, they have increased enormously in the United States and other English-speaking countries. This rise of top income shares is due not to the revival of top capital incomes, but rather to the very large increases in top wages (especially top executive

compensation). As a consequence, top executives (the "working rich") replaced top capital owners (the "rentiers") at the top of the income hierarchy during the twentieth century. Understanding why top wages have surged in English-speaking countries in recent decades, but not in continental Europe or Japan, remains a controversial question, with three broad views. First, the free market view claims that technological progress has made managerial skills more general and less firm-specific, increasing competition for the best executives from segregated within-firm markets to a single economywide market. While this view can account for U.S. trends, it cannot explain why executive pay has not changed in other countries such as Japan and France, which have gone through similar technological changes. A second view claims impediments to free markets due to labor market regulations, unions, or social norms regarding pay inequality can keep executive pay below market. Such impediments have been largely removed in the United States, but still exist in Europe and Japan. Under this view, the surge in executive compensation actually represents valuable efficiency gains. Finally, a third view claims the surge in top compensation in the United States is due to the increased ability of executives to set their own pay and extract rents at the expense of shareholders, perhaps for the same reasons as under the second view. In this case, however, there might not be any associated efficiency gains.

The relationship one might want to test, ultimately using our database, is the impact of inequality on growth. Casual examination of the series constructed suggests income concentration and growth are not systematically related. Many countries (such as France, the United States, and Japan) grew fastest in the postwar decades when income concentration was at its lowest. Thus, one can safely conclude that the enormous decline in wealth concentration that took place between 1914 and 1945 did not prevent high growth from occurring. It seems that in recent decades, however, growth and increases in inequality have been positively correlated: the United States and the United Kingdom have grown faster than continental Europe and Japan. Although cross-country analysis will always suffer from severe identifi-

cation problems, our hope is that the database will renew the analysis of the interplay between inequality and growth.

‖ REFERENCES

Atkinson, Anthony and Piketty, Thomas. *Top incomes over the twentieth century.* Oxford: Oxford University Press, 2006.

Kopczuk, Wojciech and Saez, Emmanuel. "Top Wealth Shares in the United States, 1916–2000: Evidence from Estate Tax Returns." *National Tax Journal*, 2004, *57*(2), pp. 445–87.

Kuznets, Simon. *Shares of upper income groups in income and savings.* New York: National Bureau of Economic Research, 1953.

Moriguchi, Chiaki and Saez, Emmanual. "The Evolution of Income Concentration in Japan, 1885–2002," Unpublished Paper, 2005.

Piketty, Thomas. "Income Inequality in France, 1901–1998." *Journal of Political Economy*, 2003, *111*(5), pp. 1004–42.

Piketty, Thomas and Saez, Emmanuel. "Income Inequality in the United States, 1913–1998." *Quartery Journal of Economics*, 2003, *118*(1), pp. 1–39.

Saez, Emmanuel and Veall, Michael R. "The Evolution of High Incomes in Northern America: Lessons from Canadian Evidence." *American Economic Review*, 2005, *95*(3), pp. 831–49.

12

Inequality of Wage Rates, Earnings and Family Income in the United States, 1975–2002★

PETER GOTTSCHALK AND SHELDON DANZIGER

||| I. INTRODUCTION

This paper reviews evidence on changes in inequality of four distinct income concepts: individual wage rates, individual annual earnings, family annual earnings, and family income adjusted for family size. The first two income concepts are the primary focus of labor economists. Changes in the distribution of wage rates reflect changes in labor supply and labor demand and changes in labor market institutions, including changes in government policies. Labor economists have spent considerable effort documenting increased inequality in male wage rates and the reasons for these changes, including the importance of technological changes, changes in foreign competition, changes in wage-setting institutions, such as labor unions, and changes in governmental regulations, such as the minimum wage. While there is still considerable uncertainty about the causes of these changes, there is broad consensus that wage rate inequality is considerably higher at the start of the

---

★ First published in 1965; from *Review of Income and Wealth*, Volume 51, Issue 2.

FIGURE 1 **INEQUALITY OF ADJUSTED FAMILY INCOME AND INEQUALITY OF MALE HOURLY WAGE RATES, 1975–2002 (1975 = 1.0)**

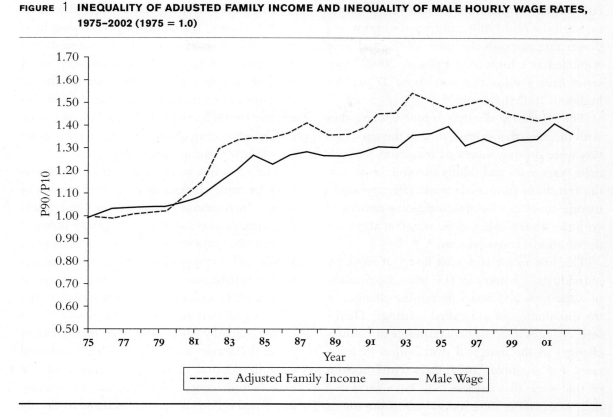

21st century than it was a quarter of a century earlier. In fact, increases in wage rate and annual earnings inequality occurred primarily in the early 1980s, and were not reversed by a prolonged economic recovery during the 1990s.

Whereas changes in wage rate inequality have been the primary focus of studies by labor economists, changes in family income inequality have been the primary focus of studies by public policy analysts interested in changes in the distribution of well-being and changes in poverty.[1] Again, there is broad consensus about the facts. Family income inequality increased

dramatically during the last quarter of the 21st century. This reflects sharp increases during the late 1970s and early 1980s that were not offset by declines during the long expansion of the 1990s.

Figure 1 shows inequality of hourly wage rates for male workers between the ages of 22 and 62 and inequality of family income (adjusted for family size) for all persons living in families with a head of household in the same age range over the period 1975–2002. While the exact timing of changes differs slightly, both follow remarkably similar patterns. Male wage

1 For example, see Danziger and Gottschalk (1995) and Burtless and Jencks (2003).

rate and family income inequality rose sharply through the mid 1980s, continued to grow at a slower rate through the early 1990s, and then stabilized at a high level through 2002. Both series have a value that was about 37 percent higher in 2002 than in 1975.

The similarity in these trends is consistent with the view that at least some of the same factors were driving increased inequality of both male wage rates and family income. However, the transition from male wage rates to family income involves a set of factors, some associated with the labor market, some not, that also have distributional consequences. ★ ★ ★

The first factor is annual hours of work by individuals. Changes in the joint distribution of wage rates and hours determine changes in the distribution of individual earnings. Therefore, changes in hours may reinforce or counter changes in the marginal distribution of wage rates. For example, individuals at the bottom of the wage distribution may have increased their hours more than individuals at the top of the wage distribution. If this were the case, it would imply that increased inequality of wage rates would be larger than increases in the dispersion of individual earnings.

The second link is from the distribution of individual earnings to the distribution of family earnings. Even if inequality in the distribution of individual earnings increases, family earnings inequality might not rise, because family earnings depend on the joint distribution of earnings of all persons in the family. For example, if the wage rates or hours of work of wives increased the most in families headed by males with low earnings, then family earnings inequality would increase less than inequality of male earnings.

This same reasoning can be applied to non-earned income. If changes in government benefits, such as welfare or other income-tested programs, led to a disproportionately small increase in non-earned income for families at the bottom of the family earnings distribution relative to the increase for other families, then family income inequality would increase more than family earnings inequality.

The objective of this paper is to systematically examine changes in inequality of each of these distributions (wage rates, individual earnings, family earnings and family income) using a consistent set of definitions and samples. While other papers have examined changes in the distribution of each income concept, it is difficult to make comparisons across studies that use different measures or samples.

We start by discussing the measurement issues that guide our analyses. This is followed by a description of changes in inequality of each income source. We conclude by discussing whether the observed increase in family income inequality was largely driven by the widely-documented increase in inequality of male wage rates or whether there were offsetting changes in hours worked by different family members or changes in the distribution of other income sources.

2. MEASUREMENT ISSUES

We use the annual March Current Population Surveys (CPS) from 1976 to 2003 to analyze changes in the levels and distributions of individual wage rates and annual earnings, family earnings and family income adjusted for family size. The availability of yearly data allows us to examine cyclical as well as secular changes. CPS person weights are used throughout.

Our primary sample includes all individuals (except those in the armed forces and those living in group quarters) between the ages of 22 and 62, who had positive weeks of work and positive wage and salary earnings in the calendar year prior to the March interview. ★ ★ ★

3. DISTRIBUTION OF INDIVIDUAL WAGE RATES

Change in Mean Wage Rate

Before turning to changes in inequality in the distribution of wage rates, we describe changes in the mean of the distribution. Figure 2 shows mean hourly wages in constant 1999 dollars for male and female workers between the ages of 22 and 62 in each year between 1975 and 2002. For men, the recovery of the 1990s represents a break in the experience of the prior two decades. While male wages increased by 3 percent between 1983 and 1989, those gains were lost during the recession of the early 1990s. The mean hourly wage (in constant 1999 dollars) was virtually the same in 1993 as it had been in 1975 ($15.39 and $15.28, respectively). In contrast, between 1993 and 2002, the mean male wage grew by 14 percent to $17.51, the first sustained increase in nearly twenty years.

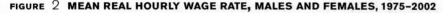

FIGURE 2 **MEAN REAL HOURLY WAGE RATE, MALES AND FEMALES, 1975–2002**

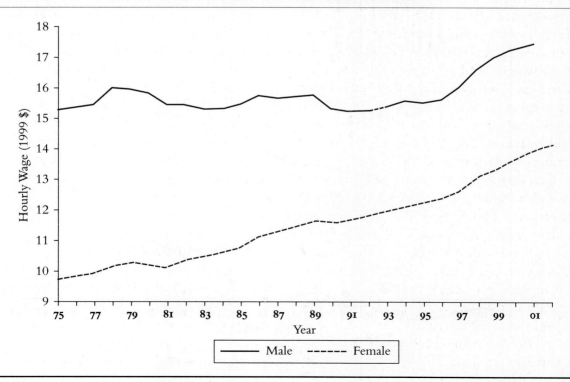

The trend in mean real wages of females over this quarter century is dramatically different from that of men. First, the overall growth rate is much more rapid. Whereas male wages were 15 percent higher in 2002 than they had been in 1975, female wages were 46 percent higher ($14.14 vs. $9.71). Second, while male wages stagnated for most of this period, female wages increased steadily. For example, female wages increased by 15 percent between 1979 and 1989 and by another 15 percent between 1989 and 1999.

Changes in Inequality of Wage Rates

These trends in mean wages mask different experiences across the distribution of workers.

Figure 3a plots the percentage change in real hourly wages between 1975 and 2002 for males and females at selected percentiles throughout the distribution. This figure shows increased wage inequality for both men and women—the lines slope upward to the right, indicating that percentage changes in wages were higher for workers at the top of the wage rate distribution than for those at the bottom of the distribution.

For men, the relationship between percentile rank and real earnings growth is nearly monotonic—the lower the rank, the smaller the increase (or the larger the decrease) in earnings. At the 10th percentile in 2002, male wages were 2 percent lower than for males at the 10th percentile a quarter century earlier ($6.68 vs.

FIGURE 3A PERCENTAGE CHANGE IN REAL HOURLY WAGES BY PERCENTILE, 1975–2002

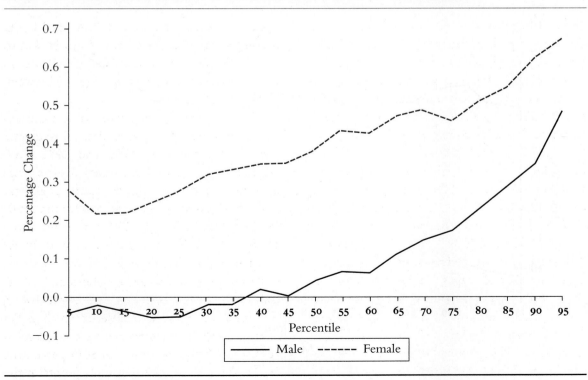

FIGURE 3B **PERCENTAGE CHANGE IN REAL HOURLY WAGES BY PERCENTILE, 1982–1989**

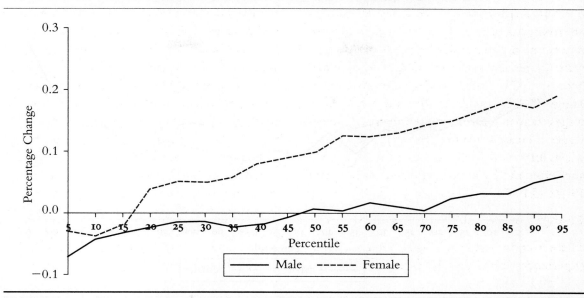

$6.83 in 1999$); the median male had wages that were 4 percent higher ($15.59 vs. $15.00). Real wages declined at every point on the distribution up to the 35th percentile. At the top of the distribution, males at the 95th percentile in 2002 had wages that were 47 percent higher than their counterparts in 1975 ($48.12 vs. $32.84). The increased wage inequality over this quarter century reflected an absolute, as well as a relative, decline at the lower end of the distribution. For male workers, the P90/P10 ratio of wage rates increased from 3.9 to 5.3 between 1975 and 2002.

For females, wage inequality also increased, even though real wages increased throughout the distribution. Growth was highest at the higher deciles and lowest at the lower deciles. For example, between 1975 and 2002, wages increased by 67 percent at the 95th percentile (from $20.22 to $33.67), by 38 percent at

the median (from $8.80 to $12.16), and by 22 percent at the 10th percentile (from $4.442 to $5.42). For female workers, the P90/P10 ratio of wage rates increased from 3.7 to 4.9 between 1975 and 2002.

Figures 3b and 3c show the same information as Figure 3a, but present data on wage rate changes for the 1982–1989 and 1993–2000 economic recoveries. Each figure depicts wage growth from the trough year to the peak year of the business cycle. The patterns for the 1990s recovery are strikingly different from those of the 1980s. First, the curves for both males and females in Figure 3c are above 9 percent at all points in the wage distribution. In contrast, wage increases in Figure 3b were only 5 percent at the 95th percentile of males in the 1980s recovery and were negative or close to zero for all workers up to the 80th percentile. For women, wages grew at most points in the

FIGURE 3C **PERCENTAGE CHANGE IN REAL HOURLY WAGES BY PERCENTILE, 1993–2000**

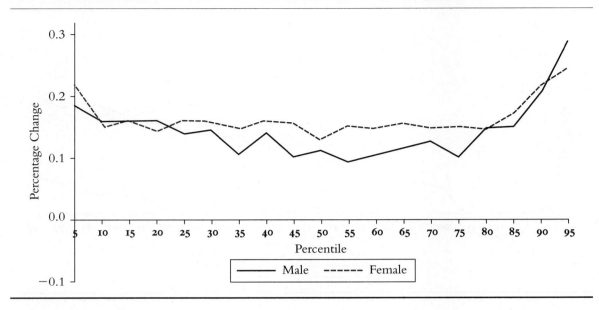

distribution during the 1980s recovery, but the rate of increase was much higher for the bottom half during the 1990s expansion.

There are also striking differences in the slopes of the two lines. The lines in Figure 3c are flatter than those in Figure 3b, indicating that wage growth was spread much more evenly throughout the distribution in the most recent economic boom than it was during the 1980s recovery. For females in the boom of the 1990s, wage growth was between 10 and 15 percent between the 10th and 80th percentile. For males during that recovery, wages rose most at the bottom and at the top of the distribution—by 22 percent at the 5th percentile, from $4.19 to $5.12, and by 27 percent at the 95th percentile, from $36.56 to $46.47. Wage growth was between 9 and 17 percent from the 10th through the 90th percentile.

To explore how recessions and recoveries differentially affect wage rate inequality, we show the time series for the P90/P10 ratios in Figure 4. To make the series for males and females comparable we index both to equal 1.00 in 1975. The ratio for men increased most rapidly during the recession of the early 1980s, rising from 4.1 in 1979 to 4.7 in 1983, but it did not decline during the subsequent recovery, remaining between 4.8 and 5.0 for the rest of the 1980s. The increase from 5.0 to 5.3 during the recession of the early 1990s does not differ much from the increase during the recovery of the 1980s, and part of this increase could be due to changes in the CPS procedures. There was a slight decline in the ratio during the later part of the recovery of the 1990s, but an increase to an historic peak at 5.5 as the economy went into recession in 2001.

FIGURE 4 **P90/P10 OF HOURLY WAGE RATES (1975 = 1.0)**

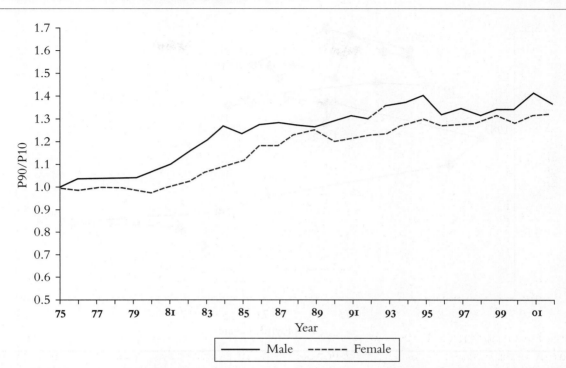

The P90/P10 series for women's hourly wage rate shows less cyclicality than the series for men, as the ratio increased steadily from 3.8 to 4.9 between 1975 and 2002. Most of the increased wage inequality occurred during the 1980s.

We distinguish between cyclical and secular changes in wage inequality by plotting the P90/Pl0 ratio of male wages against the employment rate for males over the age of 20 in Figure 5. During a recession, the economy contracts and the employment rate tends to fall, so a movement to the left indicates a recession; a movement to the right indicates a recovery. If wage inequality is affected by the business cycle, then decreases in employment rates will be accompa-nied by increased inequality, so the line would be upward sloping. Secular increases in wage inequality are reflected in upward shifts in the line, indicating that inequality is higher even when the employment rate remains constant.

Figure 5 highlights several cyclical changes and secular trends. From 1975 to 1979, the male employment rate increased from 74.8 to 76.5 percent (the high point during this quarter century) and the P90/P10 ratio increased from 3.9 to 4.1. This inequality increase does not reflect a cyclical change since it occurred during an expansion. The period from 1980 to 1983 was marked by two recessions. The employment rate fell by 5.1 points between 1979 and 1983

FIGURE 5 EMPLOYMENT RATE AND P90/P10 OF HOURLY WAGE RATE—MALES, 1975-2002

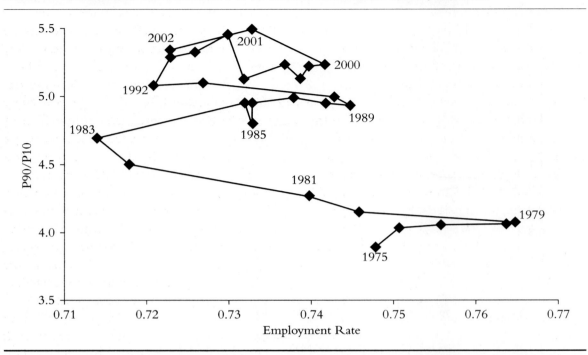

(the low point during this quarter century, 71.4 percent), and the P90/P10 reflects a cyclical increase of an additional 0.6 points to 4.7. The employment rate increased by 3.1 points during the 1983–1989 recovery, but was accompanied by another secular 0.2 point increase in the ratio to 4.9. The fact that wage inequality failed to decline during the expansion indicates that the large change in wage inequality during the early 1980s was not solely a cyclical change.

During the recession of the early 1990s, the employment rate fell again, but the P90/P10 ratio did not increase by much. There was a 0.3 point increase in wage inequality between 1992 and 1993, but this coincides with the change in CPS data collection methods. Thus, one cannot tell how much of this was due to economic changes compared to changes in measurement procedures. By the end of the 1990s expansion, the employment rate had increased back to about the same level as at the end of the 1980s expansion (74 percent). This expansion did not produce a significant decline in wage inequality (the ratio was 5.3 in 1993 and 5.2 in 2000), but lack of change was better than the increased inequality of the 1980s expansion.

Over the quarter century, about half of the increased male wage inequality occurred during the 1980s. Inequality increased most during the recession of the early 1980s, but did not decline in any subsequent expansion. We conclude that increases in wage rate inequality primarily reflect long-run secular changes in how labor markets operate, not cyclical fluctuations.

4. CHANGES IN BETWEEN-GROUP INEQUALITY

The increased wage inequality we have documented reflects changes in inequality both between groups of workers and within groups. To explore these differences, we estimated a set of standard log wage rate equations, where the independent variables include a set of education dummies (completed less than high school, some college, college, more than college), a quadratic in experience, a gender dummy, dummies for race and ethnicity and three regional dummies (Midwest, South and West). These regressions were estimated separately for each year from 1975 to 2002. (Results are available from the authors.)

From these regressions, we estimate gender and race differentials, holding education and experience constant, and we estimate returns to education and experience, holding other factors constant. Within-group inequality is the remaining variation in wage rates holding all factors constant and is measured by the standard deviation of the residuals.

As shown earlier, mean wage rates for females grew faster than those of males over the entire quarter century. As a result, the between-gender wage rate gap declined. This was partially due to increases in human capital of working women, reflected in their increased education and labor force experience, but it also reflects the increased relative wages of women, holding these characteristics constant. The coefficient on the female dummy variable shows that the gender wage gap closed steadily from 47 percent in 1975 to 27 percent in 1993.

This decline in the female/male wage rate differential halted after 1993, when real wages of men began to increase after almost 20 years of stagnation. As a result, the gender wage gap was about the same in 2002, 25 percent, as it had been at the start of the 1990s expansion.

Holding personal characteristics constant, there was little change in the black/white male and the black/white female wage differentials over the quarter century. The female gap by race had virtually closed by the mid-1970s, before increasing to 7 percent in 1993. It then fell during the 1990s recovery to 4 percent in 2002.

The black/white male wage gap is much greater than that for females in every year. It increased from 14 percent in 1975 to about 20 percent during the recession of the early 1980s; then fell to 13 percent in 1996 before rising to 15 percent in 2002. Over this quarter century there was no reduction in the racial wage gaps for men or for women.[2]

The increased wage inequality of the 1980s reflected a substantial increase in the returns to education and to a lesser degree an increase in the returns to experience among young college-educated males. Figure 6 shows the returns to a college degree relative to a high school degree

---

[2] While we can not compute hourly wage rates prior to 1975, Gottschalk (1997) reports that the black non-black gap in earnings for full-time workers declined by 2.1 percentage points per year from the mid-1960s to the mid-1970s. This is greater than the 0.4 points per year decline in the black white wage gap reported here. The difference is due, in part, to the greater cyclicality of black work hours relative to white hours. The black/non-black gap in full-time earnings declined from 40 percent in 1963 to less than 15 percent in 1975.

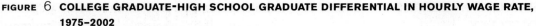

FIGURE 6 **COLLEGE GRADUATE-HIGH SCHOOL GRADUATE DIFFERENTIAL IN HOURLY WAGE RATE, 1975–2002**

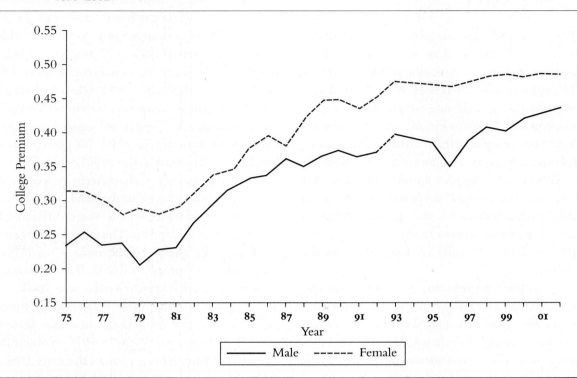

for male and female workers between the ages of 22 and 62. The college premium fell by a few percentage points between 1975 and 1979 for both men and women, before rising dramatically in the 1980s. Between 1979 and 1989 the mean wage rates of college graduates relative to high school graduates increased from 21 to 35 percent for males and from 29 to 45 percent for females. These premia rose, but at a slower rate through the end of the sample period, reaching 44 percent for males and 49 percent for females in 2002. Thus, one factor that accounted for a large portion of the rising inequality of the

1980s, the college premium, was exerting less upward pressure during the 1990s.

5. CHANGES IN WITHIN-GROUP INEQUALITY

Wage inequality increased during the 1980s, not only among those with different observable traits, such as gender, race, education and experience, but also within groups of workers with the same gender, race, education and experience. In terms of the regression framework, the growth in within-group inequality is reflected

FIGURE 7 RESIDUAL WAGE INEQUALITY: 90TH AND 10TH PERCENTILES IN HOURLY WAGES (1975 = 1.0)

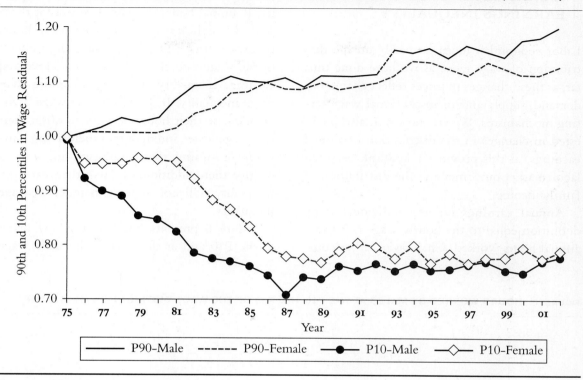

by a wider dispersion of the residuals. Figure 7 plots the P10 and P90 of residual hourly wages for males and females. Each is benchmarked to equal 1.00 in 1975, expressing changes relative to this baseline value.

The patterns are striking. For men and women at the bottom of the distribution, wage rates fell continuously from 1975 through the late-1980s, at which point a male at the 10th percentile had earnings roughly 30 percent lower than a similar worker at the 10th percentile in 1975; for women, the decline was about 25 percent. The P10 of the residuals then stabilized, remaining relatively constant for both men and women throughout the 1990s, with the value in 2002 about 20 percent lower than in 1975 for both genders.

In contrast, residual wages at the 90th percentile, increased from 1975 through the mid-1980s, at which time the P90 was roughly 10 percent higher for both males and females than in 1975. The relative positions of males and females then stabilized, rising only between 1992 and 1993, which coincides with the change in CPS procedures. This indicates that within-group inequality among people with the same characteristics stopped increasing until the end of the 1990s, when the P90 for males increased substantially from 1.15 to 1.20 between 1999 and 2002.

6. CHANGES IN INDIVIDUAL EARNINGS INEQUALITY

Labor economists focus primarily on the distribution of wage rates, as we have done thus far, as these changes in prices reflect changes in demand, supply and/or institutional wage setting mechanisms. We are, however, also interested in changes in the distribution of annual earnings, as this provides a key link between labor market outcomes and the distribution of family income.

Annual earnings for any individual is by definition equal to the hourly wage rate times annual hours worked. Changes in either component will affect annual earnings inequality. If annual hours increase the most for those with the highest wages, then changes in hours reinforce the inequality-increasing effects of the wage rate changes discussed above and earnings inequality will increase more than wage inequality. If, however, low wage earners increase their hours of work to offset their real wage losses and maintain their living standards (assuming that employers are willing to give them additional hours), then earnings inequality will not increase as much as wage inequality.

Figure 8 presents hours worked by males at the P10 and at the P90 of the male wage

FIGURE 8 **HOURS WORKED BY MALES AT THE P10 AND P90 OF THE WAGE DISTRIBUTION (1975 = 1.0)**

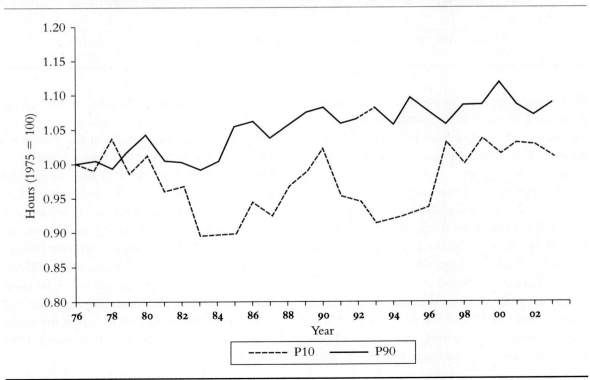

distribution. Hours are indexed to 1.00 in 1975. The increase in hours over the full period 1975 to 2002 for males at the top of the wage distribution was slightly larger than the increase in hours for males at the bottom of the wage distribution. While this secular change in hours would tend to make earnings inequality rise faster than wage inequality, the effect is likely to be small given the small change in hours.

There is, however, substantial cyclical change in the hours of males at the P10 of the wage distribution. Hours for these males fell by 10 percent between 1975 and 1983. This ground was made up during the expansion of the 1980s. The recession of the early 1990s again reduced the hours of low wage males by roughly 10 per-

cent. This decline was more than offset by the increase in hours during the sustained expansion during the rest of the 1990s. In contrast, the hours of males at the 90th percentile show little cyclical change. These patterns in hours show that earnings inequality is more cyclically sensitive than wage inequality.

This is confirmed in Figure 9 which shows the P90/P10 for male wage rates and male annual earnings. Inequality of male wage rates and male earnings both increased by 37 percent between 1975 and 2002 so secular changes in hours, which affect earnings inequality, had little impact. Figure 9 confirms that the decline in hours of males at the P10 during recessions and the increase in hours during expansions

FIGURE 9 P90/P10 OF ANNUAL EARNINGS AND HOURLY WAGE FOR MALES (1975 = 1.0)

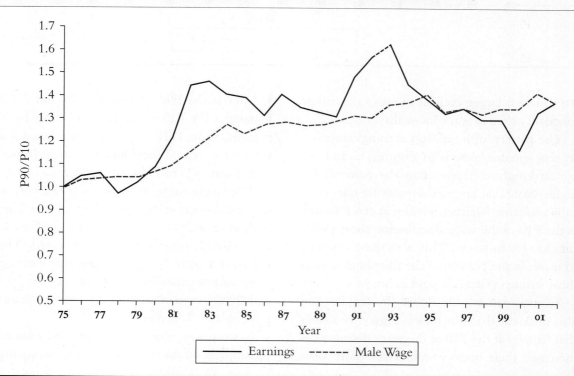

FIGURE 10 **HOURS WORKED BY FEMALES AT THE P10 AND P90 OF THE WAGE DISTRIBUTION (1975 = 1.0)**

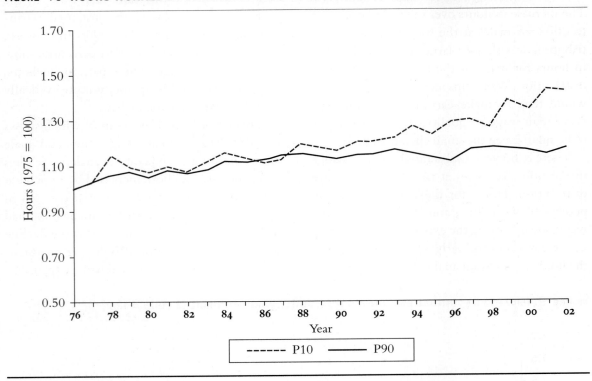

led to much larger cyclical swings in earnings inequality than in wage inequality.

The pattern of hours and earnings inequality for females, shown in Figures 10 and 11, are strikingly different than the patterns for males. Note that hours of females are not cyclically sensitive. Neither females at the P90 nor at the P10 of the wage distribution show cyclical changes in hours. This is in sharp contrast to males at the bottom of the distribution who show strong cyclical changes in hours.

Secular patterns in hours for females are also different than for males. Figure 10 shows that females at the P10 of the wage distribution increased their hours considerably more than

females at the P90. Between 1975 and 2002, females at the P10 increased their hours by 47 percent, from 1127 to 1662, while females at the P90 increased their hours by only 18 percent, from 1625 to 1916.

The larger increase in hours at the bottom of the distribution than at the top led to a sharp decline in earnings inequality among females even though wage inequality increased. This is seen in Figure 11 which shows that earnings inequality declined by 37 percent between 1975 and 2002, even though wage rate inequality increased by 32 percent.

In summary, changes in hours had substantial impacts on the trend in earnings inequality.

FIGURE 11 **P90/P10 OF ANNUAL EARNINGS AND HOURLY WAGE FOR FEMALES (1975 = 1.0)**

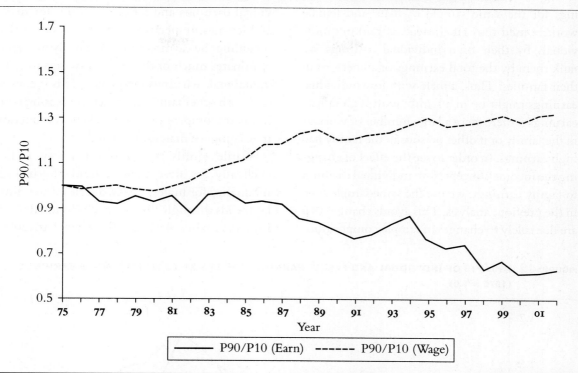

While male wage and earnings inequality have similar trends, they differ sharply over the business cycle, due to cyclical sensitivity of hours for males at the bottom of the distribution. Females do not exhibit this cyclical sensitivity in hours but the trends in wage inequality and earnings inequality differ sharply. The large increase in hours for females at the bottom of the distribution is more than enough to offset the increase in wage inequality.

7. CHANGES IN FAMILY EARNINGS INEQUALITY

We now make the transition from the distributions of annual earnings of male and female workers to the distribution of family earnings. Because family earnings is the sum of earnings of all related individuals, family earnings inequality need not change in the same direction as individual earnings inequality. The trend in family earnings inequality will depend on changes in family labor supply across the distribution of individual earners and the correlation of earnings among family members. For example, if males with high earnings have become more likely to marry females with high earnings, or if the wives of high earner males are more likely to enter the labor market, then the resulting increase in the correlation of earnings among family members would by itself increase family earnings inequality.

We now turn to the P90/P10 of family earnings for the same sample of male and female workers used thus far. Instead of ranking individuals by their own individual earnings we rank them by the total earnings of all persons in their families. Thus, a male with low individual earnings might be in a family with high family earnings if there were a large number of workers in the family or if other persons in the family had high earnings. In order to see the effect of changing the income concept from individual earnings to family earnings, we use the same sample used in the previous analysis. This avoids changes that are due solely to changes in sample composition.

Figures 12 and 13 plot inequality of individual earnings and family earnings for males and females, respectively. Figure 12 shows that including the earnings of other family members eliminates much of the cyclical swings in individual male earnings inequality. This is consistent with other family members increasing their hours to compensate for the cyclical reduction in earnings of males at the P10.

While family earnings inequality is less cyclically sensitive than individual earnings inequality for males, the two series show similar trends through 1990. Male individual earnings inequality declined from 1993 to 2000,

FIGURE 12 **P90/P10 OF INDIVIDUAL AND FAMILY EARNINGS: MALES 22–62 WITH POSITIVE EARNINGS (1975 = 1.0)**

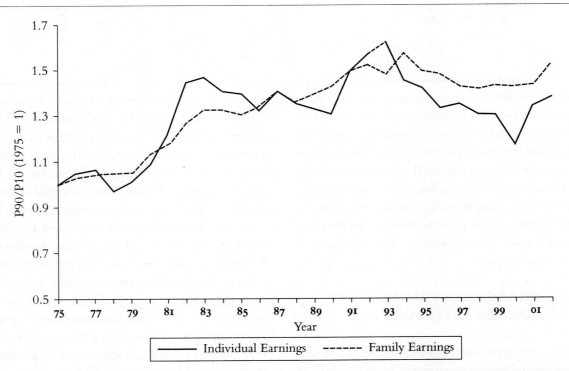

FIGURE 13 **P90/P10 OF INDIVIDUAL AND FAMILY EARNINGS: FEMALES 22–62 WITH POSITIVE EARNINGS (1975 = 1.0)**

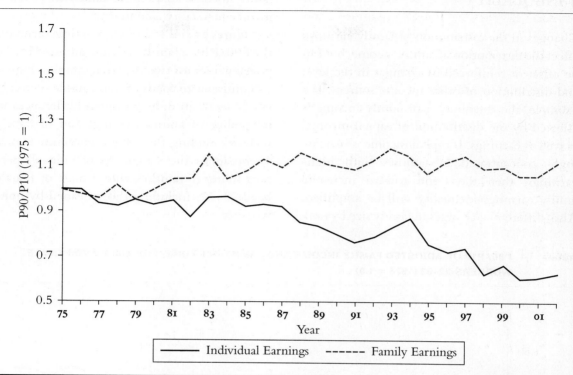

while family earnings inequality remained roughly unchanged. After the recession that began in 2000, individual earnings inequality increased again. As a result of these changes, family earnings inequality was 51 percent higher in 2002 than in 1975, while male earnings inequality was 37 percent higher. Thus, including the earnings of other family members exacerbates the increased earnings inequality of males.

The difference in trends between individual earnings and family earnings inequality is also dramatic for females. Figure 13 shows that while female earnings inequality fell by 37

percent between 1975 and 2002, family earnings inequality for these females increased by 12 percent over the same period. This again reflects changes in earnings of other family members, primarily male spouses, for whom earnings inequality was increasing. While the P10 of family earnings increased by 36 percent between 1974 and 2002, the P90 increased by 53 percent. The fact that family earnings increased more for females at the top of the distribution of family earnings is in marked contrast to Figure 11 which shows that earnings increased more at the bottom of the distribution of individual earnings.

8. CHANGES IN FAMILY INCOME INEQUALITY

Changes in the distribution of family earnings affect the distribution of family income, but can be offset or reinforced by changes in the level and distribution of other income sources. For example, the distribution of family income is affected by the distribution of capital income, as well as earnings. If capital income is increasingly concentrated in families with high-earnings, then the trend toward increased family earnings inequality will be amplified. Also, differential changes in family size by rank

in the income distribution affect inequality of family income adjusted for family size even if income inequality is constant.

Figures 14 and 15 present the time series for the P90/P10 of family income (adjusted by the poverty line) for two different samples. Figure 14 continues to focus on our sample of workers 22 to 62 in order to isolate differences in inequality of family earnings and of family income, holding the sample constant. Figure 15 broadens the sample to include all persons living in families with a male or female head 22–62, including those headed by non-workers.

FIGURE 14 **P90/P10 OF ADJUSTED FAMILY INCOME AND FAMILY EARNINGS FOR MALE AND FEMALE WORKERS 22–62 (1975 = 1.0)**

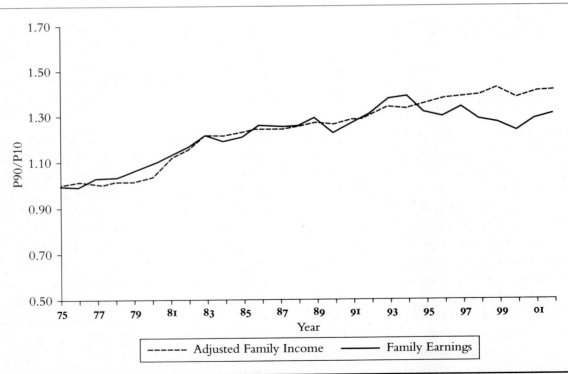

FIGURE 15 **P90/P10 OF ADJUSTED FAMILY INCOME OF ALL PERSONS VS. PERSONS IN FAMILIES WITH HEADS 22–62 (1975 = 1)**

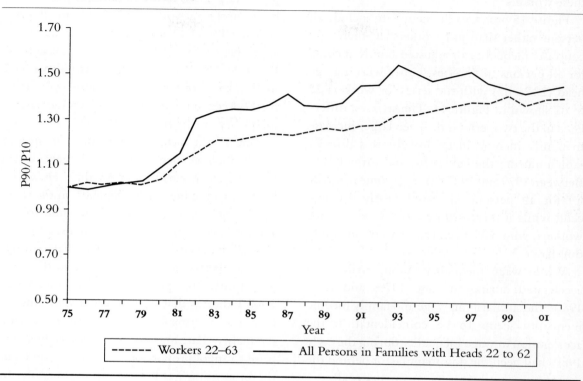

In order to contrast differences in trends in inequality that reflect differences in income concept, not differences in samples, we start by contrasting changes in the P90/P10 of family income (adjusted by the poverty line) with changes in the P90/P10 family earnings for our sample of workers 22 to 62. Figure 14 shows that while family earnings inequality did not rise particularly rapidly during the early 1980s for this sample, family income inequality did show substantial acceleration during this period when wage inequality of males was also growing rapidly (see Figure 4). Paradoxically, the changes in family income inequality in the early 1980s are more similar to changes in individual wage inequality than to changes in family earnings inequality, even though it is the latter that affects family income inequality directly. Family earnings, and family income inequality, however, closely mirror each other between 1985 and 1995.

Family income inequality and family earnings inequality again diverged after 1995. Inequality of family income (adjusted for family size) continued to increase at a moderate rate while family earnings inequality declined modestly. This implies that changes in the distribution of non-wage income and changes in family size were disequalizing after 1995 for these workers.

Figure 15 broadens the sample to include all persons rather than just workers. It, therefore, contrasts inequality of adjusted family income for all persons in families with a working age head (22 to 62) with the series for workers 22 to 62 shown in Figure 14. The striking difference in the two series is the even larger increase in family income inequality for this broader sample during the late 1970s and early 1980s. Between 1979 and 1982 family income inequality for all persons increased nearly 30 percent, while it increased by only 16 percent for workers, who have been the focus of our study thus far.

While wage inequality among males also accelerated during the late 1970s and early 1980s, the similarity in wage and family income inequality seems to be coincidental. If the acceleration in wage inequality during the early 1980s had been the dominant factor behind the rapid rise in family income inequality of all persons during the same period, then we would have expected the change in wage inequality to translate into a similar rapid rise in family earnings inequality over the same period, This did not happen. Neither individual earnings nor family earnings inequality show a particularly rapid rise during the early 1980s.

Finally, we explore whether our results for family income inequality are sensitive to the method used to adjust for top-coding. Burkhauser et al. (2004) point out that using the P90/P10 of adjusted family income may not eliminate the effects of changes in the top coding even, if the top code for family income is above the P90 in all years. They propose an alternative method which we apply to our sample of all persons living in families with a head between the ages of 22 and 62. Figure 16 presents the P90/P10 using both methods. Their adjustment shows a steeper decline in the P90/P10 after 1995 than does the method we have used throughout this paper. However, their method continues to show a sharp increase in inequality during the early 1980s.

One might have expected that changes in family income inequality were largely driven by changes in earnings inequality. However, family income inequality depends on the share of income coming from each income source and the correlations between sources, as well as inequality of each source. The fact that earnings of heads between the ages of 22 and 62 comprised only 56.7 percent of family income in 2002 indicates that other sources were important in accounting for the level of family income inequality. Earnings of heads not only comprised a small proportion of family income but the proportion has been declining steadily. In 1975, 70.6 percent of family income came from heads earnings. By 2002 this proportion had declined 56.7 percent. Over the same period, earnings of other family members (primarily working wives) increased from 19.3 percent to 34.7 percent of family income; income from government cash transfers, property income (dividends, interest and rents) and other income sources remained roughly constant.

The next step in understanding the sources of change in family income inequality would be to decompose the change in overall inequality into its component parts, using accounting identities such as those proposed by Shorrocks (1983). Such identities would isolate the other

FIGURE 16   **P90/P10 OF ADJUSTED FAMILY INCOME OF ALL PERSONS IN FAMILIES WITH HEADS 22–62**
(1979 = 1.0)

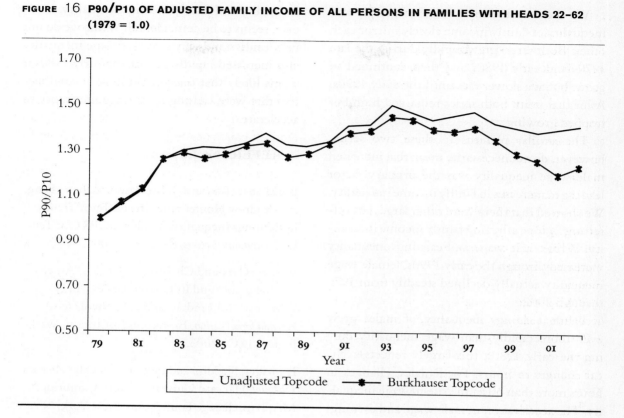

important factors that accounted for changes in family income inequality. While these decompositions would not uncover the behavioral links between changes in wage inequality and changes in family income inequality, they would focus attention on those factors that need to be explained.

||| 9. CONCLUSIONS

This paper documented changes over a quarter century in inequality of four income concepts, using consistent definitions and samples across concepts. We have focused on four conceptually

distinct distributions: the distribution of wage rates, individual earnings, family earnings and family income adjusted for family size. Labor economists have tended to focus on changes in the distribution of wage rates, the most restrictive income concept, since they are interested in changes in market and institutional forces that have altered the prices paid to labor of different types. At the other extreme, policy analysts have focused on changes in the distribution of the broadest income concept, family income adjusted for family size. This reflects their interests in changes in resources available to different groups, including the poor.

We showed that male wage inequality and inequality of family income closely mirror each other. Both series grew rapidly during the late 1970s and early 1980s and then continued to grow, but at a slower rate until the early 1990s. After that point both series remained high but stopped growing.

The similar patterns in these two series, however, do not necessarily mean that increased male wage inequality was the primary factor leading to increases in family income inequality. We showed that there were other large, but off-setting factors, affecting family income inequality. While male wage and earnings inequality increased through the early 1990s, female wage inequality actually declined steadily from 1975 through 2002.

While earnings inequality of males grew even more rapidly than wage inequality during the early 1980s, this largely reflects cyclical changes in hours. For females, changes in hours more than offset the rise in wage inequality. The acceleration in male wage and earnings inequality during the early 1980s disappears when earnings of other family members are included. Thus, changes in work hours by other family members seems to have largely offset increased male labor market inequality.

It is only when we further broaden the definition to family income that the acceleration in inequality during the early 1980s reappears. The similarity of the time series of male wage inequality and family income inequality, however, seems to be coincidental. While we do not fully understand why family income inequality also increased rapidly during the early 1980s it seems likely that one should look beyond factors that were causing male wage inequality to accelerate.

⫼ REFERENCES

Burkhauser Richard, J. Butler, Shuaizhang Feng, and Andrew Houtenville, "Long Term Trends in Earnings Inequality: What the CPS Can Tell Us," *Economic Letters*, 82, 295–9, 2004.

Burtless Gary and Christopher Jencks, "American Inequality and Its Consequences," in H. J. Aaron, J. M. Lindsay, and P. S. Nivola (eds), *Agenda for a Nation*, Brookings Institution, Washington, D.C., 2003.

Danziger, Sheldon and Peter Gottschalk, *America Unequal*, Harvard University Press, Cambridge, MA, Russell Sage Foundation, New York, NY, 1995.

Gottschalk, Peter, "Inequality, Income, Growth, and Mobility: The Basic Facts," *Journal of Economic Perspectives*, 11, 21–40, 1997.

Shorrocks, Anthony F., "The Impact of Income Components on the Distribution of Family Incomes," *Quarterly Journal of Economics*, 98, 311–26, 1983.

13

The Gender Pay Gap*

FRANCINE D. BLAU AND LAWRENCE M. KAHN

During the 1970s, when the Equal Rights Amendment campaign was at its peak, proponents lamented that women earned only 60 cents for every dollar that men earned, implying a "gender pay gap" of 40 cents (or 40 percent). Although the gender pay gap had stood at roughly that level for decades, and although the Amendment was never passed, during the 1980s a striking thing happened: the "raw" pay gap shrunk rapidly, and it has continued to shrink to this day, although the pace of change slowed in the 1990s.

Interestingly, however, whereas in 1979, a substantial portion of the gender pay gap could be accounted for by the combined effect of traditional measures of human capital—education and labor market experience, particularly women's lesser amount of labor market experience—today almost none of it can. Gender differences in industry and occupation distributions continue to be important sources of the gender pay gap. This raises some important questions: What role does gender discrimination play in determining today's wage gap? What other factors contribute to gender differences in wages?

---

* First published in 2007; from *The Economists' Voice*, Volume 4, Issue 4.

THE GENDER PAY GAP AND ITS CAUSES

Figure 1 shows estimates of the gender wage gap for full-time workers from the Current Population Surveys (CPS) for selected years from 1979 to 2004. The raw wage gap started at 35 percent in 1979, fell sharply (by nearly eight percentage points) over the next decade, and then declined at a slower pace (by four percentage points) to 1998. Between 1998 and 2004, the pace of change picked up again: The wage gap declined by 4.5 percentage points in just six years—a similar rate of decline to that which had existed in the 1980s. By 2004, the wage gap was 18 percent. What creates these wage gaps, and what influences their evolution?

Economists analyze the gender wage gap using wage regressions—that is, statistical analyses specifying the relationship between wages and productivity-related characteristics for men and women. These regressions show that some

FIGURE 1 **GENDER WAGE GAPS, BASED ON AVERAGE HOURLY EARNINGS OF FULL-TIME WORKERS (DATA FROM THE CURRENT POPULATION SURVEY)**

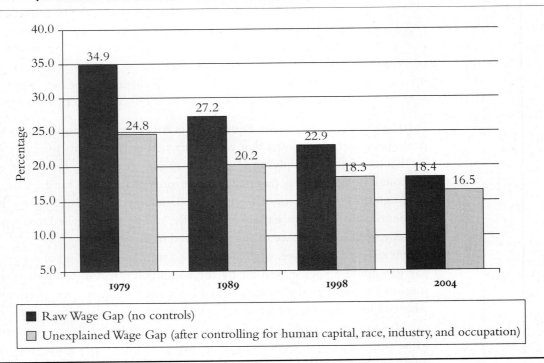

■ Raw Wage Gap (no controls)
□ Unexplained Wage Gap (after controlling for human capital, race, industry, and occupation)

NOTE: Entries are percentages of male wages, based on authors' calculations. Controls include: years of schooling, potential experience, and its square; and 21 industry and 17 occupation dummy variables. The years refer to the period during which wages and salaries were earned. Those earning less than $2 or more than $200 per hour in 2000 dollars (PCE deflator) were excluded.

of the raw wage gap is due to differences in the measured characteristics of men and women. For example, in 1979, while male and female full-time workers had about the same level of education, on average, male workers tended to have slightly more potential experience (years elapsed since completing their schooling), providing one nondiscriminatory reason that their pay was higher. Male workers were also a bit more likely to be white than female workers are, and whites earn more than nonwhites on average (a whole different kind of pay gap, potentially explained in part by a different kind of discrimination). Moreover, women were more likely to work in lower-paying occupations and industries, as teachers and clerical or service workers, for example, rather than as managers or in high-paying craft or operator jobs. In 1979, about ten cents of the wage gap was explained by these factors, particularly occupation and industry differences. In 2004, by contrast, only two cents was explained.

The CPS data set, disappointingly does not tell us about men's and women's work experience—how many years they actually worked in the past. Accordingly, in Figure 1, we use "potential" experience, a variable calculated from information about the individual's age and educational attainment. However this variable may not accurately approximate work experience, particularly for women: Traditionally, women moved in and out of the labor force depending on the needs of their families, meaning that they might end up having far less work experience than they had the potential to attain. Thus, having a good measure of prior work experience is extremely important in studying gender differences in pay. That is

why, in a recent study, we used the Michigan Panel Study of Income Dynamics (PSID), the only nationally-representative database with information on *actual* work experience, to study this issue.

As may be seen in Figure 2, using the PSID data, we found a similar pattern of declining raw gender wage gaps for full-time workers, as we had using the CPS data included in Figure 1, over 1979–98, the period covered by our study.

However, there is also a crucial contrast: Gender differences in measured human capital (education and experience) do not explain much of the gender wage gap that is displayed if we use the CPS data and the potential experience measure. (Thus, we do not show these effects separately in Figure 1). Yet we do find these differences to be important in some years in the PSID. Controlling for education and actual work experience lowered the wage gap from 37 to 29 percent in 1979, and from 26 to 18 percent in 1989, chiefly due to the control for gender differences in work experience. However, in 1998, the wage gap, controlling for human capital and race, was only slightly less than the raw gap; in other words, the traditional human capital measures explained almost none of the raw wage gap. This outcome occurred because, among full-time workers in 1998, women's higher education levels roughly counterbalanced their lower experience levels, so that in the end, the effect of these two factors was more or less a wash.

Figure 2 also shows what happens to the unexplained wage gap when we control both for human capital and for sector (industry and occupation). If women opt to take jobs in lower-paying occupations and industries, or are

FIGURE 2   **GENDER WAGE GAPS, BASED ON AVERAGE HOURLY EARNINGS OF FULL-TIME WORKERS (DATA FROM THE PANEL STUDY OF INCOME DYNAMICS)**

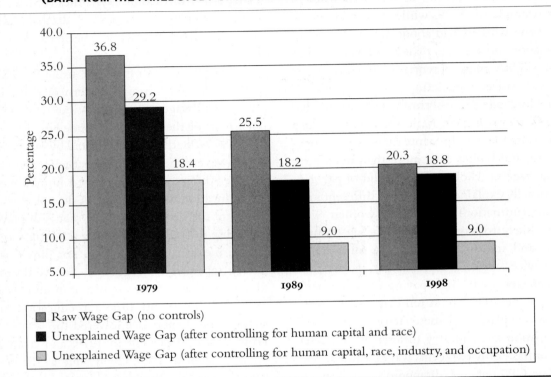

■ Raw Wage Gap (no controls)
■ Unexplained Wage Gap (after controlling for human capital and race)
■ Unexplained Wage Gap (after controlling for human capital, race, industry, and occupation)

NOTE: Entries are percentages of male wages, based on a study by Francine Blau and Lawrence Kahn. Controls for human capital include years of schooling, dummy variables for college and advanced degrees, full-time and part-time experience and their squares; controls for occupation and industry include 25 industry and 19 occupation dummy variables, and a control for collective bargaining coverage. The years refer to the period during which wages and salaries were earned. Those earning less than $1 or more than $250 per hour in 1983 dollars (PCE deflator) were excluded.

restricted by discrimination to such jobs, that too could explain the wage gap. Adding these controls makes a substantial difference in all years. Thus, with the full set of controls we have described, the unexplained wage gap had fallen to nine percent by 1989, where it remained in 1998.

The unexplained gap, with these controls, may be compared to our findings from the CPS in Figure 1, which shows larger unexplained gaps of 17 to 18 percent for 1998 and 2004. While the PSID data rely upon better measures of experience, the CPS data are more timely and have larger sample sizes. Thus, both sets of results are of interest, and both show an unexplained wage gap—of nine to 17 percent in the most recent year.

DO PAY GAPS REFLECT DISCRIMINATION?

Do these results mean that discrimination against women currently accounts for a pay gap of nine to 17 cents on the dollar, or nine to 17 percent? One might be tempted to think so. After all, if white women with two years of college education who are in managerial jobs in the transportation equipment industry make nine to 17 cents less on the dollar than white men in the same position, then discrimination seems a likely answer. Discrimination may not be the culprit, however. Perhaps omitted factors such as working conditions or motivation explain the remaining pay gap. Or, perhaps women work at lower levels of the managerial hierarchy and all employees, women or men, are paid less in these lower-level positions. In that case, the "unexplained" wage gap of 9–17 percent could overstate discrimination.

Before we become too complacent, however, we should note that discrimination could just as easily result in more than nine to 17 cents of disparity. For example, discrimination can affect employer hiring and promotion policies and decrease women's employment in highly-paid occupations and industries. Put differently, if we look at a man who is a manager and earns much more than a woman clerical worker, a regression might suggest that he earns more for being a manager, not for being a man. But what if he was made a manager *because* he was a

man? Or, thinking more broadly, if discrimination lowers women's wages relative to men's, it could influence the decisions couples make as to who will drop out of the labor force to care for children, whose career will determine the location of the family, etc. The anticipation of such discrimination or experience with it could influence women's incentives to invest in education, how much experience they accumulate, and what industries and occupations they decide to enter.

Thus, findings from wage regressions are suggestive, but they do not give us definite answers. The case that gender discrimination is still real, however, is holstered by research looking for direct evidence using an experimental approach.

David Neumark analyzed the results of a hiring "audit" in which male and female pseudo-job-seekers were given similar résumés and sent to apply for waiter or waitress jobs at the same set of Philadelphia restaurants. In high-priced restaurants where earnings of workers are generally higher than in the other establishments, a female applicant's probability of getting an interview or an offer was substantially lower than a male's. A second study by Claudia Goldin and Cecilia Rouse examined the impact of the "natural experiment" in which major symphony orchestras in the United States adopted "blind" auditions. In a blind audition, a screen is used to conceal the identity of the candidate. Using data from actual auditions, the authors found that the screen substantially increased the probability that a woman would advance out of preliminary rounds and be the winner in the final round. Both of these studies suggest the existence of discrimination in particular sectors, but, of course, they do not tell us how extensive its effects are in the economy generally.

THE EVOLUTION OF THE GENDER WAGE GAP OVER TIME

As we have seen, the gender wage gap fell sharply in the 1980s and then declined at a slower pace in the 1990s. The pace of change picked up again after that. What accounts for the increase in women's pay relative to men's over time?

In our recent study, which focused on the 1979–98 period, we found that improvements in women's human capital (for instance, through greater education and experience) accounted for some of the increase, with declining gender differences in experience playing a larger role in the 1980s, and women's rising relative educational attainment playing a larger role in the 1990s. We found that the rising occupational attainment of women relative to men also contributed to the increase, as women moved out of clerical and service jobs, and into managerial and professional occupations, and as men moved out of (or lost) relatively high-paying craft and operator jobs (the latter especially in the 1980s).

In addition, in the 1980s, but not the 1990s, our analysis indicated that a major reason for the convergence in men's and women's wages was that the "unexplained" gender-wage gap declined sharply. This suggests that, during that decade, women improved their unmeasured skills relative to men, or that discrimination against them decreased. Indeed both of these factors may have played a role. Women may

also have benefited from a shift in labor market demand favoring them, particularly in the 1980s. There has been a rise in the demand for white-collar, relative to blue-collar, workers, in part due to technological change. Women are much more likely than men to work in white-collar jobs, and therefore such a development is likely to have benefited women relative to men.

What are we to make of the recent increase in the rate of decline in the gender wage gap? It may signal a resumption of a strong long-run trend toward convergence of women's and men's pay, or it may prove to be of only short duration. One short-term factor could be the recession of 2001 and the relatively high unemployment rates that lingered in its aftermath. The demand for male workers tends to be more cyclically sensitive than that for female workers, due to their greater concentration in blue-collar jobs and durable goods manufacturing industries.

CONCLUDING COMMENTS

What does the future hold now that women earn about 80 cents for every dollar that men earn, implying a gender pay gap of 20 percent? While this represents a considerable gain from the 1970s gender pay gap of 40 percent, further gains for women are certainly possible. Women's education has been rising relative to men's, and, indeed, among younger cohorts women are now more likely to graduate college than men. This trend shows no signs of abating. And, technological change, which has likely raised women's relative wages through demand effects, will probably continue and could even accelerate.

On the other hand, the gender pay gap seems unlikely to vanish in the near term. For one thing, women continue to confront discrimination in the labor market, and, although its extent seems to be decreasing, it is unlikely to be completely eliminated soon. In addition, at least some of the remaining pay gap is surely tied to the gender division of labor in the home. Women still retain primary responsibility for housework and child care in most American families. This pattern has been slowly changing as families respond to rising labor market opportunities for women that increase the opportunity cost of such arrangements, as well as the increasing prevalence of policies, both voluntary and government-mandated, that facilitate the integration of workers' job and family responsibilities. Of course, how far such changes will go is difficult to predict.

REFERENCES

Blau, Francine D. and Lawrence M. Kahn (2006) "The US Gender Pay Gap in the 1990s: Slowing Convergence," Industrial and Labor Relations Review, 60(1):45–66. (Our recent study using data from the Panel Study of Income Dynamics.)

Blau, Francine D., Marianne A. Ferber, and Anne E. Winkler (2006) *The Economics of Women, Men, and Work*, 5th edition. Upper Saddle River, NJ: Prentice-Hall.

Goldin, Claudia and Cecilia Rouse (2000) "Orchestrating Impartiality: The Impact of 'Blind' Auditions on Female Musicians," American Economic Review, 90(4):715–41.

Neumark, David M. (1996) "Sex Discrimination in Restaurant Hiring: An Audit Study," Quarterly Journal of Economics, 111(3):915–41.

14

I'd Rather Be Rich★

LISA KEISTER

In the 1964 movie *I'd Rather Be Rich*, people were typical in their willingness to go to great lengths to get rich. In the movie, the goal was to inherit from a dying grandfather, but people have all manner of ways of trying to hit it big. There is a general sense that being rich is better than not being rich, but wealth—and the processes that lead to wealth ownership—may be even more important than most people realize.

Wealth is the things people own, including their homes, savings, investments, real estate, businesses, and vehicles. It is usually measured as net worth, the sum of assets less the sum of debts. Owning wealth has many advantages, from the obvious financial freedom it provides to the even more enduring social and political privileges and power accessible to the wealthy. These advantages and the elusive nature of true wealth make questions about who is rich and why broadly appealing. Dramatic economic changes in recent years, accompanied by rising wealth inequality, have created renewed interest in wealth. These changes have also generated speculation about new patterns

---

★ First published in 2005; from *Getting Rich: America's New Rich and How They Got That Way.*

in the ways people become wealthy. The visibility of Internet millionaires created speculation that there may be an increasing number of entrepreneurs among the wealthy, and the subsequent devaluation of technology stocks and the bankruptcy of scores of dot-com companies raised questions about the role the sectoral shifts play in wealth ownership. Through all this, an increasingly skewed wealth distribution has raised questions, at least in some corners, about why there continue to be people who accumulate little even during periods of unprecedented economic growth.

While basic facts about wealth ownership and inequality are no mystery, we still know very little about who is wealthy and why. That is, we still know very little about wealth accumulation and wealth mobility. Wealth accumulation is the way people acquire assets and debts during their lives. Wealth mobility refers to changes in relative positions within the distribution of wealth. That is, if all people were sorted according to how much wealth they have, mobility refers to how a person's position in this list changes over time. Clearly, wealth accumulation is central to these changes. Those who accumulate assets quickly are going to move upward more rapidly. Of course, wealth mobility is also related to wealth distribution. Given that wealth ownership is highly concentrated and that it has become more concentrated during the time I will be considering here, moving into the upper positions in the distribution is difficult.

Researchers have shown that there is considerable concentration of wealth ownership and have estimated trends in the growth of wealth owned by households. There are also estimates of the role that macroeconomic and demographic trends played in shaping recent changes in wealth ownership. Yet the processes by which people accumulate wealth, the way their wealth ownership changes over their lives, and the way their positions in the distribution change over time have received little attention. ★ ★ ★ How much mobility is there? Has the nature of mobility changed over time? Who is rich? Are most wealthy people entrepreneurs, did they inherit their wealth, or did they become wealthy in some other way? And what behaviors and processes in middle- and working class families propel some people out of these classes while others remain poor throughout their lives?

[My] starting point ★ ★ ★ is the notion that understanding wealth and the processes that create wealth are not only interesting but also of critical importance to understanding the way people sort themselves socially and economically. That is, understanding wealth ownership is central to understanding inequality. The approach used here directs attention primarily toward the paths people take during their lives in order to understand how these paths shape the distribution of wealth. From this perspective, life paths include the starting point as well as many of the key points of change people encounter during their lives. Being born into a wealthy family, of course, makes it easier to be wealthy as an adult. But decisions about education, work, marriage, children, and saving also matter, and these interact with each other in complex ways to create trajectories. The paths people take are also a product of circumstances and influences that individuals do not directly control but that impede or enhance these trajectories. To understand why people occupy certain positions in a distribution, it is necessary to understand how these processes interact. The objective ★ ★ ★ is to explore the life paths that underlie wealth mobility in order to better understand both the wealthy and those who never become wealthy.

WEALTH AND WELL-BEING: ARE THE RICH REALLY BETTER OFF?

There is growing evidence that having wealth, at least some wealth, is critically important to well-being. *Wealth* is the value of the property that people own. It is *net worth* or total assets less total debts. For most families, this includes tangible assets such as the family home and vehicles. Other families also own vacation homes, other real estate, and business assets. In addition, assets include financial wealth such as checking and savings accounts, stocks, bonds, mutual funds, Certificates of Deposit, and other financial assets. Debts or liabilities include mortgages on the family home, other mortgages, consumer debt, student loans, car loans, home equity loans, and other debt to institutional lenders or informal lenders such as family members. *Financial wealth* is the value of liquid assets, such as stocks and bonds, but does not include housing wealth or the value of business assets or investment in real estate. Wealth is different from income. *Income* is a flow of money over time, such as wages and salaries from work, government transfer payments, or interest and dividends earned on investments. Unlike income, wealth is not used directly to buy necessities such as food and clothing; rather, wealth is the total amount of property owned at a point in time.

Studies of inequality and the distribution of financial well-being tend to focus on income and how income changes over time. However, wealth may be an even more important indicator of well-being because it provides both direct financial benefits and other advantages. The family home, for example, provides shelter and other current services to the owner. At the same time, home ownership can be one of the most beneficial investments a family can make. Wealth also provides a financial cushion that can alleviate the impact of an emergency. For those without savings, a medical emergency, the unemployment of a primary income earner, or a family breakup can be devastating. Wealth can be used to directly generate more wealth if it is invested and allowed to accumulate. It can also be used to indirectly generate more wealth if it is used as collateral for loans for further investments, such as in the purchase of a home or business. Wealth can be used to purchase luxuries, and it can be used to buy physical protection and a safe and pleasant living environment. In the extreme, wealth can also buy leisure when its owner is able to decide whether to work or not. When family savings provide sufficient current income, income earned from wages and salaries is unnecessary.

Wealth ownership may also generate political and social influence. In a representative democracy, the distribution of political influence is often related to the distribution of wealth, and wealth carries with it social connections that can be used in important ways. Wealth expands educational and occupational opportunities for the current owner, and because wealth can be passed from one generation to the next, it often expands educational and occupational advantages intergenerationally. Of course, the truly rich may attract media attention, solicitations for donations, and other unwanted recognition. Wealth also invites security threats, may be socially isolating, and can dampen motivation. Yet the benefits of wealth ownership generally outweigh the disadvantages, and most agree that the rich are generally better off as a result of their asset ownership.

THE ALLURE OF WEALTH: WHY DOES WEALTH FASCINATE US?

The rich have perhaps always been fascinating, and dramatic changes in economic conditions in recent years created even more interest in wealth and the wealthy. Social registers and other written accounts of the lives of the wealthy captivated attention in earlier eras much like magazines and television shows that offer a glimpse into the lives of the rich do today. During the 1990s, changing economic conditions drew even more attention to wealth accumulation. Spectacular stock market booms, sustained economic growth, low inflation, low unemployment, and decreased fear of historic international rivals combined to create economic conditions that matched or surpassed numerous historic records. A subsequent economic slowdown reminded investors that good economic times must eventually become more normal. Before the downturn, however, there were important changes in the amount of wealth owned by households, changes in who owned it, and changes in how it was distributed. The magnitude of these changes generated new interest in who gets rich and how.

EXPENDING INTEREST IN WEALTH

The total wealth owned by American households began to grow in the 1960s, and it continued to expand through the 1990s. Total household assets increased more than four times during that period, from about $8 trillion in 1960 to more than $33 trillion in 1994 (all estimates are in year 2000 dollars unless otherwise noted). By the end of 1999, total household assets were valued at more than $50 trillion, decreasing to just more than $45 trillion at the end of the first quarter of 2001. Figure 1 illustrates the extent of growth of assets and liabilities held by households during the late 1990s and shows that changes in net worth reflected changes in assets more than they reflected changes in liabilities. During the 1980s and 1990s, fluctuating real estate prices increased the importance of housing assets in the portfolios of American households. There were bigger shifts, however, in the role of financial assets in the portfolio, particularly stock assets.

Indeed, changing stock market values had a relatively large effect on household wealth throughout the 1990s and beyond 2000. During the 1970s and early 1980s, the stock market was relatively stable, and middle-class families were relatively unlikely to own stocks. This changed in the late 1980s and 1990s, when stock market booms, combined with increased availability of stock mutual funds, made stock ownership both more common and more lucrative for families. The trend line imposed over Figure 1 indicates the Dow Jones Industrial Average during the period included in the graph. During the later years included there, many households watched

FIGURE 1   **TRENDS IN HOUSEHOLD WEALTH: WEALTH OWNED BY ALL U.S. HOUSEHOLDS, 1994–2003**

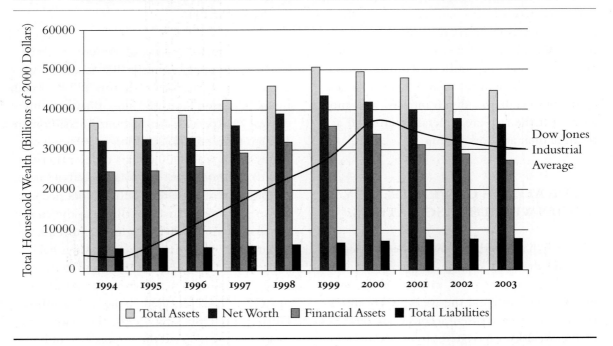

NOTE: Wealth values are from the Federal Reserve Board's *Balance Sheets of the U.S. Economy* converted to 2000 dollars using the Consumer Price Index (Federal Reserve System 2001). Dow Jones Industrial Average ranges from 3,700 in 1994 to a high of 11,400 in 2000 (scale not indicated on graph). ★ ★ ★

their portfolios expand enormously. Decreasing stock values between 2000 and 2003, however, also accounted for much of the decline in household assets at the end of the period pictured in the figure. As the economy slowed, many of the same households were forced to watch the value of their portfolios diminish almost overnight. More recently, increases in stock values are once again increasing household wealth, a testament to the importance of aggregate trends in outcomes at the household level.

Figure 2 focuses on changes in the composition of household wealth ownership that occurred between 1994 and 2003. The figure

illustrates the percentage of total household assets that was accounted for by real estate, corporate equities, and mutual fund shares during that period. Between 1994 and 1999, the relative importance of housing wealth declined while the importance of corporate equities and mutual funds increased. These trends reflected inflated stock prices and a growing propensity for households to own corporate equities and (to a lesser degree) mutual funds, rather than changes in the propensity of households to own homes. Corporate equities and mutual funds became an increasingly significant portion of American household portfolios during the

FIGURE 2 **THE RELATIVE IMPORTANCE OF REAL ESTATE AND STOCK IN FAMILY PORTFOLIOS**

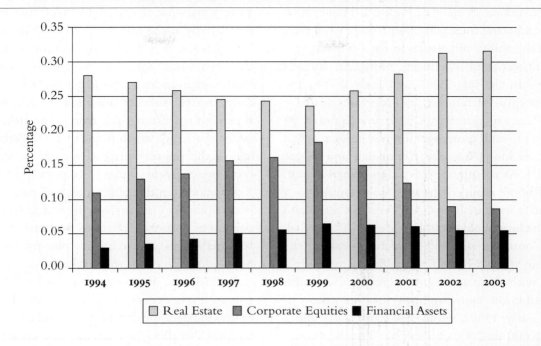

NOTE: Estimates are from the Federal Reserve Board's *Balance Sheets of the U.S. Economy* (Federal Reserve System 2001). Corporate equities are at market value. Mutual fund values are based on the market values of equities held and the book value of other assets held by mutual funds. Real estate includes vacant land and vacant homes for sale. Estimates for 1994–2002 are for end of the year; values for 2003 are for the first quarter.

1990s. At the same time, saving and investing increased during the mid-1990s because favorable economic conditions made investing more appealing, because baby boomers had begun to increase their saving for retirement around that time, and because changes to financial instruments created new opportunities for families to save. The introduction of Individual Retirement Accounts, for example, allowed some Americans to save for retirement, tax-free, in ways in which they were not able to in the past. Similarly, while mutual funds have been around

for decades, they also became easier to use during the 1990s, and more people accordingly began to save at least a small amount in mutual funds. Technological and other changes, such as the ability to invest easily on the Internet, also changed the way people save. In particular, during the 1990s, it became relatively common to buy stocks, bonds, mutual funds, Certificates of Deposit, and other financial assets online.

Beginning in 2000, the relative importance of real estate in total household wealth increased while the importance of stock ownership declined. This trend reflected declining stock values, evident in Figure 1. However, it also reflected increasing home ownership rates and the ability of families to pay off mortgages resulting from declining mortgage interest rates. In the late 1990s and early 2000s, the proportion of families owning their primary residence increased by 1.5 percent to nearly 68 percent, and mortgage interest rates reached historic lows (Aizcorbe, Kennickell, and Moore 2001). As a result, more families owned homes, and home equity increased, contributing to a relative increase in the importance of real estate in the household portfolio.

Consistent with these patterns, wealth ownership at the level of families fluctuated quite a bit, with those at the upper ends of the wealth distribution enjoying most of the gains. In the early 1960s, mean net worth was about $116,000 (in 2000 dollars), but it has been consistently greater than $170,000 since the early 1980s. Similarly, financial wealth increased from about $92,000 to more than $134,000 between the 1960s and the late 1990s. Table 1 summarizes trends in wealth ownership between 1989 and 2001. Changing stock and

housing values caused mean net worth to fluctuate somewhat dramatically over that time, particularly at the upper levels of the distribution. Median net worth (the central value in the distribution) varied less in response to stock market changes and is perhaps a better indicator of the true average household wealth. What is perhaps most noticeable from these estimates is that while net worth fluctuated, the percentage of the population that owned no wealth remained high throughout this period. In each year included in the table, at least 17 percent of households had no net worth, and at least 25 percent of households had no financial wealth. In other words, approximately one-fifth of the population owned no wealth at all.

In order to have negative net worth, of course, it is necessary to have debts. In addition to making decisions about saving and investing, families also affect their net worth by acquiring debt. Including total liabilities in Figure 2 is not particularly instructive, because the value of total debt is minimal compared to the value of total assets and trends in aggregate debt do not vary as dramatically as changes in assets. However, the composition of total household debt

TABLE 1 HOUSEHOLD WEALTH

	1989	1992	1995	1998	2001
NET WORTH					
Mean	239,110	247,340	228,751	283,230	325,180
Median	60,700	51,300	50,220	63,600	65,690
% WITH ZERO OR NEGATIVE	18	18	19	18	17
FINANCIAL WEALTH					
Mean	190,800	188,300	175,540	222,400	254,900
Median	14,200	12,300	11,100	18,650	19,800
% WITH ZERO OR NEGATIVE	27	28	29	26	25

NOTE: Estimates from the Surveys of Consumer Finances. All monetary values are in 2000 dollars.

FIGURE 3 **THE DEBT OF THE POOR: SOURCES OF HOUSEHOLD DEBT FOR THOSE WITH NEGATIVE NET WORTH (% OF TOTAL DEBT)**

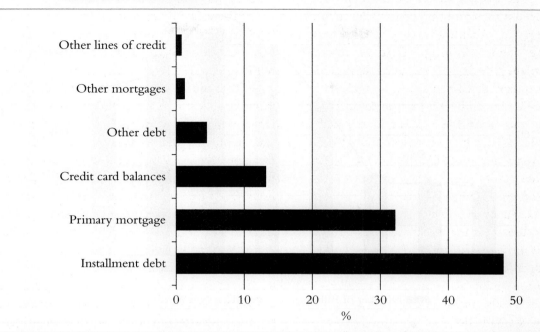

SOURCE: Survey of Consumer Finances. Net worth was estimated in 2001 dollars.

for those with negative net worth sheds light on the reasons so many families have no wealth. Figure 3 shows the debt sources of poor families for 2001. As this figure demonstrates, the largest percentage of debt is installment debt. In 2001, nearly 50 percent of the total liabilities of families with zero net worth was installment debt, and an additional 13 percent was credit card balances. Installment debt refers to loans with fixed payments and a fixed term, including student loans, automobile loans, and loans to buy furniture, appliances, and other durable goods.

When wealthy households are examined in isolation, increasing asset values are much more evident than estimates of all households. Indeed, there are more millionaires and billionaires in America than there were in the past. Figure 4 shows the increase in the number of families whose wealth is greater than $1 billion and the mean wealth of the Forbes 400. This increase is net of inflation—the estimates are derived from wealth estimates in constant (1995) dollars—suggesting that the increase in millionaires has been considerable. There is also evidence from the Forbes 400 that the wealthiest Americans have gotten even wealthier in recent years. Consistent with the fact that the largest gains in wealth ownership have been enjoyed by those who are already rich, the mean net

FIGURE 4 **HOW RICH IS RICH? NUMBER OF BILLIONAIRES AND MEAN WEALTH OF FORBES 400**

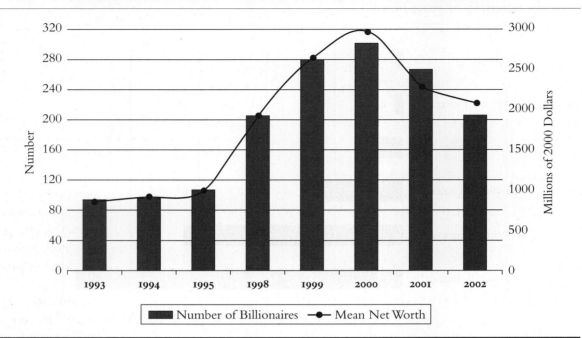

SOURCE: *Forbes* magazine. Number of those in Forbes 400 with net worth greater than $1 billion (in 2000 dollars). Mean net worth in 2000 dollars for all Forbes 400.

worth of the Forbes 400 has increased dramatically in recent decades. In the early 1980s, the mean net worth of this group of the wealthiest Americans was $408 million (in 2000 dollars). The mean increased slowly in the early 1990s, as Figure 4 indicates, and it rose dramatically between 1995 and 2000. In 2000, the mean net worth of the Forbes 400 exceeded $3.4 billion. Moreover, the number of Americans with more than $10 billion in assets has increased noticeably in recent years. In 2000, approximately 75 percent of the members of the Forbes 400 were billionaires (in 2000 dollars), whereas fewer than 10 percent were billionaires through 1986.

In 1996, only three of those in the Forbes 400 had net worth greater than $10 billion (current year dollars), while in 2000, 23 of the Forbes 400 had amassed more than $10 billion in net worth.

The wealthy are also amassing billion-dollar fortunes faster than they used to, in part because of highly valued (perhaps overvalued) Internet companies that create enormous paper fortunes when they go public. Jay Walker, the founder and CEO of the Internet auction service Priceline.com, is an interesting example. His company was worth less than $100 million in mid-1998, but after the company went public

Walker's wealth soared to more than $1 billion, and he became the fourteenth richest person in the world (Dolan 1999). Of course, not all of the very rich got that way through inflated valuations of their company's stock. Martin S. Fridson, author of *How to Be a Billionaire*, insists that frugality still plays a role in the making of fortunes. His anthology of superrich icons does point to a number of cost-cutting personal behaviors of the wealthy, including John D. Rockefeller's insistence on using old golf balls in situations in which he was likely to lose the ball. Yet this anthology of the rich ultimately underscores popular images of the changing nature of the upper class.

THE REALITY OF WEALTH INEQUALITY

Wealth has also attracted attention because its distribution is extremely unequal. Many Americans have enjoyed remarkable and increasing prosperity, but for others, reports of sensational economic conditions in recent years bore little resemblance to their own experiences. Those in the middle and lower segments of the wealth distribution have continued to own little or no wealth, and many have watched their economic standing deteriorate. Basic facts about wealth inequality throughout American history have become fairly well understood. The facts are somewhat vague before 1900, but even for early historical periods, it is possible to piece together information that shows extreme inequality. Williamson and Lindert (1980), for example, show that the percentage of total wealth held by the top 1 percent of households was at least 37 percent in six major U.S. cities prior to 1900.

TABLE 2 WEALTH INEQUALITY BEFORE 1900

Percentage Held by the Top 1%	
Baltimore (1860)	39
Boston (1848)	37
New York (1845)	40
New Orleans (1860)	43
Philadelphia (1860)	50
St. Louis (1860)	38

SOURCE: Williamson and Lindert, 1980.

Table 2 reproduces the estimates of the percentage of total wealth held by the top 1 percent of households in these cities. As the table indicates, inequality was most extreme in Philadelphia, but there was considerable inequality in each of the six metropolitan areas.

Evidence from historical records also suggests that levels of wealth inequality varied drastically during the first part of the twentieth century, but wealth inequality was consistently extreme. Lampman (1962) is usually credited as being among the first to identify wealth inequality as a source of social problems. He used estate tax data to document trends in wealth ownership and inequality in the decades between 1920 and 1960. His findings indicated that between 1922 and 1953, the top 1 percent of wealth holders owned an average of 30 percent of total household sector wealth. While inequalities varied with macroeconomic trends during the decades Lampman studied, he provided convincing evidence that inequality was consistently extreme throughout that period. Table 3 summarizes the trends in the percentage of total wealth owned by the top 1 and 5 percent of households between 1922 and 1956. Across these decades, the richest families con-

TABLE 3 **WEALTH INEQUALITY IN THE FIRST HALF OF THE 20TH CENTURY**

	Percentage Held by the	
	Top 1%	Top 0.5%
1922	31.6	29.8
1929	36.3	32.4
1933	28.3	25.2
1939	30.6	28.0
1945	23.3	20.9
1949	20.8	19.3
1953	24.3	22.7
1954	24.0	22.5
1956	26.0	25.0

SOURCE: Lampman 1962, pp. 202, 204.

sistently owned more than 20 percent of total wealth and as much as 32 percent of the total.

Other historical estimates have produced similar evidence of inequality during the early twentieth century. Wolff and Marley (1989) used various data sources to study wealth inequality over the entire 1920–1990 period. For the early part of the century, their results were consistent with Lampman's findings. They demonstrated that those in the top 1 percent of the wealth distribution owned an average of 30 percent of total net worth between 1922 and the early 1950s. The share of wealth owned by the top 1 percent increased from about 29 percent to about 32 percent between 1922 and the 1929 stock market crash. During the 1930s and 1940s, the concentration of wealth declined, so that the top 1 percent owned less than 30 percent by the late 1940s. During the 1950s, economic prosperity brought with it increased wealth inequality, and by the late 1950s, esti-

mates suggest that the top 1 percent of households owned nearly 35 percent of total wealth.

Wealth data, and the corresponding estimates of wealth distribution, began to improve in the 1960s. In 1962, the Federal Reserve Board's Survey of Financial Characteristics of Consumers (SFCC) became the first comprehensive survey of wealth holdings in the United States. Table 4 contains estimates of wealth distribution from the SFCC and SCF panels for the 1962–2001 period. These estimates demonstrate that a very small portion of households have consistently owned the vast majority of household wealth. In 1962, the top 1 percent of wealth owners owned 33.5 percent of total net worth, and the top quintile owned more than 80 percent of total net worth. Wealth remained unequally distributed but relatively constant between 1962 and the mid-1970s because of an extended stock market slump and the growth of welfare programs such as Aid to Families of

TABLE 4 **WEALTH INEQUALITY IN THE SECOND HALF OF THE 20TH CENTURY**

	Gini Coefficient	Top 1%	Next 4%	Next 5%	Next 10%	Top 20%	2nd 20%	3rd 20%	Bottom 40%
NET WORTH									
1962	0.80	33.5	21.2	12.5	14.0	81.2	13.5	5.0	0.3
1983	0.80	33.8	22.3	12.1	13.1	81.3	12.6	5.2	0.9
1989	0.85	37.4	21.6	11.6	13.0	83.6	12.3	4.8	−0.7
1992	0.85	37.2	22.9	11.8	12.0	83.9	11.4	4.5	0.2
1995	0.85	38.5	21.8	11.5	12.1	83.9	11.4	4.5	0.2
1998	0.85	38.1	21.3	11.5	12.5	83.4	11.9	45	0.2
FINANCIAL WEALTH									
1962	0.88	40.3	23.8	12.8	12.7	89.6	9.6	2.1	−1.4
1983	0.90	42.9	25.1	12.3	11.0	91.3	7.9	1.7	−0.9
1989	0.93	46.9	23.9	11.6	10.9	93.4	7.4	1.7	−2.4
1992	0.92	45.6	25.0	11.5	10.2	92.3	7.3	1.5	−1.1
1995	0.94	47.2	24.6	11.2	10.1	93.0	6.9	1.4	−1.3
1998	0.94	47.3	21.0	11.4	11.2	90.9	8.3	1.9	−1.1

NOTE: Estimates from the Survey of Consumer Finances. Cells indicate the percentage of net worth or financial wealth held by households in each segment of the distribution.

Dependent Children (AFDC) and Social Security (Smith 1987). Using estate tax data, Smith found evidence that after 1973 wealth inequality began to drop once again. Others using similar methods have found that between 1972 and 1976, the share of total wealth owned by the top 1 percent of wealth owners declined from 29 to about 19 percent of total wealth (Smith 1987; Wolff 1992).

Wealth inequality began to rise considerably after 1979, a trend that continued throughout the 1980s. By 1983, wealth inequality had returned to, and indeed surpassed on some measures, the 1962 levels. In fact, the share of wealth owned by the top 1 percent of wealth holders was 33.8 percent in 1983 and 37.4 percent by 1989. Real mean wealth grew at 3.4 percent annually during this six-year period, a rate that was nearly double the rate of wealth growth between 1962 and 1983. Others have found similar trends (Danziger, Gottschalk, and Smolensky 1989; Wolff 1993). Wolff (1993) found that mean family wealth increased 23 percent in real terms, but that median wealth grew by only 8 percent over that period. His research also suggested that the share of the top 0.5 percent of wealth owners rose by 5 percent during this period, from 26.2 percent of total household sector wealth in 1983 to 31.4 percent in 1989. The wealth of the next 0.5 percent remained relatively constant at about 7.5 percent of total household wealth, but the share of the next 9 percent decreased from 34.4 percent in 1983 to 33.4 percent in 1989.

Most striking is evidence of the decline in the wealth of the poorest 80 percent of households. The wealth of this group decreased by more than 2 percentage points between 1983 and 1989, leaving their share at just more than 16 percent at the start of the 1990s. Moreover, the top 20 percent of the distribution accumulated nearly all growth in real wealth between 1983 and 1989, and their share of total wealth grew to nearly 84 percent. Past research has also suggested that in the 1980s, wealth inequality in the United States became severe relative to that found in European nations. Studies of wealth in the 1920s suggested that wealth was much more equally distributed in the United States than in Western European nations. Yet research suggests that by the late 1980s, household sector wealth was considerably more concentrated in the United States than in Western Europe (Wolff 1995).

While mean and median household net worth declined during the 1990s, the distribution of wealth continued to worsen. The wealth of the top 1 percent of wealth holders increased from 37 percent of total wealth in 1989 to nearly 39 percent in 1995. However, between 1989 and 1998, the proportion of net worth owned by the top 1 percent of wealth owners rose from 30 percent to more than 34 percent. At the same time, the proportion of net worth owned by those in the bottom 90 percent declined from 33 percent to just over 30 percent (Wolff 1998). The average Forbes 400 member's wealth grew by 177 percent between 1990 and 2000. Between 1989 and 1998, the net worth of the median U.S. household declined by 8.6 percent. In 2000, the Forbes 400 owned as much wealth as the bottom half of the U.S. population combined. The Gini coefficient, an indicator of the degree of inequality comparable to the Gini

coefficient used to measure income inequality, increased from 0.85 in 1989 and 1992 to 0.87 in 1995. The Gini coefficient ranges from 0 to 1, with 0 indicating perfect equality and 1 indicating perfect inequality. Conceptually, if a single household were to own all wealth, the Gini coefficient would equal unity (Weicher 1995, 1997). The Gini coefficient for financial wealth, that is, when real assets such as the family home and other real estate are excluded, reached 0.94 in the late 1990s (Keister 2000b).

Yet another way to think about wealth inequality is to consider spread, or the difference between the wealthiest and the poorest households. Because there is a great deal of inequality in wealth ownership, the spread is naturally quite large. What is perhaps most striking, though, is the degree to which the spread in wealth inequality exceeds the spread in income inequality. Table 5 compares the variance (or spread) in household income to the variance in net asset ownership in three years to demonstrate the changing nature of wealth inequality and the relative size of income inequality. The estimates in this table are from the National Longitudinal Survey of Youth, 1979 Cohort (a detailed explanation of these data is given in the last section of this chapter). As the table indicates, the variance in household ownership of net assets was extremely large in each year included in the table, but particularly in 1990 when other estimates indicate that wealth inequality was at historically high levels. The spread in income inequality was also quite large, but as the ratio between the two measures indicates, inequality in wealth ownership surpasses inequality in income by tremendous margins. In 1990, for instance, variance in net asset

TABLE 5 **RATIO OF VARIANCE OF NATURAL LOG OF WEALTH TO VARIANCE OF NATURAL LOG OF INCOME**

	1985	1990	1998
Variance in income	1.56	2.01	3.38
Variance in net assets	45.18	215.80	113.21
Ratio	0.034	0.009	0.030

NOTE: Ratio is calculated using the NLS-Y79. Income is total household income; net assets is the sum of assets less the sum of debts; both wealth and income are in 2000 dollars (adjusted using the CPI). The sample size varies between income and net assets because missing values are different for the two variables.

ownership was more than 100 times greater than variance in income.

Racial inequality in wealth ownership is among the most extreme and persistent forms of stratification in general and wealth stratification in particular (Conley 1999; Keister 2000; Oliver and Shapiro 1995). Blacks and Hispanics, in particular, own considerably less wealth than whites. In 1992, while median income for blacks was about 60 percent of median income for whites, median net worth for blacks was only 8 percent of median net worth for whites. In that same year, 25 percent of white families had zero or negative assets, but more than 60 percent of black families had no wealth (Oliver and Shapiro 1995). Longitudinal estimates suggest that between 1960 and 1995, whites were twice as likely as minorities to have more wealth than income and nearly three times as likely to experience wealth mobility (Keister 2000b). Minorities are also underrepresented among the very wealthy. In 1995, 95 percent of those in the top 1 percent of wealth holders were white, while only 1 percent were black (Keister 2000b; Wolff 1998). The wealth position of nonblack minorities has attracted less attention, but there

is evidence that the wealth accumulation of whites also exceeds that of Hispanics and Asians (Campbell and Kaufman 2000; Wolff 1998).

‖ REFERENCES

Aizcorbe, Ana M., Arthur B. Kennickell, and Kevin B. Moore. 2001. "Recent Changes in U.S. Family Finances: Evidence from the 1998 and 2001 Survey of Consumer Finances." Federal Reserve Board Working Paper.

Campbell, Lori A., and Robert L. Kaufman. 2000. "Racial Differences in Household Wealth: Beyond Black and White." *American Sociological Association.*

Conley, Dalton. 1999. *Being Black, Living in the Red: Race, Wealth and Social Policy in America.* Berkeley, CA: University of California Press.

Danziger, Sheldon, Peter Gottschalk, and Eugene Smolensky. 1989. "How the Rich Fared, 1973–1987." *American Economic Review* 79:310–14.

Dolan, Kerry A. 1999. "200 Global Billionaires." *Forbes Magazine.*

Federal Reserve System, Board of Governors. 2001. *Balance Sheets For the U.S. Economy*. Washington, DC: Federal Reserve Board.

Keister, Lisa A. 2000a. "Race and Wealth Inequality: The Impact of Racial Differences in Asset Ownership on the Distribution of Household Wealth." *Social Science Research* 29:477–502.

Keister, Lisa A. 2000b. *Wealth in America*. New York: Cambridge University Press.

Lampman, Robert J. 1962. *The Share of Top Wealth-Holders in National Wealth, 1922–56*. Princeton, NJ: Princeton University Press.

Oliver, Melvin O., and Thomas M. Shapiro. 1995. *Black Wealth/White Wealth*. New York: Routledge.

Smith, James D. 1987. "Recent Trends in the Distribution of Wealth in the U.S.: Data, Research Problems, and Prospects." Pp. 72–90 in *International Comparisons of the Distribution of Household Wealth*, edited by E. N. Wolff. New York: Oxford University Press.

Weicher, John C. 1995. "Changes in the Distribution of Wealth: Increasing Inequality?" *Federal Reserve Bank of St. Louis Review* 77:5–23.

Weicher, John C. 1997. "Wealth and Its Distribution: 1983–1992: Secular Growth, Cyclical Stability." *Federal Reserve Bank of St. Louis Review* 79:3–23.

Williamson, Jeffrey G., and Peter H. Lindert. 1980. *American Inequality: A Macroweconomic History*. New York: Academic Press.

Wolff, Edward N. 1992. Changing Inequality of Wealth." *American Economic Review* 82:552–58.

Wolff, Edward N. 1993. "Trends in Household Wealth in the United States During the 1980s." Unpublished manuscript, New York University.

Wolff, Edward N. 1995. *Top Heavy: A Study of the Increasing Inequality of Wealth in America*. New York: Twentieth Century Fund.

Wolff, Edward N. 1998. "Recent Trends in the Size Distribution of Household Wealth." *Journal of Economic Perspectives* 12:131–50.

Wolff, Edward N., and Maria Marley. 1989. "Long Term Trends in U.S. Wealth Inequality: Methodological Issues and Results." Pp. 765–839 in *The Measurement of Saving, Investment, and Wealth*, edited by R. Lipsey and H. S. Tice. Chicago: University of Chicago Press.

Forty Acres and a Mule*

DALTON CONLEY

The loss of wealth is the loss of dirt.

John Heywood, circa 1564

In 1865, at the time of the Emancipation Proclamation, African Americans owned 0.5 percent of the total worth of the United States. This statistic is not surprising; most black Americans had been slaves up to that point. However, by 1990, a full 135 years after the abolition of slavery, black Americans owned only a meager 1 percent of total wealth.[1] In other words, almost no progress had been made in terms of property ownership. African Americans may have won "title" to their own bodies and to their labor, but they have gained ownership over little else.

During the nineteenth century and at the start of the twentieth, this lack of assets was nothing remarkable, for the vast majority of Americans of all races owned little if any property. But over the course of the twentieth century, there has been a dispersal of wealth[2]—limited as it may have been—with

---

* First published in 1999; from *Being Black, Living in the Red: Race, Wealth, and Social Policy in America*.

1 C. Anderson, *Black Labor, White Wealth: The Search for Power and Economic Justice* (Edgewood, Md.: Duncan and Duncan, 1994).

2 S. Spilerman, M. Semyonov, and N. Lewin-Epstein, "Wealth, Intergenerational Transfers, and Life Chances," in *Social Theory and Social Policy: Essays in Honor of James Coleman*, ed. A. Sorensen and S. Spilerman (New York: Praeger, 1993).

the result that the typical white American family in 1994 had a nest egg of assets totaling a median of $72,000. With a median net worth of approximately $9,800 in that year, the typical black family had no significant nest egg to speak of.[3] Unlike income or education levels, wealth has the particular attribute of tending to reproduce itself in a multiplicative fashion from generation to generation. More colloquially, "it takes money to make money." As a result, the black-white gap in assets has continued to grow since the 1960s, when civil rights victories were won.[4]

Black people seem to have gained little that would encourage them to maintain a realistic belief in the "American dream." In fact, this growing wealth gap may help to explain a paradox that exists with respect to race and the American dream. As a group, poor African Americans—increasingly concentrated in inner cities and relatively worse off—maintain the same level of credence in the American dream as they did in the 1960s. By contrast, the black middle class, which has achieved more in terms of income, occupation, and education since the 1960s, has grown increasingly bitter and disillusioned with the idea of the American dream. "In combination," writes Jennifer Hochschild, "these paradoxes produce the surprising result that poor blacks now believe more in the American dream than rich blacks do, which is a reversal from the 1960s."[5] For middle-class blacks, perhaps the promise of their higher education,

more prestigious occupations, and even greater incomes falls flat since they still face difficulty in achieving parity with their white counterparts in the most tangible manifestation of class identity: asset accumulation (the house, the car, the business, and so on).

||| WEALTH BY INCOME BRACKET

Differences in wealth between blacks and whites are not a result of lower earnings among the black population. As Figure 1 shows, the story does not get much better when the lower incomes of African Americans are taken into consideration. Even with data broken down by yearly income bracket, the median and mean net worths of blacks are dramatically lower than those of whites. In fact, Francine Blau and John Graham conclude that even after taking into account the lower average incomes of African American families, as much as three-quarters of the wealth gap persists.[6]

When we look at the PSID wealth distribution by race and income in Figure 1 ★ ★ ★, we find that, at every income level, blacks have substantially fewer assets than whites. Among the poorest group (annual income of $15,000 or less in 1992), whites have at least some wealth, with a median net worth of $10,000 (the mean figure is $47,214), whereas the typical black family has virtually no wealth (the median is zero, and the mean is $15,959). A full half of all poor African American families have zero (or

---

3 These figures include housing and vehicle equity.

4 M. Oliver and T. Shapiro, *Black Wealth/White Wealth: A New Perspective on Racial Inequality* (New York: Routledge, 1995).

5 J. L. Hochschild, *Facing Up to the American Dream: Race, Class, and the Soul of the Nation* (Princeton, N.J.: Princeton University Press, 1995), p. 72.

6 F. D. Blau and J. W. Graham, "Black-White Differences in Wealth and Asset Composition," *Quarterly Journal of Economics* 105 (1990): 321–39.

FIGURE 1 **MEDIAN NET WORTH IN 1994, BY RACE AND ANNUAL INCOME. AT ALL LEVELS OF ANNUAL INCOME, AFRICAN AMERICANS HAVE A LOWER MEDIAN NET WORTH THAN WHITES. * * ***

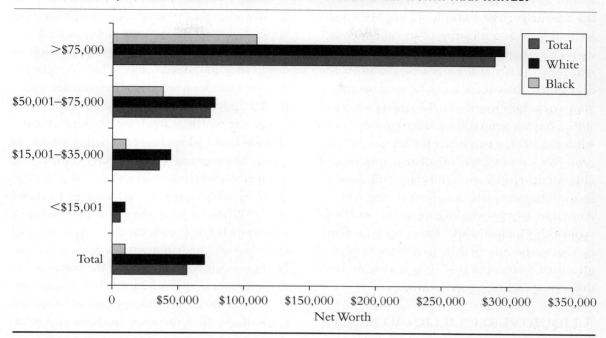

less than zero) assets, while slightly less than 23 percent of poor whites find themselves in this situation. In the middle of the income distribution—the $35,001 to $50,000 range—whites have a median figure that is slightly more than double that of blacks ($81,000 and $40,000, respectively; the mean figures are $166,185 and $74,834). At the upper end of the income ladder, whites have on average almost three times the wealth of blacks.

Examining the data graphically helps us understand the distribution by race. When viewed in this format, it becomes clear that the rate of increase of wealth as we move up the income ladder follows a curve for both blacks

and whites. At the lowest level, the percentage difference is the greatest, but the absolute difference is the lowest, given the lower amounts for both groups. The gap becomes smallest in percentage terms among the middle-income group and then widens again among the next two higher categories.

Because lower-income black families essentially have no assets, it becomes evident not only that African Americans suffer from lower asset levels as a group but also that the distribution of wealth *within* the community is far more uneven.[7] For example, if we were to scale down the entire white population of the United States to a total of one hundred families, we would

7 Also see A. Brimmer, "Income, Wealth, and Investment Behavior in the Black Community," *A.E.A. Papers and Proceedings* 78 (1988): 151–55.

find that the tenth richest family would own wealth totaling 41.5 times the amount held by the ninetieth richest family. (The 90/10 ratio is often used as a measure of income inequality.) This number, 41.5, is a large 90/10 ratio, reflecting the fact that assets are more unevenly distributed than income. (The corresponding 90/10 ratio for income was 9.4 among whites in 1992.) But as unequal as the distribution was for whites in 1994, it was worse for African Americans. We cannot even calculate a meaningful ratio for the black community since the denominator is negative (the ninetieth richest African American family would have a net worth of minus $200); meanwhile, the ratio of the tenth richest to the ninetieth richest black family as measured by income is 12.7, again higher than the corresponding figure for whites.

‖ LIQUID VERSUS ILLIQUID ASSETS

Although there is no absolutely clear line between liquid and illiquid wealth, many scholars do distinguish the two types of assets. As a general rule, liquid assets can be cashed in relatively quickly, as compared to illiquid assets. Liquid assets include stocks, bonds, and cash accounts; illiquid assets range from vehicles to real estate to business ownership. Liquid assets may prove more critical during times of crisis such as spells of unemployment, whereas illiquid assets such as a home, car, and vacation property may have more of an immediate psychological effect since they are consumptive as well as being investment instruments. A car, for example, might be necessary to commute to

work, but it can also serve as a status symbol. Owning a valuable home may place a family in a better school district and a safer neighborhood while showing off economic power as well.

In a variation of the liquid-illiquid dichotomy, Melvin Oliver and Thomas Shapiro employ a similar distinction between net worth (NW) and net financial assets (NFA). They define net worth as total wealth minus liabilities; net financial assets are defined as net worth minus housing and vehicle equity. Employing this methodology, they demonstrate that in 1984 the black–white gap was greater for net financial assets.[8] When we jump ahead a decade and use a similar dichotomy with the PSID data, we find that, overall, median assets for blacks, excluding home equity, total $2,000; the corresponding figure for whites is $28,816 ★ ★ ★. The sum of $28,000 could provide substantial leeway in times of unemployment, medical crises, or other unexpected expenses. In comparison, $2,000 would not cover many mortgage payments or months of rent. The average (mean) white family, with over $30,000 of fungible assets, could probably sustain itself for quite a while through an income shock or other financial crisis.

‖ SPENDING, SAVING, AND INVESTING: EXPLODING RACIAL STEREOTYPES

If African Americans saved less of their earnings than whites, this would provide a relatively simple explanation for the wealth difference by race. Certainly the popular stereotype is that African Americans are more likely to dis-

8 Oliver and Shapiro, *Black Wealth / White Wealth.*

play rampant consumerism. Popular culture is flooded with images of the profligate urban black; films often depict an extreme fashion consciousness among young African Americans. Since respect and a sense of identity can be hard to come by through work in the ghetto (and since jobs themselves are hard to come by), perhaps African Americans resort to consumer spending more often than whites in order to construct an identity in today's socioeconomic landscape. Maybe African Americans react to feelings of oppression by indulging in more escapist activities and thus spend a higher proportion of their incomes. A heavier reliance on spending for consumer goods and entertainment necessarily implies a lower savings rate and thus would explain racial differences in total wealth accumulation.

However enticing this explanation may be, a look at data over a five-year period (1984–89) does not indicate that blacks save a lower percentage of income than their white counterparts. In the PSID data, we find that African Americans saved an average of 11 percent of their annual income over this period, and whites saved 10 percent (not a statistically significant difference). This finding is consistent with other research that has examined black-white savings differentials (although savings can be measured many different ways).[9] For example, economist Warren Hrung reports that when permanent income is taken into consideration, there is no difference in the savings rates of blacks and whites.[10] Others have found no significant "cultural" effects (such as race might be) on savings at the individual level.[11]

Many other demographic factors, such as family size and structure, education, age, and home-ownership, affect savings levels. For instance, female-headed households tend to save less than two-parent or male headed households. Families whose members have higher education levels tend to save more. The relationship between savings and age is curvilinear: people tend to save more as they get older, until they hit a certain point—most likely, retirement age—when their savings decline and they may even move to dissaving (that is, spending down the capital).[12] Race, however, is not among the demographic factors that determine savings rates. Thus, we may conclude that the highly visible black consumerism witnessed through the lens of media stereotypes may be just that—a stereotype.

Alternatively, although it may be the case that African American adolescents disproportionately spend on particular consumer goods such as sneakers and movies, it may also be the case that these spending patterns are concentrated on

---

9 In the case of the PSID, the amount of savings is imputed through the difference between 1984 and 1989 net worth, adjusted for inheritances received, value changes in 1984 assets, and changes in household composition (people moving in or out with assets or debts). I then take that as a percentage of the inflation-adjusted, five-year average income for that period. However, windfalls and gifts may appear to be savings in this case. Alternative measures include self-reported savings as a percentage of annual income.

10 W. Hrung, "The Permanent Income Hypothesis and Black/White Savings Differentials" (Department of Economics, University of California at Berkeley, 1997).

11 C. D. Carroll, B.-K. Rhee, and C. Rhee, "Are There Cultural Effects on Saving? Some Cross-Sectional Evidence," *Quarterly Journal of Economics* 109 (1994): 695–99.

12 See, e.g., K. C. Land and S. T. Russell, "Wealth Accumulation Across the Life Course: Stability and Change in Sociodemographic Covariate Structures of Net Worth Data in the Survey of Income and Program Participation, 1984–1991," *Social Science Research* 25 (1996): 423–62.

very visible, recognizable consumer items that do not add up to much in figuring total expenditures and savings among the population as a whole. In other words, stereotypical "white" expenses might be less publicized but dearer in the final count.

Another stereotype is that African Americans have a lower propensity for entrepreneurship in the mainstream economy—that is, they are less likely to take on the risk of owning their own business or becoming self-employed. At the same time, blacks are more often depicted as "street hustlers," black-market or illicit entrepreneurs such as drug dealers, pimps, numbers runners, and so on. There is an obvious contradiction in portraying African Americans as averse to risk in the mainstream economy but willing to seek out even more dangerous gambles for profit in the underground economy. It is possible, however, that informal economic activities come to replace formal means of business development when attempts at legal business formation are repeatedly frustrated or when informal activities yield higher net profits.

It is beyond the scope of the data available in this study to analyze all the opportunities and activities available to African Americans and whites in the formal and informal economies (as well as the barriers). But it is possible to examine the data for an answer to the following question: are African Americans less likely than whites to be self-employed entrepreneurs in the mainstream economy? In the PSID data, the answer to this question is no. There is no significant racial difference in rates of self-employment. In fact, overall, African Americans have a slightly higher rate than whites ★ ★ ★.

This finding tends to obscure a more complex picture of a race–class interaction, however. When we examine the data more closely, we see that it is among the middle-income brackets that blacks are more likely to be entrepreneurs. At the highest income bracket, 10.6 percent of whites were self-employed, compared to only 2.6 percent of African Americans, a differential factor of 4. To a great extent, this group probably represents professionals such as doctors and lawyers—occupations to which blacks have only recently gained equal access. We should also keep in mind that self-employment can be defined in many ways, ranging from artisan work to business ownership to contract/temporary employee status. This variation may also explain the higher propensity of middle-income blacks to be self-employed, since those in this group may well be contract employees.

COMPETING EXPLANATIONS FOR BLACK-WHITE WEALTH INEQUALITY

If neither income differences, differential savings rates, nor propensity for entrepreneurship lead to racial inequalities in wealth accumulation, what is the source of the disparity? The reasons for the disparity may rest in the historical nature of race relations in the United States, in contemporary dynamics, or in both. Historically, low wages have meant a low savings rate in both absolute and percentage terms, while discrimination in the credit market has precluded African Americans from becoming business owners: "To a considerable extent [lack of wealth] can be traced to a long history of deprivation in this country," argues economist Andrew Brimmer. "This means that blacks have had much less opportunity than whites to earn, save or to inherit wealth. Because of this historical legacy, black families have had few opportunities to accumulate wealth and to pass it on to their descendants."[13] Whereas Brimmer attributes racial differences in wealth holdings primarily to the head start that whites have enjoyed, others claim that African Americans continue to face institutional barriers to converting their income to equity. Specifically, in their book *American Apartheid*, sociologists Douglas Massey and Nancy Denton document how black people continue to face discrimination in both housing and credit markets.[14]

The results of both these sets of forces are documented by sociologist John Henretta, who shows that during the 1970s blacks were much less likely than whites of similar incomes and ages to own their homes. Further, he demonstrates that even after accounting for a range of socioeconomic and demographic factors, the net worths of blacks were substantially lower than those of whites.[15] Additionally, Toby Parcel documents that, even among homeowners, African Americans face difficulty in converting their income to housing equity—that is, to net worth.[16] These data are quite dated by now, having been collected only half a generation after the passage of landmark civil rights legislation during the 1960s. Nonetheless, using simulation

techniques, Oliver and Shapiro more recently estimate that "institutional biases in the residential arena have cost the current generation of blacks about $82 billion."[17] In *Assets and the Poor*, Michael Sherraden sums up the two forces leading to the black-white wealth difference:

> The most obvious answer is that blacks have always earned less than whites, and, over the years, these earnings shortfalls have resulted in less savings, less investment, and less transfers to the succeeding generations. Over time, less income can result in vast differences in asset accumulation. In addition, however, there is another dimension to the explanation: social and economic institutions have systematically restricted asset accumulation among blacks.[18]

Most scholars would agree with Sherraden that both current and past circumstances lead to racial differences in net worth. But the question remains: how much of the wealth discrepancy is linked to wealth inheritance and how much to contemporary conditions? The answer has important theoretical and policy implications. If it is the socioeconomic disadvantage of the parents of the current African American generation that matters, then the answer may lie in inheritance and property tax policy. But if the lion's share of the black-white wealth gap remains after parental socioeconomic status (including net worth) is taken into

13 Brimmer, "Income, Wealth, and Investment Behavior," p. 153.

14 D. Massey and N. Denton, *American Apartheid: Segregation and the Making of the Underclass* (Cambridge, Mass.: Harvard University Press, 1993).

15 J. C. Henretta, "Race Differences in Middle-Class Lifestyle: The Role of Home Ownership," *Social Science Research* 8 (1979): 63–78; also see M. R. Jackman and R. W. Jackman,

"Racial Inequalities in Home Ownership," *Social Forces* 58 (1980): 1221–34.

16 T. Parcel, "Wealth Accumulation of Black and White Men: The Case of Housing Equity," *Social Problems* 30 (1982): 199–211.

17 Oliver and Shapiro, *Black Wealth/White Wealth*, p. 9.

18 M. Sherraden, *Assets and the Poor: A New Direction for Social Policy* (Armonk, N.Y.: Sharpe, 1991), p. 131.

consideration, then an aggressive race-based policy in the housing and credit markets may be in order. Before we directly address this issue empirically, it will be helpful to review some of the historical and contemporary issues that may be at play.

The Historical Legacy of Deprivation

There is ample evidence to suspect that historical forces and their legacy of asset bequeathment play a role in explaining the current black-white wealth gap. While there has been a paucity of data on individual African American wealth holdings until very recently, we have ample evidence that, as a group, black people have endured a long history of asset deprivation, from the first days when Africans were wrested from their families, homes, and possessions in West Africa and brought to these shores in bondage, not "owning" even their bodies or their labor, let alone any tangible wealth. In fact, for the most part, slaves were legally prohibited from ownership of any form of wealth.[19]

Some theorists have argued that the social-psychological legacy of slavery prevented habits of savings and asset accrual among African Americans. "Using a cultural argument," write Oliver and Shapiro, "[conservative scholars] assert that slaves developed a habit of excessive consumerism and not one of savings and thrift."[20] Although there may be truth to the argument that individuals who lack an opportunity to accumulate savings would develop a

more consumerist outlook, it is unlikely that such a legacy would persist a century later if blacks had not been continually prevented from accumulating assets in the postslavery era. It may even be the case that *especially* during the rough conditions of slavery, blacks had to be thrifty and resourceful in order to survive. Further, Oliver and Shapiro claim, "while slaves were not legally able to amass wealth, they did, in large numbers, acquire assets through thrift, intelligence, industry and their owners' liberal paternalism."[21]

During the antebellum period, some free black people did own property that totaled an estimated $50 million in 1860.[22] Historian Peter Kolchin has documented that even as early as the period between 1664 and 1677 (before the peak of slavery), in Northhampton County, Virginia, "at least 13 (out of 101) blacks became free landowners, most through self-purchase."[23] After the Emancipation Proclamation, rhetoric floated around regarding a potential and massive land redistribution. The Freedmen's Bureau, set up by President Andrew Johnson and administered by "good Christian" General Oliver Otis Howard, had the mission of promoting economic self-sufficiency among the former slaves. The agency, however, never delivered on its promise of dividing up plantations and giving each freed slave "forty acres and a mule" as reparation for slavery.[24]

The importance of the lack of land redistribution cannot be overstated. Historian Paul

---

19 Oliver and Shapiro, *Black Wealth/White Wealth*, p. 37.
20 Ibid.
21 Ibid.
22 E. F. Frazier, *The Free Negro Family* (Nashville: Fisk University Press, 1932), p. 35.
23 P. Kolchin, *American Slavery, 1619–1877* (New York: Hill and Wang, 1993), p. 16.
24 C. F. Oubre, *Forty Acres and a Mule: The Freedman's Bureau and Black Land Ownership* (Baton Rouge: Louisiana State University Press, 1978).

Cimbala writes, "Once established on property of their own, [the former slaves] believed, they would be truly free to pursue additional goals [such as wealth accumulation and political participation] without constantly worrying about offending those who otherwise would have been paying them wages."[25] W. E. B. Du Bois argued that if white America had made good on its promise of land repatriation to blacks, it "would have made a basis of real democracy in the United States."[26]

In many southern states where land redistribution did occur, it turned out to be only a temporary phenomenon. In Georgia, for example, Cimbala describes how land given to freed slaves by General Sherman "was restored [by General Howard] to its white claimants before the ex-slaves had even one full season to test their new status."[27] While Commissioner Howard "believed that the freedmen should have land and that the South could become reconstructed only if it became a land of small farms," according to Claude Oubre, Howard also clung to the notion that "freedmen should earn land and not receive it as a gift. He therefore encouraged freedmen to work and save money in order to purchase land." Never mind the argument that the slaves—through their servitude—had already earned the land. In the face of white southerners who refused to sell farms to blacks even if the whites could not afford to plant

crops themselves, Howard "recommended that northerners, including bureau agents, purchase or lease farms to provide work for the freedmen."[28] In fact, P. S. Peirce writes that of the confiscated plantations, "the greater number went to northerners, who hired Negroes to cultivate them."[29] In this manner, the Freedmen's Bureau may have unwittingly become a catalyst more for the enrichment of northern "carpetbaggers" than for the promotion of southern black entrepreneurship.

It was this hesitancy to "give" land to freed black slaves, combined with the wage labor/land-lease policy, that helped to foster the system of farm tenancy that dominated the South after the Civil War. Sharecropping (tenant farming) was an arrangement in which poor black farmers were provided with housing, seed, acreage, and provisions in return for cultivating the crop.[30] The black farmers did not own any of the capital (that is, the acreage or supplies) and thus were dependent on their white landlords, who kept them on the land at subsistence levels. While farm tenancy was politically different from slavery, in economic terms the end result was not much different. The recollections of Moses Burge, the daughter of black sharecroppers in Georgia, attest to this fact: "We went barefooted. My feet been frost-bitten lots of times. My dad couldn't afford to buy no shoes. He'd get in debt and he'd figure every year he

---

25 P. Cimbala, "A Black Colony in Dougherty County: The Freedman's Bureau and the Failure of Reconstruction in Southwest Georgia," *Journal of Southwest Georgia History* 4 (1986): 72.

26 Du Bois quoted in Sherraden, *Assets and the Poor*, p. 133.

27 P. Cimbala, "The Freedman's Bureau, the Freedmen, and Sherman's Grant in Reconstruction Georgia, 1865–1867," *Journal of Southern History* 55 (1989): 597–98.

28 Oubre, *Forty Acres and a Mule*, p. xiii.

29 P. S. Peirce, *The Freedman's Bureau: A Chapter in the History of Reconstruction* (New York: Haskell House, 1904), p. 22.

30 N. Lemann, *The Promised Land: The Great Black Migration and How It Changed America* (New York: Vintage, 1991), p. 11.

going to get out. . . ." But, she added, "[then] they'd tell you, 'You bought so and so.' They get through figuring it up you lacking $100 of coming clear. What the hell could you do? You living on his place, you couldn't walk off."[31]

While many southern blacks were trapped in a cycle of debt and no assets—denied the right to make deposits and get loans by banks across the region—whites were given low-interest loans to set up farms in the middle and far western United States. Those few black individuals who managed to escape sharecropping and join the westward migration with the promise of land grants found that their ownership status was "not legally enforceable" in, for example, the state of California.[32] A white person could come and lay legal claim to the land that a black individual had already settled, and the white person's title would be honored over that of the African American. "Thus," according to Oliver and Shapiro, "African Americans were largely barred from taking advantage of the nineteenth-century Federal land-grant program that helped result in an astounding three quarters of families owning their farms."[33]

In fact, the only major nineteenth-century institution that was somewhat successful in fostering wealth accumulation among African Americans was the Freedmen's Bank, part of the Freedmen's Bureau. This bank failed in 1874, however (after the Panic of 1873), largely as a result of "highly questionable no-interest loans from the bank to white companies" doled out by the white-controlled board of directors, according to Sherraden.[34] Despite its problems, the Freedmen's Bank did help some blacks acquire land and businesses. After its collapse, the rate of land ownership among black people did not rise as rapidly, and, furthermore, many blacks no longer trusted banks because many African American small investors lost all their savings when the institution failed.

Constraints on capital were not the only nineteenth-century barrier to asset accumulation for African Americans. Many southern states passed "Black Codes," laws that required blacks to have an employer or face arrest as a "vagrant." Manning Marable describes the result:

> Working independently for themselves, some Black artisans were fined, jailed and even sentenced to work as convict laborers. South Carolina's legislature declared in December 1865, that 'no person of color shall pursue or practice the art, trade, or business of an artisan, mechanic, or shopkeeper, or another trade employment or business . . . on his own account and for his own benefit until he shall have obtained a license which shall be good for one year only.' Black peddlers and merchants had to produce $100 annually to pay for the license, while whites paid nothing.[35]

Aside from such institutional and legal barriers, there always existed the not-so-subtle threat of lynching or other physical violence if an African American tried to open a business—

---

31 "From Field to Factory: Afro-American Migration, 1915–1940," Smithsonian Institution exhibition, Museum of American History, Washington, D.C., 1994.
32 Oliver and Shapiro, *Black Wealth/White Wealth*, p. 38.
33 Ibid.

34 Sherraden, *Assets and the Poor*, p. 133.
35 M. Marable, *How Capitalism Underdeveloped Black America: Problems in Race, Political Economy, and Society* (Boston: South End Press, 1983), pp. 142–43.

particularly if the business might compete with white-owned franchises.[36]

Black ownership of wealth grew slowly during the latter half of the nineteenth century, and it continued to face obstacles in the twentieth century. The land holdings belonging to the majority of black title holders at the turn of the century were small, family-run farms; the advent of large-scale farming in the twentieth century hurt blacks disproportionately. The peak of farm ownership among African Americans was reached in 1910 at 218,000 units; this figure held steady until 1920. By 1930, it had dropped to 182,000, and to 173,000 by 1940. During this period of decline, which includes the Great Depression, many farmers, both black and white, were losing their land, but there appears to have been a net transfer of land from blacks to whites. August Meier and Elliot Rudwick estimate that the rate of land loss for blacks averaged 350,000 acres per year.[37] As the number of black-owned farms dropped over the course of the first half of the century, the numbers of African Americans who migrated to the northern industrial centers grew: between 1910 and 1970, 6.5 million black Americans moved from the South to the North; 5 million of this group made the transition after 1940.[38]

Meanwhile, Old Age Insurance (Social Security), established in 1935, "virtually excluded African Americans and Latinos, for it exempted agricultural and domestic workers from coverage and marginalized low-wage workers. . . . In 1935, for example, 42 percent of black workers in occupations covered by social insurance did not earn enough to qualify for benefits compared to 22 percent for whites."[39] Not receiving Social Security benefits meant that any savings that had been accumulated by retired or disabled black Americans most likely had to be spent during old age rather than being handed down to the next generation. Further, the lack of social insurance meant that many households had to care for and support indigent, elderly family members, directly diverting the next generation's resources away from savings and capital accumulation.

Perhaps the most dramatic barrier to black-white wealth equity in the twentieth century, however, has involved residential issues and institutions. For example, the Home Owners' Loan Corporation (HOLC), founded in 1933, helped many homeowners avoid default during the Great Depression. But it was the HOLC that institutionalized the redlining technique of associating estimated risks of loan default with neighborhoods. The HOLC invariably assigned black neighborhoods the lowest rating, ensuring that no HOLC-sponsored loans went to black residents. Thus, African Americans could not as readily refinance their mortgages during the Depression, and a greater proportion of black owners lost their homes when contrasted to their white counterparts.

The story did not change after the Great Depression. The Federal Housing Authority (FHA), established in 1937, in combination with the Veterans Administration (VA)

---

36 Sherraden, *Assets and the Poor.*
37 A. Meier and E. Rudwick, *From Plantation to Ghetto* (New York: Hill and Wang, 1970).
38 Lemann, *Promised Land,* p. 6.
39 Oliver and Shapiro, *Black Wealth/White Wealth,* p. 38.

home-lending program that was part of the Servicemen's Readjustment Act of 1944, made homeownership possible for millions of Americans after World War II by guaranteeing low-interest, long-term loans for first-home buyers. But African Americans were systematically shut out of participation in these programs because loans were channeled to suburbs and away from the central cities where blacks predominantly resided. In fact, according to Massey and Denton, with FHA financing, it became "cheaper to buy new suburban homes than to rent comparable older dwellings in the central city."[40]

"In the suburb-shaping years between 1930 and 1960," write David Kirp, John Dwyer, and Larry Rosenthal, "fewer than one percent of all mortgages in the nation were issued to African Americans."[41] The FHA helped to facilitate this disparity. The *Underwriting Manual* distributed to lenders by the FHA specifically prohibited lending in neighborhoods that were changing in racial or social composition.[42] For example, "in a 1941 memorandum concerning St. Louis, the FHA proclaimed that 'the rapidly rising Negro population has produced a problem in the maintenance of real estate values.'"[43] In this manner, not only did FHA policy prevent the emergence of a new, larger class of suburban black homeowners, but the lack of loans to potential purchasers in the central city caused an accelerated decline in existing property values among African Americans, since willing sellers

could not find buyers. All these institutionalized practices set the stage for the conditions of racial segregation that are observable today and that may contribute, in large part, to the black-white wealth disparity.

Contemporary Black-White Segregation

Over and above the historical forces that may be at work to depress the wealth levels of African Americans relative to those of whites, there is also evidence that race-based dynamics in the contemporary United States play a major role in perpetuating this type of inequality. Owning one's home is the prime method of equity accumulation for most families in the United States.[44] In 1997, the overall rate of homeownership was 65.7 percent, a record high (although, according to data from the Luxembourg Income Study, this rate still falls in the middle range among Western countries; the country with the highest percentage of homeowning households is Australia).[45] But the overall U.S. figure obscures differences by race and place.

Patterns of residential segregation that lead to a disproportionate concentration of minority households in central cities mean that African Americans are less likely than whites to own the homes in which they reside. In 1997, 28 percent of whites lived in central cities, compared to 55 percent who lived in suburbs. During that same year, the corresponding figures for blacks were almost a mirror image: 64 percent for urban residence and

40 Massey and Denton, *American Apartheid,* p. 52.
41 D. L. Kirp, J. P. Dwyer, and L. A. Rosenthal, *Our Town: Race, Housing, and the Soul of Suburbia* (New Brunswick, N.J.: Rutgers University Press, 1995), p. 7.
42 Massey and Denton, *American Apartheid,* p. 54.
43 Kirp, Dwyer, and Rosenthal, *Our Town,* p. 26.
44 F. S. Levy and R. Michel, *The Economic Future of American Families* (Washington, D.C.: Urban Institute Press, 1991);

and Spilerman, Semyonov, and Lewin-Epstein, "Wealth, Intergenerational Transfers, and Life Chances."
45 Joint Center for Housing Studies, *The State of the Nation's Housing: 1997* (Cambridge: Harvard University, 1998). The Luxembourg Income Study is a dataset housed at the Centre d'Etudes de Populations, de Pauvreté et de Politiques Socio-Economiques (CEPS), Difrerdange, Luxembourg; see *http://lissy.ceps.lu/access.htm.*

31 percent for suburban residence. (These figures do not add up to 100 percent by race because they exclude rural residents.)[46] This spatial distribution is important because 72 percent of suburban residents owned their homes in 1997, compared to only 49 percent of their urban counterparts. The result of this combination is that in 1997 only 44 percent of blacks owned their homes, in contrast to 71 percent of whites, according to the Harvard Joint Center for Housing Studies.[47]

The issue of segregation is not economically benign. Housing in black neighborhoods has a lower rate of value increase (and in some cases may decrease in worth) when contrasted to similar units in predominantly white neighborhoods.[48] Therefore, not only do racially segregated housing markets hinder the efforts of African Americans to become homeowners, but also those individuals who do manage to buy a house may find that it is worth less than a comparable house owned by a white person purely because it is located in a black neighborhood. In this manner, the social-psychological realm (of racist ideology) may be directly linked to the economic arena (by determining the relative value of neighborhoods). ★ ★ ★ Property has the quality of picking up the social value conferred upon an object or idea. A rare stamp or a precious metal has no inherent productive value; rather, its value is socially conferred by the market. Likewise,

black housing may be worth less because the majority group (whites) controls the market, and thus segregation is in this group's interest. White housing is worth more precisely because it is not black housing.

This dynamic is best illustrated by the process of "white flight." White flight usually occurs when the percentage of black residents in a community reaches a certain level (roughly 20 percent) and white homeowners begin to fear that their property values will drop. Why might they drop? Values fall because white flight creates a vacuum in the market—in other words, the anticipation of a market drop in housing prices becomes a self-fulfilling prophecy. This pernicious circle sustains racist residential ideology and directly links it to economics in the housing market. The property value/racial segregation dynamic affects the life chances of black Americans in many realms since, as a result of residential segregation patterns, poor minorities are more likely to find themselves living among other poor families (that is, concentrated) than impoverished whites are.[49] Minority families are also more likely to live in areas with abandoned buildings or in units that have multiple inadequacies.[50] In addition, because school budgets are financed through local property taxes, the issue of school quality is tied to the value of property.

46 K. DeBarros and C. Bennett, "The Black Population in the United States: March 1997 (Update)," *Current Population Reports,* Series P-20, No. 508 (Washington, D.C.: U.S. Government Printing Office, 1998).

47 Joint Center for Housing Studies, *State of the Nation's Housing,* 1997.

48 F. Stutz and A. E. Kartman, "Housing Affordability and Spatial Price Variation in the United States," *Economic Geography* 58 (1982); 221–35; J. Adams, "Growth of U.S. Cities and Recent Trends in Urban Real Estate Values," in *Cities and*

Their Vital Systems, ed. J. H. Ausubel and R. Herman (Washington, D.C.: National Academy Press, 1988), pp. 108–45.

49 G. Duncan and J. L. Aber, "Neighborhood Structure and Conditions," in *Neighborhood Poverty: Context and Consequences for Child and Adolescent Development,* ed. G. Duncan, J. Brooks-Gunn, and J. L. Aber (New York: Russell Sage Foundation, 1997).

50 E. Rosenbaum, "Racial/Ethnic Differences in Home Ownership and Housing Quality, 1991," *Social Problems* 43 (1997): 403–26.

The existence of such a dual housing market—a market segregated by race, where African Americans suffer limited housing selections as a result of institutional and overt discrimination—is well documented.[51] Furthermore, some researchers have used U.S. census data to demonstrate that levels of residential segregation have increased in the period since the 1960s,[52] although at least one study claims that residential segregation seems to have peaked in the 1970s and declined slightly since then—with the largest percentage decreases of segregation indices in newer southern and western cities.[53]

While there is a sizable literature tracking and documenting the importance of continued residential segregation, few researchers have addressed the issue of racial differences in rates of homeownership directly, in order to determine whether they result from class differentials or from racial dynamics. What researchers have shown is that racial segregation *per se* and the existence of dual housing markets *cannot* be explained by class; as Massey and Denton state, "Whereas segregation declines steadily for most minority groups as socioeconomic status rises,

levels of black-white segregation do not vary significantly by social class."[54] Research by the U.S. Department of Housing and Urban Development (HUD) has shown that the dual housing market is maintained by a variety of practices such as overt discrimination on the part of real estate agents and institutional discrimination on the part of lending institutions.[55] A local study conducted in St. Louis by HUD found that African Americans paid 15 to 25 percent more than whites for similar housing.[56] Since housing quality was controlled in this study, any differences in price would be a result of race, not class. If this pattern were to hold across the entire country, we should expect a contemporary effect of race on wealth levels net of parental assets and other socioeconomic measures.

Most research documenting the effects of a dual market has focused on community-level issues such as neighborhood quality, spatial assimilation, or suburbanization.[57] Spatial assimilation is the process by which minority groups seek to convert income gains to social status through improved residential conditions, typically moving out from an urban ethnic enclave into a predominantly

51 See, e.g., R. Alba and J. Logan, "Variations on Two Themes: Racial and Ethnic Patterns in the Attainment of Suburban Residence," *Demography* 28 (1991): 431–53; Massey and Denton, *American Apartheid;* R. Farley and W. H. Frey, "Changes in the Segregation of Whites from Blacks," *American Sociological Review* 59 (1994): 23–45; E. Rosenbaum, "The Structural Constraints on Minority Housing Choices," *Social Forces* 72 (1994): 725–47.

52 S. McKinney and A. B. Schnare, "Trends in Residential Segregation by Race: 1960–1980," *Journal of Urban Economics* 26 (1989): 269–80.

53 Farley and Frey, "Changes in the Segregation of Whites from Blacks."

54 Massey and Denton, *American Apartheid*, p. 11.

55 R. E. Weink, C. E. Reid, J. C. Simonson, and F. J. Eggers, *Measuring Racial Discrimination in American Housing Markets: The Housing Market Practices Survey* (Washington, D.C.: Department of Housing and Urban Development, 1979);

M. Fix and R. Struyk, eds., *Clear and Convincing Evidence: Measurement of Discrimination in America* (Washington, D.C.: Urban Institute Press, 1993).

56 J. Yinger, G. Galster, B. Smith, and F. Eggers, *The Status of Research into Racial Discrimination and Segregation in American Housing Markets* (Washington, D.C.: U.S. Department of Housing and Urban Development, 1978).

57 D. Massey and E. Fong, "Segregation and Neighborhood Quality: Blacks, Hispanics, and Asians in the San Francisco Metropolitan Area," *Social Forces* 69 (1990): 15–32; A. Gross and D. Massey, "Spatial Assimilation Models: A Micro-Macro Comparison," *Social Science Quarterly* 72 (1991): 349–59; L. Stearns and J. Logan, "The Racial Structuring of the Housing Market and Segregation in Suburban Areas," *Social Forces* 65 (1986): 29–42; D. Massey and N. Denton, "Suburbanization and Segregation in U.S. Metropolitan Areas," *American Journal of Sociology* 94 (1988): 592–626.

white suburb. African Americans have faced
obstacles in making this transition, however.
For instance, one study reports that blacks are
less likely than Hispanics and Asian Americans
to reside in the suburbs, even after accounting
for differences in socioeconomic status.[58] When
African Americans do manage to attain suburban
residence, sociologist Emily Rosenbaum notes,
the communities into which they "move tend to
have lower income levels, higher unemployment,
lower tax bases and more of the problems common to inner-city neighborhoods."[59]

This community-level focus of the literature
is a result of the impetus for housing research.
Stimulated by the urban riots of the 1960s, the
Kerner Commission, appointed by the president,
concluded that America was "moving towards
two societies, one black, one white—separate
and unequal."[60] Subsequent analysis was concerned with the nature of minority confinement
to urban ghettos, the concentration of poverty,
neighborhood-level effects, and the making of
the underclass.[61] Massey and Denton write:

> Residential segregation is not a neutral fact; it
> systematically undermines the social and eco-
> nomic well-being of blacks in the United States.
> Because of racial segregation, a significant share
> of black America is condemned to experience a
> social environment where poverty and jobless-
> ness are the norm, where a majority of children
> are born out of wedlock, where most families

are on welfare, where educational failure prevails, and where social and physical deterioration abound. Through prolonged exposure to
such an environment, black chances for social
and economic success are drastically reduced.…
*The effect of segregation on black well-being is struc-
tural, not individual.*[62]

This focus on the macro-structural conditions that
segregation creates has neglected the mechanisms
by which housing conditions affect the individual
(and in turn contribute to the maintenance and
continuation of the structural conditions). One
important way that housing segregation may
directly affect the individual family is through
its impact on individual and family wealth accumulation. Little research has addressed the role of
segregation as it affects the economic well-being
of individual black family units.

Instead, individual-level research on race
and housing usually takes residential segregation as a given and looks at how black and white
families attain housing equity. For example,
Rosenbaum reports that, net of other socioeconomic and demographic characteristics, blacks
in the greater New York metropolitan area are
less likely to own their homes than whites (presumably as a result of spatial assimilation patterns).[63] Oliver and Shapiro analyze housing
appreciation and find that—net of inflation,
year of purchase, mortgage rate, and an indicator of hypersegregation[64]—housing owned by

58 D. Massey and N. Denton, "Trends in the Residential Segre-
    gation of Blacks, Hispanics, and Asians: 1970–1980," *Ameri-
    can Sociological Review* 52 (1987): 802–25.

59 Rosenbaum, "Racial/Ethnic Differences in Home Owner-
    ship and Housing Quality," p. 3.

60 U.S. National Advisory Commission on Civil Disorders,
    The Kerner Report (New York: Pantheon, 1988), p. 1.

61 W. J. Wilson, *The Truly Disadvantaged: The Inner City, the
    Underclass, and Public Policy* (Chicago: University of Chi-

cago Press, 1987); Massey and Denton, *American Apartheid.*
Also see C. Jencks and P. Peterson, eds., *The Urban Underclass*
(Washington, D.C.: Brookings Institution, 1991).

62 Massey and Denton, *American Apartheid,* p. 2; emphasis
    added.

63 Rosenbaum, "Racial/Ethnic Differences in Home Owner-
    ship and Housing Quality."

64 Massey and Denton define hypersegregation as the condi-
    tion of being "very highly segregated [having a black-white

blacks appreciates at a significantly lower rate than housing owned by whites. These authors also address credit issues, developing a statistical model that holds constant a number of factors (including household income and whether the loan was financed through the FHA or the VA), and demonstrate that blacks pay significantly higher mortgage interest rates than whites.[65]

In the PSID data, I find racial differences that point to the saliency of current conditions in the housing and credit markets in determining black-white wealth inequity. For example, African Americans who do own homes and attempt to get financing against their equity (a second mortgage) are much more likely to be turned down, with a 4.4 percent rejection rate in contrast to a 1.1 percent rejection rate for whites ★ ★ ★. This may be related to the finding that 11.8 percent of white applicants have had previous business with the bank to which they applied, in contrast to only 2.4 percent of their African American counterparts. As a result, black homeowners are less likely to have refinanced their mortgage (which often allows a homeowner to save money by taking advantage of a drop in interest rates). On the other hand, contemporary black homeowners are actually more likely (46.9 percent) than whites (21.7 percent) to have a government-sponsored loan. Possibly as a result of this higher rate of government backing, African Americans are less likely to have mortgage insurance (when an institution other than the lender underwrites the loan, often because of a small down payment). Some other aspects of credit financing, such as the pro-

pensity to have a fixed-interest mortgage and the likelihood of a mortgage tax, do not show sizable racial differences in the PSID data.

While these measures of credit access center around housing, they may imply that African Americans suffer from similar disadvantages when applying for business loans (for example, not having had previous business with the bank). Also important is that homeownership not only affects the quality of one's abode and neighborhood but also directly affects the amount of money left for other investing or spending.

Put simply, owning is cheaper than renting. The PSID data show that in 1996 the median rent for tenants was $400, while the median monthly mortgage payment for homeowners was only $279. Although other costs such as property taxes, insurance, and repair expenses are associated with owning, these costs are generally not enough to raise the typical owner's monthly cost over that of the median renter. The Harvard Joint Center for Housing Studies demonstrated that between 1982 and 1993, the proportion of income that went to mortgage payments in the average household declined from 34 percent to 20.2 percent, before rising modestly to 22 percent in 1996.[66] This increasing affordability of homeownership stands in contrast to rents, which have remained consistently high over the 1980s and 1990s. Thus, owning may actually free up more money for other expenses or investments. This may be part of the reason owners accumulate net worth much faster than renters.

★ ★ ★

index of dissimilarity greater than 60 percent] on at least four of the five dimensions at once" (*American Apartheid*, p. 74). The five dimensions are unevenness, isolation, clustering, concentration, and urban centralization. For a technical discussion, see D. Massey and N. Denton, "Hypersegregation

in U.S. Metropolitan Areas: Black and Hispanic Segregation Along Five Dimensions," *Demography* 26 (1989): 378–79.

65 Oliver and Shapiro, *Black Wealth/White Wealth*, p. 205.
66 Joint Center for Housing Studies, *The State of the Nation's Housing: 1996* (Cambridge: Harvard University, 1997).

Poverty

The Changing Face of Poverty

REBECCA BLANK[*]

Which of the following statements are true and which are false?

- Most of the poor are women or children in single-parent families who receive welfare.
- Most poor families have no working adults.
- The majority of poor are African American or Latino.
- The poor typically live in urban ghettos.
- The poor typically live in isolated rural areas.
- Elderly persons are disproportionately likely to be poor.
- Poor families are larger than nonpoor families.

As it turns out, all of these statements are false. The composition of the poor has been changing rapidly over the past two decades. Things that used to be true in the 1960s—the poor lived in rural areas, had larger families, and were disproportionately elderly—were not true by the 1990s. Images of the poor which we often receive in the media—that the poor are mostly black or Latino, are single mothers, live in urban ghetto areas, and don't work—are not accurate pictures.

---

* First published in 1997; from *It Takes a Nation*.

Our mental images about who the poor are, where they live, and how they live has lagged behind a changing reality. Extensive media coverage of the very real problems of urban ghetto neighborhoods—the so-called underclass areas—has led many Americans to believe that this is the dominant face of poverty, when in reality only about 12 percent of the poor live in such neighborhoods. Ongoing public discussion about the problems of welfare recipients have led many to believe that most of the poor are never-married single mothers and their children. In reality, less than half of the poor are single parents and their children; less than 20 percent of the poor live in families with never-married mothers.

In short, there is no one "face" of poverty in America. Simplistic images of the poor only lead to a misunderstanding of poverty. Some poor live in extremely dangerous and troubled urban ghetto neighborhoods, but most are in more diverse communities. Some poor engage in crime or gang activity, or use drugs, but most do not. Some poor do not work, but most live in families where at least one person works at least part-time and/or part-year.

Much of the recent discussion about poverty has emphasized certain behavioral problems as defining characteristics for poverty, such as teenage pregnancy, poor work habits, parental desertion, or involvement in drugs and crime. These behavioral images particularly emphasize the "otherness" of the poor, making it easy for middle Americans to feel little sympathy or connection with them. All of these behaviors are major problems in today's society, affecting far too many people, but they do not accurately characterize many low-income families.

The face of the poor *has* changed over time, although many of these changes are mirrored throughout society, among the middle class as well as the poor. There are many more single mothers raising children among the poor, as there are among all income groups; there are fewer elderly poor, as resources among the elderly have improved throughout society; poor families are smaller, as family size has fallen at all income levels.

These changes in the composition of the poor have created new challenges for policymakers and made many of our traditional antipoverty strategies less effective. In particular, the growing share of the poor who are single mothers with children face different problems escaping poverty than do single individuals or married-couple families. Single-mother families typically have only one adult, which means that their earning opportunities are limited to what a single person can earn. In addition, single mothers who work often earn less than adult men in married-couple families because less-skilled women typically have much lower earning levels than less-skilled men, a subject that is the focus of the next chapter. Mothers might also be seriously limited in when and how much they can work by parental responsibilities and child care availability.

Similarly, although only about 12 percent among the poor live in ghetto neighborhoods in our inner cities, the multiple problems faced by these families often make them less responsive to many antipoverty efforts. The people in these neighborhoods must deal with poorly performing public institutions (such as inadequate public schools), the absence of any economic base in their neighborhoods, and serious problems of dilapidated housing and high crime. Too many families in these areas are caught in a downward spiral of problems, with no way to escape. Policies that tend to focus on single specific issues—school reform by itself, or welfare reform by itself, or improved policing efforts alone—rarely address the range of problems that encompass these neighborhoods and are rarely effective as single efforts.

The changing face of poverty in America demands programs and policies that are appropriate to today's problems. This chapter lays the groundwork for understanding who is poor and why they are poor, a necessary first step before we can discuss policy in more detail.

1.1 WHO IS POOR IN AMERICA TODAY?

SUMMARY. *The poor are an extremely heterogenous group of persons. Half are either below the age of 18 or over the age of 65. Although poverty among the elderly is at an all-time low, poverty among children remains distressingly high, and is related to the growth in single-parent families among the poor. But even this trend is often exaggerated. Almost 40 percent of all poor families with children are still headed by married couples. The poor are both white and black, single and married, young and old.*

Different images of the poor evoke very different responses from Americans. Imagine four different pictures of poverty: (1) a group of children playing in an urban park with their mothers watching; (2) an elderly woman sitting at a table in a shabby one-room apartment; (3) three African American young men hanging out on an urban street corner; and (4) a homeless man panhandling on the corner of a downtown city. Most people will respond very differently to each of these pictures, with a different mix of sympathy and judgment. Each of these images is an accurate picture of real poverty in America today, although none of them alone is representative of all poor people. The poor are a very heterogeneous and mixed group in America; one reason our responses to poverty often seem confused and contradictory is because we react differently to different groups among the poor.

There were 38.1 million people in the United States in 1994 whose family income was below the poverty line, representing 14.5 percent of the population. These are not small numbers, and it is not surprising that they encompass a wide range of families and individuals.[1]

The eight pie charts in figure 1 show how the poor and the nonpoor were distributed in 1993 by age, race, family type, and education.[2] About 40 percent of the poor are children, while only 9 percent are elderly. The remaining half of all poor individuals are adults between the ages of 18 and 64.

Contrary to many people's perceptions, less than half the poor (48 percent) are African American or Latino. Forty-eight percent are white, and the remaining 4 percent are Native

---

1 Unless otherwise referenced, all 1994 data on poverty (the most recent year available) come from the U.S. Bureau of the Census (1995b). Unfortunately, when this book went to press, only limited 1994 data were available. Data for 1993 and ear-

lier, unless otherwise referenced, come from the U.S. Bureau of the Census (1995a).

2 Data in figures 1a through 1d are tabulated by the author from the 1994 March Current Population Survey.

FIGURE 1 **COMPOSITION OF POOR AND NONPOOR FAMILIES IN THE UNITED STATES, 1993, BY (A) AGE, (B) RACE AND ETHNICITY, (C) FAMILY TYPE, AND (D) EDUCATIONAL ATTAINMENT (AGE 25 AND UP)**

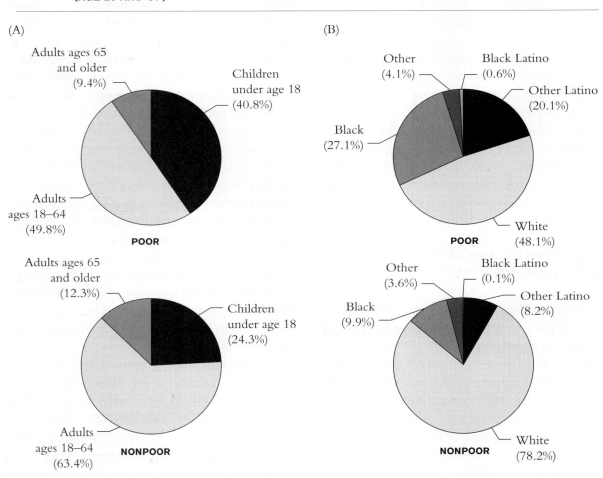

(A)

Adults ages 65 and older (9.4%)

Children under age 18 (40.8%)

Adults ages 18–64 (49.8%)

POOR

Adults ages 65 and older (12.3%)

Children under age 18 (24.3%)

Adults ages 18–64 (63.4%)

NONPOOR

(B)

Other (4.1%)

Black Latino (0.6%)

Other Latino (20.1%)

Black (27.1%)

White (48.1%)

POOR

Other (3.6%)

Black Latino (0.1%)

Black (9.9%)

Other Latino (8.2%)

White (78.2%)

NONPOOR

SOURCE: Author's tabulations from March, 1994, Current Population Survey.

Americans, Asians, and other peoples of color. While blacks and Latinos are much more likely to live in poverty than whites, a much larger share of the population is white, meaning that almost half of the poor are non-Latino white. But a comparison between the poor and non-

poor shows a disproportionate level of poverty among people of color in the United States: they compose 52 percent of the poor and only 22 percent of the nonpoor.

In terms of family structure, single-mother families are the largest (and fastest-growing)

FIGURE 1 *(CONTINUED)*

(C)

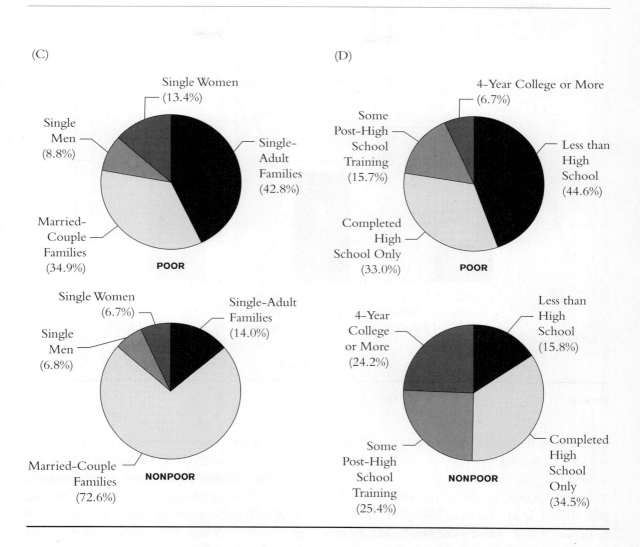

Single Women
(13.4%)

Single
Men
(8.8%)

Single-
Adult
Families
(42.8%)

Married-
Couple
Families
(34.9%)

POOR

Single Women
(6.7%)

Single-Adult
Families
(14.0%)

Single
Men
(6.8%)

Married-Couple
Families
(72.6%)

NONPOOR

(D)

4-Year College or More
(6.7%)

Some
Post-High
School
Training
(15.7%)

Less than
High
School
(44.6%)

Completed
High
School Only
(33.0%)

POOR

4-Year
College
or More
(24.2%)

Less than
High
School
(15.8%)

Some
Post-High
School
Training
(25.4%)

Completed
High
School
Only
(34.5%)

NONPOOR

family type. About 43 percent of all poor persons live in families headed by a single parent, almost all of them women. Among this group, less than half (about two out of five) are headed by never-married mothers. But many poor families are headed by married couples; another 35 percent of poor persons live in married-couple families. The remaining 22 percent of the poor are single individuals who live alone without other relatives. In the nonpoor population, there are far fewer single people, either living on their own or heading families, and far

FIGURE 2 **POVERTY RATES BY RACE AND ETHNICITY, 1994, IN TOTAL AND AMONG SINGLE-MOTHER FAMILIES**

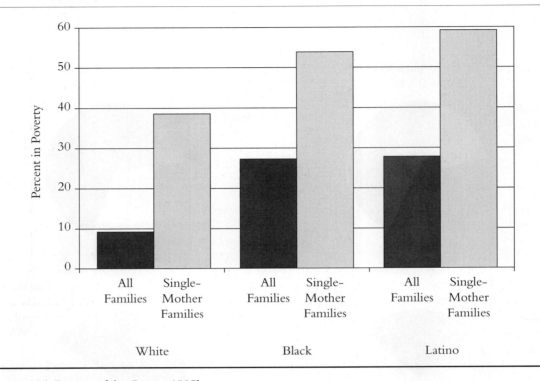

SOURCE: U.S. Bureau of the Census 1995b.

more married couples. We discuss these different groups among the poor in the rest of this section.

Finally, figure 1d shows the differences in educational levels between the poor and the nonpoor. ★ ★ ★ Among the poor, close to 80 percent have only a high school degree or are high school dropouts. Among the nonpoor, only 50 percent are in this position. Few among the poor hold college degrees.

Mothers and Children

As the number of single-parent families has grown in this country, single mothers and their children have increased as a share of the poor population. In 1970, 48 percent of poor families with children were headed by single mothers. By 1993, single mothers headed 60 percent of poor families with children. Among all age groups, race groups, and family types in America today, a single mother with children has the highest probability of being poor.

Figure 2 looks at poverty rates among single mothers and children and contrasts it to overall poverty rates among whites, blacks, and Hispanics. There is a four in ten chance that a white single mother and her children will be poor, while among black and Latina women

FIGURE 3 POVERTY RATES AMONG CHILDREN AND THE ELDERLY, 1966–1994

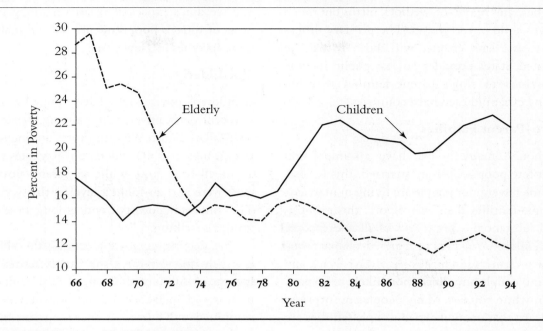

SOURCE: U.S. Bureau of the Census 1995a,b.

who are raising children on their own, six out of ten are poor. These numbers have changed little over time: single mothers have always been extremely poor. What has changed is that there are many more single mothers now than in earlier decades, and as a result, they make up a larger share of the poor. The share of single mothers who have never married is also increasing. In 1983, 27 percent of poor single mothers had never married; by 1994, 39 percent of poor single mothers had never married.[3]

The growth in single-mother families and their very high likelihood of being poor is a primary reason why child poverty rates in America are at appallingly high levels. Well over one-fifth of today's children live in families whose income is below the poverty line, as figure 3 indicates. Over half, 57 percent, of these children are in single-mother families. A white child being raised only by a mother has a better than 45 percent probability of being poor. For a black or Latino child in a single-mother household, the probability of being poor is around two-thirds.

Child poverty rates are higher in the United States than in any other industrialized country. In part, this is because the United States has somewhat higher rates of single motherhood. A

---

3 Data on never-married poor single mothers for 1983 and 1994 are tabulated from the 1983 and 1994 March Current Population Surveys. 1983 is the earliest year in which such tabula- tions can be made because earlier years contain coding errors in the ways subfamilies are defined (see Ellwood and Bane 1985).

number of European countries, however, have higher rates of out-of-wedlock births but much lower child poverty rates. The primary difference, as a later chapter will show, is that the United States provides far less public income assistance to single-parent families than do many other industrialized countries.

Two-Parent Families

Although many people have an impression that few poor people are married, this is false. While fewer poor people are living in married-couple families than ever before, this group is still substantial—35 percent of all poor people are children or adults in married-couple families, as figure 1c indicates. As always, black and Latino couples are much more likely to be poor than white couples. Many people are surprised to learn that many married-couple families are poor because the extensive public discussion about the poor tends to focus on "welfare recipients," who are typically single parents. Married couples typically receive less public assistance and less public attention. Many of these families are among the working poor.

Single Persons

Single persons among the poor tend to be either young adults or elderly singles. More poor single persons are women than men, in part because older women are more likely to outlive their husbands and often have more limited income as widows. About 6 percent of the poor are younger adults who report that they are in school full-time.[4] This is one group among the poor about whom we tend not to worry at all.

In some sense, their poverty is "self-chosen," and we don't expect it to last very long since most of today's poor students will be making good incomes in a few years.

The Elderly

If children's poverty rates have climbed steadily in recent years, poverty rates among the elderly have fallen. Figure 3 plots poverty among these two groups. In 1993, elderly poverty rates were at an all-time low, while children's poverty rates were at their highest level in thirty years. The contrast in poverty trends among these two groups is striking.

The decline in poverty among the elderly is largely due to increases in elderly retirement income. A substantial amount of this is due to increases in Social Security retirement benefits, combined with other assistance programs aimed at the elderly. (★ ★ ★ Supplemental Security Income provides cash assistance to poor elderly individuals and couples for whom Social Security does not suffice.) The United States has greatly increased its cash support to elderly families over the years and the result has been a substantial drop in poverty. Thus, the elderly are one of the biggest success stories for public policy; expansion in government benefits to the elderly has resulted in very low poverty rates.

Despite the myth that retirees receive back from Social Security only what they pay in, retirees over the past three decades have made windfall income gains from Social Security. The average person who retired in 1980 received back within the first four years of retirement everything that he or she and his or her

---

4 Author's tabulations from the 1994 March Current Population Survey.

employer had paid into Social Security.[5] This is largely due to legislative increases in Social Security benefits, far beyond those expected when these retirees were working and paying Social Security taxes in the 1950s, 1960s, and 1970s. This expansion in Social Security has increased incomes among the elderly at all income levels and reduced poverty among older low-income retirees. In addition, an expansion of private pensions among workers occurred through the early 1980s and has meant that more elderly persons receive private-pension income now than in the past.[6]

The elderly who remain poor are largely older widowed or divorced women who accrued little pension or Social Security income on their own and who have found themselves destitute following a husband's death. The growth in labor force participation among younger women means that this elderly poor female group should shrink in size over time, although continued low earnings among many women means this group will not disappear anytime soon.

Racial and Ethnic Differences among the Poor

Members of racial and ethnic minority groups in the United States are disproportionately more likely to be poor. As figure 2 shows, just under one-third of all African American or Latino individuals live in poor families, much higher than the 12 percent poverty rates among non-Hispanic white persons. Native Americans, particularly those living on reservations, often have extremely high poverty rates. Recent immigrants, like generations of immigrants before them, are also more likely to be poor.

There are many reasons for high poverty among these groups. As will be discussed further below, black Americans have been particularly subject to housing discrimination, which has prevented many black families from following the path pursued by urban white families who moved to the suburbs when jobs started shifting there from the cities. Minority workers still face exclusion and discrimination from many employers, limiting their wages and employment options. Minority workers also have lower levels of formal education on average, a problem that is more acute in the Latino population than in the African American population. More recent immigrants face cultural and language barriers as well as skill barriers when they search for a job.

While this section is designed to provide some sense of the relative presence of different groups among the poor, the bottom line is that the poor are a very mixed group of people: they are white *and* black *and* Hispanic, both single *and* married, both young *and* old. The largest group among the poor is single mothers and their children (if differentiated by race, the largest group in real numbers would be white single mothers and their children). Single-parent families also have higher poverty rates than anyone else. But single parents and their children comprise less than half of all poor individuals.

Single mothers are often a primary focus of policy concern, both because we care about the

---

5 Kollman (1995).
6 Reno (1993), table 2.

impact of poverty on the children in these families and because this group receives more public assistance than any group other than the poor elderly and disabled. In fact, one reason that many people have an inaccurate image of poverty is that *poverty* is often assumed to be synonymous with *welfare recipients.* ★ ★ ★ Welfare typically refers to the cash assistance program known as Aid to Families with Dependent Children (AFDC), available primarily to single mothers and their children. While 65 percent of single mother families receive AFDC (note that many do not!), only 25 percent of all poor families receive AFDC.[7]

[I] will talk more about single parents and their children than about some of the other groups among the poor. But even when we focus on single mothers and their children and on welfare-related policies in more detail, it is important to keep in mind that many poor people are *not* part of this population: the married couples, many of them working but poor; the single men and women among the poor; and the whole mix of poor people who live in different types of neighborhoods.

1.2 MOVING IN AND OUT OF POVERTY

SUMMARY: *We are less concerned with a family that experiences a short spell of poverty than with families who remain poor year after year. The long-term poor often experience the deepest poverty and its most sustained effects. They also use a greater share of public assistance dollars. Only a minority of those currently poor are likely to experience long-term poverty. But among black Americans and among children, the probabilities of long-term poverty are much higher. Long-term poverty among children is particularly worrisome, given its potential to limit children's cognitive and physical development. The majority of poverty spells both begin and end because of economic changes in earnings or other income sources rather than changes in family composition.*

We care not only about *who* is poor and *why* they are poor, but also how long they are poor. People who are poor for only one or two years might be considered less disadvantaged than those who are poor year after year. Those among the poor we worry about the most are those who seem unable to escape poverty. This group may be experiencing the most sustained effects of poverty, through accumulated health problems, long-term inadequate housing, and lack of access to or experience in the mainstream labor market. The long-term poor also use the most government resources and are therefore the most expensive from a taxpayer's point of view.

When we discuss the duration of poverty, we can present the picture in two quite different ways. On the one hand, most people who become poor are not poor for very long. On the other hand, there is a substantial minority of poor persons who seem to be poor for extremely long periods of time. How can both of these statements be true? Let's take a random sample of Americans and follow them over thirteen years to see how many were poor most

---

7 Author's tabulations from the 1994 March Current Population Survey. We define as a family any group of related people who live together, including single individuals (living alone or with other unrelated persons) as one-person families.

FIGURE 4 **EXTENT OF POVERTY AMONG AMERICANS, 1979–1991**

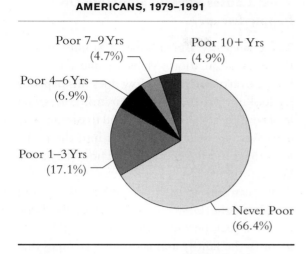

Poor 7–9 Yrs (4.7%)
Poor 10+ Yrs (4.9%)
Poor 4–6 Yrs (6.9%)
Poor 1–3 Yrs (17.1%)
Never Poor (66.4%)

SOURCE: Author's tabulations from the Panel Study of Income Dynamics.

Years of Poverty among Americans

Figure 4 shows the number of years of poverty experienced among a random sample of Americans whose income was surveyed annually over the years 1979 to 1991. For thirteen recent years, these data indicate how prevalent poverty is and how much it is concentrated in long and short spells.

Two-thirds of all persons are never in a poor family during these thirteen years. About half of those who are ever poor are poor for only one to three years. Only 1.5 percent of the population is poor all thirteen years, but 5 percent are poor for ten or more years.

Of course, among different groups, these numbers look quite different. For whites, pov-

erty is much more likely to be short term, while for blacks the duration of poverty is longer. Figure 5 shows how the extent of poverty differs among blacks and whites between 1979 and 1991. While only one-fourth of whites ever experience poverty in one of these years, almost

of those years, some of those years, or none of those years.

FIGURE 5 **EXTENT OF POVERTY AMONG WHITE AND BLACK AMERICANS, 1979–1991**

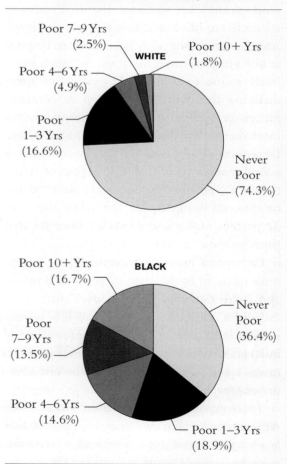

WHITE
Poor 7–9 Yrs (2.5%)
Poor 10+ Yrs (1.8%)
Poor 4–6 Yrs (4.9%)
Poor 1–3 Yrs (16.6%)
Never Poor (74.3%)

BLACK
Poor 10+ Yrs (16.7%)
Poor 7–9 Yrs (13.5%)
Poor 4–6 Yrs (14.6%)
Poor 1–3 Yrs (18.9%)
Never Poor (36.4%)

SOURCE: Author's tabulations from the Panel Study of Income Dynamics.

two-thirds of all blacks experience at least one year of poverty. Furthermore, among white families who experience poverty, two-thirds are poor for only three years or less; barely 2 percent are poor ten years or more. In sharp contrast, a shocking 17 percent of the black population is poor for ten or more of these thirteen years.

These data suggest that differences in annual poverty rates between African Americans and white Americans *understate* the differences in economic need among these two groups. Black Americans are not only more likely to be poor at any point in time, but they are much more likely to be poor for long periods of time, suffering the cumulative effects of continuing poverty. Continuous, long-term poverty might be a particular concern among children. If we look only at children who were eight or younger in 1980, a tiny proportion of white children (less than 3 percent) is poor for ten or more of the next thirteen years. But over 32 percent of black children are poor for that time.

Perhaps to no one's surprise, those groups most likely to be poor at any point in time are also more likely to be poor over time. One exception to this is the elderly. While overall poverty rates among the elderly are relatively low, when an elderly person becomes poor, he or she typically remains poor for the rest of his or her life.

The long-term poor are more likely to be African American, as we have seen, to have low levels of education, to report health problems, or to be in single-mother families. Those who are least able to support themselves through earnings are also least able to escape poverty.

What Causes Poverty and How Do People Escape?

There is clearly a great deal of fluidity among the poor population. Many people enter and leave poverty each year. How does this happen? By looking at the changing circumstances that lead families to become poor and to escape poverty, we may gain some insight into the problems that poor families face and how they solve them.

We can follow each person in our random sample of the U.S. population over the same thirteen-year period from 1979 to 1991 and identify the family and economic changes that are associated with the beginning of all observed spells of poverty between these years. (Those who never became poor or who were poor in all years obviously do not contribute any information to this calculation.) Similarly, we can also look at the events that occur when people escape poverty for all spells of poverty that end between these years. I assume that changes in marital and family status are of first importance in explaining why a spell of poverty begins or ends. Thus, even though there is often a sharp decline in earnings in families after a divorce when the husband (and his earnings) leaves and the wife becomes the head of the family, I list the cause of poverty in this case as "married couple breaks up." Only in families where the same person is the head of the family for two years in a row can "earnings of head (of family) fell" be the cause of poverty.

Figure 6 shows how people enter poverty. In about one-quarter of the cases, a person enters poverty when there is a major change in his or her family composition—either a mar-

FIGURE 6 REASONS WHY POVERTY SPELLS BEGIN

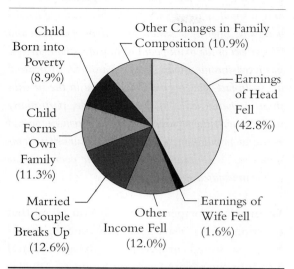

Child Born into Poverty (8.9%)

Child Forms Own Family (11.3%)

Married Couple Breaks Up (12.6%)

Other Income Fell (12.0%)

Earnings of Wife Fell (1.6%)

Earnings of Head Fell (42.8%)

Other Changes in Family Composition (10.9%)

SOURCE: Author's tabulations from the Panel Study of Income Dynamics.

ried couple breaks up, or a child who was living with his or her parents establishes an independent household. In another 10 percent of cases there are changes in family composition other than a change in the family head; for instance, an unmarried sibling who contributed earnings to the family might move out. In 9 percent of the cases, a person is born into a poor family. But in the majority of cases, poverty starts for a person when the economic situation of his or her family changes, with no changes in family composition. Almost half of all poverty spells start when the earnings of either the head or the wife fall, and another 12 percent start when other income sources are lost, such as a decline in child support, public assistance, or pension income.

In short, there are two main reasons why people become poor: either their families change composition in ways that threaten their economic security, or there is a major economic loss (usually in earnings). Most of these are job losses, where family heads experience extended unemployment. Among these two reasons, changes in economics create more poverty than changes in family composition.

Figure 7 shows equivalent information on how and why an individual leaves poverty. Over two-thirds of poor people escape poverty when a change occurs in their family's economic resources. In the majority of cases, poverty ends because either the earnings of the head or the wife increase enough to escape poverty, although increases in other income (typically government assistance) ends 16 percent of poverty spells. About 13 percent of

FIGURE 7 REASONS WHY POVERTY SPELLS END

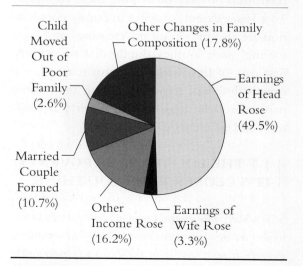

Child Moved Out of Poor Family (2.6%)

Married Couple Formed (10.7%)

Other Income Rose (16.2%)

Earnings of Wife Rose (3.3%)

Earnings of Head Rose (49.5%)

Other Changes in Family Composition (17.8%)

SOURCE: Author's tabulations from the Panel Study of Income Dynamics.

poverty spells end with major changes in who heads the family—either a couple gets married, or a child in a poor family leaves and establishes his or her own nonpoor family. Other changes in family composition occur in another 18 percent of cases.

Figure 7 again emphasizes the importance of economic opportunities and the ability of poor adults to find and hold jobs. Most people leave poverty when they or the head of their family receives more earnings. Changes in family composition are less important in escaping poverty than they are in beginning a spell of poverty; for example, a woman and her children are more likely to become poor by leaving a marriage than they are likely to escape poverty by remarrying. From the limited evidence available, marriage is declining in its importance as a way to escape poverty.

Changes in earnings and work opportunities are very important in many families, driving them into poverty or helping them to escape. To a lesser extent, changes in family composition are also important in "creating" and "dissolving" poor families. But the discussion in the first part of this section remains relevant. For some substantial minority among the poor—particularly the black poor—poverty is long-term and escape is infrequent.

1.3 THE LOCATION OF POVERTY: IT'S CLOSER THAN YOU THINK

SUMMARY. *The invisibility of modern poverty makes us less aware of its prevalence in many communities. Poverty is most visible in the extremely poor urban*

ghettos that are frequently depicted in the media. While these may be the worst places to be poor in America, only a small share of poor people live in these neighborhoods. Slightly less than 90 percent of all poor and 75 percent of the black poor live outside urban ghettos, in mixed-income urban or suburban areas or in rural areas. In fact, poverty has grown faster in the suburbs than in central cities in the last decade, particularly in the inner-ring suburbs that are experiencing loss of jobs and population to more distant suburban communities. A substantial number of the poor continue to live in isolated rural areas as well.

Where do poor people live? If you asked that question thirty years ago, most people would have mentioned rural America: the agricultural South or the isolated mining towns of Appalachia. If you ask that question today, many people will respond with images of urban ghetto poverty: high-rise public housing and abandoned buildings, with an ever-present threat of gang violence. Most Americans have become frighteningly familiar with this image of poverty in recent years, which has dominated the media presentations.

Despite these images, relatively few among the poor live in poor urban ghettos. Most poor live in mixed-income city or suburban neighborhoods. In fact, there are few city neighborhoods, suburbs or midsized towns that do not have a substantial number of low-income families. The best answer to where the poor live: they live among us and with us.

In 1962, Michael Harrington published a book that discussed the "invisibility" of poverty in America.[8] While the location of poverty has

8 Harrington (1962).

changed over the past thirty years, its invisibility has not. Walk through the nearest shopping mall in your neighborhood and try to guess the income levels of the teenagers who are hanging out there. Or try to guess the income levels of the older shoppers. It's not obvious. In most public settings, all Americans dress with similar casualness.

The rising number of single-parent families and their high probability of poverty has also been a force that fosters income mixing within neighborhoods. Divorced women with children often try to stay in the same school district, moving to less expensive apartments. Never-married women often try to live close to parents or sisters. Even the most expensive neighborhoods will contain a few low-rent garage apartments or apartment buildings.

The one exception to the invisibility of poverty occurs in our urban ghettos. Because these are the neighborhoods where poverty is the most visible, we have incorrectly come to assume that these are the neighborhoods where most poverty is located. As typically defined among researchers, urban ghettos are areas where 40 percent or more of the people who live there are poor. These areas are often referred to as "underclass" neighborhoods, and poverty is only one of their many social and economic problems. These areas experience high crime, drug, and gang activity; they often contain tracts of extremely inadequate housing; residents have low levels of education and high rates of non-participation in the mainstream economy; a high share of the population receives government assistance; and local institutions like the schools or the police function inadequately. For too many families in these neighborhoods, these are dangerous, desperate places, where children are at risk of dying from random bullets on the street, where apartments have inadequate plumbing and unsafe stairways, and where too many residents live with fear.

Without in any way trying to minimize the problems that families in these areas face, the media images of these neighborhoods in local newspapers or TV news broadcasts have often left the impression that neighborhoods filled with deprivation, danger, and fear are the face of poverty in America. For some families, this is reality. But only a small minority of the poor live in such neighborhoods, and even among those who do, there are many success stories. It is important to remember that in most of these urban ghetto neighborhoods more than half of the population is *not* poor. While the worst of these neighborhoods—the concentrated areas of high-rise public housing—dominate the news in cities like New York and Chicago, many urban ghetto neighborhoods and their residents do not fit the stereotypes. Many of these neighborhoods have strong church and community organizations supported by long-term residents; many of the families in these areas are coping effectively with their lives and raising their children well.

The most recent calculations, using data from the 1990 census, indicate that only about *12 percent* of all poor persons live in urban ghetto neighborhoods with greater than 40 percent poverty rates. Disproportionately, these neighborhoods are likely to have a high share of African American residents. Indeed, the legacy of housing segregation and discrimination has been a major cause in the creation of these neighborhoods. But even among the African

American poor, only around one-quarter live in such neighborhoods. Twenty percent of poor Hispanics are in ghetto neighborhoods. This says that almost 90 percent of the poor do *not* live in such communities. The bad news is that too many poor live in these communities, some of which are worlds where no Americans, and particularly not families with children, should live. The good news is that most poor do *not* live in these areas.

Figure 8 indicates the broader geographic composition of the poor in 1970 and 1993. In 1993, 43 percent of the poor lived in the central cities of major metropolitan areas, most of them in mixed-income neighborhoods. Another 33 percent lived in the suburbs of these cities, while one-quarter of the poor still live in small-town or rural America, outside major metropolitan areas. As figure 8 indicates, the increase in suburban poverty is greater than the increase in city poverty.

Poverty in rural America, while a shrinking share of the poor, has hardly disappeared. The poorest counties in the United States are rural counties, where many families still live isolated lives. While [I focus] heavily on poverty in more populated areas, because that is where the growth in poverty has been in recent decades, rural poverty is still very present in some parts of the country. Lack of jobs and high unemployment in these areas are often more pressing than in urban ghetto neighborhoods. For people in poor urban neighborhoods, there *are* jobs in nearby suburbs although they may not be readily accessible. In poor rural areas, there often are few jobs anywhere.

Like all Americans, the poor have been moving out of rural areas and into urban areas over

FIGURE 8 **COMPOSITION OF POOR PERSONS IN THE UNITED STATES, BY GEOGRAPHIC LOCATION, 1970 AND 1993.**

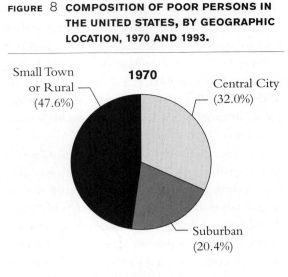

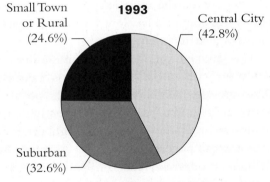

SOURCE: U.S. Bureau of the Census 1971, 1995a.

the past five decades. But over the last decade, it is not in the central cities where poverty has grown, but in the suburbs. Increasingly, the older inner-ring suburbs are experiencing rising poverty rates, much of it due to the growth of single-parent families in these areas. The growing edge of poverty is single mothers and their children living in suburban areas. This is a very different image than the hard-core urban ghetto poverty often depicted on TV. Those images are not wrong; serious poverty exists in such areas. But this does not represent the experiences of most of the poor. Most poor people live closer than many of the nonpoor realize because often they are not immediately distinguishable from their better-off neighbors.

★ ★ ★

||| REFERENCES

Ellwood, David T., and Mary Jo Bane. 1985. "The Impact of AFDC on Family Structure and Living Arrangements." *Research in Labor Economics* 7: 137–207.

Harrington, Michael. 1962. *The Other America: Poverty in the United States*. Baltimore: Penguin Books.

Kollman, Geoffrey. 1995. "Social Security: The Relationship of Taxes and Benefits for Past, Present and Future Retirees." *CRS Report for Congress*. Washington, D.C.: Library of Congress, Congressional Research Service. January 9.

Reno, Virginia P. 1993. "The Role of Pensions in Retirement Income: Trends and Questions." *Social Security Bulletin* 56(1, Spring): 29–43.

U.S. Bureau of the Census. 1995a. *Income, Poverty, and Valuation of Noncash Benefits: 1993*. Current Population Reports, Series P60–188. Washington, D.C.: U.S. Government Printing Office. February. Supplemental unpublished tables to this publication also provided by the U.S. Bureau of the Census.

U.S. Bureau of the Census. 1995b. "Press Briefing on 1994 Income and Poverty Estimates." Washington, D.C.: U.S. Bureau of the Census. October 5. Supplemental unpublished tables also provided by the U.S. Bureau of the Census.

What Does It Mean to Be Poor in America?★

MAYA FEDERMAN, THESIA I. GARNER, KATHLEEN SHORT,
W. BOWMAN CUTTER IV, JOHN KIELY, DAVID LEVINE,
DUANE McDOUGH, AND MARILYN McMILLEN

To understand the relationship between poverty and living conditions, a multifaceted understanding of what it means to be poor is required. In one sense, the answer to the question "What does it mean to be poor?" is straightforward—having cash income below the official poverty line for a given family size. In a broader sense, the living conditions of the poor are difficult to measure, both because annual cash income is only one factor related to living conditions, and because the poor are quite heterogeneous.

This article represents an effort to get closer to the answer by summarizing findings from nine national surveys that shed light on the living conditions of individuals living in poor and nonpoor families. It differs from earlier examinations of living conditions and the material well-being of American families in that it draws upon a broader set of household surveys and attempts to maximize uniformity in the definition of family types and poverty. This work represents a coordinated effort of representatives of various Federal agencies that produce and analyze data from nationally representative surveys. The aim in this process has been to produce measurements of material well-being for an expanded set of dimensions, following a methodology that would

★ First published in 1996; from *Monthly Labor Review*, Volume 119, Number 5.

promote comparability across surveys as much as possible.

||| RELATED RESEARCH

Although the official poverty measure in the United States is defined in terms of current before-tax cash income, some aspects of economic welfare can be more accurately gauged by measuring consumption or other dimensions of living conditions. Income measures ignore homeownership and other assets that can be important sources of consumption. Thus, some people, such as those who are retired or those whose incomes are only temporarily low, may be classified as poor based on income but do not have low consumption. Furthermore, the official poverty rate does not account for taxes or in-kind transfers such as food stamps or government-provided medical insurance, which improve living conditions without affecting a family's official poverty status.

★ ★ ★

||| A PORTRAIT OF THE POOR

The results for individuals living in poor and nonpoor families are divided into seven categories: income sources, spending patterns, housing, consumer durables and utilities, crime and neighborhood, health and nutrition, and education. In the first four categories, the unit of data collection is the family; thus, results are presented by family characteristic. For example, the mean total expenditures of poor families is $11,596. The unit of data collection for the last two categories is the individual in general; thus, results are for the average individual of the relevant population. For example, 27 percent of poor children aged 5 to 7 years have fewer than 10 books. The crime and neighborhood category has measures of both family (or household) and individual characteristics. The final table presents an "index of deprivation" for individuals that reflects several family characteristics.

Summary tables of all variables discussed in the text are provided for each category. The source survey for each variable is noted in each table. All differences discussed below are statistically significant at the 1-percent level.

Income Sources

Poor families differ from nonpoor families both in the levels and sources of their incomes. (See table 1.) The average poor person lives in a family whose income is about a sixth as much as the family income of the average nonpoor person ($8,501 versus $55,394). For the single-parent poor and those in families receiving welfare, average family incomes are $6,794 and $12,678.[1]

The average nonpoor person lives in a family that receives 85.1 percent of its income from wages, salaries, and self-employment earnings, compared to 52 percent for the poor and only 36 percent for those in poor, single-parent families. A larger proportion of the income of poor families comes from public assistance and welfare: 20 percent, compared with only 0.2 percent for the nonpoor. For those in poor, single-parent

---

[1] For those individuals who both are poor and receive welfare, family income is $7,769, of which 56.0 percent comes from public assistance and welfare (based on person-weighted results).

TABLE 1   INCOME AND SELECTED TAXES AND TRANSFERS OF FAMILIES IN 1993

Item	Nonpoor families	Poor families	Single-parent poor families	Families receiving welfare
Current Population Survey				
Total before-tax family income	$55,394	$8,501	$6,794	$12,678
PERCENT OF INCOME FROM:				
Wages and salaries	78.9	50.0	35.8	46.0
Self-employment earnings	6.2	1.7	.6	1.3
Public assistance/welfare	.2	20.3	39.8	34.6
SELECTED TAXES AND TRANSFERS:				
Federal income tax	$6,878	$15	$7	$268
State income tax	1,805	19	7	95
FICA payroll tax	3,093	370	187	446
Earned income tax credit	116	484	356	321
Public assistance/welfare	115	1,727	2,701	4,381
Food stamps	65	1,392	1,871	2,241

NOTE: Family-level data, person-weighted. Data collected in March 1994, with 1993 as the reference period.

families, 40 percent of family income comes from public assistance and welfare.

Not surprisingly, poor families pay less in taxes and receive more in government transfers than do the nonpoor. On average, the Earned Income Tax Credit fully offsets the Federal and State income and FICA payroll taxes for the family of the average poor person. Additional taxes, such as sales taxes, are not included in these calculations. The family of the average nonpoor person pays an estimated $11,660 in Federal and State income and FICA taxes (less the Earned Income Tax Credit). The average poor person lives in a family that receives $1,727 in public assistance

and welfare and $1,392 in food stamps. For those in poor, single-parent families, welfare and food stamp transfers are $2,701 and $1,871 ($4,381 and $2,241 for families receiving welfare).

Spending Patterns

In this section, expenditure data from the Consumer Expenditure Survey, in conjunction with the official poverty thresholds, are used to determine if an individual lives in a poor family. Individuals defined as poor using expenditure data may not have the same family characteristics as individuals identified as income-poor in other sections of this article.[2] Poverty rates, mea-

2 Garner, Johnson, and Kokoski found that 52 percent of the income-poor (based on before-tax income) had total consumer unit expenditures less than the poverty line, while 61 percent of expenditure-poor consumer units had incomes

below the thresholds. Their results are based on Consumer Expenditure Survey data from 1982–84. (See Thesia I. Garner, David S. Johnson, and Mary F. Kokoski, "Experimental Consumer Price Index for the Poor," *Monthly Labor Review,*

TABLE 2   **EXPENDITURES BY FAMILIES IN 1992–93**

Expenditures	Nonpoor families	Poor families	Single-parent poor families	Families receiving welfare
CONSUMER EXPENDITURE INTERVIEW SURVEY				
Total family expenditures	$36,926	$11,596	$9,172	$16,280
Percent of expenditures for:				
Food	15.6	29.8	34.3	25.5
Shelter	18.6	22.3	25.5	24.0
Utilities	6.9	14.0	13.7	10.8
Apparel	4.9	5.1	6.7	6.0
Transportation	20.1	10.3	6.4	13.3
Health care	5.4	2.8	1.2	2.2
Entertainment	5.4	2.8	2.8	3.9
Personal insurance and pensions	10.9	5.4	2.1	4.8

NOTE: Family-level data, person-weighted. Quarterly data collected from January 1992 to December 1993, with reference period from October 1991 to November 1993. Results are presented for expenditure nonpoor and poor families.

sured using expenditure data, are generally lower than in the other surveys, although trends across family types are similar.

Differences between the poor and the non-poor in average family expenditures are smaller than differences in average family incomes. (See table 2.) While average family incomes of the non-income-poor are over 6 times as large as those for the income-poor ($55,394 versus $8,501), average family expenditures of the non-expenditure-poor are only about 3 times as large as those for the expenditure-poor

($36,926 versus $11,596). For the single-parent poor and those in families receiving welfare, average family expenditures are $9,172 and $16,280.[3]

According to the data presented in tables 1 and 2, total family expenditures exceed total before-tax family income for all but the non-poor. Transfer benefits, such as food stamps, are not reflected in the income figures, nor are taxes paid by families. When these are accounted for in income, the spending power of poor families increases. For example, if the value of food

September 1996, 119(9), pp. 32–42.) Rogers and Gray found similar results when they examined quintiles of income and expenditure outlays. (See John Rogers and Maureen Gray, "CE data: quintiles of income versus quintiles of outlays," *Monthly Labor Review*, December 1994, pp. 32–37.)

3 It is important to point out that these are arithmetic means, and not medians or modes. If the distribution of income is positively skewed, and that of expenditures is negatively skewed, higher mean expenditures would result. Skewness is not examined for in this study, however.

stamps and the Earned Income Tax Credit are added to before-tax income, and taxes paid are subtracted, the ratio of expenditures to income becomes smaller, falling from 1.36 to 1.16 for poor families, from 1.35 to 1.04 for single-parent poor families, and from 1.28 to 1.13 for welfare families. The fact that expenditures still exceed income is likely related to how expenditures are defined ★ ★ ★, possible under-reporting of income compared to expenditures, differences in the types of families that are considered poor on the basis of income versus expenditures, and differences in income and expenditure distributions.[4]

The composition of spending also varies by family type. Not surprisingly, a greater share of poor people's total expenditures is allocated to purchasing items frequently considered necessities: food, shelter, utilities, and apparel. Seventy-one percent of poor persons' family expenditures are spent on these necessities, compared to 46 percent for the nonpoor. For those in expenditure-poor, single-parent families, an even larger share of total family expenditures, 80 percent, is spent on necessities. Spending a larger share of total expenditures on necessities leaves a smaller portion for other items such as transportation, health care, personal insurance and pensions, and entertainment (including admissions to events, television, toys, and pets).

Housing

Rates of homeownership vary dramatically across both income levels and family types. (See table 3.) Seventy-eight percent of the

nonpoor live in homes that their families own, compared with only 41 percent of the poor. For those in poor, single-parent families and those in families receiving welfare, the home-ownership rate is even lower, 24 percent. Thus, the nonpoor are 3 times more likely to live in homes they own than are those in poor, single-parent families.

The main reason for the difference in owner-ship rates between all individuals in poor families and individuals in poor, single-parent families is the high rate of ownership among individuals in poor, elderly families, 63 percent of whom live in homes they own (results not shown). In addition, 51 percent of people in poor two-parent families live in homes they own.

The poor are at greater risk of being evicted from their home or apartment, with eviction rates 5 times as high as those of the nonpoor. While only 0.4 percent of the nonpoor were evicted in the previous 12 months, 2.1 percent of the poor, 2.4 percent of the single-parent poor, and 2.6 percent of those in welfare-recipient families lost their homes. Twenty-six percent of the poor and 29 percent of those receiving welfare were in families that did not pay the full rent or mortgage at some point in the survey year. The rate for the nonpoor was much lower, only 7.5 percent.

Those in poor and nonpoor families differ according to the characteristics and condition of their housing as well. For example, poor individuals are more than twice as likely to live in crowded housing; 19 percent of those in poor families live in housing with more than one

4 Family expenditures for those individuals who both are poor and receive welfare are $11,012, and the share spent on necessities is 78.6 percent (based on person-weighted results).

TABLE 3 **HOUSING CHARACTERISTICS IN 1992 AND 1993**

Housing characteristic	Nonpoor families	Poor families	Single-parent poor families	Families receiving welfare
AMERICAN HOUSING SURVEY				
Owned home	77.6	40.8	24.3	24.9
More than one person per room (crowding)	4.2	19.2	16.7	23.6
Moderate upkeep problems	3.3	11.3	12.5	11.9
Severe upkeep problems	1.7	3.8	4.4	4.3
SURVEY OF INCOME AND PROGRAM PARTICIPATION				
Conditions in home unsatisfactory enough that one would like to move	9.5	26.6	33.5	34.5
In the past 12 months, there was a time when the household:				
Did not pay the full amount of the rent or mortgage	7.5	25.9	26.0	29.1
Was evicted from home/apartment for not paying rent/mortgage	.4	2.1	2.4	2.6

NOTE: Family-level data, person-weighted. American Housing Survey data were collected from July through December 1993, with 1993 as the reference period. Survey of Income and Program Participation data were collected from September through December of 1992, with these same months as the reference period.

person per room, compared to only 4 percent of the nonpoor. Similarly, those in poor families are about twice as likely to live in housing with upkeep problems as are the nonpoor. Eleven percent of the poor have housing with moderate upkeep problems and 4 percent have severe upkeep problems. Among persons living in nonpoor families, 4 percent have housing with moderate problems and 2 percent have severe problems.[5]

Consumer Durables and Utilities

For some major consumer durables, the poor and nonpoor differ little in access. (See table 4.) Almost all of the poor, like the nonpoor, have access to refrigerators and stoves: 98 percent versus 99.5 percent. Also, 92 percent of people in poor and in single-parent poor families and 98 percent of people living in nonpoor families have access to a color television.[6]

---

5 The U.S. Department of Housing and Urban Development defines moderate (severe) upkeep problems as the presence of 3 (5) or more of the following 6 problems: broken plaster or peeling paint, rats or mice, cracks in the wall, pipes or plumbing leaks, dents or holes in the floor, and roof, window, or basement leaks.

6 Mayer and Jencks note that color televisions are a low-cost form of entertainment for poor families. (See Susan Mayer and Christopher Jencks, "Has Poverty Really Increased Among Children Since 1970?" Working Paper 94–14 (Northwestern University, Center for Urban Affairs and Policy Research, 1995.)

TABLE 4 **DURABLE ITEMS AND UTILITIES 1992 AND 1993**

Durable or utility item	Nonpoor families	Poor families	Single-parent poor families	Families receiving welfare
SURVEY OF INCOME AND PROGRAM PARTICIPATION				
Items currently in the home or building that are in working condition:				
Washing machine	92.7	71.7	67.5	66.3
Clothes dryer	87.3	50.2	43.9	44.8
Refrigerator	99.5	97.9	98.1	98.2
Color television	98.5	92.5	92.1	92.2
Stove	99.5	97.7	97.3	98.0
Air conditioning	71.9	49.6	46.0	40.7
Telephone	97.2	76.7	69.9	67.5
In the past 12 months, there was a time when the household:				
Did not pay the full amount of the gas, oil, or electricity bill	9.8	32.4	37.0	40.7
Had service turned off by the gas, electric, or oil company	1.8	8.5	10.1	10.5
Had telephone service disconnected because payment was not made	3.2	16.0	18.0	20.3
AMERICAN HOUSING SURVEY				
Car or truck owner	97.2	76.8	64.1	65.3

NOTE: Family-level data, person-weighted. Survey of Income and Program Participation data collection and reference periods are September through December 1992. American Housing Survey data were collected between July and December 1993, with 1993 as the reference period.

For several other consumer durables, the poor have considerably lower rates of access, although for most of the items measured, their access rates are still above 50 percent. For example, 77 percent of the poor and 70 percent of the single-parent poor have access to a telephone, compared with 97 percent of the nonpoor. Similarly, 72 percent of the nonpoor live in families that have air conditioning (central or room), while 50 percent of those in poor families and 46 percent of those in poor, single-parent families do. People in poor families also are considerably less likely to have access to washing machines and apparel dryers. (Because the Survey of Income and Program Participation asks whether the family has these items in either the home or the building, actual ownership rates of some items are likely lower.) About 77 percent of the poor and 64 percent of those in poor, single-parent families have a household car or truck available, compared to 97 percent of the nonpoor.

TABLE 5 **CHARACTERISTICS OF CRIME AND NEIGHBORHOOD CONDITIONS IN 1992**

Characteristic	Nonpoor families	Poor families	Single-parent poor families	Families receiving welfare
NATIONAL CRIME VICTIMIZATION INTERVIEW SURVEY				
Violent crimes, per 1,000 people per year	26.15	53.68	87.50	....
Thefts, per 1,000 people per year	59.69	66.01	84.66	....
Household crimes, per 1,000 households per year	143.29	207.10	317.59	....
SURVEY OF INCOME AND PROGRAM PARTICIPATION (percent of persons)				
Neighborhood safe from crime	93.0	78.1	72.4	67.4
Afraid to go out	8.7	19.5	20.7	24.6
Neighborhood condition bad enough that one would like to move	6.5	18.4	24.5	27.5
Community services bad enough that one would like to move	5.5	15.1	19.7	20.5

NOTE: For the National Crime Victimization Interview Survey, results are presented for households or persons living in households, rather than for families. Family- and household-level data are person-weighted, except for data from the National Crime Victimization Interview Survey. Person-level data are presented for crimes and thefts. National Crime Victimization Interview Survey data were collected between January 1992 and June 1993, with 1992 as the reference period. Survey of Income and Program Participation data collection and reference periods are September through December 1992.

Finally, the poor are more likely to have problems paying utility bills and to have services cut off. The poor and the single-parent poor are more than 3 times as likely as the nonpoor to have not paid their utility bill at some time during a 12-month period. The poor are more than 4 times as likely to have their utilities cut off, while the single-parent poor are more than 5 times as likely. Finally, the poor are 5 times as likely as the nonpoor to have their telephone service disconnected because payments were not made, while the single-parent poor are 6 times as likely.

Crime and Neighborhood

Individuals who live in poor households,[7] especially those in poor, single-parent households, are much more likely to be victims of crime than are those who live in other households. (See table 5.) Those living in poor households

---

7 The National Crime Victimization Survey did not have measures for families available; thus, crime results are presented for individuals in poor and nonpoor households. (National Crime Victimization Survey, Bureau of Justice Statistics.)

are twice as likely as the nonpoor to be victims of violent crimes (rape, assault, and robbery); those in poor, single-parent households are more than 3 times as likely.

The difference in the incidence of personal theft between the poor and the nonpoor is not statistically significant, but those in poor, single-parent households again suffer crimes at a higher rate. Rates of theft for the nonpoor are 60 per 1,000 people per year, compared to 66 for the poor and 85 for those in poor, single-parent households. The rates of incidence for household crimes (burglary, household theft, or motor vehicle theft) are high for both the poor and the poor in single-parent families. Poor households are almost one and a half times as likely and poor, single-parent households are more than twice as likely as nonpoor households to suffer these crimes.

Consistent with the statistics on crime victimization, the poor are less likely to report living in safe neighborhoods. Ninety-three percent of the nonpoor live in families whose family head reports that the neighborhood is safe from crime, compared to only 78 percent of the poor, 72 percent of those in poor, single-parent families, and 67 percent of those in families receiving welfare. Similarly, the poor are more likely to live in families whose head reports being afraid to go out:[8] this was the case for only 9 percent of the nonpoor, compared with 19.5 percent of the poor, 21 percent of those in poor, single-parent families, and 25 percent of those in families receiving welfare.

Overall, the poor are more likely to express dissatisfaction with the communities in which they live: 18 percent of the poor and 25 percent of those in poor, single-parent families are in households that report that their neighborhood is bad enough that they would like to move, compared with only 7 percent of the nonpoor. Similarly, 15 percent of the poor and 20 percent of persons in poor, single-parent families are in families that report that community services in their neighborhoods are bad enough that they would like to move, compared with only 6 percent of the nonpoor.

Given that these measures of safety and neighborhood quality are subjective, it is plausible that differences would be greater if measured on an absolute scale, because people tend to adjust their expectations according to their experiences.[9]

Health and Nutrition

Poor mothers are much more likely than are nonpoor mothers to experience problems in birth and pregnancy. (See table 6.) The number of infant deaths within the first year is higher: 13.5 per 1,000 live births for poor mothers and 14.6 for poor, single mothers, compared to 8.3 for nonpoor mothers. Similarly, the percentage of live births with low weight and the rate of preterm births is about twice as high for poor and for single, poor mothers as for nonpoor mothers.[10]

8 The respondent reports that, in the past month, there were times when he or she wanted to go somewhere but stayed home instead because he or she thought it would be unsafe to leave home.

9 R. Janoff-Bulman, "Lottery Winners and Accident Victims: Is Happiness Relative?" *Journal of Personality and Social Psychology,* vol. 36, no. 8, pp. 917–27; and Robert H. Frank, "Frames of Reference and the Quality of Life," *American Economic Review,* May 1989, pp. 80–85.

10 The income differentials in birth outcomes hold across age groups.

TABLE 6 **HEALTH CHARACTERISTICS OF PERSONS IN 1988, 1992, AND 1993**

Characteristic	Nonpoor families	Poor families	Single-parent poor families	Families receiving welfare
NATIONAL MATERNAL AND INFANT HEALTH SURVEY				
Number per 1,000 live births:				
infant deaths in first year	8.3	13.5	14.6	14.3
Percent of live births:				
Low birth weight (less than 2,500 grams)	5.5	10.2	12.8	11.6
Preterm (gestation under 37 weeks)	7.3	13.0	15.2	15.1
Percent of mothers:				
inadequate prenatal care	15.6	43.1	48.8	42.1
NATIONAL HOUSEHOLD EDUCATION SURVEY				
Percent of children aged 3 to 7 years:				
Is there a particular clinic, health center, doctor's office, or other place the child is usually taken when *sick*?				
Yes, an emergency room	5.3	14.7	17.2	....
No	3.1	8.3	6.1	....
Child has a usual place where they are taken for *routine* care	41.8	40.1	40.2	....
Child ever had one or more disabling conditions	17.5	23.8	24.7	....
NATIONAL HEALTH INTERVIEW SURVEY				
Percent of children under age 18 who:				
Visited the doctor in the past year	84.0	80.0	....	....
Visited the dentist in the past year	62.0	41.0	....	....
CURRENT POPULATION SURVEY				
Percent of persons:				
Covered by private health insurance for all or part of the year	80.0	21.1	16.0	....
Covered by medicaid for all or part of the year	6.1	54.5	71.6	....
Not covered by health insurance at any time during the year	12.1	26.8	18.0	....
SURVEY OF INCOME AND PROGRAM PARTICIPATION				
Percent of persons living in families that had enough food in the past 4 months	98.6	89.0	86.9	85.8

NOTE: Data are for individuals, except that the Survey of Income and Program Participation results are based on family-level data, person-weighted. National Maternal and Infant Health Survey data were collected in 1989 and 1990, with 1988 as the reference period. Current Population Survey data were collected in March 1994, with 1993 as the reference period. National Household Education Survey data were collected from January through April 1993; the reference period is the period since the beginning of the 1992–93 school year, or the current period. Survey of Income and Program Participation data collection and reference periods are September through December 1992. National Health Interview Survey data were collected from January through December 1993, with the 12 months prior to the interview as the reference period.

Poor and nonpoor mothers also differ in quality of prenatal care. The Centers for Disease Control defines inadequate prenatal care as lack of prenatal doctor visits in the first trimester, a strong predictor of birth outcomes. Forty-three percent of poor mothers and 49 percent of poor, single mothers reported no prenatal doctor visits in the first trimester, compared with only 16 percent of nonpoor mothers.

Poor children are more likely to have had a disability or health impairment lasting more than 6 months: 24 percent of poor children (aged 3 through 7) suffered such problems, compared to 18 percent of nonpoor children. Similarly, 25 percent of poor children in single-parent families have had a disability.

Poor children also are less likely to have a particular clinic, health center, or doctor's office that they usually visit when sick, and are more likely to use an emergency room as their usual clinic, if they have one. Twenty-three percent of poor children usually use an emergency room or have no usual clinic when sick, compared to only 8 percent of nonpoor children. Poor and nonpoor children do not differ as to whether they have a usual place to which they go for routine care.

Poor and nonpoor children under age 18 do not differ significantly in terms of whether they had visited a doctor in the past year, perhaps because medicaid is available to poor children. However, poor children are less likely to see a dentist regularly. Sixty-two percent of nonpoor children have seen a dentist within the last year, compared with only 41 percent of the poor.

Differences also exist in the presence and source of health insurance coverage. Thirteen percent of those in nonpoor families, compared with 29 percent of those in poor families, are not covered by health insurance at any time during the year. Those in poor, single-parent families actually have a lower rate, 19 percent, than do all poor families. The higher coverage of the single-parent poor most likely results from their access to medicaid. The poor are less likely to be covered by private health insurance and are more likely to be covered by medicaid for all or part of the year. Only 24 percent of the poor (17 percent of those in poor, single-parent families) have private health insurance, while 46 percent are covered by medicaid (68 percent of the single-parent poor). In contrast, 78, percent of the nonpoor have private health insurance and only 6 percent are covered by medicaid.

Finally, the poor are more likely to live in families that report sometimes or often not having enough food to eat. Ninety-nine percent of the nonpoor live in families where the head reports having enough food to eat, compared to 89 percent of persons in poor families and 87 percent of persons in poor, single-parent families.

Education

Poor students are more likely to have repeated a grade and to have been expelled from school. (See table 7.) Thirty-one percent of poor youth (grades 3 through 12) are reported by their parents to have repeated a grade, which is twice the rate for nonpoor students, 15 percent. Poor students are more than 3 times as likely as are nonpoor students to be expelled from school, 3.4 percent versus 1.0 percent. Also, poor students are considerably more likely to attend schools with security guards and metal detectors.

Both poor and nonpoor students have high expectations that they will attend and graduate from college. Ninety percent of poor stu-

TABLE 7 **EDUCATIONAL CHARACTERISTICS OF PERSONS IN 1992-93**

Characteristic	Nonpoor families	Poor families	Single-parent families
CURRENT POPULATION SURVEY—EDUCATION SUPPLEMENT			
Percent of children under age 15:			
Children (in school) who use a computer at school	63.3	54.8	51.9
Children who use a computer at home	23.0	3.2	2.5
NATIONAL HOUSEHOLD EDUCATION SURVEY			
School Safety and Discipline Component			
Percent of students grades 3 to 12:			
Student has repeated a grade since starting school	15.4	31.3	31.6
Student has been expelled from school (at some point)	1.0	3.4	3.5
Percent of students grades 6 to 12:			
Student thinks he/she will attend school after high school	96.1	90.1	90.2
Student thinks he/she will graduate from a 4-year college	89.7	82.7	82.3
School has security guards	28.8	43.3	46.2
School has metal detectors	4.1	11.5	12.8
School Readiness Component			
Percent of prekindergarten children:			
Child not enrolled in preschool or Head Start	5.8	8.6	7.1
Child enrolled in public (not private) preschool/ Head Start program	31.0	75.5	78.2
Child attends Head Start program	11.1	48.2	54.5
Child attends a preschool program (other than Head Start)	86.2	52.9	49.3
Percent of children aged 5 to 7:			
Child has fewer than 10 books	5.4	27.2	28.5
Child watches more than 3 hours of television per day	32.9	49.4	52.3
Child watches more than 4 hours of television per day	15.1	29.2	30.8
Child moved three or more times between birth and 5th birthday	19.5	28.0	27.9
HIGH SCHOOL AND BEYOND SURVEY			
Percent of persons in 1980 sophomore cohort who:			
Attended either a 2- or a 4-year college	69.6	48.3	47.6
Completed requirements for a bachelor's degree	32.6	16.9	13.2

NOTE: Data are for individuals. Current Population Survey—Education Supplement data collection and reference periods are October 1993. National Household Education Survey data were collected from January through April 1993; the reference period is the period since the beginning of the 1992–93 school year or the current period. High School and Beyond Survey data were collected in 1992 and early 1993, with reference periods of fall of 1980 through spring of 1991 for education questions and 1992 for total household income before taxes.

dents expect to attend school after high school and 83 percent anticipate graduating. Ninety-six percent of nonpoor students expect to continue their education, and 90 percent expect to graduate college. On the other hand, actual attendance and graduation rates exhibit differences. Forty-eight percent of poor students and 70 percent of nonpoor students attend either a 2- or 4-year college; 17 percent of poor students and 33 percent of nonpoor students complete a bachelor's degree.[11]

Home computer use by children (aged 14 and younger) varies dramatically by income, although it was not prevelant for either the poor or the nonpoor. Twenty-three percent of children in nonpoor families use a computer at home, compared with only 3 percent of children in poor families and 2.5 percent of children in poor, single-parent families. Children have more equitable use of computers at school: 63 percent of nonpoor students compared with 55 percent of poor students and 52 percent of students in poor, single-parent families use a computer at school.

Most poor and nonpoor prekindergarten children are enrolled in a nursery or preschool program; only 9 percent of poor and 6 percent of nonpoor children did not attend such a program. The poor are much more likely to attend a Head Start program or other public preschool.

Young children (aged 5 to 7) in poor families watch more television than do those in nonpoor households and have fewer books. Almost one-third of them watch more than 4 hours of television per day, compared to only 15 percent of nonpoor children. Twenty-seven percent of poor children and 29 percent of poor children in single-parent families have fewer than 10 books, compared to only 5 percent of nonpoor children.

Finally, poor children change residence more often. Twenty-eight percent of poor children aged 5 to 7 move 3 or more times before their fifth birthday, compared to 20 percent of nonpoor children. The pattern is similar for older children as well.

Overall Deprivation

The previous discussion provides information on the distribution of various assets, consumption commodities, and income. However, correlations across measures are not apparent. Families with limited resources may choose different allocations of commodities in order to make ends meet. Examining one dimension of living conditions at a time probably understates the extent to which families forego important other elements of material well-being.

To address this issue, an index of deprivation was created using data from the Survey of Income and Program Participation. (See table 8.) Deprivations were defined on nine family characteristics: evicted in the past year, gas or electricity turned off in the past year, phone disconnected in the past year, did not have enough food in the past 4 months, lives in crowded housing (more than one person

TABLE 8 **OVERALL DEPRIVATION IN 1992**

Number of deprivations[1]	Nonpoor families	Poor families	Single-parent poor families	Families receiving welfare
SURVEY OF INCOME AND PROGRAM PARTICIPATION				
Percent of persons in families with:				
No deprivations	87.0	44.9	43.2	34.6
One deprivation or more	13.0	55.1	56.8	65.4
Two deprivations or more	3.2	26.9	29.8	33.6
Three deprivations or more	1.0	11.8	12.9	14.6
Four deprivations or more	.3	4.0	4.5	4.9
Five deprivations or more	.1	1.1	1.1	1.7
Six deprivations or more	.0	.1	.1	.1
Seven deprivations or more	.0	.0	.0	.0
Average number of deprivations	.19	.99	1.06	1.21

[1]Deprivation = Evicted in past year;
> Utilities disconnected in past year;
> Telephone disconnected in past year;
> Housing with upkeep problems;
> Not enough food in past 4 months;
> Crowded housing (more than 1 person per room);
> No refrigerator;
> No stove;
> No telephone

NOTE: Family-level data, person-weighted. Survey of Income and Program Participation data collection and reference periods are September through December 1992.

per room), lives in housing with moderate or severe upkeep problems,[12] lives without a refrigerator, lives without a stove, and lives without a telephone. For each individual, the number of deprivations reported is the total number of these characteristics reported by the individual's family. The number of deprivations is between 0 and 9 for each individual. Each of these hardships was chosen because it is relatively rare in the overall U.S. population and represents an element of material well-being important in day-to-day life in this country that has been forgone.[13]

The majority of the poor live with at least one of these deprivations: 55 percent of the poor, compared with 13 percent of the nonpoor. Similarly, 27 percent of the poor face two or more deprivations, compared with only 3 percent of the nonpoor. Fifty-seven percent of those in poor, single-parent families suffer at least one deprivation and 30 percent live with two or more; 65 percent of those in families receiving welfare suffer at least one deprivation and 34 percent live with two or more. Overall, the average number of deprivations for the poor, the poor in single-parent families, and those in families receiving welfare is 5 to 6 times higher than for the nonpoor.

★   ★   ★

---

12 For the Survey of Income and Program Participation, residences with moderate upkeep problems are defined as having three or four of the following: leaking roof or ceiling; toilet, hot water heater, plumbing not working; broken windows; exposed wiring; holes in the floor; cracks or holes in wall or ceiling; and rats, mice, or roaches. Problems are severe if there are five or more of the above.

13 Specifically, we include all variables, except "lives without a color television," for which 95 percent or more of nonpoor individuals do not live in families that report the deprivation.

Social Mobility

18

Social Mobility*

RICHARD BREEN AND DAVID ROTTMAN

||| INTRODUCTION

Neither the position of families nor individuals within the class structure nor that structure itself, remain constant over time. Individuals and families change their class position and the class structure itself evolves, as some occupations decline and others become more numerous. Both these sorts of change have been intensively studied by sociologists and other social scientists. Examining the development of a class structure over time involves adopting a historical perspective, as in the work of Przeworski et al. (1980) or Wright and Martin (1987). The extent and the way in which families move through the class structure—between positions in it, in other words—is the subject matter of the study of social mobility. Social mobility has long been a central topic of sociological inquiry, and has been particularly actively pursued over the past 25 years. In this chapter our aim is to explain what the study of social mobility is, to give a brief explanation of the methods used in social mobility analysis, and to summarize the main results of recent research. Before we begin,

---

* First published in 1995; from *Class Stratification: A Comparative Perspective*.

however, we need first to set the scene by saying something about the temporal dimension of social class.

★ ★ ★

‖ SOCIAL MOBILITY

When we examine social mobility—that is, how and why people or families change position in the class structure—we are usually interested in two things. First, in the nature of mobility: how much change in class position is there; how far do people move from their original class; is there more upward or downward mobility in society; how does mobility affect people's behaviour and attitudes (for example, when people are mobile out of class X and into class Y, to what extent do they continue to behave (for example to vote) in ways that are typical of class X—from which they have come—and to what extent do they take on the behaviour typical of the class to which they move—class Y?)? Second, we are interested in the consequences of mobility for the class structure. For instance, if we take one class virtually all of whose members have always been in that class and whose families were before them, and contrast it with another class which is chiefly made up of families which have been mobile into that class from outside it, how are the two likely to differ? In particular, will the members of the more 'closed' of the two classes be more likely to view themselves as constituting a class *for* themselves, in Marx's terms, than will the members of the more open class?

These two perspectives on mobility are, as we might have anticipated, not entirely distinct. Classes are, after all, made up of families and the individuals within them: they both comprise a

class and are influenced by being members of it, in much the same way that individual actions are shaped by the existence of constraints but also help, to a greater or lesser extent, to change or maintain these constraints.

‖ INTER-GENERATIONAL MOBILITY

The most commonly studied form of class mobility is termed inter-generational mobility. This takes the form of a comparison of a person's current social class with the class that his or her family occupied at the time the person was growing up.

The vast majority of studies of inter-generational mobility have analyzed data for men: typically, then, the comparison is between the class position occupied by a man's family at the time he was growing up (say, at age 16) and the class position he currently occupies. When these studies are carried out on populations or large samples the relationship between the two is shown as a two-dimensional cross-tabulation (see Table 1). This table shows us the number of men who fall into each combination of current class and the class they were part of when they were growing up. Such tables are sometimes called origin by destination tables, since the name 'class origin' is usually given to the class they occupied when they were growing up, and 'class destination' is the name given to their current class. Hence the process of mobility is conceived of rather like a journey or a flow from an origin to a destination. The labelling of the two margins of the table in this way overcomes a problem of interpretation that had caused some problems in mobility analysis; this is that, despite

TABLE 1 **THREE-CLASS MOBILITY TABLE: MEN IN ENGLAND AND WALES 1972**

		Current (destination) class			
		1	**2**	**3**	**Total**
ORIGIN CLASS	1	731	322	189	1242
	2	857	1140	1109	3106
	3	787	1386	2915	5088
	Total	2375	2848	4213	9436

NOTE: Classes are: 1 = Service; 2 = Intermediate; 3 = Working.
SOURCE: Calculated from Goldthorpe et al. (1980/87), Table 2.2.

the term 'inter-generational' mobility, the distribution of men across the origin classes did not represent the class structure as it was at any particular point in time or for any particular generation. Mobility data is gathered from a survey of men (or people) in the current population (sometimes only the current working population) and thus, if it is representative of that population, it cannot, in its distribution over the origin classes, be representative of any other population (except by chance)—such as a particular generation or age group, or even of the population of fathers or families of men currently in the workforce (Duncan 1966). Therefore, mobility tables do not show us how one generation's class distribution evolves into the next generation's; rather, they show us how the classes men start out in (their origins) relate to the class they are in at the time of the survey (class destinations[1]).

Table 1 refers to a sample of 9436 men in England and Wales interviewed in 1972 for the Oxford Mobility Study (Goldthorpe 1980/87). It is immediately evident, of course, that what the table looks like will depend very much on how many classes we identify: here we have used a three-class categorization, and, as is conventionally the case, the same three classes are identified for origins as for destinations. These three classes are termed the service, intermediate and working class, respectively ★ ★ ★.[2] The working class comprises men in largely manual occupations, whether these are considered skilled or not. The service class is made up largely of professionals, managers, administrators, supervisors of white-collar workers and owners of capital. In the middle, the intermediate class comprises other white-collar workers—such as clerical workers, salespersons, employees in services—small proprietors, such as farmers and smallholders, the self-employed (who do not employ others),

---

1 To label them class destinations may also be misleading, as Sorenson (1986) has argued. The men in a mobility sample typically range in age from 18 or 21 to retirement age or more, and their current class cannot be considered a destination (at least in the sense of final destination) for many of the younger men.

2 We could, of course, have used a finer class classification—say into seven classes, as Goldthorpe does for most of his analyses (see also Marshall 1990: Chapter 2).

TABLE 2 PERCENTAGE OUTFLOW MOBILITY TABLE: MEN IN ENGLAND AND WALES 1972

		Destination class			
		I	2	3	Total
ORIGIN CLASS	1	59	26	15	100
	2	28	37	36	101
	3	15	27	57	99

NOTE: Classes as Table 1. Percentages are by row—row totals may not add to 100 because of rounding.
SOURCE: As Table 1.

and lower-grade technicians and supervisors of manual workers.[3]

This table tells us that there are 731 men who were born into class 1 and, at the time of the survey, were in class l; there were 322 men also born into class 1 who had moved to class 2; and so forth. Since it is difficult to interpret what these numbers mean when they are presented this way, they are usually given as percentages. If we calculate the percentages along the rows, we get the percentage of all men of a given origin class in each destination class. This is termed an 'outflow' table. Such a table for the England and Wales sample looks like Table 2. This table tells us that, for example, of all men originating in the working class, 15 per cent moved into the service class; 27 per cent moved into the intermediate class; and the remaining 57 per cent stayed in the working class (they were 'immobile'). Another way of interpreting this is to say that the probability of a man, who was born into the working class moving into, say, the intermediate class, was 0.27.

The other way of percentaging the table is to do it by columns: this gives us the percentage of men in a given destination class who come from the various origin classes. This is termed an 'inflow' table. An inflow table looks like Table 3. We interpret this table by, for example, noting that, of the current occupants of the intermediate class, 11 per cent came from service-class origins; 40 per cent came from intermediate-class origins; and 49 per cent came from working-class origins.

These two different ways of percentaging a table yield different insights into mobility. The inflow table tells us about the current composition of the classes, in terms of where members of the class came from. So, they tell us how heterogenous each class is in its composition. In these data an interesting contrast is provided by the service class and the working class. The service class is very heterogenous in its composition, being made up almost equally of men from all three origin classes, while the working class is much more homogenous: over two-thirds of

3 The three-class categorization used here corresponds to that used by Goldthorpe *et al.* (1980/87) and not to that found in Erikson and Goldthorpe (1992b:38-9). In terms of the original Goldthorpe classes (as shown in Table 3.1) the three classes used here are made up as follows: Service class: I and II; Intermediate class: III, IV and V; Working class: VI and VII.

TABLE 3 **PERCENTAGE INFLOW MOBILITY TABLE: MEN IN ENGLAND AND WALES 1972**

		Destination class		
		I	2	3
ORIGIN CLASS	1	31	11	5
	2	36	40	26
	3	33	49	69
	Total	100	100	100

NOTE: Percentages are by column—column totals may not add to 100 because of rounding.
SOURCE: As Table 1.

men in this class were also born into this class. It is relevant to bear in mind that the service class expanded over this period—hence one would expect that it would be heterogenous in its composition not least because there are not enough men of service-class origins (1242 in Table 1) to fill the number of service-class destination positions (2375). Conversely, the working class destination is much smaller than the working-class origin, and the reverse argument applies. As the number of positions in this class contracted, we should expect that the remaining positions would have been filled by those with origins in that class, rather than by outsiders moving in.

We should expect, furthermore, that differences of this kind in the composition of classes would have consequences for the formation of 'class consciousness'. The members of a class which is relatively homogenous with respect to the class origins of its members are, all other things being equal, probably rather more likely to be aware of themselves as constituting a dis-

tinctive class than are the members of a class who are diverse in respect of their class origins.[4] 'In general, the greater the degree of "closure" of mobility chances—both intergenerationally and within the career of the individual—the more this facilitates the formation of identifiable classes' (Giddens 1973:107). However, shared class origins are only one factor which may contribute to an awareness of class (see ★ ★ ★ Giddens 1973).

The outflow table, on the other hand, tells us the chances of ending up in a particular destination class, given that a man started in a certain origin class. We can then make a comparison of these chances as between different origins. For example, the chances of a man born into the working class getting into the service class are 0.15 or 15 per cent; while the chances of a man of service-class origins staying in that class are 59 per cent. So, men from the service class are much more likely to be found there than are men born into the working class. Hence, the outflow table

4 Recall that ease of mobility is one of the factors that Weber uses to distinguish the existence of social classes out of groups of economic classes.

provides us with a ready means of examining class differences in mobility chances, or, to put it in slightly different terms, the strength of the relationship between where you start out in the class structure (your class origin) and where you go to (your class destination).

However, when we make these comparisons of mobility chances as between different origin classes, we do not usually do so in terms of probabilities (or percentages flowing into a particular destination class from a given origin class); rather, we calculate chances in terms of odds. This idea will be familiar to any readers with an interest in gambling. Instead of looking at the *probability* that a man of intermediate class origins ends up in the service class, we look, instead, at the *odds* that such a man ends up in the service class *rather* than another class. So the probability of being in the service-class destination is .28, while the odds of being in that destination class rather than in, say, the intermediate class are 0.75. This figure is equal to the number (or percentage) who end up in the service class divided by the number (or percentage) who end up in the intermediate class.[5] So, when we make the comparison across different origin classes, we do this in respect of the odds of being in one destination class, rather than another. If we then want to compare the mobility chances of men from service-class origins with those of men from intermediate-class origins, say, we do this in terms of the odds of their arriving at one destination class rather than another.

For example, we can compare the odds of entering the service-class destination rather than the intermediate-class destination, as between men of service-class and intermediate-class origins. In these data, then, the odds for men of service-class origins are: 731 (= number of men in service-class destination from service-class origins) divided by 322 (= number of men in intermediate-class destination from service-class origins) = 2.27; while for men of intermediate-class origins they are 857 (= number of men in the service-class destination from intermediate-class origins) divided by 1140 (= number of men in intermediate-class destination from intermediate-class origin) = 0.75. We compare these two odds by simply taking their ratio: this yields a measure called the 'odds ratio' which, in this case, is equal to 3.03.

The odds ratio is the conventional measure of inequality in access to particular class destinations from different class origins. Odds ratios are usually set up so that they measure the odds of getting into a 'higher' or more desirable destination class, relative to getting into a lower, or less desirable, class. Odds ratios can be readily interpreted as a measure of how the odds of getting into a more desirable class relative to getting into a less desirable one differ as between different origin classes. Equality of access to a more desirable, rather than a less desirable, destination class, as between different origin classes, would give rise to an odds ratio of one (since both origins would have the same odds). If the odds ratio is more than one, this reflects greater advantages to the origin class whose odds form the numerator of the ratio, while an odds ratio less than one indicates that the advantages

---

5 So 28/37 from the outflow table (Table 2) is (allowing for rounding error) equal to 857/1140 from the original table (Table 1).

TABLE 4 **ALL POSSIBLE ODDS RATIO IN THE THREE-CLASS ENGLAND AND WALES MOBILITY TABLE**

Destination class	Origin class	Odds ratio
1 v 2	1 v 2	3.03
1 v 2	1 v 3	3.98
1 v 2	2 v 3	1.32
1 v 3	1 v 2	5.03
1 v 3	1 v 3	14.33
1 v 3	2 v 3	2.85
2 v 3	1 v 2	1.65
2 v 3	1 v 3	3.54
2 v 3	2 v 3	2.15

accrue to the destination class whose odds form the denominator.

It might seem that there is likely to be a plethora of possible odds ratios that we could calculate for any table. In Table 4 we show all the possible odds ratios in the three-class table for England and Wales.[6] So, for example, the odds of being in the intermediate-class destination rather than the working-class destination are 2.15 times greater for men of intermediate class origins than for men of working-class origins. However, it turns out that not all of these odds ratios are independent of one another. In a mobility table using M classes (M = 3 in our example) there are $(M-1)^2$ independent odds ratios. So, in our three-class table, there are four independent odds ratios. If we know these, then we can calculate all the rest. So, for example if we take any pair of destination classes (say classes 1 and 3) we can calculate the odds ratio as between origin classes 2 and 3 (which is 2.85)

from a knowledge of the odds ratios involving origin classes 1 v 2 (5.03) and 1 v 3 (14.03). In this case we divide the latter by the former to yield 2.85.[7]

STRUCTURAL AND EXCHANGE MOBILITY

We have spent some time discussing odds ratios because they turn out to play a central role in mobility table analysis. We will now explain why.

Many mobility analysts have argued that the mobility we see in a mobility table can be explained as the result of two processes. These are sometimes called structural and exchange mobility. The idea behind structural mobility is quite simple. If we take a given society, the amount of inter-generational class mobility that we observe will depend, to a very great extent, upon the degree of change in the class or occupational structure of that society. So, a society which was developing rapidly should show a lot of mobility, not least because many occupations would be declining in importance and thus men whose father held one such occupation would have very great difficulty in pursuing the same occupation. They would, in a sense, be forced to be mobile out of that class or occupation by virtue of the fact that the occupational positions were not there for them to fill. Sometimes this kind of mobility is called 'forced mobility'. The difference between the origin class and destination class distributions in a mobility table is sometimes taken as a measure of the extent of this. So, in the three-class table (Table 1), we see

---

6 We could also invert all these odds ratios to yield a much larger total, but this would be of no interest.

7 We see why this follows if we write the odds ratio for any two origin classes in the form of a ratio, thus 1/2 and 1/3. It therefore follows that the ratio 2/3 is simply 1/3 divided by 1/2.

many more origin than destination positions in the working class, and rather more destination than origin positions in the service class. So, the suggestion is that men must have had to move out of the working class because it is contracting, and, equally, men must have been 'drawn into' the service class as it expanded.

It was usually argued that this process operated independently of other processes of social mobility. In particular, it operated independently of processes of exchange mobility, which was concerned with how different class origins influenced mobility, and the inequalities in mobility chances that derive from different class origins. The reason that different origins confer different chances of mobility is because they provide people with different resources for mobility. So, people born into more advantaged classes generally acquire higher levels of formal qualifications, and, in addition, may have other resources (such as kinship links or friendship networks) which they can use to help them acquire a more desirable class position. In his analysis of the English and Welsh mobility data Goldthorpe (1980/87:99) developed a mobility model in which he argued that patterns of social fluidity (in other words, patterns of inequality of access to particular class destinations as between men of different class origins) were shaped by three factors. These are, he argues, the *relative desirability* of different classes as destinations; the *barriers to entry* to these classes; and the *resources* attached to different class origins which allow these barriers to be overcome and the more desirable destina-

tions to be entered (and the less desirable ones to be avoided).[8] So, people seek to gain entry to more highly desired destination classes: to do this they must overcome a variety of barriers to entry (such as the requirement to possess certain educational or other credentials; or the acquaintance of particular individuals), using the resources that they have acquired as a result of their origin-class position.

From this it follows that if resources were more or less equally distributed (so that the resources one had for mobility did not depend upon one's origin class) there should be a good deal of inter-generational class mobility in society. Hence, an egalitarian society (in the sense of one in which there was equality of condition as between people of different class origins) should be a society displaying high rates of mobility. In particular, of course, the chances of people born into a given class staying in that class would be no better than the chances of people born outside that class entering it. Therefore more equal societies should display more social mobility.

However, we have already seen that the amount of mobility in a society also depends upon the amount and speed of occupational or class change. Hence, a society which was very unequal could, it appeared, display a high rate of mobility provided that the pace of structural change were fast enough. The problem is to disentangle these two effects: how much mobility is due to structural change, and how much reflects the degree of equality—or, as it is sometimes called, openness—in society? The posing

8   ★ ★ ★ Resources are used to overcome barriers (constraints) in order to try to secure the most desired destination (the most preferred alternative).

of this question then led to a number of attempts, by sociologists, to partition the total amount of mobility in a given observed mobility table into a component due to structural mobility (which was, in some fashion, linked to changes in the marginal distributions of the mobility table— that is, to the difference between the origin and destination distributions) and some component due to exchange mobility.[9] None of these attempts, in the 1970s and early 1980s, were particularly successful.

In the 1970s, however, a number of sociologists began to point out that odds ratios might be useful in this context, since they certainly measured inequalities in access to different class destinations arising from different class origins. Furthermore, odds ratios are independent of the marginal distributions of the mobility table. This means that, if two societies have the same level and pattern of class inequality in relative mobility chances, the fact that one of them has experienced rapid changes in the class structure (and, perhaps as a result, the origin and destination distributions are more unalike in one country's table than in another's) will not affect the fact that the pattern and magnitude of their odds ratios will

be the same. Drawing on this, Goldthorpe and his co-authors (Goldthorpe 1980/87; Erikson, Goldthorpe and Portocarero 1979, 1982) abandoned the structure/exchange distinction and replaced it with an emphasis on absolute mobility (the actual mobility observed in the mobility table) and social fluidity (measured in terms of odds ratios), sometimes called 'relative mobility'.[10] There is no attempt, in this approach, to partition absolute mobility into some part due to structural change and some to exchange mobility.[11]

Nevertheless it provides a framework in which it is possible to identify societies which display very high rates of absolute mobility, together with low social fluidity or low 'societal openness' as reflected in large odds ratios. A very good example of this is provided by social mobility data for São Paolo, Brazil, collected by Hutchinson (1958) and later presented and used by Sobel, Hout and Duncan (1985:366). This shows massively high rates of absolute mobility, arising from very rapid and large changes in the class structure together with very large odds ratios reflecting a high level of inequality in access to more desired class destinations as between men of different class origins.

---

9 Some examples include Hazelrigg 1974; Hope 1981, 1982; and McClendon 1977, 1980. For a critique of this approach see Sobel 1983.

10 It was also recognized that odds ratios, which measure social fluidity, are directly captured in the parameters of log-linear models which, since the 1970s, have been used to model mobility tables (see Fienberg 1977; Goodman 1979). The parameters that are estimated in log-linear modelling fall into two kinds: main effect parameters, and interaction, or association, parameters. These latter depend upon the nature and extent of the statistical relationship between origins and destinations. Odds ratios are functions of these parameters, and not of the main effects. So, for example, if all odds ratios are one, the association parameters of the log-linear model will all be zero (in the log form of the model).

11 The structure/exchange distinction was then revived by Sobel, Hout and Duncan (1985). They present an elegant reformulation of the concepts, arguing that exchange mobility refers to equal reciprocal flows between pairs of classes (for example the flow from origin class A to destination class B and from origin B to destination A); and that structural mobility is captured in origin-specific parameters that make such flows unequal (so that the flow from A to B may, for example, exceed that from B to A). The difficulty with this model is that it implies that the observed mobility table should display the property of 'quasi-symmetry' (see Bishop *et al.* 1975 for a definition of this technical term). While a number of mobility tables do indeed display this property, many do not. In such cases, a third type of mobility—a residual category— has to be invoked in order to account for the observed flows.

⫴ ABSOLUTE MOBILITY

The study of absolute mobility places the focus on changes in the class structure over time (such as the contraction or expansion of classes). We have already noted the major trends in this respect during this century in most of the industrialized countries of the world: the decline in farming and farm-related jobs, and in unskilled work, with increases in skilled and white-collar jobs. The timing of this transition has, however, varied. We can gain some indications of this by comparing the origin and destination distributions for a number of tables from different countries.[12] Table 5 shows this comparison for four of the European countries taken from the CASMIN data set—Sweden, England and Wales, the Republic of Ireland, and Poland. Here we have moved to a five-class classification, in order to bring out some of the salient differences between these societies. These five classes (with the Erikson and Goldthorpe 11-class schema classes in parentheses) are:

1. White-collar workers (I, II, IIIa and IIIb).
2. Petty bourgeoisie (IVa and IVb).
3. Farmers and farm workers (IVc and VIIb).
4. Skilled workers (V+VI).
5. Non-skilled workers (VIIa).

(See Erikson and Goldthorpe 1992b: 38-9.)

We have chosen these four countries because they represent four different sorts of society— England and Wales having been industrialized for a long period, Sweden being a society which has experienced a long period of social democratic government and which has, accordingly, developed possibly the world's most comprehensive system of social welfare (broadly defined). The Republic of Ireland is a late-industrializing nation that retains a substantial dependence on agriculture, and Poland was, at the time these data were collected, a state socialist country.

Many of these differences are reflected in the comparison of the origin and destination distributions of their respective mobility tables. For example, it is noticeable that in England and Wales, origin classes 1 (white-collar workers) and 4 (skilled manual workers) are much larger (in percentage terms) than in the other three countries, reflecting Britain's earlier industrialization. In Sweden the destination distribution of class 1 is of comparable size to England and Wales, but in Ireland and Poland it remains much smaller. The relative lack of men in class 2 (petty bourgeoisie) in the Polish origin and destination distributions is hardly surprising in a state socialist country. In the other countries the distributions of this class are quite similar. It is in class 3 (farmers and farm workers) that we find major variation, particularly in the destination distributions where the contrast is between the two countries which retain substantial dependence on agriculture (Ireland and Poland) and whose industrialization has been very late and the other two. However, the decline in the importance of farming in Sweden has been both recent and very rapid indeed as we can see by comparing the origin and distributions for class 3 here. Conversely, agriculture declined in significance in England and Wales long before

---

12 It is important to reiterate that this only approximates changes in the class or occupational structures over time. To examine such change formally we should compare sample surveys of the labour force at two points in time.

TABLE 5 PERCENTAGE ORIGIN- AND DESTINATION-CLASS DISTRIBUTIONS: SWEDEN, ENGLAND AND WALES, REPUBLIC OF IRELAND, POLAND

		Classes				
		1	2	3	4	5
Sweden	Origin	14	11	26	24	25
(N = 2103)	Destination	32	8	5	30	24
E & W	Origin	21	10	5	39	26
(N = 9434)	Destination	34	8	2	41	15
Republic of	Origin	11	10	39	14	27
Ireland	Destination	23	8	21	20	27
(N = 1992)						
Poland	Origin	10	3	53	18	16
(N = 32109)	Destination	20	2	25	31	22

SOURCE: CASMIN data set.

the period covered by these data: here class 3 makes up only a very small part of both the origin and destination distributions. Finally, class 5 (unskilled workers) shows a good deal of cross-national variation, particularly in a comparison of Poland with the other three countries. Here we see that it is relatively under-represented in the origins, but is the only country in which this class is larger (in relative terms) in the destination distribution. Again, it seems likely that the unusual position of Poland is associated with its post-war experience of state socialism.

Table 6 shows the percentage composition of the destination classes in terms of origin class: in other words, the table shows what percentage of men in a given class come from each of the origin classes. We limit ourselves to highlighting two points. First, the class which has shown the greatest growth in these four countries—the white-collar class 1—also shows substantial heterogeneity of composition. This is particularly striking in Ireland. Nevertheless, with the

exception of Poland, the origin class which is most over-represented among the incumbents of this destination class is class 1 itself. This is part of a more general feature of these four tables, namely that for all except the relatively small classes, it is the corresponding origin class that supplies the largest share of members of a given destination class. The exception to this is Poland, where this is true only of the farming class.

The second trend is the remarkable degree of self-recruitment and class closure in class 3 (farmers and farm workers). This is particularly pronounced in Poland and Ireland, where this class remains very large. The reasons for this high degree of self-recruitment are easy to find: by and large farms are inherited, either legally or *de facto* and the same is true of jobs as farm workers. Except in England and Wales there is a good deal of mobility from class 3 into all the other classes, reflecting the 'forced' outward mobility of those born into a declining class.

TABLE 6 **PERCENTAGE INFLOW TABLES FROM SWEDEN, ENGLAND AND WALES, REPUBLIC OR IRELAND, POLAND**

		Destination classes				
		I	2	3	4	5
(A) SWEDEN						
	1	28	13	0	9	6
	2	12	23	5	10	8
Origin class	3	17	23	84	21	32
	4	24	19	5	30	21
	5	19	22	7	31	32
(B) ENGLAND AND WALES						
	1	37	18	11	12	15
	2	10	25	5	7	11
Origin class	3	3	4	67	3	9
	4	33	34	3	49	61
	5	17	20	13	29	5
(C) REPUBLIC OR IRELAND						
	1	28	9	1	9	5
	2	15	33	1	8	7
Origin class	3	21	30	92	14	33
	4	15	7	1	33	12
	5	21	21	5	37	43
(D) POLAND						
	1	25	8	1	9	7
	2	5	18	1	3	3
Origin class	3	34	44	92	37	51
	4	21	16	2	30	16
	5	15	13	4	21	23

SOURCE: As Table 5.

On the basis of these figures, there is clearly no class in any of our four countries (class 3 excepted) in which self-recruitment could be said to lead to class closure sufficient to promote the formation of class consciousness. Class heterogeneity is particularly marked in Poland, largely because of the effects of the outflow from farming origins into the other destination classes.

||| SOCIAL FLUIDITY

Sociologists interested in social mobility devote the majority of their attention to social fluidity. Recall that in studying social fluidity we are using odds ratios to measure the differences between people of different origin classes in their chances of access to more rather than less desirable destination classes. This is, therefore, a useful measure of the degree of societal openness, since if there were no differences in this respect between men of different class origins, all odds ratios would be equal to one. Such differences as exist are usually attributed to inequalities in the possession of mobility resources as between different class origins.[13]

When we come to try to judge whether or not a society displays much or little 'openness' of this kind, we can adopt one (or both) of two yardsticks. First, we could compare the observed set of odds ratios with the yardstick of total equality where all odds ratios would equal one. The latter is sometimes called a situation of perfect mobility, and it arises when there is no relationship between class origins and class destinations—that is to say, between the class a person starts out in and the one he or she is currently in. However, since all societies are some considerable distance from displaying perfect mobility, a possibly more useful perspective is provided by international comparisons which ask: How open is one society compared with another society?

One of the most famous hypotheses in sociology addresses exactly this question. The so-called Featherman-Jones-Hauser (FJH) hypothesis argues that a basic similarity will be found in social fluidity in all industrial societies

'with a market economy and a nuclear family system' (Featherman, Jones and Hauser 1975:340). This innocuous-seeming formulation has, if it is true, some very important ramifications. Many societies have expended a good deal of effort and resources on policies designed to increase societal openness by, for example, providing free education, medical care, and, more generally, the panoply of the welfare state. The FJH hypothesis suggests that whether a state pursues such policies or not has no consequences for the level of social fluidity that it will display.

The bulk of the many papers that have used comparative data to test the FJH hypothesis have arrived at much the same conclusions. These are that, first, the greatest differences between societies in mobility are in the area of absolute mobility. This is not surprising, given the different rates of structural change in societies, as we noted earlier. Second, there are very great similarities in the degree of openness in different societies. There are statistically significant differences in fluidity between them, but these tend to be relatively small for the most part. This finding has largely been born out by the results of the most painstaking and detailed comparative mobility project yet undertaken, the CASMIN project. In discussing the results of this research, Erikson and Goldthorpe find it necessary to modify the FJH hypothesis somewhat. Their conclusion is that:

A basic similarity will be found in patterns of social fluidity ... across all nations with market

---

13 Though, clearly, they might also be (and indeed, in reality probably are) due to differences in preferences for different class destinations among men of different class origins

(in other words, in a relationship between origin class and subjective assessments of the desirability of different destinations).

economies and nuclear family systems where no sustained attempts have been made to use the power of the modern state apparatus in order to modify the processes or the outcomes of the processes through which class inequalities are intergenerationally reproduced. (Erikson and Goldthorpe 1987b:162)

What is notable about this modification is that, while retaining the emphasis on the high degree of commonality that apparently exists across industrialized nations in their pattern of social fluidity, it allows for the possible impact of state intervention. Erikson and Goldthorpe (1992b:178) argue that it is the attaining of greater equality of condition that best promotes high rates of social fluidity; that is, if inequalities in the conditions of life enjoyed by people are small, fluidity will be high. Thus, for example, policies of taxation and redistribution that seek to reduce the level of inequality in the distribution of income and in living standards, are likely, all other things being equal, to promote greater social fluidity.

||| SOCIAL FLUIDITY IN EUROPE

Differences in social fluidity will be most evident in comparisons involving the extremes. In Erikson and Goldthorpe's analysis of the CASMIN data the extremes of societal openness in Europe are represented by Sweden (most open) and Poland and the Republic of Ireland (least open), with England and Wales falling in the middle. In Table 7 we show the outflow

tables for our four countries—Sweden, England and Wales, Republic of Ireland and Poland—with a view to comparing their social fluidity.

Recall that an outflow table tells us the percentage of men from each class origin who entered each destination class. So, in Table 7 we see that, in Sweden, of men born into class 1, 64 per cent had class 1 as their destination class. The striking feature of this table is that, for both white-collar (class 1) and skilled worker (class 4) destinations in all countries, the highest probability of being found in that class is enjoyed by men who were born into it. In all countries the strength of the link between origins and destinations in the white-collar class (as measured in this way) exceeds that observed in the farming class, and, in all countries except Ireland, so does the strength of this link among the skilled working class. These figures suggest that in both these classes very effective mechanisms exist through which class position can be transmitted from father to son, despite considerable heterogeneity in the composition of these classes as destinations (particularly in the case of class 1, as revealed by the inflow table).

To undertake a proper comparison of social fluidity between these four countries would require that we model the pattern of odds ratios in each table using log-linear models, as Erikson and Goldthorpe (1987a and b, 1992b) do in their analyses. Here, however, we will compute some illustrative odds ratios.[14] So, for example, take the extreme odds ratios—that

14 As we noted earlier, odds ratios can be computed from either a table of frequency counts (Table 1 for example) or from tables of inflow or outflow percentages.

TABLE 7 **PERCENTAGE OUTFLOW TABLES FROM SWEDEN, ENGLAND AND WALES, REPUBLIC OF IRELAND, POLAND**

		Destination classes				
		1	2	3	4	5
(A) SWEDEN						
	1	64	7	0	18	11
	2	36	17	2	27	18
	3	21	7	17	24	30
	4	33	7	1	38	22
	5	24	7	2	36	31
(B) ENGLAND AND WALES						
	1	62	7	1	20	11
	2	37	21	1	25	17
	3	21	7	23	20	28
	4	29	7	0	41	23
	5	23	6	1	36	35
(C) REPUBLIC OF IRELAND						
	1	60	7	3	17	13
	2	35	28	3	15	20
	3	12	6	51	7	23
	4	25	4	1	47	24
	5	18	7	4	27	44
(D) POLAND						
	1	53	2	1	29	15
	2	30	11	9	30	21
	3	13	2	42	21	21
	4	24	2	3	51	20
	5	20	2	7	40	32

SOURCE: As Table 5.

is the odds ratio of being found in destination class 1 (white-collar workers) rather than class 5 (unskilled manual) as between men of class 1 and class 5 origins. In Sweden this is 64/11 divided by 24/31 = 7.5. In England and Wales the ratio is larger—8.6. In Ireland it is 11.3 and in Poland 5.7. On this basis, then, there is sub-

stantial inequality in competition for class 1 rather than class 5 destinations as between men of these different origins, but this inequality is least in Poland. However, the same is not true of the odds ratios of being found in class 1 rather than class 2 (petty bourgeoisie), given origins in class 1 rather than class 2. Here the figures are

4.3 for Sweden, 5.0 for England and Wales, 6.9 for Ireland and 9.7 for Poland. In other words, the disadvantages associated (in this case) with origins in the petty bourgeoisie are greatest in Poland, least in Sweden.

We could, of course, compute all the odds ratios in this table (all 100 of them) and compare them, but the general picture is as noted above. Odds ratios are, on average, smallest in Sweden, next smallest in England and Wales. Overall, Ireland has the next smallest odds ratios, followed by Poland. A simple index of this involves calculating these 100 odds ratios, taking their logarithm (so that an odds ratio of 1, indicating perfect equality, has a logged value of 0) and finding the average of the absolute values of these logged odds ratios.[15] The average for Sweden is 0.21; for England and Wales 0.24; for Ireland 0.30 and for Poland 0.33. Once again, using this particular yardstick, Sweden emerges as the society displaying the greatest social fluidity.

As we might expect, the explanation for the greater degree of social fluidity found in Sweden (not only by Erikson and Goldthorpe but by most other analysts of Swedish mobility in a comparative perspective: for example, Breen 1987; Erikson, Goldthorpe and Portocarero 1982; Erikson and Pontinen 1984) centres on the effects of a long period of social democratic government.[16] This has had the effect of reducing inequalities of condition (such as income

inequality) and increasing equality of opportunity. In addition, the commitment to maintaining full employment seems also likely to have played a significant role in fostering high rates of social fluidity (Erikson and Goldthorpe 1992b:165).

By contrast, the low level of social fluidity in the Republic of Ireland is linked to a number of factors. Most important is Ireland's position as a late industrializing, semi-peripheral state in which free post-primary education and very many other welfare state programmes were introduced only around the time that these mobility data were collected or afterwards. As a result, inequalities of condition between families were particularly marked (Breen *et al.* 1990) and thus, following Erikson and Goldthorpe's (1992b) argument cited earlier, a finding of low levels of social fluidity is perhaps not surprising.

What of Poland? Despite its post-war history Poland displays less social fluidity than either Sweden or England and Wales—but, once again, this accords with what we know of the impact of state socialism on social mobility. Broadly speaking, levels of social fluidity in state socialist societies are similar to those found in capitalist societies, albeit with some differences as to which classes are advantaged and which disadvantaged. Furthermore the persistence, in both Ireland and Poland, of a large agricultural sector in which inheritance is of overwhelming

---

15 The technicalities of this measure need not concern us: interested readers should consult Breen 1994 for details.

16 Though Erikson and Goldthorpe (1992b:177–9) are at pains to argue that although state intervention may influence fluidity in particular instances (as in Sweden) this does not allow us to conclude that rule by a particular sort of political

party (e.g. Social Democrats) will necessarily give rise to a distinctive pattern of fluidity in all countries where that kind of political party is in power. In other words, there does not exist, for example, a generic 'social democratic' pattern of social fluidity.

importance in acquiring a position as a farmer or farm worker, acts to reduce the overall level of social fluidity in these countries.

Finally, in our discussion of social fluidity we might ask: Where does America fit into this picture? A view of America as the 'land of opportunity' has existed for several centuries. In this view, America is seen as lacking the kind of rigid class structure felt to be characteristic of European societies and as presenting opportunities for personal advance that older countries could not. So, for example, the idea that class relations in America were distinctively different was found in Sombart's (1907/76) thesis of 'American exceptionalism'. While some studies can be seen as supporting this position (Miller 1960, and, particularly, Blau and Duncan 1967), recent research by Erikson and Goldthorpe (1985, 1992b:321) has led to the opposite conclusion: namely that 'no very convincing case for American exceptionalism . . . can be made out', and

> No matter how distinctive the United States . . . may be in (its) economic and social histories . . . or in the ideas, beliefs and values concerning mobility that are prevalent . . . it could not, on our evidence, be said that (it) differ(s) more widely from European nations in . . . mobility than do the European nations among themselves. (Erikson and Goldthorpe 1992b:337, parentheses added)

||| CONCLUSIONS

The study of social mobility is, we believe, a powerful research programme that tells us a great deal about the nature of modern societies and the position of classes within them.[17] However, it is hardly to be wondered at that, having been an area of active research for many years, it has generated many critiques. But what is less obvious perhaps is that the great majority of the criticisms levelled at mobility studies are not criticisms of mobility research *per se* but, rather, of the framework within which it is pursued. That is to say, most critiques of mobility research concern either the issue of the adequacy of the class classification used or the question of the appropriate unit of class composition. In this sense they are criticisms of mobility research *en passant*. ★ ★ ★

Aside from these very important questions there are two specific criticisms of mobility research itself which we should mention. The first of these concerns the neglect of women in much social mobility analysis. It has been argued (by Hayes and Miller 1993 for example) that the concentration on men distorts the picture we have of mobility in modern societies. While this would be a very damaging criticism if it were true, there is much evidence to suggest that the inclusion of women in mobility studies does not change conclusions about social fluidity based on men-only studies (for example Marshall

---

17 In this chapter we have concentrated on inter-generational mobility: however, in recent years a great deal of interest has arisen in the study of intra-generational mobility. While at its simplest this involves a tabular comparison of the class an individual occupied on entry to the labour force with the class he or she occupies at some later point in time (and is thus analogous to the origin—destination inter-generational mobility table), more sophisticated approaches are also used which seek to analyze the sequence and timing of transitions between jobs or classes that people experience during their life course (for example Allmendinger 1989).

et al. 1988). While it is very obvious that there is a marked difference in the occupational and class distributions of men and women, patterns of social fluidity among women appear to be very similar to those found among men. In other words, differences in mobility chances between women of different class origins are much the same as those found between men of different class origins.

The second criticism is one which has been made by Poulantzas (1975) who argues that mobility research is fundamentally mistaken in placing its emphasis on the movement of individuals between class positions, when what should be focused on is the structure of, and the functions carried out by, these positions. While such an argument accords well with the views of 'structural Marxists' it is difficult to credit it with any force. In its concern with absolute rates, mobility research does indeed examine the structure of class positions in society. All researchers in the area accept, for example, that the single largest 'cause' of mobility flows during the last 100 years has been the contraction in the number of positions available in agriculture. On the other hand, in any society with a division of labour linked to unequal rewards the question of how people and families are distributed over these positions will be of central significance for an understanding of the way in which life chances are allocated. Furthermore, the study of how much openness of access exists to these various positions, as measured by social fluidity, tells us something very basic about the nature of the modern nation-state. To argue, as Poulantzas seems to, that a concern for such matters is misplaced is, at best, a statement of somewhat eccentric preferences.

||| REFERENCES

Blau, P. and O.D. Duncan, 1967, *The American Occupational Structure*, New York: John Wiley.

Breen, R. 1987, 'Sources of Cross-National Variation in Mobility Regimes: English, French and Swedish data Reanalysed', *Sociology*, 22,1:75–90.

Breen, R., D.F. Hannan, D.B. Rottman, and C.T. Whelan, 1990, *Understanding Contemporary Ireland: State, Class and Development in the Republic of Ireland*, London: Macmillan.

Duncan, O.D. 1966, 'Methodological Issues in the Analysis of Social Mobility', in N.J. Smelser and S.M. Lipset (eds) *Social Structure and Mobility in Economic Development*, New York: Aldine.

Erikson, R. and J.H. Goldthorpe, 1985, 'Are American Rates of Social Mobility Exceptionally High? New Evidence on an Old Issue', *European Sociological Review*, 1, 1: 1–22.

Erikson, R. and J.H. Goldthorpe, 1987a, 'Commonality and Variation in Social Fluidity in Industrial Nations, Part II: A Model for Evaluating the "FJH Hypothesis" ', *European Sociological Review*, 3, 1: 54–77.

Erikson, R. and J.H. Goldthorpe, 1987b, 'Commonality and Variation in Social Fluidity in Industrial Nations, Part I: The Model of Core Social Fluidity Applied', *European Sociological Review*, 3, 2: 145–66.

Erikson, R. and J.H. Goldthorpe, 1992a, 'Individual or Family? Results from two Approaches to Class Assignment', *Acta Sociologica*, 35: 95–106.

Erikson R. and J.H. Goldthorpe, 1992b, *The Constant Flux: A Study of Class Mobility in Industrial Societies*, Oxford: Clarendon Press.

Erikson, R., J.H. Goldthorpe, and L. Portocarero, 1979, 'Intergenerational Class Mobility in Three Western European Societies: England, France and Sweden', *British Journal of Sociology*, 30, 4: 415–41.

Erikson, R., J.H., Goldthorpe, and L. Portocarero, 1982, 'Social Fluidity in Industrial Nations: England, France and Sweden', *British Journal of Sociology*, 33, 1: 1–34.

Erikson, R. and S. Pontinen, 1984, "Social Mobility in Finland and Sweden: A Comparison of Men and Women', in R. Alapuro (ed.) *Small States in Comparative Perspective*, Oslo: Norwegian University Press.

Featherman, D.L., F.L. Jones, and R.M. Hauser, 1975, 'Assumptions of Social Mobility Research in the US: The Case of Occupational Status', *Social Science Research*, 4: 329–60.

Giddens, A. 1973, *The Class Structure of the Advanced Societies*, London: Hutchinson.

Goldthorpe, J.H. with C. Llewellyn and C. Payne, 1980 (second edition 1987), *Social Mobility and Class Structure in Modern Britain*, Oxford: Clarendon Press.

Hayes, B.C. and R.L. Miller, 1993, 'The Silenced Voice: Female Social Mobility Patterns with Particular Reference to the British Isles', *British Journal of Sociology*, 44, 4: 653–72.

Hazelrigg, L.E. 1974, 'Partitioning Structural Effects and Endogenous Mobility Processes in the Measurement of Vertical Occupational Status Change', *Acta Sociologica*, 17, 2: 115–39.

Hope, K. 1981, 'Vertical mobility in Britain: A Structured Analysis', *Sociology*, 15, 1: 19–55.

Hope, K. 1982, 'Vertical and Non-vertical Class Mobility in Three Countries', *American Sociological Review*, 47, 1: 99–113.

Hutchinson, B. 1958, 'Structural and Exchange Mobility in the Assimilation of Immigrants to Brazil', *Population Studies*, 12: 111–20.

Marshall, G. 1990, *In Praise of Sociology*, London: Unwin Hyman.

Marshall, G., H. Newby, D. Rose and C. Vogler, 1988, *Social Class in Modern Britain*, London: Unwin Hyman.

McClendon, M.J. 1977, 'Structural and Exchange Components of Vertical Mobility', *American Sociological Review*, 42, 1: 56–74.

McClendon, M.J. 1980. 'Structural and Exchange Components of Occupational Mobility: A Cross-National Analysis', *The Sociological Quarterly*, 21: 493–509.

Miller, S.M. 1960, 'Comparative Social Mobility', *Current Sociology*, 9: 1–89.

Poulantzas, N. 1975, *Classes in Contemporary Capitalism*, London: New Left Books.

Przeworski, A., R.R. Barnett, and E. Underhill, 1980, "The Evolution of the Class Structure of France, 1901–1968', *Economic Development and Cultural Change*, 28, July: 725–52.

Sobel, M.E. 1983, 'Structural Mobility, Circulation Mobility and the Analysis of Occupational Mobility: A Conceptual Mismatch', *American Sociological Review*, 48, 6: 721–7.

Sobel, M.E., M. Hout, and O.D. Duncan, 1985, 'Exchange, Structure and Symmetry in Occupational Mobility', *American Journal of Sociology*, 91, 2: 359–72.

Sombart, W. 1907/76, *Why is there no Socialism in the United States?*, London: Macmillan.

Sorenson, A.B. 1986, 'Theory and Methodology in Social Stratification', in U. Himmelstrand (ed.) *Sociology; From Crisis to Science*, London: Sage.

Wright, E.O. and B. Martin, 1987, 'The Transformation of the American Class Structure', *American Journal of Sociology*, 93, 1: 1–29.

19

Finding Work: Some Basic Results*

MARK GRANOVETTER

How people find jobs is a prosaic problem—but exactly for this reason, it relates closely to important issues in sociology and economics. Under the rubric "labor mobility" in economics, and "social mobility" in sociology, how people move between jobs and between occupations has received much study; but surprisingly little detailed attention has been given to the question of how individuals become *aware* of the opportunities they take. Most studies are either highly aggregated or highly individualized. At the macro level, excellent monographs detail the statistics of men flowing between categories ★ ★ ★; at the micro level, other studies offer plausible psychological and economic motives for particular individuals to *want* to change jobs ★ ★ ★. Important as these concerns are, they are not those of the present study. Rather, I have chosen to concentrate on the issue of how the information that facilitates mobility is secured and disseminated. This question lies somewhere between the micro- and macro-level concerns described above, and is a potentially crucial link in their integration; it is an important part of the study of the *immediate* causes of mobility, and, as in other social science problems, failure

★ First published in 1974; from *Getting a Job: A Study of Contacts and Careers*.

to specify immediate causes leads to inability to link micro and macro levels of analysis.

★ ★ ★

PROFESSIONAL, TECHNICAL, AND MANAGERIAL (PTM) WORK

PTM workers use three basic ways of finding out about jobs: formal means, personal contacts, and direct application. Included under "formal means" are advertisements, public and private employment agencies (including those calling themselves "management consultants" or "executive search services"), interviews and placements sponsored by universities or professional associations, and placement committees in certain professions, notably in various ministries. The defining characteristic of formal means is that the job-seeker uses the services of an impersonal intermediary, between himself and prospective employers. By "impersonal" is meant either the lack of any personal contact (as in newspaper advertising), or use of an individual, who is specifically designated by himself or others, as an employment intermediary. "Personal contacts," by contrast, implies that there is some individual known personally to the respondent, with whom he *originally* became acquainted in some context *unrelated* to a search for job information, from whom he has found out about his new job, or, who recommended him to someone who then contacted him. "Direct application" means that one goes or writes directly to a firm, does not use a formal or personal intermediary, and has not heard about a *specific* opening from a personal contact. Although the three methods are distinct,

in principle, and pure cases outnumber others, the differences may become blurred in specific instances. ★ ★ ★

In the present PTM sample, personal contact is the predominant method of finding out about jobs. Almost fifty-six percent of the respondents used this method; 18.8 percent used formal means (9.9 percent advertisements, 8.9 percent other formal means) and 18.8 percent used direct application; 6.7 percent fell into miscellaneous categories (including "not ascertained.") If one takes into account the usual over-estimation of the use of "direct application" ★ ★ ★, these figures are remarkably similar to those generally found for blue-collar workers.

We must now ask, in some detail, why a given individual uses one method rather than another to find a job. Other methods may have been used, of course, besides the one that ultimately resulted in a job change. Hence, we have, to some extent, not only a question of propensity to use a method, but also one of why the respondent was able to do so successfully.

Most respondents prefer the use of personal contacts to other means. Other labor market studies indicate that employers express a similar preference for hiring methods. It follows that external economic conditions have less influence than might be supposed on the methods that connect people to jobs. In tight labor markets, employers are forced to use less preferred methods; but this is largely cancelled by the lower motivation of job-seekers or job-changers to do so. The opposite may be said of loose labor markets. Thus, studies done under various economic conditions have shown similar distributions of job-finding methods. (The statement about "cancelling" is crude, however, and ought to be subjected to more systematic investigation.)

As a first approximation, we may suppose that preferences for different methods are determined by some sort of cost-benefit analysis of job-search procedures by prospective job-changers. This is only an approximation because ★ ★ ★ the image of the job-changer as conducting a search according to rational, utility-maximizing principles needs considerable modification.

Nevertheless, the preference described above *is* roughly justified by respondents on a cost-benefit basis; findings from various other studies support their judgment. Sheppard and Belitsky, for instance, for a mostly blue-collar sample, computed the proportion of those using a given method who obtained jobs through it. They found that "friends and relatives" received by far the highest rating (1966: 94). Brown, for each method used by his respondents, college professors, computed the number of jobs accepted as a proportion of the number of jobs found by that method; this is presumably a measure of the desirability of jobs found in various ways. The top five methods on this measure were different types of personal contact (1967:141). In addition, he reported more use of personal contacts in the finding of jobs of higher rank, smaller teaching loads, higher salaries, and greater prestige of college (1965b:227; 1967:118). Next in quality of job produced was direct application ("blind letters" in most cases), followed by the various formal methods (1965b:241).

The PTM workers to whom I spoke believed that information secured through personal contacts is of higher quality than that available by other means; a friend gives more than a simple job description—he may also indicate if prospective workmates are congenial, if the boss is neurotic, and if the company is moving forward or is stagnant. (Similarly, on the demand side, evaluations of prospective employees will be trusted better when the employer knows the evaluator personally.)

Various measures of the quality of jobs held by my respondents substantiate their idea that better jobs are found via personal contacts. Table 1 shows that those using personal contacts are most likely to say that they are "very satisfied" with their current job, and least likely not to express satisfaction; direct application and formal means follow, in that order. Table 2 shows the strong association of income level with job-finding method. Nearly half (45.5 percent) of those using personal contacts report incomes over $15,000, whereas the corresponding figure for formal means is under one-third; for direct application, under one-fifth.

Jobs can also be classified by the nature of their creation. In some cases one directly replaces someone who has vacated a position; or an individual may be added on to do work similar to that which others are already doing. New positions may also be created: work may be done that has not been done before, or previously scattered tasks can be put together into one job. It seems likely that the most desirable positions would be found in the category of "newly created" jobs, since these would be most apt to have been tailored to the needs, preferences, and abilities of an incumbent. Table 3 shows that those finding a job through contacts

TABLE 1 LEVEL OF JOB SATISFACTION ATTAINED BY JOB-FINDING METHOD OF RESPONDENT

Level of satisfaction	Method used				
	Formal means	Personal contacts	Direct application	Other	Total[d]
Very satisfied	30.0%	54.2%	52.8%	47.1%	49.1%
Fairly satisfied	46.0%	36.8%	32.1%	47.1%	38.2%
Lower[a]	24.0%	9.0%	15.1%	5.9%	12.7%
N[b]	50	155	53	17	275

$$p = 0.03^c$$

[a]Includes "neither satisfied nor dissatisfied," "fairly dissatisfied," and "very dissatisfied."
[b]Two-variable tables add to 100 percent in the columns. Rather than printing "100 percent" in each case, the number of cases on which column percentages are based is given.
[c]All significance levels are by chi-square test.
[d]Omitted from this and subsequent tables are respondents from whom a usable response was not obtained on any variable in the table.

are much more likely than those using formal means or direct application, to have had jobs newly created for them.

By taking the percentages on these tables in the opposite direction, we may view the same findings from the point of view of the system of jobs. Results are parallel: The more satisfied individuals are in their jobs, the more likely they are to have found them through contacts. Jobs offer-

ing the highest salary are much more prone to be found through contacts than others: whereas less than half of jobs yielding less than $10,000 per year were found by contacts, the figure is more than three-quarters for those paying more than $25,000. The use of direct application falls steadily as the salary of a job rises; the use of formal methods is somewhat less regular in pattern, though least likely at the highest sal-

TABLE 2 LEVEL OF INCOME OF RESPONDENT IN PRESENT JOB, BY JOB-FINDING METHOD USED

Income	Method used				
	Formal means	Personal contacts	Direct application	Other	Total
Less than $10,000	28.0%	22.7%	50.0%	5.3%	27.6%
$10,000–14,999	42.0%	31.8%	30.8%	26.3%	33.1%
$15,000–24,999	24.0%	31.2%	15.4%	52.6%	28.4%
$25,000 or more	6.0%	14.3%	3.8%	15.8%	10.9%
N	50	154	52	19	275

$$p = 0.001$$

TABLE 3   **ORIGIN OF JOB, BY JOB-FINDING METHOD OF RESPONDENT**

Origin of job	Method used				
	Formal means	**Personal contacts**	**Direct application**	**Other**	**Total**
Direct replacement	47.1%	40.5%	58.0%	38.9%	44.9%
Added on	31.4%	15.7%	18.0%	27.8%	19.9%
Newly created	21.6%	43.8%	24.0%	33.3%	35.3%
N	51	153	50	18	272

$$p = 0.02$$

ary. Finally, newly created jobs are much more likely to be filled via personal contacts than are other types, and are least likely to be filled by direct application or formal means.

A related finding is that 57.9 percent of those who say they have recently thought about looking for another job found their present job through contacts, compared to 72.1 percent of those who have not considered changing ($p = 0.09$). This is parallel to the finding of Shapero et al. for aerospace engineers, that those recently leaving their company were considerably less likely to have entered via contacts than those who remained (1965:50). Discussions of labor force "attachment" would do well to consider method of recruitment. The fact that "stayers" are more likely to have been recruited through contacts than "movers" may result only from the fact that better jobs are found in this way. It may also be true, however, that the man who is thus recruited is more likely to become quickly integrated into the social circles of his workplace, having an entree in the person of his contact. The data of the present study are too limited to allow a choice between the two hypotheses.

To sum up, evidence is strong that the use of personal contacts by my respondents results in better jobs than other methods. A number of respondents even had the odd experience of being refused a job for which they applied directly, only to be accepted later for the same job through personal contacts. One postdoctoral student in biology received a letter from an institution to which he had applied for a job, saying that there were "no openings for an individual with your qualifications." But when his thesis adviser took a position there, the younger man went along as a research associate; he subsequently received an effusive letter expressing the college's delight at his appointment. An assistant professor of psychology tells a similar story; his inquiry about the position he now holds was never answered. But several months later, he received a call from someone he had once worked with, asking him if he would be interested in the position. The friend was unaware of his previous inquiry.

Since respondents prefer to find jobs through personal contacts, and this preference appears well-grounded, we must then ask why everyone did not do so. Here the influence of social structure must be probed. Some individuals have the right contacts, while others do not. If one lacks the appropriate contact, there is little he can do about it. While this is obvious enough, it is a difficult question, and a major focus of this study, to determine under what circumstances a given individual *will* have such contacts.

We may begin by asking whether groups with particular demographic characteristics are more or less prone to the use of certain methods. In this context, the standard sociological variables of religion, ethnicity, and educational background come to mind. Several studies have compared the behavior of black and white (usually blue-collar) workers; some found that blacks used formal means more than whites, others that they used them less often. (Crain, 1970; Lurie and Rayack, 1966:369; Sheppard and Belitsky, 1966:174, 178; Ullman and Taylor, 1965:283; Wilcock and Franke, 1963:130). A recent national survey of 14–24-year-old males found no racial differences in search behavior (Parnes et al., 1970:102–104). In the present PTM sample, Table 4 shows that religious background had no particular impact on likelihood of using a given method. Similarly uninteresting tables could be produced showing that ethnic background and educational level attained has no relation to incidence of these methods. (As the present sample is over 99 percent white, no data on racial differences are produced.)

This finding may be surprising insofar as one expects differences in cultural background and personality traits to have an impact on behavior. Sheppard and Belitsky (1966) explicitly tested, for example, the notion that one's degree of "achievement motivation" would affect job-seeking behavior. While they did find some effects in predicted directions, these were rather weak. I will argue, in general, that a much more important type of determinant of one's behavior is one's position in a social network. By this is meant not only the identity of the set of people one knows and his relations to them but also the

TABLE 4 **JOB-FINDING METHOD, BY RELIGIOUS BACKGROUND OF RESPONDENT**

	Religious background				
Method used	Protestant	Catholic	Jewish	None[b]	Total
Formal means	15.4%	16.9%	19.2%	16.7%	17.3%
Personal contact	55.1%	56.6%	57.6%	66.7%	56.8%
Direct application	23.1%	20.5%	16.2%	0.0%	19.2%
Other	6.4%	6.0%	7.1%	16.7%	6.8%
N	78	83	99	6	266

p = n.s.[a]

[a]Significance levels of 0.20 or less are reported; otherwise n.s. (= not significant) is indicated.
[b]Those responding "none" to religious preference were assigned to the religious preference of their parents, if any; where both respondents' and parents' preference are reported as none, the respondents' religious background is coded none.

TABLE 5 **JOB-FINDING METHOD, BY AGE OF RESPONDENT**

| | Age | | |
Method used	Under 34	Over 34	Total
Formal means	25.3%	11.9%	18.9%
Personal contacts	47.9%	64.2%	55.7%
Direct application	22.6%	14.9%	18.9%
Other	4.1%	9.0%	6.4%
N	146	134	280

$p = 0.002$

set known by that set, and so on, as well as the structure of connections among one's friends, friends' friends, and so on. The structure and dynamics of this network, though elusive and difficult to analyze, largely determine what information will reach a given person, and, to that extent, what possibilities will be open to him.

This is not to argue that culture and personality have no impact on one's position in this structure; only that the impact is not systematic or predictable. Nor is it my argument that people make no choices. Individuals clearly do not seize every job offer that reaches them; cultural and personality factors no doubt have their impact on which job one chooses to accept. A separate study would be required to do justice to this issue. The point is that if we confine ourselves to looking at jobs that people *do* accept, however the choice is made, structural factors have the largest influence on the method of uncovering those jobs. By "structural factors" I mean the properties of one's social situation

that shape his contact network; one typically has little control over these factors.

An example is the effect of age. Blue-collar studies have uniformly shown that personal contacts are particularly important to individuals in the early stages of their career—especially in finding one's first job (De Schweinetz, 1933:87, 93; Reynolds, 1951:127). In the Newton sample, the finding is reversed: Table 5 shows that those in the younger half of the sample are considerably more likely to use formal means and direct application, while nearly two-thirds of the older PTM workers find their jobs through personal contacts.[1]

This appears to be due to the greater specialization inherent in PTM occupations; not yet having worked long in the specialized field he has been trained for, the young PTM worker will have acquired few useful contacts. He must thus fall back on formal means and direct application. In the blue-collar case, however, less specialization combined with less geographic mobility make it more likely that some older

---

[1] At this point, the reader might properly wonder if the earlier finding, that those using contacts find higher-paying jobs, is merely an artifact of the overrepresentation of older PTM workers among those using contacts. This is not the case. Controlling for age, the relationship persists within each age group. Similarly, within each age group, the higher the salary, the more likely one was to have used contacts. Among those in the older half of the sample, over 80 percent of those earning $25,000 or more per year found the job through contacts.

TABLE 6 **JOB-FINDING METHOD, BY OCCUPATIONAL CATEGORY OF RESPONDENT**

	Occupation			
Method used	**Professional**	**Technical**[a]	**Managerial**	**Total**
Formal means	15.9%	30.4%	13.6%	18.8%
Personal contacts	56.1%	43.5%	65.4%	55.7
Direct application	18.2%	24.6%	14.8%	18.8%
Other	9.8%	1.4%	6.2%	6.7%
N	132	69	81	282
		$p = 0.01$		

[a]Includes all technical, engineering, and scientific workers except college professors or high school teachers of science.

friend or relative can help the young worker. In their national sample of white, out-of-school youth, aged 14–24, Parnes et al. (1970:104) similarly found that the proportion using "friends and relatives" to find their job is smallest for professional and technical work, increasing steadily to a maximum for semi- and unskilled workers.

Still another structural factor appears if we break the PTM group into its three constituent types of occupation; the results are shown in Table 6. Technical workers are least likely to use personal contacts, and most likely to use formal means and direct application. There are a particularly large number of agencies specializing in technical personnel, which makes it possible to use this route more often than for either professionals or managers; direct application may also be enhanced by the size and con-

sequent wide reputations of many firms which hire technical personnel. Another factor is more subtle, and more structural; whereas scientists and technicians may work alone or in small groups, managers, by definition, must spend a great deal of time in personal interaction. In the course of a manager's career, many more personal contacts may be established than in that of a scientist; such contacts may later be useful.[2]

Individual cases also illustrate the impact of structural factors. One respondent was an engineer, blinded about seven years ago. Unable to maintain as many contacts as formerly, he found it necessary to seek work by formal means. A recent immigrant, though an experienced scientist in Japan, knew very few people in his field in this country, and so, from the point of view of contacts, was just "starting out."

---

2 The figure for professionals must be treated with caution since 58 of the 132 professionals (43.8 percent) are college professors, an atypical situation related to the large number of colleges in the Boston area. College professors are much more likely than other professionals to find jobs through contacts: 77.6 percent do so, as compared to 54.5 percent of high school teachers and 32.7 percent of other professionals. Although older respondents and those with higher incomes are over-represented among professors, this does not explain the strong disposition to use of contacts, as the older and higher-income respondents *among* professors are not more likely than the younger and lower-income ones to use contacts—they are, actually, a little *less* likely, though one cannot take relationships seriously based on such small numbers. Note that this implies that if professors were less prominent in the sample, the general tendency for older and higher income respondents to be more likely to use contacts would be even stronger.

In general, then, Brown's statement about the job-seeking behavior of college professors applies to the present overall PTM sample: "Formal methods [including direct application] are used only after informal contacts have failed to yield a good job" (1967:117). Those who resort to these methods tend to be those who, for more or less structural reasons, lack the right personal contacts. There are, however, some positive reasons to use formal means:

Case #1: Albert W. was working for a large engineering firm, but was dissatisfied. He had personal contacts who could have been useful but did not trust them enough to tell them he was looking for a new job; he therefore went to an agency specializing in technical personnel.[3]

Mr. W. was rather bitter about his experience, however. He reports that the agency scheduled him for interviews in the same room as personnel managers from his company, who would have recognized him and realized why he was there; he covered his face and hurried from the room. He cites this obvious blunder as an example of the utter impersonality of such agencies, which makes them distasteful to deal with. Many of those who had used agencies had similar attitudes. A ghoulish set of terms reflects their evaluation of such services and those who run them: "head-hunters"; "body-snatchers"; "flesh-peddlers"; "warm-body shops."

The appointment of Jewish Conservative rabbis, brought to my attention by one respondent, is an interesting case; formal means were instituted by centralized control for ideological reasons. Before 1947, congregations seeking a rabbi, and rabbis seeking congregations operated by the three methods described above. The situation came to be viewed as intolerable, as congregations considered most desirable found themselves with thirty or forty applicants; those thought less attractive had few or none. (The market was a tight one at the time.) Rabbis found themselves in "lineups" of applicants for interviews; a congregation that had an advantageous bargaining position could bid down the salary asked. Personal connections with members of the boards of trustees were of considerable importance.

All this was considered undignified for clergymen. In 1947–48, the Rabbinical Assembly, central administrative body of the Conservative Jewish movement, asserted control over placement of all Conservative rabbis. This was possible since all such rabbis were members. A placement committee now sends each congregation looking for a rabbi a list of three names, a "panel," from whom they may either choose one, after interviews, or ask for another panel. The committee chooses these names from among those rabbis who, upon receiving the list of vacancies circulated periodically, express interest. The process continues until a rabbi is chosen. Rabbis or congregations attempting to circumvent this system are subject to effective sanctions. There appear now to be few or no exceptions to this method of placement.[4] Its success recently stimulated the Reform Jewish movement to adopt a similar system.

---

3 Anecdotal material in this study has been modified as necessary to protect the anonymity of respondents. Besides the use of fictitious names, this sometimes involves changing industry names and job titles.

4 Information on this placement procedure was secured through the courtesy of a personal interview with Rabbi Gilbert Epstein, Director of Placement, Jewish Theological Seminary, New York City.

In effect, this action approximated the creation of an internal labor market; individuals transfer from one congregation to another as if from once branch to another of the same firm. It is unlikely that the degree of central control necessary to implement such a system could be duplicated in larger, nonreligious groups. There are, at present, less than 1000 Conservative rabbis.

★ ★ ★ Personal contacts are of paramount importance in connecting people with jobs. Better jobs are found through contacts, and the best jobs, the ones with the highest pay and prestige and affording the greatest satisfaction to those in them, are most apt to be filled in this way. With a few interesting exceptions, those who do not find their jobs through personal contacts, would have liked to do so, but were prevented by "structural" factors. A few such factors were briefly sketched in this chapter, but for a deeper understanding it is necessary to ask more detailed questions about how people "use" personal contacts. ★ ★ ★

||| REFERENCES

Brown, David G. 1965a. *The Market for College Teachers*. Chapel Hill: University of North Carolina Press.

——— 1965b. *Academic Labor Markets*. Washington, D.C.: U.S. Dept. of Labor, Office of Manpower, Automation and Training.

——— 1967. *The Mobile Professors*. Washington, D.C.: American Council on Education.

Crain, Robert L. 1970. "School Integration and Occupational Achievement of Negroes." *American Journal of Sociology* 75 (January, Part 2): 593–606.

De Schweinetz, Dorothea. 1932. *How Workers Find Jobs*. Philadelphia: University of Pennsylvania Press.

Lurie, Melvin, and Elton Rayack. 1968. "Racial Differences in Migration and Job Search: A Case Study." In *Negroes and Jobs,* edited by L. Ferman, J. Kornbluth and J. Miller. Ann Arbor: University of Michigan Press.

Parnes, Herbert, R. Miljus, and R. Spitz. 1970. *Career Thresholds*, vol. 1. (Manpower Research Monograph # 16). Washington, D.C.: U.S. Dept. of Labor, Manpower Administration.

Reynolds, Lloyd. 1951. *The Structure of Labor Markets*. New York: Harper.

Shapero, A.R., Richard Howell, and J. Tombaugh. 1965. *The Structure and Dynamics of the Defense R. and D. Industry: The Los Angeles and Boston Complexes*. Menlo Park,, Cal.: Stanford Research Institute.

Sheppard, Harold L., and A. Harvey Belitsky. 1966. *The Job Hunt: Job-Seeking Behavior of Unemployed Workers in a Local Economy*. Baltimore: The Johns Hopkins Press.

Ullman, Joseph C., and David P. Taylor. 1965. "The Information System in Changing Labor Markets." *Proceedings of the Industrial Relations Research Association*: 276–289.

Wilcock, Richard C., and Walter H. Franke. 1963. *Unwanted Workers: Permanent Layoffs and Long-term Unemployment*. New York: The Free Press.

20

The American Jobs Machine:
Is the New Economy Creating Good Jobs?[*]

ERIK OLIN WRIGHT AND RACHEL DWYER

In February 2000, when the current American economic expansion passed the 107th month, President Clinton proudly announced that this expansion was the most sustained in U.S. history, surpassing even the "golden age" of the 1960s. Praise for this expansion extends well beyond our own borders. Throughout the developed world, the American economy now serves as a model of dynamic growth and job creation. European politicians look with envy at the low rate of unemployment here—half the official levels in many European countries—and marvel at all the new jobs.

To be sure, American economic performance has its critics. Some analysts argue that American and European unemployment rates are not so different, once one takes into consideration the vastly higher rate of imprisonment here.[1] Incarceration rates in the United States rose dramatically in the 1990s, and prisoners are drawn from a segment of the population with high rates of

---

[*] First published in 2000; from *Boston Review*, Volume 25, Number 6.

[1] Bruce Western and Katherine Beckett, "How Unregulated Is the U.S. Labor Market? The Penal System as a Labor Market Institution," *American Journal of Sociology*, 104, 4 (January 1999): 1030–60.

unemployment. So if prisoners were still in the labor market, U.S. unemployment rates would be higher. Adjusting the unemployment rate in the United States for incarceration rates could add as much as 2 percentage points to the unemployment rate in the mid-1990s, which would push the U.S. rate above that of a number of European countries.

A more common criticism points to the costs of the American strategy of employment growth. American success is founded on "flexible" labor markets, which allow employers—especially in the context of globalization, NAFTA, and WTO—to hire and fire employees relatively easily, reorganize employment structures in response to market conditions, and adjust wages as needed, especially in a downward direction. As a result, job growth is accompanied by persistent poverty, continuing high levels of inequality, and the growth of poorly paid, dead-end service sector jobs. While these critics acknowledge the recent American success at creating jobs, then, they also argue that the jobs are lousy—with low pay and little chance for improvement.

Are the critics right? Is the American "jobs miracle" based on the expansion of lousy jobs? More precisely, what is the distribution of job quality—the balance of good and bad—in the current expansion, and how does this distribution compare to earlier job expansions? Before celebrating the American model, and urging its emulation elsewhere, we need answers to these questions.

A "public interest" ad in the *Economist* by the Pfizer company in 1999 reports one line of response:

> But what about the quality of the new jobs created? The figures about the American labour market tell us a quite different story from the "trash-job-and-working poor" litany that we so often hear. Since 1983 about 50 percent of the new net jobs created in the U.S. economy—about 15 million—were in the managerial and professional sector, and adding the medium skilled occupation, the figure rises to over 80 percent. Furthermore, around 70% of the new net jobs were in occupations remunerated above the median income for all full-time employees.[2]

The assertions in Pfizer's ad are based on a widely cited report on the topic prepared by Joseph Stiglitz when he was chairperson of the President's Council of Economic Advisors.[3] The report is based on a study of the 1994–1996 expansion. Using Current Population Survey data provided by the U.S. Census Bureau, Stiglitz constructed an "occupation-by-sector matrix": in effect, a table listing 22 different sectors of the economy and 45 occupations in each sector. Typical examples of sectors at this level of disaggregation are durable goods manufacturing, educational services, and wholesale trade; typical examples of occupations include machine operators, teachers except college and university, secretaries, and engineers. This yielded a total of 990 potential kinds of "jobs"

---

2 Mauricio Rojas, "The End of Work Fallacy," Pfizer forum, *The Economist* (February 20–26, 1999): 28.

3 The Annual Report of the Council of Economic Advisors (Washington: United States Government Printing Office, 1997).

(cells in the matrix). After eliminating empty and small cells, some 250 or so jobs remained in the analysis, accounting for roughly 95 percent of total employment. Stiglitz and his colleagues then calculated the median weekly earnings of full-time employees in each of the 250 cells and defined "job quality" by the distribution of these cell medians. In the simplest model, "good jobs" were defined as all cells in this job matrix with median earnings above that of the median cell for the whole matrix, and "bad jobs" were defined as cells with median earnings below the median cell. The final step in the analysis was to calculate the change in the number of people in each cell for the period 1994–1996. The central finding was striking: roughly 68 percent of all net job growth was among the good jobs, and roughly 50 percent of all net job growth was in jobs in the top three deciles of the job median earnings distribution.[4] The conclusion offered in the report, and summarized in the Pfizer ad, was that the job expansion was strongly weighted toward the creation of good jobs.

The Stiglitz report received a great deal of press at the time of its release, and its influence continues. But does it present an adequate picture of changes in the American labor market and job structure in the job expansion in the 1990s? We think not, and for two principal reasons. First, while it is true that many of the newly created jobs are good, it is also true that

lots are lousy and there has been little expansion in between: in short, the story is one of *job polarization* and not simply growth at the top. Second, while job growth for white Americans has been concentrated at the good end of the spectrum, job growth for blacks and Hispanics has been concentrated at the lousy end: in short, the full story is also one of *racial division* in the labor market.

STRATEGY OF ANALYSIS

To evaluate the quality of newly created jobs in the current economic expansion, we have examined the entire period of expansion in the 1990s (recall that Stiglitz studied only 1994–1996), compared the recent period with the 1960s, and studied the role of gender and race in each period. The two pivotal tasks for exploring the distribution of job quality during these expansions are to categorize jobs and figure out how to measure the "quality" of different categories of jobs.

On the categorization, we follow Stiglitz in classifying jobs on the basis of occupation-by-sector matrices (using Current Population Survey [CPS] data)—45 occupations by 22 sectors in the 1990s (the identical categories as those used by Stigliz) and, because of limitations in the available data, 32 occupations by 21 sectors in the 1960s.[5] In principle there would be 990

---

4 It is important to note that these results refer to net job expansion rather than job creation per se. That is, there is always a simultaneous process of the creation of new jobs and the destruction of already existing jobs. When we observe that a particular cell in the occupation-by-sector job matrix increased by 10,000 over a period of time, this could mean the creation of 25,000 new jobs and the destruction of 15,000

old jobs. All that we observe is the net effect of these two processes.

5 One other note on the 1960s data: because of problems in the CPS surveys in the early 1960s we could not use the data for the first two years—1961 and 1962—of the employment expansion. Our data analysis thus covers the period 1963–1970. ★ ★ ★

jobs (45 × 22) within this matrix in the 1990s data and 672 jobs (32 × 21) in the 1960s data, but not all of these cells had any CPS survey respondents in them at both the beginning and the end of the period of job expansion under study.[6] Our analysis, therefore, is based on changes in the number of people in those cells in which there were sample cases in both the first year of the expansion and the last: 746 job categories for the 1990s, and 296 in the 1960s.

On the measurement of job quality: ideally we would like to rank order job categories from best to worst on the basis of some index of job properties, including wages, job security, working conditions, fringe benefits, career potentials. In practice, however, the only consistent indicator of job quality available is the earnings of people in these jobs. Moreover, while many other job attributes are obviously important to people, most desirable features of jobs are correlated with earnings. So, again following the general method adopted by Stiglitz, we measure job quality by the median hourly earnings of full-time employees in the job categories derived from the occupation-by-sector matrix.[7] In 1992, the best of the 746 jobs was lawyers in wholesale trade with median hourly earnings of $43.23 while the worst was the occupational category

"fabricators, assemblers, inspectors and samplers" in the "social services" sector with median earnings $4.32. (For jobs with large numbers of people in them, the best job was "health diagnosing" in the "other medical services" sector, with median hourly earnings of $30.75, and the worst was "private household service workers" in the "private household services" sector, with median hourly earnings of $5.32).

Our goal, then, is to measure the relative contributions to job expansion of jobs of differential quality defined by the median hourly earnings of job categories. In doing this, we face a methodological problem: the cells in our jobs matrix are of vastly different sizes. For example, engineers (occupation) in social services (sector) is quite small, with roughly 750 people in that job across the United States in 1999, whereas "teachers except college and university" (occupation) in "educational services" (sector) includes 3.6 million people in that year. It makes little sense, therefore, to simply chart the contribution of each cell to the overall expansion of jobs, since the large categories will tend to contribute more to job growth simply because they are bigger. We could correct for these differences in the number of people in different jobs by shifting to an analysis of the rates of growth of differ-

---

6 Stiglitz dropped all cells from this matrix with fewer than 10 cases; we have decided to include all cells in which there are cases in both of the years in any time period over which we are assessing job expansion. None of the substantive results we will report would be different if we excluded these small cells.

7 A couple of brief further technical notes: (1) We are using hourly earnings to index job quality rather than weekly earnings, as in the Stiglitz report. The results are not substantively affected by this shift, but we felt that hourly earnings was a better measure of job quality. (2) In order to rank order the cells of the occupation-by-industry matrix by median earnings as accurately as possible, we combined the CPS samples

for the entire period of a job expansion and calculated the median earnings (in constant dollars) of incumbents of these jobs for this expanded sample. This means, in effect, that the quality of jobs is being evaluated by the median earnings over the entire period of a job expansion rather than simply at the beginning. (3) In the 1960s respondents were not directly asked about their hourly earnings for the current job. Instead they were asked about their earnings for the longest job held the previous year. We therefore had to use this retrospective data to calculate the median earnings of the occupation-by-sector matrix.

ent jobs—that is, the change in employment in a cell divided by the size at the beginning of a period. But this strategy would not answer the question we are asking since the cells with the highest growth rates might typically be very small cells, which do not contribute much to the overall expansion of jobs. A massive expansion in a tiny, well-paid job cell—tripling the number of engineers in social services, for example—would not imply a large contribution to overall job growth.

Our strategy of analysis, therefore, is to group jobs of similar earnings-defined quality into larger categories with more or less equal numbers of people at the beginning of a job expansion. To do this we first rank ordered the cells in the matrix from best to worst: that is, from the highest median weekly earnings to the lowest. We then grouped this ranked-ordered set of cells into 10 ordered categories, each containing as close to 10 percent of the labor force at the beginning of a job expansion as possible.[8] We refer to these aggregated categories of jobs as "Job Quality Deciles." The bottom decile contains the roughly 10 percent of the labor force at the beginning of a job expansion that are in the jobs with the lowest median earnings, the highest decile contains the roughly 10 percent of the labor force in jobs with the highest median weekly earnings, and so on. These job quality deciles are the primary categories we will use in assessing the contributions of jobs of varying quality to the expansion of jobs in the American economy. ★ ★ ★

Not everyone will find this way of classifying jobs and job quality satisfactory. Even though we have divided the job structure into hundreds of job categories, many of these categories remain quite heterogeneous. For example, the category of "college and university teachers in the educational services sector" includes community college faculty earning $30,000 a year and professors in elite law schools earning over $250,000 a year. Similarly, "other executives, administrators and managers" in "finance, insurance, and real estate" comprises CEOs in multinational insurance corporations and executives in local real estate companies. To observe that 20 percent of the net job expansion in the 1990s was generated by the highest job quality decile, therefore, does not mean that all of this increase reflects expansion of actually high paying jobs: a big expansion in "college and university teachers in the educational services sector" might have occurred principally because community colleges were hiring new faculty.

An alternative strategy, therefore, would be to ignore occupation and sector entirely and simply treat jobs as earnings-generating employment contracts. We could then study how this job-earnings distribution changes during job expansions. The considerable research in recent years on growth of earnings inequality does precisely this. But while direct analyses of the earnings distribution are certainly important, we believe it is also important to have a clear idea of how jobs themselves are changing. Employers do not simply make

8 Since jobs come in lumpy units, it is not possible to aggregate the rank-ordered jobs into groups each containing exactly 10 percent of the labor force. Thus, for example, of the 10 deciles in 1992, 8 contained between 9.6 percent and 10.5 percent of the labor force, 1 (the lowest decile) contained 11.4 percent of the labor force and 1 (the third decile) 8.2 percent. None of the patterns we will be examining is significantly affected by these deviations from equal decile categories.

employment offers at a specified earnings level; they make job offers to do particular kinds of things (occupations) within particular kinds of firms (sectors) at particular levels of earnings. Jobs within the occupation-by-sector matrix are a rough proxy for types of jobs created by firms. What we want to know is whether or not the occupations and sectors within which jobs have the best earnings prospects—defined by median earnings—are the ones that are growing the most rapidly.

‖ PATTERNS OF JOB GROWTH

Consider, then, the distribution of job quality in the net job expansion during the long, sustained employment boom of the 1990s. Figure 1 presents the contribution of each of the job quality deciles (defined at the beginning of the employment expansion in 1992) to the growth of jobs between 1992 and 1999. The results are striking. The job quality decile that contributed most to the job expansion was the highest decile: over 20 percent of the net expansion of jobs during the 1990s job expansion came from these jobs. So far, the results seem consistent with the Stiglitz study.

The second biggest contributor, however, was the worst decile, which contributed about 17 percent of the net job expansion. Nearly 40 percent of the total net job expansion occurred among the very best and the very worst kinds of jobs in the American economy. The jobs that

FIGURE 1   **CONTRIBUTIONS OF JOB QUALITY DECILES TO NET JOB EXPANSION, 1992–1999**

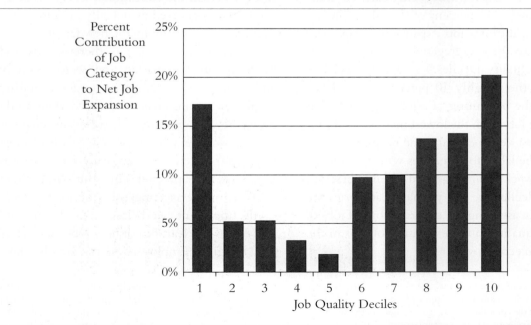

contributed least to the job expansion occur in the 2nd–5th deciles of job quality. In 1992 these accounted for just under 40 percent of the labor force, but only 14 percent of the net expansion of jobs came from these categories.

Overall, then, the 1990s job expansion is indeed dominated by the net expansion of employment among relatively good jobs—the top three deciles accounted for almost 50 percent of job expansion. But it is also marked by strong polarization in the pattern of employment growth: strong expansion at the tails of the job quality distribution, combined with weak growth among average to just below average quality jobs. So the skeptics who emphasize lousy jobs do have a point.

To bring out the force of the polarization of job growth in the 1990s, consider the contrast (indicated in Figure 2) between the pattern for the 1990s and the pattern for the 1960s. In the 1960s, the decile of job quality that contributed the least to job expansion was the lowest decile: less than 2 percent of the net job growth came from this category of jobs. The bottom four deciles, in fact, collectively generated less than 20 percent of job expansion. In the 1990s, the bottom decile alone generated 17 percent of net job expansion. In addition, while job expansion at the top of the job structure was strong in the 1960s, the top deciles did not generate quite as high a proportion of total job expansion as in the 1990s. In the earlier decade, just over

FIGURE 2 **CONTRIBUTIONS OF JOB QUALITY DECILES TO NET JOB EXPANSION, 1963–1970**

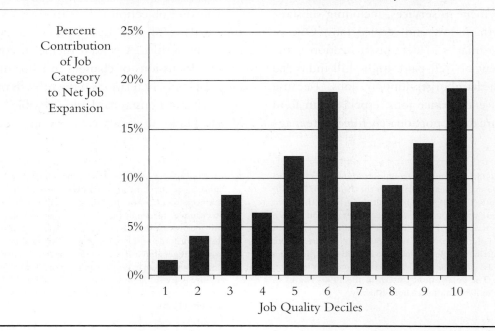

40 percent of the job expansion came from the top three job quality deciles whereas in the 1990s these categories generated nearly 50 percent of the job expansion. Finally, in the 1960s the two middle deciles of the job structure generated 30 percent of the job expansion compared to only 12 percent in the 1990s. Overall, then, the 1960s was a period of strong employment growth in the middle and upper segments of the job distribution, whereas the 1990s is characterized by much more polarized job expansion with particularly robust expansion among high-end job categories.[9]

These claims about job polarization in the 1990s might be challenged in either of two ways: by reference to problems of youth employment or numbers of part-time workers.

As has frequently been noted, the past several decades have seen a fairly steady decline of employment in manufacturing and growth of employment in services, including substantial growth in low-end service jobs. One of the iconic images of deindustrialization is the replacement of well-paid, high-skill industrial jobs with hamburger-flipping jobs. Because these low-end service jobs, especially in food services, are disproportionately filled by teenag-

ers and young adults, it is possible that the rapid expansion of the lowest paid job categories in the 1990s was largely the result of job expansion for young workers. The job polarization in Figure 1 would, perhaps, not matter so much if the rapid growth of jobs in the bottom decile was mainly due to the growth of fast-food and retail sales jobs filled by teenagers. What we would be seeing is not polarization in adult employment opportunities, but an expansion in jobs for early employment experience for teenagers.

To assess this objection, consider what happens when we confine attention to full-time employees between the ages of 30 and 55.[10] The results, shown in Figure 3, show a pattern that is virtually identical to the pattern for all full-time workers in both the 1990s and the 1960s. The polarization of job expansion in the 1990s cannot be attributed to the expansion of employment opportunities for young workers.

A second objection is that the restriction of our analysis to full-time workers could also affect the results. A central theme in contemporary discussions of changes in labor markets and employment relations is the growth of various forms of nonstandard and "flexible" work. While Figure 1 shows very strong expansion

---

9   We have conducted similar decompositions of net job expansion for the expansionary periods in the 1970s (1975–1980) and the 1980s (1983–1989). The results suggest that these two decades were transitional between the job expansion pattern of the 1960s and the 1990s. The 1975–1980 job expansion looks like a muted version of the 1960s pattern—the bottom deciles contribute somewhat more to the job expansion than in the 1960s, while the top deciles contribute a bit less than the 1960s. The polarization pattern in the 1990s begins to appear in the 1980s, although not as sharply.

10 A technical note on these results: the job quality deciles in Figure 3 are the same as in Figures 1 and 2: that is, these have been calculated on the basis of the entire full-time labor force sample, not simply the 30- to 50-year-old adult sample. This means that there is no longer 10 percent of the older adult labor force within each of these job quality "deciles" (since younger employees are more concentrated in the lower deciles). In particular, only 8.8 percent of 30- to 50-year-old employees are in the bottom decile, yet about 13.9 percent of net job expansion among mature adults comes from this category of jobs.

FIGURE 3 **CONTRIBUTION OF JOB QUALITY DECILES TO NET JOB EXPANSION AMONG EMPLOYEES AGED THIRTY, 1960S AND 1990S**

Percent
Contribution
of Each
Job Decile
to Net Job
Expansion

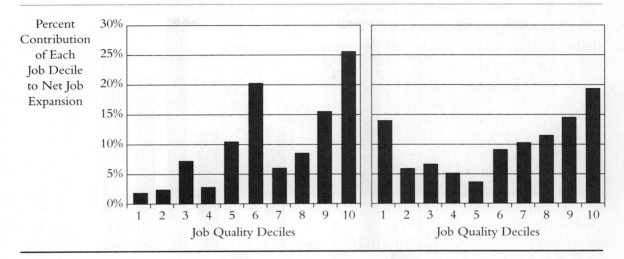

Job Quality Deciles

Job Quality Deciles

of employment in the top three deciles of the employment structure, these results could be misleading if there was a massive growth in part-time employment in jobs in the lowest deciles.

Figure 4 indicates that this, too, is not the case in the 1990s:[11] broadly there is the same kind of polarization in the net job expansion among part-time employees as among full-time employees. If anything, the contribution to net job expansion of the top deciles for part-time work is even greater than for full-time work: nearly two thirds of the net job expansion in part time work was generated by the jobs in the top three job quality deciles.[12] The pattern in Figure 1, therefore, cannot be attributed to the restriction to full-time jobs.

11 It was not possible to do a separate analysis for part-time employees using the 1960s CPS data.

12 In order to facilitate comparisons between Figure 4 for part-time jobs and Figure 1 for full-time jobs, we have used the same job quality deciles in Figure 4 as were used in Figure 1—that is, they have been calculated on the basis of median hourly earnings of jobs in the occupation-by-sector matrix for the full-time sample (rather than recalibrating these deciles just for part-time workers). This makes the results of Figure 4 particularly striking since part-time employment is more concentrated in the bottom deciles of the overall employment structure than is full-time employment. Thus, for example, only 3 percent of part-time employees were employed in the highest job quality decile in 1992 (the beginning of the 1990s job expansion), yet over 20 percent of the net job expansion of part-time work occurred in this decile. If we recalibrate the job quality deciles to reflect the distribution of job quality strictly within the part-time sample, then this growth at the top appears even stronger: roughly 45 percent of the net expansion of part-time employment in the 1990s was generated within the top job quality decile when these deciles are calculated among part-time jobs.

FIGURE 4 **CONTRIBUTIONS OF JOB QUALITY DECILES TO EXPANSION OF PART-TIME JOBS, 1992–1999**

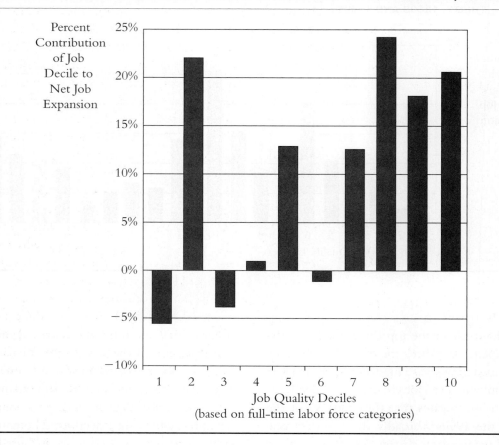

Percent Contribution of Job Decile to Net Job Expansion

Job Quality Deciles
(based on full-time labor force categories)

‖ RACE AND GENDER

To recapitulate the analysis so far: in both the "golden age" of the 1960s and the "new economy" of the 1990s, the job categories at the high earning end of the job distribution contributed disproportionately to job expansion. In the 1990s, but not the 1960s, the very bottom of the job structure also contributed substantially to job expansion, and the middle of the dis-

tribution made only a marginal contribution. The net result is a polarized job expansion in the 1990s compared to a quality-upgrading job expansion in the 1960s.

Taking race and gender into account sharpens the contrasts between the two expansions and clarifies the nature of the polarization. Thus consider the contributions of each of the job quality deciles to the net expansion of employment in the 1960s and the 1990s within each of the race-gender categories. Because of data limitations, in the 1960s we can distinguish only four categories: white males, white females, black males, and black females. In the 1990s we can divide the white racial group into Hispanic and nonhispanic whites. The results, presented in Figure 5 and Figure 6, reveal quite dramatic variations, both over time and across the various race-gender categories.[13]

In the 1960s, gender differences in the patterns of job expansion were much sharper than racial differences. Virtually none of the job expansion for white men or black men in the 1960s occurred in the bottom four job quality deciles: these four deciles accounted for −2.6 percent of the net job expansion for white men and −23.1 percent of the net job expansion for black men. In contrast, for women of both races job expansion was heavily concentrated in the bottom deciles of the job quality distribution: fully 48 percent of the net job expansion for white women and 52 percent for black women occurred in the bottom four deciles. At the other end of the job quality distribution, 67 percent of the net job expansion for white men and 44 percent of the job expansion for black men occurred in the top three deciles, compared to 12 percent of the net expansion for black women and 13 percent for white women. Although racial differences in patterns of job expansion among men were not negligible in the 1960s, they were relatively muted compared to the dramatic difference between men and women.

In contrast, in the 1990s (see Figure 6), the racial differences in patterns of net job expansion are, if anything, bigger than the gender differences. Among whites (non-Hispanic)— both men and women—job expansion is very heavily concentrated in the top deciles: in the 1990s, 62 percent of the net job expansion for white men and nearly 90 percent for white women occurred in the top three job quality deciles. The polarization we observed for the labor force as a whole in Figure 1 is *completely absent* among white men (only 6 percent of the net job expansion for white men occurred in the lowest decile of the job structure) and present only in a muted way among white women (for whom 13.4 percent of net job expansion occurred in the bottom decile of jobs).

The patterns for nonwhite men and women in the 1900s differ sharply from the pattern for whites. For all four nonwhite race-gender categories, job expansion was especially concentrated in the lower deciles of the job quality distribution: the bottom two deciles accounted for 50 percent of the net job expansion for Hispanic women, 35 percent for Hispanic men, 25 percent for black women and 28 percent for black men (compared to 15 percent of the net job expansion for white women and only 4 percent for white men). Some polarization of job expansion is also present among blacks and among Hispanic men, although not among Hispanic women.

The pattern of polarized job expansion in the 1990s we observed in Figure 2, therefore, has a

---

13 The job quality decile categories in Figures 5 and 6 are the same as those used in the analysis of the full-time labor force as a whole. This means that once we break the analysis down into separate race-gender categories then there is no longer approxi- mately 10 percent of the relevant category within each of these job quality deciles. These figures thus present, for each race-gender group, the distribution of net job expansion for that group across the job quality categories defined for the entire labor force.

FIGURE 5 **CONTRIBUTIONS OF JOB QUALITY DECILES TO NET JOB EXPANSION WITHIN RACE AND GENDER CATEGORIES, 1963–1970**

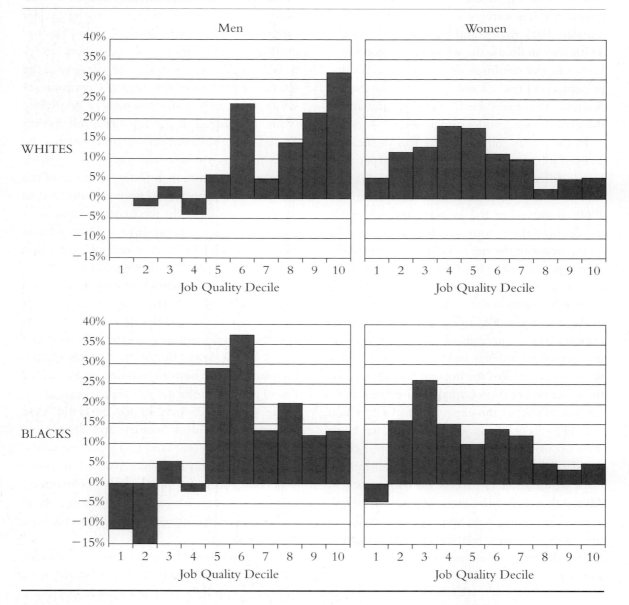

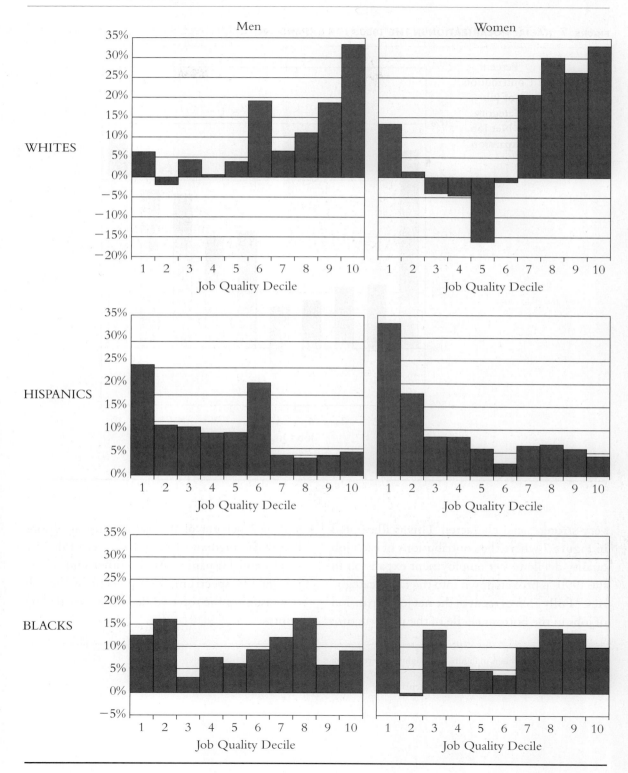

FIGURE 7   **RACIAL POLARIZATION IN THE 1990S JOB EXPANSION**

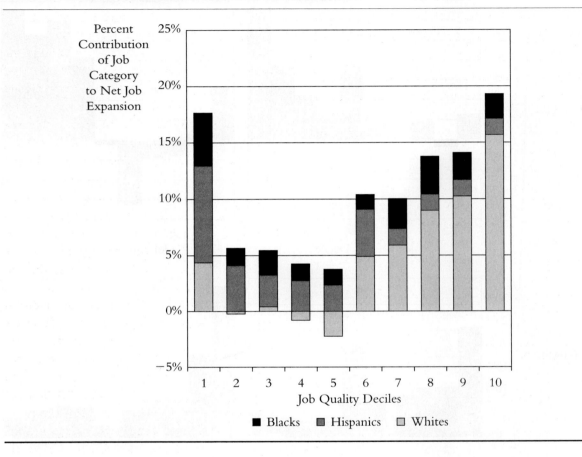

very strong racial character. This is illustrated in Figure 7 where the contributions of each job quality decile to net employment expansion in the 1990s is broken down into the racial categories.[14] Fully 75.5 percent of the net job expansion of jobs in the bottom decile of the job structure and 95.7 percent of the net expansion of jobs below the median (deciles 1–5) were filled by blacks and Hispanics. At the other end of the job quality spectrum, 77.9 percent of the job expansion in the top two deciles were filled by whites.

14 The aggregate numbers in Figure 7 are slightly different from Figure 1 since we have not included "other races" (mainly Native Americans and Asians) in the calculations.

Putting these various observations together, the race and gender patterns of job expansion in the 1960s and the 1990s can be summarized as follows:

1. The pattern of job expansion among white men is virtually the same in both decades: the job expansion is heavily weighted at the high end of the job structure with little tendency for polarization of employment growth.
2. The pattern of job expansion for white women changes dramatically across the two periods: in the 1960s this expansion was concentrated in the middle and bottom of the employment structure; in the 1990s it has been heavily concentrated at the top. Whereas in the 1960s the profile of job expansion among white men differed sharply from that among white women, in the 1990s the two patterns have substantially converged.
3. Racial differences in patterns of employment expansion have increased to the point that the 1990s can be characterized as a period of *racially polarized job expansion:* the net expansion of jobs at the bottom of the employment distribution is overwhelmingly dominated by minorities whereas the expansion of employment at the top is strongly dominated by whites.

||| CONCLUSION

Does the sustained expansion of employment in the United States in the 1990s conform, then, to the rosy picture of the "jobs miracle" touted at home and abroad? It is certainly true that masses of new jobs have indeed been cre-

ated in the United States in this period. And if one dichotomizes jobs into two simple categories—good jobs that are above the median and bad jobs that are below it—then most of the American jobs expansion in the 1990s occurred among "good jobs": about two thirds of the net expansion was among jobs in the 6th to 10th deciles of the job quality distribution. So the evidence does not support a simple summary judgment that crummy jobs dominate the job expansion.

But it should now be clear that this summary judgment tells only part of the story. In the 1960s, the sustained job expansion was unequivocally a process of upgrading the employment structure. In the 1990s, the job expansion is characterized by a polarization of employment opportunities, albeit a polarization weighted toward the high end of the job structure. Moreover, this polarized pattern of job expansion is highly racialized. Employment for whites—both men and women—has expanded sharply among the better jobs in the employment structure, whereas expanding employment for blacks and Hispanics is concentrated at the bottom of the employment structure. The sustained period of economic growth may, then, be creating masses of new jobs, and in the aggregate many of these jobs may be among the better paying kinds of jobs in the American economy, but the net effect of this employment expansion has been to increase polarization in the employment structure in a particularly racialized form.

This pattern of employment expansion has deep implications for the nature of social inequality in the United States. First, it suggests that the problem of poverty in the United States increasingly concerns the working poor rather than primarily people largely marginalized from the system of employment altogether. This is not to say that the link of poverty to unemployment and exclusion from the labor force has disappeared, but rather that an increasing proportion of poor people are working full-time in those kinds of jobs that pay below poverty-level wages. To seriously tackle poverty in America today requires more than just getting poor people into jobs; it requires changing the quality of jobs available to them.

Second, the very slow rate of growth of jobs in the lower-middle range of job quality suggests that it is likely to become increasingly difficult for people working in the very worst jobs to move up in the employment structure. Most upward job mobility is to jobs that are only modestly better than the job one holds. This means that people in the bottom decile of employment are unlikely to make a jump directly to jobs in the 6th–10th deciles. Since jobs in the 2nd–5th deciles of the employment structure have been growing at about a third the rate of the labor force as a whole, people employed in the rapidly expanding bottom job decile face very limited opportunities for improvements in employment.

Third, the pattern of job expansion in the 1990s suggests significant transformations in the structure of racial stratification. Since the 1960s there has been a considerable expansion of employment of African Americans and other racial minorities in what are loosely described as middle-class jobs. The proportion of doctors, lawyers, professors, managers, and even executives who are Africa American has increased significantly. Among higher level jobs, therefore, there has been a gradual deracialization. Among jobs at the bottom of the employment structure, on the other hand, the 1990s witnessed a process of deepening racialization. Only 2 percent of the expansion of jobs among non-Hispanic whites occurred in the jobs below the median job category compared to nearly 60 percent of net job expansion among blacks and Hispanics combined.

So, what is to be done? What sorts of public policies are suggested in light of these trends in the American employment structure? Of course, any thorough analysis of policy alternatives would have to consider many more issues in current labor market trends than simply the macro-patterns of job expansion studied here—the patterns of inequalities within these jobs categories; the problem of contingent and part-time work; the patterns of mobility across these job categories for different demographic groups; the relationship between patterns of job creation and things like firm size, technical change, linkages to the global economy, and so on. Still, we think our analysis has something to say about current government policy and potential new directions. What we offer here, therefore, is a relatively stylized discussion of a range of policy directions that bear on the specific problem of the polarized pattern of job expansion rather than a comprehensive discussion of government policies, labor markets and employment structures.

If one regards the patterns we have documented of polarized job expansion in the 1990s, particularly the racialized form of that polarization, to be a problem, then there are two broad categories of policy response: (1) Don't worry too much about job polarization per se—let the market determine the character of the jobs that are created—but in various ways ameliorate the impact of such polarization on the standards of living underwritten by these jobs. If the expansion of jobs generated by the market is economically polarized, this is because this is what the "New Economy" needs. The task of government in this context is to ensure that people in these jobs—the "working poor"—live decent lives in spite of the job polarization; the quality of lives need not be polarized even if the quality of jobs is. (2) Use public policy to directly affect the patterns of job growth, encouraging in various ways job growth in the middle of the employment structure and discouraging it at the bottom. The pattern of job expansion is not some "natural" result of the operation of efficient markets but is inevitably affected by all sorts of public policies: the nature of the tax code, the institutions of skill formation, the regulation of the employment contract and working conditions, the minimum wage, laws regulating unions, etc. The task of government is to design such policies in such a way as to rebuild mobility bridges and expand job

opportunities in the middle of the employment structure.

The first of these policy directions, if only in halting ways, has been the principle mode of response to economic polarization in the United States in recent years. The most notable example is the Earned Income Tax Credit, a provision in the tax code specifically designed to raise standards of living of the working poor above what they can get through earnings in the labor market.[15] The EITC is the one redistributive program that has seen significant expansion in the 1990s. The failed attempt at creating universal health insurance in the early 1990s can also be interpreted in this way as an attempt to partially decouple the standards of living of working people from the pattern of earnings and benefits generated by the labor market. If the EITC were further expanded and if comprehensive universal health insurance were enacted, then it would matter a lot less if the lowest paying jobs were rapidly expanding or if mobility bridges between those jobs and better paying jobs had collapsed.[16]

Policy reforms like the EITC leave the distribution of job quality generated by the labor market largely unaffected. Indeed, for many policy makers this is one of the virtues of the EITC: the

---

15 The EITC is a kind of limited negative income tax for people in the paid labor force that gives people an income supplement if their annual earnings fall below a certain level and various other criteria are satisfied.

16 A more radical policy reform to partially decouple standards of living from the labor market would be some kind of universal basic income grant that guaranteed all citizens an above-poverty standard of living regardless of their employment status. Universal Basic Income could have quite different effects from the EITC. Whereas the latter can be considered

basically a subsidy for low-wage work and thus potentially increases the supply of workers willing to work for low wages, a true basic income makes it possible for people to exit the labor market entirely, thus reducing the supply of workers for low-paid jobs. For an extended discussion of basic income, see Philippe van Parijs, *Boston Review*, in press. For a comparison of Basic Income with other related proposals, see Erik Olin Wright, "Reducing Income and Wealth Inequality: Real Utopian Proposals," *Contemporary Sociology* (January 2000): 143–55.

tax code provides income subsidies to the working poor without mucking about with the internal operation of labor markets. This would be fine if one believed that there were no negative consequences to an economically polarized employment structure. There are, however, many reasons why this kind of job polarization should be of concern, even apart from its impact on standards of living: employment polarization undermines opportunities for individual mobility; polarization is likely to reduce social solidarity; the racialized character of job polarization is likely to reinforce racist stereotypes and other forms of racial division; the amount of income-raising politically feasible through devices like the EITC are likely to be small compared to the income-raising achievable through a significant expansion of employment opportunities in the middle regions of the employment structure.

The question, then, is whether public policy can effectively shift the pattern of job creation in ways that generate jobs in greater numbers around the middle of the job quality distribution. Here there are basically two broad kinds of strategies: first, the direct intervention of the state to create certain types of jobs through publicly funded employment and, second, the creation of incentives and institutional infrastructure to encourage private employers to create such jobs.

Since the triumph of neoliberalism and the demise of Keynesian views of state intervention, the public sector employment option has been completely off the political agenda in the United States. Certainly in the immediate future, there is no real political prospect of launching a major expansion of public employment, except perhaps of public school teachers. Nevertheless, we may soon be entering a period in which a serious expansion of public works is once again politically feasible. The oft-noted neglect over the past quarter century of bridges, public transportation, public school buildings and other state-financed infrastructural public goods certainly creates a need for a considerable expansion of public works. And the large government budget surpluses generated by the economic expansion of the 1990s makes such an expansion fiscally feasible as well. Such an expansion of public works could help shift employment expansion away from personal services, retail and other low-end jobs toward the middle range of the job structure, even if, for the moment, an effective political coalition in favor of such projects does not exist. Particularly if one wants to counteract the racial polarization embedded in the current pattern of job growth, a significant expansion of public works could be important since it is easier to direct public works toward specific labor markets and populations than it is to direct private sector employment.

In a variety of ways, public policy can also have a significant impact on the extent to which private employers create low-end jobs or relatively well paid skilled jobs. This is at the heart of the discussion of "high road" versus "low road" capitalism: high road capitalism is characterized by the expansion of fairly well paid skilled jobs in the middle of the employment structure, low road capitalism by the expansion of low-skill, low-wage jobs. So, the question is: what can be done, in Joel Rogers words, "to close off the low road, help to pave the high road, and enable workers and firms stuck on one to walk the other."[17]

Two policies are especially relevant to closing off the low road: significantly raising the minimum wage and strengthening the labor movement. While modest increases in the minimum wage probably have little effect on the pattern of job creation, a substantial rise—a rise sufficient to give people in low-end jobs a "living wage"—would almost certainly dampen the expansion of jobs at the bottom of the job quality distribution. Changing labor laws in ways that would facilitate the growth of unions and strengthen their role in regulating labor markets and working conditions could also contribute to dampening low road job creation. While of course much would depend upon the specific strategies and vision adopted by unions, a strong union movement has the potential of reducing wage differentials by raising wages at the bottom, making subcontracting to low-wage firms more difficult and in other ways making "low road" strategies more costly for employers.

Closing off the low road, obviously, is not enough. Unless this is also combined with policies that encourage the expansion of middle-range jobs and the acquisition of skills needed to fill those jobs, the result will simply be a decline in job opportunities for people currently at the bottom of the job quality distribution. Improved education and expanded programs of vocational training, particularly directed toward black and Hispanic communities, are certainly part of this since an inadequate supply of skilled labor impedes the creation of skilled jobs. But simply expanding the skilled labor supply does not automatically call forth the employer demand for such labor. An effective sustained strategy for expanding middle-range employment needs to closely link such training to an industrial policy that creates real incentives for employers to invest in the right kinds of employment expansion."[18]

None of these proposals—neither the proposals to partially decouple standards of living from employment nor the various strategies to alter the pattern of job expansion itself—can be implemented in a serious way if public policy is driven by the neoliberal belief that markets should be maximally unconstrained, that the state should be minimally interventionist, and taxes should be as low as possible. Taken together, these policies would require a dramatic increase in the resources and energy of an

---

17 Joel Rogers, "The Folks Who Brought You the Weekend: Labor and Independent Politics," in *Audacious Democracy* (247–61), ed. Steve Fraser and Joshua Freeman (New York: Houghton Mifflin, 1997).

18 An example of such institutional innovation in skill formation and labor markets is the much heralded Wisconsin Regional Training Partnership (WRTP). The WRTP was formed in the mid-1990s in an effort to solve two problems in worker training in the metal working industry: (1) the problem that publicly provided training often had little to do with the actual skills needed within production, and (2)

the chronic collective action problem faced by employers in providing high-level, flexible training to employees (each employer is worried that if high levels of training are provided to employees, other employers, who have not devoted resources to training, will poach the trained workers). The WRTP solution to these problems involves firms, unions, the state vocational education program, and a university-based labor market research institute working together in collective institutions for skill formation and job upgrading. For a description of the Wisconsin Regional Training Partnership, see http://www.cows.org/projects/wrtp.html.

affirmative state committed to counteracting the inegalitarian dynamics of markets. This, in turn, would require significant increases in taxation on the beneficiaries of the long expansion of the 1990s. There is no fundamental resource constraint on pursuing such policies; the question is simply whether an effective progressive political coalition around such policies can be forged. In the absence of such a political will, the "New Economy" is likely to further deepen the polarized character of employment and earnings.

PART III

GROUP–LEVEL STRATIFICATION PROCESSES

INTRODUCTION TO PART III

The chapters in this part of the book include theoretical and empirical studies of how the stratification system in the United States is organized on the basis of group membership, especially along the lines of race, class, and gender.

The first section includes several selections that present influential theoretical accounts of group differences. The first two readings consider the role of prejudice. Herbert Blumer's famous 1958 paper on the origins of racial prejudice develops a key argument: he asserts that it is only when there is *competition* between groups that pressures for exclusionary practices and group stereotyping arise. When group competition is low, pressures for exclusion (and the strength of prejudicial attitudes) are likely to be low. This "group threat" idea has been very prominent in recent discussions. Douglas Massey's essay on the social psychology of prejudice provides a short and compelling introduction to how images of others become concrete in the mind. He argues that "out groups" are viewed across two dimensions: whether they are pitied or hated and whether they are competent or incompetent. The resulting two-by-two table highlights four general types of attitudes toward out-groups that can be held by dominant group members, and it predicts the level of discrimination different groups are likely to experience (with "hated" and "incompetent" groups suffering the most).

One place that discrimination manifests itself explicitly is in the labor market. Two readings explore this process. The queuing model developed by Barbara Reskin and Patricia Roos to explain women's disadvantage in the labor market provides one way of understanding how discrimination works: employers sort among workers on the basis of social group assets, filling open positions first from among those with the right sets of qualifications. Drawing on data from an innovative field experiment in New York City, Devah Pager and Bruce Western provide compelling empirical evidence of the extent to which such discriminatory preferences of employers in low-wage labor markets matter. Sending out matched pairs of "testers" with similar résumés and qualifications to compete for the same job, the authors found startling evidence that many employers do, in fact, have a preferred hiring queue in mind. Through their behavior, employers demonstrate a strong preference for white men (even those *with* criminal records) over black men (even those *without* criminal records), with Latinos falling somewhere in the middle.

The next two chapters focus on how group inequalities become located in organizational settings. Charles Tilly's chapter provides a sweeping theoretical overview of the sources of what he calls "durable inequality," contrasting inequality-generating processes rooted in economic exploitation from those based on processes of social exclusion (or closure). In this way, Tilly seeks to marry Marx and Weber, combining a market-based model of exploitation with an organizational theory of how status differences among groups are maintained. Tilly argues that, depending on the social setting, either exploitation or exclusion can serve as a basis for one group to dominate another. Exploitation arises from economic class power rooted in ownership of business assets (which makes it possible to "exploit" others even without excluding them). Exclusion, by contrast, arises when one group organizes to prevent one or more other groups from access to jobs, education, neighborhoods, or other desirable goods or opportunities. The novelty of Tilly's theorization is that he highlights how either exploitation or exclusion becomes "durable" when it comes to be embedded in institutions (like the market) or organizations (like firms).

Tilly's emphasis on the importance of group-based inequalities becoming built into the fabric of organizations is strikingly paralleled in the earlier work of Rossabeth Kantor. In her classic study of professional and managerial women, Kantor demonstrates how the numerical differences between men and women in these positions create difficulties for minorities in the workplace. She finds that co-workers, especially in situations where minorities constitute a very small proportion of their peers ("tokenism"), tend to pay more attention to the activities of these minority groups and judge these activities more critically. Kantor attributes these dynamics primarily to our perceptual tendency to notice difference, and she finds that as the relative size of minority groups in the workplace change (for example, as the number of women in the professional and managerial ranks increases), the stigmatizing effects of being a minority in the workplace will decrease significantly.

The chapter by the influential French sociologist Pierre Bourdieu develops a theoretical model of how individuals and groups can deploy their "assets" to claim special rewards at the expense of others. In the 1970s, Bourdieu (building on the earlier insight of economists about human capital) advances the idea that economic capital is but one type of "capital" asset an individual can possess. Bourdieu identifies social capital, cultural capital, and symbolic capital as distinct categories of assets that, like economic capital, can be accumulated and then strategically invested to maximize life chances for individuals and families. His concept of social capital has parallels to the work of Mark Granovetter (see Part II), emphasizing the importance of social networks—or social capital—as a source of access to opportunities and rewards. Cultural capital refers to the stock of cultural knowledge, linguistic skills, and dispositions that individuals can deploy in significant social settings in which they are being evaluated. Symbolic capital is a more diffuse idea, referring to the fame or status an individual may possess that can be used to win favorable positions. Individuals and groups all have more or less of each type of capital, depending on where they are located in the social structure.

The next section of essays focus on problems of class analysis. Sociologist Erik Olin Wright grapples, from within a Marxist paradigm, with the "problem" of the middle class, a widely-used but seldom defined concept. Wright embraces the concept of exploitation as the foundation for identifying classes in capitalist societies. He argues that the distinct "class" location of any individual can be identified on the basis of the kinds of assets he or she possesses, assets that provide the basis for one or another kind of "exploitation." Wright identifies three kinds of assets that allow those who possess them to exploit others: ownership assets (such as owning a company), organizational assets (having managerial authority over others), and skill/credential assets (like a college degree or a valuable and relatively scarce skill like carpentry). Anyone with such assets is in a position to gain market advantage by exploiting other people who lack those assets. His model thus identifies middle-class locations as those actors possessing some, but not all, of these assets.

Wright identifies class on the basis of resources and jobs possessed by individuals, or what might be called the "class structure" of society. But in Marx's original conceptualization of class, there is also a second meaning of class: class as active agents of historical change. In the famous preface to his 1963 study of the formation of the English working class in the early nineteenth century, British social historian E. P. Thompson argues that class "matters," or can even be said to exist, only when it provides the basis for meaningful identities or collective behavior of some sort. There was no "working class" in England until workers began to find the basis for engaging in forms of collective action to enhance their power vis-à-vis their employers and to challenge the domination of political life by the upper class. The position he stakes out, with great passion and elegance, challenges theories of class that see these groups as existing on paper as opposed to in history or in action.

The "problem" of the middle class and the role of political action in organizing class interests are further explored by Charles Derber and his colleagues in their analysis of professionals. Those working in a knowledge-based professional occupation such as lawyer, doctor, accountant, architect, or engineer are able to use their expert knowledge to create lucrative niches for themselves. To be sure, expert knowledge has always been an important part of stratification systems. In hunting and gathering societies, for example, the medicine man, or shaman, held a privileged position that was endowed with status and rewards based on their (presumed) special knowledge. But over the past hundred years, there has been a vast expansion of professional occupations and an increase in the proportion of all workers in professional occupations. This process is codified by the state and the educational system, generally at the urging of occupations seeking professional status. Derber and co-authors develop a broader theory of how knowledge can become analogous to ownership of capital as a source of market power.

The papers in the next section examine some important aspects of racial inequality (more specifically, the black/white divide). The continuing high rates of poverty among African Americans are linked to residence by sociologist William Julius Wilson, and by sociologists Douglas Massey and Nancy Denton, in their respective and widely influential work. Wilson famously argued that declining segregation since the 1960s has made it possible for the black middle class to move out of historically African-American neighborhoods, taking with them vital resources and jobs. The result, he argues, has been the rise of what he refers to as the "jobless ghetto": low-income urban neighborhoods with declining economic opportunities for its residents. Although Wilson emphasizes the effects of desegregation on the neighborhood, Massey and Denton argue that persisting racial segregation is still critical. High rates of racial residential segregation in metropolitan areas reinforces concentrated disadvantage. Massey and Denton argue that segregation also creates interacting inequalities; concentrating African Americans in "black neighborhoods" gives rise to distinctive urban speech patterns that do not serve its speakers well in education or on the labor market. These are not accidental outcomes. Massey and Denton note that the housing policies of the federal government, along with those of banks and insurance companies, work together to reinforce racial segregation and thereby concentrate disadvantage.

The next chapter explores one critical aspect of racial inequality in America: stereotypes about African Americans. Martin Gilens notes that Americans substantially overestimate the percentage of the poor and of those on welfare who are black. Where do such perceptions come from, and why do they persist? Gilens hypothesizes that media images and news reporting about African Americans may have something to do with it, something that many scholars have asserted. He shows, through a cleverly designed study coding the race of poor people and welfare recipients in the leading national news magazines, that in fact the media do significantly overrepresent African Americans among the poor. Strikingly, the news and photo editors who select such images are not themselves racists, and are not even aware of the racial bias in their depictions of the poor. The biases he finds may be all the more pernicious because they are so unrecognized by decision-making editors.

Various aspects of contemporary gender inequality are explored in the next section. In his chapter on occupational segregation by gender, Jerry Jacobs notes that segregation continues to persist even in the face of antidiscrimination laws, well-publicized advances by women into the higher ranks of professional and managerial occupations, and higher levels of education attained by women. Jacobs's data suggest slow and uneven progress in incorporating women into better-paid traditionally male jobs. He speculates that gender segregation will not noticeably improve in the near future because the "major engines of gender integration"—namely, the entrance of women into male-dominated fields at the beginning or in the middle of their careers—have not been successful in integrating the top positions.

If Jacobs's analysis suggests that the pattern of change has slowed, there have nonetheless been many important ways in which gender inequality is different from what it was a few decades ago. The complex of forces needed to produce these change are many. Economist Claudia Golden's short and forceful chapter on the gender revolution provides an intriguing overview of how complex forces of change have been. She argues that advances in reproductive technology allowed women (for the first time in human history) to control their fertility, something that facilitates their entrance into the labor market and to time career and family choices. The expansion of higher education after World War II and the concomitant growth of white-collar employment opportunities, coupled with the ability of women to equal or better men in school, also pushed along this process. Finally, she notes the importance of the changing legal environment in which explicit discrimination is outlawed. These changes together laid the foundation for one kind of gender revolution, and evidence (such as that presented by Francine Blau and Lawrence Kahn's chapter in Part II) suggests that wage inequality has indeed narrowed for at least some women.

The final three chapters in this section explore two other critical aspects of gender inequality. Arlie Hochschild's classical work examines the connection between housework and caring labor and the gender inequality in the workplace. She argues that even as beliefs in gender inequality have become widespread in American society, the actual distribution of labor inside households still reflects traditionally sexist patterns. For example, the level of inequality in caring work remains high; in most families women still do far more routine and caring work than men. This is important, Hochschild argues, because the continuing disproportionate burden most women have when it comes to caring for children or aged relatives bears on the ability of women to successfully pursue careers. In other words, the unequal burdens of the "second (unpaid) shift" contribute in important ways to gender inequalities on the "first (paid) shift."

Paula England and Barbara Kilbourne examine how and in what ways women's bargaining power inside marriage constitutes an important aspect of gender inequality. When women depend on men's earning power for their own economic well-being, they have relatively little leverage to demand equality inside the marriage. As options for women improve in the labor market, however, their bargaining power inside marriages also improves, because women have more "exit" options. The bargaining model England and Kilbourne employ usefully focuses attention on a range of issues involving marriage and how it relates to gender inequality. The final chapter explores another aspect of gender inequality: violence against women. Legal scholar Deborah Rhode convincingly argues that sexual abuse can be understood only within the context of societywide patterns of gender inequality. This inequality, according to Rhode, increases the frequency of sexual abuse—whether sexual harassment, domestic violence, or rape—and colors society's reaction to it by discouraging reports of such activity, decreasing the rates of prosecution of those who commit these crimes, and stigmatizing those who are its victims. This devaluation of the seriousness of sexual abuse, Rhode contends, is not only a consequence of existing gender stratification but also serves to entrench these inequalities even further.

The next section of Part III explores how immigration is reshaping the group bases of social stratification in the United States today. Charles Hirschman begins by taking a long view of this issue, documenting how American society has been continually transformed by the influx of immigrant populations.

Hirschman provides a general overview of immigration trends during the last century and discusses the effects of these population changes: increased population diversity, the sustenance of urban environments, the expansion of the national economy, and the transformation of politics. In short, Hirschman argues, immigrants have constantly redefined and enriched American society and, as such, have been an essential component of the ascendancy of the United States to a position of world leadership in economics and politics. In this view, the current wave of immigration is likely to produce enormous long-term benefits for American society.

Immigrants, of course, are also transformed by their move to a new country. Of particular concern to sociologists are the processes by which these immigrants, and even more so their children, assimilate into American society. In their chapter on segmented assimilation, Alejandro Portes, Patricia Fernández-Kelly, and William Haller maintain that while all of today's second-generation immigrants assimilate (learn English and adopt American culture), the segments of society into which they assimilate differ markedly. Drawing from survey and ethnographic data, the authors find that many members of the second generation are able to achieve greater educational and occupational success than their parents and move into the American mainstream. A significant number of others, however, "assimilate downward," falling into "the bottom ranks of society." These two paths of adaptation are, according to Portes and colleagues, largely determined by differences in the human and financial capital possessed by their parents, the educational opportunities available, and the degree of stigmatization and discrimination they face.

This important argument is not uncontroversial. Roger Waldinger and Cynthia Feliciano question the segmented assimilation hypothesis in their study of U.S.-born Mexican men and women. They find that the children of working-class immigrants are, on average, better educated than their parents and have lower levels of unemployment. While these second generation workers may not escape the working class, they also do not assimilate further downward. Waldinger and Feliciano contend that these new entrants into American society, much like earlier generations of immigrants, are best seen, at least provisionally, as moving ahead within the working class as their education and skill levels surpass those of their parents.

The final section of Part III includes several chapters that investigate some of the ways in which the intersection of different kinds of inequalities produce a more complex picture than studies focusing on specific group-based inequalities. The influential theoretical work of Patricia Hill Collins on the difficulties faced by black women provides an important impetus for theorizing about intersecting inequalities. In the chapter reprinted here, Collins argues that poor women of color face a triple burden: race, class, and gender. These multiple, overlapping inequalities produce a particular kind of oppression that is different from the disadvantages produced by any one domain by itself. Through this lens of intersecting inequalities, Collins shows that black women have faced hurdles that are significantly different from either white women or black men.

The broad vision that Collins develops is challenged, however, in some interesting ways in the chapter by Orlando Patterson. Patterson notes that black *men* have suffered in unique ways from the legacies of slavery, and some evidence suggests that they are worse off than black women. The huge disparity in college attendance and college graduation between black men and women (with black women more than twice as likely to attain a college degree) is one example. The startling increase in conviction rates among black men (with over one third of black men in America now having a felony conviction on their record) is another. The implicit debate between Collins and Patterson highlights some of the complexities of the problem of race and gender and how to interpret their intersection.

The last three chapters present important pieces of research highlighting other aspects of the question of how class and race and of how class and gender intersect in concrete ways. Intensively studying a group of black and white middle-class and working-class families, sociologist Annette Lareau finds ways in which both class (and, in particular, the level of "cultural capital" of the parents) and race shape the interactions between children and their schools. Middle-class parents are better able to prepare their children for school, fund extracurricular activities for their kids, and negotiate with teachers and school administrators to secure maximal advantage for their kids. But even among families with similar class locations, there are important differences between white and black families, in particular in relation to the school system.

Leslie McCall's chapter demonstrates how the diverging class interests among women have deepened in recent years. Just as William Julius Wilson famously argued in the late 1970s that class divisions among blacks were becoming increasingly consequential, McCall highlights a dynamic in which the disparities among working women have grown dramatically; women at the top have gained access to positions once closed to them, while less privileged women have made few if any gains in recent years. The ability of upper–middle–class women to purchase services, such as child–care from poor women, magnifies the growing class divide among women. Such outcomes highlight how complex inequalities become once we explore their intersecting character.

Ian Ayers and Peter Siegelman's study of race and gender differences in bargaining for a car offers yet another perspective on how race and gender can interact. Taking advantage of the well–known leeway that car dealers have in negotiating prices with buyers, Ayers and Siegelman trained a group of "testers" to use identical bargaining tactics to arrive at the best possible price for the same car from the same dealer. Their testers included white men and women, and black men and women, randomly assigned to carry out the tests. Even though the testers used the same bargaining tactics, the white male testers received a price that was on average significantly better than anyone else, with black women having to pay the highest price. The fact that there were significant differences in prices along both racial and gender lines exemplifies the complex pattern of interaction that occurs in some settings (this one being especially visible and measurable).

Social Exclusion and Group Advantage

Race Prejudice as a Sense of Group Position*

HERBERT BLUMER

In this paper I am proposing an approach to the study of race prejudice different from that which dominates contemporary scholarly thought on this topic. My thesis is that race prejudice exists basically in a sense of group position rather than in a set of feelings which members of one racial group have toward the members of another racial group. This different way of viewing race prejudice shifts study and analysis from a preoccupation with feelings as lodged in individuals to a concern with the relationship of racial groups. It also shifts scholarly treatment away from individual lines of experience and focuses interest on the collective process by which a racial group comes to define and redefine another racial group. Such shifts, I believe, will yield a more realistic and penetrating understanding of race prejudice.

There can be little question that the rather vast literature on race prejudice is dominated by the idea that such prejudice exists fundamentally as a feeling

---

* First published in 1958; from *Pacific Sociological Review* (now called *Sociological Perspectives*), Volume 1;1.

or set of feelings lodged in the individual. It is usually depicted as consisting of feelings such as antipathy, hostility, hatred, intolerance, and aggressiveness. Accordingly, the task of scientific inquiry becomes two-fold. On one hand, there is a need to identify the feelings which make up race prejudice—to see how they fit together and how they are supported by other psychological elements, such as mythical beliefs. On the other hand, there is need of showing how the feeling complex has come into being. Thus, some scholars trace the complex feelings back chiefly to innate dispositions; some trace it to personality composition, such as authoritarian personality; and others regard the feelings of prejudice as being formed through social experience. However different may be the contentions regarding the make-up of racial prejudice and the way in which it may come into existence, these contentions are alike in locating prejudice in the realm of individual feeling. This is clearly true of the work of psychologists, psychiatrists, and social psychologists, and tends to be predominantly the case in the work of sociologists.

Unfortunately, this customary way of viewing race prejudice overlooks and obscures the fact that race prejudice is fundamentally a matter of relationship between racial groups. A little reflective thought should make this very clear. Race prejudice presupposes, necessarily, that racially prejudiced individuals think of themselves as belonging to a given racial group. It means, also, that they assign to other racial groups those against whom they are prejudiced. Thus, logically and actually, a scheme of racial identification is necessary as a framework for racial prejudice. Moreover, such identification

involves the formation of an image or a conception of one's own racial group and of another racial group, inevitably in terms of the relationship of such groups. To fail to see that racial prejudice is a matter (a) of the racial identification made of oneself and of others, and (b) of the way in which the identified groups are conceived in relation to each other, is to miss what is logically and actually basic. One should keep clearly in mind that people necessarily come to identify themselves as belonging to a racial group; such identification is not spontaneous or inevitable but a result of experience. Further, one must realize that the kind of picture which a racial group forms of itself and the kind of picture which it may form of others are similarly products of experience. Hence, such pictures are variable, just as the lines of experience which produce them are variable.

The body of feelings which scholars, today, are so inclined to regard as constituting the substance of race prejudice is actually a resultant of the way in which given racial groups conceive of themselves and of others. A basic understanding of race prejudice must be sought in the process by which racial groups form images of themselves and of others. This process, as I hope to show, is fundamentally *a collective process*. It operates chiefly through the public media in which individuals who are accepted as the spokesmen of a racial group characterize publicly another racial group. To characterize another racial group is, by opposition, to define one's own group. This is equivalent to placing the two groups in relation to each other, or defining their positions *vis-à-vis* each other. It is the *sense of social position* emerging from this collective process of characterization which provides the basis of race prejudice. The following discussion will consider important facets of this matter.

I would like to begin by discussing several of the important feelings that enter into race prejudice. This discussion will reveal how fundamentally racial feelings point to and depend on a positional arrangement of the racial groups. In this discussion I will confine myself to such feelings in the case of a dominant racial group.

There are four basic types of feelings that seem to be always present in race prejudice in the dominant group. They are (1) a feeling of superiority, (2) a feeling that the subordinate race is intrinsically different and alien, (3) a feeling of proprietary claim to certain areas of privilege and advantage, and (4) a fear and suspicion that the subordinate race harbors designs on the prerogatives of the dominant race. A few words about each of these four feelings will suffice.

In race prejudice there is a self-assured feeling on the part of the dominant racial group of being naturally superior or better. This is commonly shown in a disparagement of the qualities of the subordinate racial group. Condemnatory or debasing traits, such as laziness, dishonesty, greediness, unreliability, stupidity, deceit and immorality, are usually imputed to it. The second feeling, that the subordinate race is an alien and fundamentally different stock, is likewise always present. "They are not of our kind" is a common way in which this is likely to be expressed. It is this feeling that reflects, justifies, and promotes the social exclusion of the subordinate racial group. The combination of these two feelings of superiority and of distinctiveness can easily give rise to feelings of aversion

and even antipathy. But in themselves they do not form prejudice. We have to introduce the third and fourth types of feeling.

The third feeling, the sense of proprietary claim, is of crucial importance. It is the feeling on the part of the dominant group of being entitled to either exclusive or prior rights in many important areas of life. The range of such exclusive or prior claims may be wide, covering the ownership of property such as choice lands and sites; the right to certain jobs, occupations or professions; the claim to certain kinds of industry or lines of business; the claim to certain positions of control and decision-making as in government and law; the right to exclusive membership in given institutions such as schools, churches and recreational institutions; the claim to certain positions of social prestige and to the display of the symbols and accoutrements of these positions; and the claim to certain areas of intimacy and privacy. The feeling of such proprietary claims is exceedingly strong in race prejudice. Again, however, this feeling even in combination with the feeling of superiority and the feeling of distinctiveness does not explain race prejudice. These three feelings are present frequently in societies showing no prejudice, as in certain forms of feudalism, in caste relations, in societies of chiefs and commoners, and under many settled relations of conquerors and conquered. Where claims are solidified into a structure which is accepted or respected by all, there seems to be no group prejudice.

The remaining feeling essential to race prejudice is a fear or apprehension that the subordinate racial group is threatening, or will threaten, the position of the dominant group. Thus, acts or suspected acts that are interpreted as an attack on the natural superiority of the dominant group, or an intrusion into their sphere of group exclusiveness, or an encroachment on their area of proprietary claim are crucial in arousing and fashioning race prejudice. These acts mean "getting out of place."

It should be clear that these four basic feelings of race prejudice definitely refer to a positional arrangement of the racial groups. The feeling of superiority places the subordinate people *below*; the feeling of alienation places them *beyond*; the feeling of proprietary claim excludes them from the prerogatives of position; and the fear of encroachment is an emotional recoil from the endangering of group position. As these features suggest, the positional relation of the two racial groups is crucial in race prejudice. The dominant group is not concerned with the subordinate group as such but it is deeply concerned with its position *vis-à-vis* the subordinate group. This is epitomized in the key and universal expression that a given race is all right in "its place." The sense of group position is the very heart of the relation of the dominant to the subordinate group. It supplies the dominant group with its framework of perception, its standard of judgment, its patterns of sensitivity, and its emotional proclivities.

It is important to recognize that this sense of group position transcends the feelings of the individual members of the dominant group, giving such members a common orientation that is not otherwise to be found in separate feelings and views. There is likely to be considerable difference between the ways in which the individual members of the dominant group think and feel about the subordinate group. Some may feel bitter and hostile, with strong antipathies, with an exalted sense of superiority and with a lot of spite; others may have charitable and protective feelings, marked by a sense of piety and tinctured by benevolence; others may be condescending and reflect mild contempt; and others may be disposed to politeness and considerateness with no feelings of truculence. These are only a few of many different patterns of feeling to be found among members of the dominant racial group. What gives a common dimension to them is a sense of the social position of their group. Whether the members be humane or callous, cultured or unlettered, liberal or reactionary, powerful or impotent, arrogant or humble, rich or poor, honorable or dishonorable—all are led, by virtue of sharing the sense of group position, to similar individual positions.

The sense of group position is a general kind of orientation. It is a general feeling without being reducible to specific feelings like hatred, hostility or antipathy. It is also a general understanding without being composed of any set of specific beliefs. On the social psychological side it cannot be equated to a sense of social status as ordinarily conceived, for it refers not merely to vertical positioning but to many other lines of position independent of the vertical dimension. Sociologically it is not a mere reflection of the objective relations between racial groups. Rather, it stands for "what ought to be" rather than for "what is." It is a sense of where the two racial groups *belong*.

In its own way, the sense of group position is a norm and imperative—indeed a very powerful one. It guides, incites, cows, and coerces. It should be borne in mind that this sense of group position stands for and involves a fundamental kind of group affiliation for the members of the dominant racial group. To the extent they recognize or feel themselves as belonging to that group they will automatically come under the influence of the sense of position held by that group. Thus, even though given individual members may have personal views and feelings different from the sense of group position, they will have to conjure with the sense of group position held by their racial group. If the sense of position is strong, to act contrary to it is to risk a feeling of self-alienation and to face the possibility of ostracism. I am trying to suggest, accordingly, that the locus of race prejudice is not in the area of individual feeling but in the definition of the respective positions of the racial groups.

The source of race prejudice lies in a felt challenge to this sense of group position. The challenge, one must recognize, may come in many different ways. It may be in the form of an affront to feelings of group superiority; it may be in the form of attempts at familiarity or transgressing the boundary line of group exclusiveness; it may be in the form of encroachment at countless points of proprietary claim; it may be a challenge to power and privilege; it may take the form of economic competition. Race prejudice is a defensive reaction to such challenging of the sense of group position. It consists of the disturbed feelings, usually of marked hostility, that are thereby aroused. As such, race prejudice is a protective device. It functions, however short-sightedly, to preserve the integrity and the position of the dominant group.

It is crucially important to recognize that the sense of group position is not a mere summation of the feelings of position such as might be developed independently by separate individuals as they come to compare themselves with given individuals of the subordinate race. The sense of group position refers to the position of group to group, not to that of individual to individual. Thus, *vis-à-vis* the subordinate racial group the unlettered individual with low status in the dominant racial group has a sense of group position common to that of the elite of his group. By virtue of sharing this sense of position such an individual, despite his low status, feels that members of the subordinate group, however distinguished and accomplished, are somehow inferior, alien, and properly restricted in the area of claims. He forms his conception as a representative of the dominant group: he treats individual members of the subordinate group as representative of that group.

An analysis of how the sense of group position is formed should start with a clear recognition that it is an historical product. It is set originally by conditions of initial contact. Prestige, power, possession of skill, numbers, original self-conceptions, aims, designs and opportunities are a few of the factors that may fashion the original sense of group position. Subsequent experience in the relation of the two racial groups, especially in the area of claims, opportunities and advantages, may mould the sense of group position in many diverse ways. Further, the sense of group position may be intensified or weakened, brought to sharp focus or dulled. It may be deeply entrenched and tenaciously resist change for long periods of time. Or it may never take root. It may undergo quick growth and vigorous expansion, or it may dwindle away through slow-moving erosion. It may be firm or soft, acute or dull, continuous or intermittent. In short, viewed comparatively, the sense of group position is very variable.

However variable its particular career, the sense of group position is clearly formed by a running process in which the dominant racial group is led to define and redefine the subordinate racial group and the relations between them. There are two important aspects of this process of definition that I wish to single out for consideration.

First, the process of definition occurs obviously through complex interaction and communication between the members of the dominant group. Leaders, prestige bearers, officials, group agents, dominant individuals and ordinary laymen present to one another characterizations of the subordinate group and express their feelings and ideas on the relations. Through talk, tales, stories, gossip, anecdotes, messages, pronouncements, news accounts, orations, sermons, preachments and the like definitions are presented and feelings are expressed. In this usually vast and complex interaction separate views run against one another, influence one another, modify each other, incite one another and fuse together in new forms. Correspondingly, feelings which are expressed meet, stimulate each other, feed on each other, intensify each other and emerge in new patterns. Currents of view and currents of feeling come into being; sweeping along to positions of dominance and serving as polar points for the organization of thought and sentiment. If the interaction becomes increasingly circular and reinforcing, devoid of serious inner opposition, such currents grow, fuse and become strengthened. It is through such a process that a collective image of the subordinate group is formed and a sense of group position is set. The evidence of such a process is glaring when one reviews the history of any racial arrangement marked by prejudice.

Such a complex process of mutual interaction with its different lines and degrees of formation gives the lie to the many schemes which would lodge the cause of race prejudice in the make-up of the individual—whether in the form of innate disposition, constitutional make-up, personality structure, or direct personal experience with members of the other race. The collective image and feelings in race prejudice are forged out of a complicated social process in which the individual is himself shaped and organized. The scheme, so popular today, which would trace race prejudice to a so-called authoritarian personality shows a grievous misunderstanding of the simple essentials of the collective process that leads to a sense of group position.

The second important aspect of the process of group definition is that it is necessarily concerned with *an abstract image* of the subordinate racial group. The subordinate racial group is defined as if it were an entity or whole. This entity or whole—like the Negro race, or the Japanese, or the Jews—is necessarily an abstraction, never coming within the perception of any of the senses. While actual encounters are with individuals, the picture formed of the racial group is necessarily of a vast entity which spreads out far beyond such individuals and transcends experience with such individuals. The implications of the fact that the collective image is of an abstract group are of crucial significance. I would like to note four of these implications.

First, the building of the image of the abstract group takes place in the area of the remote and not of the near. It is not the experience with concrete individuals in daily association that gives rise to the definitions of the extended, abstract group. Such immediate experience is usually regulated and orderly. Even where such immediate experience is disrupted the new definitions which are formed are limited to the individuals involved. The collective image of the abstract group grows up not by generalizing from experiences gained in close, first-hand contacts but through the transcending characterizations that are made of the group as an entity. Thus, one must seek the central stream of definition in those areas where the dominant group as such is characterizing the subordinate group as such. This occurs in the "public arena" wherein the spokesmen appear as representatives and agents of the dominant group. The extended public arena is constituted by such things as legislative assemblies, public meetings, conventions, the press, and the printed word. What goes on in this public arena attracts the attention of large numbers of the dominant group and is felt as the voice and action of the group as such.

Second, the definitions that are forged in the public arena center, obviously, about matters that are felt to be of major importance. Thus, we are led to recognize the crucial role of the "big event" in developing a conception of the subordinate racial group. The happening that seems momentous, that touches deep sentiments, that seems to raise fundamental questions about relations, and that awakens strong feelings of identification with one's racial group is the kind of event that is central in the formation of the racial image. Here, again, we note the relative unimportance of the huge bulk of experiences coming from daily contact with individuals of the subordinate group. It is the events seemingly loaded with great collective significance that are the focal points of the public discussion. The definition of these events is chiefly responsible for the development of a racial image and of the sense of group position. When this public discussion takes the form of a denunciation

of the subordinate racial group, signifying that it is unfit and a threat, the discussion becomes particularly potent in shaping the sense of social position.

Third, the major influence in public discussion is exercised by individuals and groups who have the public ear and who are felt to have standing, prestige, authority and power. Intellectual and social elites, public figures of prominence, and leaders of powerful organizations are likely to be the key figures in the formation of the sense of group position and in the characterization of the subordinate group. It is well to note this in view of the not infrequent tendency of students to regard race prejudice as growing out of the multiplicity of experiences and attitudes of the bulk of the people.

Fourth, we also need to perceive the appreciable opportunity that is given to strong interest groups in directing the lines of discussion and setting the interpretations that arise in such discussion. Their self-interests may dictate the kind of position they wish the dominant racial group to enjoy. It may be a position which enables them to retain certain advantages, or even more to gain still greater advantages. Hence, they may be vigorous in seeking to manufacture events to attract public attention and to set lines of issue in such a way as to predetermine interpretations favorable to their interests. The role of strongly organized groups seeking to further special interest is usually central in the formation of collective images of abstract groups. Historical records of major instances of race relations, as in our South, or in South Africa, or in Europe in the case of the Jew, or on the West Coast in the case of the Japanese show the formidable part played by interest groups in defining the subordinate racial group.

I conclude this highly condensed paper with two further observations that may throw additional light on the relation of the sense of group position to race prejudice. Race prejudice becomes entrenched and tenacious to the extent the prevailing social order is rooted in the sense of social position. This has been true of the historic South in our country. In such a social order race prejudice tends to become chronic and impermeable to change. In other places the social order may be affected only to a limited extent by the sense of group position held by the dominant racial group. This I think has been true usually in the case of anti–Semitism in Europe and this country. Under these conditions the sense of group position tends to be weaker and more vulnerable. In turn, race prejudice has a much more variable and intermittent career, usually becoming pronounced only as a consequence of grave disorganizing events that allow for the formation of a scapegoat.

This leads me to my final observation which in a measure is an indirect summary. The sense of group position dissolves and race prejudice declines when the process of running definition does not keep abreast of major shifts in the social order. When events touching on relations are not treated as "big events" and hence do not set crucial issues in the arena of public discussion; or when the elite leaders or spokesmen do not define such big events vehemently or adversely; or where they define them in the direction of racial harmony; or when there is a paucity of strong interest groups seeking to build up a strong adverse image for special advantage—under such conditions the sense of group position recedes and race prejudice declines.

The clear implication of my discussion is that the proper and the fruitful area in which race prejudice should be studied is the collective process through which a sense of group position is formed. To seek, instead, to understand it or to handle it in the arena of individual feeling and of individual experience seems to me to be clearly misdirected.

22

The Psychology of Social Stratification*

DOUGLAS MASSEY

* * *

||| THE PSYCHOLOGY OF SOCIAL CLASSIFICATION

Although obvious and glaring, in principle the mechanisms of stratification employed in the Jim Crow South are quite general and operate at some level in all human societies. They are ultimately social in origin and predate the emergence of the market as a means of organizing human production and consumption (Massey 2005). Instead, they follow naturally from the pursuit of core social motives common to all human beings (Fiske 2004). What has changed dramatically is the societal context within which the core social motives play out. Human interactions increasingly occur within urban environments of great size, density, and heterogeneity, and the ecological settings that individuals find themselves adapting to—psychologically, socially, cultur-

---

* First published in 2007; from *Categorically Unequal: The American Stratification System.*

ally, and physiologically—vary greatly depending on whether the individuals are rich or poor, light or dark, male or female.

In a very real way, stratification begins psychologically with the creation of cognitive boundaries that allocate people to social categories. Before categorical inequality can be implemented socially, categories must be created cognitively to classify people conceptually based on some set of achieved and ascribed characteristics. The roots of social stratification thus lie ultimately in the cognitive construction of boundaries to make social distinctions, a task that comes naturally to human beings, who are mentally hardwired to engage in categorical thought (Fiske 2004). Indeed, recent work shows that human intelligence works more through pattern recognition and inductive generalization than deductive logic or mathematical optimization (Dawes 1998). In contrast to the software and hardware of a digital computer, which work together to make decisions using a strict Boolean logic, the "wetware" of the human brain is messy, inconsistent, and often quite "illogical" in a strictly deductive sense (Dawes and Hastie 2001; Kahneman and Tversky 1973, 1979). Instead, human "rationality" has been shaped by evolution to depart in characteristic ways from strict adherence to the principles of logic and probability that are assumed by most rational choice models (Dawes 1998; Kahneman and Tversky 2000).

Our natural capacity for categorical thought evolved in this fashion because the human brain is an energy sink. Constituting just 2 percent of the body's weight, the brain uses 20 percent of its total energy (Donald 1991). In the course of thousands of years of evolution, therefore, human beings evolved ingrained mental short-

cuts to conserve cognitive resources. Operating with deductive rigor to consider all possible combinations, permutations, and contingencies before making a decision is possible for a powerful electronic computer contemplating a single problem, but if the brain were to adopt such an approach to decide the myriad of choices that human beings face in daily life, humans would waste a lot of scarce energy pondering routine situations and everyday actions that have little effect on survival. Most decisions made by humans are not perfect or optimal in any real sense; they are just "good enough" to get by and live another day, yielding the human practice of "satisficing" rather than optimizing (Simon 1981).

For this reason, human beings function mentally as "cognitive misers." They take a variety of characteristic mental shortcuts and use simple rules of thumb and shorthands to make everyday judgments (Fiske and Taylor 1991). As organisms, we tend to "satisfice" rather than optimize (Newell and Simon 1972), and we are wired cognitively to construct general categories about the world in which we live and then to use them to classify and evaluate the stimuli we encounter. These conceptual categories are collectively known as *schemas*. They represent cognitive structures that serve to interconnect a set of stimuli, their various attributes, and the relationships between them (Fiske 2004).

Since human memory is finite and cannot be expanded, if the brain is to remember more things it must combine or "chunk" bits of information into larger conceptual categories (schemas), using common properties to classify a much larger number of people, objects, and experiences into a small number of readily identifiable categories for recall. Ultimately schemas are nothing more than well-established neural pathways that have been created through the repeated firing of particular constellations of synapses, leading to the formation of an integrated assembly of neurons that function together according to a specific sequence along specific routes to produce a consistent mental representation (LeDoux 2002).

People use schemas to evaluate themselves and the social roles, social groups, social events, and individuals they encounter, a process known as social cognition (Fiske 2004). The categories into which they divide up the world may change over time and evolve with experience, but among mature human beings they always exist and people always fall back on them when they interpret objects, events, people, and situations (Fiske 2004), and they are especially reliant on categorical judgments under conditions of threat or uncertainty. Human beings are psychologically programmed to categorize the people they encounter and to use these categorizations to make social judgments.

Social schemas do not exist simply as neutral mental representations, however; they are typically associated with emotional valences. The human brain is composed of two parallel processors that, while interconnected, function independently (Carter 1998; Konner 2002; Panksepp 1998). The emotional brain is rooted in a set of neural structures that are common to all mammals and are known collectively as the limbic system, whereas the rational brain is centered in the prefrontal cortex and other areas of the neocortex (Damasio 1994, 1999). The two portions of the brain, labeled system 1 and system 2 by Daniel Kahneman (2003), are neurally interconnected, but the number and speed of the connections running from the limbic system to the neocortex are greater than the reverse, so that emotional memories stored in the limbic system, which are typically unconscious or implicit, greatly affect how human beings make use of categories that exist within the rational, conscious brain (LeDoux 1996; Zajonc 1998).

Emotions stored in the limbic system may be positive or negative, but when they are associated with particular classes of people or objects they contribute to *prejudice,* which is a predetermined emotional orientation toward individuals or objects (Fiske 2004). A prejudicial orientation for or against some social group thus contains both conscious and unconscious components (Bargh 1996, 1997). On the one hand, people may be principled racists who consciously believe that African Americans are inferior and thus rationally seek to subordinate them, consistent with their explicit beliefs. On the other hand, a person may quite sincerely believe in equal opportunity and racial justice and yet harbor unconscious anti-black sentiments and associations that were created through some process of conditioning (such as the repeated visual pairing of violent crime scenes with black perpetrators on television), even though this prejudice may be inconsistent with the person's explicit beliefs.

All human beings, whether they think of themselves as prejudiced or not, hold in their heads schemas that classify people into categories based on age, gender, race, and ethnicity (Stangor et al. 1992; Taylor et al. 1978). They cannot help it. It is part of the human condition, and these schemas generally include implicit memories that yield subconscious dispositions toward people and objects; leading to stereotypes (Fiske 1998). Moreover, although stereotypical notions are always present, people are more likely to fall back on them in making judgments when they feel challenged, face uncertainty, or experience sensory overload (Bodenhausen and Lichtenstein 1987; Bodenhausen and Wyer 1985).

In making stereotypical judgments about others, human beings appear to evaluate people along two basic psychological dimensions: warmth and competence (Fiske et al. 2002). Warmth is how likable and approachable a person is. We are attracted to people we view as high on the warmth dimension, and we seek to interact and spend time with them. We find people who are low on the warmth dimension to be off-putting, and we generally avoid them and seek to minimize the number and range of our social contacts with them; we don't like them and find them "cold." In addition to these subjective feelings of attraction and liking, we also evaluate people in terms of competence and efficacy—their ability to act in a purposeful manner to get things done. We may or may not like people who are highly competent, but we generally respect them and admire their ability to achieve.

These two dimensions of social perception come together in the *stereotype content model,* which argues that human social cognition and stereotyping involve the cognitive placement of groups and individuals in a two-dimensional social space defined by the intersection of independent axes of warmth and competence (Fiske et al. 2002). As shown in figure 1, the social space for stereotyping has four quadrants. The top-right quadrant contains people within the person's own group, along with members of groups perceived to be similar to one's own. Naturally, we think of members of our own social group as warm and competent and, hence, approachable and worthy of respect. The relevant emotion associated with in-group social perceptions is esteem or pride.

FIGURE 1 **THE STEREOTYPE CONTENT MODEL**

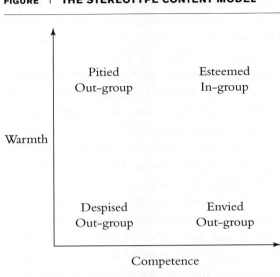

SOURCE: Author's compilation.

The intersection of the two dimensions yields three distinct kinds of out-groups, however, which vary in terms of approachability and respect. The bottom-right quadrant contains those groups that are viewed socially as competent but not warm. They are respected but not liked, and the relevant emotion that people feel toward them is envy. This quadrant embraces the classic middleman minorities, such as Jews in medieval Europe, Chinese in Malaysia, Tutsi in Rwanda, and Indians in East Africa. In a stable social structure, people show public respect for and defer to members of envied out-groups, but if the social order breaks down, these out-groups may become targets of communal hatred and violence because they are not liked and are not perceived as people "like us."

The top-left quadrant includes out-groups that are viewed as warm, and thus likable, but as not competent. Those falling into this category include people who have experienced some misfortune but are otherwise perceived as "people like me," such as the disabled, the elderly, the blind, or the mentally retarded. One could imagine being in their shoes but for an accident of fate, and so the relevant emotion is pity. We like the members of these out-groups, but recognizing their lack of competence, we also feel sorry for them and do not respect them. In a stable social structure, members of pitied out-groups tend to be looked after and cared for, but in times of social disorder they may suffer from neglect (as seen in the aftermath of Hurricane Katrina in New Orleans), though they generally do not become targets of intentional hatred or communal violence.

Finally, social groups occupying the bottom-left quadrant are perceived simultaneously as low in warmth and low in competence. Being neither likable nor capable, people within these out groups are socially despised, and the dominant emotion is disgust. This quadrant contains social outcasts such as drug dealers, lazy welfare recipients, sex offenders, and the chronically homeless. It also includes members of groups that have been subject to an ideological process of group formation and boundary definition that questions their humanity. African Americans in the Jim Crow South were perceived by whites as neither competent nor warm. They were socially labeled as inferior, even subhuman, and because they were perceived as less than fully human, they could be exploited, segregated, humiliated, and killed with near impunity.

Recent work in neuroscience has implicated a particular region of the brain as central to the process of social cognition (see Harris and Fiske 2006). Whenever individuals perceive a stimulus as a human being and therefore a potential social actor, an area of the brain known as the *medial prefrontal cortex* lights up when observed under functional magnetic resonance imagery (fMRI). Lasana Harris and Susan Fiske (2006) pretested a number of photographic images of social actors to establish the quadrant into which they fell; then they showed these images to experimental subjects so that each person saw a total of eighty images—twenty of in-group members, twenty of envied out-groups, twenty of pitied out-groups, and twenty of despised out-groups.

As they viewed the various social images, the brains of subjects were scanned under fMRI and centers of activity recorded. As expected, the investigators found that images of people representing in-groups, envied out-groups, and pitied out-groups triggered clear reactions in the medial prefrontal cortex. Startlingly, however, images of despised out-groups did not (Harris and Fiske 2006). Whereas out-groups triggering feelings of pity and envy were instantly perceived as human beings and social actors, those that were despised were not seen in social terms at all—at the most fundamental level of cognition. Despised out-groups thus become dehumanized at the neural level, and those who harbor these feelings thus have a license, in their own minds, to treat members of these out-groups as if they are animals or objects.

This basic feature of human social cognition provides the psychological foundations for exploitation and opportunity hoarding in the real world. It is reinforced by another characteristic feature of human psychology known as the *fundamental attribution error,* "the general tendency to overestimate the importance of personal or dispositional factors relative to environmental influences" in accounting for behavior (Ross, Greene, and House 1977, 184). In evaluating others, all human beings have a natural tendency to attribute behavioral outcomes to characteristics of the people involved rather than the structure of the situation. Thus, the poor are poor because they are lazy, lack a work ethic, have no sense of responsibility, are careless in their choices, or are just plain immoral, not because they lost their job or were born into a social position that did not give them the resources they needed to develop. Because of the fundamental attribution error, we are all cognitively wired and prone to blame the victim—to think that people deserve their location in the prevailing stratification system.

In parallel fashion, human beings have an opposite bias when they make attributions about themselves, at least with respect to negative outcomes. Rather than blaming themselves—something about their disposition or character—they tend to attribute personal misfortunes to specific features of the situation, a proclivity known as the *actor-observer effect* (Jones and Nisbett 1972). When *someone else* ends up on welfare, it is because he or she is lazy, careless, or irresponsible; when *I* end up on welfare, however, it is through no fault of my own but because of events beyond my control: I lost my job, got sick, was injured, got pregnant accidentally, got divorced, was widowed. Because of the actor-observer effect, we are also cognitively prone to explain our own misfortunes and outcomes in terms of the structure of the situation.

THE CREATION OF CAPITAL

The position of a group within the social space defined by warmth and competence is not fixed but malleable, varying across time, space, and culture (Leslie, Constantine, and Fiske 2006). Although social categories are ultimately constructed and maintained by individuals within their own minds, the process by which boundaries are expressed is ultimately social. Group identities and boundaries are negotiated through repeated interactions that establish working definitions of the categories in question, including both objective and subjective content, a process that sociologists have labeled *boundary work* (Gieryn 1983; Lamont and Molnar 2002). When social actors succeed in establishing the limits and content of various social categories in the minds of others, psychologists refer to the process as *framing* (Kahneman and Tversky 2000). In essence, boundary work involves defining categories in the social structure, and framing involves defining them in human cognition.

People naturally favor boundaries and framings that grant them greater access to material, symbolic, and emotional resources, and they seek to convince others to accept their favored version of social reality (Lakoff 2002; Lakoff and Johnson 2003). In general, social actors who control more resources in society—those toward the top of the stratification system—have the upper hand in framing and boundary work. Whites historically have perpetuated negative stereotypes of African Americans as unintelligent, violent, hyper-sexual, and shiftless, and rich people likewise have promoted a view of the poor as lazy, unmotivated, undisciplined, and undeserving. To the extent that such stereotypes become a part of everyday social cognition, individual members of the stereotyped out-group tend to experience discrimination and exclusion.

Nonetheless, exclusionary social distinctions and demeaning framings are always contested by people on the receiving end (Barth 1969). Those subject to exploitation by a particular framing of social reality work to oppose it and substitute an alternative framing more amenable to their interests. Likewise, when they encounter categorical boundaries that prevent them from accessing a desired resource, people work actively to resist and subvert the social definitions as best they can. Members of subjugated groups have their own expectations about how they should be perceived and treated, and even if they outwardly adapt to the social preconceptions of more powerful others, they generally work inwardly to undermine the dominant conceptual and social order in small and large ways.

Through such two-way interactions, however asymmetric they may be, people on both sides of a stratified social divide actively participate in the construction of the boundaries and identities that define a system of stratification. No matter what their position in the system, people seek to define for themselves the content and meaning of social categories, embracing some elements ascribed to them by the dominant society and rejecting others, simultaneously accepting and resisting the constraints and opportunities associated with their particular social status. Through daily interactions with individuals and institutions, people construct an understanding of the lines between specific social groups (Barth 1981).

The reification of group boundaries within human social structures creates two important resources that are widely deployed in the process of social stratification: social capital and cultural capital (Bourdieu 1986). In classical economics, of course, capital refers to anything that can be used in the production of other resources, is human-made, and is not fully consumed in the process of production (Ricardo 1996). Common examples are *financial capital,* which can be invested to generate income, and *physical capital,* which can be applied in production to increase output. Economists later generalized the concept by defining *human capital* as the skills and abilities embodied in people, notably through education and training (Schultz 1963). By investing in education, parents and societies thus create human capital in their children, and when individuals forgo income and incur costs to gain additional training, they invest in their own human capital. Individuals recoup this investment through higher lifetime earnings; societies recoup it through higher taxes and enhanced productivity; and parents recoup it by enjoying the economic independence and financial security of their adult children (Becker 1975).

Sociologists have broadened the concept of capital to embrace resources derived from social ties to people and institutions (Bourdieu 1986; Coleman 1988). *Social capital* comes into existence whenever a social connection to another person or membership in a social organization yields tangible benefits with respect to material, symbolic, or emotional resources, such as getting a job that offers higher income, greater prestige, and more access to attractive sexual partners. Most "good" jobs are not found through formal mechanisms such as paid advertisements but through informal connections with other social actors who provide information and leads (Granovetter 1974).

Because ties to friends and family do not extend very far and mostly yield redundant information, weak ties to casual acquaintances are generally more important in getting a job than close relationships to close friends or kin (Granovetter 1973).

The use of framing and boundary work to construct an advantaged social group with privileged access to resources and power creates the potential for social capital formation. Having a tie to a member of a privileged elite increases the odds of being able to access resources and power oneself. Elites implicitly recognize this fact and generally take steps to restrict social ties to other members of the elite. Marriage outside the group is discouraged; friendships are turned inward through exclusive organizations such as clubs, fraternities, and lodges; and rules of inheritance conserve elite status along family lines. To the extent that group members are successful in confining social ties to other group members, they achieve *social closure*. Outsiders trying to break into elite circles are labeled bounders or interlopers, and they are derided for acting "uppity" or "above their station."

Social closure within elite networks and institutions also creates the potential for another valuable resource known as *cultural capital* (Bourdieu 1986). In contrast to human capital, which includes knowledge, skills, and abilities that make people directly productive as individuals, cultural capital consists of knowledge and manners that do not make individuals more productive in and of themselves, but that permit them to be more effective as actors within a particular social context—in this case, elite settings. Because members of an elite tend to go to the same schools, read the same books, peruse the same periodicals, learn the same stylized manners, follow the same fashions, and develop the same accents and speech patterns, they are easily able to acquire a common set of socially defined markers that designate "good taste" and "high class," so that elite members are quickly recognizable to one another and to the masses.

The possession of cultural capital makes an individual more productive not because he or she can perform a given operation better or faster, but because he or she can navigate structures of power with greater ease, feeling relaxed and comfortable in the social settings they define and thus interacting with other persons of influence to get things done. Cultural capital represents a symbolic resource that privileged groups can manipulate through opportunity hoarding to perpetuate stratification and increase inequality.

SPATIAL BOUNDARIES

To this point, I have argued that stratification stems from a social process wherein individuals form categorical mental representations of in-groups and out-groups through framing; translate these representations into social categories through boundary work; and then establish institutional structures for exploitation and opportunity hoarding that correspond to categorical boundaries, thereby generating unequal access to resources such as financial capital, human capital, social capital, and cultural capital. To function, this system need only exist in the social and cognitive spheres. Position in a cognitively and institutionally defined social order need not correspond to any real location in physical space. If, however, social boundaries can be made to conform to geographic boundaries through a systematic process of segregation, then the fundamental processes of stratification become considerably more efficient and effective (Massey 2005).

If out-group members are spatially segregated from in-group members, then the latter are put in a good position to use their social power to create institutions and practices that channel resources away from the places where out-group members live, thus facilitating exploitation. At the same time, they can use their social power to implement other mechanisms that direct resources systematically toward in-group areas, thus facilitating opportunity hoarding. Spatial segregation renders stratification easy, convenient, and efficient because simply by investing or disinvesting in a place, one can invest or disinvest in a whole set of people (Massey and Denton 1993).

Stratification thus becomes more effective to the degree that social and spatial boundaries can be made to overlap. When members of an out-group are well integrated spatially, stratification is more difficult and costly because disinvestment in the out-group must occur on a person-by-person, family-by-family basis. Throughout history, therefore, whenever the powerful have sought to stigmatize and subordinate a particular social group, they have endeavored to confine its members to specific neighborhoods by law, edict, or practice (Wirth 1928).

The overlapping of social, cultural, economic, and spatial boundaries yields what Peter Blau (1977) calls a *consolidation of parameters*. When social parameters are consolidated—when social, economic, and spatial characteristics correlate strongly with one another—the process of stratification becomes sharper and more acute. Within a hypothetical social space made up of cells defined by the intersection of spatial status, social status,

economic status, and cultural status, within-cell relations intensify and between-cell interactions attenuate. Over time, inter-cell mobility withers, social categories reify and reproduce themselves, and the social structure as a whole grows rigid. A society defined by consolidated parameters is thus one in which the categorical mechanisms of inequality operate very effectively and social boundaries are salient and difficult to cross, yielding "durable inequality," a structural state wherein stratification replicates and reproduces itself more or less automatically over time.

★ ★ ★

||| REFERENCES

Bargh, John A. 1996. "Automaticity in Social Psychology." In *Social Psychology: Handbook of Basic Principles*, edited by E. Tory Higgins and Arie W. Kruglanski. New York: Guilford.

Barth, Fredrik. 1969. *Ethnic Groups and Boundaries: The Social Organization of Culture Difference*. Boston: Little, Brown.

———. 1981. *Process and Form in Social Life*. London: Routledge and Kegan Paul.

Becker, Gary S. 1975. *Human Capital: A Theoretical and Empirical Analysis with Special Reference to Education*. Chicago: University of Chicago Press.

Blau, Peter M. 1977. *Inequality and Heterogeneity: A Primitive Theory of Social Structure*. New York: Free Press.

Bodenhausen, Galen V., and Meryl Lichtenstein. 1987. "Social Stereotypes and Information-Processing Strategies: The Impact of Task Complexity." *Journal of Personality and Social Psychology* 52: 871–80.

Bodenhausen, Galen V., and Robert S. Wyer. 1985. "Effects of Stereotypes on Decision Making and Information-Processing Strategies." *Journal of Personality and Social Psychology* 48(2): 267–82.

Bourdieu, Pierre. 1986. "The Forms of Capital." In *Handbook of Theory and Research for the Sociology of Education*, edited by John G. Richardson. New York: Greenwood Press.

Carter, Rita. 1998. *Mapping the Mind*. Berkeley: University of California Press.

Coleman, James S. 1988. "Social Capital in the Creation of Human Capital." *American Journal of Sociology* 94(suppl.): S95–120.

Damasio, Antonio R. 1994. *Descartes' Error: Emotion, Reason, and the Human Brain*. New York: Putnam.

———. 1999. *The Feeling of What Happens: Body and Emotion in the Making of Consciousness*. New York: Harcourt Brace.

Dawes, Robyn M. 1998. "Behavioral Decision Making and Judgment." In *The Handbook of Social Psychology*, edited by Daniel T. Gilbert, Susan T. Fiske, and Gardner Lindzey. Boston: McGraw-Hill.

Dawes, Robyn M., and Reid Hastie. 2001. *Rational Choice in an Uncertain World: The Psychology of Judgment and Decision Making*. Newbury Park, Calif.: Sage Publications.

Donald, Merlin. 1991. *Origins of the Modern Mind: Three States in the Evolution of Culture and Cognition*. Cambridge, Mass.: Harvard University Press.

Fiske, Susan T. 1998. "Stereotyping, Prejudice, and Discrimination." In *The Handbook of Social Psychology*, 4th ed., vol. 1, edited by Daniel T. Gilbert, Susan T. Fiske, and Gardner Lindzey. New York: McGraw-Hill.

———. 2004. *Social Beings: A Core Motives Approach to Social Psychology*. New York: Wiley.

Fiske, Susan T., Amy J. C. Cuddy, Peter Glick, and Jun Xu. 2002. "A Model of (Often Mixed) Stereotype Content: Competence and Warmth Respectively Follow from Perceived Status and Competition." *Journal of Personality and Social Psychology* 82(6): 878–902.

Fiske, Susan T., and Shelly E. Taylor. 1991. *Social Cognition*, 2nd ed. New York: McGraw-Hill.

Gieryn, Thomas F. 1983. "Boundary-Work and the Demarcation of Science from Non-science: Strains and Interests in Professional Ideologies of Scientists." *American Sociological Review* 48(6): 781–95.

Granovetter, Mark S. 1973. "The Strength of Weak Ties." *American Journal of Sociology* 78(6):1360–80.

———. 1974. *Getting a Job: A Study of Contacts and Careers*. Cambridge, Mass.: Harvard University Press.

Harris, Lasana T., and Susan T. Fiske. 2006. "Dehumanizing the Lowest of the Low: Neuroimaging Responses to Extreme Outgroups." *Psychological Science* 17(10): 847–53.

Jones, Edward E., and Richard E. Nisbett. 1972. "The Actor and the Observer: Divergent Perceptions of the Causes of Behavior." In *Attribution:*

Perceiving the Causes of Behavior, edited by Edward E. Jones, S. Valin, and B. Weiner. Morristown, N.J.: General Learning Press.

Kahneman, Daniel. 2003. "Maps of Bounded Rationality: Psychology for Behavioral Economics." *American Economic Review* 93(5): 1449–75.

Kahneman, Daniel, and Amos Tversky. 1973. "On the Psychology of Prediction." *Psychological Review* 80: 237–51.

———. 1979. "Prospect Theory: An Analysis of Decisions Under Risk." *Econometrica* 47(2): 313–27.

———. 2000. *Choices, Values, and Frames.* New York: Cambridge University Press.

Konner, Melvin. 2002. *The Tangled Wing: Biological Constraints on the Human Spirit.* New York: Henry Holt.

Lakoff, George. 2002. *Moral Politics: How Liberals and Conservatives Think.* Chicago: University of Chicago Press.

Lakoff, George, and Mark Johnson. 2003. *Metaphors We Live By.* Chicago: University of Chicago Press.

Lamont, Michèle, and Vireg Molnar. 2002. "The Study of Boundaries in the Social Sciences." *Annual Review of Sociology* 28: 167–95.

LeDoux, Joseph. 1996. *The Emotional Brain: The Mysterious Underpinnings of Emotional Life.* New York: Simon & Schuster.

———. 2002. *Synaptic Self: How Our Brains Become Who We Are.* New York: Viking.

Leslie, Lisa M., V. S. Constantine, and Susan T. Fiske. 2006. "The Princeton Quartet: How Are Stereotypes Changing?" Unpublished paper. Princeton, N.J.: Princeton University, Department of Psychology.

Massey, Douglas S. 2005. *Strangers in a Strange Land: Humans in an Urbanizing World.* New York: Norton.

Massey, Douglas S., and Nancy A. Denton. 1993. *American Apartheid: Segregation and the Making of the Underclass.* Cambridge, Mass.: Harvard University Press.

Newell, Allen, and Herbert A. Simon. 1972. *Human Problem Solving.* Englewood Cliffs, N.J.: Prentice-Hall.

Panksepp, Jaak. 1998. *Affective Neuroscience: The Foundations of Human and Animal Emotions.* New York: Oxford University Press.

Ricardo, David. 1996. *Principles of Political Economy and Taxation.* New York: Prometheus Books.

Ross, Lee R., D. Greene, and P. House. 1977. "The False Consensus Effect: An Egocentric Bias in Social Perception and Attribution Processes." *Journal of Experimental Social Psychology* 13: 279–301.

Schultz, Theodore W. 1963. *The Economic Value of Education.* New York: Columbia University Press.

Simon, Herbert A. 1981. *Sciences of the Artificial*, 2nd ed., rev. and enl. Cambridge, Mass.: MIT Press.

Strangor, Charles, L. Lynch, C. Duan, and B. Glass. 1992. "Categorization of Individuals on the Basis of Multiple Social Features." *Journal of Personality and Social Psychology* 62(2): 207–18.

Taylor, Shelly E., Susan T. Fiske, Nancy L. Etcoff, and Audrey J. Ruderman. 1978. "Categorical Bases of Person Memory and Stereotyping." *Journal of Personality and Social Psychology* 36: 778–93.

Wirth, Louis. 1928. *The Ghetto*. Chicago: University of Chicago Press.

Zajonc, Robert B. 1998. "Emotions." In *The Handbook of Social Psychology*, edited by Daniel T. Gilbert, Susan T. Fiske, and Gardner Lindzey. Boston: McGraw-Hill.

23

Minorities and Majorities★

ROSABETH KANTER

Up the ranks in Industrial Supply Corporation [*editor's note*: a pseudonym], one of the most consequential conditions of work for women was also among the simplest to identify: there were so few of them. On the professional and managerial levels, Industrial Supply Corporation was nearly a single-sex organization. Women held less than 10 percent of the exempt (salaried) jobs starting at the bottom grades—a 50 percent rise from a few years earlier— and there were no women at the level reporting to officers. When Indsco was asked to participate in a meeting on women in business by bringing their women executives to a civic luncheon, the corporate personnel committee had no difficulty selecting them. There were only five sufficiently senior women in the organization.

The numerical distributions of men and women at the upper reaches created a strikingly different interaction context for women than for men. At local and regional meetings, training programs, task forces, casual out-of-the-office lunches with colleagues, and career review or planning sessions with managers,

---

★ First published in 1977; from *Men and Women of the Corporation*.

the men were overwhelmingly likely to find themselves with a predominance of people of their own type—other men. For men in units with no exempt women, there would be, at most, occasional events in which a handful of women would be present alongside many men. Quite apart from the content of particular jobs and their location in the hierarchy, the culture of corporate administration and the experiences of men in it were influenced by this fact of numerical dominance, by the fact that men were the *many*.

Women, on the other hand, often found themselves alone among male peers. The twenty women in a three hundred-person sales force were scattered over fourteen offices. Their peers, managers, and customers were nearly all men. Never more than two women at a time were found in twelve-person personnel training groups. There was a cluster of professional women on the floor at corporate headquarters housing employee administration and training, but all except three were part of different groups where they worked most closely with men.

The life of women in the corporation was influenced by the proportions in which they found themselves. Those women who were few in number among male peers and often had "only woman" status became tokens: symbols of how-women-can-do, stand-ins for all women. Sometimes they had the advantages of those who are "different" and thus were highly visible in a system where success is tied to becoming known. Sometimes they faced the loneliness of the outsider, of the stranger who intrudes upon an alien culture and may become self-estranged in the process of assimilation. In any case, their turn-

over and "failure rate" were known to be much higher than those of men in entry and early grade positions; in the sales function, women's turnover was twice that of men. What happened around Indsco women resembled other reports of the experiences of women in politics, law, medicine, or management who have been the few among many men.

At the same time, they also echoed the experiences of people of any kind who are rare and scarce: the lone black among whites, the lone man among women, the few foreigners among natives. Any situation where proportions of significant types of people are highly skewed can produce similar themes and processes. It was rarity and scarcity, rather than femaleness *per se,* that shaped the environment for women in the parts of Indsco mostly populated by men.

The situations of Industrial Supply Corporation men and women, then, point to the significance of numerical distributions for behavior in organizations: how many of one social type are found with how many of another. As proportions begin to shift, so do social experiences.

THE MANY AND THE FEW: THE SIGNIFICANCE OF PROPORTIONS FOR SOCIAL LIFE

Georg Simmel's classic analysis of the significance of numbers for social life argued persuasively that numerical shifts transform social interaction, as in the differences between two-person and three-person situations or between small and large groups.[1] But Simmel, and then later investigations

---

[1] Kurt H. Wolff, *The Sociology of Georg Simmel* (Glencoe, Illinois: Free Press, 1950).

in this tradition, dealt almost exclusively with the impact of absolute numbers, with group size as a determinant of form and process. We have no vocabulary for dealing with the effects of *relative* numbers, of *proportional* representation: the difference for individuals and groups that stem from particular numerical distributions of categories of people.

Yet questions of how many and how few confound any statements about the organizational behavior of special kinds of people. For example, certain popular conclusions and research findings about male-female relations or role potentials may turn critically on the issue of proportions. One study of mock jury deliberations found that men played proactive, task-oriented leadership roles, whereas women in the same groups tended to take reactive, emotional, and nurturant postures—supposed proof that traditional stereotypes reflect behavior realities. But, strikingly, *men far outnumbered women in all of the groups studied.* Perhaps it was the women's scarcity that pushed them into classical positions and the men's numerical superiority that encouraged them to assert task superiority. Similarly, the early kibbutzim, collective villages in Israel that theoretically espoused equality of the sexes but were unable to fully implement it, could push women into traditional service positions because there were *more than twice as many men as women.* Again, relative numbers interfered with a fair test of what men or women can "naturally" do, as it did in the case of the relatively few women in the upper levels

of Indsco. Indeed, recently Marcia Guttentag has found sex ratios in the population in general to be so important that they predict a large number of behavioral phenomena, from the degree of power women and men feel to the ways they cope with the economic and sexual aspects of their lives.[2]

To understand the dramas of the many and the few in the organization requires a theory and a vocabulary. Four group types can be identified on the basis of different proportional representations of kinds of people, as Figure 1 shows. *Uniform* groups have only one kind of person, one significant social type. The group may develop its own differentiations, of course, but groups called uniform can be considered homogeneous with respect to salient external master statuses such as sex, race, or ethnicity. Uniform groups have a typological ratio of 100:0. *Skewed* groups are those in which there is a large preponderance of one type over another, up to a ratio of perhaps 85:15. The numerically dominant types also control the group and its culture in enough ways to be labeled "dominants." The few of another type in a skewed group can appropriately be called "tokens," for, like the Indsco exempt women, they are often treated as representatives of their category, as symbols rather than individuals. If the absolute size of the skewed group is small, tokens can also be solos, the only one of their kind present; but even if there are two tokens in a skewed group, it is difficult for them to generate an alliance that can become powerful in the group, as we shall see later. Next, *tilted* groups begin to

2 On juries: Fred L. Strodtbeck and Richard D. Mann, "Sex Role Differentiation in Jury Deliberations," *Sociometry,* 19 (March 1956): pp. 3–11; and Fred L. Strodtbeck, Rita M. James, and Charles Hawkins, "Social Status in Jury Deliberations," *American Sociological Review,* 22 (1957) pp. 713–19. On the kibbutz: Lionel Tiger and Joseph Shepher, *Women in the Kibbutz* (New York: Harcourt, Brace Jovanovich, 1975), and my critique in terms of sex ratios, Rosabeth Moss Kanter, "Interpreting the Results of a Social Experiment," *Science,* 192 (14 May 1976): pp. 662–63. "Behavioral demography" as the study of population ratios: Marcia Guttentag, *Too Many Women* (New York: Basic Books, in press).

FIGURE 1 **THE STEREOTYPE CONTENT MODEL**

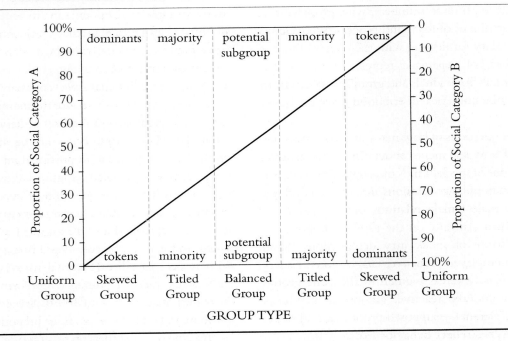

SOURCE: Author's compilation.

move toward less extreme distributions and less exaggerated effects. In this situation, with ratios of perhaps 65:35, dominants are just a "majority" and tokens become a "minority." Minority members have potential allies among each other, can form coalitions, and can affect the culture of the group. They begin to become individuals differentiated from each other as well as a type differentiated from the majority. Finally, at about 60:40 and down to 50:50, the group becomes *balanced*. Culture and interaction reflect this balance. Majority and minority turn into potential subgroups that may or may not generate actual type-based identifications. Outcomes for individuals in such a balanced peer group, regardless of type, will depend more on other structural and per-

sonal factors, including formation of subgroups or differentiated roles and abilities.

It is the characteristics of the second type, the skewed group, that underlay the behavior and treatment of professional and managerial women observed at Indsco. If the ratio of women to men in various parts of the organization begins to shift, as affirmative action and new hiring and promotion policies promised, forms of relationships and peer culture should also change. But as of the mid-1970s, the dynamics of tokenism predominated in Indsco's exempt ranks, and women and men were in the positions of token and dominant. Tokenism, like low opportunity and low power, set in motion self-perpetuating cycles that served to reinforce the low numbers of women and, in the absence of external intervention, to keep women in the position of token.

VIEWING THE FEW: WHY TOKENS FACE SPECIAL SITUATIONS

The proportional rarity of tokens is associated with three perceptual tendencies: visibility, contrast, and assimilation. These are all derived simply from the ways any set of objects are perceived. If one sees nine X's and one 0:

X X x x X X 0 X x X

the 0 will stand out. The 0 may also be overlooked, but if it is seen at all, it will get more notice than any X. Further, the X's may seem more alike than different because of their contrast with the 0. And it will be easier to assimilate the 0 to generalizations about all 0's than to do the same with the X's, which offer more examples and thus, perhaps, more variety and individuation. The same perceptual factors operate in social situations, and they generate special pressures for token women.

First, tokens get attention. One by one, they have higher visibility than dominants looked at alone; they capture a larger awareness share. A group member's awareness share, averaged over other individuals of the same social type, declines as the proportion of total membership occupied by the category increases, because each individual becomes less and less surprising, unique, or noteworthy. In Gestalt psychology terms, those who get to be common more easily become "ground" rather than "figure"; as the group moves from skewed to tilted, tokens turn into a less individually noticed minority. But for

tokens, there is a "law of increasing returns": as individuals of their type represent a *smaller* numerical proportion of the overall group, they each potentially capture a *larger* share of the awareness given to that group.

Contrast—or polarization and exaggeration of differences—is the second perceptual tendency. In uniform groups, members and observers may never become self-conscious about the common culture and type, which remain taken for granted and implicit. But the presence of a person or two bearing a different set of social characteristics increases the self-consciousness of the numerically dominant population and the consciousness of observers about what makes the dominants a class. They become more aware both of their commonalities and their difference from the token, and to preserve their commonality, they try to keep the token slightly outside, to offer a boundary for the dominants. There is a tendency to exaggerate the extent of the differences between tokens and dominants, because as we see next, tokens are, by definition, too few in numbers to defeat any attempts at generalization. It is thus easier for the commonalities of dominants to be defined in contrast to the token than in tilted or balanced groups. One person can be perceptually isolated and seen as cut off from the core of the group more than many, who begin to represent too great a share of what is called the group.

Assimilation, the third perceptual tendency, involves the use of stereotypes, or familiar generalizations about a person's social type. The characteristics of a token tend to be distorted to fit the generalization. Tokens are more easily stereotyped than people found in greater proportion. If there were enough people of the token's type to let discrepant examples occur, it is eventually possible that the generalization would change to accommodate the accumulated cases. But in skewed groups, it is easier to retain the generalization and distort the perception of the token. It is also easier for tokens to find an instant identity by conforming to the preexisting stereotypes. So tokens are, ironically, both highly visible as people who are different and yet not permitted the individuality of their own unique, non-stereotypical characteristics.

All of these phenomena occurred around the proportionally scarce women in Indsco, but there was, of course, no way to compare these same women's behavior and treatment when they were not in the token position. However, a clever and suggestive laboratory experiment showed that the same person may be perceived differently depending on whether he or she is a token in a skewed group or one of many in a balanced group. (Because the categories used in the experiment were black–white rather than male–female, it also demonstrated the generality of such perceptual tendencies beyond token women.) Shelley Taylor and Susan Fiske played a tape of a group discussion to subjects while showing them pictures of the "group," and then asked them for their impressions of group members on a number of dimensions. The tape was the same for all subjects, but the purported composition of the group varied. The pictures illustrated either an otherwise all-white male group with one black man (the "token" condition) or a mixed black–white male group. In the token condition, disproportionate attention was paid to the token, his prominence in the group was overemphasized, and his attributes were exaggerated. Similarly, the token was perceived as playing out special roles in the group, often highly stereotypical ones. By contrast, in "integrated" groups, subjects recalled no more about blacks than whites, and their attributes were evaluated about the same.[3]

Visibility, contrast, and assimilation are each associated with particular forces and dynamics that, in turn, generate typical token responses. These dynamics are, again, similar regardless of the category from which the tokens come, although the specific kinds of people and their history of relationships with dominants provide cultural content for specific communications. Visibility tends to create *performance pressures* on the token. Contrast leads to heightening of *dominant culture boundaries,* including isolation of the token. And assimilation results in the token's *role encapsulation.*

The experiences of exempt women at Industrial Supply Corporation took their shape from these processes.

PERFORMANCE PRESSURES: LIFE IN THE LIMELIGHT

Indsco's upper-level women, especially those in sales, were highly visible, much more so than their male peers. Even those who reported they felt ignored and overlooked were known in their immediate divisions and spotted when they did something unusual. But the ones who felt ignored also seemed to be those in jobs not enmeshed in the interpersonal structure of the company: for

3 Shelley E. Taylor and Susan Fiske, "The Token in the Small Group: Research Findings and Theoretical Implications," in *Psychology and Politics,* J. Sweeney, ed. (New Haven: Yale University Press, 1976).

example, a woman in public relations who had only a clerical assistant reporting to her and whose job did not occupy a space in the competitive race to the top.

In the sales force, where peer culture and informal relations were most strongly entrenched, everyone knew about the women. They were the subject of conversation, questioning, gossip, and careful scrutiny. Their placements were known and observed through the division, whereas those of most men typically were not. Their names came up at meetings, and they would easily be used as examples. Travelers to locations with women in it would bring back news of the latest about the women, along with other gossip. In other functions, too, the women developed well-known names, and their characteristics would often be broadcast through the system in anticipation of their arrival in another office to do a piece of work. A woman swore in an elevator in an Atlanta hotel while going to have drinks with colleagues, and it was known all over Chicago a few days later that she was a "radical." And some women were even told by their managers that they were watched more closely than the men. Sometimes the manager was intending to be helpful, to let the woman know that he would be right there behind her. But the net effect was the same as all of the visibility phenomena. Tokens typically performed their jobs under public and symbolic conditions different from those of dominants.

The Two-Edged Sword of Publicity

The upper-level women became public creatures. It was difficult for them to do anything in training programs, on their jobs, or even at informal social affairs that would not attract

public notice. This provided the advantage of an attention-getting edge at the same time that it made privacy and anonymity impossible. A saleswoman reported: "I've been at sales meetings where all the trainees were going up to the managers—'Hi, Mr. So-and-So'—trying to make that impression, wearing a strawberry tie, whatever, something that they could be remembered by. Whereas there were three of us [women] in a group of fifty, and all we had to do was walk in and everyone recognized us."

But their mistakes or their intimate relationships were known as readily as other information. Many felt their freedom of action was restricted, and they would have preferred to be less noticeable, as these typical comments indicated: "If it seems good to be noticed, wait until you make your first major mistake." "It's a burden for the manager who gets asked about a woman and has to answer behind-the-back stuff about her. It doesn't reach the woman unless he tells her. The manager gets it and has to deal with it." "I don't have as much freedom of behavior as men do; I can't be as independent."

On some occasions, tokens were deliberately thrust into the limelight and displayed as showpieces, paraded before the corporation's public but in ways that sometimes violated the women's sense of personal dignity. One of Indsco's most senior women, a staff manager finally given two assistants (and thus managerial responsibilities) after twenty-six years with the company, was among the five women celebrated at the civic lunch for outstanding women in business. A series of calls from high-level officers indicated that the chairman of the board of the corporation wanted her to attend a lunch at a large hotel that day, although she was given no information about the nature of the event. When she threatened not to go unless she was given more information, she was reminded that the invitation had come down from the chairman himself, and of course she would go. On the day of the luncheon, a corsage arrived and, later, a vice-president to escort her. So she went, and found she was there to represent the corporation's "prize women," symbolizing the strides made by women in business. The program for the affair listed the women executives from participating companies, except in the case of Indsco, where the male vice-presidential escorts were listed instead. Pictures were taken for the employee newsletter and, a few days later, she received an inscribed paper-weight as a memento. She told the story a few weeks after the event with visible embarrassment about being "taken on a date. It was more like a senior prom than a business event." And she expressed resentment at being singled out in such a fashion, "just for being a woman at Indsco, not for any real achievement." Similar sentiments were expressed by a woman personnel manager who wanted a pay increase as a sign of the company's appreciation, not her picture in a newspaper, which "gave the company brownie points but cost nothing."

Yet the senior woman had to go, the personnel manager had to have her picture taken, and they had to be gracious and grateful. The reaction of tokens to their notice was also noticed. Many of the tokens seemed to have developed a capacity often observed among marginal or subordinate peoples: to project a public persona that hid inner feelings. Although some junior management men at Indsco, including several fast trackers, were quite open about their lack of commitment to the company and dissatisfaction with aspects of its style, the women felt they could not afford

to voice any negative sentiments. They played by a different set of rules, one that maintained the split between public persona and private self. One woman commented, "I know the company's a rumor factory. You must be careful how you conduct yourself and what you say to whom. I saw how one woman in the office was discussed endlessly, and I decided it would be better to keep my personal life and personal affairs separate." She refused to bring dates to office parties when she was single, and she did not tell anyone at work that she got married until several months later—this was an office where the involvement of wives was routine. Because the glare of publicity meant that no private information could be kept circumscribed or routine, tokens were forced into the position of keeping secrets and carefully contriving a public performance. They could not afford to stumble.

Symbolic Consequences

The women were visible as category members, because of their social type. This loaded all of their acts with extra symbolic consequences and gave them the burden of representing their category, not just themselves. Some women were told outright that their performances could affect the prospects of other women in the company. In the men's informal conversations, women were often measured by two yardsticks: how *as women* they carried out the sales or management role; and how *as managers* they lived up to images of womanhood. In short, every act tended to be evaluated beyond its meaning for the organization and taken as a sign of "how women perform." This meant that there was a tendency for problematic situations to be blamed on the woman—on her category membership—rather than on the situation, a phenomenon noted in other reports of few women among many men in high-ranking corporate jobs. In one case of victim-blaming, a woman in sales went to her manager to discuss the handling of a customer who was behaving seductively. The manager jumped to the assumption that the woman had led him on. The result was an angry confrontation between woman and manager in which she thought he was incapable of seeing her apart from his stereotypes, and he said later he felt misunderstood.

Women were treated as symbols or representatives on those occasions when, regardless of their expertise or interest, they would be asked to provide the meeting with "the woman's point of view" or to explain to a manager why he was having certain problems with his women. They were often expected to be speaking for women, not just for themselves, and felt, even in my interviews, that they must preface personal statements with a disclaimer that they were speaking for themselves rather than for women generally. Such individuality was difficult to find when among dominants. But this was not always generated by dominants. Some women seized this chance to be a symbol as an opportunity to get included in particular gatherings or task forces, where they could come to represent all women at Indsco. "Even if you don't want *me* personally," they seemed to be saying to dominants, "you can want me as a symbol." Yet, if they did this, they would always be left with uncertainty about the grounds for their inclusion; they were failing to distinguish themselves as individuals.

Women also added symbolic consequences to each other's affairs. Upper-level women were scrutinized by those on a lower level, who dis-cussed the merits of things done by the higher-ranking women and considered them to have implications for their own careers. One woman manager who was passed over for a promotion in her department was the subject of considerable discussion by other women, who felt she should have pushed to get the opening and complained when she did not.

The extension of consequences for those in token statuses may increase their self-consciousness about their self-presentation and about their decisions, and can change the nature of the decisions that get made. Decisions about what to wear and who to sit with at lunch are not casual. One executive woman knew that her clothing and leisure choices would have impact. She deliberately wore pants one day as she walked through an office—not her own—of female clerks supervised by a man who wanted them to wear dresses, and she noted that a few women cautiously began to wear pants occasionally. She decided to let it be known that she was leaving at four p.m. for ballet lessons once a week, arguing that the men at her level did the same thing to play golf, but also knowing that ballet was going to have a very different meaning from golf. Her act was a gesture performed with an audience in mind as much as an expression of preference. The meaning of "natural" in such situations is problematic, for in doing what they might find natural as private beings, tokens as public personae are also sending messages to the organization.

Business as well as personal decisions were handled by tokens with an awareness of their extended symbolic consequences. One woman manager was faced with the dilemma of deciding what to do about a woman assistant who wanted to go back to the secretarial ranks from which she had recently been promoted. The manager felt she jeopardized her own claims for mobility and the need to open the system to more women if she let her assistant return and had to admit that a woman who was given opportunity had failed. She spent much more time on the issue than a mere change of assistants would have warranted, going privately to a few men she trusted at the officer level to discuss the situation. She also kept the assistant on much longer than she felt was wise, but she thought herself trapped.

Sometimes the thought of the symbolic as well as personal consequences of acts led token women to outright distortions. One was an active feminist in a training staff job who, according to her own reports, "separated what I say for the cause from what I want for myself." Her secret ambition was to leave the corporation within a year or two to increase her own professional skills and become an external consultant. But when discussing her aspirations with her own manager in career reviews or with peers on informal occasions, she always smiled and said, "Chairman of the board of Industrial Supply Corporation." Every time a job at the grade level above her became vacant, she would inquire about it and appear to be very interested, making sure that there was some reason at the last minute she could not take it. "They are watching me," she explained, "to see if women are really motivated or if they will be content to stay in low-level jobs. They are expecting me to prove something one way or the other."

The Tokenism Eclipse

The token's visibility stemmed from characteristics—attributes of a master status—that threatened to blot out other aspects of a token's performance. Although the token captured attention, it was often for her discrepant characteristics, for the auxiliary traits that gave her token status. The token does not have to work hard to have her presence noticed, but she does have to work hard to have her achievements noticed. In the sales force, the women found that their technical abilities were likely to be eclipsed by their physical appearances, and thus, an additional performance pressure was created. The women had to put in extra effort to make their technical skills known, and said they worked twice as hard to prove their competence.

"Both male peers and customers could tend to forget information women provided about their experiences and credentials while noticing and remembering such secondary attributes as style of dress. For example, there was this report from a salesman: "Some of our competition, like ourselves, have women sales people in the field. It's interesting that when you go in to see a purchasing agent, what he has to say about the woman sales person. It is always what kind of a body she had or how good-looking she is or "Boy, are you in trouble on this account now." They don't tell you how good-looking your competitors are if they're males, but I've never heard about a woman's technical competence or what kind of a sales person she was—only what her body was like." And a saleswoman complained in an angry outburst, "There are times when I would rather say to a man, 'Hey, listen, you can have our bodies and look like a female and have the advantage of walking in the room and being noticed.' But the noticeability also has attached to it that surprise on the part of men that you can talk and talk intelligently. Recognition works against you as well as for you." And another: "Some of the attention is nice, but some of it is demeaning to a professional. When a man gets a job, they don't tell him he's better looking than the man who was here before—but they say that to me." The focus on appearance and other non–ability traits was an almost direct consequence of the presence of very few women.

Fear of Retaliation

The women were also aware of another performance pressure: not to make the dominants look bad. Tokenism sets up a dynamic that can make tokens afraid of being too outstanding in performance on group events and tasks. When a token does well enough to "show up" a dominant, it cannot be kept a secret, since all eyes are upon the token, and therefore, it is more difficult to avoid the public humiliation of a dominant. Thus, paradoxically, while the token women felt they had to do better than anyone else in order to be seen as competent and allowed to continue, they also felt, in some cases, that their successes would not be rewarded and should be kept to themselves. They needed to toe the fine line between doing just well enough and too well. One woman had trouble understanding this and complained of her treatment by managers. They had fired another woman for not being aggressive enough, she reported; yet she, who succeeded in doing all they asked and brought in the largest amount of new business during the past year, was criticized for being "too aggressive, too much of a hustler."

The fears had some grounding in reality. In a corporate bureaucracy like Indsco, where "peer acceptance" held part of the key to success in securing promotions and prized jobs ★ ★ ★, it was known how people were received by colleagues as well as by higher management. Indeed, men down the ranks resented the tendency for some top executives to make snap judgments about people after five minutes' worth of conversation and then try to influence their career reviews and create instant stars. So the emphasis on peer acceptance in performance evaluations, a concept known to junior managers, was one way people lower down the managerial hierarchy retained some control over the climbing process, ensured themselves a voice, and maintained a system they felt was equitable, in which people of whom they approved had a greater chance for success. Getting along well with peers was thus not just something that could make daily life in the company more pleasant; it was also fed into the formal review system.

At a meeting of ten middle managers, two women who differed in peer acceptance were contrasted. One was well liked by her peers even though she had an outstanding record because she did not flaunt her successes and modestly waited her turn to be promoted. She did not trade on her visibility. Her long previous experience in technical work served to certify her and elicit colleague respect, and her pleasant but plain appearance and quiet dress minimized disruptive sexual attributes. The other was seen very differently. The mention of her name as a "star performer" was accompanied by laughter and these comments: "She's infamous all over the country. Many dislike her who have never met her. Everyone's heard of her whether or not they know her, and they already have opinions. There seems to be no problem with direct peer acceptance from people who see her day-to-day, but the publicity she has received for her successes has created a negative climate around her." Some thought she was in need of a lesson for her cockiness and presumption. She was said to be aspiring too high, too soon, and refusing to play the promotion game by the same rules the men had to use: waiting for one's turn, the requisite years' experience and training. Some men at her level found her over-rated and were concerned that their opinions be heard before she was automatically pushed ahead. A common prediction was that she would fail in her next assignment and be cut down to size. The managers, in general, agreed that there was back-lash if women seemed to advance too fast.

And a number of men were concerned that women would jump ahead of them. They made their resentments known. One unwit-tingly revealed a central principle for the suc-cess of tokens in competition with dominants: to always stay one step behind, never exceed or excell. "It's okay for women to have these jobs," he said, "as long as they don't go zooming by *me*."

One form peer retaliation against success took was to abandon a successful woman the first time she encountered problems. A dramatic instance involved a confrontation between a very digni-fied woman manager, the only woman in a man-agement position in her unit, who supervised a large group of both male and female work-ers, and an aggressive but objectively low-performing woman subordinate, who had been hired by one of the other managers and was unof-ficially "sponsored" by him. The woman man-ager had given low ratings to the subordinate on her last performance appraisal, and another review was coming up; the manager had already indicated that the rating would still be low, despite strong protests of unfairness from the worker. One day after work, the manager walked through a public lounge area where several workers were stand-ing around, and the subordinate began to hurl invectives at her, accusing her of being a "bitch, a

stuck-up snob," and other unpleasant labels. The manager stood quietly, maintaining her dignity, then left the room, fearing physical violence. Her feelings ranged from hurt to embarrassment at the public character of the scene and the talk it would cause. The response over the next few days from her male peers ranged from silence to com-ments like, "The catharsis was good for X. She needed to get that off her chest. You know, you never *were* responsive to her." A male friend told the manager that he heard two young men who were passed over for the job she was eventually given commenting on the event: "So Miss High-and-Mighty finally got hers!" The humiliation and the thought that colleagues supported the worker rather than her was enough to make this otherwise-successful woman consider leaving the corporation.

Tokens' Responses to Performance Pressures

A manager posed the issue for scarce women this way: "Can they survive the organizational scru-tiny?" The choices for those in the token posi-tion were either to over-achieve and carefully construct a public performance that minimized organizational and peer concerns, to try to turn the notoriety of publicity to advantage, or to find ways to become socially invisible. The first course means that the tokens involved are already out-standing and exceptional, able to perform well under close observation where others are ready to notice first and to attribute any problems to the characteristics that set them apart—but also able to develop skills in impressions management that permit them to retain control over the extra consequences loaded onto their acts. This choice involved creating a delicate balance between always doing well and not generating peer resentment. Such dexterity requires both job-related competence and political sensitivity that could take years to acquire. For this reason, young women just out of college had the greatest difficulty in entering male domains like the Indsco sales force and were responsible for much of the high turnover among women in sales. Women were successful, on the other hand, who were slightly older than their male peers, had strong technical backgrounds, and had already had previous experiences as token women among male peers. The success of such women was most likely to increase the prospects for hiring more women in the future; they worked for themselves and as symbols.

The second strategy, accepting notoriety and trading on it, seemed least likely to succeed in a corporate environment because of the power of peers. A few women at Indsco flaunted themselves in the public arena in which they operated and made a point out of demonstrating their "difference," as in refusing to go to certain programs, parading their high-level connections, or by-passing the routine authority structure. Such boldness was usually accompanied by top management sponsorship. But this strategy was made risky by shifting power alliances at the top; the need to secure peer cooperation in certain jobs where negotiation, bargaining, and the power of others to generate advantage or disadvantage through their use of the rules were important; and the likelihood that some current peers would eventually reach the top. Furthermore, those women who sought publicity and were getting it in part for their rarity developed a stake in not sharing the spotlight. They enjoyed their only-women status, since it gave them an advantage, and they seemed less consciously aware than the other women of the attendant dangers, pressures, psychic costs, and disadvantages. In a few instances, they operated so as to keep other women out by excessive criticism of possible new-hires or by subtly undercutting a possible woman peer (who eventually left the company), something that, we shall see later, was also pushed for by the male dominants. Thus, this second strategy eventually kept the numbers of women down both because the token herself was in danger of not succeeding and because she might keep other women out. This second strategy, then, serves to reinforce the dynamics of tokenism by ensuring that, in the absence of external pressures like affirmative action, the group remains skewed.

The third choice was more often accepted by the older generation of corporate women, who predated the women's movement and had years ago accommodated to token status. It involved attempts to limit visibility, to become "socially invisible." This strategy characterizes women who try to minimize their sexual attributes so as to blend unnoticeably into the predominant male culture, perhaps by adopting "mannish dress," as in reports by other investigators. Or it can include avoidance of public events and occasions for performance—staying away from meetings, working at home rather than in the office, keeping silent at meetings. Several of the saleswomen deliberately took such a "low profile," unlike male peers who tended to seize every opportunity to make themselves noticed. They avoided conflict, risks, or controversial situations. They were relieved or happy to step into assistant or technical staff jobs such as personnel administration or advertising, where they could quietly play background roles that kept men in the visible forefront—or they at least did not object when the corporation put them into low-visibility jobs, since for many years the company had a stake in keeping its "unusual" people hidden.

Those women preferring or accepting social invisibility also made little attempt to make their achievements publicly known or to get credit for their own contributions to problem-solving or other organizational tasks, just like other women reported in the research literature who have let men assume visible leadership or take credit for accomplishments that the women really produced—the upper corporate equivalent of the achieving secretary. In one remarkable laboratory experiment, women with high needs for dominance, paired with a man in a situation where they had to choose a leader, exercised their dominance by *appointing him* the leader.[4] Women making this choice, then, did blend into the background and control their performance pressures, but at the cost of limited recognition of their competence. This choice, too, involved a psychic splitting, for rewards for such people often came with secret knowledge—knowing what they had contributed almost anonymously to an effort that made someone else look good. In general, this strategy, like the last, also reinforces the existence of tokenism and keeps the numbers of women down, because it leads the organization to conclude that women are not very effective: low risk-takers who cannot stand on their own.

The performance pressures on people in token positions generate a set of attitudes and behaviors that appear sex-linked, in the case of women, but can be understood better as situational responses, true of any person in a token role. Perhaps what has been called in the popular literature "fear of success in women," for example, is really the token woman's *fear of visibility*. The original research that identified the fear of success concept created a hypothetical situation in which a woman was at the top of her class in medical school—a token woman in a male peer group. Such a situation is the kind that exacts extra psychic costs and creates pressures for some women to make themselves and their achievements invisible—to deny success. Replication of this research using examples of settings in which women were not so clearly proportionately scarce produced very different results and failed to confirm the sex-linked nature of this construct. Seymour Sarason also pointed out that minorities of any kind, trying to succeed in a culturally alien environment, may fear visibility because of retaliation costs and, for this reason, may try to play down any recognition of their presence, as did Jews at Yale for many years.[5] Fear of visibility, then, is one response to performance pressures in a token's situation. The token must often choose between trying to limit visibility—and being overlooked—or taking advantage of the publicity—and being labeled a "troublemaker."

★ ★ ★

---

4 Margaret Hennig, *Career Development for Women Executives,* Unpublished Doctoral Dissertation, Harvard Business School, 1970, p. vi–21. The experimental study of high-dominance women was Edwin I. Megaree, "Influence of Sex Roles on the Manifestation of Leadership," *Journal of Applied Psychology,* 53 (1969): pp. 377–82. Cynthia Epstein's book is *Woman's Place* (Berkeley: University of California Press, 1970). See also Edith M. Lynch, *The Executive Suite: Feminine Style* (New York: AMACOM, 1973); Margaret Cussler, *The Woman Executive* (New York: Harcourt, Brace, 1958).

5 See Adeline Levine and Janice Crumrine, "Women and the Fear of Success: A Problem in Replication," *American Journal of Sociology,* 80 (January 1975): pp. 967–74. Seymour Sarason's argument is in his "Jewishness, Blackness, and the Nature-Nurture Controversy," *American Psychologist,* 28 (November 1973): pp. 962–71.

24

Occupational Sex Segregation: Persistence and Change*

BARBARA RESKIN AND PATRICIA ROOS

Early in the 1980s the media took notice of a new phenomenon: women's marked progress into occupations traditionally reserved for men. Commenting on newly published data from the Department of Labor and the Bureau of the Census, media accounts such as Frank Prial's were quick to portray women's gains in "men's" occupations as dramatic:

> An increasing number of women in the United States are working at what used to be men's jobs. Despite the unemployment rate, the number of women working [for wages] in the United States has risen 21 million, or 95 percent, over the last two decades, according to a new study by the United States Department of Labor, and many of the jobs they have taken are in categories once largely the province of men. (Prial, 1982)

---

* First published in 1990; from *Job Queues, Gender Queues: Explaining Women's Inroads into Male Occupations*.

Front-page stories in leading newspapers announced women's advancement in such occupations as executive, lawyer, pharmacist, physician, veterinarian, bartender, bus driver, and baker ★ ★ ★. By 1980, for example, women represented nearly half of all bus drivers and bartenders. Moreover, as Prial noted, women had become the majority in six formerly male-dominated occupations: insurance adjusters, examiners, and investigators; bill collectors; real estate agents and brokers; photographic process workers; checkers, examiners, and inspectors; and production-line assemblers.

Published 1980 census data indeed confirmed that women had posted disproportionate gains during the 1970s in some predominantly male occupations ★ ★ ★. But close inspection of the data suggests that media accounts of women's *progress* were exaggerated—women's representational gains exceeded their growth in the labor force as a whole in only a small number of the detailed occupations for which the Census Bureau collects data, and they even lost ground in a few occupations such as heavy-equipment mechanics, lathe and turning-machine operators, and production testers (U.S. Bureau of the Census, 1984).

The phenomenon underlying these news stories and census data is the segregation of the sexes into different lines of work. Occupational sex segregation is one of the most enduring features of the U.S. labor market ★ ★ ★. As Table 1 confirms, in 1980 substantial differentiation by sex existed at the level of aggregated occupational categories. Men tend to be overrepresented in managerial and craft occupations, traditionally the best paid of the white-collar and blue-collar workforces, respectively. They also predominate

in transport operative and laboring occupations. Women are the clear majority in service occupations and in administrative-support occupations because of their predominance in clerical jobs. They are also slightly overrepresented in professional occupations because of their preponderance in the typically lower-paid female *semi*professions such as nursing, library work, social work, and teaching.

Table 1 reveals another fundamental feature of the U.S. occupational structure—its segregation by race. Blacks, whether male or female, are less likely than whites to command well-paid managerial or professional jobs. Similarly, relative to white men, black men have garnered few of the better-paid blue-collar craft occupations. Compared with white women, black women are underrepresented in sales and administrative-support occupations. Instead, blacks of both sexes are overrepresented in service, operative, and laborer occupations. Like sex segregation, race segregation is problematic because it relegates blacks to the most poorly paid occupational sectors and hence helps to perpetuate the wage disparity between blacks and whites.

The segregation of the U.S. occupational structure by race and sex extends back to the turn of the century. Gross (1968), for example, found that occupational segregation by sex, as measured by the index of segregation, remained essentially constant between 1900 and 1960, reflecting the unusual persistence of this social phenomenon ★ ★ ★. Table 2 updates Gross's occupational segregation indexes across major census groups for both sex and race between 1940 and 1981. The data reveal that occupational segregation by race declined sharply after World War II, especially for women. Nonwhite women, 81 percent of whom

TABLE 1 OCCUPATIONAL DISTRIBUTION OVER MAJOR OCCUPATIONAL GROUPS, BY SEX AND RACE, CIVILIAN LABOR FORCE, 1980

Occupational Group	Men			Women			Percent Female
	Total[a]	White[b]	Black	Total[a]	White[b]	Black	
Executive, administrative, managerial	12.1	13.2	5.4	7.2	7.7	4.5	30.5
Professional specialty	10.5	11.2	5.6	13.7	14.4	11.2	49.1
Technicians and related support	2.9	3.0	1.8	3.0	3.1	3.2	43.8
Sales occupations	8.8	9.6	3.9	11.3	12.2	6.5	48.7
Administrative support, including clerical	6.7	6.5	9.0	30.7	31.9	25.2	77.1
Service occupations	9.4	8.2	17.0	18.2	16.4	29.3	58.9
Farming, forestry, fishing	4.3	4.2	3.4	1.0	1.0	.6	14.9
Precision production, craft, repair	21.0	21.7	15.5	2.4	2.3	2.4	7.8
Machine operators, assemblers, inspectors	10.0	9.2	15.1	9.3	8.1	13.0	40.7
Transportation and material moving	7.5	7.2	11.0	.9	.9	1.0	7.8
Handlers, equipment cleaners, helpers, laborers	6.8	6.0	12.3	2.3	2.0	3.2	19.8
TOTAL[c]	100.0	100.0	100.0	100.0	100.0	100.1	42.5

[a]All races.
[b]Whites of Hispanic background not included.
[c]Sample sizes: 59,625,553 (total men), 49,633,442 (white men), 5,161,234 (black men), 44,092,523 (total women), 35,624,861 (white women), 5,058,243(black women).
SOURCE: U.S. Department of Labor, Employment and Training Administration (1982:1).

are black (U.S. Department of Labor, Employment and Training Administration, 1982:1), have gone a long way toward reducing the occupational gap between themselves and white women. However, *nonwhite women* continue to lag far behind *white men*.

★ ★ ★ Occupational *sex* segregation has been more resistant to change than race segre-gation. Despite revolutionary transformations in the industrial and occupational structures, and changes in the composition of the labor force, the degree of occupational sex segregation among whites remained essentially constant between 1940 and 1970. During the same period, with black women's movement out of domestic work, occupational sex seg-

TABLE 2 **OCCUPATIONAL SEGREGATION INDEXES ACROSS MAJOR CENSUS CATEGORIES FOR SEX AND RACE, 1940–1981**

	1940	1950	1960	1970	1981
SEGREGATION BY SEX AMONG					
Whites	46	43	44	44	41
Blacks and others	58	50	52	49	39
SEGREGATION BY RACE AMONG					
Men	43	36	35	30	24
Women	62	52	45	30	17

SOURCES: For 1940–70, Treiman and Terrell (1975:167); for 1981, Reskin and Hartmann (1986:19).

regation among blacks declined to the level of whites. Beginning in the late 1960s another "revolution"—the women's liberation movement—promised to improve women's position in the workplace. By challenging social values, the feminist movement fostered and reinforced antidiscrimination regulations, thus opening to women the doors of some traditionally male occupations. As a consequence of these and other factors, the level of occupational segregation declined at a faster rate during the 1970s than in any other decade in this century ★ ★ ★. Nonetheless, the labor force remained segregated: in 1981 at least 39 percent of black women and 41 percent of white women would have had to change to a different major occupational category to achieve distributions identical to those of men of their race across broad occupational categories (Table 2).

Thus, the 1970s represented a watershed for sex segregation. For the first time in this century women made notable gains in some occupations in which men had typically predominated. However, the level of occupational sex segrega-

tion at the end of the decade remained high. In 1980 almost half of all women and 53 percent of men worked in occupations that were at least 80 percent women and men, respectively ★ ★ ★. Women made inroads into some "male" occupations but little or no progress in integrating most others. White women were more likely than black women to enter customarily male occupations, but black women and men did advance disproportionately into some sex- and race-atypical occupations ★ ★ ★.

The variability in women's increased representation in male occupations during the 1970s raises three important questions. First, how can we explain women's disproportionate movement into some traditionally male or mixed-sex occupations during a decade in which their advancement into most male occupations was modest at best? In other words, what factors facilitated women's movement into the particular occupations in which they made pronounced numerical inroads? Second, what forms did occupational feminization take? Did women's entry yield genuine sex integration within these desegregating occupations so that women and men did the same kinds of work? Finally, did women's integration bring them closer to economic equity with male incumbents in occupations that became more female during the 1970s? ★ ★ ★

The changing race composition of occupations since 1970 ★ ★ ★ raises similar questions, and they are equally pressing. As demonstrated in Table 1, the continued segregation of blacks in low paid, low-skill occupations ensures blacks' continuing economic disadvantage. At the outset we planned to examine changing patterns of both sex and race segregation, but the depth and complexity of our research methods soon convinced us that we could not encompass both in a single volume; hence, this study emphasizes the changing sex composition of occupations. Because we believe that our theoretical approach applies equally to understanding the changing race–sex composition of occupations, however, we plan to examine that question in future work.

★ ★ ★

What led to the feminization of the customarily male occupations our research team studied? In answering that question, this chapter develops a theoretical model of occupational feminization. We begin our task by outlining a model of occupational composition that accounts for the uneven distribution of groups across occupations and hence, specifically, how occupations' sex compositions change. The most fruitful model sees occupational composition as the result of a *dual-queueing* process: *labor queues* order groups of workers in terms of their attractiveness to employers, and *job queues* rank

jobs in terms of their attractiveness to workers. Identifying how and why employers order workers within labor queues and workers rank occupations within job queues—and how these factors have changed since 1970—tells part of the story of why some customarily male and mixed-sex occupations have feminized. How the "shapes" of the two queues have changed to provide some groups with jobs that were formerly beyond their reach completes the story.

The queueing perspective is a powerful lens that makes sense of seemingly disparate results from our case studies. It encompasses a wide range of phenomena, elucidates puzzling findings, and predicts future patterns. Because we rely heavily on the queueing perspective in this chapter ★ ★ ★, we begin by examining queueing processes.

||| LABOR MARKETS AS QUEUES

Lester Thurow (1969:48) was the first social scientist to characterize the labor market explicitly as a labor queue. Blacks, Thurow hypothesized, experienced more unemployment than whites because employers ranked them below whites in the labor queue. In recognizing that the labor market functions as if it comprised ordered elements, Thurow formalized what others had already remarked. As early as 1929, a Women's Bureau bulletin (U.S. Department of Labor, Women's Bureau, 1929:13; cited in Strober and Catanzarite, 1988:10) stated:

> The history of . . . women workers in New England textile mills . . . show[s] a picture typical of such occupational changes. . . . The

moving of the New England girls of the old stock out of the mills into higher-grade occupations, and the filling of the vacant posts by Irish women, had become common enough in the latter half of the [eighteen] forties.

In examining race differences in labor market outcomes, Thurow and his successors focused on the *labor* queue. Yet implicit in the New England girls' move from the mills into higher-grade occupations is a second queue—a *job* queue that represents workers' rankings of jobs. Rotella (1981) and Strober (1984:150) and her colleagues (Strober and Arnold, 1987a:117; Catanzarite and Strober, 1988) recognized the importance of job queues, although they did not designate them as such. Rotella explained the feminization of clerical work partly in terms of the attractiveness of clerical jobs relative to women's alternatives, and Strober and her colleagues posited more generally that society grants men first choice of jobs and that men select the most attractive ones available. Job queues and labor queues govern labor market outcomes: employers hire workers from as high in the labor queue as possible, and workers accept the best jobs available to them. As a result the best jobs go to the most preferred workers, and less attractive jobs go to workers lower in the labor queue; bottom-ranked workers may go jobless, and the worst jobs may be left unfilled.

Historical accounts and studies of upwardly mobile groups bequeathing abandoned jobs to groups ranked below them illustrate the role of queueing in occupational succession. Also supporting queueing theory's applicability to labor market outcomes are statistical analyses of race differences in occupational distributions and unemployment ★ ★ ★. Thus, the research literature is consistent with the concept of labor and job queues jointly generating the uneven distribution of groups across occupations—in other words, occupational segregation.

The Structural Properties of Queues

Queues can be characterized by three structural properties: the *ordering of their elements* (that is, jobs, groups of workers), their *shape* (the relative sizes of various elements—population subgroups in the labor queue and occupations in the job queues), and the *intensity of rankers' preferences* (whether or not elements overlap). We argue below that changes in these properties redistribute groups across occupations.

By definition, queues are composed of ordered elements (occupations, jobs; subgroups of workers), and their ordering dictates which groups end up in which jobs. As Lieberson (1980:296) put it, if employers tend to favor group X, then the Xs will be concentrated in the best jobs and the non-Xs largely relegated to the least desirable ones.

The absolute and relative numbers of elements in a queue determine its shape. Thus, the number of prospective workers in each subgroup in a labor market sets the shape of the labor queue. Similarly, the number of jobs at each level in the job queue fixes its shape. Panels A and B of Figure 1 show how the shapes of labor and job queues can vary while their order remains constant. This variation influences each group's probable access to occupations of varying desirability and each occupation's chance of recruiting workers from particular groups. For example, in a society with relatively few workers in the preferred group (A2) and few very desirable jobs (for illustrative

FIGURE 1 **VARIATION IN THE SHAPE OF LABOR AND JOB QUEUES**

PANEL A. HYPOTHETICAL LABOR QUEUES ORDERED BY RACE FOR PREDOMINANTLY WHITE AND PREDOMINANTLY BLACK LABOR MARKETS

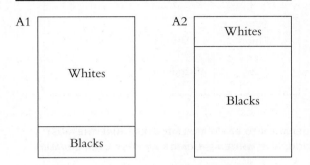

PANEL B. HYPOTHETICAL JOB QUEUES ORDERED BY NONMANUAL-MANUAL WORK FOR PREDOMINANTLY NON-MANUAL AND PREDOMINANTLY MANUAL OCCUPATIONAL STRUCTURES

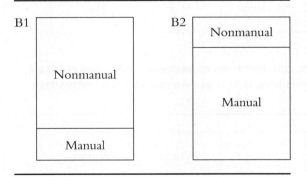

purposes, we consider nonmanual jobs preferable to manual jobs; see B2), preferred groups will monopolize the generally preferable jobs. A mismatch in the relative numbers of jobs and workers at corresponding levels of their respective queues means that some workers will get better or worse jobs than persons from their group normally garner. For example, when preferred jobs sharply

outnumber highly ranked workers, as in a situation characterized by panels A2 and B1, employers must fill some better jobs with workers from lower in the labor queue than usual. In contrast, when the job queue is bottom-heavy (as in B2), only the highest-ranked workers get desirable jobs, and workers moderately high in the labor queue must settle for less. As Lieberson (1980: 297) has shown, both the *absolute* and *relative* size of each group in the labor queue affects lower-ranked workers' chances of getting desirable jobs. The larger a subordinate group relative to the size of the preferred group, the harder employers find it to deny its members good jobs ★ ★ ★.

The intensity of raters' preferences is the third property of queues. For some employers, group membership is the paramount consideration in ordering the labor queue. When group membership is overriding, rankers invariably favor persons from the group they prefer, regardless of their qualifications; for example, some employers never hire blacks to supervise whites. Yet others are almost indifferent to group membership, using it only to break ties between otherwise equally qualified prospects. Figure 2 illustrates variation in the intensity of raters' preferences with respect to workers' race in three hypothetical labor queues. The space between the races in panel A depicts the ranking for employers who invariably hire the lowest-ranked white worker over the best black worker; the preferences for moderately qualified blacks over whites with low qualifications and for highly qualified blacks over whites with only moderate qualifications in panel B mean that raters' aversion to blacks, though weak, persists. Panel C illustrates an intermediate situation in which employers prefer average white workers over above-average

FIGURE 2 **VARIATION IN THE INTENSITY OF RATERS' PREFERENCES WITH RESPECT TO RACE: EMPLOYERS HIRE APPLICANTS FROM AS FAR RIGHT AS POSSIBLE**

PANEL A. RACIAL GROUP MEMBERSHIP IS AN OVERRIDING CONSIDERATION TO RANKERS. EMPLOYERS HIRE APPLICANTS AS QUALIFIED AS POSSIBLE BUT CHOOSE UNQUALIFIED WHITES BEFORE HIGHLY QUALIFIED BLACKS.

Blacks	Blacks	Blacks		Whites	Whites	Whites
Low	Moderate	High		Low	Moderate	High

Level of Qualification

PANEL B. RACIAL GROUP MEMBERSHIP IS A MINOR CONSIDERATION TO RANKERS. EMPLOYERS HIRE THE MOST QUALIFIED APPLICANTS BUT, WITHIN LEVELS OF QUALIFICATION, GIVE WHITE APPLICANTS AN EDGE OVER EQUALLY QUALIFIED BLACKS.

Blacks	Whites	Blacks	Whites	Blacks	Whites
Low	Low	Moderate	Moderate	High	High

Level of Qualification

PANEL C. RACIAL GROUP MEMBERSHIP IS AN INTERMEDIATE CONSIDERATION TO RANKERS. EMPLOYERS PREFER A MORE QUALIFIED WHITE TO A LESS QUALIFIED BLACK BUT WILL HIRE VERY QUALIFIED BLACKS OVER UNQUALIFIED WHITES.

Blacks	Blacks	Whites	Blacks	Whites	Whites
Low	Moderate	Low	High	Moderate	High

Level of Qualification

blacks but suppress racial biases to hire very talented blacks over mediocre whites.

Of course, workers' job preferences also vary in intensity. Some workers may have a categorical preference for any job in a high-ranked occupation over any work in what they perceive as a lower occupation (expressed, for example, in rejecting all manual jobs in favor of any nonmanual work). Others may be may be more attuned to specific job characteristics:

they may occasionally appropriate more desirable jobs within lower-ranked occupations that usually go to less preferred groups (for example, male nurses); or they may eschew jobs in occupations usually reserved for the preferred group (such as physicians in isolated rural communities), thereby making them available to workers from lower-ranked groups. We expect the former behavior from the lowest-ranked members of the preferred group (among men, for example, ethnic and racial minorities, immigrants, and inexperienced youth). The latter is most likely for nominally highly ranked occupations that are for other reasons undesirable.

Changing Occupational Composition and Queue Mismatches

Changes in size—of subgroups of workers or of various occupations—that create a mismatch between the number of workers at some level in a labor queue and the number of jobs in the corresponding level of the job queue can lead occupations' composition to change. When labor becomes scarce in top-ranked groups, either through job growth or a shrinkage in the number of customary workers, employers must be less choosy. Shortages spur occupations' composition to change because they force employers to resort to lower-ranked workers than they normally hire. For example, employers gave women semiskilled factory jobs at the end of the nineteenth century because the opportunity for freeholding, with its prospects for financial security, depleted the supply of men. Wars have often precipitated shortages of white male workers. At least since the Civil War, American minorities of both sexes and white women have won jobs that white men had dominated before

war service called them away. Nonwhite men and white women have been the first to benefit from employers' descent down their hierarchy of preference to fill white men's jobs. During World War I the shortage of male workers gave women a start in such diverse jobs as streetcar conducting, marketing, publishing, accounting, life insurance, and personnel relations. World War II replicated the process: employers hired women for traditionally male blue-collar jobs in retooled auto plants and for nonwar jobs such as bank telling and reporting ★ ★ ★. The jobs that white women and black men had abandoned for better opportunities trickled down to black women. For example, light manufacturing industries turned to black men only after they had "tap[ped] the reserve" of available white women, and they did not turn to black women until they ran out of black men (Weaver, 1946, cited in Strober and Catanzarite, 1988:11). Thus, labor shortages can create a chain of opportunities for progressively lower-ranked groups in the labor queue.

When a higher-ranked group expands—or the number of positions open to it shrinks—it spills over into jobs normally held by the less preferred. For example, as medical-school slots became scarce early in this century, schools that had been admitting women increasingly excluded them. More recently, when high unemployment in the early 1980s permitted the military to meet enlistment goals among young men, it cut female recruitment. Queueing ensures that workers from the lowest-ranked groups, as the last hired, are usually first to be fired, even without seniority rules. A shortage of jobs in occupations reserved for preferred workers or the emergence of desirable jobs in occupations usually allotted to lower-ranked workers can lead the former to usurp the latter's jobs. This is especially likely with jobs that high-ranked workers had formerly held. For example, white women, bumped from factory jobs by returning soldiers after World War I, displaced black women from domestic jobs ★ ★ ★. During the Great Depression men reclaimed banking, insurance, librarianship, and social work jobs that women had entered during World War I, and each time men have come marching home from military service, employers have restored the prewar sex (and race) composition of most occupations. However, not having held jobs in the past does not prevent higher-status groups from colonizing them if they become more attractive than "their own" jobs. For example, in Great Britain men moved into women's jobs in radiography after pay and working conditions improved ★ ★ ★. In the United States, since Title IX of the 1972 Educational Amendment raised the budgets of women's sports programs, men have been replacing female coaches for women's collegiate sports ★ ★ ★. Thus, while it is rare for men to take over female occupations, they may do so when those jobs are better than available male jobs.

How Employers Rank Male and Female Workers in Labor Queues

Before tackling the question of why labor queues change, we must take a moment to consider how employers rank workers. Classical economists contend that employers rank prospective workers in terms of potential productivity and labor costs. That these and other considerations transform the labor queue into a *gender queue* is evident in the high level of sex segregation in the workplace. Until recently, employers gave white men "first dibs" on most jobs (Strober, 1984). Thus, establishments with the most "good" jobs are the most sex and race segregated; occupations whose male workforce has grown faster than others pay best, offer more vocational training, demand less strength, and shelter incumbents from competition; and occupations' return on workers' human-capital investments is positively correlated with men's representation (Catanzarite and Strober, 1988). Of course, other factors affect employers' placement of groups of workers in the labor queue; marital and parental status also influence their evaluations of women workers, beyond any effects on women's performance.

Ever since they invented wage labor, employers have paid women less than men. Predominantly female occupations still pay less than male occupations, and men still, on average, outearn women. Recent data show that *within* many occupations women are paid about two-thirds of what men earn; in only a few does the wage ratio reach four-fifths. These disparities within occupations result largely from the segregation of women and men in different jobs, firms, and industries. Women's lower market wage not only "endear[s] them to employers" (Rotella, 1981:162); it sometimes has been a sufficient incentive for employers to rank women ahead of men and occasionally to replace male workers. A nineteenth-century student of industrialization explained that employers sought constantly to replace human labor altogether with machinery or to "diminish its cost by substituting the industry of women and children for that of men" (Scott, 1982). However, employers' preference for low-wage workers has seldom governed their ranking of the sexes. Instead, custom, the belief that women's lower productivity or other factors will offset their lower pay, and sex bias have led employers to place men ahead of women whom they could hire more cheaply. It is these factors that transform labor queues into gender queues. Let us examine the role each one plays.

First, sex labels that characterize jobs as "women's" or "men's" work influence day-to-day hiring and job assignments by affecting employers' notions of appropriate and inappropriate workers for particular jobs. The force of custom tends to blind employers to economically irrational decisions, at least until external events galvanize them to change.

Second, employers' difficulty in identifying productive workers leads them to resort to proxies such as educational attainment, experience, and group membership. Although various factors could generate differences in women's and men's productivity, sex often influences rankings through stereotypical beliefs that men outproduce women in "male" jobs because they are stronger, more rational, more mechanically adept, and so forth, or because women have higher absentee and turnover rates. Stereotypes supported by custom make employers reluctant to risk untried workers, especially for jobs involving uncertainty ★ ★ ★. In occupations in which observers can easily judge workers' performance, employers are less likely to act on group stereotypes about performance.

Third, some employers worry that male workers' negative response to female interlopers will reduce productivity or raise labor costs by increasing turnover, or lead men to demand higher wages to compensate them for working with women ★ ★ ★. Historically, like every group faced with competition from lower-paid workers, men have responded to the threat of female incursion with organized opposition: strikes, slowdowns, and on-the-job resistance. Of course, anticipated male opposition need not deter employers if enough qualified women are available to replace men, but employers can rarely feminize entire work teams. Seniority rules prevent their replacing experienced men; too few qualified women may be available; and employers may be unable to train women because male unions control training or because training takes too long. Moreover, if employers believe that the pool of women cannot meet their needs, especially for jobs that require substantial on-the-job training, they will not risk antagonizing male workers to hire women, even at bargain rates—especially if they harbor any doubt as to whether women can be as productive as men.

Fourth, some employers are not compelled to minimize wages. The level of competition they face and the share of all costs that wages constitute affect their incentive to find ways to cut wages. When labor makes up a large fraction of an organization's total costs, hiring cheaper workers can generate enough savings to compensate for opposition. In contrast, when labor constitutes a small part of all costs or when employers are buffered from concern with costs, they can ignore potential wage savings in positioning workers in the labor queue. Factors that buffer organizations from the need to minimize their wage bill include market dominance (Ashenfelter and Hannan, 1986), high profits, and nonprofit status. Rich enterprises may derive prestige from paying above-market wages and thus opt for costly workers over cheaper ones as "noneconomic amenities" (Stolzenberg, 1982; but see Rotella, 1987). Furthermore, as Jacobs (1989:180) noted, employers who pay premium wages to spur greater productivity are indifferent to the cost savings that women offer.

Finally, some employers willingly accept higher wages as the price for favoring men. The effect of bias on employers' rankings of the sexes is well established. Hartmann (1976) claimed that in preferring men for customarily male jobs, male employers seek to maintain male privileges inside as well as outside the workplace. Strober (1984, 1988; Catanzarite and Strober, 1988) proposed additional reasons for employers' preference for male workers: gender solidarity preserves sex-based privileges that all men enjoy, forestalls the possibility that women will eventually challenge owners' and managers' positions, and keeps employers in the good graces of their male friends and colleagues who demand preference for male workers even if it means a higher wage bill. To the extent that all employers abide by this patriarchal norm, Strober argued, none suffers a competitive disadvantage. Reskin (1988) advanced a more general explanation for men's monopoly of the most desirable jobs: men enforce segregation partly to sustain differentiation because it legitimates the larger sex–gender hierarchy from which almost all men benefit. Dispensing with sex differentiation at any level threatens it at every level, so ignoring sex in the labor queue challenges the advantaged positions of male employers and managers. As Cockburn (1988:41) put it, "Behind occupational segregation is gender differentiation, and behind that is male power." Of course, when labor costs are nontrivial and cutting costs is paramount, biases are less likely to affect rankings. For example, postbellum white southerners' aversion to integration did not prevent their hiring black teachers after they realized they could pay them much less than white teachers. When all employers share a bias—especially one that community values endorse—the disadvantage from the premiums they pay to hire preferred workers cancels out. Finally, even nondiscriminating employers can perpetuate discriminatory queues when they delegate hiring and job assignment to biased subordinates who lack the incentive to minimize labor costs.

In sum, expectations about performance and cost, the dictates of custom, and sex prejudice influence how employers rank the sexes within labor queues. Which considerations prevail depends partly on whether employers are insulated from economic considerations, whether performance is paramount and easily assessed, the strength of employers' biases, the cost of indulging them, and men's ability to raise the cost of employing women. Because employers tend to place greater weight on custom, stereotypes about sex differences in productivity, and anti-female or pro-male biases than they place on minimizing wages, labor queues typically operate as gender queues that favor men over women.

How Workers Rank Occupations in the Job Queue

We have emphasized the labor queue to stress employers' primary role in the labor market: ultimately, employers assign and withhold jobs. Obviously if we hope to explain groups' changing distributions across occupations, we must also specify how workers rank jobs—ranking expressed usually in their power to reject jobs. We devote less attention to this issue because readers—as past, present, and future workers—already understand this process. Most workers try to maximize income, social standing, autonomy, job security, congenial working conditions, interesting work, and the chance for advancement; and they rank occupations accordingly ★ ★ ★. Of course, specific groups (temporary migrant workers, students) may attach more or less importance to particular job attributes (job security, benefits) or prefer activities other than those sought by the majority, and these differences may lead to inconsistent rankings across groups (Lieberson, 1980).

For our purposes, the key question is whether women and men value different job characteristics. They rank income equally highly among job rewards ★ ★ ★ and differ little on why they judge a job to be good or prestigious. Some observers contend that women place a premium on jobs that are compatible with child rearing, but sociological research provides little support for the thesis that women's family roles lead them to choose different occupations than men do. Others have argued that some men value the capacity of exclusively male blue-collar occupations to confirm their masculinity. Although this claim enjoys anecdotal support, no evidence exists as to its importance relative to material rewards, and we suspect that men in low-paying or low-prestige jobs value maleness in jobs more than other men do.

In sum, job queues result from how workers rank jobs on a variety of characteristics on whose importance women and men generally agree. Overall, the sexes generally rank occupations similarly. Although many exceptions do exist, for the occupations we studied there is little question that women's rankings were similar to men's; women's increasing numbers in these occupations speak for themselves.

★ ★ ★

⫴ REFERENCES

Catanzarite, Lisa M., and Myra H. Strober. 1988. "Occupational Attractiveness and Race-Gender Segregation, 1960–1980." Paper presented at the annual meeting of the American Sociological Association, Atlanta, August.

Cockburn, Cynthia. 1988. "The Gendering of Jobs: Workplace Relations and the Reproduction of Sex Segregation." In Sylvia Walby, ed., *Gender Segregation at Work*, 29–42. Milton Keynes, U.K.: Open University Press.

Gross, Edward. 1968. "*Plus ça change. . . .* The Sexual Segregation of Occupations over Time." *Social Problems* 16:198–208.

Hartmann, Heidi I. 1976. "Capitalism, Patriarchy, and Job Segregation by Sex." *Signs* 1(3):137–70.

Jacobs, Jerry A. 1989. *Revolving Doors: Sex Segregation and Women's Careers*. Stanford, Calif.: Stanford University Press.

Lieberson, Stanley. 1980. *A Piece of the Pie*. Berkeley: University of California Press.

Prial, Frank J. 1982. "More Women Work at Traditional Male Jobs." *New York Times*, November 15, p. 1.

Reskin, Barbara F. 1988. "Bringing the Men Back In: Sex Differentiation and the Devaluation of Women's Work." *Gender & Society* 2 (March): 58–81.

Reskin, Barbara F., and Heidi I. Hartmann. 1986. *Women's Work, Men's Work: Sex Segregation on the Job*. Washington, D.C.: National Academy Press.

Rotella, Elyce. 1981 (1977). *From Home to Office: U.S. Women at Work, 1870–1930.* Ann Arbor, Mich.: UMI Research Press.

———. 1987. "Comments." In Clair Brown and Joseph Pechman, eds., *Gender in the Workplace*, 149–54. Washington, D.C.: Brookings Institution.

Scott, Joan Wallach. 1982. "The Mechanization of Women's Work." *Scientific American* 247 (September): 169–87.

Stolzenberg, Ross. 1982. "Industrial Profits and the Propensity to Employ Women Workers." Paper presented at the Workshop on Job Segregation, Women's Employment and Related Social Issues, National Research Council. Washington, D.C., May.

Strober, Myra H. 1984. "Toward a General Theory of Occupational Sex Segregation." In Barbara F. Reskin, ed., *Sex Segregation in the Workplace: Trends, Explanations, Remedies*, 144–56. Washington, D.C.: National Academy Press.

———. 1988. "The Processes of Occupational Segregation: Relative Attractiveness and Patriarchy." Paper presented at the meeting of the American Educational Research Association, New Orleans, April.

Strober, Myra H., and Carolyn L. Arnold. 1987a. "The Dynamics of Occupational Segregation among Bank Tellers." In Clair Brown and Joseph Pechman, eds., *Gender in the Workplace*, 107–48. Washington, D.C.: Brookings Institution.

———. 1987b. "Integrated Circuits/Segregated Labor: Women in Computer-Related Occupations and High-Tech Industries." In Heidi I. Hartmann, ed., *Computer Chips and Paper Clips: Technology and Women's Employment*, 2:136–82. Washington, D.C.: National Academy Press.

Strober, Myra H., and Lisa M. Catanzarite. 1988. "Changes in Black Women's Representation in Occupations and a Measure of the Relative Attractiveness of Occupations, 1960–1980." Paper presented at the meeting of the American Education Research Association, New Orleans, April.

Thurow, Lester. 1969. *Poverty and Discrimination.* Washington, D.C.: Brookings Institution.

Treiman, Donald J., and Kermit Terrell. 1975. "Women, Work, and Wages: Trends in the Female Occupational Structure since 1940." In Kenneth C. Land and Seymour Spilerman, eds., *Social Indicator Models*, 157–99. New York: Russell Sage Foundation.

U.S. Bureau of the Census. 1984. *1980 Census of Population: Detailed Occupation of the Experienced Civilian Labor Force by Sex for the United States and Regions, 1980 and 1970.* Supplementary Report PC80-S1-15. Washington, D.C.: Government Printing Office.

U.S. Department of Labor, Women's Bureau. 1929. *Negro Women in Industry in 15 States.* Bulletin 70. Washington, D.C.: Government Printing Office.

———. 1961. *Life Insurance Selling: Careers for Women as Life Underwriters.* Bulletin 279. Washington, D.C.: Government Printing Office.

25

Race at Work: Realities of Race and Criminal Record in the NYC Job Market*

DEVAH PAGER, BRUCE WESTERN, AND BART BONIKOWSKI

Racial progress since the 1960s has led some researchers and policy makers to proclaim the problem of discrimination solved. Despite low rates of employment among blacks compared to whites, many people are now skeptical that discrimination remains a significant cause of racial inequality in the U.S. labor market. Public opinion polls indicate that Americans today are much less likely to view discrimination as a major problem as were their counterparts in the 1970s. In fact, according to a recent Gallup poll, more than three-quarters of the general public believe that blacks are treated the same as whites in society.

In part, white Americans have turned their attention away from the problems of discrimination because it is difficult to observe. Contemporary forms of discrimination are often subtle and covert, making it difficult for the average observer to recognize their effects. In the present study, we adopt an experimental audit approach to more explicitly identify patterns of discrimination in the low-wage labor market of New York City. By using matched teams of individuals to apply for real entry-level jobs, it becomes possible to

---

* First published in 2005; from NYC Commission on Human Rights Conference.

directly measure the extent to which race/eth-nicity—in the absence of other disqualifying characteristics—reduce employment opportunities among equally qualified applicants.

RESEARCH METHODOLOGY

Our research design involved sending matched teams of young men (called testers) to apply for 341 real entry-level jobs throughout New York City over ten months in 2004. The testers were well-spoken young men, aged 22 to 26; most were college-educated, between 5 feet 10 inches and 6 feet in height, recruited in and around New York City. They were chosen on the basis of their similar verbal skills, interactional styles, and physical attractiveness. Additionally, testers went through a common training program to ensure uniform style of self presentation in job interviews. Testers were assigned matched ficti-tious resumes representing comparable profiles with respect to educational attainment, quality of high school, work experience, and neighbor-hood of residence. Testers presented themselves as high school graduates with steady work experience in entry-level jobs. In some conditions, testers presented additional evidence of a felony conviction.[1]

RESULTS

Our first set of results come from the three-person team in which a white, Hispanic, and black tester applied to the same set of employers presenting identical qualifications. For each

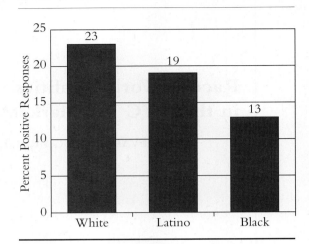

FIGURE 1 CALL-BACKS OR JOB OFFERS BY RACE/ETHNICITY

NOTE: The total number of employers audited by this team = 252. Positive response rates for Whites and Latinos are significantly different from Blacks ($p < .05$). Response rates for Latinos are marginally significantly different from Whites ($p = .07$).

set of visits, we recorded whether testers were offered the job on the spot, or, at some later point, called back for a second interview (which we refer to together as "positive responses.") As we can see in Figure 1, the proportion of positive responses depends strongly on the race of the job applicant. This comparison demonstrates a strong racial hierarchy, with whites in the lead, followed by Latinos, with blacks trailing far behind. These outcomes suggest that blacks are only slightly more than half as likely to receive consideration by employers relative to equally qualified white applicants. Latinos also pay a penalty for minority status, but they are clearly preferred relative to their black counterparts.

---

1 In this report, we study racial and ethnic discrimination using data from two teams of testers. A total of 6 teams (and 13 testers) were included in this study, allowing us to study various combinations of race, criminal background, and educational attainment. The results from the other teams will be discussed in a companion paper.

Beyond these numerical outcomes, the experiences reported by testers in the course of their interviews with employers were also revealing of the racial dynamics at work. In some cases, our minority testers received clear feedback that they were not welcome or appropriate for a particular work environment. On one occasion, for example, Dathan, an African American tester, reports his experience applying for a position at an upscale jewelry store's booth at a job fair. Waiting for the store representative to finish her conversation with another applicant, he watches her giggling with the blond female applicant in front of him. Finally it's Dathan's turn to speak with the representative. He reports the following interaction:

"[When the rep saw me] her smiley face turned into a serious business face, and I said 'Hi, I'm interested in applying for a position at [your store].' She asked, 'To do what?' I said, 'I have customer service experience and sales experience.'

She said: 'I haven't been with [company X] for too long, but I imagine they want [company X] type of people, who can represent [company X] . . .' "

In this 30 second interaction, the rep had apparently been able to size up Dathan's potential and had decided that he was not "company X type of people." In the rep's view, the employer's status—prestigious company in a prestigious retail trade—appeared to rule out the possibility of hiring a young black male.

These interactions in which race plays a role provide a small window into the process by which employers regard young African Americans as unsuitable employees. Most commonly, however, stereotyping and discrimination remain invisible to the job applicant. In fact, despite certain fairly striking examples of racial dynamics in testers' interactions with employers, the vast majority of disparate treatment occurred with little or no signs of trouble.

In one case, for example, the three test partners reported experiences that, in the absence of direct comparisons, would have revealed no evidence of discrimination. In recording his experience applying for this retail sales position, Joe, one of our African American testers, reports: *"[The employer] said the position was just filled and that she would be calling people in for an interview if the person doesn't work out."* Josue, his Latino test partner, was told something very similar: *"She informed me that the position was already filled, but did not know if the hired employee would work out. She told me to leave my resume with her."* By contrast, when Simon, their white tester, applied last, his experience was notably different: *". . . I asked what the hiring process was—if they're taking applications now, interviewing, etc. She looked at my application. 'You can start immediately?' Yes. 'Can you start tomorrow?' Yes. '10 a.m.' She was very friendly and introduced me to another woman (white, 28) at the cash register who will be training me."*

When evaluated individually, these interactions would not have raised any concern. All three testers were asked about their availability and about their sales experience. The employer appeared willing to consider each of them. But in the final analysis, it was the white applicant who walked out with the job. Incidents such as these illustrate the ease with which contemporary acts of discrimination can remain completely undetected. Without a white partner following in their footsteps, Joe and Josue would have had no indication of the degree to which their experiences, in cases like these, were being shaped by racial considerations. And yet, as the results of the study show, race remains highly consequential in determining the opportunities available for low wage work.

In a second set of analyses, we compare the magnitude of race/ethnic discrimination to another prevalent form of stigma among low-wage workers. Recent political discussions and media coverage have highlighted the plight of an increasing number of inmates being released from prison each year. We know that these men face substantial difficulties in securing employment as a result of their criminal background. Comparing the outcome of this group to minorities with no criminal background allows us to assess the relative magnitudes of criminal stigma and minority status.

Figure 2 shows the results from this second three-person team in which the white tester now presents evidence of a felony conviction. His test partners, black and Latino young men, present no criminal background. As we can see in this figure, the rate of positive responses for the white tester are substantially diminished relative to the white tester with no criminal background (from Figure 1). Nevertheless, this white applicant with a felony conviction appears to do just as well, if not better, than his black counterpart with no criminal background. These results suggest that employers view minority job applicants as essentially equivalent to whites just out of prison.

Despite the fact that these applicants presented equivalent credentials and applied for exactly the same jobs, race appears to overtake all else in determining employment opportunities.

Calibrating the magnitude of the race effects to the effects of a felony conviction presents a

FIGURE 2 CALL-BACKS OR JOB OFFERS BY RACE AND CRIMINAL RECORD

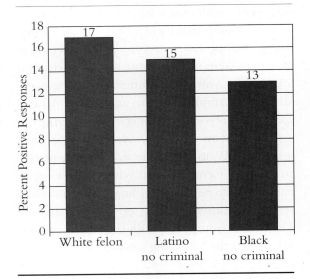

NOTE: The total number of employers audited by this team = 255. Positive response rates for White felons are not significantly different from Latinos and Blacks. Response rates for Latinos are marginally significantly different from Blacks (p = .05).

disturbing picture. Blacks remain at the very end of the hiring queue, even in relation to (white) applicants who have just been released from prison. The results here point to the striking persistence of race in the allocation of employment opportunities. Employers faced with large numbers of applicants and little time to evaluate them seem to view race as an adequate means by which to weed out undesirable applicants upon first review.

As just one example, the following case records this team's experience applying for a position at a local auto dealership. Joe, the black tester, applied first and was informed at the outset that the only available positions were for those with direct auto sales experience. When

Josue, his Latino partner, applied, the lack of direct auto sales experience was less of a problem. Josue reports: *"He asked me if I had any customer service experience and I said not really. . . . He then told me that he wanted to get rid of a few bad apples who were not performing well. He asked me when I could start. . . ."* Josue was told to wait for a call back on Monday. Keith, their white ex-felon test partner, was first given a stern lecture regarding his criminal background. *"I have no problem with your conviction, it doesn't bother me. But if I find out money is missing or you're not clean or not showing up on time I have no problem ending the relationship."* Despite the employer's concerns, and despite Keith having no more sales experience than his test partners, Keith was offered the job on the spot.

This example illustrates the ways in which race can trump even known criminality in certain cases. Indeed, far from racial considerations in employment being a thing of the past, we see that they are alive and well and actively shaping the opportunities available to members of different racial/ethnic groups.

||| RACE-CODED CHANNELING

The basic outcome of "positive responses" measured in this study quantifies the employers' willingness to consider each applicant type for a job. But the simple distinction between getting a job or not captures only one piece of the employment puzzle. In many cases employers are hiring for more than one position at the same time. Examining how employers match applicants to job types can be further revealing of the assumptions employers hold about various groups of workers.

The testers' narratives, reporting their experiences at the conclusion of each audit, provide vivid illustrations of the kinds of the channeling that takes place. In an audit of a retail clothing company, for example, one of our Hispanic testers, Josue, encounters the following:

Josue describes the various young white 20-something women running the place. One of the women interviews him and asks about past work experience. She asks him what job he's applying for—"I told her sales associate. . . . [The last serious job listed on Josue's resume was as a sales assistant at a sporting goods store].

She then told me that there was a stock position and asked if I would be interested in that."

Josue ended up getting the stocker job, and was asked to start the next day.

In another case, one of our black testers, Zuri, applied for a sales position at a lighting store. He describes the following interaction:

When she asked what position I was looking for I said I was open, but that since they were looking for a salesperson I would be interested in that. She smiled, put her head in her hand and her elbow on the table and said, "I need a stock boy. Can you do stock boy?"

Zuri's white and Hispanic test partners, by contrast, were each able to apply for the advertised sales position.

The job applications of Josue and Zuri are both coded as "positive responses" in the initial analyses. Indeed, our key concern is about access to employment of any kind. But this general focus masks some of the racial biases at play.

TABLE 1 **JOB CHANNELING BY RACE, ETHNICITY, & CRIMINAL BACKGROUND**

Original Job Title	Suggested Job
BLACKS CHANNELED DOWN	
Server	Busser
Counter person	Dishwasher/porter
Server	Busboy
Assistant manager	Entry fast food position
Server	Busboy/runner
Retail sales	Maintenance
Counter person	Delivery
Sales	Stockboy
Sales	Not specified[a]
HISPANICS CHANNELED DOWN	
Server	Runner
Sales	Stock
Steam cleaning	Exterminator
Counter person	Delivery
Sales	Stock person
WHITES CHANNELED DOWN	
Server	Busboy
HISPANICS CHANNELED UP	
Carwash attendant	Manager
Warehouse worker	Computer/office
WHITES CHANNELED UP	
Line Cook	Waitstaff
Mover	Office / Telesales
Dishwasher	Waitstaff
Driver	Auto detailing
Kitchen job	"Front of the house" job
Receptionist	Company supervisor

(a) employer told tester:"sales might not be right for you...."

Indeed, the experience of channeling was not limited to a handful of cases. A more systemic analysis of the testers' experiences provides support for these anecdotal experiences. A total of 53 cases of channeling were recorded by the testers. These cases were then individually coded as downward channeling, upward channeling, lateral channeling, or unknown, by comparing the original job title to the suggested job type. Downward channeling is defined as (1) a move from a job involving contact with customers to a job without (e.g., server to busboy); (2) a move from a white collar position to a manual position (e.g., from dispatcher to driver); or (3) a move in which hierarchy can be clearly discerned (e.g., manager to server). Upward channeling is defined as a move in the opposite direction. We focus on these two types of channeling for our current analysis. Instances of channeling in which all members of the team were channeled similarly are eliminated (e.g., the original job was filled and all subsequent job applicants were invited to apply for a different position).

The analysis of these cases reveals fairly striking patterns of racial categorization. Black applicants were channeled into lower positions in 9 cases and never channeled upwards. Hispanics were channeled down in 5 cases, whereas whites experienced downward channeling in only 1 case, and only when showing a criminal record (see Table 1).

A substantial number of these cases were restaurant jobs in which the tester applied for a position as server but was instead channeled into a position as busboy or dishwasher. Almost all were cases in which the original position required extensive customer contact while the suggested position did not (e.g., salesperson to stocker). While in some cases the limited work experiences reflected on our testers' resumes warranted movement into a lower-level position, the differential incidence by race suggests that these decisions were not based on qualifications alone.

In fact, a surprising degree of channeling among our white testers took place in the opposite direction. In at least 6 cases, white testers were encouraged to apply for jobs that were of a higher-level or required more customer contact than the initial position they inquired about. In one case, for example, a white tester applied for a position as a cleaner but was instead encouraged to apply for a clerical position. In another case the tester requested an application for the dishwasher position, but was instead channeled into applying for a job as waitstaff. In at least

one case, a white tester was encouraged to apply for a management position, despite his paltry level of work experience.

It is not the case, then, that the resumes of testers in this study prevented them from consideration in a wide range of jobs, or left them on the borderline between job classes. In fact, the testers' resumes were constructed so that they would appear highly competitive for the kinds of low-wage jobs we were targeting. Rather, the testers' race or ethnicity appears to be associated with differential levels of skill, competence, or suitability for particular kinds of work. The critical relevance of customer contact in the channeling decisions likewise suggests that employers have assumptions about what their clients expect/prefer in the appearance of those serving them.

‖ CONCLUSION

In contrast to public opinion that assumes little influence of discrimination on labor market inequality, we find that black job applicants are only two-thirds as successful as equally qualified Latinos, and little more than half as successful as equally qualified whites. Indeed, black job seekers fare no better than white men just released from prison. Discrimination continues to represent a major barrier to economic self-sufficiency for those at the low end of the labor market hierarchy. Blacks, and to a lesser extent Latinos, are routinely passed over in favor of whites for the most basic kinds of low-wage work. Indeed, discrimination has not been eliminated in the post-civil rights period as some contend, but remains a vital component of a complex pattern of racial inequality.

26

The Roots of Durable Inequality*

CHARLES TILLY

We could reasonably call James Gillray (1757–1815) Britain's first professional cartoonist. He left us unforgettable images of public and private affairs under George III. Very few handsome people figure in Gillray's caricatures. In the savage portrayals of British life he drew, etched, and colored toward 1800, beefy, red-faced aristocrats commonly tower over other people, while paupers almost invariably appear as small, gaunt, and gnarled. If Gillray painted his compatriots with malice, however, he also observed them acutely.

Take the matter of height. Let us consider fourteen-year-old entrants to the Royal Military Academy at Sandhurst to represent the healthier portion of the aristocracy and gentry, and fourteen-year-old recruits for naval service via London's Marine Society to represent the healthier portion of the city's jobless poor. At the nineteenth century's start, poor boys of fourteen averaged only 4 feet 3 inches tall, while aristocrats and gentry of the same age averaged about 5 feet 1 inch (Floud, Wachter, and Gregory 1990, 197). An average beginning military cadet stood some 10 inches taller than a newly recruited mariner. Because poor youths then matured later than

---

* First published in 1999; from "Of Essences and Bonds," in *Durable Inequality*.

rich ones, their heights converged an inch or two by adulthood. Nevertheless we can imagine their counterparts in the army: aristocratic officers glowering down half a foot or more at their plebeian troops. Such an image vivifies the phrases "high and mighty," "haughty," and "look down on someone."

Poor people have few good times. But the years around 1800 brought Britain's low-income families especially bad times. In the short run, massive diversion of resources and labor power to French Revolutionary and Napoleonic wars depleted domestic production as it drove up consumer prices. Over the longer run, the urbanization, industrialization, and sharpened inequality promoted by capitalist expansion were then aggravating the hardships faced by Western Europe's poorer households. As poor people ceased producing their own food faster than agricultural productivity rose, hardship extended to their daily bread.

In his Nobel Prize lecture, economist and economic historian Robert Fogel points out that at nutritional levels prevailing toward the end of the eighteenth century, from 3 to 10 percent of the English and French work forces had too little food to sustain any effective work at all, while a full fifth of the population commanded too little for more than a few hours of light work per day (Fogel 1994, 371–374). At those low nutritional levels, furthermore, English and French workers were extremely vulnerable to chronic disease, hence liable to work lives disrupted by illness and early death. Fogel speculates that malnutrition itself thereby accounted for the stunning proportion of beggars—up to 20 percent of the entire population—reported in various regions of eighteenth-century Europe.

Over population categories, regions, and countries, as Fogel and other researchers have recently established, material well-being and stature vary in strong relation to each other. Richard Steckel sums up:

> Stature adeptly measures inequality in the form of nutritional deprivation; average height in the past century is sensitive not only to the level of income but to the distribution of income and the consumption of basic necessities by the poor. Unlike conventional measures of living standards based on output, stature is a measure of consumption that incorporates or adjusts for individual nutritional needs; it is a net measure that captures not only the supply of inputs to health but demands on those inputs. (Steckel 1995, 1903)

Well-being and height link through food consumption; victuals invigorate. Although genes set variable limits to height distributions in human populations, childhood nutrition strongly affects the degree to which any individual approaches her or his genetic limit. Low birth weight, which typically results from a mother's illness and malnutrition, predicts reliably to a child's health problems, diminished life expectancy, and smaller adult size.

Within a given population, furthermore, short stature itself generally predicts to higher levels of morbidity and mortality—most likely not because of height's inherent advantages but because, on the whole, short stature correlates with unfavorable childhood health experiences and lesser body strength. Rising height across an entire population therefore provides one of our clearest signs that the well-being of that population is increasing, and marked adult height differentials by social category within the male or female population provide a strong indicator of durable inequality.

That average heights of adults in Western countries have typically risen 6 inches or so over the past century and a half reflects a significant rise in living standards. That even in egalitarian Sweden recent studies reveal lower birth weights for the newborn of less–educated women (in this case, most likely a joint outcome of smoking and nutrition) tells us that material inequalities persist into prosperity. That at my modest altitude I easily see over the heads of many adult males with whom I travel on New York subways—especially those speaking languages other than English—signals that in capitalist countries we still have profound inequalities of life experience to identify and explain.

Since sexual dimorphism prevails among primates and since humans commonly live in mixed-sex households whose members share food, one might suppose that female/male height differences, unlike class inequalities, derive almost entirely from genetic predisposition. Not quite. Nature and nurture are disentangled with difficulty when it comes to such matters as sex differences in body size. As James Tanner puts it:

Variation between the heights of *individuals* within a subpopulation is indeed largely dependent on differences in their genetic endowment; but the variation between the means of groups of individuals (at least within an ethnically homogeneous population) reflects the cumulative nutritional, hygienic, disease, and stress experience of each of the groups. In the language of analysis of variance, most of the within-group variation is due

to heredity, and most of the between-group variation is due to childhood environment. (Tanner 1994, 1)

What counts, however, as a subpopulation, or group? Surely not any cohabiting population, regardless of social divisions within it. For "group," read "category," to recognize that class, gender, race, ethnicity, and similar socially organized systems of distinction clearly qualify. (I will follow current conventions by speaking of "sex" in reference to X and Y chromosome-linked biological differences, "gender" in reference to social categories.) In each of these cases, differences in "nutritional, hygienic, disease, and stress experience" contribute to differences in adult stature. Researchers in the field have so far done much more with class differences, national differences, and change over time than with male/female differences.

Still, gender likewise marks distinctive childhood experiences, even when it comes to nutrition. When children in pastoral and agricultural economies begin serious work in their household enterprises, they almost always take on gender-differentiated tasks. That means their daily routines give boys and girls unequal access to food. Most of the time girls get less, and their food is of lower quality. Where men fish or hunt while females till and gather, however, the division of labor often attaches girls and women to the more reliable and continuous sources of calories. Thus in some circumstances females may actually get better nourishment than males.

The fundamental fact, then, is gender differentiation in nutrition, with the usual but not universal condition being inferior nutrition for females. We have enough episodic documentation concerning gender discrimination with respect to health care, feeding, infanticide, and general nurture, as well as slivers of evidence suggesting gender-differential patterns of improvement or decline in nutrition under the influence of broad economic fluctuations, to support hypotheses of widespread unequal treatment of males and females, of inequality in their resulting life chances, hence of a social contribution to gender differences in weight and height as well.

Below a certain threshold of food supply, most households make regular if implicit choices concerning which of their members will have adequate nourishment. Contemporary capitalist countries seem to have risen above that threshold, although we lack reliable evidence concerning nutritional inequality among capitalism's currently increasing share of poor people. But the hungry world as a whole still features gender discrimination in nutrition.

Here Fogel's line of investigation crosses the inquiries of Amartya Sen (Sen 1981, 1982, 1983, 1992). From his analyses of poverty and famine onward, Sen has sniffed out deliberately unequal treatment in the presence of resources that could ensure more general welfare. He recurrently detects gender-differentiated claims on such resources. "There is a lot of indirect evidence," he comments, "of differential treatment of women and men, and particularly of girls *vis-à-vis* boys, in many parts of the world, e.g., among rural families in Asia and North Africa. The observed morbidity and mortality rates frequently reflect differential female deprivation of extraordinary proportions" (Sen 1992, 123). The most dramatic observations concern female infanticide through direct attack or (more often) systematic neglect, which analysts have frequently reported for strongly patrilineal regions of Asia.

People of Western countries have not much practiced selective female infanticide. But Western states have often reinforced gender distinctions in nutrition and nurture, notably by confining military service to males, diverting food stocks from civilian to military use, providing superior health care for troops, and ensuring that soldiers receive better rations than the general population. Florence Nightingale, after all, more or less invented professional nursing as we know it while organizing the health care of British fighting men during the Crimean War. In the absence of powerful drugs and diagnostic instruments, Nightingale's nursing stressed cleanliness, warmth, and nourishment, comforts many women back home in Britain did not then share. If military men at war have historically faced exceptional risks of violent death and disabling disease, in recent centuries they have also typically received three square meals a day when civilians, especially female civilians, were tightening their belts.

Such socially organized differences in well-being illustrate this book's main subject: the causes, uses, structures, and effects of categorical inequality. The book does not ask what causes human inequality in general. Instead it addresses these questions: How, why, and with what consequences do long-lasting, systematic inequalities in life chances distinguish members of different socially defined categories of persons? How do categorical inequalities form, change, and disappear? Since all social relations involve fleeting, fluctuating inequalities, let us concentrate on *durable* inequalities, those that last from one social interaction to the next, with special attention to those that persist over whole careers, lifetimes, and organizational histories.

Let us concentrate, furthermore, on distinctly bounded pairs such as female/male, aristocrat/plebeian, citizen/foreigner, and more complex classifications based on religious affiliation, ethnic origin, or race. We focus on *categories* rather than on continua such as [rich . . . poor], [tall . . . short], [ugly . . . beautiful], and so on. Bounded categories deserve special attention because they provide clearer evidence for the operation of durable inequality, because their boundaries do crucial organizational work, and because categorical differences actually account for much of what ordinary observers take to be results of variation in individual talent or effort.

As Max Weber noted almost a century ago, the creation of what he called "social closure" advances efforts by the powerful to exclude less powerful people from the full benefits of joint enterprises, while facilitating efforts by underdogs to organize for the seizure of benefits denied (Weber 1968, 1:43–46, 1:341–348; Parkin 1979, 44–116). A relationship is likely to be closed, Weber remarked,

> in the following type of situation: a social relationship may provide the parties to it with opportunities for the satisfaction of spiritual or material interests. If the participants expect that the admission of others will lead to an improvement of their situation, an improvement in degree, in kind, in the security or the value of the satisfaction, their interest will be in keeping the relationship open. If, on the other hand, their expectations are of improving their position by monopolistic tactics, their interest is in a closed relationship. (Weber 1968, 1:43)

Organizations such as firms and clans use closure by drawing complete boundaries around themselves and then monitoring flows across those boundaries with care. Contrary to Weber, however, I argue that at a scale larger than a single organization completely bounded categories are rare and difficult to maintain, that most categorical inequality relies on establishment of a partial frontier and defined social relations across that frontier, with much less control in regions distant from the frontier. Yet in other regards my analysis resonates with Weber's discussion. It builds a bridge from Max Weber on social closure to Karl Marx on exploitation, and back. Crossing that bridge repeatedly, this book concerns social mechanisms—recurrent causal sequences of general scope—that actually lock categorical inequality into place. The central argument runs like this: Large, significant inequalities in advantages among human beings correspond mainly to categorical differences such as black/white, male/female, citizen/foreigner, or Muslim/Jew rather than to individual differences in attributes, propensities, or performances. In actual operation, more complex categorical systems involving multiple religions or various races typically resolve into bounded pairs relating just two categories at a time, as when the coexistence of Muslims, Jews, and Christians resolves into the sets Muslim/Jew, Muslim/Christian, and Jew/Christian, with each pair having its own distinct set of boundary relations.

Even where they employ ostensibly biological markers, such categories always depend on extensive social organization, belief, and enforcement. Durable inequality among categories arises because people who control access to value-producing resources solve pressing organizational problems by means of categorical distinctions. Inadvertently or otherwise, those people set up systems of social closure, exclusion, and control. Multiple parties—not all of them powerful, some of them even victims of exploitation—then acquire stakes in those solutions. Variation in the form and durability of inequality therefore depends chiefly on the nature of the resources involved, the previous social locations of the categories, the character of the organizational problems, and the configurations of interested parties.

Through all these variations, we discover and rediscover paired, recognized, organized, unequal categories such as black/white, male/female, married/unmarried, and citizen/noncitizen. The dividing line between such categories usually remains incomplete in two regards: first, some people (persons of mixed race, transsexuals, certified refugees, and so on) do not fit clearly on one side of the line or the other; and, second, in many situations the distinction between the members of any particular pair does not matter. Where they apply, however, paired and unequal categories do crucial organizational work, producing marked, durable differences in access to valued resources. Durable inequality depends heavily on the institutionalization of categorical pairs.

THE ROOTS OF CATEGORICAL INEQUALITY

How and why does the institutionalization of categorical pairs occur? Since the argument is unfamiliar and complicated, it may help to lay out its major elements and their causal connections even before defining crucial terms. The list will serve as a preliminary map of the wilderness [I] will explore:

1. Paired and unequal categories, consisting of asymmetrical relations across a socially recognized (and usually incomplete) dividing line between interpersonal networks, recur in a wide variety of situations, with the usual effect being the unequal exclusion of each network from resources controlled by the other.

2. Two mechanisms we may label *exploitation* and *opportunity hoarding* cause durable inequality when their agents incorporate paired and unequal categories at crucial organizational boundaries.

3. Two further mechanisms we may title *emulation* and *adaptation* reinforce the effectiveness of categorical distinctions.

4. Local categorical distinctions gain strength and operate at lower cost when matched with widely available paired and unequal categories.

5. When many organizations adopt the same categorical distinctions, those distinctions become more pervasive and decisive in social life at large.

6. Experience within categorically differentiated settings gives participants systematically different and unequal preparation for performance in new organizations.

7. Much of what observers ordinarily interpret as individual differences that create inequality is actually the consequence of categorical organization.

8. For these reasons, inequalities by race, gender, ethnicity, class, age, citizenship, educational level, and other apparently contradictory principles of differentiation form through similar social processes and are to an important degree organizationally interchangeable.

[I] will make clear what is at issue in such an organizational view of inequality-producing mechanisms. At a minimum, [I] will challenge other analysts to clarify the causal mechanisms implied by their own preferred explanations of durable inequality and then to search for evidence that those causal mechanisms are actually operating.

Although the word "organization" may call to mind firms, governments, schools, and similar formal, hierarchical structures, I mean the analysis to encompass all sorts of well-bounded clusters of social relations in which occupants of at least one position have the right to commit collective resources to activities reaching across the boundary. Organizations include corporate kin groups, households, religious sects, bands of mercenaries, and many local communities. Durable inequality arises in all of them. All of them at times incorporate categorical distinctions originating in adjacent organizations.

Humans invented categorical inequality millennia ago and have applied it to a wide range of social situations. People establish systems of categorical inequality, however inadvertently, chiefly by means of these two causal mechanisms:

- *Exploitation,* which operates when powerful, connected people command resources from which they draw significantly increased returns by coordinating the effort of outsiders whom they exclude from the full value added by that effort.
- *Opportunity hoarding,* which operates when members of a categorically bounded network acquire access to a resource that is valuable, renewable, subject to monopoly, supportive of network activities, and enhanced by the network's modus operandi.

The two mechanisms obviously parallel each other, but people who lack great power can pursue the second if encouraged, tolerated, or ignored by the powerful. Often the two parties gain complementary, if unequal, benefits from jointly excluding others.

Two further mechanisms cement such arrangements in place: *emulation,* the copying of established organizational models and/or the transplanting of existing social relations from one setting to another; and *adaptation,* the elaboration of daily routines such as mutual aid, political influence, courtship, and information gathering on the basis of categorically unequal structures. Exploitation and opportunity hoarding favor the installation of categorical inequality, while emulation and adaptation generalize its influence.

A certain kind of inequality therefore becomes prevalent over a large population in two complementary ways. Either the categorical pair in question—male/female, legitimate/illegitimate, black/white, citizen/noncitizen, and so on—operates in organizations that control major resources affecting welfare, and its effects spread from there; or the categorical pair repeats in a great many similar organizations, regardless of their power.

In the first case, organizations that produce work and wield coercive power—corporations and states, plantations and mercenary forces, textile mills and drug rings, depending on the context—take pride of place because they ordinarily control the largest concentrations of deployable resources within large populations. In some settings of ideological hegemony, religious organizations and their own categorical distinctions can also have similar effects on inequality around them.

In the second case, households, kin groups, and local communities hold crucial positions for two reasons: within a given population, they form and change according to similar principles, and they strongly influence biological and social reproduction. Gender and age distinctions, for example, do not ordinarily separate lineages from one another, but the repetition of these distinctions in many lineages lends them influence throughout the population. The basic mechanisms that generate inequality operate in a similar fashion over a wide variety of organizational settings as well as over a great range of unequal outcomes: income, wealth, power, deference, fame, privilege, and more.

People who create or sustain categorical inequality by means of the four basic mechanisms rarely set out to manufacture inequality as such. Instead they solve other organizational problems by establishing categorically unequal access to valued outcomes. More than anything else, they seek to secure rewards from sequestered resources. Both exploitation and opportunity hoarding provide a means of doing so. But, once undertaken, exploitation and opportunity hoarding pose their own organizational problems: how to maintain distinctions between insiders and outsiders; how to ensure solidarity, loyalty, control, and succession; how to monopolize knowledge that favors profitable use of sequestered resources. The installation of explicitly categorical boundaries helps to solve such organizational problems, especially if the boundaries in question incorporate forms of inequality that are already well established in the surrounding world. Emulation and adaptation lock such distinctions into place, making them habitual and sometimes even essential to exploiters and exploited alike.

To be sure, widely applicable categories accumulate their own histories and relations to other social structures: male/female distinctions have acquired enormous, slow-moving cultural carapaces yet reappear within almost all social structures of any scale, whereas in the United States the distinction Hispanic/white remains a disputed, politically driven division of uncertain cultural content. Such categorical pairs therefore operate with characteristic differences when imported into new settings. The distinction citizen/foreigner, for instance, does a variety of organizational work—separating temporary from long-term employees, differentiating access to public benefits, managing rights to intervene in political processes, and so on—but everywhere and always its existence and effectiveness depend on the present capacity of a relatively centralized government. The power of a differentiator based on membership or nonmembership in a political party (notable cases being communist parties in state socialist regimes) similarly depends on the existence of a hegemonic party exercising extensive state power and controlling a wide variety of valued resources.

Divisions based on preference for sexual partners—gay, lesbian, straight, and so on—depend far less on governmental structure. As compared to those who differentiate based on citizenship or party membership, those who install sexual preference as a local basis of inequality have less access to governmental backing as well as a lower likelihood of governmental intervention. Sexual preference distinctions, however, do import extensive mythologies, practices, relations, and understandings that significantly affect how the distinctions work within a new setting.

Categorical inequality, in short, has some very general properties. But one of those properties, paradoxically, is to vary in practical operation with the historically accumulated understandings, practices, and social relations already attached to a given set of distinctions.

Consider some quick examples. Josef Stalin knits together an effective political machine by recruiting ethnically identified regional leaders, training them in Moscow, making them regional party bosses, and giving their ethnic identifications priority within semiautonomous political jurisdictions. When the Soviet center later relaxes its grip, political entrepreneurs within regions mobilize followings around those ethnic identities, others mobilize against them, and ostensibly age–old ethnic conflicts flame into civil war.

Again, the founder of a small manufacturing firm, following models already established in the trade, divides the firm's work into clusters of jobs viewed as distinct in character and qualifications and then recruits workers for those jobs within well-marked categories. As turnover occurs and the firm expands, established workers pass word of available jobs among friends and relatives, collaborating with and supporting them once they join the work force. Those new workers therefore prove more reliable and effective than others hired off the street, and all concerned come to associate job with category, so much so that owner and workers come to believe in the superior fitness of that category's members for the particular line of work.

Another case in point. Householders in an urban neighborhood build up a precarious system of trust on the basis of common backgrounds and shared relations to third parties, live with persons and property at risk to that system of trust, and then react violently when newcomers whom they cannot easily integrate into the same networks threaten to occupy part of the territory. In the process, members of the two groups elaborate compelling stories about each other's perfidy and utter incompatibility.

Members of an immigrant stream, finally, peddle craft goods from their home region on big-city streets, and some of them set up businesses as suppliers, manufacturers, or retail merchants. New immigrants find work in the expanding trade, and not only an immigrant niche but an ethnically specific international connection provides exclusive opportunities for the next generation. In all these cases, organizational improvisations lead to durable categorical inequality. In all these cases, but with variable weight, exploitation and opportunity hoarding favor the installation of categorical inequality, while emulation and adaptation generalize its influence.

When it comes to the determinants of durable inequality, are these special cases or the general rule? [I give] reasons for thinking that categorical inequality in general results from varying intersections of exploitation, opportunity hoarding, emulation, and adaptation. [I go] farther, claiming that much of the inequality that seems to result from individual or group differences in ability actually stems from the same causes:

- Authoritatively organized categorical differences in current performance (e.g., categorically differentiated cooperation or sabotage by fellow workers, subordinates, and supervisors)
- Authoritatively organized categorical differences in *rewards* for performance (e.g., systematically lower pay for blacks than for whites doing similar work)
- Authoritatively organized differences in the acquisition of *capacities* for performance (e.g., categorically segregated and unequal schools)

[I] also [argue] that the social mechanisms which generate inequality with respect to a wide range of advantages—wealth, income, esteem, protection, power, and more—are similar. Although historical accumulations of institutions, social relations, and shared understandings produce differences in the day-to-day operation of various sorts of categories (gender, race, citizenship, and so on) as well as differences in various sorts of outcomes (e.g., landed wealth versus cash income), ultimately interactions of exploitation, opportunity hoarding, emulation, and adaptation explain them all.

Nutrition turns out to provide a useful general model for categorical inequality, since in most settings feeding differs with categorical membership, and since in many cases the cumulative effects of feeding elsewhere help to explain categorical differences in performance in the current case. In direct parallel, the information and social ties that individuals and groups can currently acquire differ categorically, but previous categorical experience also strongly affects the information and social ties these individuals and groups already have at their disposal, not to mention the means they have of acquiring new information and social ties. Unequal treatment of females and males in a wide range of social lives creates female/male differences in the qualifications and social ties prospective workers bring to workplaces; those differences interact with (and generally reinforce) gender distinctions built into the allocation and supervision of work.

Again, categorically differentiated family experience strongly affects children's school performance and teachers' evaluations of that performance, which in turn channel children into categorically differentiated, career-shaping educational streams ★ ★ ★. To the extent that teachers, employers, public officials, and other authorities differentiate their responses to performances categorically, they contribute to durable, authoritatively organized categorical differences. More generally, apparent third parties to the inequality in question—state officials, legislatures, owners of firms, and other powerholders—significantly influence the operation of categorical inequality and sometimes take the initiative in creating it. Authorities do, in fact, frequently solve their own organizational problems—how to sort students, whom to hire, what rights to honor—in categorical ways.

Feelings of identity, on one side, and intergroup hostility, on the other, may well accompany, promote, or result from the use of categorical differences to solve organizational problems. But the relative prevalence of such attitudes plays a secondary part in inequality's extent and form. Mistaken beliefs reinforce exploitation, opportunity hoarding, emulation, and adaptation but exercise little independent influence on their initiation—or so I will argue. It follows that the reduction or intensification of racist, sexist, or xenophobic attitudes will have relatively little impact on durable inequality, whereas the introduction of certain new organizational forms—for example, installing different categories or changing the relation between categories and rewards—will have great impact.

If so, the identification of such organizational forms becomes a significant challenge for social scientists. It also follows that similar organizational problems generate parallel solutions in very different settings, in articulation with very different sets of categories. Thus matches of positions with categories, and the justifications for such matches, vary much more than recurrent structural arrangements—for example, when similar clusters of jobs acquire contrasting racial, ethnic, or gender identifications in different labor markets. Causal mechanisms resemble each other greatly, while outcomes differ dramatically, thus inviting very different rationalizations or condemnations after the fact. Social scientists dealing with such durable forms of inequality must hack through dense ideological overgrowth to reach structural roots.

‖ REFERENCES

Floud, Roderick, Kenneth Wachter, and Annabel Gregory. 1990. *Height, Health, and History: Nutritional Status in the United Kingdom, 1750–1980.* Cambridge: Cambridge University Press.

Fogel, Robert W. 1994. "Economic Growth, Population Theory, and Physiology: The Bearing of Long-Term Processes on the Making of Economic Policy." *American Economic Review* 84: 369–395.

Parkin, Frank. 1979. *Marxism and Class Theory: A Bourgeois Critique.* London: Tavistock.

Sen, Amartya. 1981. *Poverty and Famines: An Essay on Entitlement and Deprivation.* Oxford: Clarendon Press.

———. 1982. *Choice, Welfare, and Measurement.* Cambridge: MIT Press.

———. 1983. "Women, Technology, and Sexual Divisions." *Trade and Development* 6: 195–223.

———. 1992. *Inequality Reexamined.* Cambridge: Harvard University Press.

Steckel, Richard H. 1995. "Stature and the Standard of Living." *Journal of Economic Literature* 33: 1903–1940.

Tanner, James M. 1994. "Introduction: Growth in Height as a Mirror of the Standard of Living." In *Stature, Living Standards, and Economic Development: Essays in Anthropometric History*, edited by John Komlos. Chicago: University of Chicago Press.

Weber, Max. 1968. *Economy and Society: An Outline of Interpretive Sociology.* Edited by Guenther Roth and Claus Wittich. 3 vols. New York: Bedminster.

27

The Forms of Capital★

PIERRE BOURDIEU

The social world is accumulated history, and if it is not to be reduced to a discontinuous series of instantaneous mechanical equilibria between agents who are treated as interchangeable particles, one must reintroduce into it the notion of capital and with it, accumulation and all its effects. Capital is accumulated labor (in its materialized form or its "incorporated," embodied form) which, when appropriated on a private, i.e., exclusive, basis by agents or groups of agents, enables them to appropriate social energy in the form of reified or living labor. ★ ★ ★ It is what makes the games of society—not least, the economic game—something other than simple games of chance offering at every moment the possibility of a miracle. Roulette, which holds out the opportunity of winning a lot of money in a short space of time, and therefore of changing one's social status quasi-instantaneously, and in which the winning of the previous spin of the wheel can be staked and lost at every new spin, gives a fairly accurate image of this imaginary universe of perfect competition or perfect equality of opportunity, a world without inertia, without accumulation, without heredity or acquired properties, in which every moment

---

★ First published in 1986; from *Handbook of Theory and Research for the Sociology of Education*, edited by John Richardson, translated by Richard Nice.

is perfectly independent of the previous one, every soldier has a marshal's baton in his knapsack, and every prize can be attained, instantaneously, by everyone, so that at each moment anyone can become anything. Capital, which, in its objectified or embodied forms, takes time to accumulate and which, as a potential capacity to produce profits and to reproduce itself in identical or expanded form, contains a tendency to persist in its being, is a force inscribed in the objectivity of things so that everything is not equally possible or impossible. And the structure of the distribution of the different types and subtypes of capital at a given moment in time represents the immanent structure of the social world, i.e., the set of constraints, inscribed in the very reality of that world, which govern its functioning in a durable way, determining the chances of success for practices.

It is in fact impossible to account for the structure and functioning of the social world unless one reintroduces capital in all its forms and not solely in the one form recognized by economic theory. Economic theory has allowed to be foisted upon it a definition of the economy of practices which is the historical invention of capitalism; and by reducing the universe of exchanges to mercantile exchange, which is objectively and subjectively oriented toward the maximization of profit, i.e., (economically) *self-interested,* it has implicitly defined the other forms of exchange as noneconomic, and therefore *disinterested.* In particular, it defines as disinterested those forms of exchange which ensure the *transubstantiation* whereby the most material types of capital—those which are economic in the restricted sense—can present themselves in the immaterial form of cultural capital or social capital and vice versa. Interest, in

the restricted sense it is given in economic theory, cannot be produced without producing its negative counterpart, disinterestedness. The class of practices whose explicit purpose is to maximize monetary profit cannot be defined as such without producing the purposeless finality of cultural or artistic practices and their products; the world of bourgeois man, with his double-entry accounting, cannot be invented without producing the pure, perfect universe of the artist and the intellectual and the gratuitous activities of art-for-art's sake and pure theory. ★ ★ ★

Depending on the field in which it functions, and at the cost of the more or less expensive transformations which are the precondition for its efficacy in the field in question, capital can present itself in three fundamental guises: as *economic capital,* which is immediately and directly convertible into money and may be institutionalized in the form of property rights; as *cultural capital,* which is convertible, on certain conditions, into economic capital and may be institutionalized in the form of educational qualifications; and as *social capital,* made up of social obligations ("connections"), which is convertible, in certain conditions, into economic capital and may be institutionalized in the form of a title of nobility.

||| CULTURAL CAPITAL

Cultural capital can exist in three forms: in the *embodied* state, i.e., in the form of long-lasting dispositions of the mind and body; in the *objectified* state, in the form of cultural goods (pictures, books, dictionaries, instruments, machines, etc.), which are the trace or realization of theories or critiques of these theories, problematics, etc.; and in the *institutionalized* state, a form of objectification which must be set apart because, as will be seen in the case of educational qualifications, it confers entirely original properties on the cultural capital which it is presumed to guarantee.

The reader should not be misled by the somewhat peremptory air which the effort at axiomization may give to my argument. The notion of cultural capital initially presented itself to me, in the course of research, as a theoretical hypothesis which made it possible to explain the unequal scholastic achievement of children originating from the different social classes by relating academic success, i.e., the specific profits which children from the different classes and class fractions can obtain in the academic market, to the distribution of cultural capital between the classes and class fractions. This starting point implies a break with the presuppositions inherent both in the commonsense view, which sees academic success or failure as an effect of natural aptitudes, and in human capital theories. Economists might seem to deserve credit for explicitly raising the question of the relationship between the rates of profit on educational investment and on economic investment (and its evolution). But their measurement of the yield from scholastic investment takes account only of *monetary* investments and profits, or those directly convertible into money, such as the costs of schooling and the cash equivalent of time devoted to study; they are unable to explain the different proportions of their resources which different agents or different social classes allocate to economic investment and cultural investment because they fail to take systematic account of the structure of the differential chances of profit which the various markets offer these agents or classes as a function of the volume and the composition of their assets (see esp. Becker 1964b). Furthermore, because they neglect to relate scholastic investment strategies to the whole set of educational strategies and to the system of reproduction strategies, they inevitably, by a necessary paradox, let slip the best hidden and socially most determinant educational investment, namely, the domestic transmission of cultural capital. Their studies of the relationship between academic ability and academic investment show that they are unaware that ability or talent is itself the product of an investment of time and cultural capital (Becker 1964a, p. 63–66). Not surprisingly, when endeavoring to evaluate the profits of scholastic investment, they can only consider the profitability of educational expenditure for society as a whole, the "social rate of return," or the "social gain of education as measured by its effects on national productivity" (Becker 1964b, pp. 121, 155). This typically functionalist definition of the functions of education ignores the contribution which the educational system makes to the reproduction of the social structure by sanctioning the hereditary transmission of cultural capital. From the very beginning, a definition of human capital, despite its humanistic connotations, does not move beyond economism and ignores, *inter alia,* the fact that the scholastic yield from educational action depends on the cultural capital previously invested by the family. Moreover, the economic and social yield of the educational qualification depends on the social capital, again inherited, which can be used to back it up.

The Embodied State

Most of the properties of cultural capital can be deduced from the fact that, in its fundamental state, it is linked to the body and presupposes embodiment. The accumulation of cultural capital in the embodied state, i.e., in the form of what is called culture, cultivation, *Bildung,* presupposes a process of em-bodiment, incorporation, which, insofar as it implies a labor of inculcation and assimilation, costs time, time which must be invested personally by the investor. Like the acquisition of a muscular physique or a suntan, it cannot be done at second hand (so that all effects of delegation are ruled out).

The work of acquisition is work on oneself (self-improvement), an effort that presupposes a personal cost (*on paie de sa personne,* as we say in French), an investment, above all of time, but also of that socially constituted form of libido, *libido sciendi,* with all the privation, renunciation, and sacrifice that it may entail. It follows that the least inexact of all the measurements of cultural capital are those which take as their standard the length of acquisition—so long, of course, as this is not reduced to length of schooling and allowance is made for early domestic education by giving it a positive value (a gain in time, a head start) or a negative value (wasted time, and doubly so because more time must be spent correcting its effects), according to its distance from the demands of the scholastic market.

This embodied capital, external wealth converted into an integral part of the person, into a habitus, cannot be transmitted instantaneously (unlike money, property rights, or even titles of nobility) by gift or bequest, purchase or exchange. It follows that the use or exploitation of cultural capital presents particular problems for the holders of economic or political capital, whether they be private patrons or, at the other extreme, entrepreneurs employing executives endowed with a specific cultural competence (not to mention the new state patrons). How can this capital, so closely linked to the person, be bought without buying the person and so losing the very effect of legitimation which presupposes the dissimulation of dependence? How can this capital be concentrated—as some undertakings demand—without concentrating the possessors of the capital, which can have all sorts of unwanted consequences?

Cultural capital can be acquired, to a varying extent, depending on the period, the society, and the social class, in the absence of any deliberate inculcation, and therefore quite unconsciously. It always remains marked by its earliest conditions of acquisition which, through the more or less visible marks they leave (such as the pronunciations characteristic of a class or region), help to determine its distinctive value. It cannot be accumulated beyond the appropriating capacities of an individual agent; it declines and dies with its bearer (with his biological capacity, his memory, etc.). Because it is thus linked in numerous ways to the person in his biological singularity and is subject to a hereditary transmission which is always heavily disguised, or even invisible, it defies the old, deep-rooted distinction the Greek jurists made between inherited properties *(ta patroa)* and acquired properties *(epikteta),* i.e., those which an individual adds to his heritage. It thus manages to combine the prestige of innate property with the merits of acquisition. Because the social conditions of its transmission and acquisition are more disguised than those of economic capital, it is predisposed to function as symbolic capital, i.e., to be unrecognized as capital and recognized as legitimate competence, as authority exerting an effect of (mis)recognition, e.g., in the matrimonial market and in all the markets in which economic capital is not fully recognized, whether in matters of culture, with the great art collections or great cultural foundations, or in social welfare, with the economy of generosity and the gift. Furthermore, the specifically symbolic logic of distinction additionally secures material and symbolic profits for the possessors of a large cultural capital: any given cultural competence (e.g., being able to read in a world of illiterates) derives a scarcity value from its position in the distribution of cultural capital and yields profits of distinction for its owner. In other words, the share in profits which scarce cultural capital secures in class-divided societies is based, in the last analysis, on the fact that all agents do not have the economic and cultural means for prolonging their children's education beyond the minimum necessary for the reproduction of the labor-power least valorized at a given moment.

Thus the capital, in the sense of the means of appropriating the product of accumulated labor in the objectified state which is held by a given agent, depends for its real efficacy on the form of the distribution of the means of appropriating the accumulated and objectively available resources; and the relationship of appropriation between an agent and the resources objectively available, and hence the profits they produce, is mediated by the relationship of (objective and/or subjective) competition between himself and the other possessors of capital competing for the same goods, in which scarcity—and through it social value—is generated. The structure of the field, i.e., the unequal distribution of capital, is the source of the specific effects of capital, i.e., the appropriation of profits and the power to impose the laws of functioning of the field most favorable to capital and its reproduction.

But the most powerful principle of the symbolic efficacy of cultural capital no doubt lies in the logic of its transmission. On the one hand, the process of appropriating objectified cultural capital and the time necessary for it to take place mainly depend on the cultural capital embodied in the whole family—through (among other things) the generalized Arrow effect and all forms of implicit transmission.[1] On the other hand, the initial accumulation of cultural capital, the precondition for the fast, easy accumulation of every kind of useful cultural capital, starts at the outset, without delay, without wasted time, only for the offspring of families endowed with strong cultural capital; in this case, the accumulation period covers the whole period of socialization. It follows that the

---

1 What I call the generalized Arrow effect, i.e., the fact that all cultural goods—paintings, monuments, machines, and any objects shaped by man, particularly all those which belong to the childhood environment—exert an educative effect by their mere existence, is no doubt one of the structural factors behind the "schooling explosion," in the sense that a growth in the quantity of cultural capital accumulated in the objectified state increases the educative effect automatically exerted by the environment. If one adds to this the fact that embodied cultural capital is constantly increasing, it can be seen that, in each generation, the educational system can take more for granted. The fact that the same educational investment is increasingly productive is one of the structural factors of the inflation of qualifications (together with cyclical factors linked to effects of capital conversion).

transmission of cultural capital is no doubt the best hidden form of hereditary transmission of capital, and it therefore receives proportionately greater weight in the system of reproduction strategies, as the direct, visible forms of transmission tend to be more strongly censored and controlled.

It can immediately be seen that the link between economic and cultural capital is established through the mediation of the time needed for acquisition. Differences in the cultural capital possessed by the family imply differences first in the age at which the work of transmission and accumulation begins—the limiting case being full use of the time biologically available, with the maximum free time being harnessed to maximum cultural capital—and then in the capacity, thus defined, to satisfy the specifically cultural demands of a prolonged process of acquisition. Furthermore, and in correlation with this, the length of time for which a given individual can prolong his acquisition process depends on the length of time for which his family can provide him with the free time, i.e., time free from economic necessity, which is the precondition for the initial accumulation (time which can be evaluated as a handicap to be made up).

The Objectified State

Cultural capital, in the objectified state, has a number of properties which are defined only in the relationship with cultural capital in its embodied form. The cultural capital objectified in material objects and media, such as writings, paintings, monuments, instruments, etc., is transmissible in its materiality. A collection of paintings, for example, can be transmitted as well as economic capital (if not better, because the capital transfer is more disguised). But what is transmissible is legal ownership and not (or not necessarily) what constitutes the precondition for specific appropriation, namely, the possession of the means of "consuming" a painting or using a machine, which, being nothing other than embodied capital, are subject to the same laws of transmission.

Thus cultural goods can be appropriate both materially—which presupposes economic capital—and symbolically—which presupposes cultural capital. It follows that the owner of the means of production must find a way of appropriating either the embodied capital which is the precondition of specific appropriation or the services of the holders of this capital. To possess the machines, he only needs economic capital; to appropriate them and use them in accordance with their specific purpose (defined by the cultural capital, of scientific or technical type, incorporated in them), he must have access to embodied cultural capital, either in person or by proxy. This is no doubt the basis of the ambiguous status of cadres (executives and engineers). If it is emphasized that they are not the possessors (in the strictly economic sense) of the means of production which they use, and that they derive profit from their own cultural capital only by selling the services and products which it makes possible, then they will be classified among the dominated groups; if it is emphasized that they draw their profits from the use of a particular form of capital, then they will be classified among the dominant groups. Everything suggests that as the cultural capital incorporated in the means of production increases (and with it the period of embodiment needed to acquire the means of appropriating it), so the collective strength of the holders of cultural capital would tend to increase—if the holders of the dominant type of capital (economic capital) were not able to set the holders of cultural capital in competition with one another. (They are, moreover, inclined to competition by the very conditions in which they are selected and trained, in particular by the logic of scholastic and recruitment competitions.)

Cultural capital in its objectified state presents itself with all the appearances of an autonomous, coherent universe which, although the product of historical action, has its own laws, transcending individual wills, and which, as the example of language well illustrates, therefore remains irreducible to that which each agent, or even the aggregate of the agents, can appropriate (i.e., to the cultural capital embodied in each agent or even in the aggregate of the agents). However, it should not be forgotten that it exists as symbolically and materially active, effective capital only insofar as it is appropriated by agents and implemented and invested as a weapon and a stake in the struggles which go on in the fields of cultural production (the artistic field, the scientific field, etc.) and, beyond them, in the field of the social classes—struggles in which the agents wield strengths and obtain profits proportionate to their mastery of this objectified capital, and therefore to the extent of their embodied capital.

The Institutionalized State

The objectification of cultural capital in the form of academic qualifications is one way of neutralizing some of the properties it derives from the fact that, being embodied, it has the same biological limits as its bearer. This objectification is what makes the difference between the capital of the autodidact, which may be called into question at any time, or even the cultural capital of the courtier, which can yield only ill-defined profits, of fluctuating value, in the market of high-society exchanges, and the cultural capital academically sanctioned by legally guaranteed qualifications, formally independent of the person of their bearer. With the academic qualification, a certificate of cultural competence which confers on its holder a conventional, constant, legally guaranteed value with respect to culture, social alchemy produces a form of cultural capital which has a relative autonomy vis-à-vis its bearer and even vis-à-vis the cultural capital he effectively possesses at a given moment in time. It institutes cultural capital by collective magic, just as, according to Merleau-Ponty, the living institute their dead through the ritual of mourning. One has only to think of the *concours* (competitive recruitment examination) which, out of the continuum of infinitesimal differences between performances, produces sharp, absolute, lasting differences, such as that which separates the last successful candidate from the first unsuccessful one, and institutes an essential difference between the officially recognized, guaranteed competence and simple cultural capital, which is constantly required to prove itself. In this case, one sees clearly the performative magic of the power of instituting, the power to show forth and secure belief or, in a word, to impose recognition.

By conferring institutional recognition on the cultural capital possessed by any given agent, the academic qualification also makes it possible to compare qualification holders and even to exchange them (by substituting one for another in succession). Furthermore, it makes it possible to establish conversion rates between cultural capital and economic capital by guaranteeing the monetary value of a given academic capital. This product of the conversion of economic capital into cultural capital establishes the value, in terms of cultural capital, of the holder of a given qualification relative to other qualification holders and, by the same token, the monetary value for which it can be exchanged on the labor market (academic investment has no meaning unless a minimum degree of reversibility of the conversion it implies is objectively guaranteed). Because the material and symbolic profits which the academic qualification guarantees also depend on its scarcity, the investments made (in time and effort) may turn out to be less profitable than was anticipated when they were made (there having been a *de facto* change in the conversion rate between academic capital and economic capital). The strategies for converting economic capital into cultural capital, which are among the short-term factors of the schooling explosion and the inflation of qualifications, are governed by changes in the structure of the chances of profit offered by the different types of capital.

SOCIAL CAPITAL

Social capital is the aggregate of the actual or potential resources which are linked to posses-sion of a durable network of more or less institutionalized relationships of mutual acquaintance and recognition—or in other words, to membership in a group—which provides each of its members with the backing of the collectivity-owned capital, a "credential" which entitles them to credit, in the various senses of the word. These relationships may exist only in the practical state, in material and/or symbolic exchanges which help to maintain them. They may also be socially instituted and guaranteed by the application of a common name (the name of a family, a class, or a tribe or of a school, a party, etc.) and by a whole set of instituting acts designed simultaneously to form and inform those who undergo them; in this case, they are more or less really enacted and so maintained and reinforced, in exchanges. Being based on indissolubly material and symbolic exchanges, the establishment and maintenance of which presuppose reacknowledgment of proximity, they are also partially irreducible to objective relations of proximity in physical (geographical) space or even in economic and social space.[2]

The volume of the social capital possessed by a given agent thus depends on the size of the network of connections he can effectively mobilize and on the volume of the capital (economic, cultural or symbolic) possessed in his own right by each of those to whom he is connected.[3] This means that, although it is relatively irreducible to the economic and cultural capital possessed

---

2 Neighborhood relationships may, of course, receive an elementary form of institutionalization, as in the Bearn—or the Basque region—where neighbors, *lous besis* (a word which, in old texts, is applied to the legitimate inhabitants of the village, the rightful members of the assembly), are explicitly designated, in accordance with fairly codified rules, and are assigned functions which are differentiated according to their rank (there is a "first neighbor," a "second neighbor," and so

on), particularly for the major social ceremonies (funerals, marriages, etc.). But even in this case, the relationships actually used by no means always coincide with the relationships socially instituted.

3 Manners (bearing, pronunciation, etc.) may be included in social capital insofar as, through the mode of acquisition they point to, they indicate initial membership of a more or less prestigious group.

by a given agent, or even by the whole set of agents to whom he is connected, social capital is never completely independent of it because the exchanges instituting mutual acknowledgment presuppose the reacknowledgment of a minimum of objective homogeneity, and because it exerts a multiplier effect on the capital he possesses in his own right.

The profits which accrue from membership in a group are the basis of the solidarity which makes them possible. This does not mean that they are consciously pursued as such, even in the case of groups like select clubs, which are deliberately organized in order to concentrate social capital and so to derive full benefit from the multiplier effect implied in concentration and to secure the profits of membership—material profits, such as all the types of services accruing from useful relationships, and symbolic profits, such as those derived from association with a rare, prestigious group.

The existence of a network of connections is not a natural given, or even a social given, constituted once and for all by an initial act of institution, represented, in the case of the family group, by the genealogical definition of kinship relations, which is the characteristic of a social formation. It is the product of an endless effort at institution, of which institution rites—often wrongly described as rites of passage—mark the essential moments and which is necessary in order to produce and reproduce lasting, useful relationships that can secure material or symbolic profits (see Bourdieu 1982). In other words, the network of relationships is the product of investment strategies, individual or collective, consciously or unconsciously aimed at establishing or reproducing social relationships that are directly usable in the short or long

term, i.e., at transforming contingent relations, such as those of neighborhood, the workplace, or even kinship, into relationships that are at once necessary and elective, implying durable obligations subjectively felt (feelings of gratitude, respect, friendship, etc.) or institutionally guaranteed (rights). This is done through the alchemy of *consecration,* the symbolic constitution produced by social institution (institution as a relative—brother, sister, cousin, etc.—or as a knight, an heir, an elder, etc.) and endlessly reproduced in and through the exchange (of gifts, words, women, etc.) which it encourages and which presupposes and produces mutual knowledge and recognition. Exchange transforms the things exchanged into signs of recognition and, through the mutual recognition and the recognition of group membership which it implies, reproduces the group. By the same token, it reaffirms the limits of the group, i.e., the limits beyond which the constitutive exchange—trade, commensality, or marriage—cannot take place. Each member of the group is thus instituted as a custodian of the limits of the group: because the definition of the criteria of entry is at stake in each new entry, he can modify the group by modifying the limits of legitimate exchange through some form of misalliance. It is quite logical that, in most societies, the preparation and conclusion of marriages should be the business of the whole group, and not of the agents directly concerned. Through the introduction of new members into a family, a clan, or a club, the whole definition of the group, i.e., its fines, its boundaries, and its identity, is put at stake, exposed to redefinition, alteration, adulteration. When, as in modern societies, families lose the monopoly of the establishment of exchanges which can lead to lasting relationships, whether socially sanctioned (like marriage) or not, they may continue to control these exchanges, while remaining within the logic of laissez-faire, through all the institutions which are designed to favor legitimate exchanges and exclude illegitimate ones by producing occasions (rallies, cruises, hunts, parties, receptions, etc.), places (smart neighborhoods, select schools, clubs, etc.), or practices (smart sports, parlor games, cultural ceremonies, etc.) which bring together, in a seemingly fortuitous way, individuals as homogeneous as possible in all the pertinent respects in terms of the existence and persistence of the group.

The reproduction of social capital presupposes an unceasing effort of sociability, a continuous series of exchanges in which recognition is endlessly affirmed and reaffirmed. This work, which implies expenditure of time and energy and so, directly or indirectly, of economic capital, is not profitable or even conceivable unless one invests in it a specific competence (knowledge of genealogical relationships and of real connections and skill at using them, etc.) and an acquired disposition to acquire and maintain this competence, which are themselves integral parts of this capital.[4] "This is one of the factors which explain why the profitability of this labor of accumulating and maintaining social capital rises in proportion to the size of the capital. Because the social capital accruing from a relationship is that much greater to the extent that the person who is the object of it is richly endowed with capital (mainly social, but also cultural and even economic capital), the possessors of an inherited social capital, symbolized by a great name, are able to transform all circumstantial relationships into lasting connections. They are sought after for their social capital and, because they are well known, are worthy of being known ("I know him well"); they do not need to "make the acquaintance" of all their "acquaintances"; they are known to more people than they know, and their work of sociability, when it is exerted, is highly productive.

Every group has its more or less institutionalized forms of delegation which enable it to concentrate the totality of the social capital, which is the basis of the existence of the group (a family or a nation, of course, but also an association or a party), in the hands of a single agent or a small group of agents and to mandate this plenipotentiary, charged with *plena potestas agendi et loquendi*,[5] to represent the group, to speak and act in its name and so, with the aid of this collectively owned capital, to exercise a power incommensurate with the agent's personal contribution. Thus, at the most elementary degree of institutionalization, the head of the family, the *pater familias*, the eldest, most senior member, is tacitly recognized as the only person entitled to speak on behalf of the family group in all official circumstances. But whereas in this case, diffuse delegation requires the great to step forward and defend the collective honor when the honor of the weakest members is threatened. The institutionalized delegation, which ensures the concentration of social capital, also has the effect of limiting the consequences of

---

4 There is every reason to suppose that socializing, or, more generally, relational, dispositions are very unequally distributed among the social classes and, within a given class, among fractions of different origin.

5 A "full power to act and speak" (translator).

individual lapses by explicitly delimiting responsibilities and authorizing the recognized spokesmen to shield the group as a whole from discredit by expelling or excommunicating the embarrassing individuals.

If the internal competition for the monopoly of legitimate representation of the group is not to threaten the conservation and accumulation of the capital which is the basis of the group, the members of the group must regulate the conditions of access to the right to declare oneself a member of the group and, above all, to set oneself up as a representative (delegate, plenipotentiary, spokesman, etc.) of the whole group, thereby committing the social capital of the whole group. The title of nobility is the form *par excellence* of the institutionalized social capital which guarantees a particular form of social relationship in a lasting way. One of the paradoxes of delegation is that the mandated agent can exert on (and, up to a point, against) the group the power which the group enables him to concentrate. (This is perhaps especially true in the limiting cases in which the mandated agent creates the group which creates him but which only exists through him.) The mechanisms of delegation and representation (in both the theatrical and the legal senses) which fall into place—that much more strongly, no doubt, when the group is large and its members weak—as one of the conditions for the concentration of social capital (among other reasons, because it enables numerous, varied, scattered agents to act as one man and to overcome the limitations of space and time) also contain the seeds of an embezzlement or misappropriation of the capital which they assemble.

This embezzlement is latent in the fact that a group as a whole can be represented, in the various meanings of the word, by a subgroup, clearly delimited and perfectly visible to all, known to all, and recognized by all, that of the *nobiles,* the "people who are known," the paradigm of whom is the nobility, and who may speak on behalf of the whole group, represent the whole group, and exercise authority in the name of the whole group. The noble is the group personified. He bears the name of the group to which he gives his name (the metonymy which links the noble to his group is clearly seen when Shakespeare calls Cleopatra "Egypt" or the King of France "France," just as Racine calls Pyrrhus "Epirus"). It is by him, his name, the difference it proclaims, that the members of his group, the liegemen, and also the land and castles, are known and recognized. Similarly, phenomena such as the "personality cult" or the identification of parties, trade unions, or movements with their leader are latent in the very logic of representation. Everything combines to cause the signifier to take the place of the signified, the spokesmen that of the group he is supposed to express, not least because his distinction, his "outstandingness," his visibility constitute the essential part, if not the essence, of this power, which, being entirely set within the logic of knowledge and acknowledgment, is fundamentally a symbolic power; but also because the representative, the sign, the emblem, may be, and create, the whole reality of groups which receive effective social existence only in and through representation.

CONVERSIONS

The different types of capital can be derived from *economic capital,* but only at the cost of a more or less great effort of transformation, which is needed to produce the type of power effective in the field in question. For example, there are some goods and services to which economic capital gives immediate access, without secondary costs; others can be obtained only by virtue of a social capital of relationships (or social obligations) which cannot act instantaneously, at the appropriate moment, unless they have been established and maintained for a long time, as if for their own sake, and therefore outside their period of use, i.e., at the cost of an investment in sociability which is necessarily long-term because the time lag is one of the factors of the transmutation of a pure and simple debt into that recognition of nonspecific indebtedness which is called gratitude. In contrast to the cynical but also economical transparency of economic exchange, in which equivalents change hands in the same instant, the essential ambiguity of social exchange, which presupposes misrecognition, in other words, a form of faith and of bad faith (in the sense of self-deception), presupposes a much more subtle economy of time.

So it has to be posited simultaneously that economic capital is at the root of all the other types of capital and that these transformed, disguised forms of economic capital, never entirely reducible to that definition, produce their most specific effects only to the extent that they conceal (not least from their possessors) the fact that economic capital is at their root, in other words—but only in the last analysis—at the root of their effects. The real logic of the functioning of capital, the conversions from one type to another, and the law of conservation which governs them cannot be understood unless two opposing but equally partial views are superseded: on the one hand, economism, which, on the grounds that every type of capital is reducible in the last analysis to economic capital, ignores what makes the specific efficacy of the other types of capital, and on the other hand, semiologism (nowadays represented by structuralism, symbolic interactionism, or ethnomethodology), which reduces social exchanges to phenomena of communication and ignores the brutal fact of universal reducibility to economics.

In accordance with a principle which is the equivalent of the principle of the conservation of energy, profits in one area are necessarily paid for by costs in another (so that a concept like wastage has no meaning in a general science of the economy of practices). The universal equivalent, the measure of all equivalences, is nothing other than labor-time (in the widest sense); and the conservation of social energy through all its conversions is verified if, in each case, one takes into account both the labor-time accumulated in the form of capital and the labor-time needed to transform it from one type into another.

It has been seen, for example, that the transformation of economic capital into social capital presupposes a specific labor, i.e., an apparently gratuitous expenditure of time, attention, care, concern, which, as is seen in the endeavor to personalize a gift, has the effect of transfiguring the purely monetary import of the exchange and, by the same token, the very meaning of the exchange. From a narrowly economic standpoint, this effort is bound to be seen as pure wastage, but in the terms of the logic of social exchanges, it is a solid investment, the profits of which will appear, in the long run, in monetary or other form. Similarly, if the best measure of cultural capital is undoubtedly the amount of time devoted to acquiring it, this is because the transformation of economic capital into cultural capital presupposes an expenditure of time that is made possible by possession of economic capital. More precisely, it is because the cultural capital that is effectively transmitted within the family itself depends not only on the quantity of cultural capital, itself accumulated by spending time, that the domestic group possess, but also on the usable time (particularly in the form of the mother's free time) available to it (by virtue of its economic capital, which enables it to purchase the time of others) to ensure the transmission of this capital and to delay entry into the labor market through prolonged schooling, a credit which pays off, if at all, only in the very long term.[6]

The convertibility of the different types of capital is the basis of the strategies aimed at ensuring the reproduction of capital (and the position occupied in social space) by means of the conversions least costly in terms of conversion work and of the losses inherent in the conversion itself (in a given state of the social power relations). The different types of capital can be distinguished according to their reproducibility or, more precisely, according to how easily they are transmitted, i.e., with more or less loss and with more or less concealment; the rate of loss and the degree of concealment tend to vary in inverse ratio. Everything which helps to disguise the economic aspect also tends to increase the risk of loss (particularly the intergenerational transfers). Thus the (apparent) incommensurability of the different types of capital introduces a high degree of uncertainty into all transactions between holders of different types. Similarly, the declared refusal of calculation and of guarantees which characterizes exchanges tending to produce a social capital in the form of a capital of obligations that are usable in the more or less long term (exchanges of gifts, services, visits, etc.) necessarily entails the risk of ingratitude, the refusal of that recognition of nonguaranteed debts which such exchanges aim to produce. Similarly, too, the high degree of concealment of the transmission of cultural capital has the disadvantage (in addition to its inherent risks of loss) that the academic qualification which is its institutionalized form is neither transmissible (like a title of nobility) nor negotiable (like stocks and shares). More precisely, cultural capital, whose diffuse, continuous transmission within the family escapes observation and control (so that the educational system seems to award its honors solely to natural qualities) and which is increas-

---

6 Among the advantages procured by capital in all its types, the most precious is the increased volume of useful time that is made possible through the various methods of appropriating other people's time (in the form of services). It may take the form either of increased spare time, secured by reducing the time consumed in activities directly channeled toward producing the means of reproducing the existence of the domestic group, or of more intense use of the time so consumed, by recourse to other people's labor or to devices and methods which are available only to those who have spent time learning how to use them and which (like better transport or living close to the place of work) make it possible to save time. (This is in contrast to the cash savings of the poor, which are paid for in time—do-it-yourself, bargain hunting, etc.) None of this is true of mere economic capital; it is possession of cultural capital that makes it possible to derive greater profit not only from labor-time, by securing a higher yield from the same time, but also from spare time, and so to increase both economic and cultural capital.

ingly tending to attain full efficacy, at least on the labor market, only when validated by the educational system, i.e., converted into a capital of qualifications, is subject to a more disguised but more risky transmission than economic capital. As the educational qualification, invested with the specific force of the official, becomes the condition for legitimate access to a growing number of positions, particularly the dominant ones, the educational system tends increasingly to dispossess the domestic group of the monopoly of the transmission of power and privileges—and, among other things, of the choice of its legitimate heirs from among children of different sex and birth rank. And economic capital itself poses quite different problems of transmission, depending on the particular form it takes. Thus, according to Grassby (1970), the liquidity of commercial capital, which gives immediate economic power and favors transmission, also makes it more vulnerable than landed property (or even real estate) and does not favor the establishment of long-lasting dynasties.

Because the question of the arbitrariness of appropriation arises most sharply in the process of transmission—particularly at the time of succession, a critical moment for all power—every reproduction strategy is at the same time a legitimation strategy aimed at consecrating both an exclusive appropriate and its reproduction. When the subversive critique which aims to weaken the dominant class through the principle of its perpetuation by bringing to light the arbitrariness of the entitlements transmitted and of their transmission (such as the critique which the Enlightenment *philosophes* directed, in the name of nature, against the arbitrariness of birth) is incorporated

in institutionalized mechanisms (for example, laws of inheritance) aimed at controlling the official, direct transmission of power and privileges, the holders of capital have an ever greater interest in resorting to reproduction strategies capable of ensuring better-disguised transmission, but at the cost of greater loss of capital, by exploiting the convertibility of the types of capital. Thus the more the official transmission of capital is prevented or hindered, the more the effects of the clandestine circulation of capital in the form of cultural capital become determinant in the reproduction of the social structure. As an instrument of reproduction capable of disguising its own function, the scope of the educational system tends to increase, and together with this increase is the unification of the market in social qualifications which gives rights to occupy rare positions.

||| REFERENCES

Becker, Gary S. *A Theoretical and Empirical Analysis with Special Reference to Education.* New York: National Bureau of Economic Research, 1964a.

————. *Human Capital.* New York: Columbia University Press, 1964b.

Bourdieu, Pierre. "Les rites d'institution." *Actes de la recherche en sciences sociales* 43 (1982): 58–63.

Grassby, Richard. "English Merchant Capitalism in the Late Seventeenth Century: The Composition of Business Fortunes." *Past and Present* 46 (1970); 87–107.

Class Analysis

28

Class Structure in Comparative Perspective*

ERIK OLIN WRIGHT

||| CLASS AND EXPLOITATION

Within the Marxist tradition of class analysis, class divisions are defined primarily in terms of the linkage between property relations and exploitation. Slave masters and slaves constitute classes because a particular property relation (property rights in people) generates exploitation (the appropriation of the fruits of labor of the slave by the slave master). Homeowners and the homeless would not constitute "classes" even though they are distinguished by property rights in housing since this division does not constitute a basis for the exploitation of the homeless by homeowners.[1]

---

* First published in 2000; from *Class Counts*.

1 If homeowners exchanged housing in vacant rooms for domestic service, then the property rights in housing might become the basis for a class relation. The sheer fact of homeownership and homelessness, however, does not itself constitute a form of exploitation and thus is not a class division. It is only when this property right is translated into a power relation between actors within which labor is appropriated that it becomes exploitative.

In capitalist society, the central form of exploitation is based on property rights in the means of production. These property rights generate three basic classes: capitalists (exploiters), who own the means of production and hire workers; *workers* (exploited), who do not own the means of production and sell their labor power to capitalists; and *petty bourgeois* (neither exploiter nor exploited), who own and use the means of production without hiring others. The Marxist account of how the capital–labor relation generates exploitation is a familiar one: propertyless workers, in order to acquire their means of livelihood, must sell their labor power to people who own the means of production.[2] In this exchange relation, they agree to work for a specified length of time in exchange for a wage which they use to buy their means of subsistence. Because of the power relation between capitalists and workers, capitalists are able to force workers to produce more than is needed to provide them with this subsistence. As a result, workers produce a surplus which is owned by the capitalist and takes the form of profits. Profits, the amount of the social product that is left over after the costs of producing and reproducing all of the inputs (both labor power inputs and physical inputs) have been deducted, constitute an appropriation of the fruits of labor of workers.

Describing this relation as exploitative is a claim about the basis for the inherent conflict between workers and capitalists in the employment relation. It points to the crucial fact that the conflict between capitalists and workers is not simply over the *level of wages,* but over the *amount of work effort* performed for those wages. Capitalists always want workers to expend more effort than workers willingly want to do. As Bowles and Gintis (1990) have argued, "the whistle while you work" level of effort of workers is always suboptimal for capitalists, and thus capitalists have to adopt various strategies of surveillance and control to increase labor effort. While the intensity of overt conflict generated by these relations will vary over time and place, and class compromises may occur in which high levels of cooperation between labor and management take place, nevertheless, this underlying antagonism of material interests remains so long as the relationship remains exploitative.

For some theoretical and empirical purposes, this simple image of the class structure may be sufficient. For example, if the main purpose of an analysis is to explore the basic differences between the class structures of feudalism and capitalism, then an analysis which revolved entirely around the relationship between capitalists and workers might be adequate. However, for many of the things we want to study with class analysis, we need a more nuanced set of categories. In particular, we need concepts which allow for two kinds of analyses: first, the analysis of the variation across time and place in the class structures of concrete capitalist societies, and second, the analysis of the ways individual lives are affected by their location within the class structure. The first of these is needed

---

2 To be somewhat more precise, in order to acquire the means of subsistence, at least some members of a propertyless family (defined as the unit of shared consumption) must sell labor power to employers. In some times and places, this has meant that the male "breadwinner" entered the labor market while the female "housewife" stayed home. In contemporary advanced capitalism, generally all adult members of households sell their labor power.

if we are to explore macro-variations in a fine-grained way; the second is needed if we are to use class effectively in micro-analysis.

Both of these tasks involve elaborating a concept of class structure in capitalist societies that moves beyond the core polarization between capitalists and workers. More specifically, this involves solving two general problems in class structural analysis: first, the problem of locating the "middle class" within the class structure, and second, locating people not in the paid labor force in the class structure.

THE PROBLEM OF THE "MIDDLE CLASS" AMONG EMPLOYEES

If we limit the analysis of class structure in capitalism to the ownership of, and exclusion from, the means of production, we end up with a class structure in which there are only three locations—the capitalist class, the working class and the petty bourgeoisie (those who own means of production but do not hire workers)—and in which around 85–90% of the population in most developed capitalist countries falls into a single class. While this may in some sense reflect a profound truth about capitalism—that the large majority of the population are separated from the means of production and must sell their labor power on the labor market in order to survive—it does not provide us with an adequate conceptual framework for explaining many of the things we want class to help explain. In particular, if we want class structure to help explain class consciousness, class formation and class conflict, then we need some way of understanding the class-relevant divisions within the employee population.

In ordinary language terms, this is the problem of the "middle class"—people who do not own their own means of production, who sell their labor power on a labor market, and yet do not seem part of the "working class." The question, then, is on what basis can we differentiate class locations among people who share a common location of nonownership within capitalist property relations? In the analyses in this book, I will divide the class of employees along two dimensions: first, their relationship to authority within production, and second, their possession of skills or expertise.

Authority

There are two rationales for treating authority as a dimension of class relations among employees. The first concerns the role of *domination* within capitalist property relations. In order to insure the performance of adequate effort on the part of workers, capitalist production always involves an apparatus of domination involving surveillance, positive and negative sanctions and varying forms of hierarchy. Capitalists do not simply *own* the means of production and *hire* workers; they also *dominate* workers within production.

In these terms, managers and supervisors can be viewed as exercising delegated capitalist class powers in so far as they engage in the practices of domination within production. In this sense they can be considered *simultaneously* in the capitalist class *and* the working class: they are like capitalists in that they dominate workers; they are like workers in that they are controlled by capitalists and exploited within production. They thus occupy what I have called *contradictory locations within class relations*. The term "contradictory" is used in this expression rather than simply "dual" since the class interests embedded in managerial jobs combine the inherently antagonistic interests of capital and labor. The higher one moves in the authority hierarchy, the greater will be the weight of capitalist interests within this class location. Thus upper managers, and especially Chief Executive Officers in large corporations will be very closely tied to the capitalist class, while the class character of lower level supervisor jobs will be much closer to that of the working class.

The second rationale for treating the authority dimension as a criterion for differentiating class locations among employees centers on the relationship between their earnings and the appropriation of surplus. The strategic position of managers within the organization of production enables them to make significant claims on a portion of the social surplus (defined in the counterfactual manner discussed above) in the form of relatively high earnings [3] In effect this means that the wages and salaries of managerial labor power are above the costs of producing and reproducing their labor power (including whatever skills they might have).

The specific mechanism through which this appropriation takes place can be referred to as a "loyalty rent." It is important for the profitability of capitalist firms that managers wield their power in an effective and responsible way. The difficulty is that a high level of surveillance and threats is generally not an effective strategy for eliciting this kind of behavior, both because managerial performance is generally rather hard to monitor and because repressive controls tend to undermine initiative rather than stimulate creative behavior. What is needed, then, is a way of generating some level of real commitment on the part of managers to the goals of the organization. This is accomplished by relatively high earnings linked to careers and promotion ladders within authority hierarchies. These higher earnings involve a redistribution of part of the social surplus to managers in order to build their loyalty to the organization. Of course, negative sanctions are still present in the background: managers are sometimes fired, they are disciplined for poor work by failing to get promotions or raises, etc. But these coercive forms of control gain their efficacy from their link to the strong inducements of earnings that, especially for higher level managers, are significantly above the costs of producing the skills of managers.[4] Managers thus not only occupy contradictory locations within class relations by

---

3 In earlier work I argued that by virtue of this appropriation of surplus by managers they should be seen as exploiters. The problem with this formulation is that managers also contribute to the surplus through their own laboring activity, and thus their surplus income may simply reflect a capacity to appropriate part of the surplus which they contribute to production. Instead of being "exploiters," therefore, many managers may simply be less exploited than other employees. Because of this ambiguity, therefore, it is better simply to see managers as occupying a *privileged* position with respect to the process of exploitation which enables them to appropriate part of the social surplus in the form of higher incomes.

4 This rent component of the earnings of managers has been recognized in "efficiency wage" theory which acknowledges

that the market-clearing wage may be suboptimal from the point of view of the goals of the employer. Because of the difficulty in enforcing labor contracts, employers have to pay employees more than the wages predicted by theories of competitive equilibria in order to gain compliance. While this mechanism may generate some small "employment rents" for all employees, it is especially salient for those employees who occupy strategic jobs requiring responsible, diligent performance of duties. For the mainstream economics discussion of efficiency wages, see Akerloff and Yellen (1986). For arguments that extend efficiency wage theory to Marxist arguments about the "extraction" of labor effort from workers, see Bowles and Gintis (1990).

virtue of domination, they occupy what might be termed a *privileged appropriation location within exploitation relations*. Both of these differentiate them from the working class.

Skills and Expertise

The second axis of class differentiation among employees centers on the possession of skills or expertise. Like managers, employees who possess high levels of skills/expertise are potentially in a privileged appropriation location within exploitation relations. There are two primary mechanisms through which this can happen. First, skills and expertise are frequently scarce in labor markets, not simply because they are in short supply, but also because there are systematic obstacles in the way of increasing the supply of those skills to meet the requirements of employing organizations. One important form of these obstacles is credentials, but rare talents could also constitute the basis for sustained restrictions on the supply of a particular form of labor power.[5] The result of such restrictions on supply is that owners of the scarce skills are able to receive a wage above the costs of producing and reproducing their labor power. This "skill rent" is a way by which employees can appropriate part of the social surplus.

Second, the control over knowledge and skills frequently renders also the labor effort of skilled workers difficult to monitor and control. The effective control over knowledge by such employees means that employers must rely to some extent on loyalty enhancing mechanisms in order to achieve desired levels of cooperation and effort from employees with high levels of skills and expertise, just as they have to do in the case of managers. Employees with high levels of expertise, therefore, are able to appropriate surplus both because of their strategic location within the organization of production (as controllers of knowledge), and because of their strategic location in the organization of labor markets (as controllers of a scarce form of labor power).

Understood in this way, the possession of skills and expertise defines a distinctive location within class relations because of a specific kind of power they confer on employees. It may also be the case that expertise, skills and knowledge are associated with various kinds of "symbolic capital" and distinctive life-styles, as Bourdieu (1984) and others have noted. While these cultural correlates of class may be of considerable explanatory importance for a variety of sociological questions, they do not constitute the essential rationale for treating skills and expertise as a dimension of class location within a materialist class analysis (except in so far as symbolic capital plays a role in acquiring skills and credentials). That rationale rests on the claim that experts, like managers, occupy a privileged appropriation location within exploitation relations that differentiates them from ordinary workers.

★ ★ ★ I frequently use "skills and expertise" as a couplet. The term "skill" by itself sometimes is taken to refer simply to manual skills,

---

5 Credentials would not constitute a restriction on the supply of a particular kind of skill if there were no obstacles for individuals acquiring the credentials. A variety of such obstacles exist: restrictions on the number of slots in the training programs; restrictions in credit markets to get loans to obtain the training; inequality in the distribution of "cultural capital" (including such things as manners, accent, appearance, etc.) and "social capital" (especially such things as access to networks and information); and, of course, inequalities in genetic endowments.

FIGURE 1 BASIC CLASS TYPOLOGY

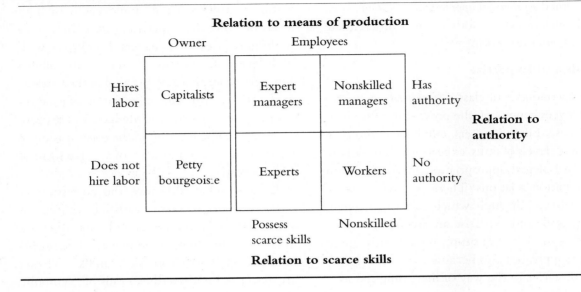

rather than the more general idea of enhanced or complex labor power, contrasted to "raw" or undeveloped labor power. This enhancement can take many forms, both physical and cognitive. It may provide great flexibility to engage in a variety of work settings, or it may be highly specialized and vulnerable to obsolescence. Enhanced labor power is often legally certified in the form of official credentials, but in some circumstances skills and expertise may function effectively without such certification. The important theoretical idea is that skills and expertise designate an asset embodied in the labor power of people which enhances their power in labor markets and labor processes.

A Map of Middle-Class Class Locations

Adding position within authority hierarchies and possession of scarce skills and expertise to

the fundamental dimension of capitalist property relations generates the map of class locations presented in Figure 1. With appropriate modifications depending upon our specific empirical objectives, this is the basic schema that underlies [my] investigations. It is important to stress that this is a map of class *locations*. The cells in the typology are not "classes" as such; they are locations within class relations. Some of these are contradictory locations within class relations, others are privileged appropriation locations within exploitation relations and still others are polarized locations within capitalist property relations. By convention the polarized locations—"capitalists" and "workers" in capitalism—are often called "classes," but the more precise terminology would be to describe these as the fundamental locations within the capitalist class structure. The typology is thus

FIGURE 2 ELABORATED CLASS TYPOLOGY

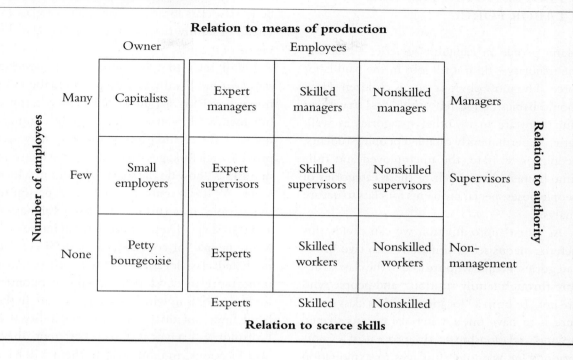

not a proposal for a six-class model of the class structure of capitalism, but rather a model of a class structure which differentiates six locations within class relations.

In some of the empirical analyses we will discuss, we will combine some of the locations in this typology, typically to generate a four category typology consisting of capitalists, petty bourgeois, "middle-class" locations (contradictory locations and privileged appropriation locations among employees) and workers. In other analyses we will modify the typology by adding intermediary categories along each of the dimensions. On the relation to means of production dimension this involves distinguishing between proper capitalists, small

employers who only have a few employees, and the petty bourgeoisie (self-employed people with no employees). On the authority dimension this means differentiating between proper managers—people who are involved in organizational decision making—and mere supervisors, who have power over subordinates but are not involved in policy-making decisions. And, on the skill dimension this involves distinguishing between occupations which typically require advanced academic degrees, and other skilled occupations which require lower levels of specialized training. The result will be the twelve-location class-structure matrix presented in Figure 2.

★ ★ ★

PEOPLE NOT IN THE PAID LABOR FORCE

Many people in capitalist societies—probably the majority—do not fill jobs in the paid labor force. The most obvious case is children. How should babies be located in the class structure? But there are many other categories as well: retirees, permanently disabled people, students, people on welfare, the unemployed and full-time homemakers. Each of these categories of people poses special problems for class structure analysis.

As a first approximation we can divide this heterogeneous set of situations into two broad categories: people who are tied to the class structure through family relations, and people who are not. To be in a "location" within class structure is to have one's material interests shaped by one's relationship to the process of exploitation. One way such linkages to exploitation are generated by class structures is through *jobs*. This is the kind of class location we have been exploring so far. I will refer to these as *direct class locations*. But there are other mechanisms by which people's lives are linked to the process of exploitation. Of particular importance are the ways in which family structures and kinship relations link an individual's material interests to the process of exploitation. Being born into a wealthy capitalist family links the child to the material interests of the capitalist class via family relations. It makes sense, then, to say that this child is "in" the capitalist class. If that child, as a young adult, works in a factory but stands to inherit millions of dollars of capitalist wealth and can rely on family resources for various

needs, then that person would simultaneously be in two class locations: the capitalist class by virtue of family ties and the working class by virtue of the job.

I will refer to these situations as *mediated class locations*. Family ties are probably the most important basis for mediated class locations, but membership in certain kinds of communities or the relationship to the state may also provide such linkages. In each case the question one asks is "how do the social relations in which a person's life is embedded link that person to the various mechanisms of class exploitation and thus shape that person's material interests?" Many people, of course, have both direct and mediated class locations. This is of particular importance in developed capitalist economies for households in which both spouses are in the labor force, for this creates the possibility that husbands and wives will have different direct class locations, and thus each of them will have different direct and mediated locations. ★ ★ ★

There are, however, people for whom family ties provide at most extremely tenuous linkages to the class structure. Most notably, this is the situation of many people in the so-called "underclass." This expression is used in a variety of ways in contemporary policy discussions. Sometimes it is meant to be a pejorative term rather like the old Marxist concept of "lumpenproletariat"; at other times it is used more descriptively to designate a segment of the poor whose conditions of life are especially desperate and whose prospects for improvement are particularly dismal. In terms of the analysis of this chapter, one way of giving this concept a more precise theoretical status is to link it to the concepts of exploitation and oppression: an "underclass" can be defined as a category of social agents who are economically oppressed but not consistently exploited within a given class system.[6]

Different kinds of class structures will generate different forms of an "underclass." In many parts of the world today and throughout much of human history, the pivotal resource which defines the underclass is land. Landlords, agrarian capitalists, peasants and exploited agrarian producers all have access to land; people who are excluded from such access constitute the underclass of agrarian societies. In these terms, many Native Americans were transformed into an underclass in the nineteenth century when they were pushed off of the land onto the reservations.

In contemporary advanced capitalism, the key resource which defines the predicament of the underclass is labor power itself. This might seem like an odd statement since in capitalism, at least since the abolition of slavery, everyone supposedly owns one "unit" of labor power, him or herself. The point is that some people do not in fact own *productively saleable* labor power. The situation is similar to a capitalist owning outmoded machines. While the capitalist physically controls these pieces of machinery, they cease to be "capital"—a capitalistically productive asset—if they cannot be deployed within a capitalist production process profitably. In the case of labor power, a person can physically control his or her own laboring capacity, but that capacity can cease to have economic value in capitalism if it cannot be deployed productively. This is the essential condition of people in the "underclass." They are oppressed because they are denied access to various kinds of productive resources, above all the necessary means to acquire the skills needed to make their labor power saleable. As a result, they are not consistently exploited.

Understood in this way, the underclass consists of human beings who are largely expendable *from the point of view of the logic of capitalism*. Like Native Americans who became a landless underclass in the nineteenth century, repression rather than incorporation is the central mode of social control directed toward them. Capitalism does not need the labor power of unemployed inner city youth. The material interests of the wealthy and privileged segments of American society would be better served if these people simply disappeared. However, unlike in the nineteenth century, the moral and political forces are such that direct genocide is no longer a viable strategy. The alternative, then, is to build prisons and to cordon off the zones of cities in which the underclass lives.

6 Although he does not explicitly elaborate the term "underclass" in terms of a theory of exploitation and economic oppression, the definition proposed here is consistent with the more structural aspects of way the term is used by William Julius Wilson (1982, 1987) in his analysis of the interconnection between race and class in American society. Wilson argues that as legal barriers to racial equality have disappeared and as class differentiation within the black population has increased, the central determining structure of the lives of many African-Americans is no longer race as such, but class. More specifically, he argues that there has been a substantial growth of an urban underclass of people without marketable skills and with very weak attachments to the labor force, living in crumbling central cities isolated from the mainstream of American life and institutions.

Marxist versus Weberian Class Analysis

As a set of empirical categories, the class structure matrix in Figures 1 and 2 could be deployed within either a Weberian or Marxist framework. The control over economic resources is central to both Marxist and Weberian class analysis, and both frameworks could be massaged to allow for the array of categories I am using. Indeed, a good argument could be made that the proposed class structure concept incorporates significant Weberian elements, since the explicit inclusion of skills as a criterion for class division and the importance accorded income privileges for both managers and credentialed experts are hallmarks of Weberian class analysis. In a real sense, therefore, the empirical categories in this book can be seen as a hybrid of the categories conventionally found in Marxist and Weberian class analysis.[7] In what sense, therefore, does this class structure analysis remain "Marxist"?

To answer this question we need to compare the theoretical foundations of the concept of class in the Marxist and Weberian traditions. The contrast between Marx and Weber has been one of the grand themes in the history of Sociology as a discipline. Most graduate school programs have a sociological theory course within which Marx versus Weber figures as a central motif. However, in terms of class analysis, posing Marx and Weber as polar opposites is a bit misleading because in many ways Weber is speaking in his most Marxian voice when he talks about class. The concept of class within these two streams of thought share a number of important features:

- Both Marxist and Weberian approaches differ from what might be called simple gradational notions of class in which classes are differentiated strictly on the basis of inequalities in the material conditions of life. This conceptualization of class underwrites the common inventory of classes found in popular discourse and the mass media: upper class, upper middle class, middle class, lower middle class, lower class, underclass. Both Marxist and Weberian class analysis define classes *relationally,* i.e. a given class location is defined by virtue of the social relations which link it to other class locations.

- Both traditions identify the concept of class with the relationship between people and economically relevant assets or resources. Marxists call this relation to the means of production; Weberians refer to "market capacities." But they are both really talking about very similar empirical phenomena.

- Both traditions see the causal relevance of class as operating, at least in part, via the ways in which these relations shape the material interests of actors. Ownership of the means of production and ownership of one's own labor power are explanatory of social action because these property rights shape the strategic alternatives people face in pursuing their

---

7 It should not be so surprising to see Marxist and Weberian elements conjoined in class analysis. After all, Weber's class analysis was deeply indebted to the Marxist legacy which was part of the general intellectual discourse of his time. In spite of the fact that Weber constantly distanced himself from Marxism, particularly because of its tendencies toward economic determinism which were especially pronounced in his day, when Weber talks of classes he is speaking in a rather Marxian voice.

material well-being. What people *have* imposes constraints on what they can do to get what they *want*. To be sure, Marxists tend to put more weight on the objective character of these "material interests" by highlighting the fact that these constraints are imposed on individuals, whereas Weberians tend to focus on the subjective conditions, by emphasizing the relative contingency in what people want. Nevertheless, it is still the case that at their core, both class concepts involve the causal connection between (a) social relations to resources and (b) material interests via (c) the way resources shape strategies for acquiring income.

How then do they differ? The pivotal difference is captured by the contrast between the favorite buzz-words of each theoretical tradition: *life chances* for Weberians, and *exploitation* for Marxists. The reason why production is more central to Marxist than to Weberian class analysis is because of its salience for the problem of exploitation; the reason why Weberians give greater emphasis to the market is because it so directly shapes life chances.

The intuition behind the idea of life chances is straightforward. "In our terminology," Weber (in Gerth and Mills 1958:181–2) writes:

> "classes" are not communities; they merely represent possible, and frequent, bases for communal action. We may speak of a "class" when (1) a number of people have in common a specific causal component of their life chances, in so far as (2) this component is represented exclusively by economic interests in the possession of goods and opportunities for income, and (3) is represented under conditions of the commodity or labor markets.

> [These points refer to "class situation," which we may express more briefly as the typical chance for a supply of goods, external living conditions and life experiences, in so far as this chance is determined by the amount and kind of power, or lack of such, to dispose of goods or skills for the sake of income in a given economic order. The term "class" refers to any group of people that is found in the same class situation] . . . But always this is the generic connotation of the concept of class: that the kind of chance in the *market* is the decisive moment which presents a common condition for the individual's fate. "Class situation" is, in this sense, ultimately "market situation."

In short, the kind and quantity of resources you own affects your opportunities for income in market exchanges. "Opportunity" is a description of the feasible set individuals face, the trade-offs they encounter in deciding what to do. Owning means of production gives a person different alternatives from owning credentials, and both of these are different from simply owning unskilled labor power. Furthermore, in a market economy, access to market-derived income affects the broader array of life experiences and opportunities for oneself and one's children. The study of the life chances of children based on parents' market capacity is thus an integral part of the Weberian agenda of class analysis.

Within a Weberian perspective, therefore, the salient issue in the linkage of people to different kinds of economic resources is the way this confers on them different kinds of economic opportunities and disadvantages and thereby shapes their material interests. One way of rep-

FIGURE 3 LEISURE VS. CONSUMPTION TRADE-OFFS FACED BY PEOPLE IN DIFFERENT ECONOMIC CLASSES

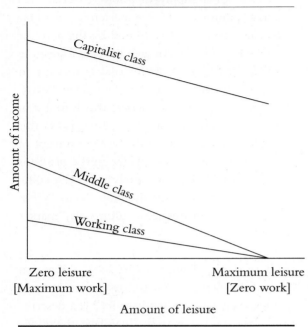

Zero leisure
[Maximum work]

Maximum leisure
[Zero work]

Amount of leisure

resenting this idea in a simple way is by examining the income-leisure trade-offs faced by people in different classes as pictured in Figure 3. In this figure, everyone faces some trade-off between leisure and income: less leisure yields more income. However, for the propertied class it is possible to have high income with no work (thus the expressions "the leisure class" or the "idle rich"), whereas for both the middle class and the working class in this stylized drawing, zero work corresponds to zero income. The middle class has "greater" opportunities (life chances) in the market than workers because the slope they face (i.e. the wage rate) is steeper. Some workers in fact might actually have a higher standard of living than some people in the middle class, but the trade-offs they face

are nevertheless less desirable. These common trade-offs, then, are the basis for a potential commonality of interests among members of a class, and thus constitute the basis for potential common action.

Within a Marxist framework, the feature of the relationship of people to economic resources which is at the core of class analysis is "exploitation." Both "exploitation" and "life chances" identify inequalities in material well-being that are generated by inequalities in access to resources of various sorts. Thus both of these concepts point to conflicts of interest over the *distribution* of the assets themselves. What exploitation adds to this is a claim that conflicts of interest between classes are generated not simply by what people *have,* but also by what people *do* with what they have. The concept of exploitation, therefore, points our attention to conflicts within production, not simply conflicts in the market.

This contrast between the Marxist and Weberian traditions of class analysis is summarized in Figure 4. Weberian class analysis revolves around a single causal nexus that works through market exchanges. Marxist class analysis includes the Weberian causal processes, but adds to them a causal structure within production itself as well as an account of the interactions of production and exchange. Part of our analysis of the class location of managers, for example, concerns the "loyalty rent" which managers receive by virtue of their position within the authority structure of production. This reflects the way in which location within the relations of production and not simply within market relations affects the "life chances" of managers. Our analysis of the shmoo—and more broadly, the analysis of such things as the way transfer

FIGURE 4 **THREE MODELS OF CLASS ANALYSIS**

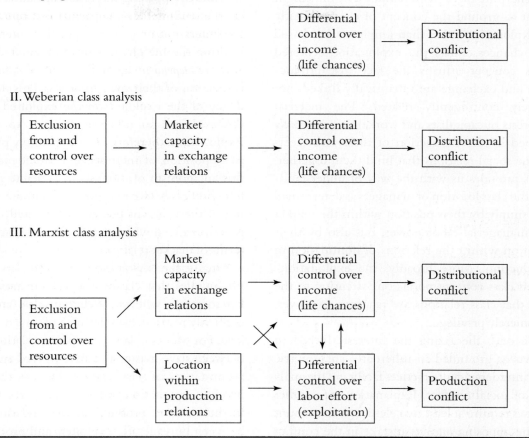

I. Simple gradational class analysis

II. Weberian class analysis

III. Marxist class analysis

payments of the welfare state affect the market capacity of workers—illustrates how market capacity has an impact on the extraction of labor effort within production. The Marxist concept of class directs our attention both theoretically and empirically towards these interactions.

A Weberian might reply that there is nothing in the Weberian idea of market-based life chances that would *prevent* the analysis of the extraction of labor effort within production. A good and subtle Weberian class analyst could certainly link the analysis of market capacities within exchange relations to power relations within the labor process, and thus explore the causal structures at the center of Marxist class analysis. In systematically joining production and exchange in this way, however, the Weberian concept would in effect become Marxianized. Frank Parkin (1979: 25), in a famous gibe, said, "Inside every neo-Marxist there seems to be a Weberian struggling to get out." One could just as easily say that inside every left-wing Weberian there is a Marxist struggling to stay hidden.

There are three main reasons why one might want to ground the concept of class explicitly in exploitation rather than simply market-based life chances. First, the exploitation-centered class concept affirms the fact that production and exchange are intrinsically linked, not merely contingently related. The material interests of capitalists and workers are *inherently* shaped by the interaction of these two facets of the social relations that bind them together. This provides us with the way of understanding the class location of managers as determined not simply by their position within the market for managerial labor power, but also by their position within the relations of domination in production. More broadly, the exploitation-based class concept points our attention to the fact that class relations are relations of power, not merely privilege.

Second, theorizing the interests linked to classes as grounded in inherently antagonistic and interdependent practices facilitates the analysis of social conflict. Explanations of conflict always require at least two elements: an account of the opposing *interests* at stake in the conflict and an account of the *capacity* of the actors to pursue those interests. A simple opposition of interests is not enough to explain active con-

flict between groups. Exploitation is a powerful concept precisely because it brings together an account of opposing interests with an account of the rudimentary capacity for resistance. Exploiters not only have a positive interest in limiting the life chances of the exploited, but also are *dependent* upon the exploited for the realization of their own interests. This dependency of the exploiter on the exploited gives the exploited an inherent capacity to resist. Exploitation, therefore, does not simply predict an opposition of interests, but a tendency for this antagonism of interests to generate manifest conflicts between classes. This understanding of the inherent power of exploited classes is marginalized when class is defined strictly in terms of market relations.

Finally, the exploitation-centered class analysis implies that classes can exist in nonmarket societies, whereas Weberian class analysis explicitly restricts the relevance of class to markets. For Marxist class analysis, the relationship between slave master and slave or lord and serf are instances of class relations because they all involve exploitation linked to property rights in the forces of production.[8] The relationship between bureaucratic exploiters and producers in command economies can also be considered a form of class relations since the capacity of the state bureaucratic elite to appropriate surplus

---

8 The classic Marxist description of feudalism is a society in which the lords appropriate surplus products directly from the serfs through the use of what is generally called "extra-economic coercion." This coercion either takes the form of forcing the peasant to work part of the week on the land of the lord, or exacting some portion of the produce of the peasant. An alternative characterization is to say that in feudalism the lord and the serf are joint owners of the labor power of the serf. This gives the lord property rights in the laboring capacity of serfs. Slavery, in these terms, is simply the limiting case in which the slave has lost all property rights in his or her own labor power. This joint ownership of the serf's labor power is reflected in the laws which tie serfs to the land and which prevent the flight of serfs to the city. Such flight is simply a form of theft: the fleeing serf, like the fleeing slave, has stolen property from the lord. The use of extra-economic coercion, then, is simply the means of enforcing these property rights, no different from the use of extra-economic coercion to prevent workers from taking over a factory. For an extended discussion of this way of understanding feudalism, see Wright (1985: 77–78).

rests on their effective control over the society's productive resources (Wright 1994: ch. 6). For Weberian class analysis these are not class relations, but rather examples of castes or estates or some other form of inequality of power, since the differences in "life chances" of the slave and slave master, the lord and serf, the bureaucratic appropriator and producer, are not the result of their meeting within a market. The Weberian restriction of the concept of class to market societies, therefore, directs our attention away from the underlying commonality of these relations across different kinds of social systems.

★ ★ ★

THE BASIC CONTOURS OF THE CLASS STRUCTURE

Figure 5 presents the distribution of the employed labor force into the twelve class locations described [earlier] for six countries: the United States, Canada, the United Kingdom, Sweden, Norway and Japan. The details of the operationalization of these categories and a discussion of a range of methodological problems in making these estimates are presented [elsewhere].We will first look at the patterns across the property dimensions of the class structure and then turn to class distributions among employees.

The Property Dimension

The capitalist class, defined as self-employed people who employ ten or more employees, comprises no more than about 2% of the labor force in any of these countries, and less than 1% in two of them (Sweden and Norway). Of course, this figure does not include those capitalists who are not technically "employers." Many people who own significant amounts of capitalist wealth may be employed as top executives of corporations, others are employed in jobs completely unrelated to their capitalist wealth, and some are formally out of the labor force, living as pure rentiers off the income from their wealth. A few are even professors. Unfortunately, with the comparative data in this project it is not possible to estimate the proportion of the population who would fall into the segment of the capitalist class which is not self-employed. In any case, this would probably only add at most a few percentage points to these figures.[9]

As would be expected, there are considerably more small employers, defined here as self-employed individuals employing two to nine employees, than proper capitalists. The range is between about 3% of the labor force in Canada and Norway and about 6% in the United States and Japan. Putting these two class locations together, between roughly 4% and 8% of the labor forces of these six developed capitalist countries are in class locations which are, to a greater or lesser extent, directly connected to the capitalist class.

Considering the differences in other aspects of the political economies of these countries

---

9 According to Lawrence Mishel and David Frankel (1991: p. 162), in the richest 1% of US households defined by the income distribution, 47.8% of household income came from capital assets in 1988. For the next richest 4%, this figure drops to 23.2%. The average assets per household for the richest 0.5% of American households in 1989 was over $8 million, and of the next 0.5% over $2.5 million. These data suggest that the wealthy capitalist class defined strictly in terms of holdings of financial assets—i.e. individuals whose livelihood is substantially dependent upon income derived from capital holdings—constitutes probably no more than 2–3% of the population.

FIGURE 5 CLASS DISTRIBUTIONS IN SIX COUNTRIES

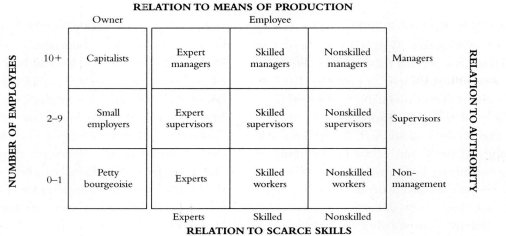

RELATION TO MEANS OF PRODUCTION

NUMBER OF EMPLOYEES / RELATION TO AUTHORITY

	Owner	Employee			
10+	Capitalists	Expert managers	Skilled managers	Nonskilled managers	Managers
2–9	Small employers	Expert supervisors	Skilled supervisors	Nonskilled supervisors	Supervisors
0–1	Petty bourgeoisie	Experts	Skilled workers	Nonskilled workers	Non-management
		Experts	Skilled	Nonskilled	

RELATION TO SCARCE SKILLS

United States (n = 1,493)

1.8	5.5	3.7	2.8	12.0
6.0	3.1	6.3	7.2	16.6
6.8	2.9	13.1	40.6	56.7
14.7	11.6	23.3	50.6	100.0

Sweden (n = 1,074)

0.7	3.2	4.1	2.3	9.6
4.7	1.3	5.0	4.2	10.5
5.4	2.7	17.4	49.1	69.2
10.7	7.2	26.5	55.6	100.0

Norway (n = 1,522)

0.8	4.8	4.1	3.5	12.4
2.9	3.7	3.8	3.4	10.9
10.3	4.2	21.0	37.4	72.6
14.0	12.7	28.9	44.3	100.0

Canada (n = 1,779)

1.0	5.3	3.9	2.5	11.7
3.2	2.2	4.9	3.7	10.8
13.5	2.8	21.7	35.4	59.9
17.7	10.3	30.5	41.5	100.0

United Kingdom (n = 1,146)

2.1	2.4	6.9	2.6	11.9
5.1	2.1	6.8	4.5	11.9
6.7	1.5	16.6	42.7	60.8
14.0	5.9	30.3	49.8	100.0

Japan (n = 612)

1.6	4.9	2.0	4.6	11.5
6.2	3.3	2.3	4.1	9.7
23.2	1.3	10.5	36.1	47.9
31.0	9.5	14.7	44.8	100.0

which might be thought relevant to the size of their capitalist classes—the size of their domestic markets, the recentness of industrialization, their position in the world economy, the role of the state—this is a relatively small range of variation. Sweden, which is arguably the least capitalistic of these six countries, still has 5.4% of its labor force in either the small employer or capitalist class location; the United States, the most purely capitalistic of these countries, has 7.8% of its labor force in these locations. This does constitute a real difference, but it is not striking.

There is much more variation across these countries in the size of the petty bourgeoisie (self-employed people with no more than one employee), which ranges from about 5% of the labor force in Sweden to over 23% in Japan. Japan is clearly the outlier. Furthermore, ★ ★ ★ this high proportion of the labor force in the petty bourgeoisie in Japan compared to the other five countries occurs within nearly every major economic sector. In most of these sectors, the percentage of people in the petty bourgeoisie is at least twice as high as in the other countries in our analysis, and in some sectors it is more than three times as high. Our first general conclusion, then, is that *Japan has a much larger petty bourgeoisie than any of the other countries, and this petty bourgeoisie is present throughout the Japanese economy.* The persistence of economic activity not directly organized by capitalist firms is thus considerably stronger in Japan than in the other advanced capitalist countries we are studying.

Among the other five countries, there are two principal contrasts in class distributions across the property boundary: Canada has somewhat larger self-employment (17.7%)

and Sweden somewhat smaller (10.7%) than the other countries. The higher rate of self-employment in Canada is entirely due to the agricultural sector: Canada has proportionately the largest agricultural sector among these five countries, and, within that sector, there is a higher rate of self-employment in Canada than elsewhere. ★ ★ ★ Within the nonagricultural sectors taken together, the rate of self-employment in Canada is only 11%, which is about the average of the other countries. The large Canadian petty bourgeoisie is therefore a consequence of the persistence of a relatively large agricultural sector that continues to be organized around relatively small family farms to a greater extent than elsewhere. The smaller Swedish rate of self-employment is also largely due to the sectoral composition of the labor force, although in the Swedish case this is not because of agriculture but because of state employment. In Sweden nearly 42% of the labor force is employed directly by the state. This is in contrast to less than 20% in the United States and intermediary levels in the other countries. Since there are no self-employed people in the state sector, all things being equal, a large sector of state employment will reduce the relative size of the petty bourgeoisie in a country. When we examine the private sector separately, the petty bourgeoisie in the United States is actually slightly smaller than that of Sweden: 8.3% of the labor force in the US compared to 9.3% in Sweden. Our second general descriptive conclusion, then, is that *among the five countries other than Japan, most of the variation in class distributions across the property dimension of the class structure is due to variations in the sectoral composition of the labor force*—specifically the size of the state sector and agricultural sector—rather than sharply different class distributions within sectors.

Employees

At first glance it appears in Figure 5 that there is a fair amount of variation in the class distributions among employees across these six countries. The expert-manager category is more than twice as large in Japan, Canada and the United States as in the United Kingdom, and the working class is more than 30% larger in Sweden than in Norway, Japan and Canada. These cross-national differences, however, may be somewhat misleading for two reasons. First, because of the variation across countries in self-employment (especially the high self-employment rate in Japan), some cross-national differences among subcategories of employees will simply reflect these broader variations in self-employment rather than anything specific to the class distributions among employees as such. This suggests that we should examine the class distributions separately among employees. Second, for reasons that are discussed in the methodological appendix, some of the differences across countries in these distributions are quite vulnerable to measurement problems, especially in the skill/expertise dimension of the class-structure matrix. It is notoriously difficult to precisely compare skill levels across different national economies, and this potentially could distort observed national differences in the relative size of certain locations in the class structure.

For purposes of comparing class distributions among employees, therefore, it may be somewhat more reliable to combine the polarized class locations with the intermediary cat-

egories immediately adjacent to them. In this modified class map of employees (Figure 6), the cross-national variability is considerably attenuated. In five of the six countries—the United States, Norway, Canada, the United Kingdom and Japan—13–15% of all employees are in the extended expert-manager class location, and 71–74% are in the extended working-class category. Given how different are the work organizations and historical experiences of these countries, it is really quite striking that their class distributions among employees are so similar.

The one country which does differ modestly from these figures is Sweden, in which 79.2% of the employee labor force is in the extended working-class location and only 9.6% is in the extended expert-manager class location. Unlike in the case of the relatively small Swedish petty bourgeoisie, this difference between Sweden and the other countries is not the result of the distribution of the Swedish labor force across economic sectors or state employment—Sweden has a higher proportion of employees in the working class and the extended working-class category than other countries within every sector. The Swedish distributions are also not the result of anything special about the relationship between class and gender in Sweden—Sweden has a higher proportion of workers among men than in all the other countries and a higher proportion among women than in all the countries except for Japan. Age composition and the size distribution of firms also do not appear to account for the difference between the Swedish class distributions and those of other countries. It appears, therefore, that the observed difference in class distributions between

FIGURE 6 **MODIFIED CLASS DISTRIBUTIONS AMONG EMPLOYEES IN SIX COUNTRIES**

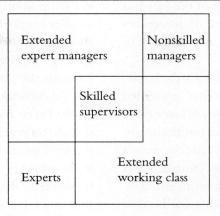

United States (n = 1,228)

14.4	4.3
7.4	
3.4	71.4

Sweden (n = 958)

9.6	2.6
5.6	
3.0	79.2

Norway (n = 1,309)

14.7	4.1
4.4	
4.9	71.8

Canada (n = 1,465)

13.9	3.0
6.0	
3.4	73.9

United Kingdom (n = 960)

13.3	3.0
7.9	
1.7	74.2

Japan (n = 391)

14.8	6.7
3.3	
1.9	73.5

Sweden and the other countries is not the result of some compositional property of the Swedish economy, but is directly a result of differences between the Swedish class structure and that of the other countries.

At the heart of the distinctiveness of the Swedish class distributions is the fact that in Sweden a smaller proportion of its employee labor force occupies manager and supervisor positions than in any of the other countries. This contrast is particularly sharp between the United States and Sweden: in the United States nearly 35% of all employees are in jobs with some kind of real workplace authority; in Sweden the figure is only 22.5%. This difference between the two countries goes a long way toward explaining why the Swedish working class is larger than the American. If the United States had the same overall distribution of authority as in Sweden, but had its current distribution of skills within categories of authority, then 56.5% of American employees would be in the working-class corner of the class-structure matrix (and 79.9% would be in the extended working class). In contrast, if the United States had the same overall distribution of skills as in Sweden, but had its current authority distribution within skill categories, the American working class would only increase to 49.1% of employees (and the extended working class would increase to 74.8%). In terms of accounting for the relative size of the working class, the central contrast between Sweden and the United States is thus the distribution of workplace authority in the two countries.

It is beyond the scope of the data in this project to explain why Swedish workplaces have smaller numbers of managers and supervisors than their American counterparts. One way of getting a limited handle on this problem is to examine the authority distributions within specific occupations. These data are presented in Table 1. For high-status occupations—professionals, technicians, teachers, managers—there is only a modestly higher proportion of people with authority in the United States compared to Sweden.[10] Except in the case of laborers, the differences between the two countries are much greater in those occupations which are usually thought of as part of the "working class"—clericals, crafts, operatives and service workers. And among these occupations, by far the biggest difference between the United States and Sweden is among craftworkers: in the US 39.2% occupy supervisory positions compared to only 8.7% in Sweden.

What these results seem to indicate is that the critical difference between Sweden and the United States is the extent to which the supervisory aspect of managerial functions has been delegated to positions which would otherwise be part of the working class. In particular, skilled working-class positions—craft occupations—tend to be assigned supervisory authority over other workers in the United States much more frequently than in Sweden.

While it is impossible to provide a rigorous explanation of these differences without looking at historical data on both structural transformations within production and political strategies

---

10 The term "manager" is used both to designate an occupation and to designate a structural location within the relations of power within authority hierarchies. Here we are referring to the percentage of employees in managerial occupations who also exercise managerial or supervisory powers. Even in the United States, nearly 15% of the people whose occupation is classified as "manager" do not appear to have any supervisory or decisionmaking powers.

TABLE 1 **DISTRIBUTION OF SUPERVISORY AUTHORITY WITHIN OCCUPATIONAL CATEGORIES**

	Percentage of employees with supervisory authority		Ratio
Occupation	United States	Sweden	US : Sweden
Professionals	54.9	51.2	1.1:1
Teachers	23.2	15.6	1.5:1
Technicians	58.3	40.2	1.45:1
Managers	85.1	79.5	1.1:1
Clerks	25.9	13.1	2.0:1
Sales	15.6	21.8	0.7:1
Foremen	93.2	75.5	1.2:1
Crafts	39.2	8.7	4.5:1
Operatives	18.6	8.9	2.1:1
Laborers	15.8	16.7	0.95:1
Skilled services	51.9	17.5	3.0:1
Unskilled services	23.3	5.9	3.9:1

of workers and capitalists in both countries, I can offer some speculations on the mechanisms at work. One important factor may center around the role and power of labor unions in the two countries. The labor movement in Sweden has been able to eliminate legal restrictions on its ability to organize wage-earners much more successfully than in the United States. In particular, in the United States employees who are part of "management" are generally legally excluded from the union bargaining unit. This means that it is in the interests of American capitalists to integrate into the lower levels of management at least some jobs within pivotal categories of wage-earners, categories which otherwise would remain working class (Institute for Labor Education and Research 1982: 315). In Sweden, since managers and supervisors also have high rates of unionization, there is no incentive for employers to use the author-

ity hierarchy as a way of undercutting the labor movement. The extension of supervisory functions to segments of the working class may thus be one facet of the general efforts by capital to weaken the union movement in the United States.

A second factor which might explain the leaner managerial hierarchies in Sweden compared to the United States centers on the nature of the "class compromise" that has been in place in Sweden over the last forty years or so. Sweden was, at least until the late 1980s, the preeminent example of what is often called the "social democratic compromise" between labor and capital. In this compromise, workers agree to moderate their militancy, especially on the shop floor, and cooperate with management in exchange for guarantees that wages will rise more or less in step with productivity increases and that unemployment will be kept at a minimum.[11] To the extent that such a compromise is firmly in place, problems of social control within the labor process will be reduced. The result is a lower need for extensive "guard labor," to use the expression of Bowles, Gordon and Weisskopf (1990: 194–196). In the United States, in contrast, there is a much more conflictual relation between labor and management on the shop floor and a much weaker "social contract" embedded in the workplace and state policies. American workplaces, therefore, typically require a fairly elaborate apparatus of social control involving intensive monitoring and a relatively heavy reliance on negative sanctions. One of the consequences is the employment of lots of supervisors, including supervisors of supervisors. There may thus be fewer supervisory employees in Sweden than in the United States at least in part because the differences in the labor movements, class compromises, and problems of labor discipline in the two countries make it less necessary for Swedish capitalists to devote so many positions and resources to social control activities.

Whatever is the explanation for the distinctiveness of the Swedish class distribution among employees, the main conclusion from the results in Figure 6 is that the differences across countries are not dramatic. The working class and the locations closest to the working class constitute around three-quarters of the employee labor force in these countries, and the privileged segments of the "middle class"—the extended expert-manager category—constitute about 10–15%.

★ ★ ★

‖ REFERENCES

Bowles, Samuel and Herb Gintis. 1990. "Contested Exchange: New Microfoundations for the Political Economy of Capitalism," *Politics & Society* 18, 2: 165–222.

Bowles, Samuel, David M. Gordon and Thomas E. Weisskopf. 1990. *After the Wasteland: A Democratic Economics for the Year 2000.* New York: M. E. Sharpe.

Gerth, Hans and C. W. Mills. 1958. *From Max Weber.* New York: Oxford University Press.

Institute for Labor Education and Research. 1982. *What's Wrong with the US Economy?* Boston: South End Press.

Mishel, Lawrence and David Frankel. 1991. *The State of Working America.* New York.

Parkin, Frank. 1979. *Marxism and Class Theory: A Bourgeois Critique.* New York: Columbia University Press.

Wilson, William Julius. 1982. *The Declining Significance of Race.* Chicago: University of Chicago Press.

———. 1987. *The Truly Disadvantaged.* Chicago: University of Chicago Press.

Wright, Erik Olin. 1985. *Classes.* London: New Left Books.

———. 1994. *Interrogating Inequality.* London: Verso.

---

11 For an extended theoretical discussion of the logic of this compromise and the conditions for its stability, see Przeworski (1985).

29

Preface to *The Making of the English Working Class*★

E.P. THOMPSON

★ ★ ★

By class I understand an historical phenomenon, unifying a number of disparate and seemingly unconnected events, both in the raw material of experience and in consciousness. I emphasise that it is an *historical* phenomenon. I do
not see class as a "structure", nor even as a "category", but as something which
in fact happens (and can be shown to have happened) in human relationships.

More than this, the notion of class entails the notion of historical relationship. Like any other relationship, it is a fluency which evades analysis if
we attempt to stop it dead at any given moment and anatomise its structure.
The finest–meshed sociological net cannot give us a pure specimen of class,
any more than it can give us one of deference or of love. The relationship
must always be embodied in real people and in a real context. Moreover, we
cannot have two distinct classes, each with an independent being, and then

---

★ First published in 1963.

bring them *into* relationship with each other. We cannot have love without lovers, nor deference without squires and labourers. And class happens when some men, as a result of common experiences (inherited or shared), feel and articulate the identity of their interests as between themselves, and as against other men whose interests are different from (and usually opposed to) theirs. The class experience is largely determined by the productive relations into which men are born—or enter involuntarily. Class-consciousness is the way in which these experiences are handled in cultural terms: embodied in traditions, value-systems, ideas, and institutional forms. If the experience appears as determined, class-consciousness does not. We can see a *logic* in the responses of similar occupational groups undergoing similar experiences, but we cannot predicate any *law*. Consciousness of class arises in the same way in different times and places, but never in *just* the same way.

There is today an ever-present temptation to suppose that class is a thing. This was not Marx's meaning, in his own historical writing, yet the error vitiates much latter-day "Marxist" writing. "It", the working class, is assumed to have a real existence, which can be defined almost mathematically—so many men who stand in a certain relation to the means of production. Once this is assumed it becomes possible to deduce the class-consciousness which "it" ought to have (but seldom does have) if "it" was properly aware of its own position and real interests. There is a cultural superstruc-

ture, through which this recognition dawns in inefficient ways. These cultural "lags" and distortions are a nuisance, so that it is easy to pass from this to some theory of substitution: the party, sect, or theorist, who disclose class-consciousness, not as it is, but as it ought to be.

But a similar error is committed daily on the other side of the ideological divide. In one form, this is a plain negative. Since the crude notion of class attributed to Marx can be faulted without difficulty, it is assumed that any notion of class is a pejorative theoretical construct, imposed upon the evidence. It is denied that class has happened at all. In another form, and by a curious inversion, it is possible to pass from a dynamic to a static view of class. "It"—the working class—exists, and can be defined with some accuracy as a component of the social structure. Class-consciousness, however, is a bad thing, invented by displaced intellectuals, since everything which disturbs the harmonious co-existence of groups performing different "social rôles" (and which thereby retards economic growth) is to be deplored as an "unjustified disturbance-symptom".[1] The problem is to determine how best "it" can be conditioned to accept its social rôle, and how its grievances may best be "handled and channelled".

If we remember that class is a relationship, and not a thing, we can not think in this way. "It" does not exist, either to have an ideal interest or consciousness, or to lie as a patient on the Adjustor's table. Nor can we turn matters upon their heads, as has been done by one authority who (in a study of class obsessively concerned

---

1 An example of this approach, covering the period of this book, is to be found in the work of a colleague of Professor Talcott Parsons: N. J. Smelser, *Social Change in the Industrial Revolution* (1959).

with methodology, to the exclusion of the examination of a single real class situation in a real historical context) has informed us:

> Classes are based on the differences in legitimate power associated with certain positions, i.e. on the structure of social rôles with respect to their authority expectations. . . . An individual becomes a member of a class by playing a social rôle relevant from the point of view of authority. . . . He belongs to a class because he occupies a position in a social organisation; i.e. class membership is derived from the incumbency of a social rôle.

The question, of course, is how the individual got to be in this "social rôle", and how the particular social organisation (with its property-rights and structure of authority) got to be there. And these are historical questions. If we stop history at a given point, then there are no classes but simply a multitude of individuals with a multitude of experiences. But if we watch these men over an adequate period of social change, we observe patterns in their relationships, their ideas, and their institutions. Class is defined by men as they live their own history, and, in the end, this is its only definition.

★ ★ ★

30

Spinning Knowledge into Gold: Knowledge as Property*

CHARLES DERBER, WILLIAM A. SCHWARTZ,
AND YALE MAGRASS

No spider can weave its web or bird construct its nest without the knowledge to do the job. The lion that does not know how to trap its prey will starve.

The same is true for humans. The silversmith cannot make buckles and the engineer cannot design bridges or computers without knowledge. Deprive the worker of knowledge and the work will grind to a halt as surely as by taking away his tools. Hunting and gathering skills were necessary for survival in early nomadic societies. Settled communities depended on agricultural knowledge. Advanced societies are based on craft and artisan skills and, increasingly, scientific ones.

To be sure, knowledge often seems more like smoke and mirrors than a real resource. For example, many dismiss as hocus pocus the psychoanalytic therapy for which people pay more than $100 an hour. But the Freudian psychologist's pursuit is impossible without the theory behind it, whether or not that theory is valid. In any economic activity, practitioners depend on some know-how, whether genuine or not, that tells them what to do. As a class

---

* First published in 1990; from *Power in The Highest Degree: Professionals and The Rise of A New Mandarin Order.*

resource, knowledge need not meet any objective standards, but only be accepted by enough employers or consumers to pay the way of the experts.

Witch doctors' magical knowledge was perceived as real in many tribal societies and led to a thriving medical practice. The leading "scientific doctor" of eighteenth-century colonial Philadelphia, Benjamin Rush, believed that there was only "one disease in the world . . . morbid excitement induced by capillary tension."[1] It had one remedy: "to deplete the body by letting blood with the lancet and emptying out the stomach and bowels with the use of powerful emetics and cathartics. . . . Patients could be bled until unconscious."[2] Today, we dismiss bloodletting as quackery. In future centuries, many ideas advanced by today's doctors will doubtless also seem bogus. But this fact scarcely weakens the power of modern medical knowledge as an economic resource today—a resource that, whatever its validity, buys expensive homes and cars for thousands of doctors.

Labor and capital—the other two basic productive resources—are also defined culturally and, like knowledge, are partly matters of perception. For centuries, adults saw children as workers. Today, child labor is outlawed in the United States. What "labor" is, and who is capable of it, is a social judgment.

The American Indians regarded gold as "yellow rock" that "makes the white man crazy."[3] The decision to base currency on the yellow rock was arbitrary. Currency of any kind—whether greenbacks or credit cards—is an artificial claim to value resting on faith. The run on banks in the Great Depression showed what can happen when such faith crumbles. Capital, like knowledge, is partly in the eye of the beholder.

||| KNOWLEDGE AND CLASS POWER

Knowledge, capital, and labor are the three basic factors of production. Each is essential to produce *all* goods and services in *all* societies and eras. If any of the three is missing, no crop can be grown, no object can be made, and no service can be delivered.

A group that controls one of the three factors of production can wield vast power. Medieval lords monopolized land—the most important form of capital in the Middle Ages—and thereby dominated the serfs. Nineteenth-century robber barons held sway over workers because they controlled the crucial capital of their age: money. Such mastery, rooted in control of a resource that everyone needs to survive, is what Karl Marx called class power. But Marx failed to recognize that monopolies of knowledge can bring class power as surely as monopolies of capital.

Much knowledge, like how to dress, walk, or turn on a light switch, is "socialized"—that is, known by most adults. It is nobody's private property, and thus does not command much influence.

Scarce or nonsocialized knowledge, in contrast, can confer great power. The humorist Art Buchwald jokes about electricians:

---

1 Quoted in Paul Starr, *The Social Transformation of American Medicine* (New York: Basic Books, 1982), p. 42.
2 Ibid.

3 Paraphrased in John G. Neihardt, *Black Elk Speaks* (New York: Pocket Books, 1959), p. 66.

I was playing tennis when I was called off the court by my wife. She said excitedly over the phone "The electrician is coming in an hour"....

When I arrived at the house, my wife was dusting the furniture and fixing the flowers. "You better shower and put on a shirt and tie. I don't want him to think we can't afford him."

I showered and put on my best dress shirt and Italian silk tie, plus the blue blazer that I save for British royalty and American workmen....

She put powder on her nose. "I hope he likes us."[4]

When a group organizes to monopolize the *general* fund of marketable skills rather than just *particular* skills, such as the electrician's, true knowledge classes can emerge.

In the simplest Robinson Crusoe economy, each person possesses the capital, labor, and knowledge needed to produce. In more complex societies, however, the three are often divided among different people, and capital and knowledge are withheld from the people who do the physical work. Let's look at the five possible ways to distribute capital, labor, and knowledge:

WHEN TWO OR THREE RESOURCES APPEAR IN THE SAME CIRCLE, IT MEANS ONE GROUP HOLDS THEM.

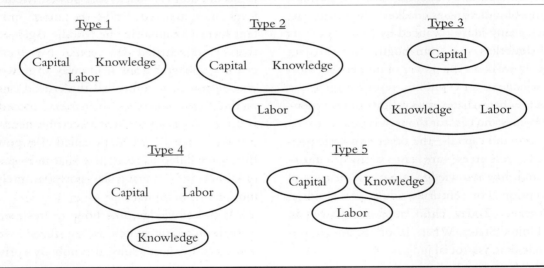

All five types of resource distribution can be found in history, each giving rise to its own class structure. In the cities of the late Middle Ages, many craftsmen, like Robinson Crusoe, owned their own tools, conceived their own work, and executed the physical tasks (Type 1), although some had apprentices and other helpers. A Robinson Crusoe economy composed solely of such producers could not be a class society. Everyone would be both entrepreneur and expert, but each would also have to do his own manual labor.

---

4 Art Buchwald, "Electrical Shocks," *Boston Globe,* 1988, p. 11.

Today, many contemporary, high-technology firms are run by scientist-entrepreneurs who supply much of the knowledge and own the business, but pay others to do unskilled tasks like cleaning the test tubes and answering the phones. These are Robinson Crusoes with Fridays (Type 2). The Fridays are doubly disenfranchised, from both capital and expertise.

In small nineteenth-century capitalist workshops, skilled craft workers often conceived and executed their own tasks, uniting knowledge and labor; their employers supplied most of the capital (Type 3). The craftsmen's expertise, we shall see, gave them great power. Where the craftsmen had no helpers, and did all their own manual work there was no class division between experts and workers, only between experts and capitalists. Exploitation based on expertise arises only when there is a separate class of unskilled people to do the dirty work that experts shun.

In the Mondragon cooperatives of Spain's Basque region, production workers own the businesses, but managers and engineers often monopolize crucial knowledge (Type 4).[5] Since laborers own the capital, they legally control their factories. But because professionals control key knowledge, they run much of the show, sometimes leading to unexpected worker alienation, even strikes.

In the United States, too, full-scale educational drives have been necessary to hold experts at bay in worker-owned companies. Some, such as publishing houses, free schools, and newspapers, require each worker-owner to learn every job, taking turns at skilled tasks while doing his or her share of the dirty work. Buying the company, experience shows, is not enough to produce true workplace democracy. Workers must acquire a knowledge portfolio as well.[6]

Factories in Yugoslavia are officially governed on a one-worker/one-vote principle. There is no capitalist class to exploit workers. But engineers, managers, and skilled workers often dominate. One scholar notes that while the skilled are a minority of the labor force, they make up "nearly three quarters of the members of the workers' councils and eighty percent of the members of the management boards."[7]

Similarly, in some Israeli kibbutzim (which are essentially collectively owned) professionalism is sabotaging democracy and creating a new governing class of experts. Despite the one-person/one-vote power of the General Assembly, one Israeli researcher writes, "professionalization brought a concentration of power into the hands of the economic coordinator and the treasurer" and a small number of other specialists.[8] The kibbutz's new class "gains decisive influence, power, prestige, authority and even material advantages . . . by creating the impression that all the other members depend on their special skills."[9]

Ironworking, munitions making, and other nineteenth-century industries yielded a true craft class: employees who jealously guarded

5 Henk Thomas and Chris Logan, *Mondragon* (London: George Allen & Unwin, 1982).

6 Paul Bernstein, *Workplace Democratization* (New Brunswick, N.J.: Transaction Books, 1976), chap. 9.

7 Paul Blumberg, *Industrial Democracy* (New York: Schocken, 1973), p. 217.

8 Amir Helman, "Professional Managers in the Kibbutz" (1986, Mimeographed), pp. 3–4.

9 G. Kresl, "To Each According to His Needs," cited in ibid., p. 5.

their secrets from a mass of unskilled workers. Here we find distinct capital, knowledge, and labor classes (Type 5). The Marxist analysis of capitalism as a two-class system pitting capitalists against labor overlooks craft workers as a potential independent knowledge class, and fails to recognize how skilled workers can exploit the unskilled.

In many modern-day American corporations, a business elite owns most of the capital; managers, professionals, skilled craft workers, and technicians hold most of the knowledge; and unskilled or semiskilled production workers do the physical labor. Here, both owners and salaried experts have the potential to exploit, although the latter are employees and usually lack formal power over other workers. Class struggle is triangular, with three-way battles over both capital and knowledge. Workers find themselves, as we will see, at the bottom of two intertwined class hierarchies.

In the class struggle over knowledge, the most essentially human gift, the right to enjoy creative thought and put one's ideas to work, becomes problematic for the mass of uncredentialed workers. Modern professionals, seeking to lock up knowledge as their private property, can set themselves against the most elementary creative needs of the rest of the population. Like individual capitalists, professionals may not consciously intend to exploit others. But monopolizing knowledge, as we shall see, inevitably restricts the opportunities of others to think. Preserving a large class of unskilled workers is the dark side of professionalism.

ENCLOSING THE MIND: LETTING ONE TRUTH BLOOM

On their road to class power, knowledge groups of all stripes—whether witch doctors or modern professionals—have to fight battles for the mind. If others lose faith in their knowledge, it ceases to be economically useful.

Experts can rarely *prove* the validity of their knowledge. Thus they must create a general perception of credibility, much as corporations do. The airlines reassure the public with images of rock-solid pilots in full-dress uniform. Pictures of shiny buses and cheerful drivers illustrate Greyhound's message that riders can relax and "leave the driving to us." Likewise, witch doctors often wore imposing headdresses. The medieval priest's robes, collars, crucifixes, even chastity vows, were symbols of virtue. Doctors, lawyers, and scientists today have their white coats, three-piece suits, certificates on the wall, and, increasingly, sophisticated advertising.

William James marvels that

> the mind is at every stage a theatre of simultaneous possibilities. . . . The mind works as a sculptor works on his block of stone. In a sense the statue stood there from eternity. But there were a thousand different ones beside it, and the sculptor alone is to thank for having extricated this one from the rest.[10]

As mental sculptors, knowledge groups chisel a particular "truth mold," offering one perspective on the problems of their clients while undermining other "simultaneous possibili-

---

10 William James. *The Principles of Psychology* (New York: Dover, 1950), pp. 284–85.

ties." In the Middle Ages, "volcanoes were supposed by many to be the mouths of hell; their rumbling was a faint echo of the moans of the damned."[11] Since "nearly every event in history was interpreted in religious terms,"[12] priests had a lot of business. Today, professionals urge us to understand not only volcanoes but virtually everything from the psyche to the economy in secular and rationalist terms—their terms.

Professionals have the same stake in a secular scientific view of the world as witch doctors did in a magical view of life and medieval priests had in a theological one. Today, as in the Middle Ages, knowledge groups have made substantial progress in creating a world where one truth blooms and an infinity of other possibilities is subordinated or weeded out.

Edward Evans-Pritchard notes that in Zandeland, many "who frequently spoke with a measure of contempt about witch-doctors have made speed to visit them when in pain."[13] The Azande may be dubious about a particular witch doctor's competency, but "cannot reason" against magic itself "because they have no other idiom in which to express their thoughts."[14] Magic provides a coherent and exclusive view of the world that is the cognitive umbrella for legitimating the witch doctor's skills:

> Were a Zande to give up faith in witch-doctorhood he would have to surrender equally his belief in witchcraft and oracles. . . . In this web of belief every strand depends upon every other strand, and a Zande cannot get out of its meshes because this is the only world he knows. The web is not an external structure in which he is *enclosed*. It is the texture of his thought and he cannot think that his thought is wrong.[15]

Magic totally encloses the mind, binding the Azande to the witch doctor. Like science, it is a comprehensive "logical system" with its "own rules of thought."[16] For the Azande, it explains everything from "blight seizing the groundnut crop"[17] to human sickness and death.[18] In both science and magic, once certain premises are accepted, much else follows inexorably: "If one's logic is that of witchcraft, it is no more possible to be persuaded that the alien logic of scientific explanation is more valid than it would be for a scientist to allow for the validity of witchcraft."[19]

Like the Azande who cannot escape the magical worldview, most of us find it difficult to escape the assumptions of scientific rationality and to challenge scientists, engineers, doctors, and other professionals. Like magic, the scientific worldview is based on assumptions that are grounded in faith.[20] The scientific version of "rational" and "objective" knowledge serves ★ ★ ★ to legitimate the modern expert's

11 Will Durant, *The Age of Faith* (New York: Simon and Schuster, 1950), p. 735.
12 Ibid., p. 737.
13 Edward Evans-Pritchard, *Witchcraft, Oracles, and Magic Among the Azande* (New York: Oxford University Press, 1957), p. 191.
14 Ibid., p. 338.
15 Ibid., pp. 194–95.
16 Edward Evans-Pritchard, cited in Judith Willer, *The Social Determination of Knowledge* (Englewood Cliffs, N.J.: Prentice-Hall, 1971), p. 46.
17 Evans-Pritchard, *Witchcraft, Oracles, and Magic Among the Azande,* p. 18.
18 Ibid.
19 G. B. Madison, *Understanding* (Westport, Conn.: Greenwood Press, 1982), p. 87.
20 Michael Polanyi, *Personal Knowledge* (Chicago: University of Chicago Press, 1958).

knowledge as fact and to cast doubt on everything else.

Edmund Husserl reminds us that scientific principles are "nothing more than a garb of ideas thrown over the world of immediate intuition and experience."[21] Like magic and religion, science offers only one version of truth: "Science's appeal to universal man or to 'all reasonable men' is an appeal to . . . one peculiar kind of man and one peculiar form of reasoning, the kind of reasoning found in the logician and in the computer but not in the poetic or religious man."[22]

Whether the facts of science are truer than the teachings of priests or witch doctors matters less for science's power as a class resource than its success in winning converts. For our purposes, magic and science, witch doctoring and modern medicine are more alike than they are different. As G. B. Madison argues, "All the human worlds are only so many semantic constructs, the mythical other-worldly world as much as the scientific this-worldly one."[23] Both are limited, since the human mind itself has limits and "any knowledge that we think we know is only an insignificant part of what we do not know, of the great unknown."[24] Moreover, knowledge useful for one set of purposes may be less so for others. Believers in science sometimes convert to religion on their deathbed, suggesting that science's strengths in approaching life are not matched in preparing for death. But in their quest to enclose the mind, magicians, priests, and scientists whittle away at competing truths.

As their own church becomes institutionalized, and their faith universalized, they are well on the road to class power.

ENCLOSING THE COMMONS: MONOPOLIZING KNOWLEDGE AS PROPERTY

If everyone had expertise to sell, separate knowledge classes could not exist. To finish the job of making knowledge into property, experts must keep secrets and create a division of mental and manual labor.

Workers have historically sought to monopolize their primary resource, the ability to labor. Unions limit who can unload ships or even dig ditches. Male workers have tried to define women as biologically unsuited for their own brawny pursuits. Similarly, white workers have excluded blacks, labeling them lazy or shiftless. But privatizing labor is difficult, and no Western working class has fully enclosed the labor commons.

Capitalists have been more successful in protecting their monopoly. The distribution of wealth in the United States has remained relatively constant for decades.[25] The creation of this monopoly, however, was an arduous struggle requiring centuries. In the Middle Ages, feudal lords routinely appropriated profits from merchants, arbitrarily slapping on "taxes" or tolls.[26] To shelter their earnings, merchants ultimately aligned with monarchs and the

21 Edmund Husserl, *Experience and Judgment* (Evanston, Ill.: Northwestern University Press, 1973), p. 43.

22 Madison, *Understanding,* p. 242.

23 Ibid., p. 258.

24 Ibid., p. 177.

25 Robert J. Lampman, *The Share of Top Wealth-Holders in National Wealth, 1922–1956* (Princeton, N.J.: Princeton University Press, 1962).

26 Michael Tigar and Madeleine R. Levy, *Law and the Rise of Capitalism* (New York: Monthly Review Press, 1977), p. 59.

developing national state to establish a unified political and legal framework for protecting private property.

It is not quite as obvious why knowledge classes require monopoly, since knowledge, unlike capital, is not zero-sum. When we give a dollar to a friend, we are a dollar poorer, but when we share an idea, we have not lost our thought; we still have it. Sharing can be the best route to accumulating ideas, even if it risks baring secrets. Someone else I confide in can help me articulate my idea more clearly and can critique it, leading to a better understanding for both of us. In practice, as we shall see, members of a knowledge group sometimes share among themselves, but others usually are excluded from the conversation.

In comparison with capital, knowledge is reproduced and communicated easily, especially through modern information technologies such as video and photocopy machines. But throughout history, experts have developed powerful strategies for privatizing their knowledge. Shamans taught that outsiders were inherently unable to learn or understand some forms of magic and witchcraft: "For the Azande, witchcraft results from the presence in the body of a certain substance. This substance (observed after death and found in the abdomen of the corpse by autopsy) is inherited and transmitted directly from parent to child."[27]

In the Middle Ages, many Europeans believed that priestly powers to ward off sins or to bless the fields and make them fertile ("every harvest is a miracle")[28] came directly from God to a chosen few, under the aegis of the church.[29] Priestly knowledge was, under some interpretations, a sign of grace. No one could steal it, any more than an ordinary Azande could steal witchcraft. This is divinely ordained private property.

Clergy have often used more worldly means to protect their secrets. In ancient Mesopotamia, the priesthood "successfully prevented any simplification of the complicated hieroglyphic writing that would make access to it any easier. The Indian Brahmans prosecuted the distribution of the Veda, the 'knowledge,' among those not entitled to it, as one of the most heinous of sins."[30] In the Middle Ages, the church saw to it that "the cost of books, and the dearth of funds for schools, produced a degree of illiteracy which would have seemed shameful to ancient Greece or Rome. North of the Alps, before 1100, literacy was almost confined to 'clerics.'"[31]

Later the church resisted translating the Bible and other sacred texts into any language other than Latin. The development of the printing press nonetheless "made the Bible a common possession"[32] and threatened aspects of priestly monopoly. Cheap printing "prepared the people for Luther's appeal from the popes to the Gospels; later it would permit the rationalist's appeal from the Gospels to reason. It ended the clerical monopoly of learning, the priestly control of education."[33]

27 Willer, *Social Determination of Knowledge,* p. 42.
28 Will Durant, *The Reformation* (New York: Simon and Schuster, 1957), p. 14.
29 Durant, *Age of Faith,* p. 739.

30 Rudolf Bahro, *The Alternative in Eastern Europe* (London: Verso, 1981), p. 75.
31 Durant, *Age of Faith,* p. 908.
32 Durant, *Reformation,* p. 160.
33 Ibid.

Because their knowledge is, by their own insistence, communicable, craftworkers and professionals had to develop monopoly strategies that differed from those of shamans and priests. At the dawn of capitalism, guilds emerged to ensure that "the secrets of each trade or craft were to be preserved inviolate by its members."[34] Practitioners were forbidden to share their techniques with anybody, except future guild members. Medieval masons would drop their tools if an outsider approached the job site. Closely guarded apprenticeships limited access to craft guilds, initiating only a lucky few noviates. Professionals today, we shall see, are committed to some of the same ends, but use their own methods.

It matters little that outsiders acquire know-how if they are not permitted to use it. Barring lay practice is the most powerful method of privatizing knowledge. This can be accomplished by legal locks such as licensing, but by far the most important strategy is the mental/manual division of labor: writing thinking out of most people's job descriptions.

Separation of brain from brawn work dates back to earliest known times. But even in primitive societies, it was not universal; in some cases,

> uniformity of occupation is the rule, and the distribution of the community into various classes of workers has hardly begun, every man is more or less his own magician . . . , the hunter, the fisher, the farmer—all resort to magical practices. . . . Thompson Indians used to lay charms on the tracks of wounded deer.[35]

Here, magical knowledge is largely socialized; more or less democratically distributed and freely used by everyone.

But in primitive societies characterized by what James Frazer calls "higher stages of savagery," a "special class of magicians" emerged, freed from the obligation of working with their hands.[36] They did not monopolize all economic knowledge, but stripped ordinary tribesmen of the authority to use magic in hunting and horticulture. Such magical proletarianization (or privatization of magical knowledge) created perhaps the world's first division of mental and manual labor.

In the early empires, the mental/manual division of labor progressed. The pyramids along the Nile were built by "a hundred thousand slaves" but designed by master architects, such as Imhotep (described by Will Durant as "the first real person in known history").[37] The slaves must have had considerable skills to "bring these vast stones six hundred miles, to raise some of them, weighing many tons, to a height of half a thousand feet," but the whole effort was planned by experts.[38]

In the last century, capitalism has not only separated "mental" occupations from "manual" ones, but also subdivided both factory tasks and office jobs in an effort to radically restrict the scope of workers' thinking.[39] "Unskilled" workers, of course, have plenty of brain power

34 John Davis, *Corporations* (New York: Capricorn Books, 1961), p. 174.

35 James Frazer, *The Golden Bough* (New York: Macmillan, 1951), pp. 52–52, 70.

36 Ibid., p. 71.

37 Will Durant, *Our Oriental Heritage* (New York: Simon and Schuster, 1954), p. 147.

38 Ibid., p. 139.

39 Harry Braverman, *Labor and Monopoly Capital* (New York: Monthly Review Press, 1974).

and knowledge, but their jobs tap little of this potential.

Shamans, priests, craftworkers, and professionals, as we shall see, also seek to enclose their commons by legally monopolizing practice, much as mercantile capitalists used state-backed charters to frustrate potential competitors.

LOGOCRACIES PAST AND FUTURE: THE CLASS INTERESTS OF KNOWLEDGE GROUPS

"Logocracy" is to magicians, priests, craftworkers, and professionals what capitalism is to capitalists, feudalism was to lords, and slavery was to ancient patricians. In logocracy, those possessing knowledge—not those who invest capital—control and profit from economic enterprises and occupy the highest seats of government.

At least since Plato, intellectuals have envisioned many possible logocracies.[40] The Republic that Plato envisioned was to be governed by philosopher-kings. As Alvin Gouldner writes, "The Platonic Complex, the dream of the philosopher-king with which Western philosophy begins . . . is [now] the deepest wish-fulfilling fantasy of the New Class."[41]

By the nineteenth century, philosophers such as Turgot, Condorcet, Saint-Simon, and Auguste Comte had become enamored with science and saw scientists as the appropriate philosopher-kings of the coming era.[42] For Condorcet, "a body of scientists [would be] supreme within the state, separate from and above all other political institutions."[43] For Saint-Simon, "theory, scientific theory, was to govern social practice . . . the new scientists-technocrats [would] become the 'priests' of this society. . . . Authority would then no longer rest upon inherited office or on force and violence—or even property—but on skill and science."[44]

Others, including those whom Steven Lukes calls "administrative syndicalists," proposed a society of numerous professional associations, each controlling its area of certified expertise.[45] Society "would come to consist of professional federations, each with its own life . . . within which each professional group would be sovereign on internal matters. The State would become absorbed into the professional groups themselves."[46] This vision might be viewed as the first manifesto of the professional class. Today, writers still forecast a new society governed by professional elites. Michael Young describes a chilling negative utopia in which IQ determines each person's social position:

> We have an elite selected according to brains and educated according to deserts. . . . we frankly realize that democracy can be no more than aspiration and have rule not so much by

40 See Gouldner's bibliographic note in Alvin Gouldner, *The Future of Intellectuals and the Rise of the New Class* (New York: Seabury Press, 1979), pp. 94–102. Also see Daniel Bell, *The Coming of Post-Industrial Society* (New York: Basic Books, 1976), chap. 1, and Krishan Kumar, *Prophecy and Progress* (Harmondsworth: Penguin Books, 1978), pp. 13–45.

41 Gouldner, *Future of Intellectuals and the Rise of the New Class,* p. 65.

42 For an excellent review of the thinking of all four men, see Kumar, *Prophecy and Progress,* pp. 13–45.

43 Cited in ibid., p. 25.

44 Cited in Gouldner, *Future of Intellectuals and the Rise of the New Class,* p. 35.

45 Steven Lukes, *Emile Durkheim: His Life and Works* (Harmondsworth: Penguin Books, 1973), pp. 536–37.

46 Ibid., p. 537.

the people as by the cleverest people; not an aristocracy of birth, not a plutocracy of wealth, but a true meritocracy of talent.[47]

Logocracy exists not only in the imagination of intellectuals, but also—imperfectly—in history. From earliest known times until the rise of capitalism, knowledge classes have, to a degree, been ruling classes.

Marx described tribal societies as "primitive communism," but some may be better characterized as "primitive logocracies." Shamans and priests often wielded great power and were sometimes formally recognized as ruling elders:

> The priest as magician had access, through trance, inspiration or esoteric prayer, to the will of the spirits or gods, and could change that will for human purposes. Since such knowledge and skill seemed to primitive men the most valuable of all, and supernatural forces were conceived to affect men's fate at every turn, the power of the clergy became as great as that of the state; and from the earliest societies to modern times the priest has vied and alternated with the warrior in dominating and disciplining men. Let Egypt, Judea and medieval Europe suffice as instances.[48]

Among the Zuñi, a Native American people of New Mexico, "the heads of the major priesthoods, with the chief priest of the sun cult and the two chief priests of the war cult, constitute the ruling body."[49] In the earliest villages of western Asia, "the city god and temple formed the center of economic organization."[50] Many villages were "ruled by men whose service to gods of the town was direct."[51] James Frazer notes that in tribal societies throughout the world the

> magician occupies a position of great influence from which, if he is a prudent and able man, he may advance step by step to the rank of a chief or king. . . . in savage and barbarous society many chiefs and kings appear to owe their authority in great measure to their reputation as magicians.[52]

Anthropologist Conrad Arensberg proposes that "the shaman is the first human leader."[53] The magician "as Minority (Knower of Power)" dominates "the hunters' Majority" in "the first, shallow, two-level incipient stratification between the wise man and the unseeing, and the first shallow, merely two-echelon human institutional pyramid: the medicine man and his client followers."[54]

Frazer makes clear that the shaman's control grew partly from monopolies of magical knowledge about economic and other practical matters, including

> the healing of diseases, the forecasting of the future, the regulation of the weather, or any other object of general utility. . . . It was

47 Michael Young, *The Rise of the Meritocracy* (Harmondsworth: Penguin Books, 1961), p. 21.

48 Durant, *Our Oriental Heritage*, p. 68.

49 Ruth Benedict, *Patterns of Culture* (New York: Houghton Mifflin, 1934), p. 67.

50 Grahame Clark and Stuart Piggott, *Prehistoric Society* (New York: Penguin, 1965), p. 216.

51 Ibid.

52 Frazer, *Golden Bough,* p. 70.

53 Conrad Arensberg, "Cultural Holism Through Interactional Systems," *American Anthropologist* 83 (September 1981): 571, 574.

54 Ibid., p. 574.

at once their duty and their interest to know more than their fellows, to acquaint themselves with everything that could aid man in his arduous struggle with nature, everything that could mitigate his sufferings and prolong his life.[55]

While their magic infused all practical activity and was, like science today, an economic source of political power, shamans did not completely monopolize economic knowledge in any tribal society. The Zande potter "selects the proper clay, kneads it thoroughly till he has extracted all grit and pebbles, and builds it up slowly and carefully"[56]—all with his own skills, not the shaman's. But the potter attributes the cracking of his pots during firing to witchcraft, and may feel the need to consult a shaman to ward off disasters. Tribal production depends on the combination of shaman and artisan knowledge, both necessary, neither sufficient. In all magical societies, "these two groups of activities possess the same degree of reality. It would be meaningless to ask . . . whether the success of the harvest depended on the skill of the farmers or on the correct performance of the New Year's festival. Both were essential to success."[57]

The shaman's magic was seen as especially important in areas where workers could not get consistently good results on their own, particularly in hunting and horticulture. Frazer catalogs scores of magical rites for growing corn alone, and hundreds of other fertility and hunting incantations. Many African tribes were ruled by rainmaking god-kings.[58] When nature was most problematic, shamans who could make rain in the desert, deliver harvests in rocky soils, or ward off periodic typhoons seemed to be particularly powerful politically. Spiritual and material knowledge were woven together in a seamless magical quilt that the shamans wrapped around themselves as a single fabric bringing power.[59]

In ancient Egypt, priests were agricultural experts who gave life to "the palm tree that shaded them amid the desert, the spring that gave them drink in the oasis, the grove where they could meet and rest, the sycamore flourishing miraculously in the sand," and all the animals that "filled the Egyptian pantheon like a chattering managerie."[60] With his secret knowledge of the Nile and the rain, the pharaoh was thought to have ultimate power over Egypt's food supply. The pharaoh, of course, also had whip-wielding slave overseers to bolster his authority. Slave rebellions, such as the one Moses led, indicated that the whip was often more important than supposed secret knowledge in securing the pharaoh's power. Slave societies such as Egypt were clearly logocracies only in part.

Ancient Egyptians, like members of tribal societies, attributed agricultural successes to practical, widely known farming techniques combined with specialized magical knowledge monopolized by priests. Frazer notes that "a

55 Frazer, *Golden Bough,* p. 71.

56 Evans-Pritchard, *Witchcraft, Oracles, and Magic Among the Azande,* p. 21.

57 H. A. Frankfort et al., *Before Philosophy* (Baltimore: Penguin Books, 1968), p. 22.

58 Clark and Piggott, *Prehistoric Society,* p. 215.

59 Evans-Pritchard, *Witches, Oracles, and Magic Among the Azande,* p. 30.

60 Durant, *Our Oriental Heritage,* pp. 198–99.

priest and his assistant went into the field and sang songs of invocation to the spirit of the corn. After that a loud rustling would be heard, which was thought to be caused by the Old Woman bringing the corn into the field."[61] This invocation was considered as essential to the harvest as the farmer's planting and hoeing skills. Such indispensible knowledge helped make priests a powerful, if not a ruling, class:

> In effect, though not in law, the office of priest passed down from father to son, and a class grew up which . . . became in time richer and stronger than the feudal aristocracy or the royal family itself. The sacrifices offered to the gods supplied the priests with food and drink; the temple buildings gave them spacious homes; the revenues of temple lands and services furnished them with ample incomes; and their exemption from forced labor, military service, and ordinary taxation left them in an enviable position of prestige and power.[62]

Among the Azande and some other peoples, magical monopolies did not produce logocracy. Evans-Pritchard notes that witch doctors can be "important people" but "have no political power. . . . Many people say that the great majority of witch-doctors are liars whose sole concern is to acquire wealth. . . . It is indeed probable that Zande faith in their witch-doctors has declined since European conquest of their country."[63] Obviously, possessing knowledge or any other crucial resource does not auto-matically produce class power. In many tribal societies, shamans lacked the will or political acumen to become ruling mandarins.

In the Middle Ages, clergymen's spiritual/material knowledge helped make them, like the Egyptian priests, something close to a logocratic ruling class. Of course, the clergy shared power with feudal lords and the king, and much of the church's own power derived not from its theology, but from its vast land holdings, army, and Inquisition. But the church unquestionably gained much of its power by providing knowledge for life's uncertainties, both spiritual and material:

> For every emergency or ill men had a friend in the skies. St. Sebastian and St. Roch were mighty in time of pestilence. St. Apollinia . . . healed the toothache; St. Blaise cured sore throat. St. Corneille protected oxen, St. Gall chickens, St. Anthony pigs. St. Medard was for France the saint most frequently solicited for rain; if he failed to pour, his impatient worshipers, now and then, threw his statue into the water, perhaps as suggestive magic.[64]

God and the devil permeated every aspect of life, and the clergy claimed a monopoly on the ability to get a good hearing from "the friendly skies." The church contributed to production directly through its monastic orders, which were a prime source of improvements in building, timekeeping, printing, record keeping, and agriculture.[65] Economic and otherworldly

---

61 Frazer, *Golden Bough*, p. 432.

62 Durant, *Our Oriental Heritage*, p. 201.

63 Evans-Pritchard, *Witchcraft, Oracles, and Magic Among the Azande*, pp. 112, 115.

64 Durant, *Age of Faith*, p. 743.

65 This was brought to our attention by James Meehan.

knowledge were fused in a seamless religious web owned and controlled by the church. From this, the clergy built one of history's most formidable empires. The church was Europe's biggest landholder, and the papacy's authority at its height dwarfed that of the kings, whom the pope annointed: "Kings and emperors held the stirrup and kissed the feet of the white-robed Servant of the Servants of God. The papacy was now the highest reach of human ambition."[66]

Scholar-officials selected by competitive examination governed the imperial Chinese empire, perhaps the purest logocracy ever seen. Begun well before the Middle Ages, it survived into the twentieth century. The scholars ruled autocratically, following Confucius' view that "the common people, the lower class" should be maintained "in an entirely subordinate position":[67]

> The class of scholar-officials [or mandarins], numerically infinitesimal but omnipotent by reason of their strength, influence, position and prestige, held all the power and owned the largest amount of land. This class possessed every privilege, above all the privilege of reproducing itself, because of its monopoly of education.[68]

Mastery of knowledge—specifically the Confucian texts and literature—was the official qualification for rule. The scholar-officials believed in and perfectly embodied Mencius' philosophy of a political mental/manual divide:

> Great men have their proper business and little men have their proper business. . . . Some labor with their minds, and some with their strength. Those who labor with their minds govern others; those who labor with their strength are governed by others. Those who are governed by others support them; those who govern others are supported by them.[69]

The mandarins carefully built and protected their knowledge monopoly. Chinese historian Dun Li notes that their paradigm gave no respect to farmers' and merchants' know-how, derogated manual work, and disparaged even mental work "outside the study of humanities."[70]

Monopoly was facilitated by the difficulty of the written Chinese language, which

> required not only the mastering of more than 10,000 separate characters and their numerous combinations but also a fair knowledge of the great accumulations of Chinese literature. Unless the learner was a born genius, it would take a considerable part of his life just to learn to write in a presentable style.[71]

According to Dun Li, "true mastery of a literary education was bound to be limited to a few. Knowledge, like commodities, commanded a high price when it was difficult to obtain."[72]

---

66 Durant, *Age of Faith,* pp. 758–59.
67 Wolfram Eberhard, "Life and Ideas of Confucius" in Molly Joel Cove, Jon Livingston, and Jean Highland, eds., *China* (New York: Bantam, 1984), p. 35.
68 Etienne Balazs, "Imperial China: The Han Dynasty," in Coye et al., *China,* p. 27.
69 Quoted in ibid., pp. 28–29.
70 Dun Li, "The Examination System," in Coye et al., *China,* p. 51.
71 Dun Li, "The Four Classes," in Coye et al., *China,* p. 49.
72 Ibid., p. 50.

The Confucian scholars justified their rule on the grounds that they alone could guide Chinese society according to its own richest intellectual and moral tradition (which, of course, they themselves had created and enshrined). But, as historian Etienne Balazs notes, the mandarins stretched their undeniable competence in the Confucian texts to a claim of universal competence, qualifying them to manage the economy and coordinate social life in every detail: "All mediating and administrative functions were carried out by the scholar-officials. They prepared the calendar, they organized transport and exchange, they supervised the construction of roads, canals, dikes, and dams."[73]

These were generalists who monopolized the knowledge now divided among all the different professions. They constituted themselves as a single ruling class in a logocratic state: "Their social role was at one and the same time that of architect, engineer, teacher, administrator and ruler. Yet these 'managers' before their time were firmly against any form of specialization. There was only one profession they recognized: that of governing."[74]

The imperfect logocracies of shamans and priests came to a crashing end in capitalist societies. Capitalism brought science and other secular knowledge as alternative wisdom to nurture people's economic destinies, if not their souls.

Spiritual/material knowledge could not compete with the rising secular/material knowledge in delivering earthly goods—and as the latter blossomed, the church's enclosure of the mind slowly weakened. The rise of scientific knowledge, as Will Durant observes, "clashes with mythology and theology. . . . Priestly control of arts and letters is then felt as a galling shackle or hateful barrier, and intellectual history takes on the character of a 'conflict between science and religion.' "[75]

Considering its predecessors, early capitalism may seem a historical aberration, since its knowledge classes, including priests and craftworkers, held comparatively little power. But as industrial production began to exploit science fully in the nineteenth century, capitalists came to depend increasingly on a new class of specialized scientists, engineers, and other professionals. Many believe that capitalism is slowly evolving into a scientific breed of logocracy. Daniel Bell suggests that knowledge is supplanting capital as the critical economic resource; universities are replacing corporations as the preeminent social institutions; professionals and scientists are gaining influence at the expense of businessmen and entrepreneurs; expertise is becoming the surest route to power.[76]

John Kenneth Galbraith's theory of the technostructure proposes that people with engineering, scientific, financial, and marketing knowledge increasingly control large corporations:

It is a shift of power as between the factors of production which matches that which occurred from land to capital in the advanced countries beginning two centuries ago. It is an occurrence of the last fifty years and is still

73 Balazs, "Imperial China," p. 27.
74 Ibid.
75 Durant, *Our Oriental Heritage*, p. 71.
76 Bell, *Coming of Post-Industrial Society*.

going on. . . . Power has, in fact, passed to what anyone in search of novelty might be justified in calling a new factor of production. This is the association of men of diverse technical knowledge, experience or other talent which modern industrial technology and planning require.[77]

James Burnham likewise argues that managers and professionals claiming expertise are supplanting owners as the rulers of economic life, in the process creating a new planned capitalism.[78]

Others argue that the Soviet Union, Czechoslovakia, Hungary, and other East European countries before the revolutions of 1989 offered another glimpse of emerging logocracy. George Konrad and Ivan Szelenyi write that "the diploma is a kind of ticket of admission to the realm of opportunity, which opens before the graduate like a gambling casino."[79] As Mikhail Bakunin foresaw a century ago, Communist Party members can become self-appointed experts, dominating rather than serving labor.[80] Milovan Djilas, a former high party official in Yugoslavia, testified to the rise of a "new class" in Eastern Europe that dominated workers as surely as capital does in the West.[81] In the 1990s, Communist planners may be supplanted by Western-trained economists, engineers, and other experts widely viewed as the key to the renaissance of a transformed Eastern Europe.

In both East and West, we have pictures of new societies dominated, or coming to be dominated, by experts. If the spirits of witch doctors and the God of the Middle Ages are dying, their ghosts are reappearing—in white coats. The specter of logocracy now haunts capitalism and socialism alike.

77 John Kenneth Galbraith, *The New Industrial State* (New York: New American Library, 1967), pp. 68–69.

78 James W. Burnham, *The Managerial Revolution* (New York: Penguin Books, 1941).

79 George Konrad and Ivan Szelenyi, *The Intellectuals on the Road to Class Power* (New York: Harcourt Brace Jovanovich, 1979).

80 Mikhail Bakunin, *Etatisme et anarchie, 1873* (Archives Bakounine, I.I.S.G., Amsterdam), ed. Arthur Lehning (Leiden: Brill, 1967).

81 Milovan *Djilas, The New Class: An Analysis of the Communist System* (New York: Praeger, 1957).

Some Peculiarities of Racial Inequality in America

3 I

Jobless Poverty: A New Form of Social Dislocation in the Inner-City Ghetto*

WILLIAM JULIUS WILSON

In September 1996 my book, *When Work Disappears: The World of the New Urban Poor,* was published. ★ ★ ★ *When Work Disappears* describes a new type of poverty in our nation's metropolises: poor, segregated neighborhoods in which a majority of adults are either unemployed or have dropped out of the labor force altogether.

What is the effect of these "jobless ghettos" on individuals, families, and neighborhoods? What accounts for their existence? I suggest several factors and conclude with policy recommendations: a mix of public and private sector projects is more effective than relying on a strategy of employer subsidies.

★ ★ ★

||| JOBLESS GHETTOS

The jobless poverty of today stands in sharp contrast to previous periods. In 1950, a substantial portion of the urban black population was poor but they were working. Urban poverty was quite extensive but people held jobs. However, as we entered the 1990s most adults in many inner-city ghetto

---

★ First published in 1999; from *A Nation Divided: Diversity, Inequality, and Community in American Society,* edited by Phyllis Moen, Donna Dempster-McClain, and Henry A. Walker.

neighborhoods were not working. For example, in 1950 a significant majority of adults held jobs in a typical week in the three neighborhoods that represent the historic core of the Black Belt in Chicago—Douglas, Grand Boulevard, and Washington Park. But by 1990, only four in ten in Douglas worked in a typical week, one in three in Washington Park, and one in four in Grand Boulevard.[1] In 1950, 69 percent of all males aged fourteen and older who lived in these three neighborhoods worked in a typical week, and in 1960, 64 percent of this group were so employed. However, by 1990 only 37 percent of all males aged sixteen and over held jobs in a typical week in these three neighborhoods.

The disappearance of work has had negative effects not only on individuals and families, but on the social life of neighborhoods as well. Inner-city joblessness is a severe problem that is often overlooked or obscured when the focus is mainly on poverty and its consequences. Despite increases in the concentration of poverty since 1970, inner cities have always featured high levels of poverty. But the levels of inner-city joblessness reached during the first half of the 1990s were unprecedented.

Joblessness versus Informal Work Activity

I should note that when I speak of "joblessness" I am not solely referring to official unemployment. The unemployment rate represents only the percentage of workers in the *official* labor force—that is, those who are *actively* looking for work. It does not include those who are outside of or have dropped out of the labor market, including the nearly six million males aged twenty-five to sixty who appeared in the census statistics but were not recorded in the labor market statistics in 1990 (Thurow 1990).

These uncounted males in the labor market are disproportionately represented in the inner-city ghettos. Accordingly, in *When Work Disappears,* I use a more appropriate measure of joblessness, a measure that takes into account both official unemployment and non–labor-force participation. That measure is the employment-to-population ratio, which corresponds to the percentage of adults aged sixteen and older who are working. Using the employment-to-population ratio we find, for example, that in 1990 only one in three adults aged sixteen and older held a job in the ghetto poverty areas of Chicago, areas representing roughly 425,000 men, women, and children. And in the ghetto tracts of the nation's one hundred largest cities, for every ten adults who did not hold a job in a typical week in 1990 there were only six employed persons (Kasarda 1993).

The consequences of high neighborhood joblessness are more devastating than those of high neighborhood poverty. A neighborhood in which people are poor but employed is much different than a neighborhood in which

---

1 The figures on adult employment are based on calculations from data provided by the 1990 U.S. Bureau of the Census (1993) and the *Local Community Fact Book for Chicago—1950* (1953) and the *Local Community Fact Book for Chicago—1960* (1963). The adult employment rates represent the number of employed individuals (aged fourteen and older in 1950 and sixteen and older in 1990) among the total number of adults in a given area. Those who are not employed include both the individuals who are members of the labor force but are not working and those who have dropped out or are not part of the labor force.

people are poor and jobless. *When Work Disappears* shows that many of today's problems in the inner-city ghetto neighborhoods—crime, family dissolution, welfare, low levels of social organization, and so on—are fundamentally a consequence of the disappearance of work.

It should be clear that when I speak of the disappearance of work, I am referring to the declining involvement in or lack of attachment to the formal labor market. It could be argued that, in the general sense of the term, "joblessness" does not necessarily mean "nonwork." In other words, to be officially unemployed or officially outside the labor market does not mean that one is totally removed from all forms of work activity. Many people who are officially jobless are nonetheless involved in informal kinds of work activity, ranging from unpaid housework to work that draws income from the informal or illegal economies.

Housework is work, baby-sitting is work, even drug dealing is work. However, what contrasts work in the formal economy with work activity in the informal and illegal economies is that work in the formal economy is characterized by, indeed calls for, greater regularity and consistency in schedules and hours. Work schedules and hours are formalized. The demands for discipline are greater. It is true that some work activities outside the formal economy also call for discipline and regular schedules. Several studies reveal that the social organization of the drug industry is driven by discipline and a work ethic, however perverse. However, as a general rule, work in the informal and illegal economies is far less governed by norms or expectations that place a premium on discipline and regularity. For all these reasons, when I speak of

the disappearance of work, I mean work in the formal economy, work that provides a framework for daily behavior because of the discipline, regularity, and stability that it imposes.

Effect of Joblessness on Routine and Discipline

In the absence of regular employment, a person lacks not only a place in which to work and the receipt of regular income but also a coherent organization of the present—that is, a system of concrete expectations and goals. Regular employment provides the anchor for the spatial and temporal aspects of daily life. It determines where you are going to be and when you are going to be there. In the absence of regular employment, life, including family life, becomes less coherent. Persistent unemployment and irregular employment hinder rational planning in daily life, a necessary condition of adaptation to an industrial economy (Bourdieu 1965).

Thus, a youngster who grows up in a family with a steady breadwinner and in a neighborhood in which most of the adults are employed will tend to develop some of the disciplined habits associated with stable or steady employment—habits that are reflected in the behavior of his or her parents and of other neighborhood adults. These might include attachment to a routine, a recognition of the hierarchy found in most work situations, a sense of personal efficacy attained through the routine management of financial affairs, endorsement of a system of personal and material rewards associated with dependability and responsibility, and so on. Accordingly, when this youngster enters the labor market, he or she has a distinct advantage over the youngsters who grow up in households without a steady breadwinner and in neighborhoods that are not organized around work—in other words, a milieu in which one is more exposed to the less disciplined habits associated with casual or infrequent work.

With the sharp recent rise of solo-parent families, black children who live in inner-city households are less likely to be socialized in a work environment for two main reasons. Their mothers, saddled with child-care responsibilities, can prevent a slide deeper into poverty by accepting welfare. Their fathers, removed from family responsibilities and obligations, are more likely to become idle as a response to restricted employment opportunities, which further weakens their influence in the household and attenuates their contact with the family. In short, the social and cultural responses to joblessness are reflected in the organization of family life and patterns of family formation; there they have implications for labor-force attachment as well.

Given the current policy debates that assign blame to the personal shortcomings of the jobless, we need to understand their behavior as responses and adaptations to chronic subordination, including behaviors that have evolved into cultural patterns. The social actions of the jobless—including their behavior, habits, skills, styles, orientations, attitudes—ought not to be analyzed as if they are unrelated to the broader structure of their opportunities and constraints that have evolved over time. This is not to argue that individuals and groups lack the freedom to make their own choices, engage in certain conduct, and develop certain styles and orientations; but I maintain that their decisions and actions occur within a context of constraints and opportunities that are drastically different from those in middle-class society.

EXPLANATIONS OF THE GROWTH OF JOBLESS GHETTOS

What accounts for the growing proportion of jobless adults in inner-city communities? An easy explanation would be racial segregation. However, a race-specific argument is not sufficient to explain recent changes in such neighborhoods. After all, these historical Black Belt neighborhoods were *just as segregated by skin color in 1950* as they are today, yet the level of employment was much higher then. One has to account for the ways in which racial segregation interacts with other changes in society to produce the recent escalating rates of joblessness. Several factors stand out: the decreasing demand for low-skilled labor, the suburbanization of jobs, the social deterioration of ghetto neighborhoods, and negative employer attitudes. I discuss each of these factors next.

Decreasing Demand for Low-Skilled Labor

The disappearance of work in many inner-city neighborhoods is in part related to the nationwide decline in the fortunes of low-skilled workers. The sharp decline in the relative demand for unskilled labor has had a more adverse effect on blacks than on whites because a substantially larger proportion of African Americans are unskilled. Although the number of skilled blacks (including managers, professionals, and technicians) has increased sharply in the last several years, the proportion of those who are unskilled remains large, because the black population, burdened by cumulative experiences of racial restrictions, was overwhelmingly unskilled just several decades ago (Schwartzman 1997).[2]

The factors involved in the decreased relative demand for unskilled labor include changes in skilled-based technology, the rapid growth in college enrollment that increased the supply and reduced the relative cost of skilled labor, and the growing internationalization of economic activity, including trade liberalization policies, which reduced the price of imports and raised the output of export industries (Schwartzman 1997). The increased output of export industries aids skilled workers, simply because they are heavily represented in export industries. But increasing imports, especially those from developing countries that compete with labor-intensive industries (for example, apparel, textile, toy, footwear, and some manufacturing industries), hurts unskilled labor (Schwartzman 1997).

Accordingly, inner-city blacks are experiencing a more extreme form of the economic marginality that has affected most unskilled workers in America since 1980. Unfortunately, there is a tendency among policy makers, black leaders, and scholars alike to separate the economic problems of the ghetto from the national and international trends affecting American families and neighborhoods. If the economic problems of the ghetto are defined solely in

racial terms they can be isolated and viewed as only requiring race-based solutions as proposed by those on the left, or as only requiring narrow political solutions with subtle racial connotations (such as welfare reform), as strongly proposed by those on the right.

Overemphasis on Racial Factors

Race continues to be a factor that aggravates inner-city black employment problems as we shall soon see. But the tendency to overemphasize the racial factors obscures other more fundamental forces that have sharply increased inner-city black joblessness. As the late black economist Vivian Henderson put it several years ago, "[I]t is as if racism having put blacks in their economic place steps aside to watch changes in the economy destroy that place" (Henderson 1975, 54). To repeat, the concentrated joblessness of the inner-city poor represents the most dramatic form of the growing economic dislocations among the unskilled stemming in large measure from changes in the organization of the economy, including the global economy.

Suburbanization of Jobs

But inner-city workers face an additional problem: the growing suburbanization of jobs. Most ghetto residents cannot afford an automobile and therefore have to rely on public transit systems that make the connection between inner-city neighborhoods and suburban job locations difficult and time consuming.

2 The economist David Schwartzman defines "unskilled workers to include operators, fabricators, and laborers, and those in service occupations, including private household workers, those working in protective service occupations, food service, and cleaning and building service." On the basis of this definition he estimates that 80 percent of all black workers and 38 percent of all white workers were unskilled in 1950. By 1990, 46 percent of black workers and 27 percent of white workers were employed in unskilled occupations (Schwartzman 1997).

Although studies based on data collected before 1970 showed no consistent or convincing effects on black employment as a consequence of this spatial mismatch, the employment of inner-city blacks relative to suburban blacks has clearly deteriorated since then. Recent research (conducted mainly by urban labor economists) strongly shows that the decentralization of employment is continuing and that employment in manufacturing, most of which is already suburbanized, has decreased in central cities, particularly in the Northeast and Midwest (Holzer 1996).

Blacks living in central cities have less access to employment (as measured by the ratio of jobs to people and the average travel time to and from work) than do central-city whites. Moreover, unlike most other groups of workers across the urban-suburban divide, less-educated central-city blacks receive lower wages than suburban blacks who have similar levels of education. And the decline in earnings of central-city blacks is related to the decentralization of employment—that is, the movement of jobs from the cities to the suburbs—in metropolitan areas (Holzer 1996).

Social Deterioration of Ghetto Neighborhoods

Changes in the class, racial, and demographic composition of inner-city neighborhoods have also contributed to the high percentage of jobless adults in these neighborhoods. Because of the steady out-migration of more advantaged families, the proportion of nonpoor families and prime-age working adults has decreased sharply in the typical inner-city ghetto since 1970 (Wilson 1987). In the face of increasing

and prolonged joblessness, the declining proportion of nonpoor families and the overall depopulation has made it increasingly difficult to sustain basic neighborhood institutions or to achieve adequate levels of social organization. The declining presence of working- and middle-class blacks has also deprived ghetto neighborhoods of key structural and cultural resources. Structural resources include residents with income high enough to sustain neighborhood services, and cultural resources include conventional role models for neighborhood children.

On the basis of our research in Chicago, it appears that what many high jobless neighborhoods have in common is a relatively high degree of social integration (high levels of local neighboring while being relatively isolated from contacts in the broader mainstream society) and low levels of informal social control (feelings that they have little control over their immediate environment, including the environment's negative influences on their children). In such areas, not only are children at risk because of the lack of informal social controls, they are also disadvantaged because the social interaction among neighbors tends to be confined to those whose skills, styles, orientations, and habits are not as conducive to promoting positive social outcomes (academic success, pro-social behavior, employment in the formal labor market, etc.) as those in more stable neighborhoods. Although the close interaction among neighbors in such areas may be useful in devising strategies, disseminating information, and developing styles of behavior that are helpful in a ghetto milieu (teaching children to avoid eye-to-eye contact with strangers and to develop a tough demeanor in the public sphere for self-protection), they may be less effective in promoting the welfare of children in society at large.

Despite being socially integrated, the residents in Chicago's ghetto neighborhoods shared a feeling that they had little informal social control over the children in their environment. A primary reason is the absence of a strong organizational capacity or an institutional resource base that would provide an extra layer of social organization in their neighborhoods. It is easier for parents to control the behavior of the children in their neighborhoods when a strong institutional resource base exists and when the links between community institutions such as churches, schools, political organizations, businesses, and civic clubs are strong or secure. The higher the density and stability of formal organizations, the less illicit activities such as drug trafficking, crime, prostitution, and the formation of gangs can take root in the neighborhood.

Few Community Institutions

A weak institutional resource base is what distinguishes high jobless inner-city neighborhoods from stable middle-class and working-class areas. As one resident of a high jobless neighborhood on the South Side of Chicago put it, "Our children, you know, seems to be more at risk than any other children there is, because there's no library for them to go to. There's not a center they can go to, there's no field house that they can go into. There's nothing. There's nothing at all." Parents in high jobless neighborhoods have a much more difficult task controlling the behavior of their adolescents and preventing them from getting involved in activities detrimental to pro-social development. Given the lack of organizational capacity and a weak institutional base, some parents choose to protect their children by isolating them from activities in the neighborhood, including avoiding contact and interaction with neighborhood families. Wherever possible, and often with great difficulty when one considers the problems of transportation and limited financial resources, they attempt to establish contacts and cultivate relations with individuals, families, and institutions, such as church groups, schools, and community recreation programs, outside their neighborhood. A note of caution is necessary, though. It is just as indefensible to treat inner-city residents as super heroes who overcome racist oppression as it is to view them as helpless victims. We should, however, appreciate the range of choices, including choices representing cultural influences, that are available to inner-city residents who live under constraints that most people in the larger society do not experience.

Effect of Joblessness on Marriage and Family

It is within the context of labor-force attachment that the public policy discussion on welfare reform and family values should be couched. The research that we have conducted in Chicago suggests that as employment prospects recede, the foundation for stable relationships becomes weaker over time. More permanent relationships such as marriage give way to temporary liaisons that result in broken unions, out-of-wedlock pregnancies, and, to a lesser extent, separation and divorce. The changing norms concerning marriage in the larger society reinforce the movement toward temporary liaisons in the inner city, and therefore economic considerations in marital decisions take on even greater weight. Many inner-city residents have negative outlooks toward marriage, outlooks that are developed in and influenced by an environment featuring persistent joblessness.

The disrupting effect of joblessness on marriage and family causes poor inner-city blacks to be even more disconnected from the job market and discouraged about their role in the labor force. The economic marginality of the ghetto poor is cruelly reinforced, therefore, by conditions in the neighborhoods in which they live.

Negative Employer Attitudes

In the eyes of employers in metropolitan Chicago, the social conditions in the ghetto render inner-city blacks less desirable as workers, and therefore many are reluctant to hire them. One of the three studies that provided the empirical foundation for *When Work Disappears* included a representative sample of employers in the greater Chicago area who provided entry-level jobs. An overwhelming majority of these employers, both white and black, expressed negative views about inner-city ghetto workers, and many stated that they were reluctant to hire them. For example, a president of an inner-city manufacturing firm expressed a concern about employing residents from certain inner-city neighborhoods:

> If somebody gave me their address, uh, Cabrini Green I might unavoidably have some concerns. *Interviewer:* What would your concerns be? *Respondent:* That the poor guy probably would be frequently unable to get to work and . . . I probably would watch him more carefully even if it wasn't fair, than I would with somebody else. I know what I should do though is recognize that here's a guy that is trying to get out of his situation and probably will work harder than somebody else who's already out of there and he might be the best one around here. But I, I think I would have to struggle accepting that premise at the beginning. (Wilson 1996, field notes)

In addition to qualms about the neighborhood milieu of inner-city residents, the employers frequently mentioned concerns about applicants' language skills and educational training. An employer from a computer software firm in Chicago expressed the view "that in many businesses the ability to meet the public is paramount and you do not talk street talk to the buying public. Almost all your black welfare people talk street talk. And who's going to sit them down and change their speech patterns?" (Wilson 1996, field notes) A Chicago real estate broker made a similar point:

> A lot of times I will interview applicants who are black, who are sort of lower class....They'll come to me and I cannot hire them because their language skills are so poor. Their speaking voice for one thing is poor . . . they have no verbal facility with the language . . . and these . . . you know, they just don't know how to speak and they'll say "salesmens" instead of "salesmen" and that's a problem....They don't know punctuation, they don't know how to use correct grammar, and they cannot spell. And I can't hire them. And I feel bad about

that and I think they're being very disadvantaged by the Chicago Public School system. (Wilson 1996, field notes)

Another respondent defended his method of screening out most job applicants on the telephone on the basis of their use of "grammar and English":

I have every right to say that that's a requirement for this job. I don't care if you're pink, black, green, yellow or orange, I demand someone who speaks well. You want to tell me that I'm a bigot, fine, call me a bigot. I know blacks, you don't even know they're black. (Wilson 1996, field notes)

Finally, an inner-city banker claimed that many blacks in the ghetto "simply cannot read. When you're talking our type of business, that disqualifies them immediately, we don't have a job here that doesn't require that somebody have minimum reading and writing skills" (Wilson 1996, field notes).

How should we interpret the negative attitudes and actions of employers? To what extent do they represent an aversion to blacks *per se* and to what degree do they reflect judgments based on the job-related skills and training of inner-city blacks in a changing labor market? I should point out that the statements made by the African American employers concerning the qualifications of inner-city black workers did not differ significantly from those of the white employers. Whereas 74 percent of all the white employers who responded to the open-ended questions expressed negative views of the job-related traits of inner-city blacks, 80 percent of the black employers did so as well.

This raises a question about the meaning and significance of race in certain situations—in other words, how race intersects with other factors. A key hypothesis in this connection is that given the recent shifts in the economy, employers are looking for workers with a broad range of abilities: "hard" skills (literacy, numerical ability, basic mechanical ability, and other testable attributes) and "soft" skills (personalities suitable to the work environment, good grooming, group-oriented work behaviors, etc.). While hard skills are the product of education and training—benefits that are apparently in short supply in inner-city schools—soft skills are strongly tied to culture, and are therefore shaped by the harsh environment of the inner-city ghetto. For example, our research revealed that many parents in the inner-city ghetto neighborhoods of Chicago wanted their children not to make eye-to-eye contact with strangers and to develop a tough demeanor when interacting with people on the streets. While such behaviors are helpful for survival in the ghetto, they hinder successful interaction in mainstream society.

Statistical Discrimination

If employers are indeed reacting to the difference in skills between white and black applicants, it becomes increasingly difficult to discuss the motives of employers: are they rejecting inner-city black applicants out of overt racial discrimination or on the basis of qualifications?

Nonetheless, many of the selective recruitment practices do represent what economists call "statistical discrimination": employers make assumptions about the inner-city black workers *in general* and reach decisions based on those assumptions before they have had a chance to review systematically the qualifications of an individual applicant. The net effect is that many black inner-city applicants are never given the chance to prove their qualifications on an individual level because they are systematically screened out by the selective recruitment process.

Statistical discrimination, although representing elements of class bias against poor workers in the inner city, is clearly a matter of race both directly and indirectly. Directly, the selective recruitment patterns effectively screen out far more black workers from the inner city than Hispanic or white workers from the same types of backgrounds. But indirectly, race is also a factor, even in those decisions to deny employment to inner-city black workers on the basis of objective and thorough evaluations of their qualifications. The hard and soft skills among inner-city blacks that do not match the current needs of the labor market are products of racially segregated communities, communities that have historically featured widespread social constraints and restricted opportunities.

Thus the job prospects of inner-city workers have diminished not only because of the decreasing relative demand for low-skilled labor in the United States economy, the suburbanization of jobs, and the social deterioration of ghetto neighborhoods, but also because of negative employer attitudes. This combination of factors presents a real challenge to policy makers. Indeed, considering the narrow range of social policy options in the "balance-the-budget" political climate, how can we immediately alleviate the inner-city jobs problem—a problem which will undoubtedly grow when the new welfare reform bill takes full effect and creates a situation that will be even more harmful to inner-city children and adolescents?

★ ★ ★

‖ REFERENCES

Bourdieu, Pierre. 1965. *Travail et Travailleurs en Algerie.* Paris: Editions Mouton.

Henderson, Vivian. 1975. "Race, Economics, and Public Policy." *Crisis* 83 (Fall): 50–55.

Holzer, Harry J. 1996. *What Employers Want: Job Prospects for Less-Educated Workers.* New York: Russell Sage.

Kasarda, John D. 1993. "Inner-City Concentrated Poverty and Neighborhood Distress: 1970–1990." *Housing Policy Debate* 4(3): 253–302.

Local Community Fact Book for Chicago—1950. 1953. Chicago: Community Inventory, University of Chicago.

Local Community Fact Book for Chicago—1960. 1963. Chicago: Community Inventory, University of Chicago.

Schwartzman, David. 1997. *Black Unemployment: Part of Unskilled Unemployment.* Westport, CT: Greenwood.

Thurow, Lester. 1990. "The Crusade That's Killing Prosperity." *American Prospect* March/April:54–59.

U.S. Bureau of the Census. 1993. *Census of Population: Detailed Characteristics of the Population.* Washington, DC: U.S. Government Printing Office.

Wilson, William Julius. 1996. *When Work Disappears: The World of the New Urban Poor.* New York: Alfred A. Knopf.

32

The Perpetuation of the Black Underclass*

DOUGLAS MASSEY AND NANCY A. DENTON

It is quite simple. As soon as there is a group area
then all your uncertainties are removed and that is,
after all, the primary purpose of this Bill [requiring
racial segregation in housing].

Minister of the Interior, Union of South Africa,
Legislative debate on the Group Areas Act of 1950

During the 1970s and 1980s a word disappeared from the American vocabulary.[1] It was not in the speeches of politicians decrying the multiple ills beset-
ting American cities. It was not spoken by government officials responsible
for administering the nation's social programs. It was not mentioned by journalists reporting on the rising tide of homelessness, drugs, and violence in
urban America. It was not discussed by foundation executives and think-tank
experts proposing new programs for unemployed parents and unwed mothers. It was not articulated by civil rights leaders speaking out against the persistence of racial inequality; and it was nowhere to be found in the thousands
of pages written by social scientists on the urban underclass. The word was
segregation.

---

* First published in 1993; from *American Apartheid: Segregation and the Making of the Underclass.*

1 Epigraph from Edgar H. Brookes, *Apartheid: A Documentary Study of Modern South Africa* (London:
Routledge and Kegan Paul, 1968), p. 142.

Most Americans vaguely realize that urban America is still a residentially segregated society, but few appreciate the depth of black segregation or the degree to which it is maintained by ongoing institutional arrangements and contemporary individual actions. They view segregation as an unfortunate holdover from a racist past, one that is fading progressively over time. If racial residential segregation persists, they reason, it is only because civil rights laws passed during the 1960s have not had enough time to work or because many blacks still prefer to live in black neighborhoods. The residential segregation of blacks is viewed charitably as a "natural" outcome of impersonal social and economic forces, the same forces that produced Italian and Polish neighborhoods in the past and that yield Mexican and Korean areas today.

But black segregation is not comparable to the limited and transient segregation experienced by other racial and ethnic groups, now or in the past. No group in the history of the United States has ever experienced the sustained high level of residential segregation that has been imposed on blacks in large American cities for the past fifty years. This extreme racial isolation did not just happen; it was manufactured by whites through a series of self-conscious actions and purposeful institutional arrangements that continue today. Not only is the depth of black segregation unprecedented and utterly unique compared with that of other groups, but it shows little sign of change with the passage of time or improvements in socioeconomic status.

If policymakers, scholars, and the public have been reluctant to acknowledge segregation's persistence, they have likewise been blind to its consequences for American blacks. Residential segregation is not a neutral fact; it systematically undermines the social and economic well-being of blacks in the United States. Because of racial segregation, a significant share of black America is condemned to experience a social environment where poverty and joblessness are the norm, where a majority of children are born out of wedlock, where most families are on welfare, where educational failure prevails, and where social and physical deterioration abound. Through prolonged exposure to such an environment, black chances for social and economic success are drastically reduced.

Deleterious neighborhood conditions are built into the structure of the black community. They occur because segregation concentrates poverty to build a set of mutually reinforcing and self-feeding spirals of decline into black neighborhoods. When economic dislocations deprive a segregated group of employment and increase its rate of poverty, socioeconomic deprivation inevitably becomes more concentrated in neighborhoods where that group lives. The damaging social consequences that follow from increased poverty are spatially concentrated as well, creating uniquely disadvantaged environments that become progressively isolated—geographically, socially, and economically—from the rest of society.

The effect of segregation on black well-being is structural, not individual. Residential segregation lies beyond the ability of any individual to change; it constrains black life chances irrespective of personal traits, individual motivations, or private achievements. For the past twenty years this fundamental fact has been swept under the rug by policymakers, scholars, and theorists of the urban underclass. Segregation is the missing link in prior attempts to understand the plight of the urban poor. As long as blacks continue to be segregated in American cities, the United States cannot be called a race-blind society.

THE FORGOTTEN FACTOR

The present myopia regarding segregation is all the more startling because it once figured prominently in theories of racial inequality. Indeed, the ghetto was once seen as central to black subjugation in the United States. In 1944 Gunnar Myrdal wrote in *An American Dilemma* that residential segregation "is basic in a mechanical sense. It exerts its influence in an indirect and impersonal way: because Negro people do not live near white people, they cannot . . . associate with each other in the many activities founded on common neighborhood. Residential segregation . . . becomes reflected in uni-racial schools, hospitals, and other institutions" and creates "an artificial city . . . that permits any prejudice on the part of public officials to be freely vented on Negroes without hurting whites."[2]

Kenneth B. Clark, who worked with Gunnar Myrdal as a student and later applied his research skills in the landmark *Brown v. Topeka* school integration case, placed residential segregation at the heart of the U.S. system of racial oppression. In *Dark Ghetto,* written in 1965, he argued that "the dark ghetto's invisible walls

have been erected by the white society, by those who have power, both to confine those who have *no* power and to perpetuate their powerlessness. The dark ghettos are social, political, educational, and—above all—economic colonies. Their inhabitants are subject peoples, victims of the greed, cruelty, insensitivity, guilt, and fear of their masters."[3]

Public recognition of segregation's role in perpetuating racial inequality was galvanized in the late 1960s by the riots that erupted in the nation's ghettos. In their aftermath, President Lyndon B. Johnson appointed a commission chaired by Governor Otto Kerner of Illinois to identify the causes of the violence and to propose policies to prevent its recurrence. The Kerner Commission released its report in March 1968 with the shocking admonition that the United States was "moving toward two societies, one black, one white—separate and unequal."[4] Prominent among the causes that the commission identified for this growing racial inequality was residential segregation.

In stark, blunt language, the Kerner Commission informed white Americans that "discrimination and segregation have long permeated much of American life; they now threaten the future of every American."[5] "Segregation and poverty have created in the racial ghetto a destructive environment totally unknown to most white Americans. What white Americans have never fully understood—but what the Negro can never forget—is that white society is

2 Gunnar Myrdal, *An American Dilemma,* vol. 1 (New York: Harper and Brothers, 1944), p. 618; see also Walter A. Jackson, *Gunnar Myrdal and America's Conscience* (Chapel Hill: University of North Carolina Press, 1990), pp. 88–271.
3 Kenneth B. Clark, *Dark Ghetto: Dilemmas of Social Power* (New York: Harper and Row, 1965), p. 11.
4 U.S. National Advisory Commission on Civil Disorders, *The Kerner Report* (New York: Pantheon Books, 1988), p. 1.
5 Ibid.

deeply implicated in the ghetto. White institutions created it, white institutions maintain it, and white society condones it."[6]

The report argued that to continue present policies was "to make permanent the division of our country into two societies; one, largely Negro and poor, located in the central cities; the other, predominantly white and affluent, located in the suburbs."[7] Commission members rejected a strategy of ghetto enrichment coupled with abandonment of efforts to integrate, an approach they saw "as another way of choosing a permanently divided country."[8] Rather, they insisted that the only reasonable choice for America was "a policy which combines ghetto enrichment with programs designed to encourage integration of substantial numbers of Negroes into the society outside the ghetto."[9]

America chose differently. Following the passage of the Fair Housing Act in 1968, the problem of housing discrimination was declared solved, and residential segregation dropped off the national agenda. Civil rights leaders stopped pressing for the enforcement of open housing, political leaders increasingly debated employment and educational policies rather than hous-

ing integration, and academicians focused their theoretical scrutiny on everything from culture to family structure, to institutional racism, to federal welfare systems. Few people spoke of racial segregation as a problem or acknowledged its persisting consequences. By the end of the 1970s residential segregation became the forgotten factor in American race relations.[10]

While public discourse on race and poverty became more acrimonious and more focused on divisive issues such as school busing, racial quotas, welfare, and affirmative action, conditions in the nation's ghettos steadily deteriorated.[11] By the end of the 1970s, the image of poor minority families mired in an endless cycle of unemployment, unwed childbearing, illiteracy, and dependency had coalesced into a compelling and powerful concept: the urban underclass.[12] In the view of many middle-class whites, inner cities had come to house a large population of poorly educated single mothers and jobless men—mostly black and Puerto Rican—who were unlikely to exit poverty and become self-sufficient. In the ensuing national debate on the causes for this persistent poverty, four theoretical explanations gradu-

6 Ibid., p. 2.
7 Ibid., p. 22.
8 Ibid.
9 Ibid.
10 A few scholars attempted to keep the Kerner Commission's call for desegregation alive, but their voices have largely been unheeded in the ongoing debate. Thomas Pettigrew has continued to assert the central importance of residential segregation, calling it the "linchpin" of American race relations; see "Racial Change and Social Policy," *Annals of the American Academy of Political and Social Science* 441 (1979):114–31. Gary Orfield has repeatedly pointed out segregation's deleterious effects on black prospects for education, employment, and socioeconomic mobility; see "Separate Societies:

Have the Kerner Warnings Come True?" in Fred R. Harris and Roger W. Wilkins, eds., *Quiet Riots: Race and Poverty in the United States* (New York: Pantheon Books, 1988), pp. 100–122; and "Ghettoization and Its Alternatives," in Paul E. Peterson, ed., *The New Urban Reality* (Washington, D.C.: Brookings Institution, 1985), pp. 161–96.
11 See Thomas B. Edsall and Mary D. Edsall, *Chain Reaction: The Impact of Race, Rights, and Taxes on American Politics* (New York: Norton, 1991).
12 For an informative history of the evolution of the concept of the underclass, see Michael B. Katz, *The Undeserving Poor: From the War on Poverty to the War on Welfare* (New York: Pantheon, 1989), pp. 185–235.

ally emerged: culture, racism, economics, and welfare.

Cultural explanations for the underclass can be traced to the work of Oscar Lewis, who identified a "culture of poverty" that he felt promoted patterns of behavior inconsistent with socioeconomic advancement.[13] According to Lewis, this culture originated in endemic unemployment and chronic social immobility, and provided an ideology that allowed poor people to cope with feelings of hopelessness and despair that arose because their chances for socioeconomic success were remote. In individuals, this culture was typified by a lack of impulse control, a strong present-time orientation, and little ability to defer gratification. Among families, it yielded an absence of childhood, an early initiation into sex, a prevalence of free marital unions, and a high incidence of abandonment of mothers and children.

Although Lewis explicitly connected the emergence of these cultural patterns to structural conditions in society, he argued that once the culture of poverty was established, it became an independent cause of persistent poverty. This idea was further elaborated in 1965 by the Harvard sociologist and then Assistant Secretary of Labor Daniel Patrick Moynihan, who in a confidential report to the President focused on the relationship between male unemployment,

family instability, and the inter-generational transmission of poverty, a process he labeled a "tangle of pathology."[14] He warned that because of the structural absence of employment in the ghetto, the black family was disintegrating in a way that threatened the fabric of community life.

When these ideas were transmitted through the press, both popular and scholarly, the connection between culture and economic structure was somehow lost, and the argument was popularly perceived to be that "people were poor because they had a defective culture." This position was later explicitly adopted by the conservative theorist Edward Banfield, who argued that lower-class culture—with its limited time horizon, impulsive need for gratification, and psychological self-doubt—was primarily responsible for persistent urban poverty.[15] He believed that these cultural traits were largely imported, arising primarily because cities attracted lower-class migrants.

The culture-of-poverty argument was strongly criticized by liberal theorists as a self-serving ideology that "blamed the victim."[16] In the ensuing wave of reaction, black families were viewed not as weak but, on the contrary, as resilient and well adapted survivors in an oppressive and racially prejudiced society.[17] Black disadvantages were attributed not

13 Oscar Lewis, *La Vida: A Puerto Rican Family in the Culture of Poverty—San Juan and New York* (New York: Random House, 1965); "The Culture of Poverty," *Scientific American* 215 (1966):19–25; "The Culture of Poverty," in Daniel P. Moynihan, ed., *On Understanding Poverty: Perspectives from the Social Sciences* (New York: Basic Books, 1968), pp. 187–220.

14 The complete text of this report is reprinted in Lee Rainwater and William L. Yancey, *The Moynihan Report and the Politics of Controversy* (Cambridge: MIT Press, 1967), pp. 39–125.

15 Edward C. Banfield, *The Unheavenly City* (Boston: Little, Brown, 1970).

16 William Ryan, *Blaming the Victim* (New York: Random House, 1971).

17 Carol Stack, *All Our Kin: Strategies of Survival in a Black Community* (New York: Harper and Row, 1974).

to a defective culture but to the persistence of institutional racism in the United States. According to theorists of the underclass such as Douglas Glasgow and Alphonso Pinkney, the black urban underclass came about because deeply imbedded racist practices within American institutions—particularly schools and the economy—effectively kept blacks poor and dependent.[18]

As the debate on culture versus racism ground to a halt during the late 1970s, conservative theorists increasingly captured public attention by focusing on a third possible cause of poverty: government welfare policy. According to Charles Murray, the creation of the underclass was rooted in the liberal welfare state.[19] Federal antipoverty programs altered the incentives governing the behavior of poor men and women, reducing the desirability of marriage, increasing the benefits of unwed childbearing, lowering the attractiveness of menial labor, and ultimately resulted in greater poverty.

A slightly different attack on the welfare state was launched by Lawrence Mead, who argued that it was not the generosity but the permissiveness of the U.S. welfare system that was at fault.[20] Jobless men and unwed mothers should be required to display "good citizenship" before being supported by the state. By not requiring anything of the poor, Mead argued, the welfare

state undermined their independence and competence, thereby perpetuating their poverty.

This conservative reasoning was subsequently attacked by liberal social scientists, led principally by the sociologist William Julius Wilson, who had long been arguing for the increasing importance of class over race in understanding the social and economic problems facing blacks.[21] In his 1987 book *The Truly Disadvantaged,* Wilson argued that persistent urban poverty stemmed primarily from the structural transformation of the inner-city economy.[22] The decline of manufacturing, the suburbanization of employment, and the rise of a low-wage service sector dramatically reduced the number of city jobs that paid wages sufficient to support a family, which led to high rates of joblessness among minorities and a shrinking pool of "marriageable" men (those financially able to support a family). Marriage thus became less attractive to poor women, unwed childbearing increased, and female-headed families proliferated. Blacks suffered disproportionately from these trends because, owing to past discrimination, they were concentrated in locations and occupations particularly affected by economic restructuring.

Wilson argued that these economic changes were accompanied by an increase in the spatial concentration of poverty within black neigh-

18 Douglas C. Glasgow, *The Black Underclass: Poverty, Unemployment, and Entrapment of Ghetto Youth* (New York: Vintage, 1981), p. 11; Alphonso Pinkney, *The Myth of Black Progress* (Cambridge: Cambridge University Press, 1984), pp. 78–80.

19 Charles Murray, *Losing Ground: American Social Policy, 1950–1980* (New York: Basic Books, 1984).

20 Lawrence M. Mead, *Beyond Entitlement: The Social Obligations of Citizenship* (New York: Free Press, 1986).

21 William Julius Wilson, *The Declining Significance of Race: Blacks and Changing American Institutions* (Chicago: University of Chicago Press, 1978).

22 William Julius Wilson, *The Truly Disadvantaged: The Inner City, the Underclass, and Public Policy* (Chicago: University of Chicago Press, 1987), pp. 1–108.

borhoods. This new geography of poverty, he felt, was enabled by the civil rights revolution of the 1960s, which provided middle-class blacks with new opportunities outside the ghetto.[23] The out-migration of middle-class families from ghetto areas left behind a destitute community lacking the institutions, resources, and values necessary for success in post-industrial society. The urban underclass thus arose from a complex interplay of civil rights policy, economic restructuring, and a historical legacy of discrimination.

Theoretical concepts such as the culture of poverty, institutional racism, welfare disincentives, and structural economic change have all been widely debated. None of these explanations, however, considers residential segregation to be an important contributing cause of urban poverty and the underclass. In their principal works, Murray and Mead do not mention segregation at all;[24] and Wilson refers to racial segregation only as a historical legacy from the past, not as an outcome that is institutionally supported and actively created today.[25] Although Lewis mentions segregation sporadically in his writings, it is not assigned a central role in the set of structural factors responsible for the culture of poverty, and Banfield ignores it entirely. Glasgow, Pinkney, and other theorists of institutional racism mention the ghetto frequently, but generally call not for residential desegregation but for race-specific policies to combat the effects of discrimination in the schools and labor markets. In general, then, contemporary theorists of urban poverty do not see high levels of black-white segregation as particularly relevant to understanding the underclass or alleviating urban poverty.[26]

[Our] purpose ★ ★ ★ is to redirect the focus of public debate back to issues of race and racial segregation, and to suggest that they should be fundamental to thinking about the status of black Americans and the origins of the urban underclass. Our quarrel is less with any of the prevailing theories of urban poverty than with their systematic failure to consider the important role that segregation has played in mediating, exacerbating, and ultimately amplifying the harmful social and economic processes they treat.

We join earlier scholars in rejecting the view that poor urban blacks have an autonomous "culture of poverty" that explains their failure to achieve socioeconomic success in American society. We argue instead that residential segregation has been instrumental in creating a structural niche within which a deleterious set of attitudes and behaviors—a culture of segregation—has arisen and flourished. Segregation created the structural conditions for the emergence of an oppositional culture that devalues work, schooling, and marriage and that stresses attitudes and behaviors that are antithetical and often hostile to success in the larger

---

23 Ibid., pp. 49–62.

24 The subject indices of *Losing Ground* and *Beyond Entitlement* contain no references at all to residential segregation.

25 The subject index of *The Truly Disadvantaged* contains two references to pre-1960s Jim Crow segregation.

26 Again with the exception of Thomas Pettigrew and Gary Orfield.

economy. Although poor black neighborhoods still contain many people who lead conventional, productive lives, their example has been overshadowed in recent years by a growing concentration of poor, welfare-dependent families that is an inevitable result of residential segregation.

We readily agree with Glasgow, Pinkney, and others that racial discrimination is widespread and may even be institutionalized within large sectors of American society, including the labor market, the educational system, and the welfare bureaucracy. We argue, however, that this view of black subjugation is incomplete without understanding the special role that residential segregation plays in enabling all other forms of racial oppression. Residential segregation is the institutional apparatus that supports other racially discriminatory processes and binds them together into a coherent and uniquely effective system of racial subordination. Until the black ghetto is dismantled as a basic institution of American urban life, progress ameliorating racial inequality in other arenas will be slow, fitful, and incomplete.

We also agree with William Wilson's basic argument that the structural transformation of the urban economy undermined economic supports for the black community during the 1970s and 1980s.[27] We argue, however, that in the absence of segregation, these structural changes would not have produced the disastrous social and economic outcomes observed in inner cities during these decades. Although rates of black poverty were driven up by the economic dislocations Wilson identifies, it was segregation that confined the increased deprivation to a small number of densely settled, tightly packed, and geographically isolated areas.

Wilson also argues that concentrated poverty arose because the civil rights revolution allowed middle-class blacks to move out of the ghetto. Although we remain open to the possibility that class-selective migration did occur,[28] we argue that concentrated poverty would have happened during the 1970s with or without black middle-class migration. Our principal objection to Wilson's focus on middle-class out-migration is not that it did not occur, but that it is misdirected: focusing on the flight of

---

27 We have published several studies documenting how the decline of manufacturing, the surburbanization of jobs, and the rise of low-wage service employment eliminated high-paying jobs for manual workers, drove up rates of black male unemployment, and reduced the attractiveness of marriage to black women, thereby contributing to a proliferation of female-headed families and persistent poverty. See Mitchell L. Eggers and Douglas S. Massey, "The Structural Determinants of Urban Poverty," *Social Science Research* 20 (1991):217–55; Mitchell L. Eggers and Douglas S. Massey, "A Longitudinal Analysis of Urban Poverty: Blacks in U.S. Metropolitan Areas between 1970 and 1980," *Social Science Research* 21 (1992):175–203.

28 The evidence on the extent of middle-class out-migration from ghetto areas is inconclusive. Because racial segregation does not decline with rising socioeconomic status, out-movement from poor black neighborhoods certainly has not been to white areas. When Kathryn P. Nelson measured rates of black out-migration from local "zones" within forty metropolitan areas, however, she found higher rates of out-movement for middle- and upper-class blacks compared with poor blacks; but her "zones" contained more than 100,000 inhabitants, making them considerably larger than neighborhoods (see "Racial Segregation, Mobility, and Poverty Concentration," paper presented at the annual meetings of the Population Association of America, Washington, D.C., March 19–23, 1991). In contrast, Edward Gramlich and Deborah Laren found that poor and middle-class blacks displayed about the same likelihood of out-migration from poor census tracts (see "Geographic Mobility and Persistent Poverty," Department of Economics, University of Michigan, Ann Arbor, 1990).

the black middle class deflects attention from the real issue, which is the limitation of black residential options through segregation.

Middle-class households—whether they are black, Mexican, Italian, Jewish, or Polish—always try to escape the poor. But only blacks must attempt their escape within a highly segregated, racially segmented housing market. Because of segregation, middle-class blacks are less able to escape than other groups, and as a result are exposed to more poverty. At the same time, because of segregation no one will move into a poor black neighborhood except other poor blacks. Thus both middle-class blacks and poor blacks lose compared with the poor and middle class of other groups: poor blacks live under unrivaled concentrations of poverty and affluent blacks live in neighborhoods that are far less advantageous than those experienced by the middle class of other groups.

Finally, we concede Murray's general point that federal welfare policies are linked to the rise of the urban underclass, but we disagree with his specific hypothesis that generous welfare payments, by themselves, discouraged employment, encouraged unwed childbearing, undermined the strength of the family, and thereby caused persistent poverty.[29] We argue instead that welfare payments were only harmful to the socioeconomic well-being of groups that were residentially segregated. As poverty rates rose among blacks in response to the economic dislocations of the 1970s and 1980s, so did the use of welfare programs. Because of racial segregation, however, the higher levels of welfare receipt

were confined to a small number of isolated, all-black neighborhoods. By promoting the spatial concentration of welfare use, therefore, segregation created a residential environment within which welfare dependency was the norm, leading to the intergenerational transmission and broader perpetuation of urban poverty.

COMING TO TERMS WITH AMERICAN APARTHEID

Our fundamental argument is that racial segregation—and its characteristic institutional form, the black ghetto—are the key structural factors responsible for the perpetuation of black poverty in the United States. Residential segregation is the principal organizational feature of American society that is responsible for the creation of the urban underclass. ★ ★ ★

High levels of black-white segregation were not always characteristic of American urban areas. Until the end of the nineteenth century blacks and whites were relatively integrated in both northern and southern cities; as late as 1900, the typical black urbanite still lived in a neighborhood that was predominantly white. The evolution of segregated, all-black neighborhoods occurred later and was not the result of impersonal market forces. It did not reflect the desires of African Americans themselves. On the contrary, the black ghetto was constructed through a series of well-defined institutional practices, private behaviors, and public policies by which whites sought to contain growing urban black populations.

---

29 See Eggers and Massey, "A Longitudinal Analysis of Urban Poverty."

The manner in which blacks were residentially incorporated into American cities differed fundamentally from the path of spatial assimilation followed by other ethnic groups. Even at the height of immigration from Europe, most Italians, Poles, and Jews lived in neighborhoods where members of their own group did not predominate, and as their socioeconomic status and generations spent in the United States rose, each group was progressively integrated into American society. In contrast, after the construction of the black ghetto the vast majority of blacks were forced to live in neighborhoods that were all black, yielding an extreme level of social isolation.

★ ★ ★ We show that high levels of black-white segregation had become universal in American cities by 1970, and despite the passage of the Fair Housing Act in 1968, this situation had not changed much in the nation's largest black communities by 1980. In these large urban areas black-white segregation persisted at very high levels, and the extent of black suburbanization lagged far behind that of other groups. Even within suburbs, levels of racial segregation remained exceptionally high, and in many urban areas the degree of racial separation between blacks and whites was profound. Within sixteen large metropolitan areas—containing one-third of all blacks in the United States—the extent of racial segregation was so intense and occurred on so many dimensions simultaneously that we label the pattern "hypersegregation."

[We also examine] why black segregation continues to be so extreme. One possibility that we rule out is that high levels of racial segregation reflect socioeconomic differences between blacks and whites. Segregation cannot be attributed to income differences, because blacks are equally highly segregated at all levels of income. Whereas segregation declines steadily for most minority groups as socioeconomic status rises, levels of black-white segregation do not vary significantly by social class. Because segregation reflects the effects of white prejudice rather than objective market forces, blacks are segregated no matter how much money they earn.

Although whites now accept open housing in principle, they remain prejudiced against black neighbors in practice. Despite whites' endorsement of the ideal that people should be able to live wherever they can afford to regardless of race, a majority still feel uncomfortable in any neighborhood that contains more than a few black residents; and as the percentage of blacks rises, the number of whites who say they would refuse to enter or would try to move out increases sharply.

These patterns of white prejudice fuel a pattern of neighborhood resegregation because racially mixed neighborhoods are strongly desired by blacks. As the percentage of blacks in a neighborhood rises, white demand for homes within it falls sharply while black demand rises. The surge in black demand and the withering of white demand yield a process of racial turnover. As a result, the only urban areas where significant desegregation occurred during the 1970s were those where the black population was so small that integration could take place without threatening white preferences for limited contact with blacks.

Prejudice alone cannot account for high levels of black segregation, however, because whites seeking to avoid contact with blacks must have somewhere to go. That is, some all-white neighborhoods must be perpetuated and maintained, which requires the erection of systematic barriers to black residential mobility. In most urban housing markets, therefore, the effects of white prejudice are typically reinforced by direct discrimination against black homeseekers. Housing audits carried out over the past two decades have documented the persistence of widespread discrimination against black renters and homebuyers, and a recent comprehensive study carried out by the U.S. Department of Housing and Urban Development suggests that prior work has understated both the incidence and the severity of this racial bias. Evidence also suggests that blacks can expect to experience significant discrimination in the allocation of home mortgages as well.

★ ★ ★ Segregation creates underclass communities and systematically builds deprivation into the residential structure of black communities. We show how any increase in the poverty rate of a residentially segregated group leads to an immediate and automatic increase in the geographic concentration of poverty. When the rate of minority poverty is increased under conditions of high segregation, all of the increase is absorbed by a small number of neighborhoods. When the same increase in poverty occurs in an integrated group, the added poverty is spread evenly throughout the urban area, and the neighborhood environment that group members face does not change much.

During the 1970s and 1980s, therefore, when urban economic restructuring and inflation drove up rates of black and Hispanic poverty in many urban areas, underclass communities were created only where increased minority poverty coincided with a high degree of segregation—principally in older metropolitan areas of the northeast and the midwest. Among Hispanics,

only Puerto Ricans developed underclass communities, because only they were highly segregated; and this high degree of segregation is directly attributable to the fact that a large proportion of Puerto Ricans are of African origin.

The interaction of intense segregation and high poverty leaves black neighborhoods extremely vulnerable to fluctuations in the urban economy, because any dislocation that causes an upward shift in black poverty rates will also produce a rapid change in the concentration of poverty and, hence, a dramatic shift in the social and economic composition of black neighborhoods. The concentration of poverty, for example, is associated with the wholesale withdrawal of commercial institutions and the deterioration or elimination of goods and services distributed through the market.

Neighborhoods, of course, are dynamic and constantly changing, and given the high rates of residential turnover characteristic of contemporary American cities, their well-being depends to a great extent on the characteristics and actions of their residents. Decisions taken by one actor affect the subsequent decisions of others in the neighborhood. In this way isolated actions affect the well-being of the community and alter the stability of the neighborhood.

Because of this feedback between individual and collective behavior, neighborhood stability is characterized by a series of thresholds, beyond which various self-perpetuating processes of decay take hold. Above these thresholds, each actor who makes a decision that undermines neighborhood well-being makes it increasingly likely that other actors will do the same. Each property owner who decides not to invest in upkeep and maintenance, for example, lowers the incentive for others to maintain their properties. Likewise, each new crime promotes psychological and physical withdrawal from public life, which reduces vigilance within the neighborhood and undermines the capacity for collective organization, making additional criminal activity more likely.

Segregation increases the susceptibility of neighborhoods to these spirals of decline. During periods of economic dislocation, a rising concentration of black poverty is associated with the simultaneous concentration of other negative social and economic conditions. Given the high levels of racial segregation characteristic of American urban areas, increases in black poverty such as those observed during the 1970s can only lead to a concentration of housing abandonment, crime, and social disorder, pushing poor black neighborhoods beyond the threshold of stability.

By building physical decay, crime, and social disorder into the residential structure of black communities, segregation creates a harsh and extremely disadvantaged environment to which ghetto blacks must adapt. In concentrating poverty, moreover, segregation also concentrates conditions such as drug use, joblessness, welfare dependency, teenage childbearing, and unwed parenthood, producing a social context where these conditions are not only common but the norm. [We argue] that in adapting to this social environment, ghetto dwellers evolve a set of behaviors, attitudes, and expectations that are sharply at variance with those common in the rest of American society.

As a direct result of the high degree of racial and class isolation created by segregation, for example, Black English has become progressively more distant from Standard American English, and its speakers are at a clear disadvantage in U.S. schools and labor markets. Moreover, the isolation and intense poverty of the ghetto provides a supportive structural niche for the emergence of an "oppositional culture" that inverts the values of middle-class society. Anthropologists have found that young people in the ghetto experience strong peer pressure not to succeed in school, which severely limits their prospects for social mobility in the larger society. Quantitative research shows that growing up in a ghetto neighborhood increases the likelihood of dropping out of high school, reduces the probability of attending college, lowers the likelihood of employment, reduces income earned as an adult, and increases the risk of teenage childbearing and unwed pregnancy.

Segregation also has profound political consequences for blacks, because it so isolates them geographically that they are the only ones who benefit from public expenditures in their neighborhoods. The relative integration of most ethnic groups means that jobs or services allocated to them will generally benefit several other groups at the same time. Integration thus creates a basis for political coalitions and pluralist politics, and most ethnic groups that seek public resources are able to find coalition partners because other groups can anticipate sharing the benefits. That blacks are the only ones to benefit from resources allocated to the ghetto—and are the only ones harmed when resources are removed—makes it difficult for them to find partners for political coalitions. Although segregation paradoxically makes it easier for blacks to elect representatives, it limits their political influence and marginalizes them within the American polity. Segregation prevents blacks from participating in pluralist politics based on mutual self-interest.

Because of the close connection between social and spatial mobility, segregation also perpetuates poverty. One of the primary means by which individuals improve their life chances—and those of their children—is by moving to neighborhoods with higher home values, safer streets, higher-quality schools, and better services. As groups move up the socioeconomic ladder, they typically move up the residential hierarchy as well, and in doing so they not only improve their standard of living but also enhance their chances for future success. Barriers to spatial mobility are barriers to social mobility, and by confining blacks to a small set of relatively disadvantaged neighborhoods, segregation constitutes a very powerful impediment to black socioeconomic progress.

Despite the obvious deleterious consequences of black spatial isolation, policymakers have not paid much attention to segregation as a contributing cause of urban poverty and have not taken effective steps to dismantle the ghetto. Indeed ★ ★ ★ for most of the past two decades public policies tolerated and even supported the perpetuation of segregation in American urban areas. Although many political initiatives were launched to combat discrimination and prejudice in the housing and banking industries, each legislative or judicial act was fought tenaciously by a powerful array of people who believed in or benefited from the status quo.

Although a comprehensive open housing bill finally passed Congress under unusual circumstances in 1968, it was stripped of its enforcement provisions as its price of enactment, yielding a Fair Housing Act that was structurally flawed and all but doomed to fail. As documentation of the law's defects accumulated in multiple Congressional hearings, government reports, and scholarly studies, little was done to repair the situation until 1988, when a series of scandals and political errors by the Reagan Administration finally enabled a significant strengthening of federal anti-discrimination law.

Yet even more must be done to prevent the permanent bifurcation of the United States into black and white societies that are separate and unequal. As of 1990, levels of racial segregation were still extraordinarily high in the nation's large urban areas, particularly those of the north. Segregation has remained high because fair housing enforcement relies too heavily on the private efforts of individual victims of discrimination. Whereas the processes that perpetuate segregation are entrenched and institutionalized, fair housing enforcement is individual, sporadic, and confined to a small number of isolated cases.

As long as the Fair Housing Act is enforced individually rather than systemically, it is unlikely to be effective in overcoming the structural arrangements that support segregation and sustain the ghetto. Until the government throws its considerable institutional weight behind efforts to dismantle the ghetto, racial segregation will persist. ★ ★ ★ We propose a variety of specific actions that the federal government will need to take to end the residential segregation of blacks in American society.

Ultimately, however, dismantling the ghetto and ending the long reign of racial segregation will require more than specific bureaucratic reforms; it requires a moral commitment that white America has historically lacked. The segregation of American blacks was no historical accident; it was brought about by actions and practices that had the passive acceptance, if not the active support, of most whites in the United States. Although America's apartheid may not be rooted in the legal strictures of its South African relative, it is no less effective in perpetuating racial inequality, and whites are no less culpable for the socioeconomic deprivation that results.

As in South Africa, residential segregation in the United States provides a firm basis for a broader system of racial injustice. The geographic isolation of Africans within a narrowly circumscribed portion of the urban environment—whether African townships or American ghettos—forces blacks to live under extraordinarily harsh conditions and to endure a social world where poverty is endemic, infrastructure is inadequate, education is lacking, families are fragmented, and crime and violence are rampant.[30] Moreover, segregation confines these unpleasant by-products of racial oppression to an isolated portion of the urban geography far removed from the experience of most whites. Resting on a foundation of segregation, apartheid not only denies blacks their rights as citizens but forces them to bear the social costs of their own victimization.

Although Americans have been quick to criticize the apartheid system of South Africa, they have been reluctant to acknowledge the consequences of their own institutionalized system of racial separation. The topic of segregation has virtually disappeared from public policy debates; it has vanished from the list of issues on the civil rights agenda; and it has been ignored by social scientists spinning endless theories of the underclass. Residential segregation has become the forgotten factor of American race relations, a minor footnote in the ongoing debate on the urban underclass. Until policymakers, social scientists, and private citizens recognize the crucial role of America's own apartheid in perpetuating urban poverty and racial injustice, the United States will remain a deeply divided and very troubled society.[31]

30 See International Defense and Aid Fund for Southern Africa, *Apartheid: The Facts* (London: United Nations Centre against Apartheid, 1983), pp. 15–26.

31 We are not the first to notice the striking parallel between the institutionalized system of racial segregation in U.S. cities and the organized, state-sponsored system of racial repression in South Africa. See John H. Denton, *Apartheid American Style* (Berkeley, Calif.: Diablo Press, 1967); James A. Kushner, "Apartheid in America: An Historical and Legal Analysis of Contemporary Racial Residential Segregation in the United States," *Howard Law Journal* 22 (1979):547–60.

33

American News Media and Public Misperceptions of Race and Poverty*

MARTIN GILENS

> The only feeling that anyone can have about
> an event he does not experience is the feeling
> aroused by his mental image of that event. That
> is why until we know what others think they
> know, we cannot truly understand their acts.
> *Walter Lippman*

As Walter Lippmann argued decades ago, our opinions and behavior are responses not to the world itself, but to our perceptions of that world. It is the "pictures in our heads" that shape our feelings and actions, and these pictures only imperfectly reflect the world that surrounds us. Just as importantly, our experience of the world is largely indirect. "Our opinions," Lippmann wrote, "cover a bigger space, a longer reach of time, a greater number of things, than we can directly observe. They have, therefore, to be pieced together out of what others have reported" (Lippmann 1960:79). Already in Lippmann's time, and even more so in our own, "reports about the world" come primarily through the mass media.

---

* First published in 2004; from *Race, Poverty, and Domestic Policy*, edited by C. Michael Henry.

To understand the roots of American public opinion, we need to understand Americans' perceptions of the social and political world they inhabit, and the role of the media in shaping those perceptions. Survey data show that public perceptions of poverty are erroneous in at least one crucial respect: Americans substantially exaggerate the degree to which blacks compose the poor. Furthermore, white Americans with the most exaggerated misunderstandings of the racial composition of the poor are the most likely to oppose welfare.

This chapter investigates the portrayal of poverty in the national news, compares these images with the reality of poverty in America, and offers some preliminary evidence that media coverage of poverty shapes public perceptions and misperceptions of the poor. Examining weekly newsmagazines and, to a lesser extent, network television news shows, I find that news media distortions coincide with public misperceptions about race and poverty, and that both are biased in ways that reflect negatively on the poor in general, and on poor African Americans in particular.

I argue below that the correspondence of public misunderstandings and media misrepresentations of poverty reflects the influence of each upon the other. On the one hand, the media are subject to many of the same biases and misperceptions that afflict American society at large, and therefore reproduce those biases in their portrayals of American social conditions. On the other hand, Americans rely heavily on the mass media for information about the society in which they live, and the media shape Americans' social perceptions and political attitudes in important ways. Media distortions of social conditions are therefore likely to result in public misperceptions that reinforce existing biases and stereotypes.

PUBLIC PERCEPTIONS OF RACE AND POVERTY

African Americans account for 29 percent of America's poor (U.S. Bureau of the Census 1990a). But recent national surveys show that the public substantially overestimates the percentage of blacks among the poor. When one survey asked "What percent of all the poor people in this country would you say are black?" the median response was 50 percent (National Race and Politics Study 1991).[1] Another survey simply asked "Of all the people who are poor in this country, are more of them black or are more of them white?" Fifty-five percent of the respondents chose black compared to 24 percent who chose white, with 21 percent volunteering "about equal" (CBS/*New York Times* Survey 1994).[2]

---

1 This datum is from the 1991 National Race and Politics Study, a nationwide random-digit telephone survey administered by the Survey Research Center at the University of California at Berkeley, and directed by Paul M. Sniderman, Philip E. Tetlock, and Thomas Piazza. Data were collected between February and November 1991 from 2,223 respondents, with a response rate of 65.3 percent (Survey Research Center 1991).

2 CBS/*New York Times* national telephone survey, conducted December 6–9, 1994. Comparing public perceptions of the poor with census bureau statistics implies that the public holds at least a roughly compatible understanding of who is included among the poor. According to census data, a decrease in the poverty threshold would result in a higher proportion of African Americans among the poor, while an increase in the pov-

The public's exaggerated association of race and poverty not only reflects and perpetuates negative racial stereotypes but it also increases white Americans' opposition to welfare. Whites who think the poor are mostly black are more likely to blame welfare recipients for their situation, and less likely to support welfare than are those with more accurate perceptions of poverty. In one national survey, 46 percent of the white respondents who thought African Americans make up more than half of the poor wanted to cut welfare spending. In contrast, only 26 percent of those who thought blacks compose less than one-quarter of the poor wanted welfare spending cut (*Los Angeles Times Poll* 1985).[3]

Americans views on poverty and welfare are colored by the belief that economic opportunity is widespread and that anyone who tries hard enough can succeed. For example, 70 percent of respondents to one survey agreed that "Amer-ica is the land of opportunity where everyone who works hard can get ahead" (Kluegel and Smith 1986:44). For those who perceive abundant opportunities, poverty itself is presumptive evidence of personal failure. Thus Americans' exaggerated association of race and poverty perpetuates long-standing stereotypes of African Americans as poor and lazy. When social scientists began studying stereotypes in the early twentieth century, they found a widespread belief that blacks are lazy,[4] and this stereotype does not appear to have faded much over the years. In 1990, the General Social Survey asked respondents to place blacks as a group on a seven-point scale with "lazy" at one end, and "hard working" at the other. Forty-seven percent of whites placed blacks on the "lazy" side of the scale, and only 17 percent chose the "hard work-ing" side (General Social Surveys 1972–90).

Negative stereotypes of African Americans as lazy, and misperceptions of the poor as

---

erty line would result in a lower proportion of blacks. Thus if the public has a lower implicit poverty threshold than the census bureau, public perceptions of the racial composition of the poor may not be as inaccurate as would otherwise appear to be the case. All evidence, however, suggests that if anything, the public has a higher (more inclusive) definition of poverty than is reflected in official government statistics. When a recent survey informed respondents that the federal poverty line for a family of four is now about $15,000 a year, 58 percent of respondents said the poverty line should be set higher, and only 7 percent said it should be set lower (Center for the Study of Policy Attitudes 1994). When asked in another survey what the level of income should be below which a family of four could be considered poor, the median response was about 15 percent higher than the official poverty line for a four-person family (General Social Survey 1993).

3   The association between perceptions of the racial composition of poverty and opposition to welfare spending does not, of course, prove that perceptions of poverty *cause* opposition to welfare. The causal influence might run in the opposite direction. That is, whites who oppose welfare for other rea-sons (such as its perceived cost to taxpayers) may come to view the poor as largely black. It is not clear, however, why such misperceptions of the poor should follow from welfare policy preferences. A more plausible alternative account of the association of perceptions of poverty and opposition to welfare is that both are consequences of a third factor. But when a number of such possible factors are controlled for, the relationship between perceptions of poverty and opposition to welfare is unaffected. In a regression equation predicting whites' opposition to welfare, the coefficient for perceived percentage black among the poor is 1.16 ($\beta = .19$) when percentage black is used as the only predictor. When age, sex, income, race, liberal/conservative ideology, and party identification are added to the model, the coefficient for percentage black barely declines to 1.08 ($\beta = .18$).

4   In one early study (Katz and Braly 1933), Princeton students were given a list of eighty-four traits and asked to select the five which were "most characteristic" of blacks. Over 75 per-cent chose "lazy" as among these five traits (second in popu-larity only to "superstitious").

predominantly black, reinforce each other. If poverty is a black problem, many whites reason, then blacks must not be trying hard enough. And if blacks are lazy in comparison with other Americans, and economic opportunities are plentiful, then it stands to reason that poverty would be a predominantly black problem. In sum, the public rather dramatically misunderstands the racial composition of America's poor, with consequences harmful to both poor people and African Americans.

PREVIOUS RESEARCH ON POVERTY IN THE NEWS

The portrayal of poverty by the American news media has never been systematically studied. There have, however, been a number of studies of minorities in the news that have some relevance to the current project. The most common such studies have examined the proportion of ethnic or racial minorities appearing in news coverage, and have consistently found that blacks are underrepresented in the American news media, whether it be television (Baran 1973), newspapers (Chaudhary 1980), or newsmagazines (Stempel 1971; Lester and Smith 1990). The underrepresentation of African Americans has decreased over time, however. Lester and Smith (1990), for example, found that only 1.3 percent of the pictures in *Time* and *Newsweek* during the 1950s were of blacks, compared with 3.1 percent in the 1960s and 7.5 percent in the 1980s. Another study looked at the representation of African Americans in news magazine advertisements

(Humphrey and Schuman 1984). Advertisements, of course, constitute a very different subject matter from news content, and we would not expect to find many poor people in advertisements. Nevertheless, 10 percent of the blacks in advertisements in *Time* magazine in 1980 were either Africans or Americans in poverty, while none of the whites in these ads were shown as poor.

DATA AND METHODS

The primary data for this chapter consist of every story on poverty and related topics appearing between January 1, 1988, and December 31, 1992, in the three leading American newsmagazines, *Time, Newsweek,* and *U.S. News and World Report.* The *Reader's Guide to Periodical Literature* was used to identify stories related to poverty and the poor. In each year the "core categories" of *poor, poverty,* and *public welfare* were examined. Any cross-references listed under these topics were then followed.[5] In total, 182 stories related to poverty were found under 31 topic headings (the topic headings and number of stories indexed under each are found in the appendix).

Specifically excluded from the list of topics are references to blacks or African Americans. The stories identified thus represent only those that are primarily focused on some aspect of poverty or poor relief. To the extent that stories which focus on African Americans also discuss poverty, the body of stories examined here will *underestimate* the true degree to which poverty is presented as a black problem.

---

5 The *Reader's Guide is* inconsistent in citing cross-references to related topics. Therefore, when a cross-reference to another topic was found in a particular year, this topic was checked for all five years under study.

Once the poverty stories were identified, each accompanying picture (if any) was examined to determine if it contained images of poor people. Of the 214 pictures containing 635 poor people, the vast majority were photographs, but a few consisted of drawings, most often as part of a chart. Finally, the race of each poor person in each picture was coded as black, nonblack, or not determinable.

Of the 635 poor people pictured, race could be determined for 560 (88 percent). To assess the reliability of the coding, a random 25 percent sample of pictures was coded by a second coder. The intercoder reliability was .97 for percentage African American in each picture.[6] In addition to race, the age of each poor person pictured was coded as under 18 years old, between 18 and 64, or over 64 years old. For this coding both the picture and any accompanying textual information (often including the exact age of the person pictured) were used. Intercoder reliability for under or over 18 years old was .98, and reliability for under or over 64 years old was .95. Finally, each poor person between 18 and 64 years old was coded as working or not. Again, textual information accompanying the picture was used. Intercoder reliability for work status was .97.

In addition to newsmagazines, coverage of poverty by network television news was also examined. Stories on poverty and related topics were identified using the *Television News Index and Abstracts,* published by Vanderbilt University (see appendix [to the chapter] for specific topics). During the five-year time frame for this study, the three weeknight network television news shows broadcast 534 stories on poverty and related topics, the equivalent of about one story every week-and-a-half per network. Although the differences among networks were not great, ABC broadcast the largest number of poverty stories (207), followed by NBC (173) and CBS (154). Of these 534 stories, 50 stories were randomly chosen for analysis. These 50 stories contained pictures of 1,353 poor people.

Television news stories typically include far more pictures of poor people than do magazine stories, but provide far less information about the individual poor people pictured. Consequently, only race of the poor was coded for the television stories on poverty. Of the 1,353 poor people in these stories, race could be coded for 1,100 (81 percent).[7] Intercoder reliability for percentage African American in each scene was .94.

---

6 Intercoder reliability was calculated on the basis of percentage African American in each picture. This is because the picture, not the individual, is the unit of analysis in the computer data file. It is possible that the intercoder reliability for individuals would be slightly lower than the figures based on pictures. For example, two coders might agree that there are 5 blacks and 5 nonblacks in a picture, but disagree on which individuals are black and nonblack. Such a scenario is unlikely to occur often, however, and the picture-based intercoder reliability coefficient is therefore very close, if not identical, to what one would find using individuals as the unit of analysis. The reliability coefficients for age and work status are picture-based as well.

7 Race coding was done by first identifying individual "scenes" within each news story. A scene was defined as one or more camera shots of the same people in the same setting (or a subgroup of the same people in the same setting). Within each scene people were then identified as poor or nonpoor based on both the information contained in the text of the story and the visual information in the scene itself. Finally, the number of black, nonblack, and nonidentifiable poor people in each scene was recorded. To assess reliability of the race coding for the television news stories, a 10-percent random sample of news scenes was selected and independently coded by two coders.

TABLE 1 **STORIES ON POVERTY IN U.S. NEWSMAGAZINES, 1988–1992**

	Number of stories	Number of pictures	Number of poor people pictured[a]	Percent African American[b]
Time	44	36	86	65%
Newsweek	82	103	294	66%
U.S. News and World Report	56	67	180	53
TOTAL	**182**	**206**	**560**	**62%**

[a]Excludes 75 people for whom race could not be determined.
[b]Difference in percentage African American across the three magazines is significant at p < .02.

||| FINDINGS

During the five-year period examined, *Newsweek* published 82 stories on poverty and related topics, an average of about one story every three weeks (Table 1). Fewer stories on poverty were found in the other two magazines, with *U.S. News and World Report* publishing 56 poverty stories over this period, and *Time* only 44. Overall, African Americans made up 62 percent of the poor people pictured in these stories, more than twice their true proportion of 29 percent. Of the three magazines, *U.S. News and World Report* showed the lowest percent-age of African Americans in poverty stories (53 percent, p < .02), but the differences between magazines were not great.[8]

A reader of these newsmagazines is likely to develop the impression that America's poor are predominantly black.[9] This distorted portrait of the American poor cannot help but reinforce negative stereotypes of blacks as mired in poverty and contribute to the belief that poverty is primarily a "black problem." Yet as problematic as this overall racial misrepresentation of the poor is, we shall see that the portrayal of poor African Americans differs from the portrayal of the nonblack poor in ways that further stigmatize blacks.

8 As traditionally understood, significance tests and probability levels are not appropriate to the data on newsmagazine photographs. Since every photograph from every poverty story during the period of interest is included in the data set, these data do not constitute a sample drawn from a larger population. Nevertheless, the operation of producing and selecting photographs can be viewed as stochastic process (for example, a given photo editor might select pictures of African Americans for particular types of stories with some specific probability). Viewed this way, the resulting set of photographs can be understood as representative of a larger hypothetical population consisting of the universe of photographs that *might* equally likely have been published in these magazines during this time period. From this perspective, significance tests illuminate the question of how likely it is that similar results would have been found if a larger set of photographs—generated by the same processes that generated the actual photographs—were available for analysis (see Henkel 1976:85–86).

9 For the next stage of this research, the percentage black among the magazine poor has been coded for the period from 1950 through 1994. Since 1965, when these magazines began to include large numbers of African Americans in their pictures of the poor, the percentage black has averaged 54 percent. Thus it appears that for the period under study in this chapter—1988 through 1992—the magazine poor are somewhat "more black" than average for the past three decades. In future analyses I will attempt to account for variation over time in the racial complexion of poverty in the news media.

TABLE 2 AGE DISTRIBUTION OF THE AMERICAN POOR AND AGE DISTRIBUTION OF THE "MAGAZINE POOR," BY RACE

	Total[a]	African American	Non-African American
TRUE POOR			
Under 18 years old	40%	47%	37%
18 to 64 years old	49%	45%	51%
Over 64 years old	11%	8%	12%
TOTAL	100%	100%	100%
MAGAZINE POOR			
Under 18 years old	43%	52%*	35%
18 to 64 years old	55%**	48%	60%***
Over 64 years old	2%***	1%***	5%***
TOTAL	100%	101%	100%
Number of magazine poor	635	345	215

[a]Includes 75 people for whom race could not be determined.
*p < .05; **p < .01; ***p < .001

Age Distribution of the "Magazine Poor"

The public is more sympathetic toward some age groups of poor people than others. Working-age adults are expected to support themselves, and poverty among this group is viewed by many Americans as indicating a lack of discipline or effort. Children and the elderly are, to a large extent, not held to blame for their poverty, and these groups are looked upon much more favorably for government assistance. In one survey, for example, respondents gave the disabled elderly the highest priority for government financial assistance, followed by the poor elderly and poor children (Cook and Barrett 1992). Respondents were much less sympathetic toward the working-age poor, who were given the lowest priority for government help of the six groups examined. Yet as Cook and Barrett point out in their study, sympathy toward poor children is often not translated into support for government aid when providing that aid means helping their working-age parents. In terms of public policy, therefore, the elderly are the only unambiguously privileged age group among the poor.

Given the public's greater willingness to help the elderly poor, and to a lesser degree poor children, public perceptions of the age distribution of the poor are likely to have an impact on overall levels of support for government anti-poverty efforts. Although dramatically off base in terms of the racial composition of the poor, news magazine portrayals of poverty are fairly accurate in showing large numbers of children among the poor. Forty-three percent of the poor people pictured were coded as under 18 years old, compared with the true figure of 40 percent of America's poor (Table 2). And newsmagazines are also accurate in showing a somewhat larger number of children among the black poor than among the nonblack poor. The census bureau reports that 47 percent of poor African Americans are under 18, while newsmagazines show 52 percent. Similarly, children make up 37 percent of the nonblack poor, while newsmagazines show 35 percent.

With regard to the elderly, however, the magazine poor and the true poor differ substantially. In reality, those over 64 years old account for 11 percent of all poor people, but they are scarcely to be found at all in magazine poverty stories (see Table 2). If newsmagazine pictures reflected the true nature of American poverty, we would expect to find about 70 elderly people among the 635 poor people pictured; instead we find a mere 13 (2 percent). (In coding the age of the magazine poor, a very lax criterion was applied, so that any poor person who could at all plausibly be thought to be over 64 years old was so coded.)

The most sympathetic age group of poor people—the elderly—while a small proportion of the true poor, are virtually invisible among the magazine poor. Furthermore, of the 13 elderly poor shown over the five-year period under study, ten are white and only two are black (the race of one person could not be determined). According to census data, those over 64 constitute 12 percent of the nonblack poor and 8 percent of poor African Americans (Table 2); but in newsmagazines, the elderly represent only 5 percent of poor nonblacks, and a scant six-tenths of one percent of the black poor. Thus the most sympathetic age category of the poor is both underrepresented in general, and reserved almost exclusively for nonblacks.

Work Status of the "Magazine Poor"

For centuries, Americans have distinguished between the "deserving poor" who are trying to make it on their own, and the "undeserving poor" who are lazy, shiftless, or drunken, and prefer to live off the generosity of others (Katz 1989). More remarkable than the tenacity of this distinction is the tendency to place a majority of the poor in the "undeserving" category. In one survey, for example, 57 percent of the respondents agreed that "Most poor people these days would rather take assistance from the government than make it on their own through hard work" (National Race and Politics Study 1991). While the true preferences of the poor are hard to measure, the fact is that 51 percent of the working-age poor (and 62 percent of poor working-age men) are employed at least part-time (Table 3).

The magazine poor are much less likely to be employed than their real-world counterparts. Overall, only 15 percent of the working-age magazine poor hold a paying job (see Table 3). If we add in all those described as looking for work, or participating in some kind of vocational training program, or even just collecting bottles and cans, the number increases to only 21 percent. Thus the clearest indication of "deservingness"—preparing for or engaging in some form of employment—is rare indeed among the magazine poor. Whatever public sympathy might accompany the perception that the poor are trying to work their way out of poverty is unlikely to emerge from these newsmagazines.

Just as newsmagazines' underrepresentation of the elderly poor is greater for African Ameri-

TABLE 3   **WORK STATUS OF THE WORKING-AGE AMERICAN POOR AND WORK STATUS OF THE WORKING-AGE "MAGAZINE POOR," BY RACE**

	Total[a]	African American	Non-African American
TRUE POOR			
Working	51%	42%	54%
Not working	49%	58%	46%
MAGAZINE POOR			
Working	15%***	12%***	27%***
Not working	85%***	88%***	73%***
Number of working-age magazine poor	351	165	129

NOTE: Significance levels indicated differences between magazine portrayals and census figures for each category. Working-age includes those 18 to 64 years old.

SOURCE: U.S. Bureau of the Census, Current Population Reports, Series P-60, No. 171, Poverty in the United States: 1988 and 1989. U.S. Government Printing Office, Washington, D.C., 1990.

[a]Includes 57 working-age poor for whom race could not be determined.

★★★p < .0001

cans than for others, so is their underrepresentation of the working poor. In reality, poor African Americans are somewhat less likely to be employed than non-African Americans, but the difference is modest: 42 percent of poor African Americans work compared with 54 percent of the non-African American poor (see Table 3). But among the magazine poor, this difference is much greater. While 27 percent of the nonblack poor are shown as working, only 12 percent of the African American poor are portrayed as workers. Thus the true proportion of poor nonblacks who work is twice as high in real life as it is in these newsmagazines (54 percent vs. 27 percent), while the true proportion working among the black poor is three-and-one-half times that shown in *Time, Newsweek,* and *U.S. News and World Report* (42 percent vs. 12 percent). Once again, the misleadingly negative portrait of the poor presented in these news stories is even more misleading and more negative for poor African Americans.

The "Magazine Poor" by Topic of Story

To examine portrayals of the poor by story topic, the thirty-one topics were grouped into nine major categories (including a residual "miscellaneous" category). The story topics shown in Table 4 relate to members of the poverty population that receive varying levels of public support or censure. For example, surveys show greater sympathy for the poor in general than for welfare recipients (Smith 1987). And we would expect more sympathetic responses to stories about poor children or poor people in employment programs than to stories about nonworking poor adults. Most of the topics shown in Table 4 are illustrated with

TABLE 4 **PERCENTAGE AFRICAN AMERICANS IN PICTURES OF THE POOR BY TOPIC OF STORY**

	Number of stories	Number of poor people pictured[a]	Percentage African American
Underclass	6	36	100%
Poor	33	147	69%
Housing/homelessness[b]	96	195	66%
Education for the poor[c]	4	17	65%
Poor children[d]	24	70	60%
Public welfare	25	97	57%
Employment programs for the poor[e]	9	52	40%
Medicaid	7	6	17%
Miscellaneous others[f]	14	13	43%
TOTAL	**182**	**560**	**62%**

NOTE: Column entries exceed totals shown because stories may be indexed under more than one topic.
[a]Excludes 75 people for whom race could not be determined.
[b]Includes housing, [city/state]; U.S.; housing projects; housing, federal aid; housing vouchers; Department of Housing and Urban Development; homeless; poor, housing; welfare hotels; Habitat for Humanity; Covenant House.
[c]Includes Head Start; poor, education.
[d]Includes child welfare; children, homeless; runaways; socially handicapped children.
[e]Includes workfare; Job Corps; American Conservation Corps.
[f]Includes MadCAPP; LIFE program; I Have a Dream Foundation; refugees; economic assistance, domestic; legal aid; relief work; unemployment insurance; Street News; entitlement spending.

approximately the same proportion of African Americans. These include "sympathetic" topics such as poor children (60 percent black) and education for the poor (65 percent black), and "unsympathetic" topics such as public welfare (57 percent black).

Of those topics that do differ substantially in percentage African American, however, fewer blacks are shown in stories on the more sympathetic topics of employment programs (40 percent black) and Medicaid (17 percent black),

while stories on the underclass—perhaps the least sympathetic topic in Table 4—are illustrated exclusively with pictures of African Americans. While the underclass lacks any consistent definition in either popular or academic discourse,[10] it is most often associated with intergenerational poverty, labor force nonparticipation, out-of-wedlock births, crime, drugs, and "welfare dependency as a way of life" (Jencks 1991).

In fact, blacks do compose a large proportion of the American underclass, just how large

10 Some argue that the very notion of an underclass is misguided at best and pernicious at worst (e.g., Reed 1991), but this is not the place to debate the utility of this concept. Because the media have adopted the term "underclass," those interested in understanding public attitudes must acknowledge its importance, irrespective of our feelings about the desirability or undesirability of the concept.

a proportion depending on how the underclass is defined. But even those definitions that result in the highest percentages of African Americans do not approach the magazine portrait of the underclass as 100 percent black. One such definition counts as members of the underclass only poor residents of census tracts with unusually high proportions of (1) welfare recipients, (2) female-headed households, (3) high school dropouts, *and* (4) unemployed working-age males (Ricketts and Sawhill 1988).[11] By this definition, 59 percent of the underclass is African American. However defined, it is clear that the American underclass contains substantial numbers of nonblacks, in contrast to the magazine underclass composed exclusively of African Americans.

With regard to topic of story, then, we find a tendency to portray a variety of subgroups of the poor as roughly similar in the proportion of African Americans. For those aspects of poverty that do differ in this regard, however, the more sympathetic groups among the poor are shown as relatively less black, while the least sympathetic element of the underclass is shown as made up completely of African Americans.

Race and Poverty in Television News Stories

The three newsmagazines examined here have a combined circulation of over ten million

(Folio 500 1994), and 20 percent of American adults claim to be regular readers of "newsmagazines such as *Time, U.S. News and World Report,* or *Newsweek.*"[12] In addition, these magazines influence how other journalists see the world. In one study, for example, magazine and newspaper journalists were asked what news sources they read most regularly (Wilhoit and Weaver 1991). Among these journalists, *Time* and *Newsweek* were the first- and second-most frequently cited news sources, far more popular than the *New York Times,* the *Wall Street Journal,* or the *Washington Post.*

Despite the broad reach of these weekly magazines, and their role as "background material" for other journalists, there can be little doubt that television is the dominant news source for most Americans. In recent surveys, about 70 percent of the American public identifies television as the source of "most of your news about what's going on in the world today" (Mayer 1993). If television news coverage of poverty were to differ substantially from that found in newsmagazines, the implications of this study would be severely limited.

Unfortunately, it is difficult to analyze television news in the way that newsmagazine coverage of poverty was analyzed above because television news typically provides far less information about the individuals pictured in poverty stories than do newsmagazines. The

11 To qualify as an underclass area based on Ricketts and Sawhill's criteria, a census tract must be at least one standard deviation above the national average on *all* four of these characteristics. By this definition, 5 percent of the American poor live in underclass areas (Ricketts and Sawhill 1988).

12 A *Times Mirror* survey of February 20, 1992, asked "I'd like to know how often, if ever, you read certain types of publica-

tions. For each that I read tell me if you read them regularly, sometimes, hardly ever or never. . . . Newsmagazines such as *Time, U.S. News and World Report,* or *Newsweek.*" Twenty percent of respondents claimed to read such magazines regularly, 38 percent sometimes, 20 percent hardly ever, and 21 percent never.

analysis of television news is therefore limited to the race of the poor people used to illustrate stories on poverty.

During the five-year period of this study (1988 through 1992), weeknight news shows on ABC, NBC, and CBS broadcast 534 stories on poverty and related topics, of which 50 stories were randomly selected for analysis. Of the 1,100 race-codable poor people in these stories, 65.2 percent were black—a slightly higher figure than the 62 percent black found in news-magazine stories on poverty. Clearly, then, the overrepresentation of African Americans in stories on poverty found in weekly newsmagazines is not unique to this particular medium, but is shared by the even more important medium of network television news.

DO MEDIA PORTRAYALS OF POVERTY INFLUENCE PUBLIC PERCEPTIONS?

Although we lack the data to demonstrate directly the impact of media portrayals of poverty on public perceptions, a variety of evidence suggests that such portrayals are likely to be important influences. First, both experimental and nonexperimental studies have demonstrated the power of the media to shape public perceptions and political preferences. Media content can affect the importance viewers attach to different political issues (Iyengar and Kinder 1987; Rogers and Dearing 1988), the standards that they employ in making political evaluations (Iyengar and Kinder 1987; Krosnick and Kinder 1990), the causes they attribute to national problems (Iyengar 1989, 1991), and

their issue positions and perceptions of political candidates (Bartels 1993).

None of these studies focused on the visual aspect of media content. Other evidence suggests, however, that visual elements of the news including the race of the people pictured are highly salient to viewers. In a study aptly titled "Seeing Is Remembering," Graber (1990) found that people were more likely to remember what they saw in a television news story than what they heard. With regard to viewers' use of race as a visual cue, Iyengar and Kinder (1987:41) presented subjects with television news stories about unemployment in which the unemployed individual pictured was either black or white. Following the unemployment story (which was included as part of a larger compilation of news stories), subjects were asked to name the three most important problems facing the nation. Of those white viewers who were randomly assigned the story about an unemployed white person, 71 percent said that unemployment was among the three most important national problems. Of those whites who saw a story about an unemployed African American, however, only 53 percent felt that unemployment was a pressing national concern.

Thus past research has shown that the mass media can exert a powerful influence on public perceptions and attitudes, that news pictures convey important information that viewers are comparatively likely to remember, and that the race of people pictured in news stories is a salient aspect of the story for many viewers. While past studies have focused largely on television news, there is no reason to think that the impact of pictures, or the salience of the race of those pictured, would be any less in newsmagazines.[13]

A second source of evidence concerning the plausibility that media portrayals shape public perceptions of the poor comes from the limited available longitudinal data. If the media drive public perceptions, then changes over time in media portrayals should be associated with changes in public beliefs. For many issues, this strategy for assessing media effects is complicated by the problem of "real-world" changes. That is, any association found between media coverage and public opinion could be due to the dependence of both upon some real change in social conditions. This is not a problem with regard to the racial composition of the poor, however, which has remained remarkably constant since the government started collecting official poverty data in the 1960s.[14]

Although the data gauging public perceptions of the racial composition of the poor are sparse, the patterns are consistent with the media effects hypothesis. Two questions asking about the racial composition of the poor are available from national surveys, each asked at two points in time. To assess the relationship between media portrayals and public per-

ceptions, I examined the percentage black among the poor in the three magazines for the six-month periods prior to each survey. The median response to a straightforward question "What percent of the poor are black?" increased from 39 percent in 1985 to 50 percent in 1991; the percentage of African Americans in media portrayals of poverty also increased across this period, from 50 percent in 1985 to 63 percent in 1991. The second survey question asked whether most poor people in this country are white or black. This question elicited a larger "most are black" response in 1982 than in 1994 (63 percent versus 55 percent), and similarly the percentage of blacks among the magazine poor decreased from 34 percent to 26 percent.[15] These corresponding patterns of change in the media and public perceptions hardly constitute proof that the media is the causal agent, but they are consistent with that hypothesis.

A final indication that the media shape perceptions of the racial composition of the poor concerns the implausibility of the alternative hypotheses. If the media are not the dominant influence on public perceptions of the racial composition of the poor, then these perceptions must be shaped by either personal encounters

---

13 In fact, the relative impact of pictures may be even greater in newsmagazines than in television news. In a newsmagazine, even those who do not read a story are likely to look at least briefly at the pictures as they browse through the magazine. In contrast, television viewers with little interest in a particular story are not likely to turn off the sound but may busy themselves with other things (like making or eating dinner) and may not bother to look at the pictures.

14 Between 1961 and 1995, the percentage of all poor people who are black fluctuated between 27 percent and 32 percent (U.S. Bureau of the Census 1993, 1996).

15 The two surveys asking for the percentage of blacks among the poor are the *Los Angeles Times* Poll 96, April 1985 (n = 2,439) and the National Race and Politics Study, February–November 1991, (n = 2,223; see note 1 for details). The surveys asking whether more of the poor are black or white are the CBS/*New York Times* Poll, March 1982 (n = 1,545) and the CBS/*New York Times* Poll, December 1994 (n = 1,147). The low percentage of blacks among the magazine poor prior to March 1982 and December 1994 (34 percent and 26 percent) are clearly anomalous. As note 9 indicates, an average of 54 percent of poor people in these magazines were African American for the period from 1965 through 1994.

with poor people or conversations about poverty with friends and acquaintances. Conversations with others might indeed be an important influence, but this begs the question of how an individual's conversation partners arrived at *their* perceptions. If personal encounters with poor people explain the public's perceptions, then variation in individuals' perceptions should correspond with variations in the racial mix of the poor people they encounter in everyday life.

Although the personal encounter thesis is plausible, survey data show that the racial makeup of the poor in an individual's state appears to have almost no impact on his or her perceptions of the country's poor as a whole. For example, residents of Michigan and Pennsylvania, where African Americans make up 31 percent of the poor, believe that 50 percent of America's poor are black.[16] In Washington and Oregon, blacks constitute only 6 percent of the poor, yet residents of these states believe that the American poor are 47 percent black. Finally, blacks make up only *1 percent* of the poor in Idaho, Montana, Wyoming, North Dakota, South Dakota, and Utah, yet survey respondents from these states think that blacks account for 47 percent of all poor people in this country. Thus, despite the large state-by-state differences in the percentage of blacks among the poor, personal experience appears to have little impact on public perceptions of the racial composition of poverty.

Not only do we find little variation in racial perceptions of the poor across states, but we

also find little variation across other population groups. Although one might expect those with more education to hold more accurate understandings of current social conditions, differences in racial perceptions of the poor are fairly small and nonmonotonic. When asked whether most poor people are white or black, for example, 47 percent of respondents who lack a high school degree chose black, compared with 59 percent of high school graduates, 57 percent of those with some college education, and 48 percent of college graduates (p < .01). A similar pattern, but with smaller (and nonsignificant) differences, was found when respondents were asked the percentage of all poor people who are black. Nor do perceptions differ for blacks and whites. Fifty-two percent of blacks and 55 percent of whites said that most poor people are black, while the average estimate of the percentage of blacks among the poor is 51 percent for black respondents and 48 percent for whites.[17]

In sum, then, previous work on related issues shows that the media can have a significant impact on public opinion. Second, changes in media portrayals over time are associated with corresponding changes in public perceptions. And finally, as judged by the similarity in public perceptions across states, differences in personal exposure to poor people of different races appears to have little impact on perceptions of the poor as a whole. Taken together, this evidence strongly suggests that the portrayals of poverty in the media do matter. At least with regard to the racial composition of the poor,

---

16 Data on public perceptions come from the 1991 National Race and Politics Study. Figures for the true percentage of blacks among the poor are from the 1990 census (U.S. Department of Commerce 1993c).

17 Figures for whether more poor people are black or white are from the CBS/*New York Times* Poll, December 1994; figures for the percentage of the poor who are black are from the 1991 National Race and Politics Study.

public perceptions appear to be shaped by the images offered by the mass media.

★ ★ ★

SUMMARY AND CONCLUSIONS

If 560 people were selected at random from among America's poor, we would expect 162 to be black. But of the 560 poor people of determinable race pictured in newsmagazines between 1988 and 1992, 345 were African American. In reality, two out of three poor Americans are nonblack, but the reader of these magazines would likely come to exactly the opposite conclusion.

Although the newsmagazines examined grossly overrepresent African Americans in their pictures of poor people as a whole, African Americans are seldom found in pictures of the most sympathetic subgroups of the poor. I found that the elderly constitute less than 1 percent of the black poor shown in these magazines (compared with 5 percent of the nonblack poor), and the working poor make up only 12 percent of poor blacks (compared with 27 percent of poor nonblacks).

I also found that stories dealing with aspects of antipoverty policy that are most strongly supported by the public are less likely to contain pictures of African Americans. Although 62 percent of all poor people pictured, African Americans make up only 40 percent of the poor in stories on employment programs, and only 17 percent in stories on Medicaid. In contrast, we find far too many African Americans in stories on the least favorable subgroup of the poor: the underclass. Every one of the 36 poor people pictured in stories on the underclass was black.

A number of explanations for the racial misrepresentation of poverty were considered in this chapter. First, the greater geographic concentration of poor blacks, in comparison with poor whites, might lead photographers to over-represent African Americans in their pictures of poor people. Second, photo editors' own misperceptions of the racial composition of American poverty can explain some of the overrepresentation of blacks among published photographs of the poor. But since neither of these factors can fully account for the dramatic distortions of the racial composition of the poor, however, two additional possibilities were considered. First, editors' conscious or unconscious indulgence of what they perceive to be the public's stereotypes could explain distortions in the portrayal of poverty. Alternatively, editors' own unconscious stereotypes concerning the nature of poverty in America could be at work. Although considerations of unconscious stereotypes must be somewhat speculative, the consistent pattern of racial misrepresentation (along with the consistently liberal nature of these editors' conscious beliefs about racial inequality)[18] strongly suggests that unconscious negative images of blacks are at work.

---

18 This characterization of the photo editors as racially liberal is based both on our general conversations about race and poverty and on their responses to survey-style questions about the causes of racial inequality. For example, when asked whether blacks or whites are primarily to blame for racial inequality, the photo editors either blamed whites alone or both blacks and whites together. In contrast, when the same question was asked of the public in the 1991 National Race and Politics Study, Americans were more likely to attribute blame for racial inequality to blacks rather than to whites.

Perhaps the most disheartening aspect of the situation is that apparently well-meaning, racially liberal news professionals generate images of the social world that consistently misrepresent both black Americans and poor people in destructive ways. Whether these distortions stem from residential patterns, conscious efforts to reflect the public's existing stereotypical expectations, or editors' own unconscious stereotypes, these racial misrepresentations reinforce the public's exaggerated association of blacks with poverty.

Whatever the processes that result in distorted images of poverty, the political consequences of these misrepresentations are clear. First, the poverty population shown in newsmagazines as primarily black, overwhelmingly unemployed, and almost completely nonelderly is not likely to generate a great deal of support for government antipoverty programs among white Americans. Furthermore, public support for efforts to redress racial inequality is likely to be diminished by the portrait of poverty found in these newsmagazines. Not only do African Americans as a whole suffer from the exaggerated association of race and poverty, but poor African Americans (who are often the intended beneficiaries of race-targeted policies) are portrayed in a particularly negative light.

A more accurate portrayal of poverty would still, of course, include a large number of blacks. But rather than portraying poverty as a *predominantly* black problem, a true reflection of social conditions would show the poverty population to be primarily nonblack. The danger, perhaps, is that a more accurate understanding of current conditions might lead some to feel the problem of racial inequality is less pressing. But current misunderstandings may pose a greater danger: that whites will continue to harbor negative stereotypes of blacks as mired in poverty and unwilling to make the effort needed to work their way out. By implicitly identifying poverty with race, the news media perpetuate stereotypes that work against the interests of both poor people and African Americans.

||| REFERENCES

Baran, S. 1973. "Dying Black/Dying White: Coverage of Six Newspapers." *Journalism Quarterly* 50:761–763.

Bartels, Larry M. 1993. "Messages Received: The Political Impact of Media Exposure." *American Political Science Review* 87:267–285.

CBS/*New York Times* Survey. 1994. National telephone survey.

Center for the Study of Policy Attitudes. 1994. "Fighting Poverty in America." National telephone survey sponsored by the Center for the Study of Policy Attitudes, October 13–16.

Chaudhary, A. 1980. "Press Portrayals of Black Officials." *Journalism Quarterly* 57:636–641.

Cook, Fay Lomax, and Edith J. Barrett. 1992. *Support for the American Welfare State.* New York: Columbia University Press.

Fishman, Mark. 1980. *Manufacturing the News.* Austin: University of Texas Press.

Folio. 1994. "Folio 500." *Folio: The Magazine for Magazine Management* 23 (12):52.

Gans, Herbert J. 1979. *Deciding What's News.* New York: Pantheon.

General Social Survey. 1990. Machine readable data file. Conducted by the National Opinion Research Center; James Davis and Tom W. Smith, principal investigators.

————. 1993. National personal interview survey conducted by the National Opinion Research Center, February 5–April 26.

Gitlin, Todd. 1980. *The Whole World Is Watching: Mass Media in the Making and Unmaking of the New Left.* Berkeley: University of California Press.

Graber, Doris A. 1990. "Seeing Is Remembering: How Visuals Contribute to Learning from Television News." *Journal of Communication* 40:134–155.

Henkel, Ramon E. 1976. *Tests of Significance.* Sage University Paper series on Quantitative Applications in the Social Sciences, 07-004. Beverly Hills, Calif.: Sage.

Humphrey, Ronald, and Howard Schuman. 1984. "The Portrayal of Blacks in Magazine Advertisements: 1950–1982." *Public Opinion Quarterly* 48:551–563.

Iyengar, Shanto. 1989. "How Citizens Think About National Issues: A Matter of Responsibility." *American Journal of Political Science* 33:878–900.

————. 1991. *Is Anyone Responsible?* Chicago: University of Chicago Press.

Iyengar, Shanto, and Donald R. Kinder. 1987. *News That Matters.* Chicago: University of Chicago Press.

Jargowsky, Paul A., and Mary Jo Bane. 1991. "Ghetto Poverty in the United States, 1970–

1980." Pp. 235–273 in *The Urban Underclass,* ed. Christopher Jencks and Paul E. Peterson. Washington, D.C.: Brookings Institution.

Jencks, Christopher. 1991. "Is the American Underclass Growing?" Pp. 28–100 in *The Urban Underclass,* ed. Christopher Jencks and Paul E. Peterson. Washington, D.C.: Brookings Institution.

Katz, D., and K. Braly. 1933. "Racial Stereotypes in One Hundred College Students." *Journal of Abnormal and Social Psychology* 28:280–290.

Katz, Michael B. 1989. *The Undeserving Poor.* New York: Pantheon Books.

Kluegel, James R., and Eliot R. Smith. 1986. *Beliefs About Inequality.* New York: Aldine de Gruyter.

Krosnick, Jon A., and Donald R. Kinder. 1990. "Altering the Foundations of Popular Support for the President Through Priming." *American Political Science Review* 84:497–512.

Lester, Paul, and Ron Smith. 1990. "African-American Photo Coverage in *Life, Newsweek* and *Time,* 1937–1988." *Journalism Quarterly* 67:128–136.

Lippmann, Walter. 1960 [1922]. *Public Opinion.* New York: Macmillan.

Los Angeles Times. 1985. Machine readable data file. Poll number 96, April.

Massey, Douglas S., and Nancy A. Denton. 1993. *American Apartheid.* Cambridge: Harvard University Press.

Mayer, William G. 1993. "Poll Trends: Trends in Media Usage." *Public Opinion Quarterly* 57: 593–611.

National Race and Politics Study. 1991. Machine readable data file. Conducted by the Survey Research Center, University of California, Berkeley. Paul Sniderman, Philip E. Tetlock, and Thomas Piazza, principal investigators.

Reed, Adolph L., Jr. 1991. "The Underclass Myth." *Progressive* 55:18–20.

Ricketts, Erol R., and Isabel V. Sawhill. 1988. "Defining and Measuring the Underclass. *Journal of Policy Analysis and Management* 7:316–325.

Rogers, Everett M., and James W. Dearing. 1988. "Agenda-Setting Research: Where Has it Been and Where is it Going?" In James A. Anderson, ed., *Communication Yearbook* vol. II. Beverly Hills, Calif.: Sage.

Smith, Tom W. 1987. "That Which We Call Welfare by Any Other Name Would Smell Sweeter." *Public Opinion Quarterly* 51:75–83.

Stempel, G. 1971. "Visibility of Blacks in News and News-Picture Magazines." *Journalism Quarterly* 48:337–339.

Survey Research Center. 1991. "National Race and Politics Study." Machine-readable data file. Survey conducted by the Survey Research Center, University of California, Berkeley. Paul M. Sniderman, Philip E. Tetlock, and Thomas Piazza, principal investigators.

U.S. Bureau of the Census. 1990a. Current Population Reports, Series P-60, No. 168, *Money Income and Poverty Status in the United States: 1989.* Washington, D.C.: U.S. Government Printing Office.

———. 1990b. Current Population Reports, Series P-60, No. 171, *Poverty in the United States: 1988 and 1989.* Washington, D.C.: U.S. Government Printing Office.

———. 1993a. *Statistical Abstract of the United States.* Washington, D.C.: U.S. Government Printing Office.

———. 1993b. *1990 Census of Population and Housing, Summary Tape File 3A,* (CD90-3C-I).

———. 1993c. *1990 Census of Population and Housing, Summary Tape File 3C,* (CD90-3C-I).

———. 1996. *Census Bureau Web Page* http://www.census.gov/ftp/pub/hhes/income/pov-sum.html.

Wilhoit, G. Cleveland, and David H. Weaver. 1991. *The American Journalist: A Portrait of U.S. News People and Their Work.* Bloomington: Indiana University Press.

APPENDIX 1 NUMBER OF MAGAZINE STORIES BY TOPIC

Poor, U.S./Poor, statistics/Poor, [city or state]/Poor, taxation	33
Economic assistance, domestic	4
Public welfare/Public welfare, U.S./Public welfare, [city or state]/Public welfare, law	5
Department of Housing and Urban Development	26
Homeless	47
Housing, [city or state]/Housing, U.S./Housing projects/Housing, federal aid/ Housing vouchers	10
Poor, housing	7
Welfare hotels	1
Habitat for Humanity	1
Covenant House	4
American Conservation Corps	2
Job Corps	1
Workfare	6
Head Start	3
Poor, education	1
Child welfare	12
Children, homeless	4
Runaways	1
Socially handicapped children	7
Legal aid/Legal service	1
Medicaid	7
Old age assistance	2
Refugees	1
Relief work	1
Unemployment insurance	3
Underclass	6
MadCAPP	1
LIFE program	1
Street News	1
I Have a Dream Foundation	1
Entitlement spending	1

Total number of magazine stories = 182

APPENDIX 2 **NUMBER OF TELEVISION STORIES BY TOPIC**

Appalachia	7
Children and youth, housing project	6
Children and youth, child care and support, low-income	1
Children and youth, medicine and health, homeless	15
Children and youth, medicine and health, hunger	2
Children and youth, poverty	40
Children and youth, runaways	2
Children and youth, welfare	1
Cities, homeless	249
Cities, inner cities	1
Covenant house	12
Employment, wages, working poor	7
Food stamps	8
Housing, programs, habitat for humanity	6
Head start	20
Housing, programs, [city or state]/Housing, programs, low income/ Housing, public housing/Housing, cities, tenements	68

Gender Inequalities

34

Detours on the Road to Equality: Women, Work, and Higher Education*

JERRY A. JACOBS

News stories about the first woman entering a field—astronaut, firefighter, professional basketball player, Ivy League university president—have largely faded, although Carly Fiorina's selection as head of Hewlett Packard was widely extolled in both the business and popular press. It is commonly assumed that the barriers that once blocked women's entry into new fields have been dismantled. But there has been less change than meets the eye. The slow but steady movement of women into formerly male-dominated occupations has tapered off, if not completely stopped, during the 1990s. Women have made greater strides, however, in their pursuit of higher education. Indeed, the second development may be the result of the roadblocks they are facing in finding employment in traditionally male fields.

||| LAYERS OF SEGREGATION

Despite highly visible exceptions, such as local television news anchor teams, most occupations remain skewed toward either men or women. For every

---

* First published in 2003; from *Contexts*, Volume 2, Number 1.

news anchorwoman, there are literally thousands of women who work in traditional female settings such as at a receptionist's desk, in an elementary school classroom, or at the take-out window of a fast-food restaurant. Whether she is a white single mother in Florida or a black empty-nester in Michigan, a woman more often works next to other women than to men. Women remain crowded in certain jobs such as secretaries or administrative assistants (99 percent female), child care workers (98 percent) or registered nurses (93 percent). Among the remaining male bastions are construction trades, such as carpenters, plumbers and electricians (3 percent female), mechanics and repairers (5 percent) and engineers (10 percent). This concentration of women and men in different jobs, occupations and industries is what sociologists mean when they refer to the gender segregation of work.

Among the highest-status professions, law, medicine and management have experienced a large influx of women. Nearly half of managers, law students and medical students are women. But within these fields, gender disparities are unmistakable. Few female managers have reached the highest echelons of large corporations, and women middle-managers are less likely than their male counterparts to have authority over staffs and budgets. Female lawyers are more likely to be found in family law or working for the government than practicing in the more lucrative specializations at major firms. And female physicians are more likely to specialize in pediatrics or family practice than surgery or anesthesiology. Indeed, the closer you look within nominally integrated occupa-

tions, the more segregation you find. Men and women are segregated by occupation, by firms within occupation, and by jobs and specializations within firms. There are "men's jobs" and "women's jobs" at all levels of education, skills, and experience, and at each level, the women's jobs tend to be paid less. Moreover, female-dominated fields pay less even when working time, qualifications and experience are taken into account.

One way to appreciate the income disparity is to compare the pay for male- and female-dominated occupations that have similar job qualifications. Women are 50 percent of bus drivers but only 3 percent of railroad conductors. Women are 71 percent of accountants and auditors but only 29 percent of securities and financial services sales representatives. Women are 88 percent of dressmakers but only 22 percent of upholsterers. In each of these cases, the male occupation pays more than the female one. These heavily-skewed numbers suggest that, despite good intentions, many jobs are not truly open to everyone.

||| EXPLAINING JOB SEGREGATION

Why do women and men end up in different occupations? A popular view is that gender distinctions at work are as natural as boys and girls playing separately on the school playground. But sociologists tend to view gender roles as social conventions rather than natural phenomena.

People are taught to distinguish men's work from women's work, just as they are taught right from wrong. Gender stereotypes in the workplace are readily apparent, even to young chil-

HIRING DISCRIMINATION

A female Assistant Attorney General called the exclusive Cipriani's restaurant in New York City requesting an interview for a job on the dining room staff and was told by a manager, on tape, "we don't hire girls." In fact, this restaurant had never hired a waitress, and the Attorney General sued for hiring discrimination. In depositions, Cipriani's claimed that there were few, if any, women with experience serving in similar establishments in New York City, despite the fact that, overall, waitresses outnumber waiters by nearly four to one. To see if comparable restaurants hire women, Sara Rab and I conducted a survey of elite restaurants in New York City. We found that two-thirds of the elite restaurants in New York hired women, but the more expensive the dinner, the fewer the women servers. We found a similar pattern in Philadelphia. Servers in our sample of elite restaurants brought home an average annual salary of about $45,000, compared with less than $20,000 in less expensive establishments. Our findings are consistent with an experiment conducted on 65 Philadelphia restaurants by economist David Neumark, who directed pairs of men and women matched for their credentials to apply for jobs as servers. In high-priced restaurants, women were 35 percent less likely than men to receive an interview, and 40 percent less likely to receive a job offer. The hiring decisions of managers clearly contribute to the disparate placement and earnings of waiters and waitresses.

dren, and are often self-perpetuating. Children in elementary school report without hesitation that nurses are usually women, and firefighters, engineers and presidents are usually men. Young girls may no longer be encouraged to stay home, but now many are encouraged to work in "suitable" jobs that emphasize helping others. Ideals pressed on boys include abstract reasoning, competitive prowess in sports and business, tinkering with things and financial success.

But persistent sex segregation at work is not the simple product of young men and women's choices. American youngsters' occupational aspirations are notoriously fickle. Occupational goals change often during the teenage years. More than half of college students change majors at least once. Even workers in their 20s and 30s continue to change occupations.

For example, women engaged in emotionally demanding jobs, such as assisting children with learning disabilities, suffer from burnout, while other women working in male-dominated fields find that such jobs are not always worth the isolation and long hours. That this turnover has failed to reduce sex segregation suggests that continued pressure to pursue sex-typed work lasts well into adulthood.

For example, working in a masculine field can raise questions about a woman's femininity. Christine Williams found that female Marines feel they need to show how tough they are on the job but also how feminine they can be off the job. Men who work as nurses face some of the same issues, and respond by emphasizing the heroic aspects of nursing. Beyond the pressure of gender expectations, a web of social factors tends to press women into traditionally female occupations and hold them there in adulthood. Women have fewer acquaintances with knowledge about openings in male-dominated settings ★ ★ ★. They often lack the co-worker support necessary to succeed. They face job tasks and hours that assume a male breadwinner with a supportive stay-at-home wife. And their family and friends are often dubious about or hostile to a new or unconventional occupation. Some of the remaining barriers to women's economic advancement are rooted in the structure of work. For example, excessive hours in a number of demanding fields limit the opportunities of those with parental and other caregiving obligations, especially mothers. Over the last 30 years, the work week has lengthened and the pace of work has intensified for many in the labor force, accentuating the strain on women.

Historical experiences also instruct us about just how flexible these gender distinctions can be. When seats in medical school classrooms became vacant during World War II, young women rushed to fill them. Other women were recruited to fill manufacturing jobs, with the media stressing how the required skills were similar to women's domestic talents. In the 1960s young women switched rapidly from education into medicine, business, and other fields as professional schools in these fields opened their doors. These examples suggest that the gender stereotypes with which women grow up do not prevent them from seizing new opportunities as they become available.

And the things men and women say they want from their jobs are more similar than different. For example, Allison Konrad has shown that men and women overlap a great deal in the specific features of jobs they rank as important. In other words, gender segregation cannot be reduced to what men and women look for in jobs.

HITTING A WALL?

The early 1980s was a period of great energy and optimism both for research and policy on occupational gender segregation. An entirely new dimension of social inequality appeared to be open for exploration—not an everyday event. Comparable worth—the idea of equalizing pay not only for the same work, but also for work of comparable value—seemed a realistic and even imminent possibility. Women were making notable strides, entering new occupations and receiving graduate training in professions such as law, medicine and business. And women's entry into male fields even helped the women who remained in female fields. Fields such as nursing and teaching now face severe shortages, which stimulate higher wages for these undervalued professions.

At that time I was confident that these trends would continue, while some other analysts feared that the rate of change was so slow that it would take many decades to rectify the gender disparities at work. As it turns out, even the skeptics were too optimistic. Progress toward greater gender integration of occupations largely ground to a halt during the 1990s. The most widely used measure of segregation is the "index of dissimilarity," which measures the proportion of women who would have to change fields in order to be represented across types of occupations in the same proportions as men are. (Zero represents complete integration; 100 complete segregation.) This index fell from 67 in 1970 to 60 in 1980 to 56 in 1990, and then to 52 by 2000. But the modest change that occurred during the 1990s was almost all due to shifts in the size of occupations, rather than greater integration within occupations. (The more integrated occupational groups—professionals, technical workers, managers and sales occupations—grew, while the more segregated occupational groups—clerical workers and craft workers—declined.) More mixing within occupations did not happen in the 1990s.

Stagnation is evident in several related areas as well. The gender gap in median weekly earnings has been stuck at the same level since 1993—76 percent in 2001—and segregation by gender across medical specialties actually inched upward during the 1990s.

Why has the gender integration of occupations slowed to a crawl? A longer view suggests that this stability is typical and it is the unusual changes of the 1970s and 1980s that need to be explained. For most of the century gender differentiation remained roughly constant, despite economic booms and depressions, revolutions in marriage, fertility, and divorce, and the incremental but inexorable entry of women into the labor force.

Social change often occurs in brief intervals followed by periods of renewed stagnation. The feminist movement of the late 1960s and 1970s challenged many traditional assumptions, but its force waned by the late 1980s. The idea that a woman could do anything a man could do had tremendous force, but gradually was contested by the notion that women have special values and strengths which should be better appreciated. And inevitably a backlash against ostensibly special treatment challenged affirmative action and other measures

designed to broaden opportunities for women and minorities.

Gender integration occurred largely through women entering formerly male-dominated settings. Few men showed interest in breaking into the pink-collar frontier. The stigma of doing "women's work," coupled with low pay, makes many jobs performed by women unattractive to men. The puzzle, of course, is why women have not left traditional female fields in even greater numbers for the better pay, benefits, promotion opportunities, and even job flexibility found in many men's occupations. Since women continue to join the labor market in ever greater numbers and take shorter and shorter breaks from work for childbearing, one would expect that they would continue to seek out avenues toward economic self-sufficiency. Such commitments to work should keep the pressure on to open male-dominated fields. Yet, while some pressure continues, many women have sought economic independence by the alternative and time-honored route of enrolling in higher education.

||| DEGREES OF DIFFERENCE

Women first surpassed men in obtaining bachelor's degrees in 1982, and the gap continues to widen. In 1998, the most current data available, 56 percent of bachelor's degrees went to women. Before long, college graduates will probably be roughly 60:40 women to men, or a 1.5 to 1 ratio of young women to young men. Women are even more disproportionately concentrated among associate degree recipients, and are at parity with men in garnering master's and professional degrees.

Women's domination of undergraduate education represents a remarkable turn of events. Just 40 years ago, men were earning two-thirds of college degrees, and just 20 years ago, men and women were at parity. While many expected and welcomed women's catching up to men in educational attainment, I am not aware of anyone—economist, sociologist or educator—who predicted that women would surpass men by so much so quickly. What happened?

The surge in women's education is probably linked to gender segregation at work in several ways. First, women realize that the low wages that they face in unskilled women's jobs do not offer a living wage. In 1998, women with a high school degree working full-time, year-round brought home a median income of $22,800 a year; high school dropouts earned $16,700. Male high school graduates made $31,200 a year on average ($24,000 for high school dropouts). Young men consequently have less of a pressing need to pursue higher education. If skilled crafts and other relatively high-wage jobs open to male high school graduates were equally open to women, it is possible that fewer women would pursue higher education.

Second, by seeking specific vocational credentials, women gain some protection against hiring discrimination. If a pharmacy position requires a master's degree, women with such a diploma can expect that they will be given serious consideration. Many women returning to higher education do so to pursue particular vocational degree programs, to become nurse's aides, to get a teacher's certificate and to update office skills. The laundry list of rationalizations for turning away women is less readily available in professional settings, especially where there is a tight market for highly specialized skills. Accordingly, sex segregation has declined more sharply for college graduates than for those with fewer educational credentials.

Finally, the educational credentials women garner are themselves segregated, which limits the financial returns they can expect. In a national survey of the college class of 1999, I found that women college seniors expected to earn 30 percent less than their male classmates when they reached age 30, and the field of the degree they were pursuing explained the largest slice of this gap.

Women are pursuing a broader set of college programs than in the past, but here too change has slowed. About 30 percent of women would have to change fields to match their male counterparts, a difference that has been roughly constant since the mid-1980s. Biology, business and math are among the fields that have reached a rough gender balance. Engineering and the physical sciences (astronomy, chemistry and physics) remain male-dominated fields while psychology, education, nursing, and the romance languages are leading feminine fields of study. Girls are increasingly taking math and science in high school and testing better in those subjects, but this convergence in courses and scores has not translated into a convergence in college majors.

||| LOOKING TOWARD 2020

While forecasting trends is treacherous, it seems safe to predict that the gender segregation of jobs in the year 2020 will resemble current patterns. The major engines of gender integration have all lost steam. There are two ways in which women enter male fields: by starting their careers there or by switching later in life. The numbers taking either route have shrunk in recent years and are no longer enough to make up for the women who drop out of male-dominated careers.

As a result, it seems unrealistic to expect total gender integration. Basic changes in the way work is structured are needed, but we are in a period of political retrenchment, with bold new proposals unlikely to gain serious attention. Further reductions in occupational segregation will take another wave of political, cultural, social and economic reforms like those initiated during the 1960s. Specific policy measures would include: vigorous enforcement of anti-discrimination laws; training programs that target highly gender-typed fields; and a broad reconsideration of the value of women's work, especially caregiving work. Restructuring of working time to make all jobs parent-friendly is needed so that responsible parents (mostly women) are not trapped in so-called "mommy track" positions or part-time jobs with no job security or employment benefits. Specifically, policies that reduce the length of the work week—especially for professionals and managers—could reduce work-family conflict, increase the time working parents can spend with their children and advance gender equal-ity at work. Reducing artificial gender barriers at work can improve economic efficiency while promoting gender equity. Recruiting more women into fields such as computer science and engineering could help to provide much needed talent in these areas, while recruiting more men to be elementary school teachers would help solve the looming national shortages we face in this area. There are many simple and effective measures that can be taken to broaden opportunities for women at work. We simply need the political will. Of course, the gender gap in voting—women were 11 percentage points more likely to vote for Gore than Bush in 2000—could return gender equality to the center of public policy discussions and put the labor force back on a course of incremental progress toward gender equality.

Most observers view the large and growing number of women in colleges and universities as yet another indication of how far women have come. But this welcome development may also have a darker side, as it reflects in part the continued obstacles women face in obtaining high-paying jobs that require no diploma. In other words, until we see more women wearing mechanic's overalls, we can expect to see more and more women marching in caps and gowns at graduation.

35

From the Valley to the Summit: A Brief History of the Quiet Revolution that Transformed Women's Work★

CLAUDIA GOLDIN

Throughout recorded history, individual women have reached summits, and their accomplishments have been touted as evidence that women could achieve greatness. But it has taken considerably longer for substantial numbers of women—more than a token few—to reach the peaks. Until recently, the vast majority of women—even college graduates—occupied the valleys, not the summits. They had jobs, not careers.

The only reason we can have a meaningful discussion today about "women at the top" is because a quiet revolution took place about 30 years ago. It followed on the heels of a noisier revolution, although the quiet one had greater long-run impact. The revolution was accomplished by many who were unaware they were part of a grand transformation that would deeply affect women and their families for decades to come. They were the unwitting foot soldiers of an upheaval that transformed women's employment and the workforce.

This transformation was startlingly rapid, thus the term "revolution," not evolution. The break occurred over a relatively brief period from the late 1960s to the early 1970s, and for women born during the 1940s and later. We can see

★ First printed in 2005; from *Regional Review, The Federal Reserve Bank of Boston*, Volume 14, Number 3.

the abruptness of the transition in a number of social and economic indicators: young women's expectations about their future work life, their college graduation rates, attainment of professional degrees, age at first marriage, and labor force participation rates all show sharp breaks and turning points during this short interval. Women's choice of college major and occupation also exhibit evidence of a shift during these years.

Perhaps it is not surprising that these factors would change around the same time, since they are all interrelated. When young women have expectations of high labor force participation, they are likely to alter their college programs and college graduation rates. Advanced degree programs, for example, are necessary for certain occupations. Particular college majors are required for certain advanced degree programs. Career aspirations will encourage women to marry and begin their families later; in turn, a later first marriage will serve to facilitate women's career development.

In the sections that follow, I present and discuss these factors. In the last section, I explore

CHANGING EXPECTATIONS ABOUT PAID WORK . . .

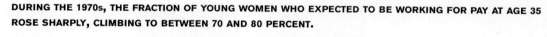

DURING THE 1970s, THE FRACTION OF YOUNG WOMEN WHO EXPECTED TO BE WORKING FOR PAY AT AGE 35 ROSE SHARPLY, CLIMBING TO BETWEEN 70 AND 80 PERCENT.

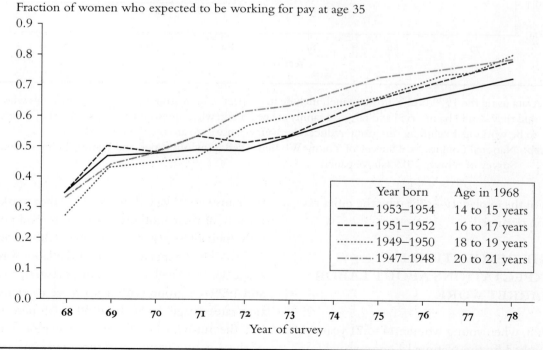

Fraction of women who expected to be working for pay at age 35

Year born	Age in 1968
—— 1953–1954	14 to 15 years
- - - - 1951–1952	16 to 17 years
········ 1949–1950	18 to 19 years
—·—· 1947–1948	20 to 21 years

Year of survey

(CONTINUED)

CHANGING EXPECTATIONS ABOUT PAID WORK . . . (*CONTINUED*)

BY 1979, THE SHIFT WAS IN PLACE, WITH VIRTUALLY NO FURTHER CHANGE DURING THE 1980s.

Fraction of women who expected to be working for pay at age 35

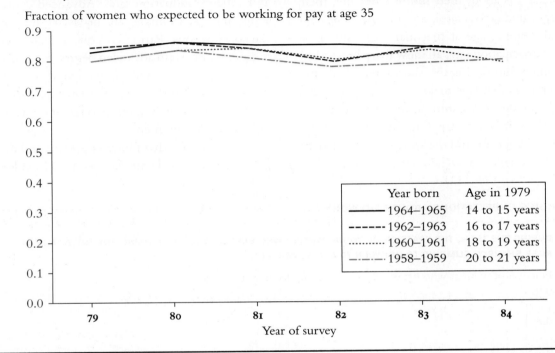

Year born	Age in 1979
1964–1965	14 to 15 years
1962–1963	16 to 17 years
1960–1961	18 to 19 years
1958–1959	20 to 21 years

Year of survey

NOTE: Data using the 1979 NLSY (lower panel) include in "expect to be working at age 35," individuals who said they would be married and raising a family at age 35 but, when questioned further, said they wanted to be working. Excluding this group reduces the average answer to around 0.65 to 0.70.

SOURCES: National Longitudinal Survey of Young Women, 1968 (previous panel) and National Longitudinal Survey of Youth, 1979 (above panel).

some of the explanations for why the quiet revolution occurred.

THE REVOLUTION IN EXPECTATIONS ABOUT LABOR MARKET WORK

In 1968, when young women 14 to 21 years old were asked by the National Longitudinal Survey (NLS) about their future labor force plans, their answers reflected the current labor market activity of their mothers, their aunts, and possibly their older sisters. Only about 30 percent said that they expected to be in the labor force at age 35. Most had mothers born between 1922 and 1929—a group with labor force participation rates at age 35 of about 30 to 35 percent. Yet the future labor force participation rates of these young women (of those ever-married born 1951 to 1954) would in fact be about

. . . LEAD WOMEN TO GREATER INVESTMENTS IN CAREER-ORIENTED EDUCATION

AS THE REVOLUTION IN EXPECTATIONS BEGINS, WOMEN ARE ALREADY INCREASINGLY ATTENDING AND GRADUATING FROM COLLEGE.

Percentage of population at age 35 that are college graduates

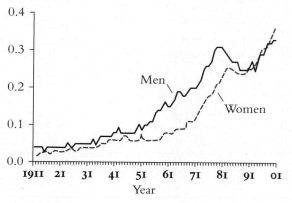

Ratio of female to male college-graduate shares of the population at age 35

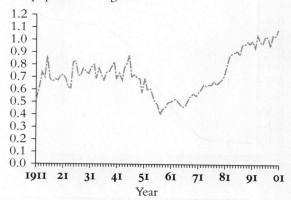

THEIR CHOICE OF COLLEGE MAJOR BECOMES MORE SIMILAR TO THEIR MALE COUNTERPARTS.

Fraction in gender-typical majors   Dissimilarity index

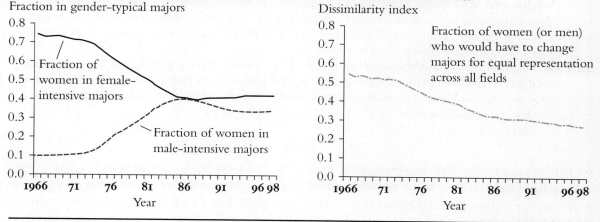

(CONTINUED)

... LEAD WOMEN TO GREATER INVESTMENTS IN CAREER-ORIENTED EDUCATION (*CONTINUED*)

ESPECIALLY NOTABLE IS THE SHARP RISE IN THE SHARE OF WOMEN MAJORING IN BUSINESS AND MANAGEMENT AND ENROLLING IN PROFESSIONAL PROGRAMS THAT HAD PREVIOUSLY BEEN ENTIRELY MALE.

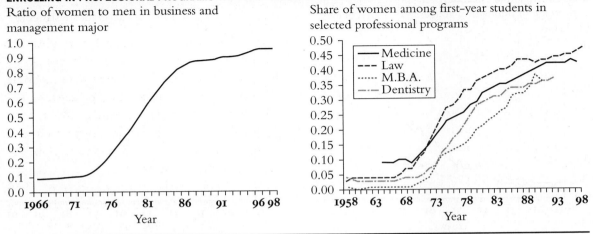

NOTES: Upper panel: College graduate is 16 years of schooling or more through 1980, and a bachelor's degree or higher in 1990 and 2000. Middle panel: Female-intensive (or male-intensive) majors are those in which the share of women (or men) is 0.5 standard deviations above the mean in 1970, using 1970 weights. Out of 53 majors, 11 were female-intensive, 31 were male-intensive, and 11 were neither. Female-intensive majors were anthropology, arts & music, non-science education, English & literature, foreign languages, health technologies, linguistics, other life sciences, social services professions, sociology, and vocational studies & home economics.

SOURCES: Integrated Public Use Microdata Series of the U.S. Censuses, 1940–1990; Current Population Survey, 1990 and 2000; National Center for Education Statistics, U.S. Department of Education; *Journal of the American Medical Association*; American Bar Association; and *Digest of Education Statistics*, U.S. Department of Education.

65 percent at age 35. That is, young women's expectations were more in line with what older women were currently doing rather than with what their own futures would actually hold.

But in the late 1960s and the early 1970s, something began to change. In 1975, the fraction of young women who expected to be working at age 35 reached 65 percent, more than double the response seven years earlier and

more in line with their future rates. Even comparing 21-year-olds in 1968 with 21-year-olds in 1975 shows an increase in expected participation of about 35 percentage points. In fact, the expectations of all cohorts increased at the same time and by about the same amount. Furthermore, this period of rapid change in expectations ended by around 1980. Responses to similar questions asked by a later version of the NLS, begun in 1979 with a group of young women 14 to 21 years old, reveal virtually no change either by age or by year from 1979 to 1984—a very different picture from the sharp increase in expectations of future employment by young women from 1968 to 1978.

Thus, by the mid-to-late 1970s young women's plans were considerably different from a decade earlier, with the turning point in the late 1960s and early-to-mid 1970s. Expectations about participation in paid work no longer mimicked the experience of their mothers, but were in line with, if not somewhat higher than, the levels they would eventually achieve.

THE SHIFT IN EDUCATION FROM CONSUMPTION TO INVESTMENT

Although not all the young women surveyed above would attend or graduate from college, the implication for professional advancement is clear. Young women (and men) who have a more accurate assessment of their future labor market involvement will invest more wisely in education and training, whether attending and graduating from college, choosing a college major, or enrolling in a professional degree program.

College Majors

In 1966, almost 75 percent of women graduating from a four-year college majored in subjects in which most of the students were female. About 10 percent specialized in a subject for which most of the students were men, about the same fraction as in 1960; and about 15 percent majored in gender "mixed" fields, such as math,

psychology, sociology, anthropology, linguistics, history, and arts & music.

Moreover, fully 40 percent of women college undergraduates majored in education—at a time when that major was 78 percent female. About 17 percent concentrated in English literature or foreign languages (combined, 68 percent female). And 3 percent were in home economics and social services professions (92 percent female). Thus, 60 percent (40 + 17 + 3) of all female undergraduates majored in one of three female-dominated concentrations (or combined concentrations).

By contrast, 50 percent of men in 1966 majored in either science (except "other life sciences"), engineering, or business & management. Most of the women's concentrations could be classified as "job" or "consumption" oriented (e.g., education and literature), whereas those of the men as "career" and "investment" oriented (e.g., engineering, and business & management).

Another way to show the separation of the sexes is to compute a standard index of dissimilarity. The index uses the full range of the 50-plus concentrations for which we have data and measures the percent of women (or men) who would have to change concentrations for equal representation across the fields. This calculation shows that more than half of all women (or men) would have had to change concentrations to create equality by sex in all fields in 1966.

But in the early 1970s, the sex segregation of undergraduate majors fell markedly. The break is especially sharp for the fraction of women in male-intensive majors, but it is also apparent for the fraction of women in female-intensive majors and in the sex segregation index.

The proximate reasons for this change can be found in the enrollments in two large concentrations: education and business & management. The relative decrease in women's enrollment in education depressed the fraction of women in female-intensive majors, while their relative increase in business & management boosted the fraction in male-intensive majors. By 1980, only about 20 percent of women were majoring in education; by 1998, the figure had dropped to 12 percent. Because of the increase in women's college participation rates, the number of women majoring in education continued to rise from 1966 to 1973. But it has declined steadily since 1973, despite the continued increase in the fraction of young women attending and graduating from college.

The reverse trend can be found in business & management. Only 2 percent of all women college graduates majored in these fields in 1966; the figure rose to 22 percent in 1988, the height of its relative popularity among all undergraduates. Because women also increased their numbers as undergraduates relative to men throughout the period, the ratio of women to men majoring in business & management majors increased at an even greater rate, climbing spectacularly from 0.12 in 1973 to 0.84 by 1986.

Therefore, beginning in the early 1970s, female undergraduates radically changed their concentrations. They moved out of majors that led to traditionally female occupations. They moved into those that were career-oriented and often led to advanced degrees. And their majors shifted to subjects that were more similar to those of their male counterparts. Differences in the college majors of men and women still exist but are considerably less significant than they once were. In 1998, about 27 percent of women (or men) would have to change majors for equality across the fields, about half the rate in 1966.

College Degrees

The fraction of women graduating from four-year institutions of higher education increased greatly for women born from 1941 to 1951. This coincided with an increase for men due, at least in part, to Vietnam War draft deferments. But enrollments for men decreased substantially for those born from 1946 to the early 1950s, while enrollments for women continued to rise. Thus the ratio of women to men graduating from college soared for those born from 1946 to 1956, rising from 0.65 to more than 0.95.

This ratio began to rise for precisely the same women that underwent the change in college majors described above—women born in the 1940s, and graduating college from the late 1960s to the early 1970s. Such a change was not unprecedented—the ratio of female to male college graduates increased from a low point for those born in 1924 to those born in the 1940s. But that increase mainly made up for the large decrease caused by men returning from World War II and taking advantage of the GI Bill to attend college. The rise in this period was due to something else, and it echoes the breaks for college majors and labor force expectations.

Professional Degrees

Women's enrollment in professional degree programs also reveals obvious turning points in the early 1970s. Women's share of first-year students in medical school, business school, and dentistry turned up around 1970; the share in law school increased sharply a year or two earlier. Similar trends can be observed in the number of women entering professional degree programs expressed as a fraction of all female four-year college and university graduates in that year. This fraction began to increase in about the same year as did the ratio of women to men among first-year professional students. However, almost all the growth in the fraction of female B.A.s continuing on to professional school occurs from 1970 to 1980, whereas the ratio of women to men in graduate programs increases throughout the period considered. Both these data series exhibit among the clearest and sharpest breaks of any shown in this paper.

THE SHIFT TO CAREERS AND DELAYED MARRIAGE

Changes in women's choices about career and family closely mirrored the changes in their labor market expectations and ill their educational investments.

Occupations and Labor Force Participation

The shift in the occupations of college-graduate women, 30 to 34 years old, closely follows that for college majors. Traditional female occupations (e.g., K through 12th grade teachers, nurses, librarians, social workers) show a sharp decrease starting around 1970 and bottom out around 1990. Nontraditional occupations (e.g., doctors, lawyers, managers, college professors) show essentially the opposite trend. The larg-

est increase in the fraction of women in nontraditional occupations occurred in the 1980s, a bit after the change in college majors, probably because advanced degrees are needed to enter these professions.

As more women majored in career-oriented subjects and entered professional and advanced degree programs, they also increased their labor force participation during their late twenties and early thirties. Participation rates among young women (under 35 years) with college degrees or more show the greatest increase for women born during the 1940s. Whereas rates for young college-educated women born in the 1930s were around 50 percent, participation rose to 80 percent for women born in 1950. That is, the greatest change in labor force participation occurred in the 1970s.

As noted above, these women college graduates were the first group to correctly anticipate that their future labor force participation would be considerably higher than that of their mothers. Furthermore, their expectations changed when they were young enough to alter their educational investments. It is likely, therefore, that their actual labor force participation was high precisely because their educational investments made their employment more lucrative and desirable.

Age at First Marriage

A host of demographic changes also occurred for this group of women. One of the most important was the trend toward delaying the age at which they married.

The age at first marriage for college-graduate women began to increase for those women born around 1950. Women born in

POSTGRADUATE

BEGINNING AROUND 1970, YOUNG COLLEGE-GRADUATE WOMEN (UNDER 35 YEARS OLD) ARE FAR MORE LIKELY TO REMAIN IN THE LABOR FORCE...

Labor force participation rate

Birth year

...WORK IN NONTRADITIONAL OCCUPATIONS...

Fraction of working college-graduate women, 30 to 34 years old, in occupation type

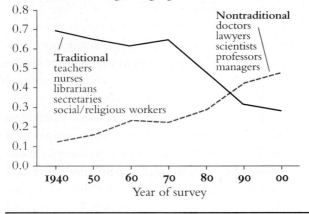

Year of survey

(CONTINUED)

1949 had a median age at first marriage of 23 years, about the same as for the previous two decades. But women born in 1957 had a median age at first marriage of 25.5. Because so many college-graduate women born in the two decades prior to 1950 married directly out of college, college had functioned, in large part, as a marriage market.

By the time the women born in 1957 married for the first time, their median age had increased by 2.5 years, a large increase in only seven years; and the median age at first marriage continued

POSTGRADUATE (CONTINUED)

...AND DELAY THE AGE AT WHICH THEY FIRST MARRY.

Median age at first marriage for white, college-graduate women

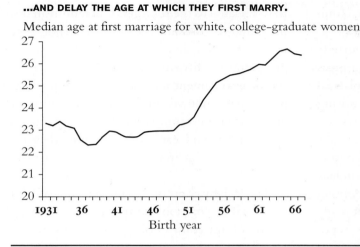

NOTES: Upper panel: Data are for white, non-Hispanic, college-graduate women, except for 1970, which includes Hispanics. College graduate is 16 years or more of schooling, except after 1990 when it is a bachelor's degree or higher. Middle panel is civilian workers. Nontraditional occupations include all professional and managerial occupations except teachers, librarians, nurses, and social and religious welfare occupations.

SOURCES: Integrated Public Use Microdata Series of the U.S. Censuses, 1940–1960; Current Population Survey, 1970–12000, and CPS Fertility and Marital History Supplement, 1990 and 1995.

to climb, although more slowly, rising to 26.5 years for women born in 1965. The age at first marriage also increased for other education groups, but the increase was somewhat smaller than for college women.

WHAT CAUSED THE REVOLUTION?

The transformations in women's work roles—from jobs to careers, from "consumption" majors to "investment" majors, and from early to later marriages—took place in an astonishingly short period of time. Labor market expectations of young women were altered beginning

in the late 1960s; and by the late 1970s, the transformation was completed. Undergraduate fields of concentration began to change around 1972, and the conversion was mostly finished by the mid 1980s. Similarly, enrollment in professional schools shifted up markedly around 1970, with the largest relative gains occurring by 1980. Changes in occupations and in labor force participation echoed changes in college majors and enrollment in professional schools. The mean age at first marriage began its upward climb with women born in the early 1950s and was completed with women born in the mid 1960s. The only reason that we are able, today, to speak about a significant group of women who are "leaders" and who are "at the top" (or who should be "at the top") is because these changes allowed women to begin their climb from the valley to the summit.

What can explain why the changes occurred?

Any set of social changes as wide-ranging as those just mentioned is not likely to be explained by a single factor, so it would not be surprising to find several contributing circumstances.

The first important clue is that the process described above was episodic rather than continuous. This suggests seeking explanations in factors that also changed discontinuously. Among the likely contenders are: (1) government mandates such as Title VII of the Civil Rights Act of 1964 that prohibited discrimination in employment practices such as in hiring and promotion, and Title IX of the Education Amendments of 1972 that required equal treatment of the sexes in educational programs, including colleges and universities; (2) social change spurred by the resurgence of feminism that followed the Civil Rights movement and was reinforced by the anti-war movement; and (3) the contraceptive innovation, known as "the Pill," which gave young women the ability to delay marriage and childbearing and plan for a career. Other candidates include abortion reform, which was decided in some states before *Roe v. Wade*; the Baby Boom which, by producing a surplus of women (relative to men) of marriageable age (since women marry younger than men), may have forced some women to postpone or forgo marriage; and the declining economy of the mid 1970s, which may have produced the same effect.

I focus on the Pill, not because government mandates and larger social change made no contribution, but because their importance has been hard to assess. To statistically prove the impact of social change, one must find a factor that is related to the resurgence of feminism but unrelated to the choice of college major, college graduation, and enrollment in professional programs—a difficult, if not impossible, task. As for government mandates, various research papers have not yet uncovered a meaningful effect of antidiscrimination laws on women's employment and earnings, although they do point to a strong impact with regard to race. ★ ★ ★

The Pill, by contrast, has proven amenable to empirical exploration and appears to have made an important contribution in changing women's careers and the age at first marriage. How did the Pill affect the expectations of young women or their desire to pursue college, male-dominated majors, and professional degrees? It lowered the costs to young, unmarried women of pursuing careers, particularly careers involving substantial, upfront investments of time.

A young college woman in the mid 1960s who was considering whether to enter a professional degree program or make other substantial career investments had to consider the impact on her personal life. Sex was highly risky in a world without effective, female-controlled, and easy-to-use contraception—and pregnancy could derail a career. The Pill was more reliable than other methods of contraception and its use was controlled by women. Thus, it might have had a *direct effect* in fostering women's careers by reducing the risk and cost of having sex.

The Pill also could have had an *indirect effect* by increasing the age at first marriage, which may in turn have influenced other decisions advancing women's careers. The Pill virtually eliminated one potent reason for early marriage and for many of the social trappings (e.g., going steady, engagements) that led to early marriage. With more men and women delaying marriage for many years after college graduation, the decision of any one woman to delay marriage meant that she would reenter a marriage market that would not be as depleted of eligible men. Thus, the Pill *could* have influenced women's careers, college majors, professional degrees, and the age at first marriage.

What are the facts? The FDA approved the Pill for contraceptive use in 1960. Married women began to use it immediately, and their use peaked within about five years. But young, single women did not gain full access until the late 1960s or early 1970s, as most were minors and needed parental consent to obtain non-life-threatening medical care. Eventually, age-of-majority laws and mature minor cases at the state level lowered the age at which a woman could legally receive family planning services by a doctor without her parent's consent. These changes were driven in large part by agitation during the Vietnam War to lower the voting age ("Old enough to die, old enough to vote," was the slogan at the time.)

Using these variations in state law and judicial rulings, Lawrence F. Katz and I were able to look at their impact on the age at first marriage and on women's careers. We find that laws allowing for greater access were strongly and positively related to the age at first marriage and strongly and positively related to the fraction of women pursuing professional careers. The availability of the Pill to young, single women does appear to have been a substantial factor in the quiet revolution.

While the Pill was an important factor, it was only one contributing factor; and it functioned within a larger changing social and economic environment for young women. Labor force participation rates had already been rising for some time, although until the late 1960s young women had not built the increases into their educational investment calculus. The appearance of the Pill may have enabled young women to view early investments in time-intensive careers as less risky. The resurgence of feminism may have awakened young women to the social changes around them and also contributed to their use of the Pill. Anti-discrimination laws affecting hiring, promotion, and education may also have contributed, on the margin, to protect women workers and to encourage schools to admit them.

Other factors appear to have been less important. Abortion reform may have mattered somewhat; but in our statistical analysis, abortion reform runs a distant second to the Pill in explaining the changes discussed above. Similarly, because women tend to marry men who are somewhat older than they are, the Baby Boom created a sex ratio bulge. But this does not explain much of the increase in the age at first marriage for the group of women analyzed here, nor can it explain the enormous increase in professional degrees for women.

Whatever the precise reasons, a great divide in college-graduate women's lives and employment occurred about 35 years ago. Before this change, women who reached the peaks made solo climbs. They became symbols and tokens demonstrating that women could achieve greatness. But real change demanded a march by the masses from the valley to the summit. That march began with women born in the late 1940s.

36

From *The Second Shift: Working Parents and the Revolution at Home**

ARLIE HOCHSCHILD

||| A SPEED-UP IN THE FAMILY

She is not the same woman in each magazine advertisement, but she is the same idea. She has that working-mother look as she strides forward, briefcase in one hand, smiling child in the other. Literally and figuratively, she is moving ahead. Her hair, if long, tosses behind her; if it is short, it sweeps back at the sides, suggesting mobility and progress. There is nothing shy or passive about her. She is confident, active, "liberated." She wears a dark tailored suit, but with a silk bow or colorful frill that says, "I'm really feminine underneath." She has made it in a man's world without sacrificing her femininity. And she has done this on her own. By some personal miracle, this image suggests, she has managed to combine what 150 years of industrialization have split wide apart—child and job, frill and suit, female culture and male.

When I showed a photograph of a supermom like this to the working mothers I talked to in the course of researching this book, many responded with an outright laugh. One daycare worker and mother of two, ages three

---

* First published in 1989.

and five, threw back her head: "Ha! They've got to be *kidding* about her. Look at me, hair a mess, nails jagged, twenty pounds overweight. Mornings, I'm getting my kids dressed, the dog fed, the lunches made, the shopping list done. That lady's got a maid." Even working mothers who did have maids couldn't imagine combining work and family in such a carefree way. "Do you know what a baby *does* to your life, the two o'clock feedings, the four o'clock feedings?" Another mother of two said: "They don't show it, but she's whistling"—she imitated a whistling woman, eyes to the sky—"so she can't hear the din." They envied the apparent ease of the woman with the flying hair, but she didn't remind them of anyone they knew.

The women I interviewed—lawyers, corporate executives, word processors, garment pattern cutters, daycare workers—and most of their husbands, too—felt differently about some issues: how right it is for a mother of young children to work a full-time job, or how much a husband should be responsible for the home. But they all agreed that it was hard to work two full-time jobs and raise young children.

How well do couples do it? The more women work outside the home, the more central this question. The number of women in paid work has risen steadily since before the turn of the century, but since 1950 the rise has been staggering. In 1950, 30 percent of American women were in the labor force; in 1986, it was 55 percent. In 1950, 28 percent of married women with children between six and seventeen worked outside the home; in 1986, it had

risen to 68 percent. In 1950, 23 percent of married women with children under six worked. By 1986, it had grown to 54 percent. We don't know how many women with children under the age of one worked outside the home in 1950; it was so rare that the Bureau of Labor kept no statistics on it. Today half of such women do. Two-thirds of all mothers are now in the labor force; in fact, more mothers have paid jobs (or are actively looking for one) than nonmothers. Because of this change in women, two-job families now make up 58 percent of all married couples with children.[1]

Since an increasing number of working women have small children, we might expect an increase in part-time work. But actually, 67 percent of the mothers who work have full-time jobs—that is, thirty-five hours or more weekly. That proportion is what it was in 1959.

If more mothers of young children are stepping into full-time jobs outside the home, and if most couples can't afford household help, how much more are fathers doing at home? As I began exploring this question I found many studies on the hours working men and women devote to housework and childcare. One national random sample of 1,243 working parents in forty-four American cities, conducted in 1965–66 by Alexander Szalai and his coworkers, for example, found that working women averaged three hours a day on housework while men averaged 17 minutes; women spent fifty minutes a day of time exclusively with their children; men spent twelve minutes. On the other side of the coin, working fathers watched television an hour

---

1 U.S. Bureau of Labor Statistics, *Employment and Earnings, Characteristics of Families: First Quarter* (Washington, D.C.: U.S. Department of Labor, 1988).

longer than their working wives, and slept a half hour longer each night. A comparison of this American sample with eleven other industrial countries in Eastern and Western Europe revealed the same difference between working women and working men in those countries as well.[2] In a 1983 study of white middle-class families in greater Boston, Grace Baruch and R. C. Barnett found that working men married to working women spent only three-quarters of an hour longer each week with their kindergarten-aged children than did men married to housewives.[3]

Szalai's landmark study documented the now familiar but still alarming story of the working woman's "double day," but it left me wondering how men and women actually felt about all this. He and his coworkers studied how people used time, but not, say, how a father felt about his twelve minutes with his child, or how his wife felt about it. Szalai's study revealed the visible surface of what I discovered to be a set of deeply emotional issues: What should a man and woman contribute to the family? How appreciated does each feel? How does each respond to subtle changes in the balance of marital power? How does each develop an unconscious "gender strategy" for coping with the work at home, with marriage, and, indeed, with life itself? These were the underlying issues.

But I began with the measurable issue of time. Adding together the time it takes to do a paid job and to do housework and childcare, I averaged estimates from the major studies on time use done in the 1960s and 1970s, and discovered that women worked roughly fifteen hours longer each week than men. Over a year, they worked an *extra month of twenty four-hour days a year.* Over a dozen years, it was an extra year of twenty-four-hour days. Most women without children spend much more time than men on housework; with children, they devote more time to both housework and childcare. Just as there is a wage gap between men and women in the workplace, there is a "leisure gap" between them at home. Most women work one shift at the office or factory and a "second shift" at home.

Studies show that working mothers have higher self-esteem and get less depressed than housewives, but compared to their husbands, they're more tired and get sick more often. In Peggy Thoits's 1985 analysis of two large-scale surveys, each of about a thousand men and women, people were asked how often in the preceding week they'd experienced each

---

2 Alexander Szalai, ed., *The Use of Time: Daily Activities of Urban and Suburban Populations in Twelve Countries* (The Hague: Mouton, 1972), p. 668, Table B. Another study found that men spent a longer time than women eating meals (Shelley Coverman, "Gender, Domestic Labor Time and Wage Inequality," *American Sociological Review* 48 [1983]: 626). With regard to sleep, the pattern differs for men and women. The higher the social class of a man, the more sleep he's likely to get. The higher the class of a woman, the less sleep she's likely to get. (Upper-white-collar men average 7.6 hours sleep a night. Lower-white-collar, skilled and unskilled men all averaged 7.3 hours. Upper-white-collar women average 7.1 hours of

sleep; lower-white-collar workers average 7.4; skilled workers 7.0 and unskilled workers 8.1.) Working wives seem to meet the demands of high-pressure careers by reducing sleep, whereas working husbands don't. ★ ★ ★

3 Grace K. Baruch and Rosalind Barnett, "Correlates of Fathers' Participation in Family Work: A Technical Report," Working Paper no. 106 (Wellesley, Mass.: Wellesley College Center for Research on Women, 1983), pp. 80–81. Also see Kathryn E. Walker and Margaret E. Woods, *Time Use: A Measure of Household Production of Goods and Services* (Washington, D.C.: American Home Economics Association, 1976).

of twenty-three symptoms of anxiety (such as dizziness or hallucinations). According to the researchers' criteria, working mothers were more likely than any other group to be "anxious."

In light of these studies, the image of the woman with the flying hair seems like an upbeat "cover" for a grim reality, like those pictures of Soviet tractor drivers smiling radiantly into the distance as they think about the ten-year plan. The Szalai study was conducted in 1965–66. I wanted to know whether the leisure gap he found in 1965 persists, or whether it has disappeared. Since most married couples work two jobs, since more will in the future, since most wives in these couples work the extra month a year, I wanted to understand what the wife's extra month a year meant for each person, and what it does for love and marriage in an age of high divorce.

★ ★ ★

Inside the Extra Month a Year

The women I interviewed seemed to be far more deeply torn between the demands of work and family than were their husbands. They talked with more animation and at greater length than their husbands about the abiding conflict between them. Busy as they were, women more often brightened at the idea of yet another interviewing session. They felt the second shift was *their* issue and most of their husbands agreed. When I telephoned one husband to arrange an interview with him, explaining that I wanted to ask him about how he managed work and family life, he replied genially, "Oh, this will *really* interest my *wife*."

It was a woman who first proposed to me the metaphor, borrowed from industrial life, of the "second shift." She strongly resisted the *idea* that homemaking was a "shift." Her family was her life and she didn't want it reduced to a job. But as she put it, "You're on duty at work. You come home, and you're on duty. Then you go back to work and you're on duty." After eight hours of adjusting insurance claims, she came home to put on the rice for dinner, care for her children, and wash laundry. Despite herself her home life *felt* like a second shift. That was the real story and that was the real problem.

Men who shared the load at home seemed just as pressed for time as their wives, and as torn between the demands of career and small children, as the stories of Michael Sherman and Art Winfield will show. But the majority of men did not share the load at home. Some refused outright. Others refused more passively, often offering a loving shoulder to lean on, an understanding ear as their working wife faced the conflict they both saw as hers. At first it seemed to me that the problem of the second shift was hers. But I came to realize that those husbands who helped very little at home were often indirectly just as deeply affected as their wives by the need to do that work, through the resentment their wives feel toward them, and through their need to steel themselves against that resentment. Evan Holt, a warehouse furniture salesman ★ ★ ★ did very little housework and played with his four-year-old son, Joey, at his convenience. Juggling the demands of work with family at first seemed a problem for his wife. But Evan himself suffered enormously from the side effects of "her" problem. His wife did the second shift, but she resented it keenly, and half-consciously expressed her frustration and rage by losing interest in sex and becoming overly absorbed with Joey. One way or another, most men I talked with do suffer the severe repercussions of what I think is a transitional phase in American family life.

One reason women take a deeper interest than men in the problems of juggling work with family life is that even when husbands happily shared the hours of work, their wives felt more *responsible* for home and children. More women kept track of doctors' appointments and arranged for playmates to come over. More mothers than fathers worried about the tail on a child's Halloween costume or a birthday present for a school friend. They were more likely to think about their children while at work and to check in by phone with the baby-sitter.

Partly because of this, more women felt torn between one sense of urgency and another, between the need to soothe a child's fear of being left at daycare, and the need to show the boss she's "serious" at work. More women than men questioned how good they were as parents, or if they did not, they questioned why they weren't questioning it. More often than men, women alternated between living in their ambition and standing apart from it.

As masses of women have moved into the economy, families have been hit by a "speed-up" in work and family life. There is no more time in the day than there was when wives stayed home, but there is twice as much to get done. It is mainly women who absorb this "speed-up." Twenty percent of the men in my study shared housework equally. Seventy percent of men did a substantial amount (less than half but more than a third), and 10 percent

did less than a third. Even when couples share more equitably in the work at home, women do two-thirds of the *daily* jobs at home, like cooking and cleaning up—jobs that fix them into a rigid routine. Most women cook dinner and most men change the oil in the family car. But, as one mother pointed out, dinner needs to be prepared every evening around six o'clock, whereas the car oil needs to be changed every six months, any day around that time, any time that day. Women do more childcare than men, and men repair more household appliances. A child needs to be tended daily while the repair of household appliances can often wait "until I have time." Men thus have more control over *when* they make their contributions than women do. They may be very busy with family chores but, like the executive who tells his secretary to "hold my calls," the man has more control over his time. The job of the working mother, like that of the secretary, is usually to "take the calls."

Another reason women may feel more strained than men is that women more often do two things at once—for example, write checks and return phone calls, vacuum and keep an eye on a three year-old, fold laundry and think out the shopping list. Men more often cook dinner *or* take a child to the park. Indeed, women more often juggle three spheres—job, children, and housework—while most men juggle two—job and children. For women, two activities compete with their time with children, not just one.

Beyond doing more at home, women also devote *proportionately more* of their time at home to housework and proportionately less of it to childcare. Of all the time men spend working at home, more of it goes to childcare. That is, working wives spend relatively more time "mothering the house"; husbands spend more time "mothering" the children. Since most parents prefer to tend to their children than clean house, men do more of what they'd rather do. More men than women take their children on "fun" outings to the park, the zoo, the movies. Women spend more time on maintenance, feeding and bathing children, enjoyable activities to be sure, but often less leisurely or "special" than going to the zoo. Men also do fewer of the "undesirable" household chores: fewer men than women wash toilets and scrub the bathroom.

As a result, women tend to talk more intently about being over-tired, sick, and "emotionally drained." Many women I could not tear away from the topic of sleep. They talked about how much they could "get by on" . . . six and a half, seven, seven and a half, less, more. They talked about who they knew who needed more or less. Some apologized for how much sleep they needed—"I'm afraid I need eight hours of sleep"—as if eight was "too much." They talked about the effect of a change in baby-sitter, the birth of a second child, or a business trip on their child's pattern of sleep. They talked about how to avoid fully waking up when a child called them at night, and how to get back to sleep. These women talked about sleep the way a hungry person talks about food.

All in all, if in this period of American history, the two-job family is suffering from a speed up of work and family life, working mothers are its primary victims. It is ironic, then, that often it falls to women to be the "time and motion expert" of family life. Watching inside homes, I noticed it was often the mother who rushed children, saying, "Hurry up! It's time to go," "Finish your cereal now," "You can do that later," "Let's go!" When a bath is crammed into a slot between 7:45 and 8:00 it was often the mother who called out, "Let's see who can take their bath the quickest!" Often a younger child will rush out, scurrying to be first in bed, while the older and wiser one stalls, resistant, sometimes resentful: "Mother is always rushing us." Sadly enough, women are more often the lightning rods for family aggressions aroused by the speed-up of work and family life. They are the "villains" in a process of which they are also the primary victims. More than the longer hours, the sleeplessness, and feeling torn, this is the saddest cost to women of the extra month a year.

MARRIAGE IN THE STALLED REVOLUTION

Each marriage bears the footprints of economic and cultural trends which originate far outside marriage. A rise in inflation which erodes the earning power of the male wage, an expanding service sector which opens up jobs for women, new cultural images—like the woman with the flying hair—that make the working mother seem exciting, all these changes do not simply go on *around* marriage. They occur *within* marriage, and transform it. Problems between husbands and wives, problems which seem "individual" and "marital," are often individual experiences of powerful economic and cultural shock waves that are not caused by one person or two. Quarrels that erupt, as we'll see, between Nancy and Evan Holt, Jessica and Seth

Stein, Anita and Ray Judson result mainly from a friction between faster-changing women and slower-changing men, rates of change which themselves result from the different rates at which the industrial economy has drawn men and women into itself.

There is a "his" and "hers" to the economic development of the United States. In the latter part of the nineteenth century, it was mainly men who were drawn off the farm into paid, industrial work and who changed their way of life and their identity. At that point in history, men became more different from their fathers than women became from their mothers. Today the economic arrow points at women; it is women who are being drawn into wage work, and women who are undergoing changes in their way of life and identity. Women are departing more from their mothers' and grand-mothers' way of life, men are doing so less.[4]

Both the earlier entrance of men into the industrial economy and the later entrance of women have influenced the relations *between* men and women, especially their relations within marriage. The former increase in the number of men in industrial work tended to increase the power of men, and the present growth in the number of women in such work has somewhat increased the power of women. On the whole, the entrance of men into indus-trial work did not destabilize the family whereas *in the absence of other changes,* the rise in female employment has gone with the rise in divorce. I will have more to say about the "his" and "hers"

of economic history [elsewhere]. Here I'll focus on the current economic story, that which hangs over the marriages I describe in this book. Beneath the image of the woman with the flying hair, there has been a real change in women without much change in anything else.

The exodus of women into the economy has not been accompanied by a cultural understand-ing of marriage and work that would make this transition smooth. The workforce has changed. Women have changed. But most workplaces have remained inflexible in the face of the fam-ily demands of their workers and at home, most men have yet to really adapt to the changes in women. This strain between the change in women and the absence of change in much else leads me to speak of a "stalled revolution."

A society which did not suffer from this stall would be a society *humanely* adapted to the fact that most women work outside the home. The workplace would allow parents to work part time, to share jobs, to work flexible hours, to take parental leaves to give birth, tend a sick child, or care for a well one. As Delo-res Hayden has envisioned in *Redesigning the American Dream,* it would include affordable housing closer to places of work, and perhaps community-based meal and laundry services. It would include men whose notion of manhood encouraged them to be active parents and share at home. In contrast, a stalled revolution lacks social arrangements that ease life for working parents, and lacks men who share the second shift.

---

4 This is more true of white and middle-class women than it is of black or poor women, whose mothers often worked outside the home. But the trend I am talking about—an increase from 20 percent of women in paid jobs in 1900 to 55 percent in 1986—has affected a large number of women.

If women begin to do less at home because they have less time, if men do little more, if the work of raising children and tending a home requires roughly the same effort, then the questions of who does what at home and of what "needs doing" become key. Indeed, they may become a source of deep tension in the marriage, tensions I explore here one by one.

The tensions caused by the stall in this social revolution have led many men and women to avoid becoming part of a two-job couple. Some have married but clung to the tradition of the man as provider, the woman as homemaker. Others have resisted marriage itself. In *The Hearts of Men,* Barbara Ehrenreich describes a "male revolt" against the financial and emotional burden of supporting and raising a family. In *Women and Love,* Shere Hite describes a "female revolt" against unsatisfying and unequal relationships with men. But the couples I focused on are not in traditional marriages and not giving up on marriage. They are struggling to reconcile the demands of two jobs with a happy family life. Given this larger economic story, and given the present stalled revolution, I wanted to know how the two-job family was progressing.

As I drove from my classes at Berkeley to the outreaching suburbs, small towns, and inner cities of the San Francisco Bay to observe and ask questions in the homes of two-job couples, and back to my own two-job marriage, my first question about who does what gave way to a series of deeper questions: What leads some working mothers to do all the work at home themselves—to pursue what I call a supermom strategy—and what leads others to press their husbands to share the responsibility and work of the home? Why do some men genuinely want to share housework and childcare, others fatalistically acquiesce, and still others actively resist?

How does each husband's ideas about manhood lead him to think he "should feel" about what he's doing at home and at work? What does he really feel? Do his real feelings conflict with what he thinks he should feel? How does he resolve the conflict? The same questions apply to wives. What influence does each person's consequent "strategy" for handling his or her feelings and actions with regard to the second shift affect his or her children, job, and marriage? Through this line of questioning, I was led to the complex web of ties between a family's needs, the sometime quest for equality, and happiness in modern marriage, the real topic of this book.

We can describe a couple as rich or poor and that will tell us a great deal about their two-job marriage. We can describe them as Catholic, Protestant, Jewish, black, Chicano, Asian, or white and that will tell us something more. We can describe their marriage as a combination of two personalities, one "obsessive compulsive," say, and the other "narcissistic," and again that will tell us something. But knowledge about social class, ethnicity, and personality takes us only so far in understanding who does and doesn't share the second shift, and whether or not sharing the work at home makes marriages happier.

When I sat down to compare one couple that shared the second shift with another three that didn't, many of the answers that would seem obvious—a man's greater income, his longer hours of work, the fact that his mother was a housewife or his father did little at home, his ideas about men and women—all these factors didn't really explain why some women work the extra month a year and others don't. They didn't explain why some women seemed content to work the extra month, while others were deeply unhappy about it. When I compared a couple who was sharing and happy with another couple who was sharing but miserable, it was clear that purely economic or psychological answers were not enough. Gradually, I felt the need to explore how *deep* within each man and woman gender ideology goes. I felt the need to understand the ways in which some men and women seemed to be egalitarian "on top" but traditional "underneath," or the other way around. I tried to sensitize myself to the difference between shallow ideologies (ideologies which were contradicted by deeper feelings) and deep ideologies (which were reinforced by such feelings). I explored how each person reconciled ideology with his or her own behavior, that of a partner, and with the other realities of life. I felt the need to explore what I call loosely "gender strategies."

The Top and Bottom of Gender Ideology

A gender strategy is a plan of action through which a person tries to solve problems at hand, given the cultural notions of gender at play. To pursue a gender strategy, a man draws on beliefs about manhood and womanhood, beliefs that are forged in early childhood and thus anchored to deep emotions. He makes a connection between how he thinks about his manhood, what he feels about it, and what he does. It works in the same way for a woman.

A woman's gender ideology determines what sphere she *wants* to identify with (home or work) and how much power in the marriage she wants to have (less, more, or the same amount). I found three types of ideology of marital roles:—traditional, transitional, and egalitarian. Even though she works, the "pure" traditional wants to identify with her activities at home (as a wife, a mother, a neighborhood mom), wants her husband to base his at work and wants less power than he. The traditional man wants the same. The "pure" egalitarian, as the type emerges here, wants to identify with the same spheres her husband does, and to have an equal amount of power in the marriage. Some want the couple to be jointly oriented to the home, others to their careers, or both of them to jointly hold some balance between the two. Between the traditional and the egalitarian is the transitional, any one of a variety of types of blending of the two. But, in contrast to the traditional, a transitional woman wants to identify with her role at work as well as at home. Unlike the egalitarian, she believes her husband should base his identity more on work than she does. A typical transitional wants to identify *both* with the caring for the home, and with helping her husband earn money, but wants her husband to focus on earning a living. A typical transitional man is all for his wife working, but expects her to take the main responsibility at home too. Most men and women I talked with were "transitional." At least, transitional ideas came out when I asked people directly what they believed.

In actuality, I found there were contradictions between what people said they believed about their marital roles and how they seemed to *feel* about those roles. Some men seemed to me egalitarian "on top" but traditional "underneath." Others seemed traditional on top and egalitarian underneath.[5] Often a person attached deep feelings to his or her gender ideology in response to what I call early "cautionary tales" from childhood, as well as in response to his or her present situation. Sometimes these feelings *reinforced* the surface of a person's gender ideology. For example, the fear Nancy Holt was to feel of becoming a submissive mother, a "doormat," as she felt her mother had been, infused emotional steam into her belief that her husband Evan should do half the second shift.

On the other hand, the dissociation Ann Myerson was to feel from her successful career undermined her ostensible commitment both to that career and to sharing the second shift. Ann Myerson's surface ideology was egalitarian; she *wanted* to feel as engaged with her career as her husband was with his. This was her view of the "proper experience" of her career. She thought she *should* love her work. She *should* think it mattered. In fact, as she confessed in a troubled tone, she didn't love her work and didn't think it mattered. She felt a conflict between what she thought she ought to feel (according to her surface ideology)—emotionally involved in her career—and what she did feel—uninvolved with it. Among other things, her gender strategy was a way of trying to resolve that conflict.

The men and women I am about to describe seem to have developed their gender ideology by unconsciously synthesizing certain cultural ideas with feelings about their past. But they also developed their ideology by taking opportunity into account. Sometime in adolescence they matched their personal assets against the opportunities available to men or women of their type; they saw which gender ideology best fit their circumstances, and—often regardless of their upbringing—they identified with a certain version of manhood or womanhood. It "made sense" to them. It felt like "who they were." For example, a woman sizes up her education, intelligence, age, charm, sexual attractiveness, her dependency needs, her aspirations, and she matches these against her perception of how women like her are doing in the job market and the "marriage market." What jobs could she get? What men? What are her chances for an equal marriage, a traditional marriage, a happy marriage, any marriage? Half-consciously, she assesses her chances—chances of an interesting, well-paid job are poor? her courtship pool has very traditional men? She takes these into account. *Then a* certain gender ideology, let's say a traditional one, will "make sense" to her. She will embrace the ideology that suits her perception of her chances. She holds to a certain version of womanhood (the "wilting violet," say). She identifies with its customs (men opening doors), and symbols (lacy dress, long hair, soft handshakes, and lowered eyes). She tries to develop its "ideal personality" (deferential, dependent), not because this is what her parents taught her, not because this corresponds to how she naturally "is," but because these particular

---

5 In a 1978 national survey, Joan Huber and Glenna Spitze found that 78 percent of husbands think that if husband and wife both work full time, they should share housework equally (*Sex Stratification: Children, Housework and Jobs.* New York: Academic Press, 1983). In fact, the husbands of working wives at most average a third of the work at home.

customs now *make sense* of her resources and of her overall situation in a stalled revolution. The same principle applies to men. However whole-hearted or ambivalent, a person's gender ideology tends to fit their situation.

Gender Strategies

When a man tries to apply his gender ideology to the situations that face him in real life, unconsciously or not he pursues a gender strategy.[6] He outlines a course of action. He might become a "superdad"—working long hours and keeping his child up late at night to spend time with him or her. Or he might cut back his hours at work. Or he might scale back housework and spend less time with his children. Or he might actively try to share the second shift.

The term "strategy" refers both to his plan of action and to his emotional preparations for pursuing it. For example, he may require himself to suppress his career ambitions to devote himself more to his children, or suppress his responsiveness to his children's appeals in the course of steeling himself for the struggle at work. He might harden himself to his wife's appeals, or he might be the one in the family who "lets" himself see when a child is calling out for help.

In the families I am about to describe, then, I have tried to be sensitive to the fractures in gender ideology, the conflicts between what a person thinks he or she ought to feel and what

he or she does feel, and to the emotional work it takes to fit a gender ideal when inner needs or outer conditions make it hard.

As this social revolution proceeds, the problems of the two-job family will not diminish. If anything, as more couples work two jobs these problems will increase. If we can't return to traditional marriage, and if we are not to despair of marriage altogether, it becomes vitally important to understand marriage as a magnet for the strains of the stalled revolution, and to understand gender strategies as the basic dynamic of marriage.

The Economy of Gratitude

The interplay between a man's gender ideology and a woman's implies a deeper interplay between his gratitude toward her, and hers toward him. For how a person wants to identify himself or herself influences what, in the back and forth of a marriage, will seem like a gift and what will not. If a man doesn't think it fits the kind of "man" he wants to be to have his wife earn more than he, it may become his "gift" to her to "bear it" anyway. But a man may also feel like the husband I interviewed, who said, "When my wife began earning more than me I thought I'd struck gold!" In this case his wife's salary is the gift, not his capacity to accept it "anyway." When couples struggle, it is seldom simply over who does what. Far more often, it is over the giving and receiving of gratitude.

---

6 The concept of "gender strategy" is an adaptation of Ann Swidler's notion of "strategies of action." In "Culture in Action—Symbols and Strategies," *American Sociological Review* 51 (1986): 273–86, Swidler focuses on how the individual uses aspects of culture (symbols, rituals, stories) as "tools" for constructing a line of action. Here, I focus on aspects of culture that bear on our ideas of manhood and womanhood, and I focus on our emotional preparation for and the emotional consequences of our strategies.

Family Myths

As I watched couples in their own homes, I began to realize that couples sometimes develop "family myths"—versions of reality that obscure a core truth in order to manage a family tension.[7] Evan and Nancy Holt managed an irresolvable conflict over the distribution of work at home through the myth that they now "shared it equally." Another couple unable to admit to the conflict came to believe "we aren't competing over who will take responsibility at home; we're just dreadfully busy with our careers." Yet another couple jointly believed that the husband was bound hand and foot to his career "because his work demanded it," while in fact his careerism covered the fact that they were avoiding each other. Not all couples need or have family myths. But when they do arise, I believe they often manage key tensions which are linked, by degrees, to the long hand of the stalled revolution.

After interviewing couples for a while, I got into the practice of offering families who wanted it my interpretations of how they fit into the broader picture I was seeing and what I perceived were their strategies for coping with the second shift. Couples were often relieved to discover they were not alone, and were encouraged to open up a dialogue about the inner and outer origins of their troubles.

Many couples [I met] worked long hours at their jobs and their children were very young: in this way their lot was unusually hard. But in one crucial way they had it far easier than most two-job couples in America: most were middle class. Many also worked for a company that embraced progressive policies toward personnel, generous benefits and salaries. If *these* middle-class couples find it hard to juggle work and family life, many other two-job families across the nation—who earn less, work at less flexible, steady, or lucrative jobs, and rely on poorer daycare—are likely to find it much harder still.

Anne Machung and I began interviewing in 1976, and accomplished most of our interviews in the early 1980s. I finished in 1988. About half of my later interviews were follow-up contacts with couples we'd talked to earlier; the other half were new.

How much had changed from 1976 to 1988? In practical terms, little: most women I interviewed in the late 1980s still do the lion's share of work at home, do most of the daily chores and take responsibility for running the home. But something was different, too. More couples *wanted* to share and imagined that they did. Dorothy Sims, a personnel director, summed up this new blend of idea and reality. She eagerly explained to me that she and her husband Dan "shared all the housework," and that they were "equally involved in raising their nine-month-old son Timothy." Her husband, a refrigerator salesman, applauded her career and "was more pleased than threatened by her high salary"; he urged her to develop such competencies as reading ocean maps, and calculating interest rates

---

7 For the term *family myth* I am indebted to Antonio J. Ferreira, "Psychosis and Family Myth," *American Journal of Psychotherapy* 21 (1967): 186–225.

(which she'd so far "resisted learning") because these days "a woman should." But one evening at dinner, a telling episode occurred. Dorothy had handed Timothy to her husband while she served us a chicken dinner. Gradually, the baby began to doze on his father's lap. "When do you want me to put Timmy to bed?" Dan asked. A long silence followed during which it occurred to Dorothy—then, I think, to her husband—that this seemingly insignificant question hinted to me that it was *she,* not he, or "they," who usually decided such matters. Dorothy slipped me a glance, put her elbows on the table, and said to her husband in a slow, deliberate voice, "So, what do *we* think?"

When Dorothy and Dan described their "typical days," their picture of sharing grew even less convincing. Dorothy worked the same nine-hour day at the office as her husband. But she came home to fix dinner and to tend Timmy while Dan fit in a squash game three nights a week from six to seven (a good time for his squash partner). Dan read the newspaper more often and slept longer.

Compared to the early interviews, women in the later interviews seemed to speak more often in passing of relationships or marriages that had ended for some other reason but of which it "was also true" that he "didn't lift a finger at home." Or the extra month alone did it. One divorcee who typed part of this manuscript echoed this theme when she explained, "I was a potter and lived with a sculptor for eight years. I cooked, shopped, and cleaned because his art 'took him longer.' He said it was fair because he worked harder. But we both worked at home, and I could see that if anyone worked longer hours I did, because I earned less with my pots than he earned with his sculpture. That was *hard* to live with, and that's really why we ended."

Some women moved on to slightly more equitable arrangements in the early 1980s, doing a bit less of the second shift than the working mothers I talked to in the late 1970s. Comparing two national surveys of working couples, F. T. Juster found the male slice of the second shift rose from 20 percent in 1965 to 30 percent in 1981, and my study may be a local reflection of this slow national trend.[8] But women like Dorothy Sims, who simply add to their extra month a year a new illusion that they aren't doing it, represent a sad alternative to the woman with the flying hair—the woman who doesn't think that's who she is.

---

8 Juster, F. T., "A Note on Recent Change in Time Use," *Studies in the Measurement of Time Allocation.* Edited by F. T. Juster and Frank F. Stafford (Ann Arbor: Institute for Social Research, 1986).

37

Markets, Marriages, and Other Mates: The Problem of Power⋆

PAULA ENGLAND AND BARBARA STANEK KILBOURNE

What is the distribution of power between husbands and wives or other heterosexual cohabitants, and what explains this distribution? This is as central a question to the study of the family as the distribution of authority is to the study of bureaucracies. After offering a definition of power and reviewing empirical research on marital power, we criticize past theorizing about power among mates. Writing by many sociologists, Marxists, and feminists has taken the link between men's higher earnings and their greater marital power to be so obvious that little theoretical explanation is needed. By contrast, neoclassical economists have ignored power differentials within the family. We suggest that neither approach is satisfactory, and seek to problematize power among mates rather than to assume it as an obvious consequence of earnings or to ignore it.

We propose an understanding of power among mates that is presented in four propositions. They explain why men generally have more power than women, and why power flows from earnings more than from domestic work. ⋆ ⋆ ⋆ Specifically, we suggest that domestic contributions are less effective in producing marital power than earnings because of (1) cultural forces that

---

⋆ First printed in 1990; from *Beyond the Marketplace: Rethinking Economy and Society*.

devalue traditionally female work and encourage women to be altruistic, (2) the fact that the beneficiaries of much domestic work are children rather than men, (3) the fact that some domestic work involves making investments that are specific to a particular relationship rather than "general," and (4) the fact that even "general" investments in domestic skills are less "liquid" than earnings because they do not ensure survival until one finds another partner.

★ ★ ★

⫼ DEFINING POWER

We begin with a definition of social power. "Social" denotes that the power has effects on at least one other person. One has more social power to the extent that one's objective situation allows the advance of one's own wishes even when this is detrimental to another person's wishes. The other we are concerned with is the spouse or cohabitant. Defining power in terms of an objective situation that allows one to advance one's own interest against another's interest permits us to distinguish between having power and exercising that power. That is, the definition admits the possibility that individuals will sometimes fail to fully exercise the power made possible by their objective position because of altruism, an egalitarian or patriarchal ideology, or a choice to leave the relationship rather than exercise power within it.

⫼ EMPIRICAL EVIDENCE ON
⫼ POWER IN MARRIAGES

Sociologists have used several approaches to measuring marital power. One approach begins by identifying a number of decision-making areas. Within each of these, the respondent is asked to report who usually makes the final decision governing this matter, with possible responses such as "husband always," "husband usually," "half and half," "wife usually," and "wife always." An early study of this genre was Blood and Wolfe's (1960) exploration of decision-making areas that included what job the husband should take, which automobile to purchase, whether or not to purchase life insurance, where to go on vacation, what house or apartment to choose, and whether or not the wife should begin or quit work outside the home. There are several problems with this method of measuring power. First, since husbands and wives typically specialize in different areas, any global measure of marital power (summed over all decision-making areas) is sensitive to which areas are chosen for study. Further, the researcher may mistake the importance of different areas to spouses' utilities, and spouses may themselves differ in this, so that it is not clear how to weight the topical areas to compute an overall measure of power. Finally, the fact that one party makes more decisions does not necessarily mean that the other has less power. Indeed, the party with more power may relegate many minor decisions to the less powerful party because of a preference to avoid menial decisions. These problems have contributed to a second strategy to measure marital power. Here respondents identify areas of conflict in the marriage, and then report who usually "wins" in these areas.

Whatever their method of measurement, sociological studies generally find that, on average, husbands have more power than wives, that male power is stronger when the wife is exclusively a homemaker than when she is employed outside the home, and that male power is less extreme when women have higher earnings. We accept this empirical generalization, but believe that it requires more theoretical interpretation than past writers have offered.

★ ★ ★

DETERMINANTS OF POWER AMONG MATES: FOUR EXPLANATIONS

Our goal is to explain why earnings provide power more readily than domestic work (in which we include fertility, child rearing, the work of making emotional or sexual accommodations to a partner, and housework), and, hence, why men have more marital power than women.

Our argument here takes the typical division of labor by sex as given, though a few words on its explanation seem warranted. One way to categorize writings that purport to explain sex differentiation is in terms of whether they see roles in the family or in employment as having greater causal priority. Many neoclassical economists have seen women's household role (which they believe to be determined by exogenous social or biological forces) as explaining the intermittent employment and low pay of women within the labor force. Another view of the life cycle also begins the causal arrow within the household, seeing early life decisions about both employment and household behavior as the determinants of adult roles within both arenas. Some sociological work emphasizing socialization agrees with this view that

social forces are exogenous to employment outcomes. Other economists and sociologists have reversed the causal arrow, pointing to discrimination against women in labor markets as affecting career plans and the division of labor at home. We would stress that the position of men and women in households and in employment has reciprocal effects. ★ ★ ★ Such reciprocal links do not completely rule out change; indeed, they mean that change in either arena will be the precursor of change in the other.

Our discussion focuses on the way in which the typical division of labor by sex across both household and employment sectors affects marital power. Yet we do not deny the possibility that marital power may affect sex differentiation as well. Some sex differentiation may *result* from men's power to avoid a more equal sharing of household and career roles, though this causal direction is not our focus.

The sexual division of labor puts men and women in different structural positions. By "structural positions" we refer to roles whose characteristics transcend those of any particular incumbents. Examples of structural positions are "homemaker," "earner," or more specific job or occupational categories. The typical marriage features men contributing the bulk of earnings and women contributing either exclusively domestic work or some combination of such work and a relatively small paycheck. Why does this arrangement yield more power to men than women?

We propose an answer that draws on a neoclassical model of implicit contracts, sociological exchange theory (Cook 1987), game theory (Schotter and Schwodiauer 1980; Binmore et al. 1986), a sociological view in which habits and preferences flow from one's structural roles (Kohn and Schooler 1983), and a view of culture taken from interdisciplinary radical/cultural feminist theory (England 1990, Chapter 6). Although we have criticized theorizing about marital power offered by writers working in some of these traditions, we think that they have much to offer the study of marital power. Let us preview the argument we present below: One's power depends on how much one contributes to a relationship, the ease with which one could leave the relationship and take the fruits of such contributions, the extent to which one is inclined toward self-interested bargaining, how much one's contributions are valued by the partner, how this compares to the value the partner places on what could be had outside this relationship, and how one compares what is had within the current relationship to what could be had outside it. The four propositions are discussed in turn below.

The Role of Culture: Devaluation of the Traditionally Feminine Sphere and Differences between "Male" and "Female" Values

We argued above that a devaluation of tasks traditionally done by women is an unacknowledged assumption of much writing on marital power, and suggested that writers contribute to such a devaluation by making it invisible. We think it important to acknowledge that Western culture has privileged the traditionally male sphere, and that these values limit women's power through limiting the value men place on what women offer in relationships. Western thought features a series of dichotomies such as rational/emotional, mind/body, active/passive, good/evil, and superordinate/subordinate. In each of these dichotomies, the first category has been valued more highly and assigned to males. Thus, men may benefit from and enjoy what women provide but have been socialized to take such benefits for granted or to find them not deserving of any credit. It is striking, for example, how classical liberal thought saw the nurturance of men and children by women as outside the sphere deserving of moral status but rather as something women "naturally" supplied (Benhabib 1987). It is the low valuation of their roles as well as the assignment to these roles that disadvantages women. This is overlooked when economists focus on "barriers to entry" and functionalist sociologists focus on social mobility as if they were the only possible mechanisms of group subordination. Since this cultural devaluation of everything associated with females has a long history, it is in part exogenous to, or at least jointly endogenous with, the structural and market realities we emphasize below.

In response to our cultural argument, one might ask how men get away with rewarding what women provide at less than is commensurate with the utility they themselves experience from receipt of these services. Couldn't women get their due by threatening to withdraw their services? Below we consider structural reasons why it is difficult for women to do this. But here we answer this query with another cultural argument: women seem disinclined to act in such a self-interested manner. Women hold a subcultural value system emphasizing connection and mutual altruism. Holding such a value system is not inherently subordinating, except if one's partner is more narrowly selfish. We believe that women do not bargain as far toward the margins of their power as men do because of a greater valuation of altruism, a value women wish that men would reciprocate. This cultural difference between men and women may itself be explained in part by women's experience in the structural role of nurturer. It may also, in part, be an act of resistance of women against the prevailing masculinist model of separative self that dominates our culture, and that radical/cultural feminists criticize ★ ★ ★. If there is, in some sense, a male and a female culture, an important question about power in intimate male-female relationships is what happens when these two styles are paired.

To explore this, suppose that there are two kinds of dispositions toward self and other coexisting in the social world: (1) Model "S" (for separative) deemphasizes empathy, sees self-interested behavior as natural, and takes advantage of being in a powerful bargaining position when it occurs. (2) Model "C" (for connective) emphasizes the rewards of emotional connection, and takes both one's own and a connected other's utility as roughly of equal importance, regardless of who is in a stronger bargaining position. One way to put this is that those who practice model S fit economic and exchange theories better than those who practice model C. Suppose further that existing social structures and socialization practices produce more males practicing S and more females practicing C. To oversimplify, suppose that all men practice S and all women practice C.

Under these assumptions, marriage would feature men pressing their bargaining harder and getting more of what they wanted as a function of the amount of their earnings relative to their wives' earnings. The extent to which wives pushed for their own way at the expense of a partner's would be uncorrelated with their earnings. Overall, the fit of men's behavior with exchange theory would be sufficient to produce the correlation between earnings and power observed in the literature, though the correlation would be less than if women, too, practiced S. In such a situation, there are two ways for women to rectify the power imbalance. The first way is through increasing their earnings and using them for bargaining power, but this requires that they abandon model C, which they do not want to do. Their second option is to persuade men to adopt model C with them, but this is a "hard sell" to men already thinking in S terms. We might think of this as the altruistic self's version of the prisoner's dilemma. That is, Model C is disadvantageous only when you cannot get your partner to collude with you and practice it too.

★ ★ ★

Women's Contributions to Children's Well-Being

If we think of marriage as an exchange in which men offer earnings and women offer household work, the language suggests that men receive the benefits of women's domestic work (e.g., Hartmann 1981). However, in the case of child rearing, the direct recipients of the work are children, not men. This work seems less something that women offer their husbands as part of reciprocal exchange, and more something they freely offer their children.

Yet several factors mitigate against work for children translating into marital power for women. First, an exchange or game-theoretic perspective implies that something one offers one's partner creates power on the assumption that offering it implies the ability to retract it. But since women usually retain custody of children in divorces, any benefits men perceive from what women do for their children will not be lost even if the marriage ends. Women cannot derive power from a credible threat to stop taking care of the children when men know that the woman's bond to and commitment to the children transcends the relationship to the men. Indeed, historian Gerda Lerner (1986) speculates that the origins of patriarchy may lie in the fact that women made better slaves than men precisely because they were likely to cooperate with their masters for the sake of their children.

Second, several factors militate against men placing a high value on the well-being that comes from the care of their children. Men will place value on women's child-rearing services to the extent that they are altruistic and empathic toward their children. The evidence suggests that men are much less altruistic toward children than are women. For example, Blumberg (1988) provides cross-cultural evidence that when women control family income they allocate more of it to children than do men. We suggest that the very fact that women not men do the nurturing of children creates sex differences in felt bonds of empathy and altruism with children. This explanation of women's limited marital power is an example of seeing values endogenous to one's structural role. It contrasts with the neoclassical assumption that preferences are exogenous to economic roles, and is more consistent with the view in sociology that sees one's psychology to be influenced by one's structural role (Kohn and Schooler 1983).

The Asymmetry of Relationship-Specific vs. Portable Investments

One reason for women's lesser power in marriage is that more of the fruits of men's invest-

ments are portable outside this particular marriage whereas more of women's than men's investments after marriage are "relationship-specific." We use the term "investment" here as economists do, to indicate incurring a cost at an earlier time that yields a benefit at a later time. Costs may be pecuniary or nonpecuniary, and they may be either directly paid or opportunity costs. By "relationship-specific" we refer to investments that not only require one to be in some relationship to pay off, but that require that one stay *in the specific relationship in which the investment was made.* Thus a relationship-specific investment will not pay off in a new marriage or in a single state.

★ ★ ★

A fundamental insight of these new ideas is that parties often make investments that will continue to benefit them only if this particular exchange relationship is continued. In labor markets, workers sometimes receive on-the-job training. This training has present costs and future benefits, and thus may be seen as an investment. The training may entail directly paid expenses for materials or teachers. Even when the training is informal, it has the opportunity-cost of foregone productivity while an experienced worker teaches a new worker. These costs are the investment the employer has made in the human capital of the workers. Neoclassical theory also suggests that employees share some of these costs by accepting lower wages at first. While some on-the-job training may provide skills that one could transfer to another company, what is central in the new theories is the training that produces knowledge and skills that are useful only in this particular firm. This is called firm-specific training; in the terms we use here it is "relationship-specific" in that it is specific to the relationship between this particular employer and employee. This training makes it more likely that the worker is more productive to the employer than workers that might be newly hired (since new workers would not have this firm-specific training), and that the worker is more productive here than at other firms (since the worker has not received the specific training of other firms). Thus, both employer and employee have invested in an asset (firm-specific human capital) that pays off to either party only if the employee continues to work there. Williamson (1988) calls this a situation of "asset specificity." Because there are no workers outside the firm who have received such training and no other firms for which the present workers have received specific training, economists see a situation of bilateral monopoly to develop after the firm-specific training has occurred. Williamson (1988) calls this passage from before to after firm-specific investment the "fundamental transformation." It is the transformation into a situation in which a competitive market model is no longer fully appropriate because each side has a sort of monopoly power over the other.

★ ★ ★

Many of the things people value in marriage are a result of relationship-specific rather than general investment. To call an investment relationship-specific means that it has value only within the current relationship, and would be of no benefit outside a relationship or in a different one. Firm-specific training is the analog in labor markets. In marriage or cohabitation, once such investments have been undertaken, both partners are likely to be better off within this relationship than they would be were they to start over with someone else. Marital invest-

ments that transfer poorly to a new relationship involve learning to deal with the idiosyncrasies of one particular partner, such as learning his or her preferences and personal history, forming attachments with in-laws, learning this partner's sexual preferences, learning how to resolve disagreements with this partner, or contributing to the felt solidarity of the marriage by investments in children. To the extent that such learning takes time and/or resources that could be profitably or enjoyably spent doing other things it has costs and can thus be viewed as an investment. Such relationship-specific investments mitigate against rapid turnover among partners just as firm-specific training mitigates against employee turnover. As with employer and employee, both parties in a marriage have an incentive to make some long-term "contract" to protect their relationship-specific investments.

★ ★ ★

Given the benefits of some long-term arrangement over the spot market, and the aforementioned problems of formal contracts, marriages can be seen as implicit contracts. This refers to the informal understandings grounded in each party's incentive to remain in and conscientiously contribute to the marriage by virtue of past relationship-specific investments. An interesting feature of relationship-specific investments (whether in employment or marriage) is that they provide incentives that "bind" *both* partners, regardless of which partner has made the investment. For example, once an employee has learned to use equipment that is idiosyncratic to one firm, this gives the firm a motivation to pay this employee more than they would a new person, thus also providing the employee with an incentive to stay with this firm. Both parties are more "bound" the more relationship-specific investments have been made, *regardless of which side paid for the investment*. Thus, in a marriage, relationship-specific investments by either partner increase the durability of the marriage.

Investments are called "general" rather than "relationship-specific" if they produce benefits outside this particular relationship. The analog in the analysis of paid employment is "general human capital," which refers to education or vocational training that provides skills of use in many different firms. When looking at marriage, there are two kinds of investments in human capital that will benefit the marriage but that are not specific to this marital relationship. The first is one's development of skills at aspects of child rearing, emotional work, and household work that could just as easily transfer to exchange in another marital relationship because they do not entail learning anything idiosyncratic to this partner. *Note, then, that although we argue below that more of the homemaker's than earner's role entails relationship-specific investments, this does not mean that all aspects of domestic work are relationship-specific.* The skills learned at housecleaning are as portable to another marriage as typing skills are to another job. A second type of investment that is portable back into the marriage market is the investment in earning power that is represented by job search, schooling, or the on-the-job training of career building. Whether or not such investments are firm-specific, their fruits are not specific to *this* marriage. Except for the typically small and badly enforced amounts of child support one may pay, earning power is entirely portable out of relationships.

Although in marriages, both partners make general and relationship-specific investments, in general, women make proportionately more of the latter. For example, women concern themselves more with the emotional work of learning this partners' idiosyncrasies. Of what use is this if the relationship terminates? Women typically invest more time forming emotional attachments to in-laws than do men. These do little for the solidarity of a future marriage. Women invest much more in the socialization of children. If one is divorced, having well-adjusted children may be appreciated by both oneself and a new partner, but not having had children might make one more valued on the marriage market and in a new marriage. Whereas women focus on these relationship-specific investments, men's general investments build portable earning power. Investments in earnings (such as schooling, on-the-job training, job search) lack specificity to this particular marriage and benefit the man whether he stays in this marriage or not.

This asymmetry in which women make proportionally less general or portable investments contributes to men's power in marriages. Both sociological exchange theory and game theory suggest that the better one's alternatives outside the relationship, and the worse one's partner's alternatives, the more one can afford to risk the other partner leaving by bargaining harder within the marriage. Game theorists express this in terms of "threat points." The threat points of a bargaining situation determine what each person would "walk away with" (and without) if the bargaining over how to allocate the surplus from the relationship-specific investment breaks down and the parties walk away from the relationship. Thus, one's threat points are more advantageous the more one's investments have been portable.

★ ★ ★

Imperfect Capital Markets and the Limited Liquidity of Women's General Domestic Investments

Women's domestic role lessens their power, not only because it entails relationship-specific investments not portable to a new relationship, but also because even *general* (rather than relationship-specific) investments in domestic skills are less "liquid" than investments in earning power. As we noted, learning domestic skills is not all a relationship-specific investment. The "on-the-job training" of being a homemaker may teach one to keep an attractive house, budget money well, develop the best in children, be a good listener and lover, and be a gracious entertainer. These skills enhance one's desirability on the "marriage market" because they are transferable to a new relationship. Yet even if there were no inequality between men and women in amount of relationship-specific investment, homemakers would still be disadvantaged in power because general investments in being a good marital partner are less "liquid" than general investments in earning power. If one leaves a marriage having made general investments in earnings, one can survive without another marriage. But if one has made general investments in skills as a marital partner, one needs to find a new partner on the marriage market to "cash in" these investments. This requires a period of search. One of the costs of marital search is the foregone income from a partner during the period of singleness.

(The analog in labor markets is the foregone earnings while one is unemployed looking for a job.) This particular search cost is less important to someone who has their own earnings while reentering the marriage market. Underlying this argument is an assumed hierarchy of needs: one can go without emotional benefits of marriage for a while during search, but one cannot meet even the most basic needs of food and shelter without earnings. This factor makes leaving a marriage more detrimental for women than for men, owing to women's absent or lower earnings. Women's "threat points" and ability to bargain within the marriage are adversely affected.

★ ★ ★

In sum, women's domestic investments often require *some* marriage even though not *this* marriage to yield their benefits in exchange. This disadvantages women's marital power, though less so than if their domestic work entailed only relationship-specific investments. Either kind of domestic investments limits women's ability to leave marriages, and hence reduces their bargaining power within.

OUTCOMES OF CHANGES IN WOMEN'S POWER: EXIT, VOICE, OR LOYALTY?

The link between earnings and power implies that recent dramatic increases in married women's employment should have increased women's average marital power. Since, compared to men, women's earnings are still less and their domestic contributions still greater, we would expect women's power to be less than men's but to be more than previously. At present this is a conjecture since data using a similar instrument to measure power at two points in time are not available. One thing that might make us doubt the increase in women's power is the fact that as women have increased their employment and earnings, men have increased the time they spend in domestic work only marginally, and, as a result, women generally enjoy less leisure than men (Miller and Garrison 1982; Shelton forthcoming). If housework is seen as onerous and leisure as enjoyable, one would expect women to use some of their new power to persuade men to do more housework. But the adjustment to female employment is generally a decrease in total housework done, rather than a substantial increase in husbands' participation. ★ ★ ★

The double burden of household and paid work of many women makes one wonder if women's well-being has really increased with the presumed increase in female power in marriage. The possibility that women's well-being in marriage could fail to increase while their marital power increased reminds us of the usefulness of defining power as the structural *ability* to act in one's own interest even against the interest of another rather than as the *outcome* of having advanced one's own interest at the expense of another's. That is, various factors such as an altruistic ideology or an acceptance of patriarchal values may prevent one from exercising one's power within the relationship and make it more likely that one will leave the relationship rather than pushing one's power within the marriage as far as it can go. Our discussion of women's versus men's culture suggests that women may leave relationships with men who practice a separative model of self hoping to find

a man who will join them in jointly practicing the model of an altruistic connective self.

Our understanding of this anomaly is aided by the insights of Albert Hirschman's (1970) classic book, *Exit, Voice, and Loyalty.* He pointed out three options people have when they are dissatisfied with a relationship: They may exit (leave the relationship), voice their disagreement through some bargaining process, or remain stoically loyal. For example, if parents are unhappy with the public schools in their city, their options are passive loyalty, an exit from the school district (either through moving their home or using private schools), or voicing their concerns through activism in things such as School Board elections and the PTA. ★ ★ ★

This distinction between exit, voice, and loyalty can be usefully applied to marriage. During the 1950s, women's limited marital power meant that even those deeply dissatisfied with their marriages generally chose loyalty because their only option was destitution. Men's greater power allowed them to respond to dissatisfaction either through "exit" (divorce or separation) or a bargaining "voice" in which their greater power usually brought them concessions. The low divorce rate of the period suggests that men generally chose "voice."

If women's power has increased due to their increased employment, women could choose either to leave unsatisfactory marriages (exit) or to utilize their new power by bargaining harder for what they want in marriage. That the two options of voice and exit go hand in hand is implied in our discussion above. We highlighted the fact that portable resources allowing one to lose less if a relationship is left also increase one's bargaining power in the relationship. The anomaly of women's continued responsibility for most household work has cast doubt on whether women are using "voice" to bargain for a more equitable distribution of work. The steep increase in divorce, correlated as it is temporally with increases in women's employment, suggests that women may be using their new power to exit more than to change their current marriages. This view is buttressed by evidence that, at least in the last decade, women predominate over men as the partner who suggests divorces and separations. Casual observation suggests that this female predominance is greater among younger couples. This would be expected from our discussion above, since younger cohorts of women have more continuous employment and higher earning prospects, and hence have more marital power to be used in either exit or voice.

Why are women using their increased power more often for exit rather than voice within marriages? To guide our answer, we might first ask what women would most like to change about their marriages if they were to use voice. We believe they would most like to change the degree to which men provide the emotional intimacy of talking about and listening to feelings ★ ★ ★ and the degree of men's participation in domestic work. Both of these things would require a significant change in the men's roles. One result of women using exit rather than voice is to protect men's roles from having to change, leading to a profound asymmetry in gender role change such that men's roles are being redefined much less than women's (England and Swoboda 1988). Thus, the question of

why exit is used rather than voice may reduce to the question of why men's roles are so much harder to change than women's even in the face of changes in some of the objective, structural arrangements of power.

★ ★ ★

This trend of large changes in women's roles, few changes in men's roles, and a high divorce rate has two important consequences. One is a reduction in the economic well-being of children who are increasingly disconnected from the earnings of men. ★ ★ ★

A second consequence of the asymmetric nature of gender role is the demise of traditionally female values of nurturing and connection. Without men joining women in a connective, altruistic notion of self, women are able to gain power only through entering traditionally male roles. Women are unable or unwilling to use their new power to bring men into traditionally female activities. The march of rationalization (to use Weberian terms), commodification (to use Marxist terms), extension of market relations (to use neoclassical terms), or masculinist values (to use feminist terms) is thus advanced rather than altered by women's changing roles. This follows from the fact that labor markets are even less organized around principles of altruism and reciprocity than are families. This consequence reminds us of the tension between liberal feminism, that would open all roles formerly monopolized by men to women, and radical/cultural feminism that would do this as well as elevate the traditionally female principles of connection, altruism, and mutual nurturance to a higher place in our priorities and reward system. Under current conditions, women's increased power results from and enhances the liberal feminist program but not the radical/cultural feminist program. If women are to live with men, the latter would require a profound change in men's roles and a redefinition of power even as women increase their relative power.

CONCLUSION

To summarize, we have argued that women's lower earnings and greater involvement in domestic work disadvantage them in marital power because (1) our culture devalues traditionally female activities and encourages men but not women to bargain self-interestedly, (2) much of women's work contributes to the well-being of children rather than men, (3) fewer investments of women than men are general rather than relationship-specific, and (4) even women's general investments lack liquidity when they can transfer to a new marriage but not provide support outside of a marriage. Given the continuing division of labor in which women do more domestic work and men have larger earnings, these factors explain why men have more marital power than women, while employed women have more marital power than homemakers. However, power implies a potential to either leave a relationship or bargain for change within it. As women's employment has brought them more power, it appears they are using this power more to leave relationships than to change them. This may be because women have thus far been unable to change the male gender role to involve more traditionally female tasks of child rearing, housework, and emotional work.

REFERENCES

Benhabib, Seyla. 1987. "The Generalized and the Concrete Other: The Kohlberg-Gilligan Controversy and Moral Theory." Pp. 154–178 in *Women and Moral Theory*, edited by Eva Feder Kittay and Diana T. Meyers. Totowa, NJ: Rowman & Littlefield.

Binmore, Ken, Ariel Rubinstein, and Asher Wolinsky. 1986. "The Nash Bargaining Solution in Economic Modelling." *Rand Journal of Economics* 17:176–188.

Blumberg, Rae Lesser. 1988. "Income under Female versus Male Control: Hypotheses from a Theory of Gender Stratification and Data from the Third World." *Journal of Family Issues* 9:51–84.

Cook, Karen. (ed.) 1987. *Social Exchange Theory*. Beverly Hills, Sage.

England, Paula. 1992. *Comparable Worth: Theories and Evidence*. New York: Aldine de Gruyter.

England, Paula and Diane Swoboda. 1988. "The Asymmetry of Contemporary Gender Role Change." *Free Inquiry in Creative Sociology* 16:157–161.

Hartmann, Heidi. 1981. "The Unhappy Marriage of Marxism and Feminism: Toward a More Progressive Union." Pp. 1–41 in *Women and Revolution*, edited by Lydia Sargent. Boston: South End Press.

Hirschman, Albert O. 1970. *Exit, Voice, and Loyalty*. Cambridge: Harvard University Press.

Kohn, Melvin and Carmi Schooler (with J. Miller, K. Miller, and R. Schoenberg). 1983.

Work and Personality: An Inquiry into the Impact of Social Stratification. Norwood, NJ: Ablex.

Lerner, Gerda. 1986. *The Creation of Patriarchy.* New York: Oxford University Press.

————. 1980. "Marriage and Household Decision-Making: A Bargaining Analysis." *International Economic Review* 21:31–44.

Miller, Joanne and Howard H. Garrison. 1982. "Sex Roles: The Division of Labor at Home and in the Workplace." *Annual Review of Sociology* 8:237–262.

Schotter, Andrew and Gerhard Schwodiauer. 1980. "Economics and the Theory of Games: A Survey." *Journal of Economic Literature* 18:479–527.

Shelton, Beth Anne. 1991. *Women, Men and Time: Gender Differences in Paid Work, House Work and Leisure.* Westport, CT: Greenwood Press.

Williamson, Oliver. 1988. "The Economics and Sociology of Organization: Promoting a Dialogue." Pp. 159–186 in *Industries, Firms, and Jobs: Sociological and Economic Approaches*, edited by G. Farkas and P. England. New York: Plenum.

38

Sex and Violence★

DEBORAH RHODE

"A bit nutty, and a bit slutty." That was journalist David Brock's description of Anita Hill after her Senate testimony regarding harassment by Supreme Court nominee Clarence Thomas. Such characterizations, somewhat more tactfully expressed, are common in cases involving sexual abuse. When the issue is harassment, acquaintance rape, or domestic violence, it is often the victim whose conduct is on trial.[1]

Matters could, of course, be worse. And have been. For most of this nation's history, most sexual abuse went unnamed, unreported, unchallenged, and unchanged. Until the last quarter-century, America had no legal term or conceptual cubbyhole for sexual harassment. There also were no rape crisis policies or battered-women's shelters, no studies on the frequency of acquaintance rape or spousal abuse, and no discussion of the link between pornography and sexual violence. All this has changed. Yet longstanding patterns of denial remain much the same. Many men and a depressingly large number of

---

★ First published in 1997; from *Speaking of Sex: The Denial of Gender Inequality.*

1 David Brock, "The Real Anita Hill," *American Spectator* (March 1992): 18.

women still discount the problem, victimize the victims, and resist the most plausible solutions.

Moreover, even those who acknowledge that sexual abuse is a serious problem often fail to see its connection to broader patterns of sexual inequality. Many Americans perceive sexual harassment, acquaintance rape, and nonviolent pornography as issues of sex, or perhaps bad sex, but not of subordination. By contrast, serious domestic assaults, stranger rapes, and slasher porn are viewed as examples of violence, not sex. What falls through the cracks are issues of power. We fail to see sexual abuse as a strategy of dominance, exclusion, control, and retaliation—as a way to keep women in their place and out of men's. Until we acknowledge the true dynamics of sexualized violence, we cannot adequately address its consequences.

||| SEXUAL HARASSMENT

Shortly after the Hill-Thomas Senate hearings, a celebrated cartoon featured a puzzled woman questioning her male coworker. "Why don't men get it? I mean how would you like it if I made lewd remarks, described scenes from porn movies or patted your behind?" He responded: "How much for all three?" This gap between men's perceptions and women's experience emerged clearly during Clarence Thomas' confirmation proceedings. Hearing Hill, and hearing her not being heard, was a unique occasion for collective consciousness raising.[2]

Yet the outpouring of personal narratives and legal complaints that followed Hill's testimony also revealed a countercurrent of denial. This resistance centers around a few basic themes:

denial that a serious problem of harassment exists ("It doesn't happen much, or it doesn't happen here");

denial that women are seriously injured ("So what if it happened?");

denial that men are responsible for women's injuries ("She provoked, enjoyed, accepted, or asked for it");

denial that legal sanctions are the answer ("You can't legislate morality," and trying to do so squelches free speech, office romances, and decent working relationships).

A closer look at these responses reveals both our progress and its limits. For centuries, women experienced harassment, but only *they* suffered the consequences: now men who harass bear some of the costs. Those in positions of power—politicians, employers, coworkers—must increasingly listen to injured women. The problem is that too many Americans still don't hear what is being said.

The insistence that "real" harassment rarely happens is a recent variation on traditional views that it didn't happen at all. The term "sexual harassment" did not even surface until the 1970s, when courts and the Equal Employment Opportunity Commission first recognized such abuse as prohibited discrimination. American law now bans two forms of conduct: "quid pro quo" harassment, which involves

2 Steve Kelly, artist, reprinted in Charles Brooks, ed., *Best Editorial Cartoons of the Year: 1991* (New York: Pelican, 1991).

unwelcome sexual advances or demands, and work environment harassment, which involves conduct that creates an intimidating, hostile, or offensive workplace. In the classic quid pro quo case, a supervisor denies a promotion to a subordinate who rejects sexual overtures. In hostile-environment claims, individuals experience everything from physical assaults to pervasive verbal degradation. Both forms of harassment involve an abuse of power, but its motivations, perpetuators, and occupational contexts differ. Quid pro cases arise when individuals feel entitled to use their superior economic and social status to impose a sexual relationship. By contrast, hostile-environment cases often reflect a desire to exclude individuals from certain positions and to remind them of their subordinate status. Women as well as men engage in such conduct, but the vast majority—over 90 percent—of reported cases involve males harassing females.[3]

Although recent highly publicized incidents have made such harassment hard to overlook, many Americans believe that it is widely exaggerated. Goaded on by "overzealous," "hypersensitive," and "neo-Puritan" "neurotics," women reportedly are flooding the courts with frivolous complaints. In harassment cases, "you can sue anybody about anything," announces talk show host John McLaughlin. And "there's a rush to judgment . . . against the male." Men are being held "liable for a look." "Unwelcome gazing," "friendly banter," harmless "horseplay," a dirty joke, or one open display of *Playboy* supposedly will bring hordes of mincing moralists down upon unwitting culprits. According to conservative commentators like John Leo and Christina Hoff Sommers, "corporate McCarthyism" and "witch trials," are the result, while feminist "PC paranoia" is to blame.[4]

Yet if the charge is exaggeration, critics, not complainants, are the worst offenders. In sifting through thousands of pages of judicial opinions and recent research, I have yet to discover the hapless individual defending himself for a look or a single tasteless joke. What emerge instead are innumerable judicial and arbitration

---

3 See *Code of Federal Regulations,* section 1604 (1981); and cases discussed in Gillian K. Hadfield, "Rational Women: A Test for Sex-Based Harassment," *California Law Review* 83 (1995): 1151, 1158–1166. For male-female complaint ratios, see Marion Crain, "Women, Labor Unions, and Hostile Work Environment Sexual Harassment: The Untold Story," *Texas Journal of Women and the Law* 4 (1995): 9, 18–21; "Man Wins $1 Million Sex-Harassment Suit," *New York Times,* 21 May 1993, A15.

4 Waiter Christopher Arbery, "A Step Backward for Equality Principles: The 'Reasonable Woman' Standard in Title VII Hostile Work Environment Sexual Harassment Claims," *Georgia Law Review* 27 (1993): 503, 544 ("overzealous" and "hypersensitive"); Gretchen Morgenson, "May I Have the Pleasure . . . ," *National Review,* 18 November 1991, 36 (dirty joke and "hypersensitive"); Orlando Patterson, "Race, Gender and Liberal Fallacies," *New York Times,* 20 October 1991,

15 ("neopuritan"); Camille Paglia, *Vamps and Tramps* (New York: Vintage, 1994), 48 ("neurotics"); Warren Farrell, *The Myth of Male Power* (New York: Simon and Schuster, 1993), 287 ("liable for look"); John McLaughlin, quoted in Deborah Epstein, "Can a 'Dumb Ass Woman' Achieve Equality in the Workplace Running the Gauntlet of Hostile Environment Harassing Speech," *Georgetown Law Journal* 84 (1996): 399, 408; John Leo, *Two Steps Ahead of the Thought Police* (New York: Simon and Schuster, 1994), 238 ("unwelcome gazing" and *Playboy*); Katherine Dowling, "Sexual Harassment Jackpot," *Los Angeles Times,* 7 September 1994, B7; Crain, "Sexual Harassment," 39 ("banter" and "horseplay"); John Leo, "An Empty Ruling on Harassment," *U.S. News and World Report,* 29 November 1993, 20 ("McCarthyism"); Christine Hoff Sommers, *Crossfire,* 4 July 1994 ("witchhunt"); Stuart Taylor, Jr., *"Real* Sexual Harassment," *Legal Times,* 6 May 1996, 23 ("PC paranoia").

proceedings in which decisionmakers deny relief because the harassment was insufficiently "malicious" or "brutal." In many judges' view, sex discrimination law is not meant to redress the "petty slights of the hypersensitive" or to "bring about a magical transformation in the social mores of American workplaces." In order to establish liability, plaintiffs must prove severe and pervasive conduct that was unwelcome and injurious, and that a reasonable person in their situation would have found offensive. One unusually candid judge expressed the attitude that many men bring to harassment claims: "So, we will have to hear [this complaint], but the Court doesn't think too much of it."[5]

Of course, borderline cases do exist, and recent changes in cultural norms have created some genuine confusion about where the boundaries are. There have also been occasional examples of overreaction—women who are offended by photographs of a bikini-clad wife, copies of *Playboy*, a Goya portrait of a nude, or classroom lectures using sexist metaphors. But these incidents almost never result in findings of harassment, and for every one of such aberrant yet oft-cited cases, there are countless illustrations of the converse problem. Male employers and judges frequently deny relief for conduct that they find isolated or trivial but that most women would not. Examples include:

a woman whose coworker masturbated in front of her and requested that she engage in sado-masochistic acts;

a woman who, after fielding repeated sexual propositions and slaps on the buttocks, requested help from her supervisor and was asked, "What will I get for it?";

an employee whose coworkers regularly referred to women as "whore," "cunt," "pussy," and "tits," who plastered the workplace with posters of naked women, who called the plaintiff a "fat ass," and who claimed that all she needed was "a good lay";

a woman who was maced, taunted, handcuffed to a toilet, and had her head pushed underwater.

Federal judges denied all of these claims. In their view, the conduct was not sufficiently pervasive, the claimant's injuries were not sufficiently serious, or her own conduct was not sufficiently blameless.[6]

Nor are these isolated examples. Although commentators like Phyllis Schlafly insist that for the "virtuous woman," sex harassment is not a problem, the most comprehensive research consistently indicates otherwise. Over half of all women experience harassment during their academic or working lives. That figure has

5 Deborah Rhode, *Justice and Gender* (Cambridge, Mass.: Harvard Univ. Press, 1989), 235, n. 14 (cases); *Zabkowicz v. West Bend Co.*, 585 F.Supp. 635 (E. D. Wisc. 1984); *Lipsett v. Rive Mora*, 669 F.Supp. 1188 (D. C. Puerto Rico, 1987); *Rabiduse v. Osceola Refining Co.*, 805 F.2d., 611, 620–621 (7th Cir., 1984); *Henson v. City of Dundee*, 682 F.2d 897, 900 n.2 (11th Cir., 1982).

6 For examples of overreaction, see Christina Hoff Sommers, *Who Stole Feminism?* (New York: Simon and Schuster, 1994), 270–271; Andrew Blum, "Profs Sue Schools on Suspensions,"

National Law Journal, 6 June 1994, A6, A7; Barry R. Gross, "Salem in Minnesota," *Academic Questions* (Spring 1992): 67, 70–71. For denials of claims, see *Foster v. Township of Hillside,* 780 F. Supp. 1026 (D. N.J. 1992), aff'd without op. *Poster v. Hillside Police Dep't.,* 977 F.2d 567 (3d Cir., 1992); *Scott v. Sears, Roebuck, & Co.,* 798 F.2d 210, 212 (7th Cir., 1986); *Rabidue v. Osceola Refining Co.,* 805 F.2d. 611 (7th Cir., 1984); *Reed v. Shepard,* 939 F.2d 484, 486–487 (7th Cir., 1991). For further examples, see Epstein, "'Dumb Ass Woman,'" 416.

changed little over the last decade, despite a substantial increase in formal remedies. Lesbians and women of color are targets of particularly virulent conduct, and suspicion of homosexual behavior increases the risk of physical assault. Immigrants are also especially vulnerable, given their unfamiliarity with American legal norms and their fear of reprisals if they submit formal complaints. Harassing conduct is frequent even by lawyers who might be expected to know what is unlawful; some 60 percent of surveyed female attorneys report experiencing such abuse. And in branches of the military that claim "zero tolerance" for harassment, 90 percent of female personnel under age fifty indicate that they have endured it—more than half in the preceding year.[7]

For the vast majority of sex harassment complaints, underreporting, not overreaction, is the norm. Only 5 to 10 percent of women experiencing abuse make formal complaints and fewer still can afford the financial and psychological costs of litigation. In the rare successful lawsuit, damages are usually quite small, averaging only about three thousand dollars. Conservative critics who worry about legal hypochondria and who advise women to "just lighten up" should look at the data and take their own advice.[8]

Many individuals' failure to see sexual harassment as a serious problem results partly from the failure to understand its consequences. The traditional "boys will be boys" response frequently reveals the gap between men's assumptions and women's experiences. "At least you weren't raped," has been some judges' and arbitrators' response to workplace abuse. From this perspective, women like Anita Hill are at fault for trying to turn a simple flirtation into a

7 Phyllis Schlafly, quoted in Nancy C. McGlen and Karen O'Connor, *Women's Rights: The Struggle for Equality in the Nineteenth and Twentieth Centuries* (New York: Praeger, 1983), 186. For the frequency of harassment, see Epstein, " 'Dumb Ass Woman,' " 403–404; Mary P. Koss, Lisa Goodman, Angela Browne, Louise F. Fitzgerald, Gwendolyn Puryear Keita, and Nancy Felipe Russo, *No Safe Haven: Male Violence against Women at Home, at Work and in the Community* (Washington, D.C.: American Psychological Association, 1994), 112, 124–126; Louise F. Fitzgerald and Alayne J. Omerod, "Breaking Silence: The Sexual Harassment of Women in Academia and the Workplace," in Florence L. Denmark and Michelle A. Paludi, eds., *Psychology of Women: A Handbook of Issues and Theories* (Westport, Conn.: Greenwood, 1993), 558. For women of color, see Kimberle Crenshaw, "Whose Story Is It Anyway? Feminist and Antiracist Appropriations of Anita Hill," in Toni Morrison, ed., *Raging Justice, Engendering Power: Essays on Anita Hill, Clarence Thomas, and the Construction of Social Reality* (New York: Pantheon, 1992): 402. For lesbians, Beth E. Schneider, "Put Up and Shut Up: Workplace Sexual Assaults," in Pauline B. Bart and Eileen Gail Moran, eds., *Violence against Women: The Bloody Footprints* (Newbury Park, Calif.: Sage, 1993), 57, 62–63. For immigrants and other especially vulnerable groups, see National Council for Research on Women, *Sexual Harassment: Research and Resources* (New York: National Council for Research on Women, 1995), 29–32. For lawyers, see ibid., 26–27; Kerry Segrave, *The Sexual Harassment of Women in the Workplace* (Jefferson, N.C.: McFarland, 1994), 204. For military personnel, see Timothy Egan, "A Battleground of Sexual Conflict," *New York Times,* 15 November 1996, A10; Eric Schmitt, "Study Says Sex Harassment Persists at Military Academies," *New York Times,* 5 April 1995, B8; Alison Bass, "Military Remains Lair of Sexual Harassment," *San Francisco Chronicle,* 5 May 1995, 3. See Department of Defense News Briefing, *Results of the 1995 Sexual Harassment Study* (Washington, D.C.: Department of Defense, 1996).

8 For complaints, see Louise F. Fitzgerald, Suzanne Swan, and Karla Fischer, "Why Didn't She Just Report Him? The Psychological and Legal Implications of Women's Responses to Sexual Harassment," *Journal of Social Issues* 51 (1995): 117; Koss et al., *No Safe Haven,* 135; American Management Association, *Sexual Harassment: Policies and Procedures* (New York: American Management Association, 1996). For awards, see Fitzgerald, Swan, and Fischer, "Why Didn't She Just Report Him?" 123. For advice by critics, see Robert Grant, president of the American Freedom Coalition, quoted in Jane Gross, "Suffering in Silence No More, Women Fight Back on Sexual Harassment," *New York Times,* 14 July 1992.

federal case. After all, "he never touched her." If her career didn't suffer, why should his?[9]

Variations on this theme play out in men's defenses to formal sex harassment charges. "Who can tell," they complain, "where courtship stops and coercion starts?" Defenders of Senator Robert Packwood were incensed that "gender avengers" pressured the Senate Ethics Committee into punishing "crude" but innocent "office gropings." As Packwood himself put it, "I don't know how you decide ahead of time what is going to be offensive . . . If you don't try, how do you know?"[10]

Men in genuine doubt could consult any of the countless publications or training programs that report what leading research confirms: about two-thirds of surveyed women, but fewer than 15 percent of surveyed men, would find an unsolicited invitation for sex offensive. Women are also far more likely than men to object to sexist jokes and repeated requests for dates. But it should not require formal training to recognize that the conduct triggering harassment complaints rarely qualifies as harmless seduction. For example, in Packwood's case, the Senate Ethics Committee found at least eighteen instances of abuse not easily dismissed as "flirtation." As law professor Stephen Gillers observes, "Grabbing someone by surprise . . . pushing your tongue into her mouth, and put-

ting your hands on her buttocks is not ambiguous conduct. Penal codes have names for these acts: they're called sexual assault."[11]

★ ★ ★

Even when the victim wins in court, she often loses in life. The minimal remedies usually available may not compensate for risks of retaliation, such as transfers, demotion, informal blacklisting, physical threats, and vandalism. In a survey of women who filed harassment complaints, a third felt that complaining made things worse, and only a fifth believed that such complaints were handled fairly. As one summary of such studies concludes, an "assertive" response to harassment generally results in "negative outcomes" for complainants. Many of these individuals confront a no-win situation. Those who complain promptly are "whiners," or "troublemakers." Those who wait until the situation becomes unbearable are no longer credible. If the harassment was really bad, why didn't they say so sooner? Even substantial damage awards may fail to compensate for the stress, humiliation, and career suicide involved in a lawsuit. As one "successful" litigant put it, "I wouldn't really recommend this to anybody."

A further reason sexual harassment remains common is that many Americans deny the need to strengthen legal responses. Conservatives frequently see harassment law as one more

9 For judges and arbitrators, see Koss et al., *No Safe Haven,* 154; Crain, "Sexual Harassment," 55. For comments on Hill, see Camille Paglia, quoted in "Think Tank with Ben Wattenberg," *Federal News Service,* 4 November 1994, 30.

10 Robert Packwood, quoted in Peter J. Boyer, "The Ogre's Tale," *New Yorker,* 4 April 1994, 37.

11 Barbara Gutek, *Sex and the Workplace* (San Francisco: Jossey-Bass, 1985), 19; Daniel Goleman, "Sexual Harassment: It's about Power, Not Lust," *New York Times,* 22 October 1991, Cl; Robert S. Adler and Ellen R. Peirce, "The Legal, Ethical, and Social Implications of the 'Reasonable Woman' Standard in Sexual Harassment Cases," *Fordham Law Review* 61 (1993): 773, 776; Stephen Gillers, quoted in Ruth Rosen, " 'Boys Will Be Boys' No Longer Cuts It," *Los Angeles Times,* 29 April 1993, B7 (quoting Gillers).

ineffective and intrusive form of government regulation. Liberals often are troubled by the free speech implications of monitoring offensive expression. And individuals of all political persuasions worry about expanding opportunities for vindictive litigation. While these are all legitimate concerns, critics tend to exaggerate one set of problems at the expense of ignoring others.

★ ★ ★

Even with a significantly improved legal process, however, most victims are unlikely to file claims, because of the expense, embarrassment, and evidentiary hurdles. More efforts should focus on other strategies, such as clear workplace policies, well-designed educational programs, adequate legal representation, informal but unbiased complaint channels, and effective sanctions by employers.

Yet in the long run, we cannot respond adequately to sexual harassment without also responding to the institutional structures that perpetuate it. If we want to change the conditions that make women vulnerable to such abuse, we need to focus on job training, glass ceilings, affirmative action, pay equity, parental and childcare policies, and sex-role stereotypes. We also must see harassing conduct as a symptom as well as a cause of broader patterns of gender inequality. The dynamics of male entitlement, dominance, and control that foster harassment also contribute to more serious forms of abuse, such as domestic violence

and rape. Only by acknowledging these connections are we likely to deal with the cultural forces that make sexual coercion seem sexy.

||| DOMESTIC VIOLENCE

The reason I don't believe [you need a protective order] is because I don't believe that anything like this could happen to me. If I was you and someone had threatened me with a gun, there is no way that I would . . . take that kind of abuse from them. Therefore, since I would not let that happen to me, I can't believe that it happened to you.
Maryland trial judge[12]

For many Americans, the O. J. Simpson case challenged deeply ingrained patterns of denial. When the story broke about Nicole Simpson's nine desperate and ultimately ineffectual telephone calls to the police, the public finally heard how battered women are in fact not heard. What for centuries had been a largely private matter at last surfaced as a major public issue.

The statistics are sobering. Domestic violence is the leading cause of injury to women and claims an estimated four million victims each year. Between one-third and one-half of all women are assaulted by a spouse or partner at some point during their lifetime. One-third of all female homicide victims are killed by a husband or boyfriend. The American Medical Association estimates that the cost of domestic violence totals somewhere between $5 billion

12 *Gender Bias in the Courts: Report of the Special Joint Committee on Gender Bias in the Courts* (Annapolis, Md.: Committee on Gender Bias in the Courts, 1989), 2–3.

and $10 billion per year in health care, absences, lost wages, litigation, and incarceration.[13]

★ ★ ★

Despite these increasingly well-publicized facts, many Americans still underestimate the seriousness of violence against women. Denial is pervasive among the two groups most responsible for the problem: men who batter and the law enforcement officials who fail to deter it. Virtually every study of male batterers finds that they discount women's injuries even as they describe them:

"I never beat my wife. I responded physically to her."

"Maybe I'd whack her once or twice but I wasn't going to kill her."

"She bruises easily."

"I only pushed her. She just happened to be at the top of the stairs at the time."[14]

Such trivialization of women's injuries was all too apparent in the *Simpson* proceedings. A familiar series of euphemisms surfaced to describe the defendant's history of violence. Simpson himself described his brutal marital assaults as "get[ting] physical." His lawyer, Johnnie Cochran, referred to the beating that led to Simpson's earlier conviction as an "unfortunate incident" and noted that "nobody's perfect." A dismissed juror, Michael Knox, was equally forgiving of the same assault, which he saw as part of the normal "ups and downs with spouses and girlfriends."[15]

Judges often share these views. One consistent finding of some two dozen reports on gender bias in the courts involves the denial and devaluation of domestic violence. In a representative California survey, a majority of male judges agreed that women's allegations of domestic abuse were often exaggerated. Three-fourths of the female judges disagreed. Male judges use many of the same euphemisms as male batterers: the beating was just a "whack"; the woman wasn't really "bruised"; things couldn't have been "as bad as she claims, or she would have left." Even when the severity of the violence is undeniable, such as when the victim is dead, some judges still give a "domestic discount" in sentencing for the crime. From their perspective, abusers look like otherwise normal and upstanding citizens with "unblemished" records, apart from the "unfortunate" or

13 For the frequency of domestic violence, see Antonio C. Novella, "A Medical Response to Domestic Violence," *Journal of the American Medical Association* 267 (1992): 3132; Koss et al., *No Safe Haven,* 42; Staff of Senate Committee on the Judiciary, 102nd Congress, 2nd Session, *Violence against Women: A Week in the Life of America* (Washington, D.C.: Government Printing Office, 1992), 3. For homicides, see United States Department of Justice, *Murder in Families* (Washington, D.C.: Government Printing Office, 1994). For costs, see NOW Legal Defense Fund, *Stop Violence against Women: Strategies for Ending Violence against Women* (New York: NOW Legal Defense Fund, 1994).

14 James Ptacek, "Why Do Men Batter Their Wives?" in Kersti Yllo and Michele Bogard, eds., *Feminist Perspectives on Wife Abuse* (Newbury Park, Calif: Sage, 1988): 133, 146; Jan Hoffman, "When Men Hit Women," *New York Times Magazine,* 16 February 1992, 23–24; Adam Jukes, *Why Men Hate Women* (London: Free Association Books, 1993), 274; David Olive, *GenderBabble* (New York: Putnam, 1993), 157.

15 O. J. Simpson, quoted in Frank Rich, "The Second Word," *New York Times,* 14 October 1995, A19; Johnnie Cochran, quoted in Ann Jones, "I Object, Mr. Cochran," *New York Times,* 11 October 1995, E13; Michael Knox, quoted in Katha Pollitt, "Subject to Debate," *The Nation,* 23 October 1995, 457.

"tragic" incidents at issue. Crimes that in other contexts appear brutal and inhumane seem to matter less when they are "family matters."[16]

★ ★ ★

Despite recent improvements, too many police officers and prosecutors still see domestic "incidents" as diversions from their "real" criminal work. Violence against women of color, particularly those in poor communities, often remains a low priority. Even officials who would like to invest more resources in domestic violence see little point when others in the system are unwilling to do the same. Police blame prosecutors, prosecutors blame judges, and everyone blames battered women. Why should an officer make an arrest in a case that won't be pursued? Why should prosecutors go forward with complaints when the judge won't impose a significant sanction or the woman may not testify? And why should women risk the physical retaliation and financial hardship of filing a complaint if no one is taking them seriously?[17]

The result of this self-perpetuating cycle is that an estimated 90 percent of domestic assaults and a majority of domestic-violence arrests never result in prosecution. Two-thirds of battering complaints are classified as simple misdemeanors, even though most involve serious injuries. In recently surveyed cities, fewer than 10 percent of men arrested for domestic assault serve any jail time.[18]

---

16 For denials and devaluation, see *Maryland Report,* 2–3; "Report of the New York Task Force on Women in the Courts," *Fordham Urban Law Journal* 15 (1987): 11, 28–33; Karen Czapansky, "Domestic Violence, the Family, and the Lawyering Process: Lessons from Studies on Gender Bias in the Courts," *Family Law Quarterly* 27 (1993): 247, 252–255. For the survey, see California Judicial Council Advisory Committee on Gender Bias in the Courts, *Achieving Equal Justice for Women and Men in the Courts,* Draft Report (San Francisco: Judicial Council of California, 1990), 92–93. For euphemistic discussions, see Ptacek, "Why Do Men Batter?," 155; Martha Mahoney, "Victimization or Oppression? Women's Lives, Violence and Agency," in Martha Albertson Fineman and Roxanne Mykitiuk, eds., *The Public Nature of Private Violence: The Discovery of Domestic Abuse* (New York: Routledge, 1994), 78; *Blair v. Blair,* 154 Vt. 201, 203–204 (1990). For homicide sentences, see Elizabeth Rapaport, "The Death Penalty and the Domestic Discount," in Fineman and Mykitiuk, eds., *Public Nature,* 224, 230–233

17 For police and prosecutors' views, see Lisa Frohmann and Elizabeth Mertz, "Legal Reform and Social Construction: Violence, Gender and the Law," *Law and Social Inquiry* 19 (1994): 829, 837; Eve S. Buzawa and Carl G. Buzawa, "The Scientific Evidence Is Not Conclusive: Arrest Is No Panacea," in Gelles and Loseke, eds., *Current Controversies,* 340. For racial bias, see Linda L. Ammons, "Mules, Madonnas, Babies, Bathwater, Racial Imagery and Stereotypes: The African-American Woman and the Battered Woman Syndrome," *Wisconsin Law Review* (1995): 1003; Kimberle Crenshaw, "Mapping the Margins: Intersectionality, Identity Politics, and Violence against Women of Color," *Stanford Law Review* 43 (1991): 1241. For lack of support from other officials and the resulting cycle of blame, see Pamela Jenkins and Barbara Davidson, "Battered Women in the Criminal Justice System: An Analysis of Gender Stereotypes," *Behavioral Sciences and the Law* 8 (1990): 161; Susan Sward, "O. J. Simpson Case Throws Spotlight on Domestic Violence," *San Francisco Chronicle,* 24 June 1994, A1, A6. Donald G. Dutton, with Susan K. Golant, *The Batterer* (New York: Basic Books, 1995), 11.

18 For prosecution rates, see Adele Harrell, *A Guide to Research on Family Violence, Prepared for Courts and Communities* (Washington, D.C.: Urban Institute, 1993), 41. For misdemeanor classification, see NOW Legal Defense Fund, *Stop Violence against Women,* 5. In some jurisdictions, 90 percent of family violence cases are filed as misdemeanors. Bettina Boxall and Frederick M. Muir, "Prosecutors Taking Harder Line toward Spouse Abuse," *Los Angeles Times,* 11 July 1994, A1, A16. For jail time, see Ann Jones, *Next Time She'll Be Dead: Battering and How to Stop It* (Boston: Beacon, 1994), 143. In one study, *The American Lawyer* tracked all the domestic-violence arrests that occurred in eleven jurisdictions on Father's Day, 1995. Half the offenders were never prosecuted, and only 10 percent served jail time. Alison Frankel, "Domestic Disaster," *The American Lamyer* (June 1996): 55, 56.

This trivialization of women's injuries is not lost on women themselves, who often have other reasons to discount abuse. Many of these individuals depend on their batterers for economic support, social identity, and emotional attachment. According to some recent estimates, women who leave an abusive relationship have a 50 percent likelihood of some period of poverty, and account for half of all homeless women. Even where severe economic hardship is not an issue, many individuals have difficulty acknowledging the violence in their relationships, especially in cases where the man later appears loving and promises to change.[19]

Certain stereotypes associated with battered women—passivity, helplessness, and disfiguring injuries—also encourage individuals to deny or discount their own vulnerability. Many women who actively resist violence also resist labeling themselves as victims and their partners as batterers. The pressures for denial are particularly great for certain groups. Some racial and ethnic communities have ties to cultures where private violence is rarely a matter for public intervention. Immigrant women often lack information and language skills, fear contact with American governmental agencies, and risk shame, isolation, and retaliation if they make formal complaints. Many elderly and disabled women are physically as well as emotionally and economically dependent on an abusive caregiver, and their batterers' awareness of that vulnerability increases the risk of assault. So too, lesbians often are reluctant to risk the homophobia and the lack of gay-community support that may follow disclosure of a violent same-sex relationship. Such concerns help account for the gross underreporting of domestic assault; most surveys estimate that well over 90 percent of battering incidents never reach police attention.[20]

★ ★ ★

The way we frame these questions is itself part of the problem. If we want to know why more women don't leave, we should first ask whether they have somewhere safe to go. The answers are not encouraging. Half of all interspousal homicides and most serious injuries occur after the victim does in fact leave. As experts like Martha Mahoney note, men's fear of abandonment is one of the most common motivations for violence. Although individuals at risk of abuse are entitled to protective orders,

19 For women's needs, see Lee H. Bowker, "A Battered Woman's Problems Are Social, Not Psychological," in Gelles and Loseke, eds., *Current Controversies,* 154, 158. For risks of poverty and homelessness, see Margie Laird McCue, *Domestic Violence: A Reference Handbook* (Santa Barbara, Calif.: ABC-CLIO, 1995), 106–107, 113; Gretchen P. Mullins, "The Battered Woman and Homelessness," *Journal of Law and Policy* 3 (1994): 237. For men's promises, see Dutton, *The Batterer,* 49–57; Raoul Felder and Barbara Victor, *Getting Away with Murder* (New York: Simon and Schuster, 1996), 256.

20 For women's aversion to stereotypical images, see Mahoney, "Women's Lives," 78, 84; Elizabeth Schneider, "The Violence of Privacy," *Connecticut Law Review* 23 (1991): 973, 984. For immigrant and Asian American women, see Leslye E. Orloff, Deeana Jang, and Catherine F. Klein, "With No Place to Turn: Improving Legal Advocacy for Battered Immigrant Women," *Family Law Quarterly* 29 (1995): 313; Kimberly A. Huisman, "Wife Battering in Asian American Communities," *Violence against Women* 2 (1996): 260. For lesbians, see Mary Eaton, "Abuse by Any Other Name: Feminism, Difference, and Intralesbian Violence," in Fineman and Mykutiuk, eds., *Public Nature,* 195; Ruthann Robson, "Lavender Bruises: Intralesbian Violence, Law, and Lesbian Legal Theory," *Golden Gate University Law Review* 20 (1990): 567. For disabled women, see Dick Sobsey, *Abuse in the Lives of People with Disabilities* (Baltimore: Paul H. Brookes, 1994), 163–166. For underreporting, see Buzawa and Buzawa, "Scientific Evidence," 345; Center for Women for Policy Studies, *Violence against Women: Fact Sheet* (Waslungton, D.C.: Center for Women for Policy Studies, 1994).

most of these mandates are violated and violators are seldom prosecuted. In some states, such safeguards are not even available for same-sex partners.[21]

Moreover, shelters and related social services for battered women are chronically underfunded. Despite recent progress, including modest federal subsidies authorized in the 1994 Violence Against Women Act, we are nowhere close to providing adequate assistance. About half of all counties have no formal resources for battered women. This nation provides only a small part of necessary housing, childcare, legal aid, and related assistance. We offer least to those who need help most: low-income, poor, nonwhite, elderly, disabled, and immigrant women.[22]

★ ★ ★

‖ RAPE

By even the most conservative estimates, the United States has the highest rate of reported rape in the Western industrial world. According to government and crime center research, between two-thirds and four-fifths of these rapes involve acquaintances. But the problem of "date rape" is commonly dismissed as the "mass psychosis" of feminist fanatics. Well-publicized books and leading media accounts condemn "rape hype" and "rape hysteria." And child sexual abuse, which experts estimate affects 13 to 23 percent of American girls, evokes equally widespread disbelief.[23]

With no apparent sense of irony, critics often caricature antirape activists in far more extremist rhetoric than that used by the activists themselves. To commentators like Katie Roiphe, Camille Paglia, Mary Matalin, John Leo, and Neil Gilbert, "delusional" "yuppie feminist[s]" with "simpering prom-queen" sensibilities and "neopuritan preoccupation[s]" are determined to "transform the act of seduction into the crime of rape." In the process, these antirape activists supposedly exaggerate dangers, entrench sexist stereotypes, trivialize real rape, and erode female responsibility. By casting all women as "powerless, innocent victims" and all men as "overpowering, sex-crazed barbarians," femi-

21 Mahoney, "Legal Images," 64–65; Dutton, *The Batterer,* 14–15, 45–46. For protective orders, see Peter Finn, "Civil Protection Orders: A Flawed Opportunity for Intervention," in Michael Steinman, ed., *Woman Battering* (1991), 155–157; *Domestic Violence: Not Just a Family Matter,* Hearing before the Subcommittee on Crime and Criminal Justice, Committee on the Judiciary, House of Representatives, 103rd Congress, 2nd Session, (30 June 1994); Adele Harrell et al., *Court Processing and the Effects of Restraining Orders for Domestic Violence Victims* (Washington; D.C.: Urban Institute, 1993), 49, 61.

22 Koss et al., *No Safe Haven,* 105. For women of color, see Crenshaw, "Mapping the Margins," 1245–1250; Huisman, "Wife Battering"; Orloff, Jang, and Klein, "With No Place to Turn."

23 For cross-cultural comparisons, see United Nations Development Programme, *Human Development Report, 1993* (New York: Oxford University Press, 1993), 192, table 3. For acquaintance rape, see Joel Epstein and Stacia Langenbahn, *The Criminal Justice and Community Response to Rape* (Washington, D.C.: U.S. Department of Justice, Office of Justice Programs, 1994); National Victim Center and the Crime Victims Research and Treatment Center, *Rape in America: Report to the Nation* (Arlington, Va.: National Victim Center, 1992); *Crime Victimization Survey Report* (Rockville, Md.: Bureau of Justice Statistics Clearinghouse, 1995). For denials, see Paglia, *Vamps and Tramps,* 24; Katie Roiphe, *The Morning After: Sex, Fear, and Feminism on Campus* (Boston: Little, Brown, 1993), 52; Susan Faludi, "Whose Hype?" *Newsweek,* 25 October 1993, 61. For child sexual abuse, see Dean D. Knudsen, "Child Sexual Coercion," in Elizabeth Grauerholz and Mary A. Koralewski, eds., *Sexual Coercion: A Sourcebook on Its Nature, Causes and Prevention* (Lexington, Mass.: Lexington Books, 1991).

nists reportedly are resurrecting mid-Victorian prejudices that work against gender equality.[24]

What is most telling about the 1990s rape hype controversy is not that it offers new and persuasive insights, but rather that it builds so successfully on old and unfounded prejudices. Traditional understandings of rape reflect a pronounced sexual schizophrenia. For centuries, one form of assault—intercourse forced by a stranger on a chaste white woman—has been treated as the archetypal antisocial crime. By contrast, coercive sex that has departed from this paradigm frequently has been denied or discounted. The attitude, well captured by a popular army slogan, has been that "it never happened, and what's more [she] deserved it." Despite two decades of educational and law reform efforts, these attitudes remain resilient. As legal scholar Susan Estrich notes, most Americans continue to believe the standard stories about what "real rape" is and isn't. These beliefs, as they play out in bedrooms, locker rooms, and courtrooms, account for much of America's difficulty in combating sexual assault. Our principal problem is not that we exaggerate the problem and demonize men, but that we so often deny the problem and blame women.[25]

The most common strategy of denial starts from the common assumption that "normal" men don't rape; "barbarians" do. "Nice girls" aren't assaulted; "loose" and "careless" women are. Much, however, depends on how we define "normal" and what we consider an assault.[26]

Under most criminal statutes, rape involves sexual penetration against a person's consent through the use of force or threat of bodily harm, or through incapacitation. By that definition, the most comprehensive studies find that between 12 and 25 percent of women have experienced rape and another 12 to 20 percent have experienced attempted rape. The vast majority of these assaults, including over 85 percent of completed rapes, are not reported to the police. Women of color are most likely to be victimized, and least likely to make a formal complaint.[27]

Contrary to popular assumptions, most rapes do not involve strangers, weapons, or sexually deviant offenders. Moreover, virtually every study of "normal" college-age men has found that substantial numbers, typically around one-third, acknowledge that they would commit rape if they could he sure of not being caught. About half would force a woman to have sex

24 Paglia, *Vamps and Tramps,* 24, 32; Roiphe. *The Morning After;* John Leo, "Don't Oversimplify Date Rape," *U.S. News and World Report,* 11 February 1991, 17; Neil Gilbert, "Counterpoint: A Few Women Want to Speak for Both Sexes," *San Francisco Chronicle,* 26 June 1991, A17; Mary Matalin, "Stop Whining!" *Newsweek,* 25 October 1993, 63.

25 Rhode, *Justice and Gender,* 245; Susan Estrich, *Real Rape* (Cambridge, Mass.: Harvard University Press, 1987).

26 Lance Morrow, "Men: Are They Really That Bad?" *Time,* 14 February 1994, 52; Margaret D. Bonilla, "Cultural Assault: What Feminists Are Doing to Rape Ought to be a Crime," *Policy Review,* October 1993, 22; Paglia, *Vamps and Tramps,* 36–37.

27 For the frequency of rape and attempted rape, see National Victim Center, *Rape in America* (New York: Vintage, 1994); Patricia A. Harney and Charlene Muehlenhard, "Rape," in Grauerholz and Koralewski, eds., *Sexual Coercion,* 3; Mary P. Koss and Mary R. Harvey, *The Rape Victim: Clinical and Community Interventions,* 2nd ed. (Newbury Park, Calif.: Sage, 1991), 19–27, 262–263. For underreporting, see U.S. Senate, Committee on the Judiciary, Majority Staff Report, 103rd Congress, 1st Session, *The Response to Rape: Detours on the Road to Equal Justice* (Washington, D.C.: Government Printing Office, 1993), 8. For women of color, see Koss et al., *No Safe Haven,* 203; Patricia H. Collins, *Black Feminist Thought: Knowledge, Consciousness and the Politics of Empowerment* (New York: Routledge, 1991), 178.

if they could get away with it, although apparently they do not consider this rape. A majority of surveyed men report engaging in some sexually coercive behaviors, and 10 to 15 percent admit having forced sex on a date.[28]

The point is not what critics caricature as *the* feminist position—that "all men are rapists." It is rather that many Americans view some degree of sexual coercion as "normal" and that many "normal" individuals find it erotic. This perception helps account for the unwillingness on the part of both men and women (80 percent and 75 percent in one representative survey) to label forced sex between acquaintances as rape.[29]

To alter those attitudes, we need to address both the individual motivations and societal structures that encourage rape. Profiles of rapists indicate that many are primarily attracted to power; they want the feeling of domination, adventure, and self-esteem that comes from coercive sex. Other men emphasize anger; rape is a means to punish or avenge some wrong by a particular woman, women in general, or another adversary. Most rapists blame their victims, and some stress situational influences such as peer pressure or drug and alcohol abuse. Exposure to family violence during childhood increases the likelihood that men will engage in sexually violent activities as adults.[30]

Of course, these explanations provide only part of the story. An equally critical question is why so many men in America, but not in all societies, channel their desires for power, revenge, and peer approval into sexual assaults. The answer has much to do with the long-standing family, media, and law enforcement influences that reinforce or fail to restrain male aggression.[31]

Such influences underpin many Americans' refusal to hold men accountable for coercive sex in dating contexts. In celebrated cases like the Los Angeles Spur Posse, where male high school students were awarded points for sexual conquests,

---

28 For characteristics of the offense and offenders, see Laurie Bechhofer and Andrea Parrot, "What Is Acquaintance Rape?" in Bechhofer and Parrot, eds., *Acquaintance Rape: The Hidden Crime* (New York: Wiley, 1991), 9–11; Isla L. Lottes, "Sexual Socialization and Attitudes toward Rape," in Ann Wolbert Burgess, ed., *Rape and Sexual Assault, II* (New York: Garland, 1988), 195; Susan B. Sorenson and Jacquelyn W. White, "Adult Sexual Assault: Overview of Research," *Journal of Social Issues* 48 (1992): 1; Lynn H. Schafran, "Writing and Reading about Rape: A Primer," *St. John's Law Review* 66 (1993): 979, 1003; For surveys of men, see Lynne Henderson, "Rape and Responsibility," *Law and Philosophy* 11 (1993): 127, 170; Gregory Matoesian, *Reproducing Rape: Domination through Talk in the Courtroom* (Chicago: University of Chicago Press, 1993), 9; Robin Warshaw, *I Never Called It Rape: The Ms. Report on Recognizing, Fighting, and Surviving Date and Acquaintance Rape* (New York: Harper and Row, 1988), 11–14 (describing Mary Koss's research); Susan Basow, *Gender: Stereotypes and Roles* (Pacific Grove, Calif.: Brooks/Cole, 1992), 318.

29 For statements blurring the distinction between rape and sex see Morrow, "Men: Are They Really That Bad?" For the unwillingness to label rapes, see Warshaw, *I Never Called It Rape;* Koss and Harvey, *The Rape Victim.* For the normalcy of offenders, see Judith Lewis Herman, "Considering Sex Offenders: A Model of Addiction," in Patricia Searles and Ronald J. Berger, *Rape and Society* (Boulder, Colo.: Westview, 1996), 74, 77–79.

30 Diana Scully, *Understanding Sexual Violence: A Study of Convicted Rapists* (Boston: Unwim Hyman, 1990); Eugene J. Kanin, "Date Rape: Unofficial Criminals and Victims," *Victimology: An International Journal* 9 (1984): 95; Barry Burkhart and Mary Ellen Fromuth, "Individual Psychological and Social Psychological Understandings of Sexual Coercion," in Grauerholz and Koralewski, eds., *Sexual Coercion,* 79–83; Julie A. Allison and Lawrence S. Wrightsman, *Rape: The Misunderstood Crime* (Newbury Park, Calif.: Sage, 1993), 29.

31 Peggy Reeves Sanday, *Female Power and Male Dominance: On the Origins of Sexual Inequality* (New York: Cambridge University Press, 1981); Matoesian, *Reproducing Rape,* 8–12.

voluntary or not, parents defended their sons as "all men" and "virile specimens." Similarly, in a gang rape case in Glen Ridge, New Jersey, the defense attorney shrugged off evidence indicating that the defendants had sexually assaulted a retarded girl with a baseball bat. According to the lawyer, the defendants were just "pranksters" responding to "basic boyish needs." And after all, "boys will be boys."[32]

Judges and juries frequently share these views, together with the assumption that attractive males don't need to rape. The trial of William Kennedy Smith highlighted attitudes that leading prosecutors like Linda Fairstein repeatedly encounter. After Smith's acquittal, juror Lea Haller told the media: "I think he's too charming and too good-looking to have to resort to violence for a night out." In fact, research on rapists consistently shows that few men "need" to rape. The vast majority are involved in consensual intimate relationships and are more sexually active than the average male. Rape is not about sexual deprivation; it is about domination.[33]

A further way of denying the problem is to discount the injuries that follow from it. A common, although not always explicit, assumption is that forced sex is not all that harmful if the parties know each other and if no other injuries result. Some male politicians and athletic coaches have captured widespread views with the quip that "if rape is inevitable," women should just "relax and enjoy it." According to one Missouri mayor, "the only difference between rape and seduction is salesmanship." Referring to conduct that a jury later found to be rape, Michael Tyson defended himself by saying that, after all, "I didn't hurt anyone—no black eyes, no broken bones."[34]

The Tyson case was, however, exceptional. Prosecutors usually are unwilling to file date rape charges in the absence of other physical injury; they assume (with good reason) that to most juries, if "there aren't bruises . . . then it isn't rape." In one representative case, the lawyer for three college basketball players successfully rebutted gang rape charges on the grounds that the woman had no other injuries; indeed, her "hair was not [even] messed up." Many judges hold similar views. In explaining his light sentence for a rapist, a Massachusetts trial court noted, "It's not like [the victim] was tortured or chopped up." And in the case of a man convicted of forcibly sodomizing a retarded woman, a Manhattan judge justified leniency "on the ground that there was no violence here."[35]

---

32 For the spur posse, see Nelson, *The Stronger Women Get, the More Men Love Football,* 82, Mariah Burton Nelson (New York: Harper Collins, 1995), 82. For the Glen Ridge rape, see Michael Querques, quoted in Karen Houppert, "Boystown," *Village Voice,* 10 November 1992, 11; Joseph Phalon, "It Happened—But Could She Consent?" *National Law Journal,* 28 December 1992, 8.

33 Lea Haller, quoted in Lynn Hecht Schafran, "The Importance of Voir Dire in Rape Trials," *Trial* (August 1992): 26. For research and examples, see ibid.; also Linda Fairstein, *Sexual Violence: Our War against Rape* (New York: William Morrow, 1993), 135.

34 Bobby Knight, quoted in Nelson, *The Stronger Women Get,* 87; Clayton Williams, quoted in *Ms.,* January–February 1991, 15; Missouri mayor quoted in Allison and Wrightsman, *Rape,* 2; Tyson, quoted in Don Bickley, "Agony and Ecstasy," *Chicago Sun-Times,* 27 December 1992, 20.

35 Epstein and Langenbahn, *The Criminal Justice and Community Response to Rape,* 66 (bruises); Nelson, *The Stronger Women Get,* 154 (hair); Massachusetts Supreme Court Justice Jerome Marks, quoted in Anthony M. DeStefano, "Judge Outlasts Outcry: Recertified Despite Feminist Protest," *Newsday,* 3 July 1989, A8 (torture); *New York v. Garay* (Sup. Ct., March 11, 1992), discussed in Lynn Schafran, "Maiming the Soul: Judges, Sentencing, and the Myth of the Nonviolent Rapist," *Fordham Urban Law Journal* 20 (1993): 439, 440 (violence).

Such attitudes help explain the relatively light penalties that follow most complaints of sexual assault. Eighty-five percent of reported rapes end up with no convictions, and almost 90 percent result in no incarceration. About half of convicted rapists receive probation or jail sentences of less than one year. In theory, our criminal justice system treats rape as one of the most serious offenses. In practice, we reserve such treatment for a small category of "real rapes," usually those involving violence, strangers, and white complainants. A Texas study illustrates the extent of racial biases. It found that the median sentence for a black man who raped a white woman was nineteen years; for a white man who raped a white woman, it was five years.[36]

Cases involving youthful offenders and acquaintances, even gang rapes, seldom result in serious sanctions. In one 1993 case, defendants convicted of "sexual misconduct" for raping a woman who had passed out in a bar were sentenced to pay a $750 fine and complete 250 hours of community service. Yet when law enforcement officials treat criminal conduct as "youthful indiscretions," they discourage victim reports and perpetuate the attitudes that perpetuate the problem. In the brutal Glen Ridge rape of a retarded girl, many trial observers and jurors expressed shock that the convicted defendants would serve less than two years in juvenile facilities. But as some experts noted, what *should* shock people is that such sentences are close to the national average.[37]

The trivialization of women's injuries in these cases rests on deep-seated cultural attitudes. To many Americans, date rape is little more than bad sex. As Camille Paglia puts it, when feminist "rape ranters" are unable to distinguish the "drunken fraternity brother from the homicidal maniac, women are in trouble." When critics like Paglia document these legions of "ranters," we should start to worry. Until then, we should share the concern of virtually all respected researchers in the field. They find that fraternity rape is a serious problem and that it often involves brutal premeditated assaults, not sexual "miscommunication" or consensual intimacy that goes "a little too far."[38]

Of course, many women do experience what another critic derisively labels "icky sex"; it happens when their partner was "clumsy," they let him "get carried away," they wanted to "avoid a hassle," and so forth. But critics' further claims that these women "feel that they have been raped" runs counter to virtually all recent research. Although there may be some ambiguity at the boundaries, few individuals appear unable to distinguish between a bad choice and no choice at all. The vast majority of surveyed women are reluctant to label forced sex rape if it

36 Senate Judiciary Committee, *The Response to Rape,* 12; Schafran, "Primer," 1005–1006; Ray F. Herndon, "Race Tilts the Scales of Justice," *Dallas Times Herald,* 9 August 1990, A1.

37 Sheila James Kuehl, "Legal Remedies for Teen Dating Violence," in Barrie Levy, ed., *Dating Violence: Young Women in Danger* (Seattle: Seal Press, 1991), 209–222; Rachel Singer, "Journey to Justice," *Ms.,* November–December 1994; Epstein and Langenbahn, *The Criminal Justice Response,* 137.

38 Paglia, *Vamp and Tramps,* 25, 33; Peggy Reeves Sanday, *Fraternity Gang Rape* (New York: New York University Press, 1990), and Peggy Reeves Sanday, A *Woman Scorned: Acquaintance Rape on Trial* (New York: Doubleday, 1996).

involves acquaintances, even when it meets the statutory definition.[39]

The common assumption that date rapes or "nonviolent" rapes do not involve serious injury is similarly inconsistent with the evidence. Research from the Department of Justice and the National Crime Center indicates that although most rapes do not involve physical injury apart from the assault itself, they often produce debilitating and enduring psychological trauma. Rape by an acquaintance is no less harmful than other assaults, because it calls into question a woman's behavior, judgment, and sense of trust in ways that random acts by strangers do not.[40]

Many individuals also overlook the way that fear of rape reinforces broader structures of inequality. According to Roiphe, "considering how many things there are to be afraid of and how many are not fair, being frightened to walk around [a college campus] . . . late at night does not seem like one of God's greatest injustices." If the comparison is battle sites in Bosnia or gang warfare zones in urban ghettos, she is undoubtedly right. But why should these be the relevant comparisons? Why are we so judgmental about the women who want to feel safe, instead of about the men who make it impossible? Golda Meir made a similar point when, during her term as Israeli prime minister, a cabinet official proposed a curfew for women. Meir responded, "But it's the men who are attacking . . . If there's to be a curfew, let the men stay home, not the women."[41]

It is fair to complain, as do other critics, that a disproportionate amount of tax dollars for rape services go to college campuses, rather than to low-income communities with more assaults. But it does not follow that the solution is less money and less concern about the campuses. Among American women under thirty-five, rape provokes more fear than any other crime, including murder or robbery. That was true long before any alleged feminist fanaticism set in. Sexual assault is unique in its capacity for terror, degradation, shame, and recurring trauma. Until this registers more fully in the national consciousness, boys will go on being boys, and girls will pay the price.[42]

★ ★ ★

Harassment, battery, rape, and pornography all raise common questions. What makes sexual abuse sexy? What accounts for its pervasiveness and persistence? Why have we managed to accomplish so much in changing consciousness and changing law, but so little in changing cultural practices? Answering these questions requires us to look more deeply not only at the

39 Compare Marcia Pally, *Sex and Sensibility: Reflections on Forbidden Mirrors and the Will to Censor* (Hopewell, N.J.: Ecco, 1994), 151, with Henderson, "Rape and Responsibility," 165–166. See also Warshaw, *I Never Called It Rape;* Koss and Harvey, *The Rape Victim.*

40 Schafran, "Primer," 978–985; National Victim Center, *Rape in America* (70 percent of rapes involve no other physical injury); Bonnie L. Katz, "The Psychological Impact of Stranger Versus Nonstranger Rape on Victims' Recovery," in Bechhofer and Parrot, eds., *Acquaintance Rape,* 251–253;

Christine A. Gidycz and Mary P. Koss, "The Effects of Acquaintance Rape on the Female Victim," ibid., 270.

41 Roiphe, *The Morning After,* 45; Meier, quoted in Dianne Herman, "The Rape Culture," in Jo Freeman, ed., *Women: A Feminist Perspective,* 2nd ed. (Palo Alto, Calif.: Mayfield, 1979), 41, 53.

42 Sommers, *Who Stole Feminism?* 120; Margaret T. Gordon and Stephanie Riger, *The Female Fear* (New York: Free Press, 1989).

dynamics of sexual abuse but also at the structures of social power.

American culture eroticizes male violence and objectifies female bodies. These practices are so omnipresent that it is difficult even to imagine a sexual ideology that excludes them. Yet part of our challenge is to make such an alternative realistic and appealing. As feminist theorist Carol Vance notes, it is "not enough to move women away from danger and oppression." We must also move women "toward something: toward pleasure, agency, self-definition." Not only must we promote a more egalitarian vision of sexuality; we must create the conditions that will make it possible. Women are trapped both by the social construction of sexuality and the social constraints on choice. As long as their status and economic security depend so much on relationships with men, the conditions for sexual abuse will persist. Social inequality increases physical vulnerability. To change the dynamics of men's aggression, we also must increase women's capacities for resistance.[43]

Pointing this out, of course, often gives feminism a bad press. Whining about "whiners" is in fashion; it is less threatening to dismiss all those victim-mongering messengers than to hear their messages. And so the denials persist. We refuse to believe that sexual abuse is common, that victims aren't somehow responsible, and that we could do more about it. Nor will we admit that whatever happens in our workplace, in our family, and in our relationships is part of the problem. Until we recognize how our denials perpetuate abuse, there will be plenty of abuse to deny.

---

43 Carole S. Vance, *Pleasure and Danger* (Boston: Routledge, 1984), 24.

Immigration and Inequality in Contemporary America

39

Immigration and the American Century[*]

CHARLES HIRSCHMAN

Once I thought to write a history of the
immigrants in America. Then I discovered that
immigrants were American history.
Oscar Handlin (1973:3)

The importance of this stream (immigration) for
the economic growth of the United States is still
not fully understood or completely analyzed,
much of the past literature having concentrated
on difficulties of adjustment and assimilation have
been biased by reformers concerned with
short-term problems rather than long-term gains.
Simon Kuznets (1971:21)

---

[*] First published in 2005; from *Demography*, Volume 42, Number 4.

The twentieth century is sometimes referred to as the American Century, which is generally interpreted to mean the rise of the United States to world leadership, first through its economic ascendancy in the first half of the century and then through its political and military hegemony in the post–World War II era. If these characteristics were all that mattered, then the American Century would be a rather fleeting moment in historical perspective. There is a long history of political and economic empires, remembered most often for their excesses and eventual decline. I suggest, however, that America's symbolic position in the twentieth century is at least as important as its economic and military dominance, and this symbolic role is likely to be the dominant historical legacy.

This symbolic role has many components, but one of the most influential is that American identity is not rooted in nationhood but rather in the welcoming of strangers. Kasinitz (2004:279) has argued that over the course of the twentieth century, the Statue of Liberty replaced Revolutionary War icons as the preeminent national symbol. The founding fathers did not intend for the United States to become a nation of immigrants, but that is what happened. The Statue of Liberty was given to the American people by France to commemorate the 100th anniversary of the independence of the United States. Although the statue was intended to symbolize Franco-American friendship and the freedom of American society, the statue has acquired a new identity—as a beacon of welcome for people seeking new and better lives for themselves and their children (Higham 1984: chap. 3). This interpretation owes much to the poem by Emma Lazarus, which celebrates Lady Liberty as the Mother of Exiles who welcomes the huddled masses and the homeless from other lands. Although the American government and people have not always embraced immigrants, the image of the United States as a land of opportunity and refuge has become its preeminent national identity at home and abroad.

In this article, my aim is not to recount what immigrants have experienced or how they have become "American," though that is part of the story. My primary objective is to explain how American society—its institutions and culture—has changed as immigrants have become active participants as workers, political actors, and creators of culture. To paraphrase Handlin (1973:3), immigration is not simply a part of American history; rather immigration is a principal wellspring from which so much of America's dynamic character and identity have originated.

This survey of the impact of immigration on American society is a preliminary one with ideas and data drawn from various quarters. I begin with an overview of the magnitude and patterns of immigration to the United States and then review the evidence of the influence of immigration on population diversity, cities, the economy, and American politics and culture. I even argue that immigration, along with preexisting sources of population diversity, has created a more cosmopolitan and tolerant society that is much less susceptible to monolithic claims of American nationalism.

A word on terminology—I use the terms *immigrants* and *the foreign born* as synonyms, although technically and legally they are quite different. *The second generation* refers to the children of immigrants, and the balance of the population is referred to as the third and higher generations or the native born of native parentage.

||| HISTORICAL TREND

The 1880 to 1924 age of mass migration, primarily from Europe, and the post-1965 wave of immigration, primarily from Latin America and Asia, are bookends of the twentieth century, but they represent a longer history that began in the seventeenth century and that may well continue far into the future (Hirschman, Kasinitz, and DeWind 1999; Jones 1992; Min 2002; Portes and Rumbaut 1996).

Figure 1 shows the trend in immigration from 1850 to 2000. The bars show the absolute count of the foreign born population enumerated in each decennial census. In absolute numbers, the size of the foreign-born population more than tripled from about 4 million in 1860 to just shy of 14 million in 1920. Following the near closing of the immigration door to southern and eastern Europe in the 1920s (it closed even earlier to peoples from Asia), the numbers of the foreign born fell steadily for the next half-century to less than 10 million persons in 1960 and 1970.

The curved line shows the foreign born as a proportion of the total U.S. population at each census. In 1860, after a decade of the larg-

FIGURE 1 **NUMBER OF FOREIGN BORN (IN MILLIONS) AND PERCENTAGE FOREIGN BORN OF THE U.S. POPULATION: 1850–2000**

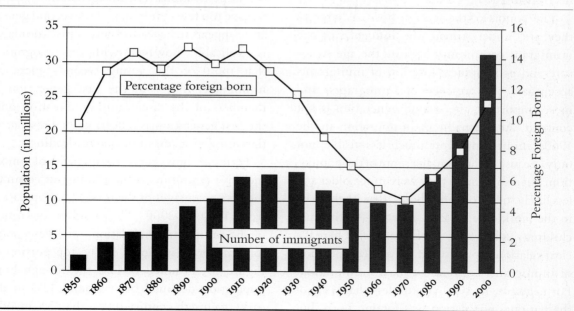

SOURCES: Gibson and Lennon (1999: table 1); Malone et al. (2003: table 1).

est (relative) immigration in American history, about 13% of the population was foreign born. For the next 60 years, the ratio of immigrants to the population remained around the same level—about 13%, to 14%, or about 1 in 7 Americans. Then, the relative size of the foreign-born population declined precipitously, and only 1 in 20 Americans alive in 1970 was an immigrant.

With the return of immigration to the main stage of American society in the last three decades of the century, the number of foreign-born persons tripled from less than 10 million in 1970 to more than 30 million in 2000, and proportionately, the percentage foreign born increased to over 11% of the population (the most recent available estimate of the foreign born in 2004 is 34 million, which is just shy of 12% of the total U.S. population; see U.S. Census Bureau 2005).

The counts of the foreign born, as large as they are, underestimate the influence of the immigrant community because the age structure and geographical location of immigrants accentuate the presence of immigrants, and more important, the second generation is not counted. At the nadir of immigration in the 1960s, immigrants were much less visible, not only because of their smaller share of the population, but also because they were much older and less likely to be "out and about" (less likely to be in the workforce, at PTA meetings with small children, and in other public venues). There is a clear relationship between the age composition of immigrants and eras of mass immigration. For example, in 1900, a little less than 14% of the national population was foreign born, but

21% of workers were foreign born (Ruggles et al. 2004). In 2000, the 11% foreign-born population translated into 14% of the labor force (King, Ruggles, and Sobek 2003). The visibility of immigrants also depends on geography. Most immigrants live in cities, while old-stock, native-born Americans are more likely to live in rural areas and small towns.

The most significant limitation of the standard demographic statistics on immigration is the exclusion of the native-born children of immigrants. The children of immigrants are reared, at least in part, in the social and cultural world of their immigrant families. The values, stories, and languages of immigrants are part of the cultural heritage of the children of immigrants. Figure 2 shows the unusual age distributions of the first and second generations, relative to the "normal" age distribution of the third and higher generations. The first generation appears to have too few children, and the second generation appears to have too many. This "anomaly" is explicable, however, with the recognition that most of the young second-generation immigrants live with the first generation as members of the same families. Treating only the first generation as reflecting the presence of the immigrant community is misleading.

Figure 3 shows three components of a more inclusive definition of the immigrant community as percentages of the total U.S. population from 1880 to 2000. The standard definition of the immigrant population—the percentage foreign born—is shown in the top portion of Figure 3. As noted earlier, the foreign-born population declined from around 14% in the early twentieth century to less than 5% in 1970

FIGURE 2 AGE COMPOSITION OF THE U.S. POPULATION, BY GENERATION: 2004

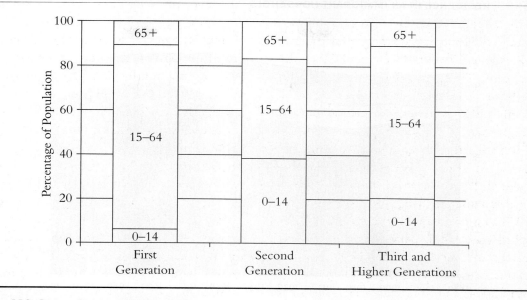

SOURCE: U.S. Census Bureau (2005: table 5.1).

and then bounced back to over 11% in 2000. The second component of the immigrant community—in the figure, the white area below the foreign born—includes the native born who live in households with an immigrant householder (or head of household). Most of this segment is composed of the dependent children of immigrant parents, but it also includes native-born spouses of immigrants and other relatives in immigrant households. Defining the immigrant community as inclusive of the families of foreign-born householders is probably close to the popular image.

A more expansive definition of the immigrant community includes the second generation who do not live in immigrant households—the third area from the top in Figure 3. Although some of the second generation may have no identification with their parents' birthplaces, many probably have some sense of belonging to the immigrant world, perhaps from hearing stories about life in the old country and their immigrant parents' struggles to make it in America.

In this broadest definition of the immigrant community (including all three areas at the top of Figure 3), the current share of the population with recent familial roots in the cultures and languages of other countries is closer to one-fifth or one-fourth of the national population, in contrast to the typical estimate of only slightly over 10% (counting only the foreign

FIGURE 3 **PERCENTAGE DISTRIBUTION OF THE U.S. POPULATION, BY IMMIGRANT GENERATION AND RESIDENCE IN AN IMMIGRANT HOUSEHOLD**

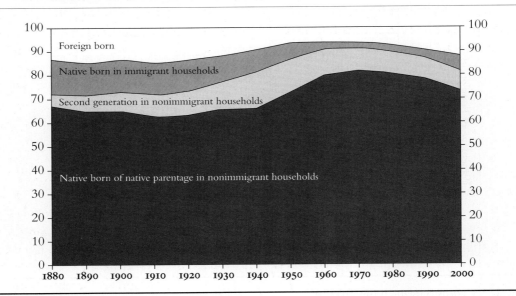

NOTES: The 1890, 1930, 1980, and 1990 second-generation populations (by immigrant household) are interpolations between censuses (or the merged 1998 to 2002 CPS file). The foreign-born populations reported here include the small number of persons born abroad of U.S.-born parents and those born in U.S. territories. The NA responses to nativity in the 1940 and 1950 census files and the merged 1998–2002 CPS file are adjusted pro rata across the first, second, and third generations. "Living in a foreign-born household" indicates that a respondent lived with a foreign-born householder or foreign-born head of household. Estimates of the third generation living in foreign-born households are higher than expected in 1940 and 1950. Nearly half this population are younger than age 15 and are most likely to be children in multifamily households.

SOURCES: Author's tabulations from Gibson and Lennon (1999); King et al. (2003); and Ruggles et al. (2004).

born). For the non-South (the North, Midwest, and West), the immigrant share of the population was closer to one-third in 2000 and was almost one half of the non-South population in the early decades of the twentieth century. The size of the immigrant population, the relative size in particular, creates the potential for a much more pervasive influence of immigration on American society than is generally realized.

THE IMPACT OF IMMIGRATION ON POPULATION DIVERSITY

Immigration has been the primary cause of the growth of the American population from a little less than 4 million in 1790 to over 270 million in 2000. Edmonston and Passell (1994:61) estimated that the current American population would be only a little more than one-third of its current size if it included only the descendents of those who arrived before 1800. Beyond population size, the most notable impact of immigration has been the broadening of the social and cultural diversity of the American population.

Colonial America was probably more diverse than the conventional portrait of the population of the 13 colonies as primarily of English origin. African Americans (both slave and free) constituted over one-fifth of the 1790 population (Gibson and Jung 2002: table 1), and there was a substantial American Indian population, many of whom were living in independent settlements and were not enumerated in censuses (Archdeacon 1983:2–4). There has even been a spirited debate among historians on the degree of diversity among the white population of Colonial America. One study, based on the method of assigning ethnic origins from assumptions about the nationality of surnames reported in the 1790 census, concluded that more than 80% of the 1790 white population was of English origin (U.S. Bureau of the Census 1909: 117). A follow-up study, using a stricter interpretation of unambiguously English names, lowered the estimate of the English origin to 60% of the 1790 white population (American Council of Learned Societies 1932). More recent scholarship has questioned the methods of these studies and concluded that there were probably much higher fractions of Celtic (Scottish and Irish), German, and other European nationalities present during the colonial era (see Akenson 1984; McDonald and McDonald 1980; and Purvis 1984).

Although variations among populations of European descent may seem relatively trivial at present, many Americans of English origin during the colonial era were concerned about too much ethnic diversity. In 1751, Benjamin Franklin complained about the "Palatine Boors" who were trying to Germanize the province of Pennsylvania and refused to learn English (Archdeacon 1983:20). These fears may have been accentuated by several major waves of immigration to the colonies in the eighteenth century, including a quarter million Scotch-Irish in the decades before the American Revolution (Fischer 1989:606–608; Jones 1992: chap. 2). The cultural diversity among the American peoples during the colonial era, however, pales when compared with the heterogeneity introduced by subsequent waves of immigration.

Table 1 provides a summary portrait of ethnic diversity, by immigrant generation, of the American population in 1900, 1970, and 2000. From our current perspective on race and ethnicity, the U.S. population appears to have been very homogenous in 1900. Altogether, American Indians, Asian Americans, and Latinos made up only about 1% of the American population in 1900. African Americans were 12% of the population in 1900, but they were regionally concentrated in the South—mostly in the rural South (Farley 1968:248).

The most visible manifestation of diversity in 1900 was the multitude of nationalities, languages, and cultures within the white population. A century ago, more than one-third of the U.S. population was composed of immigrants from Europe and their children. About half the immigrants in 1900 were considered to be "old immigrants," meaning that they came from the traditional sending countries of Great Britain and northwestern Europe. The rest,

TABLE 1   **PERCENTAGE DISTRIBUTION OF THE U.S. POPULATION, BY RACE/ETHNICITY AND IMMIGRANT GENERATION: 1900, 1970, AND 2000**

Race/Ethnicity and Immigrant Generation	1900 (%)	1970 (%)	2000 (%)
White (non–Hispanic)	87.3	83.3	69.6
Third and higher generations	53.8	69.0	62.4
First and second generation	33.5	14.3	7.2
American Indian/Native American	0.3	0.3	1.0
African American	11.7	10.9	12.9
Third and higher generations	11.7	10.7	11.4
First and second generation	0.1	0.3	1.5
Latino/Hispanic/Spanish	0.5	4.6	11.5
Third and higher generations	0.2	2.1	3.1
First and second generation	0.3	2.5	8.5
Asian American and Pacific Islander	0.2	1.2	4.9
Third and higher generations	0.0	0.2	0.5
First and second generation	0.1	1.0	4.5
TOTAL	100.0	100.0	100.0
Population (in thousands)	75,186	203,302	274,709

SOURCES: Author's tabulations of IPUMS census files from Ruggles et al. (2004); King et al. (2003).

including Italians, Slavs, Greeks, Poles, East European Jews, and many other groups from southern and eastern Europe, were labeled "new immigrants." If we consider the percentage of the majority population without recent foreign roots—the third and higher generation whites—as an index of homogeneity of the American population, then the United States were more diverse in 1900 than it was in 2000. Only 54% of the population in 1900 was native-born white of native parentage, compared with 62% in 2000.

In the early decades of the century, the "new immigrants" were often considered to be non-white and encountered considerable prejudice and hostility. Cities, where most immigrants settled, were derided and feared as places filled with dangerous people and radical ideas (Hawley 1972:521). These sentiments were often formulated by intellectuals, but they resonated with many white Americans who were reared in rather parochial and homogenous rural and small-town environments. Baltzell (1964:111) noted that most old-stock Americans in the late nineteenth century were appalled at the growing evils of industrialization, immigration, and urbanization. While some reformers, such as Jane Addams, went to work to alleviate the many problems of urban slums, others, such as Henry Adams, the descendent of two American presidents and a noted man of letters, expressed virulent nativism and anti-Semitism (Baltzell 1964:111). Henry Ford, who as much as anyone created the American automobile age, "looked upon big cities as cesspools of iniquity, soulless, and artificial" (Higham 1988:283). Through his general magazine, the *Dearborn Independent*, Henry Ford spread his hatred of the "international Jewish conspiracy" to a mass audience during the 1920s. Muller (1993:41) observed that, "Speeches by Ku Klux Klan members (against immigrants) were virtually indistinguishable in substance and language, if not in style, from the writings of many university professors."

People from a variety of groups and affiliations, ranging from the Ku Klux Klan to the Progressive movement, old-line New England aristocrats, and the eugenics movement, were among the strange bedfellows in the campaign to stop the immigration that was deemed undesirable by old-stock white Americans (Higham 1988; Jones 1992: chap. 9). The passage of immigration restrictions in the early 1920s ended virtually all immigration except from northwestern Europe (Bernard 1981).

In spite of the hostility against the new immigrants and the vitriolic campaign against continued immigration, the children and grandchildren of eastern and southern European immigrants experienced considerable socioeconomic mobility during the middle decades of the twentieth century (Lieberson 1980). By the 1950s and 1960s, white ethnic communities in the United States encountered only modest socioeconomic disadvantages (Duncan and Duncan 1968; Hirschman and Kraly 1988, 1990). Alba and Nee (2003:102) noted the amazing progress of Italian Americans, who were considered to be a community in distress in the 1930s but who had entered the economic mainstream by the 1970s. Although there is

not a simple comprehensive explanation for the socioeconomic assimilation of white ethnics in the middle decades of the twentieth century, several plausible reasons have been advanced in the literature, including rising levels of education of the second generation, the expansion of occupational opportunities, declines in residential segregation, unionization, the nation-building experience of two world wars, and the growing presence of African American workers who filled the bottom rungs of employment in industrial cities (Alba and Nee 2003: chap. 3; Lieberson 1980).

Another major factor that erased the stark divisions between old-stock Americans and the southern and eastern European communities was intermarriage. In the early decades of the century, there was virtually no intermarriage between the new immigrants and the native born (Pagnini and Morgan 1990), but by mid-century, only a minority of the descendents of white ethnics were not of mixed parentage (Alba and Golden 1986). The one white ethnic group that remained primarily endogamous for a much longer period was Jewish Americans, but by the late 1980s, almost half of Jews were marrying persons of different faiths (Alba and Nee 2003:92; Kosim and Lachman 1993:246–47). Although ethnic, religious, and cultural divisions persist at modest levels for whites of European origin, these are only an echo of early twentieth-century patterns of inequality, segregation, and xenophobia.

In 1970, more than 8 out of 10 Americans were non-Hispanic whites, and almost 7 out of 10 were third or higher generation non-Hispanic whites. The immigrant roots of the white population were a distant memory and were evoked only for parades on St. Patrick's Day and Columbus Day and other symbolic rituals. The study of immigrants had largely disappeared from sociology textbooks and was barely kept alive by a dwindling band of immigration historians. Diversity was a term that had not yet come into everyday discourse.

The only component of diversity on the national agenda in 1970 was the pervasive inequality between white and black America. The stark differences between the gradual processes of integration and inclusion experienced by the descendents of white immigrants and the persistence of discrimination and segregation experienced by African Americans led to a focus on the apparent immutable reality of race as opposed to a more permeable notion of ethnicity (Lieberson 1980; Massey and Denton 1994).

With the renewal of immigration from 1970 to 2000, there has been a renaissance of new forms of population diversity, including English spoken with accents by peoples from dozens of countries from around the globe (Portes and Rumbaut 1996). Initially confined to California, Texas, the New York region, Chicago, and southern Florida, the new immigration wave is now reaching across the country. From 1970 to 2000, the overall share of the national population composed of American Indians, African Americans, Latinos, and Asian Americans increased from less than 13% to over 30%.

The national share of African Americans inched up from 11% to 13%, largely owing to immigration. The relative share of Latinos and Asians grew by 7 and 4 percentage points, respectively, almost entirely because of immigration. These sharp increases have been accompanied by the expansion of new immigrants beyond their places of historical concentration. Mexican Americans have become a national minority with a presence in most cities, even in many southern rural areas that have not experienced immigration in over 200 years. Puerto Ricans and Cubans have spread beyond New York and Miami to nearby suburban areas and beyond. Asian Americans have become part of the national landscape and a visible presence on almost every college and university campus. By the century's end, national-origin groups that scarcely existed in the American imagination in 1970, such as Asian Indians and Vietnamese, had established all the trademarks of American ethnic communities, including recognizable areas of settlement, newspapers and periodicals in their home languages, and popular cuisines whose reach extends far into middle America (Min 2005).

The second half of the twentieth century witnessed two countervailing trends. The first trend was the almost complete "Americanization" of the white population as the foreign-born segment of white America largely disappeared. The second trend was a resurgence of immigration, beginning around 1970, that led to an expansion of diversity, with the establishment of Latinos and Asians as part of the American ethnic panorama. In addition to immigration, late twentieth-century diversity also has domestic roots. In 1900, the American Indian population was thought to be on the verge of disappearing, but natural increase and greater self-identification have led to a current population of 2.5 or 4.1 million in 2000, depending on whether an American Indian heritage is defined as a sole or joint racial identity (Ogunwole 2002; Snipp 2002).

Will the new immigrant populations in the twenty-first century follow the path experienced by the new immigrants from southern and eastern Europe in the middle decades of the twentieth century? A number of studies have found that, overall, most contemporary immigrants and their children have made socioeconomic gains, especially in education (Alba and Nee 2003; chap. 6; Card 2004; Hirschman 2001). Assuming continued socioeconomic mobility and moderately high levels of intermarriage, history might repeat itself, and the children of the post-1965 wave of immigrants may well be absorbed into the American mainstream. My only hesitation in making such a prediction comes from the disinvestment in inner-city public schools and other institutions that have historically fostered the social mobility of the children of immigrants.

Robert Merton (1994), perhaps the most celebrated sociologist of the twentieth century, described the rich quality of public institutions available to him as the child of working-class eastern European immigrants. Merton grew up in Philadelphia in the 1920s close to a public library and to public schools that were staffed by dedicated women concerned for his education and welfare. The nearby settlement house brought opportunities for artistic development and even chamber music performed by members of the Philadelphia Orchestra. Merton (1994:7) claimed that as a youngster in a seemingly deprived south Philadelphia slum, he was able to acquire the social, cultural, and human capital that facilitated socioeconomic mobility.

A recent ethnographic account described some of the high schools in New York City attended by first- and second-generation West Indian immigrants in the 1990s as "places of despair, fear, and resignation to low standards" (Waters 1999:217). There are, of course, many opportunities for contemporary upward mobility, but some scholars have posed the question of "second-generation decline" because of the loss of good unionized manufacturing jobs for immigrants and the lure of an inner-city street culture that discourages education aspirations among the second generation (Gans 1992; Portes and Zhou 1993).

★ ★ ★

IMMIGRANTS AND THE AMERICAN ECONOMY

Immigration adds more workers, and just as with the addition of any factor of production, immigration contributes to an expansion of the national economy. However, there are widespread popular beliefs, including many influential voices within public policy circles, that immigration is harmful to the economic welfare of the country and especially to native-born Americans (Borjas 1999; Bouvier 1992; Briggs 1984; Brimelow 1995). However, neither economic theory nor empirical evidence supports such negative assessments.

A report of the National Research Council (NRC) panel on the demographic and economic impacts of immigration, drawing on the theoretical and empirical research conducted by the leading specialists in labor economics and public finance, concluded that there were relatively modest effects of immigration on the American economy (Smith and Edmonston 1997, 1998). Economic theory predicts that immigration will expand labor supply and increase competition for jobs and lower wages for native-born workers who are substitutes for immigrants. But a corollary of this thesis is that immigrants expand total production (national income) and increase the incomes that accrue to native-born workers who are complements to immigrants (Smith and Edmonston 1997: chap. 4).

The indeterminate part of the theory is the division of native-born workers into those who are substitutes and those who are complements (to immigrants). The simplistic interpretation is that workers are substitutes and that capitalists are complements; these categories, however, are not necessarily people, but sources of income. Many workers have direct or indirect income from capital through their savings, ownership of property, and pension programs. Moreover, a substantial share of ordinary workers have jobs that appear to be complementary to immigrant labor, not competitive with it. This means that many native-born workers may get "pushed up" rather than being "pushed out" with the arrival of unskilled immigrant labor (Lieberson 1980: chap. 10). Regardless of the complexities of economic theory, the overwhelming body of empirical research finds little evidence of negative effects (Bean, Lowell, and Taylor 1988; Borjas 1994; Friedberg and Hunt 1995; Hamermesh 1993: 119–27).

The NRC report (Smith and Edmonston 1997) summarized the empirical findings of this literature in labor economics: "The weight of the empirical evidence suggests that the impact of immigration on the wages of competing native born workers is small—possibly only reducing them by 1 or 2%" (p. 220). "The evidence also indicates that the numerically weak relationship between native wages and immigration is observed across all types of native workers, white and black, skilled and unskilled, male and female" (p. 223).

These findings have led to a revisionist hypothesis that immigration does not adversely affect low-skilled native-born workers in locations with many immigrants—say, Los Angeles or New York—but that the negative effect is observed in the national labor market, which adjusts through internal migration (Borjas 2000:5–6; Borjas, Freeman, and Katz 1996; Frey 1995). In other words, the negative impact of immigration is experienced by migrants who leave Los Angeles or New York or by those who would have migrated to Los Angeles or New York in the absence of immigration. There is no consensus in this very complex and contested area of research, but Card and his colleagues (Card 2001, 2004; Card, DiNardo, and Estes 2000) have found little evidence that low-skilled native-born workers are disproportionately leaving high-immigration areas, nor that the wage gap between native-born high school dropouts (the group that is assumed to be in competition with immigrants) and workers with higher education is widening.

What might really resolve this debate would be an experiment in which a large number of immigrants were suddenly added to a city's workforce. History provided a natural experiment along these lines when about 125,000 Cubans, mostly unskilled workers, arrived in Miami, Florida, in September 1980 during the "Mariel Boatlift." Although the workforce of Miami was instantly increased by about 7%, there were almost no measurable changes in wages and employment of the native working class in Miami, including the African American population (Card 1990).

Immigration, as with other economic forces such as technological change and international trade, certainly leads to the displacement of native-born workers in some sectors (e.g., taxis drivers or construction workers in some cities). However, immigrants also stimulate the economy through their roles as consumers, investors, and entrepreneurs. Moreover, a good share of the "savings" gained through the lower wages of immigrant workers is passed on to native-born consumers through lower prices and to native-born workers in sectors of the economy that experience added demand. The observed net effect of immigration of about zero on the employment and wages of the native-born workers is the composite of these positive and negative effects.

The other major economic issue addressed by the 1997 NRC report was the impact of immigration on the governmental fiscal system—the balance between taxes paid and the value of government services received (Clune 1998; Garvey and Espenshade 1998; Lee and Miller 1998; Smith and Edmonston 1997: chaps. 6 and 7). The NRC researchers reported that the average native-born household in New Jersey and California (and probably in other states with many immigrants) pays more in state and local taxes as a result of the presence of immigrants (Smith and Edmonston 1997: chap. 6). These results are largely determined by the lower wages of immigrants and the demographic composition of immigrant households, which tend to be younger and have more children than the native-born population. The largest component of local and state government budgets is

schooling, and immigrant households, with more children per household than native-born households, are disproportionately beneficiaries of state support for schooling.

The conclusion that native-born households are subsidizing immigrant households through the provision of public education rests on a number of debatable assumptions. First, educational costs could be considered an investment as well as an expenditure. A more-educated local workforce should lead to higher incomes and higher tax revenues in the coming years, all other things remaining equal. Second, if the costs of educating the children of immigrants are considered to be a public transfer from the native born, then the balance sheet should also count the subsidy from immigrants' countries of origin, which have reared and educated immigrants coming to the United States. Finally, the bulk of the state and local educational expenditures are the salaries of teachers, administrators, and staff who are employed in the education sector, most of whom are native born.

Regardless of the debate over the net transfer of revenues at the local and state level, an accounting of the federal fiscal system shows that immigrants (and their descendants) contribute more in taxes than they receive in benefits (Smith and Edmonston 1997: chap. 7). Just as the age structure of immigrant households makes them disproportionately the beneficiaries of public education, the relative youth of immigrants also means they are less likely to be beneficiaries of social security and Medicare (and Medicaid for the institutionalized elderly). Immigrants also help to relieve the per capita fiscal burden of native born for the national debt, national security, and public goods, which are major federal expenditures that are only loosely tied to population size. An intergenerational accounting that counts the future taxes paid by the children of immigrants concludes that immigration helps, rather than hurts, the nation's fiscal balance (Lee and Miller 1998; Smith and Edmonston 1997: chap. 7).

There is a continuing debate on the impact of immigration on aggregate economic growth and the per capita income growth of native-born workers during the age of industrialization. Hatton and Williamson (1998: chap. 8) concluded that the mass migration from Europe in the two decades before World War I did not fill labor shortages, but rather lowered wages in unskilled jobs and displaced native-born workers (also see Goldin 1994). On the other hand, Carter and Sutch (1998) argued that many of Hatton and Williamson's conclusions were determined by their assumptions and model specifications. Carter and Sutch (1998:314–44) observed that economic growth did not slow during the years of mass immigration to the United States (also see Rees 1961). They also argued that immigrants contributed to economic growth (and rising real wages of the native born) through a variety of mechanisms, including increased national savings, a faster rate of inventive activity and technological innovation, and increasing economies of scale, both in the production and in consumer markets.

In his analysis of long swings, or Kuznets cycles, Easterlin (1968) found that immigration, which contributed to population growth and family formation, stimulated economic growth through increasing demand for housing, urban development, and other amenities. This association was strongest, Easterlin observed, before

the post–World War II era, when the federal government assumed more responsibility for maintaining aggregate demand. Although there are conflicting findings and debates in the literature, I do not see any unambiguous evidence for the negative effects of immigration on the American economy, past or present.

★ ★ ★

||| CONCLUSIONS

In conventional accounts of American history and contemporary American society, immigrants are considered a part of the story, indeed a very important part of the story. The tales of how peoples from different parts of the world arrived in a new land with relatively few resources but, through dint of hard work and family sacrifice, eventually joined the American mainstream is part of the national epic. The story line is one of how immigrants become Americans. In this article, I offer an alternative interpretation of the relationship between immigration and American society. Immigrants do, of course, adapt and become more similar to other Americans over time (or at least across generations). The complementary point is that twenty-first century American society and culture are not simply products of continuity from eighteenth-century origins, but have been continually reshaped by successive waves of immigrants and their descendants.

Beyond the English language and certain eighteenth-century political ideals, the cultural legacy and influence of the American "founding population" have eroded over the years. The proportion of the American population that reported English ancestry declined from 22% in 1980 to 13% in 1990 and then to only 9% in 2000 (Brittingham and de la Cruz 2004:4; Lieberson and Waters 1988:34). Fashion, as much as genealogy, determines the subjective responses to census questions about ancestry and ethnicity. To measure the popularity of different ancestries, Waters (1990:33–36) compared the 1980 census reports of the ethnicity/ancestry of children (presumably by older family members who filled out the census form) who had mothers and fathers of different ancestries. The popularity of an English ancestry was about average but far below the preference of identification with Italian ancestry. Persons of English origin are even underrepresented in elite positions, as measured by listings in Who's Who (McDermott 2002:147). With few national myths and a founding population that no longer holds demographic, symbolic, or real power, the image of the United States as a nation of immigrants has become the primary national identity and ideology.

This was not meant to be. The United States has always had an ambivalent response to immigration. Even though immigrants played a prominent role in Colonial America and the American Revolution, the fear of foreign influences and spies led to the passage of the Alien and Sedition laws shortly after independence (Jones 1993:72–77). In the 1840s and 1850s, the "Know Nothing Party" attracted a mass following with its attacks on Catholic Irish immigrants. In 1855, the Know Nothing Party elected six governors, dominated several state legislatures, and elected a bloc of representatives to Congress (Jones 1992:134).

In spite of these flare-ups, there was generally an open immigration policy during the nineteenth century. After the land had been wrested from its original owners, the American frontier presented virtually unlimited opportunities, and most immigrants were generally thought to be pretty similar to the original founding stock of the nation. Tolerance of open immigration ended, however, with the arrival of Asian immigrants on the West Coast in the 1850s and 1860s and of southern and eastern European immigrants in subsequent decades. The Chinese Exclusion Act of 1882 was the first step toward a closed society. Four decades later, the door to southern and eastern European immigrants was also closed. Passing the national origins quotas in the early 1920s was a victory for the old guard of American society, which staked the claim that old-stock Americans of English Protestant origins were the founding population that defined the national character. With nativist fears to arouse the masses and pseudo-scientific eugenics to convince the educated, the proponents of immigration restriction in the 1920s seemed to be firmly in charge (Higham 1988: chap. 10).

Their victory, however, was ephemeral. Only four decades later, the immigration door was reopened, and American cities were again buzzing with new arrivals from around the world. Immigration restriction was doomed because of the tens of millions of "new immigrants" who arrived from 1880 to 1924. These immigrants and their descendants have profoundly altered the structure and culture of American society, and after they had their turn in American politics, they overturned the national-origins quotas (Reimers 1985: chap. 3). The legacy of the 1880–1924 immigration includes a major role in the development of the modern industrial economy and the reorientation of the Democratic Party that led to the New Deal and the Great Society.

The new immigrants and their children have also made important contributions to the development of American culture and identity. The Hollywood theme "that anyone can make it in America" is a particularly Americanized version of the rags-to-riches story—one that is appealing to people, such as immigrants, who are striving for upward mobility. Many Hollywood and Broadway productions have also given us poignant accounts of outsiders who struggle to be understood and accepted. Not all the American creative arts draw on the aspirations and creative energies of immigrants, but first- and second-generation Americans have been very influential in defining and popularizing American culture.

The new immigrants who have arrived since 1965 are also changing the structure and culture of American society in new directions that cannot yet be clearly seen. One important direction, I believe, is the creation of a more cosmopolitan and tolerant society. Many new immigrants and their children have mastery of difficult-to-learn languages, and they have opened up new cultural horizons through ethnic cuisines, music, and the arts. International issues, such as the conflicts in the Middle East and Eastern Europe, the political currents in Mexico and Central America, and the spread of the Asian economic miracle, are matters of particular interest and concern to Americans who maintain familial, social, and even economic ties to the lands of their birth.

The children of immigrants inevitably lose many distinctive attributes, including language skills and personal knowledge of their countries of origin. However, the children of immigrants often broaden the base of the cosmopolitan society through the creation of multicultural families. The majority of young native-born Japanese and Chinese marry outside their communities (Alba and Nee 2003:92–93). Estimates of the intermarriage rates of other specific Asian American and Hispanic American groups range from 25% to 50% (Edmonston, Lee, and Passel 2002:239–42; Farley 1999; Qian 1997; Stevens and Tyler 2002)—patterns that are comparable to the historical experience of white ethnic groups (Alba and Golden 1956). The children of intermarried couples are likely to be an important bridge to a more tolerant society. Having both an Italian and Irish ancestry may make one somewhat less likely to accept jingoistic claims about the depravity of foreign cultures and societies. Having both an Eastern European Jewish heritage and a Korean Buddhist family may make one less likely to believe that religion is destiny or that American society should be monolithic in terms of its cultural traditions.

In sum, the presence of immigrants is a hedge against the parochial view of us versus them. Each intermarriage not only affects the identity choices of the children but also creates the potential of interethnic ties among a much larger number of persons in the extended families of the intermarried couple (Goldstein 1999). It is more difficult to hold onto ethnic stereotypes when the "other" is a nephew, niece, cousin, or grandchild.

The twentieth century was conceived in the era of nationalism and the belief that each national-origin population should have its homeland and state. However, as McNeill

(1984:17) observed, "the barbarian ideal of an ethnically homogenous nation is incompatible with the normal population dynamics of civilization." The pernicious ideology of ethnonationalism has been used to legitimate much of the conflict and misery of the past century, or as Hobsbawn (1992:134) expressed it, "The homogeneous territorial nation could now be seen as a program that could only be realized by barbarians, or at least by barbarian means."

The evolution of American society as an immigrant society, with moderately high levels of social mobility and intermarriage, has created a population of blended ancestries, united with a common civic identity. Although unintended, the American example of nationhood, open to all peoples, may be the real legacy of the American Century.

||| REFERENCES

Akenson, D.H. 1984. "Why the Accepted Estimates of the American People, 1790, Are Unacceptable." *William and Mary Quarterly* 41:109–19.

Alba, R. and R. Golden. 1986. "Patterns of Ethnic Marriage in the United States." *Social Forces* 65:202–23.

Alba, R. and V. Nee. 2003. *Remaking the American Mainstream: Assimilation and Contemporary Immigration*. Cambridge, MA: Harvard University Press.

American Council of Learned Societies. 1932. "Report of Committee on Linguistic and National Stocks in the Population of the United States." Pp. 107–441 in *American Historical Association Annual Report for 1931*. Washington, DC: American Historical Association.

Archdeacon, T.J. 1983. *Becoming American: An Ethnic History*. New York: Free Press.

Baltzell, E.D. 1964. *The Protestant Establishment: Aristocracy and Caste in America*. New York: Vintage Books.

Bean, F.D., B.L. Lowell, and L.J. Taylor. 1988. "Undocumented Mexican Immigrants and the Earnings of Other Workers in the United States." *Demography* 25:35–52.

Bernard, W.S. 1981. "Immigration: History of U.S. Policy." Pp. 486–95 in *Harvard Encyclopedia of American Ethnic Groups*, edited by S. Thernstrom. Cambridge, MA: Harvard University Press.

Borjas, G. 1994. "The Economics of Immigration." *Journal of Economic Literature* 32:1667–717.

———. 1999. *Heaven's Door: Immigration Policy and the American Economy*. Princeton, NJ: Princeton University Press.

———, ed. 2000. *Issues in the Economics of Immigration*. Chicago: University of Chicago Press.

Borjas, G.J., R.B. Freeman, and L. Katz. 1996. "Searching for the Effect of Immigration on the Labor Market." *American Economic Review* 86:246–51.

Bouvier, L.F. 1992. *Peaceful Invasions*. Lanham, MD: University Press of America.

Briggs, V. 1984. *Immigration Policy and the American Labor Force*. Baltimore, MD: Johns Hopkins University Press.

Brimelow, P. 1995. *Alien Nation: Common Sense About America's Immigration Disaster*. New York: Random House.

Brittingham, A. and G.P. de la Cruz. 2004. *Ancestry: 2000.* Census 2000 brief. Washington, DC: U.S. Census Bureau, Available online at http://www.census.gov/prod/2004pubs/c2kbr-35.pdf

Card, D. 1990. "The Impact of the Mariel Boatlift on the Miami Labor Market." *Industrial and Labor Relations* 43:245–57.

———. 2001. "Immigrant Inflows, Native Outflows and the Local Labor Market Impacts of Higher Immigration." *Journal of Labor Economics* 19:22–64.

———. 2004. "Is the New Immigration Really So Bad?" Discussion Paper No. 1119. Institute for the Study of Labor, Bonn, Germany. Available online at http://www.iza.org

Card, D., J. DiNardo, and E. Estes. 2000. "The More Things Change: Immigrants and the Children of Immigrants in the 1940s, the 1970s and the 1990s." Pp. 227–69 in *Issues in the Economics of Immigration*, edited by G. Borjas. Chicago: University of Chicago Press.

Carter, S. and R. Sutch. 1998. "Historical Background to Current Immigration Issues." Pp. 289–366 in *The Immigration Debate: Studies on the Economic, Demographic, and Fiscal Effects of Immigration*, edited by J.P. Smith and B. Edmonston. Washington, DC: National Research Council.

Clune, M.S. 1998. "The Fiscal Impacts of Immigrants: A California Case Study." Pp. 120–82 in *The Immigration Debate: Studies on the Economic, Demographic, and Fiscal Effects of Immigration*, edited by J.P. Smith and B. Edmonston, Washington, DC: National Research Council.

Duncan, B. and O.D. Duncan. 1968. "Minorities and the Process of Stratification." *American Sociological Review* 33:356–64.

Easterlin, R. 1968. *Population, Labor Force, and Long Swings in Economic Growth: The American Experience.* New York: Columbia University Press.

Edmonston, B., S.M. Lee, and J. Passel. 2002. "Recent Trends in Intermarriage and Immigration and Their Effects on the Future Racial Composition of the U.S. Population." Pp. 227–55 in *The New Race Question: How the Census Counts Multiracial Individuals*, edited by J. Perlmann and M.C. Waters. New York: Russell Sage Foundation.

Edmonston, B. and J. Passel, eds. 1994. *Immigration and Ethnicity: The Integration of America's Newest Arrivals.* Washington, DC: Urban Institute Press.

Farley, R. 1968. "The Urbanization of Negroes in the United States." *Journal of Social History* 1:241–58.

———. 1999. "Racial Issues: Recent Trends in Residential Patterns and Intermarriage." Pp. 85–128 in *Diversity and Its Discontents: Cultural Conflict and Common Ground in Contemporary American Society*, edited by N.J. Smelser and J.C. Alexander. Princeton, NJ: Princeton University Press.

Fischer, D.H. 1989. *Albion's Seed: Four British Folkways in America.* New York: Oxford University Press.

Foner, N. 2000. *From Ellis Island to JFK: New York's Two Great Waves of Immigration*. New Haven: Yale University Press.

Frey, W. 1995. "Immigration and Internal Migration Flight From U.S. Metropolitan Areas: Toward a New Demographic Balkanization." *Urban Studies* 32:733–57.

Friedberg, R. and J. Hunt. 1995. "The Impact of Immigrants on Host Country Wages, Employment and Growth." *Journal of Economic Perspectives* 9:23–44.

Gans, H. 1992. "Second Generation Decline—Scenarios for the Economic and Ethnic Futures of the Post-1965 American Immigrants." *Ethnic and Racial Studies* 15:173–92.

Garvey, D.L. and T.J. Espenshade. 1998. "Fiscal Impacts of Immigrant and Native Households: A New Jersey Case Study." Pp. 66–119 in *The Immigration Debate: Studies on the Economic, Demographic, and Fiscal Effects of Immigration*, edited by J.P. Smith and B. Edmonston. Washington, DC: National Research Council.

Gibson, C. and K. Jung. 2002. "Historical Census Statistics on Population Totals by Race, 1790 to 1990, and by Hispanic Origin, 1790 to 1990, for the United States, Regions, Divisions, and States." Population Division Working Paper No. 56. Population Division, U.S Census Bureau, Washington, DC. Available online at http://www.census.gov/population/www/documentation/twps0056.html

Gibson, C. and E. Lennon. 1999. "Historical Census Statistics on the Foreign-Born Population of the United States: 1850–1990." Working Paper No. 29. Population Division, U.S. Census Bureau, Washington, DC. Available online at http://www.census.gov/population/www/documentation/twps0029/twps0029.html

Goldin, C. 1994. "The Political Economy of Immigration Restriction in the United States, 1890 to 1921." Pp. 223–57 in *The Regulated Economy: A Historical Approach to Political Economy*, edited by C. Golden and G.D. Libecap. Chicago: University of Chicago Press.

Goldstein, J.R. 1999. "Markers of Racial and Ethnic Identity Kinship Networks That Cross Racial Lines: The Exception or the Rule?" *Demography* 36:399–407.

Hamermesh, D. 1993. *Labor Demand*. Princeton, NJ: Princeton University Press.

Handlin, O. 1973. *The Uprooted: The Epic Story of the Great Migrations that Made the American People*. 2nd ed. Boston: Little Brown and Company. (Orig. pub. 1951.)

Hatton, T.J. and J.G. Williamson. 1998. *The Age of Mass Migration: Causes and Economic Impact*. New York: Oxford University Press.

Hawley, A. 1972. "Population Density and the City." *Demography* 9:521–29.

Higham, J. 1984. *Send These to Me: Immigrants in Urban America*. Revised ed. Baltimore, MD: Johns Hopkins University Press.

———. 1988. *Strangers in the Land: Patterns of American Nativism, 1860–1925*. 2nd ed. New Brunswick, NJ: Rutgers University Press. (Orig. pub. 1955.)

Hirschman, C. 2001. "The Educational Enrollment of Immigrant Youth: A Test of the Segmented-Assimilation Hypothesis." *Demography* 38:317–36.

Hirschman, C., P. Kasinitz, and J. DeWind. 1999. *The Handbook of International Migration: The American Experience.* New York: Russell Sage Foundation.

Hirschman, C. and E. Kraly, 1988. "Immigrants, Minorities and Earnings in the United States in 1950." *Ethnic and Racial Studies* 11:332–65.

———. 1990. "Race and Ethnic Inequality in the United States, 1940 and 1950: The Impact of Geographic Location and Human Capital." *International Migration Review* 24:4–33.

Hobsbawm, E.J. 1992. *Nations and Nationalism Since 1780: Programme, Myth and Reality.* 2nd ed. Cambridge, England: Cambridge University Press.

Jones, M.A. 1992. *American Immigration.* 2nd ed. Chicago: University of Chicago Press. (Orig. pub. 1960.)

Kasinitz, P. 2004. "Race, Assimilation, and 'Second Generations,' Past and Present." Pp. 278–98 in *Not Just Black and White: Historical and Contemporary Perspectives on Immigration, Race, and Ethnicity in the United States*, edited by N. Foner and G. Fredrickson, New York: Russell Sage Foundation.

King, M., S. Ruggles, and M. Sobek, 2003. *Integrated Public Use Microdata Series, Current Population Survey: Preliminary Version 0.1.* Minneapolis, MN: Minnesota Population Center, University of Minnesota. Available online at http://beta.ipums.org/cps

Kosim, B.A. and S.P. Lachman, 1993. *One Nation Under God: Religion in Contemporary American Society.* New York: Harmony Books.

Kuznets, S. 1971. "Notes on the Pattern of U.S. Economic Growth." Pp. 17–24 in *The Reinterpretation of American Economic History*, edited by R.W. Fogel and S.L. Engerman. New York: Harper and Row. (Orig. pub. 1964.)

Lee, R.D. and T.W. Miller, 1998. "The Current Fiscal Impact of Immigrants and Their Descendents: Beyond the Immigrant Household." Pp. 183–205 in *The Immigration Debate: Studies on the Economic, Demographic, and Fiscal Impacts of Immigration*, edited by J. Smith and B. Edmonston. Washington, DC: National Academy Press.

Lieberson, S. 1980. *A Piece of the Pie: Blacks and White Immigrants Since 1880.* Berkeley, CA: University of California Press.

Lieberson, S. and M. Waters. 1988. *From Many Strands: Ethnic and Racial Groups in Contemporary America.* New York: Russell Sage Foundation.

Malone, N., K.F. Baluja, J.M. Costanzo, and C.J. Davis. 2003. *The Foreign-Born Population: 2000.* Census 2000 brief. Washington, DC: U.S. Census Bureau. Available online at http://www.census.gov/prod/2003pubs/c2kbr-34.pdf

Massey, D. and N. Denton, 1994. *American Apartheid: Segregation and the Making of the Underclass.* Cambridge, MA: Harvard University Press.

McDermott, M. 2002. "Trends in the Race and Ethnicity of Eminent Americans." *Sociological Forum* 17:137–60.

McDonald, F. and E. Shapiro McDonald, 1980. "The Ethnic Origins of the American People, 1790." *William and Mary Quarterly* 37:179–99.

McNeill, W.H. 1984. "Human Migration in Historical Perspective." *Population and Development Review* 10:1–18.

Merton, R.K. 1968. *Social Theory and Social Structure.* Enlarged ed. New York: Free Press.

———. 1994. *A Life of Learning.* Charles Homer Haskins Lecture. ACLS Occasional Paper, No. 25. American Council of Learned Societies, New York.

Min, P.G., ed. 2002. *Mass Migration to the United States: Classical and Contemporary Periods.* Walnut Creek, CA: Altmira Press.

———, ed. 2005. *Asian Americans: Contemporary Trends and Issues.* 2nd ed. Thousand Oaks, CA: Pine Forge Press.

Muller, T. 1993. *Immigrants and the American City,* New York: New York University Press.

Ogunwole, S.U. 2002. *The American Indian and Alaska Native Population: 2000.* Census brief. Washington, DC: U.S. Census Bureau. Available online at www.census.gov/prod/2002pubs/c2kbr01-15.pdf

Pagnini, D. and S.P. Morgan. 1990. "Intermarriage and Social Distance Among Immigrants at the Turn of the Century." *American Journal of Sociology* 96:405–32.

Portes, A. and R. Rumbaut. 1996. *Immigrant America: A Portrait.* 2nd ed. Berkeley, CA: University of California Press.

Portes, A. and M. Zhou. 1993. "The New Second Generation: Segmented Assimilation and Its Variants." *Annals of the American Academy of Political and Social Sciences* 530:74–96.

Purvis, T.L. 1984. "The European Ancestry of the United States Population, 1790." *William and Mary Quarterly* 41:85–101.

Qian, Z. 1997. "Breaking the Racial Barriers: Variation in Interracial Marriages Between 1980 and 1990." *Demography* 34:263–76.

Rees, A. 1961. *Real Wages in Manufacturing.* Princeton, NJ: Princeton University Press.

Reimers, D.M. 1985. *Still the Golden Door: The Third World Comes to America.* New York: Columbia University Press.

Ruggles, S., M. Sobek, T. Alexander, C.A. Fitch, R. Goeken, P.K. Hall, M. King, and C. Ronnander. 2004. *Integrated Public Use Microdata Series: Version 3.0* [Machine-readable database]. Minneapolis, MN: Minnesota Population Center [producer and distributor]. Available online at http://www.ipums.org

Smith, J.P. and B. Edmonston, eds. 1997. *The New Americans: Economic, Demographic, and Fiscal Impacts of Immigration.* Washington, DC: National Academy Press.

———, eds. 1998. *The Immigration Debate: Studies on the Economic, Demographic, and Fiscal Impacts of Immigration.* Washington, DC: National Academy Press.

Snipp, C.M. 2002. "American Indians: Clues to the Future of Other Racial Groups." Pp. 189–214 in *The New Race Question: How the Census Counts Multiracial Individuals,* edited by J. Perlmann and M. Waters. New York: Russell Sage Foundation.

Stevens, G. and M.K. Tyler. 2002. "Ethnic and Racial Intermarriage in the United States: Old and New Regimes." Pp. 221–42 in *American Diversity: A Demographic Challenge for the Twenty-First Century,* edited by N.A. Denton and S.E. Tolnay. Albany, NJ: State University of New York Press.

U.S. Bureau of the Census. 1909. *A Century of Population Growth, 1790–1900.* Washington, DC: U.S. Government Printing Office.

———. 1933. *Fifteenth Census of the United States: 1930,* Vol. 2. *Population. General Report. Statistics by Subjects.* Washington, DC: U.S. Government Printing Office.

———. 1965. *U.S. Census of Population: 1960. Subject Reports. Nativity and Parentage.* PC(2)-1A. Washington, DC: U.S. Bureau of the Census.

———. 1975. *Historical Statistics of the United States, Colonial Times to 1970.* Parts 1 and 2.

Washington, DC: U.S. Government Printing Office.

U.S. Census Bureau. 2003. *2000 Census of Population and Housing. United States Summary: 2000.* Part 2. Washington, DC: U.S. Census Bureau. Available online at http://www.census.gov/prod/cen2000/phc-2-1-pt2.pdf

———. 2005. "The Foreign-Born Population of the United States Current Population Survey—March 2004. Detailed Tables (PPL-176)." Washington, DC: U.S. Census Bureau. Available online at http://www.census.gov/population/www/socdemo/foreign/pp1-176.html

Waters, M. 1990. *Ethnic Options: Choosing Identities in America.* Berkeley, CA: University of California Press.

———. 1999. *Black Identities: West Indian Immigrant Dreams and American Realities.* New York and Cambridge, MA: Russell Sage and Harvard University Press.

40

Segmented Assimilation on the Ground: The New Second Generation in Early Adulthood★

ALEJANDRO PORTES, PATRICIA FERNÁNDEZ-KELLY,
AND WILLIAM HALLER

To a greater extent than at the beginning of the twentieth century, second-generation youths confront today a pluralistic, fragmented environment that simultaneously offers a wealth of opportunities and major dangers to successful adaptation. In this situation, the central question is not whether the second generation will assimilate to American society, but *to what segment* of that society it will assimilate. The past literature has identified three major challenges to educational achievement and career success by today's children of immigrants. The first is the persistence of racial discrimination; the second is the bifurcation of the American labour market and its growing inequality; and the third is the consolidation of a marginalized population in the inner city.

These challenges will be summarized below and evidence for each will be presented. This is important because the traditional normative view of assimilation as a uniform process is still strong, tending to distort our understanding of what is taking place on the ground.

★ ★ ★

★ First published in 2005; from *Ethnic and Racial Studies*, Volume 28, Number 6.

CHALLENGES CONFRONTED BY TODAY'S SECOND GENERATION

Contrary to an all-inclusive characterization of the "mainstream," it is evident that what immigrants aspire to for their children, if not for themselves, are the levels of occupational status and income making possible the enviable lifestyles of the mostly white upper middle class. The promise of American society, which makes so many foreigners come lies in the access it provides to well-remunerated professional and entrepreneurial careers and the affluent lifestyles associated with them. At the same time, it is obvious that not everyone gains access to these positions and that, at the opposite end of society, there is a very unenviable scenario of youth gangs, drug-dictated lifestyles, premature childbearing, imprisonment, and early death. This is the scenario confronted by minority populations trapped in the American inner cities and described, in poignant detail, in the urban poverty literature.

Immigrant families navigate between these opposite extremes, seeking to steer their youths in the direction of the true mainstream. They do so, however, with very different material resources and skills and confronting very different social contexts. Differences in class background, in physical features, and in contexts of reception all have decisive bearing on the resources that immigrant families can muster. It is such cleavages that a homogenous view of assimilation obscures rather than clarifies.

a. Race

One of the key features that children inherit from their parents is their race. Defined by contemporary standards, the majority of today's second generation is non-white, being formed by children of Asian immigrants, blacks from the West Indies and Africa, and blacks, mulattos, and mestizos from Latin America. The minority of white immigrants also come from Latin America and, in declining numbers, from Europe and Canada. Figure 1 presents the racial self-identities of second-generation youths in late adolescence, based on the follow-up survey of the Children of Immigrants Longitudinal Study [CILS]. As shown, only a minority identified themselves as white, the majority seeing themselves as Asian, Hispanic, Latino, Black, or Multiracial.

Children of Asian, black, mulatto, and mestizo immigrants cannot escape their ethnicity and race, as defined by the mainstream. Their enduring physical differences from whites and the equally persistent strong effects of discrimination based on those differences, especially against black persons, throws a barrier in the path of occupational mobility and social acceptance. Immigrant children's identities, their aspirations, and their academic performance are affected accordingly. As Waters (1996, pp. 10–11) remarks in the case of West Indians:

> The teens experience racism and discrimination constantly, and develop perceptions of the overwhelming influence of race on their lives and life chances that differ from their parents' views. These teens experience being hassled by police and store owners, being turned down for jobs they apply for, and being attacked on the street if they venture into white neighborhoods.

As Alba and Nee (2003, p. 54) rightly note, civil rights legislation prohibiting ethnic and racial discrimination has effectively eliminated

FIGURE 1 **THE RACIAL IDENTITIES OF CHILDREN OF IMMIGRANTS, 1996**

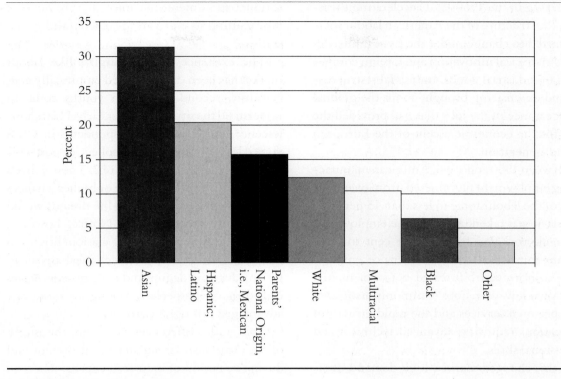

*CILS full sample. N = 5262.

the most overt manifestations of these attitudes on the part of employers and the native mainstream population. This does not mean, however, that such attitudes disappear or cannot be expressed in other, equally destructive forms. An extensive sociological and anthropological literature has documented these subtler, but often worse forms of discrimination. Not surprisingly, over 60 per cent of CILS respondents of Mexican and black Caribbean origin reported having experienced discrimination against themselves and up to 60 per cent of the latter believe that they would experience discrimination in the future "no matter how much

education I get" (Portes and Rumbaut 2001, pp. 39–41).

b. Bifurcated Labour Markets

A second major barrier to successful adaptation, identified in earlier work, is the deindustrialization and progressive bifurcation of the American labour market. As the prime industrial power of its time, the United States generated a vast demand for industrial labour during the first three decades of the twentieth century. Indeed, this was the reason why European immigrants first and southern black migrants second were recruited and came in such vast numbers to northern American cities. Beginning in the 1960s and accelerating thereafter, the structure of the American labour market started to change under the twin influences of technological innovation and foreign competition in industrial goods. Industrial restructuring and downsizing brought about the gradual disappearance of the jobs that had provided the basis for the economic ascent of the European second-generation.

Between 1950 and 1996, American manufacturing employment plummeted, from over one-third of the labour force to less than 15 per cent. The slack was taken up by service employment which skyrocketed from 12 per cent to close on one-third of all workers. Service employment is, however, bifurcated between menial and casual low-wage jobs commonly associated with personal services and the rapid growth of occupations requiring advanced technical and professional skills.

In this changed market, high demand exists at the low end for unskilled and menial service workers and at the high-end, for professionals and technicians, with diminishing opportunities in-between. Adult immigrants, especially those with low levels of education confront this new *hourglass* labour market by crowding into low-wage service jobs. On the other hand, their children, imbued with American-style status consciousness and consumption aspirations, are generally not satisfied with the same roles. A bifurcated labour market implies that, to succeed socially and economically, children of immigrants must cross *in the span of one generation* the educational gap that took their predecessors, descendants of European immigrants, several generations to bridge. They cannot simply improve on their parents' modest educational attainment, but must sharply increase it by gaining access to an advanced training and skills.

The existence of an hourglass-like labour market has been demonstrated empirically and, certainly, second-generation youths come to understand the situation rather early. In late adolescence, the majority of respondents in CILS voiced lofty aspirations for a college or post-college degree, as shown in Figure 2. They realized that without a college degree or higher, chances for fulfilling their career and life dreams would be seriously compromised. Notice, however, the wide differences among nationalities and the wide discrepancies between ideal *aspirations* for an advanced degree and realistic *expectations* of getting one, especially among the more disadvantaged immigrant groups.

The stark differences between the shape of the American labour market at present and during its period of industrial expansion a century ago is another *prima facie* indicator of the qualitative distinctness in the process of second-generation adaptation yesterday and today. Contrary to the "nothing has changed" school, the very high educational expectations voiced by children of immigrants today are at variance with what was aspired and actually achieved by most children of Italian or Polish peasants a century ago (Thomas and Znaniecki [1918–20] 1984; Child 1943; Alba 1985).

c. Poverty and Crime

The final external challenge confronting children of immigrants is that the social context they encounter, in American schools and neighbourhoods, may promote a set of undesir-

FIGURE 2 **EDUCATIONAL ASPIRATIONS AND EXPECTATIONS OF CHILDREN OF IMMIGRANTS, SELECTED NATIONALITIES, 1996**

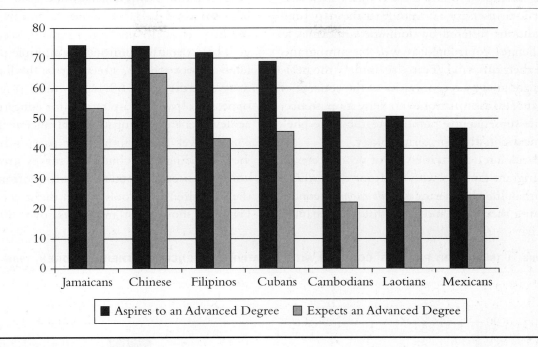

CILS full sample. N = 5262.

able outcomes inimical to successful integration such as dropping out of school, joining youth gangs, and using and selling drugs. This alternative path has been labelled *downward assimilation* because exposure to American society and entry into its social circles does not lead, in these cases, to upward mobility, but exactly to the opposite. The widespread poverty in American inner cities and the high incidence of crime and deviant lifestyles in them are linked to the transformation of the labour market that did away with the ladder of blue-collar jobs facilitating the upward mobility of earlier children of immigrants. The first victims of this trans-

formation were not members of today's second generation, but the children and grandchildren of their predecessors—Southern blacks, Mexicans and Puerto Ricans—who were brought to fill the labour needs of the American industrial economy during and after World War I.

It must be clear that entrapment of these populations in central cities is the structural condition that underlies the proliferation of pathologies of which they are the first victims—the flight of the middle class, the deterioration of schools, the proliferation of gangs, and the occupation of the streets by the drug industry. ★ ★ ★ When it comes to the second generation, however, some mainstream authors have attempted to skip these realities, believing that it is insensitive to point to the structural conditions suffered by domestic minorities as challenges confronted as well by immigrants and their offspring. This is seemingly the position adopted by recent critics of the concept of downward assimilation who deny its existence, while subsequently pointing to the same phenomenon in different terminology.

Academic sensitivities are of no concern to immigrant families who confront the realities of urban life in America as a *fait accompli*, conditioning their own and their children's chances for success. Because of their poverty, a large proportion of immigrant families (close to 40 per cent as of the latest count) cluster in central city areas. In that environment, second-generation youths confront the multiple problems of poor schools, street crime, the lure of drugs, and the option offered by youth gangs, all opposed to parental aspirations for educational achievement and occupational advancement.

The over 2,500 immigrant parents interviewed during the second CILS survey strongly voiced concerns about the perils confronting their children in schools and in the streets. As Figure 3 shows, vast majorities, over 80 per

FIGURE 3 **IMMIGRANT PARENTS' CONCERN WITH NEGATIVE INFLUENCES ON THEIR CHILDREN, 1996**

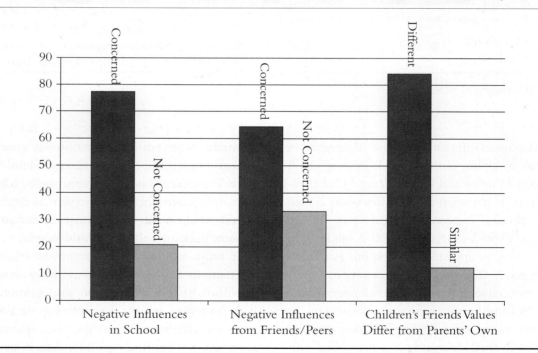

CILS full parental sample. N = 2442.

cent, were preoccupied about the negative influences their children receive in school and the gap between their own goals and values and those of their children's friends. Perlmann and Waldinger (1997) speculate that these parental concerns may be exaggerated because the dangers confronting second-generation adolescents today are not too different from those faced by their European predecessors. While there is little hard evidence to establish this comparison, the key factor is that whatever the conditions were in the past, they do not make those at present any less real. When a number of immigrant families take the rather desperate measure of sending their children home to be educated in the care of kin in order to protect them from the dangers of American streets, we can be certain of facing actual fact. The observations of many parents interviewed in the course of the CILS survey exemplify these concerns and the realities that underlie them:

> Why? Why? Why should this country, the richest in the world, have such low educational standards and disruptive behaviour? It is so sad to see this country's children smoking grass or wearing their hair in spikes ...You can wear anything to school, you can talk in class ... no one can stop you.
>
> *Roger, 38, Nicaraguan father living in Miami*

> This is a bad area to live in because of the many homeboys using alcohol and drugs. Every night there is the sound of the police sirens ... I want to move but the rent is cheap here. I am concerned about my younger children. I'm afraid they will join with the homeboys ... I

feel I cannot control the peer pressure; when they step out of the house, it's all over them.

> *Botum, Cambodian mother of six living in San Diego* (Portes and Rumbaut 2001, p. 97).

Similar observations abound in the scholarly and even in the journalistic literature. A lengthy *New Yorker* report about Mexican-American farm workers living in the Yakima Valley of Washington State remarked about the peculiar attitude of "Juan," the U.S.-born son of one such family whose parents had become increasingly involved in protests against the exploitative practices of their employers:

> The unhappy truth is that the rock-video culture that forms so much part of Juan's world view simply provides no referent for his parents' kind of heroism. The dignity of labour is no longer even a minor value in the devouring consumerism of the America Juan has grown up in.
>
> *(Finnegan 1996, p. 67).*

Segmented assimilation emerges from the different ways in which second-generation youths approach these challenges and the resources that they bring to the encounter. Figure 4 reproduces the typology of adaptation paths across generations, developed on the basis of prior CILS results. It relates systematically parental human capital, family structure, and modes of immigrant incorporation to expected patterns of mobility. The following section clarifies the three ideal types of inter-generational mobility presented in this figure and provides new evidence about their determinants on the ground.

FIGURE 4   **PATHS OF MOBILITY ACROSS GENERATIONS**

Background Determinants	First Generation	Second Generation	Third Generation and Higher
• Human Capital	Achievement of middle class status →	Professional and entrepreneurial occupations; full acculturation →	Complete integration into social and economic mainstream
• Family Structure	Working class status and strong co-ethnic communities →	Selective acculturation; attainment of middle class status through education →	Full acculturation and integration into the mainstream
• Modes of Incorporation	Working class status and weak co-ethnic communities →	Dissonant acculturation and low educational achievement	Marginal working class communities; reactive ethnicity
			Downward assimilation to underclass; reactive ethnicity

SOURCE: Portes and Rumbaut 2001:283.

||| CONFRONTING THE CHALLENGE

a. First Narrative

Fast forward to the Entenza family who just came back from helping their son move into his own apartment in Princeton, New Jersey. The Entenzas are being interviewed in their comfortable home in the Miami suburb of Coral Gables. They are first-generation Cubans. Ariel, who is 25, has always lived with his parents, following custom for unmarried Cuban children. The parents are owners of a medium-sized hardware store catering to a mostly Latin clientele. Ariel's mother, Teresa, came from Cuba with her family after the Castro government expropriated the department store they

owned in Havana. Scraping together his savings and with the help of friends, Teresa's father was able to get himself into business. After she married Esteban, he went to work in his father-in-law's store. After the father passed away, Esteban took over the business. Teresa and Esteban have always lived in Miami, close to other Cuban families, always worked in the same business, and always attended the same church. They are both devout Roman Catholics.

As a child, Ariel Entenza attended Belen Prep, a Jesuit school transplanted from Havana and favoured by middle-class Cuban families. Afterwards, he moved to Florida International University, where he completed a degree in finance. First, he went to work in the same store founded by his grandfather, but his dad encouraged him to move on. "We did not make all these sacrifices for him to be just a small businessman," the father says. Ariel first went to work for a local firm and then accepted a well-paid job in the accounting department of a New Jersey firm. Leaving Miami and his home was a traumatic step, but his future career prospects required it.

Mario, Ariel's brother, joined the Marines and then went on to work for the sheriff's department of nearby Broward County (Ft. Lauderdale) where he is currently a sergeant. He says that he feels "more Cuban than the old-timers." During the protests following the forced removal of the child Elian Gonzalez to Cuba in 2000, he called his police station sick and stayed at home. "I would do anything for this country, but I could not repress my neighbors," he says. "If I were not a cop, I would have been there protesting with them."

b. Human Capital and Social Capital

Not all families possess the means to promote educational success and ward off the threats posed by discrimination, bifurcated labour market options, and street gangs and consumerism. Resources necessary to achieve this goal are of two kinds: 1) those that provide access to economic goods and job opportunities; 2) those that reinforce parental normative controls. Parents with high levels of education are in a better position to support their children's education for two reasons: first, they have more information about opportunities and pitfalls in the surrounding environment; and second, they earn higher incomes, giving them access to strategic goods. A home in the suburbs, a private school

education, a summer trip back home to reinforce family ties are all expensive propositions, not within reach of the average immigrant family. Families able to afford them can confront the challenges faced by their children with a measure of equanimity.

Yet immigrant parents' human capital and family composition do not exhaust the range of forces moulding types of acculturation and subsequent adaptation outcomes. The outside environment supplies the other key factor. When a favourable reception by the government and society-at-large promotes the emergence of strong ethnic communities, the social capital grounded on ethnic networks, provides a key resource in confronting obstacles to successful adaptation. The Entenza family illustrates a situation mid-point between the first and second adaptation paths portrayed in Figure 4: Despite modest resources and a parental education reaching only to junior college, the family succeeded because of its strong co-ethnic networks. Growing up in the midst of the Cuban middle-class enclave, Ariel and Mario never had to contend with drugs and were never approached by a gang. So well-ensconced were they in the community where they were born that it was a difficult decision for Ariel to move north in pursuit of his career and an impossible one for Mario to repress his neighbours.

c. The Immigrant Community

Community social capital depends less on the economic or occupational success of immigrants than on the *density* of ties among them. It makes little difference whether fellow nationals are highly educated and wealthy if they feel no obligation towards one another. It does not matter either that doctors and business owners come from the same country when they are physically dispersed or otherwise unreachable. On the other hand, modest but solidary communities can be a valuable resource, because their networks support parental guidance and parental aspirations for their children. Among immigrants of limited means, this function of social capital is vital.

In a foreign land, parental controls can wane fast when confronted with the sustained challenges of deviant lifestyles, media-driven consumerism, and peer influences. For isolated families, the situation can easily devolve into a pattern of parental powerlessness, early abandonment of school by children, and involvement in gangs and drugs. Alternatively, when parental expectations are reinforced by others in the community, the probability of successful adaptation increases. This is the situation that James Coleman (1988) labelled "closure." In densely integrated communities, where children have internalized the goals of occupational success through high educational achievement, the threat of downward assimilation effectively disappears.

||| THE EVIDENCE

The third wave of the Children of Immigrants Longitudinal Study [CILS] was completed in 2002. The average age of the sample was 24 by this time. ★ ★ ★ An ethnographic module was added to the survey in the summer of 2002. In South Florida, a sample of fifty-five respondents, stratified by socio-economic status, gender and nationality were selected for intensive study. The story of the Entenza family and those presented below come from this module. Survey data from South Florida are used subsequently to document patterns of adaptation in the second generation and compare them with alternative theoretical perspectives.

a. Second Narrative

Eddie Cifuentes was born in Havana and came to the U.S. as a young child in the Mariel exodus of 1980. He is now twenty-five. His father, an auto mechanic, worked in a succession of odd jobs. So did his mother but, shortly after arriving in the U.S., the couple divorced and the mother "took everything." Eddie stayed with his father and attended a succession of public schools. Until the ninth grade, his education went normally and his grades were good, but then things went downhill. He fell in with "the wrong kind of crowd" and, at seventeen, began to steal cars. He learnt the necessary skills from other kids at a junkyard. Later he began to deal drugs:

> I was still 17 when I quit my first job and pretty much quit everything, left home, left school. At that time, it didn't bother me to do all those things. I was using drugs a little. Ecstasy wasn't around yet, but Ruthanol was already a big rave drug and it was a mind-eraser. I couldn't remember anything later.

To support himself and a growing drug habit, Eddie organized a regular business with about thirty customers. By the time he was nineteen, he was selling practically anything customers would want including cocaine, marijuana, ruthanol, and crack. On a typical Friday, as people prepared to party, he made more than twenty deliveries and grossed up to $8,000. Every month, he cleared at least $10,000.

His father disapproved of what Eddie was doing but, holding down three jobs himself, there was little that he could do. Besides, the boy had moved out of his father's home to lead a life of luxury. He bought two cars and supported his girlfriend, a former drugstore cashier, lavishly. He tried to launder his earnings by putting them in accounts in her name. At twenty, he was manufacturing crack and selling it to anyone, including pregnant women. The cops started trailing his Nissan Altima and he was eventually caught and convicted for theft, drug manufacturing, and racketeering. He served three years at a correctional institution.

Time in jail went more smoothly than Eddie had anticipated, that was "only because I was Spanish . . . like everywhere there were cliques—your whites, your Spanish, your Asians: If you mess with someone, you're messing with three or four of his buddies." Blacks were the majority, but Eddie often enjoyed the protection of prison guards, "some real rednecks." A fair-complexioned young man with striking blue eyes, Eddie had little trouble getting guards on his side and putting blame on others when fights broke out.

In prison, Eddie finally earned his GED. He also established a friendship with Ramon Ruiz, a 55-year-old lifer who took him under his wing. Eddie says that he learnt a lot from Ruiz. "First of all, I learned family values; then I learned self-respect." He came out of prison a transformed man, going to work first in his father's auto repair business. However, his prison record made things difficult for him when trying to find a better job. Eventually,

through an acquaintance, he found a job doing electrical work for Artistic Dome Ceilings. The $500 to $800 a week he brings home are a far cry from his former earnings as a dealer, but is enough to support himself. Despite his record, he is expecting to become manager of the firm when its owner and current manager retires.

Eddie does not feel particularly Cuban nor does he have any significant ties to his ethnic community. Further, he has no strong feelings against Castro, having left the island as a baby. He vaguely sees himself as American and says that this country stands for freedom. Alone in the world, save for his stranded parents and a new Venezuelan girlfriend, with no economic resources, and a prison record, Eddie still sees the future with optimism. He puts all his hopes in eventually owning the small firm in which he works. "I am so close to success, I can almost taste it," he says.

b. The Second Generation at a Glance

The story of Eddie Cifuentes serves well to introduce our survey results because it illustrates the complexities of second-generation adaptation as it occurs on the ground. Quantitative data alone cannot do this. Living not three miles from where Ariel Entenza grew up, the views and the life prospects of the two young men are worlds apart: one securely ensconced in his community and with a solid educational record to his credit; the other, torn from these moorings and navigating a turbulent society as best he can, with only a weak high school education and a criminal past. Although both are Cuban, their parents' modes of incorporation were quite different: the Entenzas were part of the well-received and highly solidary early exile waves; the Cifuentes, part of the chaotic and stigmatized Mariel exodus. Although the young men probably do not know it, their families' contrasting contexts of reception have a great deal to do with their life paths. Yet both of them look at the future with optimism; success that "almost can be tasted," although their chances of achieving it are quite different.

Segmented assimilation may be defined empirically as a set of strategic outcomes in the lives of young second-generation persons. One such outcome is educational attainment, in terms of both completed years of education and whether the person is still in school. A second includes employment, occupation and income; a third, language use and preferences. Indicators of downward assimilation include dropping out of school, premature childbearing, and being arrested or incarcerated for a crime. The CILS-III survey contains measures of all these variables. The results for the South Florida sample, unadjusted and adjusted for sample selection bias, as described in the introductory article, are presented in Table 1.

Adjusted means are generally quite close to the unadjusted figures and do not alter the substantive conclusions in any case. On average, figures show that the immigrant second generation is doing well with a mean of education of two years of college and with over half the respondents still attending school. High-school dropouts are less than 5 per cent, a figure below that reported for the Miami-Dade School System as a whole in 2000–2001 (5.8%). Another 16 per cent of respondents have only completed high school, which would put them at a disadvantage in the labour market. However, some in this category (9.9%) are still enrolled in school.

About one-third of our respondents have already graduated from college and, of these, 8.5 per cent have or are pursuing an advanced degree. Although these figures contrast markedly with the 44 per cent who seven years earlier said that they expected to achieve such a degree (Portes and Rumbaut 2001, p. 217), they still indicate that a sizable proportion of the sample is poised to attain professional and other high-status occupations. Over half the respondents are still in school on a full- or part-time basis so that the number of college graduates can be expected to increase in the future.

Already two-thirds of the sample is employed full-time and 8 per cent are unemployed, a figure that is about average for the population of this age cohort in South Florida. Since half our respondents are still attending school, a substantial number of these young people (26%) is both going to school and working full-time. Over 5 per cent have become entrepreneurs, a figure that is average for their age cohort, although detailed interviews in the ethnographic module revealed a widespread aspiration to do so.

At over $58,000 per year, average family income is high relative to the comparable 2000 census figure for the Miami metropolitan area ($54,939). The median family income is considerably lower, which is a statistical indication that the arithmetic mean is "pulled" upwards by very high incomes. Family incomes only partially reflect respondents' personal earnings since the majority (52.9%) still live at home with their parents, so that reported figures are often the sum of parents' and children's incomes. Still this result is important because it reveals that, on average, second-generation young adults in South Florida live in comfortable, middle-class surroundings.

TABLE 1 **KEY ADAPTATION OUTCOMES IN EARLY ADULTHOOD: CHILDREN OF IMMIGRANTS, IN SOUTH FLORIDA, 2002**

Variable	Unadjusted Mean/Per cent	Adjusted Mean/Per cent
Demographics:		
Age	24.2	–
Sex (Female)	55.2	–
Per cent Living with Parents	52.4	–
Education:		
Average Years Completed	14.5	14.3
Per cent Less than High School	4.0	4.0
Per cent High School Only	15.7	16.8
Per cent College Graduate or More	29.8	30.0
Per cent Still Attending School	52.0	52.0
Employment:		
Per cent Employed Full-time	65.7	67.1
Per cent Unemployed	6.6	7.0
Per cent Self-employed	4.9	5.1
Occupational Prestige Score[a]	47.2	47.3
Income:		
Average Family Income, $	58,345	58,425
Median Family Income, %	44,185	–
Per cent >$75,000	22.2	21.3
Per cent <$20,000	16.5	16.5
Per cent Received Cash Assistance, Last Year	3.2	3.4
Average Personal Income, $	23,172	23,136
Median Personal Income, $	19,200	–
Per cent >$50,000	4.7	4.7
Per cent <$15,000	32.6	32.0
Language:		
Percent Prefers English	65.9	64.7
Percent Prefers Other Language	1.9	2.2
Percent Prefers Children Bilingual	81.7	82.0
Legal:		
Per cent Arrested, Last Five Years	9.6	10.4
Per cent Had Kin Arrested, Last Five Years	18.3	19.4
Per cent Incarcerated or Sentenced, Last Five Years	5.4	6.4
Per cent Males Incarcerated or Sentenced	9.6	11.1
Family:		
Per cent Married	17.9	17.9
Per cent Cohabiting	5.2	5.2
Per cent with Children	17.6	17.6
Average Number of Children[b]	1.4	1.6

[a]Average scores for employed respondents in Treiman Occupational Prestige Scores. Range is from 0 to 100.
[b]Among respondents with children.

Over 20 per cent report average incomes that exceed $75,000 per year. On the other hand, 175 youths, representing 16 per cent of the sample, have to survive with yearly family incomes of less than $20,000. Personal incomes of our respondents are less than half of the family incomes, indicating the weight of parental income in the average figures above. About one-third of these youths had personal incomes of less than $15,000 which, in the absence of parental support, would place them at or below the poverty line.

Language use is a major indicator of assimilation. Results from the earlier CILS surveys showed that second-generation youths are universally fluent in English. They also showed that the vast majority prefers this language (Portes and Rumbaut 2001, p. 123). Present results confirm that pattern: two-thirds of CILS-III respondents indicated that they preferred communicating in English, in comparison with just 2 per cent in favour of their parents' language. However, the number of youths that prefer to be bilingual *increased* from adolescence into early adulthood: in CILS-II when the sample's average age was 17, less than 12 per cent indicated a linguistic preference for anything other than English. At age 24, however, 33 per cent said that they preferred bilingualism. This tendency is still stronger when respondents were asked in what language they wanted to educate their own children.

In addition to dropping out of school and being unemployed, a key indicator of downward assimilation is running afoul of the law and, in particular, being sentenced or incarcerated for a crime. We asked our respondents if they had been arrested or had been incarcerated during the past five years. We also asked them if

a family member had been arrested for a crime during the same period. In addition, we visited the Florida Department of Corrections website where data on all current felons, incarcerated or on probation, are published. By matching personal identifiers from prior surveys, it was possible to trace sample members who were behind bars or on probation at the time of the third survey, even if they had not returned a questionnaire or had not been interviewed.

For the sample as a whole, 10 per cent were arrested during the preceding five years and double that figure reported that other family members had been arrested. These figures compare with Federal Bureau of Investigation's [FBI] arrest statistics for the Miami Metropolitan Area which show an arrest index of 8.8 per cent for adolescents (age 10–17) and of 6.4 per cent for adults. Since persons can be arrested for minor infractions (such as vagrancy or disorderly conduct), a more relevant indicator is having been sentenced and incarcerated (or placed on probation) for a crime. Over 5 per cent of the sample had been incarcerated during the past five years or were currently in jail or on probation. Among males, the figure increases to almost 10 per cent. These results can be compared with those reported by Western (2002) for the population of the United States. Males imprisoned by age 40 represented 7.8 of the relevant national cohort in 1998 (Western 2002, p. 530). The CILS South Florida male incarceration rate thus exceeds the national figure, even though its members only average 24 years of age.

A final indicator of downward assimilation is premature child-bearing. At average age 24, our respondents confront multiple challenges to completing their education and moving ahead in the occupational world. Having children at this early age represents a significant burden in terms of time and money when many youths can least afford them. For the sample as a whole, over 20 per cent were already married or cohabiting in their early twenties and 18 per cent had at least one child. This last figure compares with an almost identical proportion among the same age cohort, 18–30, nationwide (18.2%). Thus a significant minority of this age cohort, including its second-generation members, confront a family situation that imperils their long-term educational and occupational success.

★ ★ ★

||| CONCLUSION

a. Third Narrative

Jessica Wynters was born in Miami. Her father is originally from Jamaica. He worked as a shipmate arriving first in the U.S. in 1976. Now 55 years old, he is serving an eight-year prison sentence in Louisiana for illegal re-entry and smuggling. She has many half brothers and sisters on both sides of the family. Jessica had a difficult childhood. In junior high, she joined "the wrong crowd." She believes kids get in trouble because they try to rebel against the rules. By tenth grade, her grades had recovered somewhat but then she became pregnant. She first considered abortion but her mother, Carolyn, disapproved. Jessica delivered a son, Erik, who is now six years old. Five months ago, she was delivered of another child, this time a daughter whom she named Tess.

Tess' father, Kalongi, is now working in a lumberyard somewhere in Georgia while saving money to marry. He sends Jessica money regularly to support their child. Jessica met Kalongi in Overtown, Miami's poorest slum district, where she lived with her grandmother after Carolyn became a crack addict. During that period, the mother was in and out of jail all the time. She finally found religion and they both now regularly attend Mount Antioch Missionary Baptist Church in North Miami. Jessica plans to raise her children religiously.

Jessica did not graduate from high school, but despite all obstacles, she persisted and got her GED. She wanted to major in criminal justice as a first step to becoming a lawyer or, at least, a law enforcement officer. She started taking courses at Miami-Dade Community College but could not complete even one semester. Living alone with her child, she could not afford the time to study. Since then, she has held a succession of low-paid jobs and has been on and off welfare, although she does not like it: "The agents get into your personal life. It's humiliating . . . you feel like a beggar."

Jessica continues to dream of a career in law enforcement, although her chances of returning to school are dim. Another possibility is to become self-employed by buying goods in Miami—like clothing, shoes, and perfume—for sale in Jamaica. She already attempted this once although, as seen next, the results were catastrophic. Jessica calls herself Jamaican-American and believes that the United States is the land of opportunity and freedom. Despite all her troubles, she does not think that circumstances played a part in shaping her life. She strongly agrees that "we are all masters of our destiny."

About a year ago, in her efforts to become self-supporting, Jessica rented a Nissan Maxima, to shop for goods to re-sell in Jamaica. She rented it for a week. A friend who is also

entrepreneur in his high-rise luxury office in Miami Beach, as when one visits a person who ten years ago was a child full of dreams for the future and who is today in prison.

From these results, it is evident that most of the new second generation is not joining the bottom ranks of society, but that a sizable minority is poised to do so. Since second-generation children are the fastest growing component of American youth, we ignore the forces leading to downward assimilation at our own peril. Rather than forcing immigrants and their offspring into a uniform assimilation path while otherwise abandoning them to their own resources, programmes that support selective acculturation—learning English while upholding the value of parents' language and culture—and that offer compensatory resources to deal with poverty and outside discrimination are needed to ward off the challenges confronted today by immigrant families. Theoretical positions that dismiss these challenges by asserting that there is really "nothing new" only help to compound these problems.

||| REFERENCES

Alba, Richard and Victor Nee. 2003. *Remaking the American Mainstream: Assimilation and Contemporary Immigration*, Cambridge, MA: Harvard University Press.

Alba, Richard D. 1985. *Italian Americans: Into the Twilight of Ethnicity*, Englewood Cliffs, NJ: Prentice Hall.

Child, Irvin L. 1943. *Italian or American? The Second Generation in Conflict*, New Haven, CT: Yale University Press.

Coleman, James. 1988. "Social capital in the creation of human capital," *American Journal of Sociology*, vol. 94, no. (Supplement), pp. S95–121.

Finnegan, William. 1996. "The New Americans," A Reporter at Large section of *The New Yorker* (March 25), pp. 52–71.

Perlmann, Joel. 2004. "The Mexican-American Second Generation in Census 2000: Education and Earnings," paper presented at the Conference on the Next Generation: Immigrant Youth and Families in Comparative Perspective, Radcliffe Institute for Advanced Studies, Harvard University, October.

———— and Roger Waldinger. 1997. "Second generation decline? Immigrant children past and present—a reconsideration," *International Migration Review*, vol. 31, pp. 893–922.

Portes, Alejandro and Ruben G. Rumbaut. 2001. *Legacies: The Story of the Immigrant Second Generation*, Berkeley, CA: University of California Press and Russell Sage Foundation.

Thomas, William I. and Florian Znaniecki. [1918–1920] 1984. *The Polish Peasant in Europe and America 1918–1920*, Chicago: University of Illinois Press.

Waters, Mary C. 1996. "West Indian Family Resources and Adolescent Outcomes," paper presented at the meetings of the American Association for the Advancement of Science, Baltimore, February.

Western, Bruce. 2002. "The impact of incarceration on wage mobility and inequality," *American Sociological Review*, vol. (August), pp. 526–546.

41

Will the New Second Generation Experience 'Downward Assimilation'? Segmented Assimilation Re-Assessed*

ROGER WALDINGER AND CYNTHIA FELICIANO

Concern with the prospects and experience of the "new" second generation stands at the top of the immigration research agenda in the United States. The emergence of the second generation has naturally occurred with a lag, given the protracted nature of immigrant settlement and the gradual process by which the foreign-born population has grown over the past forty years. But demography does not automatically shape minds. The intellectual catalyst for the shift in orientation was delivered by Portes and Zhou with their seminal article on "segmented assimilation (1993)." With the more recent appearance of Portes and Rumbaut's landmark study, *Legacies* (2001), based on a longitudinal survey of immigrant children in Florida and California, as well as *Ethnicities* (Rumbaut and Portes 2001), a companion volume on individual ethnic groups, the conceptual framework sketched out more than a decade ago has gained considerable reinforcement.

Portes, Zhou and Rumbaut have argued that the children of today's immigrants will assimilate in several ways—as opposed to the single, straight-line path supposedly followed by earlier immigrant waves. The offspring of

---

* First published in 2004; from *Racial and Ethnic Studies*, Volume 27, Issue 3.

middle-class immigrants will move sprightly ahead, using the resources linked to their parents' class and the opportunities furnished by the U.S.'s system of higher education to join the American "main-stream" at a pace unequalled by the second generation of old. But the children of low-skilled immigrants, visibly identifiable and entering a mainly white society still not cured of its racist afflictions, face a different, more difficult set of options. While immigrant parents arrive willing to do the jobs that natives won't hold, the children want more: not clear is whether the children's careers can live up to "their U.S.-acquired aspirations" (Portes and Zhou 1993, p. 85)? The conundrum of the contemporary second generation is heightened by the continuing transformation of the U.S. economy. Though low-skilled jobs persist, occupational segmentation has "reduced the opportunities for incremental upward mobility through well-paid, blue-collar positions." The advent of the hourglass economy confronts the immigrant children with a cruel choice: either acquire the college, and other advanced degrees needed to move into the professional/managerial elite, or else accept the same menial jobs to which the first generation was consigned. However, the children's experience of growing up as stigmatized strangers, exposed to the "adversarial culture" of native-born minorities, may lead them to act in ways that imperil school success. And without extended schooling, the immigrant offspring will be relegated to jobs at the bottom of the queue—to which, if they have absorbed the consumption norms of the American mainstream, and the oppositional values of the U.S. underclass, they may simply say, "no thanks."

Thus, the hypothesis of segmented assimilation yields a distinctive prediction: as clearly specified by Portes and Rumbaut in their recent book (2001, p. 59), the children of peasant and working-class immigrants are at risk of "downward assimilation." In this "alternative path," immigrant offspring face the prospect of dropping :from their "parents" modest starting position (Portes and Rumbaut 2001, p. 59) into "a new rainbow underclass . . . at the bottom of society" (Portes and Rumbaut 2001, p. 45). Though not always stated with the clarity one might desire, it is not difficult to infer just who makes up the "masses of the dispossessed . . . in America's inner cities (Portes and Rumbaut 2001, p. 45)": the existing native-born underclass of urban, low-skilled African-Americans, and their less numerous Puerto Rican counterparts. That contention is what this article seeks to assess, focusing on the experience of Mexicans, the overwhelmingly largest of today's second-generation groups, and a population of predominantly working- or lower-class origins, which makes it the perfect case for a test of this particular point of view.

★ ★ ★

MEXICAN IMMIGRANTS AND THEIR OFFSPRING: THE CRUCIAL TEST CASE

★ ★ ★ The hypothesis of "segmented assimilation" tells us that not all immigrant children are equally at risk. While the offspring of the large population of middle-class immigrants are "slated for a smooth transition into the mainstream" (Portes and Rumbaut 2001, p. 45), trouble, however, awaits the children of working-class immigrants.

The national origins of these children of working-class immigrants are exceedingly diverse. But Portes and his associates tell us that there is one crucial case, at once standing out from all others and exemplifying the theoretical claims that the hypothesis of segmented assimilation seeks to advance: the Mexicans. As noted in the final concluding chapter of *Legacies*: "Mexican immigrants represent *the* textbook example of theoretically anticipated effects of low immigrant human capital combined with a negative context of reception" (Portes and Rumbaut 2001, p. 277; emphasis in the original) Reviewing the book's findings, as regards the offspring of Mexican immigrants, Portes and Rumbaut conclude that the "cumulative results clearly point to a difficult process of adaptation and to the likelihood of downward assimilation . . ." (p. 279) and insist that these results warrant special attention, "given the size of the Mexican immigrant population and its all but certain continuing growth in future years." As further pointed out by Lopez and Stanton-Salazar, the authors of an article on Mexican Americans in the companion volume, *Ethnicities*, the Mexican case is of "unique importance," especially in California and the southwest, where Mexicans are "by far the largest minority and are rapidly becoming the single-largest ethnic group . . ." (Lopez and Stanton-Salazar 2001, pp. 58–9).

If the Mexican experience provides the benchmark against which the theory of segmented assimilation should be assessed, the social character of Mexican migration to the United States provides ample reason for scepticism, as regards the theory's claims. After all,

the master narrative of contemporary Mexican migration to the United States tells a story of the inexorable and progressive implantation of immigrant networks (Massey *et al*, 1987; 1994). Instability at the bottom of the labour market creates vacancies for bottom-level jobs, which immigrants, impelled by a different set of tastes and expectations than natives, are especially likely to obtain. Immigrant ranks quickly proliferate, as veterans tap the newest arrival to fill each subsequent vacancy; the process consolidates, once the best established among the immigrants moves up the pecking order, gaining influence over hiring decisions, a factor which further opens the door to kith and kin. As the immigrant network expands, and immigrant niches proliferate, immigrants are only mildly penalized for the few skills they possess, but are rewarded instead for *whom* they know. In the memorable phrase coined by Douglas Massey and his collaborators, landless Mexican *campesinos* "may be poor in financial resources, but they are wealthy in social capital, which they can readily convert into jobs and earnings in the United States" (Massey *et al*. 1987).

Of course, it is one thing when brand new immigrants, having crossed over to *el otro lado*, then take advantage of the support and information furnished by their established kin and *paisanos*. What is in dispute is the possibility that those same processes could operate in ways that facilitate labour force attachment among the second generation.

One can certainly imagine a scenario characterized by inter-generational discontinuity, as suggested by the hypothesis of segmented assimilation, but we caution against going down that road too fast. The analogy does seem overdrawn: East Los Angeles bears little resemblance to the south side of Chicago, in either its past or present incarnations. If the concept of social capital has any meaning at all, it implies that social structure has an independent effect (as argued by Coleman 1988, S96). While the children of Mexican immigrants may grow up in high poverty areas, those same places are characterized by high immigrant job-holding rates, quite in contrast to the pattern among African-Americans, where high poverty is associated with low levels of employment (Johnson *et al.*, 2000). Following Portes and Rumbaut, who tell us that "social capital depends less on the relative economic or occupational success of immigrants than on the density of ties among them (p. 65)," we should therefore expect higher employment rates among Mexican second-generation school-leavers or high school completers, as compared to their African-American counterparts.

It is also worth recalling that the embedding of immigrant communities is, at least in part, a response to employers' favourable views of the work ethic and behaviour of the foreign-born; for that reason, one can expect that immigrant children enter a reception context quite different from that encountered by their African-American counterparts. The penetration of immigrant networks is also now very deep, which, in southern California or Texas, means that there are still plenty of Mexican sweepers and sewing machine operators, but also quite a few foremen and skilled workers, which in turn provides the second generation

with access to job opportunities well above the bottom. As immigration itself generates ample needs for bilingual speakers (whether in hospitals, department stores, or factories), it creates positions for which the children of immigrants are ideally suited (Waldinger and Lichter 2003). Consequently, the social embedding of Mexican migration, with densely knit ties that span the population and connect it to workplaces, provides ground for thinking that first- to second-generation trajectories may take the form well known to the working-class, labour migrations from Eastern and Southern Europe in the century before ours. At the very least, contentions of likely "downward assimilation" warrant sceptical examination: it is this task to which we shall now turn.

COMPARISONS, INDICATORS, DATA

Comparisons

The argument that the children of Mexican immigrants may be joining the ranks of a "rainbow underclass" suffers from all the ideological problems associated with the underclass concept itself, as we have noted above. Nonetheless, the two literatures in question—on the second generation and on the "underclass"—make the identities of the relevant contrast groups clear. As we are interested in the *within group* comparison *across generations*, we will contrast a first generation born and raised in Mexico with a second generation born in the United States of Mexican immigrant parents.[1] Simultaneously,

---

1 Members of the second generation were identified using two criteria: if the father was born in Mexico; or, in those cases in which the father was born in the United States, if the mother was born in Mexico.

we want to pursue *across group* comparisons, focusing first on those native-born populations whose patterns of labour force activity are likely to exemplify the "rainbow underclass" future forecast by the hypothesis of "segmented assimilation." In keeping with the concerns of the "underclass" literature, we examine African-Americans, here defined as non-hispanic "black" native-born persons born to native parents of native parentage. The relevant contrast to native-born minorities also encompasses mainland-born Puerto Ricans. Though this group is relatively small, its disadvantaged situation has led many observers to worry that a disproportionately large number of Puerto Ricans may be falling into the "underclass" (Tienda 1989). The Puerto Rican case also plays a role in the segmented assimilation literature: Portes and Rumbaut have explicitly drawn attention to Philippe Bourgois' (1995) ethnographic study of a small group of Puerto Rican youth in New York's East, which, in their view, "exemplifies this . . . oppositional ideology . . . reinforcing the very blockage of opportunities that it denounces (2001, p. 60)."[2] We extend the across group comparison to include native-born "whites" born to native-born parents. In addition, we examine *within group* and *across group* differences *across gender*.

Indicators

In assessing the hypothesis that the Mexican second generation might experience "down-ward assimilation," we need to remember that the Mexican first generation is concentrated in jobs that lie at the very bottom of the labour market. From that standpoint, "downward" really means *out* of the labour market, a statement consistent with the view that an "underclass" emerges "when work disappears." Since the relevant spotlight, therefore, should be cast on the working-age population, we restrict our discussion to prime age adults, 25–64 years old; following Jencks (1992), we focus on three indicators of labour market attachment:

First, we examine differences in (1) *employment*, a dichotomous category separating those people with a job from those who are either out of work and looking for a job as well as those who are out of the labour force altogether. This indicator, alone, however, is likely to be too restrictive. If low-skilled workers experience high levels of frictional unemployment, as suggested by the literature on segmented labour markets (Doeringer and Piore 1971), a snapshot taken at any one point in time is likely to miss a recent, previous experience of employment. Consequently, we also examine differences in (2) *average weeks of work employed in the previous year for all those with at least one week of employment during that period.* As opposed to workers caught in the secondary labour market, where they churn from one job to another with a high frequency, persons in an "underclass" would experience long-term, chronic joblessness. Thus, to capture the population with the

---

2 For the purposes of this article, "Puerto Ricans" refers to Puerto Ricans born in the continental United States, unless otherwise indicated.

weakest attachment to the labour market, we examine differences in the proportion with (3) *no weeks of employment during the previous year.*

Following the literature, the terms of the comparison reflect those factors that put the groups at risk, most notably space and skill. On the one hand, low-skilled workers are at risk, marginalized by the decline of manufacturing and its replacement by a new economy, whose employers demand a mix of "hard" and "soft" skills that even high school educated workers— let alone drop-outs—are unlikely to possess. On the other hand, these transformations yield their greatest impact in the nation's metropolitan centres, with the most severe effects felt in inner cities (Holzer 1996; Holzer and Danziger, 2000; Moss and Tilly 2001).

However, the literature leaves considerable ambiguity as to how controls for these factors should affect the comparison to native-whites. The hypotheses of skills and spatial mismatches, from which the underclass literature derives, imply that disparities should diminish *after* application of the relevant controls. From the standpoint of segmented assimilation, however, "downward assimilation" entails a distinctively subcultural component; if less skilled members of the second generation adopt an "adversarial culture" inimical to sustained work effort, immigrant offspring should show lower levels of employment, and more chronic forms of joblessness than comparably educated native whites. Consequently, the segmented assimilation hypothesis implies that disparities should

either *persist* or *widen* after application of controls for education and location.

If the underclass literature emphasizes the importance of skills and space, and the hypothesis of "segmented assimilation" underscores the additional role of ethnicity, neither has much to say about gender. By contrast, we hypothesize that acculturation should lead to labour force patterns among second-generation women that converge with those of their third generation white counterparts, as opposed to the divergent patterns characteristic of the foreign-born. Since access to employment is affected by the presence of children, which in turn systematically differs among the groups in question, we add an additional set of controls for children under 18 in the household, when examining women.

Data

This article uses data collected as part of the March demographic files of the Current Population Survey [CPS] a monthly survey of a national probability sample of approximately 60,000 households, conducted by the U.S. Bureau of the Census. Since 1994, questions about place of birth and parents' place of birth are a permanent feature of each month's survey, making the CPS the only, large-scale, dataset capable of identifying foreign-born, U.S. born of foreign-parentage, and U.S. born of U.S. born parentage subgroups within the larger population.[3] Though the CPS universe is far smaller than the Census, one can

---

3 Since 1994, the Current Population Survey [CPS] has often been used for studies of the second generation. Other nota-

ble studies drawing on the CPS include: Card *et al.*, 2000; Hirschman 2001; Zhou 2001; Farley and Alba 2002.

combine surveys from subsequent years to build up a sample of very respectable size; this article makes particular use of a combined sample concatenating observations from the 1996 through 2001 Current Population Surveys. The CPS retains respondents during a two-year period, interviewing individuals for four consecutive months, dropping them from the sample for the next eight months, and then re-interviewing them for another four consecutive months, after which time they are dropped from the sample completely. Consequently, half of the persons interviewed in any given month reappear in the following year's sample in the same month. To avoid duplicate cases, we have retained non-overlapping halves of the 1996, 1997, 1998, 1999 and 2000 samples, and have included the entire 2001 sample. This procedure produces a sample of 239,255 prime age adults, 172,000 more than the number available in any single year.

Our contrast of the five groups in question proceeds through a set of cross-tabulations, in which we first show the zero-order difference, relative to native whites, and then apply a set of successive controls, derived from the relevant literature. For some groups, the additional controls create sample size problems; we therefore excluded from the analysis any subgroups with less than 100 cases. We also standardized for age, based on the age distributions of white men and women, to adjust for any confounding influences of age. After showing the net difference for each indicator, we first display differences for the two least skilled categories (high school graduates with no further schooling and less than high school). Within each of these two educational categories, we then show differences by place, moving from total U.S., to the twenty-seven largest metropolitan regions, and then to the central cities of those regions.[4] When examining women, the presence of children in the home provides the first axis of variation; we then apply the skill and locational controls to women with children in the household.

FINDINGS

Men

Our discussion begins with men. To reiterate, the hypothesis of segmented assimilation forecasts that levels of labour force attachment among Mexican-origin men will diminish as generational status increases, leading to convergence with the patterns for native-born minorities. By contrast, we hypothesize continuity among the two groups of Mexican-origin men, leading to persistent difference in labour force attachment as compared to native-born minorities.

---

4 As noted by a reviewer of this article, the Current Population Survey shares many of the shortcomings that afflict other similar sources of official data used for the study of immigration: in particular, it does not ask about legal status. However, this lacuna is unlikely to matter for the purposes at hand, which entail studying those children of immigrants who are born in the United States, and for whom U.S. citizenship is a birthright status. While it is true that legal status affects the foreign-born, it is unlikely that a problem in measuring legal status would account for some of this article's most basic findings: that low-skilled, Mexican-born men have high employment rates and very low rates of chronic unemployment. As concerns this essay, the first generation is of interest only insofar as it provides a baseline against which the situation of the second generation can be assessed; the article is not concerned with the first generation in and of itself.

FIGURE 1 **PERCENTAGE DIFFERENCE IN EMPLOYMENT RATES: COMPARISONS TO NATIVE-BORN WHITE MEN**

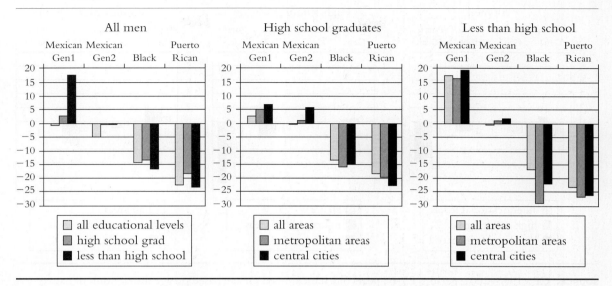

SOURCE: CPS 1996–2001; persons 25–64 years old; standardized for age based on age distribution of native whites.

1) Employment

As Figure 1 shows, the comparison between native whites and Mexican immigrants shows only slight, if any difference; employment rates for Mexican second-generation men marginally fall below those of whites. By contrast, employment levels for all black and all Puerto Rican men fall considerably short of the pattern characteristic of native whites. The literature offers little guidance to this initial comparison: given the highly unfavourable skill levels of the Mexican-origin groups, we should expect that the gap in employment rates should exceed the disparity evinced in the black and Puerto Rican cases. Applying educational controls barely affects the native minority groups, and actually enlarges the gap at the lowest skill lev-

els. For the Mexican-*born*, however, the same procedure yields far greater impact and in the opposite direction, as the least educated sustain employment rates well above the level achieved by comparable native whites. As for the second generation, applying educational controls yields effects in the same direction, reducing the second-generation/native white gap to near zero.

The next two frames in the figure, which repeat the same exercise, though now controlling for space among two categories of less skilled men, yield similar and similarly counterintuitive results. Spatial factors modestly increase the native minority/native white gap; the impact is greater for all metropolitan residents as opposed to those living in central cities

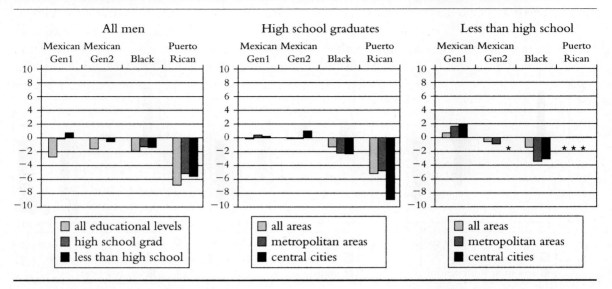

SOURCE: CPS 1996–2001; persons 25–64 years old; standardized for age based on age distribution of native whites.

*Subgroup N < 100; excluded from analysis.

only; likewise, location[5] has a more powerful effect on the very least skilled workers. The effect of space for the Mexican-origin groups contradicts the argument that metropolitan or inner-city locations is a source of exposure to risk. Regardless of location, employment rates among the Mexican-born workers compare favourably with their white counterparts, with the disparity widest among the least skilled workers located in central cities. Among male high school graduates, employment rates for Mexican second-generation workers are the same as those enjoyed by native-born whites, but then exceed the native white level with

each locational control. Regardless of location, the *least* skilled second-generation Mexicans display slightly higher employment rates than do comparable native-whites.

2) Weeks worked

Notwithstanding their very low skills, male Mexican immigrants maintain high employment rates, and regardless of location, as demonstrated by Figure 1. But, as Figure 2 shows, this snapshot taken at a single point at a time obscures the vulnerabilities associated with the labour markets on which these foreign-born workers converge: namely, the unstable nature

---

5 The metropolitan areas included are Los Angeles, New York, San Francisco, Chicago, Miami, Boston, Cincinnati, Cleveland, Dallas, Denver, Detroit, Houston, Milwaukee, Phila-

delphia, Portland, Sacramento, Seattle, Washington, Atlanta, Kansas City, Minneapolis, Norfolk, Phoenix, Pittsburgh, St. Louis, San Diego, and Tampa.

of the jobs and their susceptibility to short-term shifts in demand, whether of a seasonal or cyclical nature. Thus, on average, Mexican-origin men work fewer weeks than do native whites, a disparity that hits its widest point when the contrast compares all Mexican first generation and white native-born men. The disparity, however, either diminishes or reverses direction once controls for schooling are applied, suggesting that the lesser instability of employment among Mexicans principally stems from the inherent vulnerability associated with their very low skills. Controls for location further reduce the advantages enjoyed by native whites, a change consistent with the pure spatial mismatch hypothesis, though one that leaves one wondering why central cities should be the places where the lowest skilled Mexican-origin men are particularly likely to work more weeks than comparable native whites. Similarly, Mexican second-generation men lag behind white native men by a gap of almost two weeks. But the disparity virtually disappears when the contrast is restricted to high school graduates, and, while reappearing among those without a high school degree, takes a more modest form. Controlling for spatial differences among the high school graduates leave Mexican second-generation men at an advantage in precisely that location where they should be most vulnerable: central cities. By contrast, the high school dropouts experience a very slight disadvantage, nationwide and in all metropolitan areas, relative to the native whites. Most crucially, the situation of second-generation Mexican high school graduates and non-completers compares very favourably to the patterns shown by native minority men. Not only do all black and Puerto

Rican men work fewer weeks than do all native white men; application of educational controls leaves a substantial gap. The same holds true for the locational controls, a factor that actually widens the disparity experienced by Puerto Rican high school graduates, as predicted by the spatial mismatch hypothesis.

3) Chronic joblessness

Figure 3, which shows differences in long-term joblessness, provides the mirror image of Figure 1. Among *all* men, long-term joblessness is only slightly higher among the Mexican-born group as among native whites. But once the comparison narrows to men of lower skills, advantage passes to the immigrants, and by a very considerable margin among those in the least educated category. As in the previous contrasts, locational controls work in favour of Mexican immigrants. Overall, the Mexican second generation displays a slightly higher rate of chronic joblessness than appears among native whites. Among the least educated and among high school graduates in central cities, however, the balance shifts in favour of the Mexican second generation. By contrast, chronic joblessness is far more prevalent among blacks and Puerto Ricans than among whites or either Mexican-origin group. Moreover, that disparity widens significantly, as one shifts the comparison to less skilled groups, and within skill groups, from the entire U.S. population to those in metropolitan regions.

Women

Much of the underclass literature concerns women, but through a prism that sees their destinies largely determined by the fate of "their" men. The skills and spatial mismatch

FIGURE 3 **PERCENTAGE DIFFERENCE IN LONG-TERM JOBLESSNESS: COMPARISON TO NATIVE WHITE MEN**

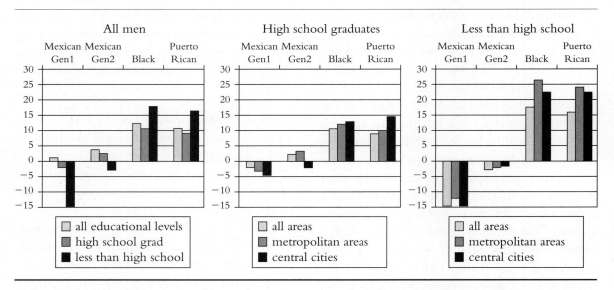

SOURCE: CPS 1996–2001; persons 25–64 years old; standardized for age based on age distribution of native whites.

literatures, from which the Wilsonian underclass view derives, make much of the baleful consequences of the decline of the heavy manufacturing industries with their well-paying jobs —but those were never the places in which women found work. The same point holds for the "segmented assimilation" hypothesis, which claims that today's new economy will impede the gradual transition from labourer to well-paid blue-collar worker enjoyed by the second generation of old. Perhaps, perhaps not; but in any case, only a delimited subset of yesterday's second generation got ahead this way. Unlike their menfolk, Italian, Polish, and Slovak second-generation women mainly worked in light industry, service, or low level clerical jobs—in other words, not so different a mix than that available to the adult immigrant offspring of the early twenty-first century.

There are further ironies to the way in which the entire discussion has been framed, While Mexican men enjoy high rates of employment and labour force participation, Mexican immigrant and -origin women have historically displayed the opposite pattern. If the argument implies that the behaviour of the second generation shifts as a result of "acculturation" into the norms of native minorities, then it is the historically high labour force participation rates of African-American women that should provide the model for their second-generation Mexican-origin counterparts.

1) Employment

Thus, the literature does not prepare us well for Figure 4, which displays employment rates, distinguishing between women with children under 18 in the household, and those without.

FIGURE 4 **PERCENTAGE DIFFERENCE IN EMPLOYMENT RATES: COMPARISON TO NATIVE WHITE WOMEN**

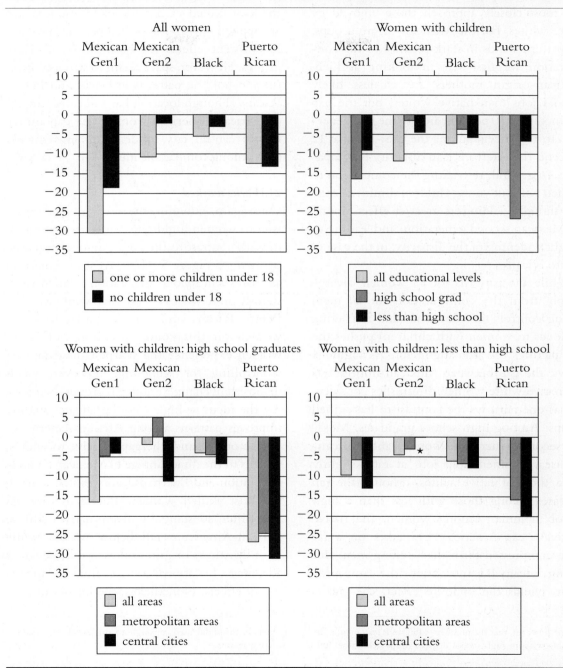

SOURCE: CPS 1996–2001; persons 25–64 years old; standardized for age based on age distribution of native whites.

Of all the groups, black mothers work at rates that most closely approach those enjoyed by native whites. For the Mexican-origin groups, the pattern stands in stark contrast to the configuration we first saw in looking at men. Mexican-origin mothers are all less likely to hold jobs than native whites, but the gap declines from 30 per cent among the first generation to 11 per cent among the U.S.-born; at 12 per cent, the Puerto Rican disparity is comparable. In general, restricting the comparison to women without young children diminishes the gap, though yielding its greatest effect among the Mexican second generation, and leading to a slight widening of the disparity, in the case of Puerto Ricans.

While the patterns for *all* women diverge sharply from the configuration for *all* men, adding controls for education (and restricting the focus to women with children) pushes the two pictures towards alignment. As Figure 4 shows, the gap between Mexican immigrants and native white women diminishes considerably as one narrows the contrast to less skilled groups. Among high school graduates, Mexican second generation women and African-American women hold jobs at rates slightly below those of native whites, although the gap increases among those with less than a high school diploma. Among women, the native white/African-American gap takes on a far more compressed form than among men. But among Puerto Rican women, the same procedure yields the opposite effect: the gap is greatest for high school graduates and less for the least skilled.[6] Controls for location, which are applied only to less skilled persons, produce inconsistent effects for both Mexican-origin groups. However, space seems to strongly affect the job-holding patterns of blacks and Puerto Ricans. Though location has a negative impact on African-American women, the gap among female central city residents remains smaller than among comparable men.

2) Weeks worked

Once again, extending the inter-group comparison to women highlights a pattern that stands in stark contrast to the configuration displayed by men. As Figure 5 shows, African-American and Mexican second-generation women work slightly more weeks overall than white women; Puerto Rican women look similar to white women on this count; Mexican immigrant women experience the sharpest disadvantage. Controlling for schooling, however, yields inconsistent change among all groups. Narrowing the focus to high school graduates slightly improves patterns among African-Americans; on the other hand, the gap, relative to whites, widens to the disadvantage of Mexican second-generation and Puerto Rican women. Among the least skilled women, Puerto Ricans do not differ substantially from native whites, African-Americans fall below whites, while both Mexican-origin groups are at a slight advantage. Locational controls also yield inconsistent effects. Nonetheless, the impact of cen-

---

6 Note, however, that the number of Puerto Rican men in the sample without high school degrees drops below the 100- person threshold used, throughout this article, for making comparisons.

FIGURE 5 **DIFFERENCE IN AVERAGE WEEKS WORKED; WOMEN WITH CHILDREN, COMPARISON TO COMPARABLE WHITE WOMEN**

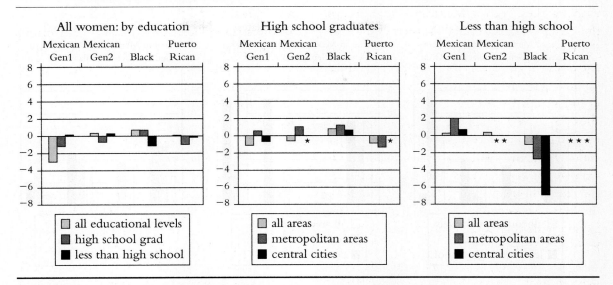

SOURCE: CPS 1996–2001; persons 25–64 years old; standardized for age based on age distribution of native whites.

*Subgroup N < 100: excluded from analysis.

---

tral city location exercises its greatest, negative effect on the least skilled black and Puerto Rican women.

3) Chronic joblessness

This last indicator, which identifies the population with the weakest attachment to the labour market, underscores the generational changes at work among Mexican-origin women. As we have seen, job holding among Mexican immigrant women falls substantially below the native white level; when we turn to chronic joblessness, however, we observe a gap of virtually the same size, but in the opposite direction. As shown in Figure 6, the gap narrows sub-

stantially as one moves from first- to second-generation Mexican-origin women, who in turn, do slightly worse than black women, among whom chronic joblessness is 5 per cent higher than the level recorded by whites. Controlling for education alters inter-group differences, clearly reducing the gap in the case of the Mexican immigrants, on the one hand, and yielding inconsistent effects for the other groups. In the case of Mexican second-generation women, the gap declines substantially when the contrast narrows to high school graduates, a finding that is surely relevant if we argue it is when *work* disappears that the "underclass" emerges. Subsequent controls for location

FIGURE 6 **PERCENTAGE DIFFERENCE, LONG-TERM JOBLESSNESS: WOMEN WITH CHILDREN, COMPARISON TO COMPARABLE WHITE WOMEN**

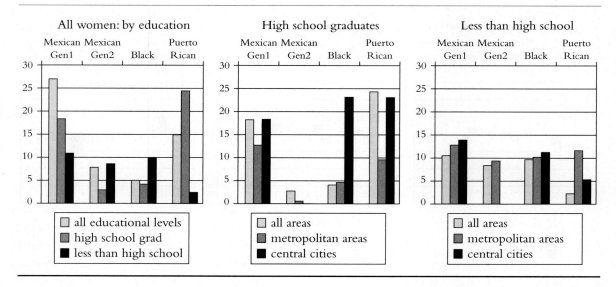

produce varying and inconsistent effects across group and skilled category. The most notable pattern is the one observed among the Mexican first generation, where joblessness bears little relationship to location, suggesting that the barriers to employment derive largely, if not entirely, from some other source.

||| CONCLUSION

The recent scholarship on the "new" second generation has begun on a note of inflected pessimism, of which the hypothesis of "segmented assimilation" is the best and most influential example. Concern for the prospects of the children of today's immigrants is certainly warranted. While low-skilled immigrants are moving to the United States in large numbers, they are entering an economy that provides

little reward for workers of modest schooling, regardless of ethnic stripes. The liabilities associated with foreign-birth exercise a further penalty, adding to the difficulties that derive from low schooling as such. And although the migration process operates in such a way as to connect immigrants—or at least the men among them—to employers, the social capital that generates attachment seems less able to produce the skill acquisition needed for occupational mobility. So if less skilled immigrants make up a working poor, locked into low wage jobs, and therefore confined to inner cities and their failing school systems, can we expect that their U.S.-born and -raised children will find progress?

The hypothesis of "segmented assimilation" suggests that the answer should be no. But this article, comparing first- and second-generation Mexicans with African-Americans, Puerto

Ricans, and native whites, finds little support for the point of view that the offspring of working-class immigrants will experience "downward assimilation." While U.S.-born Mexican men do not retain the extraordinary job-holding rates of the foreign-born generational groups, the shift takes them to the levels that characterize native-born whites. As the second generation is significantly better educated than the first, U.S.-born men find jobs associated with lower levels of frictional unemployment, as indicated by the smaller gap, compared to native whites, in weeks worked. Most importantly, the U.S.-born and -raised groups display patterns that consistently diverge from those observed among African-Americans or Puerto Ricans, that is to say, those groups comprising the putative "rainbow underclass" whose ranks today's second generation are supposedly fated to join.

Taking gender into account, not considered in any of the formulations in which the hypothesis of "segmented assimilation" has been developed, alters the picture still more. The segmented assimilation story line is one of diminishing labour force attachment as one moves from foreign-born to U.S.-raised to U.S.-born generations, a scenario that might be plausible for men, but immediately runs into problems in the case of Mexican women, among whom rates of labour force participation have historically been low. As we have shown, the labour force behaviour of U.S.-born Mexican-origin women looks a good deal more like the pattern evident among native whites. Though a gap persists on all three of the indicators that we have examined, the disparity is of greatly diminished proportions.

So if the Mexican second generation is not travelling the road of "downward assimilation" into a "rainbow underclass," what type of future can one forecast? In our view, the evidence compiled in this article suggests that the experience of today's second generation is consistent with the earlier pattern, in which the children of immigrants progressed by moving ahead within the working class. To begin with, the second generation enters the labour market with levels of education that greatly exceed the schooling obtained by the parental generation. Yes, levels of schooling are not such as to produce parity with native whites, but they do mitigate the negative effects associated with the very low skills of the foreign-born and -raised generations. And one needs also to take account of the changes at work among women—among whom the increase in average schooling levels is greater still—which implies that the effect of higher levels of labour force activity are amplified by the greater earnings power generated by further education. If the high rates of marriage, characteristic of the first generation, persist among women, and fertility falls, the levels of living enjoyed by second-generation families, not quite so large as among the first, and in which mothers are a good deal more likely to work, should compare favourably with the pattern that characterizes the first generation. While the empirical evidence needed to make this case convincing requires another article, we do note support in the literature. For example, Vilma Ortiz's (1996) study of the Mexican experience in Los Angeles underscored the persistent disadvantage endured by the region's Mexican Americans, all the while pointing out that the native-born population had evolved into a group that was of distinctly working-class character. Ortiz's conclusions resonated with the findings of an earlier effort to assess the relevance of the underclass hypothesis for Latinos (Moore and Pinderhughes 1993), which concluded that the sources of Latino poverty had far more to do with the problems of the working-poor, as opposed to the difficulties experienced by those for whom "work has disappeared." And the historically minded reader can turn to the pages of Douglas Monroy's (1999) history of the Mexican American second generation of the 1920s and 1930s, which shows that Americanization powerfully affected this earlier group of immigrant offspring, and in contemporary-sounding ways, without ever producing an "underclass" along the lines projected today.

★ ★ ★

‖ REFERENCES

Bourgois, Philippe. 1995. *In Search of Respect: Selling Crack in El Barrio*, New York: Cambridge University Press.

Card, David, John Dinardo, and Eugena Estes. 2000. "The more things change: immigrants and the children of immigrants in the 1940s, 1970s, and 1990s," pp. 227–71 in George J. Borjas (ed.), *Issues in the Economics of Immigration*, Chicago: University of Chicago Press.

Coleman, James S. 1988. "Social capital in the creation of human capital," *American Journal of Sociology*, vol. 94, S95–S120.

Doeringer, Peter B. and Michael J. Piore. 1971. *Internal Labor Markets and Manpower Analysis*, Lexington, MA: Heath Lexington Books.

Farley, Reynolds and Richard Alba. 2002. "The new second generation in the United States" *International Migration Review*, vol. 36, no. 2, pp. 669–701.

Gans, Herbert. 1962. *The Urban Villagers*, New York: Free Press.

———. 1992. "Second-generation decline: scenarios for the economic and ethnic futures of the post-1965 American immigrants" *Ethnic and Racial Studies*, vol. 15, no. 2.

Hirschman, Charles. 2001. "The educational enrollment of immigrant youth: A test of the segmented–assimilation hypothesis," *Demography*, vol. 38, no. 3, pp. 318–38.

Holzer, Harry. 1996. *What Employers Want: Job Prospects for Less-educated Workers*, New York: Russell Sage Foundation.

Holzer, Harry and Sheldon Danziger. 2000. "Are jobs available for disadvantaged workers in the United States," in Lawrence Bobo, Alice O'Connor, and Chris Tilly (eds), *Urban Inequality in the United States: Evidence from Four Cities,* New York: Russell Sage Foundation.

Jencks, Christopher. 1992. *Rethinking Social Policy: Race, Poverty, and the Underclass*, Cambridge: Harvard University Press.

Johnson, James H. Jr., Walter Farrell Jr., and Jennifer A. Stoloff. 2000. "African American males in decline: A Los Angeles case study," pp. 315–38, in Lawrence Bobo, Melvin L. Oliver, James H. Johnson, Jr., and Abel Valenzuela (eds), *Prismatic Metropolis*, New York: Russell Sage.

Lopez, David and Ricardo Stanton-Salazar. 2001. "The new Mexican second generation," in Rubén Rumbaut and Alejandro Portes (eds). 2001. *Ethnicities: Children of Immigrants in America,* Berkeley: University of California Press.

Massey, Douglas *et al.* 1987. *Return to Aztlan,* Berkeley: University of California Press.

————. 1994. "Continuities in transnational migration: An analysis of 19 Mexican communities," *American Journal of Sociology,* May, pp. 1492–1533.

Monroy, Douglas. 1999. *Rebirth: Mexican Los Angeles from the Great Migration to the Great Depression,* Berkeley: University of California Press.

Moore, Joan and Raquel Pinderhughes (eds). 1993. *In the Barrios: Latinos and the Underclass Debate,* New York: Russell Sage Foundation.

Moss, Philip and Chris Tilly. 2001. *Stories Employers Tell: Race, Skill, and Hiring in America,* New York: Russell Sage Foundation.

Neckerman, Kathryn M., Prudence Carter, Jennifer Lee. 1998. "Segmented assimilation and minority cultures of mobility," *Ethnic and Racial Studies,* vol. 22, no. 6, pp. 945–65.

Ortiz, Vilma. 1996. "The Mexican-origin population: Permanent working-class or emerging middle class?," pp. 247–78, in Roger Waldinger and Mehdi Bozorgmehr (eds), *Ethnic Los Angeles,* New York: Russell Sage.

Portes, Alejandro and Rubén Rumbaut. 1996. *Immigrant America,* Berkeley: University of California Press.

————. 2001. *Legacies: The Story of the Immigrant Second Generation,* Berkeley: University of California Press.

Portes, Alejandro and Min Zhou. 1993. "The new second generation: segmented assimilation and its variants among post-1965 immigrant youth," *Annals* No. 530, pp. 74–96.

Rumbaut, Rubén and Alejandro Portes (eds). 2001. *Ethnicities: Children of Immigrants in America,* Berkeley: University of California Press.

Tienda, Marta. 1989. "Puerto-Ricans and the underclass debate," *Annals of the American Academy of Political and Social Science,* vol. 501, pp. 105–19.

Waldinger, Roger and Michael Lichter. 2003. *How the Other Half Works: Immigration and the Social Organization of Labor,* Berkeley: University of California Press.

Ware, Caroline. [1935] 1965. *Greenwich Village, 1920–1930: A Comment on American Civilization in the Post-War Years,* New York: Harper.

Zhou, Min. 2001. "Progress, Decline, Stagnation? The New Second Generation Comes of Age," pp. 272–307, in Roger Waldinger (ed.), *Strangers at the Gates: New Immigrants in Urban America,* Berkeley: University of California Press.

Complex Inequalities: The Intersection of Gender, Race, and Class

42

Race, Class, and Gender as Categories of Analysis and Connection*

PATRICIA HILL COLLINS

★ ★ ★ While many of us have little difficulty assessing our own victimization within some major system of oppression, whether it be by race, social class, religion, sexual orientation, ethnicity, age or gender, we typically fail to see how our thoughts and actions uphold someone else's subordination. Thus, white feminists routinely point with confidence to their oppression as women but resist seeing how much their white skin privileges them. African-Americans who possess eloquent analyses of racism often persist in viewing poor White women as symbols of white power. The radical left fares little better. "If only people of color and women could see their true class interests," they argue, "class solidarity would eliminate racism and sexism." In essence, each group identifies the type of oppression with which it feels most comfortable as being fundamental and classifies all other types as being of lesser importance.

Oppression is full of such contradictions. Errors in political judgment that we make concerning how we teach our courses, what we tell our children, and which organizations are worthy of our time, talents and financial support

---

* First published in 1993; from *Race, Gender & Class*, Volume 1, Number 1.

flow smoothly from errors in theoretical analysis about the nature of oppression and activism. Once we realize that there are few pure victims or oppressors, and that each one of us derives varying amounts of penalty and privilege from the multiple systems of oppression that frame our lives, then we will be in a position to see the need for new ways of thought and action.

To get at that "piece of the oppressor which is planted deep within each of us," we need at least two things. First, we need new visions of what oppression is, new categories of analysis that are inclusive of race, class, and gender as distinctive yet interlocking structures of oppression. Adhering to a stance of comparing and ranking oppressions—the proverbial, "I'm more oppressed than you"—locks us all into a dangerous dance of competing for attention, resources, and theoretical supremacy. Instead, I suggest that we examine our different experiences within the more fundamental relationship of damnation and subordination. To focus on the particular arrangements that race or class or gender take in our time and place without seeing these structures as sometimes parallel and sometimes interlocking dimensions of the more fundamental relationship of domination and subordination may temporarily ease our consciences. But while such thinking may lead to short term social reforms, it is simply inadequate for the task of bringing about long term social transformation.

While race, class and gender as categories of analysis are essential in helping us understand the structural bases of domination and subordination, new ways of thinking that are not accompanied by new ways of acting offer incomplete prospects for change. To get at that "piece of the oppressor which is planted deep within each of us," we also need to change our daily behavior. Currently, we are all enmeshed in a complex web of problematic relationships that grant our minor images full human subjectivity while stereotyping and objectifying those most different than ourselves. We often assume that the people we work with, teach, send our children to school with, and sit next to in conferences such as this, will act and feel in prescribed ways because they belong to given race, social class or gender categories. These judgments by category must be replaced with fully human relationships that transcend the legitimate differences created by race, class and gender as categories of analysis. We require new categories of connection, new visions of what our relationships with one another can be.

Our task is immense. We must first recognize race, class and gender as interlocking categories of analysis that together cultivate profound differences in our personal biographies. But then we must transcend those very differences by reconceptualizing race, class and gender in order to create new categories of connection.

My presentation today addresses this need for new patterns of thought and action. I focus on two basic questions. First, how can we reconceptualize race, class and gender as categories of analysis? Second, how can we transcend the barriers created by our experiences with race, class and gender oppression in order to build the types of coalitions essential for social exchange? To address these questions I contend that we must acquire both new theories of how race, class and gender have shaped the experiences not just of women of color, but of all groups. Moreover, we must see the connections between these categories of analysis and the personal issues in our everyday lives, particularly our scholarship, our teaching and our relationships with our colleagues and students. As Audre Lorde points out, change starts with self, and relationships that we have with those around us must always be the primary site for social change.

HOW CAN WE RECONCEPTUALIZE RACE, CLASS AND GENDER AS CATEGORIES OF ANALYSIS?

To me, we must shift our discourse away from additive analyses of oppression (Spelman 1982; Collins 1989). Such approaches are typically based on two key premises. First, they depend on either/or, dichotomous thinking. Persons, things and ideas are conceptualized in terms of their opposites. For example, Black/White, man/woman, thought/feeling, and fact/opinion are defined in oppositional terms. Thought and feeling are not seen as two different and interconnected ways of approaching truth that can coexist in scholarship and teaching. Instead, feeling is defined as antithetical to reason, as its opposite. In spite of the fact that we all have "both/and" identities, (I am both a college professor and a mother—I don't stop being a mother when I drop my child off at school, or forget everything I learned while scrubbing the toilet), we persist in trying to classify each other in either/or categories. I live each day as an African-American woman—a race/gender specific experience. And I am not alone. Everyone in this room has a race/gender/class specific identity. Either/or, dichotomous thinking is especially troublesome when applied to theo-

ries of oppression because every individual must be classified as being either oppressed or not oppressed. The both/and position of simultaneously being oppressed and oppressor becomes conceptually impossible.

A second premise of additive analyses of oppression is that these dichotomous differences must be ranked. One side of the dichotomy is typically labeled dominant and the other subordinate. Thus, Whites rule Blacks, men are deemed superior to women, and reason is seen as being preferable to emotion. Applying this premise to discussions of oppression leads to the assumption that oppression can be quantified, and that some groups are oppressed more than others. I am frequently asked, "Which has been most oppressive to you, your status as a Black person or your status as a woman?" What I am really being asked to do is divide myself into little boxes and rank my various statuses. If I experience oppression as a both/and phenomenon, why should I analyze it any differently?

Additive analyses of oppression rest squarely on the twin pillars of either/or thinking and the necessity to quantify and rank all relationships in order to know where one stands. Such approaches typically see African-American women as being more oppressed than everyone else because the majority of Black women experience the negative effects of race, class and gender oppression simultaneously. In essence, if you add together separate oppressions, you are left with a grand oppression greater than the sum of its parts.

I am not denying that specific groups experience oppression more harshly than others— lynching is certainly objectively worse than being held up as a sex object. But we must be careful not to confuse this issue of the saliency of one type of oppression in people's lives with a theoretical stance positing the interlocking nature of oppression. Race, class and gender may all structure a situation but may not be equally visible and/or important in people's self-definitions. In certain contexts, such as the antebellum American South and contemporary South America, racial oppression is more visibly salient, while in other contexts, such as Haiti, El Salvador and Nicaragua, social class oppression may be more apparent. For middle class White women, gender may assume experiential primacy unavailable to poor Hispanic women struggling with the ongoing issues of low paid jobs and the frustrations of the welfare bureaucracy. This recognition that one category may have salience over another for a given time and place does not minimize the theoretical importance of assuming that race, class and gender as categories of analysis structure all relationships.

In order to move toward new visions of what oppression is, I think that we need to ask new questions. How are relationships of domination and subordination structured and maintained in the American political economy? How do race, class and gender function as parallel and interlocking systems that shape this basic relationship of domination and subordination? Questions such as these promise to move us away from futile theoretical struggles concerned with ranking oppressions and towards analyses that assume race, class and gender are all present in any given setting, even if one appears more visible and salient than the others. Our task becomes redefined as one of reconceptualizing oppression by uncovering the connec-

tions among race, class and gender as categories of analysis.

1. Institutional Dimension of Oppression

Sandra Harding's contention that gender oppression is structured along three main dimensions—the institutional, the symbolic, and the individual—offers a useful model for a more comprehensive analysis encompassing race, class and gender oppression (Harding 1989). Systemic relationships of domination and subordination structured through social institutions such as schools, businesses, hospitals, the work place, and government agencies represent the institutional dimension of oppression. Racism, sexism and elitism all have concrete institutional locations. Even though the workings of the institutional dimension of oppression are often obscured with ideologies claiming equality of opportunity, in actuality, race, class and gender place Asian-American women, Native American men, White men, African-American women, and other groups in distinct institutional niches with varying degrees of penalty and privilege.

★ ★ ★ Let us assume that the institutions of American society discriminate, whether by design or by accident. While many of us are familiar with how race, gender and class operate separately to structure inequality, I want to focus on how these three systems interlock in structuring the institutional dimension of oppression. To get at the interlocking nature of race, class and gender, I want you to think about the antebellum plantation as a guiding metaphor for a variety of American ˉsocial institutions. Even though slavery is typically analyzed as a racist institution, and occasionally as a class institution, I suggest that slavery was a race, class, gender specific institution. Removing any one piece from our analysis diminishes our understanding of the true nature of relations of domination and subordination under slavery.

Slavery was a profoundly patriarchal institution. It rested on the dual tenets of White male authority and White male property, a joining of the political and the economic within the institution of the family. Heterosexism was assumed and all Whites were expected to marry. Control over affluent White women's sexuality remained key to slavery's survival because property was to be passed on to the legitimate heirs of the slave owner. Ensuring affluent White women's virginity and chastity was deeply intertwined with maintenance of property relations.

Under slavery, we see varying levels of institutional protection given to affluent White women, working class and poor White women, and enslaved African women. Poor White women enjoyed few of the protections held out to their upper class sisters. Moreover, the devalued status of Black women was key in keeping all White women in their assigned places. Controlling Black women's fertility was also key to the continuation of slavery, for children born to slave mothers themselves were slaves.

A.frican-American women shared the devalued status of chattel with their husbands, fathers and sons. Racism stripped Blacks as a group of legal rights, education, and control over their own persons. African-Americans could be whipped, branded, sold, or killed, not because they were poor, or because they were women, but because they were Black. Racism ensured that Blacks would continue to serve Whites and

suffer economic exploitation at the hands of all Whites.

So we have a very interesting chain of command on the plantation—the affluent White master as the reigning patriarch, his White wife helpmate to serve him, help him manage his property and bring up his heirs, his faithful servants whose production and reproduction were tied to the requirements of the capitalist political economy, and largely propertyless, working class White men and women watching from afar. In essence, the foundations for the contemporary roles of elite White women, poor Black women, working class White men, and a series of other groups can be seen in stark relief in this fundamental American social institution. While Blacks experienced the most harsh treatment under slavery, and thus made slavery clearly visible as a racist institution, race, class and gender interlocked in structuring slavery's systemic organization of domination and subordination.

Even today, the plantation remains a compelling metaphor for institutional oppression. Certainly the actual conditions of oppression are not as severe now as they were then. To argue, as some do, that things have not changed all that much denigrates the achievements of those who struggled for social change before us. But the basic relationships among Black men, Black women, elite White women, elite White men, working class White men and working class White women as groups remain essentially intact.

A brief analysis of key American social institutions most controlled by elite White men should convince us of the interlocking nature of race, class and gender in structuring the institutional dimension of oppression. For example, if you are from an American college or university, is your campus a modem plantation? Who controls your university's political economy? Are elite White men over represented among the upper administrators and trustees controlling your university's finances and policies? Are elite White men being joined by growing numbers of elite White women helpmates? What kinds of people are in your classrooms grooming the next generation who will occupy these and other decision-making positions? Who are the support staff that produce the mass mailings, order the supplies, fix the leaky pipes? Do African-Americans, Hispanics or other people of color form the majority of the invisible workers who feed you, wash your dishes, and clean up your offices and libraries after everyone else has gone home?

If your college is anything like mine, you know the answers to these questions. You may be affiliated with an institution that has Hispanic women as vice-presidents for finance, or substantial numbers of Black men among the faculty. If so, you are fortunate. Much more typical are colleges where a modified version of the plantation as a metaphor for the institutional dimension of oppression survives.

The Symbolic Dimension of Oppression

Widespread, societally-sanctioned ideologies used to justify relations of domination and subordination comprise the symbolic dimension of oppression. Central to this process is the use of stereotypical or controlling images of diverse race, class and gender groups. In order to assess the power of this dimension of oppression, I want you to make a list, either on paper or in your head, of "masculine" and "feminine" characteristics. If your list is anything like that compiled by most people, it reflects some variation of the following:

Masculine	Feminine
aggressive	passive
leader	follower
rational	emotional
strong	weak
intellectual	physical

Not only does this list reflect either/or dichotomous thinking and the need to rank both sides of the dichotomy, but ask yourself exactly which men and women you had in mind when compiling these characteristics. This list applies almost exclusively to middle class White men and women. The allegedly "masculine" qualities that you probably listed are only acceptable when exhibited by elite White men, or when used by Black and Hispanic men against each other or against women of color. Aggressive Black and Hispanic men are seen as dangerous, not powerful, and are often penalized when they exhibit any of the allegedly "masculine" characteristics. Working class and poor White men fare slightly better and are also denied the allegedly "masculine" symbols of leadership, intellectual competence, and human rationality. Women of color and working class and poor White women are also not represented on this list, for they have never had the luxury of being "ladies." What appear to be universal categories representing all men and women instead are unmasked as being applicable to only a small group.

It is important to see how the symbolic images applied to different race, class and gender groups interact in maintaining systems of domination and subordination. If I were to ask you to repeat the same assignment, only this time, by making separate lists for Black men, Black women, Hispanic women and Hispanic men, I suspect that your gender symbolism would be quite different. In comparing all of the lists, you might begin to see the interdependence of symbols applied to all groups. For example, the elevated images of White womanhood need devalued images of Black womanhood in order to maintain credibility.

While the above exercise reveals the interlocking nature of race, class and gender in structuring the symbolic dimension of oppression, part of its importance lies in demonstrating how race, class and gender pervade a wide range of what appears to be universal language. Attending to diversity in our scholarship, in our teaching, and in our daily lives provides a new angle of vision on interpretations of reality thought to be natural, normal and "true." Moreover, viewing images of masculinity and femininity as universal gender symbolism, rather than as symbolic images that are race, class and gender specific, renders the experiences of people of color and of non-privileged White women and men invisible. One way to dehumanize an individual or a group is to deny the reality of their experiences. So when we refuse to deal with race or class because they do not appear to be directly relevant to gender, we are actually becoming part of someone else's problem.

Assuming that everyone is affected differently by the same interlocking set of symbolic images allows us to move forward toward new analyses. Women of color and White women have different relationships to White male authority and this difference explains the distinct gender symbolism applied to both groups. Black women encounter controlling images such as the mammy, the matriarch, the mule and the whore, that encourage others to reject us as fully human people. Ironically, the negative nature of these images simultaneously encourages us to reject them. In contrast, White women are offered seductive images, those that promise to reward them for supporting the status quo. And yet seductive images can be equally controlling. Consider, for example, the views of Nancy White, a 73-year old Black woman, concerning images of rejection and seduction:

> My mother used to say that the black woman is the white man's mule and the white woman is his dog. Now, she said that to say this: we do the heavy work and get beat whether we do it well or not. But the white woman is closer to the master and he pats them on the head and lets them sleep in the house, but he ain't gon' treat neither one like he was dealing with a person. (Gwaltney, 148)

Both sets of images stimulate particular political stances. By broadening the analysis beyond the confines of race, we can see the varying levels of rejection and seduction available to each of us due to our race, class and gender identity. Each of us lives with an allotted portion of institutional privilege and penalty, and with varying levels of rejection and seduction inherent in the symbolic images applied to us. This is the context in which we make our choices. Taken together, the institutional and symbolic dimensions of oppression create a structural backdrop against which all of us live our lives.

The Individual Dimension of Oppression

Whether we benefit or not, we all live within institutions that reproduce race, class and gender oppression. Even if we never have any contact with members of other race, class and gender groups, we all encounter images of these groups and are exposed to the symbolic meanings attached to those images. On this dimension of oppression, our individual biographies vary tremendously. As a result of our institutional and symbolic statuses, all of our choices become political acts.

Each of us must come to terms with the multiple ways in which race, class and gender as categories of analysis frame our individual biographies. I have lived my entire life as an African-American woman from a working class family and this basic fact has had a profound impact on my personal biography. Imagine how different your life might be if you had been born Black, or White, or poor, or a different race/class/gender group than the one with which you are most familiar. The institutional treatment you would have received and the symbolic meanings attached to your very existence might differ dramatically from what you now consider to be natural, normal and part of everyday life. You might be the same, but your personal biography might have been quite different.

I believe that each of us carries around the cumulative effect of our lives within multiple structures of oppression. If you want to see how much you have been affected by this whole thing, I ask you one simple question—who are your close friends? Who are the people with whom you can share your hopes, dreams, vul-nerabilities, fears and victories? Do they look like you? If they are all the same, circumstance may be the cause. For the first seven years of my life I saw only low income Black people. My friends from those years reflected the composition of my community. But now that I am an adult, can the defense of circumstance explain the patterns of people that I trust as my friends and colleagues? When given other alternatives, if my friends and colleagues reflect the homogeneity of one race, class and gender group, then these categories of analysis have indeed become barriers to connection.

I am not suggesting that people are doomed to follow the paths laid out for them by race, class and gender as categories of analysis. While these three structures certainly frame my opportunity structure, I as an individual always have the choice of accepting things as they are, or trying to change them. As Nikki Giovanni points out, "we've got to live in the real world. If we don't like the world we're living in, change it. And if we can't change it, we change ourselves. We can do something" (Tate 1983, 68). While a piece of the oppressor may be planted deep within each of us, we each have the choice of accepting that piece or challenging it as part of the "true focus of revolutionary change."

★ ★ ★

||| REFERENCES

Butler, Johnnella. 1989. "Difficult Dialogues." *The Women's Review of Books* 6, no. 5.

Collins, Patricia Hill. 1989. "The Social Construction of Black Feminist Thought." *Signs.* Summer 1989.

Harding, Sandra. 1986. *The Science Question in Feminism.* Ithaca, New York: Cornell University Press.

Gwalatney, John Langston. 1980. *Drylongso: A Self-Portrait of Black America.* New York: Vintage.

Lorde, Audre. 1984. *Sister Outsider.* Trumansberg, New York: The Crossing Press.

————. 1985 "Sisterhood and Survival." Keynote address, conference on the Black Woman Writer and the Diaspora, Michigan State University.

Jordan, June. 1985. *On Call: Political Essays.* Boston: South End Press.

Spelman, Elizabeth. 1982. "Theories of Race and Gender: The Erasure of Black Women." *Quest* 5: 32–36.

Tate, Claudia, ed. 1983. *Black Women Writers at Work.* New York: Continuum.

43

Broken Bloodlines:
The External Gender Environment[*]

ORLANDO PATTERSON

THE EXTERNAL GENDER ENVIRONMENT: ASPECTS OF THE DOUBLE BURDEN

Afro-American women writers and leaders have long claimed that they share a double burden, being victims of both their gender and their ethnicity. This sociological trope originated in the middle of the nineteenth century with the ex-slave writer Harriet A. Jacobs when she wrote of Afro-American women in general: "Superadded to the burden common to all, *they* have wrongs, and sufferings, and mortifications peculiarly their own."[1] In today's terms, added to the burden of racism is the "double jeopardy" of mainstream gender discrimination.[2] All this is well taken.

---

[*] First published in 1998; from *Rituals of Blood: Consequences of Slavery in Two American Centuries*.

[1] Harriet Jacobs, *Incidents in the Life of a Slave Girl, Written by Herself* (Cambridge: Harvard University Press, 1987), 77.

[2] Frances Beale, "Double Jeopardy: To Be Black and Female," in Toni Cade Bambara, ed., *The Black Woman* (New York: New American Library, 1970), 90–100.

My only problem with this view is the assumption that it applies exclusively to Afro-American women. It was always the case in America that "superadded" to the burden of being a male slave or a male laborer was the burden of the assault on Afro-American men's integrity and identity as men. ★ ★ ★ Racist oppressors were virulently obsessed with the maleness of the Afro-American male and brutally sought to extinguish any hint of manhood in him.

With the remarkable changes in the attitudes of Euro-Americans and the condition of Afro-Americans over recent decades, the situation has now become rather more complex. When we examine the facts carefully, we find that Afro-American men are now, by many indicators, the gender at greater risk among Afro-Americans, while by others Afro-American women clearly continue to bear the greater burden. These factors affect the lives of Afro-Americans separately and interactively in complex ways. We must attempt to sort them out prior to our examination of the history and present internal problems of gender relations between Afro-American men and women.

There can be no denying what has been called the feminization of poverty for a large minority of Afro-American women.[3] As Figure 1 shows, in both individual and familial terms, women of all ethnic groups experience higher levels of poverty than men. As is well known, households headed by single women,

which now constitute the single largest category among Afro-Americans, are at high risk of poverty compared with other kinds of households: 46.4 and 53.5 percent for Afro-American and Latino ethnicities, respectively. There is no doubt that there is a gender burden here, but whether an added "racial" burden can be claimed is questionable.

As I argued in *The Ordeal of Integration*, while "race" is obviously the decisive factor in explaining the origins of the acute problems of the Afro-American poor, it is not at all clear that it has much to do with explaining contemporary poverty levels among either men or women. Latinos were never enslaved here; the majority of them are of European ancestry; and a substantial minority descended from slaveholders—uncomfortable facts too often glossed over in multicultural rhetoric—yet, as Figure 1 shows, their poverty levels are higher than Afro-Americans'.

What about the majority of Afro-American women, who are not poor? In terms of equal pay for equal work and qualifications, how do they fare in the labor market when compared with men and Euro-American women? This is a complex issue. In most respects Afro-American women share with their Euro-American counterparts a persistent burden of gender prejudice. In one or two areas there is also an ethnic discrepancy. However, in most respects there is little evidence of a double burden of gender and ethnic prejudice. When cur-

3 See Orlando Patterson, *The Ordeal of Integration: Progress and Resentment in America's "Racial" Crisis* (Washington, DC: Civitas/Counterpoint, 1997), chap. 1; Rebecca M. Blank, *It Takes a Nation: A New Agenda for Fighting Poverty* (New York: Princeton University Press, 1997); Irwin Garfinkel and Sara

S. McLanahan, *Single Mothers and Their Children: The New American Dilemma* (Washington, DC: Urban Institute Press, 1986); Diane Pearce, "The Feminization of Poverty: Women, Work, and Welfare," *Urban and Social Change Review* 11: 1/2 (1978), 28–36.

FIGURE 1 **PERCENTAGES OF INDIVIDUALS AND FAMILIES IN POVERTY BY GENDER, MARCH 1997**

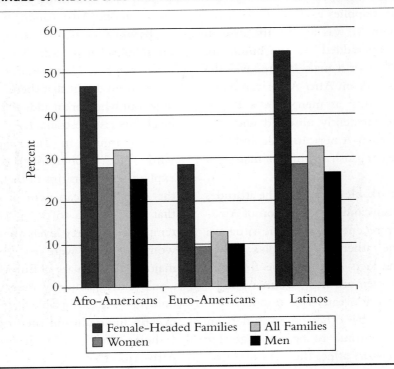

SOURCE: Author's tabulation of data from U.S. Bureau of the Census (Internet release, June 26, 1997).

rent trends are projected, there is every reason to believe that Afro-American women will soon surpass Afro-American men in median income. Indeed, when we take account not just of median income but of the numbers and proportions of Afro-American women in desirable occupations, it is already the case that they have outperformed Afro-American men in absolute terms and Euro-American women in relative terms.

Figure 2 shows an unambiguous pattern of gender discrepancy in annual earnings for both groups of women at every educational level. This, of course, is not necessarily proof of gender prejudice; much depends on the work his-

tories, as well as the occupational and industrial locations, of men and women. However, there is now good reason to believe that even after controlling for these factors, substantial gender discrepancies remain between the earnings of equally educated full-time working men and women.

We see also that for each educational level there is a discrepancy between the earnings of Afro-American and Euro-American women, albeit much smaller than the gender discrepancy for either group. Figure 3 recalculates, in terms of income ratios, the absolute figures given in Figure 2. Is this evidence of a double burden? Seen in static terms, the answer is "yes." But the

FIGURE 2 **MEDIAN EARNINGS BY EDUCATIONAL ATTAINMENT, ETHNICITY, AND GENDER, 1995**

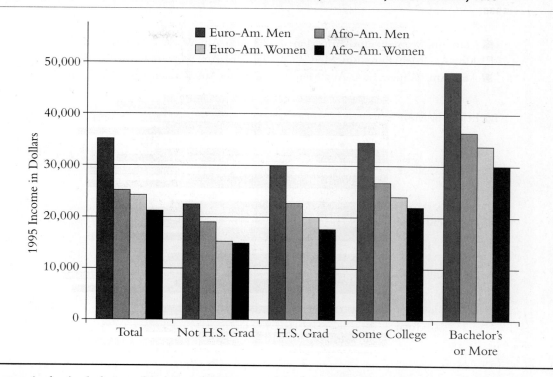

SOURCE: Author's tabulation of data from U.S. Bureau of the Census (Internet release, June 26, 1997).

discrepancy between the incomes of the two women's groups is largely a reflection of past ethnic prejudices in favor of Euro-American women, especially at the higher educational levels. The proportion of Euro-American women with college degrees who are now at or near their maximum earning capacity is much larger than that of Afro-American women. The impressive growth in the numbers and proportions of Afro-American women with "some college" or "bachelor's degree or more" levels of education, discussed below, is a post–1970 phenomenon. In fact, young Afro-American

female college graduates now earn more than their Euro-American counterparts.

Comparing the economic returns to women of different groups is difficult because of important differences in their economic activities. Thus, Afro-American women have traditionally had higher labor-force participation rates, but higher unemployment rates, than Euro-American women; they work more hours per week but roughly the same number of hours per year.[4] A lot depends on what measures one uses to make comparisons between the two groups. Using mean, rather than median,

4 See "Blacks in the Economy," in Gerald D. Jaynes and Robin M. Williams Jr., eds., *A Common Destiny: Blacks and American*

Society (Washington, DC: National Academy Press, 1989), chap. 6.

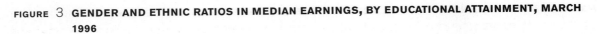

FIGURE 3 **GENDER AND ETHNIC RATIOS IN MEDIAN EARNINGS, BY EDUCATIONAL ATTAINMENT, MARCH 1996**

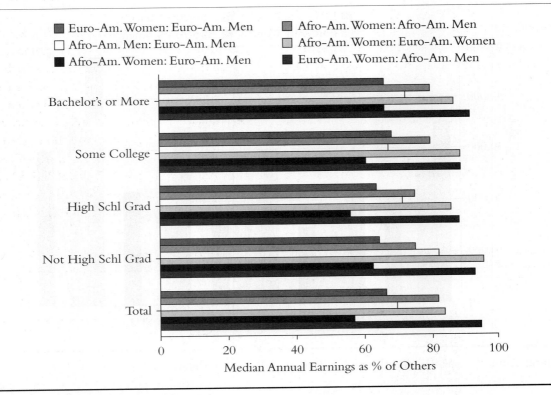

NOTE: Includes only year-round, full-time workers, ages 25 or older.

SOURCE: Author's tabulation of data from U.S. Bureau of the Census (Internet release, June 26, 1997).

earnings, one can show that there is no remaining gap. Emphasizing income rather than earnings reveals persisting ethnic differences. On yet another measure, estimated lifetime earnings, the gap has nearly vanished. On the whole, it is safe to say that ethnic differences in the economic experiences of Afro-American and Euro-American women have either disappeared or are on the verge of becoming insignificant. Afro-American women continue to suffer serious gender biases in the economy, but they suffer them equally with Euro-American women. Appearances to the contrary, there is no double burden of race and gender in economic matters.

Life, however, is a great deal more than economic activity. When we compare the life-chances and actual experience of Afro-American men and women in recent years, we are forced to question the conventional wisdom that Afro-American women are somehow more destructively burdened by the system than their male counterparts. It cannot be denied that when it comes to evaluating life's burdens, vital statistics are the ultimate tests. How long we live, the rate at which we can expect to die at given years of life, and the rate of survival—all are bottom-line assessments of just how well or badly a given group is doing in relation to others. On every one of these indicators, Afro-American men are not only far behind their Euro-American counterparts but also significantly worse off than Afro-American women. In contrast, Afro-American women not only have far better life-chances than Afro-American and Euro-American men but are fast catching up with Euro-American women on most indicators, and in a few cases are doing better.

Thus, as Figure 4 shows, in 1994 (the most recent data available), Afro-American male life expectancy at birth was 64.9 years, which was 8.4 years less than for Euro-American men, 9 years less than for Afro-American women, and 14.7 years less than for Euro-American women. This figure is not only shocking for an advanced industrial society, it is, in fact, significantly lower than that for men of several Third World societies such as Cuba and the Afro-Caribbean states of Jamaica, Barbados, and Trinidad—all

FIGURE 4 **AVERAGE EXPECTANCY AT BIRTH, BY GENDER AND ETHNICITY, 1994**

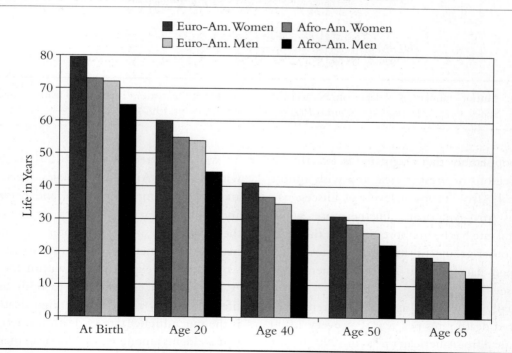

SOURCE: Author's tabulation of data from U.S. National Center for Health Statistics, "Births and Deaths: United States, 1996," *Monthly Vital Statistics Report* 46:1, Suppl. 2 (Sept. 1997).

FIGURE 5 **EXPECTANCY AT BIRTH, BY GENDER AND ETHNICITY, 1970–1995, AND PROJECTIONS FOR 1995–2010**

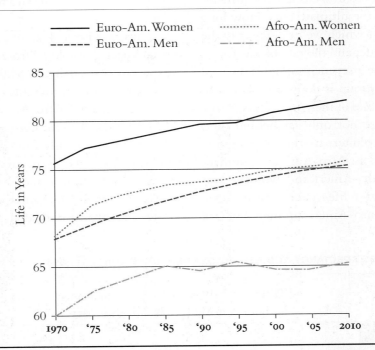

SOURCE: Author's tabulation of data from National Center for Health Statistics, "Births and Deaths, United States, 1995," *Monthly Vital Statistics Report* 46: 1, Suppl. 2 (Sept. 1997).

with populations that originated in exactly the same regions of West Africa, and with almost identical Afro-European levels of miscegenation, as Afro-Americans. Furthermore, while this vital rate has been improving over the years for all other groups in the United States, it has remained flat for Afro-American men since 1985 (see Figure 5).

Equally distressing are the differences in expected death rates per year. For every 1,000 live male Afro-American births in 1990, almost

20 were expected to die by 1991, compared with 16 Afro-American females, between 8 and 9 Euro-American males, and between 6 and 7 Euro-American females. At age twenty the differences are even greater; 3.8 times as many Afro-American men as Afro-American women could expect to die within the year.[5] A major factor contributing to both the low life-expectancy rates and the high death rates is the much higher rate of death from violence and accidents among Afro-American men. Fre-

5 U.S. National Center for Health Statistics, *Life Tables, Actuarial Tables, and Vital Statistics for 1990* (Washington, DC: U.S. National Center for Health Statistics, 1998).

FIGURE 6 **DEATH RATES FROM ACCIDENTS AND VIOLENCE, BY AGE GROUP, GENDER, AND ETHNICITY, 1990**

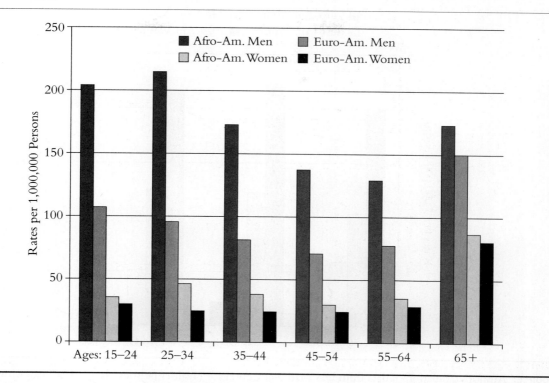

SOURCE: Author's tabulation of data from Center for Health Statistics, "Report of Final Mortality Statistics, 1995," *Monthly Vital Statistics Report* 45: 11, Suppl. 2 (1997):Table 7.

quent public commentary has tended to focus attention on violence among youth, but as Figure 6 demonstrates, Afro-American men die from violent and accidental causes at disproportionately greater levels throughout all age categories. Note, in contrast, that the gap between Euro-American and Afro-American women is negligible for most age groups and virtually disappears after age sixty-five.

Among the causes of death, suicide is often singled out as especially indicative of social anomie and despair, and there has been anguished recent commentary on the growing rate among young Afro-American men. However, suicide rates, as all sociologists know from one of the discipline's founding fathers,[6] are complex and must be treated with great caution. In nearly all Western societies, more prosperous classes have tended to experience higher suicide rates than less prosperous ones. Because they have less to

6 I refer to the French sociologist Emile Durkheim, whose classic study, *Suicide*, published in 1897, is a virtual foundation text of the discipline. Although most of Durkheim's empirical findings have been either rejected or sharply qualified, the theoretical issues he raised are still central to sociology.

FIGURE 7 **SUICIDE RATES, BY GENDER AND ETHNICITY, 1980–1994**

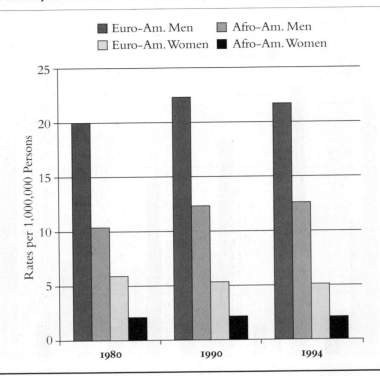

SOURCE: Author's tabulation of data from U.S. National Center for Health Statistics, "Report of Final Mortality Statistics, 1995," *Monthly Vital Statistics Report*, 45: 11, Suppl. 2 (June 1997).

lose and make fewer demands on themselves, poorer people tend to experience catastrophic feelings of failure and despair less often. Partly for this reason too, men have typically experienced much higher rates than women. Nonetheless, even after taking all these factors into account, the suicide rate for Afro-American men is unusually high. Figure 7 shows that in 1994 the Euro-American male rate was 4.3 times that for Euro-American females, while Afro-American men committed suicide at 6.2 times the rate at which Afro-American women did. What is more, Afro-American men are the only group for whom the rate is rising steadily. As dismal as these figures are, it is likely that the situation is actually much worse, not only because of underreporting for Afro-American youth, which according to J. T. Gibbs and A. M. Hines may be as high as 82 per 100,000,[7] but because of the masking effect of what R. H. Seiden calls "victim precipitated" homicide, in which young Afro-American men

7 J. T Gibbs and A. M. Hines, "Factors Related to Sex Differences in Suicidal Behavior among African-American Youth," *Journal of Adolescent Research* 4: 2 (1989):152–72.

FIGURE 8 **BACHELOR'S DEGREES CONFERRED ON AFRO-AMERICANS, BY GENDER, 1976–1995**

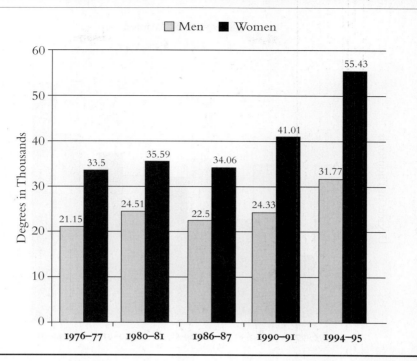

SOURCE: Author's tabulation of data from U.S. Dept. of Education, National Center for Education Statistics (HEGIS) (Internet data release, 1997).

commit suicide the "macho" way by inciting violence against themselves.[8] The gender difference, according to specialists on the subject, stems from the much greater involvement of women with institutions in the Afro-American community, such as church organizations, other support networks, and remaining kin ties. Indeed, the suicide rate for Afro-American women is among the lowest in the nation.

Beyond these vital statistics, we find that in almost every area of educational and skills acquisition Afro-American women are far outperforming Afro-American men. It is well known that females do better than males in the primary, secondary, and, more recently, undergraduate levels of the educational system. However, the gender differences between Afro-American men and women now bear little comparison with those in other groups. Between 1977 and 1995, Afro-American women almost doubled the gender gap in bachelor's degrees conferred, from 12,300 to 23,600 (see Figure 8). In all other ethnic groups, women have been catching up with, and surpassing, men in the

8 R. H. Seiden, "We're Driving Young Blacks to Suicide," *Psychology Today*, vol. 4 (1970): 24–28.

FIGURE 9 **FIRST PROFESSIONAL DEGREES CONFERRED ON AFRO–AMERICANS, BY GENDER, 1976–1995**

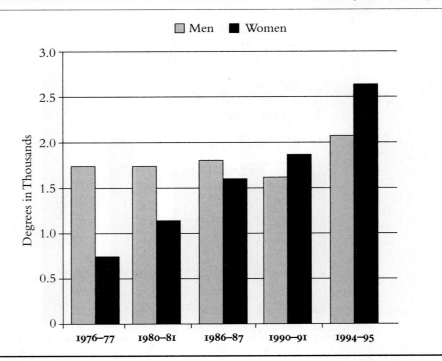

SOURCE: Author's tabulation of data from U.S. Dept. of Education, National Center for Education Statistics (HEGIS) (Internet data release, 1997).

acquisition of bachelor's degrees since about the early eighties. Afro-American women had passed this milestone years earlier and simply widened the gap with the enhanced opportunities that came with the seventies.

There are many other respects in which the Afro-American gender differences in education depart from those of other ethnic groups. Thus, Afro-Americans are the only ethnic group in which women outperform men in most of the hard sciences, especially physics, math, and computer science; engineering is an exception, but Afro-American women are fast catching up. Of even greater significance for the future

gender composition of the Afro-American middle class is the unusual trend in the acquisition of first professional degrees. In 1977 Afro-American men received twice as many professional degrees as women (see Figure 9). A decade later, women took the lead, and since then the gap has been widening substantially each year. Figure 10 indicates that this trend is unique among ethnic groups. With the exception of Asian Americans in the legal profession, where both genders are near parity, only among Afro-Americans do we find men substantially below parity in the fields of medicine, dentistry, law, and business.

FIGURE 10 **MALE/FEMALE RATIOS IN ATTAINMENT OF SELECTED PROFESSIONAL DEGREES, BY ETHNICITY, 1995**

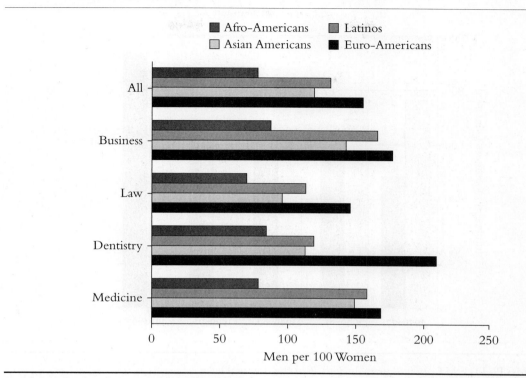

SOURCE: Author's tabulation of data from U.S. Dept of Education, National Center for Educational Statistics (IPEDS) (Internet data release, 1997).

The same trends hold for the acquisition of doctorates between 1977 and 1995. Afro-American women are at the head of a trend toward gender parity in the attainment of doctorates. Their situation is unique in two respects. First, in 1987 they became the first women to outperform the men of their group in achieving doctorates. Second, the Afro-American gender gap comes not only from women gaining more doctorates but, as Figure 11 shows, from men gaining fewer such advanced degrees. Between 1977 and 1987 there was a 37 percent fall in the number of Afro-American men gaining doctorates, a disastrous decline from which Afro-American men are yet to recover fully; in 1995 they still obtained 35 fewer doctorates than they did in 1977.

How do we explain all this? Why are the fortunes of Afro-American men declining so precipitously while those of Afro-American women are getting better? Why, in particular, are Afro-American women now poised to assume leadership in almost all areas of the Afro-American community and to outperform

FIGURE 11 **DOCTORATES CONFERRED ON AFRO-AMERICANS, BY GENDER, 1976–1995**

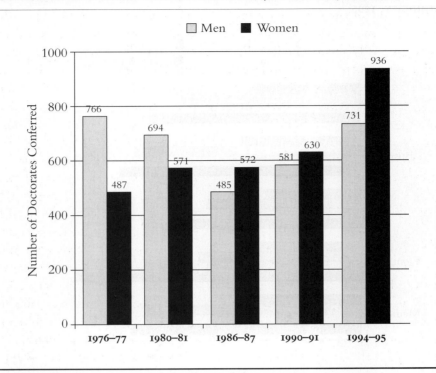

NOTE: Includes Ph.D., Ed.D., and comparable degrees at the doctoral level.
SOURCE: Author's tabulation of data from U.S. Dept of Education, National Center for Education Statistics (IPEDS) (Internet data release, 1997).

Afro-American men at middle- and upper-middle-class levels of the wider society and economy? Has the double burden been eliminated for Afro-American women?

It clearly has not, but it is perhaps time to think again, more carefully, about the nature of the burdens that each gender has had to face. Being burdened, having to work harder than others, is not in itself a necessarily bad thing, as the workaholic behavior of the nation's Fortune 500 executives attests. From the days of the Puritan founders, Americans have always prided themselves on being hardworking; people have competed with each other for the privilege of being burdened with great responsibilities and with the necessity to work long hours. Some burdens, in other words, we not only welcome but consider generative and empowering.

Without in any way underplaying the enormous problems that poor Afro-American women face, I want to suggest that the burdens of poor Afro-American men have always been oppressive, dispiriting, demoralizing, isolating, and soul killing, whereas those of women, while physically and emotionally no doubt as great, have always also been at least *partly* generative, empowering, and humanizing. Furthermore, as I will document later, the experience of Afro-American women during both the past and the present has nearly always entailed their incorporation into the norms, values, and work habits of the dominant culture, while the experience of Afro-American men has been until recently one of unmitigated exclusion.

Take, first, the role of mother. As Patricia Hill Collins correctly observes: "Some women view motherhood as a truly burdensome condition that stifles creativity, exploits their labor, and makes them partners in their own oppression. Others see motherhood as providing a base for self-actualization, status in the Black community, and a catalyst for social activism.[9] One of the great tragedies of Afro-American men was that for the great majority of them, for most of their history, fatherhood was rarely a "base for self-actualization." Indeed, to the degree that slavery, and later racial discrimination in the employment sector, prevented them from meeting their material obligations as providers, and to the degree that their own inner failings and distorted masculine values (on which more later) prevented them from meeting their social and emotional obligations to their offspring, to that extent was fatherhood a site of shame and humiliation.

Second, even under slavery and Jim Crow, the Afro-American woman, in her roles as domestic, nanny, nurse, and clerk, has always had greater access to the wider, dominant Euro-American world. As Fran Sanders has

written, with little exaggeration, "For two hundred years it was she who initiated the dialogue between the white world and the African American."[10] Today, Afro-American scholars and intellectuals are inclined to speak contemptuously about the job of domestic, but it is clearly wrong to project such attitudes onto the past. In spite of its unpleasant association with slavery and the often exploitative terms of employment, what Afro-American and Euro-American domestics always hated was not the job itself but live-in domestic work. When done on a regular basis with civilized employers and a decent wage in both kind and money, the job was a modestly secure one in which the Afro-American woman, unlike her male counterpart in the fields or factories, to quote Jacqueline Jones, "wielded an informal power that directly affected the basic human services provided within the white households."[11]

Domestic and other employment in the service sector also brought the Afro-American woman into direct contact with the most intimate areas of the dominant culture. This intimacy was sometimes deepened by another factor peculiar to women: that in America, as in most human societies, women of different statuses and ethnic groups can and often do establish close relationships, where men so separated cannot or will not. The knowledge thus acquired was valuable cultural capital, a point explicitly stated by many of the domestics interviewed by Bonnie Thornton Dill; these women "saw work as an ability rather than a

9 Patricia Hill Collins, *Black Feminist Thought* (New York: Routledge, 1991), 118.

10 Fran Sanders, "Dear Black Man," in Cade Bambara, ed., *The Black Woman*, 73.

11 Jacqueline Jones, *Labor of Love, Labor of Sorrow: Black Women, Work, and Family from Slavery to the Present* (New York: Basic Books, 1985), 134.

burden. Work was a means for attaining [their] goals; it provided [them] with the money [they] needed to be an independent person, and it exposed [them] and [their] children to 'good' things—values and a style of life which [they] considered important."[12]

It has been suggested that this cultural capital was selectively transmitted only to daughters and not to sons, for reasons that were complex but may have had to do with the differing realistic expectations Afro-American mothers had of their daughters and sons in light of the dominant labor market and its gender and ethnic biases. The less successful daughter could be expected to pursue a job as a domestic; the more successful daughter, to become a schoolteacher or nurse. In both cases, the cultural skills acquired from the dominant culture would be an asset. No such transmissions were considered important for lower-class boys, who had few prospects beyond manual work. Some ethnographic and psychological studies suggest that this pattern continues today among the lower classes.[13] However, the most recent survey data I have analyzed indicate that, at least in expressed attitudes, this is no longer the case. When asked in the HWPK survey conducted in the fall of 1997 whether parents should have different expectations for boys and girls, the

great majority of Afro-Americans responded that parents should have the same expectations. Men did respond positively to this question nearly twice as often as women (22 percent versus 11.8 percent), but the difference was not statistically significant in this sample. However, the question whether boys and girls should be raised differently yielded a significant difference in responses according to income group. A third of the poorest Afro-Americans thought they should be raised differently, while nearly all better off Afro-Americans thought they should be raised alike.[14] The responses of the poorest Afro-Americans may well be a vestige of a time, not so long ago, when all Afro-American parents raised boys and girls with different sets of expectations.

The attitudes and prejudices of the dominant group have also played an important role in generating gender disparities among Afro-Americans. Euro-Americans have always been more willing to accept Afro-American women than Afro-American men. Greater fear of Afro-American men, induced by racist sexual attitudes,[15] and greater familiarity with Afro-American women in the course of growing up made it much easier for Afro-American women to find jobs in clerical, and later in professional, Euro-American settings.

12 Bonnie Thornton Dill, "'The Means to Put My Children Through': Child-Rearing Goals and Strategies among Black Female Domestic Servants," in La Frances Rodgers-Rose, ed., *The Black Woman* (Beverly Hills: Sage, 1980), 115.

13 See P. J. Bowman and C. Howard, "Race-Related Socialization, Motivation, and Academic Achievement: A Study of Black Youths in Three-Generation Families," *Journal of the American Academy of Child Psychiatry* 24: 2 (1985): 131–141. Diane K. Lewis admits that there was a strong preference for and greater tendency to promote girls in the past but speculates that, with growing economic opportunities for men,

this should change: "The Black Family: Socialization and Sex Roles," *Phylon* 36: 3 (1975):221–231.

14 The relationship between income and attitude to child rearing was significant at the .03 probability level. It was not significant for other groups. Bear in mind though, that two-thirds of even the poorest group of Afro-Americans did hold that boys and girls should be raised alike.

15 For the classic exploration of such racist fears and fantasies about Afro-American men, see John Dollard, *Caste and Class in a Southern Town* (1937; reprint, New York: Doubleday Anchor, 1949), 160–163 and, more generally, chaps. 15–16.

There is good evidence that these attitudes and expectations persist toward all classes of Afro-Americans. The economist Harry J. Holzer recently documented a marked preference for Afro-American women over Afro-American men among suburban and inner-city employers. This preference is most striking where noncollege jobs require cognitive-interactive skills. The difference in employment cannot be explained solely in terms of qualifications (although this is indeed a factor) because less skilled and educated Afro-American women and Latino men are persistently placed ahead of Afro-American men in urban job queues.[16] In middle-class occupations this preference may well be interacting with affirmative action to reinforce the traditional bias in favor of Afro-American women. It is not simply that firms under pressure to meet affirmative action guidelines can achieve both gender and ethnic targets when they employ Afro-American women. Even more important, it has been found that in the professional and corporate world the intersection of "race" and gender benefits Afro-American career women, when compared not only with Afro-American men but with Euro-American women. Corporate Euro-American men are less inclined to view Afro-American women as sex objects, as women "out to get a husband," and are therefore more inclined to take them seriously as fellow professionals. The highly successful Afro-American women interviewed by sociologist Cynthia Epstein in the early 1970s almost

all agreed that being female "reduced the effect of the racial taboo" against Afro-Americans in corporate positions and that the combination of being Afro-American, female, and educated created a unique social space for them, enhancing their self-confidence and motivation.[17]

In the quarter of a century since Epstein's study, Afro-American women have expanded that social space impressively, in the process not only catching up with Euro-American women in many important areas but numerically surpassing Afro-American men in all the top occupational categories (see Figure 12). Among executive, administrative, and managerial workers, there are now 127 Afro-American women for every 100 Afro-American men; among professionals, 151 for every 100. By way of contrast, there are, respectively, only 64 and 85 Euro-American women for every 100 Euro-American men in these two categories of occupations.

From what has been said, it should now be clear that the claim that Afro-American women peculiarly and uniquely suffer a double burden in this society both misleads and obscures the realities of the Afro-American condition. For some Afro-American women, especially among the poor, the assertion is correct; but it is equally true that for an equally substantial minority of Afro-American men, a similar double burden can be claimed. As we have seen, the intersection of ethnicity and gender has deadly consequences for a large and growing minority of lower-class Afro-American men,

---

16 Harry J. Holzer, *What Employers Want: Job Prospects for Less-Educated Workers* (New York: Russell Sage Foundation, 1996), 80–105.

17 Cynthia F. Epstein, "Positive Effects of the Multiple Negatives: Explaining the Success of Black Professional Women," *American Journal of Sociology* 78 (1973):912–935.

FIGURE 12 **FEMALE/MALE RATIOS IN TOP FOUR CATEGORIES OF OCCUPATIONS OF LONGEST JOB, BY ETHNICITY**

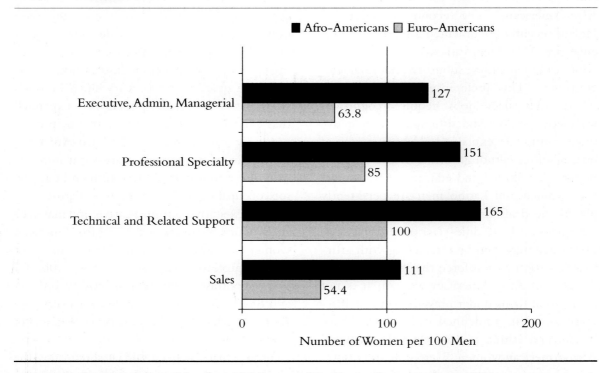

SOURCE: Author's tabulation of data from U.S. Bureau of the Census (Internet release, 1997).

reflected in the Third World levels of their vital statistics. Afro-American women, like their Euro-American counterparts, suffer serious gender discrimination. But, ironically, when gender and ethnicity interact, this sometimes works to the benefit of Afro-American women, especially those of the middle classes, as their increasing outperformance of Afro-American men in higher learning, white collar occupations, and the professions attests.

But as I suggested earlier, the very success of Afro-American women in the wider world exacerbates what is their greater gender problem—that between them and Afro-American males in all their sex roles and at all periods of the lifespan.

★ ★ ★

44

Invisible Inequality: Social Class and Childrearing in Black Families and White Families⋆

ANNETTE LAREAU

In recent decades, sociological knowledge about inequality in family life has increased dramatically. Yet, debate persists, especially about the transmission of class advantages to children. Kingston (2000) and others question whether disparate aspects of family life cohere in meaningful patterns. Pointing to a "thin evidentiary base" for claims of social class differences in the interior of family life, Kingston also asserts that "class distinguishes neither distinctive parenting styles or distinctive involvement of kids" in specific behaviors (p. 134).

★ ★ ★

I draw on findings from a small, intensive data set collected using ethnographic methods. I map the connections between parents' resources and their children's daily lives. My first goal, then, is to challenge Kingston's (2000) argument that social class does not distinguish parents' behavior or children's daily lives. I seek to show empirically that social class does indeed create distinctive parenting styles. I demonstrate that parents differ by class in the ways they define their own roles in their children's lives as well as in how they perceive the nature of childhood. The middle-class parents, both white

---

⋆ First published in 2002; from *American Sociological Review*, Volume 67, Number 5.

and black, tend to conform to a cultural logic of childrearing I call "concerted cultivation." They enroll their children in numerous age-specific organized activities that dominate family life and create enormous labor, particularly for mothers. The parents view these activities as transmitting important life skills to children. Middle-class parents also stress language use and the development of reasoning and employ talking as their preferred form of discipline. This "cultivation" approach results in a wider range of experiences for children but also creates a frenetic pace for parents, a cult of individualism within the family, and an emphasis on children's performance.

The childrearing strategies of white and black working-class and poor parents emphasize the "accomplishment of natural growth." These parents believe that as long as they provide love, food, and safety, their children will grow and thrive. They do not focus on developing their children's special talents. Compared to the middle-class children, working-class and poor children participate in few organized activities and have more free time and deeper, richer ties within their extended families. Working-class and poor parents issue many more directives to their children and, in some households, place more emphasis on physical discipline than do the middle-class parents. These findings extend Kohn and Schooler's (1983) observation of class differences in parents' values, showing that differences also exist in the *behavior* of parents *and* children.

Quantitative studies of children's activities offer valuable empirical evidence but only limited ideas about how to conceptualize the mechanisms through which social advantage is transmitted. Thus, my second goal is to offer "conceptual umbrellas" useful for making comparisons across race and class and for assessing the role of social structural location in shaping daily life.

Last, I trace the connections between the class position of family members—including children—and the uneven outcomes of their experiences outside the home as they interact with professionals in dominant institutions. The pattern of concerted cultivation encourages an *emerging sense of entitlement* in children. All parents and children are not equally assertive, but the pattern of questioning and intervening among the white and black middle-class parents contrasts sharply with the definitions of how to be helpful and effective observed among the white and black working-class and poor adults. The pattern of the accomplishment of natural growth encourages an *emerging sense of constraint*. Adults as well as children in these social classes tend to be deferential and outwardly accepting in their interactions with professionals such as doctors and educators. At the same time, however, compared to their middle-class counterparts, white and black working-class and poor family members are more distrustful of professionals. These are differences with potential long-term consequences. In an historical moment when the dominant society privileges active, informed, assertive clients of health and educational services, the strategies employed by children and parents are not equally effective across classes. In sum, differences in family life lie not only in the advantages parents obtain for their children, but also in the skills they transmit to children for negotiating their own life paths.

Kalongi's niece offered to take care of Erik during Jessica's absence. She also offered to keep the car while Jessica went to Jamaica and return it after a week. Unfortunately, the friend did not do so and also kept the money that Jessica had given her for the rental. As a result, Jessica was charged with grand theft upon her return from Jamaica, since her signature was on the rental agreement. The charge was later changed to failure to return a rental vehicle.

Jessica is currently under a three-year probation sentence and ordered to pay $3,700 in restitution. Her probationary status prevents her from leaving the state to join Kalongi in Georgia or attempt another business trip to Jamaica. The same status would keep her from working in any field related to law enforcement. She has no resources to hire a lawyer. "It's been tough," she says, "but things will get better."

b. Lessons for the Future

Downward assimilation does not emerge from the stories of our respondents as a deliberate path, but as an outgrowth of a web of constraints, bad luck, and limited opportunities. Jessica Wynters shares with other members of our sample a police record derived from an original attempt to muster the resources to build a business. Her case also illustrates how difficulties with the law further entrap young persons. She cannot obtain a decent job and cannot pursue her life dream—ironically a career in law enforcement. Given her situation, it is striking that Jessica's value system is so utterly normative. There is something truly moving in her belief, shared with others in similar situations, that she can be "master of her own destiny." Against all odds, she keeps holding on to her dreams. Her recent return to church, along with her repentant mother, reinforces these hopes. In reality, chances of her breaking loose from the circle of poverty, pregnancy, and poorly-paid jobs are dim.

Results from our study are almost frightening in revealing the power of structural factors—family human capital, family composition, and modes of incorporation—in shaping the lives of these young men and women. While we stop short of the conclusion that "context is destiny," there is little doubt that the opportunities for a successful career and a respected standing in society are widely divergent. The power of pervasive American racism and the dearth of compensatory programmes for the most disadvantaged members of society comes forth with unusual force in the divergent adaptation paths followed by second-generation youths and in their individual stories of success and failure.

★ ★ ★

It makes little sense to speak of a uniform assimilation path for the second generation when such different outcomes are observed. It is equally useless to adopt an optimistic outlook where "assimilation" can be each and all things. The challenges and traumas confronted by many children of immigrants reflect the realities of American society as it is today, on the ground. This divergence is not chaotic but follows, by and large, predictable channels: resources—intellectual, material, and social—build on each other and lead to ever greater advantages within and across generations; lack of skills, poverty, and a hostile context of reception also accumulate into frequently insurmountable difficulties. Segmented assimilation is a reality that assumes equally strong contours when one interviews a successful 24-year-old

||| METHODOLOGY

Study Participants

This study is based on interviews and observations of children, aged 8 to 10, and their families. The data were collected over time in three research phases. Phase one involved observations in two third-grade classrooms in a public school in the Midwestern community of "Lawrenceville."[1] After conducting observations for two months, I grouped the families into social class (and race) categories based on information provided by educators. I then chose every third name, and sent a letter to the child's home asking the mother and father to participate in separate interviews. Over 90 percent of parents agreed, for a total of 32 children (16 white and 16 African American). A black graduate student and I interviewed all mothers and most fathers (or guardians) of the children. Each interview lasted 90 to 120 minutes, and all took place in 1989–1990.

Phase two took place at two sites in a northeastern metropolitan area. One school, "Lower Richmond," although located in a predominantly white, working-class urban neighborhood, drew about half of its students from a nearby all-black housing project. I observed one third-grade class at Lower Richmond about twice a week for almost six months. The second site, "Swan," was located in a suburban neighborhood about 45 minutes from the city center. It was 90 percent white; most of the remaining 10 percent were middle-class black children.

There, I observed twice a week for two months at the end of the third grade; a research assistant then observed weekly for four more months in the fourth grade. At each site, teachers and parents described their school in positive terms. The observations took place between September 1992 and January 1994. In the fall of 1993, I drew an interview sample from Lower Richmond and Swan, following the same method of selection used for Lawrenceville. A team of research assistants and I interviewed the parents and guardians of 39 children. Again, the response rate was over 90 percent but because the classrooms did not generate enough black middle-class children and white poor children to fill the analytical categories, interviews were also conducted with 17 families with children aged 8 to 10. (Most of these interviews took place during the summers of 1996 and 1997.) Thus, the total number of children who participated in the study was 88 (32 from the Midwest and 56 from the Northeast).

||| FAMILY OBSERVATIONS

Phase three, the most intensive research phase of the study, involved home observations of 12 children and their families in the Northeast who had been previously interviewed. Some themes, such as language use and families' social connections, surfaced mainly during this phase. Although I entered the field interested in examining the influence of social class on children's daily lives, I incorporated new themes as they

---

1 All names of people and places are pseudonyms. The Lawrenceville school was in a white suburban neighborhood in a university community a few hours from a metropolitan area.

The student population was about half white and half black; the (disproportionately poor) black children were bused from other neighborhoods.

"bubbled up" from the field observations. The evidence presented here comes mainly from the family observations, but I also use interview findings from the full sample of 88 children where appropriate.

Nine of the 12 families came from the Northeastern classroom sample. The home observations took place, one family at a time, from December 1993 to August 1994. Three 10-year-olds (a black middle-class boy and girl and a white poor boy) who were not part of the classroom sample were observed in their homes during the summer of 1995.

The research assistants and I took turns visiting the participating families daily, for a total of about 20 visits to each home, often in the space of one month. The observations went beyond the home: Fieldworkers followed children and parents as they participated in school activities, church services and events, organized play, visits to relatives, and medical appointments. Observations typically lasted three hours, but sometimes much longer (e.g., when we observed an out-of-town funeral, a special extended family event, or a long shopping trip). Most cases also involved one overnight visit. We often carried tape recorders and used the audiotapes for reference in writing field notes. Writing field notes usually required 8 to 12 hours for each two- or three-hour home visit. Participating families each were paid $350, usually at the end of the visits.

★ ★ ★

CONCERTED CULTIVATION AND NATURAL GROWTH

The interviews and observations suggested that crucial aspects of family life *cohered*. Within the concerted cultivation and accomplishment of natural growth approaches, three key dimensions may be distinguished: the organization of daily life, the use of language, and social connections. ("Interventions in institutions" and "consequences" are addressed later in the paper.) These dimensions do not capture all important parts of family life, but they do incorporate core aspects of childrearing (Table 1). Moreover, our field observations revealed that behaviors and activities related to these dimensions dominated the rhythms of family life. Conceptually, the organization of daily life and the use of language are crucial dimensions. Both must be present for the family to be described as engaging in one childrearing approach rather the other. Social connections are significant but less conceptually essential.

All three aspects of childrearing were intricately woven into the families' daily routines, but rarely remarked upon. As part of everyday practice, they were invisible to parents and children. Analytically, however, they are useful means for comparing and contrasting ways in which social class differences shape the character of family life. I now examine two families in terms of these three key dimensions. I "control" for race and gender and contrast the lives of two black boys—one from an (upper) middle-class family and one from a family on public assistance. I could have focused on almost any of the other 12 children, but this pair seemed optimal, given the limited number of studies reporting on black middle-class families, as well as the aspect of my argument that suggests that race is less important than class in shaping childrearing patterns.

TABLE 1 SUMMARY OF DIFFERENCES IN CHILDREARING APPROACHES

	Childrearing Approach	
Dimension Observed	Concerted Cultivation	Accomplishment of Natural Growth
Key elements of each approach	Parent actively fosters and assesses child's talents, opinions, and skills	Parent cares for child and allows child to grow
Organization of daily life	Multiple child leisure activities are orchestrated by adults	Child "hangs out" particularly with kin
Language use	Reasoning/directives	Directives
	Child contestation of adult statements	Rare for child to question or challenge adults
	Extended negotiations between parents and child	General acceptance by child of directives
Social connections	Weak extended family ties	Strong extended family ties
	Child often in homogenous age groupings	Child often in heterogeneous age groupings
Interventions in institutions	Criticisms and interventions on behalf of child	Dependence on institutions
	Training of child to intervene on his or her own behalf	Sense of powerlessness and frustration
		Conflict between childrearing practices at home and at school
Consequences	Emerging sense of entitlement on the part of the child	Emerging sense of constraint on the part of the child

Developing Alexander Williams

Alexander Williams and his parents live in a predominantly black middle-class neighborhood. Their six-bedroom house is worth about $150,000. Alexander is an only child. Both parents grew up in small towns in the South, and both are from large families. His father, a tall, handsome man, is a very successful trial lawyer who earns about $125,000 annually in a small firm specializing in medical malpractice cases. Two weeks each month, he works very long hours (from about 5:30 A.M. until midnight)

preparing for trials. The other two weeks, his workday ends around 6:00 P.M. He rarely travels out of town. Alexander's mother, Christina, is a positive, bubbly woman with freckles and long, black, wavy hair. A high-level manager in a major corporation, she has a corner office, a personal secretary, and responsibilities for other offices across the nation. She tries to limit her travel, but at least once a month she takes an overnight trip.

Alexander is a charming, inquisitive boy with a winsome smile. Ms. Williams is pleased that Alexander seems interested in so many things:

Alexander is a joy. He's a gift to me. He's very energetic, very curious, loving, caring person, that, um . . . is outgoing and who, uh, really loves to be with people. And who loves to explore, and loves to read and . . . just do a lot of fun things.

The private school Alexander attends has an on-site after-school program. There, he participates in several activities and receives guitar lessons and photography instruction.

Organization of Daily Life

Alexander is busy with activities during the week and on weekends (Table 2). His mother describes their Saturday morning routine. The day starts early with a private piano lesson for Alexander downtown, a 20-minute drive from the house:

It's an 8:15 class. But for me, it was a tradeoff. I am very adamant about Saturday morning TV. I don't know what it contributes. So . . . it was . . . um . . . either stay at home and fight on a Saturday morning [laughs] or go do something constructive. . . . Now Saturday mornings are pretty booked up. You know, the piano lesson, and then straight to choir for a couple of hours. So, he has a very full schedule.

Ms. Williams's vehement opposition to television is based on her view of what Alexander needs to grow and thrive. She objects to TV's passivity and feels it is her obligation to help her son cultivate his talents.

Sometimes Alexander complains that "my mother signs me up for everything!" Generally, however, he likes his activities. He says they make him feel "special," and without them life would be "boring." His sense of time is thoroughly entwined with his activities: He feels disoriented when his schedule is not full. This unease is clear in the following field-note excerpt. The family is driving home from a Back-to-School night. The next morning, Ms. Williams will leave for a work-related day trip and will not return until late at night. Alexander is grumpy because he has nothing planned for the next day. He wants to have a friend over, but his mother rebuffs him. Whining, he wonders what he will do. His mother, speaking tersely, says:

You have piano and guitar. You'll have some free time. [Pause] I think you'll survive for one night. [Alexander does not respond but seems mad. It is quiet for the rest of the trip home.]

Alexander's parents believe his activities provide a wide range of benefits important for his development. In discussing Alexander's piano lessons, Mr. Williams notes that as a Suzuki student, Alexander is already able to read music. Speculating about more diffuse benefits of Alexander's involvement with piano, he says:

I don't see how any kid's adolescence and adulthood could not but be enhanced by an awareness of who Beethoven was. And is that Bach or Mozart? I don't know the difference between the two! I don't know Baroque from Classical—but he does. How can that not be a benefit in later life? I'm convinced that this rich experience will make him a better person, a better citizen, a better husband, a better father—certainly a better student.

Ms. Williams sees music as building her son's "confidence" and his "poise." In interviews and casual conversation, she stresses "exposure."

TABLE 2 **PARTICIPATION IN ACTIVITIES OUTSIDE OF SCHOOL: BOYS**

Boy's Name/Race/Class	Activities Organized by Adults	Informal Activities
MIDDLE CLASS		
Garrett Tallinger (white)	Soccer team	Plays with siblings in yard
	Traveling soccer team	Watches television
	Baseball team	Plays computer games
	Basketball team (summer)	Overnights with friends
	Swim team	
	Piano	
	Saxophone (through school)	
Alexander Williams (black)	Soccer team	Restricted television
	Baseball team	Plays outside occasionally with
	Community choir	two other boys
	Church choir	Visits friends from school
	Sunday school	
	Piano (Suzuki)	
	School plays	
	Guitar (through school)	
WORKING CLASS		
Billy Yanelli (white)	Baseball team	Watches television
		Visits relatives
		Rides bike
		Plays outside in the street
		Hangs out with neighborhood kids
Tyrec Taylor (black)	Football team	Watches television
	Vacation Bible School	Plays outside in the street
	Sunday school (off/on)	Rides bikes with neighborhood
		boys
		Visit relatives
		Goes to swimming pool
POOR		
Karl Greeley (white)	Goes to swimming pool	Watches television
	Walks dogs with neighbor	Plays Nintendo
		Plays with siblings
Harold McAllister (black)	Bible study in neighbor's	Visits relatives
	house (occasionally)	Plays ball with neighborhood kids
	Bible camp (1 week)	Watches television
		Watches videos

She believes it is her responsibility to broaden Alexander's worldview. Childhood activities provide a learning ground for important life skills:

> Sports provide great opportunities to learn how to be competitive. Learn how to accept defeat, you know. Learn how to accept winning, you know, in a gracious way. Also it gives him the opportunity to learn leadership skills and how to be a team player. . . . Sports really provides a lot of really great opportunities.

Alexander's schedule is constantly shifting; some activities wind down and others start up. Because the schedules of sports practices and games are issued no sooner than the start of the new season, advance planning is rarely possible. Given the sheer number of Alexander's activities, events inevitably overlap. Some activities, though short-lived, are extremely time consuming. Alexander's school play, for example, requires rehearsals three nights the week before the opening. In addition, in choosing activities, the Williamses have an added concern— the group's racial balance. Ms. Williams prefers that Alexander not be the only black child at events. Typically, one or two other black boys are involved, but the groups are predominantly white and the activities take place in predominantly white residential neighborhoods. Alexander is, however, part of his church's youth choir and Sunday School, activities in which all participants are black.

Many activities involve competition. Alex must audition for his solo performance in the school play, for example. Similarly, parents and children alike understand that participation on "A," "B," or "All-Star" sports teams signal different skill levels. Like other middle-class children in the study, Alexander seems to enjoy public performance. According to a field note, after his solo at a musical production in front of over 200 people, he appeared "contained, pleased, aware of the attention he's receiving."

Alexander's commitments do not consume *all* his free time. Still, his life is defined by a series of deadlines and schedules interwoven with a series of activities that are organized and controlled by adults rather than children. Neither he nor his parents see this as troublesome.

Language Use

Like other middle-class families, the Williamses often engage in conversation that promotes reasoning and negotiation. An excerpt from a field note (describing an exchange between Alexander and his mother during a car ride home after summer camp) shows the kind of pointed questions middle-class parents ask children. Ms. Williams is not just eliciting information. She is also giving Alexander the opportunity to develop and practice verbal skills, including how to summarize, clarify, and amplify information:

> As she drives, [Ms. Williams] asks Alex, "So, how was your day?"
>
> Alex: "Okay. I had hot dogs today, but they were burned! They were all black!"
>
> Mom: "Oh, great. You shouldn't have eaten any.
>
> Alex: "They weren't *all* black, only half were. The rest were regular."
>
> Mom: "Oh, okay. What was that game you were playing this morning? . . .
>
> Alex: "It was [called] 'Whatcha doin?'"
>
> Mom: "How do you play?"
>
> Alexander explains the game elaborately— fieldworker doesn't quite follow. Mom asks

Alex questions throughout his explanation, saying, "Oh, I see," when he answers. She asks him about another game she saw them play; he again explains.... She continues to prompt and encourage him with small giggles in the back of her throat as he elaborates.

Expressions of interest in children's activities often lead to negotiations over small, home-based matters. During the same car ride, Ms. Williams tries to adjust the dinner menu to suit Alexander:

Alexander says, "I don't want hot dogs tonight."

Mom: "Oh? Because you had them for lunch."

Alexander nods.

Mom: "Well, I can fix something else and save the hot dogs for tomorrow night."

Alex: "But I don't want any pork chops either."

Mom: "Well, Alexander, we need to eat something. Why didn't you have hamburgers today?"

Alex: "They don't have them any more at the snack bar."

Mom asks Alexander if he's ok, if he wants a snack. Alexander says he's ok. Mom asks if he's sure he doesn't want a bag of chips?

Not all middle-class parents are as attentive to their children's needs as this mother, and none are *always* interested in negotiating. But a general pattern of reasoning and accommodating is common.

Social Connections

Mr. and Ms. Williams consider themselves very close to their extended families. Because the Williams's aging parents live in the South, visiting requires a plane trip. Ms. Williams takes Alexander with her to see his grandparents twice a year. She speaks on the phone with her parents at least once a week and also calls her siblings several times a week. Mr. Williams talks with his mother regularly by phone (he has less contact with his stepfather). With pride, he also mentions his niece, whose Ivy League education he is helping to finance.

Interactions with cousins are not normally a part of Alexander's leisure time. (As I explain below, other middle-class children did not see cousins routinely either, even when they lived nearby.) Nor does he often play with neighborhood children. The huge homes on the Williams's street are occupied mainly by couples without children. Most of Alexander's playmates come from his classroom or his organized activities. Because most of his school events, church life, and assorted activities are organized by the age (and sometimes gender) of the participants, Alexander interacts almost exclusively with children his own age, usually boys. Adult-organized activities thus define the context of his social life.

Mr. and Ms. Williams are aware that they allocate a sizable portion of time to Alexander's activities. What they stress, however, is the time they *hold back*. They mention activities the family has chosen *not* to take on (such as traveling soccer).

Summary

Alexander's parents engaged in concerted cultivation. They fostered their son's growth through involvement in music, church, athletics, and academics. They talked with him at length, seeking his opinions and encouraging his ideas. Their approach involved considerable direct expenses (e.g., the cost of lessons and equipment) and large indirect expenses (e.g., the cost of taking time off from work, driving to practices, and foregoing adult leisure activities). Although Mr. and Ms. Williams acknowledged the importance of extended family, Alexander spent relatively little time with relatives. His social interactions occurred almost exclusively with children his own age and with adults. Alexander's many activities significantly shaped the organization of daily life in the family. Both parents' leisure time was tailored to their son's commitments. Mr. and Ms. Williams felt that the strategies they cultivated with Alexander would result in his having the best possible chance at a happy and productive life. They couldn't imagine themselves *not* investing large amounts of time and energy in their son's life. But, as I explain in the next section, which focuses on a black boy from a poor family, other parents held a different view.

Supporting the Natural Growth of Harold McAllister

Harold McAllister, a large, stocky boy with a big smile, is from a poor black family. He lives with his mother and his 8-year-old sister, Alexis, in a large apartment. Two cousins often stay overnight. Harold's 16-year-old sister and 18-year-old brother usually live with their grandmother, but sometimes they stay at the McAllister's home. Ms. McAllister, a high school graduate, relies on public assistance (AFDC). Hank, Harold and Alexis's father, is a mechanic. He and Ms. McAllister have never married. He visits regularly, sometimes weekly, stopping by after work to watch television or nap. Harold (but not Alexis) sometimes travels across town by bus to spend the weekend with Hank.

The McAllister's apartment is in a public housing project near a busy street. The complex consists of rows of two- and three-story brick units. The buildings, blocky and brown, have small yards enclosed by concrete and wood fences. Large floodlights are mounted on the corners of the buildings, and wide concrete sidewalks cut through the spaces between units. The ground is bare in many places; paper wrappers and glass litter the area.

Inside the apartment, life is humorous and lively, with family members and kin sharing in the daily routines. Ms. McAllister discussed, disdainfully, mothers who are on drugs or who abuse alcohol and do not "look after" their children. Indeed, the previous year Ms. McAllister called Child Protective Services to report her twin sister, a cocaine addict, because she was neglecting her children. Ms. McAllister is actively involved in her twin's daughters' lives. Her two nephews also frequently stay with her. Overall, she sees herself as a capable mother who takes care of her children and her extended family.

Organization of Daily Life

Much of Harold's life and the lives of his family members revolve around home. Project residents often sit outside in lawn chairs or on front stoops, drinking beer, talking, and watching children play. During summer, windows are frequently left open, allowing breezes to waft through the units and providing vantage points from which residents can survey the neighborhood. A large deciduous tree in front of the McAllister's apartment unit provides welcome shade in the summer's heat.

Harold loves sports. He is particularly fond of basketball, but he also enjoys football, and he follows televised professional sports closely. Most afternoons, he is either inside watching television or outside playing ball. He tosses a football with cousins and boys from the neighboring units and organizes pick-up basketball games. Sometimes he and his friends use a rusty, bare hoop hanging from a telephone pole in the housing project; other times, they string up an old, blue plastic crate as a makeshift hoop. One obstacle to playing sports, however, is a shortage of equipment. Balls are costly to replace, especially given the rate at which they disappear—theft of children's play equipment, including balls and bicycles, is an ongoing problem. During a field observation, Harold asks his mother if she knows where the ball is. She replies with some vehemence, "They stole the blue and yellow ball, and they stole the green ball, and they stole the other ball."

Hunting for balls is a routine part of Harold's leisure time. One June day, with the temperature and humidity in the high 80's, Harold and his cousin Tyrice (and a fieldworker) wander around the housing project for about an hour, trying to find a basketball:

> We head to the other side of the complex. On the way . . . we passed four guys sitting on the step. Their ages were 9 to 13 years. They had a radio blaring. Two were working intently on fixing a flat bike tire. The other two were dribbling a basketball.
>
> Harold: "Yo! What's up, ya'll."
> Group: "What's up, Har." "What's up?" "Yo."
>
> They continued to work on the tire and dribble the ball. As we walked down the hill, Harold asked, "Yo, could I use your ball?"

> The guy responded, looking up from the tire, "Naw, man. Ya'll might lose it."

Harold, Tyrice, and the fieldworker walk to another part of the complex, heading for a makeshift basketball court where they hope to find a game in progress:

> No such luck. Harold enters an apartment directly in front of the makeshift court. The door was open. . . . Harold came back. "No ball. I guess I gotta go back."

The pace of life for Harold and his friends ebbs and flows with the children's interests and family obligations. The day of the basketball search, for example, after spending time listening to music and looking at baseball cards, the children join a water fight Tyrice instigates. It is a lively game, filled with laughter and with efforts to get the adults next door wet (against their wishes). When the game winds down, the kids ask their mother for money, receive it, and then walk to a store to buy chips and soda. They chat with another young boy and then amble back to the apartment, eating as they walk. Another afternoon, almost two weeks later, the children—Harold, two of his cousins, and two children from the neighborhood—and the fieldworker play basketball on a makeshift court in the street (using the fieldworker's ball). As Harold bounces the ball, neighborhood children of all ages wander through the space.

Thus, Harold's life is more free-flowing and more child-directed than is Alexander Williams's. The pace of any given day is not so much planned as emergent, reflecting child-based interests and activities. Parents intervene in specific areas, such as personal grooming, meals, and occasional chores, but they do not continuously direct and monitor their children's leisure activities. Moreover, the leisure activities Harold and other working-class and poor children pursue require them to develop a repertoire of skills for dealing with much older and much younger children as well as with neighbors and relatives.

Language Use

Life in the working-class and poor families in the study flows smoothly without extended verbal discussions. The amount of talking varies, but overall, it is considerably less than occurs in the middle-class homes. Ms. McAllister jokes with the children and discusses what is on television. But she does not appear to cultivate conversation by asking the children questions or by drawing them out. Often she is brief and direct in her remarks. For instance, she coordinates the use of the apartment's only bathroom by using one-word directives. She sends the children (there are almost always at least four children home at once) to wash up by pointing to a child, saying one word, "bathroom," and handing him or her a washcloth. Wordlessly, the designated child gets up and goes to the bathroom to take a shower.

Similarly, although Ms. McAllister will listen to the children's complaints about school, she does not draw them out on these issues or seek to determine details, as Ms. Williams would. For instance, at the start of the new school year, when I ask Harold about his teacher, he tells me she is "mean" and that "she lies." Ms. McAllister, washing dishes, listens to her son, but she does not encourage Harold to support his opinion about his new teacher with more examples, nor does she mention any concerns of her own. Instead, she asks about last year's teacher, "What was the name of that man teacher?" Harold says, "Mr. Lindsey?" She says, "No, the other one." He says, "Mr. Terrene." Ms. McAllister smiles and says, "Yeah. I liked him." Unlike Alexander's mother, she seems content with a brief exchange of information.

Social Connections

Children, especially boys, frequently play outside. The number of potential playmates in Harold's world is vastly higher than the number in Alexander's neighborhood. When a fieldworker stops to count heads, she finds 40 children of elementary school age residing in the nearby rows of apartments. With so many children nearby, Harold could choose to play only with others his own age. In fact, though, he often hangs out with older and younger children and with his cousins (who are close to his age).

The McAllister family, like other poor and working-class families, is involved in a web of extended kin. As noted earlier, Harold's older siblings and his two male cousins often spend the night at the McAllister home. Celebrations such as birthdays involve relatives almost exclusively. Party guests are not, as in middle-class families, friends from school or from extracurricular activities. Birthdays are celebrated enthusiastically, with cake and special food to mark the occasion; presents, however, are not offered. Similarly, Christmas at Harold's house featured a tree and special food but no presents. At these and other family events, the older children voluntarily look after the younger ones: Harold plays with his 16-month-old niece, and his cousins carry around the younger babies.

The importance of family ties—and the contingent nature of life in the McAllister's world—

is clear in the response Alexis offers when asked what she would do if she were given a million dollars:

> Oh, boy! I'd buy my brother, my sister, my uncle, my aunt, my nieces and my nephews, and my grandpop, and my grandmom, and my mom, and my dad, and my friends, not my friends, but mostly my best friend—I'd buy them all clothes . . . and sneakers. And I'd buy some food, and I'd buy my mom some food, and I'd get my brothers and my sisters gifts for their birthdays.

Summary

In a setting where everyone, including the children, was acutely aware of the lack of money, the McAllister family made do. Ms. McAllister rightfully saw herself as a very capable mother. She was a strong, positive influence in the lives of the children she looked after. Still, the contrast with Ms. Williams is striking. Ms. McAllister did not seem to think that Harold's opinions needed to be cultivated and developed. She, like most parents in the working-class and poor families, drew strong and clear boundaries between adults and children. Adults gave directions to children. Children were given freedom to play informally unless they were needed for chores. Extended family networks were deemed important and trustworthy.

The Intersection of Race and Class in Family Life

I expected race to powerfully shape children's daily schedules, but this was not evident (also see Conley 1999; Pattillo-McCoy 1999). This is not to say that race is unimportant. Black parents were particularly concerned with monitoring their children's lives outside the home for signs of racial problems. Black middle-class fathers, especially, were likely to stress the importance of their sons understanding "what it means to be a black man in this society" (J. Hochschild 1995). Mr. Williams, in summarizing how he and his wife orient Alexander, said:

> [We try to] teach him that race unfortunately is the most important aspect of our national life. I mean people look at other people and they see a color first. But that isn't going to define who he is. He will do his best. He will succeed, despite racism. And I think he lives his life that way.

Alexander's parents were acutely aware of the potential significance of race in his life. Both were adamant, however, that race should not be used as "an excuse" for not striving to succeed. Mr. Williams put it this way:

> I discuss how race impacts on my life as an attorney, and I discuss how race will impact on his life. The one teaching that he takes away from this is that he is never to use discrimination as an excuse for not doing his best.

Thus far, few incidents of overt racism had occurred in Alexander's life, as his mother noted:

> Those situations have been far and few between. . . . I mean, I can count them on my fingers.

Still, Ms. Williams recounted with obvious pain an incident at a birthday party Alexander had attended as a preschooler. The grandparents of the birthday child repeatedly asked, "Who is that boy?" and exclaimed, "He's so dark!" Such experiences fueled the Williams's resolve always to be "cautious":

> We've never been, uh, parents who drop off their kid anywhere. We've always gone with him. And even now, I go in and—to school in the morning—and check [in]. . . . The school environment, we've watched very closely.

Alexander's parents were not equally optimistic about the chances for racial equality in this country. Ms. Williams felt strongly that, especially while Alexander was young, his father should not voice his pessimism. Mr. Williams complained that this meant he had to "watch" what he said to Alexander about race relations. Still, both parents agreed about the need to be vigilant regarding potential racial problems in Alexander's life. Other black parents reported experiencing racial prejudice and expressed a similar commitment to vigilance.

Issues surrounding the prospect of growing up black and male in this society were threaded through Alexander's life in ways that had no equivalent among his middle-class, white male peers. Still, in fourth grade there were no signs of racial experiences having "taken hold" the way that they might as Alexander ages. In terms of the number and kind of activities he participated in, his life was very similar to that of Garrett Tallinger, his white counterpart (see Table 2). That both sets of parents were fully committed to a strategy of concentrated cultivation was apparent in the number of adult-organized activities the boys were enrolled in, the hectic pace of family life, and the stress on reasoning in parent-child negotiations. Likewise, the research assistants and I saw no striking differences in the ways in which white parents and black parents in the working-class and poor homes socialized their children.

Others (Fordham and Ogbu 1986) have found that in middle school and high school, adolescent peer groups often draw sharp racial boundaries, a pattern not evident among this study's third- and fourth-grade participants (but sometimes present among their older siblings). Following Tatum (1997:52), I attribute this to the children's relatively young ages (also see "Race in America," *The New York Times*, June 25, 2000, p. 1). In sum, in the broader society, key aspects of daily life were shaped by racial segregation and discrimination. But in terms of enrollment in organized activities, language use, and social connections, the largest differences between the families we observed were across social class, not racial groups.

DIFFERENCES IN CULTURAL PRACTICES ACROSS THE TOTAL SAMPLE

The patterns observed among the Williams and McAllister families occurred among others in the 12-family subsample and across the larger group of 88 children. Frequently, they also echoed established patterns in the literature. These patterns highlight not only the amount of time spent on activities but also the quality of family life and the ways in which key dimensions of childrearing intertwine.

Organization of Daily Life

In the study as a whole, the rhythms of family life differed by social class. Working-class and poor children spent most of their free time in informal play; middle-class children took part in many adult-organized activities designed to develop their individual talents and interests. For the 88 children, I calculated an average score for the most common adult-directed, organized activities, based on parents' answers to interview questions. Middle-class children averaged 4.9 current activities (N = 36), working-class children averaged 2.5 activities (N = 26), and poor children averaged 1.5 (N = 26). Black middle-class children had slightly more activities than white middle-class children, largely connected to more church involvement, with an average of 5.2 (N = 18) compared with 4.6 activities for whites (N = 18). The racial difference was very modest in the working-class group (2.8 activities for black children [N = 12] and 2.3 for white children [N = 14]) and the poor group (1.6 activities for black children [N = 14] and 1.4 for white children [N = 12]). Middle-class boys had slightly more activities than middle-class girls (5.1 versus 4.7, N = 18 for both) but gender did not make a difference for the other classes. The type of activity did however. Girls tended to participate in dance, music, and Scouts, and to be less active in sports. This pattern of social class differences in activities is comparable to other, earlier reports (Medrich et al. 1982): Hofferth and Sandberg's (2001a, 2000b) recent research using a representative national sample suggests that the number of children's organized activities increases with parents' education and that children's involvement in organized activities has risen in recent decades.

The dollar cost of children's organized activities was significant, particularly when families had more than one child. Cash outlays included paying the instructors and coaches who gave lessons, purchasing uniforms and performance attire, paying for tournament admission and travel to and from tournaments, and covering hotel and food costs for overnight stays. Summer camps also were expensive. At my request, the Tallingers added up the casts for Garrett's organized activities. The total was over $4,000 per year. Recent reports of parents' expenditures for children's involvement in a single sport (e.g., hockey) are comparably high (Schemari 2002). Children's activities consumed time as well as money, co-opting parents' limited leisure hours.

The study also uncovered differences in how much time children spent in activities controlled by adults. Take the schedule of Melanie Handlon, a white middle-class girl in the fourth grade (see Table 3). Between December 8 and December 24, Melanie had a piano lesson each Monday, Girl Scouts each Thursday, a special Girl Scout event one Monday night, a special holiday musical performance at school one Tuesday night, two orthodontist appointments, five special rehearsals for the church Christmas pageant, and regular Sunday commitments (an early church service, Sunday school, and youth choir). On weekdays she spent several hours after school struggling with her homework as her mother coached her step-by-step through the worksheets. The amount of time Melanie spent in situations where her movements were controlled by adults was typical of middle-class children in the study.

The schedule of Katie Brindle, a white fourth-grader from a poor family, contrasts sharply, showing few organized activities between December 2 and 24. She sang in the

TABLE 3 PARTICIPATION IN ACTIVITIES OUTSIDE OF SCHOOL: GIRLS

Girl's Name/Race/Class	Activities Organized by Adults	Informal Activities
MIDDLE CLASS		
Melanie Handlon (white)	Girl Scouts	Restricted television
	Piano	Plays outside with neighborhood
	Sunday school	kids
	Church	Bakes cookies with mother
	Church pageant	Swims (not on swim team)
	Violin (through school)	Listens to music
	Softball team	
Stacey Marshall (black)	Gymnastics lessons	Watches television
	Gymnastic teams	Plays outside
	Church	Visits friends from school
	Sunday school	Rides bike
	Youth choir	
WORKING CLASS		
Wendy Driver (white)	Catholic education (CCD)	Watches television
	Dance lessons	Visits relatives
	School choir	Does housework
		Rides bike
		Plays outside in the street
		Hangs out with cousins
Jessica Irwin (black father/	Church	Restricted television
white mother)	Sunday school	Reads
	Saturday art class	Plays outside with neighborhood
	School band	kids
		Visit relatives
POOR		
Katie Brindle (white)	School choir	Watches television
	Friday evening church group	Visits relatives
	(rarely)	Plays with Barbies
		Rides bike
		Plays with neighborhood kids
Tara Carroll (black)	Church	Watches television
	Sunday school	Visits relatives
		Plays with dolls
		Plays Nintendo
		Plays with neighborhood kids

school choir. This involved one after-school rehearsal on Wednesdays; she walked home by herself after these rehearsals. Occasionally, Katie attended a Christian youth group on Friday nights (i.e., December 3). Significantly, all her activities were free. She wanted to enroll in ballet classes, but they were prohibitively expensive. What Katie did have was unstructured leisure time. Usually, she came home after school and then played outside with other children in the neighborhood or watched television. She also regularly visited her grandmother and her cousins, who lived a few minutes away by bus or car. She often spent weekend nights at her grandmother's house. Overall, Katie's life was centered in and around home. Compared with the middle-class children in the study, her life moved at a dramatically less hectic pace. This pattern was characteristic of the other working-class and poor families we interviewed.

In addition to these activities, television provided a major source of leisure entertainment. All children in the study spent at least some free time watching TV but there were differences in when, what, and how much they watched. Most middle-class parents we interviewed characterized television as actually or potentially harmful to children; many stressed that they preferred their children to read for entertainment. Middle-class parents often had rules about the amount of time children could spend watching television. These concerns did not surface in interviews with working-class and poor parents. Indeed, Ms. Yanelli, a white working-class mother, objected to restricting a child's access to television, noting, "You know, you learn so much from television." Working-class and poor parents did monitor the content

of programs and made some shows off-limits for children. The television itself, however, was left on almost continuously (also see Robinson and Godbey 1997).

Language Use

The social class differences in language use we observed were similar to those reported by others (see Bernstein 1971; Hart and Risley 1995; Heath 1983). In middle-class homes, parents placed a tremendous emphasis on reasoning. They also drew out their children's views on specific subjects. Middle-class parents relied on directives for matters of health and safety, but most other aspects of daily life were potentially open to negotiation: Discussions arose over what children wore in the morning, what they ate, where they sat, and how they spent their time. Not all middle-class children were equally talkative, however. In addition, in observations, mothers exhibited more willingness to engage children in prolonged discussions than did fathers. The latter tended to be less engaged with children overall and less accepting of disruptions (A. Hochschild 1989).

In working-class and poor homes, most parents did not focus on developing their children's opinions, judgments, and observations. When children volunteered information, parents would listen, but typically they did not follow up with questions or comments. In the field note excerpt below, Wendy Driver shares her new understanding of sin with the members of her white working-class family. She is sitting in the living room with her brother (Willie), her mother, and her mother's live-in boyfriend (Mack). Everyone is watching television:

Wendy asks Willie: "Do you know what mortal sin is?"

Willie: "No."

Wendy asks Mom: "Do you know what mortal sin is?"

Mom: "What is it?"

Wendy asks Mack: "Do you know what it is?"

Mack: "No."

Mom: "Tell us what it is. You're the one who went to CCD [Catholic religious education classes]."

Wendy: "It's when you know something's wrong and you do it anyway."

No one acknowledged Wendy's comment. Wendy's mother and Mack looked at her while she gave her explanation of mortal sin, then looked back at the TV.

Wendy's family is conversationally cooperative, but unlike the Williamses, for example, no one here perceives the moment as an opportunity to further develop Wendy's vocabulary or to help her exercise her critical thinking skills.

Negotiations between parents and children in working-class and poor families were infrequent. Parents tended to use firm directives and they expected prompt, positive responses. Children who ignored parental instructions could expect physical punishment. Field notes from an evening in the home of the white, working-class Yanelli family capture one example of this familiar dynamic. It is past 8:00 P.M. Ms. Yanelli, her son Billy, and the fieldworker are playing *Scrabble*. Mr. Yanelli and a friend are absorbed in a game of chess. Throughout the evening, Billy and Ms. Yanelli have been at odds. She feels Billy has not been listening to her. Ms. Yanelli wants her son to stop playing *Scrabble*, take a shower, and go to bed.

Mom: "Billy, shower. I don't care if you cry, screams."

Billy: "We're not done with the *Scrabble* game."

Mom: "You're done. Finish your homework earlier." That evening, Billy had not finished his homework until 8:00 P.M. Billy remains seated.

Mom: "Come on! Tomorrow you've got a big day." Billy does not move.

Mom goes into the other room and gets a brown leather belt. She hits Billy twice on the leg.

Mom: "Get up right now! Tomorrow I can't get you up in the morning. Get up right now!"

Billy gets up and runs up the steps.

Ms. Yanelli's disciplinary approach is very different from that of the middle-class parents we observed. Like most working-class and poor parents we observed, she is directive and her instructions are nonnegotiable ("Billy, shower" and "You're done."). Using a belt may seem harsh, but it is neither a random nor irrational form of punishment here. Ms. Yanelli gave Billy notice of her expectations and she offered an explanation (it's late, and tomorrow he has "a big day"). She turned to physical discipline as a resource when she felt Billy was not sufficiently responsive.

Social Connections

We also observed class differences in the context of children's social relations. Across the sample of 88 families, middle-class children's involvement in adult-organized activities led to mainly weak social ties. Soccer, photography classes, swim team, and so on typically take place in 6 to 8 week blocks, and participant turnover rates are relatively high. Equally important, middle-class children's commitment to organized activities generally pre-empted visits with extended family. Some did not have relatives who lived nearby, but even among those who did, children's schedules made it difficult to organize and attend regular extended-family gatherings. Many of the middle-class children visited with relatives only on major holidays.

Similarly, middle-class parents tended to forge weak rather than strong ties. Most reported having social networks that included professionals: 93 percent of the sample of middle-class parents had a friend or relative who was a teacher, compared with 43 percent of working-class parents and 36 percent of poor families. For a physician friend or relative, the pattern was comparable (70 percent versus 14 percent and 18 percent, respectively). Relationships such as these are not as deep as family ties, but they are a valuable resource when parents face a challenge in childrearing.

Working-class and poor families were much less likely to include professionals in their social networks but were much more likely than their middle-class counterparts to see or speak with kin daily. Children regularly interacted in casually assembled, heterogeneous age groups that included cousins as well as neighborhood children. As others have shown (Lever 1988), we observed gender differences in children's activities. Although girls sometimes ventured outside to ride bikes and play ball games, compared with boys they were more likely to stay inside the house to play. Whether inside or outside,

the girls, like the boys, played in loose coalitions of kin and neighbors and created their own activities.

Interactions with representatives of major social institutions (the police, courts, schools, and government agencies) also appeared significantly shaped by social class. Members of white *and* black working-class and poor families offered spontaneous comments about their distrust of these officials. For example, one white working-class mother described an episode in which the police had come to her home looking for her ex-husband (a drug user). She recalled officers "breaking down the door" and terrifying her eldest son, then only three years old. Another white working-class mother reported that her father had been arrested. Although by all accounts in good spirits, he had been found dead in the city jail, an alleged suicide. Children listened to and appeared to absorb remarks such as these.

Fear was a key reason for the unease with which working-class and poor families approached formal (and some informal) encounters with officials. Some parents worried that authorities would "come and take [our] kids away." One black mother on public assistance interviewed as part of the larger study was outraged that school personnel had allowed her daughter to come home from school one winter day without her coat. She noted that if *she* had allowed that to happen, "the school" would have reported her to Child Protective Services for child abuse. Wendy Driver's mother (white working-class) complained that she felt obligated to take Wendy to the doctor, even when she knew nothing was wrong, because Wendy had gone to see the school nurse. Ms. Driver felt she had to be extra careful because she didn't want "them" to come and take her kids away. Strikingly, no middle-class parents mention similar fears about the power of dominant institutions.

Obviously, these three dimensions of childrearing patterns—the organization of daily life, language use, and social connections—do not capture all the class advantages parents pass to their children. The middle-class children in the study enjoyed relatively privileged lives. They lived in large houses, some had swimming pools in their backyards, most had bedrooms of their own, all had many toys, and computers were common. These children also had broad horizons. They flew in airplanes, they traveled out of state for vacations, they often traveled an hour or two from home to take part in their activities, and they knew older children whose extracurricular activities involved international travel.

Still, in some important areas, variations among families did *not* appear to be linked to social class. Some of the middle-class children had learning problems. And, despite their relatively privileged social-class position, neither middle-class children nor their parents were insulated from the realities of serious illness and premature death among family and friends. In addition, some elements of family life seemed relatively immune to social class, including how orderly and tidy the households were. In one white middle-class family, the house was regularly in a state of disarray. The house was cleaned and tidied for a Christmas Eve gathering, but it returned to its normal state shortly thereafter. By contrast, a black middle-class family's home was always extremely tidy, as were some, but

not all, of the working-class and poor homes. Nor did certain aspects of parenting, particularly the degree to which mothers appeared to "mean what they said," seem linked to social class. Families also differed with respect to the presence or absence of a sense of humor among individual members, levels of anxiety, and signs of stress-related illnesses they exhibited. Finally, there were significant differences in temperament and disposition among children in the same family. These variations are useful reminders that social class is not fully a determinant of the character of children's lives.

IMPACT OF CHILDREARING STRATEGIES ON INTERACTIONS WITH INSTITUTIONS

Social scientists sometimes emphasize the importance of reshaping parenting practices to improve children's chances of success. Explicitly and implicitly, the literature exhorts parents to comply with the views of professionals (Bronfenbrenner 1966; Epstein 2001; Heimer and Staffen 1998). Such calls for compliance do not, however, reconcile professionals' judgments regarding the intrinsic value of current childrearing standards with the evidence of the historical record, which shows regular shifts in such standards over time (Aries 1962; Wrigley 1989; Zelizer 1985). Nor are the stratified, and limited, possibilities for success in the broader society examined.

I now follow the families out of their homes and into encounters with representatives of dominant institutions—institutions that are directed by middle-class professionals. Again, I focus on Alexander Williams and Harold

McAllister. (Institutional experiences are summarized in Table 1.) Across all social classes, parents and children interacted with teachers and school officials, healthcare professionals, and assorted government officials. Although they often addressed similar problems (e.g., learning disabilities, asthma, traffic violations), they typically did not achieve similar resolutions. The pattern of concerted cultivation fostered an *emerging sense of entitlement* in the life of Alexander Williams and other middle-class children. By contrast, the commitment to nurturing children's natural growth fostered an *emerging sense of constraint* in the life of Harold McAllister and other working-class or poor children. (These consequences of childrearing practices are summarized in Table 1.)

Both parents and children drew on the resources associated with these two childrearing approaches during their interactions with officials. Middle-class parents and children often customized these interactions; working-class and poor parents were more likely to have a "generic" relationship. When faced with problems, middle-class parents also appeared better equipped to exert influence over other adults compared with working-class and poor parents. Nor did middle-class parents or children display the intimidation or confusion we witnessed among many working-class and poor families when they faced a problem in their children's school experience.

Emerging Signs of Entitlement

Alexander Williams's mother, like many middle-class mothers, explicitly teaches her son to be an informed, assertive client in interactions with professionals. For example, as she drives Alexander to a routine doctor's appointment, she coaches him in the art of communicating effectively in healthcare settings:

> Alexander asks if he needs to get any shots today at the doctor's. Ms. Williams says he'll need to ask the doctor. . . . As we enter Park Lane, Mom says quietly to Alex: "Alexander, you should be thinking of questions you might want to ask the doctor. You can ask him anything you want. Don't be shy. You can ask anything."
>
> Alex thinks for a minute, then: "I have some bumps under my arms from my deodorant."
>
> Mom: "Really? You mean from your new deodorant?"
>
> Alex: "Yes."
>
> Mom: "Well, you should ask the doctor."

Alexander learns that he has the right to speak up (e.g., "don't be shy") and that he should prepare for an encounter with a person in a position of authority by gathering his thoughts in advance.

These class resources are subsequently *activated* in the encounter with the doctor (a jovial white man in his late thirties or early forties). The examination begins this way:

> Doctor: "Okay, as usual, I'd like to go through the routine questions with you. And if you have any questions for me, just fire away." Doctor examines Alex's chart: "Height-wise, as usual, Alexander's in the ninety-fifth percentile."

Although the physician is talking to Ms. Williams, Alexander interrupts him:

> Alex: "I'm in the what?" Doctor: "It means that you're taller than more than ninety-five

out of a hundred young men when they're, uh, ten years old."

Alex: "I'm not ten."

Doctor: "Well, they graphed you at ten . . . they usually take the closest year to get that graph."

Alex: "Alright."

Alexander's "Alright" reveals that he feels entitled to weigh-in with his own judgment.

A few minutes later, the exam is interrupted when the doctor is asked to provide an emergency consultation by telephone. Alexander listens to the doctor's conversation and then uses what he has overheard as the basis for a clear directive:

Doctor: "The stitches are on the eyelids themselves, the laceration? . . . Um . . . I don't suture eyelids . . . um . . . Absolutely not! . . . Don't even touch them. That was very bad judgment on the camp's part. . . . [Hangs up.] I'm sorry about the interruption."

Alex: "Stay away from my eyelids!"

Alexander's comment, which draws laughter from the adults, reflects this fourth grader's tremendous ease interacting with a physician.

Later, Ms. Williams and the doctor discuss Alexander's diet. Ms. Williams freely admits that they do not always follow nutritional guidelines. Her honesty is a form of capital because it gives the doctor accurate information on which to base a diagnosis. Feeling no need for deception positions mother and son to receive better care:

Doctor: Let's start with appetite. Do you get three meals a day?"

Alex: "Yeah."

Doctor: "And here's the important question: Do you get your fruits and vegetables too?"

Alex: "Yeah."

Mom, high-pitched: "Ooooo. . . ."

Doctor: "I see I have a second opinion. " [laughter]

Alex, voice rising: "You give me bananas and all in my lunch every day. And I had cabbage for dinner last night."

Doctor: "Do you get at least one or two fruits, one or two vegetables every day?"

Alex: "Yeah."

Doctor: "Marginally?"

Mom: "Ninety-eight percent of the time he eats pretty well."

Doctor: "OK, I can live with that. . . ."

Class resources are again activated when Alexander's mother reveals she "gave up" on a medication. The doctor pleasantly but clearly instructs her to continue the medication. Again, though, he receives accurate information rather than facing silent resistance or defiance, as occurred in encounters between healthcare professionals and other (primarily working-class and poor) families. The doctor acknowledges Ms. Williams's relative power: He "argues for" continuation rather than directing her to execute a medically necessary action:

Mom: "His allergies have just been, just acted up again. One time this summer and I had to bring him in."

Doctor: "I see a note here from Dr. Svennson that she put him on Vancinace and Benadryl. Did it seem to help him?"

Mom: "Just, not really. So, I used it for about a week and I just gave up." Doctor, sitting forward in his chair: "OK, I'm actually going to argue for not giving up. If he needs it, Vancinace is a very effective drug. But it takes at least a week to start. . . ."

Mom: "Oh. OK. . . ."

Doctor: "I'd rather have him use that than heavy oral medications. You have to give it a few weeks. . . ."

A similar pattern of give and take and questioning characterizes Alexander's interaction with the doctor, as the following excerpt illustrates:

Doctor: "The only thing that you really need besides my checking you, um, is to have, um, your eyes checked downstairs."

Alex: "Yes! I love that, I love that!"

Doctor laughs: "Well, now the most important question. Do you have any questions you want to ask me before I do your physical?"

Alex: "Um.... only one. I've been getting some bumps on my arms, right around here [indicates underarm]."

Doctor: "Underneath?"

Alex: "Yeah."

Doctor: "OK. . . . Do they hurt or itch?"

Alex; "No, they're just there."

Doctor: "OK, I'll take a look at those bumps for you. Um, what about you—um . . ."

Alex: "They're barely any left."

Doctor: "OK, well, I'll take a peek. . . . Any questions or worries on your part? [Looking at the mother]

Mom: "No. . . . He seems to be coming along very nicely."

Alexander's mother's last comment reflects her view of him as a project, one that is pro-

gressing "very nicely." Throughout the visit, she signals her ease and her perception of the exam as an exchange between peers (with Alexander a legitimate participant), rather than a communication from a person in authority to his subordinates. Other middle-class parents seemed similarly comfortable. During Garrett Tallinger's exam, for example, his mother took off her sandals and tucked her legs up under her as she sat in the examination room. She also joked casually with the doctor.

Middle-class parents and children were also very assertive in situations at the public elementary school most of the middle-class children in the study attended. There were numerous conflicts during the year over matters small and large. For example, parents complained to one another and to the teachers about the amount of homework the children were assigned. A black middle-class mother whose daughters had not tested into the school's gifted program negotiated with officials to have the girls' (higher) results from a private testing company accepted instead. The parents of a fourth-grade boy drew the school superintendent into a battle over religious lyrics in a song scheduled to be sung as part of the holiday program. The superintendent consulted the district lawyer and ultimately "counseled" the principal to be more sensitive, and the song was dropped.

Children, too, asserted themselves at school. Examples include requesting that the classroom's blinds be lowered so the sun wasn't in their eyes, badgering the teacher for permission to retake a math test for a higher grade, and demanding to know why no cupcake had been saved when an absence prevented attendance at a classroom party. In these encounters, children were not simply complying with adults' requests or asking for a repeat of an earlier experience. They were displaying an emerging sense of entitlement by urging adults to permit a customized accommodation of institutional processes to suit their preferences.

Of course, some children (and parents) were more forceful than others in their dealings with teachers, and some were more successful than others. Melanie Handlon's mother, for example, took a very "hands-on" approach to her daughter's learning problems, coaching Melanie through her homework day after day. Instead of improved grades, however, the only result was a deteriorating home environment marked by tension and tears.

Emerging Signs of Constraint

The interactions the research assistants and I observed between professionals and working-class and poor parents frequently seemed cautious and constrained. This unease is evident, for example, during a physical Harold McAllister has before going to Bible camp. Harold's mother, normally boisterous and talkative at home, is quiet. Unlike Ms. Williams, she seems wary of supplying the doctor with accurate information:

Doctor: "Does he eat something each day—either fish, meat, or egg?"
Mom, response is low and muffled: "Yes."
Doctor, attempting to make eye contact but mom stares intently at paper: "A yellow vegetable?"
Mom, still no eye contact, looking at the floor: "Yeah."

Doctor: "A green vegetable?" Mom, looking at the doctor: "Not all the time." [Fieldworker has not seen any of the children eat a green or yellow vegetable since visits began.]
Doctor: "No. Fruit or juice?"
Mom, low voice, little or no eye contact, looks at the doctor's scribbles on the paper he is filling out: "Ummh humn."
Doctor: "Does he drink milk everyday?" Mom, abruptly, in considerably louder voice: "Yeah."
Doctor: "Cereal, bread, rice, potato, anything like that?"
Mom, shakes her head: "Yes, definitely." [Looks at doctor.]

Ms. McAllister's knowledge of developmental events in Harold's life is uneven. She is not sure when he learned to walk and cannot recall the name of his previous doctor. And when the doctor asks, "When was the last time he had a tetanus shot?" she counters, gruffly, "What's a tetanus shot?"

Unlike Ms. Williams, who urged Alexander to share information with the doctor, Ms. McAllister squelches eight-year-old Alexis's overtures:

Doctor: "Any birth mark?"
Mom looks at doctor, shakes her head no.
Alexis, raising her left arm, says excitedly: "I have a birth mark under my arm!"
Mom, raising her voice and looking stern: "Will you cool out a minute?" Mom, again answering the doctor's question: "No."

Despite Ms. McAllister's tension and the marked change in her everyday demeanor, Harold's whole exam is not uncomfortable. There are moments of laughter. Moreover, Harold's mother is not consistently shy or passive. Before the visit begins, the doctor comes into the waiting room and calls Harold's and Alexis's names. In response, the McAllisters (and the fieldworker) stand. Ms. McAllister then beckons for her nephew Tyrice (who is about Harold's age) to come along *before* she clears this with the doctor. Later, she sends Tyrice down the hall to observe Harold being weighed; she relies on her nephew's report rather than asking for this information from the healthcare professionals.

Still, neither Harold nor his mother seemed as comfortable as Alexander had been. Alexander was used to extensive conversation at home; with the doctor, he was at ease initiating questions. Harold, who was used to responding to directives at home, primarily answered questions from the doctor, rather than posing his own. Alexander, encouraged by his mother, was assertive and confident with the doctor. Harold was reserved. Absorbing his mother's apparent need to conceal the truth about the range of foods he ate, he appeared cautious, displaying an emerging sense of constraint.

We observed a similar pattern in school interactions. Overall, the working-class and poor adults had much more distance or separation from the school than their middle-class counterparts. Ms. McAllister, for example, could be quite assertive in some settings (e.g., at the start of family observations, she visited the local drug dealer, warning him not to "mess with" the black male fieldworker). But throughout the fourth-grade parent-teacher conference, she kept her winter jacket zipped

up, sat hunched over in her chair, and spoke in barely audible tones. She was stunned when the teacher said that Harold did not do homework. Sounding dumbfounded, she said, "He does it at home." The teacher denied it and continued talking. Ms. McAllister made no further comments and did not probe for more information, except about a letter the teacher said he had mailed home and that she had not received. The conference ended, having yielded Ms. McAllister few insights into Harold's educational experience.

Other working-class and poor parents also appeared baffled, intimidated, and subdued in parent-teacher conferences. Ms. Driver, who was extremely worried about her fourth-grader's inability to read, kept these concerns to herself. She explained to us, "I don't want to jump into anything and find it is the wrong thing." When working-class and poor parents did try to intervene in their children's educational experiences, they often felt ineffectual. Billy Yanelli's mother appeared relaxed and chatty in many of her interactions with other adults. With "the school," however, she was very apprehensive. She distrusted school personnel. She felt bullied and powerless. Hoping to resolve a problem involving her son, she tried to prepare her ideas in advance. Still, as she recounted during an interview, she failed to make school officials see Billy as vulnerable:

Ms. Yanelli: I found a note in his school bag one morning and it said, "I'm going to kill you . . . you're a dead mother-f-er. . . ." So, I started shaking. I was all ready to go over there. [I was] prepared for the counselor. . . . They said the reason they [the other kids] do what they do is because Billy makes them do it. So they had an answer for everything.

Interviewer: How did you feel about that answer?

Ms. Yanelli: I hate the school. I hate it.

Working-class and poor children seemed aware of their parents' frustration and witnessed their powerlessness. Billy Yanelli, for example, asserted in an interview that his mother "hate[d]" school officials.

At times, these parents encouraged their children to resist school officials' authority. The Yanellis told Billy to "beat up" a boy who was bothering him. Wendy Driver's mother advised her to punch a male classmate who pestered her and pulled her ponytail. Ms. Driver's boyfriend added, "Hit him when the teacher isn't looking."

In classroom observations, working-class and poor children could be quite lively and energetic, but we did not observe them try to customize their environments. They tended to react to adults' offers or, at times, to plead with educators to repeat previous experiences, such as reading a particular story, watching a movie, or going to the computer room. Compared to middle-class classroom interactions, the boundaries between adults and children seemed firmer and clearer. Although the children often resisted and tested school rules, they did not seem to be seeking to get educators to accommodate their own *individual* preferences.

Overall, then, the behavior of working-class and poor parents cannot be explained as a manifestation of their temperaments or of overall passivity; parents were quite energetic in intervening in their children's lives in other spheres. Rather, working-class and poor parents generally appeared to depend on the school (Lareau 2000), even as they were dubious of the trustworthiness of the professionals. This suspicion of professionals in dominant institutions is, at least in some instances, a reasonable response. The unequal level of trust, as well as differences in the amount and quality of information divulged, can yield unequal *profits* during an historical moment when professionals applaud assertiveness and reject passivity as an inappropriate parenting strategy (Epstein 2001). Middle-class children and parents often (but not always) accrued advantages or profits from their efforts. Alexander Williams succeeded in having the doctor take his medical concerns seriously. Ms. Marshall's children ended up in the gifted program, even though they did not technically qualify. Middle-class children expect institutions to be responsive to *them* and to accommodate their individual needs. By contrast, when Wendy Driver is told to hit the boy who is pestering her (when the teacher isn't looking) or Billy Yanelli is told to physically defend himself, despite school rules, they are not learning how to make bureaucratic institutions work to their advantage. Instead, they are being given lessons in frustration and powerlessness.

WHY DOES SOCIAL CLASS MATTER?

Parents' economic resources helped create the observed class differences in child-rearing practices. Enrollment fees that middle-class parents dismissed as "negligible" were formidable expenses for less affluent families. Parents also paid for clothing, equipment, hotel stays, fast food meals, summer camps, and fundraisers. In 1994, the Tallingers estimated the cost of Garrett's activities at $4,000 annually, and that figure was not unusually high. Moreover, families needed reliable private transportation and flexible work schedules to get children to and from events. These resources were disproportionately concentrated in middle-class families.

Differences in educational resources also are important. Middle-class parents' superior levels of education gave them larger vocabularies that facilitated concerted cultivation, particularly in institutional interventions. Poor and working-class parents were not familiar with key terms professionals used, such as "tetanus shot." Furthermore, middle-class parents' educational backgrounds gave them confidence when criticizing educational professionals and intervening in school matters. Working-class and poor parents viewed educators as their social superiors.

Kohn and Schooler (1983) showed that parents' occupations, especially the complexity of their work, influence their childrearing beliefs. We found that parents' work mattered, but also saw signs that the experience of adulthood itself influenced conceptions of childhood. Middle-class parents often were preoccupied with the pleasures and challenges of their work lives. They tended to view childhood as a dual opportunity: a chance for play, and for developing talents and skills of value later in life. Mr. Tallinger noted that playing soccer taught Garrett to be "hard nosed" and "competitive," valuable workplace skills. Ms. Williams mentioned the value of Alexander learning to work with others by playing on a sports team. Middle-class parents, aware of the "declining fortunes" of the middle class, worried about their own economic futures and those of their children (Newman 1993). This uncertainty increased their commitment to helping their children develop broad skills to enhance their future possibilities.

Working-class and poor parents' conceptions of adulthood and childhood also appeared to be closely connected to their lived experiences. For the working class, it was the deadening quality of work and the press of economic shortages that defined their experience of adulthood and influenced their vision of childhood. It was dependence on public assistance and severe economic shortages that most shaped poor parents' views. Families in both classes had many worries about basic issues: food shortages, limited access to healthcare, physical safety, unreliable transportation, insufficient clothing. Thinking back over their childhoods, these parents remembered hardship but also recalled times without the anxieties they now faced. Many appeared to want their own youngsters to concentrate on being happy and relaxed, keeping the burdens of life at bay until they were older.

Thus, childrearing strategies are influenced by more than parents' education. It is the interweaving of life experiences and resources, including parents' economic resources, occupational conditions, and educational backgrounds, that appears to be most important in leading middle-class parents to engage in concerted cultivation and working-class and poor parents to engage in the accomplishment of natural growth. Still, the structural location of families did not fully determine their childrearing practices. The agency of actors and the indeterminacy of social life are inevitable.

In addition to economic and social resources, are there other significant factors? If the poor and working-class families' resources were transformed overnight so that they equaled those of the middle-class families, would their cultural logic of childrearing shift as well? Or are there cultural attitudes and beliefs that are substantially independent of economic and social resources that are influencing parents' practices here? The size and scope of this study preclude a definitive answer. Some poor and working-class parents embraced principles of concerted cultivation: They wished (but could not afford) to enroll their children in organized activities (e.g., piano lessons, voice lessons), they believed listening to children was important, and they were committed to being involved in their children's schooling. Still, even when parents across all of the classes seemed committed to similar principles, their motivations differed. For example, many working-class and poor parents who wanted more activities for their children were seeking a safe haven for them. Their goal was to provide protection from harm rather than to cultivate the child's talents per se.

Some parents explicitly criticized children's schedules that involved many activities. During the parent interviews, we described the real-life activities of two children (using data from the 12 families we were observing). One schedule resembled Alexander Williams's: restricted television, required reading, and many organized activities, including piano lessons (for analytical purposes, we said that, unlike Alexander, this child disliked his piano lessons but was not allowed to quit). Summing up the attitude of the working-class and poor parents who

rejected this kind of schedule, one white, poor mother complained:

> I think he wants more. I think he doesn't enjoy doing what he's doing half of the time (light laughter). I think his parents are too strict. And he's not a child.

Even parents who believed this more regimented approach would pay off "job-wise" when the child was an adult still expressed serious reservations: "I think he is a sad kid," or, "He must be dead-dog tired."

Thus, working-class and poor parents varied in their beliefs. Some longed for a schedule of organized activities for their children and others did not; some believed in reasoning with children and playing an active role in schooling and others did not. Fully untangling the effects of material and cultural resources on parents and children's choices is a challenge for future research.

||| DISCUSSION

The evidence shows that class position influences critical aspects of family life: time use, language use, and kin ties. Not all aspects of family life are affected by social class, and there is variability within class. Still, parents do transmit advantages to their children in patterns that are sufficiently consistent and identifiable to be described as a "cultural logic" of childrearing. The white and black middle-class parents engaged in practices I have termed "concerted cultivation"—they made a deliberate and sustained effort to stimulate children's development and to cultivate their cognitive and social skills. The working-class and poor parents viewed children's development as spontaneously unfolding, as long as they were provided with comfort, food, shelter, and other basic support. This commitment, too, required ongoing effort; sustaining children's natural growth despite formidable life challenges is properly viewed as an accomplishment.

In daily life, the patterns associated with each of these approaches were interwoven and mutually reinforcing. Nine-year-old middle-class children already had developed a clear sense of their own talents and skills, and they differentiated themselves from siblings and friends. They were also learning to think of themselves as special and worthy of having adults devote time and energy to promoting them and their leisure activities. In the process, the boundaries between adults and children sometimes blurred; adults' leisure preferences became subordinate to their children's. The strong emphasis on reasoning in middle-class families had similar, diffuse effects. Children used their formidable reasoning skills to persuade adults to acquiesce to their wishes. The idea that children's desires should be taken seriously was routinely realized in the middle-class families we interviewed and observed. In many subtle ways, children were taught that they were entitled. Finally, the commitment to cultivating children resulted in family schedules so crowded with activities there was little time left for visiting relatives. Quantitative studies of time use have shed light on important issues, but they do not capture the interactive nature of routine, everyday activities and the varying ways they affect the texture of family life.

In working-class and poor families, parents established limits; within those limits, children were free to fashion their own pastimes. Children's wishes did not guide adults' actions as frequently or as decisively as they did in middle-class homes. Children were viewed as subordinate to adults. Parents tended to issue directives rather than to negotiate. Frequent interactions with relatives rather than acquaintances or strangers created a thicker divide between families and the outside world. Implicitly and explicitly, parents taught their children to keep their distance from people in positions of authority, to be distrustful of institutions, and, at times, to resist officials' authority. Children seemed to absorb the adults' feelings of powerlessness in their institutional relationships. As with the middle class, there were important variations among working-class and poor families, and some critical aspects of family life, such as the use of humor, were immune to social class.

The role of race in children's daily lives was less powerful than I had expected. The middle-class black children's parents were alert to the potential effects of institutional discrimination on their children. Middle-class black parents also took steps to help their children develop a positive racial identity. Still, in terms of how children spend their time, the way parents use language and discipline in the home, the nature of the families' social connections, and the strategies used for intervening in institutions, white and black middle-class parents engaged in very similar, often identical, practices with their children. A similar pattern was observed in white and black working-class homes as well as in white and black poor families. Thus my data indicate that on the childrearing dynamics studied here, compared with social class, race was less important in children's daily lives. As they enter the racially segregated words of dating, marriage, and housing markets, and as they encounter more racism in their interpersonal contact with whites (Waters 1999), the relative importance of race in the children's daily lives is likely to increase.

Differences in family dynamics and the logic of childrearing across social classes have long-term consequences. As family members moved out of the home and interacted with representatives of formal institutions, middle-class parents and children were able to negotiate more valuable outcomes than their working-class and poor counterparts. In interactions with agents of dominant institutions, working-class and poor children were learning lessons in constraint while middle-class children were developing a sense of entitlement.

★ ★ ★

‖ REFERENCES

Aries, Philippe. 1962. *Centuries of Childhood: A Social History of the Family*. Translated by R. Baldick. London, England: Cape.

Bernstein, Basil. 1971. *Class, Codes, and Control: Theoretical Studies towards a Sociology of Language*. New York: Schocken Books.

Bronfenbrenner, Urie. 1966. "Socialization and Social Class through Time and Space." Pp. 362–77 in *Class, Status and Power,* edited by R. Bendix and S. M. Lipset. New York: Free Press.

Conley, Dalton. 1999. *Being Black, Living in the Red: Race, Wealth, and Social Policy in America*. Berkeley, CA: University of California Press.

Epstein, Joyce. 2001. *Schools, Family, and Community Partnerships*. Boulder, CO: Westview.

Fordham, Signithia and John U. Ogbu. 1986. "Black Students' School Success: Coping with the 'Burden of Acting White.' " *The Urban Review* 18:176–206.

Hart, Betty and Todd Risley. 1995. *Meaningful Differences in the Everyday Experience of Young American Children*. Baltimore, MD: Paul Brooks.

Heath, Shirley Brice. 1983. *Ways with Words*. London, England: Cambridge University Press.

Heimer, Carol A. and Lisa Staffen. 1998. *For the Sake of the Children: The Social Organization of Responsibility in the Hospital and at Home*. Chicago, IL: University of Chicago Press.

Hochschild, Arlie Russell. 1989. *The Second Shift: Working Parents and the Revolution at Home*. New York: Viking.

Hochschild, Jennifer L. 1995. *Facing Up to The American Dream*. Princeton, NJ: Princeton University Press.

Hofferth, Sandra and John Sandberg. 2001a. "Changes in American Children's Time, 1981–1997." Pp. 193–232 in *Advances in Life Course Research*, vol. 6, *Children at the Millennium: Where Have We Come From, Where Are We Going?,* edited by S. Hofferth and T. Owens. Oxford, England, Elsevier Science Ltd.

———. 2001b. "How American Children Spend Their Time." *Journal of Marriage and the Family* 63:295–308.

Kingston, Paul. 2000. *The Classless Society*. Stanford, CA: Stanford University Press.

Kohn, Melvin and Carmi Schooler, eds. 1983. *Work and Personality: An Inquiry into the Impact of Social Stratification*. Norwood, NJ: Ablex.

Lareau, Annette. 2000a. *Home Advantage: Social Class and Parental Intervention in Elementary Education*. 2d ed. Lanham, MD: Rowman and Littlefield.

Medrich, Elliot, Judith Roizen, Victor Rubin, and Stuart Buckley. 1982. *The Serious Business of Growing Up*. Berkeley, CA: University of California Press.

Newman, Kathleen. 1993. *Declining Fortunes: The Withering of the American Dream*. New York: Basic Books.

Pattillo-McCoy, Mary. 1999. *Black Picket Fences: Privilege and Peril among the Black Middle-Class*. Chicago, IL: University of Chicago Press.

Robinson, John P. and Geoffry Godbey. 1997. *Time for Life: The Surprising Ways Americans Use Their Time*. University Park, PA: The Pennsylvania State Press.

Schemari, James. 2002. "Practice Makes Perfect (and Poorer Parents)." *The New York Times,* January 27, p. 11.

Tatum, Beverly Daniel. 1997. *Why Are All the Black Kids Sitting Together in the Cafeteria?And Other Conversations about Race*. New York: Basic Books.

Waters, Mary. 1999. *Black Identities: West Indian Immigrant Dreams and American Realities*. New York: Russell Sage Foundation.

Wrigley, Julia. 1989. "Do Young Children Need Intellectual Stimulation? Experts' Advice to Parents, 1900–1985." *History of* Education 29:41–75.

Zelizer, Vivianna. 1985. *Pricing the Priceless Child: The Changing Social Value of Children*. New York: Basic Books.

45

Increasing Class Disparities among Women and the Politics of Gender Equity★

LESLIE MCCALL

Issues of gender and class inequality are rarely considered together. This chapter's primary objective is to make the case for why they should be. In particular, I focus on the need for contemporary gender inequality to be understood within the context of rising earnings and income inequality in the United States, or what I will refer to as rising class inequality because I consider earnings and income to be among the central components of one's class position (along with assets, education, and occupation, which I also discuss briefly).

Income and earnings inequalities among women, men, and families are greater now than they were three decades ago, and by some measures, more than they have been since the eve of World War II. As women's experiences in the paid labor force and in the families in which they live have become more divergent by class, so potentially has the nature of gendered economic inequality. Economic justice for women may therefore require more of an emphasis on class-specific strategies than now exists. This includes class-specific strategies that are tailored to reducing the high and rising levels of

---

★ First published in 2007; from *The Sex of Class: Women Transforming American Labor*, edited by Dorothy Sue Cobble.

earnings and income inequality that the United States and many other countries around the world are experiencing.

To demonstrate the increasing importance of class inequality in understanding recent shifts in gender inequality, this chapter provides an overview of trends in both forms of inequality over the past three decades. ★ ★ ★

Because this is a large agenda for a short chapter, my approach is to provide a brief review of existing research in each of these areas through the particular lens of class disparities among women. This lens is useful because it incorporates two additional themes alongside the more typical theme of women's changing economic status relative to men: (1) differences in the absolute progress of women in different class positions, and (2) differences in the pathways to achieving relative equality with men for women in different class positions.

By absolute progress, I am referring to women's achievement of significant increases in earnings, educational, and occupational attainment even if men have had similar increases. Such a scenario implies a decline in some forms of absolute discrimination—through, for example, wider opportunities for women to enter the professions—even as substantial relative discrimination appears to persist when comparisons are made to similarly situated men. A contrasting scenario is one in which absolute progress among women is more limited but relative progress is greater as a result of disproportionate losses among similarly situated men—through, for example, the decline in real earnings for men in the bottom half of the earnings distribution. Both scenarios have in fact occurred in the United States. I therefore give equal attention and weight to the achievement of women's absolute and relative progress and to the differences by class in the pathways to greater gender equity that these imply.

★ ★ ★

EARNINGS INEQUALITY BY GENDER

The resurgence in class inequality and women's faster growth in earnings do not mean that gender inequality has been eliminated or reduced to trivial levels. Women's wages are still lower than men's, by approximately 20 percent at the median. This represents a 50 percent decline in the median gender gap since 1973. Unfortunately, there has been little attention to whether (and if so, why) the earnings gap between men and women differs for different classes (cf. Blau and Kahn 1997, 2004; McCall 2001). The bulk of the evidence suggests that such differences in the gender gap are *less* now than they were several decades ago, so that the average gender gap is more similar to the gap at the top and bottom than it used to be. Much more research needs to be done to clarify these trends, however, and the increasing similarity in the gender gap across class lines is not the entire story. Something different is occurring at the extremes, among low-wage workers and workers with an advanced degree as well as among racial/ethnic groups. This redirects our attention once again away from an analysis of average trends and levels and toward an analysis of differences in the character of gender inequality by class as well as race. I first examine trends at the median, then at the bottom and among racial/ethnic groups, and finally at the top.

FIGURE 1   **CHANGES IN THE RATIO OF FEMALE TO MALE HOURLY WAGES BY WAGE PERCENTILE, 1973–2003**

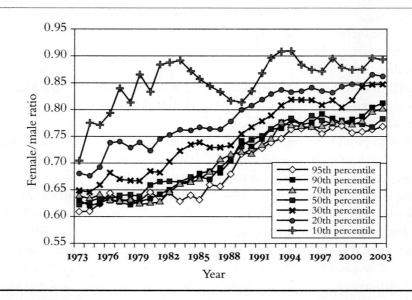

NOTE: The sample includes part-time and full-time, 18- to 64-year-old individuals with valid wage and salary earnings. The unincorporated self-employed are excluded (see Mishel Bernstein, and Allegretto 2005, app. B).
SOURCE: Data from Mishel, Bernstein, and Allegretto (2005, tables 2.7 and 2.8).

Except for a few notable exceptions, wage growth over the last three decades of the twentieth century was greater for women than for men throughout the entire distribution of workers, leading to a near universal decline in the gender gap between men and women and an increase in the ratio of female to male wages (the typical measure of gender inequality that is used here as well). As shown in figures 1 and 2, there is a remarkable degree of similarity in the female/male wage ratio for the upper 50 percent of the distribution and for all education groups but the top one (those with an advanced degree). For these groups, the ratio grew by at least fifteen percentage points—a sign that women's wages

were becoming more similar to men's and thus inequality was declining—from a range of 0.61–0.63 in the early 1970s to a range of 0.77–0.81 in 2003. The ratio was relatively stable in the 1970s, increased substantially in the 1980s, and leveled off in the late 1990s. Because the spreading out of wages for women was similar to the spreading out of wages for men in the top half of the distribution ★ ★ ★, there were similar proportionate increases in the ratio of women's to men's wages as well. At the median, this occurred through modest growth in women's wages and declines in men's wages, whereas, at the 90th percentile, it occurred through faster growth rates for women than for men.

FIGURE 2 CHANGES IN RATIO OF FEMALE TO MALE HOURLY WAGES BY EDUCATION, 1973–2003

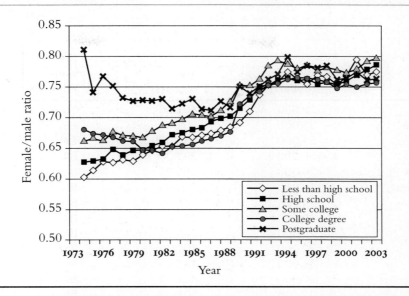

NOTE: The sample includes part-time and full-time, 18- to 64-year-old individuals with valid wage and salary earnings. The unincorporated self-employed are excluded (see Mishel Bernstein, and Allegretto 2005, app. B).
SOURCE: Data from Mishel, Bernstein, and Allegretto (2005, tables 2.18 and 2.19).

We get a different picture if we look at low-wage workers, however. First of all, gender inequality is lower at the bottom that at the top or in the middle. The female/male ratio is particularly distinctive at the 10th percentile. This ratio increased dramatically over the 1970s and early 1980s and then decreased precipitously over the rest of the 1980s. This roller-coaster pattern is explained by changes in the minimum wage, which greatly affects women's wages at the bottom (Dinardo, Fortin, and Lemieux 1996). The minimum wage was raised several times in the 1970s and then was not raised at all until 1990. The roller-coaster pattern is also explained by the steep declines in men's wages at the bottom, which were con-

centrated in the early 1980s. Wage equity for low-wage women, then, is highly sensitive to wage-setting policies and is somewhat illusory because low-wage men—the comparison group—have faired so poorly in the labor market.

This latter point also pertains to interpretations of gender equity within minority racial groups, in which minority male wages are relatively low as well. Because the gender gap tends to be lower among low-wage and minority groups, a more appropriate standard of comparison is needed for low-wage and minority women. For example, the median for white men rather than same-race/ethnicity men can be used to gauge the economic progress of

TABLE 1   MEDIAN ANNUAL EARNINGS FOR U.S. WOMEN AND MEN BY RACE AND ETHNICITY, 1999[a]

Race/ethnicity	Women (dollars)	Men (dollars)	Women's earnings as percentage of	
			Men's of same race/ethnicity	White men's
White (only)	28,000	40,000	70	70
African American	25,000	30,000	83	63
Hispanic (any)	21,000	25,000	84	53
Mexican	20,000	23,900	84	50
Puerto Rican	25,000	30,000	83	63
Central American	18,000	22,500	80	45
South American	24,000	30,000	80	60
Cuban	26,000	31,000	84	65
Dominican	20,000	24,700	81	50
Asian (any)	30,000	40,000	75	75
Chinese	34,000	43,000	79	85
South Asian	30,300	35,000	87	76
Filipina	32,300	50,000	65	81
Southeast Asian	23,100	30,000	77	58
Korean	35,000	48,500	72	88
Japanese	27,700	38,000	73	69
American Indian	24,000	30,000	80	60
Pacific Islander	25,000	30,000	83	63

SOURCE: Cotter, Hermsen, and Vanneman (2004).
[a]Earnings calculated for men and women ages 25–54, employed full-time/year-round.

minority racial and ethnic groups of women. Table 1 provides these comparisons.

For many groups, the ratio of women's to men's earnings is much higher within the same racial/ethnic group than it is across racial/ethnic groups, with white men as the cross-racial/ethnic comparison group. For example, the median earnings of Mexican American women are 84 percent of the earnings of Mexican American men but only 50 percent of the earnings of white men. We find differences of this kind that are at least twenty percentage points in magnitude for women who are African American, Hispanic, Southeast Asian, American Indian, and Pacific Islander. Although some of these ratios would increase if differences in human capital were accounted for, they would remain substantial nonetheless. For several Asian groups, however, earnings ratios within racial/ethnic groups are either comparable to or less than those with white men. Filipinas, for example, earn 65 and 81 percent of the earnings of Filipinos and white men, respectively, because Filipinos earn more than white men. Clearly, then, there is much variation in the economic standing of different racial/ethnic groups of women that a simple mean or median analysis between whites and nonwhites would miss.

One of the reasons why some Asian groups of women have earnings that are comparable to those of white men is that they have very high levels of education. If we were to compare such groups with comparably educated groups of whites, it is not clear that they would fare as well. This is suggested by the seemingly atypical lack of improvement—let alone substantial improvement—in the hourly wage ratio between men and women with advanced degrees (refer again to fig. 2). In fact, the ratio fell from 0.81 in 1973 to 0.76 in 2003. At the beginning of the period, the ratio was nearly 20 percentage points higher than the median ratio, whereas at the end of the period it was lower. Thus, in relative terms— that is, if we think of gender equity as a relative achievement rather than an absolute one—the most educated women, whose average earnings are at the 90th percentile but include women across a wider range, have fared the worst of all in the past three decades. They have made strong absolute progress but virtually no relative progress.

What are we to make of these patterns, and, most important, what are the implications for gender wage justice today? One possible explanation for (or speculation about) the lack of progress toward relative gender equity among those with advanced degrees is disquieting. The argument begins with the observation that the working women who were most

like working men in the earlier period and who are most like working men today are those with advanced degrees. Because of their substantial investment in education and strong earnings potential, their commitment to work has been relatively high and constant. A change in the female/male ratio for that group, then, is more likely to reflect changes in how they are compensated relative to men and less likely to reflect the impact of increasing education and experience, factors that are more consequential for other groups of women (Mulligan and Rubenstein 2004). It follows, then, that the stable level of gender inequality among those with an advanced degree reflects a stable level of relative discrimination. As Blau and Kahn (1997) put it in an analogous study of the wage distribution by percentile (rather than by education group), women in the top percentiles have been "swimming upstream" to keep up with a moving target (men in the top percentiles), one that is more and more distant from the middle or even upper-middle ranks in an increasingly unequal hierarchy.

In contrast, the closing of the gender pay gap in the rest of the distribution is more readily attributable to improvements in women's human capital in both absolute terms and relative to the human capital of similar men. Once these improvements have been made in the population of women workers as a whole, however, and more educated and experienced cohorts replace less educated and experienced cohorts, relative progress may stall. This is especially likely if the disadvantages faced by men at the bottom and in the middle reverse, as they did in the late 1990s, leaving the bulk of working women to swim upstream as their upper-class sisters did beginning in the 1980s. According to this explanation, then, the gender gap has narrowed because women's skills and orientation toward work have grown more similar to those of men and not because women are treated more equitably relative to men of the same caliber.

In sum, one of the key distinctions that is easier to appreciate today than a generation ago is the difference between relative and absolute progress for women. On the one hand, a remarkably similar level of relative gender inequality exists across education groups today. Yet those with the most education have made the least relative progress, and the relative progress that has been made appears to be slowing. From this perspective, there has been a consolidation of a particular regime of relative gender discrimination, especially for women in the higher-income brackets. What some are increasingly identifying as the lynchpin of this regime—the gender difference in family care, or family-based discrimination—is perhaps more visible today than in the past when other barriers were just as formidable. On the other hand, progress has been substantial for women at the top, in absolute terms and relative to all other groups (including most men).

In contrast, the greatest disparities for women at the bottom are not with men of their same standing but with women and men in more privileged class and racial/ethnic groups. Moreover, the gender pay gap at the very bottom, although smaller than for other groups,

has not changed much since the early 1980s when men's wages bottomed out and increases in the minimum wage topped out. From this view, absolute progress and mobility for women at the bottom have been stymied by increasing class inequality in tandem with ongoing racial and gender discrimination. Consequently, the problems that women at the bottom face cannot be attributed solely to the workings of gender-based discrimination.

INCOME INEQUALITY AMONG FAMILIES

Because the economic needs of individuals are met by the earnings of the people they live with in addition to their own earnings, we need to consider whether rising inequality has permeated family life as much as it has work life. On the one hand, transformations in the family could have offset the growing level of inequality among individuals in U.S. society. Specifically, the increasing share of wives and mothers in the paid work force could have been concentrated in the families that were most exposed to the fall in men's earnings potential; in that case, income inequality among families may be less of an issue than the earnings inequality among individuals.[1] If so, the more salient issue may be a time squeeze between family and work. If widespread enough, the time squeeze—and the lack of family-friendly policies that would alleviate family-based discrimination against

---

[1] Roughly 40 percent of all mothers with children under 18 were in the paid work force in 1970; this increased to 70 percent in 2000 (U.S. Bureau of the Census 2006, table 579).

women—could serve as the basis for increasing similarities in the gender dynamics of families (Williams 2000).

On the other hand, some transformations in family life tend to reinforce rather than topple existing social conventions such as class distinctions. An important way this is accomplished is through homogamy (or assortative mating), the propensity to marry someone with like education, family background, race, or other characteristics (Sweeney and Cancian 2004). Increasing individual inequality can therefore serve as a source of increasing bifurcation in the residential, educational, and social environments of U.S. families (e.g., Lareau 2003). This growing inequality and segregation could in turn shape how families from different class backgrounds resolve the time bind between work and family. In particular, the affluent may be more likely to support the current system of private care because it provides high-quality services by costly but still relatively low-paid workers. Consequently, inequality—in the form of a low-wage, deregulated, private-care market, on the one hand, and a high-wage class of consumers of care work, on the other— could minimize the potential for commonalities among families in their orientation toward the time squeeze (Morgan 2005; Duffy 2005).

So which of these predictions is the more accurate one? Have increasing class inequalities among individuals been attenuated or accentuated by gendered and class shifts in the family? Overall, income inequality among families

has in fact increased as a result of increasing inequality among individuals, especially husbands. The good news, however, is that this growth was attenuated by the equalizing effect of wives' increasing contribution to family income. Women in the top two-fifths of families log more hours of work per year (roughly 1,450) than women in the bottom two-fifths (between 800 and 1,200), but these disparities have been decreasing over time. Unquestionably, wives' earnings have contributed to absolute increases in real family income, countering declines in the earnings of husbands at the bottom and in the middle (Mishel, Bernstein, and Boushey 2003, 107, 110–111; Cancian, Danziger, and Gottschalk 1993).

Yet there are countervailing trends. A relative increase in single motherhood among low-income groups, an increase in assortative mating, and a relative increase in the rates of employment of wives with high-earning husbands can each spur further growth in inequality among families. All of these have occurred. First, single parenthood has increased most for women with low education and low income, due in part to the falling economic position of low-education men and thus their declining attractiveness as marriage partners (Ellwood and Jencks 2004). Second, there has been an increase in the correlation of both earnings and educational attainment among spouses over time.[2]

Finally, and perhaps most important, despite a net equalizing effect thus far of increasing employment among wives, the rate of increase

2 Preliminary work by Schwartz and Mare (2005) suggests that overall educational homogamy seems to have stabilized in the

1990s. This appears to be true as well for marital homogamy by income (McCall 2007).

in employment since the 1960s has been the greatest for wives with high-income husbands. This reverses the historical pattern in which the wives of low-income husbands were the most likely to work and the wives of high-income husbands were the least likely, a clear indication that when choices were limited married women worked out of necessity rather than choice.[3]

Although it is hard to predict, the labor force attachment of the high-skilled wives of high-income husbands is not likely to decline, except among the highest income families that can get by just fine without two earners (Goldin 2006). As we saw in the previous section, women with college and advanced degrees are more likely to work and to work longer hours than those with less education because their investment in education and earnings power is so high. Moreover, managerial and professional jobs are more rewarding and also demand more hours of work per week than most other jobs, setting in motion a time divide between overworked high-status workers and underworked low-status workers that results in an even greater income divide (Jacobs and Gerson 2004). The heroic increase in work by married mothers appears to be approaching a plateau in which these hours disparities may become locked in. For all income groups, the rate of growth in wives' hours declined in the 1990s, relative to the 1980s, by at least one-third. Overall, then, women's work behavior has tended to mitigate the class gap among families so far, but it may not do so in the future.

||| EXPLANATIONS

In this section, I explore some of the reasons for recent changes in the contemporary class and gender structure of U.S. society. As shown in table 2, I present only two categories of explanations: gender-specific explanations that have been developed to explain gender inequality and class-specific explanations that have been developed to explain rising class inequality. Some factors have had cross-over effects into the other domain. Although both are important and their effects are difficult to empirically measure, I argue that gender-specific factors have been more important in advancing women's absolute progress at the top, whereas class-specific factors have been more important in advancing women's relative progress in the middle and at the bottom. Put another way, absolute progress has been greater than relative progress for women at the top, but the converse has been true for women at the bottom and in the middle. This suggests that, in the future, relative progress will be a more important goal for women at the top and absolute progress will be a more important goal for women in the middle and at the bottom.

At the top, absolute improvements dominate relative ones. Women with high education and earnings potential entered the labor force at a faster rate than other women despite the fact that the men they tended to marry had the highest earnings growth, especially over the 1970s and 1980s. Moreover, because of a greater

---

3 Cancian, Danziger, and Gottschalk (1993) show that these shifts are for whites only. The employment rate for wives of husbands in the 10th, 50th, and 90th percentiles of income were roughly 32, 30, and 15 percent in 1959, respectively; 43, 41, and 25 percent in 1969; and 58, 68, and 60 percent in 1989 (Juhn and Murphy 1997, 85).

TABLE 2 **EXPLANATIONS OF IMPROVEMENTS IN ABSOLUTE AND RELATIVE GENDER EQUALITY**

Explanations	Improvements in women's economic status	
	Absolute progress	Relative progress
Gender-specific (e.g., anti-discrimination law and affirmative action)	Declining discrimination in managerial and professional schools and occupations leads to occupational gender integration and earnings growth for women at the top.	Globalization, deunionization, and postindustrial employment shifts disadvantage men and favor women in the middle.
Class-specific (e.g., shifts in wage structure and wage-setting institutions)	Rising returns to and demand for high skills draws high-skill women into the paid labor force.	Minimum wage benefits women more than men at the bottom and tight labor markets benefit both men and women in the middle and bottom.

increase in supply, such women ought to have had lower earnings growth than other women, but they did not, suggesting a strong demand for high-skilled women. These women also delayed childbearing more than women with middle and lower levels of education, an indication that the relative payoffs to pursuing work versus family shifted in favor of the former more for women at the top than for others.

It is therefore likely that eroding discriminatory barriers in education and employment worked in tandem with expanding managerial and professional opportunities—including increasing returns to working in these occupations as a result of rising inequality—to spur greater labor force preparation and attachment among women who were best able to take advantage of this new environment (Black and Juhn 2000). Other evidence supports this conclusion as well, such as a greater decline in

occupational segregation in middle-class occupations than in the working-class occupations that grew less rapidly (Cotter, Hermsen, and Vanneman 2004; Charles and Grusky 2005). Relative inequality persists, however, and by some accounts never declined, in part because men at the top have been advancing at a fast pace as well and because of persistent practices of exclusion in high-powered positions that demand extremely long hours of work.

In contrast, at the bottom and in the middle of the distribution, relative improvements dominate absolute ones, with gender-specific factors appearing to be less important than they are in explaining women's progress at the top. The most significant absolute increases in earnings for women in the middle (at the median) and at the bottom (at the 10th percentile) came during the tight labor markets of the late 1990s. For women at the bottom, increases in the minimum wage in the 1970s also meant absolute increases as well as reduced inequality with men at the bottom and with women at the median. Declines in the gender pay gap were also helped by declining real wages among men in the entire bottom half of the distribution in the 1980s. These declines were the result of industrial shifts, an increase in globalization, and a decline in unionization that all disproportionately hurt men relative to women in the lower half (Blau and Kahn 1997, 2004; Black and Brainerd 2004). The only period in which absolute improvements were greater than relative ones was in the late 1990s, when both women's and men's earnings improved at the bottom. The dynamic that characterizes the top throughout the entire period, in which women are swimming upstream to catch up to high-achieving men, becomes a possibility for women in the bottom half only in the late 1990s.

Thus, women's absolute progress in the bottom half occurred in fits and starts, but was modest compared to that of women at the top. Despite the early intent of antidiscrimination advocates to open up male-dominated blue-collar jobs to women, neither the absolute nor relative long-term progress of women in the bottom half appears to be linked in any strong way to an opening up of job opportunities because of a decline in gender discrimination. New job opportunities for working-class women were concentrated in sectors that were either already female-dominated, such as clerical and office work, or were becoming less remunerative as they became less male-dominated (Reskin and Roos 1991). For women outside the top rung, both absolute and relative progress is strongly affected by federal policies

that are non-gender-specific and structural economic factors that are either detrimental to men or relatively constant, such as the declining earnings of low-income and minority men. Overall, then, a burning issue for women in the middle and at the bottom is absolute job quality, including, most significantly, absolute wage growth, concerns that they share with men in similar class positions.

★ ★ ★

‖ REFERENCES

Black, Sandra E. and Elizabeth Brainerd. 2004. "Importing Equality? The Impact of Globalization on Gender Discrimination." *Industrial and Labor Relations Review* 57(4):540–559.

Black, Sandra and Chinhui Juhn. 2000. "The Rise of Female Professionals: Are Women Responding to Skill Demand?" *American Economic Review* 90(2):450–455.

Blau, Francine D. and Lawrence Kahn. 1997. "Swimming Upstream: Trends in the Gender Wage Differential in the 1980s." *Journal of Labor Economics* 15(1):1–42.

Blau, Francine D. and Lawrence Kahn. 2004. "The US Gender Pay Gap in the 1990s: Slowing Convergence." Working Paper 10853. Cambridge, MA: National Bureau of Economic Research.

Cancian, Maria, Sheldon Danziger, and Peter Gottschalk. 1993. "Working Wives and Family Income Inequality Among Married Couples." Pp. 195–222 in S. Danziger and P. Gottschalk, eds., *Uneven Tides: Rising Inequality in America*. NY: Russell Sage Foundation.

Charles, Maria, and David Grusky. 2005. *Occupational Ghettos: The Worldwide Segregation of Women and Men.* Stanford University Press.

Cobble, Dorothy Sue. 2003. "Having the Double Day." *New Labor Forum* 12(3): 63–72.

Cotter, David A., Joan M. Hermsen, and Reeve Vanneman. 2004. *Gender Inequality at Work.* NY and Washington, DC: Russell Sage Foundation and Population Reference Bureau.

Dinardo, John, Nicole Fortin, and Thomas Lemieux. 2004. "Labor Market Institutions and the Distribution of Wages, 1973–1992: A Semiparameteric Approach." *Econometrica* 64(5): 1001–44.

Duffy, Mignon. 2005. "Reproducing Labor Inequalities: Challenges for Feminists Conceptualizing Care at the Intersections of Gender, Race, and Class." *Gender & Society* 19(1): 66–82.

Ellwood, David T. 2000. "Winners and Losers in America: Taking the Measure of the New Economic Realities." Pp. 1–41 in D. Ellwood, R. M. Blank, J. Blasi, D. Kruse, W. Niskanen, and K. Lynn-Dyson, *A Working Nation.* NY: Russell Sage Foundation.

Ellwood, David T. and Christopher Jencks. 2004. "The Uneven Spread of Single-Parent Families: What Do We Know? Where Do We Look for Answers?" Pp. 3–78 in K. M. Neckerman, ed., *Social Inequality.* NY: Russell Sage Foundation.

Fitzgerald, Joan. 2006. *Moving Up in the New Economy: Career Ladders for U.S. Workers.* Ithaca, NY: Cornell University Press.

Goldin, Claudia. 2006. "The Quiet Revolution that Transformed Women's Employment, Education, and Family." Working Paper 11953. Cambridge. MA: National Bureau of Economic Research.

Jacobs, Jerry and Kathleen Gerson. 2004. *The Time Divide.* Cambridge, MA: Harvard University Press.

Jacoby, Sanford. 2005. "Corporate Governance and Society." *Challenge* 48(4): 69–87.

Juhn, Chinhui and Kevin M. Murphy. 1997. "Wage Inequality and Family Labor Supply." *Journal of Labor Economics* 15(1):72–97.

Lareau, Annette. 2003. *Unequal Childhoods.* Berkeley, CA: University of California Press.

MacLean, Nancy. 2006. *Freedom Is Not Enough: The Opening of the American Workplace.* Cambridge, MA and New York: Harvard University Press and Russell Sage Foundation.

McCall, Leslie. 2001. *Complex Inequality: Gender, Class, and Race in the New Economy.* NY: Routledge.

McCall, Leslie. 2004. *The Inequality Economy: How New Corporate Practices Redistribute Income to the Top.* Working Paper, Demos: A Network for Ideas and Action.

McCall, Leslie. 2007. "What Does Class Inequality Among Women Look Like? A Comparison with Men and Families, 1970–2000." In D. Conley and A. Lareau, eds., *Social Class: How Does it Work?.* NY: Russell Sage Foundation.

Mishel, Lawrence, Jared Bernstein, and Sylvia Allegretto. 2005. *The State of Working America, 2004/2005.* Ithaca, NY: ILR Press.

Mishel, Lawrence, Jared Bernstein, and Heather Boushey. 2003, *The State of Working America, 2002/2003*. Ithaca, NY: ILR Press.

Morgan, Kimberly. 2005. "The 'Production' of Child Care: How Labor Markets Shape Social Policy, and Vice Versa." *Social Politics* 12(2): 243–263.

Mulligan, Casey and Yona Rubenstein. 2004. "The Closing of the Gender Gap as a Roy Model Illusion." National Bureau of Economic Research Working Paper #10892.

Reskin, Barbara, and Patricia Roos. 1991. *Job Queues, Gender Queues: Explaining Women's Inroads into Male Occupations*. Philadelphia, PA: Temple University Press.

Schwartz, Christine R. and Robert D. Mare. 2005. "Trends in Educational Assortative Marriage from 1940 to 2003." *Demography* 42(4):621–646.

Sweeney, Megan M. and Maria Cancian. 2004. "The Changing Importance of White Women's Economic Prospects for Assortative Mating." *Journal of Marriage and the Family* 66:1015028.

Waldfogel, Jane. 1997. "The Effect of Children on Women's Wages." *American Sociological Review* 62: 209–217.

Williams, Joan. 2000. *Unbending Gender.* New York: Oxford University Press.

46

Gender and Race Discrimination in Retail Car Negotiations*

IAN AYRES AND PETER SIEGELMAN

Of the "untitled" retail markets, the new car market is particularly ripe for civil rights scrutiny for three reasons, First, it is an important market. The acquisition of a new car is a substantial purchase: apart from buying a home, new car purchases represent for most Americans their largest consumer investment.[1] Moreover, the transportation that automobiles provide is often necessary for a number of other major life activities (such as driving to work). Second, competition among sellers and purposive sorting by buyers may not be effective in driving out discrimination. ★ ★ ★ The private results of individualized negotiations might prevent consumers from discovering whether dealers discriminate, thus giving dealers the discretion to do so. Third, controlled audit testing is relatively straightforward. The fact that new

---

* First published in 2001; from *Pervasive Prejudice? Unconventional Evidence of Race and Gender Discrimination*.

1 See Bureau of Economic Analysis, U.S. Dep't of Commerce, *The National Income and Product Accounts of the United States,* 1929–82, at 105 (1986) (table 2.3) (showing annual personal expenditures on cars consistently to be one of the largest categories of expenditures): see also Bureau of the Census, U.S. Dep't of Commerce. *Statistical Abstract of the United States* 465 (119th ed. 1999) (same, with respect to 1990–97). In 1997, for example, American consumers spent $86.2 billion on new cars. See id.

cars (in contrast to, say, Persian rugs) are relatively standardized and homogenous products facilitates interretailer comparison.

This chapter reports the results of using audit testing[2] to examine whether new car dealerships in the Chicago area discriminated in negotiating against women and minorities. More than four hundred independent negotiations at more than two hundred dealerships were conducted in 1990 to examine how dealerships bargain. Testers of different races and genders entered new car dealerships separately and bargained to buy similar new cars, using a uniform negotiation strategy. The focus of the study was whether automobile retailers would react differently to this uniform strategy when potential buyers differed only by gender or race.

The tests revealed systematic disparate treatment.[3] Dealerships offered white males significantly lower prices than blacks and women. As detailed below, the average prices offered white women were more than \$200 higher than the offers to white men, the offers to black women were more than \$400 higher than those to white men, and the offers to black men were more than \$900 higher.

A central purpose of the Civil Rights Act of 1866 was to guarantee that "a dollar in the hands of a Negro will purchase the same thing as a dollar in the hands of a white man."[4] ★ ★ ★ The standard argument against vigorous enforcement or extension of our civil rights laws to retail consumer markets has been grounded in the conviction that the impersonal forces of market competition will limit race and gender discrimination to the traditionally protected markets, in which there is significant interpersonal contact.[5] The results of this study, however, challenge such an unquestioning faith in competition: in stark contrast to congressional objectives, blacks and women simply could not buy the same car for the same

---

2 Since the Fair Housing Act of 1968 outlawed discrimination in the sale and rental of housing, numerous studies have tested whether minorities and whites are treated differently in the housing market. ★ ★ ★ The empirical analysis in this chapter broadly borrows the methodology of fair housing audit tests, in which a black tester and a white tester separately approach a real estate agent or seller and express an interest in the same housing. The test of discrimination is simply whether they are treated similarly: Are they shown the same houses, in the same neighborhoods, for the same prices?

3 We use "discrimination" or "disparate treatment" interchangeably to refer to the evidence that black and female testers were treated differently from white male testers. The term *discrimination*, although surely a literal characterization, unfortunately connotes to many the notion of animus (even though in antitrust, for example, "price discrimination" is not taken to imply any hatred by sellers). "Disparate treatment," in contrast, connotes to some a strictly technical legal meaning developed in civil rights case law. For our purposes, the terms *discrimination* and *disparate treatment* are both used to refer to the result that sellers' conduct was raw- and gender-dependent; in other words, sellers took race and gender into account and

treated differently testers who were otherwise similarly situated. Paul Brest has similarly defined race discrimination in terms of "race-dependent decisions and conduct." Paul Brest, The Supreme Court, 1975 Term—Foreword: In Defense of the Antidiscrimination Principle, 90 Harv. L. Rev. 1, 6 (1976). These terms are not meant to imply that salespeople harbored any animus based on race or gender.

4 Jones v. Alfred H. Mayer Co., 392 U.S. 409, 443 (1968).

5 The increasingly accepted conception of "relational contract," Ian Macneil, The New Social Contract 10 (1980), runs counter to the notion that all unprotected markets are discrete exchanges and therefore immune to animus-based discrimination. Indeed, it is difficult at a theoretical level to see why retail purchases of personal property involve less personal contact than many public accommodations. Although the uniform pricing of many consumer goods eliminates the possibility of price discrimination, the ongoing relational nature of exchange may allow gender-based or racial animus to be reflected along other dimensions of product or service quality. And even in markets with more discrete exchanges, women and minorities can be disadvantaged when there is gender- or race-based product differentiation.

price as could white men using identical bargaining strategies. The fact that different prices were quoted by the car dealers to consumers following identical scripts implicates basic notions of equity and indicates that the scope of the civil rights laws has been underinclusive. The process of bargaining, already inefficient in many ways, becomes all the more problematic when it works to the detriment of traditionally disadvantaged members of our society.

★ ★ ★

‖ I. METHODOLOGY OF THE TEST

This study used an audit technique in which pairs of testers (one of whom was always a white male) were trained to bargain uniformly and then were sent to negotiate for the purchase of a new automobile at randomly selected Chicago-area dealerships.[6] The goal was to have the testers differ only by race and/or gender (that is, present an otherwise uniform appearance and uniform behavior) so that any systematic differences in treatment could be attributed to the dealers' race- and/or gender-dependent decisionmaking.[7] The white male results provide a benchmark against which we measure the disparate treatment of the other (nonwhite, nonmale) testers. Thirty-eight testers (eighteen white males, seven white females, eight black females, and five black males) bargained for approximately four hundred cars comprising nine car models[8] at 242 dealerships.[9] Dealerships were selected randomly, testers were assigned to dealerships randomly, and the choice of which

---

6 The testers did not inform the salespeople that they were participating in a test. This lack of disclosure raises significant ethical concerns, as the salesperson's time is spent without chance of a sale. The study has several features designed to mitigate the problem of wasting the salespersons' time during the negotiation process. Most important, the testers visited the dealerships during the least busy times of the week (from the hours of 9:00–12:00 and 1:00–5:00 Monday through Friday). During these times few people shop for cars, and there are often several salespeople without customers to serve. In addition, testers were instructed that if all the salespeople of a dealership were busy, they should return to the dealership at another time. In only 1 of more than 180 visits did the testers have to discontinue the test because of crowding. Steps were also taken to minimize the time that the testers spent with the salespeople. The test itself was designed to be completed in ten to fifteen minutes and the testers were instructed to spend no more than an hour at a dealership.

   The Federal Judicial Center Advisory Committee on Experimentation in the Law has proposed guidelines for limiting the use of deception in legal experimentation. The committee concluded that "[d]eception requires (1) that the concealment itself be indispensable to the validity of experimental results, and (2) that the burden of justification for the practice concealed not merely be met, but met by a clear and convincing margin." Advisory Comm. on Experimentation

in the Law, Fed. Judicial Center, *Experimentation in the Law* 46 (1981). The first requirement is easily met: asking salespeople if they could be tested for race and gender discrimination would certainly change their behavior. Whether the study meets the secondary burden of justification is a closer question. As reported below, blacks in this study were often forced to pay two to three times the markup of white males. If similar measurements of discrimination hold for all sales in the United States, blacks annually would pay $150 million more for new cars than do white males. The benefits from documenting such potentially significant discrimination seem to meet the burden of justification. The tests have been given approval by the Human Subject Research Committees of both the American Bar Foundation and Northwestern University. See Letter from Northwestern University Institutional Review Board (June 12, 1989); oral approval from American Bar Foundation (May 1988).

   Deceptive tests of new car sales have been conducted by other researchers. ★ ★ ★ In other fields, social scientists have feigned to be, among other things, cancer patients in hospitals and potential buyers in shoe stores. See, e.g., Eric Schaps, Cost, Dependency, and Helping, 21 J. Personality & Soc. Psychol. 74 (1972) (involving accomplices posing as shoe store customers). The Supreme Court itself has condoned similar deception by giving fair housing testers standing. See, e.g., Havens Realty Corp. v. Coleman, 455 U.S. 363 (1982).

tester in the pair would first enter the dealership was made randomly.[10]

Each tester followed a bargaining script designed to frame the bargaining in purely distributional terms: the only issue to be negotiated was the price.[11] The script instructed the tester to focus quickly on a particular car[12] and offer to provide his or her own financing.[13] After eliciting an initial price from the dealer,[14] the tester waited five minutes before respond-

ing with an initial counteroffer that equaled an estimate of the dealer's marginal cost.[15] As discussed later, making an initial offer at the dealer's cost reveals to the dealer that the tester is a fairly sophisticated buyer.

After the tester's initial counteroffer,[16] the salesperson could do one of three things: (1) accept the tester's offer, (2) refuse to bargain further, or (3) make a lower offer. If the salesperson attempted to accept the tester's offer or

---

7 Some commentators have had difficulty accepting that testers could be controlled. For example, see the discussion in chapter 5 of Mike Royko's criticism of the pilot study.

8 The nine models ranged from compacts to standard cars, and included both imports and domestic makes. Human-subject review committees—seeking to protect the privacy of the dealers as human subjects in these tests—prevented us from disclosing the car models.

9 Because of discarded tests and scheduling difficulties, 98 of the 404 observations are unpaired negotiations in which only one tester visited a particular dealership. Sample selection problems are always a concern in such situations. Chow tests on the two regression equations reported in table 1 cannot reject pooling the paired and unpaired observations, however, so there is little reason to believe that the unpaired audits are systematically different from the paired audits. See Ian Ayres & Peter Siegelman, Race and Gender Discrimination in Bargaining for a New Car, 85 Am. Econ. Rev. 304 (1995) (finding similar results from analysis of paired data alone).

10 That is, the white male tester was at times the first tester and at times the second tester to bargain at a dealership. The paired testers usually visited the dealership on the same day (and within at most four days of each other).

11 This distributional context removes collaboration and problem solving as measures of effective bargaining. See Roger Fisher & William Ury, *Getting to Yes* 73–79 (1981). For example, the bargaining was structured so that the players (the testers and salespeople) could not collaboratively bargain over financing to enhance the gains from trade. In many real-world bargaining contexts, collaborative or "win-win" solutions do not exist. See James White, The Pros and Cons of "Getting to Yes" (Book Review), 34 J. Legal Educ. 115, 116 (1954). The bargaining instead resembles the classic "split-the-dollar" game in which two contestants can share a dollar if they can agree on how to divide it between them. See Eric Rasmusen, *Games and Information* 227–29 (1989).

12 If the salesperson showed the tester more than one car, the script instructed the tester: "[W]ithin two or three minutes

focus your attention on the car with the lowest sticker price. This will be the car that you will then bargain over. You should indicate this by saying: "I'm interested in buying this car." Tester Script 4 (Nov. 8, 1990).

13 Testers were instructed to respond to questions such as "Will you need help with a loan?" by saying, "No, I can provide my own financing." Id. at 11.

Initially, some testers were instructed to volunteer that they would be moving to California in the coming month. This representation, suggested by Mitch Polinsky, sought to reduce dealers' inferences about repeat sales, referral sales, or repair service. However, dealers encountering two customers moving to California looking for the same car on the same day were more likely to suspect that the two consumers were shopping in tandem. Because of the dealer expressions of suspicion, the California representation was quickly abandoned and the tests in which the representation was made were discarded. This example illustrates a general tension between increased controls and maintaining verisimilitude so as not to alert dealers that they were being tested.

14 If the salesperson failed to quote an initial price, testers would ask, "How much would the car cost me to buy it [sic] today, including taxes and other fees" Id. at 5.

15 Because sellers will seldom sell below their marginal cost, the marginal cost counteroffer established an initial position that approximated the seller's reservation price (the minimum amount for which a seller could sell to make any profit). Estimates of dealer cost were obtained from *Consumer Reports Auto Price Service* (Mar. 2, 1990) (computer printout) and *Edmund's 1990 New Car Prices* (Nov. 1990).

16 It should be noted that the testers did not make legally binding counteroffers. The testers were carefully trained not to sign anything so that they would be protected by the statute of frauds. See U.C.C. § 2-201 1987) (invalidating oral contracts for more than $500). Moreover, the testers did not make actual counteroffers but merely invited additional offers by saying: "would you sell me this car today for $ . . . ?"

refused to bargain further, the test was over (and the tester left the dealership). If the salesperson responded by making a lower offer, the test continued, with the tester's next counteroffer scripted in one of two ways. At some dealerships, the pairs of testers used a "split-the-difference" strategy in which the tester's counteroffer was raised so as to halve the difference between the dealer's offer and the tester's last offer.[17] At other dealerships, the testers used a "fixed-concession" strategy in which the testers' counteroffers were independent of the sellers' behavior. Testers began, as before, by making their first counteroffer at marginal cost. Regardless of how much the seller conceded, each of the tester's subsequent counteroffers increased his or her previous offer by 20 percent of the gross markup.[18]

Under either bargaining strategy, each tester continued to alternate offers with the dealer until the dealer either (1) attempted to accept the tester's offer, or (2) refused to bargain further. Testers jotted down each offer and counteroffer, as well as options on the car and the sticker price. Upon leaving the dealership, the testers completed a survey recording information about the test.[19]

This design produced results that permit two tests for discrimination. The first, "short test" of discrimination simply compares the dealer's response to the testers' initial question, "How much would I have to pay to buy this car?" The "long test" of discrimination, on the other hand, compares instead the final offers given to testers after the multiple rounds of concessionary bargaining. By focusing on the initial offer, the short test is well controlled because salespeople had little information about the prospective buyers from which to draw inferences. By focusing on the final offer, the long test isolates more accurately the price a real consumer would pay, but it increases the risk that individual differences among the testers influenced the results.

In order to minimize the possibility of nonuniform bargaining, particular attention was

---

17 Consider, for example, a seller who initially offers to sell a car for $13,000. The tester counters at $10,000 (an estimate of the car's marginal cost). If the salesperson lowered the initial offer to $12,000, the tester would wait five minutes and split the difference by offering $11,000 (12,000 + 10,000) / 2). The split-the-difference strategy was identical to the script used in the pilot study. See Ian Ayres, Fair Driving: Gender and Race Discrimination in Retail Car Negotiations, 104 Harv. L. Rev. 817 (1991).

18 That is, if the car had a sticker price of SP and the tester's last offer was LO, then the tester's next offer would be LO + 0.2 × (SP − LO). Because the gross margin (SP − LO) decreases as the bargaining continues, the fixed-concession strategy produced smaller concessions in each subsequent round. The testers did not have to calculate the fixed-concession offers. The appropriate sequence was supplied to them in advance.

19 In addition to the types of factors described above, the script also controlled ancillary aspects of the bargaining. For example, testers waited in the center of the showroom to be approached by a salesperson. Significantly, the script allowed the testers to be steered to different cars and different salespeople. Forcing the second tester to seek out the same car or the same salesperson as the first tester would have introduced nonuniformity in the testers' bargaining strategies. Moreover, the study was designed to test for disparate treatment using the car dealership as the unit of analysis. Allowing testers to bargain with different salespeople afforded a test of whether dealerships engage in more sophisticated forms of discrimination by steering classes of testers to particular kinds of cars or particular kinds of salespeople. ★ ★ ★

For ethical reasons, the testers did not tape the bargaining sessions. Because the individual testers were the only observers of the field bargaining sessions, there are two potential types of experimental error in the results. First, the testers may have failed accurately to observe and describe their own behavior; second, the testers may have failed accurately to observe and describe the behavior of the salesperson. The training and initial tester observation were used to minimize both types of errors.

paid to issues of experimental control. A major part of the study was choosing uniform testers and training them to behave in a standardized manner. Testers were chosen to satisfy the following criteria for uniformity:

1. Age: All testers were twenty-four to twenty-eight years old.
2. Education: All testers had three or four years of college education.
3. Dress: All testers were dressed similarly during the negotiations. Testers wore casual sportswear: the men wore polo or button-down shirts, slacks, and loafers; the women wore straight skirts, blouses, minimal makeup, and flats.
4. Transportation: All testers drove to the dealerships in similar used rental cars of the same model and year. Using similar modes of transportation prevented the dealers from making inferences based on the kind of car the tester drove or the way the tester reached the dealership.
5. Economic Class: Testers volunteered that they could finance the car themselves.
6. Occupation: If asked by a salesperson, each tester said that he or she was a young urban professional (for example, a systems analyst for First Chicago Bank).
7. Address: If asked by the salesperson, each tester gave a fake name and an address in an upper-class, Chicago neighborhood (Streeterville).

8. Attractiveness: Applicants were subjectively ranked for average attractiveness.

The testers were trained for two days before visiting the dealerships. They were not told that the research was intended to test for race and gender discrimination.[20] Nor did they know that another tester would be negotiating at each of the dealerships. The testers were told only that the research was investigating how dealers negotiate. The training included not only memorizing the tester script but also participating in mock negotiations designed to help testers gain confidence and learn how to negotiate and answer questions uniformly. The training emphasized uniformity in cadence and inflection of tester response. In addition to spoken uniformity, the study sought to achieve tester uniformity in nonverbal behavior.[21]

The script was also designed to promote tester uniformity through silence. The testers volunteered very little information and were trained to feel comfortable with periods of silence. The script anticipated that the salespeople would ask questions and gave the testers a long list of contingent responses to questions that might be asked.[22] The study sought to let the salespeople completely control the bargaining process without letting them know they had such control.[23] At the beginning and end of the

20 In the pilot study the testers knew the study's purpose, and it is possible that this knowledge affected their expectations or behavior. Both studies, however, yielded similar results.

21 Testers were sensitized to issues of body language and nonverbal cues. For example, they were told to avoid eye contact and not to cross their arms.

22 The script provided an all-purpose default or residual response for questions not otherwise anticipated. For example, if the salesperson asked the tester a detailed question about the tester's career or personal background, the tester was instructed to respond: "I don't mean to be rude, but I'm kind of pressed for time, and would rather just talk [about] buying a car."

23 This aspect of the script can be analogized to the party game in which one person is told to leave the room so that the group can make up a story about him or her. When the person returns to the room, he or she asks yes or no questions in order to construct the story. The trick to the game is that the group never constructs a story, but simply decides to answer "yes" to any question ending in a vowel (and "no" to any question ending in a consonant). The questioner in the game thus effectively constructs a story revealing what's on his or her own mind.

testing process, project coordinators accompanied the testers to dealerships and observed how the testers bargained to determine whether they were following the script and accurately reporting the bargaining process.

Despite these attempts to control for uniform tester behavior, some differences between testers undoubtedly remained. Salespeople may have, for example, offered certain testers a higher price not because of their race or gender, but because they blinked more often or opened the car door more quickly. Two important questions about such residual differences must then be asked. First, are they likely to be correlated with race or gender? If not, the remaining nonuniformity should not influence our conclusion that it is race and gender that generate different outcomes for the testers. Second, are the residual differences large enough to explain the *amount* of discrimination that is reported below? Readers should focus, therefore, not merely on

statistical significance but also on the amount of the reported discrimination.[24] Although perfect control of such complex bargaining is impossible, the amounts of discrimination reported in the next section of this chapter cannot be plausibly explained by race- or gender-correlated divergences from the uniform bargaining behavior called for in our script.

III II: RESULTS OF THE TEST

A. Price Discrimination

Table 1 reports regressions testing whether dealers treated testers differently. Because the testers were trained to follow an identical bargaining script, any statistically significant difference in the offers made to distinct race–gender types can be ascribed to disparate treatment by the dealers. In particular, the regressions—after controlling for the effects of several variables that varied across the audits[25]—test whether the

---

24 Statistical significance measures how probable it is that the observed result occurred purely by random chance. To say, for example, that the average final offers sellers made to black and white testers are statistically different at a 5 percent significance level means that the differences would only be produced randomly 5 percent of the time (one out of twenty times). If a sample size is large enough, even small absolute differences in price (of, say, $5) will be statistically significant. Cf. 29 C.F.R. § 1607.4(D) (1990) (generally defining adverse impact for purposes of an Equal Employment Opportunity Commission (EEOC) finding of employment discrimination as existing only when disparities are both statistically significant and proportionally large).

25 Beside the three tester race and gender dummy variables—WHITE FEMALE, BLACK MALE, and BLACK FEMALE—the regression attempted to discover what aspects of the bargaining caused dealers to demand a particular level of profit in their initial and final offers. In particular, the regression focused on the relationship between the profits the dealers would have made on their offers and the following variables:

SPLIT   = 1, if tester used split-the-difference negotiating strategy, or 0, if fixed-concession strategy

MODEL$_j$ = dummy variables for each different model type

DAY_k = dummy variables for each day of the week
$WEEK_l$ = dummy variables for each week of the month
TIME   = number of days since start of testing
EXPERIENCE   = number of prior tests by this tester
FIRST   = 1, if tester was the first in the pair to visit dealership, or 0, otherwise
unpaired   = 1, if test was an unpaired observation, or 0, if test was part of a paired audit

The regression equation took the following form:

$$PROFIT = CONSTANT + \Sigma_i \beta_i (TESTER\ RACE/GENDER\ TYPE_i)$$
$$+ \Sigma_j \gamma_j MODEL_j + \Sigma_K \delta_K DAY_K + \Sigma_L \eta_L WEEK_L$$
$$+ \theta TIME + \nu SPLIT + \lambda EXPERIENCE + \mu FIRST$$
$$+ \nu UNPAIRED + \epsilon$$

where epsilon is an error term that is assumed to be independent and identically distributed.

Although a thorough review of econometric theory is beyond the scope of this chapter, a few concepts may be of use to the reader. The ordinary least square (OLS) regression technique produces estimates for the constant and the greek-letter coefficients, β, γ, and so on in the regression equation, except for the error term. A "dummy variable" resembles an on-off switch, assuming values of 0 or 1. By

TABLE 1 **REGRESSIONS EVALUATING EFFECTS OF TESTERS' RACE/GENDER TYPE AND CONTROL VARIABLES ON DEALERS' INITIAL AND FINAL PROFITS[a] (N = 404; T-STATISTICS IN PARENTHESES)[b]**

	Initial Profit ($)	Final Profit ($)
Constant	724.61*	417.52*
	(7.23)	(6.62)
TESTER RACE–GENDER		
White female	209.62	215.69
	(1.54)	(1.85)
Black male	962.32*	1,132.59*
	(6.75)	(9.28)
Black female	470.05*	446.30*
	(3.90)	(4.32)
CONTROL VARIABLES		
Split	−240.19	−262.59
	(−1.55)	(−1.97)
Tester experience	4.76	3.41
	(0.66)	(0.55)
First	88.23	138.48
	(0.91)	(1.67)
Unpaired	−100.62	−161.02
	(−1.00)	(1.87)
SUMMARY STATISTICS		
Adjusted R^2	0.27	0.33
SSR × 10^{-3}	263,758	193,706

★Significantly different from zero at the 5 percent level.

[a]None of the coefficients of the MODEL, DAY, WEEK, and TIME variables were statistically significant. These variables were omitted from table 1 to save space.

[b]The ratio of the coefficient to the standard error of the estimate is called the t-statistics. As a rule of thumb, a t-statistic greater than two suggests there is less than a 5 percent chance that the observed effect occurred purely by chance.

assigning dummy variables to all but one category, we can compare differences between any two categories. Thus, for the group of four mutually exclusive and exhaustive tester race–gender types, we assign a dummy variable to three of these four categories, and the regression provides us with the estimated coefficients for each variable; white men form the benchmark omitted category. The estimated dummy coefficients represent the amount by which membership in the associated category increases or decreases the dependent variable as compared to the benchmark category. See Ian Ayres & Joel Waldfogel, A Market Test for Race Discrimination in Bail Setting, 46 Stan. L. Rev. 987, 1009 n.84 (1994). For example, the $962 coefficient in table 1 associated with the black male dummy variable suggests that the dealer profit on initial offers made to BLACK MALE testers was $962 higher than the profit on initial offers made to white male testers, the omitted benchmark category.

dealers' initial and final offers to black and/or female testers were higher than offers to white male testers.

The final offer of each test was the lowest price offered by a dealer after the multiple rounds of bargaining.[26] By comparing these initial and final offers with independent estimates of dealer cost,[27] it was possible to calculate the dealer profit associated with each type of offer (for example, initial profit equals initial offer minus dealer cost).

The regressions reported in table 1 show that dealer profits for both initial and final offers were substantially lower for white male testers than for other race–gender groups.[28] While the estimates from these two regressions (reported in the two right-hand columns of table 1) may look forbidding, they are easily explained. The estimates for the CONSTANT represent the amounts of profit that white male testers were asked on average to pay: $725 and $418 on initial and final profits, respectively. Dealerships asked black males, however, to pay much more than white males: an extra $962 on initial offers and a whopping additional $1,133 on final offers, after controlling for other variables.

---

26 The lowest price offered by a dealer could come either when the dealer attempted to accept a tester's final offer or when a dealer refused to lower his last offer.

27 The cost estimate, obtained from *Consumer Reports* and *Edmund's*, is one of marginal cost, in that the dealer's fixed and overhead costs are not included. These cost estimates ignore "hold backs," "incentives," and other types of manufacturer refunds that reduce the dealer's net marginal cost. Domestic car manufacturers traditionally (and foreign car manufacturers recently) have periodically refunded approximately 3 percent of the dealer's original cost as a so-called holdback. See Remar Sutton, *Don't Get Taken Every Time* 23 (1986). In addition, manufacturers at times will institute "dealer incentives"—additional refunds to dealers for sales. See, e.g., Weekly Incentive Survey, *Automotive News*, Mar. 5, 1990, at 38. Because the exact size of these hold backs and incentives is not public knowledge, the cost estimates were not discounted to reflect these amounts.

28 Ancillary tests of discrimination also buttress the results reported in this chapter. Three research assistants joined the [first] author of this [chapter] in a "beat the boss contest" in the actual purchase of an automobile. The research group consisted of one white male (the author), one black male, one white female, and one black female. Members of the group individually bargained for a specific car model at Chicago dealerships. I offered my research assistants a prize of $50 or half the amount by which they could undercut my best offer, whichever was greater. The contest lacked the controls of this chapter's study but had other advantages: the testers were bargaining for an actual sale and thus had real financial incentives to get the best deal.

The results of the contest are largely consistent with the results of the larger study:

Results of Research Group Contest

Dealership Profits

Tester Type	Best Offer ($)	Average Offer ($)
White male	139	548
White female	439	806
Black male	879	1,051
Black female	878	1,185

The contest produced the same ordinal ranking of discrimination, but there seem to be returns to the greater sophistication of the bargainers who were not constrained to follow a script.

A controlled phone survey of dealerships was also conducted. A white male tester and a black female tester each called more than one hundred dealerships and, following a uniform script, bargained for cars over the phone. The results of the phone survey disclose a different form of disparate treatment. The black female tester had greater success in eliciting initial offers (95 percent versus 79 percent) and on average received lower final offers. These results, however, may have been caused by the dealers' greater willingness to quote "low-ball" prices to the female tester over the phone. Dealers make low-ball or below-cost prices to induce potential customers into the car lot, where it may then be possible to "bump" the price quoted over the phone. When dealers quoted prices below cost, they quoted lower prices to the female tester. When they quoted prices above cost, they quoted higher prices to the female tester:

Black males in essence were asked to pay more than double the markup of white males initially ($1,687 versus $725) and almost four times the markup offered to white males in the dealers' final offers ($1,550 versus $418).

The numbers reported in the parentheses underneath each of the coefficient estimates test whether the estimate is statistically different than zero. These "t-statistics" measure the number of standard deviations that the estimated coefficient is from zero. Estimates that are more than two standard deviations from zero (either > 2 or > -2) are generally considered to be statistically significant. These black male/white male differentials (represented by BLACK MALE coefficients) are thus highly statistically significant: six to nine times their standard errors.[29] This means that as a statistical matter, we can reject the hypothesis that the difference in prices offered was merely the by-product of the random variation of the sample.

Table 1 also shows that dealers' initial and final offers to black females were roughly $470 and $446 higher than comparable offers to white males. Black female testers were asked initially to pay a markup that was 65 percent higher than white males' initial markup, and finally asked to pay a markup that was more than twice the white male final markup ($864 versus $418). These coefficients are again highly significant in both regressions.

The disparate treatment of white females, in comparison, is less pronounced. Dealers' initial and final offers to white females were roughly $200 more than to white males. The dealers in effect asked white females to pay an initial markup almost 29 percent higher, and ultimately demanded a markup more than 50 percent higher ($633 versus $418). The initial profit differential, however, is not statistically significant and the final profit differential is only marginally significant ($p < 0.065$).[30]

The discrimination encountered by black female testers cannot be allocated to race or gender discrimination in a nonarbitrary way. It is impossible to say to what extent dealerships treated them differently because of their race or gender. Consequently, it is impossible to estimate a pure race or gender discrimination effect. Rather, consonant with modern scholarship,[31] it is more productive to think of black

Dealership Profits Based on Telephone Survey

Average Dealership Profits

Tester Type	Offers above Cost ($)	Offers below Cost ($)
Female tester	940	−732
Male tester	290	−383

Thus, it seems that dealers implement one of two strategies against female customers—either quoting them large markup prices or very low "low-ball" prices.

29 Recall that a ratio greater than two is considered statistically significant. See table 1, note b.

30 The WHITE FEMALE coefficient on the initial profit regression had a *p*-value equaling 0.124.

31 See, e.g., Tonya M. Evans, Comment, In the Title IX Race toward Gender Equity, the Black Female Athlete Is Left to Finish Last: The Lack of Access for the "Invisible Woman," 42 Howard L.J. 105, 1078 (1998); Kimberle Crenshaw, Mapping the Margins: Intersectionality, Identity Politics, and Violence against Women of Color, 43 Stan. L. Rev. 1241 (1991).

females as a separate group that is exposed to discriminatory treatment distinct from either white females or black males.

The statistically significant differences in the dealerships' initial offers provides particularly strong evidence of disparate treatment. Even if the final price offered is the more relevant measure of economic harm, the analysis of initial offers, as noted above, provides a "short test" of disparate treatment because the dealer's behavior is tested at the beginning of the negotiation—when there have been fewer opportunities for testers to deviate from the script.

The reliability of these results is buttressed by an analysis of the relative unimportance of individual tester effects. The average dealer profits on the nonwhite, nonmale testers were statistically different from the average profits on the white males at a 5 percent significance level. The average initial and final profits for the eighteen individual white males were, however, not significantly different from each other. This last result lends support to the proposition that the idiosyncratic characteristics of at least the white male testers did not affect the results.[32]

The regressions in table 1 also tested the success of several procedural controls. For example, we expected the coefficients on the EXPERIENCE, FIRST, and UNPAIRED variables not to be statistically different from zero.[33] The table shows that none of these coefficients was significant at the traditional 5 percent level and that additional tester experience added a trivial amount ($3.41) to dealers' final offers. But the size of the FIRST coefficient in the final profit regression is troubling even though not statistically significant: it suggests that a dealer's final offer to the first tester in a pair was $138 higher than to the second tester. This result might mean that some dealers realized a test was being conducted and artificially lowered the offer to the second testers.[34]

We also expected that the tester's use of a split-the-difference strategy or a fixed-concession strategy would not affect the dealer's initial offer, for the simple reason that the tester elicited the dealer's initial offer before the

---

32 See Ayres & Siegelman, *supra* n. 9, at 311. The training and selection of the testers were designed to eliminate as much intertester variation as possible. Thus, we would expect to find little or no evidence of individual-tester effects in our data. For reasons described above, however, we cannot test for the presence of individual-tester effects that are correlated with testers' race or gender. A fixed-effects specification with one dummy variable for each individual tester is equivalent to subtracting the tester-specific mean for each variable. This means that any variables that do not vary over time for each individual tester (including the tester race and gender dummies) are indistinguishable from the individual-tester fixed effect and cannot be used.

33 If testers faithfully followed the script, those who had previously completed more tests would not be treated differently. If the testers were successful at concealing the auditing, we would not expect the first tester to receive systematically different treatment than the second tester bargaining at the same

dealership. Finally, if the unpaired audits were representative of the larger sample, we would not expect systematically different results from these tests.

34 Manufacturers, rival dealers, and U.S. Census officials at times audit dealerships to determine the real cost of purchasing a new car. Telephone Interview with Margerie Yonsura, Wordsmith Relations (Sept. 1, 1992). Alternatively, the dealer may have lowered its offer after failing to sell to the initial tester.

We were also concerned that the dealers' final offers on the unpaired bargaining sessions were $161 lower than the final offers on bargaining sessions that were paired. This finding suggests that the dealership conditions that caused one of the tests to fail may have affected the results of the other, now unpaired, tester who was included in the regression sample. To control for this possible flaw, we reran the regression using only the paired data and found that the amount and significance of discrimination was not affected.

tester began implementing either one of these counteroffer strategies. The SPLIT coefficient was unexpectedly negative, indicating that dealers' initial offers to testers using the split-the-difference-strategy were $240 less than the initial offers to testers using a fixed-concession strategy, but again this difference was not statistically significant.

The data also confirmed that the finding of discrimination is not merely an artifact of the split-the-difference negotiation strategy. When testers' counteroffers split the difference, discrimination in early rounds may force dealers' final offers to be discriminatory as well. For example, if the dealer's second offer to a black male includes a $1,000 profit while the dealer's offer to a white male includes only a $400 profit, then any subsequent bargaining will reflect discrimination because under a split-the-difference strategy the black male tester will counter with a price based an a $500 profit that is higher than the dealer's earlier $400 profit offer to the white male.

We found, however, that dealers continued to discriminate even when the testers adopted a fixed concession strategy.[35] Table 1 in fact suggests that the split-the-difference approach might be the more effective of the two strategies because it led to dealer final offers that were $262 lower than the fixed-concession strategy,

even though this result was not quite statistically significant at the 5 percent level.[36]

We also investigated whether our findings of race and gender discrimination might be linked to the fact that the dealerships' final offers were sometimes refusals to bargain further and sometimes acceptances of tester offers.[37] By adding an ACCEPT dummy (= 1 if the seller attempted to accept a tester offer) to the regressions reported in table 1, we found that sessions ending in attempted acceptances had an approximately $400 lower final profit than those that ended in a refusal to bargain (and this result was statistically significant). The size of this acceptance effect, however, was the same for all testers; interacting the ACCEPT dummy with the tester type yielded small and insignificant coefficients.[38] The willingness of dealers to offer lower prices to white males was reflected in a greater willingness to continue bargaining until an acceptable tester offer was made. When the tester was a white male, 25.6 percent of the tests ended in an attempted seller acceptance; this figure was only 14.9 percent for the other tester types. The fact that sellers are more likely to accept offers from white males actually biases our estimates *against* finding discrimination, however, because acceptances only provide an upper bound for sellers' reservation prices. That is, in those cases where dealers attempted

---

35 Separate regressions found no difference in the amount of discrimination for the fixed-concession negotiations. See *supra* n. 9 (describing the fixed-concession strategy).

36 A 5 percent level of significance would require a t-statistic with an absolute value greater than 1.98. As shown in table l, the coefficient estimate for the SPLIT variable has a t-statistic of 1.97 and so is almost significant at the standard 5 percent level.

37 In a parallel effort, we examined whether our results were affected by the fact that sellers sometimes made unsolicited initial offers and sometimes needed to have offers elicited by

the testers. Logit regressions indicated that dealers were less likely to make an unsolicited initial offer to white males than to other tester types, but that this difference was not statistically significant. Solicited initial offers were significantly larger than unsolicited initial offers, but there was no statistical difference in final offers between tests that began with elicited initial offers and those that began with unsolicited offers by the seller.

38 The ACCEPT variable may not be exogenous in these regressions, because higher profitability may cause the dealer to accept a tester's offer.

TABLE 2 **PERCENTAGE OF TESTS IN WHICH WHITE MALES OBTAINED THE BETTER RESULT**

	Initial Profits	Final Profits
White males vs. all others (153 pairs)	68.0	66.7
White males vs. white females (53 pairs)	58.4	56.6
White males vs. black males (40 pairs)	87.5	85.0
White males vs. black females (60 pairs)	63.3	61.7

NOTE: All values are significantly different from 50 percent at the 1 percent level using a likelihood ratio test $\chi_{(1)}^2$.

to accept an offer from a white male tester, the dealers might have been willing to make an even lower offer, which would have increased our measure of discrimination. Overall, our findings of discrimination do not seem to be sensitive to the fact that most negotiations did not end in an attempted seller acceptance.[39]

In addition to the linear regressions in table 1, nonparametric tests also strongly support the finding of disparate treatment. If race or gender were unrelated to the prices quoted to testers, we would expect that the benchmark white male testers would get lower offers than their audit partners half the time, while faring worse than their counterparts in the remaining half of the tests. As table 2 indicates, however, this was not the case. Overall, white males did better than others in roughly two-thirds of the paired tests (for both initial and final offers). A

likelihood-ratio test reveals that the differences from 50 percent were all statistically significant at the 5 percent level.

The disparities are even larger in dollar terms. In paired tests in which white male testers received the lower final offer, on average they did $897 better than their counterparts. Where the nonwhite males did better, they beat white males by only $167.[40] Moreover, in 43.5 percent of the tests, white males received an *initial* offer that was lower than the *final* offer made to the nonwhite male testers.

B. Non-Price Discrimination

Another potentially important form of disparate treatment concerns the sellers' willingness to bargain. Consumers are hurt if sellers either refuse to bargain[41] or force the consumers to spend more time bargaining to achieve the

39 [Elsewhere we analyze] the subsample of our negotiations that end in dealer refusals to bargain.

40 Wilcoxon signed-ranks tests similarly reveal that the median final and initial profits with white males were significantly lower than those with the other tester types. For a description of such tests, see Morris H. Degroot, *Probability and Statistics* 573–76 (2d ed. 1986). This suggests that white males did better on average not simply because a few of them received very low offers, but because the entire distribution of offers to white males was lower than the distributions for the other tester types.

41 In the sale of housing, for example, sellers generally discriminate in order to discourage blacks from purchasing. See Rose

Helper, *Racial Policies and Practices of Real Estate Brokers* 42–46 (1969). Refusals to bargain and the steering of black consumers are the classic methods of achieving this end. Even in the sale of housing, however, there are numerous cases detailing discrimination with the intent to sell at a higher price, and such discrimination was explicitly outlawed by the Fair Housing Act. 42 U.S.C. § 3604(b) (1933). See, e.g., United States v. Pelzer Realty Co., 484 F.2d 438, 442–43 (5th Cir. 1973) (finding illegal a realtor's requirement that black home buyers either bring the realtor additional business or pay higher prices). See generally Robert G. Schwemm, *Housing Discrimination Law* 155–56 (1983) (summarizing the requirements of § 3604(b)'s prohibition on discriminatory terms).

TABLE 3 **DIFFERENCES IN ROUNDS**

	Average Number of Rounds	Average Length of Test (Minutes)	Average Length per Round (Minutes)
White Male	2.75	36.2	13.2
White female	2.98	49.1	16.5
Black male	2.96	39.7	13.4
Black female	2.71	35.2	13.0

same price. Critics might argue that the black and female testers would not have received a higher price if, at the end of the test, they had given the dealership a "take it or leave it" price. But why should black and female consumers have to expend additional effort to gain the same lower price that our white male testers received without screwing up their courage to make a "take-it-or-leave-it" ultimatum? It may be that black and female testers could also have received the price quoted to white males if they had executed twenty push-ups during the course of bargaining. If so, the fact that white male testers did not have to execute the push-ups to receive the better price would clearly constitute discrimination.

Our testing uncovered very little evidence of outright refusals to bargain and no evidence that dealerships were less likely to bargain with non-white male testers. Indeed, as summarized in table 3, if anything the dealers displayed a willingness to bargain longer with black male and white female testers—in terms of both number of bargaining rounds and number of minutes.[42] Although black male testers clearly had to pay the most for cars, it was not because dealers refused to spend time bargaining with them.

Indeed, the sellers' insistence on bargaining longer with black men may be an indirect attempt to enhance their market power by reducing their potential competition. If the hourly costs to consumers of searching for a car increase with the time spent searching, then the longer a dealership keeps customers bargaining in its showroom, the less likely they will visit other dealerships. In other words, dealers may intentionally try to bargain for more rounds with certain types of consumers, if doing so is particularly likely to reduce the chance that they will visit other dealerships.[43] This data on willingness to bargain (particularly the time spent

---

42 These black male, black female, and white female averages were statistically different from the white male average ($p < 0.1$). A chi-square analysis failed to reject a joint test that the number of rounds was the same for different tester types ($p = 0.1465$), but did reject the null hypothesis that the average length of bargaining was the same for different tester types and length was the same for different tester types ($p = 0.00003$).

43 Using ordered statistics, one can estimate the expected gains that different testers would experience by searching for the minimum price at additional dealerships. The more prices vary from dealer to dealer, the more likely it becomes that a search will turn up better offers. See George Stigler, *The Organization of Industry* 173–75 (1968).

negotiating) is used [elsewhere] together with the basic data on initial and final offers to help distinguish between different causal theories.

The initial pilot study conducted in 1989 also examined other ways in which sellers may have treated the testers differently. Although these data are not as authoritative (based as they are on a smaller sample of only approximately 180 negotiations), they illuminate ancillary ways that deals can facilitate price discrimination. Moreover, these comparisons suggest something about the racial and sexual perceptions that determine the behavior of salespeople. In the pilot study, the testers recorded how often they were asked specific types of questions. Statistical tests were then conducted to evaluate whether sellers asked nonwhite, nonmale testers certain questions significantly more or less often than white male testers. These tests indicated the following:

- Sellers asked black female testers more often about their occupation, about financing, and whether they were married.
- Sellers asked black female testers less often whether they had been to other dealerships and whether they had offers from other dealers.
- Sellers asked black male testers less often if they would like to test drive the car, whether they had been to other dealerships, and whether they had offers from other dealers.
- Sellers asked white female testers more often whether they had been to other dealerships.
- Sellers asked white female testers less often what price they would be willing to pay.

These differences may indicate ways that dealers try to sort consumers in order to price discriminate effectively. For example, the fact that salespeople asked black testers less often about whether they had been to other dealerships (or had other offers) may indicate that salespeople do not think that interdealer competition is as much of a threat with black customers as with white customers. Because the price that sellers are willing to offer any customer may be sensitive to that customer's responses, the disparity among whom is questioned may facilitate a seller's attempt to price discriminate.

In the pilot study, the testers also recorded the different tactics that the salespeople used in trying to sell the car. Test statistics were calculated to evaluate whether particular sales tactics were used significantly more or less often with white male testers than with their nonwhite, nonmale counterparts. These tests indicated the following:

- Salespeople tried to sell black female testers more often on gas mileage, the color of the car, dependability, and comfort, and asked them more often to sign purchase orders.
- Salespeople tried to sell white female testers more often on gas mileage, the color of the car, and dependability.
- With black male testers, salespeople more often offered the sticker price as the initial offer and forced the tester to elicit an initial offer from the seller. Salespeople asked black male testers to sign a purchase order less often.

These tests suggest that salespeople believe women are more concerned than men with gas mileage, color, and dependability. The tests also indicate that salespeople try to "sucker" black males into buying at the sticker price by offering the sticker price or refusing to make an initial offer until asked.

Finally, the script for the pilot study also elicited information about the dealers' willingness

TABLE 4 DISCLOSURE OF COST DATA

Tester Type	Percentage of Salespeople Disclosing Cost Figure
All Testers	35
White male	47
White female	42
Black male	25
Black female	0

TABLE 5 SELLER MISREPRESENTATION OF COST DATA

Tester Type	Average Misrepresentation ($)
White male	849
White female	1,046
Black male	752
Black female	—

to reveal their marginal cost to consumers. In half of the bargaining sessions, the testers were told to ask the seller (at the end of the test) what the dealer had paid the car manufacturer. Thirty-five percent of the sellers represented a specific dollar cost in response to the testers' inquiries. These disclosures, however, were not evenly distributed across the tester groups. Disaggregated by tester type, the disclosure rates indicated that salespeople were less willing to disclose cost data to black testers, especially black female testers, as shown in table 4.

Instead of disclosing their cost information to black testers, the salespeople were more likely to dissemble and claim that they did not know the car's cost. To the extent that such cost disclosure is valuable,[44] the failure to disclose costs to black buyers would undermine their ability to bargain as effectively as whites and thus facilitates price discrimination based on race. Based on this sample, however, it is unclear whether such disclosure would actually put white testers at a competitive advantage. When the seller did reveal his cost, the represented cost was substantially higher than independent estimates of seller cost for the same models, as seen in table 5. Thus, although salespeople are more likely to disclose cost figures to white testers, they systematically overstate their costs. The greatest misrepresentations were made to white female testers.

★ ★ ★

---

44 Consumers rationally value information concerning a seller's costs in "thin markets," in which the infrequency of transactions makes the competitive price hard to determine. ★ ★ ★

PART FOUR

POLITICAL INEQUALITY

INTRODUCTION TO PART IV

The chapters in Part IV turn to an examination of the political underpinnings of inequality. It opens with a short selection by Gosta Esping-Andersen, drawn from his classical 1990 work on the differences between the welfare states of "social democratic" countries such as Sweden and Norway; "Christian democratic" welfare states such as those in Germany, France, and Italy; and the liberal democratic welfare states of Anglo-American countries. The identification of distinct welfare state "worlds" was an important development in understanding how and why welfare states differ. Esping-Andersen shows that there are important and distinctive features of each regime type. The social democratic countries favor universal programs, the Christian democratic countries build social policies around traditional family structures, and the liberal democratic states favor means-testing for cash benefits and employment-based benefit provision. The social democratic countries have the highest spending levels and the most equality, followed by the Christian democratic countries; the liberal democracies are the most inegalitarian. Although later scholarship has refined and developed Esping-Andersen's original "three worlds" model, it continues to influence how we understand the welfare state.

There are, as we noted in the introduction, a number of ways in which the United States is unique, even among the liberal democratic countries, in doing less to reduce poverty and inequality than other rich democracies. The chapter by Claude Fischer and colleagues provides an overview of this issue, describing a range of sometimes hidden policy choices that America makes that blunt the potential egalitarian impact of welfare state institutions. America may spend a lot on social programs, many of those expenditures benefit middle-class people as much or more than the poor. These policies include such things as the homeowner tax deduction (which provides the largest benefits to the richest homeowners), subsidized private health insurance, and the federal highway system (a costly program primarily benefiting suburban homeowners and developers).

The chapters by G. William Domhoff, Dan Clawson, Jeff Manza, Richard Freeman, and Jill Quadagno all offer other answers to the puzzle of why the United States does less to reduce poverty and inequality than other countries. Domhoff argues that domination of the government by a narrow group drawn from the ranks of the corporate community and its satellite policy formation organizations is critical. This power elite stands independent of the particular party in office, as its members may divide over peripheral questions such as social issues and foreign policy. But whichever party is in office, power elite influence tends to constrain the adoption of higher taxes or expensive redistributive spending programs. Domhoff notes the existence, but weakness of countervailing groups like organized labor that in other capitalist countries provide a much more vigorous opposition to the power elite. Freeman's chapter documents the decline of organized labor in the United States. As the most likely source of pressure for more redistributive social programs, unions have frequently played an important role in supporting greater wage equality as well as public policies benefiting working-class families. But as unions in the United States have declined in strength, they have become increasingly less important actors in the economic and political system. Their very survival, at least in the private sector, is now in question; new strategies for organizing and changes in American labor laws are essential if unions are to be rebuilt.

In her chapter, Quadagno argues that American political institutions and political parties are different from those of other rich capitalist democracies because they took shape in a racialized context: slavery, then the Civil War and Reconstruction, and later in the long struggle to end the institutions of Jim Crow culminating in the upheavals of the 1960s. It was during this period that the last major effort undertaken by the federal government to expand the antipoverty policy was undertaken. Quadagno argues that the efforts of American liberals to expand the welfare state to make it more like those of western Europe foundered because of a federal political system and local racial politics in urban political environments. Manza focuses on another set of questions rarely discussed: how the right to vote influences the patterning of political inequality. Although America was an early mover in establishing a universal right to vote for white men. He notes some of the ways in which the patterning of the right to vote has been linked to the politics of race. Today, America is unique internationally for disenfranchising millions of nonincarcerated criminal offenders, and with a growing population of legal (as well as unauthorized) immigrants who cannot participate, eligibility has emerged as a major source of political inequality. As the percentage of the poorest Americans who are not eligible to vote in democratic elections goes up, the collective voice of the poor declines.

In the final chapter of this section, Dan Clawson discusses yet another unique aspect of the American political system: the enormous amount of money donated to political candidates, disproportionately from businesses and affluent individuals. Clawson argues that while money does not buy votes directly—legislators rarely literally sell votes, although it does happen in a few widely publicized cases—donors do gain something else of value: access. They gain the opportunity to bend the ear of the legislators (and sometimes presidents) they give money to, giving them a privileged opportunity to shape legislation or create beneficial tax breaks or loopholes.

47

The Three Political Economies of the Welfare State⋆

GOSTA ESPING–ANDERSEN

★ ★ ★

‖ A RESPECIFICATION OF THE WELFARE STATE

Few can disagree with T.H. Marshall's (1950) proposition that social citizenship constitutes the core idea of a welfare state. What, then, are the key principles involved in social citizenship? In our view, they must involve first and foremost the granting of social rights. This mainly entails a de-commodification of the status of individuals vis-à-vis the market. Secondly, social-citizenship involves social stratification; one's status as a citizen will compete with, or even replace, one's class position. Thirdly, the welfare state must be understood in terms of the interface between the market, the family, and the state. These principles need to be fleshed out prior to any theoretical specification of the welfare state.

⋆ First published in 1989; from *Canadian Review of Sociology*, Volume 26, Number 1.

Rights and De-commodification

As commodities in the market, workers depend for their welfare entirely on the cash-nexus. The question of social rights is thus one of de-commodification, that is of granting alternative means of welfare to that of the market. De-commodification may refer either to the service rendered, or to the status of a person, but in both cases it signifies the degree to which distribution is detached from the market mechanism. This means that the mere presence of social assistance or insurance may not necessarily bring about significant de-commodification if they do not substantially emancipate individuals from market dependence. Means-tested poor relief will possibly offer a security blanket of last resort. But if benefits are low and attached with social stigma, the relief system will compel all but the most desperate to participate in the market. This was precisely the intent of the 19th century poor laws. Similarly, most of the early social insurance programs were deliberately designed to maximize labor market performance (Ogus, 1979). Benefits required long contribution periods and were tailored to prior work effort. In either case, the motive was to avert work-disincentive effects.

There is no doubt that de-commodification has been a hugely contested issue in welfare state development. For labor, it has always been a priority. When workers are completely market dependent, they are difficult to mobilize for solidaristic action. Since their resources mirror market inequalities, divisions emerge between the "ins" and the "outs," making labor movement formation difficult. De-commodification strengthens the worker and weakens the absolute authority of the employer. It is for exactly this reason that employers always opposed de-commodification.

De-commodified rights are differentially developed in contemporary welfare states. In social assistance dominated welfare states, rights are not so much attached to work performance as to demonstrable need. Needs-tests and typically meagre benefits, however, serve to curtail the de-commodifying effect. Thus, in nations where this model is dominant (mainly in the Anglo-Saxon countries), the result is actually to strengthen the market since all but those who fail in the market will be encouraged to contract private sector welfare.

A second dominant model espouses compulsory state social insurance with fairly strong entitlements. Yet, again, this may not automatically secure substantial de-commodification, since this hinges very much on the fabric of eligibility and benefit rules. Germany was the pioneer of social insurance, but over most of the century can hardly be said to have brought about much in the way of de-commodification through its social programs. Benefits have depended almost entirely on contributions and, thus, work and employment. In fact, before the Second World War, average pensions in the German insurance system for workers were lower than prevailing poverty assistance rates (Myles, 1984). The consequence, as with the social assistance model, was that most workers would chose to remain at work rather than retire. In other words, it is not the mere presence of a social right, but the corresponding rules and preconditions that dictate the extent to which welfare programs offer genuine alternatives to market dependence.

The third dominant model of welfare, namely, the Beveridge-type citizens benefit, may, at first glance, appear the most de-commodifying. It offers a basic, equal benefit to all irrespective of prior earnings, contributions or performance. It may indeed be a more solidaristic system, but not necessarily de-commodifying since, only rarely, have such schemes been able to offer benefits of such a standard that they provide recipients with a genuine option to that of working.

De-commodifying welfare states are, in practice, of very recent date. A minimalist definition must entail that citizens can freely, and without potential losses of job, income, or general welfare, opt out of work under conditions when they, themselves, consider it necessary for reasons of health, family, age or even educational self-improvement; when, in short, they deem it necessary for participating adequately in the social community.

With this definition in mind, we would, for example, require of a sickness insurance that individuals be secured benefits equal to normal earnings, the right to absence with minimal proof of medical impairment, and for the duration that the individual deems necessary. These conditions, it is worth noting, are those usually enjoyed by academics, civil servants and higher-echelon white-collar employees. Similar requirements would be made of pensions, maternity leave, parental leave, educational leave, and unemployment insurance.

Some nations have moved towards this level of de-commodification, but only recently and, in many cases, with significant exemptions. Thus, in almost all nations benefits were upgraded to equal normal wages in the late 1960s and early 1970s. But, in some countries, for example, prompt medical certification in case of illness is still required; in others, entitlements depend on long waiting periods of up to two weeks; and, in still others, the duration of entitlements is very short (in the United States, for example, unemployment benefit duration is maximally six months, compared to 30 in Denmark). Overall, the Scandinavian welfare states tend to be the most de-commodifying; the Anglo-Saxon the least.

The Welfare State as a System of Stratification

Despite the emphasis given to it in both classical political economy and in T.H. Marshall's pioneering work, the relationship between citizenship and social class remains severely neglected, both theoretically and empirically. Generally speaking, the issue has either been assumed away (it has been taken for granted that the welfare state creates a more egalitarian society), or it has been approached narrowly in terms of income distribution or in terms of whether education promotes upward social mobility. A more basic question, it seems, is what kind of stratification system is promoted by social policy. The welfare state is not just a mechanism that intervenes in, and possibly corrects, the structure of inequality; it is, in its own right, a system of stratification. It orders actively and directly social relations.

Comparatively and historically, we can easily identify alternative systems of stratification embedded in welfare states. The poor relief tradition, and its contemporary means-tested social assistance offshoot, was conspicuously designed for purposes of stratification. By punishing and stigmatizing recipients, it promotes severe social dualisms, especially within the ranks of the working classes. It comes as no surprise that this model of welfare has been a chief target of labor movement attacks.

The social insurance model promoted by conservative reformers such as Bismarck and von Taaffe was also explicitly a form of class politics. It sought, in fact, to achieve two simultaneous stratification results. The first was to consolidate divisions among wage earners by legislating distinct programs for different class and status groups, each with its own conspicuously unique set of rights and privileges designed to accentuate the individual's appropriate station in life. The second objective was to tie the loyalties of the individual directly to the monarchy, or central state authority. This was Bismarck's motive when he promoted a direct state supplement to the pension benefit. This state-corporativist model was pursued mainly in nations such as Germany, Austria, Italy, and France and often resulted in a labyrinth of status-specific insurance funds (in France and Italy, for example, there exist more than 100 status-distinct pension schemes).

Of special importance in this corporatist tradition was the establishment of particularly privileged welfare provisions for the civil service ("Beamten"). In part, this was a means of rewarding loyalty to the state and in part, a way of demarcating this group's uniquely exalted social status. We should, however, be careful to note that the corporatist status-differentiated model springs mainly from the old guild tradition. The neo-absolutist autocrats, such as Bismarck, saw in this tradition a means to combat the rising labor movements.

The labor movements were as hostile to the corporatist model as they were to poor relief—in both cases for obvious reasons. Yet, the alternatives first espoused by labor were no less problematic from the point of view of uniting the workers as one solidaristic class. Almost invariably, the model that labor first pursued was that of the self-organized friendly societies or equivalent union- or party-sponsored fraternal welfare plan. This is not surprising. Workers were obviously suspicious of reforms sponsored by a hostile state, and saw their own organizations not only as bases of class mobilization, but also as embryos of an alternative world of solidarity and justice, as a microcosm of the socialist haven to come. Nonetheless, these microsocialist societies often became problematic class ghettos that divided rather than united workers. Membership was typically, restricted to the strongest strata of the working class and the weakest—who needed protection most—were most likely outside. In brief, the fraternal society model contradicted the goal of working-class mobilization.

The socialist ghetto approach was an additional obstacle when socialist parties found themselves forming governments and having to pass the social reforms they so long had demanded. For reasons of political coalition building and broader solidarity, their welfare model had to be recast as welfare for the "people." Hence, the socialists came to espouse the principle of universalism and, borrowing from the liberals, typically designed on the lines of the democractic flat-rate, general revenue-financed, Beveridge model.

As an alternative to means-tested assistance and corporatist social insurance, the universalistic system promotes status equality. All citizens are endowed with similar rights, irrespective of class or market position. In this sense, this system is meant to cultivate cross-class solidarity, a solidarity of the nation. But, the solidarity of flat-rate universalism presumes a historically peculiar class structure; one in which the vast majority of the population are the "little people" for whom a modest, albeit egalitarian, benefit may be considered adequate. Where this no longer obtains, as occurs with growing working-class prosperity and the rise of the new middle classes, flat-rate universalism inadvertently promotes dualism because the better off turn to private insurance and to fringe-benefit bargaining to supplement modest equality with what they have decided are accustomed standards of welfare. Where this process unfolds (as in Canada or the United Kingdom), the result is that the wonderfully egalitarian spirit of universalism turns into a dualism similar to that of the social assistance state: the poor rely on the state, and the remainder on the market.

It is not only the universalist, but in fact all historical welfare state models which have faced the dilemma of class-structural change. But, the response to prosperity and middle-class growth has been varied and so, therefore, has been the stratificational outcome. The corporatist insurance tradition was, in a sense, best equipped to manage new and loftier welfare state expectations since the existing system could technically be upgraded quite easily to distribute more adequate benefits. Adenauer's 1957 pension reform in Germany was a pioneer in this respect. Its avowed purpose was to restore status differences that had eroded due to the old insurance system's incapacity to provide benefits tailored to expectations. This it did simply by moving from contribution- to earnings-graduated benefits without altering the framework of status-distinctiveness.

In nations with either a social assistance or a universalistic Beveridge-type system, the option was whether to allow the market or the state to furnish adequacy and satisfy middle-class aspirations. Two alternative models emerged from this political choice. The one typical of Great Britain and most of the Anglo-Saxon world was to preserve an essentially modest universalism in the state and allow the market to reign for the growing social strata demanding superior welfare. Due to the political power of such groups, the dualism that emerges is not merely one between state and market, but also between forms of welfare state transfers: in these nations, one of the fastest growing components of public expenditure is tax-subsidies for so-called "private" welfare plans. And the typical political effect is eroding middle-class support for what is less and less a universalistic public sector transfer system.

Yet another alternative has been to seek a synthesis of universalism and adequacy outside of the market. This road has been followed in the countries where, by mandating or legislation, the state includes the new middle classes by erecting a luxurious second-tier, universally inclusive, earnings related insurance scheme on top of the flat-rate egalitarian one. Notable examples are Sweden and Norway. By guaranteeing benefits tailored to expectations, this solution reintroduces benefit inequalities, but effectively blocks off the market. It thus succeeds in retaining universalism and, therefore, also the degree of political consensus required to preserve broad and solidaristic support for the high taxes that such a welfare state model demands.

Welfare State Regimes

Welfare states vary considerably with respect to their principles of rights and stratification. This results in qualitatively different arrangements between state, market, and the family.

The welfare state variations, we find, are therefore not linearly distributed, but clustered by regime-types.

In one cluster, we find the "liberal" welfare state, in which means-tested assistance, modest universal transfers, or modest social insurance plans predominate. These cater mainly to a clientele of low-income, usually working-class, state dependents. It is a model in which, implicitly or explicitly, the progress of social reform has been severely circumscribed by traditional, liberal work-ethic norms; one where the limits of welfare equal the marginal propensity to demand welfare instead of work. Entitlement rules are therefore strict and often associated with stigma; benefits are typically modest. In turn, the state encourages the market, either passively by guaranteeing only a minimum, or actively by subsidizing private welfare schemes.

The consequence is that this welfare state regime minimizes de-commodification-effects, effectively contains the realm of social rights, and erects a stratification order that blends a relative equality of poverty among state welfare recipients, market-differentiated welfare among the majorities, and a class-political dualism between the two. The archetypical examples of this model are the United States, Canada, and Australia. Nations that approximate the model are Denmark, Switzerland, and Great Britain.

A second regime-cluster is composed of nations such as Austria, France, Germany, and Italy. Here, the historical corporatist-statist legacy was upgraded to cater to the new "post-industrial" class structure. In these "corporatist" welfare states, the liberal obsession with market efficiency and commodification was never pre-eminent and, as such, the granting of social rights was hardly ever a seriously contested issue. What predominated was the preservation of status differentials; rights, therefore, were attached to class and status. This corporativism was subsumed under a state edifice perfectly ready to displace the market as a provider of welfare; hence, private insurance and occupational fringe benefits play a truly marginal role in this model. On the other hand, the state's emphasis on upholding status differences means that its redistributive effects are negligible.

But, the corporativist regimes are also typically shaped by the Church, and therefore influenced by a strong commitment to the preservation of traditional family patterns. Social insurance typically excludes non-working wives, and family benefits encourage motherhood. Day care, and similar family services, are conspicuously underdeveloped, and the "subsidiarity principle" serves to emphasize that the state will only interfere when the family's capacity to service its members is exhausted. An illustrative example is German unemployment assistance. Once a person has exhausted his/her entitlement to normal unemployment insurance, eligibility for continued assistance depends on whether one's family commands the financial capacity to aid the unfortunate; this obtains for persons of any age.

The third, and clearly smallest, regime-cluster is composed of those countries in which the principles of universalism and de-commodifying social rights were extended also to the new middle classes. We may call it the "social democratic" regime-type since, in these nations, social democracy clearly was the dominant force behind social reform. Norway and Sweden are the clearest cases, but we should also consider Denmark and Finland. Rather than tolerate a dualism between state and market, between working class and middle class, the social democrats pursued a welfare state that would promote an equality of the highest standards, rather than an equality of minimal needs as was pursued elsewhere. This implied, first, that services and benefits be upgraded to levels commensurable to even the most discriminate tastes of the new middle classes; and, secondly, that equality be furnished by guaranteeing workers full participation in the quality of rights enjoyed by the better off.

This formula translates into a mix of highly de-commodifying and universalistic programs that, nonetheless, are tailored to differentiated expectations. Thus, manual workers come to enjoy rights identical to those of salaried white-collar employees or civil servants; all strata and classes are incorporated under one universal insurance system; yet, benefits are graduated according to accustomed earnings. This model crowds out the market and, consequently, inculcates an essentially universal solidarity behind the welfare state. All benefit, all are dependent, and all will presumably feel obliged to pay.

The social democratic regime's policy of emancipation addresses both the market and the traditional family. In contrast to the corporatist-subsidiarity model, the principle is not to wait until the family's capacity to aid is exhausted, but to pre-emptively socialize the costs of familihood. The ideal is not to maximize dependence on the family, but capacities for individual independence. In this sense, the model is a peculiar fusion of liberalism and socialism. The result is a welfare state that grants transfers directly to the children, and takes direct caring responsi-bilities for children, the aged and the helpless. It is, accordingly, committed to a heavy social service burden, not only to service family needs, but also to permit women to chose work rather than the household.

Perhaps the most salient characteristic of the social-democratic regime is its fusion of welfare and work. It is, at once, a welfare state genuinely committed to a full employment guarantee, and a welfare state entirely dependent on its attainment. On the one side, it is a model in which the right to work has equal status to the right of income protection. On the other side, the enormous costs of maintaining a solidaristic, universalistic and de-commodifying welfare system means that it must minimize social problems and maximize revenue income. This is obviously best done with most people working, and the fewest possible living off social transfers.

While it is empirically clear that welfare states cluster, we must recognize that no single case is pure. The social-democratic regimes of Scandinavia blend crucial socialist and liberal elements. The Danish and Swedish unemployment insurance schemes, for example, are still essentially voluntarist. Denmark's labor movement has been chronically incapable of pursuing full employment policies due in part to trade union resistance to active manpower policies. And in both Denmark and Finland, the market has been allowed to play a decisive role in pensions.

Neither are the liberal regimes pure. The American social security system is redistributive, compulsory and far from actuarial. At least in its early formulation, the New Deal was a social democratic as was contemporary Scandinavian social democracy. In contrast, the Australian welfare state would appear exceedingly close to the bourgeois-liberal ideal-type, but much of its edifice has been the co-responsibility of Australian labor. And, finally, the European corporatist regimes have received both liberal and social democratic impulses. Social insurance schemes have been substantially destratified and unified in Austria, Germany, France and Italy. Their extremely corporativist character has thus been reduced.

Notwithstanding the lack of purity, if our essential criteria for defining welfare states have to do with the quality of social rights, social stratification, and the relationship between state, market and family, the World is composed of distinct regime-clusters. Comparing welfare states on scales of more or less or, indeed, better or worse, will yield highly misleading results.

★ ★ ★

||| REFERENCES

Marshall, T.H. 1950. *Citizenship and Social Class.* Cambridge: Cambridge University Press.

Myles, J. 1984. *Old Age in the Welfare State.* Boston: Little, Brown.

Ogus, A. 1979. "Social Insurance, Legal Development and Legal History." In H.F. Zacher (ed.), *Bedingungen fur die Entstehung von Socialversicherung.* Berlin: Duncker and Humboldt.

48

How Unequal? America's Invisible Policy Choices*

CLAUDE S. FISCHER, MICHAEL HOUT,

MARTIN SANCHEZ JANKOWSKI, SAMUEL R. LUCAS,

ANN SWIDLER, AND KIM VOSS

Americans can significantly alter how much inequality there is among them. ★ ★ ★ Such fluidity results in large measure from changes and variations in *policy*. In this chapter we focus on several specific American policy choices that shape inequality.

Obvious redistributive programs, such as welfare spending, are not the only policies, or even the most important ones, that affect inequality. Many "invisible" practices are more significant. For example, American housing and road-building programs have largely subsidized the expansion of suburban homeownership for the middle class. Other largely unnoticed policies set the ground rules for the competition to get ahead. Just as in baseball, where the height of the pitcher's mound affects whether pitchers or batters have the advantage, so in the marketplace laws and regulations favor some competitors and disadvantage others. ★ ★ ★ The United States has the greatest inequality in earnings among full-time workers and that that inequality has increased since 1970.

★ First published in 1996; from *Inequality by Design*.

Some policies narrow inequality and some widen it. Again and again we will see that the basic dimensions of social inequality—how rich the rich are and how poor the poor are, and even who becomes rich or poor—are a result of our social and political choices. Many of our policies operate indirectly, and hence invisibly. The programs that help the poor are glaringly obvious, but those that aid the rich and middle class tend to be invisible. Obscured even more are the policies that set the rules of "the game" for the labor market. In this chapter, we will reveal some of the many ways that social policy shapes inequality.

We will begin by looking at one general pattern of American social policy, which is to provide, with one hand, limited direct help to some of the poor and indirectly to subsidize, with another, the middle class and the wealthy. Next, we will uncover one of the most hidden arenas of social policy, the regulation of the labor market, and show how the ground rules shape inequality. Finally, through an examination of higher education, we will look at some of the diverse ways in which public investment also molds inequality. In the end, we will better understand the major reasons why inequality is historically so inconstant and why inequality in America is so high.

VISIBLE POLICY: REDUCING POVERTY THROUGH REDISTRIBUTION

Over the last century, American government has done much to help those left poor by the market. Public health programs, school lunches,

food stamps, Aid to Families with Dependent Children (AFDC), and survivors' benefits have reduced the inequality left by earnings differences. Yet Americans have chosen not to pursue such programs as far as citizens in other affluent nations have (and the programs are being sharply cut back as we write). Most industrial societies provide "family allowances" to all families with children and some form of universal health care or health insurance to all residents. In such ways, the numbers and problems of the very poor are sharply reduced by government policies that are directed toward everyone and that do not single out the poor. Most American welfare programs, in contrast, are "means-tested"—available only to those who can prove that they are poor and that they are otherwise deserving. These targeted programs consequently lack wide political support and are vulnerable to budget-cutting. Only social security and Medicare, nearly universal entitlements for the elderly, have largely survived cutbacks in recent years. Most other nations, unlike the United States, also substantially subsidize housing for many moderate-income citizens, provide stipends for students who make it into higher education, and support the long-term unemployed.

Recent American antipoverty programs have had some success, but mostly in reducing poverty among the elderly, largely through social security and Medicare, and in taking the edge off misery. We can see the emphasis on the elderly by looking at the percentage of Americans who are pulled above the poverty line by all government financial programs (tax-ation, unemployment support, welfare, social security, etc.) put together. In 1992, 22 percent of Americans would have had incomes below the poverty line if all that had been available to them were their families' earnings. Government taxes and transfers reduced that to 12 percent, a drop of ten points in the proportion of poor Americans. For the elderly, taxes and transfers reduced the proportion by *forty points,* from the 50 percent who would have been poor based on nongovernmental income alone to the 10 percent who were poor after including governmental income and taxes. For children, however, the net effect of taxes and transfers was to reduce poverty rates by only *seven points,* from 24 percent to 17 percent. For young adults, the drop was merely five points, from 21 percent to 16 percent.[1] This generational imbalance is, in part, the outcome of policy changes during the 1980s that weakened the equalizing effects of taxes and transfers.[2] (As of yet, we have no data on the effects of the 1993 Clinton tax changes that raised the earned income tax credit for low-income families and raised the income tax rates for the very wealthiest households. Presumably, these laws shifted net incomes toward equality a little. But the changes enacted by the Republican Congress elected in 1994 will shift incomes away from equality.)

If we list all the programs that helped nonelderly Americans with low income—food stamps, AFDC, Women, Infants and Children (WIC—a nutrition program), Medicaid, SSI disability, the earned income tax credit, etc.—they sound like a lot. Adding together these programs and adding in as well a variety of federal, state, and local spending directed not just at the poor but also at many people who are above the poverty line, such as college loans, job retraining, and energy assistance, the total expenditures for "persons with limited income" in 1992 amounted to almost $290 billion. As sizable as that figure is, it represents less than 12 percent of all government expenditures at all levels that year. It comes to about $5,900 per low-income person. Almost half of this total, $134 billion, was for medical care, largely Medicaid. Nonmedical spending came to about $3,200 per limited-income person, of which about $2,100 was in the form of cash or food stamps. That $2,100 is roughly what the typical American family spent on eating out in 1992; it is within a few hundred dollars of what typical homeowners saved on their federal income taxes by being able to deduct mortgage interest. Even after this government spending—which is probably a high-end estimate of what America spent to aid low-income people in 1992—over 14 percent of Americans, 21 percent of American children, remained poor.

We can best evaluate the effort to redress poverty comparatively. Low-income American children are worse off than low-income children in any other industrial nation. In the 1980s, for example, about 20 percent of American children lived in poverty, while 9 percent of Canadian children and of Australian children were poor, 7 percent of children in the United Kingdom, and even fewer in France, West Germany, and Sweden, respectively.[3]

---

1 U.S. Bureau of the Census, "Measuring the Effect of Benefits and Taxes," table 2, definitions 2 and 13. (Full citations can be found in the reference list at the end of the chapter.)

2 Smeeding, "Why the U.S. Antipoverty System Doesn't Work"; Gramlich, et al., "Growing Inequality in the 1980s."

3 Burtless, "Public Spending on the Poor."

Why are so many American children poor? Charles Murray claimed in an earlier book that American children are poor because welfare policies encourage poor women to have more children. He is wrong. Careful studies by demographers demonstrate minimal effects, if any, of AFDC on childbearing. Rather, young parents are more susceptible to poverty, and their poverty makes their children poor. American children are more often poor, first, because American adults are more unequal in both wealth and income than people in any other industrial society. Second, children suffer especially because the incomes of young men have fallen so sharply since the mid-1970s. More young men cannot earn enough to keep their children out of poverty, and many then refuse to take on the responsibilities of marriage, leaving young mothers and children even poorer.

We can see how American government compares with others in dealing with poverty by turning again to the Luxembourg Income Study. Lee Rainwater and Timothy Smeeding calculated, for eighteen nations, the percentage of children who were poor. (To be able to compare across countries, "poor" was defined as being in a household with real purchasing power less than half that of the median in the nation. Half the median is roughly what the poverty line in the United States was in the 1960s when it was first calculated.) Figure 1 shows the percentage of children who were poor before and then after including taxes and government transfer payments in the calculations. Again, we look only at the populous nations. Before government intervention, a relatively high percentage of American children were poor, but not as high as in France and the United King-

dom. After counting taxes and government payments, however, the poverty rate for American children was substantially higher than that elsewhere (including nine other nations not shown in the figure). Even those countries with higher before-government child poverty than the United States managed to reduce their poverty levels to far below the level here.

Two objections might be raised to the evidence that America leaves so many of its children in poverty. One is that so many American children are poor because so many live in single-parent families. That is true. However, Rainwater and Smeeding also looked separately at children in two-parent and in single-parent families. In each case, the same pattern appears as in figure 1: American children were exceedingly likely to be left poor after government action. The other objection is that being poor in America, being below 50 percent of the median, is in material terms not as terrible as being poor elsewhere. Unfortunately, that is not so. Rainwater and Smeeding calculated how much real purchasing power children at the 10th, 50th, and 90th percentiles of the income distribution had available in each country. American children near the top and at the middle did, indeed, have more real income than did children near the top and at the middle elsewhere. But American children near the bottom had *less* real income than children in the other nations, 25 percent less than poor Canadian children and 40 percent less than poor West German children. And again, the researchers did not count some of the in-kind resources provided to poor children overseas.

The United States does less than any other advanced nation to reduce poverty through government benefits. In addition, our spend-

FIGURE 1 PERCENTAGE OF CHILDREN WHO ARE POOR, BEFORE AND AFTER GOVERNMENT ACTION, IN EIGHT NATIONS

GOVERNMENT IN THE UNITED STATES DOES THE LEAST TO REDUCE THE PROPORTION OF CHILDREN WHO ARE POOR: PERCENT OF CHILDREN POOR BEFORE AND AFTER GOVERNMENT ACTION.

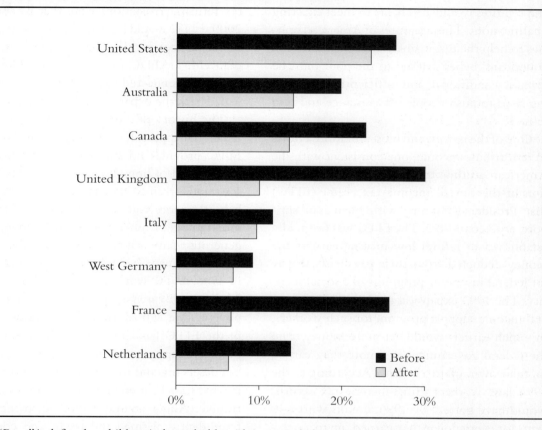

NOTE: "Poor" is defined as children in households with incomes below 50 percent of the national median household income. Government action includes all taxes and all cash and "near-cash" transfers.
SOURCE: Adapted from *Rainwater and Smeeding*, "Doing Poorly," table A-2.

ing to aid the poor is precarious. Assistance is a donation: it is not a right, as it is elsewhere, and it is therefore politically vulnerable. For example, the main program that supports children, AFDC, has been repeatedly cut such that the monthly benefits dropped 25 percent in real value between 1980 and 1993.[4] And it will continue to decline as the federal government transfers responsibility for welfare to the state governments. Also, unlike aid to the poor

4 U.S. Bureau of the Census, *Statistical Abstract 1995*, tables 609 and 762.

in most other nations, these programs form an overlapping, conflicting, and sometimes impenetrable morass. One reason they do is that each program was targeted to a specific need and requires would-be clients to meet exacting qualifications. These features of American policies to help the unfortunate are consistent with Americans' belief that aid to the poor must be limited, conditional, and sufficiently unappealing so as to push people off assistance and into jobs.

One of the newest and most ambitious efforts to redistribute income, one consistent with the American attitude toward aid, was the expansion of the earned income tax credit (EITC) that President Clinton, with bipartisan support, enacted in 1993. The EITC was originally established to refund low-income earners the money deducted from their paychecks to pay for federal insurance programs like social security. The 1993 expansion turned it into a general income support program for such workers, in which earners would get more money from the federal government the more they earned on their own, up to a ceiling. According to the 1993 law, workers filing income tax returns would have gotten, by 1996, credits worth 40 cents for every dollar they earned, up to a maximum refund of about $3,500. (That would have been for a family of four with earnings in the $8,400-$11,000 range; a fully employed worker earning the minimum wage grosses under $9,000.) Beyond $11,000 in earnings, the EITC would gradually shrink until reaching zero for families earning $27,000. Expansion of the EITC was initially popular among conser-

vatives because it rewards working and among liberals because it provides the working poor with supplementary income in a nonstigmatizing way (applicants need only fill out an income tax return). Projections were that by the year 2000, EITC would have transferred $30 billion a year to poor and low-income families, more than either AFDC or food stamps. However, the changes enacted by the 1995–96 Congress scaled back the expansion of the EITC.

The history of the EITC sheds light on the American approach to redistribution. First, the EITC provides no support at all for families whose head of household is, for whatever reason, not working. One must earn and *deserve* the help; the more you get in the marketplace, the more you get from government. Second, more generous than most programs, it is still limited. By one estimate, had it been fully implemented in 1996, EITC would have moved only about 25 percent of *working* poor families above the poverty line. Third, the design and discussion of the EITC has largely focused, not on how best to reduce poverty, but on how to aid only the deserving and to reward work effort. That is why, fourth, it encountered serious political trouble. Anger at unqualified recipients who fraudulently claimed the credit and concerns that the rebate structure may lead some workers near the top of the eligibility range to cut back on their work hours—together with efforts to balance the federal budget—propelled Congress to scale back the EITC.[5]

Overall, then, American government policy *does* reduce inequality by aiding the poor. The New Deal and the Great Society programs sub-

5 Peterson, "GOP Seeking to Curb Tax Break for Poor"; Novack, "The Worm in the Apple"; "IRS Appears Successful in Efforts to Curb Fraud," *Wall Street Journal,* June 9, 1995, p. 16; "The War on Work," *Newsweek,* October 2, 1995, p. 66.

stantially helped the elderly and reduced some of the misery for others—all that the programs were ever designed to do.[6] This mix of policies may be what most American voters wish. There are prominent voices arguing that even this amount of redistribution to the nonelderly poor is too much, that it hurts the economy and even hurts the poor by undermining their self-reliance. Our point here is that in the case of our most visible policies, ones to aid the poor, Americans have *chosen* to do less rather than more, have designed greater inequality.

INVISIBLE POLICIES I: SUBSIDIZING THE MIDDLE CLASS

In contrast to the highly visible, if limited, direct aid given to the poor, American social policy tends to subsidize the middle class more generously, but indirectly and less visibly. The effects of these indirect policies have generally been to simultaneously *decrease* inequality between the middle class and the wealthy and to *increase* the gap between the middle class and low-income Americans.

Subsidizing Homeownership

The mortgage interest deduction is a quintessential example of the invisible ways American policy subsidizes the middle class and the wealthy and, indeed, offers a greater benefit the wealthier one is. A person too poor to buy a house receives no housing subsidy (unless he or she is so poor as to qualify for welfare), while a wealthy homeowner with a mansion and a vacation house may receive a subsidy worth tens of thousands of dollars. For example, someone carrying a million-dollar mortgage would get tax breaks worth over $33,000 *a year*.

It might seem odd to think of the mortgage interest deduction as a "subsidy," because it is the taxpayer's own income that he or she keeps. But a subsidy it is, because it is a tax that the government forgoes in its effort to encourage homeownership. Had the taxpayer with the million-dollar mortgage rented the same home instead of buying it, he or she would have had to pay $33,000 more a year in taxes. If United States tax policy treated mortgage expenses the same way it treats other living expenses, like food, rent, cars, or clothes (for which no deductions can be taken), the government would have far greater revenues. Policy experts thus refer to deductions like mortgage interest as "tax expenditures," an awkward term, but one that accurately indicates that tax deductions cost the government money—which is to say that *they cost other taxpayers money*. Whatever one person saves on taxes, others must make up in taxes, or government debt, or reduced government services. By the early 1990s, the cost of the mortgage interest and property tax deductions amounted to more than $60 billion annually, over four times as much as was spent on direct housing assistance for low-income families.[7]

6 Mayer and Jencks, "War on Poverty."

7 Grigsby, "Housing Finance and Subsidies in the United States"; Coontz, *The Way We Never Were*, p. 87. Dreier and Atlas, "Housing Policy's Moment of Truth," p. 70, lists the following expenditures (in billions):

Mortgage interest and property tax deductions for homeowners—$64

HUD subsidies to public agencies, private developers, and landlords—$26

Tax breaks for investors in rental housing and mortgage bonds—$13

Military subsidies to house personnel—$10

Welfare payments—$7

Rural subsidies—$3

(This expenditure was untouched in budget-balancing legislation of 1995–96.)

And even these figures do not fully measure the subsidy homeowners receive from the government. The government underwrites much of the real estate industry by insuring and regulating private mortgage lenders. Before the Great Depression, when the government first began guaranteeing and monitoring home loans, banks typically required a 50 percent down payment on homes and normally issued mortgages for only five or ten years. Not surprisingly, under those conditions, homeownership was beyond the means of many middle-class families. Only with government intervention in the housing finance system, through the Federal Housing Authority (FHA) and the Veteran's Administration (VA), did thirty-year mortgages at relatively low interest rates become common. And these long-term, low-rate mortgages, along with the mortgage tax deduction, are what has enabled so many middle-class Americans to buy their own homes.

Another government aid to homeownership has been its massive road construction effort. For many years, but most especially in the 1950s, the federal government began ambitious projects to build tens of thousands of miles of new highways. Partly because of these highways, 85 percent of the new housing built after World War II was erected in the suburbs, where land was plentiful and relatively inexpensive.[8] Many of the new highways connected the suburbs to the downtown business districts of large cities, making it possible for middle-class Americans to buy a home in the suburbs and commute to work. Yet other government policies contributed to the expansion of middle-class homeownership in the postwar decades. Federal GI benefits allowed veterans to purchase their homes with a single dollar down. And government-funded research provided the plywood paneling, aluminum siding, and prefabricated walls and ceilings featured in the affordable housing of the 1950s and 1960s.[9]

Before World War II, many fewer Americans owned homes than do today. Nonfarm homeownership was confined primarily to the affluent. It was government policy that brought homeownership to large numbers of middle-class Americans.[10] Homeownership gave these middle-class Americans independence, real property to pass on to their children, and an opportunity to make the kind of financial investment that once only the wealthy had been able to afford.

Government subsidy of homeownership is a much-applauded policy that has shrunk some of the gap in the standard of living between wealthy Americans and middle-class Americans. But it has not yet worked that way for lower-income Americans who cannot afford to enter the housing market at all. Also, in recent years, this system has worked more to the advantage of the especially wealthy. After World War II and into the 1970s, tax expen-

---

8 Jackson, *The Crabgrass Frontier;* Coontz, *The Way We Never Were,* p. 24. See also Schneiderman, "The Hidden Handout."

9 See Jackson, *The Crabgrass Frontier;* Coontz, *The Way We Never Were,* p. 77. On the GI Bill, see Chafe, *The Unfinished Journey.*

10 Jackson, *The Crabgrass Frontier;* Coontz, *The Way We Never Were;* Chafe, *The Unfinished Journey.*

HOW AM I SUBSIDIZED? LET ME COUNT THE WAYS

Americans pride themselves on their independence. We admire the "self-made" millionaire, and we all like to think that we achieved our success on our own. These may be admirable values, but they can lead us to misunderstand our own lives and to be harsh toward the less fortunate. What would happen if a middle-class American, someone like the authors or the likely readers of this book, simply tried to count all the ways he or she was "subsidized" by the larger society?

All of us born in the United States were indirectly subsidized at birth. The public health measures that reduced disease, that eliminated smallpox and nearly wiped out polio, that provide us with safe drinking water, and that regulate hospitals and medical practice have been provided by public agencies. Then, in childhood, all of us received a vast subsidy in the form of public schooling.

Even those things we "earn" through our own effort or ability are often subsidized directly and indirectly. College education, for example, is subsidized for most people. Almost all public universities and most junior colleges charge much less in tuition than a student's education really costs. And most top private universities spend money generated by their endowments (accumulated from tax-deductible gifts and bequests) to provide students with a more expensive education than even full tuition would pay for. Only proprietary schools, like barber colleges and secretarial schools, and private colleges without endowments charge students as much as it actually costs to educate them (and even some of them receive indirect subsidies).

Businesspeople who employ highly educated workers, such as graduates of state engineering schools, receive a subsidy because their employees are trained at public expense. Businesses also depend on the indirect subsidy that supports the physical infrastructure, from roads and bridges to sidewalks and parking spaces.

These subsidies, as well as the mortgage deduction and the tax subsidy for health insurance, are for the most part to the good. Societies are joint endeavors in which each of us necessarily depends on many others, sometimes directly and often indirectly through the provision of public services ranging from national parks to sewer lines. One difficulty, however, is when these subsidies largely help those already well-off, such as the mortgage subsidy. Another difficulty comes when we imagine that we stand alone; that no one has ever done anything for us; and that we owe nothing to anyone else.

ditures for mortgage interest deductions helped the middle class about as much as they aided the wealthy. By the late 1980s, however, these tax expenditures benefited those at the top of the income distribution far more than those in the middle. The most recent statistics show that 44 percent of the mortgage subsidy goes to the 5 percent of taxpayers with incomes above $100,000 a year and that half of all homeowners receive no deductions at all.[11]

Other affluent nations have gone further than the United States in equalizing housing. Like the United States, they subsidize the middle class and the wealthy through tax deductions

11 *Business Week,* May 11, 1992, p. 20; Dreier and Atlas, "Housing Policy's Moment of Truth," p. 74.

for mortgage interest payments. But elsewhere tax deductions are a part of comprehensive programs that also include relatively generous housing support for low- and moderate-income households. In most European countries, for example, governments provide rent assistance for many working-class and poor families, and in many of these countries governments also finance the construction of new housing.[12] By providing subsidies to a larger percentage of the population, and especially to those at the lower end of the income scale, European governments have tended to lessen inequality across the board.

Housing and Discrimination

American policies that promoted middle-class homeownership decreased the distance between the wealthy and the middle class. But these government programs, which made such an enormous difference to the security and well-being of generations of Americans, were essentially denied to black Americans.

Before the federal government would guarantee a loan through the FHA or the VA, it required a professional appraisal. Appraisers always rated black neighborhoods in the lowest of the four possible categories (indicated by the color red on the maps used by federal appraisers—hence the term "redlining") and usually rated neighborhoods near a black dis-

trict in the next-to-worst category. Either designation was enough to render a property ineligible for FHA- or VA-guaranteed loans.[13] Other policies directly blocked African Americans from moving into white neighborhoods. Berkeley sociologist Troy Duster notes that "in 1939, the Federal Housing Authority's manual . . . stated that loans should not be given to any family that might 'disrupt the racial integrity' of a neighborhood. Indeed . . . the FHA manual went so far as to say that 'if a neighborhood is to retain stability, it is necessary that properties shall be continued to be occupied by the same social and racial classes.'" By the late 1940s, the FHA was recommending that developers use racially restrictive covenants as a way to ensure the financial viability of neighborhoods.[14]

Duster goes on to note that as a result of these policies, whites were able to get government-supported mortgages at 3 to 5 percent interest, "while blacks were routinely denied such loans. For example, of 350,000 new homes built in Northern California between 1940 and 1960 with FHA support, fewer than 100 went to blacks." By 1962 the VA and FHA had financed more than $120 billion in new housing, but less than 2 percent was available to nonwhite families, and most of that only in segregated neighborhoods.[15]

Other housing and development policies also widened class and racial divisions. Loan poli-

---

12 Heisler, "Housing Policy and the Underclass"; and Headey, *Housing Policy in the Developed Economy.* Coontz (*The Way We Never Were,* p. 87) points out that in the United States publicly owned housing accounts for only 1 percent of the housing market, while 37 percent of housing is publicly owned in France and 46 percent in England.

13 Jackson, "Race, Ethnicity, and Real Estate Appraisal" and "The Spacial Dimensions of Social Control"; Sugrue, "The

Structures of Urban Poverty"; Massey and Denton, *American Apartheid.*

14 Duster, "The Advantages of White Males." See also Abrams, "The Housing Problem."

15 Duster, "The Advantages of White Males"; Quadagno, *The Color of Welfare,* p. 91.

cies favored the expansion of suburbia, as did the building of the interstate highway system. The suburbs welcomed the jobs and stores that moved out with middle-class whites, while setting financial and racial barriers to city blacks who might try to move out. As a result, most blacks remained in urban ghettoes, far from growing centers of employment. Also, federal and local governments placed large-scale public housing projects, which concentrated the poor, in those same redlined neighborhoods. The contemporary isolation, concentration, and separation of poor blacks in inner cities is not simply the result of market forces, or even of market forces in combination with private racial discrimination. Rather, government policies directly contributed to widening inequality between those who were able to buy homes and move to the suburbs during the postwar housing boom (almost exclusively whites) and those who were too poor to receive government help or who, like most minorities, were excluded from programs that subsidized new housing.

The ramifications of discriminatory policies and practices go beyond housing and segregation. Housing is most Americans' major financial asset; it can be used to leverage credit from lenders; and it can be the major inheritance left to the next generation. While almost two-thirds of white households have home equity, at a median value of $45,000, only two-fifths of black households do, at a median value of $31,000. Blacks who have graduated from college earn 76 percent as much as whites who have graduated from college, but they have only 23 percent as much net worth.[16] Part of the reason for these gaps is the legacy—and continuation, too—of housing discrimination.

Health and Health Care

Health care is another arena in which social policy invisibly benefits better-off citizens while neglecting the needs of many of the less advantaged. Critics have noted how much Americans now spend on health care—more per person than any other nation.[17] Less often noticed is that the dominant way we provide health care here—private insurance, most often through plans offered by employers—tends disproportionately to subsidize high earners. As one expert notes, the tax system encourages health insurance through employers because employers' share of the insurance premiums does not count as part of employees' taxable income. But those who are too poor to pay any income taxes at all receive no subsidy for health insurance. They are therefore unlikely to be insured, because each dollar diverted to health insurance represents a full dollar less that they, lacking any tax break, might have gotten in wages. The estimated 1992 value of the federal tax subsidy—the untaxed employer contribution—was $270 for households in the bottom 20 percent of the income distribution, $525 for those in the next 20 percent, and $1,560 for those in the top 20 percent.[18] No wonder most of the poorly

---

16 Oliver and Shapiro, *Black Wealth/White Wealth,* tables 5.1, 5.2.

17 Wolfe, "Reform of Health Care," pp. 253–54. Americans spent $631 per person on health care in 1960 and $2,566 in 1990 (both in 1990 dollars), while health expenditures as share of GNP increased from 5.3 percent of GNP in 1960 to 12.2 percent in 1990, with conservative estimates that we will be spending at least 15 percent of GNP on health care by the year 2000.

18 Ibid., p. 254.

paid go without insurance even when they are employed—half of fully employed poor Americans lacked health insurance in 1993[19]—while most of those in high-paying jobs are insured through their employers.

Health policy has improved the lives of some of the poor. Since the 1960s, elderly Americans and the disabled who receive social security benefits have been insured through Medicare, the federal health care program, while Medicaid, a joint federal-state program, pays for the health care of some disabled and low-income persons. As we noted earlier, Medicaid accounts for roughly half of government spending on nonelderly low-income people. In 1990 Medicaid covered about 18 percent of all American children and about 61 percent of poor children.[20] Barbara Wolfe notes that before Medicaid, "children in families with high incomes saw physicians 67 percent more often than children in low-income families," while after the introduction of the Medicaid program, "children in families with high incomes saw physicians only 20 percent more often than children in low-income families."[21] These are widely supported programs that have measurably reduced substantive inequality.

However, this medical coverage is so spotty that it leaves many uninsured. Young adults (who are not covered by Medicare and are unlikely to be covered by Medicaid), low-income earners not quite poor enough to qualify for Medicaid, and especially blacks and Hispanics are likely to be among America's 37 million uninsured. Among low-income families above the poverty line, more than one in five remains uninsured all year. This very uneven distribution of access to health care has real consequences. Adults in the poorest fifth of the population have more than three times the number of health conditions that limit their activities (including work) as those in the top half of the income distribution.

The United States and South Africa are the only two countries in the industrialized world that fail to provide medical insurance for all their citizens. Universal coverage, of course, reduces inequality in standards of living. The system in place in the United States is more capricious and less equalizing. Americans who work for employers offering medical insurance, or who are over sixty-five, or who are so poor that they receive welfare all have subsidized access to health care. But those Americans who work for employers who do not provide health insurance, most of whom are younger, poorer, and darker skinned, receive inadequate health care and often are in worse health as a result.

Subsidizing Families

Family policy is another realm in which social policy quietly supports middle-class and wealthy Americans while providing limited benefits to poor Americans. The primary way the United States has supported families is through *tax deductions* for children. Through 1995 the deduction amounted to about $2,400 for each dependent child, which was worth about $750 in a tax refund per child for affluent families who were in the 31 percent income tax

---

19 U. S. Bureau of the Census, *Population Profile,* p. 37.
20 Wolfe, "Reform of Health Care," p. 255.

21 Ibid., p. 265.

bracket. It was worth less to families in lower brackets, and the deductions were worth nothing to families that are too poor to pay income taxes.[22] (The child tax credit passed by the 1995–96 Congress is less skewed toward the wealthy because it is worth the same to all taxpayers. But it still amounts to nothing for families too poor to pay taxes.) The earned income tax credit discussed earlier redresses this imbalance only partly.

In other advanced countries, flat cash allowances are paid instead. Rich and poor families receive the same amount per child. Of course, those amounts make a greater difference in the lives of poorer families.

In the United States, even child-care support flows disproportionately to the affluent, in the form of the dependent care tax credit. This tax credit, as of 1995, allows families to use pretax money for child care, up to a tax savings of $1,440. As with other tax-based federal subsidies, those who earn so little that they pay little or no income taxes receive no benefit. In 1994 "Depcare" cost about $2.8 billion in forgone taxes, close to the $3.3 billion budgeted for Head Start, the school-preparation program targeted to poor children.[23]

As with homeownership and health care, American policy for children narrows economic inequality in America, especially between the middle class and the wealthy. This confirms that inequality is within our control. However, with children, health care, and homeownership, American policy remains consid-

erably less equalizing than policies elsewhere in the developed world. Many American policies, in fact, subsidize the affluent instead of those with lower incomes. Most of these subsidies for the middle class and higher are nearly invisible, while those to the poor bear the flashing neon light, "WELFARE."

INVISIBLE POLICIES II: SUBSIDIZING THE WEALTHY

Another set of subsidies also often goes unremarked: those that directly or indirectly help the very wealthy. While policies that help the middle class reduce inequality between them and the rich, these subsidies clearly increase inequality altogether by elevating the rich above everyone else.

Corporate Welfare

American public policy promotes inequality through tax breaks and subsidies for corporations. While newspapers report sensational details like $2.9 million to help the Pillsbury Corporation advertise abroad and $263,000 for a Smokey Robinson concert given by Martin Marietta at taxpayers' expense,[24] direct subsidies and tax breaks to corporations take such myriad forms that it is hard to measure their full extent. Perhaps the best-known subsidies are those to farmers. These are programs that support the prices of basic commodities, pay farmers not to plant some of their acreage, or subsidize the price of farm products exported abroad. While

---

22 Garfinkel and McLanahan, "Single-Mother Families, Economic Insecurity, and Government Policy," p. 210.

23 U.S. Bureau of the Census, *Statistical Abstract 1995,* tables 523 and 524.

24 "Right, Left Call for Cuts to Corporate 'Aid,'" *San Francisco Chronicle,* March 7, 1995; "A Hard Look at Corporate 'Welfare,'" *New York Times,* March 7, 1995, p. C1.

the programs were designed originally to help low- and moderate-income family farmers, large-scale farmers and agribusiness are the big winners. The Progressive Policy Institute, in a report joined by the libertarian Cato Institute and the conservative Heritage Foundation, estimated that cutting, not eliminating, such agricultural subsidies would save $31 billion over five years.[25] A second major set of subsidies goes to energy producers and other natural resource firms. Federally owned hydroelectric plants sell electricity to utilities at below-market rates; the Forest Service builds roads into national forests for the timber industry; and the federal government finances research for the nuclear and fossil fuels industries that these industries could pay for themselves.[26]

Overall, the Cato Institute estimates that "at least 125 separate programs providing subsidies to particular industries and firms" cost taxpayers some $85 billion per year.[27] Analysts recognize the need for vital national investments—building highways and bridges, constructing irrigation systems that aid agribusiness, supporting research and development in start-up industries, funding mass transit. But they argue that most existing subsidies soak up resources that would otherwise go to productive investment, public or private. Current federal subsidies to industry are mostly historical legacies of no-longer-pressing problems (like the subsidies to miners and cattle ranchers meant to encourage settling the West) or are responses to lobbying by powerful interest groups.

The federal government *indirectly* subsidizes many industries by providing free regulatory services that are crucial to doing business. The Federal Aviation Administration provides such vital functions as the system of air traffic control to airlines as a free good. It is a subsidy to their business operations (and indirectly to airplane travelers). Coast Guard rescue and enforcement activities subsidize commercial boat companies and pleasure boat operators. The Securities and Exchange Commission's fees charged to financial firms do not cover the full costs of registering and monitoring securities transactions. Businesses using inland waterways do not pay what it costs the federal government to maintain and operate them.[28]

Industry subsidies also operate indirectly through special exemptions and deductions written into tax codes. The best known is the oil depletion allowance, which allows oil and natural gas companies to deduct a percentage of their gross income for tax purposes. (Unlike other industries, oil, gas, and mineral firms are also allowed to deduct fully some of their capital costs, rather than depreciating them over the life of the investment.) It is estimated that reforms to eliminate these and many other tax breaks for oil, gas, and mineral producers, the financial industry, the construction industry, agribusiness, the timber industry, and many others would save another $101.8 billion over five years.[29]

In even less obvious ways, the federal government supports the infrastructure that main-

---

25 Shapiro, *Cut-and-Invest*, pp. 17–18.

26 Ibid., pp. 19–20.

27 Moore and Stansel, "Ending Corporate Welfare as We Know It."

28 Shapiro, *Cut-and-Invest*, pp. 20–21.

29 Ibid., pp. 22–24.

tains the livelihoods of the wealthy—from maintaining the regulatory apparatus that keeps the stock market functioning smoothly to the enormous costs of the savings and loan bail-out. One might argue that these expenditures are good for the economy as a whole and ultimately good for everyone. That may well be so, but they do redistribute wealth upward. In the end, they most benefit the shareholders of the corporations that are subsidized. Since the highest-earning 5 percent of families own over half of American corporate stock but pay less than a third of all the taxes, they are the big winners in this redistribution—by tens of billions of dollars.[30]

Taxes

Recent changes in tax laws are another set of political choices that have helped push inequality in America to a level that leads the West. The great investigator of recent tax reforms and their effects on inequality is not a left-wing radical but Republican commentator Kevin Phillips, concerned that resentment of growing inequality will produce a populist backlash. In a pair of deliberately unsettling books, *The Politics of Rich and Poor,* published in 1990, and *Boiling Point,* published in 1993, Phillips drew a devastating portrait of changes in the fate of the American middle class between the postwar period and the present.

Phillips traces the explosion in income inequality to the decade of the 1980s. Between 1977 and 1990 the average income, in constant dollars, of the bottom tenth of American families fell by 11 percent, while the average income of the top tenth rose 20 percent to $133,200. (See table 1 ★ ★ ★.) Even more dramatically, the income of the top 1 percent of families rose 45 percent to $463,800 by 1990.[31] Most American families fell behind in real income—despite the fact that more and more wives began bringing home a paycheck—while the very wealthy made spectacular gains.

How did this happen? Phillips points to the "soak the middle" effects of the early Reagan administration's tax changes. While the first Reagan-era tax cut of 1981 reduced the average family's federal income taxes by 25 percent over three years and indexed them against inflation, increases in the social security tax and then the 1986 "tax simplification" package increased the tax burden on the middle class, while substantially decreasing taxes on the wealthy.[32] Despite what were hailed as tax cuts, the *effective* federal tax rate (income tax plus FICA) for the median American family increased from 23.7 percent in 1980 to 24.6 percent in 1990. Meanwhile, the effective federal tax rate for the highest-earning 1 percent fell dramatically, from 35.5 percent in 1980 to 26.7 percent in 1989. The 1986 Tax Reform Act saved the family in the $10,000 to $20,000 tax bracket $69 in taxes and saved the family in the million-dollar-plus bracket $281,000. A longer historical view shows an even more dramatic shift: The steeply progressive federal tax system that was in place from World War II until 1970—millionaires in 1960

30 Ibid., pp. 15–16. Shapiro assumes that any job protection for workers in assisted companies is offset by job losses to other companies that must compete with the subsidized firm for workers and investment.

31 Phillips, *Boiling Point,* p. 28.
32 Ibid., pp. 43–44.

TABLE 1 **BETWEEN 1977 AND 1990 THE FAMILY INCOME OF THE BOTTOM 60% OF AMERICAN FAMILIES DECLINED, WHILE THAT OF THE TOP GROUPS INCREASED**

Decile	Average Income Level (1988 dollars)		Percent Change 1977–1990
	1977	1990	
First	$4,277	$3,805	−11.0
Second	8,663	8,251	−4.8
Third	13,510	13,110	−3.7
Fourth	18,980	18,200	−4.1
Fifth	24,520	23,580	−3.8
Sixth	30,430	29,490	−3.1
Seventh	36,880	36,890	0.0
Eighth	44,820	46,280	3.3
Ninth	56,360	59,860	6.2
Tenth	111,100	133,200	19.9
Top 5%	149,500	187,400	25.4
Top 1%	319,100	436,800	45.4

SOURCE: Phillips, "Boiling Point," p. 28. Data from Congressional Budget Office, House Ways and Means Committee, 1992, *Green Book.*

NOTE: Income includes capital gains income.

had an official federal tax rate of more than 85 percent, although many loopholes made that only a nominal rate—became nearly flat in the late 1980s.[33]

Federal tax and spending cuts also had two indirect, unequalizing results. First, cuts in federal spending shifted burdens to state and local governments, whose taxes and user fees increased sharply. The percentage of average families' incomes going for state and local taxes increased from 9 to 10 percent, and the relative burden on poorer families increased even more.[34] Subsequent cuts in local government meant sharp cutbacks in such amenities as library hours, road repair, police patrols, and

primary education; steep increases in user fees for everything from junior college to bus fares and garbage pickup put further stress on the pocketbooks of the middle class and the poor.

Second, the most striking impact of changes in federal tax policy was to increase the *pretax* incomes of the very wealthy. In the early 1980s, the maximum tax rates on income from investments (capital gains and unearned income) dropped sharply. This increased the net value of stocks, bonds, and other financial assets, sparking a boom in the prices of such assets and the income their owners received. This in large measure explains why the richest 1 percent saw a 90 percent growth in their incomes in the

33 Ibid., pp. 110, 113.

34 Ibid., p. 117.

1980s. Between 1978 and 1988 the number of individuals with million–dollar annual incomes soared from 2,041 to 65,303.[35] Millionaires did not multiply overnight because there was a sudden increase in individual talent. Political choices in the 1980s, in large part choices about tax policy, reshaped inequality in America.

★ ★ ★

INVISIBLE POLICIES III: REGULATING THE LABOR MARKET

Thus far, we have seen that how the government collects and spends tax dollars affects inequality in America. But social policy begins shaping inequality long before the tax bills come due and the social security checks are mailed out. The market itself is structured by policy choices, by how we set the "rules of the game." We noted this briefly [elsewhere], pointing to rules such as licensing requirements and laws protecting corporations. Here, we will take a closer look at how ground rules help determine who wins and who loses and how much they win and lose.

Consider, again, the large increase in income inequality that occurred in America in the 1980s. The real losers were less–educated workers. They lost ground not only relative to their college-educated peers, as we have seen, but also compared with their counterparts a decade earlier ★ ★ ★. Market forces alone cannot explain the increase in inequality in the 1980s. If so, one would expect other advanced industrial countries to have experienced similar increases in inequality in the 1980s. They participate in the same world markets, use similar technologies, and have similar types of industries and occupations. Yet these other countries experienced neither the same large increases in wage inequality nor the drops in the real earnings of the less skilled. In Canada, Japan, and Sweden wage inequality grew, but much more modestly than it did in the United States. In France and Italy, inequality changed hardly at all.[36] (Only in Great Britain did the gap between professionals and blue-collar workers increase as much as it did in the United States, and there only because of gains at the top; the pay for people with low wages rose in Great Britain, just not as quickly.) Low-wage workers in the United States now earn only about half as much relative to American high-wage workers as low-wage workers in Europe earn relative to high-wage ones there.

Why did other advanced industrial countries experience less wage inequality in the 1980s than the United States did? Because, in large part, they made different policy choices. In particular, other advanced countries have different rules about unionization and have different wage-setting institutions.

★ ★ ★

Union Rules

Economists Richard Freeman of Harvard and David Card of Princeton estimate that the sharp decline in the percentage of unionized workers in the 1980s explains at least one-fifth of the growth in wage differentials among male workers in the United States. This is because unions reduce the pay gap between higher- and lower-ranking workers. In the United States

35 Ibid., p. 112.

36 Freeman and Katz, "Rising Wage Inequality," pp. 36–43.

in the 1980s, there were simply too few union members to offset growing inequality. Between 1970 and 1990 the proportion of the labor force that was unionized dropped more than 45 percent to only 11 percent of the private sector, virtually the lowest unionization rate in the industrialized world.

Unionization, in turn, has declined so precipitously in the United States largely because of the unusually hostile political and legal environment here. Especially instructive is the comparison with Canada, because Canada and the United States share similar cultures, economic institutions, and standards of living. In the 1940s Canadians revised their labor laws to resemble the United States' 1935 Wagner Act, which established legal procedures for labor organization and collective bargaining here. Since then, however, Canadian labor laws have become more favorable to unions while American labor laws have become less favorable. Under current Canadian law, a union is established once a majority of workers sign a card indicating their support. Under current American law, after a majority of workers have signed such cards, unions must still go through a long election campaign, often facing management consultants hired by employers to convince workers that they do not want a union after all. Also, it is illegal in Canada for employers to replace strikers permanently, but it is permissible to do so in the United States. This was brought to the consciousness of many Americans during the baseball strike that ran from August 1994, to March 1995. The Canadian government forbade foreign replacement workers, and Ontario provincial law prohibited hiring any replacements at all. The Toronto Blue Jays were forced to schedule their possible 1995 "replacement baseball" season in Florida.

In the 1950s and 1960s, when labor laws and practices were most similar in the two countries, unionization rates were also similar, but since then unionization rates have risen in Canada and dropped sharply in the United States. By the early 1990s the percentage unionized in the private sector in Canada was almost three times larger than in the United States. Partly because of these differences in unionization rates, wage inequality grew much less in Canada than in the United States in the 1980s.

Unions and Plant Relocation

In the 1980s some major American companies busted their unions in celebrated cases (after President Reagan had defeated the air traffic controllers' union). More often, however, employers escaped union pressure by moving from one state to another or out of the United States altogether. The scale of movement during the decade of the 1980s alone is staggering. University of North Carolina sociologist John Kasarda estimated that the northern and midwestern states lost 1.5 million manufacturing jobs and $40 billion in pay between 1980 and 1990. One-third of the jobs ended up in southern and western states; some of the rest moved overseas; some were lost to automation; and some were simply lost as firms stopped producing goods.

The competition among localities for jobs-on-the-move is intense. (The struggle to land sports franchises is a vivid illustration.) The competition among cities and states for firms usually turns on tax concessions, capital commitments, and promises to regulate union activity. But the costs to the victors are significant. They do not necessarily increase their tax bases, because the bidding frequently requires giving away tax revenues; also, local taxpayers often contribute to firms' relocation costs. National policy allows states to differ greatly in laws protecting labor and thus to compete on the basis of who has the weakest ones, thus encouraging the shift of jobs to weakly unionized—and lower-paying—states.

Wage Setting

In the United States, workers' wages are negotiated either by an individual employee with his or her employer or by a local union with a specific employer. In many jobs, the employer simply offers the job at a preset wage; little or no negotiation is involved. This is an extremely decentralized system, and one result is that differences in the wages of similar workers tend to be high. The variation in wages for workers of the same age, education, gender, and occupation is much greater in the United States than it is in countries with more centralized wage-setting systems.[37] That means greater earnings inequality here.

In countries like Norway and Austria, national employer associations, made up of employers in different industries, bargain with representatives of all the national unions to determine wage levels for workers in each sector of the economy. Local employers and unions are then allowed to increase (but not decrease) wages above the national level if they agree to. In countries like France and Germany, bar-

gaining goes on between unions and employers' associations in each industry or region; the government then routinely extends these collective agreements to nonunion workers and firms in the relevant industry or region. These kinds of centralized arrangements diminish the amount of wage inequality. They do so by setting a wage floor for those at the bottom of the pay scale and a wage ceiling for those at the top of the wage scale, particularly executives.

Centralized wage setting practices are one reason why the disparity between what a typical European CEO makes and what an average European worker makes is so much less than the difference between what a typical American CEO reaps and what an average American worker earns. While top American managers might claim that their enormous compensation packages are justified by their productivity, researchers have found only a weak relation between executive compensation and productivity.[38] And, Western Europe's economic growth outpaced ours between 1970 and 1990.[39]

One way to think about the policy choices different countries have made in the face of economic pressures during recent years is this: The Europeans have generally chosen to keep workers' real wages up, even if that means a slightly higher level of unemployment (because employers will hire fewer workers at those wages). Part of that decision is a commitment to sustain the basic living standards of the long-term unemployed through government transfers and services. The United States

---

37 Freeman, "How Labor Fares in Advanced Economies."
38 Crystal, *In Search of Excess.*

39 U.S. Bureau of Census, *Statistical Abstract 1994,* table 1370.

has decided—by default—to allow real wages to drop, so that slightly more people are working but in lower-paying, less-secure, and often benefit-shorn jobs. Since no provision has been made to assist the workers in these poorer jobs, income inequality has widened more in the United States.

Both unionization rules and wage-setting practices are the result of policy choices. And these policy choices have profound effects on the amount of inequality we see in American society today. Recent statistics show that before 1974 American workers' increases in productivity were rewarded by increased wages. Since 1974, this has no longer been true. Productivity in both manufacturing and services increased by over 50 percent since then, but wages in both sectors have been essentially flat. The last twenty years' gain in productivity instead fueled gains in executive compensation and in stock prices. American workers received no greater slice of the growing pie because they had no place at the table.[40]

PUBLIC INVESTMENTS: THE CASE OF HIGHER EDUCATION

Public investment decisions also shape inequality. Some investments, like clean water or public parks, improve everyone's quality of life up and down the income ladder. Other investments benefit some of us more than others. Roads that go from suburbs to downtown business areas of our large cities, for example, tend to advantage middle- and upper-class commuters more than they do central-city residents. One of the most important public investments that affects all of us, but in different ways, is public higher education.

In a crucial but not too visible manner, Americans a generation ago made a choice that moved the United States toward greater equality. From the 1950s to the 1970s, America invested enormously in higher education. In 1945 there were enough slots in postsecondary education for only one of five Americans aged eighteen to twenty-two. By 1992 the number had grown to about *four* for every five. The expansion is especially impressive because it happened while baby-boomers were entering their college years. Higher education expanded enough to serve an ever greater proportion of a growing population of young people.[41]

Expansion was achieved through a generous commitment of *public* resources. Indeed, private college and university enrollments grew only slightly faster than the eligible population, while enrollments in public colleges and universities soared. States like California and New York built elaborate systems of higher education: junior colleges, state colleges, and university campuses in California, and campus after campus of the State University of New York. Other public universities increased greatly in size—the University of Michigan from 20,000 to 45,000; Ohio State from 15,000 in 1955 to 62,000 in 1975. These political choices, made largely at state and local levels, expressed Americans' optimism and belief in opportunity, the aspirations of states and cities for prestige and

40 U.S. Bureau of Labor Statistics, "New Productivity Data," tables 3–6.

41 Hout, "The Politics of Mobility," p. 10.

economic expansion, and parents' desires to assure their children's futures.

Those who believed in the link between higher education and the expansion of opportunity were right. For those fortunate enough to earn one, a four-year-college degree levels out family advantages and disadvantages in a way that increases equal access to good jobs. Among college graduates, there is *no* connection between the occupational status of their parents and their own. Children of the working class are as likely to land prestigious jobs as are children of the middle class once they have a diploma.[42] So when higher education expanded from 1960 to 1980, the intergenerational inheritance of socioeconomic status dropped dramatically. How much a father's place on the economic ladder determined what his son's or daughter's place would be was cut by half, nearly all of this decline attributable to the rise in the proportion of the workforce with college degrees.[43] (The weakening of the connection between parents' and children's statuses directly contradicts Herrnstein and Murray's argument that a genetically based intelligence is becoming more important in the modern economy. If they were right, the correlation between parents' and children's statuses should have grown stronger during those years. There are signs, however, that, with increasing tuitions and stagnating investments in higher education, the pattern of expanding opportunity is beginning to reverse.)

Expansion of higher education increased equality of *opportunity* by weakening the connection between parental and child status. But overall equality of *income* depends on whether expansion of higher education keeps pace with the economy's demand for educated workers. The great development of colleges in the 1950s and 1960s increased the supply of educated workers, reducing each graduate's claim on high wages. The number of managerial and professional jobs available fell from 2.2 for each college diploma-holder in 1952 to 1.6 in the mid-1970s.[44] Better-educated workers could still bump less-educated workers from jobs farther down the ladder, but overall income equality increased.

After the mid-1970s, however, the supply of educated workers that colleges provided rose more slowly than the demand for them. Thus, as we first pointed out in chapter 5, the wages of college graduates rose relative to those of nongraduates. And inequality of income between those who had and those who had not graduated college increased again. Today, those who do not graduate from college—and even more so, those who have a high school education or less—face bleak prospects. The earnings of college graduates are rising at a time when the earnings of high school graduates who did not attend college are falling.[45] Between 1979 and 1989 the ratio of earnings for college graduates to earnings for high school graduates who did not go to college (the "B.A. premium")

---

42 Hout, "Expanding Universalism, Less Structural Mobility."

43 Mare, "Changes in Educational Attainment and School Enrollment"; Hout et al., "Making the Grade"; Hout, "Expanding Universalism, Less Structural Mobility."

44 Levy, *Dollars and Dreams,* p. 123.

45 Levy, "Incomes and Income Inequality."

rose from 1.45 to 1.65. Growth in high-tech manufacturing, health services, legal services, and the like increased the demand for college graduates. Meanwhile the decline of traditional manufacturing, bookkeeping, and commerce reduced the demand for workers with a high school education. These shifts in the kinds of jobs available in the United States economy do not account for all of the increase in earnings inequality in the 1980s, but they do account for the increased B.A. premium.[46] It is a trend, we emphasize, that reversed an earlier one and that reflects not just the market demand for workers, but also the supply provided by our decisions about investing in higher education.

In addition, American policy regarding postsecondary education is distinctive. Most of our trading partners provide students who do not go to college with more vocational training than we do. Successful systems link schools and firms. Firms can explain their labor needs to schools, and schools can draw on firms for technology and job placement.[47] The United States has given little systematic attention to vocational education, although recent research shows that vocational programs tailored to the labor market notably increase workers' earnings.[48]

Overall, then, America's investment decisions about education have had important—if complicated—effects on inequality. The expansion of higher education after World War II reduced inequality, both because it gave more youngsters who were less affluent the opportunity to attain high-paying jobs and because

the growth of the supply of educated workers tended to reduce the B.A. premium. Retreats since those days have increased inequality. At the same time, the failure of the United States to invest as generously in vocational training (or in primary and secondary education) has increased inequality here relative to other advanced countries where public investment in these kinds of education has been greater.

CONCLUSION: THE "FREE" MARKET AND SOCIAL POLICY

Influential commentator George Will, responding to headlines about growing inequality in America, voiced what many Americans believe: Inequality is not bad if it results from a free and fair market.

> A society that values individualism, enterprise and a market economy is neither surprised nor scandalized when the unequal distribution of marketable skills produces large disparities in the distribution of wealth. This does not mean that social justice must be defined as whatever distribution of wealth the market produces. But it does mean that there is a presumption in favor of respecting the market's version of distributive justice. Certainly there is today no prima facie case against the moral acceptability of increasingly large disparities of wealth.[49]

However, "the market's version of distributive justice" results not from a natural market

---

46 Ibid.
47 Müller and Karle, "Social Selection in Educational Systems in Europe."

48 Arum and Shavit, "Secondary Vocational Education."
49 Will, "What's Behind Income Disparity."

but from complex political choices, many of them hidden. Some policies determine how unequal the starting points are of those who enter the market's competition; other policies determine how the market selects winners and losers. For example, African Americans in the 1950s were prevented by private discrimination and explicit government policy from purchasing homes and thereby lost out on subsidized loans and mortgage deductions. They were also unable to leave substantial assets to their children. As another example, think of the businesses in industries that receive subsidies. The market is not a neutral game that distributes just rewards to the worthy; it is a politically constructed institution with built-in biases.

As we have shown here, the enormous prosperity and rising equality of post–World War II America resulted in part from many government policies, some legacies of the New Deal, policies that provided old-age security, encouraged homeownership, gave labor increased bargaining power, built massive physical infrastructure, and financed an enormous expansion of public education. Since the late 1970s, however, public investment of these sorts has slowed and sometimes actually reversed. At the same time, inequality has dramatically increased.

The kinds of inequalities we see reemerging in America are neither natural nor inevitable, nor do they reflect the distribution of individual talents. Through our politics, Americans have chosen to increase equality of opportunity (expanding higher education, for example) or equality of result (subsidies for homeownership, Medicaid, and Medicare, for instance), but to do so to a far more limited extent than citizens in other nations have chosen. We extend support to fewer of our citizens, largely the elderly and the middle class; and we extend less support. For example, we provide medical insurance for some residents; most nations provide medical care for all. We provide a tax deduction for children of taxpayers; most nations provide family allowances. Americans have also made choices that increased inequality, such as the tax changes of the 1980s and the rules on unionization we have accepted. We have structured many programs to help the well-off more than the less well-off, such as the subsidies for homeownership and medical insurance.

What all this implies is that the inequality we see today in America is in great measure a result of policy decisions Americans have made—or chosen not to make. Generally, we have chosen to do far less to equalize life conditions than have other Western people. We have chosen to reduce the inequality between the middle class and the upper class somewhat, but to do far less to reduce the gap between the lower class and other Americans—with the notable exception of older people. And in the last couple of decades, our choices have moved us farther from equality. Some criticize these choices; others, like George Will, may applaud them. Either way, Americans constructed the inequality we have.

‖ REFERENCES

Abrams, Charles. 1966. "The Housing Problem and the Negro." *Daedalus* 95:64–76.

Arum, Richard, and Yossi Shavit. 1995. "Secondary Vocational Education and the Transition from School to Work." *Sociology of Education* 68:187–204.

Burtless, Gary. 1994. "Public Spending on the Poor: Historical Trends and Economic Limits," pp. 51–84 in Sheldon H. Danziger, Gary D. Sandefur, and Daniel H. Weinberg (eds.), *Confronting Poverty: Prescriptions for Change.* Cambridge: Harvard University Press.

Coontz, Stephanie. 1992. *The Way We Never Were: American Families and the Nostalgia Trap.* New York: Basic Books.

Crystal, Graef A. 1991. *In Search of Excess: The Overcompensation of American Executives.* New York: W. W. Norton.

Dreier, Peter, and John Atlas. 1995. "Housing Policy's Moment of Truth." *The American Prospect* 22 (Summer): 68–77.

Duster, Troy. 1995. "The Advantages of White Males." *San Francisco Chronicle,* January 19.

Freeman, Richard B. 1994. "How Labor Fares in Advanced Economies," pp. 1–28 in Richard Freeman (ed.), *Working under Different Rules.* New York: Russell Sage Foundation.

Freeman, Richard B., and Lawrence F. Katz. 1994. "Rising Wage Inequality: The United States vs. Other Advanced Countries," pp. 29–62 in Richard Freeman (ed.), *Working under Different Rules.* New York: Russell Sage.

Garfinkel, Irwin, and Sara McLanahan. 1994. "Single-Mother Families, Economic Insecurity, and Government Policy," pp. 205–25 in Sheldon H. Danziger, Gary D. Sandefur, and Daniel H. Weinberg (eds.), *Confronting Poverty: Prescrip-*

tions for Change. Cambridge: Harvard University Press.

Grigsby, Williams G. 1990. "Housing Finance and Subsidies in the United States," *Urban Studies* 27:831–45.

Headey, Bruce. 1987. *Housing Policy in the Developed Economy: The United Kingdom, Sweden, and the United States.* New York: St. Martin's Press.

Heisler, Barbara Schmitter. 1990. "Housing Policy and the Underclass: The United Kingdom, Germany, and the Netherlands." *Journal of Urban Affairs* 16 (3): 203–20.

Hout, Michael. 1988. "Expanding Universalism, Less Structural Mobility: The American Occupational Structure in the 1980s." *American Journal of Sociology* 93 (May): 1358–1400.

———. 1995. "The Politics of Mobility," pp. 301–25 in Alan C. Kerckhoff (ed.), *Generations and the Lifecourse.* Boulder: Westview Press.

Hout, Michael, Adrian E. Raftery, and Eleanor O. Bell. 1993. "Making the Grade: Educational Stratification in the United States, 1925–1989," pp. 25–50 in Yossi Shavit and Hans Peter Blossfeld (eds.), *Persistent Inequality: Changing Educational Attainment in 13 Countries.* Boulder: Westview Press.

Jackson, Kenneth. 1980. "Race, Ethnicity, and Real Estate Appraisal: The Home Owner's Loan Corporation and the Federal Housing Administration," *Journal of Urban History* 6:419–52.

Jackson, Kenneth. 1985. *The Crabgrass Frontier: The Suburbanization of the United States.* New York: Oxford University Press.

Levy, Frank. 1987. *Dollars and Dreams: The Changing American Income Distribution.* New York: Russell Sage Foundation.

Mare, Robert D. 1995. "Changes in Educational Attainment and School Enrollment," pp. 155–213 in Reynolds Farley (ed.), *State of the Nation: America in the 1990s,* vol. 1. New York: Russell Sage Foundation.

Mayer, Susan, and Christopher Jencks. 1995. "War on Poverty: No Apologies, Please." *New York Times,* November 9.

Moore, Steven, and Dean Stansel. 1995. "Ending Corporate Welfare as We Know It," Cato Institute, draft report, March 6.

Müller, Walter, and Wolfgang Karle. 1993. "Social Selection in Educational Systems in Europe." *European Sociological Review* 9:1–23.

Novack, Janet. 1994. "The Worm in the Apple." *Forbes,* November 7: 96ff.

Oliver, Melvin L., and Thomas M. Shapiro. 1995. *Black Wealth/White Wealth: A New Perspective on Racial Inequality.* New York: Routledge.

Peterson, Jonathan. 1995. "GOP Seeking to Curb Tax Break for Poor." *Los Angeles Times,* May 13: A1.

Phillips, Kevin. 1994. *Boiling Point: Democrats, Republicans and the Decline of Middle-Class Prosperity.* New York: Harper Collins.

Quadagno, Jill. 1994. *The Color of Welfare: How Racism Undermined the War on Poverty.* New York: Oxford University Press.

Shapiro, Robert J. 1995. *Cut-and-Invest: A Budget Strategy for the New Economy.* Progressive Policy Institute, Policy Report no. 23, March.

Smeeding, Timothy M. 1992. "Why the U.S. Antipoverty System Doesn't Work Very Well," *Challenge* 35 (January): 30–36.

U.S. Bureau of Labor Statistics. 1996. "New Productivity Data: 1949–1994." BLS home page: www.bls.gov/data.

U.S. Bureau of the Census. 1993. "Measuring the Effect of Benefits and Taxes on Income and Poverty: 1992." Current Population Reports, series P-60–186RD. Washington, D.C.: USGPO.

———. 1995. *Population Profile of the United States: 1995.* Current Population Reports, series P23–189. Washington: USGPO.

———. 1995. *Statistical Abstract of the United States 1995.* Washington, D.C.: USGPO.

Will, George. 1995. "What's Behind Income Disparity." *San Francisco Chronicle,* April 24: A15.

Wolfe, Barbara L. 1994. "Reform of Health Care for the Nonelderly Poor," pp. 253–88 in Sheldon H. Danziger, Gary D. Sandefur, and Daniel H. Weinberg (eds.), *Confronting Poverty: Prescriptions for Change.* Cambridge: Harvard University Press.

49

Power*

G. WILLIAM DOMHOFF

Power structure research, the study of the way in which power is organized and distributed in any human society, emerged suddenly in the 1950s in the work of sociologists Floyd Hunter (1953), who showed how business elites dominated the city of Atlanta, and C. Wright Mills (1956), who argued that a triumvirate of corporate executives, appointees to the executive branch of the federal government, and top military brass dominated the United States, with little or no influence from political parties, voluntary groups, or public opinion. Their claims were immediately rejected by the mainstream social science theorists of their day, who saw the United States as a country with dispersed inequalities that is run by shifting coalitions of interest groups, with ample room for public opinion to have an impact through political parties and lobbying efforts. They were also criticized by the Marxists, the main opponents of the mainstreamers, who believe that power structures always revolve around an unending class struggle between owners and non-owners, with everything else as a sideshow.

---

* Original essay prepared for this volume.

The challenges by these rival theorist groups were understandable because power structure research differs fundamentally from mainstream social science and Marxism. It assumes that power is rooted first and foremost in a few essential organizations found in all societies. These organizations, which are discussed in the next section, are top-down power structures in and of themselves that can only be challenged when the overwhelming majority who are outside the power structure are able to organize themselves sufficiently to take advantage of the cracks and openings that exist in most power structures. This emphasis on organizations as the starting point for a general theory of power can encompass every form of society from hunting and gathering societies to large-scale societies such as the United States. But what do we mean by power, and how is it organized?

POWER: A DEFINITION AND BRIEF HISTORY

Power is the ability to achieve desired social outcomes. It has two intertwined dimensions. First, power is the overall capacity of a group, class, or nation to be effective and productive. Here the stress is on power as the degree to which a "collectivity" has the technological resources, organizational forms, and social morale to achieve its general goals. In that sense, most nations have become more powerful in recent decades than they were in the past. Second, power is also the ability of a group, class, or nation to be successful in conflicts with other groups, classes, or nations on issues of concern to it. Here the stress is on "power over," which is also called "distributive power."

Definitions aside, both collective and distributive power have the same organizational base. Organizations at their most basic are simply sets of rules and roles developed so a human group can accomplish a particular purpose. Put even more simply, they are ways in which people do something together in a routine fashion. Religious ceremonies, for example, are routines that become the basis for the institutions called churches. The established routines for face-to-face economic exchanges—my sandwich for your jelly beans--become one basis for the more complex economic system of markets. Since human beings have a vast array of "purposes," they have formed an appropriately large number of organizations. But only four of these purposes and organizations weigh heavily in terms of generating societal power: economic organizations, political organizations, military organizations, and religious organizations. All of them enhance the collective power of their members, but at the same time they can quickly become very hierarchical when they begin to grow larger or face an outside threat.

The early outlines of these four main bases of power can already be seen in small hunting and gathering societies when hunting parties are organized (economic organization, with meat shared equally among all members of the society), when communal gatherings are called in an attempt to defuse interpersonal disputes that threaten to rip apart the whole group (political organization, which is fundamentally about regulating human interactions within a specific territory), when the men band together to do battle with rival groups or clans (military organization), and when rituals of religious solidarity are performed to deal with the anxiety, guilt, and fear of death that have been part of daily existence for most people since the dawn of humanity (religious organization). The claim that these four main forms of collective power can become the basis for distributive power is supported by the fact that even in small-scale societies men use them to exclude or subjugate women. The secretive men's huts in which religion is practiced often exclude women on pain of gang rape or death, and men will band together to kill women who resist changes in the social order (Gregor 1985; Sanday 1990). Generally speaking, women have had little or no power in most societies until the last 200 years in Western Europe and North America, which is a commentary on the pervasiveness of power structures in and of itself.

Generally speaking, however, these nascent and temporary forms of organization do not become the basis for distributive power in hunting and gathering or tribal-level societies. Collective power is still ascendant because the "rank-and-file" members of those societies are able to be surprisingly and subtly vigilant against would-be power-seekers, who are controlled through gossip, chastisement, shunning, and if necessary, assassination. Contrary to the image of these societies as lacking a power structure, an image that is embodied in the Christian idea of the Garden of Eden and the Marxist idea of primitive communism, it seems more plausible that they have an "inverted power structure" in which people are able to maintain an egalitarian social structure through the kinds of collective actions against potential organizationally based dominators that are spelled out in the previous sentence (Boehm 1999).

However, when the level of organization reaches a large enough scale over a long enough period of time within the context of accumulating material abundance, a permanent division of labor develops that can further increase an organization's collective power due to a specialization of function at all of its levels. Since this division of labor makes sense in terms of collective power, it clearly increases the ability of a society to grow larger and defend itself when necessary, but it also contains the potential for a more hierarchical distribution of power because "those who occupy supervisory and coordinating positions have an immense organizational superiority over the others" (Mann 1986b, pp. 6–7). As many theorists of varying persuasions have noted, those at the top can then turn the organization into a power base for themselves due to the information and material resources they control, their ability to reshape the structure of the organization, their power to hire and fire underlings, and their opportunities to make alliances with other organizational leaders. These alliances then generate a power structure that uses its combined organizational resources to develop barriers that make it harder for people outside or on the bottom of these organizations to participate in the governance of the society in general (see Gaventa 1980, for an excellent synthesis of how these various processes are carried out in the United States).

At this point ordinary members of the society are organizationally outflanked, no longer able to maintain the more informal inverted power structures that kept pre-civilized societies largely egalitarian (Boehm 1999). They become trapped in the form of society called "civilization" by means of a gradual process that can be seen at about its midpoint through the ways in which chiefs come to political power in many large tribal societies by using a variety of strategies to create chiefdoms that weave together the growing economic, military, and religious power bases in unique ways (Earle 1997). Indeed, sociologists sometimes use the image of a "caged" population as part of their definition of civilization, which starts with a network of economic activities that generate large surpluses that are coordinated and stored in religious institutions (Mann 1986b; Weber 1904/1958, p. 181). These religious centers soon evolve into city-states that have somewhat separate religious and "state" institutions—and then into empires of domination that have large armies. Once these power bases are intertwined, they have even more potential to greatly increase collective power. This is most directly observed in the case of state and military organizations, which can increase the collective power of economic organizations through activities as varied as protecting trade routes and making it possible to employ coerced or slave labor. At the same time, the mobilization of greater collective power comes to depend on the resolution of prior questions about distributive power arrangements. Who has power over whom has to be settled within organizations, cities, or nation-states before collective power can be exercised in any useful way, as the collapse of ruling classes, armies, and states over the centuries amply demonstrates.

Furthermore, as the brief consideration of hunting and gathering societies showed, no one network comes first or is somehow more "basic" than the others. That is, each one always has presupposed the existence of the others from the beginning of human history. However, that does not mean that the networks are of necessity equal in their importance. To add further complexity, one kind of organizational power can be turned into any one of the others. Economic power can be turned into political power. Religious power can generate military power. Military power can conquer political power. In that sense, power is like the idea of "energy" in the natural sciences: it cannot be reduced to one primary form. This complexity is one of the main reasons why it is necessary to do power structure studies. Generalizations from society to society or historical epoch to historical epoch are risky if not impossible.

Finally, no firm generalizations can be made about how the development of the two types of power, collective and distributive, affects the importance of one or the other. Although collective and distributive power usually increased hand-in-hand in the first several thousand years of Western civilization, this is not always the case. For example, the economic transformations of the eighteenth and nineteenth centuries had a large impact on collective economic power, but none on distributive power, whereas the increased collective power of governments during the same time period actually helped to decrease the distributive power of political elites. More generally, Mann (1993, p. 16) finds a "surprising continuity of distributive power" in Western Europe and the United States between 1760 and 1914 despite the vast increases in collective power, except that women began to gain power in relation to men (Mann 1986a).

ANALYZING POWER STRUCTURES

Power structure research is based on a combination of network analysis—more specifically, "membership network analysis"—and content analysis, and it makes use of four power indicators: (1) what organization, group, or class in the social structure under study receives the most of what people seek for and value (who benefits?); (2) what organization, group, or class is over-represented in key decision-making positions (who sits in the seats of government power?); (3) what organization, group, or class wins in the decisional arena? (who wins?); and (4) who is thought to be powerful on the basis of interviews with knowledgeable observers and peers (who has a reputation for power?). A "power structure" is then defined as the network of people and institutions that stands at the top in any given city or nation on the combination of power indicators it has been possible to utilize. This straightforward methodology makes it possible for power structure researchers to uncover any concentration or configuration of power. It can find that power is highly concentrated or more dispersed, depending on the degree of difference between rival organizations, groups, or classes on the power indicators. It can show that some organizations, groups, or classes have power in one arena, some in another arena. It can reveal changes in a power structure over time by changes in the power indicators.

Once the power networks have been mapped, the substance of the policies and ideologies preferred by leaders and factions within the power structure can be determined through content analyses of the verbal and written "output" of strategically located people or organizations in the network, that is, through the examination of speeches, policy statements, campaign literature, and proposed legislation. Content analyses are not always done formally, but content analysis is what investigators are doing, even if they are high-level post-modern theorists who "interrogate" texts, when they infer on the basis of a speech, policy statement, or abstract theoretical document that a person or organization has specific values or policy preferences (see Domhoff 2006, Appendix A, for a detailed statement of the methodology of power structure research).

After a brief look at American history, we will see what this methodology has produced for the contemporary United States.

THE AMERICAN POWER STRUCTURE: PAST, PRESENT, AND FUTURE

Several familiar and taken-for-granted aspects of American history are basic starting points in understand the country's current power structure. First, America did not have a feudal past, so its capitalists were not hindered by a rival economic class of landed aristocrats that had to be battled, assimilated, or deferred to in attempting to dominate government. Conversely, the absence of such a rival economic elite meant that government officials could not play off one strong economic class against another in an attempt to gain autonomy from the economic elites. Second, there is no institutionalized church that can compete with economic elites. The historical role of the fragmented religious network churches also has been limited through the separation of church and state by the Founding Fathers, reflecting both the weak nature of the church network at the time and the Founders' own secular tendencies. True, churches have influence on some political issues, and can impact political parties, but they never have been strong enough to be anything but a minor factor in the overall power structure.

Third, the United States does not have a strong centralized state for a variety of historical reasons that are very familiar. The pre-revolutionary history of the United States as a set of separate colonial territories led to a federal form of government with many government functions located at the state as compared to the national level. The state level in turn ceded some of its power to the city level, where landed elites—"place entrepreneurs"—have been able to form growth coalitions that persuade local governments to protect and enhance their interest in intensifying land use (Logan and Molotch 2007; Molotch 1976; Molotch 1979).

The rivalries among the economic elites of the various states within the new United States were a second major factor in keeping the American national government limited in its scope until at least the 1930s. The Founding Fathers created a system of checks and balances at the national level that has made the powerful legislative branch of the American government very accessible to elite economic groups. In particular, the plantation capitalists of the South worked very hard to keep the federal government small out of concern that it might challenge their enslavement of their African-American workforce until 1860 and their dominance of that workforce through complete segregation and random violence from 1878 to 1964. The small size of the nineteenth-century American state meant there were powerful corporations before there was a large national government, another contrast of major importance in comparison with the stronger central governments found in many European countries (Mills 1956, p. 272). The corporate elites that arose after the Civil War thus had a big role in shaping new government institutions—it was state-building by the capitalist class, contrary to the mainstream belief that state elites enlarged the American government independently of the economic elite. With the coming of World War II and the Cold War, there was no choice but to expand the state dramatically, but that expansion also was completely controlled by the corporate capitalists (Domhoff 1996, Chapter 6).

Finally, the lack of any dangerous rival states on American borders, along with the protection from European states provided by the British navy throughout most of the 19th century, meant that the capitalist class in the United States did not have to contend with a "permanent military establishment" until World War II (see Mills 1956, Chapter 8, for an excellent historical account). The American government most certainly had an army that played a large role historically in taking territory from Native Americans, Spain, and Mexico, but it was so small after the Civil War that the increasingly ascendant corporations often created their own organizations of violence to break strikes or resist unions, or else hired private specialists in such work. The largest of the private armies in that era, the Pinkerton Detective Agency, "had more men than the U.S. Army" (Mann 1993, p. 646). The military establishment was never big enough for long enough until World War II to be considered a serious contender for power. By that time civilian traditions were long established. Presidents and the corporate leaders appointed to government positions make war in the United States, not the military leaders.

From the Social Upper Class to the Power Elite

The foregoing history of power in the United States suggests what cannot be spelled out in detailed here: rival Northern and Southern economic elites were at the center of most political disputes from 1780 to the Civil War and a national corporate elite dominated the country from the 1770s to 1932. Such are very general and they may not hold any longer. Is it possible to be more specific? This is where power structure research enters into the picture.

We begin with the concept of "class," which has two meanings. First, the term refers to both a specific role and an underlying set of relationships in the economic system. "Owners" of businesses and the "employees" of those businesses are the most obvious examples of economic classes in the nation-states of the Western world, including the United States. Second, class is a social "category" that refers to the people who belong to the same in-group social institutions, develop personal relationships, and share a common lifestyle due to their many common activities. This is what Max Weber ("Class, Status, and Party," in this book) meant by a "status group," but most American social scientists prefer the term "social class." Class as a set of intertwined economic categories is always operating, but the people in any given "economic class" may or many not be part of a "social class." Historically, it is the members

of the ownership class in a society who most frequently organize themselves socially and develop a common class awareness that is an important part of their social identity.

Studies of shared private school experiences, overlapping social club memberships, participation in exclusive retreats, and home ownership in high-status vacation areas established long ago that there is a small nationwide social upper class—less than 1% of the overall population—in the United States (Baltzell 1958; Baltzell 1964; Domhoff 1974; Domhoff 1970). Several of the most revealing of the studies that make this point focus on the social institutions and activities of women of the upper class, who direct many of the nonprofit voluntary and cultural associations that have as one primary goal trying to keep government involvement in American life at a minimum (Daniels 1988; Kendall 2002; Ostrander 1984). Generally speaking, the rituals and retreats of the upper class, including the highly ritualized nature of debutante balls, demonstrate social cohesion and class consciousness through respect for traditions and the insistence upon proper conduct (Ostrander 1980).

Another set of studies looks at the relationships among corporations, as examined most readily and objectively through an analysis of "interlocking" directorships, leading to the conclusion that the largest corporations are closely enough related to be considered a "corporate community" (e.g., Barnes and Ritter 2001; Mizruchi 1982). Common stock ownership by wealthy families, along with shared bankers, accountants, and corporate lawyers, also contribute to this corporate cohesion (Dunn 1980). Still other studies reveal there is an overlap between the directors of the interlocked corporations and membership in the interconnected social institutions that constitute the upper class, which demonstrates that the corporate community and social upper class are by and large two sides of the same coin (Domhoff, 2006, for summaries of this research). In terms of the critical issue of how the social upper class/corporate community is able to organize in order to influence government, the upshot of these studies is that social cohesion facilitates political and policy cohesion when members of the upper class and corporate executives gather in more formal settings; however, it needs to be emphasized that sustained policy discussions rarely if ever happen in social settings.

Building on the studies of the upper class and corporate community, detailed tracings of the linkages among individuals, institutions, financial donations, policy proposals, and the federal government demonstrate that there are four relatively distinct, but overlapping processes through which the corporate community controls the public agenda and then wins on most issues that appear on it. In terms of Weber's definition of a "party," as the means by which a class, status group, or coalition of groups tries to influence communal action in a planned manner, these four networks constitute the "party," that is, the means of wielding power, for the intertwined social upper class and corporate community. In other words, the two major political parties in the United States are a secondary matter; the upper class and corporate community have been able to have influence in both political parties through their own four-network "party." These networks are called the *special-interest process*, the *policy-planning process*, the *opinion-shaping process*, and the *candidate-selection process*.

The special-interest process deals with the narrow and short-run policy concerns of wealthy families, specific corporations, and specific business sectors. It operates primarily through lobbyists, company lawyers, and trade associations, with a focus on congressional committees, departments of the executive branch, and regulatory agencies. This is the process that is usually focused upon by the news media and those who study the American government. There are literally thousands of such studies by now that explain the hows and whys of corporate victories in this arena. Most of the time these "special interests" win, but sometimes one or another trade association will lose out to a coalition of liberals, labor unions, and civil rights groups (Domhoff 2006, for a discussion of wins and losses for corporations with this process).

The policy-planning process formulates the general interests of the corporate community. It operates through a policy-planning network of foundations, think tanks, and policy-discussion groups, with a focus on the White House, relevant Congressional committees, and the high-status newspapers and opinion magazines published in New York and Washington. Historically, the most important foundations in the network were the Rockefeller Foundation, Carnegie Corporation, and Ford Foundation, but they have been joined by a host of others in the past three decades. Think tanks are best exemplified by one of the earliest, The Brookings Institution, founded in 1929, which has steered right and left of center in its long history, and by the American Enterprise

TABLE 1 EXAMPLES OF MODERATE-CONSERVATIVE AND ULTRA-CONSERVATIVE GROUPS IN THE POLICY NETWORK

Moderate Conservative Groups	Ultra-Conservative Groups
Policy-discussion groups	
Business Roundtable	U.S. Chamber of Commerce
Committee For Economic Development	National Association of Manufacturers
Think Tanks	
Brookings Institution	American Enterprise Institute
Urban Institute	Heritage Foundation

Institute, which came into prominence in the 1970s as an ultra-conservative counter to the government-oriented solutions to social problems that emerged in the 1970s (Peschek 1987). The key policy-discussion groups, which bring together corporate leaders, experts from think tanks and universities, journalists, and current and former government employees for sustained consideration of specific issues, include the Council on Foreign Relations, the Committee for Economic Development, and the Conference Board (e.g., Burris 1992; Moore, Sobieraj, Whitt, Mayorova, and Beaulieu 2002; Salzman and Domhoff 1983) Those corporate leaders who are members of policy-discussion groups are more likely to be tapped for government service than other corporate leaders, suggesting that such groups are a proving grounds as well as an educational forum (Useem 1980; Useem 1984) It is an important to note that this network has been shown to have overlapping centrist (moderate conservative) and rightist (ultra-conservative) cliques within it.

The efforts within the special-interest and policy-planning processes are supplemented and sometimes made a little easier by a third process, the *opinion-shaping process*, which attempts to influence public opinion and keep some issues off the legislative agenda. Often drawing on policy positions, rationales, and statements developed within the policy-planning process, it operates through the public relations departments of large corporations, general public relations firms, and many small opinion-shaping organizations, with a focus on middle-class voluntary organizations, educational institutions, and the mass media. In discussing the opinion-influencing network, the emphasis has to be on its "attempts" to influence public opinion, not on its successes, because there is ample evidence that the American public makes up its own mind on most issues and often holds to opinions that are more liberal than those of the power elite, especially on economic issues (Page 2002; Page and Shapiro 1992).

The organizations that constitute the corporate community and its affiliated nonprofit networks provide the institutional underpinnings for the leadership group that looks out for the overlapping interests of the upper class and the

FIGURE 1 **A VENN DIAGRAM VIEW OF HOW MEMBERS OF THE POWER ELITE ARE DRAWN FROM THREE OVERLAPPING NETWORKS OF PEOPLE AND INSTITUTIONS: THE CORPORATE COMMUNITY, THE SOCIAL UPPER CLASS, AND THE POLICY-FORMATION NETWORK. THE POWER ELITE IS DEFINED BY THE THICK LINES.**

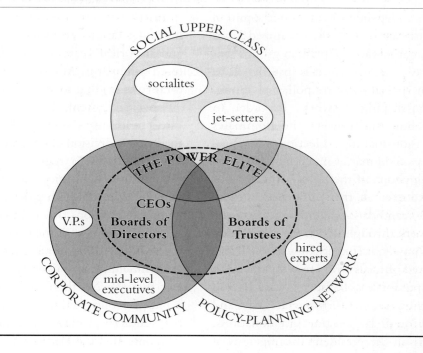

corporate community. These leaders are collectively called the "power elite." As illustrated in Figure 1, they are either members of the upper class who have taken on leadership roles in the corporate community or the nonprofit network, or they are high-level employees in corporations and corporate-connected nonprofit organizations. More formally, the power elite are the people who serve as directors or trustees in profit and nonprofit institutions controlled by the corporate community through stock ownership, financial support, or a predominant role on the board of directors. This definition includes the top-level employees who are asked to join the boards of the organizations that employ them. It has proven useful for research purposes in tracing corporate involvement in voluntary associations, the media, political parties, and government (Domhoff 2006, pp. 103–104). The concept of a power elite is also useful because it makes it possible to combine class and organizational insights into a single theoretical framework, with boards of directors providing the main formal setting in which class and organizational imperatives are discussed and integrated (DiTomaso 1980; Ostrander 1987). In that regard, power structure research is a hybrid theory that incorporates ideas that are empirically supported whatever their theoretical origins.

Coping With and Winning Elections

Due to the independence of public opinion and the existence of liberals, organized labor and various conservative Christian groups that have agendas of their own, it is insufficient to look to the special-interest, policy-planning, and opinion-shaping networks in order to understand how the power elite dominates federal decision-making. Elections do matter, and they could matter much more to average working people if the power elite did not have ways to exercise their influence in these arenas. The candidate-selection process, the fourth network through which the power elite exercises its power, is concerned with the selection of elected officials who are sympathetic to the agenda put forth in the special-interest and policy-planning processes. It operates first and foremost through large campaign donations, with a focus on the presidential campaigns of both major political parties and the Congressional campaigns of the Republican Party. The importance of campaign finance is especially important in the party primaries, which long ago were rightly described as a "choke point" in American politics (Heard 1960, p. 34). Then too, many individuals who work in the special-interest and opinion-shaping networks take direct roles as consultants and strategists in the campaigns of candidates in both parties. However, there are many other ways that members of the power elite involve themselves in the careers of the politicians they favor, including employing them and paying them huge sums

for speeches at the outset of their careers, or rewarding them with high-paying jobs as lobbyists within the special-interest process when their political careers are over.

In discussing the candidate-selection process, it is important to stress that there are structural and historical reasons why money has mattered so much in American politics. The electoral rules leading to a strong tendency toward a two-party system, that is, the single member district plurality system, when combined with the historic division of the country into Northern and Southern regions with very different political economies, adds up to a situation where until recently the parties have been such complex coalitions that it was not always clear to voters what one or the other stood for. From the 1870s until the 1960s, control of the federal government by the power elite started with the fact that the Northern industrial and finance capitalists controlled the Republican Party and the Southern plantation and merchant capitalists controlled the Democrats (Domhoff 1990, Chapter 9). To the degree to which the liberal-labor coalition that developed during the New Deal could exercise any power, it had to do so inside the Democratic Party and in the context of a bargain with the segregationist Southern Democrats that included acquiescence in elite domination of the low-wage labor force in the South, especially African Americans. It also meant tacit acceptance of the exclusion of African Americans from craft unions and good jobs in the North, which assuaged the feelings of the many Northern white workers who saw African Americans as racially inferior or as potential threats to their job security. Given this state of affairs, personalities, and name recognition could matter a great deal, which provided the opening for campaign finance to help boost one candidate over another.

Thus, the liberal–labor coalition, with fewer than a majority of senators and only 100 or so seats in the House, had far less power within the Democratic Party than liberal analysts and historians usually suggest. When it came to domestic government spending, the liberal–labor coalition had to agree that the South received more than its share of the pork and that the Southern whites could exclude African Americans if they so desired (Brown, 1999). On the occasions when the Northern liberals could convince the urban machine Democrats to support them on an issue in opposition to the Southerners, the Southerners joined with Northern Republicans after 1938 in a highly successful conservative voting bloc, defined as a majority of Southern Democrats voting with a majority of Northern Republicans, to stop any legislation they did not like, which usually involved issues related to control of labor markets in both the North and the South (Manley 1973; Patterson 1981; Shelley 1983).

Leaning Moderate, Turning Right

There are two critical junctures in recent American history that provide crucial challenges for rival theories of power in the United States. The first involves the policy responses to the Great Depression, the most important and enduring of which are the Agricultural Adjustment Act, the National Labor Relations Act, and the Social Security Act of 1935. The second concerns the right turn that began in the mid-1970s. Case studies show the importance of the policy-planning network on all three of the New Deal legislative initiatives because the key ideas and institutional arrangements that they embody all came from that network (Domhoff 1990, 1996). To take the example of the Social Security Act, it was not the work of liberals and labor leaders, as currently believed due to the fact that liberals defend it and conservatives dislike it. Instead, it was created by industrial relations experts who worked for foundations, consulting firms, and think tanks funded by several of the largest corporations of the 1930s.

Even the National Labor Relations Act, which gave life and hope to trade unions and made them important power actors for the next 40 years, was in part the result of a series of institutional innovations in 1933 that emerged from proposals made by the same corporate moderates who supported the Social Security Act. However, this case is more complicated than the first two because militant union leaders and Communists created the strikes and work stoppages that started the ball rolling, and then liberal corporate lawyers and law school professors working temporarily for the government's National Labor Relations Board crafted a new set of regulations based on case law that carried the program several steps beyond what the corporate moderates would accept. Somewhat ironically, the corporate moderates ended up leading the opposition to the legislation for which their earlier ideas had provided legitimacy. Moreover, the act passed because the corporate moderates were deserted by the Southern Democrats in a rare act of class disloyalty on a labor issue, which was made possible by the New Dealers' willingness to exclude agricultural and domestic labor from the provisions of the act.

However, this victory for the liberal-labor coalition was in good part reversed over the next 15 years when Southern plantation capitalists and their Democratic representatives in Congress founds ways to hamstring the enforcement provisions of the act. This process began when the Southerners turned against it in 1937 and 1938 due to their opposition to integrated organizing in the South and the use of sit-down strikes in the North by the militant Congress of Industrial Organizations. The handwriting was on the wall as early as 1939 when the Southern Democrats entered into negotiations with the ultra-conservatives in the National Association of Manufacturers and the leaders of the American Federation of Labor, which was by then feeling threatened by its fast-growing rival, the Congress of Industrial Organizations. This unusual coalition then agreed upon the changes in the law that became the Taft-Hartley Act in 1947, which has numerous provisions that limited the capacity of workers to organize unions. This handwriting was temporarily obscured by the need to delay the counterattack on labor until the successful completion of World War II, by which time the American Federation of Labor tried to oppose the new legislation, but to no avail (Gross 1981).

In the case of the right turn in the 1970s, it was based on two intertwined factors that first manifested themselves in the 1960s. First, and most important, the civil rights movement dynamited the New Deal coalition built on the exclusion of African Americans. This unexpected turn of events was made possible by

what turned out to be a surprisingly resourceful and resilient organizational base—the black churches of the South, which provided organizational skills, money, cultural and social solidarity, and charismatic leadership (Morris 1984). However, the churches did not act alone. Traditionally black colleges and universities and the sleeping car porters union also provided power resources that power analysts of all theoretical persuasions had overlooked. When combined with the brilliant use of strategic non-violence, and with the help of a handful of white allies, many of them religious leaders, the result was great pressure on the political system and the passage of the Civil Rights Act of 1964 and the Voting Rights Act of 1965.

The second new ingredient in the power equation was a renewal of the power elite's attacks on the National Labor Relations Board because a decision in 1962 by a board dominated by Democratic appointees reversed an earlier decision by a Republican-dominated board and gave unions the right to bargain over outsourcing. Interpreting that decision as a direct challenge to their right to manage and to invest resources when and where they pleased, the moderate conservatives within the power elite filed a suit that brought the matter all the way to the Supreme Court, where they lost. They then organized a very determined counteroffensive to reverse the decision within the labor board itself. Obtaining a reversal necessitated a Republican president in order to insure that all labor board appointees would be anti-union, which gradually moved moderate corporate leaders within the power elite out the Democratic Party for many years to come. It was victory in this battle, finally achieved in the early

1970s, that spelled the beginning of the end for the limited power labor unions had achieved. Within the context of civil rights militancy on the one hand and renewed capital-labor conflict on the other, the old power arrangements fractured. The fracturing began with the abandonment of the Democratic Party by the Southern rich because it could no longer keep African Americans powerless due to the fact that they could vote against the worst racists in Democratic Party primaries. They had been anticipated to some extent in this switch by a majority of white Southerners based on their racial resentments and religious fundamentalism.

But it was not just racial conflict in the South that destroyed the New Deal coalition. It was also racial conflict in the North, as historians are now revealing in detail as they reexamine the documents and press releases showing that the words later used by right-wingers in the late 1960s were already being said quite openly by the many white trade unionists who were not prepared to share jobs or power with African Americans (Sugrue 2001; Sugrue 2008). There were a few notable exceptions, of course, and many union leaders supported the civil rights movement at the legislative level, but enough of the rank-and-file resisted integration in housing, schooling, and unions to put the Democrats on the defensive in the North as well as the South. This point is seen most dramatically in the votes for Alabama Governor George Wallace, an avowed segregationist, in the Democratic presidential primaries as early as 1964—30% in Indiana, 34% in Wisconsin, and 47% in the former slave state of Maryland, where he won 16 of 23 counties, the state capitol, and the "ethnic" neighborhoods of Balti-

more (Carter 2000, p. 215). In 1972, mixing tirades against busing and welfare with revivalist religious appeals, Wallace then presaged the more coded and symbolic racist politics of the Christian Right by winning Democratic primaries in Michigan and Maryland just when he was forced to drop out of the race by the assassination attempt that left him paralyzed and in excruciating pain (Carter 2000).

Nor was it just racial conflict that led rank-and-file union members to aid unwittingly in the weakening of their movement at a time when it was beginning to come under siege from a power elite intent upon asserting its right to manage. Many of them did not like the feminists or environmentalists either, whom they thought of as competitors for their jobs or as threats to their status as respected white males. Moreover, many white union members did not like what they saw as the anti-Americanism of the anti-war movement. Although I strongly believe that racism was the primary issue, all of these factors contributed to the disintegration of the liberal-labor coalition and made it possible for President Richard Nixon and his right-wing allies to attract more and more white Americans (blue collar and white collar, union and nonunion) into the Republican Party. For several reasons, then, enough white Americans of modest or low incomes switched to the Republicans to solidify a new corporate-conservative coalition that then got what it wanted from President Nixon and future Republican presidents in terms of a National Labor Relations Board that would legitimate outsourcing and in other ways continue to undercut the union movement, a story that is best told by Gross (1995). From the point of view of power structure research, it was these crucial power dynamics that started the decline of the union movement in the 1970s. This analysis is also supported by the fact that the unions have not declined nearly as far or as fast in Canada and Western Europe, where working classes are far more powerful because they could develop their own political parties, thanks in fair measure to the parliamentary system of government.

The nationwide white turn to the Republicans also made it possible for the moderate conservatives in the power elite to make a right turn on other policy issues in the 1970s because the streets were free of disruptions by African Americans in the inner city and anti-war protests had ended. At that point the corporate leaders in the Business Roundtable, a new policy organization created to do battle with organized labor, took advantage of the internal conflicts within the liberal–labor coalition to deal with new economic problems caused by spiking oil prices, inflation, and rising unemployment. They also used their role in the new coalition to reverse the economic reforms that had been forced upon them by the social movements of the 1960s. We know in detail about this decision to turn right because the issues were debated in the policy-planning network, thereby making content analyses of their policy intentions possible (Jenkins and Eckert 2000; Peschek 1987). The inner tensions and disagreements over the degree to which policy should change also are revealed by the deliberations at a moderate-conservative policy-discussion group, the Committee for Economic Development, where the majority of corporate trustees turned their backs on the mildly liberal line they said taken from 1960 to 1974 and said no to permanent wage and price controls as well as to

the other plans for greater government involvement in the economy that some members had been entertaining (Frederick 1981).

The right turn was then solidified by the election of Ronald Reagan in 1980 in the context of rising unemployment, continuing inflation, and the Iranian hostage crisis. For the next 25 years, the power elite was united in taking a rightist direction on most issues. Even the centrist Democratic President Bill Clinton, taking the advice of advisors from Wall Street, continued the push for "free trade," which from a power point of view primarily involves agreements to ship union shops to low-wage countries and then import the goods they make into the United States. Clinton also accepted key steps in the financial deregulation that contributed to the further concentration of the wealth and income distributions and to the economic meltdown that began in 2005–2006. As the crisis of 2005–2008 unfolded, with Wall Street and the entire economics profession ignoring the huge housing bubble that was frequently pointed out to them by concerned regulators and a few liberal economists, many detailed accounts appeared in the *New York Times* and *Washington Post* that explained the ways in which the investment bankers, corporate executives and economists who controlled the Department of the Treasury and the Federal Reserve Board during the Clinton and Bush administrations actively squelched attempts by lower-level government officials to save the economy from a crash.

What Ended The Right Turn

When I surveyed the American power structure in early 2006, I concluded that there were no organized groups in the country that could counter the corporate-conservative coalition that had gained complete domination of the executive, legislative, and judicial branches of the federal government. The unions were divided and in decline, and the Democrats could not overcome rightist appeals to racial, religious, and social issues in the electoral arena. Only forces far stronger than liberals and what remained of organized labor could change the course the power equation: ". . . it may be that the only real limits on the corporate-conservative coalition will be set by the length and ferocity of the war in Iraq, and the reaction of financial and currency markets to the growing budget deficits and increasing federal debt" (Domhoff 2006, p. 198). I thought the war might have an impact because of studies showing that rising casualties in unpopular wars, such as the Korean and Vietnam Wars, turned public opinion against the party in power, which was slowly happening in 2005 even though most people ignored the left-wing anti-war movement (Mueller 1973; Mueller 2005).

Within this context, the 2006 midterm elections are an excellent example of how elections can matter despite all the resources that the power elite has to finance conservative candidates and shape public opinion. The unexpected Democratic victory, giving Democrats control of the House and Senate, almost totally due to the rejection of the war by moderate and independent voters, hobbled the right wing of the power elite. But it wasn't just the anti-war vote that won for the Democrats, as important as that was. They also won because the various social issues that have been a major key to Republican success—the religious, morality, and gun-control issues on which social liberals and social conservatives strongly differ—were

neutralized in this election. This happened in three ways, all of which involved extreme breaks with the past 45 years. First, the Democrats supported candidates in socially conservative areas who were opposed to gun control or abortion. They also fielded candidates who openly professed their religious faith. However, social issues were neutralized in a second way as well, courtesy of the Republicans, who were saddled with several Congressmen and candidates who appeared "corrupt" by taking money illegally from lobbyists or "immoral" through various sexual/marital scandals. Third, Democrats won because the touchiest social issue of them all—race—was not on the table in most districts or states in this election.

THE 2008 ELECTIONS AND BEYOND

The Bush Administration essentially thumbed its nose at the American people by escalating the war in Iraq shortly after the 2006 elections under cover of the claim that the escalation was a temporary "surge." But the troops were still there, even if being killed slightly less often, as the presidential elections became a burning issue in 2008. Moreover, the faltering economy headed toward a crash in the summer and fall just before the elections, leading the conservative Wall Street bankers and Ivy League economists in charge of financial policy to make unprecedented use of government monies to save the financial sector, with little concern for ordinary Americans with mortgage problems. When the ongoing war and the economic crisis were combined with the brilliant campaign waged by Barack Obama and the incredible recklessness of 72-year-old cancer survivor

John McCain in putting an inexperienced and socially conservative governor from Alaska on the Republican ticket, the result was a sweeping Democratic victory that has the ingredients to be a major turning point in American history in terms of both racial relations and greater government social support for low-income people of all ages and colors. In particular, the economic crisis forced white Americans in the Midwest to choose between their pocketbooks and their skin color, and they chose their pocketbooks.

However, it is important to stress in terms of the findings from power structure research that President Obama's victory is not quite the major break with the past that it may seem to be. First, he is a biracial American with a white mother and Kenyan father he never knew while he was growing up. Second, he was raised in a completely white environment, so he is comfortable with white Americans and can put them at ease because he does not fit any of the white stereotypes about black Americans. In addition, he also understands and has the same style as the upper-middle and upper-class white Americans with whom he has spent his life since the age of 10, when he went to live with his white grandparents in Honolulu at a time when his grandmother was on her way to becoming the first women to be a vice president in a large Honolulu bank. During those years in Honolulu President Obama also attended Punahou, one of the wealthiest preparatory schools in the country, where he learned an upper-class style (now called "cultural capital") and developed a network of wealthy and well-educated friends (now called "social capital") (see the Bourdieu article in this volume). He next went to Occidental College, a small liberal arts college in Los Angeles, for two years and then moved on to Columbia University, a sure sign that he had big ambitions at this point. After a stint as a community organizer in Chicago, he graduated from Harvard Law School and went to work for a high-status corporate law firm in Chicago. He soon left the law firm to teach in the prestigious law school at the University of Chicago, where he picked up more cultural and social capital, while he pursued his political career. Except for his skin color and his father's ancestry, he is a typical—albeit brilliant and even tempered–upper-middle-class American lawyer who decided to go into politics.

Moreover, President Obama gained the trust and support of some of the wealthiest people in Chicago, who helped him raise the enormous amount of money from the corporate rich that is still necessary to launch a serious statewide or national campaign even in a day when smaller sums can be raised from millions of people on the internet. They in turn reached out to other moderates in the power elite in other parts of the country, assuring them that President Obama was a sensible person. Finally, President Obama made clear that his main advisors were centrist multimillionaires and billionaires such as Warren Buffet, the richest man in the United States in 2008, along with corporate executives and policy experts from the policy-planning network.

However, this does not mean that the changes in the United States are likely to be minor or merely symbolic. Barack Obama's presidency could make a large difference in the lives of the many Americans who have little or no wealth and work for very low wages. This is especially the case if the economic crisis continues and unemployment rises to high levels. Such conditions might bring unrest and disruption that might be responded to with government-supported health care, better pensions, and better unemployment benefits, all of which would mean somewhat higher taxes on the wealthy few. There also could be major changes in American foreign policy, especially if moderates in the power elite believe what I suspect they believe, which is that they cannot win the war in Iraq and that they can make peace with Iran fairly easily if they choose to do so. (In the case of the tensions between the United States and Iran, it must be remembered that they are due to the fact that the United States refused to recognize the new Iranian government created in 1979 by revolutionaries who overthrew the dictatorial government that had been installed by the American government through a coup in 1953.)

For all the new possibilities, it remains the case that strong labor unions and government provision of social welfare are opposed by the wealthy centrists who are the major financial supporters of the Democratic Party, as well as by the more conservative parts of the power elite. It will take a prolonged and increasingly serious economic crisis, along with better strategies and tactics than used in the past by those who are to the left of President Obama's coalition, for the United States to move very far off center.

||| CONCLUSION

The combination of economic power, policy expertise, and continuing political success makes the corporate owners and executives a *dominant class*, not in the sense of complete and absolute power, but in the sense that they have the power to shape the economic and political frameworks within which other groups and classes must operate. The major policy conflicts between the corporate-conservative and liberal-labor coalitions are best described as *class conflicts* because they concern the distribution of profits and wages, the rate and progressivity of taxation, the usefulness of labor unions, and the degree to which business should be regulated by government. The liberal-labor side wants corporations to pay higher wages to employees and higher taxes to government. It wants government to regulate a wide range of business practices and help employees to organize unions. The corporate-conservative side rejects all these policy objectives, claiming they endanger the freedom of individuals and the efficient workings of the economic marketplace. The conflicts these disagreements generate can manifest themselves in many different ways: workplace protests, strikes, industry-wide boycotts, massive demonstrations in cities, pressure on Congress, and voting preferences.

Despite their preponderant power in the federal government and the many useful policies it carries out for them, leaders within the corporate community are constantly critical of government because of its potential independence and its ability to aid their opponents. In particular, they are wary of the federal government due to its capacity to aid average Americans by (1) creating government jobs for the unemployed, (2) making health, unemployment, and social security benefits more generous, (3) helping employees gain greater workplace rights and protections, and (4) supporting efforts by employees to form unions. These possibilities are opposed by the corporate community on the grounds that they might increase taxes, impede economic growth, or limit freedom. However, the major issue is not really taxes or government spending. The deeper issue is power. Corporations oppose any government support for unions because unions are a potential organizational base for advocating a whole range of polices that threaten corporate power. In a phrase, *control of labor markets* is the crucial issue in the eyes of the corporate community, which rightly worries that government policies could alter the power over labor markets it now enjoys.

Social conflict over abortion, same-sex marriage, and other social issues favored by liberals and vigorously opposed by the Christian Right are not part of this overall class conflict. Whatever way these issues are decided, they do not affect the power of the corporate community. They are therefore of little or no concern to most of the policy-planning organizations funded by corporate leaders. However, these social issues have been an important part of the competition between the corporate-conservative and liberal-labor coalitions in the electoral arena for the past 40 years, where they were raised by conservatives in an attempt to win over voters who were liberal on economic issues. Although the social issues seemed to be tamed in the 2006 and 2008 elections, with the issue of gay marriage providing the important exception, the historical record tells us that no academic expert, newspaper columnist, or television pundit has ever made a correction prediction about the future. The truth is that anything can happen even though mainstream social scientists and liberal media commentators now assure us, after the fact, that demographic trends or new internet technologies or whatever made the recent return to the center inevitable.

‖ REFERENCES

Baltzell, E. Digby. 1958. *Philadelphia gentlemen: The making of a national upper class.* New York: Free Press.

———. 1964. *The Protestant establishment: Aristocracy and caste in America.* New York: Random House.

Barnes, Roy C. and Emily R. Ritter. 2001. "Networks of corporate interlock: 1962–1995." *Critical Sociology* 27:192–220.

Boehm, Christopher. 1999. *Hierarchy in the forest: The evolution of egalitarian behavior.* Cambridge: Harvard University Press.

Burris, Val. 1992. "Elite policy-planning networks in the United States." *Research in Politics and Society* 4:111–134.

Carter, Dan T. 2000. *The politics of rage: George Wallace, the origins of the new conservatism, and the transformation of American politics.* Baton Rouge: Louisiana State University Press.

Daniels, Arlene Kaplan. 1988. *Invisible careers: Women civic leaders from the volunteer world.* Chicago: University of Chicago Press.

DiTomaso, Nancy. 1980. "Organizational analysis and power structure research." Pp. 255–268 in *Power Structure Research*, edited by G. W. Domhoff. Beverly Hills: Sage.

Domhoff, G. W. 1970. *The higher circles.* New York: Random House.

———. 1974. *The Bohemian Grove and other retreats; a study in ruling-class cohesiveness.* New York: Harper & Row.

———. 1990. *The power elite and the state: How policy is made in America.* Hawthorne, NY: Aldine de Gruyter.

———. 1996. *State autonomy or class dominance? Case studies on policy making in America.* Hawthorne, NY: Aldine de Gruyter.

———. 2006. *Who rules America? Power, politics, and social change.* New York: McGraw-Hill.

Dunn, Marvin. 1980. "The family office: Coordinating mechanism of the ruling class." Pp. 17–45 in *Power Strcuture Research*, edited by G. W. Domhoff. Beverly Hills: Sage.

Earle, Tim. 1997. *How chiefs come to power: The political economy in prehistory.* Stanford, CA: Stanford University Press.

Frederick, William. 1981. "Free Market vs. Social Responsibility: Decision Time at the CED." *California Management Review* 23:20–28.

Gaventa, John. 1980. *Power and powerlessness: Quiescence and rebellion in and Appalachian valley.* Chicago: University of Illinois Press.

Gregor, Thomas. 1985. Anxious pleasures: *The sexual lives of an Amazonian people.* Chicago: University of Chicago Press.

Gross, James A. 1981. *The reshaping of the National Labor Relations Board.* Albany: State University of New York Press.

Heard, Alexander. 1960. *The Costs of Democracy.* Chapel Hill: University of North Carolina Press.

Hunter, Floyd. 1953. *Community power structure: A study of decision makers.* Chapel Hill: University of North Carolina Press.

Jenkins, Craig and Craig Eckert. 2000. "The right turn in economic policy: Business elites and the new conservative economics." *Sociological Forum* 15:307–338.

Kendall, Diana. 2002. *The power of good deeds: Privileged women and the social reproduction of class.* Lanham, MD: Rowman and Littlefield.

Logan, John and H. Molotch. 2007. *Urban fortunes: The political economy of place.* Berkeley: University of California Press.

Manley, John F. 1973. "The conservative coalition in congress." *American Behavioral Scientist* 17:223–247.

Mann, Michael. 1986a. "A crisis in stratification theory? Persons, households/families/lineages, genders, classes, and nations." Pp. 42–56 in *Gender and stratification*, edited by R. Crompton and M. Mann. Cambridge: Polity Press.

———. 1986b. *The sources of social power: A history of power from the beginning to A.D. 1760*, Vol. 1. New York: Cambridge University Press.

———. 1993. *The sources of social power: The rise of classes and nation-states, 1760–1914*, Vol. 2. New York: Cambridge University Press.

Mills, C. Wright. 1956. *The power elite.* New York: Oxford University Press.

Mizruchi, M. 1982. *The American corporate network*, 1904–1974. Beverly Hills: Sage Publications.

Molotch, Harvey. 1976. "The city as a growth machine." *American Journal of Sociology* 82:309–330.

———. 1979. "Capital and neighborhood in the United States: Some conceptual links." *Urban Affairs Quarterly* 14:289–312.

Moore, G., S. Sobieraj, J. Whitt, O. Mayorova, and D. Beaulieu. 2002. "Elite interlocks in three U.S. sectors: Nonprofit, corporate, and government." *Social Science Quarterly* 83:726–744.

Morris, Aldon D. 1984. *The origins of the civil rights movement : Black communities organizing for change.* New York: Free Press.

Mueller, John E. 1973. *War, presidents, and public opinion.* New York: Wiley.

———. 2005. "The Iraq Syndrome." *Foreign Affairs,* November/December, pp. 44–54.

Ostrander, Susan A. 1980. "Upper-class women: Class consciousness as conduct and meaning." Pp. 73–96 in *Power Structure Research,* edited by G. W. Domhoff. Beverly Hills: Sage.

———. 1984. *Women of the upper class.* Philadelphia: Temple University Press.

———. 1987. "Elite domination in private social agencies: How it happens and how it is challenged." Pp. 85–102 in *Power Elites and Organizations,* edited by G. W. Domhoff and T. Dye. Beverly Hills: Sage.

Page, B. 2002. "The semi-sovereign public." Pp. 325–344 in *Navigating public opinion: Polls, policy, and the future of American democracy,* edited by J. Manza, F. Cook, and B. Page. New York: Oxford University Press.

Page, B. and R. Y. Shapiro. 1992. *The rational public: Fifty years of trends in Americans' policy preferences.* Chicago: University of Chicago Press.

Patterson, James T. 1981. *Congressional conservatism and the New Deal: The growth of the conservative coalition in Congress, 1933–1939.* Lexington: University of Kentucky Press.

Peschek, Joseph G. 1987. *Policy-planning organizations: Elite agendas and America's rightward turn.* Philadelphia: Temple University Press.

Salzman, Harold and G. William Domhoff. 1983. "Nonprofit organizations and the corporate community." *Social Science History* 7:205–216.

Sanday, Peggy. 1990. *Fraternity gang rape: Sex, brotherhood, and privilege on campus.* New York: New York University Press.

Shelley, Mack C. 1983. *The permanent majority: The conservative coalition in the United States Congress.* Tuscaloosa.: University of Alabama Press.

Sonquist, John and Thomas Koenig. 1975. "Interlocking directorates in the top U. S. corporations." *Insurgent Sociologist* 5:196–229.

Sugrue, Thomas. 2001. "Breaking through: The troubled origins of affirmative action in the workplace." Pp. 31–52 in *Color lines: Affirmative action, immigration, and civil rights options for America,* edited by J. Skrentny. Chicago: University of Chicago Press.

———. 2008. *Sweet land of liberty: The forgotten struggle for civil rights in the North.* New York: Random House.

Useem, Michael. 1980. "Which business leaders help govern?" Pp. 199–225 in *Power Structure Research,* edited by G. W. Domhoff. Beverly Hills: Sage.

———. 1984. *The inner circle: Large corporations and the rise of business political activity in the U.S. and U.K.* New York: Oxford University Press.

Weber, Max. 1904/1958. *The Protestant ethic and the spirit of capitalism.* New York: Charles Scribner.

50

Money and Politics⋆

DAN CLAWSON

A basic contradiction of capitalist democracies is that in the political realm each person is supposed to be equal, with one and only one vote, but in the marketplace the people with the most money are supposed to have the most impact. It is difficult or impossible to maintain a barrier between the political and economic realms. In a society with enormous disparities of wealth and income the individuals and organizations with the most money will exercise disproportionate influence both on election campaigns and on the shaping of public policy.

If political influence depends on wealth, then in the United States today the top 1 percent of the population will have more "votes" than the bottom 90 percent, and Bill Gates by himself will have more votes than the 100 million poorest Americans.[1] In practice, every capitalist democracy has rules to

⋆ Published in English here for the first time; a French-language version was published in *Actes de la Recherche en Sciences Sociales*, Number 138 (June, 2001).

1 See Edward N. Wolff, "How the Pie Is Sliced: America's Growing Concentration of Wealth," *American Prospect* 22 (Summer 1995):58–64 and his *Top Heavy: A Study of Increasing Inequality of Wealth in America and What Can Be Done about It* (New York: New Press, 1996). The top 10 percent of the U.S. population controls more than two-thirds of the nation's wealth; the top 1 percent controls 42 percent.

limit the political influence of wealth, and in every case those with wealth nonetheless find ways to use their money to exercise disproportionate influence. In recent years campaign finance problems have generated significant public attention and controversy not only in the United States, but also in France, Germany, Japan, Italy, and numerous other societies.

The 2000 election was the closest in U.S. history. Media attention focused primarily on ballot confusion and the limited number of people who were actively excluded from voting. This is insignificant compared to the fact that half the U.S. population does not vote in major national elections (and a far higher proportion does not vote in local elections).[2] In the nineteenth century U.S. voter turnout averaged around 80 percent, but the election of 1896 realigned politics and introduced a series of changes whose intent and effect was to drastically reduce voter turnout. These included the introduction of voter registration, a system under which voters must go to city hall at least thirty days before the election to register to vote. Voter registration initially applied only in major metropolitan areas where immigrant populations were concentrated. The consequences were immediate and dramatic: voter turnout fell from 77.9 percent in 1896 to 63.9 percent in 1904 and 55.7 percent in 1912.[3] Voter turnout increased during the 1930s, but in the last 40 years turnout has declined again, such that in each presiden-

tial election for more than 20 years only about half of American adults voted. Non-voting is strongly related to education and income. Republican voter participation levels are also highly correlated with social class, but Democratic voter participation is *not* class correlated. As Walter Dean Burnham argues, "The whole range of data suggests that if there is class struggle in American politics, it is almost entirely one-sided." To put it another way, "the 'party of nonvoters' fills up approximately to the extent that the Democratic party loses coherence and drifts away from the leftward end of our narrow political spectrum."[4] If the Democratic party presents candidates and policies similar to those of the Republican party, the most significant shift in voting patterns is an increase in the number of people who choose not to vote, and an increase in the class skew of voter turnout.

Why does this situation persist? Why wouldn't Democratic party candidates shift to the left and thereby motivate and mobilize the large numbers of working class people who choose not to vote? The reason is simple: at least in the U.S. system, electoral success depends heavily on campaign spending. The United States has weak political parties, which means that each candidate runs more-or-less on his or her own, and most races are heavily influenced by individual personal appeal. In most cases, neither the political parties nor alter-

2 Frances Fox Piven and Richard A. Cloward, *Why Americans Don't Vote* (New York: Pantheon, 1988).

3 See Walter Dean Burnham, "The System of 1896: An Analysis," pp. 147–202 in Paul Kleppner et al., eds. *The Evolution of American Electoral Systems* (Westport, CT: Greenwood Press, 1981), p. 193, for figures on turnout decline. See also Burn-

ham, *Critical Elections and the Mainsprings of American Politics* (New York: W.W. Norton & Company, 1970), and Burnham, "The Changing Shape of the American Political Universe," *American Political Science Review* 1965, vol. 59 no. 1: 7–28.

4 Walter Dean Burnham, *The Current Crisis in American Politics* (New York: Oxford University Press, 1982), pp. 188–189.

native organizations have the organizational capacity to establish personal contact with more than a small fraction of the voters. This means that races typically rely heavily on the mass media, but candidates are *not* given any free radio or television time.[5] In congressional races, for example, congressional candidates for the House of Representatives "who headed into the final three weeks with the most in combined spending and cash on hand won 93 percent of the time."[6] Candidates (and the Democratic party) have concluded that their first priority must be to raise large sums of money; in order to do so they adopt "moderate" stands that will not offend big-money donors. As a consequence many people conclude that the difference between the two parties is not important enough to make it worthwhile voting, that both parties give priority to wealthy donors and don't care about ordinary voters. Three-quarters (77 percent) of Americans believe that members of Congress listen more to major donors from outside their state than they do to voters in the state.[7] Political insiders consider "the real campaign" to be the race for money; even during the heat of the campaign, candidates spend "at least half a day, two or three days a week, on the telephone asking for money" in addition to the time they spend at fundraising gatherings.[8]

In the current American system, the most important fundraising distinction is between "hard money" and "soft money." Legislation supposedly sets strict limits on campaign contributions: only individuals, not organizations, can give money, and they can give no more than $1,000 per candidate in an election. "Hard money" is the term used for contributions that stay within these rules. Both politicians and big donors want to evade the law. In 1979 they found a loophole in the law: donations given for "party building" or for "get out the vote drives," they argued, were not covered by existing legislation. Therefore, donors could give unlimited amounts for these activities. Not only could individuals do so, but so could corporations and unions. These donations, given outside the rules, are called "soft money."

The Democratic party's priority has been to match the Republican party in fundraising, and they have come close to doing so. In the 2000 election, for example, spending for Congress was almost exactly even, as was "soft money." The Republicans had a distinct edge in "hard money" party fundraising and in the presidential race. (See Table 1.) Other parties and candidates were far behind. In the presidential race, Ralph Nader raised only $8.7 million and Patrick Buchanan $42.7 million.

The crucial financial disparity was not between political parties, but rather between business and labor. Although 1970s data are not fully comparable to that of recent years, in 1974 business was outspent by labor (.76 to 1) but by 1980 business outspent labor by 2.66 to 1.[9] Over time the funding advantage has tilted more and more toward business; currently business

---

5 The presidential debates are a partial exception.

6 *Boston Globe,* November 8, 1997, p. A26.

7 Princeton Survey Research Associates, "Money and Politics Survey: Summary and Overview," 1997.

8 *New York Times,* November 1, 1996, p. A1.

9 Gary C. Jacobson, "Money in the 1980 and 1982 Congressional Elections," pp. 38–69 in Michael J. Malbin, editor, *Money and Politics in the United States* (Chatham, NJ: Chatham House Publishers, 1984).

TABLE 1 **TOTALS RAISED, 2000 ELECTION (IN MILLIONS OF U.S. DOLLARS)**

	Republicans	Democrats
President	191.6	132.6
Congress	508.2	506.0
Senate	202.3	228.9
House of Representatives	305.9	277.1
Political parties	691.8	513.1
Hard money	447.4	269.9
Soft money	244.4	243.1

SOURCE: www.opensecrets.org, based on Federal Election Commission reports.

TABLE 2 **TOTALS BY SOURCE, 2000 ELECTION (IN MILLIONS OF U.S. DOLLARS)**

Source of funds	Republicans	Democrats
Business	496.0	340.3
Labor	3.8	52.4
Ideological groups	16.4	17.5
Other and unknown	112.6	60.3

SOURCE: www.opensecrets.org.

outspends labor by 15 to 1. (See Table 2.) The Republicans get almost no money from labor, but today even the Democrats receive *six times* as much from business as from labor. Democratic fundraisers do not wish to lose the $52 million they received from labor, but are far more concerned to maintain the $340 million they receive from business, and this makes the Democratic party extremely cautious about taking any positions calling for progressive economic policies, certainly any that involve a redistribution of wealth and income. How did we get to this situation, and what are its consequences?

||| RULES AND HISTORY

Campaign finance reform was enacted in response to the Watergate scandals, especially the discovery that the Nixon campaign had coerced many corporations to make secret contributions of $100,000 each. The system adopted in 1974 had these key provisions:[10]

1. **Disclosure**—All contributions of $200 or more must be publicly disclosed.
2. **Donation limits**—No individual may contribute more than $1,000 per candidate per

10 For a presentation and analysis of the rules governing campaign finance, including details not covered here, see Frank J. Sorauf, *Inside Campaign Finance: Myths and Realities* (New Haven: Yale University Press, 1992).

election, nor more than $25,000 per year in total. Individuals may also contribute up to $5,000 to a political action committee (PAC) and $5,000 to a political party. PACs may contribute up to $5,000 per candidate per election, with no limit on the total they may contribute to all candidates.

3. **Voluntary and by individuals**—All political contributions must come from voluntary decisions by individuals. Corporations, unions, or other associations may form PACs to collect voluntary donations from their members or employees, and may pay all the costs of operating the PAC (rent, phone, salaries for staff), but may not give the organization's money (profits for corporations, member dues for unions).

4. **Candidates unlimited**—Candidates running for office may spend unlimited amounts of their own money, thus providing an incentive to nominate candidates rich enough to finance their own election. Jon Corzine of Goldman Sachs and New Jersey won his 2000 Senate race—as a *Democrat*—on the basis of $61 million of his own money.

The campaign finance law thus limited the amount of money a donor could give but not the amount a candidate could collect. No donor may give a candidate more than a small fraction of the total amount needed to run a winning race. The intent and effect of this system is that political candidates are dependent on the capitalist class as a whole, but not on a specific individual or company. Campaign contributions are to be spent on political campaigns and campaign-related activities, but in practice this

is loosely interpreted: one candidate bought a luxury car and another paid himself $57,000 in campaign funds to rent part of his home as a campaign headquarters.[11] In the past two decades Congress has not modified the law at all, but in practice the law has changed drastically; soft money is by far the most important loophole, but by no means the only one. "Soft money" eliminates the two most important provisions of the initial legislation (donation limits and voluntary individual contributions). Soft money initially involved relatively trivial amounts (an estimated $19.1 million in 1980 and $21.6 million in 1984), but expanded rapidly (to $232 million in 1996 and $463 million in 2000). Beginning with the 1992 election, soft money itself was regulated to the extent of requiring that donors be disclosed and imposing some rules on the ways it can be spent; this makes the distinction between "hard" and "soft" money problematic. The money cannot be used for a message specifically urging people to *vote* for a specific candidate, but the entire advertisement can present a candidate's views and/or attack an opponent as long as the advertisement does not specifically say "vote for [this candidate]." In recent years, further forms of evasion have been perfected and are assuming ever greater importance: if soft money is prohibited (as proposed by the McCain-Feingold legislation), these new forms of evasion will expand dramatically.

||| THE MONEY AND ITS EFFECTS

The amounts of money involved are enormous from the perspective of a candidate but trivial

---

11 *New York Times*, November 12, 1990, p. A18.

from that of a business donor. In congressional races, the candidate with more money is elected 90 percent of the time. Money is most important to challengers; incumbents can almost always raise enough to be competitive, but challengers rarely can.[12] A challenger hoping to win a seat in the House of Representatives has less than one-half of 1 percent of a chance of winning unless he or she raises at least half a million dollars; far more is required to win a Senate race. In four out of five congressional races the challenger can't raise half as much as the incumbent; only 3 percent of those races are even competitive (decided by margins of 55–45 percent or closer). In the one out of five races where the challenger spent at least half as much as the incumbent, 39 percent of the races were competitive.[13]

The current system effectively excludes any candidate that cannot raise large amounts of money. This "money primary" eliminates potential candidates as decisively as the election primaries. From the point of view of the capitalist class the system is extremely effective: unless a candidate can attract significant support from those with money, he or she is excluded from public debate and stands almost no chance of being elected. It is important to be clear that the current U.S. money-election system is an effective technology of power: media-driven campaigns, based on extensive polling, directed by highly paid political consultants, are able to beat candidates who attempt to substitute popular participation for money. This is, of course, as much a measure of the weakness of oppositional culture and organization as it is a measure of the strength of the money-election system.

Increasingly incumbents use money to win elections before voters get involved. If candidates can raise enough money well in advance, no "serious" candidate will challenge them. Senator Rudy Boschwitz wrote a secret post-election analysis explaining his campaign strategy:

> Nobody in politics (except me!) likes to raise money, so I thought the best way of discouraging the toughest opponents from running was to have a few dollars in the sock. *I believe it worked. . . . From all forms of fund-raising I raised $6 million plus and got 3 or 4 (maybe even 5) stories and cartoons* that irked me. In retrospect, I'm glad I had the money.[14]

This strategy is highly effective and increasingly common.[15] In March 1996 Bill Paxon, chair of the House Republican campaign committee, said, "We've been pounding on members [of Congress] to raise more money by the fil-

12 Gary C. Jacobson, *Money in Congressional Elections* (New Haven: Yale University Press, 1980). See also his "The Effects of Campaign Spending in House Elections: New Evidence for Old Arguments," *American Journal of Political Science* (May 1990), Vol. 34, No. 2, pp. 334–362.

13 Dan Clawson, Alan Neustadtl, and Denise Scott, *Money Talks: Corporate PACs and Political Influence* (New York: Basic Books, 1992), p. 203, and Dan Clawson, Alan Neustadtl, and Mark Weller, *Dollars and Votes: How Business Campaign Contributions Subvert Democracy* (Philadelphia: Temple University Press, 1998), pp. 1–4.

14 Senator Rudy Boschwitz, quoted in Brooks Jackson, *Honest Graft: Big Money and the American Political Process* (New York: Knopf, 1988), pp. 251–52.

15 See David Epstein and Peter Zemsky, "Money Talks: Deterring Quality Challengers in Congressional Elections," *American Political Science Review* 89:295–308, and Peverill Squire, "Preemptive Fund-raising and Challenger Profile in Senate Elections," *Journal of Politics* 1991, vol. 53:1150–64.

ing deadline; if they show a good balance, that could ward off opponents."[16] As a result many U.S. congressional races are not contested at all, or involve only token opposition. Of course it doesn't *always* work—in his next election, Boschwitz raised so much money that all the "serious" candidates refused to challenge him, and although Boschwitz outspent his opponent by 5 to 1, the opponent (maverick Paul Wellstone) won nonetheless.

Although the amounts of money look enormous to candidates, from the perspective of business profits these are small donations; business could easily contribute far more money. The advertising budget for the top 50 corporate advertisers is more than $25 billion a year. If just these 50 corporations shifted 10 percent of their advertising budgets into campaign finance, in a two-year election cycle they would provide more money than the cost of *both* sides of *all* the races for Congress and the presidency.[17] It is not economic constraints that keep them from doing so, but rather concerns about legitimacy and fear that such massive donations would lead to a popular reaction.

Why do large donors give? Some do so because they support the candidate's positions on the issues and hope their donation will increase the candidate's chance of winning. Most business donations, however, are given to gain "access." Critics of the campaign finance system present these donations as market transactions: a donation is given to buy a vote. As in the market, they seem to believe, direct equivalents are exchanged, the transaction is balanced, minimal trust is required, and no enduring obligations are created. The most common alternative to this market metaphor is the claim, often presented by the donors themselves, that they give selflessly to promote good government and top quality leadership. The bulk of the literature on campaign finance, *both* popular *and* academic, is framed in this fashion, with the academics attempting to test such theories.[18] Donors insist that they do not and cannot "buy" the vote of a member of Congress. As the senior vice president of a major defense contractor told me: "You certainly aren't going to be able to buy anybody for $500 or $1,000 or $10,000. It's a joke."[19] The politicians who solicit contributions

16 Quoted in Elizabeth Drew, *Whatever it Takes: The Real Struggle for Political Power in America* (New York: Viking, 1997), pp. 19–20.

17 See Dan Clawson, Alan Neustadtl, and Mark Weller, *Dollars and Votes: How Business Campaign Contributions Subvert Democracy* (Philadelphia: Temple University Press, 1998), p. 124.

18 For popular exposes see Philip M. Stern, *The Best Congress Money Can Buy* (New York: Pantheon, 1988) and Lars-Erik Nelson, *The Buying of the Congress* (1998). For scholarly assessments see Janet M. Grenzke, "PACs and the Congressional Supermarket: The Currency Is Complex," *American Journal of Political Science* 1989, vol. 33:1–24 and Thomas Romer and James M. Synder, Jr., "An Empirical Investigation of the Dynamics of PAC Contributions," *American Journal of Political Science* 1994, vol. 38:745–69. For a largely

theoretical argument that in fact politicians extort money from innocent companies, see Fred S. McChesney, *Money for Nothing: Politicans, Rent Extraction, and Political Extortion* (Cambridge, MA: Harvard University Press, 1997).

19 This quotation, and all other unidentified quotations from corporate executives, comes from interviews I conducted with key officials at leading companies, typically vice presidents or senior vice presidents. Informants were promised confidentiality for themselves and their companies; on this basis they permitted me to tape record the interviews. For further background on methods see Dan Clawson, Alan Neustadtl, and Denise Scott, *Money Talks: Corporate PACs and Political Influence* (New York: Basic Books, 1992) and Dan Clawson, Alan Neustadtl, and Mark Weller, *Dollars and Votes: How Business Campaign Contributions Subvert Democracy* (Philadelphia: Temple University Press, 1998).

agree: Representative Tony Coelho, the greatest Democratic fundraiser in the interval between Lyndon Johnson and Bill Clinton, warned contributors "Don't ever try to create the impression with me, or ever say it—if you say it, it's all over—that your money has bought you something. It hasn't."[20] Academic research supports this position, if the issue is whether there is a direct exchange of equivalents: quantitative studies that try to link donations to roll-call votes find little or no relationship.

Campaign contributions are best understood as gifts, given to create a generalized sense of obligation. Marcel Mauss wrote that "in Scandinavian and many other civilizations contracts are fulfilled and exchanges of goods are made by means of gifts."[21] These gifts, Mauss argued, are supposedly "voluntary, disinterested and spontaneous" but in fact are "obligatory and interested." A gift creates an enduring relationship, one that lasts at least until it is reciprocated. Corporations thus prefer to contribute to candidates in advance, before they have any favor to request, with the intent of creating a generalized sense of obligation. Moreover, as Mauss argued, "the presentation of a gift is an imposition of identity." Given the small size of most donations ($1,000 to $2,000 to candidates for Congress), corporations happily give to candidates for years simply on the chance that at some point in the future they may want legislation tailored to their needs. As Mauss explained, "ritualized gift giving, in any soci-

ety, is a method of dealing with important but insecure relationships, whereby gifts are offered to persons or collectivities whose goodwill is needed but cannot be taken for granted."

If campaign finance donations were given simply to influence election outcomes, donors would not need to be recognized. Because donations are in reality part of a complex gift exchange system that creates networks of obligation, donors insist that they must always present the money in person. Typically they do so at a fundraising gathering and use the occasion to become acquainted with the politician and his or her staff. As the vice president of a major Texas company explained to me, "If we are making a contribution to somebody who doesn't know it, we're screwing up. . . . If we are just sending money out to somebody and they are not aware of it, we've got no business giving them a contribution because they are not doing any good." As a result, corporate government relations officials attend dozens—in some cases hundreds—of fundraisers each election cycle. The fundraiser provides an opportunity to talk to the candidate on an issue of interest to the corporation, to talk to the candidate's staff, to talk to other members of Congress (especially the leadership) who show up to support the candidate, and of course also to network with representatives of other corporations.

Even if corporations are enemies in the marketplace, they often work together in politics.[22] One corporate executive explained that his

20 Quoted in Brooks Jackson, *Honest Graft: Big Money and the American Political Process* (New York: Knopf, 1988), p. 105.
21 Marcel Mauss, *The Gift: Forms and Functions of Exchange in Archaic Societies* (New York: W. W. Norton, 1925/1967; translated by Ian Cunnison), p. xiv.
22 See Mark Mizruchi, *The Structure of Corporate Political Action: Interfirm Relations and Their Consequences* (Cambridge, MA: Harvard University Press, 1992); Dan Clawson, Alan Neustadtl, and James Bearden, "The Logic of Business Unity," *American Sociological Review* 1986, vol. 51, no. 6, pp.797–811.

company, a pharmaceutical manufacturer, had a particularly bitter rival: "You couldn't get more competitive. We're suing each other all the time. . . . We hate each other, but I have a very good relationship with them down here [in Washington DC], and often we work together on the Hill for certain bills." Corporate executives frequently serve on a candidate's fundraising committee, and in that capacity get 5 or 10 other corporations to donate to the candidate. The solicited corporation contributes as a favor to the soliciting executive or corporation, and may do so even if they dislike the *candidate*. This process allows a corporation to be responsible (and gain credit with the candidate) for raising far more money than the corporate PAC could itself give, and yields "hard money" which can be used for any purpose (as opposed to "soft money" whose uses are restricted in various ways).

||| ACCESS

The purpose of giving the money, attending the fundraisers, and the networking process it facilitates, is to make it possible to gain "access" to the relevant member of Congress when the corporation wants something. "Access" is a euphemism for a process that involves much more than a chance to talk. Although the relatively small donations permitted by law are not enough to determine a member's vote on a highly visible roll call bill, the corporation uses its access to get the member to make a minor change in the wording of an obscure provision of the bill, effectively exempting the corporation from the full force of the law. For example, the Tax Reform Act of 1986 contained a provision limited to a single company, identified as a "corporation incorporated on June 13, 1917, which has its principal place of business in Bartlesville, Oklahoma." As is the case with this provision, the language in the bill typically does not identify the corporation by name (so someone reading the bill cannot tell it applies to Phillips Petroleum), nor does it give any sense of the dollar impact, nor is there any way of knowing which member of Congress inserted the provision. Many U.S. bills are hundreds of pages long, with a large fraction of the total taken up with these sorts of provisions. The consequence is that the "Tax Reform Act" doesn't really reform taxes and the "Clean Air Act" leaves the air polluted. The head of government relations at a major chemical company that is also a heavy-duty polluter told me: "I spent seven years of my life trying to stop the Clean Air Act." Nonetheless, he was perfectly willing to make corporate contributions to legislators who voted in favor of the Clean Air Act—as ultimately, almost all of them did—because "how a person votes on the final piece of legislation often is not representative of what they have done." Some of the legislators who voted for the final bill in fact helped to undermine its effectiveness: "During the process some of them were very sympathetic to some of our concerns" this executive explained.

To get the provisions they want, corporations may need to visit many representatives and may need to re-work the provision. The senior vice president of a steel manufacturer explained this process:

They [members of Congress] say, "Here's what I think, here's what you think, can you rework

---

SOFT MONEY: THE CLINTON COFFEES

A $100,000 contribution entitled donors to attend a small-group coffee with President Clinton and other top officials, held in the White House. Selected larger donors were invited to spend the night in the White House, sleeping in the Lincoln Bedroom, and often eating breakfast with the Clintons.

Typical of the Clinton coffees is the one held May 13, 1996, with Terry Murray, president and CEO of Fleet Bank; John McCoy, chairman of Banc One; Paul Hazen, chairman and CEO of Wells Fargo Bank; and Thomas G. Labrecque, chairman and CEO of Chase Manhattan Bank, as well as Treasury Secretary Robert E. Rubin, Comptroller of the Currency Eugene A. Ludwig, Democratic National Committee Chairman Don Fowler, party Finance Chairman Marvin S. Rosen, and of course President Clinton. John P. Manning, president and CEO of Boston Capital Partners, explains that at the coffees he has attended "There was give and take on a number of business and economic issues."★

Perhaps the most unusual coffee participants were two representatives of the Cheyenne-Arapaho tribes of Oklahoma. The tribe has 11,000 members, more than 60 percent of whom were unemployed, and those with jobs earned an average annual income of $6,074. At great hardship, they came up with the $100,000 to attend a coffee and tell President Clinton about their problem: Their land was taken from them in 1883 by President Chester A. Arthur's executive order, which specified, however, that the land was to be returned to the tribe as soon as it was no longer used for military purposes. The fort was closed in 1948, but the land was never returned. The land "includes unmarked graves, ritual dance grounds and an estimated $500 million in oil and gas reserves." The tribe had earlier tried to see their U.S. senator, but had been denied a meeting. President Clinton listened to their concerns, looked them in the eye, and said "We'll see what we can do to help you." In fact, he did nothing. When they complained and went to the press the money was returned to them, but the government kept their land.†

★*Boston Globe*, January 25, 1997, p. A6.
†*New York Times*, August 12, 1997, p. A18.

---

this out so I can give you a little piece of the pie and still not screw the other 93 percent of my district who want it the other way?" And we say, "Yes, if you can just do this. It doesn't change the bill, but at least it allows us to do this." It's the fun of the game.

The senior vice president of one of the nation's largest financial companies was blunt about it:

We are not big on voting records . . . because frequently the final vote on a particular bill isn't really important. . . . Probably what's more important is what's thrashed out internally in some of the important committees in Congress. And it doesn't much matter how people vote afterwards.

Corporate executives say that essentially *all* members of Congress participate in this process; ultra-conservatives who insist on "no government interference with the market" will insert provisions to provide government handouts, as will well known liberals with a reputation for being "anti-business." A mid-level official at a utility company told me that "You have guys that will hold rallies right outside this building here, hold news conferences and picket lines periodically, every year," attacking the company and its policies. But once in Congress those same people cooperate with the company: "I don't want to say that they are the best friends we have in government, but you can go to them."

Individual and PAC contributions are the normal routes to "access" to ordinary members of Congress; soft money has become the route to access to national party officials and the president. President Clinton defended the White House coffees he held: "I look for ways to have genuine conversations with people. I learn things when I listen to people."[23] But the people to whom President Clinton was listening were not exactly a cross-section of the population: the price for admission to the coffees was $100,000. Reportedly, most discussions at coffees focused primarily on background and general policy, rather than on the direct insertion of loopholes, and involved CEO-level officials (as opposed to the vice presidents and managers who typically talk to members of Congress and to congressional staff). One coffee participant defended the coffees by explaining that President Clinton "really seemed to want businessmen's perspective on what he was doing on the economy, tax, health care."[24] (See Box 1.)

||| IDEOLOGY

Corporations also give campaign contributions for ideological reasons. A few corporations follow an almost exclusively ideological approach, and many corporations pay at least some attention to ideological concerns. An "access" strategy means that corporations contribute to incumbents, regardless of political party and generally without regard to a candidate's professed ideology (since in practice all legislators participate in this access process) or whether they even have an opponent. Ideological corporations want to change Congress and so give to pro-business challengers (in practice almost all of them Republicans) who are in tight races where contributions could influence the election outcome. The 1980 election differed from all others: a large proportion of all corporations pursued an aggressively ideological strategy for that election. If we look at corporations contributing 30 percent or more of their money to Republican challengers, more did so in 1980 than in all the other elections from 1976 to 2000 *combined*. The executive vice president of one corporation explained:

> There was a genuine movement, the closest thing I've ever seen on the part of business in this country, almost a phenomenon that occurred in that year and a half or two years of that particular election. It was a genuine virtual fervor. Let's go out there and we can do it, we can change the system.

Immediately after the 1980 Republican victories, Democratic strategists (led by Representative Tony Coelho, later Al Gore's campaign chairman) aggressively re-shaped the party and went to business seeking donations for Democrats. Coelho pointed out to business executives that Democrats (at that time) still controlled the House of Representatives, and therefore "I don't think it makes good business sense for you to try

---

23 *New York Times,* March 8, 1997, p. 9.

24 *Boston Globe,* January 25, 1997, p. A6.

to destroy us."[25] Coelho notes that in 1980 "we had our butts kicked" and is convinced that if he and others had not courted business, the Republicans "would have completed the job." As a result, most corporations reverted to predominantly access-driven contribution strategies.

The few corporations which remain ideological are furious at the access strategy of other corporations. A member of the Board of Directors of a leading manufacturer said: "I can't figure out what their motive is. I just look at it and look at it, and I just can't figure it out." Such corporations, he said, are shoving money at candidates "who don't need the money and who couldn't lose if they were caught in *flagrante delicto* with the governor's wife in the public square of the capital. " In his view, "the behavior of corporate PACs is absolutely fucking disgraceful. . . . And stupid and shortsighted beyond measure."

Most corporate executives, however, prefer the current situation, where *both* major parties are strongly "pro-business" and heavily dependent on business campaign contributions. One executive, formerly a party official but now in charge of an oil company's political contributions, explained to me: "I don't do this for myself, I do it for the company. I don't really feel I have a party now. I think it is foolish for anybody in this business to profess an affiliation with a party. I don't think that is very healthy." As a result, *both* major American parties depend primarily on business for campaign contributions. For soft money donations, for example, the *Democrats* receive more than *six* times as much from corporations as from labor unions.

Republicans made huge advances in the 1994 elections and took control of both houses of Congress. The easy assumption would be that this was because business had once again mobilized as it had done in 1980, and some left analysts made such claims. Thomas Ferguson, for example, wrote that "A sea of money that had been flowing reliably to congressional Democrats and the party that controlled the White House abruptly reversed direction and began gushing in torrents to Republican challengers."[26] In fact, however, there is no truth to this claim: corporate campaign contributions in 1994 are essentially the same as they were in every election from 1982 on. The contrast with 1980 is stark. In 1980, Republican challengers received 28.6 percent of all the money contributed by corporations; in 1994, they received only 5.7 percent.[27] The 1994 Republican victories were *not* the consequence of a massive business mobilization, nor did business fund Republican challengers in 1996—which may well explain why President Clinton was easily re-elected in 1996, and why the Republicans won so few policy changes from their 1994 victories.[28]

★ ★ ★

25 Thomas Byrne Edsall, "Coelho Mixes Democratic Fund-Raising, Political Matchmaking." *Washington Post,* December 1, 1985, pp. A17–18. See also Edsall, "The Reagan Legacy," in *The Reagan Legacy,* edited by Sidney Blumenthal and Edsall, pp. 3–50 (New York: Pantheon), and Brooks Jackson, *Honest Graft: Big Money and the American Political Process* (New York: Knopf, 1988).

26 Thomas Ferguson, "GOP Money Talked: Did Voters Listen?" *The Nation* December 26, 1994, p. 792.

27 Dan Clawson, Alan Neustadtl, and Mark Weller, *Dollars and Votes: How Business Campaign Contributions Subvert Democracy* (Philadelphia: Temple University Press, 1998), p. 160.

28 In 1996 business did increase its contributions to Republican incumbents (since they were now the majority in Congress, and would control the key committees), but not to Republican challengers. Ibid.

LESSONS

Public debate and media reports usually discuss U.S. campaign finance in terms of whether campaign contributions do or do not buy politicians' votes. This fundamentally misunderstands the way the system operates. There is little correlation between campaign contributions and high visibility roll call votes. Even for low visibility issues settled through "minor" wording changes in obscure provisions of bills, the process is much looser and more uncertain than a market transaction. The problem is not outright bribery, but rather the creation of a network of obligations; the addition of one or two or three new regulations will not significantly alter this process.

At least in the U.S. context, full public disclosure of contributions has had little effect in regulating behavior. Data on campaign contributions are publicly available on the Web,[29] but this has had few consequences for behavior. It is possible that would be different in a more class conscious society, but I know of no evidence to that effect.

Another common reform proposal, an effort to limit the size of donations to amounts so small that they would be unlikely to influence behavior, also seems unlikely to be effective. It is true that today, especially for soft money, most of the money comes from a few large donors. In 1996, of 27,596 soft money donors, 19,670 gave $1,000 or less; they were 71.3 percent of the donors but accounted for only 3.6 percent of the money. On the other hand, the 487 donors who gave $100,000 or more were only 1.8 percent of the contributors but accounted for 49.9% of the money.[30] Nonetheless, the most likely effect of donation limits would be that businesses would organize to increase the number of donors, just as corporations today often contribute because another corporation asks them to do so.

Because business has vastly more resources than any other group, over time it has come to more and more fully dominate campaign finance. In 1974 labor contributed more than business, and labor opposed public financing of elections, believing its large base of small donors would give it political muscle. The advantage has steadily shifted to business, until by now it outspends labor 15 to 1. Only in the last few years has labor accepted the fact it will not be able to compete; this has led it to switch its strategy and support full public funding of campaigns.

Business is not concerned about strategies that involve imposing additional regulations. Corporations are confident they will find new loopholes faster than Congress can impose new regulations. The only reform strategy that concerns business, or that has demonstrated much potential to fundamentally alter the system, is full public financing at a level sufficient to run a viable campaign. Partial public financing will make little difference: the current U.S. presidential elections receive public financing, but candidates are permitted to raise additional sums, and that private money provides the margin of victory.

29 At the Federal Election Commission website, www.fec.gov, and at that of the non-partisan watchdog group the Center for Responsive Politics, www.crp.org.

30 Dan Clawson, Alan Neustadtl, and Mark Weller, *Dollars and Votes: How Business Campaign Contributions Subvert Democracy* (Philadelphia: Temple University Press, 1998), p. 114; based on Federal Election Commission data.

The Right to Vote and Unequal Participation in American Politics*

JEFF MANZA

Writing in 1949, the political scientist V.O. Key famously asserted that "the blunt truth is that politicians are under no compulsion to pay much heed to classes and groups of citizens that do not vote" (Key 1964 [1949], p. 527). Key's comment captures one of the enduring dilemmas of American democracy. Elections are supposed to produce some approximation of the will of the people. But this has always been complicated by large differences in participation rates among groups of citizens, with people who have more resources voting at much higher rates than those without. Such differences arise for two reasons: first, because many people are unable or choose not to participate in politics; second, because legal barriers to participation make some people *ineligible* to participate. Because nonvoters in America are *not* drawn evenly from across American society, but rather are concentrated among disadvantaged groups, the voting public is quite different from the entire population.

This chapter explores these differences, their sources, and their implications for American democracy. Political inequalities have long been the subject of analysis by scholars and writers, but the intensity of concern has risen

---

* Original essay prepared for this volume.

in recent years. In particular, the failure of the American political system to effectively respond to rising inequality and encourage greater sharing of the benefits of economic growth raises questions about how and why public policy is being made. Evidence of the issue is widespread. For example, the American welfare state stands out among the rich democracies for low levels of public spending. The United States currently devotes about 14 percent of its gross domestic product (GDP) on social spending programs, versus an average of 26.5 percent in the western European welfare state and 18 percent in the other Anglo-American democracies frequently grouped together as "liberal" welfare states (Brooks and Manza 2007, chap. 1). There are numerous other examples of the failure of the political system to respond to rising inequality: repeated tax cutting for the superrich at a time when high-income households are already receiving unprecedented shares of national income; a pointed refusal of Congress and the White House to adjust the federal minimum wage for a decade after 1997, contributing to a cumulative decline in real value of 36 percent between 1979 and 2006. And there is evidence that when the rich and poor disagree on significant policy questions, the rich are much more likely to get what they want (Gilens 2005; Bartels 2008, chap. 9).

These political outcomes raise, in a particularly sharp way, one of the classical puzzles of democracy: why don't the (vastly more numerous) poor and middle classes simply elect governments who would redistribute income downward by, for example, taxing the rich and increasing benefits for everyone else? This puzzle arises in all democracies to one degree or another, and a wide variety of answers have been proposed. But in the specific context of American society where inequalities have grown so sharply in recent years, the puzzle is both deeper and more in need of explanation. One answer to the puzzle focuses on the widening disparities in the "inputs" flowing into the political system. Political money—discussed by Dan Clawson in the previous chapter— is the most obvious example. As the amounts and shares of income received by households at the top have increased over the past three decades, the amount of money the rich have at their disposal to give to support political causes has increased dramatically. To the extent that members of Congress vote according to the priorities of their donors, there may be a significant bias toward the interests of the rich and powerful. Yet when social scientists carefully seek out evidence of such a relationship, they frequently find it difficult to identify one (see Ansolabehere et al. 2003; Burstein 2003). My review of the vast literature suggests that while the need to raise large amounts of money may influence who runs for office and while donating money does make it easier to get access to elected officials—two nontrivial effects—in most other respects it is less clear that campaign contributions lay at the heart of the problem (see Manza, Brooks, and Sauder 2004).

Another approach focuses on which party is in charge of the government. Careful research has demonstrated that economic gains are shared more equally when the Democrats are in office (Bartels 2008). And, indeed, the political environment since the early 1980s has been one in which a business-oriented Republican Party has largely—although not completely—shaped the policy-making agenda, cutting taxes and blocking the adoption of most new spending programs aimed to address rising inequality. Republican dominance in the contemporary era of inequality represents an important historic shift in partisan power and influence. The Democratic Party controlled both houses of Congress (with but a brief interruption in the early 1950s) for nearly half a century between 1932 and 1980, as well as a majority of state houses across the country. Throughout the entire period from World War II to the early 1970s, American society became more equal on most dimensions, with an improved social safety net, especially for the aged, affirmative-action policies benefiting minorities and women, a rising minimum wage, and a vast expansion of higher education to give ever-growing numbers of young Americans opportunities to develop skills needed in a postindustrial economy (Krugman 2007).

Beginning in 1980, however, Republicans gained and maintained control of the White House (except for the Clinton years between 1993 and 2001), the U.S. Senate for most of the 1980s, and both houses of Congress from 1994 to 2006. For the first time in a couple of generations, they also won control of a majority of state governments and used that power to aggressively remake the political map during the redistricting following the 2000 Census (Hacker and Pierson 2005). No mere summary of these partisan shifts alone can fully capture the magnitude of the political earthquake since the Reagan years. The Republicans have become an increasingly probusiness, antitax party, embracing a national policy agenda that has pushed back against the direction of the more redistributive policies of the New Deal/Great Society eras. The egalitarian policy initiatives of the earlier era were brought to a halt or, in some cases, reversed.

But attributing the failure of the political system to respond to rising inequality to a shifting partisan environment (and the rise of a national Republican majority) does not, I would argue, capture the full range of factors behind the shifting terrain of the politics of inequality in the United States since the 1970s. In this chapter, I develop an argument about democracy and political inequality in America that centers on political participation. The right to vote and participate in elections has never been true for all adults living in the United States, but a variety of social and demographic changes over the past thirty years has magnified the importance of eligibility rules. Further, changes in who participates, with a growing underrepresentation of the poor in the electorate, has meant that the voting public is more likely to overrepresent those with policy preferences for smaller government and less redistribution.

||| THE RIGHT TO VOTE

Let's start with some basics. As noted, democratic political systems are based on the principle that all citizens should have equal opportunities to shape the composition of their elected government. Universal suffrage—the right of each citizen to cast one, and only, ballot for each contested election—is an essential precondition for asserting the existence of democracy. Of course universal suffrage is not enough to guarantee democracy, but it is an important starting point.

Other things—freedom of the press, freedom to run for office, fair administration and counting of the vote, and respect for the legitimacy of the outcome—are necessary features as well. But whether all citizens are allowed to vote in the first place is one critical bedrock of democratic legitimacy.

Unlike virtually all other democratic constitutions around the world, the American constitution does not guarantee universal suffrage. When the Framers met to draft the Constitution, there were no models to draw on. Some participants floated the idea of declaring the vote a "natural right." Against such radically democratic ideas were various conceptions of stakeholder democracy, in which only property owners or taxpayers would be allowed to participate. The most commonly expressed justification for this was that only "stakeholders" had a material interest in the well-being of the community and thus would exercise the franchise wisely. In the end, the drafters compromised, leaving it to the states to determine who could exercise the franchise. This power remains in the hands of the states, although a series of constitutional amendments later curtailed some of that power. States can no longer discriminate based on race, sex, or age (for those eighteen years of age or older), nor can they impose poll taxes as a precondition of voting.

Given the freedom to set their rules, states adopted a variety of legal regimes regulating access to the ballot. In the late eighteenth and early nineteenth centuries, most states adopted some kind of property restriction on the exercise of the franchise, allowing only those white men who owned property to vote. Throughout the first half of the nineteenth century,

however, property and most other restrictions against white men tended to fall. By 1840, largely property restrictions had been eliminated. On the eve of the Civil War in 1860, the main barriers to participation were those preventing women and African Americans from participating. Black men could vote in only six states, and women were excluded everywhere. Women's suffrage arrived first at the state level, especially in the newer states in the West, and later nationally with the adoption of the Nineteenth Amendment in 1920. For African Americans, the adoption of the Fifteenth Amendment in 1870, which explicitly banned the states from using race as a reason to exclude individuals from participating. Despite the promise of the Fifteenth Amendment in 1870, however, suffrage was not fully secured for African Americans in the South until the adoption of the Voting Rights Act in 1965, a full century after the end of the Civil War. Beginning in the late nineteenth century, Southern states adopted a variety of legal means to keep black citizens from casting ballots. These restrictions included requiring prospective voters to pass literacy tests administered in frequently arbitrary ways by local officials, poll taxes, notorious "grandfather clauses" (in which citizens were eligible to vote only if they could show evidence of having had a grandfather eligible to vote), and white-only primaries. These devices collectively suppressed participation of black voters across the South. And the impact persisted, even as some of the most extreme measures (like the white-only primary) were abolished.

The triumphal passage of the Voting Rights Act (VRA) in 1965—after the dramatic March to Selma, Alabama, led by Martin Luther King

Jr. highlighted for the nation the full extent to which southern officials would go to deny voting rights to African Americans—brought an end to the use of such devices. The fact that by the early 1960s, the mass migration of African Americans from the South to northern cities had created large and powerful voting blocs was a crucial part of the story. The enfranchisement of black voters proceeded thereafter with surprisingly little further violence. It would have an enormous political impact in southern states, one that is still being felt to this day, with newly enfranchised black voters finding their voice and electing thousands of African Americans across the South, and white voters defecting in droves from the Democratic Party.

The story of exclusion after the Civil War and into the first part of the twentieth century is not simply about the enfranchisement of women and continuing disenfranchisement and eventual enfranchisement of African Americans in the South. Several new disenfranchising steps were undertaken in this period. As Alexander Keyssar (2000) shows in his masterly history of the right to vote in America, from the late nineteenth century onward, northern states joined the South in experimenting with and imposing literacy tests on prospective registrants. For example, a 1911 constitutional amendment in California excluded those "who shall not be able to read the Constitution in the English language and write his or her name," while Connecticut specified in 1902 that the prospective voter must "read at least three lines of the Constitution or of the statutes of this State, other than the title or enacting clause, in such manner as to show that he is not prompted nor reciting from memory." States like Maine (1893),

Massachusetts (1892), New Hampshire (1902), New York (1921), Oregon (1924), and Washington (1912) adopted similar measures.

In this same era, states adopted new voter registration requirements, sometimes with onerous burdens of proof of residence and frequently with long residency requirements targeted specifically at urban voters. Before the large-scale introduction of voter registration requirements, voters could simply show up at the polls with some form of identification or with witnesses to vouch for the voter. The introduction of registration requirements had a "good government" rationale, in the face of real or manufactured evidence of electoral fraud. While it is difficult to adjudicate the evidence about how widespread electoral fraud was, there is little question that requiring voters to register before the election introduced a system that would make it more difficult for millions to vote (and the percentage of registered voters among the poor and working class would fall substantially behind that of the middle class).

All of these exclusions, which operated as a de facto legal bar on participation for many otherwise eligible voters, had an especially significant impact on newer immigrants who were less likely to be able to read English and pass a literacy test, or could prove sufficiently long residency in the state. How well enforced these various restrictions were is unclear, but there is good reason to think that they contributed substantially to the decline in voter participation after 1900.

Voting Rights Since 1965

The contested history of the legal right to vote has suggested to many observers that the American political system did not fully meet the requisites of democracy until after 1965. But since 1965, and the passage of the VRA, the right to vote for citizens has been more or less a taken-for-granted fact of American political life, one that nearly all informed observers have agreed. In 1995, for example, the leading study of political participation in American politics asserted that "at least since the voting rights reforms of the 1960s, political rights have been universalized in the United States. With relatively insignificant exceptions, all adult citizens have the full complement of political rights" (Verba, Scholzman, and Brady 1995, p. 11).

Today, an illiterate, homeless, propertyless, African American woman on government assistance, who has unpaid debts, and who moved to a new state just three months ago cannot be denied the right to register to vote. But once upon a time, each of those attributes would have been sufficient to deny her the right to vote in one or more states. So times have, indeed, changed. Over the past two hundred years, virtually all restrictions on the right to vote have melted away. No state would be legally entitled, or normatively justified, in using any one of those criteria to deny the right to vote. Yet two increasingly important exceptions to this broad and widely accepted generalization persist: legal (and illegal) immigrants and convicted felons. The year 1965 was important for voting rights not only because of the adoption of the VRA but also because of the expansion of legal immigration with the passage of new federal immigration law, which allowed millions of new permanent legal immigrants (and their families) to enter the United States. Over time, this law has enabled millions of non-native

adults to become part of the voting age population, but only the naturalized subset among them has the right to vote.

The United States does not stand out internationally in denying voting rights in national elections to noncitizen residents; in fact, no democratic country allows noncitizens to vote in national elections (although many allow immigrants to vote in local elections). But the upshot of the rapid growth of the immigrant population since 1965 has been a steady increase in the proportion of voting age adults without the right to vote, with the proportion of legal immigrants as a percentage of the voting age population growing from 2.6 percent to 7.8 percent between 1972 and 2004 (McCarty et al. 2006, pp. 115–16).

The second excluded group are convicted felons. Because many states have maintained laws restricting voting rights for most current felons and many ex-felons, the rising incarceration and conviction rates over the past 35 years have disenfranchised millions of citizens (Manza and Uggen 2006). The patchwork state laws regulating felon voting rights across the country do not lend themselves to easy summary (and indeed, many state laws regulating voting rights for convicted felons have changed very recently, rendering any quick summary a hazardous undertaking). Nonetheless, a few key distinctions are worth noting. All but two states (Vermont and Maine) disenfranchise current inmates and the vast majority disenfranchise some or all nonincarcerated felons (those out on probation and parole), and ten states disenfranchise not only current felons but also many or all of their ex-felon population (former offenders who have completed their sentences). As a result of the rapid increase in conviction and incarceration after 1972, the disenfranchised felon population has grown steadily (Manza and Uggen [2006, p. 78] estimate that there were 1.2 million disenfranchised felons in 1976 and 5.3 million at the time of the 2004 presidential election). About 2.75 percent of the voting-eligible population were disenfranchised at the time of the 2004 election because of a past or current felony conviction.

Because both of these groups of the disenfranchised—immigrants and felons—tend to be drawn from the bottom of the class structure, rising rates of disenfranchisement mean a skewing of the eligible electorate upward. In their important recent study, Nolan McCarty and his colleagues (2006) present historical evidence showing that rising rates of immigration are frequently associated with rising inequality. Asking why, they hypothesize that one mechanism is political exclusion of a subset of the electorate. They show that in the early 1970s, disenfranchised immigrants were a relatively small group and, in terms of income, markedly different from what they are today. In 1972, noncitizens reported higher median incomes than citizens and had an average household income that was 82 percent of that of citizens. By 2000, by contrast, the much larger group of noncitizen residents had an average household income that was only 65 percent of that of citizens. Because noncitizens are by law disenfranchised, their rising share of the overall voting age population and declining economic status has meant that the composition of the electorate has changed. Similarly, the felon population is disproportionately poor, is African American, and has low levels of education, and the

vast increase in the convicted felon population since the early 1970s has magnified the impact of existing disenfranchising measures.

Looking at the big picture, the extent to which the overall right to vote has been influenced by these changes can be seen in Figure 1, which charts the estimated growth of the disenfranchised population. In 1976, long before the full impact of the 1965 immigration reform would be felt and when the rate of felon disenfranchisement was relatively low, less than 4 percent of the adult voting age population could not vote. By 2004, a little over 10 percent—one in ten—of adults living legally in the United States could not vote. Because of the concentration of the disenfranchised among the poorest and most disadvantaged in American society, a growing share of the poor cannot express them-

FIGURE 1 INELIGIBLE ADULTS LIVING IN THE UNITED STATES, 1980–2004

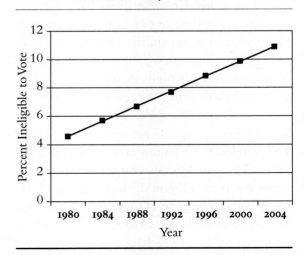

SOURCE: Adjusted by author from data originally developed by Michael McDonald; see http://elections/gmu.edu/voter_turnout.

selves politically. And the overall national figure masks enormous regional variation: the disenfranchised and the migrant population are not distributed evenly across the country but tend to be more heavily concentrated in a handful of states such as California, Texas, and Florida.

These trends pose powerful challenges for the future of American democracy. While it is certain that many current legal immigrants and their children will eventually gain citizenship (and perhaps, depending on the outcome of current debates over immigration reform, some illegal immigrants as well), the tide of new immigration into the United States is unlikely to abate any time soon. And although there has been some slowing of the rate of increase in the felon population in recent years, because some states continue to disenfranchise after the sentence is completed, it is likely (barring significant changes in state laws) that the disenfranchised felon population will continue to be very large. As a consequence, the share of the total adult population in the United States without the right to vote is likely to grow in the foreseeable future.

POLITICAL PARTICIPATION IN AMERICA

If the right to vote provides a baseline condition for participation, how many citizens actually partake of that right is also critical to understanding inequalities in political participation in America. There are large and persisting disparities in participation among the eligible, whether we are talking about voting in elections or for many other types of political activity. These disparities represent a very

important source of political inequality in the United States. The naked facts of low turnout are startling enough. One recent international survey shows that turnout in U.S. national elections ranks an extraordinary 138th highest among the 170 democratic countries surveyed, far lower than all similar capitalist democracies except Switzerland (which ranked 137th) (International Institute for Democracy and Electoral Assistance 1997; see also Freeman 2004). Figure 2 illustrates some of these differences, comparing turnout in recent American elections with those of other rich democracies most like the United States. We find turnout rates approaching or exceeding 75 percent in many countries.

In addition to having very low rates of turnout, the United States is unusual for having very large differences in rates of political participation. For example, there is often a turnout gap of as much as 25 percent or more between the high turnout groups versus low turnout groups (such as professionals versus unskilled workers, or whites and Hispanics in the case of race/ethnicity) (Lijphart 1997; Manza and Brooks 1999, chap. 7; Freeman 2004).

Why does the United States have such low levels of turnout? In the social science literature on who votes, there are two broad streams of explanation: individual-level explanations (such as education level, race/ethnicity, class, religion, community, and knowledge/interest in politics), and political and/or institutional explanations. Individual attributes are powerful predictors of who votes, but by themselves they cannot account for the comparatively low rates of turnout (Americans are no less educated or interested in or knowledgeable about politics

FIGURE 2 **TURNOUT IN ADVANCED INDUSTRIAL DEMOCRACIES, 1945–1998**

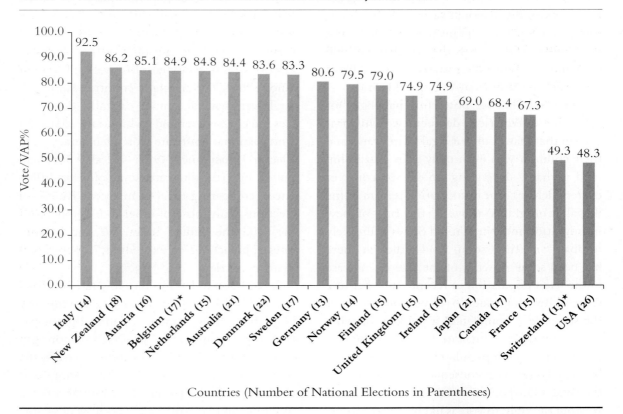

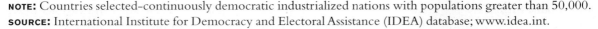

Countries (Number of National Elections in Parentheses)

NOTE: Countries selected–continuously democratic industrialized nations with populations greater than 50,000.
SOURCE: International Institute for Democracy and Electoral Assistance (IDEA) database; www.idea.int.

than citizens in other countries with much higher rates of participation).

Political and institutional explanations, by contrast, point to a set of factors that are more distinctive about the United States. Institutional constraints on participating, such as requiring voters to register ahead of time, the timing of elections, and the narrow range of meaningful choices presented to voters through the party system provide some examples. Holding elections on a working day (the first Tuesday after

the first Monday in November), is clearly one institutional source of reduced turnout. Cross-national estimates of the negative impact of holding elections on a working day (versus a weekend or holiday) are around 5 percent, with the penalty hurting turnout among workers with the least autonomy in their jobs and single parents the most.

The level and type of mobilization efforts undertaken by social movements and party organizations provides another set of explanations for why turnout is lower and the skew in participation higher in the United States. Low-turnout groups are effected more influence by mobilization efforts than higher turnout groups. As with other participatory inequalities, the United States stands out for its lack of equalizing vehicles. In other democratic countries, strong unions and social democratic parties encourage poor and working class voters to participate in elections. The United States has very weak unions and completely lacks a social democratic or labor party. As a result, voter mobilization efforts are much more of a patchwork, with social movement organizations (including those based in churches) playing a disproportionate role. While such organizations can have beneficial effects on turnout (Leighley 2001), they cannot substitute for the embedded organizational strength of strong unions and social democratic parties.

The upshot has been that the United States has participation inequalities that are far greater than elections in other countries. But the problem may be even worse than this implies: participation inequalities in American politics extend beyond voting to other types of political engagement—such as working on a political campaign, participating in a protest event, writing a letter to an elected official, and civic volunteerism of any kind. Here we also find large inequalities between resource-rich groups and disadvantaged groups. The definitive study in this area remains that of Sidney Verba, Kay Lehman Scholzman, and Henry Brady (1995), who found evidence of even larger disparities than in voting in most other types of political activity. For example, while 17 percent of those earning over $75,000 a year (in 1989) reported working on a political campaign, only 4 percent of those earning under

$15,000 did so; 73 percent of the former report being a member of a political organization, but only 29 percent of the latter; 50 percent of the affluent group wrote to an elected official at least once in the previous year, but only 25 percent of the low-income group did so.

MAKING SENSE OF PARTICIPATION INEQUALITIES

Does it matter that the right to vote in America excludes so many people and that turnout rates among the eligible poor and working class are so much lower than those of more resource rich groups? One way is to imagine what would happen in the counterfactual scenario in which everyone participated. Would outcomes be different?

The most systematic recent work on this question, by Jan Leighley and Jonathan Nagler (2007), suggests that it would, at least with respect to class-related policy questions. Survey respondents who said they would not vote in the 2004 election were more likely, for example, to support national health insurance (+7.2 percent), a federal guarantee of jobs for all who want one (+11.9 percent), or to make union organizing easier (+13.8 percent). To be sure, nonvoters were not necessarily more likely to be Democratic Party partisans or more ideologically liberal in their stated preferences than the voting public. But current attitudes and beliefs of nonvoters might well shift closer to their policy preferences in the process of their incorporation into the political system.

Getting current nonvoters into the political process might itself be an important source of equalizing pressures. With more citizens at the bottom of the income and education distribution available to be mobilized, the major parties would, at least potentially, have to pay more attention to figuring out how to win their support. The converse of the V.O. Key quote at the beginning of this chapter suggests that politicians do have to pay attention to the concerns of the voting public, because their careers partially depend on it. It is thus reasonable to think that an expanded electorate would force politicians to think harder about problems of poverty and inequality than they do today.

||| REFERENCES

Ansolabehere, Stephen, John M. de Figueiredo, and James M. Synder. 2003. "Why Is There So Little Money in U.S. Politics?" *Journal of Economic Perspectives* 17: 105–30.

Bartels, Larry. 2008. *Unequal Democracy.* New York: Russell Sage Foundation.

Brooks, Clem, and Jeff Manza. 2007. *Why Welfare States Persist.* Chicago: University of Chicago Press.

Freeman, Richard B. 2004. "What, Me Vote?" In *Social Inequality,* ed. Kathryn Neckerman, pp. 703–28. New York: Russell Sage Foundation.

Gilens, Martin. 2005. "Inequality and Democratic Responsiveness." *Public Opinion Quarterly* 69: 778–96.

Hacker, Jacob, and Paul Pierson. 2005. *Off Center.* New York: Oxford University Press.

Key, V.O. 1964 [1949]. *Southern Politics in State and Nation.* Cambridge: Harvard University Press.

Keyssar, Alexander. 2000. *The Right to Vote.* New York: Basic Books.

Krugman, Paul. 2007. *The Conscience of a Liberal.* New York: Norton.

Leighley, Jan. 2001. *Strength in Numbers? The Political Mobilization of Racial and Ethnic Minorities.* Princeton: Princeton University Press.

Leighley, Jan and Jonathan Nagler. 2007. "Who Votes Now? And Does It Matter?" Paper presented to the Midwest Political Science Association Meetings, Chicago, Illinois, April 12–15.

Lijphart, Arend. 1997. "Unequal Participation: Democracy's Unresolved Dilemma." *American Political Science Review* 91: 1–14.

Manza, Jeff, and Clem Brooks. 1999. *Social Cleavages and Political Change: Voter Alignments and U.S. Party Coalitions.* New York: Oxford University Press.

Manza, Jeff, Clem Brooks, and Michael Sauder. "Money, Participation, and Votes: Social Cleavages and Electoral Politics." In *Handbook of Political Sociology,* ed. Thomas Januski et al., pp. 201–26. New York: Cambridge University Press.

Manza, Jeff, and Christopher Uggen. 2006. *Locked Out: Felon Disenfranchisement and American Democracy.* New York: Oxford University Press.

McCarty, Nolan, Keith Poole, and Howard Rosenthal. 2006. *Polarized America: The Dance of Ideology and Unequal Riches.* Cambridge: MIT Press.

Piven, Frances Fox, and Richard Cloward. 2000. *Why Americans Still Don't Vote.* New York: The New Press.

Verba, Sidney, Kay Lehman Scholzman, and Henry Brady. 1995. *Voice and Equality.* Cambridge: Harvard University Press.

52

Where Have All the Unions Gone . . . Long Time Passing?*

RICHARD FREEMAN

Trade unions are the primary worker institution in capitalist economies. They replace market wage setting with collective bargaining and management control over workplaces with "industrial jurisprudence"—rules and negotiated procedures to deal with workplace problems. They guarantee workers a voice at the workplace and make sure that management hears workers' views on issues.

For the past half-century, unions have been dying in the United States. Year after year, the proportion of wage and salary workers in unions has fallen. In 2005 union density in the private sector was 7.9 percent of employed wage and salary workers—comparable to the level in the 1880s. Density in the public sector was 36.4 percent; this is over four times the private-sector level, but the public sector accounts for just 15 percent of the U.S. workforce.[1] As a result, economywide density was 12.5 percent. But it could go lower.

---

* First published in 2007; from *America Works*.

[1] U.S. Department of Labor, "Union Members in 2005," table 1, available at: http://www.bls.gov/news.release/union2.t01.htm.

In the state with the lowest rate of unionization, North Carolina, density fell from 5.3 percent in 1990 to 2.7 percent in 2005.[2] Because the United States does not extend collective bargaining contracts beyond the signatories, the low level of membership translates into the smallest proportion of workers covered by collective bargaining among advanced countries. In response to the failure of the AFL-CIO to find a way to reverse the decline in membership, some large trade unions left the federation in 2005 to form Change to Win, a trade union coalition dedicated to organizing new workers.

Why have unions lost representation in the private sector? What are the consequences for workers and the economy? Can unions rise like the phoenix from the ashes, or is the United States on the verge of reaching the union-free environment that anti-union zealots have long hoped for?

This chapter tells the story of the decline of unionism in the United States and offers radical suggestions on how to give workers collective voice to represent their interests despite this decline. I began researching unionism in the 1980s and have done more work on unions than on any other topic. My 1984 book *What Do Unions Do?* (with James Medoff) has been the center of union research since its publication. In 2004–2005 the *Journal of Labor Research* held a twentieth-anniversary review in which two dozen or so researchers assessed the book's findings and arguments in light of ensuing analysis and events. The symposium led to *What Do Unions Do? A Twenty-Year Perspective,* which is much larger than the original.[3] To my relief, the review concluded that the work had stood the test of time, which is more than can be said for the union movement. In 2007 Beijing University Press will publish a Chinese edition as one of the modern classics in economics. But is *What Do Unions Do?* about a live institution, or is it paleontology about a dinosaur that has failed the market test in the United States?

‖ THE FALLING HOUSE OF LABOR

The United States has a checkered record with unions. Employers have violently opposed worker efforts to unionize in the past. Courts have challenged the right of workers to unionize even after Congress enacted legislation meant to legitimize unions. On the union side, the United States is the only advanced country where the mob has run major unions, ripping off workers and firms, as the movie *On the Waterfront* highlighted in 1954. During the Depression, Congress enacted the National Labor Relations Act to move the struggle to unionize from the streets and factories to the ballot box. If a majority of workers voted for a union to represent them, firms had to recognize and bargain with that union. Many workers voted for unions in government-sponsored elections during the Depression and World War II and the Korean War, and many joined unions without going through the process. In 1955, when the AFL and CIO merged into a

---

2 For 2004, see ibid.; for 1990, see www.trinity.edu/bhirsch/unionstats/. The rate in the private sector in North Carolina fell from 3.8 percent in 1990 to 2.1 percent in 2003.

3 Kauffman and Bennett, *What Do Unions Do? A Twenty-Year Perspective.*

single federation, 37 percent of private-sector workers were unionized, and many non-union firms mimicked union agreements to keep their workers from joining unions. It was the era of Big Labor.

Whether union representation of the workforce increases or decreases over time is determined by the number of new workers organized by unions minus the number they lose owing to the closure or shrinkage of unionized workplaces and the growth of the workforce. When the workforce grows, unions must organize more workers to maintain their share of employment even if no members leave. Assuming roughly constant attrition of membership and growth of the workforce, the key factor in how union density changes is the number of workers organized by unions relative to the workforce. From the mid-1950s through the mid-1960s, unions organized from 0.5 percent to 0.7 percent of the private-sector workforce through National Labor Relations Board elections. This fell short of the rate of organizing needed to maintain union density, but that did not trouble union leaders, since unions were expanding greatly into the public sector. In 1972 AFL-CIO head George Meany dismissed concerns about organizing new workers: "I don't know, I don't care. . . . Why should we worry about organizing groups of people who do not appear to want to be organized? . . . I used to worry about . . . the size of the membership. . . . I stopped worrying because to me it doesn't make any difference. . . . The organized

fellow is the fellow that counts."[4] Foresight was not one of Meany's virtues.

In the 1970s and 1980s, the proportion of the workforce in union electoral victories fell to less than 0.2 percent.[5] These statistics imply a massive drop in union density over time. Why was the rate of organization falling? Could anything be done to make it easier for workers to be organized? I went to Lane Kirkland, Meany's successor as head of the AFL-CIO, and offered to bring together diverse researchers, some friendly and some unfriendly to unions, for an academic conference on these questions. Kirkland shook his head and told me that the AFL-CIO would not cooperate with such a meeting. He did not want to include researchers unfriendly to unionism. And academic studies were not important in any case. He was going to use the union's political clout to get Congress to enact labor law reform that would make it easier to organize workers.

In the 1990s and early 2000s, the proportion of the workforce organized through elections fell below 0.1 percent, or barely 100,000 workers unionized per year; in an economy with some 145 million workers, that is effectively no one. Unions gained more members outside the electoral process, but still not enough to staunch the fall in density. At last, union leaders recognized that the decline was spelling the death of unionism in the United States. In 1995 national union leaders forced Kirkland to resign and elected John Sweeney to invigorate organizing efforts.[6] Sweeney's "New Voice" team called for

---

4 Buhle, *Taking Care of Business.*
5 Freeman, "Why Are Unions Faring Poorly in NLRB Representation Elections?"

6 Dark, "Decline: The 1995 Race for the AFL-CIO Presidency."

unions to spend larger shares of their revenues on organizing. Some unions did. Some unions elected organizing directors as union presidents. But many internationals and locals did not increase their organizing budgets, while others could not find fruitful campaigns on which to spend the money they had. Union density continued to fall. In 2005 several major unions, led by the Service Employees International Union (SEIU) and the Teamsters, withdrew from the AFL-CIO because they felt the federation was incapable of reversing the decline in density. These unions set up the Change to Win coalition to increase union resources for organizing and jump-start a turnaround in union density. Perhaps competition among unions would spur more successful organizing than the unified house of labor.

WHY HAS UNIONISM DECLINED?

The decline of private-sector unionism is not a mechanical story of employment shifting from blue-collar mining and manufacturing, where unions had great strength, to white-collar service sectors, where unions were weaker. The fall in union density has been ubiquitous across occupations and industries in the private sector. From 1983 to 2005, density fell in durable manufacturing, in transportation, in mining, in utilities, in nondurable manufacturing, and in construction. Less than 20 percent of the

decline was associated with a change in the composition of jobs.[7]

The decline in unionism is also not a mechanical story of labor supply shifting from men who join unions to women who do not, or from high school graduates who unionize to college graduates who do not.[8] In 2005 women were as likely to be union members as men, and college graduates are more likely than high school graduates or dropouts to be union members. Persons with postcollege education have over two and a half times the union density of persons with less than a high school education. Unionized workers in the United States are disproportionately teachers, nurses, airline pilots, entertainers and athletes, machinists, police, firefighters, craft workers, and other highly skilled workers. The less skilled cannot gain union representation even when they want it.

The story of the decline of unionism is an economic story about the incentives and behavior of firms, unions, and workers interacting in the framework set by U.S. labor law of the Depression era. This framework gives workers and firms a stark choice for representation: a collective bargaining union or nothing. This contrasts with the wider selection of forms of representation available in virtually all other advanced countries, including Canada. Counter to the original purpose of the National Labor Relations Act, the legal framework, as interpreted by the courts, forces the union-

---

7 On unionization by industry and occupation, see CPS data at "Union Membership and Coverage Database," www.trinity.edu/bhirsch/unionstats/. Riddell and Riddell (2003) find that at most 20 percent of the drop in union density from 1984 to 1998 was associated with shifts in the composition of employment by industry or occupation.

8 Data on unionization by demographic characteristics are tabulated from the MORG files available at NBER, "CPS Merged Outgoing Rotation Groups."

ization issue into a conflict situation that pits unions and workers who seek unions against management.

There are three suspects for doing in the unions: management, the unions themselves, and workers. If we look for motivation, as economists generally do, the most likely suspect is management. Unions raise wages and benefits for workers in organized workplaces, and these increases lower profits. If we look for institutional competence, as organizational sociologists do, the likely suspects are the unions themselves. Union leaders failed to address declining density until it reached crisis proportions. If we look at who votes on union representation, the likely suspects are workers. Perhaps workers decided that unions did not serve their interests in the modern information economy.

||| IT'S MANAGEMENT

Managers in the United States fight hard against unions that seek to organize their workforces. Management campaign tactics include: making captive-audience speeches in which management orders all employees to listen to anti-union messages while forbidding union supporters to make their case; making "forecasts" (threats are illegal) that unionization will lead to closure and job loss; bombarding workers with company campaign material; denying unions access to workers on company property; and ordering supervisors to hold one-on-one anti-union meetings with workers. All of these actions are legally permissible under the National Labor Relations Act. If management is uncertain about how to fight unions, it can hire consultants simply by Googling "union prevention" or "labor-management consultants" or "union busters." Going beyond legally permissible tactics, some managers fire or illegally discipline union activists in NLRB elections. One study estimates almost one-in-five union organizers or activists can expect to be fired as a result of their activities in a union election campaign.[9]

Particular tactics aside, it is the confrontational tone that management adopts when workers seek to unionize that most strongly influences the election process. Three-quarters of workers believe that an employee organization can be effective *only if* management cooperates with it. Nearly two-thirds of workers say that they prefer an organization that has little nominal power but does have management cooperation over an organization that has "more power, but [that] management oppose[s]."[10] By letting workers know that management opposes unions and will not cooperate with any union, management can discourage worker efforts to organize.

Indicative of the effort that management puts into defeating unions, my employer, Harvard University, battled for over a decade to keep workers from unionizing. Harvard got the NRLB to change the election district for voting from the medical school, where the technicians who started the union drive worked, to

9 Schmidt and Zipperer (2007). In an earlier study, Brofenbrenner (2000) found that as many as 25 percent of *employers* facing a union drive fire at least one worker for union activity.

10 Freeman and Rogers, *What Workers Want,* 2nd ed., exhibit 3.8.

the entire university workforce, which included worksites as far away as Maine. Although the president of the university, Derek Bok, was a leading labor law scholar whose writings favored collective bargaining, Harvard did everything possible to convince employees that a union would be bad for them. If nonprofit Harvard under a pro-union president battled so hard to keep unions out, imagine what profit-seeking businesses do.

Managements in other countries do not fight unions with anything like the resources and zeal of American managers, if they fight them at all. In Britain most managers are neutral when workers seek to organize.[11] If workers want to be represented by a union, it is their choice. Throughout Europe management deals with unions and accepts union efforts to sign up workers. The divergent attitude of American and European management toward unions was driven home to me in 1988, when I visited Danish union and business leaders courtesy of the labor attaché at the U.S. embassy. Because I was interested in management opposition to unions, I asked the attaché to arrange for meetings with companies opposed to unions. She said she could not do that because there were no anti-union firms. No anti-union employers? Impossible! Then take me to the small employers' association, I said, certain that small Danish firms, like their U.S. counterparts, would be in the forefront of opposition to unions. I was stunned when the Danish small business association said that they preferred to operate with collective bargaining. By negotiating wages and

conditions throughout the economy, unions reduced the need for small firms to worry about those issues. Collective bargaining leveled the playing field for firms to compete on nonwage dimensions, where small employers could excel.

American and European businesses differ in their attitude toward unions not because American managers are reactionaries who reject the right of workers to form unions while Europeans are social democrats who view unions as the best thing since sliced bread. It is the economics of their situations that creates the difference in attitudes. In the United States, where unions cover only a small proportion of the workforce and bargain for higher wages, pensions, and health insurance, the unionized firm has higher costs. Management does what it can to improve productivity, but it generally cannot find ways to improve the operation of the firm enough to cover the higher costs of labor and thus ends up with lower profits. In Europe, where almost all firms pay the collectively bargained rate and health care is provided nationally, unions do not create a competitive disadvantage for an organized employer. Since unions do not affect the bottom line, why worry if workers choose to unionize?

||| IT'S THE UNIONS

Unions are the second set of suspects for causing the decline of unionization. The unions that left the AFL–CIO in the summer of 2005 complained that the federation had done too little to

---

11 Bryson and Freeman, "Worker Needs and Voice in the U.S. and U.K."

galvanize organizing efforts and spent too much dues money on Washington political activity. They advocated a huge increase in organizing budgets. Such an increase is necessary for unions to have a chance of unionizing large numbers of workers. But even with additional resources, unions have to find more creative ways to gain members than battling employers at the workplace. Management opposition has raised the cost of union organizing to such an extent that unions would have to devote the bulk of their budgets to organizing to win enough workers to maintain their 2005 density, much less to increase density.[12] And as density falls, it becomes more costly for members to fund organizing campaigns big enough to raise density. The reason is arithmetic: at low levels of density, there are relatively few members to pay for the campaign and many nonmembers to organize. What the unions need is some great organizing innovation and triumph—such as convincing Wal-Mart to welcome unions—that sparks a wave of low-cost organizing success. Slogging it out with firms that have deeper pockets is unlikely to get unions much.

WHAT WORKERS WANT

The purpose of unions or any other workplace organization is to meet the needs of employees. It is what workers want, not what union functionaries want or what management wants, that should determine whether workers have a union or some other organization or no organization representing them at their workplace. If workers are happy with management human resource policies, legislated protections, and the option to quit a bad workplace and get a new job, there is no place for unions.[13] If workers seek some form of collective representation in dealing with workplace problems, there is a place for unions or some other worker organization in the labor market. So the key question that has motivated much research is whether or not workers want some institutional protection or collective voice at their workplace.

To answer this question, Joel Rogers and I, in what we boldly described as the "mother of all workplace surveys," asked workers in the mid-1990s about their workplace experiences and desires for union or non-union representation and participation.[14] In our Workplace Representation and Participation Survey (WRPS), we found that 32 percent of *non-union* private-sector workers wanted a trade union at their workplace and that 90 percent of union workers wanted to maintain their union. If workers had their way, private-sector union density would be on the order of 40 percent—three to four times the rate in the sample in our study. Similar surveys conducted after our study came up with higher estimates of the proportion of non-union workers who wanted unions. Figure 1 shows that the proportion of non-union workers who said they would vote union exceeded 50 percent in 2003 and 2005.

12 Farber and Western, "Ronald Reagan and the Politics of Declining Union Organization"; Freeman and Rogers, "Open-Source Unionism."
13 Flanagan, "Has Management Strangled U.S. Unions?"; Farber, "Trends in Worker Demand for Union Representation"; McLennan, "A Management Perspective on *What Do Unions Do?*"
14 Freeman and Rogers, *What Workers Want,* 2nd ed.

FIGURE 1 **LIKELIHOOD OF NON-UNION WORKERS VOTING IN UNION REPRESENTATION ELECTION, PETER HART SURVEYS, 1984–2005**

IF AN ELECTION WERE HELD TOMORROW TO DECIDE WHETHER YOUR WORKPLACE WOULD HAVE A UNION OR NOT, DO YOU THINK YOU WOULD DEFINITELY VOTE FOR FORMING A UNION, PROBABLY VOTE FOR FORMING A UNION, PROBABLY VOTE AGAINST FORMING A UNION, OR DEFINITELY VOTE AGAINST FORMING A UNION?

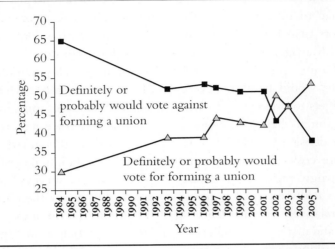

SOURCE: Richard B. Freeman and Joel Rogers, exhibit I.6 *What Workers Want,* 2nd ed. (Ithaca; N.Y: Cornell University Press, 2006.) Data from Hart Research Associates, various polls, except 1984; data for 1984 are from Harris, on a slightly differently worded question: "If an election were held tomorrow to decide whether your workplace would be unionized or not, do you think you would definitely vote for a union, probably vote for a union, probably vote against a union, or definitely vote against a union?"

Our survey also asked workers about worker organizations beyond unions. More workers said that they wanted a non-union organization at their workplace to discuss issues with management than said they wanted unions. (The unions did not like this survey result.) In fact, most workers wanted an organization to be "run jointly by employees and management." Again, surveys that followed ours confirmed these findings. Hart Research Associates asked workers in 1997, 1999, and 2001: "Suppose there was a proposal to form an employees' organization that was not a union in your workplace but that would represent the interests of employees and meet regularly with management to discuss important workplace issues." Seventy-eight percent of workers said that they would definitely or probably vote for such an organization.[15] In short, not only is there unfilled demand for unions, but there is even

---

15 Following up these results, Hart Research Associates asked workers in 1997, 1999, and 2001 about their desires for a non-union mode of meeting with management to discuss workplace issues and found a similar result; see Freeman and Rogers, *What Workers Want,* 2nd ed., introduction.

greater unfilled demand for worker organizations to discuss issues with management outside of collective bargaining.

||| WHY WORKERS WANT UNIONS

The workers who want unions want them to deal with workplace problems that they believe management does not resolve adequately or fairly. Figure 2 displays a measure of the number of needs or problems that non-union workers perceive at their workplace and the proportion of workers who would vote for a union in a union representation election. The measure of needs or problems is the sum across multiple items of the number of times workers said there was a problem at their workplace or expressed a strong desire for an improvement that management was not dealing with. The desire for unionism is strongly related to the number of needs. Among workers with no needs, 26 percent say that they would favor a union; among those with four needs, 45 percent say that they would favor a union; among those with seven or more needs, 81 percent favor unions.

The close tie between workers' desire for unionism and their perception that management is not taking care of workers can be seen starkly in two questions that asked workers to grade management on a standard A to F school mark. On a question about managerial *concern for workers,* 71 percent of non-union workers who gave management an F said that they would vote for the union, whereas barely one-third of workers who gave higher grades reported such a preference. On a question about management

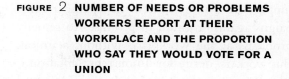

FIGURE 2 **NUMBER OF NEEDS OR PROBLEMS WORKERS REPORT AT THEIR WORKPLACE AND THE PROPORTION WHO SAY THEY WOULD VOTE FOR A UNION**

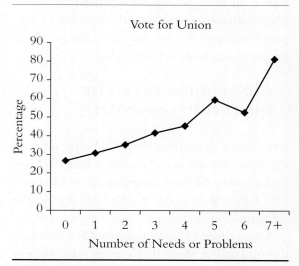

SOURCE: Tabulated from Worker Representation and Participation Survey, available at: http://www.nber.org/~freeman/wrps.html.

being *willing to share power* with workers, 69 percent of those who gave management an F grade said that they would vote for a union, compared to 47 percent who gave management a D grade, 35 percent who gave management a C grade, and just 20 percent who gave management an A or B grade.

In short, the workers who say that they want unions are responding to real problems at their workplace. They are not giving a quick, ill-informed "telephone answer to a hypothetical question."[16] Some undoubtedly reconsider their

---

16 McLennan ("A Management Perspective on *What Do Unions Do?*") suggests that this might be the case for many respondents.

support for a union when management campaigns against a union or promises to remedy problems at the workplace without a union. But workers' desire for union representation is rooted in their workplace situation. A workplace with lots of problems produces lots of support for unions. A workplace with few problems produces little support for unions.

CONSEQUENCES OF THE DECLINE IN UNIONISM

Are American workers better or worse off with the declining rate of unionization than if unions had maintained their representation of the private sector at, say, the heady rates during the Reagan administration?

Studies from *What Do Unions Do?* through the mid-2000s show that unions raise the pay of workers, reduce inequality, increase pension coverage, provide health insurance, and give workers a democratic voice at their workplace. By bargaining for defined-benefit pension systems, unions create a way for workers to defer compensation into savings and provide for secure retirements. On the basis of these findings, we would expect declining union density to be associated with sluggish growth of real earnings for most workers, increased inequality, reductions in defined-benefit pensions, and more expensive and reduced health insurance. These are all areas in which workers have in fact lost ground. The decline of unions explains part of the declining economic position of U.S. workers, though it is by no means the main factor behind these changes.

Do unions raise or reduce productivity? To many economists, this is the $64 million question. Since anything that reduces productivity is prima facie bad, one of the major charges against unions has been that they reduce productivity. The evidence is clear: they do not. We know this with some certainty because researchers have used meta-statistical methods to collapse the results from a large number of studies into summary statistics. Meta-statistics is widely used in medical research to combine the results from small trials of medicines by doctors to give the appropriate statistical summary of all the studies taken together. In the union case, these analyses show that unions have slight positive impacts on productivity, but with wide variation among sectors.[17]

Going beyond productivity, studies find that unions reduce investments in capital and R&D and lower employment or employment growth in the organized sector. In the 1970s, some analysts argued that unions were partly responsible for some of the inflation of the period. The decline of unionism makes this discussion moot. If oil shocks or other factors induce a burst of inflation in the United States in the 2000s, no one will blame unions, since they no longer affect wage determination in the economy as a whole. On the other hand, the absence of a counterforce to management within firms has given management greater control over firms, so the decline of unionism should be associated with corporate excesses. Hello, Enron, AIG, Global Crossing . . .

Historically, unions used their political muscle to gain higher minimum wages, progressive

---

17 Doucouliagos and Laroche, "What Do Unions Do to Productivity?"

taxes, and other legislation favorable to workers. As the union share of the workforce has fallen, so too has the union share of the electorate and union political influence, although much more slowly because so many of today's retirees worked during the heyday of unions.[18] Good-bye, national minimum-wage increases and strong legislation to control managerial excess.

Overall, is the economy better or worse off from the decline of unionism? If you are a worker below the top 10 percent of earners, you are worse off, having lost a force that operated on your behalf. If you are in the top 10 percent but below the top 1 percent or 0.1 percent, you probably are doing better than you would otherwise. Ah, but if you are in the upper 1 percent or upper 0.1 percent, it could not get much better, though if you are a movie or recording star or a professional athlete, you would surely suffer if you lost your union.

THE FUTURE OF WORKER REPRESENTATION

Workers in the United States want some form of collective voice inside firms and in society. While unions have been the main institutional form for giving workers a say at their workplace in years past, perhaps some non-union form can substitute for unions in the future. Workers in other advanced countries where union membership is falling have not lost their say at the workplace, in part because those countries permit or require firms to establish non-union institutions through which workers can express their collective interests to the firm. European countries mandate that firms set up works councils—elected committees of employees with specified rights—to meet and discuss workplace problems with management. Japan has a system of consultation and meetings with workers before management makes decisions. The Anglo-American countries whose institutions are closest to those of the United States—the United Kingdom, Australia, New Zealand, Ireland, and Canada—have staff associations, worker committees, and firm-sponsored non-union groups that provide representation and participation for employees.[19] Such non-union forms are illegal in the United States under section 8(a)(2) of the National Labor Relations Act, which outlaws company unions and has been legally interpreted to mean that any employer-supported group that discusses worker issues is a company union. The employee involvement committees and quality circles and teams at U.S. workplaces focus on productivity and quality of output issues that improve profits; they cannot legally discuss improvements in wages and work conditions.

Some non-union organizations have tried to fill the gap in worker representation created by the decline of unions.[20] Public-interest legal organizations help workers in the enforcement of employment laws, and human rights activists campaign for labor standards. But workers do not elect either of these types of groups, so they are not the voice of workers. Membership-based organizations such as the Industrial Areas

18 Freeman, "What Do Unions Do to Voting?"
19 Freeman, Boxall, and Haynes, *What Workers Say.*
20 Jolls, "The Role and Functioning of Public-Interest Legal Organizations in the Enforcement of the Employment Laws"; Kimberly and Freeman, *Can Labor Standards Improve Under Globalization?*

Foundation, which organizes low-income communities to give voice to workers, and workers' centers for immigrants have the potential for representing the views of those they seek to aid.[21] The most comprehensive review of these non-union institutions concluded, however, that as of the early 2000s they had not developed the scale to substitute community-based voice for worker representation and participation in the labor market, nor were they likely to do so.[22]

Putting aside non-union alternatives, can traditional unionism resuscitate itself in the United States? Most experts believe that it cannot, which makes meetings on the future of unionism resemble wakes, even for researchers who do not particularly care for unions. (After all, the decline of unions means less interest in their work.) But unionism has been at the abyss before. In 1933, before the Depression-era growth in unionism, the president of the American Economic Association, George Barnett, declared that unions had no future. In the 1950s, just before unionism came to the public sector, George Meany declared that public-sector workers were non-organizable in the United States.

The problem with projecting the future of unions is that unions grow in discontinuous "spurts" in periods of social crisis, and nothing is more difficult to predict in the social sciences than discontinuous changes.[23] The social and economic factors associated with past union spurts do not produce easy generalization about what could bring about a future spurt. Union growth during World Wars I and II occurred during a tight wartime labor market that shifted the balance of power from business to workers and induced governments, which feared that industrial disputes would disrupt wartime production, to adopt policies that helped unions organize. Union growth during the Depression reflected a different dynamic: loss of faith in business leadership and economic desperation. The 1970s oil shock crisis led to union growth in Western Europe as workers sought protection against inflation through collective bargaining, but not in the United States, where the decline in private-sector unionism continued unabated. Perhaps U.S. division over the Vietnam War, which pitted many natural supporters of unionism against the AFL-CIO, diverted activists from organizing in response to the oil-price-induced inflation.

Each of these spurts was associated with *changes in union form* that attracted groups of workers whom experts believed to be non-organizable or with *institutional or legal changes* that weakened employer opposition. In the 1880s, the new form was the geographic lodge associated with the Knights of Labor. In the Depression, the new form was the industrial union. In World War II and earlier in World War I, labor boards and the compulsory arbitration of disputes over unionization compelled firms to accept them. The public-sector spurt transformed existing non-union associations, such as the National Education Association, into collective bargaining organizations. The

---

21 Osterman, *Gathering Power;* Fine, *Worker Centers.*

22 Freeman and Hersch, introduction to Freeman, Hersch, and Mishel, *Emerging Labor Market Institutions.*

23 Freeman, "Spurts in Union Growth."

associated legal change was the enactment of public-sector collective bargaining laws that forced public-sector employers to bargain collectively.

The lesson from labor history is that to recover from the endangered species list, unionism needs a new growth spurt associated with a new union form and new mode of operating.

‖ OPEN-SOURCE UNIONISM TO THE RESCUE?

I have a solution to offer, based on the innovative ways in which some U.S. and U.K. unions have used the Internet and door-to-door canvassing to enlist new workers into labor activities. The solution is *open-source unionism*—a new union form that, like open-source programming, operates through networks rather than traditional bureaucracies. An open-source union enlists workers as members regardless of whether they can achieve majority-status unionism or collective contracts and, per its computer name, uses the Internet to connect those workers and deliver information and services to them at low cost. It brings workers together face to face in a geographic area rather than at an employer-dominated workplace. The Communication Workers of America, the United Automobile Workers, the Machin-ists, and the Steelworkers, among others, have developed such forms.[24] But the most successful open-source innovation in the early 2000s was the AFL-CIO's non-collective bargaining "community affiliate to unionism": Working America.[25]

The AFL-CIO started Working America in the summer of 2004 by sending four hundred canvassers in ten cities to neighborhoods with many union members on the notion that residents there would have pro-union attitudes and thus be willing to join a union "affiliate."[26] Working America gathered the home addresses, telephone numbers, and email addresses of workers who wanted to join. The organization promised members that they would help determine policy through online ballots. The rate at which persons joined the organization stunned the federation: two-thirds of those canvassed signed up. Moreover, many had a political or social orientation that differed from that of most persons in the union movement: one-third were born-again Christians, 70 percent were conservatives or moderates in politics, and 32 percent supported the National Rifle Association (NRA). One-quarter of the members gave their email address, which allows Working America to communicate with them weekly. In 2005 and 2006, Working America spread its organizing drive to other cities in the country.

---

24 The affiliates of the Communication Workers Union (CWU) are: Alliance@IBM, a minority union within IBM; Washington Alliance of Technology Workers, another Communication Workers affiliate based on IT workers in northern California and Washington; and the National Writers Union, an affiliate of the United Automobile Workers, which organizes freelance writers around the country. See Diamond and Freeman, "Will Unionism Prosper in Cyberspace?" The Communication Workers Union has expanded its effort to connect IT workers (www.techsunite.org) and developed a five-city organizing campaign associated with this website. The Machinists established CyberLodge (www.cyberlodge.org), and the Steelworkers initiated a "new form of individual membership—open to anyone regardless of employment," that offered modest services at modest dues.

25 See Working America, www.workingamerica.org.

26 Greenhouse, "Labor Federation Looks Beyond Unions."

As of this writing, Working America has two million members, which makes it the fastest-growing labor organization in U.S. history.

The key question that faces this new form is what it can do for its members outside of collective bargaining. Working America organizes campaigns on issues relevant to workers in their community. It encourages them to vote for candidates favorable to employees. It provides them with information. When the Bush administration changed the administrative rules governing overtime in August 2004, Working America added a page, "Is Your Overtime Pay at Risk?" to its website and hired a young lawyer to answer questions about the new ruling. As a result, Working America recruited over two thousand members per week via the Internet—a conversion rate of 7 percent of visitors to the site, about as high as any site can do.

The success of Working America validates the survey evidence that the United States has a vast untapped market for a labor organization to give voice to workers. Whether it or some comparable organization can develop a workplace presence or sufficient support services for workers to meet the unfilled demand for unionism is unclear. The split in the AFL-CIO may embolden the federation to pour more resources into Working America as its entry into the market for representation and participation. Or the split may lead the financially strapped federation to use Working America for political campaign purposes only.

||| CONCLUSION: WHAT NEXT?

In sum, the decline in unionism in the United States has left most workers without an insti-tution to represent their interests at the workplace. U.S. labor law does not allow firms to develop non-union initiatives like those in other advanced countries for fear that they will become bogus company-dominated organizations. At the same time, the law allows firms to effectively veto most efforts by unions to organize workers. The result is a massive and unprecedented unfilled demand for unionism. If unionism were a normal good or service, some smart organization or entrepreneur would step forward and find ways to meet the unfilled demand. Internet- and community-based open-source unions that operate outside of collective bargaining seem to offer the best chance for U.S. unions to expand membership and fill the massive representation and participation gap in the country.

||| REFERENCES

Bronfenbrenner, Kate. 2000. *Uneasy Terrain: The Impact of Capital Mobility on Workers, Wages, and Union Organizing.* Washington: Trade Deficit Review Commission.

Bryson, Alex, and Richard Freeman. 2006. "Worker Needs and Voice in the U.S. and U.K." Working paper 12310. Cambridge, Mass.: National Bureau of Economic Research (June).

Buhle, Paul. 1999. *Taking Care of Business: Samuel Gompers, George Meany, Lane Kirkland, and the Tragedy of American Labor.* New York: Monthly Review Press.

Dark, Taylor E. 1999. "Decline: The 1995 Race for the AFL-CIO Presidency—American Federation of Labor and Congress of Industrial Organizations." *Labor History* 40(3):323–43.

Diamond, Wayne J., and Richard B. Freeman. 2002. "Will Unionism Prosper in Cyberspace? The Promise of the Internet for Employee Organization." *British Journal of Industrial Relations* (Blackwell Publishers/London School of Economics) 40(3):569–96.

Doucouliagos, Chris (Hristos), and Patrice Laroche. 2003. "What Do Unions Do to Productivity? A Meta-Analysis." *Industrial Relations* 42(October):650–91.

Farber, Henry S. 1989. "Trends in Worker Demand for Union Representation." *American Economic Review* (papers and proceedings of the 101st meeting) 70(2):166–71.

Farber, Henry S., and Bruce Western. 2002. "Ronald Reagan and the Politics of Declining Union Organization," *British Journal of Industrial Relations* 40(3):385–401.

Fine, Janice. 2006. *Worker Centers: Organizing Communities at the Edge of the Dream.* Ithaca, N.Y.: Cornell University/ILR Press.

Flanagan, Robert J. 2005. "Has Management Strangled U.S. Unions?" *Journal of Labor Research* 26(1):33–63.

———. 1985. "Why Are Unions Faring Poorly in NLRB Representation Elections?" In *Challenges and Choices Facing American Labor,* edited by Tom Kochan. Cambridge, Mass.: MIT Press.

———. 1998. "Spurts in Union Growth: Defining Moments and Social Processes." In *The Defining Moment: The Great Depression and the American Economy in the Twentieth Century,* edited by Michael Bordo, Claudia Goldin and Eugene White. Chicago: University of Chicago Press/ National Bureau of Economic Research.

———. 2003. "What Do Unions Do to Voting?" Working paper 9992. Cambridge, Mass.: National Bureau of Economic Research (September).

Freeman, Richard B., Peter Boxall, and Peter Haynes, eds. Forthcoming. *What Workers Say: Employee Voice in the Anglo-American World.* Ithaca, N.Y.: Cornell University Press.

Freeman, Richard, and Joni Hersch. 2005. Introduction to *Emerging Labor Market Institutions for the Twenty-first Century,* edited by Richard B. Freeman, Joni Hersch, and Lawrence Mishel. Chicago: University of Chicago Press.

Freeman, Richard B., and Joel Rogers. 2002. "Open-Source Unionism: Beyond Exclusive Collective Bargaining." *WorkingUSA: The Journal of Labor and Society* 7(2):3–4. Available at: http://www.workingusa.org.

———. 2006. *What Workers Want,* 2nd ed. Ithaca, N.Y.: Cornell University Press.

Greenhouse, Steven. 2004. "Labor Federation Looks Beyond Unions." *New York Times,* July 11.

Jolls, Christine. 2005. "The Role and Functioning of Public-Interest Legal Organizations in the Enforcement of the Employment Laws." In *Emerging Labor Market Institutions for the Twenty-first Century,* edited by Richard B. Freeman, Joni Hersch, and Lawrence Mishel. Chicago: University of Chicago Press.

Kauffman, James T., and Bruce E. Bennett, eds. 2007. *What Do Unions Do? A Twenty-Year Perspective.* New Brunswick, N.J.: Transaction Publishers.

Kimberly, Elliott, and Richard Freeman. 2003. *Can Labor Standards Improve Under Globalization?* Washington, D.C.: Institute for International Economics (June).

McLennan, Kenneth. 2007. "A Management Perspective on *What Do Unions Do?*" In *What Do Unions Do? A Twenty-Year Perspective*, edited by James T. Kauffman and Bruce E. Bennett. New Brunswick, N.J.: Transaction Publishers.

Osterman, Paul. 2003. *Gathering Power: The Future of Progressive Politics in America.* Boston: Beacon Press.

Riddell, Chris, and W. Craig Riddell. 2003. "Changing Patterns of Unionization: The North American Experience, 1984–1998," University of British Columbia, Department of Economics, September. Available at: http://www.econ.ubc.ca/ine/papers/wp007.pdf

Schmitt, John, and Ben Zipperer. 2007. "Dropping the Ax: Illegal Firings During Union Election Campaigns," Center for Economic and Policy Research Report, Washington, D.C. (January). Available at: http://www.cepr.net/index.php?option=com_content&task=view&id=775&ltemid=8.

———. 2006. "Union Members in 2005." *News* USDL 06-99 (January 20). U.S. Equal Employment Opportunity Commission. n.d. "Disability Discrimination." Available at http://www.eeoc.gov/types/ada.html.

53

Explaining American Exceptionalism*

JILL QUADAGNO

Half a century ago the Carnegie Foundation invited the Swedish econo-mist Gunnar Myrdal to take a hard look at American race relations. Myrdal was not only an eminent scholar but also a foreigner, capable of scrutinizing American society with an objectivity no native could muster. Captivated by a nation he saw as simultaneously energetic, moral, rational, pragmatic, and above all, optimistic, Myrdal nonetheless discerned a disturbing contradic-tion between what he termed "the American creed" and the treatment of blacks.[1] Rooted in an abiding liberal ethos, the American creed embodied ideals of liberty, justice, and equality of opportunity. Americans espoused this creed with a remarkable unanimity, regardless of national origin, race, or social class. Their country, they proudly told Myrdal, was the land of the free, the cradle of liberty, the home of democracy. How then, Myrdal puzzled, could these champions of liberty and equality of opportunity engage in rigid

---

* First published in 1996; from *The Color of Welfare: How Racism Undermined the War on Poverty*.

1 Gunnar Myrdal, *An American Dilemma* (New York: McGraw Hill, 1944), Chapter 1.

racial discrimination that negated every aspect of the creed? How could a nation that espoused a democratic ideology and adhered to a constitution that provided the most democratic state structure in the world establish political, social, and economic institutions around a deep racial divide? For Myrdal, "The subordinate position of the Negro [was] perhaps the most glaring conflict in the American conscience and the greatest unsolved task for American democracy."[2]

Although Myrdal, a foreigner, readily identified this fundamental characteristic of American society, it has been disregarded by most other observers. Political theorists who attempt to trace the grand panorama of American politics generally fail to recognize how racial inequality has continually reshaped the nation's social, economic, and political institutions. James Morone, for example, argues that the central dynamic of American society is the expansion of the state bureaucracy and the resultant democratic impulse to limit this threat to civic liberty.[3] For Walter Dean Burnham, it is the arrested development of political parties.[4] For Kevin Phillips, it is an intensification in the concentration of wealth.[5]

I believe that only Gunnar Myrdal has correctly identified the more important motor of change, the governing force from the nation's founding to the present: the politics of racial inequality. The upheavals that periodically alter the nation's institutional arrangements stem from the contradictions between an egalitarian ethos and anti-democratic practices that reproduce racial inequality.

The pattern can be observed during the decades from the Revolutionary War to the Civil War. In those years, an industrialized North with an expanding base of free labor contained within its borders a separate nation, a cotton-producing South dependent for profit on slave labor. After the Civil War officially ended slavery, American state formation remained fettered by the unique configuration of North and South. The North had an organized working class, full political democracy (after 1920), and a competitive two-party system. A nation within a nation, the South remained primarily agricultural, distinguished politically by a one-party system and disfranchisement of blacks and economically by sharecropping, an arrangement that guaranteed planters control over a subservient, primarily black labor force. Few workers in the South organized into unions, and the unions that did exist were greatly weakened by their refusal to admit black workers.

The New Deal represented a breakthrough toward a more social democratic, Keynesian welfare state. It also set in motion a great migration of blacks out of the South. The migration undermined the political compromise that had allowed the South to function as a separate nation and forced all Americans to confront the impediments to racial equality that had previ-

---

2 Myrdal, *An American Dilemma,* p. 21.

3 James Morone, *The Democratic Wish: Popular Participation and the Limits of American Government* (New York: Basic Books, 1990).

4 Walter Dean Burnham, *Critical Elections and the Mainsprings of American Politics* (New York: W. W. Norton, 1970).

5 Kevin Phillips, *The Politics of Rich and Poor: Wealth and the American Electorate in the Reagan Aftermath* (New York: Random House, 1990).

ously been considered "the southern problem." That confrontation occurred during the 1960s when the civil rights movement demanded that Americans live up to their political ideology and guarantee full democratic rights to all, regardless of race. In the following section, I analyze what happened during the nation's one attempt to reconstruct its racial politics in the context of other theories of American exceptionalism.

RACE AND THEORIES OF AMERICAN EXCEPTIONALISM

The Polity-Centered Approach

Polity-centered theorists view the sequence of democratization and bureaucratization as crucial to understanding the timing and structure of the welfare state. They argue that in nations where government bureaucracies were installed before citizens won the right to vote, state bureaucrats instituted regulations that protected their positions from partisan use. As a result, when the working class began to mobilize politically, party activists could not use the "spoils of office" to attract voters. Instead parties had to rely on programmatic appeals to the emerging electorate.[6] Because national welfare provisions had wide programmatic appeal, they became a resource for securing party loyalty.

By contrast, in the United States electoral democratization preceded state bureaucratization. The civil administration was not protected from partisan use, and parties and factions used government jobs and resources to mobilize their personal clienteles and reward activists. Instead of attracting the electorate through programmatic appeals such as national welfare benefits, politicians waged battles over the spoils of office, which were distributed in a particularistic manner to loyal constituents.[7]

This argument helps explain the late onset of a national welfare state in the United States. During the first three decades of the twentieth century, patronage abuses in Civil War pensions made Americans suspicious of allowing the federal government to administer any national spending programs. The legacy of patronage abuses continued to haunt New Deal reformers, who only partially succeeded in instituting civil service reforms and extending the bureaucracy. Some programs of the Social Security Act of 1935 did set national regulations and national eligibility criteria but significant departures from these standards were allowed in other programs. Ann Orloff argues that this failure to create uniformity

> reflected the inability of Roosevelt administration officials to overcome the deep resistance of Congress and some congressional constituencies to reform and, ultimately, the large obstacles represented by the legacies of American state-building and state structure. . . . The patronage practices initially encouraged by early mass democracy and the

---

6 Ann Shola Orloff, *The Politics of Pensions: A Comparative Analysis of Britain, Canada, and the United States, 1880–1940* (Madison: University of Wisconsin Press, 1993), p. 88.

7 See Ann Shola Orloff and Theda Skocpol, "Why Not Equal Protection: Explaining the Politics of Public Social Spending in Britain, 1900–1911 and the United States, 1880s–1920s."

American Sociological Review, 49 (December, 1984): 726–750; Theda Skocpol, *Protecting Soldiers and Mothers: The Political Origins of Social Policy in the United States* (Cambridge: Harvard University Press, 1992).

lack of bureaucratic state-building deprived reformers of readily available institutional capacities for carrying out new social spending activities.[8]

The federal bureaucracy's incomplete authority over the New Deal welfare state was not primarily a legacy of patronage politics, however, but rather a legacy of incomplete democracy. The confrontations between the New Deal bureaucracy and the states were not struggles over regulating patronage *per se* but struggles over the way patronage inhibited basic democratic rights. A limited bureaucracy allowed the southern states to operate autonomously from central government authority and to deprive African Americans of the social rights extended to other citizens. Programs with national regulations and national eligibility criteria excluded African Americans; programs for which blacks were eligible remained under the jurisdiction of local welfare authorities. Other New Deal programs actively used the federal bureaucracy to suppress democracy. Federal housing programs tacitly endorsed racial segregation, while federal labor laws ignored racial discrimination by employers and trade unions.

The second phase of bureaucratic state-expansion occurred during the 1960s. Instead of building upon the New Deal, the War on Poverty challenged its bureaucratic legacies. It established new patronage networks that bypassed anti-democratic political structures. In distributing federal funds for job training, housing, and community improvement, the War on Poverty helped extend social rights to

African Americans. However, these resources also unintentionally fueled struggles over civil and political rights—the right to work and the right to participate in politics. Ironically, then, whereas bureaucracy repressed democracy, patronage provided the means for democratic institutions to emerge.

Polity-centered theorists rightly argue that the development of the welfare state must be analyzed in the context of broader processes of state formation. But in concentrating on the war against patronage abuse, they neglect the war waged for democracy. Among the distinctive features of American state formation, none is more salient than the failure to extend full citizenship to African Americans. It is this characteristic, more than any other, that has influenced the development of the welfare state. The battle over racial equality delayed national welfare programs, limited the reach of the federal bureaucracy, and shaped the structure of the programs that were developed in the two key periods—the New Deal and the War on Poverty

Working Class Weakness

A second explanation of American exceptionalism is the legacy of a weak working class. Andrew Martin captures the essence of this argument:

> [T]he failure of organized labor to develop sufficiently to provide the basis for a union-party formation . . . has been a decisive factor in the failure of cohesive parties to develop. In the absence of such parties, it is difficult

---

8 Orloff, *The Politics of Pensions*, p. 298.

to see what can substantially overcome the fragmented, or archaic, character of public authority in the United States. Under the circumstances, it can hardly be surprising that the role of the public sector in the American economy has lagged behind that in the industrially advanced West European countries.[9]

But when we consider the unique role race has played in American working-class politics, it becomes clear that this view ignores the importance of racial conflict in weakening the labor movement and undermining support for the welfare state.

From the Civil War to the New Deal, workers fought a losing battle to organize into trade unions. Factors that weakened labor included the consolidation of corporate power, the emergence of new industries—rubber, automobiles, chemicals—that depended largely on unskilled labor, and the migration of older industries to the South.[10] During the New Deal, resistance by skilled workers to integrating trade unions thwarted working-class solidarity and divided the labor movement. Trade union discrimination festered for decades until complaints from civil rights advocates forced the AFL to confront its discriminatory policies. Even then the skilled trades refused to yield.

These practices made it impossible for trade unions to institute a pro-labor political agenda during its one historic opportunity. That opportunity arose during the 1960s when, according to J. David Greenstone, organized labor's political influence most closely approximated the European model:

> [T]he American labor movement's role in the national Democratic party represented a partial equivalence to the Social Democratic [formerly socialist] party-trade union alliances in much of Western Europe. This equivalence obtained with respect to its activities as a party campaign [and lobbying] organization, its influence as a party faction, and its welfare state objectives.[11]

Yet instead of realizing a full employment policy and new social programs to fill in the gaps in the welfare state, organized labor made no gains in the 1960s. Instead, the government first instituted tax cuts and then embarked on an anti-poverty effort targeted to African Americans.

The failure of the working class to unite behind the welfare state resulted from racial tensions that surfaced over job training programs and housing policy. The skilled trade unions opposed federal job training programs for several reasons. The programs not only provided an alternative to union apprenticeships, they also became the means by which the government could pressure the skilled trades to integrate. The consequences were harmful to the long-term vitality of the union movement. In taking the indefensible position of defending racist policies, the skilled trade unions undermined union solidarity and provided a

9 Andrew Martin, "The Politics of Economic Policy in the United States: A Tentative View from a Comparative Perspective." *Comparative Politics Series,* Sage Professional Papers in Comparative Politics (Beverly Hills, CA: Sage Publications, 1973), p. 47.

10 Jill Quadagno, *The Transformation of Old Age Security: Class and Politics in the American Welfare State* (Chicago: University of Chicago Press, 1988), p. 55.

11 J. David Greenstone, *Labor in American Politics* (New York: Alfred A. Knopf, 1969), p. 361.

Republican administration with a weapon to further intervene in union prerogatives.

Racial tension also sapped working class strength in another more subtle way. In the United States working-class politics have largely been played out in the community rather than at the workplace.[12] From the 1930s to the present, high levels of neighborhood racial concentration have eroded the basis for a racially integrated working-class politics. Yet when the federal government sought to integrate housing, resistance to the programs undermined working-class support for national housing policy. The result was increased racial concentration in urban ghettos, or hyperghettos, and further isolation of poor blacks. As sociologists Loic Wacquant and William Julius Wilson write:

> If the "organized" or institutional ghetto of forty years ago described so graphically by Drake and Cayton imposed an enormous cost on blacks collectively, the "disorganized" ghetto, or hyperghetto, of today carries an even larger price. For now, not only are ghetto residents, as before, dependent on the will and decisions of outside forces that rule the field of power—the mostly white, dominant class, corporations, realtors, politicians, and welfare agencies—they have no control over and are forced to rely on services and institutions that are massively inferior to those of the wider society.[13]

The creation of hyperghettos, in turn, has isolated black political leaders, prevented them from keeping federal funds flowing to the cities, and destroyed possibilities for wider political coalitions between the city and suburbs. Thus, when the federal government abandoned efforts to integrate the suburbs, a new era of racial politics was established, one based on concentrated isolation of the poor.

Has the weakness of the American labor movement allowed opponents of big government to thwart efforts to expand the welfare state? Certainly, some evidence supports this argument. During the War on Poverty, however, labor's own resistance proved to be the greater impediment to welfare state expansion. Organized labor's opposition originated in racial divisions, which made the movement hostile to programs that pursued equality of opportunity. One outcome of the confrontation over social policy was the loss of working-class support for job training and for housing programs. Another outcome was further fragmentation of the labor movement.

The weakness of the American labor movement has thus been both a product and a producer of racial divisions. And a divided labor movement has been less capable of promoting social programs that enhance working-class solidarity.

Liberal Values

There is a long tradition in political theory that states that Americans oppose government intervention of all forms because of a legacy of strong, liberal values. According to the "values"

---

12 Ira Katznelson, *City Trenches: Urban Politics and the Patterning of Class in the United States* (Chicago: University of Chicago Press, 1981), p. 19.

13 Loic J. D. Wacquant and William Julius Wilson, "The Cost of Racial and Class Exclusion in the Inner City." *Annals of the American Academy of Political and Social Science,* 501 (January, 1989), p. 15.

argument, America's classic liberal tradition was born in rebellion against British rule, as the lack of strong class divisions or a feudal heritage nurtured an encompassing liberal culture. In liberal thought individual rights are sacred, private property is honored, and state authority is distrusted. It is this distrust of state authority that has been the chief obstacle to the development of American social programs.[14]

But as I noted previously, Americans have often supported massive government intervention in the form of social programs such as veteran's pensions, Social Security, and Medicare. Conflicts over the welfare state derive not from a deeply ingrained distrust of the state but from competing definitions of liberty: liberty as the positive freedom to act on one's conscious purposes versus the negative freedom from external constraints on speech, behavior, and association.[15]

The experience of the War on Poverty shows that public antagonism to most of the antipoverty programs only minimally concerned opposition to government intervention *per se.* Reducing government intervention became a rallying point only when social programs threatened the negative liberties of white Americans. But the evidence also indicates a more complex historical transformation, a redefinition of the very meaning of liberalism.

The Democrats took office in 1932 with a popular mandate to develop a new approach to economic and social problems that the Depression had brought painfully into focus. As government began monitoring malpractice among corporations, supporting the rights of workers to organize into unions, and using the state to alleviate the suffering of poor children, the unemployed, the elderly, and the disabled, the New Deal liberalism of the Democratic party came to mean active, positive intervention for the public good. Public support was high for programs that protected the many against the abuses of the few and taxed the few for the benefit of the many.[16]

During the 1960s, liberalism was redefined. Instead of government intervention for the common good, what defined the new liberalism, racial liberalism, was the premise of government intervention for civil rights. Government intervention for civil rights meant that the struggle for equal opportunity came to permeate issues of social policy. Nearly every social program—welfare, job training, community action, housing—became more than components of the welfare state that one supported or reviled depending upon whether one favored government intervention (a liberal) or opposed it (a conservative). Rather, because the reconstruction of race relations became inextricably woven into the very fabric of the Great Society, support for social programs came to mean support for integration. It also meant that if one opposed government intervention on behalf of civil rights, then one also opposed the social programs that helped enforce them.

---

14 An excellent summary of this perspective appears in Skocpol, *Protecting Soldiers and Mothers,* pp. 15–23.

15 Charles Lockhart, *Gaining Ground: Tailoring Social Programs to American Values* (Berkeley: University of California Press, 1989), p. 48.

16 Kevin Phillips, *The Emerging Republican Majority* (New York: Doubleday, 1970), p. 38.

This reconstruction of liberalism had concrete political consequences, for the War on Poverty activated the inherent conflict between positive and negative liberty. The positive liberties it extended to African Americans were viewed by the working class as infringements on their negative liberties, the liberty for trade unions to discriminate in the selection of apprentices and to control job training programs; the liberty to exclude minorities from representation in local politics; the liberty to maintain segregated neighborhoods. The resentment these infringements triggered destroyed the New Deal coalition of northern wage workers and southern racial conservatives, the stable Democratic party base for three decades.

As this coalition splintered over the racial issue, Republicans learned to capitalize on the racial hostilities civil rights enforcement had generated. In the 1964 election Barry Goldwater opposed federal intervention to end segregation and won only five states. Just four years later, Richard Nixon staked out a middle ground, remaining publicly committed to racial equality while opposing forceful implementation of civil rights legislation. By 1980 Republicans had artfully forged racial hostility with conservative economic policy into a New Right coalition, and their candidate Ronald Reagan "articulated a public philosophy directed at drawing into the Republican party citizens with the kinds of economic, social and racial concerns that could be addressed in terms of a free-market conservative doctrine."[17]

Republicans became the party of racial conservativism, while Democrats retained the liberal label inherited from their New Deal grandparents, expanded to include racial connotations.[18]

Over the past three decades, opponents of government spending for social welfare have found an anti-government ideology effective in undermining support for the welfare state. But opposition to government invention is not the central element in public antagonism to social programs. Initially, public approval of the War on Poverty was high. It was not until the anti-poverty programs became linked to the pursuit of civil rights that support waned. The idea that liberal values have inhibited the development of the American welfare state remains, at best, an overly simple explanation of how values are connected to the formation of social programs. An anti-government ideology has generated most antagonism to the welfare state when it has been associated with racial issues.

AMERICA'S WELFARE REGIMES

Over the past century the United States has instituted three "welfare state regimes." Each has had different consequences for racial equality. The first national welfare programs of the New Deal protected the working class against the exigencies of old age and unemployment. The price of this protection was a compromise with the American creed. As this compromise proved unworkable, the programs of the War on Poverty provided the means to undo the

---

17 Thomas Edsall and Mary Edsall, *Chain Reaction: The Impact of Race, Rights, and Taxes on American Politics* (New York: W. W. Norton, 1991), p. 138,

18 Edsall and Edsall, *Chain Reaction,* p. 198; Chandler Davidson, *Race and Class in Texas Politics* (Princeton: Princeton University Press, 1990); E. J. Dionne, *Why Americans Hate Politics* (New York: Simon and Schuster, 1991).

New Deal legacy and extend equal opportunity. Instead of finally instituting full democratic rights, however, the policies enacted in that turbulent decade left a disturbing legacy of "what might have been."

The community action programs that might have provided a precedent for extensive intervention in the inner cities and prevented the spiral of decline so painfully visible to observers on all sides of the political spectrum became instead embroiled in the task of extending political rights to African Americans. That proved their undoing. Rather than responding to the need for jobs, housing, and social services that the black migration brought to the urban centers, the nation turned its back on the cities.

The job training programs might have bolstered a full employment policy. They could have established a partnership between the federal government and given the trade unions a solid footing in national policymaking. Instead, job training became the source of internecine warfare within the trade union movement and between skilled workers and African Americans, hastening the decline of trade unionism. The irony of this historical outcome is that a nation that most abhors government handouts does least to prepare its citizens for work.

The funds for housing that briefly poured into the inner cities might have improved the quality and expanded the quantity of the nation's housing supply. However, the racial backlash that ensued when integration became linked to housing undermined public support for a national housing agenda.

No social programs could better have served the families of the emerging postindustrial order than a guaranteed annual income and national child care. Yet demands for welfare reform were triggered by the expanding welfare rolls and the threat of urban disorder. And child care was inextricably linked to welfare reform. When the policy agenda turned from the expansion of the welfare state to the repression of disorder, this grand opportunity to protect the family, especially families headed by women, was lost. Instead of initiating a new era of race relations, the War on Poverty became a transitional phase on the road to benign neglect. The equal opportunity welfare state was replaced by a welfare state that encouraged racial isolation and the concentration of the black poor in inner cities.

The failure of America's domestic policy agenda reflects a failure to live up to the values of the American creed, to create a nation that not only guarantees liberty but also democratic rights—the right to work, the right to participate in the political process, and the right to economic security. In the 1960s Americans sought to resolve the American dilemma and grant these basic rights. Three decades later that task remains unfinished.

PART FIVE

GLOBALIZATION AND INEQUALITY

INTRODUCTION TO PART V

The chapters in Part V examine some aspects of the global character of contemporary inequalities. Economist Robert Pollin's chapter provides a broad and incisive overview of the historical trends and major sources of global inequality today. He starts by mapping the rise of the "neoliberal" era of the present, in which free trade and governmental austerity have been successfully promoted by the major lending institutions (the World Bank and the IMF in particular) in the developing world. Pollin shows that aside from China, which has experienced extraordinary growth in the last 20 years, and a few other countries (such as India and Brazil), most of the less-developed world has experienced economic stagnation since the 1980s (and the rise of the "neoliberal" system). Pollin then charts the contours of the new economies that have emerged in these countries, highlighting the role of sweatshops in creating a new international division of labor, with very low-wage jobs becoming increasingly important in poor countries.

Virtually, all analysts of the contemporary era of globalization agree that increasing trade and changing patterns of economic development and technology tend to create winners and losers. Two contrasting images of these patterns are reflected in the chapters by sociologists Douglas Massey and Glenn Firebaugh. Massey argues that one critical aspect of the process of creating winners and losers has been the growing *concentration* of wealth and poverty. Increasingly, he argues, the world's rich live in gated enclaves, while the poor are huddled together in growing urban ghettos. The concentration of poverty in low-income urban areas is of special importance. There are a number of especially deleterious consequences of such concentration, including exposing residents to poor schools, high risk of crime, poor environmental and health conditions, and few economic opportunities. The concentration of advantage and disadvantage becomes self-perpetuating because disadvantages interact with one another. For example, as a neighborhood gets a reputation for a high crime rate, businesses may flee or choose not to locate in the area, depriving residents of economic opportunities.

The careful recent research of Glenn Firebaugh on the patterning of global inequality provides something of an alternative view to Pollin and Massey's stark visions, endorsing some but also challenging some of the theoretical claims in the globalization literature. Firebaugh agrees with Pollin and Massey that intracountry inequalities are increasing. But he disagrees that this means that inequalities across the globe are rising, and he also highlights how long-run trends across the globe have led to improved living standards. One of Firebaugh's critical insights is that in trying to assess the overall pattern of inequality across the globe, we should adjust for population size when making comparisons among countries. Because some very large previously poor but very large countries like China and India are growing very rapidly, their vast populations (currently around 1.2 billion in China and 900 million in India) have seen their average incomes approach the worldwide average. With nearly one-third of the world's population in these two countries, the fact that many small countries have not all seen the same improvements does not undercut Firebaugh's point that the world's population as a whole is actually getting more equal on average.

54

The Landscape of Global Austerity★

ROBERT POLLIN

"The decadent international but individualistic capitalism, in the hands of which we found ourselves after the War, is not a success. It is not intelligent, it is not beautiful, it is not just, it is not virtuous—and it doesn't deliver the goods. In short, we dislike it and are beginning to despise it."

John Maynard Keynes 1933

"When I give food to the poor they call me a saint. When I ask why the poor have no food, they call me a Communist."

Brazilian Archbishop Dom Helder Camara

||| FROM DEVELOPMENTAL STATE TO NEOLIBERALISM

Why speak about a landscape of global austerity in the year 2003? For most people today, including those living in developing countries, living standards are well above what would have seemed possible a hundred years ago. For example,

---

★ First published in 2003; from *Contours of Descent: U.S. Economic Fractures and the Landscape of Global Austerity.*

as of 1900, the average life span of someone living in Great Britain, the wealthiest of the imperialist powers at that time, was 50 years. Today in India—which had been Britain's largest colony and remains at present among the world's poor countries—the average life span is 60 years, a full decade beyond the British standard from the colonialist epoch.

But since the period beginning around 1980, the eclipse of state-directed development policies and the ascendancy of neoliberalism have produced dramatic upheavals in the world's poor and middle-income countries. This chapter describes a fundamental link in this transformation: the ways in which the rise of neoliberalism is responsible for the spread of global austerity. But who is responsible for neoliberalism in less developed countries? ★ ★ ★ Neoliberalism is advanced aggressively throughout the less developed countries by the "Washington Consensus" of the U.S. government, the International Monetary Fund and the World Bank. But governments in less developed countries do also support neoliberal policies. We therefore will need to consider the processes through which the priorities of the Washington Consensus institutions ideas get transmitted into political platforms and policies throughout the less developed world.

We begin with an overview of the transition from developmental planning to neoliberal policies in developing countries, and the impact of this transition on overall growth, inequality and poverty. We then consider the emergence throughout the developing world of sweatshop labor conditions in manufacturing industries. We close by considering what the impact would be of two widely discussed policy approaches for reversing the rise of global austerity—increasing development aid contributions from the wealthy countries and raising the economic growth rates in the developing countries themselves.

The Rise of the Developmental State

The first thirty years after World War II, from roughly the late 1940s to the late 1970s, was the epoch of both decolonization and the Cold War. Correspondingly, it was also the period in developing countries in which governments pursued active interventionist policies to promote economic growth and, in many cases, increasing equality.

The specific forms that these policies took varied widely by region and country. Given that this was the Cold War era, it is certainly the case that state socialism was both the most influential, as well as most bitterly contested, alternative development model. It dominated economic thinking in China and much of Southeast Asia, as well as, of course, the Soviet Union, Eastern Europe and Cuba. It also had strong adherents in parts of Africa, following the model of "ujamma" (collective self-sufficiency) advanced by Julius Nyerere in Tanzania. The government in these countries owned virtually all productive assets and economic activity was directed through a government-established comprehensive plan. State socialist governments were committed to maintaining high employment and relative equality in the distribution of income, health care, housing and educational opportunities.

A second approach was the "import-substituting industrialization" model practiced most actively throughout most of Latin America. The fundamental idea behind import substitution industrialization was that developing economies should take active measures to strengthen national capacity to produce manufactured goods for their domestic markets. This meant protecting domestic manufacturers from foreign competition while also providing them with cheap credit to finance their investments in new productive plants and equipment. The import-substituting industrialization model would also benefit from a buoyant domestic market, since the domestic producers of manufactured goods would need local buyers for these goods. The import substitution model was therefore compatible with the idea of rising living standards for Latin America's workers and poor. At the same time, in contrast to the state socialist model, it presented no challenge to the privileged economic positions of domestic capitalists and landed elite.

The East Asian economies—initially Japan, then the "tigers" including South Korea, Taiwan, Malaysia, Singapore and Thailand—created their own, third variant of state-directed development. The great myth about the achievements of the Asian tigers was that they were paragons of free market virtue. Thus, with typical hyperbole, Ronald Reagan said in his 1985 State of the Union Message, "Many countries in East Asia and the Pacific have few resources other than the enterprise of their own people. But through . . . free markets they've soared ahead of the centralized economies." In fact, the government's authority in the East Asian economies in terms of overall planning and strategic financing had always been at least as extensive as in the Latin import-substituting countries, and was, in many ways, more closely comparable to that of the centrally planned state socialist countries. The major distinction between the East Asian and Latin American models was that the East Asian approach was focused on promoting firms that could succeed as exporters. This alternative Asian approach had its historical roots in the fact that the governments in this region were able to discipline the corporations they protected and subsidised. In particular, the private firms would only continue to receive protections and subsidies from the government if they could meet product and quality standards necessary to penetrate export markets. The government's authority, in turn, resulted from the U.S.-backed land reforms in these countries after World War II, which weakened the power of landed elites and their big business allies to an extent that never occurred in Latin America.[1]

The Great U-Turn

Each of these state-directed developmental approaches did also include major failings, and these weaknesses became increasingly apparent with time. The fundamental problem with state socialism was not simply that it was brutally repressive, but that this repressive apparatus was necessary as a means of maintaining the

---

1 The literature on the alternative development models in less developed countries is voluminous. Some important examples include Alice Amsden, *The Rise of "the Rest": Challenges to the West from Late-Industrializing Economies,* New York: Oxford University Press, 2001; Ha-Joon Chang, *Kicking Away the Ladder: Development Strategy in Historical Perspective,* London: Anthem Press, 2002; Walden Bello and Stephanie Rosenfeld, *Dragons in Distress,* San Francisco: Institute for Food and Development Policy, 1990; and Robert Pollin and Diana Alarcon,

"Debt Crisis, Accumulation Crisis and Economic Restructuring in Latin America," *International Review of Applied Economics,* vol. 2, No. 2, 1988, pp. 127–154. Alexander Cockburn and I tried to summarize some of the main historical lessons and myths in the transition to ascendent neoliberalism in "Capitalism and its Specters: The World, The Free Market, and the Left," *The Nation,* 2/25/91, pp. 224–36. The quotations from Ronald Reagan and Michael Manley presented in this section are taken from this earlier article.

government's prohibition of virtually all forms of market transactions and private enterprise. Under the import substitution model, many companies grew jealous in guarding their protectionist privileges, even to the extent of lobbying the government against domestic competitors seeking similar protection. The large government bureaucracies that formed under these policies also encouraged pervasive corruption. The Latin governments were particularly vulnerable to this precisely because, unlike in East Asia, the nationalist governments never broke the power of the landed elite who had traditionally relied on special favors, as opposed to productive activity, as a means of expanding their wealth. Finally, the East Asian economies, like the Latin import substitution policies, did also fall back onto "crony capitalism" in handing out subsidised credit and protection from competitors. It also relied on repression of labor movements for keeping production costs down, and thus, maintaining international competitiveness.

These and other problems with the three main developmental models certainly created an imperative for adjustments, renovations, and, in many cases, fundamental restructuring. But it never followed that there should be only one approach to rethinking development policy—that being to abandon outright the very idea of a significant state presence to promote growth and equality, and replace this approach with neoliberalism. But this is what in fact occurred. Beginning in the 1980s and continuing through the 1990s, governments throughout Latin America, Africa and Asia, came to accept the position expressed in the triumphal pronouncement of former British Prime Minister Margaret Thatcher, that "there is no alternative"

to neoliberalism, either in Britain or anywhere else.

Yet this transformation of economic thinking throughout the world was not simply a matter of ideological persuasion. The influence of coercion needs also to be recognized. Governments in developing countries believed that they could not restructure successfully without substantial aid, credit and foreign investment. This could come only from the advanced capitalist countries and international lending institutions, and such support in turn depends on receiving a seal of approval from the Washington Consensus, and specifically the IMF and World Bank. The only way to qualify for such support was through demonstrating a commitment to the neoliberal model.

As such, by the late 1980s, even such previously committed social democrats as Jamaica's then Prime Minister Michael Manley pronounced that "we are making a radical change in direction" that will "among other things, involve the free play of market forces in the determination of prices." These same pressures remain in force up to the present. This has been most apparent with the election in October 2002 of Luiz Inácio Lula da Silva—Lula—as President of Brazil, the ninth largest economy in the world. A former steelworker and militant union–organizer, Lula was the candidate of the leftist Workers Party, and won the election with a landslide 61 percent majority. Nevertheless, immediately upon celebrating his victory, Lula "sent a message to uneasy financial markets, reiterating his pledge to respect Brazil's international agreements and stick to anti–inflationary policies." He then quickly nominated well-known orthodox financial market figures as both finance minister and central bank president. The *New York Times* reported that these choices were attempts by Lula "to demonstrate that his Workers' Party is dumping leftist policies and shifting to the political center." What will actually transpire during Lula's presidency remains to be seen, but the forces pushing him away from the program on which he was overwhelming elected are obvious.[2]

There has been one major counterexample to the pattern of neoliberal ascendancy in the developing world. This is the case of China, which, given that it constitutes 20 percent of the world's population, obviously renders it as an extremely important exception. As with East Asia, there is considerable irony in the mainstream interpretation of the Chinese experience. After the death of Mao Zedong in 1976, the still Communist Party-led government of Deng Xiaoping did indeed take dramatic steps away from a rigid state socialist model in the late 1970s. It has been hailed ever since for achieving remarkable economic success through embracing a free market economy, even while maintaining a repressive political system. But in fact, in sharp contrast with the rest of the former state socialist countries, China undertook virtually no privatization of either industry or land and other agricultural assets until the early 1990s, and even over the past decade has proceeded cautiously with these measures. By the late 1990s, state owned enterprises continued to produce about 30 percent of total industrial output. Individual farms did replace agricultural communes in the rural sector. But land, agricultural equipment, and rural enterprises have all remained under collective ownership. It is also

true that since the late 1990s, the Chinese government has substantially accelerated the pace of privatization and liberalization, and as well as more fervently espousing the rhetoric of neoliberalism. Still, the record for the 1980s and most of the 1990s stands in sharp contrast to the neoliberal transformations that occurred throughout most of the rest of the developing world.[3]

||| FIGURES OF DESCENT

What has been the impact of this transition from big government to the neoliberal framework? To provide an initial overall perspective, it will be useful to examine some general statistics on economic growth, inequality and poverty.

Growth

Table 1 shows figures on economic growth in both the developmental state and neoliberal eras for the low and middle income countries of the world—i.e. the average annual rate of gross domestic product—both in terms of overall GDP data and measuring growth on a per capita basis. Following previous discussions, I have set 1980 as the most appropriate point to mark the transition out of the post World War II era of developmental state policies and the ascendancy of neoliberalism. I have also included China separately since it had not pursued a neoliberal policy path by the end of the 1990s. Otherwise, these figures are calculated by adding up the overall GDP figures for all low and middle-income countries. This way, the

2 Tony Smith, "Brazil's President Elect Picks a Central Banker," *New York Times*, 12/13/02, p. W1. The previous quote reporting the message Lula sent to financial markets is from Agence France Presse, 10/28/02.
3 See Minqi Li, *Three Essays on China's State Owned Enterprises:* *Towards an Alternative to Privatization,* doctoral dissertation, University of Massachusetts Amherst, 2002, for an outstanding analysis of China's economic policy directions since the 1980s, as well as a discussion of the alternatives being considered for the future.

TABLE 1 TWO ERAS OF ECONOMIC GROWTH IN DEVELOPING COUNTRIES (FIGURES ARE AVERAGE ANNUAL GROWTH RATES, IN PERCENTAGES)

	Developmental state era 1961–80	Neoliberal era 1981–99
LOW AND MIDDLE INCOME COUNTRIES, EXCLUDING CHINA		
Overall growth rate	5.5	2.6
Per capita growth rate	3.2	0.7
CHINA		
Overall growth rate	4.5	9.8
Per capita growth rate	2.5	8.4

SOURCE: World Bank, *World Development Indicators*, 2001 CD-ROM.

patterns for large countries, like India, Brazil or Egypt, will carry more weight in the calculations than those for small countries like Bolivia, Uganda or Singapore.[4]

The overall growth pattern is unambiguous: there has been a sharp decline in growth in the neoliberal era relative to the developmental state period, from 5.5 to 2.6 percent, measured on average annual basis. Measured per capita—that is, the average increase in GDP relative to the growth in population—the downward growth trend is even more dramatic, with the growth rate in the neoliberal era at only 0.7 percent. This means that the average increase in overall income in the poor and middle-income countries just barely stayed ahead of population growth, after having increased 3.2 percent faster than population growth during the developmental state period.

Growth patterns do vary significantly by region, with various parts of Asia, including India (as we discuss more below), performing much better than Latin America or Africa prior to the Asian financial crisis of 1997–98. The table also shows the unique experience of China, where the average growth rate more than doubled during the 1981–98 period relative to 1961–80. It would not be possible, nor, for the most part even desirable, for the Chinese experience to be lifted out of its particular context and replicated elsewhere. Still, this performance should offer other developing economies some sense of the possibilities achievable through maintaining a strong public sector presence along with encouraging the spread of a vibrant private sector.[5]

4 Mark Weisbrot, Dean Baker, Egor Kraev and Judy Chen present a similar data analysis on growth in less developed countries in, "The Scorecard on Globalization: Twenty Years of Diminished Progress," Center for Economic and Policy Research, July 2001, <http://www.cepr.net/globalization/scorecard on_globalization.htm>.

5 It is also true that when we include China within the group of low and middle income countries, the overall growth patterns we observe are modified but do not change dramatically. Thus, per capita GDP growth for low and middle income countries including China is 3.2 percent for 1961–80 and 1.4 percent for 1981–99.

TABLE 2 **GLOBAL INCOME DISTRIBUTION TRENDS**

AVERAGE ANNUAL PER CAPITA INCOME GROWTH IN WEALTHY AND DEVELOPING COUNTRIES

	Developmental state era 1961–80	Neoliberal era 1981–99
1) Wealthy OECD economies	3.5	2.0
2) Developing economies, excluding China	3.2	0.7
3) Growth differential between regions (row 1–2)	0.3	1.3

Percent change in growth differential between eras = 333 percent
[(1.3% differential − 0.3% differential)/0.3]

SOURCE: World Bank, *World Development Indicators* 2001 CD-ROM.

• •

CHANGE IN GLOBAL DISTRIBUTION OF INCOME BETWEEN 1980–98

	Including China	Excluding China
Income of richest 50% as share of poorest 50%	14% more equal	4% more unequal
Income of richest 20% as share of poorest 20%	30% more equal	8% more unequal
Income of richest 10% as share of poorest 10%	5% more unequal	19% more unequal
Income of richest 1% as share of poorest 1%	68% more unequal	77% more unequal

SOURCE: Bob Sutcliffe, *A More or Less Unequal World*, full citation in note 7.

Distribution

There are two ways of measuring changes in income distribution throughout the world— changes that occur between countries and those that occur within each country. Both of these are relevant for our discussion.

Even though neoliberal policies have generated a decline in the developing countries' aver-age growth rate, this does not mean that these countries have necessarily become worse off relative to the wealthier countries. This would obviously depend on the growth experience in the wealthy countries as well. In fact, however, as we see in the upper panel of Table 2, growth in the developing countries has indeed been slower than in the wealthy countries during the neoliberal era, despite the declining growth in the wealthy countries themselves. The table reports the same growth rates on a per capita basis for developing countries, excluding China, that we saw in Table 1, now alongside the comparable per capita growth figures for what the World Bank calls the "high income OECD countries," which basically includes North America, Western Europe, Japan and Australia. As the table shows, the difference in the per capita growth rates between the wealthy OECD and developing countries was, on average, only 0.3 percent per year during 1961–80. But this annual differential rises to 1.3 percent during the neoliberal era—that is, an increase in the average growth differential between the wealthy and developing regions of *more than 300 percent* between the two periods.

As for inequalities within countries, most features of the neoliberal model should encourage these to rise as well. Cutting tax rates for the wealthy will obviously increase inequality, while liberalizing financial markets and selling off state assets means more opportunities for wealthy investors to reap huge gains on buying and selling publicly traded companies. Weakening labor market regulations will tend to reduce wages for workers in the lower half of the income

distribution. Cutbacks in government spending will produce greater disparities in public funds spent on health and education. Other features of a neoliberal policy environment can promote greater equality—for example, if successful manufacturing exporters in poor countries raise wages for their workers in line with the firm's growth in sales. But such factors are not likely to outweigh those encouraging greater inequality.[6]

One faces a range of difficult technical problems when trying to measure within country inequalities, or even more extensively, total income distribution throughout the world—in other words, considering overall distribution in terms of a single, borderless world economy. A large number of studies have been produced on this topic in recent years, and they have reached sharply divergent conclusions—that is, some studies find inequality increasing and others show it decreasing. However, in his extremely careful recent survey of this literature, Professor Bob Sutcliffe of the University of the Basque Country shows the ways through which these divergent conclusions are driven by different ways of organizing the statistical evidence.[7] Sutcliffe also shows that cross-currents are operating within the overall global economy—in particu-

---

6 These considerations are drawn out more fully in Francis Stewart and Albert Berry, "Globalization, Liberalization, and Inequality: Expectations and Experience," in Andrew Hurrell and Ngaire Woods eds., *Inequality, Globalization and World Politics,* New York, Oxford University Press, pp. 150–186. See also Christian E. Weller and Adam Hirsh, "The Long and the Short of It: Global Liberalization, Poverty, and Inequality," Economic Policy Institute, October, 2002.

7 Bob Sutcliffe, "A More or Less Unequal World? World Income Distribution in the 20th Century," *Indicators,* 2003, <http://www.umass.edu/peri/pdfs/WP54.pdf>. The figures in Table 2 on global distribution exclusive of China are not based on figures in Professor Sutcliffe's paper. Professor Sutcliffe

kindly supplied the necessary underlying figures to me on request. Professor Sutcliffe has also pointed out correctly that the figures in Table 1 and the top panel of Table 2 do not adjust national income figures based on calculations of purchasing power parities (PPP) between national currencies, while the figures in the lower panel of Table 2 are adjusted based on PPP. This inconsistency in methodologies was unavoidable because of gaps in the availability of PPP-adjusted data for the 1961–80 period. Moreover, as Prof. Sutcliffe pointed out in a private exchange, from the PPP-adjusted data we do have for these years, it appears that this methodological inconsistency does not have any significant effect on the data patterns presented in Tables 1 and 2.

lar, that there are more people clustering close to the 1998 world average income level of around $2,350, while, at the same time, there are growing disparities between those with very high incomes and those living in poverty (the richest 1 percent earned an average of $62,212 in 1998 while the poorest 1 percent earned $193).[8] Sutcliffe's review also makes clear that, by far, the single greatest equalizing force in the neoliberal era has been the rapid income growth of China. When one separates out the Chinese experience, as we have done above with the statistics on economic growth, it becomes unambiguous that inequality has been growing over the neoliberal era.

All of this becomes clear in the lower panel of Table 2, which presents a summary of representative figures from Professor Sutcliffe's review of the literature. The table presents figures on the change in the global distribution of income between 1980 and 1998, with 1998 being the last date on which reliable figures are available. I present the figures in two ways—both through including and excluding China from the overall sample of the world's population. I then report changes in global income distribution according to four separate distributional categories:

- The richest 50 percent of the world's population relative to the poorest 50 percent
- The richest 20 percent relative to the poorest 20 percent
- The richest 10 percent relative to the poorest 10 percent; and

- The richest one percent relative to the poorest one percent.

Considering first the figures that include China, we see that income distribution has become 14 percent more equal between 1980–98 if we compare the richest half to the poorest half of the world's population, and 30 percent more equal if we compare the richest 20 percent to the poorest 20 percent. At the same time, if we compare the richest to the poorest 10 percent, inequality rose over this period, though only by a modest 5 percent. However, in comparing the richest to the poorest 1 percent, we observe a sharp 68 percent increase in inequality, i.e. even when we keep China in the overall sample.

Considering now these same categories exclusive of China, we observe that inequality is growing according to each of the categories. Not surprisingly, the rise in inequality is more modest in the broader income categories and sharpens when the income categories become more differentiated. Thus, in considering the richest and poorest 50 percent of the world's population exclusive of China, inequality grew by 4 percent between 1980–98. But inequality grew by 19 percent in considering the difference between the richest and poorest 10 percent over this same period, and by a full 77 percent with respect to the richest and poorest 1 percent.

In short, there is no ambiguity that the world has experienced increasing disparities between the very rich and poor—that is, the top and bottom 1 percent of the world's population—

---

8 The world "average" figure is the median expressed in 1990 dollars after adjusting for purchasing power parities. The figures for the richest and poorest 1 percent are means for their groupings in 1990 dollars adjusted for purchasing power parities. I am grateful to Professor Sutcliffe for supplying these figures to me on request.

over the neoliberal era. The only real debate is whether one should consider China in a separate category because they did not practice neoliberal policies during the neoliberal era. When we do include China in our measures, we see that its rapid economic growth has pulled a large share of the world's population out of deep poverty, and has moved them increasingly toward the middle of global income distribution. On the other hand, when we consider the neoliberal era exclusive of the Chinese experience, there is, again, no ambiguity that rising global inequality has accompanied the ascendancy of neoliberalism.

Poverty Reduction

If, as we have seen, economic growth in most developing countries outside China has slowed substantially while income distribution has become more unequal, then it would follow that poverty in the developing world has either worsened or, at best, that the rate of poverty reduction has slowed. The logic is simple: if we imagine a total income pie for a country, the trend for increasing inequality means that the *share of the pie* going to the least well off will be getting smaller. Whether the *total amount of pie* going to the poor is also shrinking depends on how fast the whole pie is growing. Countries that have been the hardest hit by the slow growth in the neoliberal era would therefore be the countries where we would expect poverty trends to be worsening. China and a few other fast-growing developing countries should have experienced some poverty reduction.

I introduce this simple logical exercise into the discussion because, even more than with the data on income distribution, matters can become murky once one gets into actual measurement issues of poverty trends. There is, first, the issue of simply defining poverty in an appropriate way. Do we measure it as an absolute standard of basic minimum needs to stay alive, or as a standard of relative deprivation in any given society? There are legitimate considerations on behalf of each standard. The poverty figures discussed earlier for the United States combines both factors.

Focusing on absolute minimum needs poverty for developing countries, the World Bank in recent years has established a threshold at $1.08 per day per person. But their technique in deriving this threshold has been widely criticized by other experts. For example, Sanjay Reddy of Barnard College and Thomas Pogge of Columbia University argue that the $1.08 threshold is arbitrary, and that this threshold "may have led to a substantial understatement in the extent of world poverty."[9] According to Reddy and Pogge's own estimates, the percentage of people in poverty in a representative set of developing countries in the mid-1990s is probably in the range of 50 percent as opposed to the World Bank's estimate of about 35 percent.

Despite these controversies, what is surprisingly not in dispute is the basic conclusion of rel-

---

9 Sanjay G. Reddy and Thomas W. Pogge, "How Not to Count the Poor," version 4.4, August 15, 2002, p. 4, <http://www.columbia.edu/~sr793/count.pdf>.

evance to our present discussion: that little to no progress in reducing poverty has been made over the neoliberal period. Even the World Bank's own experts Shaohua Chen and Martin Ravallion acknowledge that "in the aggregate, and for some large regions, all our measures suggest that the 1990s did not see much progress against consumption poverty in the developing world." In explaining the pattern they observe, Chen and Ravallion write,

> We point to two main proximate causes of the disappointing rate of poverty reduction: too little economic growth in many of the poorest countries and persistent inequalities that inhibited the poor from participating in the growth that did occur (p. 1).

In other words, referring back to our simple exercise above, Chen and Ravallion observe that both the overall income pie was growing too slowly and that the share of the pie going to the least well off was shrinking. The IMF also recognized this basic pattern in their May 2000 *World Economic Outlook,* reporting that "progress in raising real incomes and alleviating poverty has been disappointingly slow in many developing countries, and the relative gap between the richest and poorest countries has continued to widen."[10] Beyond this, Reddy and Pogge believe that the negative poverty trends in developing countries may be significantly more severe than the World Bank and IMF authorities conclude.

★ ★ ★

SWEATSHOPS AND GLOBAL MANUFACTURING PRODUCTION

Probably the most widely publicized feature of the landscape of global austerity in recent years has been the spread of sweatshop labor conditions throughout the world, especially in the production of clothing and footwear.

In the U.S., the reports that first attracted widespread media attention were about the production of Nike athletic shoes, beginning with a 1992 story in *Harper's* that described workers in Indonesia assembling nearly fourteen pairs of Nike shoes every day and earning fourteen cents per hour, less than the Indonesian government's standard for "minimum physical need" for a full-time worker. The next heavily reported revelations concerned the clothing line endorsed by TV personality Kathie Lee Gifford, whose popular appeal rested heavily on her wholesome image. In April 1996, Charles Kernaghan of the New York-based National Labor Committee told a U.S. Congressional committee that Gifford's clothes were made by Honduran girls earning 31 cents per hour laboring in sweatshops.[11]

Similar reports have continued. For example, an October 2, 2000 *Business Week* story titled "A

---

10 Shaohua Chen and Martin Ravallion, "How Did the World's Poorest Fare in the 1990s?" <http://www.worldbank.org/research/povmonitor/pdfs/methodology.pdf>; and International Monetary Fund, *World Economic Outlook,* May 2000, Chapter 4, p. 1, <http://www.imf.org/external/pubs/ft/weo/2000/01/pdf/chapter4.pdf>.

11 The rise of anti-sweatshop activism in the U.S. is chronicled in Randy Shaw, *Reclaiming America: Nike, Clean Air, and the New National Activism,* Berkeley: University of California Press, 1999.

Life of Fines and Beatings" described conditions in Chinese factories that make products for Wal-Mart, among other Western companies. One handbag-producing firm profiled in the story employs 900 workers. It charged workers $15 a month for food and lodging in a crowded dormitory, which the article describes as a "crushing sum" given that a newly hired worker would clear $22 in their first month. The company also forced new workers to relinquish their personal identity cards, so "workers risked arrest if they ventured out of their immediate neighborhood."

These news reports detailing conditions in individual production sites are also consistent with more extensive and systematic studies of labor practices in the global apparel and footwear industry sponsored by, among others, the International Labor Organization of the United Nations, and various U.S. university groups. These reports found extremely low pay, dangerous and unhealthy working conditions, and restrictions on workers' basic rights—i.e. all features that we commonly associate with the term "sweatshop"—to be common in the apparel and footwear industry in the developing world.[12]

But certainly an abundance of poorly-paid jobs and bad working conditions are hardly novel phenomena in less-developed countries. Indeed, these are among the main features that define a country as being "less developed." Is there really anything new about the sweatshop labor conditions that have been widely publicized in recent years? Or is it simply a matter of the media in rich countries suddenly paying more attention to a long-standing and pervasive situation?

In fact, the current high level of attention to global sweatshop conditions does reflect more than just a rise in awareness. The underlying reality behind the rise in sweatshops is the extremely rapid increase over the past twenty-five years in less-developed countries producing manufactured products for export markets. We can see this pattern in Figure 1, showing the share of manufacturing exports as a percentage of total exports for the less-developed countries. As the figure shows, manufacturing exports amounted to 17.7 percent of total exports for less developed countries as recently as 1980. By 1998, the figure had risen to 71.6 percent. The most rapid growth in exports among these countries has been in Asia—especially China, South Korea, Taiwan, Thailand, Malaysia, Indonesia and India. But Latin American and African countries have also experienced significant increases in their export markets.

Of course, not all manufactured exports from less-developed countries are produced under sweatshop conditions. But the strategy of many business owners in less-developed countries—just as in the advanced countries—is to gain a competitive advantage through squeezing workers, and thereby driving down labor costs as far as possible. In many countries, business firms are able to proceed unchecked with such "race to the bottom" employment practices because of a lack of reasonable laws governing mini-

---

12 This literature is summarized briefly in Robert Pollin, Justine Burns and James Heintz, "Global Apparel Production and Sweatshop Labor: Can Raising Retail Prices Finance Living Wages," *Cambridge Journal of Economics,* 2004, <http://www.umass.edu/peri/pdfs/WP19.pdf>.

FIGURE 1 **MANUFACTURING EXPORTS IN LESS DEVELOPED COUNTRIES (MANUFACTURING EXPORTS AS SHARE OF TOTAL EXPORTS)**

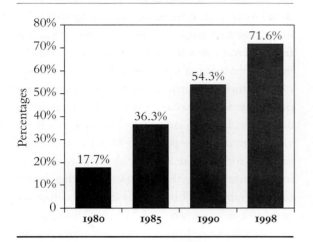

SOURCE: World Bank, *World Development Indicators* CD-Rom 2001.

mum wages, working conditions, and the basic rights of workers. Perhaps even more frequently, reasonable labor standards do exist on paper in less-developed countries but are not enforced in practice. These are the conditions that have fostered the rapid spread of sweatshops throughout the developing world.

Are Sweatshops Really So Bad?

But recognizing the existence of sweatshops is one thing: is it reasonable to also assume that sweatshops are a problem for less-developed countries? In fact, many well-known economists and other commentators consider the spread of sweatshops in these regions as a highly favorable development. This view is expressed straightforwardly in a September 24, 2000 *New York Times Magazine* article titled "Two Cheers for Sweatshops," by Nicholas Kristof and Sheryl WuDunn, focusing on conditions in Asia. Kristof and WuDunn write:

Fourteen years ago, we moved to Asia and began reporting there. Like most Westerners, we arrived in the region outraged at sweatshops. In time, though, we came to accept the view supported by most Asians: that the campaign against sweatshops risks harming the very people it is intended to help. For beneath their grime, sweatshops are a clear sign of the industrial revolution that is beginning to reshape Asia.

This is not to praise sweatshops. Some managers are brutal in the way they house workers in firetraps, expose children to dangerous chemicals, deny bathroom breaks, demand sexual favors, force people to work double shifts or dismiss anyone who tries to organize a union. Agitation for improved safety conditions can be helpful, just as it was in 19th-century Europe. But . . . the simplest way to help the poorest Asians would be to buy more from sweatshops, not less.

Jeffrey Sachs, a leading economist at Columbia University expresses this same perspective even more emphatically when he says that the problem is "not that there are too many sweatshops, but that there are too few." Also endorsing this view, the Princeton economist and *New York Times* columnist Paul Krugman explains that "the result [of sweatshop employment] has been to move hundreds of millions of people from abject poverty to something still awful but nonetheless significantly better," and thus, that "the growth of sweatshop employment is tremendous good news for the world's poor."

However else one might react to such perspectives, they do bring attention to a simple, but extremely important fact about sweatshops: that the single most important reason that sweatshops exist is that people accept these jobs. True, once workers are hired into sweatshop firms, they are often forced to stay on the job through harsh forms of compulsion, as the *Business Week* story quoted above makes clear. Still, for the most part, workers could escape sweatshop conditions simply by refusing to show up at work. The fact that they do show up means that sweatshop employment represents an option for hundreds of millions of workers in developing countries that is superior to their next best alternative. Presumably, this is the sense in which Kristof and WuDunn offer "two cheers" for sweatshops, Professor Sachs calls for more sweatshops, and Professor Krugman praises them as "tremendous good news" for the world's poor.[13]

But is it actually true that there is no alternative to creating ever more sweatshops if developing countries are to reduce poverty and succeed economically? In fact, this perspective is seriously misguided, because it ignores some crucial facts about the way that conditions have changed dramatically under neoliberal globalization.

Surplus Workers in Less-Developed Countries[14]

At least since World War II, rural workers in developing countries have been migrating out of agricultural employment. This migration has freed up more workers to contribute toward the production of non-agricultural goods and services, which, in turn, has generally contributed positively to economic growth in developing countries. But this migration out of agriculture also created a new problem: that the supply of workers moving out of agriculture was exceeding the demand for these workers in other forms of employment. This pattern led to the formation of a massive pool of "surplus" workers— people who were forced to scramble for a living any way they could. A high proportion of them migrated into the queue for jobs in the manufacturing sectors in developing countries with virtually nothing as an alternative fallback position. These are the conditions under which poor working people might well regard a sweatshop factory job as a better option than any immediately practical alternative.

This pattern has worsened under neoliberal globalization, resulting from the interaction of several factors. First, the reduction or elimination of tariffs on agricultural products has enabled cheap imported grains and other agricultural products to capture a growing share of the developing countries' markets. This has made it

---

13 The quotations from Sachs and Krugman are cited in an excellent essay by Professor John Miller of Wheaton College, "Why Economists Are Wrong About Sweatshops and the Antisweatshop Movement," *Challenge,* January–February 2003, pp. 93–122.

14 These issues are developed more fully, with citations, in Robert Pollin, "Globalization and the Transition to Egalitarian Development," Political Economy Research Institute Working Paper #42, <http://www.umass.edu/peri/pdfs/WP42.pdf>.

increasingly difficult for small-scale farmers in developing countries to survive in agriculture, which, in turn, has accelerated the migration into the non-agricultural labor market. Neoliberal policies have also brought reductions, if not outright elimination, of agricultural subsidies to smallholders ★ ★ ★. As conditions have thus worsened for small-scale agricultural producers, their opportunities for finding jobs in manufacturing have also been limited by several factors also associated with neoliberal policies. The first has been the overall decline in economic growth and average incomes in most developing countries in the neoliberal era. As income growth fell, so did the expansion of domestic markets, and thus also the expansion of jobs producing goods for domestic consumers.

But what about the sharp rise in manufacturing exports by developing countries? In fact, even this development has not generally translated into a comparable rise in jobs producing goods for export markets (with some important exceptions, notably China again, but also Malaysia and Chile). Many of the countries that are now manufacturing exporters—in particular the large Latin American economies, Mexico, Argentina and Brazil—did already have large-scale manufacturing sectors in operation, though these earlier-vintage manufacturing sectors, under the import substitution model, concentrated on producing for their domestic markets. The liberalization of trade policies has therefore produced improvements in their exporting capacity, but, concurrently, a corresponding increase in the penetration of their own domestic markets by foreign imports. Moreover, firms in the relatively new export

manufacturing countries have been forced to appropriate higher productivity production methods in order to compete in the global market. This has made their operations more efficient, but has also entailed reducing the number of workers they employ.

Workers in developing countries thus face a double squeeze: diminishing opportunities to continue earning a living in agriculture, but nothing close to a compensating growth of job opportunities outside of agriculture. These are the circumstances that have pushed more working people in developing countries into a desperate situation where they must accept a sweatshop job to continue to live. But this situation can hardly be construed as "tremendous good news for the world's poor," as Paul Krugman put it. They are simply the raw facts of life for hundreds of millions of people under global neoliberalism.

Sweatshop Jobs vs. No Jobs: No Alternatives?

In fact, there is evidence in considering the pattern of manufacturing production in less-developed countries that offers grounds for optimism about alleviating sweatshop conditions. The argument that sweatshops are "tremendous good news for the world's poor" is based on a simple premise: that if working conditions in developing countries were to become more desirable—that is, if wages were to rise, workplaces to become cleaner and safer, and workers were able to exercise basic rights—then labor costs in these countries would become excessive. The firms producing in developing countries would then be out-competed on global markets, and job opportunities for the poor would dry up, despite the best intentions of anti-sweatshop activists. But this simple premise is contradicted by the actual patterns between wage and employment growth in the apparel industries of developing countries. Table 3 offers evidence that speaks to this question.

More specifically, Table 3 gives data on the relationship between real wage and employment growth in the apparel industries for twenty-two developing countries between 1988–97 (these twenty-two developing countries were the only ones for which adequate data were available). I have grouped the countries into four categories, those in which:

1. employment and real wage growth *rose* together;
2. employment and real wage growth *fell* together;
3. employment *fell* while real wage growth *rose;* and
4. employment *rose* while real wage growth *fell.*

As we can see from the table, the countries in which employment and real wages rose together, shown in panel A, is the largest category—both in terms of the total of eight countries included in this category, and in terms of the 1.2 million workers employed in these countries as of 1997. These figures clearly contradict the notion, at least in the apparel industry, that developing countries must maintain labor costs as low as possible in order for job opportunities to grow. It is true that wages rose only modestly in most of the eight countries listed. But the fact that they are rising at all demonstrates that factors other than maintaining sweatshop working conditions are contributing to the growth of jobs. Some of these other factors are the productivity levels in the apparel plants, the quality of the local transportation and communications infrastructure, and the effectiveness of the marketing channels through which the newly manufactured clothing items reach retail markets.

Panel B includes three countries—Kenya, Guatemala and Barbados—in which apparel workers' wages fell over 1988–97, but employment nevertheless declined as well. This is a small grouping of countries, which also employs a small number of workers. But it is still useful to observe examples in which pushing wages down did not succeed in stimulating job growth.

Panel C shows the countries in which wages rose while employment declined. But these cases need to be interpreted carefully. South Korea, for example, experienced the fastest real wage growth of the twenty-two countries in the sample, at an average annual rate of 8.3 percent, while the number of jobs in the apparel industry was declining at a 5.7 percent annual rate. Two developments explain this pattern: rising productivity among apparel producers; and growing strength by the country's labor movement, which pushed successfully for higher wages while operating in a democratic environment for the first time. Jobs in which both wages and productivity are rising rapidly should be considered as a positive development. But it does still create a challenge at the same time: that job opportunities be created elsewhere in the Korean economy, to prevent unemployment from rising. ★ ★ ★

The countries in Panel D conform most closely in their experiences to the claims of sweatshop enthusiasts: they experienced employment growth while wages declined. But this

TABLE 3 RELATIONSHIP BETWEEN EMPLOYMENT AND REAL WAGE GROWTH IN DEVELOPING COUNTRIES' APPAREL INDUSTRIES

	Total apparel employment in 1997	Employment growth average annual rate 1988–97 (percentages)	Real wage growth average annual rate 1988–97 (percentages)
A) COUNTRIES IN WHICH EMPLOYMENT AND REAL WAGES ROSE TOGETHER			
(LISTED ACCORDING TO TOTAL EMPLOYMENT LEVELS IN 1997)			
1) Indonesia	393,300	+17.4	+1.3
2) India	270,000	+29.9	+0.7
3) Philippines	161,300	+4.8	+1.2
4) Morocco	116,900	+10.3	+2.3
5) Colombia	66,700	+3.7	+1.2
6) Malaysia	60,500	+4.4	+3.8
7) Costa Rica	32,900	+4.1	+2.9
8) Chile	13,800	+1.6	+6.5
Total employment for all countries	1,215,400		
B) COUNTRIES IN WHICH EMPLOYMENT AND REAL WAGES FELL TOGETHER			
1) Kenya	7,300	−1.2	−1.9
2) Guatemala	1,900	−2.1	−10.3
3) Barbados	1,300	−3.1	−6.1
Total employment for all countries	10,500		
C) COUNTRIES IN WHICH EMPLOYMENT FELL WHILE REAL WAGES ROSE			
1) South Korea	151,500	−5.7	+8.3
2) South Africa	126,300	−0.5	+2.1
3) Mauritius	66,400	−1.3	+7.0
4) Mexico	24,500	−2.1	+1.8
5) Puerto Rico	20,100	−3.6	+0.3
6) Singapore	8,100	−11.5	+4.8
7) Panama	4,300	−0.7	+1.8
Total employment for all countries	401,200		
D) COUNTRIES IN WHICH EMPLOYMENT ROSE WHILE REAL WAGES FELL			
1) Uruguay	11,300	+0.2	−6.3
2) Jordan	4,900	+8.7	−3.3
3) Ecuador	3,900	+1.5	−10.2
4) Bolivia	2,200	+18.5	−1.9
Total employment for all countries	22,300		

SOURCE: World Bank, *World Development Indicators*, 2001 CD-ROM.

grouping consisted of only four countries, employing 22,300 workers.

The overall point is that there is no single formula that will deliver a successful manufacturing sector in developing countries. Maintaining sweatshop working conditions and other "race to the bottom" business practices may indeed be successful in driving down costs and thereby enhancing competitiveness. But the evidence presented here also shows that 1) there are other ways to establish a growing manufacturing sector in developing countries; and 2) pushing labor costs down will, in itself, guarantee nothing.

There is another important consideration at play here: the fact that consumers in the United States and other wealthy countries express strong preferences to not purchase products made under sweatshop conditions, the entreaties of sweatshop enthusiasts notwithstanding. Consider the results of a 1999 survey of U.S. consumers sponsored by the National Bureau of Economic Research. This poll found that, on average, consumers were willing to pay 28 percent more on a $10 item and 15 percent more on a $100 item to ensure that the products they bought were made under "good working conditions."[15]

These polling results are especially striking, given the findings from a study I conducted with co-workers Justine Burns and James Heintz. We estimated how much retail prices in the United States would have to rise in order to fully finance a 100 percent wage increase for apparel production workers in Mexico.[16] We recognized that a one-time, 100 percent wage increase for Mexican workers—a doubling of existing wage rates—was well beyond what was likely to result even in a political environment dominated by a broadly shared commitment to eliminating sweatshops. But for the purposes of the exercise, it was important that we not err by underestimating how much labor costs might have to rise to eliminate sweatshops. The result we obtained was that retail prices in the U.S. clothing market would have to rise by only *1.8 percent to fully cover this 100 percent wage increase.* Consider, for example, the case for a $100 sports jacket. To finance a 100 percent wage increase for Mexican workers producing this jacket, the retail price of the jacket would have to rise by $1.80, to $101.80. At the same time, the National Bureau of Economic Research poll finds that U.S. consumers would be willing to pay $115 for this jacket if they could be assured that it had not been made under sweatshop conditions.

Of course, by itself, this simple exercise does not demonstrate that sweatshop labor conditions could be readily wiped out through modest increases in consumer prices. The world is obviously more complex than our exercise allows. Take just one additional layer of complexity. If the jacket's retail price really did rise from $100 to $101.80 in the U.S. market because U.S. consumers want their clothes manufactured under non-sweatshop conditions, how would the con-

---

15 The poll results are in Elliot, K. A. and R. B. Freeman (2000) "White Hats or Don Quixotes? Human Rights Vigilantes in the Global Economy," National Bureau of Economic Research Conference on Emerging Labor Market Institutions, <http:// www.nber.org/~confer/2000/si2000/elliot.pdf>.

16 Pollin, Barns, and Heintz, op. cit. Our study examined the case for Mexico only because, among developing countries, it provides the most comprehensive government statistics on production costs in its apparel industry.

sumers actually know whether that extra $1.80 that they spent on the jacket is actually getting channeled back to the production-level workers in Mexico, as opposed to getting pocketed by the owners of their local J.C. Penney outlet? There is no airtight answer to this or several other similar questions. Nevertheless, the exercise still gives important support on behalf of an important conclusion: that the spread of sweatshop working conditions need not be considered as an inevitable, much less desirable, feature of the global economic landscape.

FOREIGN AID AND ECONOMIC GROWTH

We see that the relentless spread of sweatshops is not the only way to create jobs in developing countries. But what about the broader pathologies in the less developed countries associated with the neoliberal era, i.e. declining growth, increased inequality and lack of progress in reducing poverty? World leaders set clear goals for poverty eradication at the United Nations Millennium Summit: to cut in half by 2015 the proportion of people whose income is less than one dollar a day, who suffer from hunger, or who are unable to reach or afford safe drinking water.[17] Are there any measures through which these goals could conceivably be met?

One obvious and widely discussed initiative would be for the wealthy countries to simply increase the amount of aid they provide for poor countries. This approach has received widespread attention in recent years, most visibly

from the admirable, energetic efforts of rock star Bono, the lead singer of the group U2. Bono's mission has led him to, among other things, tour areas of Africa in May 2002 with the first Treasury Secretary of the Bush-2 administration, Paul O'Neill. Bono emphasized the need for increased aid during the Africa tour, while former Secretary O'Neill espoused the virtues of free market economic policies as the single most powerful anti-poverty weapon for the continent.

Of course, what former Secretary O'Neill managed to neglect during this joint tour are the ways in which neoliberal economic policies have worsened poverty and inequality throughout most of Africa, as well as in Argentina, rural India and elsewhere. Indeed it would be illuminating to consider the Bono/O'Neill tour from another perspective. Let's allow that Bono's efforts at persuading the rich countries to substantially increase their aid to developing countries were to completely succeed. How large would the benefits be of this dramatic policy shift relative to the less developed countries pursuing the *opposite* of what former Secretary O'Neill proposed, that is, to abandon neoliberalism in favor of policy measures that could restore growth to something akin to the 1961–80 era of developmental states? Here are some figures that offer a rough answer to this question.

Increasing Foreign Aid

In the early 1970s, the wealthy countries committed themselves to provide 0.7 percent of their

---

17 The U.N. Millennium goals are presented at <http://www.un.org/millenniumgoals/index.html>.

annual GDP for development aid. The March 2002 United Nations Conference on Financing for Development affirmed that a dramatic increase in aid is necessary if there was to be any possibility to achieve the Millennium Summit poverty goals. As U.N. Secretary General Kofi Annan wrote during the Monterrey conference, "all economic studies indicate that to achieve the Millennium Development Goals, we need an increase of about $50 billion a year in worldwide official aid—a doubling of present levels."[18] But as of 1999, the average amount given by the wealthy countries was only 0.32 percent of each country's GDP. The United States was the least generous by a substantial amount, allocating only 0.1 percent of its GDP to development aid.[19]

Indeed, even Annan's call for a $50 billion increase in development aid is well below the amount that would be generated if the wealthy countries did actually uphold their earlier commitment to providing 0.7 percent of GDP in aid. Considering the years 1995–99, the 0.7 percent of GDP foreign aid pledge would have meant an average annual aid contribution of $160 billion/

year, an average increase of $105 billion over the approximately $55 billion per year that the wealthy countries did contribute in these years.

Clearly an increase in aid of $105 billion, or even $50 billion, would represent an implausible leap in generosity for most of the rich countries, especially the United States, given their evident willingness to disregard earlier pledges on this matter. But at least we have now established some outer bound figures as to how much additional income to the developing countries could be generated by increased foreign aid—the far outer limit figure being $105 billion, while even the $50 billion called for by Secretary General Annan also representing an improbable goal.[20]

Returning to Developmental Era Growth

The U.N. Conference on Financing for Development was also clear that "a crucial task" for meeting its poverty reduction goals is "to enhance the efficiency, coherence, and consistency of macroeconomic policies."[21] But the official conference document provides no specif-

---

18 Kofi A. Annan, "Trade and Aid in a Changed World," *New York Times,* 3/19/02, <http://www.un. org/News/ossg/sg/stories/sg-19mar2002.htm>.

19 Figures for development assistance provided by OECD countries is at <http://www.oecd.org/pdf/M00022000/M00022968.pdf>.

20 This $105 billion figure does not take account of a longstanding controversy regarding the effects of foreign aid, i.e. whether a dollar of aid to a poor country will actually produce something close to a dollar of additional income for the recipient country. Critics of aid programs from both the political right (e.g. Milton Friedman and Peter Bauer) and left (e.g. Keith Griffin and Teresa Hayter) have argued, for different reasons, that aid inhibits the development of productive activities in a less developed country. An alternative perspective, taking account of standard "multiplier effects" of increased income, would suggest that a dollar of aid could increase development by something more than the dollar of aid provided, The most recent formal statistical studies on

this question acknowledge that they are unable to reach any firm conclusions, though they provide suggestive, if fragile, evidence that aid may enhance growth in the short run but that such positive effects could turn negative within a longer-term framework. (Henrik Hansen and Finn Tarp, "Aid and Growth Regressions" *Journal of Development Economics,* 64, 2001, pp. 547–570 and Robert Lensink and Howard White "Are there negative returns to aid?" *Journal of Development Studies,* 37(6), 2001: 42–65.) Taking account of these arguments and findings, the most reasonable working assumption for our purposes is also the simplest: that a dollar of aid will produce roughly a dollar of additional national income—that is, a dollar of aid will have the same proportional effect on national income as an increase in the country's growth rate generated by some other means.

21 United Nations, *Report of the International Conference on Financing For Development,* Monterrey, Mexico, March, 2002, p. 3, <http://ods-dds-nyun.org/doc/UNDOC/GEN/N02/392/67/PDF/N0239267.pdf?OpenElement>.

ics as to what should constitute such "efficient, coherent, and consistent" macroeconomic policies. As a simple starting point for addressing this issue, what if we allowed that the developing countries were able to return to something like their average rate of economic growth during the era of developmental states? As we have seen earlier (see Table 1), the less developed countries (excluding China) grew at an average annual rate of 5.5 percent between 1961–80 but this rate dropped to 2.6 percent between 1981–99. The decline in the average growth rate for less developed countries was therefore 2.9 percent per year during the neoliberal era.

To give a rough estimate of how important such a shift in their growth path would be for the less developed countries, I have estimated the effects of raising the average growth rate for these countries by 2.9 percent per year over the years 1995–99 only. The specific question we are asking is: if the poor and middle income countries grew from 1995–99 at an average rate that was 2.9 percent faster than the rate at which they actually grew, how much additional national income would they have generated?

The answer is that, for the full five-year period, the poor and middle-income countries, exclusive of China, would have produced an additional $2.4 trillion in income. The average total income increase over the five-year period would therefore be $480 billion per year—that is, an amount that is nearly five times larger than what would be generated by an implausible outer limit increase of $105 billion in foreign aid. It is important to emphasize that this result does not rely on assuming that the less-developed countries achieve anything unprecedented in their growth performance, but simply that they return to their *average* rates of growth during the era of

developmental states. In other words, if the less developed countries abandoned the neoliberal policies that have inhibited their growth for the past generation, and established a new policy environment that promoted growth to an extent comparable to the levels they achieved in the 1960s and 1970s—but to no more than the average levels of this earlier period—they would have generated by 1999 gains in national income nearly five times larger than what they would attain by even an implausibly generous increase in aid from the wealthy countries.

To put it another way: if economic policies concerning less developed countries were to embrace the arguments of both Bono and former Bush Treasury Secretary Paul O'Neill—that is, for aid to dramatically increase while neoliberalism remained the dominant policy approach—incomes in developing countries would still be around $400 billion a year *less* than what could be achieved through eschewing neoliberalism in favor of something approximating the economic policies that guided the era of developmental states. Figure 2 summarizes the relative effects of the three options: 1) a Bono-level of increased aid support, versus 2) a return to a developmental state period growth performance, versus 3) Bono-level aid plus continuation of neoliberal rates of growth.

How Much Does $480 Billion Matter?

$480 billion is an immensely large figure, but what would it mean concretely for people's lives? How important would this amount be, for example, as a means of reducing poverty in the developing countries? To get some rough sense of this, it will be helpful to examine in a bit more detail the case of a single developing country. Brazil is a good case study for this purpose, since it is a large

FIGURE 2   **THE RELATIVE BENEFITS OF AID AND GROWTH FOR DEVELOPING COUNTRIES (AVERAGE ANNUAL GAINS BASED ON 1995–1999 DATA)**

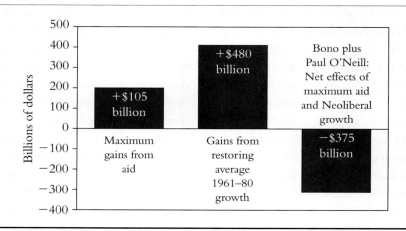

SOURCE: Calculations based on figures in World Bank, *World Development Indicators* CD-Rom, 2001.

and important developing economy and because its own growth experience during the developmental state and neoliberal periods parallels the average experience for the developing countries as a whole.

The average per capita income in Brazil between 1995–99 was about $4,500 per year. If Brazil's growth rate over these five years rose by 2.9 percent per year over the actual growth experience, this would generate an average increase in income of $415 per person—that is, the average Brazilian would enjoy roughly a 9 percent increase in income over the five-year period. But what about the poor specifically? Between 1995–99, the poorest 10 percent of Brazil's population lived on an average of $375 per year, that is, putting this segment of the population almost exactly at the United Nations' minimal global poverty threshold of one dollar per day of income (i.e. $375 per

year/365 days). Thus, if Brazil's poorest 10 percent were to receive a benefit from Brazil's accelerated economic growth equal to the average for the whole society, their additional $415 in annual income would represent more than a doubling of their living standard. Note that this example does not entail that Brazil's poor somehow begin receiving a proportionate share of the country's *total national income,* but only a proportionate share of its *increased* income generated by accelerated growth. Everyone in Brazil would still be better off through this equal distribution of the gains from growth, with the average-income person still enjoying a roughly 9 percent income gain.

But we also need to recognize that Brazil's income distribution is one of the most unequal in the world. Short of major political upheaval, one should not reasonably expect that Brazil's growth dividend would be divided equally.

However, even if we assumed that Brazil's poor received a gain from growth only one-fourth as large as the average person, that would still mean that the income of the poor would rise by 28 percent, or roughly $100. The federal government of Brazil defines what it terms as a "basic food basket" for an adult as costing approximately $56 per month. Thus, even the $100 in additional income would mean that Brazil's poor could purchase for themselves nearly two additional months of this basic food basket.

More generally then, even allowing for a highly unequal distribution of the gains from accelerated economic growth, the benefits of returning to something akin to the growth experience of the 1960s and 1970s would bring major benefits to the poor, both in Brazil and throughout the less developed world. At the same time, a major feature of any concerted poverty-reducing effort—an effort, for example, that takes seriously the anti-poverty commitments made at the U.N. Millennium Summit—would include measures for equalizing the gains from accelerated economic growth. In this regard, policies to eliminate sweatshops and guarantee workers decent, if still modest, minimum wages are good examples of measures that would enable the dividends from improved economic growth to be shared equitably.

55

The Age of Extremes: Concentrated Affluence and Poverty in the Twenty-First Century*

DOUGLAS S. MASSEY

Poverty is old news. For thousands of years the great majority of human beings have lived and labored at a low material standard of living. In the first hunter-gatherer societies that emerged on the savannahs of Africa, in the agrarian villages that later appeared in the highlands of the fertile crescent, in the great agricultural empires that arose in Mesopotamia, the Mediterranean area, India, and China, most people were very poor. This iron fact of life prevailed in all human societies until quite recently.

Despite universal material deprivation, human societies evolved cultures and social structures that permitted people to live and reproduce in relative peace. Social order was possible in conditions of pervasive poverty because of one fundamental condition: The deprivation existed at low geographic densities. Under this circumstance, the socially disruptive correlates of poverty occurred infrequently and could be managed, more or less, through informal means; and because the poverty-stricken masses rarely came into contact with the tiny elite, they did not perceive the full extent of their relative deprivation.

---

* First published in 1996; from *Demography*, Volume 33, Number 4.

The one place where rich and poor families came into direct contact was in cities, but preindustrial urban centers were few in number and never contained more than a tiny fraction of the human population. In premodern cities, moreover, the wealthy were constantly exposed to the poor and their privations, because preindustrial technologies permitted neither the separation of work from residence nor the segregation of the elite from the masses. Class integrity was maintained largely through social means, not physical separation. Indeed, the coexistence of poverty and wealth at high densities created problems of social order, as any student of ancient Rome can attest.

The industrial revolution of the nineteenth century upset the apple cart by creating and distributing wealth on a grand scale, enabling affluence and poverty to become geographically concentrated for the first time. Through urbanization, the rich and the poor both came to inhabit large urban areas. Within cities new transportation and communication technologies allowed the affluent to distance themselves spatially as well as socially from the poor, causing a rise in the levels of class segregation and a new concentration of affluence and poverty.

For a short time after World War II, mass social mobility temporarily halted the relentless geographic concentration of affluence and poverty in developed countries. The postwar economic boom that swept Europe, Japan, and the United States created a numerically dominant middle class that mixed residentially with both the upper and the lower classes. After 1970, however, the promise of mass social mobility evaporated and inequality returned with a vengeance, ushering in a new era in which the privileges of the rich and the disadvantages of the poor were compounded increasingly through geographic means.

In the coming century, the fundamental condition that enabled social order to be maintained in the past—the occurrence of affluence and poverty at low geographic densities—will no longer hold. In the future, most of the world's impoverished people will live in urban areas, and within these places they will inhabit neighborhoods characterized by extreme poverty. A small stratum of rich families meanwhile will cluster in enclaves of affluence, creating an unprecedented spatial intensification of both privilege and poverty.

As a result of this fundamental change in the geographic structure of inequality, the means by which the undesirable correlates of poverty were managed in the past will break down. The juxtaposition of geographically concentrated wealth and poverty will cause an acute sense of relative deprivation among the poor and heightened fears among the rich, resulting in a rising social tension and a growing conflict between the haves and the have-nots. As I demonstrate below, we have entered a new age of inequality in which class lines will grow more rigid as they are amplified and reinforced by a powerful process of geographic concentration.

THE SPATIAL CONCENTRATION OF POVERTY

Poverty is notoriously difficult to define; statistics on its incidence are unreliable and difficult to acquire, especially in the developing world. Tabatabai and Fouad (1993) conducted a survey of poverty estimates in developing countries for

FIGURE 1   **DISTRIBUTION OF THE POOR BY RURAL-URBAN STATUS: LATIN AMERICA, 1970–1990**

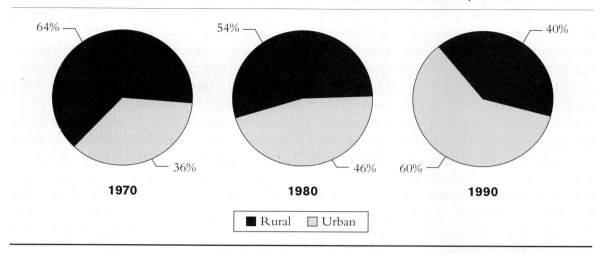

the International Labour Office and found that most regions lacked statistics dating back more than a few years. In Latin America, however, they were able to assemble reasonably accurate estimates of poverty rates beginning in 1970. To illustrate trends in the geographic concentration of poverty in developing countries, I apply rates of rural and urban poverty estimated by Tabatabai and Fouad for Latin America to rural and urban populations estimated for this region by the United Nations (1995). The resulting distribution of poverty by rural-urban status is shown in Figure 1 for 1970, 1980, and 1990.

In 1970 most of Latin America's poor—nearly two-thirds—lived in the countryside, typically in isolated farming communities, small agrarian villages, and tiny rural hamlets. In the ensuing two decades, however, the poor urbanized rapidly. By 1980 the balance of rural and urban poverty was approaching parity, and by 1990 a substantial majority (60%) of Latin America's poor lived in urban areas. This

transformation of the geographic structure of human deprivation was so quick that the ratio of rural-to-urban poverty in 1990 was almost precisely opposite the ratio that had prevailed only 20 years earlier.

Therefore, in this hemisphere, poverty is already well on the way to complete urbanization. The typical poor Latin American of the twenty-first century will not live in a village or town but in a city, and most likely a very large one. Although data limitations prevent me from demonstrating this fact for other regions of the developing world, projected trends in urbanization suggest that a majority of the world's poor will soon live in cities.

The urban concentration of poverty is already well advanced in developed countries. ★ ★ ★ By 1970 U.S. poverty was already predominantly urban; 56% of all poor persons lived either in central cities or in suburbs. Nonetheless, a large plurality of the poor (44%) lived in nonmetropolitan areas only two decades ago.

Over the next 20 years, however, the percentage of poor people living in nonmetropolitan areas dropped steadily, to 31% in 1980 and to 28% in 1990; thus by the early 1990s, 72% of America's poor lived in urban areas. Not only was poverty becoming more urbanized, however; it was also becoming more highly concentrated in the urban core. The proportion of poor people who lived in central cities stood at 34% in 1970, but the figure rose to 39% in 1980 and to 43% in 1990. Meanwhile the percentage of the poor living in suburbs, after rising during the 1970s, *fell* slightly during the 1980s and reached 29% in 1990.

While American poverty was becoming more concentrated in central cities, it was also concentrating in already-poor urban neighborhoods. John Kasarda (1993:265) recently computed the share of poor persons living in poor and very poor neighborhoods at different points in time. He defined a poor neighborhood as one with a tract poverty rate from 20% to 40%, and a very poor neighborhood as one with a tract poverty rate of more than 40%; nonpoor neighborhoods had a tract poverty rate below 20%.

★ ★ ★

In 1970, 45% of central-city poor people lived in a neighborhood that was *not* poor, whereas 55% lived in a poor or very poor neighborhood (38% in the former and 17% in the latter). Over the next two decades, however, the concentration of poor people in poor places increased sharply. From 1970 to 1990, the percentage of central-city poor people living in nonpoor areas declined from 45% to 31%, while the percentage living in poor neighborhoods increased from 38% to 41%. Meanwhile the share living in very poor neighborhoods grew markedly,

from 17% to 28%. As of 1990, more than two-thirds of all central-city poor people lived in poor or very poor neighborhoods.

Elsewhere Mitchell Eggers and I argue that the P★ isolation index popularized by Stanley Lieberson (1980, 1981) provides a reliable and accurate summary measure of poverty concentration (Massey and Eggers 1990). This index gives the rate of poverty in the neighborhood of the average poor person. The left-hand side of Figure 2 presents isolation indices for poor inhabitants of the nation's 10 largest metropolitan areas in 1970, 1980, and 1990, using data recently published by Abramson, Tobin, and VanderGoot (1995).

FIGURE 2 **CONCENTRATION OF AFFLUENCE AND POVERTY IN THE 10 LARGEST METROPOLITAN AREAS: UNITED STATES, 1970–1990**

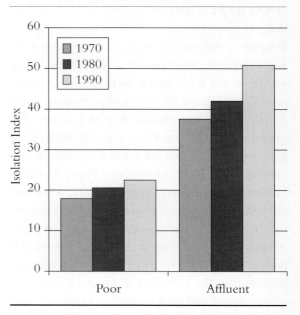

Over the past two decades, class isolation among the poor has risen steadily, growing by 21% between 1970 and 1990. As of 1990, the average poor resident of the nation's largest metropolitan areas lived in a neighborhood where roughly one-quarter of his or her neighbors were also poor. Analyses performed by Abramson and colleagues show that this geographic concentration of human poverty was remarkably widespread, and in some metropolitan areas reached extreme levels. By 1990 the average poor person in New York, Chicago, and Detroit lived in a neighborhood where 29% of the people were poor; the typical poor resident of New Orleans lived in a neighborhood where the poverty rate was a remarkable 35%. Over the past two decades, the social environment of the poor shifted to higher and higher densities of poverty.

THE SPATIAL CONCENTRATION OF AFFLUENCE

Despite a substantial and growing effort to study concentrated poverty, remarkably little attention has been given to the concentration of affluence. Since the dawn of urbanism, however, the elite have always clustered in cities for purposes of command and control. Indeed, in pre-industrial times they tended to settle in and around the city center (Sjoberg 1960). Because communications were rudimentary, effective administration required face-to-face interaction that could be achieved only through physical propinquity. Moreover, because transportation technologies were limited, goods and services required by the elite had to be produced, distributed, and sold near their places of residence.

The core of pre-industrial cities thus tended to house a variety of social classes, generating considerable face-to-face interaction across class lines. Although the rich may have been centralized, they were not separated physically from the masses, and although a wide social gulf separated them from the poor, affluence itself was not spatially concentrated (see Hershberg 1981; Zunz 1982).

This residential status quo was terminated in the nineteenth century by improvements in technology. Advances in transportation, communication, and construction led to an increase in density at the urban core, a separation of work from residence, and new possibilities for physical separation between the classes. Especially in the United States, the middle and upper classes began to leave central cities for affluent suburbs on the urban periphery early in the twentieth century, first axially along rail lines and then, as the automobile became more widely available, concentrically throughout a wide hinterland. The working classes meanwhile clustered in factory zones adjacent to the central business district, creating the spatial structure made so famous by my predecessor at the University of Chicago, Ernest Burgess (1925).

Although we have no direct measure of income segregation before 1940, we know that ethnic segregation increased substantially during the late nineteenth and early twentieth centuries in response to the changed ecological structure of the city (see Hershberg 1981; Massey 1985; Massey and Denton 1993). It is reasonable to surmise that class segregation also increased. After World War II, however, both class and ethnic segregation clearly declined (Massey 1985; Simkus 1978), fueled by an ongoing process of generational succession, social assimilation, and mass economic mobility unleashed by the postwar boom (Alba 1981).

As shown in seminal work by Blau and Duncan (1967) and Featherman and Hauser (1978), a remarkably fluid and open stratification system emerged in the United States during the years of World War II. Socioeconomic status came to depend less on one's social origins than on one's achievements; the result was a sustained decline in income inequality and an unprecedented rise in living standards. From 1947 to 1973, U.S. families doubled their incomes, while inequality declined by 5% (Levy 1987). According to James Smith (1988), the share of families with middle-class incomes grew from a minority of 40% of the population in 1940 to two-thirds of the population in 1970, while the poverty rate fell from 34% to 11%. In only 25 years the United States became a middle-class society structured meritocratically.

This broader trend toward socioeconomic equality was expressed spatially, as the degree of residential segregation between the upper and the lower classes was reduced sharply. According to calculations by Albert Simkus (1978), residential dissimilarity between high- and low-status workers declined markedly between 1960 and 1970. In the metropolitan areas he studied, the average dissimilarity index between professionals and laborers decreased by 19% from 1960 to 1970, while that between managers and service workers decreased by 17%. At the same time, residential dissimilarity between managers and laborers dropped by 23%, and that between managers and service workers by 17%. Therefore, during the 1960s, people located

at the extremes of the American occupational structure were moving rapidly together in residential terms, and observers at the time thought class segregation was on the wane.

Sometime during the mid-1970s, however, this pattern was reversed, and the classes once again began to pull apart socially and spatially. Just as we observe an increase in the concentration of poverty between 1970 and 1990, we also encounter a remarkable increase in the concentration of affluence. The right-hand side of Figure 2 shows P★ isolation indices for affluent persons in the 10 largest metropolitan areas of the United States. This index gives the proportion affluent in the neighborhood of the average affluent person. The figures for 1970 and 1980 come from work I published earlier with Mitchell Eggers (Massey and Eggers 1993); the figure for 1990 was computed especially for this address by Nancy Denton. Following James Smith (1988), I define the affluent as persons living in families whose incomes are at least four times the poverty level for a family of four—about $54,000 in 1990 dollars.

As Figure 2 clearly shows, affluence is even more highly concentrated spatially than poverty. Whereas the average poor person lived in a neighborhood that was 19% poor in 1970, the typical affluent person lived in a neighborhood that was 39% affluent. In the ensuing years, this already high concentration of affluence became even more intense: The isolation index increased to 43 in 1980 and to 52 in 1990. By the beginning of the present decade, in other words, the typical affluent person lived in a neighborhood where more than half the residents were also rich; the outcome was a social environment that was far more homogeneously privileged than at any time in the previous 20 years. In their daily lives, affluent residents of U.S. urban areas were increasingly likely to interact only with other affluent people, and progressively less likely to interact with other classes, especially the poor.

THE NEW WORLD ORDER

The hallmark of the emerging spatial order of the twenty-first century will be a geographic concentration of affluence and of poverty. Throughout the world, poverty will shift from a rural to an urban base; within urban areas poor people will be confined increasingly to poor neighborhoods, yielding a density of material deprivation that is historically unique and unprecedented. As poverty grows more geographically concentrated over time, its harmful by-products also will become more highly concentrated, intensifying social problems that the affluent will naturally seek to escape. Class segregation will increase, ratcheting up the concentration of affluence and poverty in self-reinforcing fashion.

This new ecological structure stems from deep and powerful forces operating in the world today. Simply put, concentrated poverty follows from any process that gathers poor people together in space and then inpedes their socioeconomic and residential mobility. At the end of the twentieth century, poor people are being assembled geographically through an ongoing process of urbanization that is already well advanced. Their social mobility is blocked by the emergence of a global economic structure characterized by stagnant mean incomes, rising inequality, and growing class rigidity; and their spatial mobility is stymied by a rising

tide of class segregation that is exacerbated, in many places, by an ongoing pattern of deliberate racial and ethnic exclusion. Welcome to the new world order.

THE URBANIZATION OF POVERTY

In a world where the great majority of people live in cities, poverty perforce will be urbanized. Figure 3 shows projected trends in the level of urbanization from 1970 to 2020 in developed regions, developing nations, and the United States (from United Nations 1995). Obviously most inhabitants of developed countries already live in urban areas: The proportion urban in the developed world was 74% in 1990 and is projected to reach 82% by 2020; in the United States the respective figures are 75% and 84%. Therefore, among developed nations, poverty already is highly urbanized, and this concentration will increase slowly but steadily in the coming decades.

The potential for change is considerably greater in the developing world. As late as 1970, only one-quarter of its population was urban; in 1990 the figure was only 35%. The path of urbanization, however, generally follows a logistic curve, beginning slowly and then accelerating rapidly for a time before leveling off and gradually approaching an upper asymptote (Preston 1979; United Nations 1980). Developing countries are now in that segment of the logistic curve characterized by rapid growth; the percentage urban is projected to rise rapidly in the next two decades, reaching 41% by the turn of the century and 47% in 2010.

Sometime between 2010 and 2020 the developing world as a whole will cross a significant

FIGURE 3 LEVEL OF URBANIZATION IN DEVELOPED AND DEVELOPING COUNTRIES, 1970–2020

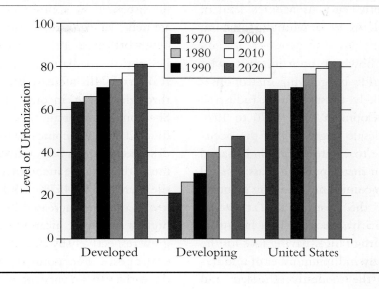

dividing line: For the first time, a majority of its population will live in cities. Because the great majority of these new urbanites will be impoverished by any standard, this event implies that poverty also will become concentrated in urban areas. Therefore, early in the next century, the typical poor citizen of Planet Earth will cease to inhabit a small town or rural village, and instead will live in a large city. Because there is no precedent for a reversal of urbanization once it has begun, the future of human poverty almost certainly lies in cities. Barring a catastrophe that wipes out much of the world's urban population, poverty will become progressively urbanized during the next century, and nobody can do much to change this fundamental fact.

THE RETURN OF INEQUALITY

Urbanization stems entirely from rural–urban migration rather than from natural increase within cities (Preston 1979; United Nations 1980). Historically much of this urbanizing population movement was internal, with peasants leaving rural areas for cities in their own countries, but a substantial part has always been directed to urban destinations overseas. Such was the case in Europe as it underwent development in the nineteenth century (Hatton and Williamson 1994; Nugent 1992); much the same is occurring in developing nations today (Massey 1988).

When they arrived in cities, rural inmigrants of the past took advantage of numerous ladders of mobility to climb out of poverty and into the working, middle, and even upper classes (Alba 1981, 1990; Hutchinson 1956; Lieberson 1980). Through the mid-1970s a pattern of widespread social mobility prevailed for in-migrants to cities, not only in developed countries such as the United States (Blau and Duncan 1967; Featherman and Hauser 1978;

Hauser and Featherman 1977) but also in developing societies such as Mexico (Balán, Browning, and Jelin 1973; Muñoz, Oliveira, and Stern 1977).

In the future, however, poor migrants who arrive in the world's burgeoning metropolises will be more likely to stay poor. Industrial growth and development from 1870 to 1970 produced a wholesale upgrading of the occupational structure to create a diamond-shaped status distribution that supported mass upward mobility, rising income, and declining inequality; in contrast, the postindustrial transformation since 1973 has produced an hourglass economic structure of high-paying jobs for the well-educated, a dwindling number of middle-income jobs for the modestly schooled, and many, many poorly paid jobs for those with little schooling. Such a structure creates few opportunities for mobility and carries great potential for inequality.

We are thus in an era of high and rising inequality (see Braun 1991; Levy 1995; Oliver and Shapiro 1995; Wolff 1995). ★ ★ ★ During the 1980s, inequality increased most sharply in Anglophone countries such as Australia, Ireland, Britain, and the United States, where the Gini rose from 33 to 36. The index also rose in Scandinavia (Finland, Norway, and Sweden) and western Europe (Austria, Belgium, Germany, and the Netherlands). Only the relatively poor countries of southern Europe—Italy, Spain, and Portugal, where incomes were lower and inequality was greater to begin with—opposed the trend toward greater inequality. The shifts in Gini coefficients may appear modest, but they conceal a rather profound transformation in underlying economic structure.

The nature of this transformation may be discerned by a closer look at trends in the United States during two contrasting eras: 1949–1969 and 1973–1991. During the earlier period, median family income doubled in real terms; this increase was shared by families throughout the income distribution. When Sheldon Danziger and Peter Gottschalk (1995) divided family incomes by the poverty line and observed changes between 1949 and 1969, they found that relative incomes in the bottom quintile increased by 457%, while those in the next lowest quintile increased by 169%. In the two highest quintiles, meanwhile, relative incomes grew respectively by 102% and 93%. Therefore, in the postwar economy that prevailed through the early 1970s, everyone did better—the poor as well as the rich. A rising tide lifted all boats, and the poverty rate dropped from 40% to 14% while the Gini index fell from 38 to 35 (Levy 1987).

After 1973, however, the median family income stagnated in real terms, ending only 6% higher in 1991. This stagnation in average income was produced by divergent trends at the extremes of the distribution. From 1973 to 1991, relative incomes for families in the two bottom quintiles declined by 19% and 8% respectively, whereas those for families in the two top quintiles increased by 21% and 22% (Danziger and Gottschalk 1995). Rather than a rising tide that lifted all boats, after 1973 Danziger and Gottschalk found uneven tides that elevated the yachts of the rich but beached the dinghies of the poor.

As a result of these contrasting trends, the shape of the income distribution changed gradually. As Martina Morris and her colleagues have shown, the middle categories shrank while the extremes expanded (Morris, Bernhardt, and Handcock 1994). After 1973 the poverty rate stopped falling in the United States, and the Gini index for family income rose from 35 to 40 by 1991 (Levy 1995). This 14% increase in inequality over the course of 18 years wiped out the entire postwar decline, and by 1991 had produced a more skewed distribution of income than existed in 1947!

Similar trends were occurring elsewhere in the developed world. Except for Australia and the United Kingdom, however, they were less dramatic than in the United States (Atkinson et al. 1995). In continental Europe, the new economic order was expressed more strongly as stagnating employment than as a decline in real wages. Income inequality rose slightly in European countries during the 1970s and 1980s, but unemployment increased fivefold between 1973 and 1985 (Krugman 1994). Despite population growth, European employment fell in absolute terms between 1973 and 1985, yielding a jobless rate whose degree and permanence were unprecedented in the postwar era.

It is much more difficult to make factual statements about trends in inequality in developing countries. Certainly in Mexico, the one developing country I know well, prospects for socioeconomic mobility seem bleak. From 1980 to 1989, the real minimum wage declined by 47%, GDP per capita declined by 9%, and the percentage of families earning less than twice the minimum wage, a rough indicator of poverty, rose to include 60% of the population (Sheahan 1991). According to conservative estimates, 48% of all Mexicans lived in poverty by 1989 (Escobar Latapí 1996); by 1996 Mexican wages

had lost 68% of their 1982 value (Equipo Pueblo 1996). Over the course of the 1980s, Mexico's standard of living fell to levels last seen in the 1960s. In just five years, from 1984 to 1989, income inequality increased enough to cancel out half of the decline achieved over the two previous decades (Cortés and Rubalcava 1992); it would have increased even more if not for the massive entry of additional household workers into the informal workforce (Cortés 1994; González de la Rocha 1986). Rates of occupational mobility increased during the 1980s, but most of the movement was downward (Escobar Latapí 1995).

Therefore, whether they stay in Mexico or come to the United States, therefore, poor Mexicans migrating from rural communities will face dim prospects for social mobility wherever they go, be it Los Angeles or Guadalajara. On both sides of the border, rural–urban migrants will confront a socioeconomic structure that offers few ladders of mobility, little access to high-wage employment, and, for those without education, the strong possibility of an enduring place at the bottom of the income distribution.

★ ★ ★

THE POLITICAL ECOLOGY OF INEQUALITY

Unless there is a radical departure from recent trends, poverty and affluence are almost certain to become geographically concentrated at high levels throughout the world early in the next century. Increasingly the poor and the rich will inhabit large urban areas, and within these places they will concentrate in separate neighborhoods. This ecological structure constitutes a radical departure from the past, and creates the potential for a new geopolitical order capable of compounding the benefits and liabilities of class by superimposing administrative segmentation on economic segregation.

Whether or not this potential is realized depends on how political districts are constructed. Insofar as the boundaries of local governmental units can be arranged to approximate the geographic contours of concentrated affluence and poverty, and insofar as the financing and delivery of public services can be shifted down the political hierarchy, the potential for reinforcing class advantages and disadvantages will be maximized.

In a society where most people live in small towns and villages, rich and poor families must mix socially, share the same public services, and inhabit the same political units. In such a geopolitical structure, the poor benefit from public institutions to which the rich are committed by reason of self-interest. When poverty and affluence become urbanized and geographically concentrated, however, the affluent acquire a means to separate themselves politically from the poor through the judicious drawing of political lines in space. If they can create separate governmental and administrative districts that encompass concentrations of poverty, and if they can force these poor districts to supply and pay for their own services, then the affluent will be able to insulate themselves from the economic costs imposed on society by the poor.

In the United States, the poor are isolated politically by the segmentation of metropolitan regions into a patchwork of separate municipalities. The concentration of affluence in certain suburbs generates high real estate values that allow the affluent to tax themselves at low rates while offering generous, even lavish municipal services. The concentration of poverty in central cities and some inner suburbs generates a high demand for services but yields low property values; thus, higher tax rates are required to support generally inferior services. The end result is a vicious cycle whereby city taxes are raised to maintain deficient services; consequently families with means are driven out; property values then decline further; the result is more tax increases and additional middle-class flight, which further exacerbate the concentration of poverty.

Under an ecological regime of concentrated affluence and poverty, efforts to decentralize government and shift the financing and provision of services to local government represent a means of enhancing the social and economic well-being of the rich at the expense of the poor. Political decentralization is progressive and democratic only in a world where all classes live together in small communities; this antiquated model of society no longer prevails, however, although it appears frequently in the writings of conservative thinkers (see Herrnstein and Murray 1994). In today's world of dense, urban agglomerations characterized by pronounced income inequality and increasing class segregation, political decentralization is punitive and regressive, forcing the poor to bear most of the cost of their own disadvantage. In a world of small towns and modest communities, political decentralization yields the social world of Andy Hardy; in a class-segregated world of large urban areas it produces the bleak vision of the Blade Runner.

Many mechanisms compound class advantages and disadvantages in the new ecology of inequality, but perhaps the most significant occurs through schools. Education is the most important single resource presently traded on global labor markets: In recent years workers with college and post-graduate degrees have seen their earnings rise, while high school graduates' and dropouts' wages have fallen. Access to high-quality education thus has become the crucial factor determining one's position in the postindustrial pecking order.

Because the emerging ecological structure concentrates the best-prepared students in areas of resource abundance while gathering the least well-prepared students in areas of resource scarcity, it necessarily exacerbates class inequities and promotes a more rigid stratification of society. Students from low-income families with poorly educated parents, little experience with books or reading, and multiple social problems attend schools with the fewest resources to help them learn, while students from affluent families with well-educated parents, extensive experience with books and reading, and few social problems attend well-funded schools that are most able to promote learning. The spatial concentration of affluence and poverty thus raises the odds that affluent children will receive a superior education while poor children will get inferior schooling.

THE CULTURAL ECOLOGY OF INEQUALITY

Until recently, poverty, though endemic, was spread uniformly in space and rarely occurred at high densities. Most impoverished families lived in small rural communities where the range of material well-being was limited. The few affluent families that were present locally were not especially affluent, and they tended to be closely related to others in the community. Truly wealthy families in the governing elite lived far away; the prevalent atmosphere in most places was one of collective poverty and shared deprivation.

In such settings, proclivities toward violence, crime, and other maladies exacerbated by material deprivation could be held in check by informal means. In small rural communities, as generations of cultural anthropologists have shown, everyone knows everyone else, either directly through personal experience or indirectly through ties of kinship or friendship. Through social networks, rewards and punishments are meted out to reinforce and maintain accepted standards of behavior. Age-old devices such as gossip, ridicule, shame, and ostracism, backed occasionally by physical discipline, are employed to punish public departures from accepted behavior, whereas praise, esteem, and prestige are accorded to those who conform (see Foster 1967; Lewis 1951).

★ ★ ★

The advent of geographically concentrated affluence and poverty as the dominant spatial structure of the twenty-first century has profound implications for the nature of social life. Not only will the informal means by which past societies preserved public order break down and ultimately disappear under the onslaught of urbanization; they will be replaced by new cultural forms rooted in the ecological order of concentrated affluence and poverty.

Just as poverty is concentrated spatially, anything correlated with poverty is also concentrated. Therefore, as the density of poverty increases in cities throughout the world, so will the density of joblessness, crime, family dissolution, drug abuse, alcoholism, disease, and violence. Not only will the poor have to grapple with the manifold problems due to their own lack of income; increasingly they also will have to confront the social effects of living in an environment where most of their neighbors are also poor. At the same time, the concentration of affluence will create a social environment for the rich that is opposite in every respect from that of the poor. The affluent will experience the personal benefits of high income; in addition, they will profit increasingly from the fact that most of their neighbors possess these advantages as well.

Therefore, in the emerging ecology of inequality, the social worlds of the poor and the rich will diverge to yield distinct, opposing subcultures. Among those at the low end of the income distribution, the spatial concentration of poverty will create a harsh and destructive environment perpetuating values, attitudes, and behaviors that are adaptive within a geographic niche of intense poverty but harmful to society at large and destructive of the poor themselves. At the other end of the hierarchy, a contrasting subculture of privilege will emerge from the spatial niche of concentrated affluence to confer additional advantages on the rich, thereby consolidating their social and economic dominance.

★ ★ ★

The contrasting ecologies of affluence and poverty will also breed opposing peer subcultures among rich and poor youths. As affluence grows more concentrated, the children of the privileged will socialize increasingly with other children of well-educated and successful parents. Knowledge of what one does to prepare for college and an appreciation of the connection between schooling and socioeconomic success will be widespread in the schools of the affluent. Students will arrive in the classroom well prepared and ready to learn. School officials need only build on this base of knowledge and motivation by using their ample resources to hire well-informed guidance counselors and enthusiastic, talented teachers.

Meanwhile, the children of the poor increasingly will attend schools with children from other poor families, who themselves are beset by multiple difficulties stemming from a lack of income. Parents will be poorly educated and will lack adequate knowledge about how to prepare for college. Children will not fully appreciate the connection between education and later success. Supervision and monitoring of students will be difficult because so many come from single-parent families, and the schools will be unable to offset this deficit because of funding limitations. Students will arrive in the classroom poorly prepared, and neither the dispirited guidance counselors nor the overworked, underpaid teachers will expect much from the students.

In such settings an alternative status system is almost certain to develop. Under circumstances where it is difficult to succeed according to conventional standards, the usual criteria for success typically are inverted to create an oppositional identity (Ogbu, 1978, 1983). Children formulate oppositional identities to preserve self-esteem when expectations are low and when failure by conventional standards is likely. Thus, in areas of concentrated poverty, students from poor families will legitimize their educational failures by attaching positive value and meaning to outcomes that affluent children label deviant and unworthy. In adapting to the environment created by concentrated poverty, success in school will be devalued, hard work will be regarded as selling out, and any display of learning will be viewed as uncool.

Oppositional subcultures already have become entrenched in many black inner-city areas of the United States, where high levels of racial segregation have produced unusually high concentrations of poverty and educational distress (Fordham and Ogbu 1986). Once such a subculture becomes established, it acquires a life of its own that contributes independently to the perpetuation of educational failure, the reproduction of poverty, and the cultural transmission of low socioeconomic status from person to person, family to family, and group to group (see Anderson 1990; Portes 1995).

||| INTO THE AGE OF EXTREMES

Thus a new age of extremes is upon us. In the social ecology now being created around the globe, affluent people increasingly will live and interact with other affluent people, while the poor increasingly will live and interact with other poor people. The social worlds of the rich and the poor will diverge, creating the potential for radical differences in thought, action, values, tastes, and feelings, and for the construction of a new political geography that divorces the interests of the rich from the welfare of the poor. For the first time in human history, the advantages and disadvantages of one's class position in society will be compounded and reinforced by a systematic process of geographic concentration.

★ ★ ★

How does the future look to me? Bleak, because I know that it is in the elite's narrow self-interest to perpetuate the status quo. Addressing serious issues such as increasing income inequality, growing class segregation, racial prejudice, and the geographic concentration of poverty will inevitably require sacrifice, and the immediate course of least resistance for affluent people will always be to raise the walls of social, economic, and geographic segregation higher in order to protect themselves from the rising tide of social pathology and violence.

If the status quo indeed is the most likely outcome, inequality will continue to increase and racial divisions will grow, creating a volatile and unstable political economy. As class tensions rise, urban areas will experience escalating crime and violence punctuated by sporadic riots and increased terrorism as class tensions rise. The poor will become disenfranchised and alienated from mainstream political and economic institutions, while the middle classes will grow more angry, more frustrated, and more politically mobilized. The affluent will continue to withdraw socially and spatially from the rest of society, and will seek to placate the middle classes' anger with quick fixes and demagogic excesses that do not change the underlying structure responsible for their problems.

This scenario is by no means inevitable, and I sincerely hope it will not come to pass. Yet we are headed in this direction unless self-conscious actions are taken to change course. A principal motivation for my pessimistic candor and perhaps overly brutal frankness is to galvanize colleagues, students, politicians, and reporters into action. Until now, neither the nature of the new ecological order nor its social implications have been fully realized; my purpose here is not to offer facile solutions to difficult problems, but to begin a process of serious thought, reflection, and debate on the new ecology of inequality, from which solutions ultimately may emerge. Until we begin to face up to the reality of rising inequality and its geographic expression, no solution will be possible.

||| REFERENCES

Abramson, A.J., M.S. Tobin, and M.R. Vander-Goot. 1995. "The Changing Geography of Metropolitan Opportunity: The Segregation of the Poor in U.S. Metropolitan Areas, 1970–1990." *Housing Policy Debate* 6:45–72.

Alba, R.D. 1981. "The Twilight of Ethnicity among American Catholics of European Ancestry." *Annals of the American Academy of Political and Social Science* 454:86–97.

———. 1990. *Ethnic Identity: The Transformation of White Identity.* New Haven: Yale University Press.

Alegría, T. 1994. "Segregación Socioespacial Urbana: El Ejemplo de Tijuana." *Estudios Demográficos y Urbanos* 9:411–28.

Anderson, E. 1990. *Streetwise: Race, Class, and Change in an Urban Community.* Chicago: University of Chicago Press.

———. 1994. "The Code of the Streets." *Atlantic Monthly* 273(3): 80–94.

Aronowitz, S. and W. DiFazio. 1994. *The Jobless Future: Sci-Tech and the Dogma of Work.* Minneapolis: University of Minnesota Press.

Atkinson, A.B., L. Rainwater, and T.M. Smeeding. 1995. *Income Distribution in OECD Countries: Evidence from the Luxembourg Income Study.* Paris: Organisation for Economic Cooperation and Development.

Balán, J., H.L. Browning, and E. Jelin. 1973. *Men in a Developing Society: Geographic and Social Mobility in Monterrey, Mexico.* Austin: University of Texas Press.

Banfield, E.C. 1967. *The Moral Basis of a Backward Society.* New York: Free Press.

Bernstein, M.A. and D.E. Adler. 1994. *Understanding American Economic Decline.* Cambridge, UK: Cambridge University Press.

Blau, P.M. and O.D. Duncan. 1967. *The American Occupational Structure.* New York: Free Press.

Bourgois, P. 1995. *In Search of Respect: Selling Crack in El Barrio.* Cambridge, UK: Cambridge University Press.

Braun, D. 1991. *The Rich Get Richer: The Rise of Income Inequality in the United States and the World.* Chicago: Nelson-Hall.

Burgess, E.W. 1925. "The Growth of the City: An Introduction to a Research Project." Pp. 47–62 in *The City,* edited by R.E. Park and E.W. Burgess. Chicago: University of Chicago Press.

Cortés, F. 1994. "La Evolución de la Desigualdad del Ingreso Familiar Durante la Década de los Ochenta." Unpublished manuscript, Centro de Estudios Sociológicos, El Colegio de México.

Cortés, F. and R.M. Rubalcava. 1992. "El Ingreso Familiar: Su Distribución y Desigualdad 1984–1989." *Demos: Carta Demografica sobre México* 5:28–30.

Danziger, S. and P. Gottschalk. 1995. *America Unequal.* Cambridge, MA: Harvard University Press.

Delgado, J. 1990. "De los Anillos de la Segregación: La Ciudad de México 1950–1987." *Estudios Demográficos y Urbanos* 5:237–74.

Denton, N.A. 1994. "Are African Americans Still Hypersegregated?" Pp. 49–81 in *Residential Apartheid: The American Legacy,* edited by R.D. Bullard, J.E. Grigsby III, and C. Lee. Los Angeles: CAAS Publications, University of California.

Drake, St.C. and H.R. Cayton. 1945. *Black Metropolis: A Study of Life in a Northern City.* New York: Harcourt, Brace.

Durkheim, E. [1893]1933. *The Division of Labor in Society,* translated by G. Simpson. Glencoe, IL: Free Press.

Equipo Pueblo. 1996. "Salaries Continue to Plummet." *Mexico Update* 69, April 23, p. 1.

Escobar Latapí, A. 1995. "Movilidad, Restructuración, y Clase Social on México: El Caso de Guadalajara." *Estudios Sociológicos* 13:231–60.

———. 1996. "Mexico: Poverty as Politics and Academic Disciplines." Pp. 539–66 in *Poverty: A Global Review,* edited by E. Oyen, S.M. Miller, and S.A. Samad. Oslo: Scandinavian University Press.

Farley, R. and W.H. Frey. 1994. "Changes in the Segregation of Whites from Blacks during the 1980s: Small Steps toward a More Integrated Society, *"American Sociological Review* 59:23–45.

Featherman, D. and R.M. Hauser. 1978. *Opportunity and Change.* New York: Academic Press.

Fischer, C.S. 1975. "Toward a Subcultural Theory of Urbanism." *American Journal of Sociology* 80:1319–41.

———. 1982. *To Dwell among Friends: Personal Networks in Town and City.* Chicago: University of Chicago Press.

———. 1995. "The Subcultural Theory of Urbanism: A Twentieth-Year Assessment." *American Journal of Sociology* 110:543–77.

Fordham, S. and J.U. Ogbu. 1986. "Black Students' School Success: Coping with the 'Burden of Acting White.' " *Urban Review* 18:176-206.

Foster, G.M. 1967. *Tzintzuntzan: Mexican Peasants in a Changing World.* Boston: Little, Brown.

Frank, R.H. and P.J. Cook. 1995. *The Winner-Take-All Society.* New York: Free Press.

Freeman, R.B. 1993. "How Much Has De-Unionization Contributed to the Rise in Male Earnings Inequality?" Pp. 133–63 in *Uneven Tides: Rising Inequality in America,* edited by S. Danziger and P. Gottschalk. New York: Russell Sage Foundation.

Gans, H.C. 1962. *The Urban Villagers: Group and Class in the Life of Italian Americans.* New York: Free Press.

Garrett, L. 1994. *The Coming Plague: Newly Emerging Diseases in a World out of Balance.* New York: Farrar, Straus, and Giroux.

Goleman, D. 1995. *Emotional Intelligence: Why It Can Matter More Than IQ.* New York: Bantam Books.

González de la Rocha, M. 1986. *Los Recursos de la Probeza: Familias de Bajos Ingresos de Guadalajara.* Guadalajara: El Colegio de Jalisco.

Gould, P. 1993. *The Slow Plague: A Geography of the AIDS Pandemic.* Cambridge, UK: Blackwell.

Harrison, B. 1995. *Lean and Mean: The Changing Landscape of Corporate Power in the Age of Flexibility.* New York: Basic Books.

Hatton, T.J. and J.G. Williamson. 1994. "What Drove the Mass Migrations from Europe?" *Population and Development Review* 20:533–61.

Hauser, R.M. and D.L. Featherman. 1977. *The Process of Stratification: Trends and Analysis.* New York: Academic Press.

Herrnstein, R.J. and C. Murray. 1994. *The Bell Curve: Intelligence and Class Structure in American Life.* New York: Free Press.

Hershberg, T. 1981. *Philadelphia: Work, Space, Family, and Group Experience in the 19th Century.* New York: Oxford University Press.

Hutchinson, E.P. 1956. *Immigrants and Their Children, 1850–1950.* New York: Wiley.

Jargowsky, P.A. Forthcoming. "Take the Money and Run: Economic Segregation in U.S. Metropolitan Areas." *American Sociological Review,* forthcoming.

Kasarda, J.D. 1993. "Inner-City Concentrated Poverty and Neighborhood Distress: 1970–1990." *Housing Policy Debate* 4:253–302.

———. 1995. "Industrial Restructuring and the Changing Location of Jobs." Pp. 215–68 in *State of the Union: America in the 1990s,* edited by R. Farley. New York: Russell Sage Foundation.

Kaus, M. 1992. *The End of Equality.* New York: Basic Books.

Krivo, L., R.D. Peterson, H. Rizzo, and J.R. Reynolds. 1996. "Race, Segregation, and the Concentration of Disadvantage: 1980–1990." Presented at the annual meetings of the Population Association of America, New Orleans.

Krivo, L. and R.D. Peterson. Forthcoming. "Extremely Disadvantaged Neighborhoods and Urban Crime." *Social Forces.*

Krugman, P. 1994. *The Age of Diminished Expectations.* Cambridge, MA: MIT Press.

Lasch, C. 1995. *The Revolt of the Elites and the Betrayal of Democracy.* New York: Norton.

LeDoux, J. 1986. "Sensory Systems and Emotion." *Integrative Psychiatry* 4:237–43.

Levy, F. 1987. *Dollars and Dreams: The Changing Distribution of American Income.* New York: Russell Sage Foundation.

———. 1995. "Incomes and Income Inequality." Pp. 1–58 in *State of the Union: America in the 1990s,* edited by R. Farley. New York: Russell Sage Foundation.

Lieberson, S. 1980. *A Piece of the Pie: Blacks and White Immigrants since 1880.* Berkeley: University of California Press.

———. 1981. "An Asymmetrical Approach to Segregation." Pp. 61–82 in *Ethnic Segregation in Cities,* edited by C. Peach, V. Robinson, and S. Smith. London: Croom Helm.

Lind, M. 1995. *The Next American Nation: The New Nationalism and the Fourth American Revolution.* New York. Free Press.

Maddrick, J. 1995. *The End of Affluence: The Causes and Consequences of America's Economic Dilemma.* New York: Random House.

Massey, D.S. 1985. "Ethnic Residential Segregation: A Theoretical Synthesis and Empirical Review." *Sociology and Social Research* 69:315–50.

———. 1988. "International Migration and Economic Development in Comparative Perspective." *Population and Development Review* 14:383–414.

———. 1990. "American Apartheid: Segregation and the Making of the Underclass." *American Journal of Sociology* 96:329–58.

———. 1995. "Getting Away with Murder: Segregation and Violent Crime in Urban America." *University of Pennsylvania Law Review* 143:1203–32.

———. Forthcoming. "The Residential Segregation of Blacks, Hispanics, and Asians: 1970 to 1990." In *Immigration and Race Relations,* edited by G.D. Jaynes. New Haven: Yale University Press.

Massey, D.S., G.A. Condran, and N.A. Denton. 1987. "The Effect of Residential Segregation on Black Social and Economic Well-Being." *Social Forces* 66:29–57.

Massey, D.S. and N.A. Denton. 1989. "Hypersegregation in U.S. Metropolitan Areas: Black and Hispanic Segregation along Five Dimensions." *Demography* 26:373–93.

———. 1993. *American Apartheid: Segregation and the Making of the Underclass.* Cambridge, MA: Harvard University Press.

Massey, D.S. and M.L. Eggers. 1990. "The Ecology of Inequality: Minorities and the Concentration of Poverty, 1970–1980." *American Journal of Sociology* 95:1153–89.

———. 1993. "The Spatial Concentration of Affluence and Poverty during the 1970s." *Urban Affairs Quarterly* 29:299–315.

Massey, D.S., A.B. Gross, and M.L. Eggers. 1991. "Segregation, the Concentration of Poverty, and the Life Chances of Individuals." *Social Science Research* 20:397–420.

Massey, D.S. and K. Shibuya. 1995. "Unravelling the Tangle of Pathology: The Effect of Spatially Concentrated Joblessness on the Well-Being of African Americans." *Social Science Research* 24:352–66.

Miles-Doan, R. and S. Kelly. 1996. "Neighborhood Contexts of Assaultive Violence: A Tract-Level Study of Disaggregated Rates in Duval County, Florida—1992." Presented at the annual meetings of the Population Association of America, New Orleans.

Morris, M., A.D. Bernhardt, and M.S. Handcock. 1994. "Economic Inequality: New Methods for New Trends." *American Sociological Review* 59:205–19.

Muñoz, H., O. de Oliveira, and C. Stern. 1977. *Migración y Desigualdad Social en la Ciudad de México.* México, DF: Universidad Nacional de México y Colegio de México.

Nugent, W. 1992. *Crossings: The Great Transatlantic Migration, 1870–1914.* Bloomington: Indiana University Press.

Ogbu, J.U. 1978. *Minority Education and Caste: The American System in Cross-Cultural Perspective.* New York: Academic Press.

———. 1983. "Minority Status and Schooling in Plural Societies." *Comparative Education Review* 27:168–90.

Oliver, M.L. and T.M. Shapiro. 1995. *Black Wealth/White Wealth: A New Perspective on Racial Inequality.* New York: Routledge.

Ousseimi, M. 1995. *Caught in the Crossfire: Growing Up in a War Zone.* New York: Walker.

Portes, A. 1995. "Children of Immigrants: Segmented Assimilation and Its Determinants." Pp. 248–80 in *The Economic Sociology of Immigration: Essays on Networks, Ethnicity, and Entrepreneurship,* edited by A. Portes. New York: Russell Sage Foundation.

Preston, S.H. 1979. "Urban Growth in Developing Countries: A Demographic Reappraisal." *Population and Development Review* 5:195–216.

Rifkin, J. 1995. *The End of Work: The Decline of the Global Labor Force and the Dawn of the Post-Market Era.* New York: Putnam.

Rubalcava, R.M. and M. Schteingart. 1985. "Diferenciación Socioespacial Intraurbana en el Area Metropolitana de la Ciudad de México." *Estatdios Sociológicos* 3:21–85.

Sheahan, J. 1991. *Conflict and Change in Mexican Economic Strategy: Implications for Mexico and Latin America.* La Jolla: Center for U.S.-Mexican Studies, University of California, San Diego.

Simkus, A.A. 1978. "Residential Segregation by Occupation and Race in Ten Urbanized Areas, 1950–1970." *American Sociological Review* 43:81–93.

Sjoberg, G. 1960. *The Preindustrial City: Past and Present.* New York: Free Press.

Smith, J.P. 1988. "Poverty and the Family." Pp. 141–72 in *Divided Opportunities: Minorities, Poverty, and Social Policy,* edited by G.D. Sandefur and M. Tienda. New York: Plenum.

Stack, C. 1974. *All Our Kin: Strategies of Survival in a Black Community.* New York: Harper and Row.

Stalker, P. 1994. *The Work of Strangers: A Survey of International Labour Migration.* Geneva: International Labour Office.

Suttles, G.D. 1968. *The Social Order of the Slum: Ethnicity and Territory in the Inner City.* Chicago: University of Chicago Press.

Tabatabai, H. and M. Fouad. 1993. *The Incidence of Poverty in Developing Countries: An ILO Compendium of Data.* Geneva: International Labour Office.

U.S. Bureau of the Census. 1973. *1970 Census of Population Subject Reports: Low-Income Population.* PC(2)-9A. Washington, DC: U.S. Government Printing Office.

———. 1983. *1980 Census of Population, General Social and Economic Characteristics, Part 1: U.S. Summary.* PC80-1-C1. Washington, DC: U.S. Government Printing Office.

———. 1993. *1990 Census of Population, Social and Economic Characteristics: Metropolitan Areas.* CP-2-1B. Washington, DC: U.S. Government Printing Office.

United Nations. 1980. *Patterns of Urban and Rural Population Growth*. Population Studies, No. 68. New York: United Nations.

———. 1995. *World Urbanization Prospects: 1994 Revision*. New York: United Nations.

Wallace, R. and D. Wallace. 1995. "U.S. Apartheid and the Spread of AIDS to the Suburbs: A Multi-City Analysis of the Political Economy of a Spatial Epidemic." *Social Science Medicine* 36:1–13.

Walton, J. 1978. "Guadalajara: Creating the Divided City." Pp. 25–50 in *Metropolitan Latin America: The Challenge and the Response,* edited by W.A. Cornelius and R.V Kemper. Beverly Hills: Sage.

Whyte, W.F. 1955. *Street Corner Society*. Chicago: University of Chicago Press.

Wilson, W.J. 1987. *The Truly Disadvantaged: The Inner City, the Underclass, and Public Policy*. Chicago: University of Chicago Press.

Wirth, L. 1938. "Urbanism as a Way of Life." *American Journal of Sociology* 44:3–24.

Wolff, E.N. 1995. "The Rich Get Increasingly Richer: Latest Data on Household Wealth during the 1980s." Pp. 33–68 in *Research in Politics and Society,* Vol. 5, edited by R.E. Ratcliff, M.L. Oliver, and T.M. Shapiro. Greenwich, CT: JAI.

Zunz, O. 1982. *The Changing Face of Inequality: Urbanization, Industrial Development, and Immigrants in Detroit, 1880–1920*. Chicago: University of Chicago Press.

56

Massive Global Income Inequality: When Did It Arise and Why Does It Matter?*

GLENN FIREBAUGH

At the time of the first Industrial Revolution, Thomas Malthus (1960 [1798]) and other classical economists feared that humans might be doomed to near-subsistence levels of living. A century earlier Thomas Hobbes had warned that a powerful sovereign was needed lest life be "solitary, poor, nasty, brutish, and short" (Hobbes 1962 [1651], p. 100). Malthus was even more pessimistic, warning that poverty is the likely human lot with or without a powerful ruler. Malthus's fear was based on a population-trap model positing that economic growth is unlikely to outpace population growth over the long run. In this model, economic gains are short-lived, because the geometric growth of population inevitably catches up with linear economic gains. Unless there are other checks on population growth, income per person will inevitably return to a low equilibrium level. A new round of economic expansion will upset that equilibrium in the short run, but in the long run income per capita will track back down to its preexpansion level. In other words, economic growth will serve to increase the size of the human population, but it will not boost living standards over the long run.

---

* First published in 2003; from *The New Geography of Global Income*.

THE GROWING WORLD INCOME PIE

The pace of population growth and economic growth over the last two centuries has proved Malthus right about the expansion of the human population but wrong about the population trap. In line with Malthus, the productivity gains of the Industrial Revolution were accompanied by an era of unprecedented population growth. In 1820 the world's population was about 1.1 billion (Maddison 1995, table 1.1a). Today the world's population has surpassed 6 billion. But contrary to Malthus's warning that rapid population growth will undermine economic growth, the quintupling of the world's population has not resulted in stagnant incomes and living standards. The economic historian Richard Easterlin recently wrote that "a revolution in the human condition is sweeping the world. Most people today are better fed, clothed, and housed than their predecessors two centuries ago. . . . Although the picture is not one of universal progress, it is the greatest advance in the condition of the world's population ever achieved in such a brief span of time" (Easterlin 2000, p. 7). In the face of unprecedented growth in world population, world income has grown even faster. In fact economic growth over the past two centuries has so greatly outpaced population growth that, according to the standard source for such historical comparisons, income per capita for the world as a whole has, in constant dollars, increased roughly eightfold since 1820 (Maddison 1995, table 1.1a).

So over the past two centuries a world population explosion has been outdone by a world income explosion. The world income pie has expanded not only in an absolute sense, but also in a per capita sense, as most people today enjoy a much higher standard of living than their ancestors had in the preindustrial world. Although scholars have tended to pay more attention to the population explosion than to the income explosion, the growth in per capita income is the defining feature of our historical epoch. Moreover, the remarkable growth in world per capita income has shown no signs of leveling off in recent decades. As Robert Lucas (2000, p. 159) notes, "The real income of an average person has more than doubled since World War II and the end of the European colonial age." Before that time, during the first half of the twentieth century and during the nineteenth century, there is strong evidence (despite the fact that income estimates before 1950 tend to be less reliable than those after 1950) that world income growth was not doubling as rapidly (see Maddison 1995, table G-3).

The best estimates of world and regional incomes over the last two centuries are from the economic historian Angus Maddison. Maddison's (1995) monumental income series begins with 1820, and Figure 1 depicts Maddison's estimates of per capita income for the whole world for 1820, 1950, and 1990. The figures are in 1990 U.S. dollars, so the observed growth is not due to inflation. Although the estimates for the nineteenth century in particular are based on gross approximations for many nations, the general pattern of sustained growth is unmistakable. As these figures indicate, recent growth has been especially remarkable. In terms of absolute change, average income in the world increased twice as much over the 40-year period 1950–1990 as it did over the previous 130 years

FIGURE 1 **WORLD AVERAGE INCOME IN 1990 U.S. DOLLARS: 1820, 1950, AND 1990**

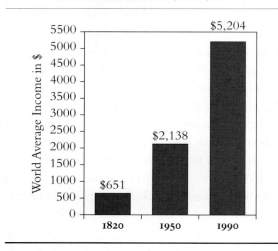

SOURCE: Based on Maddison (1995).

combined (an increase of $3,066 from 1950 to 1990 versus an increase of $1,487 from 1820 to 1950). The 1950–1990 interval also exhibits a faster growth rate, as average income increased by a factor of 2.4 over the 40 years from 1950 to 1990 after increasing by a factor of 3.3 over the much longer period of 1820 to 1950.

OTHER WELFARE CHANGES

In addition to rising incomes over the past two centuries, there are two other significant changes that bear on the issue of changing human welfare. The first is that we tend to live longer now than before. Life expectancy today is estimated to be sixty-six years at birth for the world as a whole (World Almanac 2001), which is likely almost double what it was at the beginning of the twentieth century.[1] This dramatic increase in life expectancy is one of the singular features of the past hundred years. Not only do people live better than before, they also live much longer—a fact not captured by statistics on income growth per se. No doubt most people agree with C. P. Snow's (1963, p. 78) statement that "it seems to me better that people should live rather than die . . . [and] that they shouldn't have to watch their children die." Although it is difficult to place a dollar value on longer life, most would agree that length of life is part of human welfare. Because [my] analysis focuses on change in per capita income without also factoring in rising life expectancy, one could argue that I in fact understate the rise in human welfare since the early nineteenth century. Moreover, the change in average income fails to capture the increased welfare that results from the new choices that we have in the twenty-first century that were not available earlier. Our ancestors in the early nineteenth century knew nothing of automobiles, computers, telephones, air travel, and other inventions of the past two centuries. So if human welfare is largely about options and freedom—as Amartya Sen (1999) has argued—then on that basis the estimated rates of income growth given above most likely understate the rise in material welfare over the last century, since they fail to factor in the new choices available to many today.

---

[1] For most nations of the world we lack good estimates on life expectancy for the first half of the twentieth century. Life expectancy for female babies was 43.7 years in Japan in 1899, 43.7 in Italy and 49.4 in England and Wales in 1901, and 32.5 in Chile in 1909, with males having a life expectancy about 3–4 years less (Preston, Keyfitz, and Schoen 1972). Of these nations, probably life expectancy in Chile was the nearest to that for the world as a whole at the turn of the century. If so, then life expectancy virtually doubled in the twentieth century.

THE RISE IN INCOME DISPARITIES OVER THE NINETEENTH AND TWENTIETH CENTURIES

There are two big stories about world income trends over the past two centuries. The first story is the remarkable growth in the world's average income, just described. The second story is that the growth has disproportionately benefited different regions of the world, with richer regions generally benefiting much more than poorer regions. As a result global income

inequality has worsened dramatically since the early nineteenth century. (In this [essay] the terms "global income inequality" and "world income inequality" are used as synonyms to refer to the total level of income inequality across all the world's people.) A central message of [mine] is that the enormous growth in global inequality occurred during the period of Western industrialization, that is, during the nineteenth century and the first half of the twentieth century. Today, during the period of Asian industrialization, global inequality is no longer growing. (A note on terminology: "Period of

FIGURE 2A **AVERAGE INCOMES IN MAJOR REGIONS OF THE WORLD, 1820 (IN 1990 U.S. DOLLARS)**

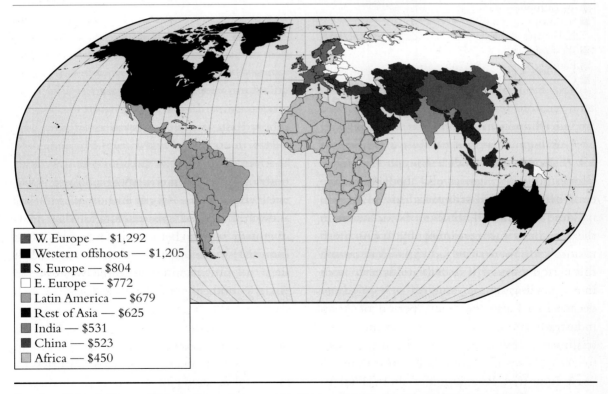

- W. Europe — $1,292
- Western offshoots — $1,205
- S. Europe — $804
- E. Europe — $772
- Latin America — $679
- Rest of Asia — $625
- India — $531
- China — $523
- Africa — $450

Based on Table 1. "Rest of Asia" refers to Asia outside China and India; "E. Europe" includes Russia.

FIGURE 2B **AVERAGE INCOMES IN MAJOR REGIONS OF THE WORLD, 1990 (IN 1990 U.S. DOLLARS)**

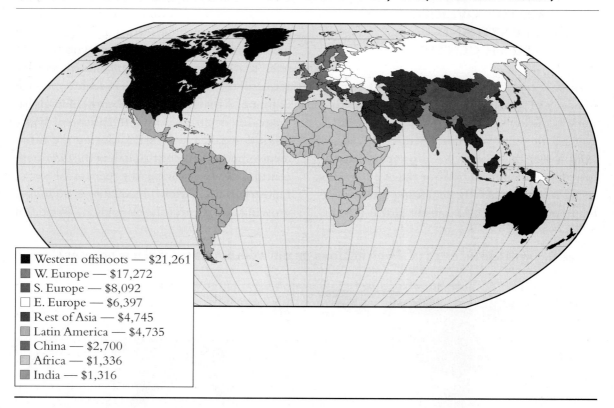

- ■ Western offshoots — $21,261
- ■ W. Europe — $17,272
- ■ S. Europe — $8,092
- ☐ E. Europe — $6,397
- ■ Rest of Asia — $4,745
- ■ Latin America — $4,735
- ■ China — $2,700
- ■ Africa — $1,336
- ■ India — $1,316

Based on Table 1. "Rest of Asia" refers to Asia outside China and India; "E. Europe" includes the Soviet Union.

Western industrialization" is shorthand for the era when industrialization was led by Western nations. Not all industrialization occurred in the West during this era, of course, but Western nations took the lead in industrializing during this period. Similarly, Asian nations have been industrializing the most aggressively in recent decades, so I use the term "period of Asian industrialization," even though recent industrialization obviously has not been restricted to Asia. Historians sometimes distinguish a "first Industrial Revolution"—about 1760 to 1830, centered in England—from a "second Industrial Revolution"—about 1860 to 1900, occurring simultaneously in the United States and Europe—but in the case of global inequality, the distinction between the first and second Industrial Revolutions is much less significant than the distinction between the Western and Asian periods of industrialization, as we shall see.)

[I focus] on the second story, the unevenness of the income growth. The remarkable rise in average income over the past two centuries has produced massive global income inequality, as income growth in the world's richer regions and

TABLE 1 WORLD "TRIFURCATION" SINCE 1820: AVERAGE INCOME IN MAJOR REGIONS OF THE WORLD IN 1820, 1950, AND 1990

Region	Income per capita			Income growth	
	1820	1950	1990	1950/1820	1990/1950
HIGH-INCOME GROUP					
Western Europe (23 nations)	$1,292	$5,126	$17,272	4.0	3.4
Western offshoots (4 nations)	1,205	9,255	21,261	7.7	2.3
MIDDLE-INCOME GROUP					
Southern Europe (7 nations)	804	2,021	8,092	2.5	4.0
Eastern Europe (9 nations)	772	2,631	6,397	3.4	2.4
Latin America (44 nations)	679	2,487	4,735	3.7	1.9
LOW-INCOME GROUP					
Asia (56 nations)					
China	523	614	2,700	1.2	4.4
India	531	597	1,316	1.1	2.2
Rest of Asia	625	1,081	4,745	1.7	4.4
Africa (56 nations)	450	830	1,336	1.8	1.6
World totals	651	2,138	5,204	3.3	2.4

SOURCE: Calculated from Maddison (1995), tables G-1 and G-3 for regional data; tables A-3e and D-1e for data for China and India.

NOTE: Regional incomes are population-weighted averages, in 1990 U.S. dollars. The ratios 1950/1820 and 1990/1950 are calculated from the income data. "Western offshoots" refers to Australia, Canada, New Zealand, and the United States. "Asia" includes Oceania.

nations has outpaced growth in poorer regions and nations. The practical implication for individuals is that in today's world, one's income is determined largely by one's residence. Figure 2 shows the magnitude of the regional disparity in incomes by disaggregating the world averages for 1820 and 1990 and mapping the regional averages with China and India separated out from the rest of Asia. These maps, based on the data in Table 1, reveal at a glance not only the striking growth in world per capita income over the past two centuries but also the striking uneven-

ness of that growth across space. Incomes have surged ahead in Europe and lagged behind in Africa and (until recently) in Asia. So the eight-fold increase in average world income since 1820 is easy to misinterpret, because it masks huge differences in income growth across the world's major regions.

An important part of the global inequality story is that the world has divided into three income camps. As Table 1 shows, although the three camps were discernible in 1820, the divisions are much sharper today. It is important to note, however, that the divisions are no longer becoming more and more distinct, because the era of global "trifurcation" in income occurred during the period of Western industrialization and now appears to be behind us. Compare the two columns under Income Growth in Table 1. If we rank regions on the basis of their estimated income levels in 1820, we find that over the course of the nineteenth century and first half of the twentieth century the initially richer regions got richer much faster than the poorer regions did (first column under Income Growth). From 1820 to 1950—the period of Western industrialization—per capita income increased by a multiple of 4.0–7.7 for the initially higher-income regions, by a multiple of 2.5–3.7 for the middle-income regions, and by a multiple if 1.8 or less for the lower-income regions. Since 1950—the period of Asian industrialization—income growth rates no longer line up with initial incomes. Some regions in the low-income group have been growing faster than some regions in the high-income group. These results point to the possibility that the era of big-time growth in global income inequality may be ending.

In the meantime the legacy of the big-time growth in inequality remains. To appreciate the unevenness of the income growth across regions during the period of Western industrialization, compare income growth in the Western off-shoots (Australia, Canada, New Zealand, and the United States) to income growth in Africa from 1820 to 1950. Average income is estimated to have been about $1,200 in the Western offshoots in 1820 compared with about $450 in Africa in

1820—a ratio of less than 3 to 1 at the early stages of Western industrialization.[2] By 1950 the ratio had ballooned to about 11 to 1 ($9,255 versus $830). Unless income estimates are wildly off the mark, regional differences in average incomes are profound.

In sum, the world income pie has expanded greatly over the past two centuries, but not everyone's piece has expanded at the same rate. Because incomes tended to grow more rapidly in the richer regions in the nineteenth and early twentieth centuries, income inequality has increased across the world's major regions.

★ ★ ★

THE REVERSAL OF HISTORICAL INEQUALITY TRENDS

★ ★ ★ The new geography of inequality—not to be confused with the "new economic geography" that arose in economics in the 1990s (Fujita, Krugman, and Venables 1999)—refers to the new pattern of global income inequality caused by the recent phenomenon of declining inequality across nations accompanied by (in many places) rising inequality within nations. This phenomenon, which began in the last third of the twentieth century and continues today, results in a "new geography" because it represents the reversal of trends that trace back to the early stages of Western industrialization. Put in the perspective of an individual, the new geography of global income inequality means that national location—while still paramount—is

---

2 The use of 1820 as the beginning point is dictated by data availability, since Maddison's income series begins with 1820.

declining in significance in the determination of one's income.

Despite a recent surge of interest in global inequality, researchers have largely overlooked its changing contour. Studies of global income inequality over the last decades of the twentieth century have been preoccupied with the problem of global divergence, that is, the presumed problem of worsening income inequality for the world as a whole. This preoccupation with global divergence is misguided, first, because global income inequality almost certainly declined over this period and, second, because the focus on the level of global income inequality has diverted attention from the changing nature of global income inequality in recent decades. Global income inequality is no worse today than it was in the 1960s and 1970s, but global income inequality is nevertheless changing—it is gradually shifting from inequality across nations to inequality within nations. The rising importance of within-nation inequality and declining importance of between-nation inequality represents a historic change, since it involves the reversal of a trend that began with the uneven industrialization of the world that started more than two centuries ago.

This chapter contrasts the New Geography Hypothesis with the popular view that globalization—by which I mean the increased interconnectedness of localities, particularly the deepening of economic links between countries—has led to growing global income inequality:

Globalization → global inequality.

For short, I call this popular view the Trade Protest Model, because the protests against the World Trade Organization in Seattle and elsewhere were driven at least in part by the assumption that global trade is exacerbating global inequality. To place the New Geography Hypothesis in context, it is useful first to examine five myths that underlie the globalization → global inequality model.

MYTHS OF THE TRADE PROTEST MODEL

Under the heading "Siege in Seattle," the December 13, 1999, issue of the U.S. magazine *Newsweek* gave this account of the protests surrounding the meeting of the World Trade Organization in Seattle, Washington:

> Until last week, not so many Americans had even heard of the WTO. Fewer still could have identified it as the small, Geneva-based bureaucracy that the United States and 134 other nations set up five years ago to referee global commerce. To Bill Clinton, it is a mechanism that can allow America to do well and good at the same time. But to many of the 40,000 activists and union members who streamed into Seattle—a clean, scenic city that has grown rich on foreign trade—the WTO is something else again: a secretive tool of ruthless multinational corporations. They charge it with helping sneaker companies to exploit Asian workers, timber companies to clear-cut rain forests, shrimpers to kill sea turtles and a world of other offenses.

Media accounts grappled with the sheer diversity of the protesters, from leaders of U.S. labor to members of environmental groups to a leading

Chinese dissident. The common thread seemed to be, as the *New York Times* (1999) put it, the view that the WTO is a "handmaiden of corporate interests whose rulings undermine health, labor and environmental protections around the world." According to *The Economist* (1999), "The WTO has become a magnet for resistance to globalisation by both old-fashioned protectionists and newer critics of free trade."

Some of the protest groups emphasized rising inequality as among the most noxious consequences of increasing trade globalization. For example, Ralph Nader's Public Citizen group portrays the WTO as a tool of big business "which is harming the environment and increasing inequality" (*The Economist* 1999), and representatives of 1,448 nongovernmental organizations protesting the WTO signed a statement claiming that "globalisation has three serious consequences: the concentration of wealth in the hands of the multinationals and the rich; poverty for the majority of the world's population; and unsustainable patterns of production and consumption that destroy the environment" (*New Scientist* 1999). Note that two of the three consequences—concentration of wealth and impoverishment of the majority—tie globalization directly to growth in inequality.

Global income inequality is the result of the interplay of multiple causes, of course, so serious analyses are unlikely to give an unqualified endorsement to the notion that globalization has automatically resulted in an explosion in global income inequality. Global inequality existed before the recent growth in world trade, and it would persist if nations suddenly stopped trading. Nonetheless, popular literature on globalization has tended to fuel the belief in a globalization-led explosion in global income inequality by making claims that purport to be grounded in the findings of serious scholarly analyses. Upon closer inspection, however, many of the claims fly in the face of available empirical evidence. This section examines the key myths that underlie the globalization → global inequality model.

Myth 1. The Myth of Exploding Global Income Inequality

A steady drumbeat of reports and articles claims that the world's income is becoming more and more unequally distributed. Here is a sample:

- "Globalization has dramatically increased inequality between and within nations" (Jay Mazur, 2000, in *Foreign Affairs*).
- "The very nature of globalization has an inherent bias toward inequality. . . . One would have to be blind not to see that globalization also exacerbates the disparity between a small class of winners and the rest of us" (Paul Martin, Canada's prime minister, June 1998, quoted in Eggertson 1998).
- "Along with ecological risk, to which it is related, expanding inequality is the most serious problem facing world society" (Anthony Giddens, 1999).
- "Thus, overall, the ascent of informational, global capitalism is indeed characterized by simultaneous economic development and underdevelopment, social inclusion and social exclusion. . . . There is polarization in the distribution of wealth at the global level, differential evolution of intra-country income inequality, and substantial growth of poverty and misery in the world at large" (Manuel Castells, 1998, p. 82, emphasis omitted).

What we will find subsequently is that global income inequality has not exploded but in fact leveled off and then declined in the last part of the twentieth century. Although income inequality rose somewhat in the average nation, income inequality declined across nations. Since between-nation inequality is the larger component of global income inequality, the decline in between-nation income inequality more than offset the rise in within-nation income inequality. As a result, global income inequality declined in the last years of the twentieth century. Sherlock Holmes was right: it *is* a capital mistake to theorize in advance of the facts (Doyle 1955, p. 507). With respect to global income inequality, much mischief has been done by theorizing about global income inequality on the basis of the views expressed above. Theorizing based on the widespread view of exploding global income inequality is theorizing based on facts that aren't.

Myth 2. The Myth of Growing Income Inequality Across Nations, as Rich Nations Surge Ahead and Poor Nations Fall Further Behind

The first myth—exploding global inequality—is based on a second myth, the myth that inequality is growing across nations. The second myth is as widespread as the first, and it has been fueled by widely circulated reports of international agencies:

- "Figures indicate that income inequality between countries has increased sharply over the past 40 years" (World Bank 2000, *World Development Report 2000/2001*, p. 51).
- "The average income in the richest 20 countries is 37 times the average in the poorest

20—a gap that has doubled in the past 40 years" (International Monetary Fund 2000, p. 50).
- "Gaps in income between the poorest and richest people and countries have continued to widen. In 1960 the 20% of the world's people in the richest countries had 30 times the income of the poorest 20%—in 1997, 74 times as much ... Gaps are widening both between and within countries" (United Nations Development Program 1999, *Human Development Report 1999*, p. 36).
- "It is an empirical fact that the income gap between poor and rich countries has increased in recent decades" (Ben-David, Nordström, and Winters 1999, World Trade Organization special study, p. 3).
- "In 1960, the Northern countries were 20 times richer than the Southern, in 1980 46 times... .[I]n this kind of race, the rich countries will always move faster than the rest" (Sachs 1992, *The Development Dictionary*, p. 3).

The myth of growing income inequality across nations is based in large part on a misinterpretation of the widely cited finding (for example, World Bank 2000b, p. 50) that income growth has tended to be slower in poor nations than in rich nations. This positive cross-country association between income level and income growth rate conceals the critical fact that the poor nations that are falling badly behind contain no more than 10 percent of the world's population, whereas the poor nations that are catching up (largely in Asia) contain over 40 percent of the world's population. When nations are weighted by population size—as they must be if we want to use between-nation inequality to draw conclusions about global income inequality—we find that income inequality across nations peaked sometime around 1970 and has been declining since. This peaking of between-nation income inequality circa 1970 is particularly interesting in light of Manuel Castells's (1998, p. 336) well-known claim that a "new world" originated in the late 1960s to mid-1970s. Ironically, though, Castells characterizes the world born in this period as a world of sharply increasing global inequality, and many other globalization writers make the same error.

★ ★ ★

Myth 3. The Myth That Globalization Historically Has Caused Rising Inequality Across Nations

Contrary to this myth, the trend in between-nation inequality historically has not followed changes in the trend in world economic integration. First, although it is true that between-nation income inequality increased dramatically over the nineteenth and early twentieth centuries, Peter Lindert and Jeffrey Williamson (2000) argue that the period of rising inequality across nations began *before* the period of true globalization started, so globalization apparently did not cause the upturn. Second, the sharp decline in globalization between World War I and World War II did not result in declining inequality across nations (to the contrary, between-nation income inequality shot up rapidly over the period). Finally, ★ ★ ★ income inequality across nations has declined in recent decades, during a period when globalization has presumably reached new heights. (I say "presumably" because globalization is itself a contentious issue: see Guillén 2001. Nonethe-

less virtually all agree that the world has become more economically integrated over recent decades, even if the degree of globalization is often overstated, as Chase-Dunn, Kawano, and Brewer 2000, among others, have noted.) In short, the rise in global inequality predates the rise in globalization, global inequality has risen while globalization was declining, and currently global inequality is declining while globalization is rising. It is hard then to make the case historically that globalization is the cause of rising income inequality across nations (O'Rourke 2001).

Myth 4. The Myth of a Postindustrial World Economy

In reading the globalization literature it is easy to lose sight of the fact that, until recently, most of the world's people were engaged in agriculture. So the world's workforce is barely postagricultural, much less postindustrial. [I make] the point that the primary engine still driving the growth in world production is more manufacturing. A new information age might be on the way, but it is not here yet—at least it is not here for most of the world's people. It is important to look ahead, of course, and it is hard to argue against the view that the world will eventually be postindustrial. The death of industrialization is nonetheless much exaggerated, as is the view that we are rapidly approaching an information-based global economy (Quah 1997). Estimates of the composition of global output, albeit rough approximations, rule out the claims of some globalization writers that we live in a new economic era quite unlike the era of the last generation. Industrialization was important in the nineteenth century, it was important in the twentieth century, and it remains important in most regions of the world in the twenty-first century. A preoccupation with postindustrialization in the face of the continuing diffusion of industrialization results in an incomplete and distorted story of global income inequality that deemphasizes the critical role of the continuing spread of industrialization to all regions of the world. Computers are important, but they are not all-important. In accounting for recent trends in global income inequality, the bigger story is industrial growth in Asia, not technological growth in the West.

Myth 5. The Myth of International Exchange as Inherently Exploitative

Globalization involves increased exchange over national boundaries. One might posit that increased exchange worsens global inequality under some historical conditions and reduces it under other conditions. Until those historical conditions are identified and understood, the effect of globalization on global income inequality at any point in time is an open question to be settled empirically.

But if international exchange is inherently exploitative, as some theories of world stratification insist, then rising exchange implies rising exploitation, and the Trade Protest Model is true virtually by definition. The Trade Protest Model then becomes:

> Globalization → more exploitation of poor nations by rich nations → greater global inequality.

Note that this elaboration of the Trade Protest Model reveals how high the theoretical stakes are with regard to empirical tests of the global-

ization → global income inequality model, since the failure of globalization to lead to rising global income inequality would undermine exploitation theories (for example, dependency theories) as well as undermining the Trade Protest Model.

[However,] increasing international exchange over recent decades has been accompanied by declining—not rising—income inequality across nations. Other studies also document declining between-nation income inequality over recent decades. The decline in between-nation inequality has significant theoretical implications. The assumption of inherent exploitation favoring rich nations in international exchange is the linchpin of some theoretical schools. But if international exchange were inherently exploitative, we would not expect to observe declining inequality across nations during a period of rising international trade. Yet the assumption persists, suggesting that in some theories the notion of inherent exploitation is so essential that it enjoys creedal status as a doctrine to be believed rather than as a hypothesis to be tested.

CAUSES OF THE REVERSAL: AN OVERVIEW

I argue that the world's spreading industrialization and growing economic integration in the late twentieth century and the early twenty-first have reversed the historical pattern of uneven economic growth favoring richer nations. The conventional view, just elaborated, is that globalization has exacerbated global income inequality. The evidence presented here challenges that view. In reality globalization has offsetting effects—by spurring industrialization in poor nations, globalization raises inequality within many nations and compresses inequality across nations. The net effect has been a reduction in global income inequality in recent decades, since the reduction in between-nation income inequality has more than offset the growth in within-nation income inequality.

The new pattern of rising within-nation and falling between-nation income inequality has multiple causes. The most important cause is spreading industrialization—the diffusion of industrialization to the world's large poor nations. The diffusion of industrialization to poor regions compresses inequality across nations and boosts inequality within them. The effect of spreading industrialization on between-nation inequality is reinforced by the effect of the growing integration of national economies. Growing economic integration tends to dissolve institutional differences between nations. The convergence of institutional economic goals and policies compresses inequality across nations by (in some instances at least) removing impediments to growth in poor nations.

There are at least four other significant causes of the new geography of global inequality. The first is technological change that reduces the tyranny of space in general and more particularly reduces the effect of labor immobility across national boundaries. This technological change works to reduce inequality across nations. The second is a demographic windfall that has benefited some poor Asian nations in recent decades and promises to benefit other poor nations in the near future. This effect also operates to compress global income inequality, by reducing between-nation inequality. The third is the rise of the ser-

vice sector, especially in richer nations. Growth in this sector has boosted income inequality within nations, and it is likely to do so in the future as well. The fourth is the collapse of communism, which also boosted within-nation inequality. This is a nonrecurring event, however, so its effect on within-nation inequality is limited to a specific point in history, the 1990s.

In short, the decline in between-nation income inequality that began in the late twentieth century was caused by deepening industrialization of poor nations, by growing economic integration that dissolves institutional differences between nations, by technological change that reduces the effects of labor immobility across national boundaries, and by a demographic windfall that has benefited some poor nations and promises to benefit others in the future. The growth in within-nation income inequality was caused by the deepening industrialization of poor nations, by the growth of the service sector, and by the collapse of communism. ★ ★ ★

‖ THE INEQUALITY TRANSITION

The industrialization of richer nations in the nineteenth century and first half of the twentieth caused income inequality across nations to explode. As a result, global income inequality shifted from inequality within nations to inequality across nations. Now, however, poorer nations are industrializing faster than richer ones are, and between-nation inequality is declining while within-nation inequality appears to be rising. If this turnaround continues, future historians will refer to an inequality transition that accompanied world industrialization. That transition is from within-nation inequality to between-nation inequality back to within-nation inequality, with the late twentieth century as the period when the shift back to within-nation income inequality began.

Phase 1 of the Transition: From Within- to Between-Nation Inequality

Phase 1 of the inequality transition coincides with the period of Western industrialization that began in the late eighteenth century and ended in the second half of the twentieth century. The first phase of the inequality transition was characterized by unprecedented growth in income inequality across nations. As Lant Pritchett (1996, p. 40) puts it, "the overwhelming feature of modern economic history is a massive divergence in per capita incomes between rich and poor countries." The evidence is incontrovertible. First, it is clear that current levels of between-nation income inequality would not have been possible earlier in human history. Again quoting Pritchett (1997, pp. 9–10): "If there had been no divergence, then we could extrapolate backward from present income of the poorer countries to past income assuming they grew at least as fast as the United States. However, this would imply that many poor countries must have had incomes below $100 in 1870 [in 1985 U.S. dollars]. Since this cannot be true, there must have been divergence."

Second, Pritchett's conclusion that "there must have been divergence" is supported by estimates of between-nation income inequality in the nineteenth century. Consider the recent estimates of Bourguignon and Morrisson (1999). Bourguignon and Morrisson use the Maddison (1995) data to estimate changes in the level of between-nation income inequality from 1820 to 1992. Because their objective is to estimate total world income inequality—not just between-nation income inequality—Bourguignon and Morrisson begin by disaggregating national income data into vintiles (5 percent groups, that is, twenty income groups per nation). National boundaries have changed over the past two centuries, of course, and nations have come and gone over the past two centuries. Even in nations where boundaries remained constant, we do not always have income data for the entire period. To overcome these problems, Bourguignon and Morrisson grouped the 199 nations with income data in 1992 into 33 homogeneous groups, each of which represented at least 1 percent of the world population or world GDP in 1950. The 33 groups include single nations (such as China and the United States) as well as large groups of small nations and small groups of medium-sized nations. From these 660 data points (33 nation groups × 20) it is a straightforward matter to apply the population-weighted formulas for the Theil index and the mean logarithmic deviation (MLD)—two measures of inequality—to calculate summary measures of the world's total inequality for different years. By collapsing the 199 nations into 33 groups, Bourguignon and Morrisson are able to extend their inequality series back to 1820. Note that, to the extent that their grouping strategy introduces bias, the bias is in the direction of underestimating between-nation inequality and inflating within-nation inequality, since some of the inequality within the nation groups is actually between-nation inequality. But that bias should not affect our basic conclusions about the relative growth in between-nation and within-nation income inequality over the past two centuries.[3]

The results are striking (Figure 3). Two facts stand out. First, the *B/W* ratio—the ratio of between-nation to within-nation income inequality—is much higher now than it was in the early stages of Western industrialization. The increase in the *B/W* ratio reflects both a rise in between-nation income inequality and a decline in within-nation income inequality since 1820 (Table 2). By far the greater change is in between-nation income inequality, however. The Theil index for between-nation income inequality (actually, inequality between nation *groups*) shot up from 0.061 in 1820 to 0.513 in 1992, and the MLD shot up from 0.053 in 1820 to 0.495 in 1992. As anticipated, then, the Industrial Revolution of the past two centuries has increased income inequality across nations, but the magnitude of the increase is stunning. There has been a metamorphosis from a world where poverty was the norm in all nations to a richer world with much lower poverty rates (Bourguignon and Morrisson 1999, table 1) but also with much greater income inequality across nations. Because the steep rise in between-nation income inequality was not accompanied by an increase in inequality within nations, where you live—your nation—is much more important in determining your income in today's world than it was in the preindustrial world.

The second fact that stands out is that the growth in the *B/W* ratio stalled in the second

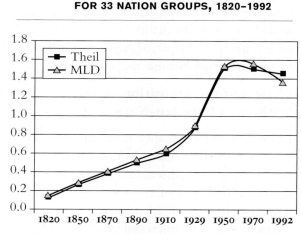

FIGURE 3 **RATIO OF BETWEEN-NATION TO WITHIN-NATION INCOME INEQUALITY FOR 33 NATION GROUPS, 1820–1992**

Based on Table 1. Theil and MLD are measures of inequality.

half of the twentieth century. The *B/W* ratio stopped growing in the second half of the twentieth century because growth in inequality across the nation groups has slowed dramatically since 1950. In the four decades after 1950, income inequality across the nation groups increased by 6 percent using the Theil index and by 5 percent using the MLD. Over the four decades prior to 1950, the Theil had grown about 60 percent and the MLD had grown about 75 percent. Apparently the most dramatic effects of Western industrialization on between-nation inequality are over. After more than a century of sharp divergence in national incomes, the trend has been much more stable

---

3 In estimating global inequality, the key is the reliability of the data for larger nations, since global income inequality is driven largely by patterns in those nations.

TABLE 2   **TRENDS IN INCOME INEQUALITY BETWEEN AND WITHIN 33 HOMOGENEOUS NATION GROUPS, 1820–1992**

Year	Between nation groups		Within nation groups	
	Theil	MLD	Theil	MLD
1820	.061	.053	.472	.388
1850	.128	.111	.477	.393
1870	.188	.162	.485	.399
1890	.251	.217	.498	.408
1910	.299	.269	.500	.413
1929	.365	.335	.413	.372
1950	.482	.472	.323	.309
1970	.490	.515	.324	.330
1992	.513	.495	.351	.362

SOURCE: Bourguignon and Morrisson (1999), table 3.

ESTIMATES: Between nation groups: From Bourguignon and Morrisson (1999), based on Maddison (1995) data set. Within nation groups: From Bourguignon and Morrisson (1999), based on updating of Berry, Bourguignon, and Morrisson (1983a,b) for the post–World War II period and on various sources (for example, Lindert 1999; Morrison 1999) for the pre–World War II period.

NOTE: Income measures are adjusted for purchasing power parity, and inequality measures are based on income vintiles (see Bourguignon and Morrisson 1999 for elaboration).

in recent years. This finding is in line with the findings of others (for example, Schultz 1998; Firebaugh 1999; Melchior, Telle, and Wiig 2000; Goesling 2001) who, drawing on data for individual nations instead of nation groups, find that between-nation income inequality is no longer rising. As we shall see later, between-nation income inequality declined in the late twentieth century when income data for the 1990s are added to data for the 1970s and 1980s.

Finally, it should be emphasized that the results here are so strong that the historical story they tell of increasing inequality across nations and of a rising *B/W* ratio cannot be dismissed as due to error in the data. To be sure, income estimates for the nineteenth century are gross approximations for many nations. But even if we make the extreme assumption that incomes are so drastically overstated for poorer nations in 1820 (or so drastically understated for richer nations in 1820) that the Theil and the MLD estimates understate between-nation income inequality in 1820 by a factor of three, that would still mean that between-nation income inequality tripled from 1820 to 1992 (from 0.18 to 0.51 based on the Theil index and from 0.16 to 0.50 for the MLD), and the *B/W* ratio still would have more than tripled for both inequality measures.

Phase 2 of the Transition: From Between-nation Back to Within-nation Inequality

The second phase of the inequality transition began in the second half of the twentieth century, with the stabilization of between-nation income inequality in the 1960–1990 period and the decline in between-nation inequality beginning in earnest in the 1990s. Social scientists hardly have a stellar track record for predictions, especially with regard to sweeping predictions such as the one made here. Nonetheless there is sufficient theory and evidence that we can plausibly forecast that the *B/W* ratio will continue to decline in the twenty-first century.

The prediction of a declining *B/W* ratio is based on two separate conjectures. The first conjecture is that between-nation income inequality will decline, and the second conjecture is that within-nation income inequality will rise, or at least will not decline. These conjectures are based on the causes of the current trends, which I expect to continue and in some cases to intensify. (I am assuming that there will be no cataclysmic upheaval in the twenty-first century, such as a global war or a worldwide plague.) Recall the causes listed earlier for the inequality turnaround in the late twentieth century. I expect the major causes to continue, so between-nation income inequality will decline because of the continued industrialization of poor nations, because of the continued convergence of national economic policies and

institutions arising from growing economic integration of national economies, because of the declining significance of labor immobility across national borders, and because of a demographic windfall for many poor nations. Within-nation income inequality will rise—or at least not decline—because of the continued industrialization of poor nations and because of continued growth in the service sector. Because between-nation inequality is the larger component, global income inequality will decline.

The conjecture of declining global income inequality is out of step with much of the globalization literature. A recurring theme in that literature is that we have entered a new information-based economic era where productive activity is becoming less dependent on physical space, as a rising share of the world's economic output is produced in electronic space that knows no national borders. This phenomenon is possible because of the emergence of a global economy where income—and hence income inequality—is becoming increasingly rooted in knowledge rather than in capital goods. What do these developments imply for global income inequality? For many globalization writers, the answer is clear: global inequality is bound to worsen because of the growing "global digital divide" that enlarges the gap between the "haves" and the "have-nots."

Empirical evidence presented subsequently suggests otherwise, however, and the theoretical argument that a shift to a knowledge-based global economy would worsen global income inequality is shaky as well. It is not hard to think of reasons why the shift from an industrial-based to a knowledge-based global economy would reduce, not increase, inequality across nations. Knowledge is mobile, especially with today's telecommunication technologies that permit virtually instant worldwide codification and distribution of knowledge. In addition, because knowledge can be given away without being lost, the notion of property rights is more problematic in the case of knowledge, so it is harder to concentrate and monopolize knowledge across nations than it is to concentrate and monopolize capital goods across nations. Hence the switch to a knowledge-based global economy should mean that one's income is increasingly determined by how much knowledge one obtains and uses as opposed to where one lives. The tighter link between knowledge and income in turn implies declining income inequality across nations and rising inequality within nations since—absent institutional barriers—the variance in individuals' ability to obtain and benefit from knowledge is greater within nations than between them.

The issue of how the new information age will affect global inequality in the near term is not as decisive as often imagined, since as already noted, the coming of the information age is often much exaggerated. What is still most important in today's world is industrialization for the many, not digitization for the few. Historically the spread of industrialization has been the primary force driving the growth in between-nation income inequality. The initially richer nations of the West were the first to industrialize, and the poorer nations of Asia and Africa lagged behind. The new geography of inequality is also driven by the spread of industrialization, but the effects are different today: now the spread of industrialization means the diffusion of manufacturing technology to the world's largest poor regions. In recent decades inequality has declined across nations as industrialization has been an engine of growth in the most populous poor regions of the world, especially East Asia. That growth has worked both to compress inequality across nations (Figure 4) and to boost inequality within the industrializing nations.

The significance of this continuation of world industrialization has been lost in much of the literature on globalization, because of preoccupation with the idea that we are witnessing the emergence of a new knowledge-based

FIGURE 4 INDUSTRIALIZATION AND BETWEEN-NATION INCOME INEQUALITY: HISTORICALLY AND IN THE LATE TWENTIETH CENTURY

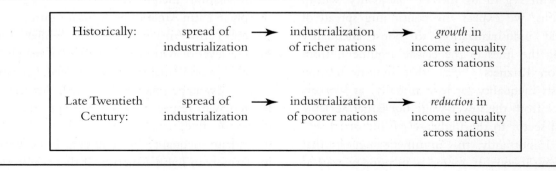

| Historically: | spread of industrialization | → | industrialization of richer nations | → | *growth* in income inequality across nations |
| Late Twentieth Century: | spread of industrialization | → | industrialization of poorer nations | → | *reduction* in income inequality across nations |

technology regime. To be sure, in the categories used to classify world production, the output of the so-called service sector is estimated to exceed the output of the industrial sector for the world as a whole (World Bank 1997, table 12). Yet much of the service sector—an amorphous sector that includes wholesale and retail trade, the banking industry, government, the transportation industry, the commercial real estate industry, and personal services (including health care and education)—has arisen to grease the wheels of industry. Aside from the growth in personal services and government, much of the growth in the service sector has been for services for producers, not consumers—for example, the rise of an engineering industry to design better machines, and the growth of a banking industry and a commercial real estate industry for commercial transactions. In addition, many of the other so-called service industries—the transportation industry that distributes manufactured goods, for example, and the specialized retailing industry that sells the goods—benefit producers as well as consumers. In short, a significant portion of the growth in service industries over the past century can be seen as ancillary to the industrialization process.

With regard to income inequality within nations, we expect the continuing spread of world industrialization to boost inequality along the lines of the classic argument, from Simon Kuznets (1955), that industrialization boosts inequality (at least initially) as workers move from the lower-wage but larger agricultural sector to the higher-wage industrial sector. Importantly, this argument suggests that income inequality increases in poor nations as they industrialize because of income gains, not income losses. In other words, inequality grows not because some people are becoming poorer but because some people are becoming richer, so the growth in income inequality in poor nations as they industrialize reflects rising rather than declining fortunes. If the industrialization of large poor nations does boost income inequality in those nations, at this juncture in history the continued spread of industrialization implies growth in income inequality in the average nation, because those nations are home to such a large fraction of the world's population. And there are no obvious counterforces on the horizon. Although the jump in income inequality following the collapse of communism in Eastern Europe and the former USSR is not likely to be repeated, there is no good reason to expect income inequality in those nations to fall in the near future. Nor is there any good reason to expect income inequality to decline notably in the West in the near future, either. We lack reliable inequality data for many African nations, but even if inequality were falling rapidly (which is unlikely), the effect of falling within-nation inequality in Africa would not offset the effect of rising within-nation inequality in Asia, given the relative sizes of the two regions. Few expect within-nation income inequality to decline sharply in Latin America in the near future, even though Latin America currently exhibits the highest level of within-nation income inequality of the world's major regions. Indeed, because of the advantage enjoyed by North American farmers with respect to some types of produce, economic integration in the Americas could exacerbate inequality by removing protections for farmers in Latin America. If that reasoning is correct, there is merit in the concern of WTO protesters that globalization may exacerbate income inequality within some poor nations by driving down incomes in the lower-income agricultural sector. But the bigger story is that industrialization (not the collapse of farm prices) will tend to drive up inequality within nations, at least initially. Because many nations are still on the part of the Kuznets (1955) curve where migration from farm to factory boosts inequality, we can anticipate further growth in within-nation income inequality in the early decades of the twenty-first century.

||| REFERENCES

Ben-David, Dan, Håkan Nordström, and L. Alan Winters. 1999. *Trade, Income Inequality, and Poverty.* WTO Special Study no. 5. Geneva: World Trade Organization.

Berry, Albert, François Bourguignon, and Christian Morrisson. 1983a. "Changes in the world distribution of income between 1950 and 1977." *Economic Journal* 93:331–350.

———. 1983b. "The level of world inequality: How much can one say?" *Review of Income and Wealth* 29:217–241.

Bourguignon, François, and Christian Morrisson. 1999. "The size distribution of income among world citizens: 1820–1990." Draft. June.

Castells, Manuel. 1998. *End of Millennium.* Malden, Mass.: Blackwell.

Chase-Dunn, Christopher, Yukio Kawano, and Benjamin D. Brewer. 2000. "Trade globalization since 1795: Waves of integration in the world-system." Special millennium issue, edited by Glenn Firebaugh, of the *American Sociological Review* 65:77–95.

Easterlin, Richard A. 1996. *Growth Triumphant: The Twenty-first Century in Historical Perspective.* Ann Arbor: University of Michigan.

———. 2000. "The Worldwide Standard of Living since 1800." *Journal of Economic Perspectives* 14:7–26.

The Economist. 1999. "The battle in Seattle." U.S. edition. November 27.

Eggertson, Laura. 1998. "Rich-poor gap next issue for Martin." *Toronto Star.* June 3, p. A6.

Firebaugh, Glenn. 1999. "Empirics of world income inequality." *American Journal of Sociology* 104:1597–1630.

Fujita, Masahisa, Paul Krugman, and Anthony J. Venables. 1999. *The Spatial Economy: Cities, Regions, and International Trade.* Cambridge: MIT Press.

Giddens, Anthony. 1999. "Globalization: An irresistible force." *The Daily Yomiuri,* June 7, p. 8.

Goesling, Brian. 2001. "Changing income inequalities within and between nations: New evidence." *American Sociological Review* 66:745–761.

Guillén, Mauro F. 2001. "Is globalization civilizing, destructive, or feeble? A critique of five key debates in the social science literature." *Annual Review of Sociology* 27:235–260.

Hobbes, Thomas. 1962 [1651]. *Leviathan: Or, the Matter, Forme, and Power of a Commonwealth, Ecclesiasticall and Civil.* New York: Simon and Schuster.

International Monetary Fund (IMF). 2000. "How we can help the poor." *Finance and Development* (December). (http://www.imf.org/external/pubs.)

Lindert, Peter, and Jeffrey G. Williamson. 2000. "Does globalization make the world more unequal?" Paper presented at the "Globalization in Historical Perspective" preconference, National Bureau of Economic Research, Cambride, Mass. November.

Lucas, Robert E., Jr. 2000. "Some macroeconomics for the twenty-first century." *Journal of Economic Perspectives* 14:159–168.

Maddison, Angus. 1995. *Monitoring the World Economy, 1820–1992.* Paris: OECD.

Malthus, Thomas R. 1960 [1798]. *On Population.* New York: Modern Library.

Mazur, Jay. 2000. "Labor's new internationalism." *Foreign Affairs* 79:79–93.

Melchior, Arne, Kjetil Telle, and Henrik Wiig. 2000. *Globalization and Inequality: World Income Distribution and Living Standards, 1960–1998.* Studies on Foreign Policy Issues. Oslo: Royal Norwegian Ministry of Foreign Affairs.

Morrisson, Christian. 1999. "Historical perspectives on income distribution: The case of Europe." In *Handbook of Income Distribution,* ed. A. B. Atkinson and F. Bourguignon. Amsterdam: Elsevier.

New Scientist. 1999. Editorial. December 4.

New York Times. 1999. "National guard is called to quell trade talk protests." December 1.

O'Rourke, Kevin H. 2001. "Globalization and inequality: Historical trends." National Bureau of Economic Research. Draft. April.

Pritchett, Lant. 1996. "Forget convergence: Divergence past, present, and future." *Finance and Development* (June):40–43.

Quah, Danny T. 1997. "Increasingly weightless economies." *Bank of England Quarterly Bulletin* (February):49–55.

Sachs, Wolfgang, ed. 1992. *The Development Dictionary: A Guide to Knowledge as Power.* London: Zed Books.

Schultz, T. Paul. 1998. "Inequality in the distribution of personal income in the world: How is it changing and why." *Journal of Population Economics* 11:307–344.

Sen, Amartya. 1999. *Development as Freedom.* New York: Knopf.

Snow, Charles Percy. 1963. *The Two Cultures: And a Second Look.* New York: Mentor.

World Almanac. 2001. *The World Almanac and Book of Facts.* Mahwah, N.J.: World Almanac Education Group.

World Bank. 1997. *World Development Report 1997: The State in a Changing World.* Oxford: Oxford University Press.

———. 2000. *World Development Report 2000/2001: Attacking Poverty.* New York: Oxford University Press.

PART SIX

CONSEQUENCES OF INEQUALITY

INTRODUCTION TO PART VI

In the final part of the book, we return to the question we posed at the beginning: why should we study inequality? Should we be concerned about *rising* inequality? The chapter included here by the Nobel-Prize-winning economist and *New York Times* columnist Paul Krugman notes that the American economy has grown quite significantly in the past thirty-five years, and, *average* incomes have grown handsomely. Yet this does not mean that all Americans have benefitted. A powerful example he points to is how the average income of patrons in a bar goes up the minute billionaire Bill Gates walks into the room, without anyone else in the bar being made better off. As the Gates example suggests, average incomes are inflated by higher incomes at the top, and most American households have seen very modest or no benefits from economic growth in the past thirty years. Krugman argues that the American stratification system has functioned in such a way as to place most of the new income and wealth from economic growth in the pockets of very rich individuals and households, some benefits to the upper-middle class, and few or no benefits to everyone else. The resulting lack of shared prosperity is thus one important cost of inequality.

Lawrence Jacobs and Theda Skocpol focus on another potential cost: the implications of rising inequality for democracy. By giving more affluent households and corporations greater resources to invest in politics, the potential for disproportionate influence grows. Jacobs and Skocpol headed an American Political Science Association task force to consider the issue. The resulting investigation raised questions about disproportionate influence over elections, policy-making processes, and government regulation. In all of these areas, there is a danger that democratic control can weaken in an age of rising inequality.

Robert Frank's short essay examines another telling concern about inequality: to the extent that people envy those who have more than they do, they never feel completely satisfied with the possessions they do own. Taking off from Thorstein Veblen's insights about invidious comparison and conspicuous consumption, Frank discusses the effects of what he calls "spending cascades," processes by which increases in consumption at the top of the income hierarchy spur greater consumption by everyone else as they try to maintain their relative standing. This cascade has stimulated demand for bigger vehicles, larger homes, and other luxury items but has done little to increase people's level of overall happiness. Moreover, these increases in spending on items of conspicuous consumption come at the expense of resources allocated to public goods and services. This reduction in "inconspicuous consumption" leads to a host of negative long-term consequences such as lower-quality healthcare, the deterioration of the nation's highways and bridges, more dangerous foods, and dirtier air (not to mention sharp cuts to Head Start, school lunch programs, and homeless shelters).

The last two chapters explore some of what we might call the "collateral consequences" of inequality. The elegant writings and ideas of Nobel Prize–winning economist Amartya Sen have perhaps done more than anyone else to highlight how poverty and inequality produce harmful and frequently overlooked side effects. In the selection reprinted here, Sen notes that inequality produces not just low incomes but also the capacities of individuals to reach their full potential. In other words, high levels of poverty deprive the poor of things like sufficient food or adequate healthcare to maximize their intellectual and physical growth potentials. Further, poverty kills. Mortality rates are much higher in poor countries and even higher within poor regions within poor countries. High rates of unemployment not only cause poverty but persistant unemployment deprives the unemployed of opportunities to develop skills and capacities that decent jobs afford. In many poor countries, a vast *informal* economy consisting of street sellers and illegal activities of all kinds may provide a means of subsistence. But it rarely affords its participants any security or opportunity to build wealth or assets, no matter how hard they work.

The final chapter by sociologist Christopher Jencks provides an authoritative yet cautionary note about how we think about the larger impact of inequality and the rising levels of inequality in the United States. Reviewing recent research—his own and that of others—Jencks finds evidence that some important outcomes, like educational aspirations and attainment and political influence, become more unequal when economic inequality grows. But the evidence is thinner in relation to other types of outcomes that are sometimes linked to inequality, such as crime rates and mortality. Looking at the big picture, Jencks notes that although there are some outcomes for which inequality makes things worse and others for which it has no effect, there are virtually no cases in which high or growing inequality is associated with positive outcomes. One of the important points Jencks makes is his caution against overreacting to recent trends in inequality. We must not assume that inequality is always and everywhere bad, but rather we have to establish when and under what circumstances it is harmful and then target precious resources to combat those consequences.

57

The Great Divergence*

PAUL KRUGMAN

Medieval theologians debated how many angels could fit on the head of a pin. Modern economists debate whether American median income has risen or fallen since the early 1970s. What's really telling is the fact that we're even having this debate. America is a far more productive and hence far richer country than it was a generation ago. The value of the output an average worker produces in an hour, even after you adjust for inflation, has risen almost 50 percent since 1973. Yet the growing concentration of income in the hands of a small minority has proceeded so rapidly that we're not sure whether the typical American has gained *anything* from rising productivity.

The great postwar boom, a boom whose benefits were shared by almost everyone in America, came to an end with the economic crisis of the 1970s—a crisis brought on by rising oil prices, out-of-control inflation, and sagging productivity. The crisis abated in the 1980s, but the sense of broadly shared economic gains never returned. It's true that there have been periods of optimism—Reagan's "Morning in America," as the economy recovered from the severe slump of the early eighties, the feverish get-rich-quick era of the late

---

* First published in 2007; from *The Conscience of a Liberal*.

nineties. Since the end of the postwar boom, however, economic progress has always felt tentative and temporary.

Yet *average* income—the total income of the nation, divided by the number of people—has gone up substantially since 1973, the last year of the great boom. We are, after all, a much more productive nation than we were when the boom ended, and hence a richer nation as well. Think of all the technological advances in our lives since 1973: personal computers and fax machines, cell phones and bar-code scanners. Other major productivity-enhancing technologies, like freight containers that can be lifted directly from ship decks onto trucks and trains, existed in 1973 but weren't yet in widespread use. All these changes have greatly increased the amount the average worker produces in a normal working day, and correspondingly raised U.S. average income substantially.

Average income, however, doesn't necessarily tell you how most people are doing. If Bill Gates walks into a bar, the average wealth of the bar's clientele soars, but the men already there when he walked in are no wealthier than before. That's why economists trying to describe the fortunes of the typical member of a group, not the few people doing extremely well or extremely badly, usually talk not about *average* income but about *median* income—the income of a person richer than half the population but poorer than the other half. The median income in the bar, unlike the average income, doesn't soar when Bill Gates walks in.

As it turns out, Bill Gates walking into a bar is a pretty good metaphor for what has actually happened in the United States over the past generation: Average income has risen substantially, but that's mainly because a few people have

gotten much, much richer. Median income, depending on which definition you use, has either risen modestly or actually declined.

About the complications: You might think that median income would be a straightforward thing to calculate: find the American richer than half the population but poorer than the other half, and calculate his or her income. In fact, however, there are two areas of dispute, not easily resolved: how to define the relevant population, and how to measure changes in the cost of living. Before we get to the complications, however, let me repeat the punch line: The fact that we're even arguing about whether the typical American has gotten ahead tells you most of what you need to know. In 1973 there wasn't a debate about whether typical Americans were better or worse off than they had been in the 1940s. Every measure showed that living standards had more or less doubled since the end of World War II. Nobody was nostalgic for the jobs and wages of a generation earlier. Today the American economy as a whole is clearly much richer than it was in 1973, the year generally taken to mark the end of the postwar boom, but economists are arguing about whether typical Americans have benefited at all from the gains of the nation as a whole.

Now for the complications: It turns out that we can't just line up all 300 million people in America in order of income and calculate the income of American number 150,000,000. After all, children don't belong in the lineup, because they only have income to the extent that the households they live in do. So perhaps we should be looking at households rather than individuals. If we do that we find that median household income, adjusted for inflation, grew modestly from 1973 to 2005, the most recent year for which we have data: The total gain was about 16 percent.

Even this modest gain may, however, overstate how well American families were doing, because it was achieved in part through longer working hours. In 1973 many wives still didn't work outside the home, and many who did worked only part-time. I don't mean to imply that there's something wrong with more women working, but a gain in family income that occurs because a spouse goes to work isn't the same thing as a wage increase. In particular it may carry hidden costs that offset some of the gains in money income, such as reduced time to spend on housework, greater dependence on prepared food, day-care expenses, and so on.

We get a considerably more pessimistic take on the data if we ask how easy it is for American families today to live the way many of them did a generation ago, with a single male breadwinner. According to the available data, it has gotten harder: The median inflation-adjusted earnings of men working full-time in 2005 were slightly lower than they had been in 1973. And even that statistic is deceptively favorable. Thanks to the maturing of the baby boomers today's work force is older and more experienced than the work force of 1973—and more experienced workers should, other things being equal, command higher wages. If we look at the earnings of men aged thirty-five to forty-four—men who would, a generation ago, often have been supporting stay-at-home wives—we find that inflation-adjusted wages were 12 percent *higher* in 1973 than they are now.

Controversies over defining the relevant population are only part of the reason economists manage to argue about whether typical Americans have gotten ahead since 1973. There is also a different set of questions, involving the measurement of prices. I keep referring to "inflation-adjusted" income—which means that income a generation ago is converted into today's dollars by adjusting for changes in the consumer price index. Now some economists argue that the CPI overstates true inflation, because it doesn't fully take account of new products and services that have improved our lives. As a result, they say, the standard of living has risen more than the official numbers suggest. Call it the "but they didn't have Netflix" argument. Seriously, there are many goods and services available today that either hadn't been invented or weren't on the market in 1973, from cell phones to the Internet. Most important, surely, are drugs and medical techniques that not only save lives but improve the quality of life for tens of millions of people. On the other hand, in some ways life has gotten harder for working families in ways the official numbers don't capture: there's more intense competition to live in a good school district, traffic congestion is worse, and so on.

Maybe the last word should be given to the public. According to a 2006 survey taken by the Pew Research Center, most working Americans believe that the average worker "has to work harder to earn a decent living" today than he did twenty or thirty years earlier.[1] Is this just nostalgia for a remembered golden age? Maybe, but there was no such

---

[1] "Public Says Work Life Is Worsening, but Most Workers Remain Satisfied with Their Jobs," Pew Center for People and Press, Labor Day, 2006, http://pewresearch.org/assets/social/pdf/Jobs.pdf.

nostalgia a generation ago about the way America was a generation before *that*. The point is that the typical American family hasn't made clear progress in the last thirty-something years. And that's not normal.

||| WINNERS AND LOSERS

As I've suggested with my Bill-Gates-in-a-bar analogy, ordinary American workers have failed to reap the gains from rising productivity because of rising inequality. But who were the winners and losers from this upward redistribution of income? It wasn't just Bill Gates—but it was a surprisingly narrow group.

If gains in productivity had been evenly shared across the work-force, the typical worker's income would be about 35 percent higher now than it was in the early seventies.[2] But the upward redistribution of income meant that the typical worker saw a far smaller gain. Indeed, everyone below roughly the 90th percentile of the wage distribution—the bottom of the top 10 percent—saw his or her income grow more slowly than average, while only those above the 90th percentile saw above-average gains. So the limited gains of the typical American worker were the flip side of above-average gains for the top 10 percent.

And the really big gains went to the really, really rich. In Oliver Stone's 1987 movie *Wall Street,* Gordon Gekko—the corporate raider modeled in part on Ivan Boesky, played by

Michael Douglas—mocks the limited ambition of his protégé, played by Charlie Sheen. "Do you want to be just another $400,000 a year working Wall Street stiff, flying first class and being *comfortable*?"

At the time an income of $400,000 a year would have put someone at about the 99.9th percentile of the wage distribution—pretty good, you might think. But as Stone realized, by the late 1980s something astonishing was happening in the upper reaches of the income distribution: The rich were pulling away from the merely affluent, and the super-rich were pulling away from the merely rich. People in the bottom half of the top 10 percent, corresponding roughly to incomes in the $100,000 to $150,000 range, though they did better than Americans further down the scale, didn't do all that well—in fact, in the period after 1973 they didn't gain nearly as much, in percentage terms, as they did during the postwar boom. Only the top 1 percent has done better since the 1970s than it did in the generation after World War II. Once you get way up the scale, however, the gains have been spectacular—the top tenth of a percent saw its income rise fivefold, and the top .01 percent of Americans is seven times richer than they were in 1973.

Who are these people, and why are they doing so much better than everyone else? In the original Gilded Age, people with very high incomes generally received those incomes due to the assets they owned: The economic elite

---

2 Dean Baker of the Center for Economic Policy Research estimates that "usable" productivity growth—the increase in the net value produced per U.S. worker-hour adjusted for rising consumer prices—was 47.9 percent between 1973 and 2006. However, nonwage labor costs rose due to rising payroll taxes, rising health care costs, and other factors, so that the amount available for wages rose about 36 percent. Dean Baker, "The Productivity to Paycheck Gap: What the Data Show," at www.cepr.net, Apr. 2007,

owned valuable land and mineral resources or highly profitable companies. Even now capital income—income from assets such as stocks, bonds, and property—is much more concentrated in the hands of a few than earned income. So is "entrepreneurial income"—income from ownership of companies. But ownership is no longer the main source of elite status. These days even multimillionaires get most of their income in the form of paid compensation for their labor.

Needless to say we're not talking about wage slaves toiling for an hourly rate. If the quintessential high-income American circa 1905 was an industrial baron who owned factories, his counterpart a hundred years later is a top executive, lavishly rewarded for his labors with bonuses and stock options. Even at the very top, the highest-income 0.01 percent of the population—the richest one in ten thousand—almost half of income comes in the form of compensation. A rough estimate is that about half of the wage income of this superelite comes from the earnings of top executives—not just CEOs but those a few ranks below—at major companies. Much of the rest of the wage income of the top 0.01 percent appears to represent the incomes of sports and entertainment celebrities.

So a large part of the overall increase in inequality is, in a direct sense, the result of a change in the way society pays its allegedly best and brightest. They were always paid well, but now they're paid incredibly well.

The question, of course, is what caused that to happen. Broadly speaking there are two competing explanations for the great divergence in incomes that has taken place since the 1970s. The first explanation, favored by people who want to sound reasonable and judicious, is that a rising demand for skill, due mainly to technological change with an assist from globalization, is responsible. The alternative explanation stresses changes in institutions, norms, and political power.

THE DEMAND FOR SKILL

The standard explanation of rising inequality—I'm tempted to call it the safe explanation, since it's favored by people who don't want to make waves—says that rising inequality is mainly caused by a rising demand for skilled labor, which in turn is driven largely by technological change. For example, Edward Lazear, chairman of the Council of Economic Advisers in 2006, had this to say:

> Most of the inequality reflects an increase in returns to "investing in skills"—workers completing more school, getting more training, and acquiring new capabilities. . . . What accounts for this divergence of earnings for the skilled and earnings for the unskilled? Most economists believe that fundamentally this is traceable to technological change that has occurred over the past two or three decades. In our technologically-advanced society, skill has higher value than it does in a less technologically-advanced society . . . with the growing importance of computers, the types of skills that are required in school and through investment in learning on the job become almost essential in making a worker productive. The typical job that individuals do today requires a much higher level of

technical skills than the kinds of jobs that workers did in 1900 or in 1970.[3]

To enlarge on Lazear's remarks: Information technology, in the form of personal computers, cell phones, local area networks, the Internet, and so on, increases the demand for people with enough formal training to build, program, operate, and repair the new gadgets. At the same time it reduces the need for workers who do routine tasks. For example, there are far fewer secretaries in modern offices than there were in 1970, because word processing has largely eliminated the need for typists, and networks have greatly reduced the need for physical filing and retrieval; but there are as many managers as ever. Bar-code scanners tied to local networks have reduced the number of people needed to man cash registers and the number required to keep track of inventory, but there are more marketing consultants than ever. And so on throughout the economy.

The hypothesis that technological change, by raising the demand for skill, has led to growing inequality is so widespread that at conferences economists often use the abbreviation SBTC—skill-biased technical change—without explanation, assuming that their listeners know what they're talking about. It's an appealing hypothesis for three main reasons. First, the timing works: The upward trend in inequality began about the same time that computing power and its applications began their great explosion. True, mainframe computers—

large machines that sat in a room by themselves, crunching payrolls and other business data—were in widespread use in the sixties. But they had little impact on how most workers did their jobs. Modern information technology didn't come into its own until Intel introduced the first integrated circuit—the first computer chip—in 1971. Only then could the technology become pervasive. Second, SBTC is the kind of hypothesis economists feel comfortable with: it's just supply and demand, with no need to bring in the kinds of things sociologists talk about but economists find hard to incorporate in their models, things like institutions, norms, and political power. Finally SBTC says that the rise in inequality isn't anybody's fault: It's just technology, working through the invisible hand.

That said, there's remarkably little direct evidence for the proposition that technological change has caused rising inequality. The truth is that there's no easy way to measure the effect of technology on markets; on this issue and others, economists mainly invoke technology to explain things they can't explain by other measurable forces. The procedure goes something like this: First, assume that rising inequality is caused by technology, growing international trade, and immigration. Then, estimate the effects of trade and immigration—a tendentious procedure in itself, but we do at least have data on the volume of imports and the number of immigrants. Finally, attribute whatever isn't explained by these measurable factors to

3 Edward Lazear, speech given at the Hudson Institute, "The State of the U.S. Economy and Labor Market," Washington, D.C., May 2, 2006.

technology. That is, economists who assert that technological change is the main cause of rising inequality arrive at that conclusion by a process of exclusion: They've concluded that trade and immigration aren't big enough to explain what has happened, so technology must be the culprit.

As I've just suggested, the main factors economists have considered as alternative explanations for rising inequality are immigration and international trade, both of which should, in principle, also have acted to raise the wages of the skilled while reducing those of less-skilled Americans.

Immigration is, of course, a very hot political issue in its own right. In 1970, almost half a century after the Immigration Act of 1924 closed the door on mass immigration from low-wage countries, less than 5 percent of U.S. adults were foreign born. But for reasons that remain somewhat unclear,[4] immigration began to pick up in the late 1960s, and soared after 1980. Today, immigrants make up about 15 percent of the workforce. In itself this should have exerted some depressing effect on overall wages: there are considerably more workers competing for U.S. jobs than there would have been without immigration.

Furthermore, a majority of immigrants over the past generation have come from Latin America, and many of the rest from other Third World countries; this means that immigrants, both legal and illegal, are on average considerably less educated than are native-born work-ers. A third of immigrants have the equivalent of less than a high-school diploma. As a result the arrival of large numbers of immigrants has made less-educated labor more abundant in the United States, while making highly educated workers relatively scarcer. Supply and demand then predicts that immigration should have depressed the wages of less-skilled workers, while raising those of highly skilled workers.

The effects, however, are at most medium-size. Even the most pessimistic mainstream estimates, by George Borjas and Larry Katz of Harvard, suggest that immigration has reduced the wages of high-school dropouts by about 5 percent, with a much smaller effect on workers with a high school degree, and a small positive effect on highly educated workers. Moreover, other economists think the Borjas–Katz numbers are too high.

[Elsewhere I] argue that immigration may have promoted inequality in a more indirect way, by shifting the balance of *political* power up the economic scale. But the direct economic effect has been modest.

What about international trade? Much international trade probably has little or no effect on the distribution of income. For example, trade in automobiles and parts between the United States and Canada—two high-wage countries occupying different niches of the same industry, shipping each other goods produced with roughly the same mix of skilled and unskilled labor—isn't likely to have much effect on wage

---

4 Changes in immigration law in 1965 made family reunification the central goal of immigration policy, shifting the focus away from the attempt to restrict immigration mainly to Western Europe. But economists studying Mexican immigration find that there were relatively few barriers even before 1965.

inequality in either country. But U.S. trade with, say, Bangladesh is a different story Bangladesh mainly exports clothing—the classic labor-intensive good, produced by workers who need little formal education and no more capital equipment than a sewing machine. In return Bangladesh buys sophisticated goods—airplanes, chemicals, computers.

There's no question that U.S. trade with Bangladesh and other Third World countries, including China, widens inequality. Suppose that you buy a pair of pants made in Bangladesh that could have been made domestically. By buying the foreign pants you are in effect forcing the workers who would have been employed producing a made-in-America pair of pants to look for other jobs. Of course the converse is also true when the United States exports something: When Bangladesh buys a Boeing airplane, the American workers employed in producing that plane don't have to look for other jobs. But the labor embodied in U.S. exports is very different from the labor employed in U.S. industries that compete with imports. We tend to export "skill-intensive" products like aircraft, supercomputers, and Hollywood movies; we tend to import "labor-intensive" goods like pants and toys. So U.S. trade with Third World countries reduces job opportunities for less-skilled American workers, while increasing demand for more-skilled workers. There's no question that this widens the wage gap between the less-skilled and the more-skilled, contributing to increased inequality. And the rapid growth of trade with low-wage countries, especially Mexico and China, suggests that this effect has been increasing over the past fifteen years.

What's really important to understand, however, is that skill-biased technological change, immigration, and growing international trade are, at best, explanations of a rising gap between less-educated and more-educated workers. And despite the claims of Lazear and many others, that's only part of the tale of rising inequality. It's true that the payoff to education has risen—but even the college educated have for the most part seen their wage gains lag behind rising productivity. For example, the median college-educated man has seen his real income rise only 17 percent since 1973.

That's because the big gains in income have gone not to a broad group of well-paid workers but to a narrow group of extremely well-paid people. In general those who receive enormous incomes are also well educated, but their gains aren't representative of the gains of educated workers as a whole. CEOs and schoolteachers both typically have master's degrees, but schoolteachers have seen only modest gains since 1973, while CEOs have seen their income rise from about thirty times that of the average worker in 1970 to more than three hundred times as much today.

The observation that even highly educated Americans have, for the most part, seen their incomes fall behind the average, while a handful of people have done incredibly well, undercuts the case for skill-biased technological change as an explanation of inequality and supports the argument that it's largely due to changes in institutions, such as the strength of labor unions, and norms, such as the once powerful but now weak belief that having the boss make vastly more than the workers is bad for morale.

INSTITUTIONS: THE END OF THE TREATY OF DETROIT

The idea that changes in institutions and changes in norms, rather than anonymous skill-biased technical change, explain rising inequality has been gaining growing support among economists, for two main reasons. First, an institutions-and-norms explanation of rising inequality today links current events to the dramatic *fall* in inequality—the Great Compression—that took place in the 1930s and 1940s. Second, an institutions-and-norms story helps explain American exceptionalism: No other advanced country has seen the same kind of surge in inequality that has taken place here.

The Great Compression in itself—or more accurately, its persistence—makes a good case for the crucial role of social forces as opposed to the invisible hand in determining income distribution. ★ ★ ★ The middle-class America baby boomers grew up in didn't evolve gradually. It was constructed in a very short period by New Deal legislation, union activity, and wage controls during World War II. Yet the relatively flat income distribution imposed during the war lasted for decades after wartime control of the economy ended. This persistence makes a strong case that anonymous market forces are less decisive than Economics 101 teaches. As Piketty and Saez put it:

> The compression of wages during the war can be explained by the wage controls of the war economy, but how can we explain the fact

that high wage earners did not recover after the wage controls were removed? This evidence cannot be immediately reconciled with explanations of the reduction of inequality based solely on technical change. . . . We think that this pattern or evolution of inequality is additional indirect evidence that nonmarket mechanisms such as labor market institutions and social norms regarding inequality may play a role in setting compensation.[5]

The MIT economists Frank Levy and Peter Temin have led the way in explaining how those "labor market institutions and social norms" worked.[6] They point to a set of institutional arrangements they call the Treaty of Detroit—the name given by *Fortune* magazine to a landmark 1949 bargain struck between the United Auto Workers and General Motors. Under that agreement, UAW members were guaranteed wages that rose with productivity, as well as health and retirement benefits; what GM got in return was labor peace.

Levy and Temin appropriate the term to refer not only to the formal arrangement between the auto companies and their workers but also to the way that arrangement was emulated throughout the U.S. economy. Other unions based their bargaining demands on the standard set by the UAW leading to the spread of wage-and-benefit packages that, while usually not as plush as what Walter Reuther managed to get, ensured that workers shared in the fruits of progress. And even nonunion workers were strongly affected, because the

---

5 Thomas Piketty and Emmanuel Saez, "Income Inequality in the United States, 1913–1998," *Quarterly Journal of Economics*, vol. 118, no. 1 (Feb. 2003), pp. 1–39.

6 Frank Levy and Peter Temin, "Inequality and Institutions in 20th–Century America," MIT Department of Economics, working paper, no. 07–17, June 2007.

threat of union activity often led nonunionized employers to offer their workers more or less what their unionized counterparts were getting: The economy of the fifties and sixties was characterized by "pattern wages," in which wage settlements of major unions and corporations established norms for the economy as a whole.

At the same time the existence of powerful unions acted as a restraint on the incomes of both management and stockholders. Top executives knew that if they paid themselves huge salaries, they would be inviting trouble with their workers; similarly corporations that made high profits while failing to raise wages were putting labor relations at risk.

The federal government was also an informal party to the Treaty of Detroit: It intervened, in various ways, to support workers' bargaining positions and restrain perceived excess at the top. Workers' productivity was substantially lower in the 1960s than it is today, but the minimum wage, adjusted for inflation, was considerably higher. Labor laws were interpreted and enforced in a way that favored unions. And there was often direct political pressure on large companies and top executives who were seen as stepping over the line. John F. Kennedy famously demanded that steel companies, which had just negotiated a modest wage settlement, rescind a price increase.

To see how different labor relations were under the Treaty of Detroit from their state today, compare two iconic corporations, one of the past, one of the present.

In the final years of the postwar boom General Motors was America's largest private employer aside from the regulated telephone monopoly. Its CEO was, correspondingly, among America's highest paid executives: Charles Johnson's 1969 salary was $795,000, about $4.3 million in today's dollars—and that salary excited considerable comment. But ordinary GM workers were also paid well. In 1969 auto industry production workers earned on average almost $9,000, the equivalent of more than $40,000 today. GM workers, who also received excellent health and retirement benefits, were considered solidly in the middle class.

Today Wal-Mart is America's largest corporation, with 800,000 employees. In 2005 Lee Scott, its chairman, was paid almost $23 million. That's more than five times Charles Johnson's inflation-adjusted salary, but Mr. Scott's compensation excited relatively little comment, since it wasn't exceptional for the CEO of a large corporation these days. The wages paid to Wal-Mart's workers, on the other hand, do attract attention, because they are low even by current standards. On average Wal-Mart's nonsupervisory employees are paid about $18,000 a year, less than half what GM workers were paid thirty-five years ago, adjusted for inflation. Wal-Mart is also notorious both for the low percentage of its workers who receive health benefits, and the stinginess of those scarce benefits.[7]

What Piketty and Saez, Levy and Temin, and a growing number of other economists argue is that the contrast between GM then and Wal-Mart now is representative of what

---

7 See, for example, Reed Abelson, "Wal-Mart's Health Care Struggle Is Corporate America's, Too," *New York Times*, October 29, 2005.

has happened in the economy at large—that in the 1970s and after, the Treaty of Detroit was rescinded, the institutions and norms that had limited inequality after World War II went away, and inequality surged back to Gilded Age levels. In other words, the great divergence of incomes since the seventies is basically the Great Compression in reverse. In the 1930s and 1940s institutions were created and norms established that limited inequality; starting in the 1970s those institutions and norms were torn down, leading to rising inequality. The institutions-and-norms explanation integrates the rise and fall of middle-class America into a single story.

The institutions-and-norms explanation also correctly predicts how trends in inequality should differ among countries. Bear in mind that the forces of technological change and globalization have affected every advanced country: Europe has applied information technology almost as rapidly as we have, cheap clothing in Europe is just as likely to be made in China as is cheap clothing in America. If technology and globalization are the driving forces behind rising inequality, then Europe should be experiencing the same rise in inequality as the United States. In terms of institutions and norms, however, things are very different among advanced nations: In Europe, for example, unions remain strong, and old norms condemning very high pay and emphasizing the entitlements of workers haven't faded away So if institutions are the story, we'd expect the U.S. experience of rising inequality to be exceptional, not echoed in Europe.

And on that comparison, an institutions-and-norms explanation wins: America is unique. The clearest evidence comes from income tax data, which allow a comparison of the share of income accruing to the economic elite. These data show that during World War II and its aftermath all advanced countries experienced a Great Compression, a sharp drop in inequality. In the United States this leveling was reversed beginning in the 1970s, and the effects of the Great Compression have now been fully eliminated. In Canada, which is closely linked to the U.S. economy, and in Britain, which had its own period of conservative dominance under Margaret Thatcher, there has been a more limited trend toward renewed inequality. But in Japan and France there has been very little change in inequality since 1980.[8]

There's also spottier and less consistent information from surveys of household incomes. The picture there is fuzzier, but again the United States and, to a lesser extent, Britain stand out as countries where inequality sharply increased, while other advanced countries experienced either minor increases or no change at all.[9]

There is, in short, a strong circumstantial case for believing that institutions and norms, rather than technology or globalization, are the big sources of rising inequality in the United States. The obvious example of changing institutions is the collapse of the U.S. union movement. But what do I mean when I talk about changing norms?

---

8 Thomas Piketty and Emmanuel Saez, "The Evolution of Top Incomes: A Historical and International Perspective," (National Bureau of Economic Research, working paper, no. 11955, Jan. 2006).

9 See Andrea Brandolini and Timothy Smeeding, "Inequality Patterns in Western-Type Democracies: Cross-Country Differences and Time Changes" (Luxembourg Income Study working paper no. 458, Apr. 2007). An attempt to systematize the survey data, yielding results similar to Piketty and Saez, is http://www.tcf.org/list.asp?type=NC&pubid=1403.

NORMS AND INEQUALITY: THE CASE OF THE RUNAWAY CEOS

When economists talk about how changing norms have led to rising inequality, they often have one concrete example in mind: the runaway growth of executive pay. Although executives at major corporations aren't the only big winners from rising inequality, their visibility makes them a good illustration of what is happening more broadly throughout the economy.

According to a Federal Reserve study, in the 1970s the chief executives at 102 major companies (those that were in the top 50 as measured by sales at some point over the period 1940–1990) were paid on average about $1.2 million in today's dollars. That wasn't hardship pay, to say the least. But it was only a bit more than CEOs were paid in the 1930s, and "only" 40 times what the average full-time worker in the U.S. economy as a whole was paid at the time. By the early years of this decade, however, CEO pay averaged more than $9 million a year, 367 times the pay of the average worker. Other top executives also saw huge increases in pay, though not as large as that of CEOs: The next two highest officers in major companies made 31 times the average worker's salary in the seventies, but 169 times as much by the early 2000s.[10]

To make some sense of this extraordinary development, let's start with an idealized story about the determinants of executive pay.[11] Imagine that the profitability of each company depends on the quality of its CEO, and that the bigger the company, the larger the CEO's impact on profit. Imagine also that the quality of potential CEOs is observable; everyone knows who is the 100th best executive in America, the 99th best, and so on. In that case, there will be a competition for executives that ends up assigning the best executives to the biggest companies, where their contribution matters the most. And as a result of that competition, each executive's pay will reflect his or her quality.

An immediate implication of this story is that at the top, even small differences in perceived executive quality will translate into big differences in salaries. The reason is competition: For a giant company the difference in profitability between having the 10th best executive and the 11th best executive may easily be tens of millions of dollars each year. In that sense the idealized model suggests that top executives might be earning their pay. And the idealized model also says that if executives are paid far more today than they were a generation ago, it must be because for some reason—more intense competition, higher stock prices, whatever—it matters more than it used to to have the best man running a company.

But once we relax the idealized premises of the story, it's not hard to see why executive pay is a lot less tied down by fundamental forces of supply and demand, and a lot more subject to changes in social norms and political power, than this story implies.

First, neither the quality of executives nor the extent to which that quality matters are hard numbers. Assessing the productivity of

10 Carola Frydman and Raven Saks, "Historical Trends in Executive Compensation, 1936–2003," Federal Reserve Bank of New York, 2005.

11 See Xavier Gabaix and Augustin Landier, "Why Has CEO Pay Increased So Much?" (National Board of Economic Research working paper no. 12365), July 2006.

corporate leaders isn't like measuring how many bricks a worker can lay in an hour. You can't even reliably evaluate managers by looking at the profitability of the companies they run, because profits depend on a lot of factors outside the chief executive's control. Moreover profitability can, for extended periods, be in the eye of the beholder: Enron looked like a fabulously successful company to most of the world; Toll Brothers, the McMansion king, looked like a great success as long as the housing bubble was still inflating. So the question of how much to pay a top executive has a strong element of subjectivity, even fashion, to it. In the fifties and sixties big companies didn't think it was important to have a famous, charismatic leader: CEOs rarely made the covers of business magazines, and companies tended to promote from within, stressing the virtues of being a team player. By contrast, in the eighties and thereafter CEOs became rock stars—they defined their companies as much as their companies defined them. Are corporate boards wiser now than they were when they chose solid insiders to run companies, or have they just been caught up in the culture of celebrity?

Second, even to the extent that corporate boards correctly judge both the quality of executives and the extent to which quality matters for profitability, the actual amount they end up paying their top executives depends a lot on what *other* companies do. Thus, in the corporate world of the 1960s and 1970s, companies rarely paid eye-popping salaries to perceived management superstars. In fact companies tended to see huge paychecks at the top as a possible source of reduced team spirit, as well as a potential source of labor problems. In that environment even a corporate board that *did* believe that hiring star

executives was the way to go didn't have to offer exorbitant pay to attract those stars. But today executive pay in the millions or tens of millions is the norm. And even corporate boards that aren't smitten with the notion of superstar leadership end up paying high salaries, partly to attract executives whom they consider adequate, partly because the financial markets will be suspicious of a company whose CEO isn't lavishly paid.

Finally, to the extent that there is a market for corporate talent, who, exactly, are the buyers? Who determines how good a CEO is, and how much he has to be paid to keep another company from poaching his entrepreneurial know-how? The answer, of course, is that corporate boards, largely selected by the CEO, hire compensation experts, almost always chosen by the CEO, to determine how much the CEO is worth. It is, shall we say, a situation conducive to overstatement both of the executive's personal qualities and of how much those supposed personal qualities matter for the company's bottom line.

What all this suggests is that incomes at the top—the paychecks of top executives and, by analogy, the incomes of many other income superstars—may depend a lot on "soft" factors such as social attitudes and the political background. Perhaps the strongest statement of this view comes from Lucian Bebchuk and Jesse Fried, authors of the 2004 book *Pay Without Performance*. Bebchuk and Fried argue that top executives in effect set their own paychecks, that neither the quality of the executives nor the marketplace for talent has any real bearing. The only thing that limits executive pay, they argue, is the "outrage constraint": the concern that very high executive compensation will create a backlash from usually quiescent shareholders, workers, politicians, or the general public.[12]

To the extent that this view is correct, soaring incomes at the top can be seen as a social and political, rather than narrowly economic phenomenon: high incomes shot up not because of an increased demand for talent but because a variety of factors caused the death of outrage. News organizations that might once have condemned lavishly paid executives lauded their business genius instead; politicians who might once have led populist denunciations of corporate fat cats sought to flatter the people who provide campaign contributions; unions that might once have walked out to protest giant executive bonuses had been crushed by years of union busting. Oh, and one more thing. Because the top marginal tax rate has declined from 70 percent in the early 1970s to 35 percent today, there's more incentive for a top executive to take advantage of his position: He gets to keep much more of his excess pay. And the result is an explosion of income inequality at the top of the scale.

The idea that rising pay at the top of the scale mainly reflects social and political change, rather than the invisible hand of the market, strikes some people as implausible—too much at odds with Economics 101. But it's an idea that has some surprising supporters: Some of the most ardent defenders of the way modern executives are paid say almost the same thing.

Before I get to those defenders, let me give you a few words from someone who listened to what they said. From Gordon Gekko's famous speech to the shareholders of Teldar Paper in the movie *Wall Street*:

> Now, in the days of the free market, when our country was a top industrial power, there was accountability to the stockholder. The Carnegies, the Mellons, the men that built this great industrial empire, made sure of it because it was their money at stake. Today, management has no stake in the company! . . . The point is, ladies and gentlemen, that greed—for lack of a better word—is good. Greed is right. Greed works.

What those who watch the movie today may not realize is that the words Oliver Stone put in Gordon Gekko's mouth were strikingly similar to what the leading theorists on executive pay were saying at the time. In 1990 Michael Jensen of the Harvard Business School and Kevin Murphy of the University of Rochester published an article in the *Harvard Business Review,* summarizing their already influential views on executive pay. The trouble with American business, they declared, is that "the compensation of top executives is virtually independent of performance. On average corporate America pays its most important leaders like bureaucrats. Is it any wonder then that so many CEOs act like bureaucrats rather than the value-maximizing entrepreneurs companies need to enhance their standing in world markets?" In other words, greed is good.[13]

Why, then, weren't companies linking pay to performance? Because of social and political pressure:

---

12 Lucian Bebchuk and Jesse Fried, *Pay Without Performance: The Unfulfilled Promise of Executive Compensation* (Harvard University Press, 2004).

13 Michael C. Jensen and Kevin J, Murphy, "CEO Incentives— It's Not How Much You Pay, but How," *Harvard Business Review* (May/June 1990), pp. 138–53.

Why don't boards of directors link pay more closely to performance? Commentators offer many explanations, but nearly every analysis we've seen overlooks one powerful ingredient—the costs imposed by making executive salaries public. Government disclosure rules ensure that executive pay remains a visible and controversial topic. The benefits of disclosure are obvious; it provides safeguards against "looting" by managers in collusion with "captive" directors.

The costs of disclosure are less well appreciated but may well exceed the benefits. Managerial labor contracts are not a private matter between employers and employees. Third parties play an important role in the contracting process, and strong political forces operate inside and outside companies to shape executive pay. Moreover, authority over compensation decisions rests not with the shareholders but with compensation committees generally composed of outside directors. These committees are elected by shareholders but are not perfect agents for them. Public disclosure of "what the boss makes" gives ammunition to outside constituencies with their own special-interest agendas. Compensation committees typically react to the agitation over pay levels by capping—explicitly or implicitly—the amount of money the CEO earns.[14]

In other words Jensen and Murphy, writing at a time when executive pay was still low by today's standards, believed that social norms, in the form of the outrage constraint, were holding executive paychecks down. Of course they saw this as a bad thing, not a good thing. They dismissed concerns about executive self-dealing, placing "looting" and "captive" in scare quotes. But their implicit explanation of trends in executive pay was the same as that of critics of high pay. Executive pay, they pointed out, had actually fallen in real terms between the late 1930s and the early 1980s, even as companies grew much bigger. The reason, they asserted, was public pressure. So they were arguing that social and political considerations, not narrowly economic forces, led to the sharp reduction in income differences between workers and bosses in the postwar era.

Today the idea that huge paychecks are part of a beneficial system in which executives are given an incentive to perform well has become something of a sick joke. A 2001 article in *Fortune*, "The Great CEO Pay Heist,"[15] encapsulated the cynicism: "You might have expected it to go like this: The stock isn't moving, so the CEO shouldn't be rewarded. But it was actually the opposite: The stock isn't moving, so we've got to find some other basis for rewarding the CEO." And the article quoted a somewhat repentant Michael Jensen: "I've generally worried these guys weren't getting paid enough. But now even I'm troubled."[16] But no matter: The doctrine that greed is good did its work, by helping to change social and political norms. Paychecks that would have made front-page news and created a furor a generation ago hardly rate mention today.

Not surprisingly, executive pay in European countries—which haven't experienced

---

14 Ibid.

15 http://money.cnn.com/magazines/fortune/fortune_archive/2001/06/25/305448 /index.htm.

16 Ibid.

the same change in norms and institutions—has lagged far behind. The CEO of BP, based in the United Kingdom, is paid less than half as much as the CEO of Chevron, a company half BP's size, but based in America. As a European pay consultant put it, "There is no shame factor in the U.S. In Europe, there is more of a concern about the social impact."[17]

To be fair, CEOs aren't the only members of the economic elite who have seen their incomes soar since the 1970s. Some economists have long argued that certain kinds of technological change, such as the rise of the mass media, may be producing large salary gaps between people who seem, on the surface, to have similar qualifications.[18] Indeed the rise of the mass media may help explain why celebrities of various types make so much more than they used to. And it's possible to argue that in a vague way technology may help explain why income gaps have widened among lawyers and other professionals: Maybe fax machines and the Internet let the top guns take on more of the work requiring that extra something, while less talented professionals are left with the routine drudge work. Still, the example of CEO pay shows how changes in institutions and norms can lead to rising inequality—and as we've already seen, international comparisons suggest that institutions, not technology, are at the heart of the changes over the past thirty years.

||| THE REASON WHY

Since the 1970s norms and institutions in the United States have changed in ways that either encouraged or permitted sharply higher inequality. Where, however, did the change in norms and institutions come from? The answer appears to be politics.

Consider, for example, the fate of the unions. Unions were once an important factor limiting income inequality, both because of their direct effect in raising their members' wages and because the union pattern of wage settlements—which consistently raised the wages of less-well-paid workers more—was, in the fifties and sixties, reflected in the labor market as a whole. The decline of the unions has removed that moderating influence. But why did unions decline?

The conventional answer is that the decline of unions is a result of the changing structure of the workforce. According to this view, the American economy used to be dominated by manufacturing, which was also where the most powerful unions were—think of the UAW and the Steelworkers. Now we're mostly a service economy, partly because of technological change, partly because we're importing so many manufactured goods. Surely, then, deindustrialization must explain the decline of unions.

Except that it turns out that it doesn't. Manufacturing has declined in importance, but most of the decline in union membership comes from a collapse of unionization *within* manufacturing, from 39 percent of workers in 1973 to 13 percent in 2005. Also, there's no economic law saying that unionization has to be restricted to manufacturing. On the contrary, a company like Wal-Mart, which doesn't face foreign competition, should be an even better target for

---

17 "U.S.-Style Pay Deals for Chiefs Become All the Rage in Europe," *New York Times,* June 16, 2006, p. Al.

18 Sherwin Rosen, "The Economics of Superstars," *American Economic Review* 71, no. 5 (Dec. 1981), pp. 845–58.

unionization than are manufacturing companies. Think how that would change the shape of the U.S. economy: If Wal-Mart employees were part of a union that could demand higher wages and better benefits, retail prices might be slightly higher, but the retail giant wouldn't go out of business—and the American middle class would have several hundred thousand additional members. Imagine extending that story to other retail giants, or better yet to the service sector as a whole, and you can get a sense of how the Great Compression happened under FDR.

Why, then, isn't Wal-Mart unionized? Why, in general, did the union movement lose ground in manufacturing while failing to gain members in the rising service industries? The answer is simple and brutal: Business interests, which seemed to have reached an accommodation with the labor movement in the 1960s, went on the offensive against unions beginning in the 1970s. And we're not talking about gentle persuasion, we're talking about hardball tactics, often including the illegal firing of workers who tried to organize or supported union activity. During the late seventies and early eighties at least one in every twenty workers who voted for a union was illegally fired; some estimates put the number as high as one in eight.

The collapse of the U.S. union movement that took place beginning in the 1970s has no counterpart in any other Western nation. Table 1 shows a stark comparison between the United States and Canada. In the 1960s the U.S. workforce was, if anything, slightly more unionized than Canada's workforce. By the end of the 1990s, however, U.S. unions had been all but driven out of the private sector, while Canada's union movement was essentially intact. The difference, of course, was politics; America's

TABLE 1 PERCENTAGE OF UNIONIZED WAGE AND SALARY WORKERS

	United States	Canada
1960	30.4	32.3
1999	13.5	32.6

SOURCE: David Card, Thomas Lemieux, and W. Craig Riddell, *Unionization and Wage Inequality: A Comparative Study of the U.S., the U.K., and Canada* (National Bureau of Economic Research working paper no. 9473, Jan. 2003).

political climate turned favorable to union busting, while Canada's didn't.

I [have] described ★ ★ ★ the centrality of anti-unionism to Barry Goldwater's rise, and the way opposition to unions played a key role in the consolidation of movement conservatism's business base. By the second half of the 1970s, movement conservatives had enough political clout that businesses felt empowered to take on unions.

And once Ronald Reagan took office the campaign against unions was aided and abetted by political support at the highest levels. In particular, Reagan's suppression of the air traffic controllers' union was the signal for a broad assault on unions throughout the economy. The rollback of unions, which were once a powerful constraint on inequality, was political in the broadest sense. It was an exercise in the use of power, both within the government and in our society at large.

To understand the Great Divergence, then, we need to understand how it was that movement conservatism became such a powerful factor in American political life.

58

American Democracy in an Era of Rising Inequality*

LAWRENCE R. JACOBS AND THEDA SKOCPOL

Equal political voice and democratically responsive government are widely cherished American ideals—yet as the United States aggressively promotes democracy abroad, these principles are under growing threat in an era of persistent and rising inequalities at home. Disparities of income, wealth, and access to opportunity are growing more sharply in the United States than in many other nations, and gaps between races and ethnic groups persist. Progress toward expanding democracy may have stalled, and in some arenas reversed.

Generations of Americans have worked to equalize citizen voice across lines of income, race, and gender. Today, however, the voices of American citizens are raised and heard unequally. The privileged participate more than others and are increasingly well organized to press their demands on government. Public officials, in turn, are much more responsive to the privileged than to average citizens and the less affluent. The voices of citizens with lower or moderate incomes are lost on the ears of inattentive government

---

* First published in 2005; from *Inequality and American Democracy*.

officials, while the advantaged roar with a clarity and consistency that policymakers readily hear and routinely follow. The scourge of overt discrimination against African Americans and women has been replaced by a more subtle but potent threat—the growing concentration of the country's wealth, income, and political influence in the hands of the few.

These are the conclusions that the Task Force on Inequality and American Democracy established by the American Political Science Association in 2002 reached. As one of several task forces recently formed to enhance the public relevance of political science, this group of scholars was charged with reviewing and assessing the best current scholarship about the health and functioning of U.S. democracy over recent decades, in a era of expanding social rights yet rising economic inequality.[1] Speaking in its own voice and on the authority of the task force members alone, the group drew conclusions after surveying available evidence about three important, interlinked areas of concern: citizen participation, government responsiveness, and the impact of public policies on social inequalities and political participation.

★ ★ ★ Although Americans tolerate varied fortunes produced by the market, they worry when economic disparities threaten equal citizen voice and undermine government respon-

siveness to the needs and values of the majority. Americans want their democracy to ensure and expand equal opportunity for all citizens. The research reviewed [here] speaks to basic concerns about the health and prospects of U.S. democracy.

★ ★ ★

CONSEQUENCES FOR DEMOCRACY

How concerned should we be about persistent and rising socioeconomic inequalities? Few normative theorists propose a genuinely equal distribution of economic resources as either desirable or feasible. Most of the debate is about the consequences and tolerability of various degrees of economic inequality. Some theorists are comfortable with significant inequalities, which they see as a just reflection of greater rewards going to people who work harder and contribute specialized skills or capital investments to the economy. Those who accept high inequalities also fear that efforts to alter economic distributions will come at an excessive cost to liberty. Others are concerned whenever the life chances of citizens in a democracy become too divergent. If disparities become too great, how can people retain a sense of community and shared fate and engage in informed

---

[1] Nominated by Theda Skocpol, president of the American Political Science Association (APSA) from 2002 to 2003, and chaired by Lawrence Jacobs of the University of Minnesota, the Task Force on Inequality and American Democracy was appointed by the APSA in the fall of 2002. With support from the APSA and the Russell Sage Foundation, it began meeting in January 2003 and issued its report in June 2004. Fifteen scholars were appointed, of whom two were eventually unable to participate for personal reasons. In addition to Jacobs and

Skocpol, the members were Ben Barber (University of Maryland); Larry Bartels (Princeton University); Morris Fiorina (Stanford University); Jacob Hacker (Yale University); Rodney Hero (Notre Dame University); Hugh Heclo (George Mason University); Suzanne Mettler (Syracuse University); Benjamin Page (Northwestern University); Dianne Pinderhughes (University of Illinois at Urbana-Champaign); Kay Lehman Schlozman (Boston College); and Sidney Verba (Harvard University).

decisionmaking? And how can political equality be realized when citizens have increasingly divergent resources?

Theorists are not the only ones who disagree about the consequences of economic inequality. Citizens in various advanced-industrial societies differ as well. Our investigations take cues from the special concerns of Americans, which focus on the consequences of inequalities for democratic politics more than on the simple existence of economic disparities as such.

Concerns of Americans

According to opinion surveys, Americans are much more likely than Europeans to accept substantial disparities of income and wealth. In the United States, unequal economic outcomes are seen as largely reflecting differences among individuals rather than flaws in the economic system. Americans support private property and free enterprise, and see much of the skewed distribution of wealth and income as a legitimate result of differences in individual talent and effort.

Tolerance of economic inequality by Americans is not unambiguous, however. Two caveats come into play (Page and Shapiro 1992; Weakliem, Andersen, and Heath 2003). First, Americans accept economic inequalities only when they are sure that everyone has an equal chance to get ahead—to achieve the best possible life for the individual and family. Research and news accounts document that the rise in economic inequality is short-circuiting the pathway to

the American Dream—the hope that opportunities to prosper are within the reach of every individual willing to work hard and accept the sacrifice. Upward mobility continues, but the number of Americans who are able to enjoy the fruits of upward mobility are few in number and do not come close to offsetting the economic disparities among the many (Gottschalk 1997; Michaels 2004; Smeeding 2004). A narrowing of opportunities for getting ahead contradicts public hopes and expectations and raises concerns about what government is doing, or can do, to further equal opportunity.

Indeed, the second situation that raises public concern is when rising economic inequalities threaten to impinge on ideals of equal citizen voice and government responsiveness to the majority. Americans fervently believe that everyone should have an equal say in our democratic politics. They embrace wholeheartedly the ideal enunciated by the Declaration of Independence that "all men are created equal," which in our time means that every citizen, regardless of income, gender, race, or ethnicity, should have an equal voice in representative government.

According to the National Elections Studies (NES) and other evidence, Americans are increasingly worried about disparities of participation, voice, and government responsiveness.[2] Citizens are much less likely than they were four decades ago to trust government to "do the right thing." Between 1964 and 1994 the proportion of Americans who only trusted

---

2 Unless otherwise noted, the data cited in this paragraph is from NES. A valuable discussion of these patterns appears in Nye, Zelikow, and King (1997), especially the chapters by Gary Orren (1997), "Fall from Grace: The Public's Loss of Faith in Government," and Robert J. Blendon and others (1997), "Changing Attitudes in America."

the federal government "some" or "none of the time" more than tripled from 22 percent to 78 percent. Although the terrorist attacks on September 11 precipitated a decline in distrust to 46 percent in 2002, distrust increased to 53 percent in 2004. The proportion of Americans who felt that the government is "run by a few big interests looking out only for themselves" more than doubled from 29 percent in 1964 to 76 percent in 1994. This proportion declined to 50 percent in 2002 following the 9/11 attacks (still nearly double the 1964 level) before rising to 56 percent in 2004. In addition, the number who believed that "public officials don't care about what people like me think" nearly doubled, growing from 36 percent in 1964 to 66 percent in 1994. While this proportion dropped to 29 percent in 2002 after the 9/11 attacks, the suspicion rebounded to 50 percent in 2004. Surveys in 1995 and 2000 found that more than six in ten respondents cited too much influence by special interests as a reason for not trusting government.[3]

Looking Ahead to Our Findings

The evidence suggests that citizens are right to be concerned about the health of American democracy. We find disturbing inequalities in the political voice expressed through elections and other avenues of participation. We find that our governing institutions are much more responsive to the privileged and well-organized narrow interests than to other Americans. And we find that the policies our government fashions today may be doing less than celebrated programs of the past to promote equal opportunity and security and enhance citizen dignity and participation, reinforcing the suspicion of many in the American public that government officials "don't care" about the needs and values of ordinary citizens.

★ ★ ★ Only about a third of eligible voters regularly participate in mid-term congressional elections and only a little more than half regularly turn out for contemporary presidential elections. While the intensely competitive presidential election of 2004 increased turnout to its highest level since 1968—60 percent of individuals living in the United States who are 18 and over[4]—the United States remains a turnout laggard compared to other advanced industrialized countries. As Richard Freeman (2004, 703) puts it, on "a world scale, the United States ranks 138th in turnout among countries that hold elections—far below every other advanced democracy save for Switzerland." Overall, the U.S. electorate has contracted since the 1960s, and the well-educated and well-to-do are much more likely to vote than the least educated and economically privileged. Stratified voting was not, of course, created by any recent increases in economic disparities. But recently growing economic inequalities may reinforce voting differentials, counteracting major reforms that

---

3 1995 survey is discussed in Blendon and others (1997, 210), and the 2000 poll was conducted by International Communications Research.

4 Most media discussion of turnout focuses on the number of ballots that are cast as a proportion of the number of individuals living in the United States who are 18 and older

(Committee for the Study of the American Electorate 2004). The disenfranchisement of felons and other factors reduce the number of Americans who are actually eligible to vote (McDonald and Popkin 2001). Voter turnout in 2004 did rise, however, regardless of which method is used.

otherwise should have greatly expanded voter turnout. Reforms that should have done much to mitigate voting stratification include the Voting Rights Act of 1965, which brought millions of African Americans into the electorate; simplified processes for registering and casting absentee ballots; and the spread of formal education, which instills the skills and values that encourage voting. Analysts disagree as to whether voting has become more unequal by class over recent decades or has simply remained as it was (see Leighley and Nagler 1992 and the careful reanalysis by Freeman 2004). Certainly, however, voting has not become more equal, despite many factors that should have pushed it in that direction.

Despite all of the limitations in voter turnout, casting a ballot remains the most common political activity. Far fewer Americans take part in more demanding and costly political activities, from protest to giving money. The direct impact of rising economic inequality may be most directly apparent in campaign contributions. As wealth and income have become more concentrated and the flow of money into elections has grown, wealthy individuals and families have opportunities for political clout not open to those of more modest means. Stratification in participation is also evident in a range of other activities, such as joining and supporting a voluntary association or interest group, working in an electoral campaign, getting in touch with a public official, getting involved in an organization that takes political stands, and taking part in a protest or demonstration. Well-developed theory shows that exercising the rights of citizenship requires not only individual resources of income, time, and education, but also skills of the sort that privileged occupations disproportionately bestow on the economically well-off. Managers, lawyers, doctors, and other professionals enjoy not only higher education and salaries but also greater confidence and abilities to speak and organize.

With socioeconomic inequality on the increase, there are some theoretical reasons to believe that the political participation of the less privileged should actually increase (see Brady 2004). But much depends on the role of organizations and political parties in mediating social interests. Although the sheer number of organizations in Washington that speak for once-underrepresented preferences and constituencies has grown, blue-collar trade unions have weakened and are thus less likely to mobilize working-class voters (Radcliff and Davis 2000). Corporate managers and professionals have also increased their organized presence in Washington and enhanced their capacities to speak loudly and clearly to government officials. Even political parties—which the APSA and generations of political activists and observers have held out as a vehicle for an inclusive form of democracy that counteracts the advantage of the better off—may nowadays skew participation in U.S. politics. Along with contemporary professionally managed interest groups, today's major parties target resources on recruiting those who are already the most privileged and involved (Schier 2000; Skocpol 2004a, 2004b). Democrats and Republicans alike have come to depend heavily on campaign contributors and middle-class activists, and have gotten used to competing for just over half of a shrinking universe of voters.

The stratification of political clout and voice interacts with the emergence of a new group of political activists harboring views more intense and extreme than the average citizen's. Operating through interest groups swirling in and around the major political parties, such activists are not only themselves likely to be higher-income and well-educated individuals. On a range of important matters from abortion to tax cuts, activists are also often resistant to government compromises that respond to the more ambiguous or middle of the road opinions of average citizens (Fiorina 1999; Skocpol 2003, chaps. 5 and 6). Even liberal "public interest" advocates, moreover, are likely to focus on the concerns and values of the middle class, than on those of the poor or working Americans (Berry 1999, 55–57).

Disparities in political participation and voice matter because they affect who governs and how these elected officials respond to citizen preferences. Research documents that campaign contributions influence who runs for government office—and therefore who sits in the halls of government. The notion that monetary contributions can directly "buy" votes on the floor of Congress is *not* supported by rigorous empirical research that controls for a variety of other relevant factors (Ansolabehere, Figueiredo, and Snyder 2003; Wright 1985, 1990). But wealthy citizens and moneyed interests who make big contributions do gain privileged access to send clear signals about their political demands and support. Money and its increasingly unequal distribution buys the rare opportunity to present self-serving information or raise problems that can be addressed through a host of helpful, low-profile actions—inserting a rider into an omnibus bill, for example, expediting the scheduling of a bill that has been languishing in committee, or making sure that threatening regulatory legislation receives minimal funding for implementation (Gopoian 1984; Hall and Wayman 1990; Kroszner and Stratmann 1998; Langbein 1986).

Scholars are beginning to document the exact degree to which skewed political demands and support are converted by the governing process into policies and activities that disproportionately respond to business, the wealthy, and the organized and vocal. Recent research (Bartels 2002) documents that the votes of U.S. senators are almost three times more likely to correspond with the policy preferences of their most privileged constituents than with the preferences of their least privileged constituents, even though the latter are of course much more numerous. Bias in government responsiveness is evident not only in Congress but also in national government policy more generally. Government officials who design policy changes are more than twice as responsive to the preferences of the rich as to those of the least affluent (Gilens 2003). Business and other elites also exert far more influence than the public on U.S. foreign policy, which not only guides the country's diplomatic and defense affairs but also has powerful consequences for domestic economic conditions through decisions on trade and the protection and promotion of American jobs and enterprise (Jacobs and Page 2005).

We also need to consider the impact of public policies, once enacted, on social stratification and further political activities. ★ ★ ★ Dramatic changes in private markets have increased economic inequality in a number of advanced industrialized nations—yet nations differ considerably in the degree to which, and ways in which, they use public policies to modify or counteract market-generated disparities. Governments in Canada, Germany, Sweden, France, and other U.S. trading partners have limited increases in economic inequality and built floors under the least privileged through the use of regulations and tax policy as well as social programs. By contrast, government policies and actions in the United States have been especially responsive to the values and interests of the most privileged Americans and therefore have often not undertaken active and effective steps to mute or offset market inequalities.

What the U.S. government does—and does not do—about economic disparities and insecurities influences political participation as well as social outcomes. Research shows that broad social programs such as the G.I. Bill of 1944 and the Social Security Act (as updated through the early 1970s) not only distributed economic benefits, but also encouraged ordinary citizens to increase their political participation (Mettler 2002; Campbell 2003). Recent social programs are likely to be narrowly targeted and to work in complex and relatively invisible ways through the tax code. Such programs may do less than major social programs of the past to boost the political engagement of ordinary Americans, especially those who are not elderly.

The effects of government inaction in the face of rising market-generated inequality are particularly evident in the economic and political conditions of less privileged minorities and women. One of the great stories of the past century in the United States has been the reduction of overt discrimination that once excluded millions of Americans from the core of politi-cal, economic, and social life. Well-educated women and minorities have benefited greatly from the removal of discriminatory barriers. In recent years, however, the reduction of overt discrimination has been countered by growing gaps in income and wealth, which have undermined economic progress and political inclusion for many, nonelite African Americans, Latinos, and women, even as equal opportunity and citizenship is also imperiled for many white men. Subsequent chapters demonstrate a general pattern of stalled progress and persistent political disparities: The political playing field remains highly unequal, and the immediate gains of the rights revolution have not yielded a sustained widening of political voice and influence in the governing process.

[Elsewhere we] discuss many more developments and assess the contributions of many more factors than we have been able to mention in this brief overview. Furthermore, and as these snapshots suggest, [we do] not present a simple picture of the impact of widening economic disparities on U.S. politics and government. Some relationships are relatively direct. Individual participation is socially stratified, for reasons that are increasingly well understood. And in a period when monetary contributions to politicians, parties, and interest groups are more and more important, the ability to give large chunks of money equips the growing ranks of the most affluent with a potent mechanism to express individual voice. Less privileged citizens may (or may not) find ways to band together to give money as well as votes, but as individuals their clout is less.

Other ways in which rising economic disparities may matter are less clear-cut, however, because socioeconomic shifts often work in complex interaction with slowly changing political institutions or with other ongoing changes that cannot be reduced to economic trends. New information technologies, for example, may magnify the effects of individuals and groups that are economically privileged enough to deploy them intensively. And longstanding "checks and balances" built into U.S. political institutions might promote pluralism under some socioeconomic conditions, but further entrench privilege under others—especially if the majority needs new government initiatives to mitigate effects of rising economic inequality and insecurity.

Indeed, in the final analysis, rising economic inequalities may have served primarily to counteract otherwise equalizing influences. As we have suggested, stasis in the situation of many African Americans may have resulted from the ways in which relative economic losses for less-privileged people have undercut the undoubted democratic gains of the Civil Rights movement.

An overriding theme of this volume is examination of the interconnections among economic and social inequalities, politics and governance, and public policies. This [analysis] resists the all-too-common tendency of social science research to compartmentalize the study of American politics into discrete cubby holes (for research developments in political science see Task Force on Inequality and American Democracy 2004). We investigate the discrete aspects of American politics to assess the overall vitality and health of U.S. democracy in an age of rising inequality. Understanding the democratic political system requires persistent inves-

tigation into complex interrelationships with an eye toward consequences for society and polity.

The various ways in which rising inequality matters, either directly or indirectly, require careful unpacking with the benefit of the latest empirical research. ★ ★ ★ As the discussions of existing evidence and currently developed literatures make clear, the data we have to answer important questions are incomplete. Much additional theorizing and analysis remains for those who would unpack the complex, two-way relationships between socioeconomic change and politics. In our conclusion to this volume, we look toward the future, offering thoughts on the challenges that remain to be tackled by scholars determined to continue to probe the health and functioning of American democracy in an era of rising inequality.

‖ REFERENCES

Ansolabehere, Stephen, John M. Figueiredo, and James M. Snyder. 2003, "Why Is There So Little Money in U.S. Politics?" *Journal of Economic Perspectives* 17(1): 105–30.

Bartels, Larry. 2002. "Economic Inequality and Political Representation." Paper presented at the Annual Meeting of the American Political Science Association, Boston, Mass. Available at: http://www.princeton.edu/~bartels/papers (accessed April 20, 2005).

Berry, Jeffrey M. 1999. *The New Liberalism: The Rising Power of Citizen Groups.* Washington, D.C.: Brookings Institution Press.

Blendon, Robert J., John M. Bensons, Richard Morin, Drew E. Altman, Mollyann Brodie,

Marios Brossard, and Matt James. 1997. "Changing Attitudes in America." In *Why People Don't Trust Government,* edited by Joseph S. Nye Jr., Philip D. Zelikow, and David C. King. Cambridge, Mass.: Harvard University Press.

Brady, Henry E. 2004. "An Analytical Perspective on Participatory Inequality and Income Inequality." In *Social Inequality,* edited by Kathryn M. Neckerman. New York: Russell Sage Foundation.

Burtless, Gary. 1999. "Growing American Inequality: Sources and Remedies." In *Setting National Priorities: The 2000 Election and Beyond,* edited by Henry J. Aaron and Robert D. Reischauer. Washington, D.C.: Brookings Institution Press.

Campbell, Andrea Louise. 2003. *How Policies Make Citizens: Senior Political Activism and the American Welfare State.* Princeton, N.J.: Princeton University Press.

Committee for the Study of the American Electorate. 2004. "President Bush, Mobilization Drives, Propel Turnout to Post-1968 High." November. Available at: http://www.fairvote.org/reports/CSAE2004electionreport.pdf (accessed April 20, 2005).

Fiorina, Morris P. 1999. "Extreme Voices: A Dark Side of Civic Engagement." In *Civic Engagement in the United States,* edited by Theda Skocpol and Morris P. Fiorina. Washington, D.C., and New York: Brookings Institution Press and the Russell Sage Foundation.

Freeman, Richard, ed. 1994. *Working Under Different Rules.* A National Bureau of Economic Research project report. New York: Russell Sage Foundation.

———. 2004. "What, Me Vote?" In *Social Inequality,* edited by Kathryn M. Neckerman. New York: Russell Sage Foundation.

Gilens, Martin. 2003. "Unequal Responsiveness." Paper presented at conference on Inequality and American Democracy, Princeton University. November. Available at: http://www.princeton.edu/~csdp/events/pdfs/Gilens.pdf (accessed April 20, 2005).

Gopoian, J. David. 1984. "What Makes PACs Tick? An Analysis of the Allocation Patterns of Economic Interest Groups." *American Journal of Political Science* 28(2): 259–81.

Gottschalk, Peter. 1997. "Inequality Income Growth, and Mobility: The Basic Facts." *Journal of Economic Perspectives* 11(2): 21–40.

Hacker, Jacob S. 2002. *The Divided Welfare State: The Baffle over Public and Private Benefits in the United States.* New York: Cambridge University Press.

Hall, Richard L., and Frank W. Wayman. 1990. "Buying Time: Moneyed Interests and the Mobilization of Bias in Congressional Committees." *American Political Science Review* 84(3): 797–820.

Heclo, Hugh. 1974. *Modern Social Politics in Britain and Sweden.* New Haven, Conn.: Yale University Press.

Jacobs, Lawrence, and Benjamin Page. 2005. "Who Influences U.S. Foreign Policy Over Time?" *American Political Science Review* 99(1):107–24.

Kennickell, Arthur. 2003. "A Rolling Tide: Changes in the Distribution of Wealth in the U.S., 1989–2001." Federal Reserve Board,

September 2003. Available at: http://www.federalreserve.gov/pubs/oss/oss2/papers/concentration.2001.10.pdf (accessed April 20, 2005).

Kroszner, Randall S., and Thomas Stratmann. 1998. "Interest Group Competition and the Organization of Congress: Theory and Evidence from Financial Services Political Action Committees." *American Economic Review* 88(5): 1163–87.

Langbein, Laura, 1986. "Money and Access: Some Empirical Evidence." *Journal of Politics* 48(4): 1052–62.

Leighley, Jan, and Jonathan Nagler. 1992. "Socioeconomic Class Bias in Turnout, 1964–1988: The Voters Remain the Same." *American Political Science Review* 86(3): 725–36.

McDonald, Michael P., and Samuel Popkin. 2001. "The Myth of the Vanishing Voter." *American Political Science Review* 95(4): 963–74.

Mettler, Suzanne. 2002. "Bringing the State Back In to Civic Engagement: Policy Feedback Effects of the G.I. Bill for World War II Veterans." *American Political Science Review* 96(2): 351–65.

Michaels, Walter Benn. 2004. "Diversity's False Solace." *New York Times Magazine,* April 11: 12–14.

Mishel, Larry, Jared Bernstein, and Heather Boushey. 2003. *The State of Working America, 2002–2003.* Ithaca, N.Y.: Cornell University Press.

Nye, Joseph S., Jr., Philip D. Zelikow, and David C. King, eds. *Why People Don't Trust Government.* Cambridge, Mass.: Harvard University Press.

Oliver, Melvin, and Thomas Shapiro. 1997. *Black Wealth, White Wealth.* New York: Routledge.

Orren, Gary. 1997. "Fall from Grace: The Public's Loss of Faith in Government." In *Why People Don't Trust Government,* edited by Joseph S. Nye Jr., Philip D. Zelikow, and David C. King. Cambridge, Mass.: Harvard University Press.

Page, Benjamin I., and Robert Y. Shapiro. 1992. *The Rational Public: Fifty Years of Trends in Americans' Policy Preferences.* Chicago: University of Chicago Press.

Pierson, Paul. 1993. "When Effect Becomes Cause: Policy Feedback and Political Change." *World Politics* 45(4): 595–628.

Piketty, Thomas, and Emmanuel Saez. 2003. "Income Inequality in the United States, 1913–1998." *Quarterly Journal of Economics* 118(1):1–39.

Radcliff, Benjamin, and Patricia Davis. 2000. "Labor Organization and Electoral Participation in Industrial Democracies." *American Journal of Political Science* 44(1):132–41.

Schier, Steven E. 2000. *By Invitation Only: The Rise of Exclusive Politics in the United States.* Pittsburgh, Penn.: University of Pittsburgh Press.

Skocpol, Theda. 2003. *Diminished Democracy: From Membership to Management in American Civic Life.* Norman: University of Oklahoma Press.

———. 2004a. "Voice and Inequality: The Transformation of American Civic Democracy." *Perspectives on Politics* 2(1): 3–20.

———. 2004b. "Civic Transformation and Inequality in the Contemporary United States." In *Social Inequality,* edited by Kathryn M. Neckerman. New York: Russell Sage Foundation.

Skrentny, John D. 2002. *The Minority Rights Revolution*. Cambridge, Mass.: Harvard University Press.

Smeeding, Timothy. 2004. "Public Policy, Economic Inequality, and Poverty: The United States in Comparative Perspective." Revised version of paper presented at the conference on Inequality and American Politics, Maxwell School, Syracuse University (February). Available at: http://www-cpr.maxwell.syr.edu/faculty/smeeding/pdf/campbell%20paper_5.17.04.pdf (accessed April 21, 2005).

Task Force on Inequality and American Democracy. 2004. "American Democracy in an Age of Rising Inequality." *Perspectives on Politics* 2(4): 651–66.

Verba, Sidney, Kay Lehman Schlozman, and Henry E. Brady. 1995. *Voice and Equality: Civic Voluntarism in American Politics*. Cambridge, Mass.: Harvard University Press.

Weakliem, David L., Robert Andersen, and Anthony F. Heath. 2003. "The Directing Power? A Comparative Study of Public Opinion and Income Distribution." Unpublished paper, University of Connecticut, Storrs.

Wright, John R. 1985. "PACs, Contributions, and Roll Calls: An Organizational Perspective." *American Political Science Review* 79(2): 400–14.

———. 1990. "Contributions, Lobbying, and Committee Voting in the U.S. House of Representatives." *American Political Science Review* 84(2): 417–38.

59

How the Middle Class Is Injured by Gains at the Top*

ROBERT H. FRANK

Suppose you had to choose between two worlds: World A, where you earn $110,000 a year and everyone else earns $200,000, and World B, where you earn $100,000 and everyone else earns $85,000.

Most neoclassical economists would have an easy time deciding. Neoclassical economics, long the dominant wing of the profession, tends to equate personal well-being with absolute income, or purchasing power. By that standard, World A wins hands down: even as the low earner on the totem pole, you would be doing 10 percent better there than in World B. In other words, you could have 10 percent more food, clothes, housing, airplane travel, or whatever else you wanted.

And yet, when the choice is put to American survey respondents, many seem torn, and most actually end up opting for World B. Is this just an amusing example of human irrationality? Are people so preoccupied with status and rank that they lose sight of objective reality? Or could it be the neoclassical economists who have missed something?

---

* First published in 2005; from *Inequality Matters: The Growing Economic Divide in America and Its Poisonous Consequences*, edited by James Lardner and David A. Smith.

For a glimpse of the possible downside of World A, it may help to consider Wendy Williams, a lanky, soft-spoken adolescent living in a trailer park in an upscale Illinois community during the boom years of the late 1990s. Every morning, according to reporter Dirk Johnson's account in the *New York Times*, Wendy shares a school bus ride with a group of more affluent classmates, who "strut past in designer clothes" while she sits silently, "wearing a cheap belt and rummage-sale slacks:" She is known as Rabbit because of a slight overbite—"a humiliation she once begged her mother and father to avoid by sending her to an orthodontist."

Most children have been counseled not to measure their financial circumstances against the circumstances of others. That advice can sometimes be easier to dispense than to follow, however. Wendy Williams makes a game effort to bridge the socioeconomic gap. "That's a really awesome shirt," she tells one of the other girls on the bus. "Where did you get it?"

But teenagers can be cruel. "Why would you want to know?" the other girl replies with a laugh.

It is odd that economists who call themselves disciples of Adam Smith should be so reluctant to introduce the psychological costs of inequality into their discussions. Smith himself recognized such concerns as a basic component of human nature. Writing more than two centuries ago, he introduced the important idea that local consumption standards influence the goods and services that people consider essential—the "necessaries," as Smith called them:

By necessaries I understand not only the commodities which are indispensably necessary for the support of life, but whatever the custom of the country renders it indecent for creditable people, even of the lowest order, to be without. A linen shirt, for example, is, strictly speaking, not a necessary of life. The Greeks and Romans lived, I suppose, very comfortably though they had no linen. But in the present times, through the greater part of Europe, a creditable day-labourer would be ashamed to appear in public without a linen shirt, the want of which would be supposed to denote that disgraceful degree of poverty which, it is presumed, nobody can well fall into without extreme bad conduct. Custom, in the same manner, has rendered leather shoes a necessary of life in England. The poorest creditable person of either sex would be ashamed to appear in public without them.

The absolute standard of living in the United States today is of course vastly higher than it was in Adam Smith's eighteenth-century Scotland. And higher living standards create a whole new set of necessaries. For a teenager in an affluent suburb, it is no stretch to imagine that these might include straight teeth. Looking good is an irreducibly relative concept; but it is one, we all know, that sometimes has objective consequences. No one would accuse you of foolish vanity if you went to a job interview with IBM wearing your best suit and tie rather than a tank top and jeans. Impressions count.

And impressions are not the only reason to be conscious of other people's choices. Think about buying a car. Thirty years ago, a middle-class family with kids might have been content with a four-door sedan of modest size. Imagine the grown-up child of that family, with children of her own, facing the same decision. She might be tempted to say, "A 2,500-pound sedan was good enough for my mom, so it's good enough for me." But on today's roads, surrounded by 6,000-pound Lincoln Navigators and 7,500-pound Ford Excursions, a 2,500-pound Honda Civic doesn't simply look a lot smaller and frailer than it did in 1975. It's objectively more dangerous. The odds of being killed in a collision rise roughly fivefold if you're driving such a vehicle and the other party sits at the helm of a Ford Excursion. In sheer self-defense, you might want a bulkier—and costlier—car than Mom's.

In the housing market, as in the automobile market, you don't have to be a spendthrift to feel pressured into overspending. Imagine a young couple who buy a house in a prosperous suburb, taking on mortgage payments that commit them to working nights and weekends and leave them with no margin of safety in the event of a health or professional setback. We might consider them reckless if they assumed these burdens just to get a few hundred extra square feet of floor space, a Jacuzzi, and the bragging rights that go with an address in Pinnacle Heights. But if, in addition to spacious houses, Pinnacle Heights offered an outstanding school system for their children, we would probably judge them less harshly.

The housing and car markets present two possible instances of what I have termed a "spending cascade," in which top earners—the people who have fared the best in the current economy—initiate a process that leads to increased expenditures on down the line, even among those whose incomes have not risen. Logic suggests that growing inequality of income and wealth might encourage additional spending in this way. Empirical evidence suggests it, too.

Two small midwestern cities, Danville, Indiana, and Mount Vernon, Illinois, make the case pretty clearly. The median income in Mount Vernon was more than $10,000 higher than it was in Danville in the year 2000, but Danville's incomes were much more unequally distributed. In Danville, a family at the ninety-fifth percentile mark earned more than $141,000, while the equivalent family in Mount Vernon earned just over $83,000. Despite its much smaller median income, Danville's median house price was almost $131,000—more than double the Mount Vernon median. It turns out that Danville and Mount Vernon follow the pattern of other American communities: median house prices depend not only on median incomes, but also on income inequality.

The Danville–Mount Vernon story illustrates how the huge income gains accruing to top earners in the United States in recent decades have imposed costs on those in the middle. Of course, nobody is *forced* to buy an expensive house or car. But inequality may be creating an increasing number of situations in which we are forced to choose between unpleasant alternatives. And through a series of decisions that make good sense for us individually, we appear to be moving in a direction that makes little sense for us as a society.

The family that overspends on housing at the cost of heavy debt, long working hours, financial anxiety, and a scarcity of family time is not just a familiar anecdote, but also a fair description of where middle-class America as a whole has been going. The median size of a newly constructed house in the United States was 1,600 square feet in 1980. By 2001, it was more than 2,100 square feet. Meanwhile, commutes were getting longer and roads more congested, savings rates were plummeting, personal bankruptcy filings were climbing to an all-time high, and there was at least a widespread perception of a sharp decline in employment security and autonomy.

Happiness is not as easy to measure as house size. Nevertheless, there is evidence that house size doesn't do much for it. If you move from a 2,000- to a 3,000-square-foot house, you may be pleased, even excited, at first. In time, however, you are likely to adapt and simply consider the larger house the norm—especially if other houses have been growing, too. Yet the sacrifices we make in order to pay for bigger houses often take a lasting toll.

One strategy of cash-strapped families is to limit their mortgage payments by commuting from longer distances. Your adaptation to a long trip from home to work through heavy traffic will probably not be as complete as your adaptation to a bigger house. Even after a long period, most people experience long commutes as stressful. In this respect, the effect is similar to that of exposure to noise and other irritants. A large increase in background noise at a constant, steady level seems less intrusive as time passes; nonetheless, prolonged exposure produces lasting elevations in blood pressure. If the noise is not only loud but intermittent, people remain conscious of their heightened irritability even after extended periods, and their symptoms of central nervous system distress become more pronounced. This pattern has been seen, for example, in a study of people living next

to a newly opened highway. Interviewed four months after the highway opened, 21 percent of the residents said they were not annoyed by the noise; that figure dropped to 16 percent when the same residents were interviewed a year later.

The prolonged experience of commuting stress is also known to suppress immune function and shorten longevity. Even daily spells in traffic as brief as fifteen minutes have been linked to significant elevations of blood glucose and cholesterol, and to declines in blood coagulation time—factors that are positively associated with cardiovascular disease. Commuting by automobile is also linked with the incidence of various cancers, especially cancer of the lung (possibly because of heavier exposure to exhaust fumes). The incidence of these and other illnesses rises with the length of commute, and is significantly lower among those who commute by bus or rail, and lower still among noncommuters. Finally, the risk of death and injury from accidents varies positively with the length of commute and is higher for those who commute by car than for those who use public transport.

Among rush-hour travelers, the amount of time wasted in stalled traffic increased from 16 hours to 62 hours per year between 1982 and 2000; the daily window of time during which travelers might experience congestion increased from 4.5 hours to 7 hours; and the volume of roadways where travel is congested grew from 34 percent to 58 percent. The Federal Highway Administration predicts that the extra time spent driving because of delays will rise from 2.7 billion vehicle hours in 1985 to 11.9 billion in 2005.

If long commutes are so hazardous, why do people put up with them? It may be because they have unconsciously allowed their spending decisions to lean toward conspicuous consumption (in the form of larger houses) and away from what, for want of a better term, I call "inconspicuous consumption"—freedom from traffic congestion, time with family and friends, vacation time, and a variety of favorable job characteristics.

Can we attribute this to rising inequality? Although there is no simple way to prove or disprove the hypothesis, it is consistent with a substantial body of research. In a 2005 study, for example, Bjornulf Ostvik-White, Adam Levine, and I found that areas with higher inequality—specifically, with higher ratios between the income of households in the ninety-fifth and fiftieth percentiles—had significantly higher personal bankruptcy rates, divorce rates, and average commute times. Analyzing international data over time, Samuel Bowles and Yongjin Park found that total hours worked were positively associated with higher inequality.

The wealthy are spending more now simply because they have more money. But their spending has led others to spend more as well, including middle-income families. If the real incomes of middle-class families have grown only slightly, how have they financed this additional consumption? In part by working longer hours, but mainly by saving less and borrowing more. American families carry an average of more than $9,000 in credit card debt, and personal bankruptcy filings are occurring at seven times the 1980 rate. Medical expenses account for a significant share of that debt. Some forty-five million Americans have no health insurance— five million more than when Bill Clinton took office. The national personal savings rate was negative in several recent years, including a few of the peak years of the 1990s economic boom. Millions of Americans now face the prospect of retirement at sharply reduced living standards. Increased spending by top earners may not be the sole cause of financial distress among middle-income families. But it has clearly been an important contributor.

Spending cascades are also an indirect cause of the median voter's growing reluctance to support expenditures for what were once considered essential public goods and services. Nationwide, more than 50 percent of our major roads and highways are in "backlog," which means they will cost from two to five times as much to repair as those that are maintained on time. We face an $84 billion backlog in the repair and replacement of the nation's bridges. Between blown tires, damaged wheels and axles, bent frames, misaligned front ends, destroyed mufflers, twisted suspension systems, and other problems, potholes on American roads cause an average of $120 worth of damage per vehicle each year, and untold numbers of deaths and injuries.

Americans spend less than we once did to assure the safety of the food we eat. Despite growing instances of contamination from E. coli 0157, listeria, and other highly toxic bacteria, the Food and Drug Administration had resources sufficient to conduct only five thousand inspections of meat-processing plants in 1997, down from twenty-one thousand in 1981. And although food imports have doubled since the 1980s, FDA inspections of imports have fallen by half. Exposure to E. coli alone causes an estimated twenty thousand infections a year, and between two hundred and five hundred deaths.

We have been woefully slow to upgrade our municipal water-supply systems. The century-old pipes in many systems are typically cast-iron fittings joined by lead solder. As these conduits age and rust, lead, manganese, and other toxic metals leach into our drinking water. According to one estimate, some forty-five million of us are currently served by water systems that deliver potentially dangerous levels of toxic metals, pesticides, and parasites.

We have grown reluctant to invest in cleaner air. The Environmental Protection Agency recently proposed a tightening of standards for concentrations of ozone and particulate matter that would prevent more than 140,000 cases of acute respiratory distress each year and save more than fifteen thousand lives. The EPA proposal drew intense and immediate political fire, and bills were introduced in both houses of Congress to repeal the new standards, which have yet to be implemented.

Although spending on public education has not declined relative to historical norms, here, too, important inputs have not kept pace. For example, the national average starting salary for primary- and secondary-school teachers fell from 118 percent of the average salary of college graduates in 1963 to only 97 percent in 1994, a period that saw a significant decline in the average SAT scores of people who chose public-school teaching as a profession. And although we know that children learn more effectively in small classes than in large ones, we have offered fiscal distress as the reason for allowing class

sizes to grow steadily larger during that same period.

We have slashed funding not only for services that benefit middle- and upper-income families, but also for the Head Start program, the school lunch program, homeless shelters, inner city hospitals, and a host of other low-overhead programs that make life more bearable for the poor. We cut these programs not because they did not work, not because they destroyed incentives, but because the median voter decided that he couldn't afford them. And that perception was, in large part, a consequence of the growing income gap.

When we choose between conspicuous and inconspicuous consumption, we confront a conflict between individual and social welfare that is structurally identical to that of a military arms race. We become like the superpowers during the heyday of the Cold War, robotically obedient to the doctrine of mutually assured destruction (with its memorable acronym MAD). The person who stays at the office two hours longer each day to afford a house in a better school district has no conscious intention of making it more difficult for others to achieve the same goal. But that is an inescapable consequence of her action. The best response available to others may be to work longer hours as well, thereby preserving their current positions. Yet the ineluctable mathematical logic of musical chairs assures that only 10 percent of all children can occupy top-decile school seats, no matter how many hours their parents work.

A family can choose how much of its own money to spend, but it cannot choose how much others spend. Buying a smaller-than-average vehicle means a greater risk of dying in an accident. Spending less on an interview suit means a greater risk of not landing the best job. Spending less than others on a house means a greater risk of sending your children to inferior schools. Yet when all spend more on heavier cars, more finely tailored suits, and larger houses, the results tend to be mutually offsetting, just as when all nations spend more on missiles and bombs. Spending less frees up money for other pressing uses, but only if everyone does it.

If it is hard for nations to unwind from such a spiral, it is surely no easier for individuals. But the first steps are probably the same: We need to look at ourselves. We need to think about our actions in relation to their consequences. We need to talk.

60

Development as Freedom★

AMARTYA SEN

Development can be seen, it is argued here, as a process of expanding the real freedoms that people enjoy. Focusing on human freedoms contrasts with narrower views of development, such as identifying development with the growth of gross national product, or with the rise in personal incomes, or with industrialization, or with technological advance, or with social modernization. Growth of GNP or of individual incomes can, of course, be very important as *means* to expanding the freedoms enjoyed by the members of the society. But freedoms depend also on other determinants, such as social and economic arrangements (for example, facilities for education and health care) as well as political and civil rights (for example, the liberty to participate in public discussion and scrutiny). Similarly, industrialization or technological progress or social modernization can substantially contribute to expanding human freedom, but freedom depends on other influences as well. If freedom is what development advances, then there is a major argument for concentrat-

---

★ First published in 1999.

ing on that overarching objective, rather than on some particular means, or some specially chosen list of instruments. Viewing development in terms of expanding substantive freedoms directs attention to the ends that make development important, rather than merely to some of the means that, inter alia, play a prominent part in the process.

Development requires the removal of major sources of unfreedom: poverty as well as tyranny, poor economic opportunities as well as systematic social deprivation, neglect of public facilities as well as intolerance or overactivity of repressive states. Despite unprecedented increases in overall opulence, the contemporary world denies elementary freedoms to vast numbers—perhaps even the majority—of people. Sometimes the lack of substantive freedoms relates directly to economic poverty, which robs people of the freedom to satisfy hunger, or to achieve sufficient nutrition, or to obtain remedies for treatable illnesses, or the opportunity to be adequately clothed or sheltered, or to enjoy clean water or sanitary facilities. In other cases, the unfreedom links closely to the lack of public facilities and social care, such as the absence of epidemiological programs, or of organized arrangements for health care or educational facilities, or of effective institutions for the maintenance of local peace and order. In still other cases, the violation of freedom results directly from a denial of political and civil liberties by authoritarian regimes and from

imposed restrictions on the freedom to participate in the social, political and economic life of the community.

★ ★ ★

POVERTY AS CAPABILITY DEPRIVATION

In analyzing social justice, there is a strong case for judging individual advantage in terms of the capabilities that a person has, that is, the substantive freedoms he or she enjoys to lead the kind of life he or she has reason to value. In this perspective, poverty must be seen as the deprivation of basic capabilities rather than merely as lowness of incomes, which is the standard criterion of identification of poverty.[1] The perspective of capability-poverty does not involve any denial of the sensible view that low income is clearly one of the major causes of poverty, since lack of income can be a principal reason for a person's capability deprivation.

Indeed, inadequate income is a strong predisposing condition for an impoverished life. If this is accepted, what then is all this fuss about, in seeing poverty in the capability perspective (as opposed to seeing it in terms of the standard income-based poverty assessment)? The claims in favor of the capability approach to poverty are, I believe, the following.

1. Poverty can be sensibly identified in terms of capability deprivation; the approach

---

[1] This view of poverty is more fully developed in my *Poverty and Famines* (Oxford: Clarendon Press, 1981) and *Resources, Values and Development* (Cambridge, Mass.: Harvard University Press, 1984), and also in Jean Drèze and Amartya Sen, *Hunger and Public Action* (Oxford: Clarendon Press, 1989), and in Sudhir Anand and Amartya Sen, "Concepts of Human Development and Poverty: A Multidimensional Perspective," in *Human Development Papers 1997* (New York: UNDP, 1997).

concentrates on deprivations that are *intrinsically* important (unlike low income, which is only *instrumentally* significant).

2. There are influences on capability deprivation—and thus on real poverty—*other* than lowness of income (income is not the only instrument in generating capabilities).

3. The instrumental relation between low income and low capability is *variable* between different communities and even between different families and different individuals (the impact of income on capabilities is contingent and conditional).

★ ★ ★

What the capability perspective does in poverty analysis is to enhance the understanding of the nature and causes of poverty and deprivation by shifting primary attention away from *means* (and one particular means that is usually given exclusive attention, viz., income) to *ends* that people have reason to pursue, and, correspondingly, to the *freedoms* to be able to satisfy these ends. The examples briefly considered here illustrate the additional discernment that results from this basic extension. The deprivations are seen at a more fundamental level—one closer to the informational demands of social justice. Hence the relevance of the perspective of capability-poverty.

INCOME POVERTY AND CAPABILITY POVERTY

While it is important to distinguish conceptually the notion of poverty as capability inade-quacy from that of poverty as lowness of income, the two perspectives cannot but be related, since income is such an important means to capabilities. And since enhanced capabilities in leading a life would tend, typically, to expand a person's ability to be more productive and earn a higher income, we would also expect a connection going from capability improvement to greater earning power and not only the other way around.

The latter connection can be particularly important for the removal of income poverty. It is not only the case that, say, better basic education and health care improve the quality of life directly; they also increase a person's ability to earn an income and be free of income-poverty as well. The more inclusive the reach of basic education and health care, the more likely it is that even the potentially poor would have a better chance of overcoming penury.

The importance of this connection was a crucial point of focus of my recent work on India, done jointly with Jean Drèze, dealing with economic reforms.[2] In many ways, the economic reforms have opened up for the Indian people economic opportunities that were suppressed by overuse of control and by the limitations of what had been called the "license Raj."[3] And yet the opportunity to make use of the new possibilities is not independent of the social preparation that different sections of the Indian community have. While the reforms were overdue, they could be much more productive if the social facilities were there to support the economic opportunities for all sections of the community.

---

2 Jean Drèze and Amartya Sen, *India: Economic Development and Social Opportunity* (Delhi: Oxford University Press, 1995).

3 See the collection of papers in Isher Judge Ahluwalia and I.M.D. Little, eds., *India's Economic Reforms and Development:* *Essays for Manmohan Singh* (Delhi: Oxford University Press, 1998). See also Vijay Joshi and Ian Little, *Indian Economic Reforms, 1991–2001* (Delhi: Oxford University Press, 1996).

Indeed, many Asian economies—first Japan, and then South Korea, Taiwan, Hong Kong, and Singapore, and later post-reform China and Thailand and other countries in East Asia and Southeast Asia—have done remarkably well in spreading the economic opportunities through an adequately supportive social background, including high levels of literacy, numeracy, and basic education; good general health care; completed land reforms; and so on. The lesson of opening of the economy and the importance of trade has been more easily learned in India than the rest of the message from the same direction of the rising sun.[4]

India is, of course, highly diverse in terms of human development, with some regions (most notably, Kerala) having much higher levels of education, health care and land reform than others (most notably, Bihar, Uttar Pradesh, Rajasthan and Madhya Pradesh). The limitations have taken different forms in the different states. It can be argued that Kerala has suffered from what were until recently fairly anti-market policies, with deep suspicion of market-based economic expansion without control. So its human resources have not been as well used in spreading economic growth as they could have been with a more complementary economic strategy, which is now being attempted. On the other hand, some of the northern states have suffered from low levels of social development, with varying degrees of control and market-based opportunities. The need for seizing the relevance of complementarity is very strong in remedying the diverse drawbacks.

It is, however, interesting that despite the rather moderate record in economic growth, Kerala seems to have had a faster rate of reduction in income poverty than any other state in India.[5] While some states have reduced income poverty through high economic growth (Punjab is the most notable example of that), Kerala has relied a great deal on expansion of basic education, health care and equitable land distribution for its success in reducing penury.

While these connections between income poverty and capability poverty are worth emphasizing, it is also important not to lose sight of the basic fact that the reduction of income poverty alone cannot possibly be the ultimate motivation of antipoverty policy. There is a danger in seeing poverty in the narrow terms of income deprivation, and then justifying investment in education, health care and so forth on the ground that they are good means to the end of reducing income poverty. That would be a confounding of ends and means. The basic foundational issues force us, for reasons already discussed, toward understanding poverty and deprivation in terms of lives people can actually lead and the freedoms they do actually have. The expansion of human capabilities fits directly into these basic considerations. It so happens that the enhancement of human capabilities also tends to go with an expansion of productivities and earning power. That connection establishes an important indirect linkage through which capability improvement helps both directly and indirectly in enriching human lives and in making human deprivations

---

4 These arguments are more fully developed in Drèze and Sen, *India: Economic Development and Social Opportunity* (1995).

5 See G. Datt, *Poverty in India and Indian States: An Update* (Washington, D.C.: International Food Policy Research Institute, 1997). See also World Bank, *India: Achievements and Challenges in Reducing Poverty,* report no. 16483 IN, May 27, 1997 (see particularly figure 2.3).

more rare and less acute. The instrumental connections, important as they are, cannot replace the need for a basic understanding of the nature and characteristics of poverty.

★ ★ ★

UNEMPLOYMENT AND CAPABILITY DEPRIVATION

That the judgments of inequality in the space of incomes can be quite different from those related to important capabilities can easily be illustrated with examples of some practical importance. In the European context, this contrast is particularly significant because of the wide prevalence of unemployment in contemporary Europe.[6] The loss of income caused by unemployment can, to a considerable extent, be compensated by income support (including unemployment benefits), as it typically is in Western Europe. If income loss were all that were involved in unemployment, then that loss could be to a great extent erased—for the individuals involved—by income support (there is, of course, the further issue of social costs of

fiscal burden and incentive effects involved in this compensation). If, however, unemployment has other serious effects on the lives of the individuals, causing deprivation of other kinds, then the amelioration through income support would be to that extent limited. There is plenty of evidence that unemployment has many far-reaching effects other than loss of income, including psychological harm, loss of work motivation, skill and self-confidence, increase in ailments and morbidity (and even mortality rates), disruption of family relations and social life, hardening of social exclusion and accentuation of racial tensions and gender asymmetries.[7]

Given the massive scale of unemployment in contemporary European economies, the concentration on income inequality only can be particularly deceptive. Indeed, it can be argued that at this time the massive level of European unemployment constitutes at least as important an issue of inequality, in its own right, as income distribution itself. An exclusive focus on income inequality tends to give the impression that Western Europe has done very much better than the United States in keeping inequality down and in avoiding the kind of

---

6 In my paper "Inequality, Unemployment and Contemporary Europe" (presented at the Lisbon conference on "Social Europe" of the Calouste Gulbenkian Foundation, May 5–7, 1997, published in *International Labour Review,* 1997), I have discussed the relevance of this contrast for contemporary policy issues in Europe. The importance that the unemployed themselves attach to the loss of freedom and capability as a result of unemployment is illuminatingly analyzed (with Belgian data) by Eric Schokkaert and L. Van Ootegem, "Sen's Concept of Living Standards Applied to the Belgian Unemployed," *Recherches Economiques de Louvain 56* (1990).

7 See the literature cited in my "Inequality, Unemployment and Contemporary Europe" (1997). On the psychological and other "social harms" of unemployment, see Robert Solow, "Mass

Unemployment as a Social Problem" in *Choice, Welfare and Development,* edited by K. Basu, P. Pattanaik and K. Suzumura (Oxford: Clarendon Press, 1995), and A. Goldsmith, J. R. Veum and W Darity Jr., "The Psychological Impact of Unemployment and Joblessness," *Journal of Socio-Economics* 25 (1996), among other contributors. See also the related literature on "social exclusion"; good introductions to the literature can be found in Gerry Rodgers, Charles Gore and J. B. Figueiredo, eds., *Social Exclusion: Rhetoric, Reality, Responses* (Geneva: International Institute for Labour Studies, 1995); Charles Gore et al., *Social Exclusion and Anti-Poverty Policy* (Geneva: International Institute for Labour Studies, 1997); Arjan de Haan and Simon Maxwell, *Poverty and Social Exclusion in North and South,* special number, *Institute of Development Studies Bulletin* 29 (January 1998).

increase in income inequality that the United States has experienced. In the space of incomes, Europe does indeed have a clearly better record both in terms of levels and trends of inequality, as is brought out by the careful investigation reported in the OECD (Organization for Economic Cooperation and Development) study prepared by A. B. Atkinson, Lee Rainwater and Timothy Smeeding.[8] Not only are the usual measures of income inequality higher in the United States than is the case, by and large, on the European side of the Atlantic, but also the U.S. income inequality has gone up in a way that has not happened in most countries in Western Europe.

And yet if we shift our gaze from income to unemployment, the picture is very different. Unemployment has risen dramatically in much of Western Europe, whereas there has been no such trend in the United States. For example, in the period 1965–1973, the unemployment rate was 4.5 percent in the United States, while Italy had 5.8 percent, France 2.3 percent, and West Germany below 1 percent. By now all three—Italy, France, and Germany—have unemployment rates that hover around 10 to 12 percent, whereas the U.S. unemployment rate is still between 4 and 5 percent. If unemployment batters lives, then that must somehow be taken into account in the analysis of economic

inequality. The comparative trends in *income* inequality give Europe an excuse to be smug, but that complacency can be deeply misleading if a broader view is taken of inequality.[9]

The contrast between Western Europe and the United States raises another interesting—and in some ways a more general—question. American social ethics seems to find it possible to be very non-supportive of the indigent and the impoverished, in a way that a typical Western European, reared in a welfare state, finds hard to accept. But the same American social ethics would find the double-digit levels of unemployment, common in Europe, to be quite intolerable. Europe has continued to accept worklessness—and its increase—with remarkable equanimity. Underlying this contrast is a difference in attitudes toward social and individual responsibilities, to which I shall return.

HEALTH CARE AND MORTALITY: AMERICAN AND EUROPEAN SOCIAL ATTITUDES

The inequality between different racial groups in the United States has received considerable attention recently. For example, in the space of incomes African Americans are decidedly poorer than American whites. This is very

8 A. B. Atkinson, Lee Rainwater and Timothy Smeeding, *Income Distribution in OECD Countries* (Paris: OECD, 1996).

9 The need for new policy initiatives is particularly strong at this time. See Jean-Paul Fitoussi and R. Rosanvallon, *Le Nouvel âge des inégalités* (Paris: Sevil, 1996); Edmund S. Phelps, *Rewarding Work: How to Restore Participation and Self-Support to Free Enterprise* (Cambridge, Mass.: Harvard University Press, 1997). See also Paul Krugman, *Technology, Trade and Factor Prices,* NBER Working Paper no. 5355 (Cambridge,

Mass.: National Bureau of Economic Research, 1995); Stephen Nickell, "Unemployment and Labor Market Rigidities: Europe versus North America," *Journal of Economics Perspectives* II (1997); Richard Layard, *Tackling Unemployment* (London: Macmillan, 1999); Jean-Paul Fitoussi, Francesco Giavezzi, Assar Lindbeck, Franco Modigliani, Beniamino Moro, Dennis J. Snower, Robert Solow and Klaus Zimmerman, "A Manifesto on Unemployment in the European Union," mimeographed, 1998.

often seen as an example of *relative* deprivation of African Americans within the nation, but not compared with poorer people in the rest of the world. Indeed, in comparison with the population of third world countries, African Americans may well be a great many times richer in terms of incomes, even after taking note of price differences. Seen this way, the deprivation of the American blacks seems to pale to insignificance in the international perspective.

But is income the right space in which to make such comparisons? What about the basic capability to live to a mature age, without succumbing to premature mortality? ★ ★ ★ In terms of that criterion the African American men fall well behind the immensely poorer men of China, or the Indian state of Kerala —and also of Sri Lanka, Costa Rica, Jamaica and many other poor economies. It is sometimes presumed that the remarkably high death rates of African Americans apply only to men, and again only to younger men, because of the prevalence of violence. Death from violence is indeed high among young black men, but this is by no means the whole story. Indeed, black women too fall not only behind white women in the United States but also behind Indian women in Kerala, and come very close to falling behind Chinese women as well. ★ ★ ★ American black *men* continue to lose ground vis-à-vis the Chinese and the Indians over the years—well past the younger ages when death from violence is common. More explanation is needed than violent deaths can provide.

Indeed, even if we take higher age groups (say, that between thirty-five and sixty-four years), there is evidence of enormously greater mortality for black men vis-à-vis white men, and black women vis-à-vis white women. And these differentials are not wiped out by adjustment for income differences. In fact, one of the more careful medical studies related to the 1980s shows that the black-white mortality differential remains remarkably large for women even after adjustment for income differentials. Figure 1 presents the ratios of the mortality rates of blacks and whites for the country as a whole (based on a sample survey).[10] While U.S. black men have 1.8 times the mortality rate of white men, black women have nearly three times the mortality of white women in this survey. And adjusted for differences in family income, while the mortality rate is 1.2 times higher for black men, it is as much as 2.2 times higher for black women. It, thus, appears that even after full note is taken of income levels, black women die young in very much larger proportions than white women in the contemporary United States.

The broadening of the informational base from income to the basic capabilities enriches our understanding of inequality and poverty in quite radical ways. When we focused on the ability to be employed and to have the associated advantages of employment, the European picture looked quite dismal, and as we turn our attention to the ability to survive, the picture of American inequality is remarkably intense. Underlying these differences and the respective

10 Data from M. W. Owen, S. M. Teutsch, D. E. Williamson and J. S. Marks, "The Effects of Known Risk Factors on the Excess Mortality of Black Adults in the United States," *Journal of the American Medical Association* 263, number 6 (February 9, 1990).

FIGURE 1 **MORTALITY RATE RATIOS OF BLACKS TO WHITES (AGED 35–54) ACTUAL AND ADJUSTED FOR FAMILY INCOME**

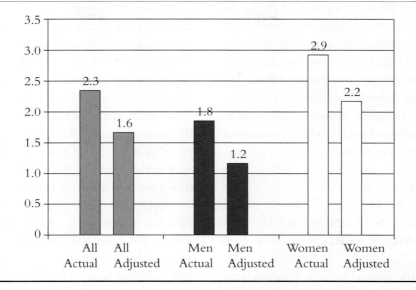

SOURCE: M. W. Owen, S. M. Teutsch, D. F. Williamson and J. S. Marks, "The Effects of Known Risk Factors on the Excess Mortality of Black Adults in the United States," *Journal of the American Medical Association* 263, no. 6 (February 9, 1990).

policy priorities associated with them, there may be an important contrast in the attitudes to social and individual responsibilities on the two sides of the Atlantic. In American official priorities, there is little commitment to providing basic health care for all, and it appears that many millions of people (in fact more than 40 million) are without any kind of medical coverage or insurance in the United States. While a considerable proportion of these uninsured people may have volitional reasons for not taking such insurance, the bulk of the uninsured do, in fact, lack the ability to have medical insurance because of economic circumstances, and in some cases because of preexisting medical conditions that private insurers shun. A comparable situation in Europe, where medical coverage is seen as a basic right of the citizen irrespective of means and independent of preexisting conditions, would very likely be politically intolerable. The limits on governmental support for the ill and the poor are too severe in the United States to be at all acceptable in Europe, and so are the social commitments toward public facilities varying from health care to educational arrangements, which the European welfare state takes for granted.

On the other hand, the double-digit unemployment rates that are currently tolerated in Europe would very likely be political dynamite in America, since unemployment rates of that magnitude would make a mockery of people's ability to help themselves. I believe no U.S. government could emerge unscathed from the doubling of the present level of unemployment, which incidentally would still keep the U.S. unemployment ratio below what it currently is in Italy or France or Germany. The nature of the respective political commitments—and lack thereof—would seem to differ fundamentally between Europe and America, and the differences relate closely to seeing inequality in terms of particular failures of basic capabilities.

POVERTY AND DEPRIVATION IN INDIA AND SUB-SAHARAN AFRICA

Extreme poverty is now heavily concentrated in two particular regions of the world: South Asia and sub-Saharan Africa. They have among the lowest levels of per capita income among all the regions, but that perspective does not give us an adequate idea of the nature and content of their respective deprivations, nor of their comparative poverty. If poverty is seen, instead, as the deprivation of basic capabilities, then a more illuminating picture can be obtained from information on aspects of life in these parts of the world.[11] A brief analysis is attempted below,

based on a joint study with Jean Drèze, and on two follow-up works of this author.[12]

Around 1991 there were fifty-two countries where the expectation of life at birth was below sixty years, and those countries had a combined population of 1.69 billion.[13] Forty-six of these countries are in South Asia and sub-Saharan Africa—only six are outside these two regions (viz. Afghanistan, Cambodia, Haiti, Laos, Papua New Guinea and Yemen), and the combined population of these six is only 3.5 percent of the total population (1.69 billion) of the fifty-two low-life-expectancy countries. The *whole* of South Asia except Sri Lanka (i.e., India, Pakistan, Bangladesh, Nepal and Bhutan) and the *whole* of sub-Saharan Africa except South Africa, Zimbabwe, Lesotho, Botswana, and a collection of tiny islands (e.g., Mauritius and the Seychelles) belong to the group of the other forty-six low-life-expectancy countries. Of course, there are variations *within* each country. Well-placed sections of the population of South Asia and sub-Saharan Africa enjoy high longevity, and as was discussed earlier, parts of the population of countries even with very high average life expectancy (such as the United States) may have survival problems that compare with conditions in the third world. (For example, American black men in U.S. cities

---

11 On this see my *Commodities and Capabilities* (1985). UNDP's *Human Development Reports* have provided important information and assessment regarding this way of seeing poverty, especially in *Human Development Report 1997*. See also Sudhir Anand and Amartya Sen, "Concepts of Human Development and Poverty: A Multidimensional Perspective" (1997).

12 Drèze and Sen, *India: Economic Development and Social Opportunity* (1995); Amartya Sen, "Hunger in the Modern World," Dr. Rajendra Prasad Memorial Lecture, New Delhi, June 1997; and "Entitlement Perspectives of Hunger," World Food Programme, 1997.

13 For sources of this information and of other information used in this section, see Drèze and Sen, *India: Economic Development and Social Opportunity* (1995), chapter 3 and statistical appendix. The picture here focuses on 1991, for reasons of data availability. There has, however, been a considerable increase in literacy just reported in the latest Indian National Sample Survey. There are also some important policy departures announced by some of the state governments, such as West Bengal and Madhya Pradesh.

such as New York, San Francisco, St. Louis, or Washington, D.C., have life expectancies well below our cut-off point of sixty years.[14]) But in terms of country averages, South Asia and sub-Saharan Africa do indeed stand out as the regions where short and precarious lives are concentrated in the contemporary world.

Indeed, India alone accounts for more than half of the combined population of these fifty-two deprived countries. It is not by any means the worst performer on average (in fact, average life expectancy in India is very close to sixty years and according to latest statistics has just risen above it), but there are large regional variations in living conditions *within* India. Some regions of India (with populations as large as—or larger than—most countries in the world) do as badly as any country in the world. India may do significantly better on average than, say, the worst performers (such as Ethiopia or Zaire, now renamed the Democratic Republic of Congo) in terms of life expectancy and other indicators, but there are large areas within India where life expectancy and other basic living conditions are not very different from those prevailing in these most-deprived countries.[15]

Table 1 compares the levels of *infant mortality* and *adult literacy* in the least-developed regions of sub-Saharan Africa and India.[16] The table presents the 1991 estimates of these two variables not only for India and sub-Saharan Africa as a whole (first and last rows), but also for the three worst-performing countries of sub-Saharan Africa, the three worst-performing Indian states, and the worst-performing districts of each of these three states. It is remarkable that there is no country in sub-Saharan Africa—or indeed in the world—where estimated infant mortality rates are as high as in the district of Ganjam in Orissa, or where the adult female literacy rate is as low as in the district of Barmer in Rajasthan. Each of these two districts, incidentally, has a larger population than Botswana or Namibia, and the combined population of the two is larger than that of Sierra Leone, Nicaragua or Ireland. Indeed, even entire states such as Uttar Pradesh (which has a population as large as that of Brazil or Russia) do not do much better than the worst-off among the sub-Saharan countries in terms of these basic indicators of living quality.[17]

It is interesting that if we take India and sub-Saharan Africa as a whole, we find that the two regions are not very different in terms of either adult literacy or infant mortality. They do differ in terms of life expectancy, though. The expectation of life in India around 1991 was about sixty years, while it was much below that

14 See C.J.L. Murray et al., *U.S. Patterns of Mortality by County and Race: 1965–1994* (Cambridge, Mass.: Harvard Center for Population and Developmental Studies, 1998), table 6d, p. 56.

15 The severity of India's failure to devote resources and efforts to social development is convincingly and movingly discussed by S. Guhan, "An Unfulfilled Vision," *IASSI Quarterly* 12 (1993). See also the collection of essays in his honor: Barbara Harriss-White and S. Subramanian, eds., *Illfare in India: Essays on India's Social Sector in Honour of S. Guhan* (Delhi: Sage, 1999).

16 This is taken from table 3.1 in Drèze and Sen, *India: Economic Development and Social Opportunity* (1995). See also Saraswati Raju, Peter J. Atkins, Naresh Kumas and Janet G. Townsend, *Atlas of Women and Men in India* (New Delhi: Kali for Women, 1999).

17 See also A. K. Shiva Kumar, "UNDP's Human Development Index: A Computation for Indian States," *Economic and Political Weekly,* October 12, 1991, and Rajah J. Chelliah and R. Sudarshan, eds., *Indian Poverty and Beyond: Human Development in India* (New Delhi: Social Science Press, 1999).

TABLE 1 **INDIA AND SUB-SAHARAN AFRICA: SELECTED COMPARISONS, 1991**

Infant mortality rate comparisons

Region	Population (millions)	Infant mortality rate (per 1,000) live births
INDIA	India	846.3	80
"Worst" three	Orissa	31.7	124
Indian states	Madhya Pradesh	66.2	117
	Uttar Pradesh	139.1	97
"Worst" district of	Ganjam (Orissa)	3.2	164
each of the "worst"	Tikamgarh (Madhya Pradesh)	0.9	152
Indian states	Hardoi (Uttar Pradesh)	2.7	129
"Worst" three	Mali	8.7	161
countries of sub-	Mozambique	16.1	149
Saharan Africa	Guinea-Bissau	1.0	148
SUB-SAHARAN AFRICA	Sub-Saharan Africa	488.9	104

Adult literacy rate comparisons

Region	Population (millions)	Adult literacy rate★ (female/male)
India	846.3	39/64
Rajasthan	44.0	20/55
Bihar	86.4	23/52
Uttar Pradesh	139.1	25/56
Barmer (Rajasthan)	1.4	8/37
Kishanganj (Bihar)	1.0	10/33
Bahraich (Uttar Pradesh)	2.8	11/36
Burkina Faso	9.2	10/31
Sierra Leone	4.3	12/35
Benin	4.8	17/35
Sub-Saharan Africa	488.9	40/63

NOTE: The age cutoff is 15 years for African figures, and 7 years for Indian figures. Note that in India, the 7+ literacy rate is usually higher than the 15+ literacy rate (e.g., the all-India 7+ literacy rate in 1981 was 43.6%, compared with 40.8% for the 15+ literacy rate).

SOURCE: J. Drèze and A. Sen, *India: Economic Development and Social Opportunity* (Delhi: Oxford University Press, 1995), table 3.1.

figure in sub-Saharan Africa (averaging about fifty-two years).[18] On the other hand, there is considerable evidence that the extent of undernourishment is much greater in India than in sub-Saharan Africa.[19]

There is thus an interesting pattern of contrast between India and sub-Saharan Africa in terms of the different criteria of (1) mortality and (2) nutrition. The survival advantage in favor of India can be brought out not only by comparisons of life expectancy, but also by contrasts of other mortality statistics. For example, the median age at death in India was about thirty-seven years around 1991; this compares with a weighted average (of median age at death) for sub-Saharan Africa of a mere five years.[20] Indeed, in as many as five African countries, the median age at death was observed to be three years or below. Seen in this perspective, the problem of premature mortality is enormously sharper in Africa than in India.

But we get a very different balance of disadvantages if we look at the prevalence of *undernourishment* in India via-à-vis Africa.

Calculations of general undernourishment are much higher in India than in sub-Saharan Africa on the average.[21] This is so despite the fact that it is India, rather than sub-Saharan Africa, that is self-sufficient in food. Indian "self-sufficiency" is based on the fulfillment of market demand, which can be, in normal years, easily met by domestically produced supply. But the market demand (based on purchasing power) understates the food needs. Actual undernourishment seems to be much higher in India than in sub-Saharan Africa. Judged in terms of the usual standards of retardation in weight for age, the proportion of undernourished children in Africa is 20 to 40 percent, whereas the proportion of undernourished children in India is a gigantic 40 to 60 percent.[22] About half of all Indian children are, it appears, chronically undernourished. While Indians live longer than sub-Saharan Africans, and have a median age at death much higher than Africans have, nevertheless there are many more undernourished children in India than sub-Saharan Africa—not just in absolute terms but also as a proportion of all children.[23] If we add to it the fact that gender

18 See World Bank, *World Development Report 1994* (Oxford: Oxford University Press, 1994), table 1, p. 163.

19 On this see the extensive comparison made by Peter Svedberg, *Poverty and Undernutrition: Theory and Measurement* (Oxford: Clarendon Press, 1997). Svedberg also scrutinizes alternative approaches to measuring undernutrition, and the conflicting pictures generated by different statistics, but arrives at a firm conclusion against India in terms of undernutrition vis-à-vis sub-Saharan Africa.

20 See World Bank, *World Development Report 1993* (Oxford: Oxford University Press, 1993), table A.3. Mortality rates have worsened with the spread of the AIDS epidemic.

21 See Svedberg, *Poverty and Undernutrition* (1997). See also C. Gopalan, ed., *Combating Undernutrition* (New Delhi: Nutrition Foundation of India, 1995).

22 See Nevin Scrimshaw, "The Lasting Damage of Early Malnutrition," in R. W. Fogel et al., *Ending the Inheritance of*

Hunger (Rome: World Food Programme, 1997). See also the papers of Robert W. Fogel, Cutberto Garza and Amartya Sen in the same volume.

23 This is not to deny that each of the standard criteria of undernourishment admits some room for doubt, but indicators based on health and physique do have some advantages over measures that simply look at food input. It is also possible to make use of the available medical and functional knowledge to improve the criteria to be used. On these and related issues, see Portha Dasgupta, *An Inquiry into Well-Being and Destitution* (Oxford: Clarendon Press, 1993); S. R. Osmani, ed., *Nutrition and Poverty* (Oxford: Clarendon Press, 1993); Scrimshaw, "The Lasting Damage of Early Malnutrition," and Robert W. Fogel, "The Global Struggle to Escape from Chronic Malnutrition since 1700," in Fogel et al., *Ending the Inheritance of Hunger* (1997).

bias at death is a substantial problem in India, but not so in sub-Saharan Africa, we see a picture that is much less favorable to India than to Africa.[24]

★ ★ ★

CONCLUDING REMARKS

Economists are sometimes criticized for concentrating too much on efficiency and too little on equity. There may be some ground for complaint here, but it must also be noted that inequality has received attention from economists throughout the history of this discipline. Adam Smith, who is often thought of as "the Father of Modern Economics," was deeply concerned with the gulf between the rich and the poor ★ ★ ★. Some of the social scientists and philosophers who are responsible for making inequality such a central subject of public attention (such as Karl Marx, John Stuart Mill, B. S. Rowntree and Hugh Dalton, to take writers belonging to very different general traditions) were, in terms of substantive involvement, devoted economists, no matter what else they might also have been. In recent years, economics of inequality as a subject has flourished, with major leadership coming from such writers as A. B. Atkinson.[25] This is not to deny that the focus on efficiency to the exclusion of other considerations is very evident in some works in economics, but economists as a group cannot be accused of neglecting inequality as a subject.

If there is a reason to grumble, it rests more on the relative importance that is attached, in much of economics, to inequality in a very narrow domain, viz., *income inequality*. This narrowness has the effect of contributing to the neglect of other ways of seeing inequality and equity, which has far-reaching bearing on the making of economic policy. Policy debates have indeed been distorted by overemphasis on income poverty and income inequality, to the neglect of deprivations that relate to other variables, such as unemployment, ill health, lack of education, and social exclusion. Unfortunately, the identification of economic inequality with income inequality is fairly common in economics, and the two are often seen as effectively synonymous. If you tell someone that you are working on economic inequality, it is quite standardly assumed that you are studying income distribution.

★ ★ ★

The distinction, however, between income inequality and economic inequality is important.[26] Many of the criticisms of economic egalitarianism as a value or a goal apply much more readily to the narrow concept of income inequality than they do to the broader notions of economic inequality. For example, giving a larger share of income to a person with more needs—say, due to a disability—can be seen as

---

24 See Svedberg, *Poverty and Undernutrition* and the literature cited there. See also United Nations Development Programme, *Human Development Report 1995* (New York: Oxford University Press, 1995).

25 See particularly A. B. Atkinson, *Social Justice and Public Policy,* (Brighton: Wheatsheaf; Cambridge, Mass.: MIT Press, 1983), and his *Poverty and Social Security* (New York: Wheatsheaf, 1989).

26 I have discussed different aspects of this distinction in "From Income Inequality to Economic Inequality," *Southern Economic Journal* 64 (1997).

militating against the principle of equalizing *incomes,* but it does not go against the broader precepts of economic equality, since the greater need for economic resources due to the disability must be taken into account in judging the requirements of economic equality.

Empirically, the relationship between income inequality and inequality in other relevant spaces can be rather distant and contingent because of various economic influences other than income that affect inequalities in individual advantages and substantive freedoms. For example, in the higher mortality rates of African Americans vis-à-vis the much poorer Chinese, or Indians in Kerala, we see the influence of factors that run in the opposite direction to income inequality, and that involve public policy issues with strong economic components: the financing of health care and insurance, provision of public education, arrangements for local security and so on.

Mortality differences can, in fact, serve as an indicator of very deep inequities that divide races, classes and genders, as the various illustrations in this chapter bring out. For example, the estimations of "missing women" show the remarkable reach of female disadvantage in many parts of the contemporary world, in a way that other statistics may not adequately reflect. Also, since the incomes earned by family members are shared by others in the family, we cannot analyze, gender inequality primarily in terms of income differences. We need much more information than is usually available on the division of resource use within the family

to get a clearer idea of inequalities in economic affluence. However, statistics on mortality rates as well as other deprivations (such as undernourishment or illiteracy) can directly present a picture of inequality and poverty in some crucial dimensions. This information can also be used to relate the extent of relative deprivation of women to the existing inequalities in opportunities (in earning outside income, in being enrolled in schools and so on). Thus, both descriptive and policy issues can be addressed through this broader perspective on inequality and poverty in terms of capability deprivation.

Despite the crucial role of incomes in the advantages enjoyed by different persons, the relationship between income (and other resources), on the one hand, and individual achievements and freedoms, on the other, is neither constant nor in any sense automatic and irresistible. Different types of contingencies lead to systematic variations in the "conversion" of incomes into the distinct "functionings" we can achieve, and that affects the lifestyles we can enjoy. I have tried to illustrate in this chapter the different ways in which there can be systematic variations in the relationship between incomes earned and substantive freedoms (in the form of capability to lead lives that people have reason to value). The respective roles of personal heterogeneities, environmental diversities, variations in social climate, differences in relational perspectives and distributions within the family have to receive the serious attention they deserve for the making of public policy.

61

Does Inequality Matter?★

CHRISTOPHER JENCKS

The economic gap between rich and poor has grown dramatically in the United States over the past generation and is now considerably wider than in any other affluent nation. This increase in economic inequality has no recent precedent, at least in America. The distribution of family income was remarkably stable from 1947 to 1980. We do not have good data on family incomes before 1947, but the wage gap between skilled and unskilled workers narrowed dramatically between 1910 and 1947, which probably means that family incomes also became more equal. The last protracted increase in economic inequality occurred between 1870 and 1910.

The gap between the rich and the rest of America has widened steadily since 1979. The Census Bureau, which is America's principal source of data on household incomes, does not collect good data from the rich, but the Congressional Budget Office (CBO) has recently combined census data with tax records to track income trends near the top of the distribution. Figure 1 shows that the share of after-tax income going to the top 1 percent of American households almost doubled between 1979 and 1997. The top 1 percent

---

★ First published in 2002; from *Daedalus*, Volume 131, Number 1.

FIGURE 1 **CHANGES IN THE PERCENT OF HOUSEHOLD INCOME GOING TO THE RICHEST 1 PERCENT OF AMERICAN HOUSEHOLDS, 1979–1997**

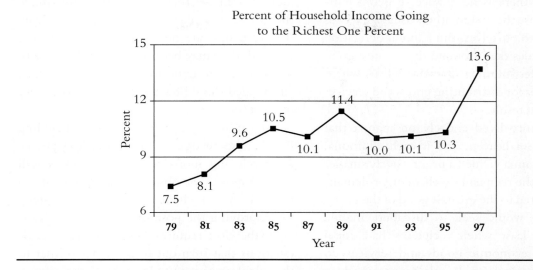

SOURCE: Congressional Budget Office, *Historical Effective Tax Rates, 1979–1997*, September 2001. Table G–1c.

included all households with after-tax incomes above $246,000 in 1997. The estimated purchasing power of the top 1 percent rose by 157 percent between 1979 and 1997, while the median household's purchasing power rose only 10 percent. The gap between the poorest fifth of American households and the median household also widened between 1979 and 1997, but the trend was far less dramatic.

To liberals who feel that economic inequality is unjust or socially destructive, its growth is evidence that America has been headed in the wrong direction. To conservatives who feel either that riches are the best way of rewarding those who contribute the most to prosperity or that a generous welfare state encourages idleness and folly among the poor, the growth of inequality seems either innocuous or desir-

able. The debate over inequality involves both moral and empirical claims, but because the empirical claims are hard to assess, both sides tend to emphasize moral arguments. But treating inequality as a moral issue does not make the empirical questions go away, because the most common moral arguments for and against inequality rest on claims about its consequences. If these claims cannot be supported with evidence, skeptics will find the moral arguments unconvincing. If the claims about consequences are actually wrong, the moral arguments are also wrong.

The connection between moral obligations and empirical evidence is most obvious in the case of utilitarian morality, which requires everyone to follow rules consistent with the greatest good of the greatest number. Utilitarian morality tells us, for example, that we should not litter even when there is no chance of being punished, because the cost to others usually exceeds the benefit to ourselves. But a moral obligation to follow rules that promote the greatest good of the greatest number does not tell us which specific rules for distributing goods and services produce that result.

If humanity lived entirely on manna that dropped from heaven, and if each additional pound of manna yielded a progressively smaller increase in the recipient's well-being, rulemakers committed to the greatest good of the greatest number would seek to distribute manna equally, at least when recipients had equal needs, But economic goods and services do not drop from heaven. People have to produce these goods and services in order to sell them to one another. How much people produce depends partly on how generously their efforts are rewarded. Rulemakers therefore have to make tradeoffs between the needs of consumers, which are relatively equal, and the motives of producers, who usually produce more when extra effort leads to higher rewards.

The most widely discussed alternative to the utilitarian theory of justice is the theory proposed by John Rawls.[1] Rawls claimed that when uncertainty is great and downside risks are high, people are—or should be—absolutely risk averse. This assumption led Rawls to believe that if people did not know what position they would occupy in a society they would want to organize the society so as to maximize the well-being of the society's least advantaged members. If this claim is correct, utilitarian logic also implies that society should maximize the well-being of the least advantaged. Even if most people are not as risk averse as Rawls claimed, they may be sufficiently risk averse to feel that maximizing the position of the least advantaged should be given very high priority in a just society.

But most thoughtful liberals, including Rawls, also recognize that rewarding people for producing more goods and services will often improve the absolute well-being of the least advantaged. Identifying the best strategy for improving the position of the least advantaged therefore requires complex empirical calculations that turn out to be rather similar to the calculations required to achieve the greatest good of the greatest number. The rest of this article assesses various empirical claims about how economic inequality affects both the mean level of well-being and the position of the least advantaged.

Some of the potential costs and benefits of inequality emerge when we contrast the United States with other rich democracies. One simple way to describe income inequality in different countries is to compute what is called the "90/10 ratio." To calculate this ratio we rank households from richest to poorest. Then we divide the income of the household at the ninetieth percentile by the income of the household at the tenth percentile. (Comparing the ninetieth percentile to the tenth percentile is better

1 John Rawls, *A Theory of Justice* (Cambridge, Mass.: Harvard University Press, 1971).

than, say, comparing the ninety-ninth percentile to the first percentile, because few countries collect reliable data on the incomes of either the very rich or the very poor.)

The Luxembourg Income Study (LIS), which is the best current source of data on economic

inequality in different countries, has calculated 90/10 ratios for fourteen rich democracies in the mid-1990s. Table 1 shows the results. To keep differences between these fourteen countries in perspective I have also included data on two poorer and less democratic countries,

TABLE 1 INCOME INEQUALITY AND ECONOMIC OUTPUT IN VARIOUS COUNTRIES DURING THE 1990s

Country (and year of the ninetieth to the tenth percentile	Ratio of holdhold income at the 90th to 10th percentile[a]	GDP per capita as a percent of U.S. level in 1998[b]	Life expectancy at birth (1995 est.)[c]
SCANDINAVIA[d]	2.8	75	77.2
Sweden (1995)	2.6	68	78.9
Finland (1995)	2.7	68	76.6
Norway (1995)	2.8	85	77.8
Denmark (1992)	2.9	79	75.4
WESTERN EUROPE	3.6	73	77.5
Nether. (1994)	3.2	75	77.5
Germany (1994)	3.2	71	76.6
Belgium (1996)	3.2	74	76.4
France (1994)	3.5	66	78.4
Switz. (1992)	3.6	84	78.5
Italy (1995)	4.8	67	77.6
BRIT. COM.	4.3	73	77.7
Canada (1994)	4.0	78	78.2
Australia (1994)	4.3	75	78.0
U.K. (1995)	4.6	67	77.0[e]
U.S. (1997)	5.6	100	75.7
MIDDLE-INCOME LIS NATIONS			
Russia (1995)	9.4	21 (?)	65.0
Mexico (1998)	11.6	25	NA

[a]From <http://lisweb.ceps.lu/key/figures/ineqtable.htm> (8/13/01).
[b]From U.S. Bureau of the Census, Statistical Abstract of the United States, 2000. Government Printing Office, Table 1365. GDP is converted to $U.S. using purchasing power parity.
[c]National center for Health Statistics, Health United States, 2000. Government Printing Office, 2000, Table 27.
[d]All area averages are unweighted arithmetic means.
[e]England and Wales.

Mexico and Russia. If we set aside Mexico and Russia, the big English-speaking democracies are the most unequal, the Scandinavian democracies are the most equal, and Western European democracies fall in the middle. (Italy looks more unequal than the other continental democracies, but the Italian data is somewhat suspect.) Within the English-speaking world the United States is the most unequal of all. The 90/10 ratio in the United States is twice that in Scandinavia. But even the United States is nothing like as unequal as Russia, Mexico, or many other Latin American countries.

America's unusually high level of inequality is not attributable to its unusually diverse labor force. Years of schooling are more equally distributed in the United States than in the European countries for which we have comparable data (Sweden, the Netherlands, and Germany). Adult test scores are more unequally distributed in the United States than Europe, partly because American immigrants score so poorly on tests given in English. But disparities in cognitive skills turn out to play a tiny role in explaining cross-national differences in the distribution of earnings. If one compares American workers with the same test scores and the same amount of schooling, the Americans' wages vary more than the wages of *all* Swedish, Dutch, or German workers.[2]

Almost everyone who studies the causes of economic inequality agrees that by far the most important reason for the differences between rich democracies is that their governments adopt different economic policies. There is no agreement about *which* policies are crucial, but there is a fairly standard list of suspects. A number of rich countries have centralized wage bargaining, which almost always compresses the distribution of earnings. Many rich democracies also make unionization easy, which also tends to compress the wage distribution. Some rich democracies transfer a lot of money to people who are retired, unemployed, sick, or permanently disabled, while others are far less generous. The United States is unusually unequal partly because it makes little effort to limit wage inequality: the minimum wage is low, and American law makes unionization relatively difficult. In addition, the United States transfers less money to those who are not working than most other rich democracies.

The fact that the American government makes so little effort to reduce economic inequality may seem surprising in a country where social equality is so important. American politicians present themselves to the public as being just like everyone else, and once they step outside their offices, Americans all wear jeans. The way Americans talk and the music they listen to are also affected by egalitarian impulses. But while the tenor of American culture may be democratic, Americans are also far more hostile to government than the citizens of other rich democracies. Since egalitarian economic policies require governmental action, they win far

---

2 Francine Blau and Lawrence Kahn, "Do Cognitive Test Scores Explain Higher U.S. Wage Inequality?" Cambridge: National Bureau of Economic Research, April 2001; and Dan Devroye and Richard Freeman, "Does Inequality in Skills Explain Inequality in Earnings Across Advanced Countries?" Cambridge: National Bureau of Economic Research, February 2001.

less support in the United States than in most other rich democracies.

Conservatives have argued for centuries that trying to limit economic inequality inevitably reduces both the incentive to work and the efficiency with which work is organized. As a result, they think egalitarian societies have fewer goods and services to distribute than societies that allow the market to determine household incomes. One simple way to test the claim is to ask whether countries that tolerate a high level of inequality really do enjoy a higher standard of living.

Measuring a country's standard of living is not easy. The most widely used measure is probably per capita Gross Domestic Product (GDP), converted to American dollars using what is known as "purchasing power parity"—a system designed to measure what different currencies actually buy in the countries where they are used. Column 2 of Table 1 shows GDP per capita for the fourteen rich democracies on which LIS provides distributional data. At first glance the data seem to support the conservative case, because the most unequal country, the United States, also has the highest GDP per capita. That fact makes a strong impression on most Americans. But if you compare the other thirteen rich democracies in Table 1 you will find no systematic relationship between inequality and per capita GDP. Britain and Italy, for example, rank just below the United States in terms of inequality, but their GDP per capita is lower than any other country but France. The fact that egalitarian economic policies have no obvious correlation with per capita GDP within Europe or the Commonwealth makes a strong impression on egalitarians in those countries. It also

suggests that America's high output per capita may be traceable to something other than our tolerance for economic inequality.

Notice, too, that no rich democracy is as unequal as Mexico or Russia. Some think this is because the combination of affluence and democracy always leads countries to adopt somewhat egalitarian economic policies. Others think the causal arrow runs the other way, and that extreme inequality retards economic growth. This debate is unlikely to be settled soon, because it requires historical evidence that is hard to find in poor countries.

If inequality does not account for America's high GDP per capita, what does? A first step toward answering this question is to decompose economic output into two components: the number of hours worked in different countries ("effort") and the value of the goods and services that workers produce per hour ("efficiency"). Table 2 shows such statistics for the United States and six other rich democracies. Americans are more likely to have paid jobs than people in the other six countries, but except in the case of France the difference is fairly small. American workers also seem to put in more hours per year than workers elsewhere, although data on hours worked is not collected in the same way in all countries, so the numbers must be treated gingerly. Still, the estimates of output per hour suggest that while the United States is considerably more efficient than Canada, Australia, Great Britain, and Sweden, it is slightly less efficient than France and Germany.

One obvious objection to this comparison is that unemployment is higher in France and Germany than in the United States. One way to correct for this waste of human resources is to

TABLE 2 **ESTIMATES OF ECONOMIC INEQUALITY, OUTPUT, EFFORT, & EFFICIENCY IN SEVEN RICH DEMOCRACIES FOR 1998**

	U.S.	U.K.	Australia	Canada	France	Germany	Sweden
Inequality (1994–1997)							
line 1: 90/10 ratio	5.6	4.6	4.3	4.0	3.5	3.2	2.6
Output (1998)							
line 2: GDP per capita	$32,184	$21,673	$24,192	$25,179	$21,132	$23,010	$21,799
Effort (1998)							
line 3: % of pop. employed	48.6	45.9	45.8	46.6	38.1	43.5	45.1
line 4: Hrs per worker per yr.	1864	1731	1860	1779	1567	1510	1629
Efficiency (1998)							
line 5: GDP per worker	$60,106	$44,280	$47,558	$49,007	$55,714	$50,616	$44,000
line 6: GDP per hr.	$32.25	$25.58	$25.57	$27.55	$35.55	$33.52	$27.01
line 7: GDP per "available" hr.	$30.81	$23.95	$23.51	$25.26	$31.38	$30.38	$24.77

SOURCE BY LINE: *Lines 1 and 2:* see Table 1. *Line 3:* see *Statistical Abstract 2000,* Table 1376. *Line 4:* see Organization for Economic Cooperation and Development, *OECD Employment Outlook, Statistical Annex,* 2001, 225. *Line 5* = line 3/line 4. *Line 6* = line 5/line 4. *Line 7* = line 6 adjusted to include hours available from those not working but seeking work, assuming that they wanted to work the same number of hours as those actually employed.

divide economic output by what Table 2 labels "available" hours—the number of hours actually worked plus the estimated number of hours that those looking for jobs in a given week wanted to work. The last row of Table 2 shows the results of this calculation. After this adjustment is made, the United States, France, and Germany look about equally efficient. If we set the United States to one side, moreover, there is again no obvious correlation between inequality and efficiency in the other six countries.

Another objection to the calculations in Table 2 is that they take no account of cross-national differences in the stock of physical and human capital. This is true, but since one major rationale for tolerating a high level of inequality is that this supposedly encourages capital accumulation and investment, holding America's advantages in these domains constant would bias the results in favor of equality. The calculations in Table 2 also ignore national differences in natural resources, but such an adjustment would almost surely make America look worse, not better. Perhaps the most fundamental objection of all is that statistics on GDP take little account of differences in the quality of the services in different countries, since these differences are almost impossible to measure. If America's service sector produces more satisfied customers than the service sector in France or Germany, Table 2 may understate the benefits of inequality.

If American managers had organized the economy in an unusually efficient way, so that American workers were producing significantly more (or better) goods and services per hour than their counterparts in other rich democracies, it would be fairly easy to argue that they deserved their fabulous salaries. Table 2 is obviously not the last word on this issue, but it does not suggest that American workers are producing significantly more per hour than their counterparts in other rich countries. Comparisons that adjust for the stock of physical and human capital show the same thing.[3] America's high standard of living seems to depend as much on long hours as clever management or clever workers.

The fact that Americans spend so much time working is rather surprising for an affluent nation with a reputation for hedonism. Workers in Germany, France, Japan, and Britain have cut their hours substantially since 1980. Americans cut their hours earlier in the twentieth century but have not done so since 1980. Americans tell pollsters that they would like to work fewer hours, but when they have a choice between shorter hours and more consumer goods, they mostly seem to opt for consumer goods rather than family time or leisure. This is a legitimate choice, but it has nothing to do with economic efficiency.

Until fairly recently the United States was so much richer than other countries that even the poor lived better in America than elsewhere, leading conservatives to argue that laissez-faire

policies benefited everyone in the long run. Today, however, the American poor are no longer the world's most affluent. Tim Smeeding, who directs the LIS, and Lee Rainwater, a Harvard sociologist, have compared the purchasing power of households at the tenth percentile of the income distribution in thirteen rich democracies covered by the LIS. These comparisons provide a pretty good indication of how the poor fare in different countries. Table 3, which is based on their work, shows that the American poor are better off than the poor in Britain or Australia but marginally worse off than the poor in Sweden, Canada, and Finland, and substantially worse off than the poor in Western Europe.

Conservatives often blame American poverty on the existence of an "underclass" that rejects mainstream social norms, does little paid work, and has children whom neither parent can support. It is certainly true that poor American households include fewer working adults than affluent American households. This is true in every rich country for which we have data. But when Lars Osberg, an economist at Dalhousie University, compared poor households in the United States, Canada, Britain, Sweden, France, and Germany, he found that the poor American households worked far more hours per year than their counterparts in the other five countries.[4] This finding suggests that what distinguishes the United States from the other rich democracies is not the idleness of the American poor but the anger that idleness inspires in more

---

3 Robert Hall and Charles Jones, "Why Do Some Countries Produce So Much More Output per Worker than Others," *Quarterly Journal of Economics* 114 (1999): 83–116.

4 Lars Osberg, "Labour Supply and Inequality Trends in the U.S.A. and Elsewhere," available at <http://is.dal.ca/~osberg/home.html>.

TABLE 3 **PURCHASING POWER OF HOUSEHOLDS AT THE 10TH AND 90TH PERCENTILES OF EACH NATION'S DISTRIBUTION RELATIVE TO HOUSEHOLDS AT THE SAME PERCENTILE IN THE UNITED STATES IN THE SAME YEAR, 1992–1997**

| Country (and year) | Purchasing power as a percent of the U.S. level in the same year | | |
	10th percentile	90th percentile	Average of all percentiles
SCANDINAVIA	112	57	77
Sweden (1995)	103	49	67
Finland (1995)	105	53	73
Norway (1995)	128	68	88
Denmark (1995)	110	59	80
WESTERN EUROPE	119	73	88
Neth. (1994)	110	64	76
Germany (1994)	113	67	82
Belgium (1996)	121	73	80
France (1994)	110	71	84
Switz. (1992)	141	89	116
COMMONWEALTH	94	73	80
Canada (1994)	105	80	92
U.K. (1995)	85	68	72
Australia (1994)	87	71	76
U.S. (1997)	100	100	100

SOURCE: Columns 1 and 2 are from Timothy Smeeding and Lee Rainwater, "Comparing Living Standards Across Countries: Real Incomes at the Top, the Bottom, and the Middle" (paper prepared for a conference on "What Has Happened to the Quality of Life in America and Other Advanced Industrial Nations?" Levy Institute, Bard College, Annandale-on-Hudson, N.Y., June 2001). Local currencies were converted to dollars using their estimated purchasing power parity. Area averages are unweighted arithmetic means. Column 3 is calculated from the national means of the logarithms of after-tax household income, using data provided by Rainwater.

affluent Americans, which helps explain the stinginess of the American welfare state.

If Rawls is right, disinterested rulemakers in all societies should be trying to maximize the well-being of the least advantaged. If you accept that claim, Table 3 suggests that Western European countries are doing a better job than the United States and that Western European countries are more just. But if you are a utilitarian whose goal is to maximize the average level of well-being, the situation is not so clear. If you want to compare the average level of well-being in countries with different distributions of income, you need some way of comparing the value people at different points in the income distribution assign to additional after-tax income. Table 3 suggests, for example, that poor Canadians have 5 percent more purchasing power than their American counterparts, while affluent Americans have 25 percent more purchasing power than affluent Canadians. If your goal is to achieve "the greatest good of the greatest number," you need some way of deciding whether the 25 percent advantage of affluent Americans over affluent Canadians should count for more or less than the 5 percent advantage of poor Canadians over poor Americans.

When employers want to reward all members of a hierarchical work group equally, they usually raise every member's wage by the same percentage. When social scientists measure economic inequality, they too assume that inequality has not changed if everyone's income has risen by the same percentage. Such practices suggest that many people think a 1 percent increase in income is equally valuable to the rich and the poor, even though a 1 percent increase represents a much larger absolute increase for the rich. In what follows I will refer to the assumption that a 1 percent gain is equally valuable at all income levels as the "One Percent Is Always The Same" rule, or the OPIATS rule for short.

The OPIATS rule implies that if my income is $100,000 and I give $20,000 of it to the poor, my well-being falls by a fifth. If I divide my $20,000 equally between ten people with incomes of $10,000, ten people's well-being will rise by a fifth. The gains from this gift will thus exceed the losses by a factor of ten. The utilitarian case for governmental redistribution almost always reflects this logic: taxing the rich won't do them much harm, and helping the poor will do them a lot of good. If you look at the actual relationship between income and outcomes like health and happiness, the OPIATS rule seldom describes the relationship perfectly, but it comes far closer than a "One Dollar Is Always The Same" rule, which is the only rule under which income inequality does not affect health or happiness.

If we apply the OPIATS rule to the tenth and ninetieth percentiles in Table 3, the percentage gains accruing to those at the ninetieth percentile from living in the United States almost always exceed the percentage gains accruing to those at the tenth percentile from living in Western Europe or Canada. Switzerland is a notable exception. Americans near the bottom of the distribution would have gained far more from living in Switzerland in 1992 than Americans near the top would have lost. Column 3 of Table 3 generalizes this logic by comparing households at every point in each country's income distribution to those at the same point in other countries and averaging the percentage differences. Averaging across the entire income distribution, Switzerland again does substantially better than the United States in 1992, but all the other rich democracies in Table 3 do somewhat worse than the United States.

Up to this point I have been focusing exclusively on what people can afford to buy. While economic goods and services are obviously important, many people believe that inequality also affects human welfare in ways that are independent of any given household's purchasing power. Even if my family income remains constant, the distribution of income in my neighborhood or my nation may influence my children's educational opportunities, my life expectancy, my chance of being robbed, the probability that I will vote, and perhaps even my overall happiness. The remainder of this article tries to summarize what we know about such effects.

EDUCATIONAL OPPORTUNITIES

Increases in economic inequality have raised the value of a college degree in the United States. If all else had remained equal, making a college degree more valuable should increase both teenagers' interest in attending college and their parents' willingness to pay for college. But the growth of economic inequality in America has been accompanied by a change in the way we finance public higher education. Tax subsidies play a smaller role than they once did, and tuition plays a larger role. Since 1979 tuition at America's public colleges and universities has risen faster than most parents' income.

If American high-school graduates were as well informed and farsighted as economic theory assumes, they would have realized that the monetary value of a college degree was rising even faster than tuition. College attendance would have risen both among children whose parents offered to pay the bills and among children who cover their own costs, who would either have borrowed more or worked longer hours to earn a degree.

But while some students clearly respond to changes in the long-term payoff of a college degree, many do not. Indeed, the reason affluent parents offer to pay their children's college expenses rather than just giving their children cash is that parents fear that if the children got the cash they might spend it on something with more short-term payoff, like a flashy car or a trip around the world. If affluent parents are right in thinking that their seventeen-year-olds have short time horizons, the same is probably true for less affluent high-school graduates whose parents cannot pay their college expenses. Such students are likely to be far more sensitive to changes in tuition than to a change in the hypothetical lifetime value of a BA. Tuition is easily observed and has to be paid now. The lifetime value of a BA is always uncertain and cannot be realized for a long time. Among students who pay their own bills, higher tuition could easily reduce college attendance even when the long-run returns of a college degree are rising.

Table 4 is taken from work by two economists, David Ellwood at Harvard and Thomas Kane at UCLA. It shows changes between 1980–1982 and 1992 in the fraction of high school graduates from different economic backgrounds entering four-year colleges. Among students from the most affluent families, the proportion entering a four-year college rose substantially. Among students from middle-income families, whose families often help with children's college expenses but seldom pay the whole bill, attendance rose more modestly. Students from the poorest quartile were no more likely to attend a four-year college in 1992 than in 1980–1982. This pattern, in which enrollment rises more at the top than at the bottom, is just what we would expect if parents respond to changes in the long-term benefits of college

TABLE 4 **PERCENT OF HIGH SCHOOL GRADUATES ENROLLING IN A 4-YEAR COLLEGE OR SOME OTHER FORM OF POSTSECONDARY EDUCATION WITHIN 20 MONTHS OF GRADUATION, BY INCOME QUARTILE: 1980–1982 AND 1992**

Income quartile	Entered a 4-year college			Entered some other form of post-secondary education		
	1980–82	1992	Change	1980–82	1992	Change
Lowest	29	28	−1	28	32	4
Second	33	38	5	30	32	2
Third	39	48	9	33	32	−1
Highest	55	66	11	26	24	−2
All	39	45	6	29	30	1

SOURCE: David Ellwood and Thomas Kane, "Who Is Getting a College Education? Family Background and the Growing Gaps in Enrollment," in Sheldon Danziger and Jane Waldfogel, eds., *Securing the Future* (New York: Russell Sage, 2000).

while students respond to changes in short-term costs. It is important to emphasize, however, that the poorest quartile's chances of attending college did not fall appreciably; they just failed to rise. The poorest quartile was worse off only insofar as higher education constitutes a "positional" good, whose value depends not just on how much you have but how much others have. That remains a contested issue.

If rising economic inequality explained the trends in Table 4, the correlation between parental income and college attendance should have grown fastest in those states where economic inequality grew fastest. Susan Mayer, a sociologist at the University of Chicago, has shown that that is exactly what happened during the 1970s and 1980s.[5] Overall, growing economic inequality in a state raised college attendance, partly because it was accompanied by increased spending on all levels of public education. The positive effects of growing inequality on college attendance persisted even when Mayer took account of changes in the payoff of schooling in the student's home state. But in the states where inequality grew the most, the effect of parental income on educational attainment also grew.

Mayer has also shown that the increase in economic inequality between 1970 and 1990 led to greater economic segregation between neighborhoods.[6] When the rich got richer they evidently moved to affluent suburbs where other rich people were also moving. Income disparities *within* neighborhoods hardly changed. Economic segregation is likely to be impor-

5 Susan E. Mayer, "How Did the Increase in Economic Inequality between 1970 and 1990 Affect Children's Educational Attainment?" *American Journal of Sociology,* 107(2001): 1–32.

6 Susan Mayer, "How the Growth in Income Inequality Increased Economic Segregation," Irving Harris Graduate School of Public Policy Studies, University of Chicago, 2001, available at <http://www.jcpr.org>.

tant, because a school's ability to attract effective teachers turns out to depend largely on its socioeconomic mix. Even when districts with a lot of poor children pay better than nearby districts, as they sometimes do, they seldom attract teachers who are good at raising children's test scores. Increasing economic segregation is therefore likely to reduce the chances that low-income students will get good teachers.

||| LIFE EXPECTANCY

People live longer in rich countries than in poor countries, but the relationship flattens out as national income rises. Indeed, the statistics in Table 1 show that life expectancy and GDP per capita are not strongly related in rich democracies. In particular, life expectancy is lower in the United States than in almost any other rich democracy.

Within any given country people with higher incomes also live longer. This relationship flattens out near the top of the income distribution, but the gap between richer and poorer families does not seem to narrow when everyone's standard of living rises. Despite both rising incomes and the introduction of Medicare and Medicaid, for example, the effects of both income and education on mortality increased in the United States between 1960 and 1986.[7] Class differences in mortality also widened in England between 1930 and 1960, even though the overall standard of living rose and the National Health Service equalized access to medical care.[8] Such facts suggest that the linkage between income and health involves more than material deprivation. Otherwise, doubling everyone's purchasing power would narrow the gap between the top and the bottom.

One reason for the persistent correlation between income and health is that poor health lowers people's earning power. In addition, big medical bills can deplete a family's savings, lowering its unearned income in later years. But while poor health clearly affects income, studies that follow the same individuals over time suggest that income, occupational position, and education also affect people's health. One reason is that members of affluent households are more likely to follow the medical profession's advice. Affluent Americans now smoke far less than poor Americans, for example. Affluent Americans also get a bit more exercise than the poor and are less likely to be overweight. But even when we take these differences into account, much of the correlation between income and life expectancy remains unexplained. Experimental studies that manipulate a monkey's rank in the hierarchy of its troop suggest that rank affects health, and the same is pretty clearly true for humans. But we do not know how much of the association between income and health can be explained in this way.

In 1992 Richard Wilkinson wrote an influential article arguing that a more equal distribution of income improved life expectancy in rich

7 See Harriet Orcutt Duleep, "Measuring Socioeconomic Mortality Differentials over Time," *Demography* 26 (May 1989): 345–351, and G. Pappas, S. Queen, W. Hadden, and G. Fisher, "The Increasing Disparity in Mortality between Socioeconomic Groups in the United States, 1960 and 1986," *New England Journal of Medicine* 329 (1993): 103–109.

8 See Elsie Pamuk, "Social Class Inequality in Mortality from 1921 to 1972 in England and Wales," *Population Studies* 39 (1985): 17–31.

countries.[9] Subsequent work showed that mortality was also lower in American states and metropolitan areas where incomes were more equal. One explanation for this phenomenon is the OPIATS rule. A 1 percent increase in income lowers the odds of dying before the age of sixty-five by roughly the same amount, regardless of what your initial income is. This means that adding $1,000 to the income of a million poor families while subtracting $1,000 from the incomes of a million richer families should lower overall mortality. It follows that countries, states, or cities with the same mean income should have lower death rates when this income is more equally distributed. But if this were the only way in which income inequality affected life expectancy, the difference between the United States and Sweden would be quite small.

Wilkinson and his followers believe that inequality also lowers life expectancy independent of its effect on any given household's income, because it changes the social context in which people live. According to Wilkinson, inequality erodes the social bonds that make people care about one another and accentuates feelings of relative deprivation (the social-science term for what people used to call envy). Other epidemiologists take what they call a "materialist" position, arguing that inequality kills because it affects public policy, altering the distribution of education, health care, environmental protection, and other material resources. Either way, if we compare people with the same income—say $50,000 a year—those who live in places where incomes are more unequal should die younger.

Recent research has raised serious doubts about such claims. As data on more countries and more time periods have become available, the cross-national correlation between economic inequality and life expectancy has fallen perilously close to zero. If you look at Table 1 and simply contrast America with other rich democracies, the idea that inequality kills seems to make sense. But if you compare the other rich democracies with one another, you find no consistent association between inequality and life expectancy. Incomes are far more unequal in Canada, Australia, and Great Britain than in Scandinavia, for example, but life expectancy is about the same in these two groups of countries.

Recent work has also raised doubts about the causal link between inequality and life expectancy in American states and cities. In America, both economic inequality and life expectancy are correlated with the percentage of African Americans in a state or city. Blacks die younger than whites no matter where they live, so states with large black populations have above-average mortality rates no matter how their residents' income is distributed. American whites also die younger when they live in a state or a metropolitan area with a large African American population. Once one takes the effects of race into account, the correlation between economic inequality and mortality tends to disappear.[10]

---

9 Wilkinson summarized his thinking on this issue in *Unhealthy Societies: The Afflictions of Inequality* (London: Routledge, 1996).

10 See also Angus Deaton and Darren Lubotsky, "Mortality, Inequality, and Race in American Cities and States," Cambridge: National Bureau of Economic Research, June 2000.

If we want to know whether egalitarian policies would improve people's health, however, we need to ask whether *changes* in economic inequality at the national, state, or local level are associated with *changes* in life expectancy. The answer to this question is "sometimes." When Andrew Clarkwest and I analyzed changes in economic inequality within American states during the 1980s, we found that white mortality rates fell least in the states where inequality increased fastest. That finding was consistent with the Wilkinson hypothesis, although the effect could have been due to chance. But when we extended our analysis back to 1970, the relationship was reversed. That relationship could also have been due to chance.

When Clarkwest and I looked at changes in economic inequality within the rich democracies that participate in the Luxembourg Income Study (LIS), we found that life expectancy had risen everywhere, but it has risen less rapidly in those countries where economic inequality was rising fastest.).[11] This was consistent with the Wilkinson hypothesis, and in this case the relationship was too large to blame on chance, at least using conventional statistical standards. Nonetheless, the relationship was weak. Economic inequality in the United States rose by about a sixth between 1979 and 1997. Life expectancy in the United States rose by three years during this period. Had inequality not increased, the LIS data implied that life expectancy in the United States would have risen by an additional 0.3 years. To keep this number in

perspective, it helps to remember that Americans in the top 5 percent of the income distribution can expect to live about nine years longer than those in the bottom 10 percent. The apparent effect of even a fairly large change in a nation's income distribution pales by comparison.

We also need to bear in mind that the cross-national correlation between changes in economic inequality and changes in life expectancy may not be causal. Countries that restrained the growth of economic inequality after 1980 were dominated by political parties that felt either politically or morally obligated to protect the interests of their less affluent citizens. Such countries may have done all sorts of other things that made people live longer, like reducing the work week or ensuring that more people got the health care they needed.

||| HAPPINESS

The relationship between income and happiness is much like the relationship between income and health, except that it is easier to tell whether someone has died than whether they are unhappy. Almost every year since 1972 the General Social Survey (GSS) has asked national samples of American adults the following question:

> Taken all together, how would you say things are these days? Would you say that you are very happy, pretty happy, or not too happy?

Those with higher incomes tend to say they are happier than those with lower incomes. This

---

11 See Andrew Clarkwest, "Notes on Cross-National Analysis of the Relationship between Mortality and Income Inequality," Malcolm Wiener Center for Social Policy, Harvard University, 2000, available at <http://www.ksg.harvard.edu/socpol/MWCstdntresearch.htm>.

relationship flattens out near the top of the distribution, but not enough to suggest that making the American distribution of income like Sweden's would have a big effect on happiness. Just as with health, equalizing the distribution of income is only likely to have large effects on happiness if it changes the social context in which people live. If equality strengthens social ties or reduces envy, for example, that could reduce unhappiness significantly.

Empirical evidence for a correlation between equality and happiness remains thin. Michael Hagerty, a social psychologist at the University of California, Davis, has shown that Americans are less likely to say they are happy when they live in cities where incomes are more unequal, but his analysis does not take account of the correlation between economic inequality and racial mix. A team of economists at Harvard and the London School of Economics has shown that Europeans become less satisfied with their lot when their country's income distribution becomes more unequal, but this effect is confined to respondents who identify with the political Left.[12] All this evidence is suggestive, but hardly definitive.

CRIME

Several studies have found that violent crime is higher in American metropolitan areas where the distribution of income is more unequal. But these studies have not looked at whether *increases* in inequality are associated with *increases* in crime. For the United States as a whole, trends in economic inequality do not match trends in violent crime at all closely. Inequality hardly changed during the 1960s, when violent crime rose sharply. Inequality rose in the early 1980s, when violent crime fell. Inequality rose more slowly in the late 1980s, when violent crime rose again. Inequality near the top of the distribution rose in the 1990s, while violent crime fell. None of this proves that changes in the distribution of income have no effect on crime, but it does suggest that trends in violent crime depend largely on other influences.

POLITICAL INFLUENCE

Americans are less likely to vote today than in the 1960s. The Left sometimes blames this decline in turnout on the fact that almost all the benefits of economic growth have been going to a small minority. Parties of the Left in most other countries have made sure that the benefits of growth were more equally distributed. In America, the Democrats have barely discussed the problem. As a result, voters are said to have become convinced that neither party cares about their problems.

Nonetheless, growing economic inequality cannot explain the decline in turnout, because this decline occurred in the early 1970s, well before inequality began to grow. Turnout

12 See Michael Hagerty, "Social Comparisons of Income in One's Community: Evidence from National Surveys of Income and Happiness," *Journal of Personality and Social Psychology* 78 (2000): 764–771, and Alberto Alesina, Rafael Di Tella, and Robert MacCulloch, "Inequality and Happiness: Are Europeans and Americans Different?" Cambridge: National Bureau of Economic Research, April 2001.

has hardly changed since 1980.[13] If growing inequality has affected turnout, it must have done so by perpetuating a decline that occurred for other reasons.

The most obvious causal link between turnout and equality runs the other way. If everyone votes, the electorate is by definition representative of the population and politicians need to keep all income groups happy. When people stop voting, turnout almost always falls the most among the poorest and least educated. As the income gap between those who vote and the population as a whole widens, politicians have less incentive to push legislation that benefits the lower half of the income distribution. Richard Freeman, an economist at Harvard, has shown that class disparities in presidential turnout increased between 1968 and 1972 and that the same thing happened between 1984 and 1988.[14] I have not seen any evidence on what has happened since 1988.

American political campaigns have also changed in ways that make it riskier for politicians to upset the rich. Until the 1960s most political candidates relied largely on volunteers to staff their campaign offices and contact voters. Now they rely largely on paid staff and television advertising. This change reflects the fact that politicians can raise more money today than in the past. Political contributions

have probably risen because government affects more aspects of our lives, so both voters and corporations are willing to spend more money to influence government regulations and spending patterns. Whatever the explanation, people who can contribute money now have more political weight, and people who can contribute time have less. Politicians also know that the easiest way to raise the money they need is to court affluent contributors. When the share of income going to the top 1 percent rises, politicians have more incentive to raise money from this group. If politicians had to rely exclusively on contributions of less than $100, they would also have to rely more on volunteers to do a lot of their campaign work.

I began this inquiry by arguing that America does less than almost any other rich democracy to limit economic inequality. As a result, the rich can buy a lot more in America than in other affluent democracies, while the poor can buy a little less. If you evaluate this situation by Rawlsian standards, America's policies are clearly inferior to those of most rich European countries. If you evaluate the same situation using a utilitarian calculus, you are likely to conclude that most American consumers do better than their counterparts in other large democracies. Much of this advantage is due to

---

13 About 62 percent of the voting-age population cast ballots in the three presidential elections conducted during the 1960s. Turnout fell to 55 percent in 1972, 54 percent in 1976, and 53 percent in 1980. Since 1980 presidential turnout has averaged 52 percent, with no clear trend. Off-year congressional elections have followed the same trajectory (U.S. Bureau of the Census, *Statistical Abstract of the United States, 2000*, Government Printing Office, 2000, Table 479). If one allows for

the fact that citizens constitute a declining fraction of the voting-age population and the fact that more citizens are disenfranchised because they are—or have been—in prison, turnout among eligible voters may actually have increased slightly since 1980.

14 Richard Freeman, "What, Me Vote?" paper presented at the Workshop on Inequality and Social Policy, Kennedy School of Government, June 2001.

the fact that Americans spend more time work-ing than Europeans do, but that may not be the whole story.

I also looked at evidence on whether eco-nomic inequality affects people's lives indepen-dent of its effects on their material standard of living. At least in the United States, the growth of inequality appears to have made more people attend college but also made educational oppor-tunities more unequal. Growing inequality may also have lowered life expectancy, but the evi-dence for such an effect is weak and the effect, if there was one, was probably small. There is some evidence that changes in inequality affect happiness in Europe, but not much evidence that this is the case in the United States. If inequality affects violent crime, these effects are swamped by other factors. There is no evidence that changes in economic inequality affect political participation, but declining political participa-tion among the less affluent may help explain why American politicians remained so passive when inequality began to grow after 1980.

My bottom line is that the social con-sequences of economic inequality are sometimes negative, sometimes neutral, but seldom—as far as I can discover—positive. The case for inequality seems to rest entirely on the claim that it promotes efficiency, and the evidence for that claim is thin. All these judgments are very tentative, however, and they are likely to change as more work is done. Still, it is worth-while to ask what they would imply about the wisdom of trying to limit economic inequality if they were, in fact, correct.

Readers' answers to that question should, I think, depend on four value judgments. First, readers need to decide how much weight they assign to improving the lot of the least advan-taged compared with improving the average level of well-being. Second, they need to decide how much weight they assign to increasing material well-being compared with increasing "family time" or "leisure." Third, they need to decide how much weight they assign to equal-izing opportunities for the young as against maximizing the welfare of adults. Fourth, they need to decide how much value they assign to admitting more people from poor countries such as Mexico to the United States, since this almost inevitably makes the distribution of income more unequal.

If you are a hard-core Rawlsian who thinks that society's sole economic goal should be to improve the position of the least advantaged, European experience suggests that limiting inequality can benefit the poor. If you are a hard-core utilitarian, European experience suggests—though it certainly does not prove—that limiting inequality lowers consumption. But European experience also suggests that low-ering inequality reduces consumption partly by encouraging people to work fewer hours, which many Europeans see as a good thing. If you care more about equal opportunity for children than about consumption among adults, limiting economic inequality among parents probably reduces disparities in the opportunities open to their children.

All things considered, the case for limiting inequality seems to me strong but not over-whelming. That is one reason why most rich societies are deeply divided about the issue. Yet given the centrality of redistribution in modern politics, it is remarkable how little effort rich societies have made to assemble the kinds of evidence they would need to assess the costs and benefits of limiting inequality. Even societies that redistribute a far larger fraction of their GDP than the United States spend almost nothing on answering questions of this kind. Answering such questions would require collecting better evidence, which costs real money. It would also require politicians to run the risk of being proven wrong. Nonetheless, moral sentiments uninformed by evidence have done incalculable damage over the past few centuries, and their malign influence shows no sign of abating. Rich democracies can do better if they try.

AUTHOR BIOGRAPHIES

Ian Ayres is the William K. Townsend Professor of Law at Yale Law School. His most recent book is *Super Crunchers: Why Thinking-By-Numbers Is the New Way to Be Smart* (Bantam, 2007).

Simone de Beauvoir (1908–1986) was a French philosopher and writer. Her book *The Second Sex* (1949) is widely regarded as one of the founding texts of modern feminist thought.

Rebecca Blank is Robert S. Kerr Senior Fellow at the Brookings Institution. Her most recent book (with Sheldon Danzinger and Robert Schoeni) is *Working and Poor: How Economic and Policy Changes Are Affecting Low-Wage Workers* (Russel Sage, 2006).

Francine Blau is Frances Perkins Professor of Industrial and Labor Relations and Labor Economics, School of Industrial and Labor Relations, Cornell University. Her most recent book (with Mary C. Brinton and David B. Grusky) is *The Declining Significance of Gender?* (Russell Sage, 2006).

Herbert Blumer (1900–1987) was an American sociologist who taught at the University of Chicago and founded the sociology department at the University of California–Berkeley in the early 1950s. His work pioneered the theory and application of symbolic interactionism, an influential theory in the development of the field of social psychology.

Bart Bonikowski is a PhD student in sociology at Princeton University.

Pierre Bourdieu (1930–2002) was a French sociologist who held the Chair in Sociology at the College de France. He was among the most influential sociologists in the world in the last quarter of the twentieth century, pioneering theoretical ideas and empirical research across a vast array of topics that sought to bridge some of the most important conventional divides in the field, such as the relationship between individual action and social structure.

Richard Breen is a professor of sociology at Yale University. His most recent book is *Social Mobility in Europe* (Oxford, 2004).

Dan Clawson is a professor of sociology at the University of Massachusetts at Amherst. His most recent book is *The Next Upsurge: Labor and the New Social Movements* (Cornell, 2003).

Patricia Hill Collins is Distinguished University Professor at the University of Maryland. Her most recent book is *From Black Power to Hip Hop: Essays on Racism, Nationalism, and Feminism* (Temple, 2006).

Dalton Conley is University Professor of the Social Sciences and Chair of Sociology at New York University. His most recent book is *Elsewhere, U.S.A.* (Pantheon, 2009).

Sheldon Danzinger is Henry J. Meyer Distinguished University Professor, Gerald R. Ford School of Public Policy. His most recent book (with Cecilia Rouse) is *The Price of Independence: The Economics of Early Adulthood* (Russell Sage, 2007)

Kingsley Davis (1908–1997) was a pioneer in the field of demography. He taught in sociology departments at several universities during his long career, including the University of California–Berkeley from 1955–1977. He developed many of the most influential theories about population growth and development, which laid the foundation for the field of population research.

Nancy Denton is a professor of sociology at SUNY–Albany. Her most recent book (with Stewart Tolnay) is *American Diversity: A Demographic Challenge for the Twenty-first Century* (SUNY, 2002).

Charles Derber is a professor of sociology at Boston College. His most recent book is *The New Feminized Majority* (Paradigm Publishers, 2008).

G. William Domhoff is a professor of sociology at the University of California–Santa-Cruz. His most recent book is *Who Rules America: Power, Politics, & Social Change*, Fifth Edition, (McGraw-Hill, 2005).

W. E. B. Du Bois (1869–1963) was an interdisciplinary social science scholar, writer, and journalist who made vital contributions as a civil rights activist (including co-founding the NAACP). Du Bois's many contributions to the study of racial inequality and the development of sociological research include important field studies of urban communities undertaken in the late nineteenth and early twentieth centuries, his many influential essays on aspects of the racial problem in America, and important historical investigations such as his account of Reconstruction in *Black Reconstruction* (1935).

Rachel Dwyer is an assistant professor of sociology at Ohio State University.

Paula England is a professor of sociology at Stanford University. Her most recent book is *Comparable Worth: Theories and Evidence* (Aldine, 1992).

Gosta Esping-Andersen is a professor of sociology at the Universitat Pompeu Fabra. His most recent book is *Family Formation and Low Fertility* (BBVA, 2006).

Maya Federman is an associate professor of economics at Pitzer College.

Cynthia Feliciano is an assistant professor of sociology and Chicano/Latino Studies at the University of California–Irvine. Her most recent book is *Unequal Origins: Immigrant Selection and the Education of the Second Generation* (LFB Scholarly Publishing, 2006).

Glenn Firebaugh is Distinguished Professor of Sociology and Demography at Pennsylvania State University. His most recent book is Seven *Rules for Social Research* (Princeton, 2008).

Claude Fischer is a professor of sociology at the University of California–Berkeley. His most recent book (with Michael Hout) is *Century of Difference: How America Changed in the Last One Hundred Years* (Russell Sage, 2006).

Robert Frank is the H. J. Louis Professor of Management and Professor of Economics at Cornell University. His most recent book is *Falling Behind: How Income Inequality Harms the Middle Class* (California, 2007).

Richard Freeman holds the Herbert Ascherman Chair in Economics at Harvard University. His most recent book is *America Works: Critical Thoughts on the Exceptional U.S. Labor Market* (Russell Sage, 2007).

James K. Galbraith is Lloyd M. Bentsen Jr. Chair in Government/Business Relations and a professor of government at the University of Texas. His most recent book is *Predator State: How Conservatives Abandoned the Free Market and Why Liberals Should Too* (The Free Press, 2008).

Martin Gilens is an associate professor of politics at Princeton University. His most recent book is *Why Americans Hate Welfare* (Chicago, 1999).

Claudia Goldin is the Henry Lee Professor of Economics at Harvard University. Her most recent book (with Lawrence Katz) is *The Race between Education and Technology* (Harvard, 2008).

Peter Gottschalk is a professor of economics at Boston College. His most recent book (with Sheldon Danzinger) is *America Unequal* (Harvard/Russell Sage, 1995).

Mark Granovetter is the Joan Butler Ford Professor in the School of Humanities and Sciences at Stanford University. His most recent book (with Richard Swedberg) is *The Sociology of Economic Life*, second edition, (Westview Press, 2001).

William Haller is an assistant professor of sociology at Clemson University.

Charles Hirschman is the Boeing International Professor of Sociology and Public Affairs at the University of Washington and recently president of the Population Association of America.

Arlie Hochschild is a professor of sociology at University of California–Berkeley. Her most recent book is *The Commercialization of Intimate Life: Notes From Home and Work* (California, 2003).

Michael Hout is a professor of sociology at the University of California–Berkeley. His most recent book (with Claude Fischer) is *Century of Difference: How America Changed in the Last One Hundred* (Russell Sage, 2006).

Jerry Jacobs is the Merriam Term Professor of Sociology at the University of Pennsylvania. His most recent book (with Ann Boulis) is *Women Becoming Doctors: Women's Entry in the Medical Profession in the United States, 1970–2000* (Cornell, 2008).

Lawrence Jacobs is Walter F. and Joan Mondale Chair for Political Studies at the University of Minnesota. His most recent book (with Benjamin Page) is *Class War? Economic Inequality and the American Dream* (Chicago, 2009).

Martin Sanchez Jankowski is a professor of sociology and Director of the Center for Urban Ethnography at University of California–Berkeley. His most recent book is *Cracks in the Pavement: Social Change and Resilience in Poor Neighborhoods* (California, 2008).

Christopher Jencks is the Malcolm Wiener Professor of Social Policy at Harvard University. His most recent book (with Meredith Phillips) is *The Black-White Test Score Gap* (Brookings, 1998).

Lawrence Kahn is a professor at the Labor Economics and Collective Bargaining at the School of Industrial and Labor Relations at Cornell University. His most recent book (with Francine Blau) is *At Home and Abroad: U.S. Labor Market Performance in International Perspective* (Russell Sage, 2002).

Rosabeth Moss Kanter is the Ernest L. Arbuckle Professor at the Harvard Business School. Her most recent book is *America the Principled* (Crown, 2007).

Lisa Keister is a professor of sociology at Duke University. Her most recent book is *Getting Rich: America's New Rich and How the Got That Way* (Cambridge, 2005).

Patricia Fernandez Kelly is a senior lecturer of sociology at Princeton University. Her most recent book (with Alejandro Portes) is *Exceptional Outcomes: Achievement in Education and Employment among Children of Immigrants* (Sage, 2009).

Barbara Stanek Kilbourne is a professor of sociology at Tennessee State University.

Paul Krugman is a professor of economics and public affairs at Princeton University and an op-ed columnist for *The New York Times*. His most recent book is *The Return of Depression Economics and the Crisis of 2008* (Norton, 2008).

Annette Lareau is Stanley I. Sheerr Professor of Sociology at the University of Pennsylvania. Her most recent book (with Dalton Conley) is *Social Class: How Does it Work?* (Russell Sage, 2008).

Samuel Lucas is an associate professor of sociology at University of California–Berkeley. His most recent book is *Theorizing Discrimination in an Era of Contested Prejudice* (Temple, 2008).

Yale Magrass is Chancellor Professor in the Department of Sociology and Anthropology at the University of Massachusetts, Dartmouth. His most recent book is *Morality Wars* (Paradigm Publishers, 2008).

T. H. Marshall (1893–1981) was a sociologist who taught at the London School of Economics from 1925–1956. He made early contributions to the field of population research in Britain. His writings on the development of citizenship and the rise of the welfare state, collected in his 1950 book *Citizenship and Social Class,* have been and continue to be widely influential.

Karl Marx (1818–1883) was born in Germany and lived in Paris before settling in London. He was a leading mid-nineteenth-century thinker and a founding figure in the world socialist movement. His many books and articles covered topics in philosophy, economics, politics, and history. He is most known for his analysis of capitalism as an economic system in his three-volume *Das Kapital* (first published in 1867) and *The Communist Manifesto* (first published in 1848, co-authored with Friedrich Engels).

Douglas Massey is the Henry G. Bryant Professor of Sociology and Public Affairs at Princeton University. His most recent book is *Categorically Unequal: The American Stratification System* (Russell Sage, 2008).

Leslie McCall is an associate professor of sociology at Northwestern University. She is the author of *Complex Inequalities* (Routledge, 2001).

C. Wright Mills (1919–1962) was an American sociologist and social critic. He taught at Columbia University. His most famous books are *White Collar* (1951), *The Power Elite* (1956), and *The Sociological Imagination* (1959).

Wilbert Moore (1914–1987) was a sociologist and demographer who taught at Princeton University. He is the author of *Order and Change: Essays in Comparative Sociology* (1967).

Devah Pager is an associate professor of sociology at Princeton University. She is the author of *Marked: Race, Crime, and Work in Low-Wage Labor Markets* (University of Chicago Press, 2007).

Orlando Patterson is the John Cowles Professor of Sociology at Harvard University. His most recent book is *Rituals of Blood: Consequences of Slavery in Two American Centuries* (Basic Books, 1999).

Thomas Piketty is a professor of economics at the Paris School of Economics. His most recent book (with A. B. Atkinson) is *Top Incomes over the Twentieth Century: A Contrast between European and English-Speaking Countries* (Oxford, 2007).

Robert Pollin is a professor of economics and the co-author of the Political Economy Research Institute at the University of Massachusetts–Amherst. His most recent book is *Contours of Descent* (Verso, 2003).

Alejandro Portes is the Howard Harrison and Gabrielle Snyder Beck Professor of Sociology, Princeton University. His most recent book is *Economic Sociology: Assumptions, Concepts, and a Mid-Range Agenda* (Princeton University Press, 2009).

Barbara Reskin is the S. Frank Miyamoto Professor of Sociology at the University of Washington. Her most recent book (with Irene Padavic) is *Women and Men at Work*, Second Edition, (Pine Forge, 2002).

Deborah Rhode is the Ernest W. McFarland Professor of Law at Stanford University. Her most recent book (with Barbara Kellerman) is *Women and Leadership: The State of Play and Strategies for Change* (Jossey-Bass, 2007).

Patricia Roos is a professor of sociology and labor studies and employment relations at Rutgers University. Her most recent book (with Barbara Reskin) is *Job Queues, Gender Queues: Explaining Women's Inroads into Male Occupations* (Temple, 1990).

David Rottman is Principal Court Research Consultant, National Center for State Courts, Williamsburg, Virginia. His most recent book (with M. Sviridoff, D. Rottman, B. Ostrom, and R. Curtis) is *Dispensing Justice Locally: The Implementation and Effects of the Midtown Community Court* (Gordon and Breach, 2000).

Jill Quadagno is the Mildred and Claude Pepper Eminent Scholar in Social Gerontology at Florida State University. Her most recent book is *One Nation, Uninsured: Why the U.S. Has No National Health Insurance* (Oxford, 2005).

Emmanuel Saez is a professor of economics at University of California–Berkeley.

Theda Skocpol is the Victor S. Thomas Professor of Government and Sociology at Harvard University. Her most recent book is *What a Mighty Power We Can Be: African American Fraternal Groups and the Struggle for Racial Equality* (Princeton, 2008).

Amartya Sen is Thomas W. Lamont University Professor and a professor of economics and philosophy at Harvard University. His most recent book is *Identity and Violence: The Illusion of Destiny* (Norton, 2006).

Adam Smith (1723–1790) was a Scottish moral philosopher and one of the founding figures of modern political economy. His book *The Wealth of Nations* (1776) famously developed a case for free markets and free trade that quickly became one of the most influential discussions about the relationship between markets and governments.

Jon Stiles is Director of Research at California Census Research Data Center, University of California–Berkeley.

William A. Schwartz is a graduate student in sociology at Boston College and the co-author of *The Nuclear Seduction* (University of California Press, 1993).

Ann Swidler is a professor of sociology at University of California–Berkeley. Her most recent book is *Talk of Love: How Culture Matters* (Chicago, 2001).

E. P. Thompson (1924–1993) was a British historian and antiwar activist. His book *The Making of the English Working Class* (1963) helped launch the field of social history (or "history from below").

Charles Tilly (1929–2008) was a sociologist who taught at the University of Michigan, The New School, and Columbia University. He was an influential social science historian and an analyst of social movements, collective action, and the rise of modern states.

Thorstein Veblen (1857–1929) was an economist and sociologist who wrote pioneering works in institutional economics, including studies of the rise of the modern corporation. His social criticisms of wealth and inequality in the late Gilded Age were developed most famously in his book *The Theory of the Leisure Class* (1899).

Kim Voss is a professor of sociology at University of California–Berkeley. Her most recent book (with Rick Fantasia) is *Hard Work: Remaking the American Labor Movement* (California, 2004).

Roger Waldinger is a professor of sociology at UCLA. His most recent book (with Michael Lichter) is *How the Other Half Works: Immigration and the Social Organization of Labor* (California, 2003).

Max Weber (1864–1920) was a German sociologist and one of the "founding fathers" of the discipline of sociology. His most famous work includes *The Protestant Ethic and the Spirit of Capitalism* (1904) and the theoretical and historical essays in his posthumously published two-volume *Economy and Society* (1922).

Bruce Western is a professor of sociology and Director of the Multidisciplinary Program in Inequality and Social Policy at Harvard University. His most recent book is *Punishment and Inequality in America* (Russell Sage, 2006).

William Julius Wilson is Lewis P. and Linda L. Geyser University Professor at Harvard University. His most recent book is *More than Just Race: Being Black and Poor in the Inner City* (Norton, 2009).

Erik Olin Wright is a professor of sociology at the University of Wisconsin. His most recent book (with Archon Fung) is *Deepening Democracy: Institutional Innovations in Empowered Participatory Governance* (Verso, 2003).

CREDITS

INDEX